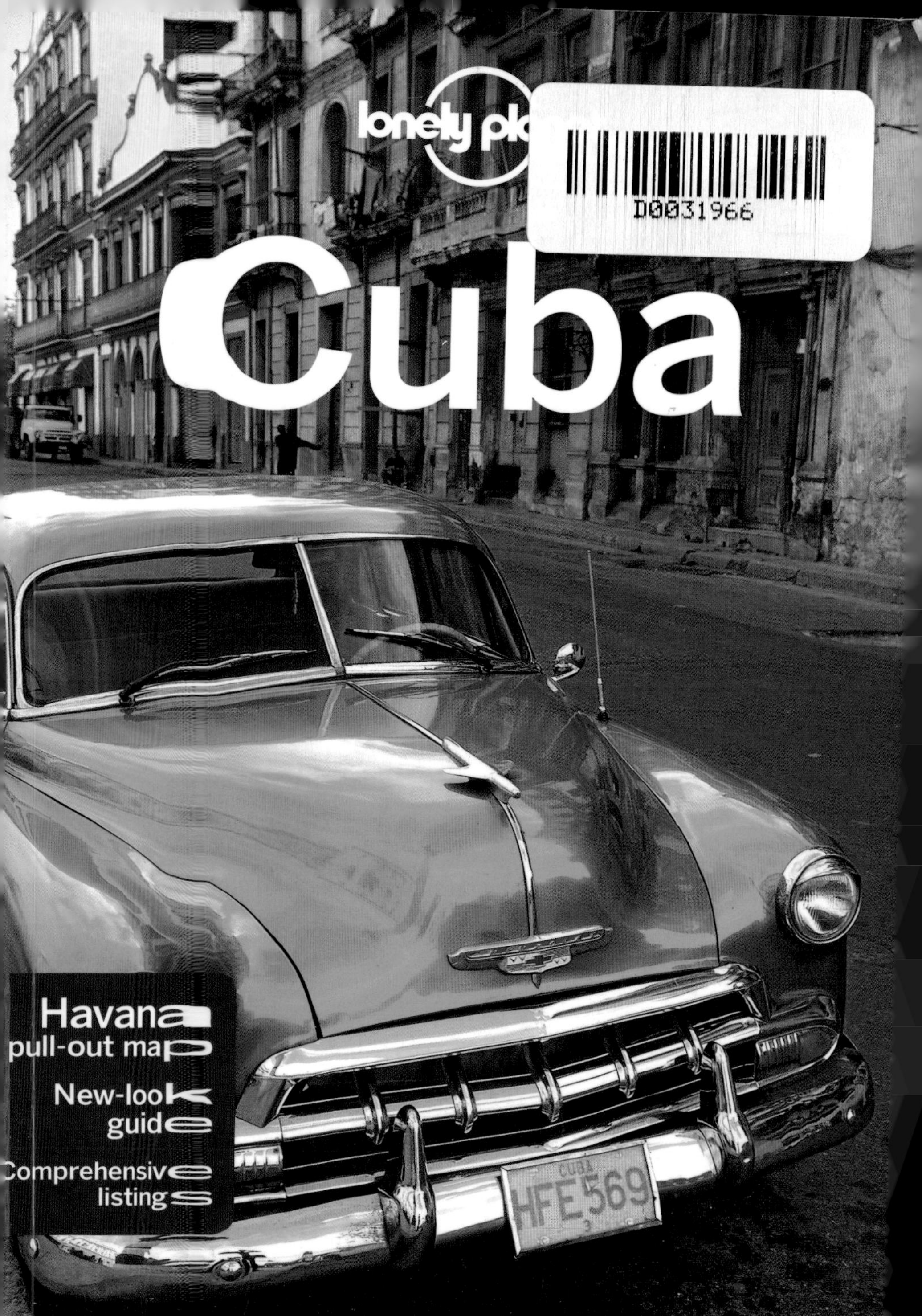
lonely pl
D0031966
Cuba
Havana
pull-out map
New-look
guide
Comprehensive
listings
CUBA
HFE 569

"All you've got to do is decide to go and the hardest part is over. So go!"

TONY WHEELER, COFOUNDER – LONELY PLANET

PAGE 1

PLAN YOUR TRIP

YOUR PLANNING TOOL KIT

Photos, itineraries, lists and suggestions to help you put together your perfect trip

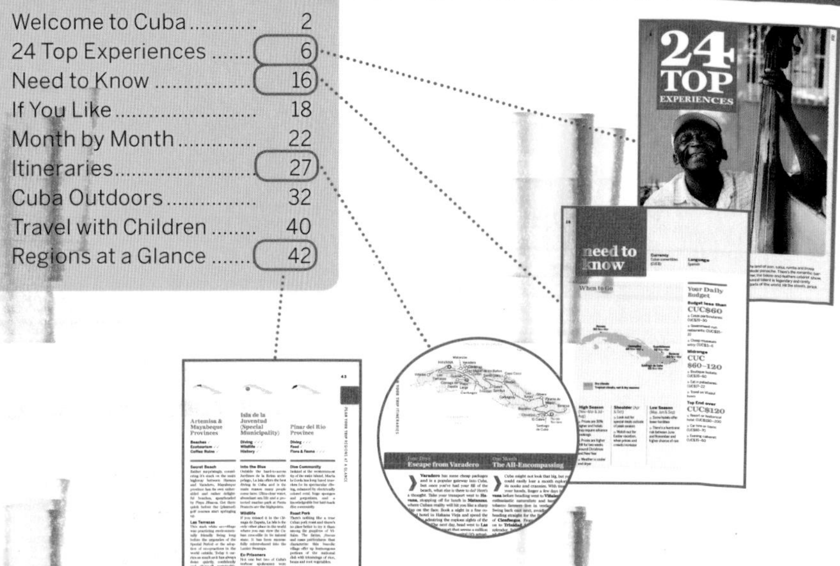

PAGE 443

UNDERSTAND CUBA

GET MORE FROM YOUR TRIP

Learn about the big picture, so you can make sense of what you see

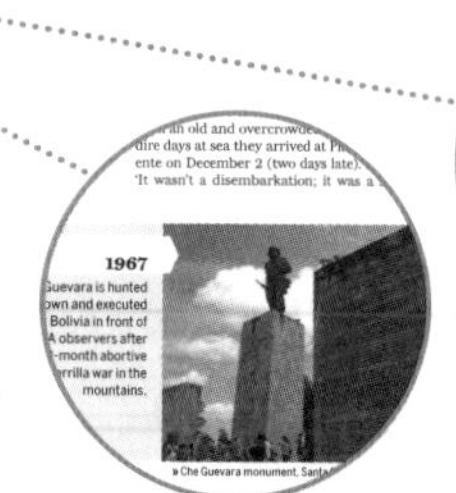

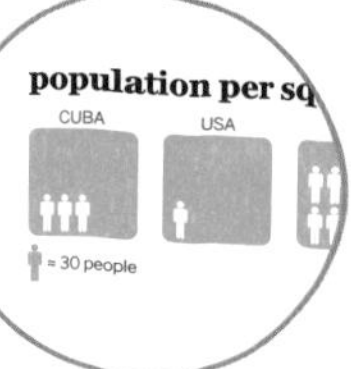

ISBN 978-1-74179-802-9

PAGE 48

ON THE ROAD

YOUR COMPLETE DESTINATION GUIDE
In-depth reviews, detailed listings and insider tips

PAGE 497

SURVIVAL GUIDE

VITAL PRACTICAL INFORMATION TO HELP YOU HAVE A SMOOTH TRIP

Language

THIS EDITION WRITTEN AND RESEARCHED BY

Brendan Sainsbury

Luke Waterson

welcome to Cuba

Mildewed Magnificence

There ought to be a banner in the arrivals hall at Havana airport that reads 'Abandon preconceptions, all ye who enter here.' Get ready for shocks, surprises, and eye-opening epiphanies. Twenty-first century Cuba promises to be like nowhere else you've ever visited: economically poor, but culturally rich; visibly mildewed, but architecturally magnificent; infuriating, yet at the same time, strangely uplifting. If the country were a book, it would be James Joyce's *Ulysses;* layered, hard to grasp, serially misunderstood, but – above all – a classic.

Cuba's intricacies are a result of its history, a troubled saga of external interference and internal strife that has bred genocide, slavery, invasion, counterinvasion, and popular revolution. Floating halfway between the US to the north and Latin America to the south, the archipelago has long struggled to work out where it fits in. Even its ecology, as German scientist Alexander von Humboldt once observed, is decidedly weird, a kind of 'Caribbean Galápagos' where contradictory phenomena coexist.

A Certain Romance

For half a century Cuba has been infamous for its politics, dominated by the increasingly wrinkled visage of Fidel Castro, who only has to cough for the world media to go on red alert. But the polemics hide deeper secrets. Most visitors are surprised to arrive

BRENT WINEBRENNER / LONELY PLANET IMAGES ©

Cuba is a continuing education. Just when you think you've figured it out, it confounds you with another brow-beating riddle. That essentially is its underlying attraction.

(left) Classic American car in the streets of Habana Vieja, Havana
(lbelow) Musicians playing traditional Cuban music in a bar, Havana.

SHANNON NACE / LONELY PLANET IMAGES ©

in Havana and find, not some grey communist dystopia, but a wildly exuberant place where the taxi drivers quote Hemingway and even hardened cynics are ensnared by the intrigue and romance.

Cuba's romance isn't of the candlelit, dinner-for-two variety. Here, in a country of few material possessions, life can be raw, in your face, and rough around the edges. But, the austerity is only half the story. Cuba is crammed with innumerable impossible-to-buy riches. Ponder the Latin Lotharios holding court on Havana's Malecón, the ingenious DIY-merchants fine-tuning their hybridized Russian-American cars, or the old ladies in rollers conjuring culinary miracles out of nothing.

The Spirit of Survival

That Cuba has survived is a miracle in itself. That it can still enthrall travelers from around the globe with its beaches, bays, mountains, rum, music, and impossibly verdant landscapes is an even greater achievement. The key lies in the Cubans themselves: survivors and improvisers, poets and dreamers, cynics and sages. Defying all logic, it is the people who have kept the country alive as the infrastructure has crumbled; and it is they also who have ensured that Cuba continues to be the fascinating, perplexing, paradoxical nation it is. Such uniqueness is a vanishing commodity in an increasingly globalized world. Grab it while it's still there.

Cuba

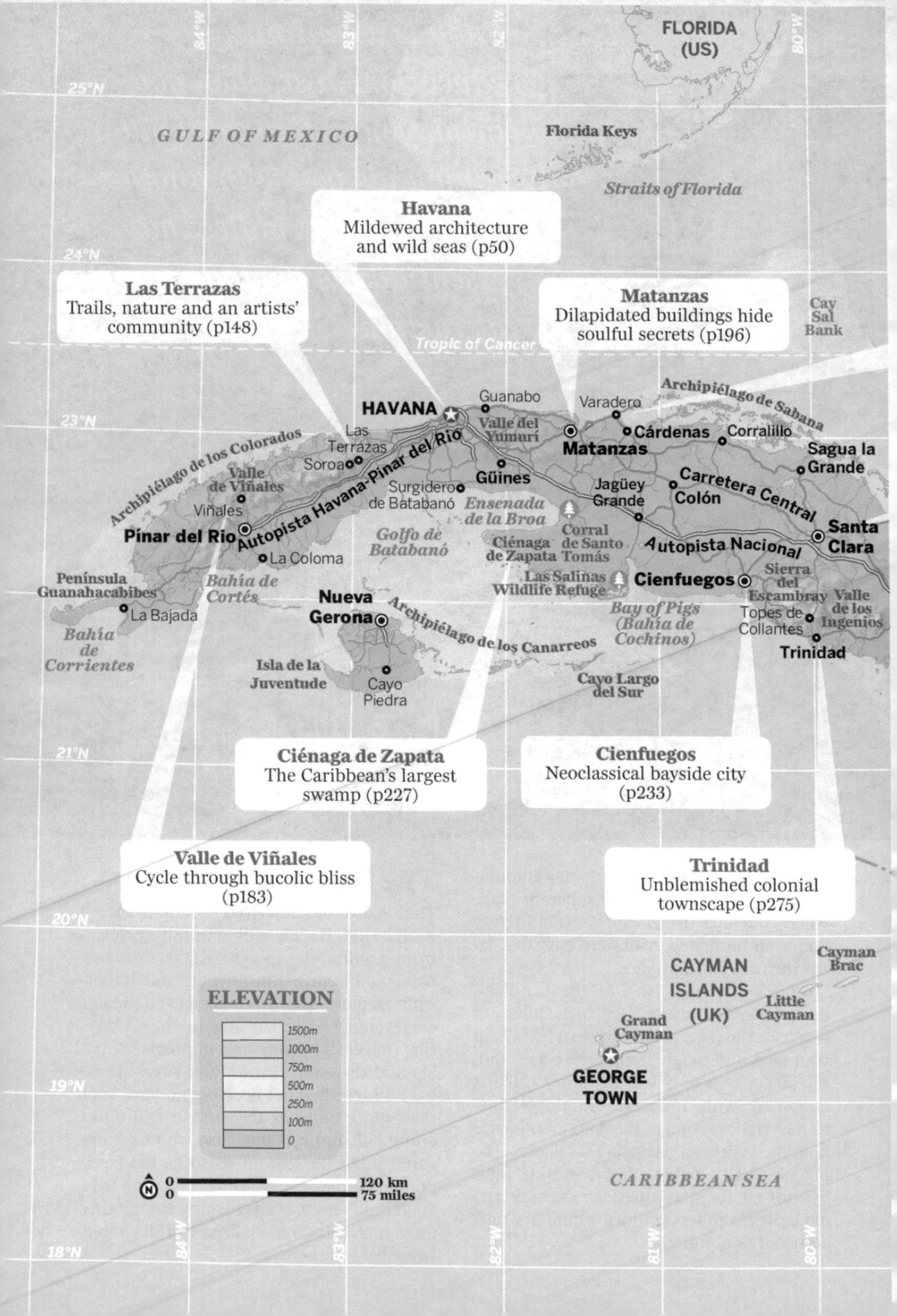

Havana
Mildewed architecture and wild seas (p50)

Las Terrazas
Trails, nature and an artists' community (p148)

Matanzas
Dilapidated buildings hide soulful secrets (p196)

Ciénaga de Zapata
The Caribbean's largest swamp (p227)

Cienfuegos
Neoclassical bayside city (p233)

Valle de Viñales
Cycle through bucolic bliss (p183)

Trinidad
Unblemished colonial townscape (p275)

FLORIDA (US)
GULF OF MEXICO
Florida Keys
Straits of Florida
Cay Sal Bank
Tropic of Cancer
Archipiélago de Sabana
Archipiélago de los Colorados
HAVANA
Guanabo
Varadero
Valle del Yumurí
Matanzas
Cárdenas
Corralillo
Sagua la Grande
Las Terrazas
Soroa
Güines
Valle de Viñales
Viñales
Autopista Havana-Pinar del Río
Surgidero de Batabanó
Ensenada de la Broa
Jagüey Grande
Carretera Central
Colón
Corral de Santo Tomás
Pínar del Río
Golfo de Batabanó
Ciénaga de Zapata
Autopista Nacional
Santa Clara
La Coloma
Las Salinas Wildlife Refuge
Cienfuegos
Sierra del Escambray
Península Guanahacabibes
Bahía de Cortés
Valle de los Ingenios
Bay of Pigs (Bahía de Cochinos)
Topes de Collantes
La Bajada
Nueva Gerona
Archipiélago de los Canarreos
Trinidad
Bahía de Corrientes
Isla de la Juventude
Cayo Piedra
Cayo Largo del Sur
CAYMAN ISLANDS (UK)
Cayman Brac
Little Cayman
Grand Cayman
GEORGE TOWN
CARIBBEAN SEA

ELEVATION
1500m
1000m
750m
500m
250m
100m
0

0 120 km
0 75 miles

25°N
24°N
23°N
21°N
20°N
19°N
18°N
84°W
83°W
82°W
81°W
80°W

Top Experiences ›

24 TOP EXPERIENCES

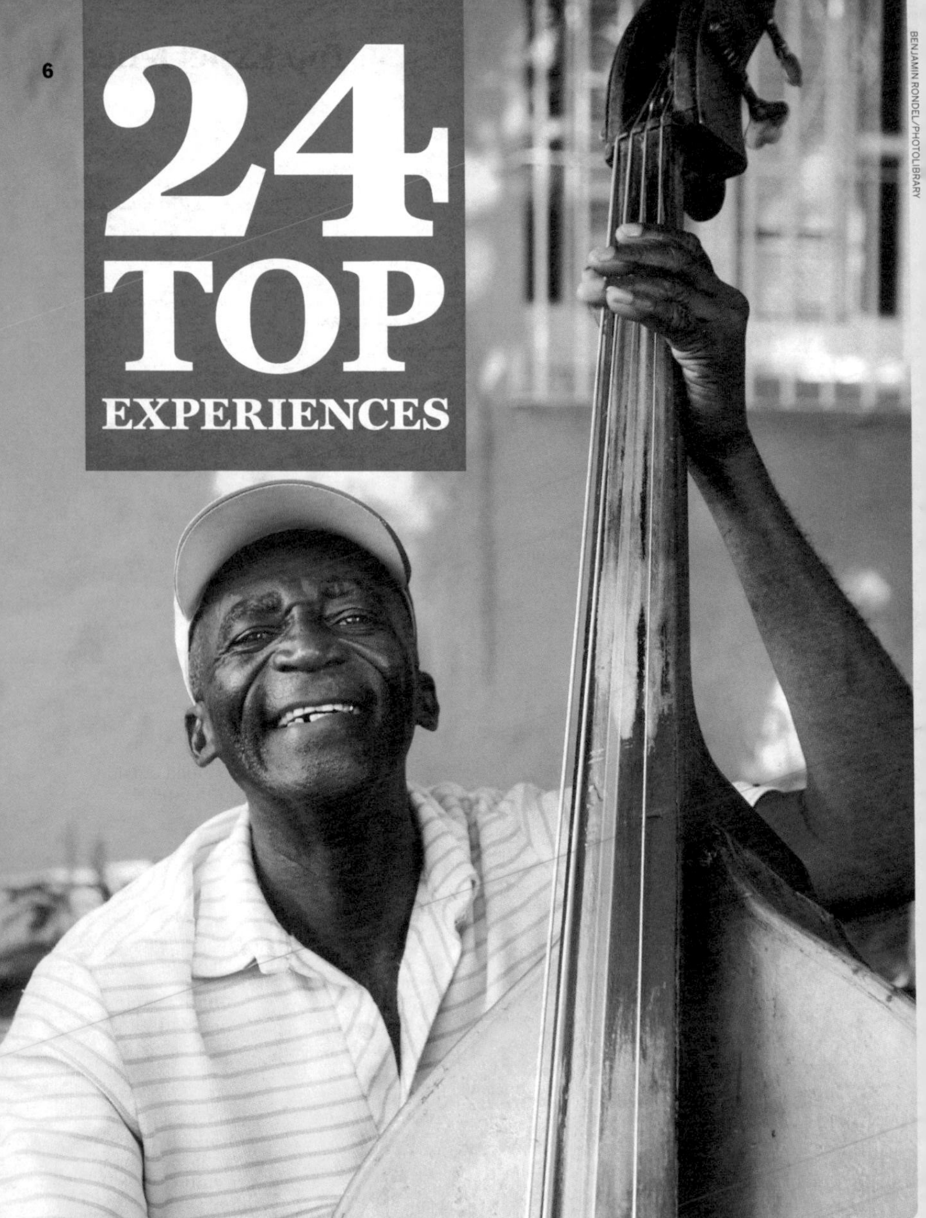

Live Music Scene

1 In Cuba piped music is considered a cop-out. Here in the land of *son*, salsa, rumba and *trova* everything is spontaneous, live and delivered with a melodic panache. There's the romantic bar-crawling troubadour, the gritty street-based rumba drummer, the bikini-and-feathers cabaret show, the late-night *reggaetón* party – the list goes on. Cuba's musical talent is legendary and rarely comes with the narcissistic 'star status' common in other parts of the world. Hit the streets, prick up your ears and let the music lure you in. Street musician, Santiago de Cuba

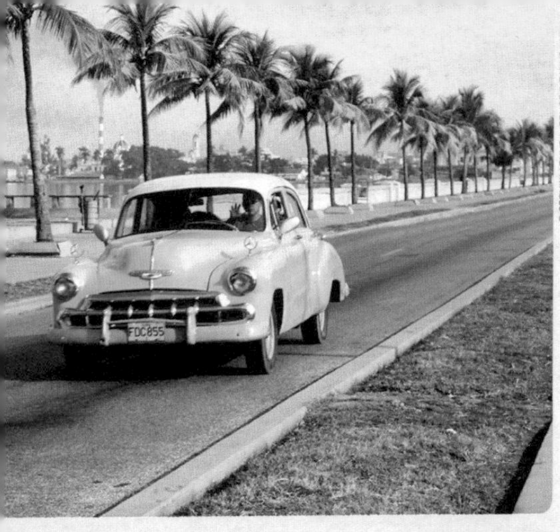

FRANK CARTER/LONELY PLANET IMAGES ©

Havana's Malecón

2 Only a fool comes to Havana and misses out on the Malecón sea drive (p78), 8km of shabby magnificence that stretches the breadth of the city from Havana Vieja to Miramar and acts as a substitute living room for tens of thousands of cavorting, canoodling, romance-seeking *habaneros*. Traverse it during a storm when giant waves breach the wall, or tackle it at sunset with Benny Moré on your mp3 player, a bottle of Havana Club in your hand and the notion that anything is possible come 10pm.

Cuba's Casas Particulares

3 Picture the scene: there are two rocking chairs creaking on a polished colonial porch, a half-finished bottle of rum being passed amiably between guest and host, and the sound of lilting music drifting ethereally through the humid tropical darkness. It could be any casa particular in any street in any town, they're all the same. Shrugging off asphyxiating censorship and bleak Cold War–style totalitarianism, Cuba can be one of the most candid countries on earth if you opt out of the government-sponsored resorts and stay in a casa particular.

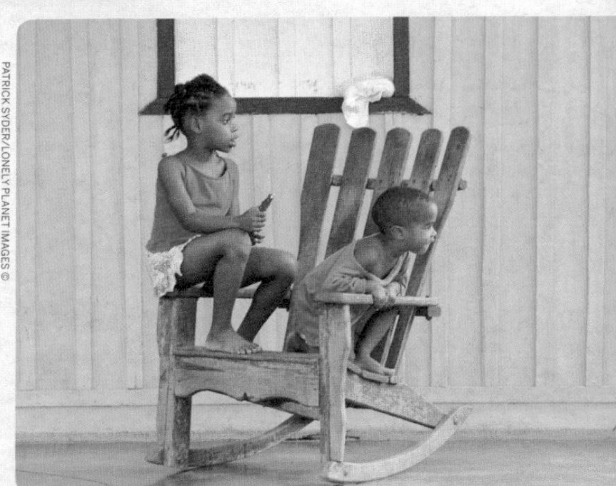

PATRICK SYDER/LONELY PLANET IMAGES ©

Eclectic Architecture

4 Cuba's architecture mirrors its ethnic heritage. Take a muscular slice of Spanish baroque, sprinkle in some French classicism, a generous portion of North American art deco and a hint of European art nouveau. Now add the sweat of Afro-Cuban slave labor, and the odd spark of creative modernism, and there you have it. Sometimes extreme yet rarely constant, Cuban architecture retains certain binding threads, a definable 'Cuban-ness' that sets it markedly apart from other genres. Visit the Unesco-listed cities of Havana, Trinidad, Cienfuegos and Camagüey to see for yourself.

Gran Teatro de la Habana and Hotel Inglaterra (p67), Havana, left

CHRISTOPHER GROENHOUT/LONELY PLANET IMAGES ©

Idyllic Beach Escapes

5 There's the big showy one in the resort and the wild, windswept one on the north coast; the sheltered palm-fringed one on a paradisiacal key and the unashamedly nudist one on a secluded southern island. Cuba's beaches come in all shapes, sizes and shades. Search around long enough and you're sure to find your own slice of nirvana. Although resorts have hijacked the best strips of sand, isolated havens remain. Highlights include Playa Pilar (p306) on Cayo Guillermo, Playa Maguana (p441) near Baracoa, and Playa Ancón (p286) in Sancti Spíritus province. Playa Ancón, right

FRANK CARTER/LONELY PLANET IMAGES ©

RICHARD I'ANSON/LONELY PLANET IMAGES ©

Lounging in Varadero

6 If you've ever been hit with a lazy desire to do nothing but lie on a comfortable sun-lounger, devour a few chapters of Dostoyevsky and drink minty mojitos until the sand flies come home, look no further. All this and more is possible in sun-drenched Varadero (p205), Cuba's manufactured modern beach resort. Hosting over 50 hotels on a 20km-long beach-embellished peninsula, Varadero is a place apart from the rest of the island, but it offers a slew of sporty activities that are nigh on impossible elsewhere. Windsurfing at Varadero, left

Bird-Watching

7 Crocodiles aside, Cuba has little impressive fauna, but the paucity of animals is more than made up for by the abundance of birdlife. Approximately 350 species inhabit the shores of this distinct and ecologically weird tropical archipelago, a good two dozen of them endemic. Look out in particular for the colorful *tocororo*, the tiny bee hummingbird, the critically endangered ivory-billed woodpecker and the world's largest flamingo nesting site. Guided bird-watching trips are a national specialty.

FGI/IMAGEBROKER

ANDREA THOMPSON/PHOTOLIBRARY

Cuba's Revolutionary Heritage

8 An improbable escape from a shipwrecked leisure yacht, handsome bearded guerrillas meting out Robin Hood–style justice and a classic David v Goliath struggle that was won convincingly by the (extreme) underdogs: Cuba's revolutionary war reads like the pages of a – ahem – Steven Soderbergh movie script. Better than watching it on the big screen is the opportunity to visit the revolutionary sites in person. Little changed in over 50 years are the disembarkation point of the Granma and Fidel's wartime HQ at mountaintop Commandancia de la Plata (p373). Che Guevara mural, Havana, above

KARL BLACKWELL/LONELY PLANET IMAGES ©

Havana's Colonial Hotels

9 Never in the field of architectural preservation has so much been achieved by so many with so few resources. When sitting in your tranquil colonial Havana hotel say a fleeting *gracias* to Havana City Historian, Eusebio Leal, whose planning and foresight launched an improbable restoration program and allowed over a dozen once-dilapidated buildings to be refashioned into the colonial jewels they once were. If your budget can take it, splash out on a sleepover in Habana Vieja (p54). It's a magical experience.

Diving & Snorkeling in the Caribbean

10 There'll be protestations, no doubt, but let's say it anyway: Cuba is home to the best diving in the Caribbean. The reason: unrivaled water clarity, virgin reefs and sheltered Caribbean waters that teem with millions of fish. Accessibility for divers varies from the swim-out walls of the Bay of Pigs to the hard-to-reach underwater nirvana of the Jardines de Reina archipelago. For repeat visitors Punta Francés (p159) on Isla de la Juventud – host of an annual underwater photography competition – reigns supreme.

MICHAEL LAWRENCE/LONELY PLANET IMAGES ©

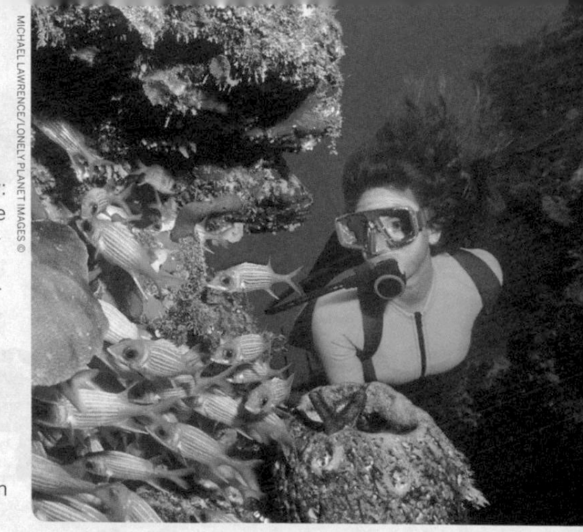

VINCENT MACNAMARA/ALAMY

Hemingway's Favorite Fishing Spots

11 When it comes to rating the planet's best deep-sea fishing spots, it's hard to argue with legendary fisherman, Cuba-phile and Nobel Prize–winning author, Ernest Hemingway. Papa adored Cuba for many reasons, not least for the quality of its offshore fishing, enhanced by its location abutting the fast-flowing waters of the Gulf Stream. Cuba's best deep-sea fishing waters hug the abundant north coast keys and few are finer than the archetypal 'island in the stream,' Cayo Guillermo (p307).

Ciénaga de Zapata's Wildlife

12 One of the few parts of Cuba that has never been truly tamed, the Zapata Swamp (p227) is as close to pure wilderness as the country gets. This is the home of the endangered Cuban crocodile, various amphibians, the bee hummingbird and over a dozen different plant habitats. It also qualifies as the Caribbean's largest wetlands, protected in numerous ways, most importantly as a Unesco Biosphere Reserve and Ramsar Convention Site. Come here to fish, bird-watch, hike and see nature at its purest. Turtles, Ciénaga de Zapata

ANDREA INNOCENTI/ALAMY

CHRISTOPHER BAKER /LONELY PLANET IMAGES ©

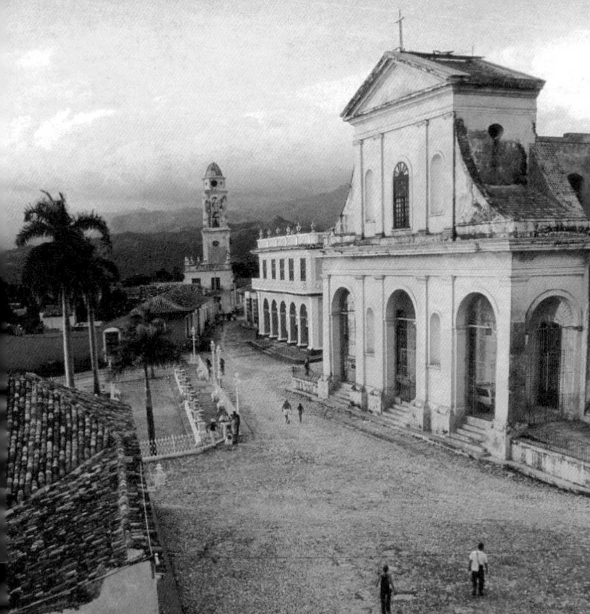

Time-Warped Trinidad

14 Soporific Trinidad went to sleep in 1850 and never really woke up. This strange twist of fate is good news for modern travelers who can roam freely through the perfectly preserved mid-19th-century sugar town like voyeurs from another era. Though it's no secret these days, the time-warped streets still have the power to enchant with their grand colonial homestays, easily accessible countryside and exciting live music scene. But this is also a real working town loaded with all the foibles and fun of 21st-century Cuba. Iglesia Parroquial de la Santísima, Trinidad (p 278), left

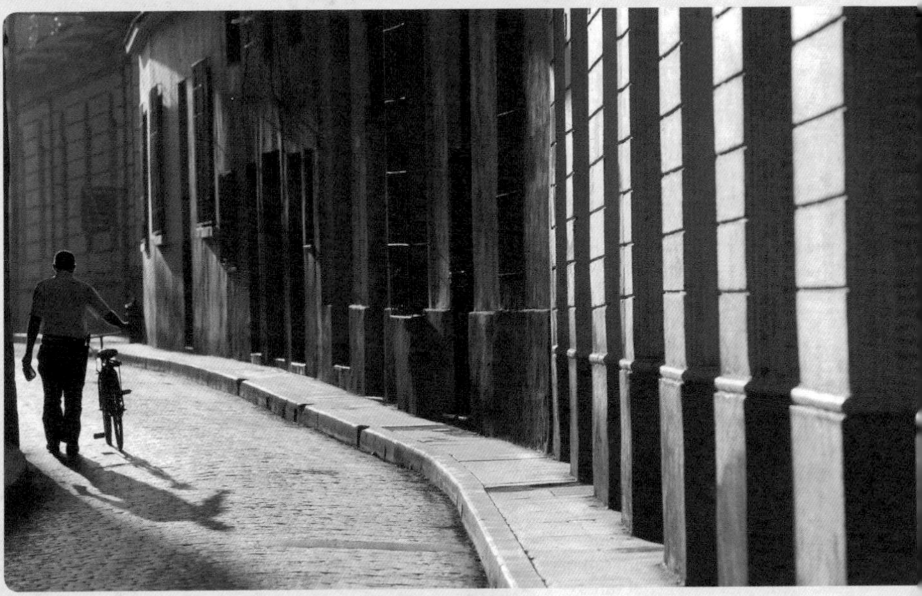

PETER ADAMS/ALAMY

Labyrinthine Streets of Camagüey

13 Get lost! No, that's not an abrupt British put-down; rather it's a savvy recommendation for any traveler passing through the city of *tinajones*, churches and erstwhile pirates – aka Camagüey. A perennial rule-breaker, Camagüey was founded on a street grid that deviated from almost every other Spanish colonial city in Latin America. Here the lanes are as labyrinthine as a Moroccan medina, hiding Catholic churches and triangular plazas, and revealing left-field artistic secrets at every turn.

Cycling Through the Valle de Viñales

JERRY ALEXANDER/LONELY PLANET IMAGES ©

15 With less traffic on the roads than 1940s Britain, Cuba is ideal for cycling and there's no better place to do it than in one of its most quintessential rural environments – the Viñales Valley (p183). Viñales offers all the ingredients of a tropical Tour de France: craggy *mogotes*, impossibly green tobacco fields, bucolic *campesino* huts and spirit-lifting viewpoints at every gear change. Fortunately the terrain is relatively flat and, if you can procure a decent bike, your biggest dilemma will be where to stop for your sunset-toasting mojito.

FRANK CARTER/LONELY PLANET IMAGES ©

Cienfuegos' Classical French Architecture

16 There's a certain *je ne sais quoi* about bay-side Cienfuegos, Cuba's self-proclaimed 'Pearl of the South.' Through hell, high water and an economically debilitating Special Period, this is a city that has always retained its poise. The elegance is best seen in the architecture, a homogenous cityscape laid out in the early 19th century by settlers from France and the US. Dip into the cultural life around the city center and its adjacent garden suburb of Punta Gorda to absorb the Gallic refinement.

Las Terrazas' Eco-Village

17 Back in 1968, when the fledgling environmental movement was a bolshie protest group for long-haired students in duffle coats, the prophetic Cubans – concerned about the ecological cost of island-wide deforestation – came up with rather a good idea. After saving hectares of denuded forest from an ecological disaster, a group of industrious workers built their own eco-village, Las Terrazas, and set about colonizing it with artists, musicians, coffee growers and the architecturally unique Hotel Moka (p149).

WOLFGANG KAEHLER/PHOTOLIBRARY

RICHARD I'ANSON/LONELY PLANET IMAGES ©

Revolutionary Billboards & Wall Art

18 While the directional signage in Cuba is famously thin on the ground, there are no lack of pointers toward socialism, the 'battle of ideas' and Fidel Castro's face. In a country devoid of gaudy advertising, billboards have become the preserve of political propagandists. You can't travel far in Cuba without encountering a Che motto, a rebuke to the *Yanquis* or a quasi-biblical poem extolling the heroic virtues of José Martí. Whatever your position on the diplomatic finger-wagging, this is part of the fabric of the Cuban countryside. Che Guevara billboard, Cienfuegos

JOHN HARDEN/CORBIS

Youthful Energy of Santa Clara

19 Check your preconceived ideas about this country at the city limits. Santa Clara is everything you thought Cuba wasn't. Erudite students, spontaneous nightlife, daring creativity and private home-stays in abodes stuffed with more antiques than the local decorative-arts museum. Pop into the drag show at Club Mejunje (p256) or hang out for a while with the enthusiastic students in La Casa de la Ciudad (p251). Musicians rehearsing, La Casa de la Cuidad, Santa Clara, above

Unlocking the Secrets of Matanzas

20 Matanzas is the *Titanic* of Cuba, a sunken liner left to languish in the murky depths, but where flickers of an erstwhile beauty still remain. After manicured Varadero, the city hits you like a slap in the face but, with a little time, its gigantic historical legacy will teach you more about the real Cuba than 20 repeat visits to the resorts. Matanzas' refined culture congregates in the Teatro Sauto (p198), while its African 'soul' manifests itself in the energetic rumba that takes off in Plaza de la Vigía (p198).

Cuba's Ebullient Festivals

21 Through war, austerity, rationing and hardship, the Cubans have retained their infectious joie de vivre. Even during the darkest days of the Special Period, the feisty festivals never stopped, a testament to the country's capacity to put politics aside and get on with the important business of living. The best shows involve fireworks in Remedios, *folklórico* dancing in Santiago de Cuba, movies in Gibara and every conceivable genre of music in Havana. Arrive prepared. Fireworks at Las Parrandas festival (p26), Remedios

Baracoa's Spicy Food & Culture

22 Over the hills and far away on the easternmost limb of Guantánamo province lies isolated Baracoa, a small yet historically significant settlement, weird even by Cuban standards for its fickle Atlantic weather, eccentric local populace and unrelenting desire to be – well – different. Watch locals scale coconut palms, listen to bands play *kiribá*, the local take on *son*, and – above all – enjoy the infinitely spicier, richer and more inventive food, starting with the sweet treat *cucuruchu*. Young men playing dominoes, Baracoa

BRUNO MORANDI/ALAMY

Folklórico Dance in Santiago de Cuba

23 Ah...there's nothing quite as transcendental as the hypnotic beat of the Santería drums summoning up the spirits of the *orishas* (African deities). But, while most Afro-Cuban religious rites are only for initiates, the drumming and dances of Cuba's *folklórico* troupes are open to all. Formed in the 1960s to keep the ancient slave culture of Cuba alive, *folklórico* groups enjoy strong government patronage, and their energetic and colorful shows remain spontaneous, true to their roots and grittily authentic. Dance school, Santiago de Cuba

PABLO CORRAL VEGA/CORBIS

Pico Turquino – Cuba's Highest Mountain

24 The trek up Cuba's highest mountain, Pico Turquino (p376), is a rare privilege. Guides are mandatory for this tough two- to three-day 17km trek through the steep broccoli-green forests of the Sierra Maestra that acts a kind of history lesson, nature trail and bird-watching extravaganza all rolled into one. Revolutionary buffs should make a side trip to Fidel's wartime jungle HQ on the way up. Palm trees near Pico Turquino, Sierra Maestra range

need to know

Currency

» Cuban convertibles (CUC$)

Language

» Spanish

When to Go

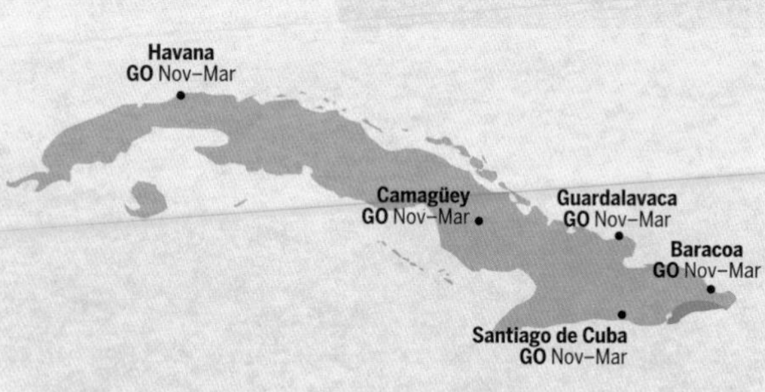

High Season (Nov–Mar & Jul–Aug)

» Prices are 30% higher and hotels may require advance bookings

» Prices are higher still for two weeks around Christmas and New Year

» Weather is cooler and dryer

Shoulder (Apr & Oct)

» Look out for special deals outside of peak season

» Watch out for Easter vacation, when prices and crowds increase

Low Season (May, Jun & Sep)

» Some hotels offer fewer facilities

» There's a hurricane risk between June and November and higher chance of rain

Your Daily Budget

Budget less than
CUC$60

» Casas particulares: CUC$20–30

» Government-run restaurants: CUC$15–20

» Cheap museum entry: CUC$3–6

Midrange
CUC $60–120

» Boutique hotels: CUC$35–60

» Eat in paladares: CUC$17–22

» Travel on Viazul buses

Top End over
CUC$120

» Resort or historical hotel: CUC$150–200

» Car hire or taxis: CUC$60–70

» Evening cabaret: CUC$35–60

Money

» Cuba is primarily a cash economy. Credit cards are accepted in resort hotels and work in most ATMs. ATMs rarely accept debit cards.

Visas

» A travel card valid for 30 days is usually included in your flight package. US travelers are prohibited from spending money in Cuba.

Cell Phones

» Limited coverage. You can prebuy services from the state-run phone company, Cubacel.

Transport

» Good system of intercity Viazul buses. Trains are slow and uncomfortable. Car hire is widely available but pricey.

Websites

» **AfroCuba Web** (www.afrocubaweb.com) Everything on Cuban culture

» **BBC** (www.bbc.co.uk) Interesting correspondent reports on Cuba

» **Cuba Absolutely** (www.cubaabsolutely.com) Art, culture, business and travel

» **Cubacasas.net** (www.cubacasas.net) Information, photos and contact details for casas particulares

» **LonelyPlanet.com** (www.lonelyplanet.com/cuba) Destination information, hotel bookings, traveler forum and more

Exchange Rates

Argentina	ARS$1	CUC$0.23
Australia	A$1	CUC$0.92
Canada	C$1	CUC$0.91
Europe	€1	CUC$1.23
Japan	¥100	CUC$1.25
Mexico	MXN$1	CUC$0.08
New Zealand	NZ$1	CUC$0.82
UK	£1	CUC$1.46
US	US$1	CUC$0.93

For current exchange rates see www.xe.com.

Important Numbers

To call between provinces, dial ☎0 + area code + number.

Emergency	☎106
Directory assistance	☎113
Police	☎106
Fire	☎105

Arriving in Cuba

» **Havana – Aeropuerto Internacional José Martí**

There are no regular buses or trains running direct from the airport into the city center. Taxis cost CUC$20 to CUC$25 and take 30 to 40 minutes to reach most of the city center hotels.

You can change money at the bank in the arrivals hall.

Double Economy

» Cuba has a double economy, whereby convertibles and Cuban pesos circulate simultaneously. In theory, tourists are only supposed to use convertibles, but in practice, there is nothing to stop you walking into a Cadeca (change booth) and swapping your convertibles into *moneda nacional* (Cuban pesos). With an exchange rate of 25 pesos per convertible, there are good saving opportunities with pesos if you're willing to sacrifice a little (or a lot!) in quality, service and/or comfort.

» Tellingly, the double economy cuts both ways. Cubans, who earn between 200 and 800 pesos (CUC$8 and CUC$32) a month, have to survive in an entirely different economy from outsiders; a financial minefield where access to valuable convertibles is a daily crapshoot between tips, personal guile and who you know.

if you like...

White-Sand Beaches

Combine the words 'Caribbean' and 'island' and you'll get more than a hint of Cuba's dazzling beach potential. The best scoops of sand are situated mainly – though not exclusively – on the north coast. Some occupy paradisiacal *cayos*, others have been turned into megaresorts. For the antisocial, plenty of remoter spots survive untainted.

Playa Pilar Hemingway's favorite is now a much-decorated travel mag photo opportunity backed by big dunes but – as yet – no hotels (p306).

Playa Maguana Wind-whipped waves and bruised clouds all add to the ethereal ambience of Baracoa's finest beach (p441).

Playa Pesquero Walk for 200m through clear bathwater-temperature ocean and still only be up to your waist (p353).

Playa Sirena Huge football-field-sized beach on what is essentially a private tourist island where the dress code is 'bare all' (p167).

Playa Los Pinos Just you, some driftwood, a good book and perhaps the odd local offering cooked lobster for lunch (p324).

Amazing Architecture

When Castro pressed the pause button on Cuban history in 1959 he inadvertently did the colonial buildings a big favor. Protected from the tentacles of modern development, old architectural heirlooms have survived and – in some cases – found new life in meticulous redevelopment projects.

Habana Vieja Like an old attic full of dusty relics, Havana is a treasure chest of eclectic architecture awaiting rediscovery (p54).

Cienfuegos Cuba's most architecturally homogenous city is a love letter to French neoclassicism, full of elegant cupolas and refined columns (p233).

Camagüey Unlike any other town in Cuba, Unesco-listed Camagüey has an unusual street plan of labyrinthine lanes and baroque spires that hide a devout Catholic soul (p310).

Trinidad Quite possibly one of the most beguiling and best-preserved towns in the Caribbean, tranquil Trinidad is a riot of colonial baroque (p275).

Nightlife & Dancing

'Two fatherlands I have: Cuba and the night,' wrote José Martí. He wasn't far wrong. Cuba is a different place after dark, an atmospheric mélange of passion and pathos. If you want to feel as if you've wandered unknowingly onto the set of a 1950s film noir, you've come to the right place.

Santa Clara This is the city where the 'next big thing' happens first: drag shows, rock 'n' roll music and everything in between (p255).

Cabarets A flamboyant mix of the kitschy and the cool, cabarets are one of the few elements of opulent prerevolutionary life that refused to die (p108).

Casas de la Trova Cuba's old-fashioned spit-and-sawdust music houses are determined to keep the essence of traditional Cuban music alive (p477).

Uneac Imagine a cultural center full of latent artistic talent where entry is free and everyone greets you like a long-lost friend. Welcome to the Unión de Escritores y Artistas de Cuba (Union of Cuban Writers and Artists), *amigos* (p468).

BRENT WINEBRENNER/LONELY PLANET IMAGES ©

» Contrasting architectural styles in Habana Vieja, Havana (p54)

Islands

Though often referred to as an island, Cuba is actually an archipelago. Its largest outlying landmass is La Isla de la Juventud, the sixth-largest island in the Caribbean, but there are plenty of smaller, remoter islets and *cayos* to keep you occupied for – oh – at least a year.

Cayo Jutías Tree Rat Island's name doesn't really do justice to its exotic location – not to mention its beach – just off the north coast of Pinar del Río province (p191).

Cayo Saetia A surreal outpost in Holguín province that sports one rustic hotel and a reserve full of exotic, nonindigenous animals (p362).

Cayo Guillermo Of the 4000 or so islands off Cuba's north coast, Guillermo was Hemingway's favorite – and who's going to argue with that? (p307).

Cayo Sabinel With no population but plenty of gorgeous beaches, the solitude on Sabinel probably has a shelf life. Get there while it lasts (p324).

Under the Radar

Sometimes the power fails, the public transport is awful and the buildings look more like demolition jobs than dreamy ruins. Welcome to the real Cuba, where friendships are forged, ideas exchanged, politics debated and realities observed.

Gibara The home of the 'poor man's film festival' is rich in wild, ocean-side scenery and creeping Holguín magic (p351).

Marea del Portillo Turn right outside the resorts and go for a wander in the magnificent mountains, untouched since the *Granma* yacht ran aground in 1956 (p382).

Matanzas Varadero's outcast sibling lacks sun-loungers and stuff-yourself-silly buffets, but it has soul *socios* – if you're willing to look for them (p196).

Las Tunas Cuba's least-visited provincial capital defies its 'boring' stereotype on Saturday nights when there's a rodeo in town (p330).

Holguín *Jinetero*-free streets, an underrated baseball team nicknamed 'the dogs' and a beer-drinking donkey named Pancho. Anyone up for a day out in Holguín (p339)?

Wildlife-Watching

Since it rehabilitated its declining crocodile population in the 1970s and '80s, Cuba's fauna has regained its luster. There are no big land mammals here, but you can get acquainted with the world's smallest hummingbird, the tiniest of all frogs and birds migrating from both North and South America.

Ciénaga de Zapata A microcosm of Cuban wildlife, including the critically endangered Cuban crocodile (p224), in a 66-sq-km swamp.

Parque Nacional Alejandro de Humbolt Sky-high levels of endemism make Humboldt, home to the world's smallest frog, an ecological rarity (p442).

Sierra del Chorrillo Nonindigenous exotic animals, including zebra and deer, in a quintessentially Cuban grassland setting (p321).

Río Máximo Behold the largest colony of nesting flamingos in the world on Camagüey's north coast (p323).

Guanahacabibes Crabs and iguanas do battle with jeep traffic on Cuba's windswept western wilderness (p181).

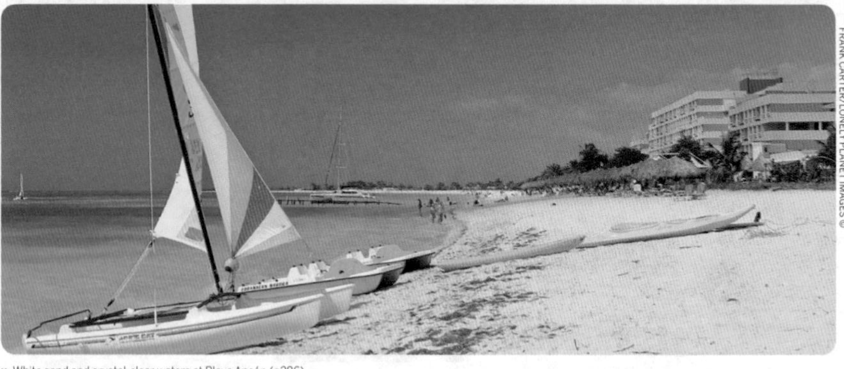

FRANK CARTER/LONELY PLANET IMAGES ©

» White sand and crystal-clear waters at Playa Ancón (p286)

Diving & Snorkeling

Diving in Cuba is a trip in its own right. The clearest, most pristine spots hug the more sheltered Caribbean waters off the south coast, while the north is kissed by one of the largest coral reefs in the world.

Isla de la Juventud Worth the effort to get there, La Isla is famed for its clear water and hosts an underwater photography competition (p165).

Jardines de la Reina This heavily protected archipelago has zero infrastructure and safeguards the most unspoiled reefs in the Caribbean (p307).

María la Gorda Over 50 dive sites and easy access off Cuba's western tip make this small resort 'diver's central' (p181).

Bahia de los Cochinos Once infamous for another reason, the Bay of Pigs has rediscovered its raison d'être – damn good diving (p228).

Playa Santa Lucía It's worth braving this rather tacky resort strip to experience the best diving on Cuba's north coast (p325).

Relaxing at a Resort

Resorts suck up a huge proportion of Cuba's annual visitors, most of whom fly in during the winter when the weather turns ugly in Europe and North America. Varadero is the big one, with over 50 hotels, and is a world apart from the rationed reality found elsewhere. Further east, three more big resort areas hug the northern littoral, while the south coast remains less developed outside the tourist island of Cayo Largo del Sur.

Varadero The biggest resort in Cuba isn't to everyone's taste, but it's still insanely popular (p205).

Cayo Coco An island getaway linked to the mainland by a causeway, Cayo Coco is low-rise and more subtle than Varadero (p303).

Guardalavaca Three separate enclaves on Holguín's north coast offer three different price brackets, with Playa Pesquero selling the poshest packages (p354).

Cayo Santa Maria The still-developing *cayos* of Villa Clara province retain a refreshingly tranquil feel (p262).

Pirates & Forts

As the prized jewel in Spain's once-lucrative Caribbean empire, Cuba was a dangling carrot for pirates in the 16th and 17th centuries, who regularly terrorized its beleaguered coastline. Today, the legacy of past battles can be witnessed in a cache of remarkably well-preserved forts.

Havana's Forts Four of the finest examples of 16th-century military architecture in the Americas are preserved in their almost original state (p64).

Camagüey Moved twice to avoid the attentions of pirates, Camagüey was once sacked by Welshman Henry Morgan; the locals redesigned the streets to prevent a repeat job (p310).

La Roca Two hundred years in the making and never really used for its original purpose, Santiago's La Roca is today a Unesco World Heritage Site (p400).

Baracoa The 'first city' has three small but stalwart forts that are today home to a museum, a hotel and a restaurant (p434).

If you like... churches, you'll find the most varied stash in Camagüey (p316), Cuba's Catholic heart.

Revolutionary History

Picture January 1959: pistols at dawn, dark shadows descending from the Sierra Maestra Mountains and Batista's New Year's Eve party interrupted by a posse of unwashed, bearded guerrillas. Cuba's revolution sounds like the script of a 1950s movie; but – lest we forget – it started long before Fidel Castro rolled triumphantly into Havana atop a jeep.

Santa Clara 'Che City' is the home of Guevara's mausoleum, myriad statues and a fascinating open-air museum (p263).

Bayamo The understated capital of Granma province, where Cuba's first revolution was ignited in 1868 (p372).

Sierra Maestra Flecked with historical significance, including the mountain ridge HQ where Castro directed operations during the revolutionary war (p373).

Santiago de Cuba The self-proclaimed 'City of Revolutionaries' has potent reminders of past battles on almost every street corner (p387).

Museo de la Revolución Cuba's most comprehensive museum is a one-stop immersion on all things revolutionary (p108).

Live Music

No introduction required. Cuba hemorrhages music of all types: *son*, salsa, *songo*, *reggaetón*, opera, classical, jazz – and that's just the above-ground stuff. You could quite happily plan multiple trips around music alone – and many do. Undertake some homework beforehand and earmark the styles and genres that best suit your taste.

La Casa de la Música The trendy choice. Casas de la Música mix live music with late-night dancing and pull in big names like Los Van Van (p109).

Casas de la Trova The traditional choice. *Son* and boleros give an old-fashioned lilt to these cultural houses that characterize every Cuban provincial town (p477).

La Tumba Francesa The esoteric choice. Mysterious *folklórico* dance troupes in Guantánamo and Santiago de Cuba provinces perform musical rites with a Haitian influence (p407).

Street Rumba Salt-of-the-earth Havana and Santiago specialize in gritty street rumba – mesmerizing drumming and dance rituals that can summon up the spirit of the *orishas* (p475).

Protected Areas

Once dubbed the world's most sustainable country by the World Wildlife Foundation (WWF), Cuba's dearth of 21st-century-style consumerism has had some positive repercussions for its environment. There are six Unesco Biosphere Reserves here, plus 13 national parks and numerous other flora and fauna refuges.

Ciénaga de Zapata This primary wilderness area is an uninhabited swamp that supports over four different ecosystems, along with copious birds, crocs and amphibian creatures (p224).

Parque Nacional Alejandro de Humboldt Humboldt is a wilderness area that protects one of the largest remaining tracts of natural rainforest in the Caribbean (p442).

Sierra del Rosario A one-time ecological disaster area that was turned around by far-sighted Cuban planners in the 1970s and '80s (p148).

Topes de Collantes Cuba's most accessible natural zone is replete with wondrous rainforest, waterfalls and multiple-day hikes (p289).

month by month

Top Events

1. **Carnaval de Santiago de Cuba,** July
2. **Festival Internacional de Cine Pobre,** April
3. **Las Parrandas,** December
4. **Festival Internacional de Jazz,** February
5. **Hemingway Marlin Fishing Tournament,** May

January

The tourist season hits full swing, and the whole country has added buoyancy and life. Cold fronts bring occasionally chilly evenings.

Día de la Liberación

As well as seeing in the New Year with roast pork and a bottle of rum, Cubans celebrate January 1st as the triumph of the Revolution, the anniversary of Fidel Castro's 1959 victory.

February

The peak tourist season continues and high demand can lead to overbooking, particularly in the rental-car market. Calm seas and less fickle weather promote better water clarity, making this an ideal time to enjoy diving and snorkeling.

Feria Internacional del Libro

First held in 1930, the International Book Fair is headquartered in Havana's Fortaleza de San Carlos de la Cabaña, but it later goes on the road to other cities. Highlights include book presentations, special readings and the prestigious Casa de las Américas prize.

Festival Internacional de Jazz

The International Jazz Festival is staged in the Karl Marx, Mella and Amadeo Roldán Theaters in Havana and draws in top figures from around the world.

Diving with Clarity

Calm conditions promote clear water for diving, particularly on Cuba's south coast. The country's prime diving nexus, La Isla de la Juventud, consequently holds the annual Fotosub International Underwater Photography competition.

March

Spring offers Cuba's best wildlife-watching opportunities, particularly for migrant birds. With dryer conditions, it is also an ideal time to indulge in hiking, cycling or numerous other outdoor activities.

Fiesta de la Toronja

Famous for its citrus plantations, Isla de la Juventud celebrates the annual grapefruit harvest with this animated excuse for a party in Nueva Gerona where the *guachi* (grapefruit schnapps) flows freely.

Festival Internacional de Trova

Held since 1962 in honor of *trova* pioneer Pepe Sánchez, this festival invades the parks, streets and music houses of Santiago de Cuba in a showcase of the popular genre.

Bird-Watching

March is a cross-over period when migrant birds from both North and South America join Cuba's resident endemics en route for warmer or colder climes. There's no better time to polish off your binoculars.

April

Economy-seeking visitors should avoid the Easter holiday, which sees another spike in tourist numbers and prices. Otherwise April is a

pleasant month with good fly-fishing potential off the south coast.

Semana de la Cultura

During the first week of April, Baracoa commemorates the landing of Antonio Maceo at Duaba on April 1, 1895, with a raucous Carnaval along the Malecón.

Festival Internacional de Cine Pobre

Gibara's celebration of low- and no-budget cinema (see boxed text, p353) has been an annual event since 2003, when it was inaugurated by late Cuban film director Humberto Sales. Highlights include film-showing workshops and discussions on movie-making with limited resources.

Bienal Internacional del Humor

You can't be serious! Cuba's unique humor festival takes place in San Antonio de los Baños in out-of-the-way Artemisa province. Headquartered at the celebrated Museo del Humor (p144), talented scribblers try to outdo each other by drawing ridiculous caricatures. Hilarious!

May

Possibly the cheapest month of all, May is the low point between the foreign crowds of winter and the domestic barrage of summer. Look out for special deals offered by resort hotels and significantly cheaper prices all around.

Romerías de Mayo

This religious festival takes place in the city of Holguín during the first week of May and culminates with a procession to the top of the city's emblematic Loma de la Cruz, a small shrine atop a 275m hill.

Cubadisco

An annual get-together of foreign and Cuban record producers and companies, Cubadisco hosts music concerts, a trade fair and a Grammy-style awards ceremony that encompasses every musical genre from chamber music to pop.

Hemingway International Marlin Fishing Tournament

Famously won by Fidel in 1960, this annual contest was set up by Ernest Hemingway in 1951 and runs out of the eponymous Havana marina. Teams of up to four use catch-and-release methods.

June

The Caribbean hurricane season begins inauspiciously. A smattering of esoteric provincial festivals keeps June interesting. Prices are still low and, with the heat and humidity rising, travelers from Europe and Canada tend to stay away.

Jornada Cucalambeana

Cuba's celebration of country music, and the witty 10-line *décimas* (stanzas) that go with it, takes place about 3km outside unassuming Las Tunas at Motel Cornito (p331), the former home of erstwhile country-music king, Juan Fajardo 'El Cucalambé.'

Festival Internacional 'Boleros de Oro'

Organized by Uneac (Unión de Escritores y Artistas de Cuba; Union of Cuban Writers and Artists), the Boleros de Oro was created by Cuban composer and musicologist José Loyola Fernández in 1986 as a global celebration of this distinctive Cuban musical genre. Most events take place in Havana's Teatro Mella.

Fiestas Sanjuaneras

This feisty carnival in Trinidad on the last weekend in June is a showcase for the local *vaqueros* (cowboys), who gallop their horses through the narrow cobbled streets.

July

High summer is when Cubans vacation; expect the beaches, campismos and cheaper hotels to be mobbed. The July heat also inspires two of the nation's hottest events: Santiago's carnaval and the annual polemics of July 26th.

Festival del Caribe, Fiesta del Fuego

The so-called Festival of Caribbean Culture, Fire Celebration in early July kicks off an action-packed month for Santiago with exhibitions, song, dance, poetry and religious-tinged rituals from all around the Caribbean.

Día de la Rebeldía Nacional

On July 26th the Cubans 'celebrate' Fidel Castro's failed 1953 attack on Santiago's Moncada Barracks (see boxed text, p394). The event is a national holiday and – in days when he enjoyed better health – Castro was famous for making five-hour speeches. Expect *un poco* (a little) politics and *mucho* (much) eating, drinking and being merry.

Carnaval de Santiago de Cuba

Arguably the biggest and most colorful carnival in the Caribbean, the famous Santiago shindig (p401) at the end of July is a riot of floats, dancers, rum, rumba and more. Come and join in the very *caliente* (hot) action.

August

While Santiago retires to sleep off its hangover, Havana gears up for its own annual shindig. Beaches and campismos still heave with holidaying Cubans while tourist hotels creak under a fresh influx of visitors from Mediterranean Europe.

Festival Internacional 'Habana Hip-Hop'

Organized by the Asociación Hermanos Saíz – a youth arm of Uneac – the annual Havana Hip-Hop Festival is a chance for the island's young musical creators to improvise and swap ideas.

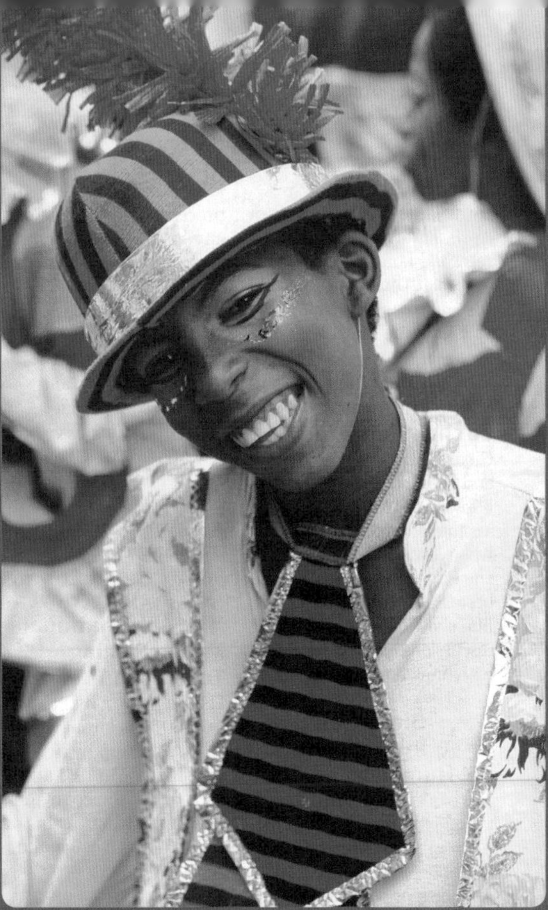

TIM HUGHES/LONELY PLANET IMAGES ©

(Above) Young boy dressed up for Carnaval celebrations, Santiago de Cuba
(Below) Dancers performing in the Carnaval parade, Havana

RACHEL LEWIS/LONELY PLANET IMAGES ©

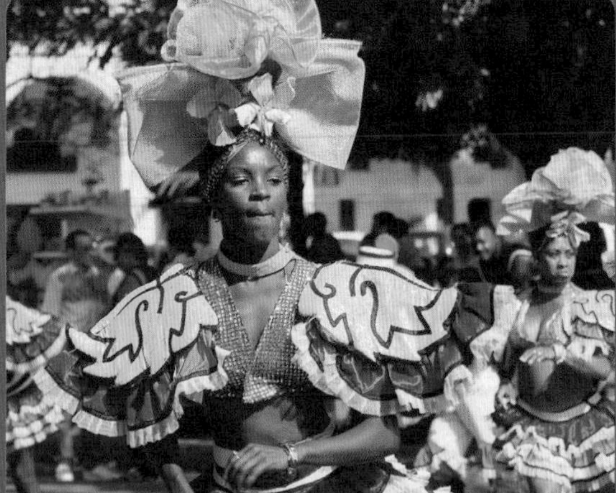

Carnaval de la Habana

Parades, dancing, music, colorful costumes and striking effigies – Havana's annual summer shindig might not be as famous as its more rootsy Santiago de Cuba counterpart, but the celebrations and processions along the Malecón leave plenty of other city carnivals in the shade.

September

It's peak hurricane season. The outside threat of a 'big one' sends most Cuba-philes running for cover and tourist numbers hit a second trough. The storm-resistant take advantage of cheaper prices and near-empty beaches. But, beware – some facilities close down completely.

Festival Internacional de Música Benny Moré

The Barbarian of Rhythm is remembered in this biannual celebration of his suave music, headquartered in the singer's small birth town of Santa Isabel de las Lajas in Cienfuegos province (see boxed text, p244).

Fiesta de Nuestra Señora de la Caridad

Every September 8th religious devotees from around Cuba partake in a pilgrimage to the Basílica de Nuestra Señora del Cobre (p419), near Santiago, to honor Cuba's venerated patron saint (and her alter ego, the Santería *orisha*, Ochún).

October

Continuing storm threats and persistent rain keep all but the most stalwart travelers away until the end of the month. While the solitude can be refreshing in Havana, life in the peripheral resorts can be deathly quiet and lacking in atmosphere.

Festival Internacional de Ballet de la Habana

Hosted by the Cuban National Ballet, this annual festival brings together dance companies, ballerinas and a mixed audience of foreigners and Cubans for a week of expositions, galas, and classical and contemporary ballet. It has been held in even-numbered years since its inception in 1960.

Festival del Bailador Rumbero

During the 10 days following October 10th, Matanzas rediscovers its rumba roots with talented local musicians performing in the city's Teatro Sauto.

November

Get ready for the big invasion from the north – and an accompanying hike in hotel rates! Over a quarter of Cuba's tourists come from Canada; they start arriving in early November, as soon as the weather turns frigid in Vancouver and Toronto.

Fiesta de los Bandas Rojo y Azul

Considered one of the most important manifestations of Cuban *campesino* (country person) culture, this esoteric fiesta in the settlement of Majagua, in Ciego de Ávila province, splits the town into two teams (red and blue) that compete against each other in boisterous dancing and music contests.

Marabana

The popular Havana marathon draws between 2000 and 3000 competitors from around the globe. It's a two-lap course, though there is also a half-marathon and races for 5km and 10km distances.

December

Christmas and the New Year see Cuba's busiest and most expensive tourist spike. Resorts nearly double their prices and rooms sell out fast. The nation goes firework-crazy in a handful of riotous festivals. Book ahead!

Festival Nacional de Changüí

Since 2003, Guantánamo has celebrated its indigenous music in this rootsy music festival held in early December. Look out for Elio Revé Jr and his orchestra.

Festival Internacional del Nuevo Cine Latinoamericano

This internationally renowned film festival (www.habanafilmfestival.com), held in cinemas across Havana, illustrates Cuba's growing influence in Latin American cinema around the world.

Procesión de San Lázaro

Every year on December 17th, Cubans descend en masse on the venerated Santuario de San Lázaro (p134) in Santiago de las Vegas, on the outskirts of Havana. Some come on bloodied knees, others walk barefoot for kilometers to exorcize evil spirits and pay off debts for miracles granted.

Las Parrandas

A firework frenzy that takes place every Christmas Eve in Remedios (p259) in Villa Clara province, Las Parrandas sees the town divide into two teams that compete against each other to see who can come up with the most colorful floats and the loudest bangs!

Las Charangas de Bejucal

Didn't like Las Parrandas? Then try Bejucal's Las Charangas, Mayabeque province's cacophonous alternative to the firework fever further east. The town splits into the exotically named Espino de Oro (Golden Thorn) and Ceiba de Plata (Silver Silk-Cotton Tree).

itineraries

Whether you've got six days or 60, these itineraries provide a starting point for the trip of a lifetime. Want more inspiration? Head online to lonelyplanet.com/thorntree to chat with other travelers.

Two Weeks
The Classic

Fall in love with classic Cuba in **Havana**, with its museums, forts, theaters and rum. Head southeast next, via the **Bay of Pigs**, to French-flavored **Cienfuegos**, an architectural monument to 19th-century neoclassicism. After a night of Gallic style, travel a couple of hours down the road to colonial **Trinidad**, with its cache of easily reachable beaches and more museums per head than anywhere else in Cuba. **Santa Clara** is a rite of passage for Che pilgrims but also great for smart private rooms and an upbeat nightlife. Further east, **Camagüey** lures you with its maze of Catholic churches and giant *tinajones* (clay pots). Skip over Las Tunas, and hightail it to gritty **Holguín** for a slice of workaday Cuba. Laid-back **Bayamo** is where the Revolution was ignited, but allow plenty of time for the cultural nexus of **Santiago de Cuba**, where the seditious plans were first hatched. Save the best till last with a long but by no means arduous journey over the hills and far away to **Baracoa** for coconuts, chocolate and other tropical treats.

Four Days
Escape from Varadero

Varadero has some cheap packages and is a popular gateway into Cuba, but once you've had your fill of the beach, what else is there to do? Here's a thought. Take your transport west to **Havana**, stopping off for lunch in **Matanzas**, where Cuban reality will hit you like a sharp slap on the face. Book a night in a fine colonial hotel in Habana Vieja and spend the next day admiring the copious sights of the old quarter. The next day, head west to **Las Terrazas**, an eco-resort that seems a million miles from the clamorous capital (it's actually only 55km). Going back east, keep on the green theme in **Guamá**, a reconstructed Taíno village and crocodile farm, before procuring accommodation in **Playa Larga**, where you can either dive or plan forays into the **Ciénaga de Zapata**. A couple of hours east lies the city of **Cienfuegos**, an elegant stopover whatever the season. A more secretive Cuba can be found in **Colón**, back in Matanzas province, and a dustier, time-warped one in half-ruined **San Miguel de los Baños**, an erstwhile spa. Last stop before returning to your Varadero sun-lounger is **Cárdenas**, home to three superb museums.

One Month
The All-Encompassing

Cuba might not look that big, but you could easily lose a month exploring its nooks and crannies. With time on your hands, linger a few days in **Havana** before heading west to **Viñales**, where enthusiastic naturalists and hard-working tobacco farmers live in verdant harmony. Swing back east next, avoiding Havana and heading straight for the French-themed city of **Cienfuegos**. From here you can press on to **Trinidad** for three days of colonial splendor. Schedule one night in understated **Sancti Spíritus**, and linger at least 48 hours in **Santa Clara** before diverting to **Morón**, where you can plan sorties on **Cayo Coco**. **Camagüey** is on everyone's schedule – pencil in two nights – but **Las Tunas** attracts only the time-rich (that's you). Stop for a day to admire the sculptures. Devote three days to Holguín province, where you can visit beguiling **Gibara** and enjoy pine-scented air in the **Pinares del Mayarí**. Stop off for a night in **Bayamo** on your way to **Santiago de Cuba**, which you can use for a base for excursions to **El Cobre**, **Chivirico** and **Parque Baconao**. Reserve three days at the end to make the obligatory pilgrimage to **Baracoa**.

KARL BLACKWELL / LONELY PLANET IMAGES ©

VERONICA GARBUTT / LONELY PLANET IMAGES ©

» (above) Arco de Triunfo, Parque José Martí, Cienfuegos (p234)
» (left) White-sand beach, Varadero (p205).

10 Days
Around the Oriente

The Oriente is a different country; they do things differently there, or so they'll tell you in Havana. This circuit allows you to bypass the Cuban capital and make your base in **Santiago de Cuba**, city of revolutionaries, culture and *folklórico* dance troupes. Regular buses travel east into the mountains of Guantánamo province. Pass a night in **Guantánamo** to suss out the *changüí* music before climbing the spectacular 'Farola road' into **Baracoa**, where three days will bag you the highlights. Heading north via Moa is a tough jaunt, with taxis or rental cars required to get you to **Cayo Saetia**, a wonderful key where lonesome beaches embellish a former hunting reserve. **Pinares de Mayarí** sits in the pine-clad mountains of the Sierra Crystal amid huge waterfalls and rare flora. Take an urban break in hassle-free **Bayamo**, before tackling **Manzanillo**, where Saturday nights in the main square can get feisty. More adventurous transport options will lead you down to Niquero and within striking distance of the largely deserted **Parque Nacional Desembarco del Granma**. Spend a couple of nights in **Marea del Portillo** before attempting the spectacular but potholed road back to Santiago.

Two Weeks
Central Cuba Circuit

Focusing on central Cuba allows you to visit places that many itineraries leave out due to lack of time and/or information. Make a base in **Trinidad**, colonial city extraordinaire, and branch out to the historical and equally beguiling **Valle de los Ingenios**. Make for the Sierra del Escambray next, where the muddy trails and clear pools of **Topes de Collantes** justify at least a two-night stopover. A rough road continues on to **Lago de Hanabanilla**, where you can hike some more or net a largemouth bass. **Santa Clara** reintroduces you to urbanity with its museums and nightlife, and there's more of the same in **Remedios**, if on a smaller scale. The quiet northeastern route enables pit stops in **Yaguajay**, with its interesting Museo Camilo Cienfuegos, and **Florencia**, where a peaceful reservoir invites bucolic contemplation. After a day or two in **Morón**, get back on the Carretera Central and hit **Camagüey**, Cuba's third city and a cornucopia of unique architecture. Thirty kilometers to the southeast is the **Hacienda la Belén**, a nature reserve renowned for its birdlife, which makes for an excellent side trip. Finish off in **Holguín** and enjoy a couple of days' beach time in nearby **Guardalavaca**.

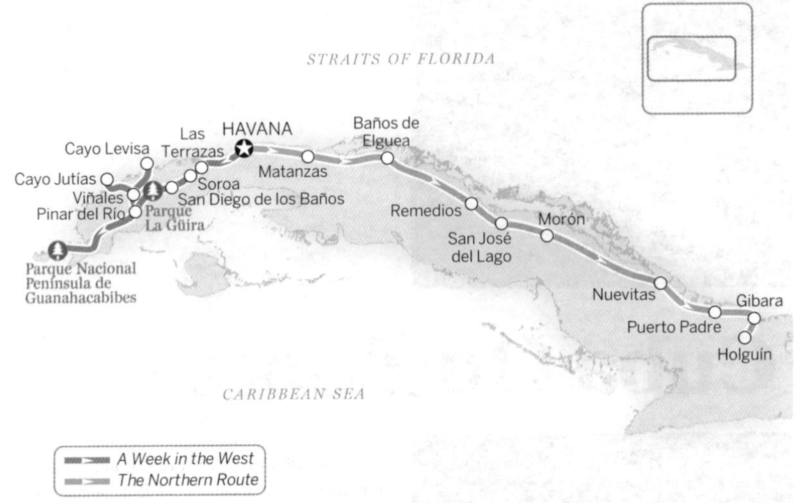

One Week
A Week in the West

West of **Havana**, green Pinar del Río often gets neglected by travelers taking the classic route east. You can rectify this by heading to **Las Terrazas**, Cuba's most successful environmental project that created a Unesco Biosphere Reserve out of a near ecological disaster. Nearby, **Soroa** is famed for its orchids and waterfalls and can be explored from the same base. Track further west on day two past faded 'spa,' **San Diego de los Baños**, toward **Parque La Güira**, where you can spot birds in between visiting the cave where Che Guevara pitched camp during the Cuban Missile Crisis. The town of **Pinar del Río** deserves a lunch stop, but the real beauty lies 25km to the north in the unique landscape of **Viñales**, prime tobacco-growing country and one of the most instantly picturesque places in the Caribbean. Tour operators in Viñales offer some enticing excursions north to uninhabited **Cayo Jutías** and equally sublime **Cayo Levisa**, both adorned with pristine beaches. If time allows, schedule a visit to Cuba's remote western tip, renowned for its world-class diving and ecologically well-stocked **Parque Nacional Península de Guanahacabibes** before heading back to Havana.

Two Weeks
The Northern Route

For Cuba veterans who've already done the 'classic' tour – or adventurers keen to keep off the tourist trail – try this alternative trek east via a little-used northern route (bike or car required). After soaking up the obvious draws of **Havana**, follow the rising sun to **Matanzas**, a gritty city with an interesting culture and the resort-phobe's antidote to Varadero. From here, a web of narrow, potholed roads lure you east, via the isolated spa of **Baños de Elguea**, to the architectural dreamscape of **Remedios**, with its quiet charm and noisy festivals. Further east, **San José del Lago** is another spa, visited primarily by Cubans, close to little-explored forests where Castro's guerrillas once roamed. **Morón** is a good place to relax for a day or two, with fishing lakes and the beaches of Cayo Coco nearby. Camagüey province's northern coast is semideserted until you arrive in **Nuevitas**, an understated industrial town close to the beach. **Puerto Padre** is a salt-of-the-earth Cuban town loved by purists, while **Gibara** is a wonderfully weathered seaside settlement with *mucho* magic. Finish your sojourn in **Holguín**, city of bar crawls, a bolshie baseball team and plenty of other surprises.

Cuba Outdoors

Best Eco-Lodges

Hotel Moka (p150)
Hotel Horizontes el Saltón (p420)
Hacienda la Belén (p321)
Villa Pinares de Mayarí (p361)

Useful Websites

www.ecoturcuba.co.cu
www.cubamarviajes.tur.cu
www.gaviota-grupo.com
www.nauticamarlin.com
www.climbingcuba.com

Where to See a Rodeo

Parque Lenin, Havana (p132)
Isla Turiguanó, Ciego de Ávila (p302)
Parque 26 de Julio, Las Tunas (p334)

Accessibility

Access to many parks and protected areas in Cuba is limited and can only be negotiated with a prearranged guide or on an organized excursion. If in doubt, consult Ecotur (www.ecoturcuba.co.cu) travel agency.

Doubters of Cuba's outdoor potential need only look at the figures: 5746km of coastline, six Unesco Biosphere Reserves, two *natural* Unesco World Heritage Sites, thousands of caves, three sprawling mountain ranges, copious bird species, the world's second-largest coral reef, barely touched tropical rainforest and swaths of unspoiled countryside.

Adventurers who feel that they've had their fill of rum, cigars and all-night salsa dancing can hit the highway on a bike, fish (as well as drink) like Hemingway, hike on guerrilla trails, jump out of an airplane or rediscover a sunken Spanish shipwreck off the shimmering south coast.

Thanks to the dearth of modern development, Cuba's outdoors is refreshingly green and free of the smog-filled highways and ugly suburban sprawl that infect many other countries.

While not on a par with North America or Europe in terms of leisure options, Cuba's facilities are well established and improving. Services and infrastructure vary depending on what activity you are looking for. The country's diving centers are generally excellent and its instructors of an international caliber. Naturalists and ornithologists in the various national parks and flora and fauna reserves are similarly conscientious and well qualified. Hiking has traditionally been limited and frustratingly rule-ridden, but opportunities have expanded in recent years, with companies such as Ecotur offering a wider variety of hikes in previously untrodden areas and even some multiday trekking. Cycling is refreshingly DIY, and all the bet-

CUBA'S BEST DIVE SITES

SITE NAME	NUMBER OF BUOYED SITES	NUMBER OF QUALIFIED INSTRUCTORS	FEATURES
Jardines de la Reina	32	5	virgin marine ecosystems, swim with sharks
Punta Francés	56	5	swim-throughs, tunnels, wrecks, clear water and huge variety of marine life
María la Gorda	39	9	caves, walls, black coral, clear and calm water conditions
Bay of Pigs	16	4	wall with a 70-80m drop-off 50m offshore, saltwater caves or cenotes
Playa Santa Lucía	35	7	part of 2nd-largest reef in world, huge variety of fish, shipwrecks and a shark-feeding show
Chivirico	23	2	crags, interconnecting tunnels and sunken ships, including some from the 1898 Spanish-Cuban-American War

ter for it. Canyoning and climbing are new sports in Cuba that have a lot of local support, but little official backing – as yet.

It's possible to hire reasonable outdoor gear in Cuba for most of the activities you will do (cycling excepted). But if you do bring your own supplies, any gear you can donate at the end of your trip to individuals you meet along the way (headlamps, snorkel masks, fins etc) will be greatly appreciated.

Diving

If Cuba has a blue ribbon activity, it is scuba diving. Even Fidel (in his younger days) liked to don a wet suit and escape beneath the iridescent waters of the Atlantic or Caribbean (his favorite dive site was – apparently – the rarely visited Jardines de la Reina archipelago). Indeed, so famous was the Cuban leader's diving addiction that the CIA allegedly once sponsored an assassination plot that involved inserting an explosive device inside a conch and placing it on the seabed.

Excellent dive sites are so numerous in Cuba that you could quite easily plan a whole trip around this one activity alone. The more sheltered south coast probably has the edge in terms of water clarity and dependable weather, though the north coast, offering easy access to one of the world's largest reefs, is no slouch.

What makes diving in Cuba special are its unpolluted seas, clear water conditions (average underwater visibility is 30m to 40m), warm seas (mean temperature is 24°C), abundant coral and fish, simple access (including a couple of excellent swim-out reefs) and fascinating shipwrecks (Cuba was a nexus for weighty galleons in the 17th and 18th centuries, and rough seas and skirmishes with pirates sunk many of them).

Where to Dive

For untamed purity head for the Jardines de la Reina, a heavily protected mini-archipelago off the south coast of Ciego de Ávila and Camagüey provinces. It's practically virgin and has no infrastructure bar an eight-room floating hotel. Diving privileges here must be booked in advance, in part to protect the magnificence of the setting. The rewards are a seabed replete with life and color unblemished since the age of Columbus. Also competing for 'best diving in the Caribbean' honors are Punta Francés on the Isla de la Juventud (see boxed text, p159) and María la Gorda (p182) in the far west of Pinar del Río province, both renowned for their calm seas, excellent water clarity (the Isla holds an annual underwater photography competition) and the profusion of all kinds of sea life. Not surprisingly, both areas, though relatively isolated, have excellent international dive centers with recompression chambers and in-house instruction available.

The Bahía de Cochinos (Bay of Pigs), on the south coast of Matanzas, offers the island's most accessible diving, with a plunging 35km coral wall located within about 50m of the shore. There are also a number of freshwater or saltwater cenotes (sinkholes) here, providing unique diving opportunities for the curious and the brave.

The longest coral reef in Cuba (and one of the longest in the world) sits 1.5km off Playa Santa Lucía (p325) on the north coast of Camagüey province, making this another mecca for divers from around the globe. The pièce de résistance here is the underwater shark-feeding show that takes place off nearby Playa los Cocos.

Guajimico (p246) in Cienfuegos province is a large campismo (with dive outfit) that offers good, cheap accommodations and in excess of 20 diving sites about 20 minutes away by boat. The area is renowned for its coral gardens.

The big north coast resorts of Varadero, Cayo Coco and Guardalavaca all have well-organized, professional dive centers that run trips to nearby reefs. Varadero boasts *El Neptuno,* a Russian ship purposely sunk in the 1940s; Cayo Coco has La Jaula with a profusion of gorgonians; and Guardalavaca offers La Corona (the Crown), a colorful coral wall.

Cuba's best wreck dive is the *Cristóbal Colón,* a Spanish warship sunk by the US in 1898. It's off the coast of Santiago de Cuba province and is accessible from dive sites in Chivirico and Parque Baconao (p417).

Diving Centers

In all, Cuba has 25 recognized diving centers spread over 17 different areas. The majority of the centers are managed by **Marlin Náutica y Marinas** (www.nauticamarlin.com), though you'll also find representation from **Gaviota** (www.gaviota-grupo.com), **Cubanacán Náutica** (www.cubanacan.cu) and **Cubamar** (www.cubamarviajes.cu). Though equipment does vary between installations, you can generally expect safe, professional service with back-up medical support. Environmentally sensitive diving is where things can get wobbly, and individuals should educate themselves about responsible diving. As well as being Scuba Schools International (SSI), American Canadian Underwater Certification (ACUC) and Confédération Mondiale de Activités Subaquatiques (CMAS) certified, most dive instructors are multilingual, speaking a variety of Spanish, English, French, German and Italian. Because of US embargo laws, Professional Association of Diving Instructors (PADI) certification is generally not offered in Cuba.

Dives and courses are comparably priced island-wide, from CUC$30 to CUC$45 per dive, with a discount after four or five dives. Full certification courses are CUC$310 to CUC$365, and 'resort' or introductory courses cost CUC$50 to CUC$60.

Cycling

Riding a bike in Cuba is *the* best way to discover the island in close-up. Decent and quiet roads, wonderful scenery and the opportunity to get off the beaten track and meet Cubans make cycling here a pleasure, whichever route you take. For less dedicated pedalers, daily bike rental is sometimes available in hotels, resorts and cafes for about CUC$3 to CUC$7 per day, but don't bank on it. The bigger resorts in Varadero and Guardalavaca are more reliable and will often include bike use as part of the all-inclusive package, though it's unlikely the bikes will have gears. Alternatively, if you're staying in a casa particular, your host will generally be able to rig something together

USEFUL AGENCIES

» **Ecotur** (www.ecoturcuba.co.cu) Runs organized hiking, trekking, fishing and bird-watching trips to some of the country's otherwise inaccessible corners. It has offices in every province and a main HQ in Havana.

» **Cubamar Viajes** (www.cubamarviajes.tur.cu) Runs Cuba's 80+ campismos (rural chalets). It has Reservaciones de Campismo offices in every provincial capital and a helpful head office in Havana.

TOP BIKE RIDES

» **Guardalavaca to Banes** Escape the big resorts on this undulating ride through quintessential rural Cuba to one of its most understated towns.

» **Santiago to Marea del Portillo** A tough but rewarding two- to three-day trek along Cuba's most deserted yet spectacular road, with the Sierra Maestra on one side and the azure Caribbean on the other.

» **Valle de Viñales** Circumnavigate craggy, haystack-shaped hills as you glide past tobacco fields, caves and Cuba's friendliest villages.

» **Bayamo to El Saltón** A hilly ride into a little-explored corner of the Sierra Maestra to an eco-resort deep in the mountain greenery.

» **La Farola** Take the rollercoaster 'lighthouse road' from arid Cajobabo to tropical Baracoa through numerous different ecosystems.

» **Morón to Remedios** This slower alternative to the Carretera Central puts you in touch with unsung towns and under-the-radar sights still unmarked on most maps.

(sometimes quite literally) in order to get you from A to B.

The main problem with Cuban bikes is that they're usually substandard, and when they're combined with poor roads, you'll often feel like you're sitting atop an improvised coat hanger and not a well-oiled machine. Serious cyclists should bring boxed bikes with them on the airplane, along with plenty of spare parts. Since organized bike trips are common here, customs officials, taxi drivers and hotel staff are used to dealing with them.

Cycling highlights include the Valle de Viñales (p190), the countryside around Trinidad, including the flat spin down to Playa Ancón (p279), the quiet lanes that zigzag through Guardalavaca (p356), and the roads out of Baracoa (p440) to Playa Maguana (northwest) and Boca de Yumurí (southeast). For a bigger challenge try La Farola (see p441) between Cajobabo and Baracoa (21km of ascent), the bumpy but spectacular coast road between Santiago and Marea del Portillo – best spread over three days with overnights in Brisas Sierra Mar los Galeones (p420) and Campismo la Mula (p422) – or, for real wheel warriors, the insanely steep mountain road from Bartolomé Masó to Santo Domingo in Granma province.

With a profusion of casas particulares offering cheap, readily available accommodation, cycle touring is a joy here as long as you keep off the Autopista and steer clear of Havana.

Off-road biking has not yet taken off in Cuba and is generally not permitted.

Fishing

Deep-Sea Fishing

Hemingway wasn't wrong. Cuba's fast-moving Gulf Stream along the north coast supports prime game fishing for sailfish, tuna, mackerel, swordfish, barracuda, marlin and shark pretty much year-round. Deep-sea fishing is a rite of passage for many and a great way to wind down, make friends, drink beer, watch sunsets and generally leave the troubles of the world behind. Not surprisingly, the country has great facilities for sport anglers, and every Cuban boat captain seems to look and talk as if he's walked straight from the pages of a Hemingway classic.

Cuba's best deep-sea fishing center is Cayo Guillermo (p307), the small island (then uninhabited) that featured in Hemingway's *Islands in the Stream*. Papa may no longer be in semiresidence, but the fish still swim freely. Another good bet is Havana, which has two marinas, one at Tarará (p138) and the other – better one – at Marina Hemingway (p124) to the west.

Elsewhere, all of Cuba's main resort areas offer deep-sea-fishing excursions for similar rates. Count on paying approximately CUC$280 per half-day and CUC$450 per full day for four people, including crew and open bar.

Fly-Fishing

Just as the north coast is a haven for deep-sea fisherfolk, the south coast is a fly-fishing paradise without equal – one boat will ply 100 sq km of water, invariably on its own.

This type of fishing is undertaken mainly on shallow sand flats easily reached from the shoreline. Classic areas to throw a line are Las Salinas in the Ciénaga de Zapata (p263), the protected waters surrounding Cayo Largo del Sur (p166), parts of the Isla de la Juventud (p 156) and – most notably – the uninhabited nirvana of the Jardines de la Reina archipelago (p308). The archipelago is a national park and heavily protected. It is not unheard of to catch 25 different species of fish in the same day here.

A 'grand slam' for fly-fishers in Cuba is to bag tarpon, bonefish and permit in the same day; bag a snook as well and they call it a 'superslam'. The best fishing season in this part of Cuba is February to June. The remoteness of the many islands, reefs and sand flats means fishing trips are usually organized on boats that offer on-board accommodations. They are coordinated through a company called **Avalon** (www.cubafishingcenters.com).

The north coast hides a couple of good fly-fishing havens. Most noted are the still uninhabited keys of Cayo Romano and Cayo Cruz in the north of Camagüey province. Trips are coordinated by **Ecotur** (www.ecoturcuba.co.cu) and are based at an attractive lodge in the mainland town of Brasil (p323).

Freshwater Fishing

Freshwater fishing in Cuba is lesser known than fly-fishing but equally rewarding, and many Americans and Canadians home in on the island's numerous lakes. Fly-fishing is superb in vast Ciénaga de Zapata (p227) in Matanzas, where enthusiasts can arrange multiday catch-and-release trips. *Trucha* (largemouth bass) was first introduced into Cuba in the early 20th century by Americans at King's Ranch and the United Fruit Company. Due to favorable environmental protection, the fish is now abundant in many Cuban lakes, and experts believe the next world-record bass (currently 9.9kg) will come from Cuba. Good places to cast a line are the Laguna del Tesoro (p226) in Matanzas, the Laguna de la Leche and Laguna la Redonda (p301) in Ciego de Ávila province, Embalse Zaza (p272) in Sancti Spíritus and Embalse Hanabanilla (p259) in Villa Clara – 7.6kg specimens have been caught here! To meet other fisherfolk, head for Hotel Morón (p300), Hotel Zaza (p272) in Sancti Spíritus or Hotel Hanabanilla (p259) in Villa Clara province.

Snorkeling

You don't have to go very deep to enjoy Cuba's tropical aquarium: snorkelers will feel like divers along the south coast from Playa Larga to Caleta Buena (p228), around Cienfuegos (p243) and along the Guardalavaca reef (p356). In Varadero, daily snorkeling tours sailing to Cayo Blanco (p208) promise abundant tropical fish and good visibility. If you're not into the group thing, you can don a mask at Playa Coral (p208), 20km away.

Good boat dives for snorkeling happen around Isla de la Juventud (see p159) and Cayo Largo (p167) especially, but also in Varadero (p208) and in the Cienfuegos (p243) and Guajimico (p245) areas. If you intend to do a lot of snorkeling, bring your own gear, as the rental stuff can be tattered and buying it in Cuba will mean you'll sacrifice both price and quality.

Bird-Watching

Cuba offers a bird-watching bonanza year-round and no serious ornithologist should enter the country without their binoculars close at hand. Your experience will be enhanced by the level of expertise shown by many of Cuba's naturalists and guides in the key bird-watching zones. Areas with specialist bird-watching trails or trips include the Cueva las Perlas trail (p190) in Parque Nacional Península de Guanahacabibes, the Maravillas de Viñales trail (p190) in Parque Nacional Viñales, the Sendero la Serafina (p150) in the Reserva Sierra del Rosario, the Observación de Aves tour (p227) in Gran Parque Natural Montemar, Parque Natural el Bagá (p303) on Cayo Coco, and the Sendero de las Aves (p321) in Hacienda la Belén in Camagüey province.

Must-sees include the *tocororo* (Cuban trogon), the *zunzuncito* (bee hummingbird), the Cuban tody, the Cuban parakeet, the Antillean palm swift, the *cartacuba* (an indigenous Cuban bird) and, of course, the flamingo – preferably in a flock. Good spots for some DIY bird-watching are on Cayo Romano (see p324) and adjacent Cayo Sabinal, although you'll need a car to get there. Specialists and ivory-billed-woodpecker seekers will enjoy Parque Nacional Alejandro de Humboldt.

OVERVIEW OF BEST HIKES

HIKE	SOLO OR GUIDED	START/FINISH	DISTANCE	GRADE	FEATURES
Pico Turquino	guided	Alto del Naranjo/Las Cuevas	17km	hard	mountain, birdwatching
Salto del Caburní	solo	Topes de Collantes	6km	medium	waterfall, natural swimming pool
El Guafe	solo	Parque Nacional Desembarco del Granma	3km	easy	flora, archaeological sites
Balcón de Iberia	guided	Parque Alejandro de Humboldt	6km	easy	flora, fauna, natural swimming pool
San Claudio	guided	Las Terrazas	13km	medium	eco-forest, birdwatching, natural swimming pool
El Yunque	guided	Campismo el Yunque	8km	medium-hard	mountain, flora

Hiking & Trekking

European hikers and North American wilderness freaks take note: while Cuba's trekking potential is enormous, the traveler's right to roam is restricted by badly maintained trails, poor signage, a lack of maps and rather draconian restrictions about where you can and cannot go without a guide. Cubans don't undertake hiking for enjoyment in the same way as Canadians or Germans. Instead, they tend to assume that all hikers want to be led by hand along short, relatively tame trails that are rarely more than 5km or 6km in length. You'll frequently be told that hiking alone is a reckless and dangerous activity, despite the fact that Cuba harbors no big fauna and no poisonous snakes. The best time of year for hiking is outside the rainy season and before it gets too hot (December to April).

The dearth of available hikes isn't always the result of nit-picking restrictions. Much of Cuba's trekkable terrain is in ecologically sensitive areas, meaning access is carefully managed and controlled. Another reason is the lack of any real hiking culture (and thus demand) among Cubans themselves. Walking from A to B for the fun of it is often viewed with mirth in many Latin American countries, and Cuba is no exception. Rather than spend all day bushwhacking along a path in order to reach a beautiful waterfall, the Cubans would much rather pack some beers, load up the car and drive there.

Multiday hiking in Cuba has improved in the last couple of years, and though information is still hard to get, you can piece together workable options in the Sierra Maestra and the Escambray Mountains. The most popular by far is the three-day trek to the summit of Pico Turquino (p421), followed by the overnight San Claudio trail (p149) in the Reserva Sierra del Rosario.

More challenging day hikes include El Yunque (p440), a mountain near Baracoa; the Balcón de Iberia circuit in Parque Nacional Alejandro de Humboldt (p442); and some of the hikes around Las Terrazas and Viñales.

Topes de Collantes (p289) probably has the largest concentration of hiking trails in its protected zone (a natural park). Indeed, some overseas groups organize four- to five-day treks here, starting near Lago Hanabanilla and finishing in Parque el Cubano (p279). Inquire in advance at the Carpeta Central information office (p289) in Topes de Collantes if you are keen to organize something on behalf of a group.

Other tamer hikes include Cueva las Perlas and Del Bosque al Mar in the Península de Guanahacabibes (p190), the guided trail in Parque Natural el Bagá (p303), El Guafe trail in Parque Nacional Desembarco del Granma (p380) and the short circuit in Reserva Ecológica Varahicacos (p208) in Varadero. Some of these hikes are guided and all require the payment of an entry fee.

If you want to hike independently, you'll need patience, resolve and an excellent sense of direction. It's also useful to ask the locals in your casa particular. Try experimenting first with Salto del Caburní or Sendero la Batata in Topes de Collantes (p289) or the various hikes around Viñales (p190). There's a beautiful, little-used DIY hike on a good trail near Marea del Portillo (p383) and some gorgeous options around Baracoa – ask the locals!

Horseback Riding

Cuba has a long-standing cowboy culture, and horseback riding is available countrywide in both official and unofficial capacities. If you arrange it privately, make sure you check the state of the horses and equipment first. Riding poorly kept horses is both cruel and potentially dangerous.

The state-owned catering company Palmares owns numerous rustic ranchos across Cuba that are supposed to give tourists a feel for traditional country life. All of these places offer guided horseback riding, usually for around CUC$5 per hour. You'll find good ranchos in Florencia (p302) in Ciego de Ávila province and Hacienda la Belén (p321) in Camagüey province.

La Guabina (p179) is a horse-breeding center near the city of Pinar del Río that offers both horse shows and horseback-riding adventures.

Boating & Kayaking

Kayaking as a sport is pretty low-key in Cuba, where it is treated more as a beach activity in the plusher resorts. Most of the tourist beaches will have *náutica* points that rent out simple kayaks, good for splashing around in but not a lot else. Boat rental is also available on many of the island's lakes. Good options include the Laguna de la Leche and Laguna la Redonda (p301), both in Ciego de Ávila province; Embalse Zaza (p272) in Sancti Spíritus province; and the Liberación de Florencia (p303) in Ciego de Ávila.

One of Cuba's best rivers is the Río Canímar (p199) near Matanzas. You can rent rowboats and head up between the jungle-covered banks of this mini-Amazon.

IN THE FOOTSTEPS OF THE GRANMA SURVIVORS

Though few know it, a fascinating web of little-used paths connects the sites visited by the exhausted survivors of the *Granma* Yacht, which ran aground 70m offshore at Las Coloradas in the present-day Parque Nacional Desembarco del Granma on December 2, 1956. The route taken by the 82-strong rebel army began with a 1.5km crawl through a mangrove forest to dry land. Today you can follow their approximate path on a more comfortable raised concrete walkway. Once on terra firma, the army headed east to a clearing known as Alegria del Pio, where they were engaged and ultimately scattered by Batista's army. This 30km trek (which took the rebels four days) can be done in seven to eight hours under modern conditions, but must be undertaken with a guide arranged through either Ecotur (p371) or the park authorities. The pristine wilderness it traverses is notable, not only for its evocative revolutionary history, but for its uplifted marine terraces and unusual endemic flora.

From Alegria del Pio, keen hikers can press on further (with an organized guide), following in the footsteps of the now-depleted army to Cinco Palmas, the point where a handful of the rebels, including Fidel, Raúl and Che Guevara, regrouped on December 15, 1956. From here, over a period of two or three days, you can ascend to their ultimate goal: Comandancia la Plata in the Sierra Maestra, Fidel's wartime HQ from 1957–58.

This multiday hike is still little known in Cuba, and foot traffic is very light. As there are no signposts and a variety of different paths, it should not be attempted alone. Arrange a guide through Ecotur well in advance and be prepared to rough it. There are no facilities en route.

Rock Climbing

The Valle de Viñales (p183) has been described as having the best rock climbing in the Western hemisphere. There are more than 150 routes now open (at all levels of difficulty, with several rated as YDS Class 5.14) and the word is out among the international climbing crowd, who are creating their own scene in one of Cuba's prettiest settings. Independent travelers will appreciate the free rein that climbers enjoy here.

Though you can climb here year-round, the heat can be oppressive, and locals stick to an October-to-April season, with December to January being the optimum months. For more information, visit **Cuba Climbing** (www.cubaclimbing.com) or head straight to Viñales.

It is important to note that, though widely practiced and normally without consequence, climbing in the Valle de Viñales is still not technically legal. You're unlikely to get arrested or even warned, but take extreme care and do not under any circumstances do anything that damages the delicate Parque Nacional Viñales ecosystem.

Caving

Cuba is riddled with caves – more than 20,000 and counting – and cave exploration is available to both casual tourists and professional speleologists. The Gran Caverna de Santo Tomás (p191), near Viñales, is Cuba's largest cavern, with over 46km of galleries; the Cueva de los Peces (see p228), near Playa Girón, is a flooded cenote with colorful snorkeling; and the Cueva de Ambrosio (p207) and Cuevas de Bellamar (p199), both in Matanzas, have tours daily.

Caving specialists have virtually unlimited caves from which to choose. With advance arrangements, you can explore deep into the Gran Caverna de Santo Tomás or visit the Cueva Martín Infierno (p246), which has the world's largest stalagmite. Also ask about San Catalina, near Varadero, which has unique mushroom formations. Speleo-diving is also possible, but only for those already highly trained. Interested experts should contact Angel Graña, secretary of the **Sociedad Espeleológica de Cuba** (☎7-209-2885; angel@fanj.cult.cu) in Havana. The **Escuela Nacional de Espeleología** (☎48-77-10-14) in Moncada, just at the entrance to the Gran Caverna de Santo Tomás, is another good resource for professionals.

Travel with Children

Best Regions for Children

Havana

The streets of Habana Vieja can't have changed much since the days of the *Pirates of the Caribbean*, so your kids' imaginations will be allowed to run wild in forts, squares, museums and narrow streets. Havana also has Cuba's largest amusement park (Isla del Coco), and its best aquarium.

Varadero

Cuba's biggest resort has the largest – if most predictable – stash of specifically tailored kids' activities, including nighttime shows, organized sports, beach games and boat trips.

Trinidad

The south coast's southern gem is awash with economic casas particulares, an ideal opportunity for your kids to mix and mingle with Cuban families. Throw in an excellent beach (Playa Ancón), easily accessible snorkeling waters and a profusion of pleasant pastoral activities (horseback riding is popular) and you've got the perfect nonresort family option.

Cuba for Kids

Get ready kids! Cuba is like nothing you've ever seen before. Children on this sun-dappled Caribbean archipelago are encouraged to talk, sing, dance, think, dream and play, and they are integrated into all parts of society: you'll see them at concerts, restaurants, churches, political rallies (giving speeches even!) and parties.

Children's Highlights

Forts & Castles

» **Fortaleza de San Carlos de la Cabaña** Havana's huge fort has museums, battlements and a nightly cannon ceremony with soldiers in period costume.

» **Castillo de San Pedro de la Roca del Morro** Santiago's Unesco-listed fort is best known for its exciting pirate museum.

» **Castillo de la Real Fuerza** This centrally located Havana fort has a moat, lookouts and scale models of Spanish galleons.

Kids' Playgrounds

» **Parque Maestranza** Bouncy castles, fairground rides and sweet snacks overlooking Havana harbor.

» **Isla del Coco** Huge, new-ish, Chinese-funded amusement park in Havana's Playa neighborhood.

» **Parque Lenin** More playground rides, boats, a minitrain and horses for rent in Havana.

WHAT TO BRING

BABIES/TOTS

- ☐ Diapers (nappies)
- ☐ Car seat (for taxis and rental cars)
- ☐ Easily foldable pushchair (stroller)
- ☐ Foldable highchair for restaurants
- ☐ Pediatric medicines
- ☐ Travel crib
- ☐ Copy of long birth certificate

OLDER KIDS

- ☐ Notebook and crayons
- ☐ Sunscreen, hat
- ☐ Vitamin tablets
- ☐ A baseball, glove, shirt
- ☐ Swim floats
- ☐ Books
- ☐ Medicines
- ☐ Toilet paper
- ☐ Antiseptic hand-wash

Animal Encounters

» **Acuario Nacional** Daily dolphin shows and a decent restaurant are the highlights of the nation's main aquarium in Havana's Miramar district.

» **Criaderos de Cocodrilos** Of the half-dozen croc farms spread across the country, the best is in Guamá, Matanzas province.

» **Horseback riding** Possible all over Cuba and usually run out of rustic *fincas* in rural areas such as Pinar del Río and Trinidad.

Snorkeling

» **Bay of Pigs** Some of the best snorkeling in Cuba is accessible directly from the shore in southern Matanzas province.

» **Trinidad** Decent reefs lie about 500m off divine Playa Ancón; local boats run excursions.

» **Playa Coral** The nearest shore snorkeling to Varadero lies approximately 20km to the west in this well-run, protected park.

Festivals

» **Las Parrandas** Fireworks, smoke and huge animated floats: Remedios' Christmas Eve party is a blast for kids *and* adults.

» **Carnaval de Santiago de Cuba** A colorful celebration of Caribbean culture with floats and dancing that takes place every July.

» **Carnaval de la Habana** More music, dancing and effigies, this time along Havana's Malecón.

Planning

Travelers with kids are not unusual in Cuba and the trend has proliferated in recent years with more Cuban-Americans visiting their families with offspring in tow; these will be your best sources for on-the-ground information. Aspects of the local culture that parents might find foreign (aside from the material shortages) are the physical contact and human warmth that are so typically Cuban: strangers ruffle kids' hair, give them kisses or take their hands with regularity. Chill, it's all part of the Cuban way.

Your kids shouldn't need any specific pre-trip inoculations for Cuba, though you may want to check with your doctor about individual requirements before departing. Medicines are in short supply in Cuba, so take all you think you might need. Useful stuff to have is acetaminophen, ibuprofen, antinausea medicines and cough drops. Insect repellent is also helpful in lowland areas.

Car seats are not mandatory in Cuba, and taxi and rental-car firms don't carry them. Bring your own if you're planning on renting a car. High chairs in restaurants are also almost nonexistent, though waiters will try to improvise. If you're unsure, bring an easily storable high chair with you. The same goes for travel cribs. Cuba's pavements (sidewalks) weren't designed with pushchairs (strollers) in mind. If your child is small enough, carry him/her in a body harness. Otherwise bring the smallest/lightest pushchair possible, or do without.

Eating with Kids

With a dearth of exotic spices and an emphasis on good, plain, nonfancy food, kids in Cuba are often surprisingly well accommodated. The family-orientated nature of life on the island certainly helps. Few eating establishments turn away children, and waiters and waitresses in most cafes and restaurants will, more often than not, dote on your boisterous young offspring and go out of their way to try to accommodate unadventurous or childish tastes. Rice and beans are good staples, and chicken and fish are relatively reliable sources of protein. The main absent food group – though your kid probably won't think so – is a regular supply of fresh vegetables.

regions at a glance

Cuba's provinces are splayed end to end across the main island, with the oft-forgotten comma of La Isla de la Juventud hanging off the bottom. All of them have coast access and all are embellished with beautiful beaches, the best hugging the north coast. Equally ubiquitous are the vivid snippets of history, impressive colonial architecture and potent reminders of the 1959 Revolution. The country's highest mountain range, the Sierra Maestra, rises in the east with another significant range, the Escambray, positioned south-central. Cuba's main wilderness areas are the Zapata swamps, the marine terraces of Granma, the tropical forests of Guantánamo and the uninhabited (for now) northern keys. Urban highlights include Havana, Santiago de Cuba, Camagüey and colonial Trinidad.

Havana

Museums ✓✓✓
Architecture ✓✓✓
Nightlife ✓✓✓

Casco Histórico
The capital's 4-sq-km historic center has history wherever you look and museums dedicated to everything from silverware to Simón Bolívar. Kick off with the Museo de la Revolución, garner more cultural immersion in the Museo de la Ciudad and schedule at least half a day for the fine Museo Nacional de Bellas Artes.

Eclecticism
Havana's architecture is not unlike its flora and fauna: hard to categorize and sometimes a little – well – weird. Stroll the streets of Habana Vieja and Centro Havana and choose your own highlights.

Life's a Cabaret
Every Cuban music style is represented in Havana, from street rumba to glitzy cabaret, making it the best place in the country for live concerts, spontaneous busking and racy nightlife.

p50

Artemisa & Mayabeque Provinces

Beaches ✓
Ecotourism ✓✓
Coffee Ruins ✓

Secret Beach
Rather surprisingly, considering it's stuck on the main highway between Havana and Varadero, Mayabeque province has its own unheralded and rather delightful beaches, spearheaded by Playa Jibacoa. Get there quick before the (planned) golf courses start springing up.

Las Terrazas
This stark white eco-village was practicing environmentally friendly living long before the urgencies of the Special Period or the adoption of eco-practices in the world outside. Today it carries on much as it has always done: quietly, confidently and – above all – sustainably.

Coffee Ruins
Las Terrazas has dozens of them, half-covered by encroaching jungle, while Artemisa has its own Antiguo Cafetal Angerona, a larger, more refined, but no-less-weathered ruin that once functioned as a coffee plantation employing 500 slaves.

p142

Isla de la Juventud (Special Municipality)

Diving ✓✓✓
Wildlife ✓✓
History ✓

Into the Blue
Outside the hard-to-access Jardines de la Reina archipelago, La Isla offers the best diving in Cuba and is the main reason many people come here. Ultra-clear water, abundant sea life and a protected marine park at Punta Francés are the highpoints.

Wildlife
If you missed it in the Ciénaga de Zapata, La Isla is the only other place in the world where you can view the Cuban crocodile in its natural state. It has been successfully reintroduced into the Lanier Swamps.

Ex-Prisoners
Not one but two of Cuba's verbose spokesmen were once imprisoned on the archipelago's largest outlying island that also doubled up as a big jail: José Martí and Fidel Castro. Not surprisingly both their former incarceration sites are riddled with historical significance.

p156

Pinar del Río Province

Diving ✓✓✓
Food ✓
Flora & Fauna ✓✓✓

Dive Community
Isolated at the westernmost tip of the main island, María la Gorda has long lured travelers for its spectacular diving, enhanced by electrically colored coral, huge sponges and gorgonians, and a knowledgeable but laid-back dive community.

Roast Pork
There's nothing like a true Cuban pork roast and there's no place better to try it than among the *guajiros* of Viñales. The farms, *fincas* and casas particulares that characterize this bucolic village offer up humongous portions of the national dish with trimmings of rice, beans and root vegetables.

Muy Verde
With more protected land than any other province, Pinar is a green paradise. Go hiking in Parque Nacional Viñales, spot a sea turtle in Parque Nacional Península de Guanahacabibes or train your binoculars on the feathered action around Cueva de los Portales.

p170

Matanzas Province

Diving ✓✓
Flora & Fauna ✓✓✓
Beaches ✓

Accessible Dives

Bahía de Cochinos (Bay of Pigs) might not have Cuba's best diving, but it certainly has its most accessible. You can glide off from the shore here and be gawping at coral-encrusted drop-off walls within a few strokes. There's more impressive shore diving from Playa Coral, on the north coast.

Swamp-Life

In contrast to the resort frenzy on the north coast, Matanzas' southern underbelly is one of Cuba's last true wildernesses and an important refuge for wildlife, including Cuban crocodiles, manatees, bee hummingbirds and tree rats.

Varadero

Even if you hate resorts, there's still one reason to go to Varadero – an unbroken 20km ribbon of golden sand that stretches the whole length of the Península de Hicacos. It's arguably the longest and finest beach in Cuba.

p195

Cienfuegos Province

Architecture ✓✓
Music ✓✓
Diving ✓✓

French Classicism

Despite its position as one of Cuba's newer cities, founded in 1819, Cienfuegos retains a remarkably homogenous urban core full of classical facades and slender columns that carry the essence of 19th-century France, where it drew its inspiration.

Benny Moré

'La ciudad que más me gusta a mí' ('the city I like the best'), once quipped Benny Moré, Cuba's most adaptable and complete musician, who ruled the clubs and dance halls in the 1940s and '50s. Come and see if you agree and, on the way, visit the village where he was born.

Guajimico

Welcome to one of Cuba's least-discovered diving spots, run out of a comfortable campismo on the warm, calm south coast and renowned for its coral gardens, sponges and scattered wrecks.

p232

Villa Clara Province

Beaches ✓✓
History ✓✓
Nightlife ✓✓✓

Spectacular Keys

Cuba's newest resorts on the keys off the coast of Villa Clara hide some stunning and still relatively uncrowded beaches, including the publicly accessible Las Salinas on Cayo las Brujas and the more-refined Playa el Mégano and Playa Ensenachos on Cayo Ensenachos.

Che Guevara

Love him or hate him, his legacy won't go away, so you might as well visit Santa Clara to at least try to understand what made the great *guerrillero* tick. The city hosts Che's mausoleum, a museum cataloguing his life and the historic site where he ambushed an armored train in 1958.

Student Scene

The city of Santa Clara has the edgiest and most contemporary nightlife scene in Cuba, where local innovators are constantly probing for the next big thing.

p247

Sancti Spíritus Province

Museums ✓✓✓
Hiking ✓✓
Music ✓✓✓

Revolution to Romance
Trinidad has more museums per square meter than anywhere outside Havana, and they're not token gestures either. Themes include history, furniture, counter-revolutionary wars, ceramics, contemporary art and romance.

Topes is Tops
Topes de Collantes has the most comprehensive trail system in Cuba and showcases some of the best scenery in the archipelago, with waterfalls, natural swimming pools, precious wildlife and working coffee plantations. Further trails can be found in the less-heralded Alturas de Banao and Jobo Rosado reserves.

Spontaneous Sounds
In Trinidad – and to a lesser extent Sancti Spíritus – music seems to emanate out of every nook and cranny, much of it spontaneous and unrehearsed. Trinidad in particular has the most varied and condensed music scene outside Havana.

p266

Ciego de Ávila Province

Fishing ✓✓✓
Beaches ✓✓✓
Festivals ✓✓

Hemingway's Haunts
Cayo Guillermo has all the makings of a fishing trip extraordinaire: a warm tropical setting; large, abundant fish; and the ghost of Ernest Hemingway to follow you from port to rippling sea and back. Pack a box of beer and follow the Gulf Stream.

Pilar Paradise
Colorados, Prohibida, Flamingo and Pilar – the beaches of the northern keys lure you with their names as much as their reputations and, when you get there, there's plenty of room for everyone.

Fiestas & Fireworks
No other province has such a varied and – frankly – weird stash of festivals. Ciego is home to an annual cricket tournament, rustic country dancing, strange voodoo rites and explosive fireworks.

p293

Camagüey Province

Diving ✓✓
Architecture ✓✓✓
Beaches ✓✓

Feeding Sharks
OK, the resorts aren't exactly refined luxury, but who cares when the diving's this good? Playa Santa Lucía sits astride one of the largest coral reefs in the world and is famous for its shark-feeding show.

Urban Maze
Camagüey doesn't conform to the normal Spanish colonial building manual when it comes to urban layout, but that's part of the attraction. Lose yourself in Cuba's third-largest city that, since 2008, has been a Unesco World Heritage Site.

Limitless Sand
The beaches on the province's north coast are phenomenal. There's 20km-long Playa Santa Lucía, Robinson Crusoe–like Playa Los Pinos on Cayo Sabinel and the shapely curve of Playa los Cocos at the mouth of the Bahía de Nuevitas.

p309

Las Tunas Province

Beaches ✓
Art ✓
Festivals ✓✓

Eco-Beaches
Hardly anyone knows about them, but they're still there. Las Tunas' northern eco-beaches are currently the preserve of local Cubans, seabirds and the odd in-the-know outsider. Come and enjoy them before the resort-building bulldozers wreck the tranquility.

City of Sculptures
The city of Las Tunas' sculpture isn't of the grandiose, in-your-face Florentine variety, but scout around the congenial streets of the provincial capital and you'll uncover an esoteric collection of revolutionary leaders, two-headed Taíno chiefs and oversized pencils crafted in stone.

Country Music
The bastion of country music in Cuba, Las Tunas hosts the annual Cucalambeana festival, where songwriters from across the country come to recite their quick-witted satirical *décimas* (verse).

p328

Holguín Province

Beaches ✓✓
Ecotourism ✓✓
Archaeology ✓

Unknown Beaches
Most tourists gravitate to the well-known beaches of Playa Pesquero and Guardalavaca that are now backed by big resorts. Less touted, but equally *linda* (pretty), are Playa Caleta near Gibara and Las Morales near Banes.

Mountains & Keys
Weirdly, for a province that hosts Cuba's largest and dirtiest industry (the Moa nickel mines), Holguín has a profusion of green escapes tucked away in pine-clad mountain retreats or hidden on exotic keys. Discover Cayo Saetia and visit Pinares de Mayarí.

Pre-Columbian Culture
Holguín preserves Cuba's best stash of archaeological finds. The region's long-lost pre-Columbian culture is showcased at the Museo Chorro de Maita and its adjacent reconstructed Taíno village. There are more artifacts on display at the Museo Indocubano Bani in nearby Banes.

p338

Granma Province

History ✓✓✓
Hiking ✓✓✓
Festivals ✓✓

Revolutionary Sites
History is never as real as it is in Cuba's most revolutionary province. Here you can hike up to Castro's 1950s mountaintop HQ, visit the sugar mill where Céspedes first freed his slaves or ponder the poignant spot where José Martí fell in battle.

Bagging a Peak
With the Sierra Maestra overlaying two national parks, Granma has tremendous hiking potential, including the trek up to the top of the nation's highest peak, Pico Turquino.

Street Parties
Granma is famous for its street parties. Towns such as Bayamo and Manzanillo have long celebrated weekly alfresco shindigs with whole roast pork, chess tournaments and music provided by old-fashioned street organs.

p363

Santiago de Cuba Province

Dance ✓✓✓
History ✓✓✓
Festivals ✓✓✓

Folklórico Groups

As magical as they are mysterious, Santiago's *folklórico* dance troupes are a throwback to another era when slaves hid their traditions behind a complex veneer of singing, dancing and syncretized religion.

Historical Sites

Cuba's hotbed of sedition has inspired multiple rebellions and many key sites can still be visited. Start at Moncada Barracks and head south through the birth houses of local heroes Frank País and Antonio Maceo, to the eerily named Museo de la Lucha Clandestina (Clandestine War Museum).

Caribbean Culture

Santiago has a wider variety of annual festivals than any other Cuban city. July is the top month, with the annual Carnaval preceded by the Festival del Caribe, celebrating the city's rich Caribbean culture.

p384

Guantánamo Province

Flora & Fauna ✓✓✓
Hiking ✓✓
Food ✓✓

Endemism

Guantánamo's historical isolation and complex soil structure has led to high levels of endemism, meaning you're likely to see plant and animal species here that you'll see nowhere else in the archipelago. Aspiring botanists should gravitate towards Parque Nacional Alejandro de Humboldt.

Growing Potential

As Baracoa grows as an ecological center, hiking possibilities are opening up. Try the long-standing treks up El Yunque or into Parque Nacional Alejandro de Humboldt, or tackle newer trails around the Duaba River or to the beaches near Boca de Yumurí.

Coconuts, Coffee & Cocoa

What do you mean you didn't come to Cuba for the food? Baracoa is waiting to blow away your culinary preconceptions with a sweet-and-spicy mélange of dishes concocted from the locally ubiquitous cocoa, coffee, coconuts and bananas.

p424

Look out for these icons:

Our author's recommendation

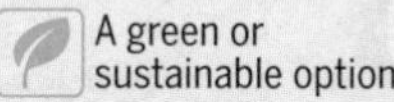
A green or sustainable option

No payment required

See the Index for a full list of destinations covered in this book.

On the Road

Havana

☎07 / POP 2,141,652

Includes »

Best Places to Eat

- Los Nardos (p102)
- Paladar la Guarida (p103)
- Restaurante el Templete (p99)
- Restaurante la Divina Pastora (p102)
- La Imprenta (p99)

Best Places to Stay

- Hostal Condes de Villanueva (p83)
- Hotel NH Parque Central (p86)
- Hotel San Felipe y Santiago de Bejúcal (p83)
- Hotel Meliá Habana (p124)
- Hotel Victoria (p97)

Why Go?

Ah...Havana, city of jarring paradoxes and unfathomable contradictions where seductive beauty sidles up to spectacular decay and revolutionary iconography is juxtaposed with sun, sea, sand, sex and a diluting slice of austere socialism. There's fascinating history here, wrapped up in erudite museums and foresighted restoration projects, and tremendous music too, from gritty street rumba to kitschy cabaret. But Havana's greatest allure is its street theater, the raw snippets of everyday life that go on all around you: the mother in rollers and the baseball-playing schoolkids, the wandering troubadours and the cigar-smoking doctor trying to jump-start his 1951 Plymouth. The attraction is the authenticity. *Habaneros* (the people of Havana) don't just survive: they duck and dive, scheme and dream, create and debate, but most of all, they *live* – with a rare passion.

When to Go

One of Havana's most outstanding music festivals is the Festival Internacional de Jazz, which is held each year in February. Don't miss it! Havana's summer heat can be stifling. To avoid it, come in October, a wonderfully quiet month when there's still plenty to do – such as enjoy the annual Festival Internacional de Ballet. Busier (for a reason) is December, when people line up for the Festival del Nuevo Cine Latinoamericano, Cuba's premiere movie shindig.

History

In 1514 San Cristóbal de La Habana was founded on the south coast of Cuba near the mouth of the Río Mayabeque by Spanish conquistador Pánfilo de Narváez. Named after the daughter of a famous Taíno Indian chief, the city was moved twice during its first five years due to mosquito infestations and wasn't permanently established on its present site until December 17, 1519. According to local legend, the first Mass was said beneath a ceiba tree in present-day Plaza de Armas.

Havana is the most westerly and isolated of Diego Velázquez' original villas, and life was hard in the early days. Things didn't get any better in 1538 when French pirates and local slaves razed the city.

It took the Spanish conquest of Mexico and Peru to swing the pendulum in Havana's favor. The town's strategic location, at the mouth of the Gulf of Mexico, made it a perfect nexus for the annual treasure fleets to regroup in its sheltered harbor before heading east. Thus endowed, its ascension was quick and decisive, and in 1607 Havana replaced Santiago as the capital of Cuba.

The city was sacked by French pirates led by Jacques de Sores in 1555; the Spanish replied by building the La Punta and El Morro forts between 1558 and 1630 to reinforce an already formidable protective ring. From 1674 to 1740, a strong wall around the city was added. These defenses kept the pirates at bay but proved ineffective when Spain became embroiled in the Seven Years' War with Britain, the strongest maritime power of the era.

On June 6, 1762, a British army under the Earl of Albemarle attacked Havana, landing at Cojímar and striking inland to Guanabacoa. From there they drove west along the northeastern side of the harbor, and on July 30 they attacked El Morro from the rear. Other troops landed at La Chorrera, west of the city, and by August 13 the Spanish were surrounded and forced to surrender. The British held Havana for 11 months. (The same war cost France almost all its colonies in North America, including Québec and Louisiana – a major paradigm shift.)

When the Spanish regained the city a year later in exchange for Florida, they began a crash building program to upgrade the city's defenses in order to avoid another debilitating siege. A new fortress, La Cabaña, was built along the ridge from which the British had shelled El Morro, and by the time the work was finished in 1774, Havana had become the most heavily fortified city in the New World, the 'bulwark of the Indies.'

The British occupation resulted in Spain opening Havana to freer trade. In 1765 the city was granted the right to trade with seven Spanish cities instead of only Cádiz, and from 1818 Havana was allowed to ship

HAVANA IN...

Two Days

Explore Habana Vieja by strolling the streets between the four main colonial squares. There are a plethora of museums, so you'll want to weed out the good ones. The **Museo de la Ciudad** is a highlight in the colonial core, while in Centro Havana don't miss the **Museo de la Revolución** and the dual-sited **Museo de Bellas Artes**. You can cover a lot of ground on Havana's open-topped bus tour, although the **Malecón sea drive** is best plied on foot. For nightlife, soak up the nocturnal essence of Habana Vieja, dipping into bars on **Calle Obispo** and **Plaza Vieja**.

Four Days

With two extra days, make sure you check out the '50s-era kitsch of the Vedado neighborhood. Essential stops are the **Hotel Nacional** for a mojito on the alfresco terrace and **Plaza de la Revolución** for a look at the Che mural and the Memorial a José Martí. Stick around in the evening for some excellent nightlife in jazz clubs, lounge bars and cabarets.

One Week

Three more days gives you time to get out to suburban sights such as the **Museo Hemingway**, the historic colonial forts on the east side of the harbor and the **Aquarium** in Miramar.

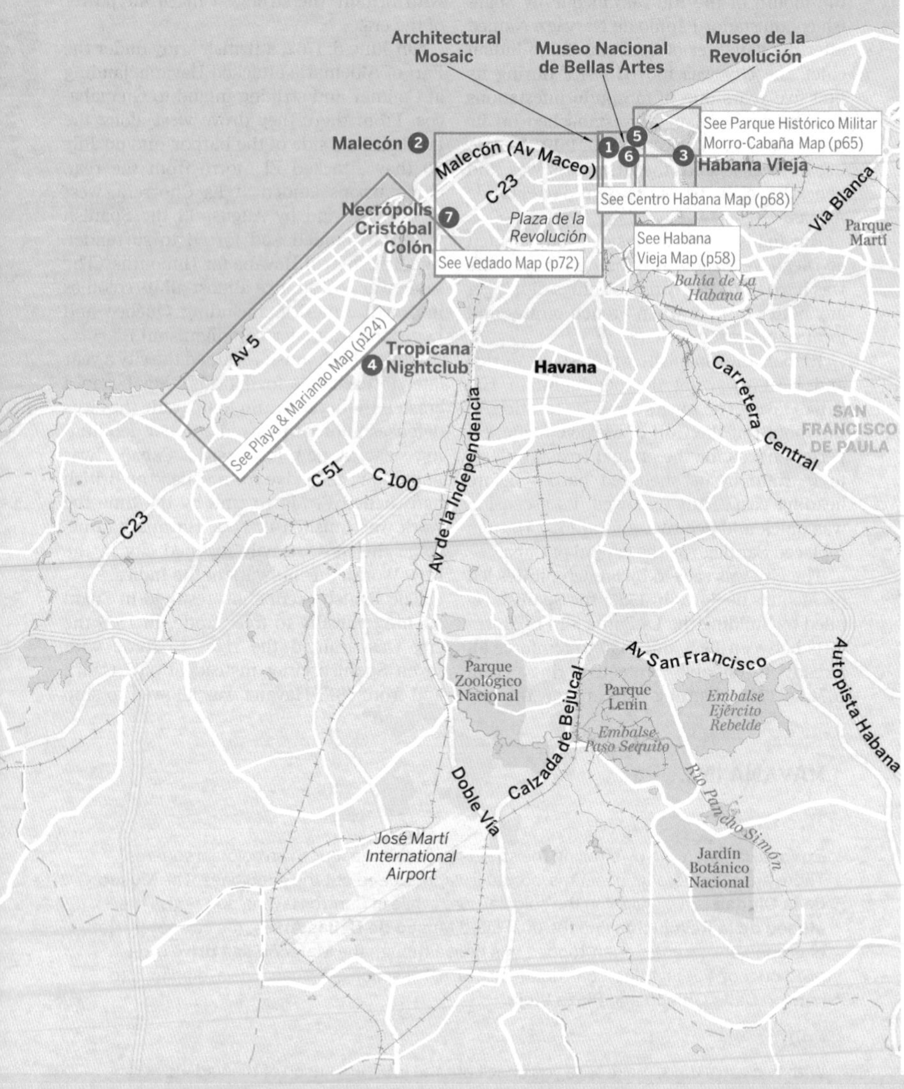

Havana Highlights

1. Stroll through Havana's mosaic of art deco, colonial baroque and neoclassical **architecture** (p84)
2. Take in the dramatic sweep of the **Malecón** (p78) at sunset
3. See how tourist money has helped to rehabilitate **Habana Vieja** (p80)
4. Rediscover kitsch at the **Tropicana Nightclub** (p130)
5. Storm the gates of the **Museo de la Revolución** (p70)
6. Trace the history of Cuban painting in the **Museo Nacional de Bellas Artes** (p67)

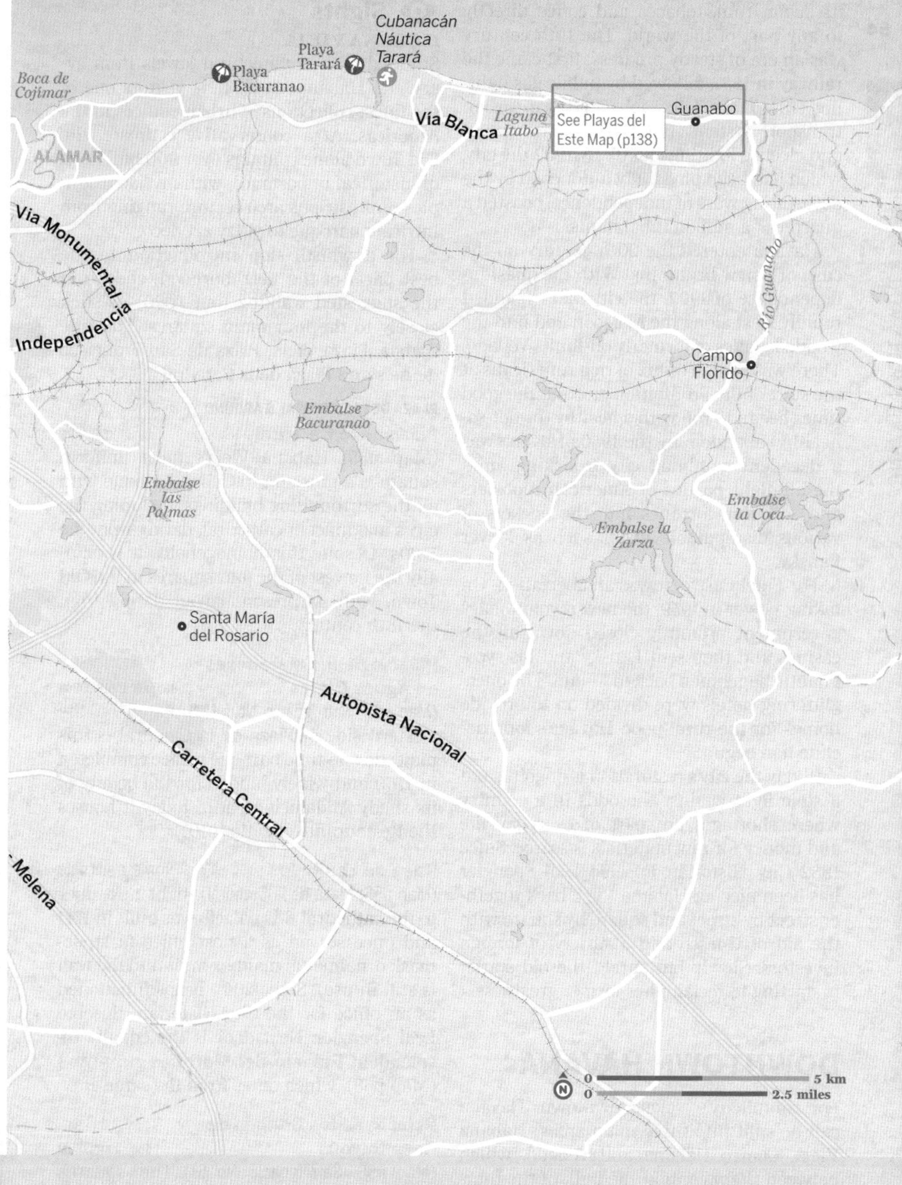

7 Try not to get spooked in the strangely beautiful **Necrópolis Cristóbal Colón** (p78)

its sugar, rum, tobacco and coffee directly to any part of the world. The 19th century was an era of steady progress: first came the railway in 1837, followed by public gas lighting (1848), the telegraph (1851), an urban transport system (1862), telephones (1888) and electric lighting (1890). By 1902 the city, which had been physically untouched by the devastating wars of independence, boasted a quarter of a million inhabitants.

Havana entered the 20th century on the cusp of a new beginning. With the quasi-independence of 1902, the city had expanded rapidly west along the Malecón and into the wooded glades of formerly off-limits Vedado. There was a large influx of rich Americans at the start of the Prohibition era, and the good times began to roll with a healthy (or not-so-healthy) abandon; by the 1950s Havana was a decadent gambling city frolicking amid the all-night parties of American mobsters and scooping fortunes into the pockets of various disreputable hoods such as Meyer Lansky.

For Fidel Castro, it was an aberration. On taking power in 1959, the new revolutionary government promptly closed down all the casinos and then sent Lansky and his sycophantic henchmen back to Miami. The once-glittering hotels were divided up to provide homes for the rural poor. Havana's long decline had begun.

Today the city's restoration is ongoing and a stoic fight against the odds in a country where shortages are part of everyday life and money for raw materials is scarce. Since 1982 City Historian Eusebio Leal Spengler has been piecing Habana Vieja back together street by street and square by square with the aid of Unesco and a variety of foreign investors. Slowly but surely, the old starlet is starting to reclaim her former greatness.

DOWNTOWN HAVANA

For simplicity's sake downtown Havana can be split into three main areas: Habana Vieja, Centro Habana and Vedado, which between them contain the bulk of the tourist sights. Centrally located Habana Vieja is the city's atmospheric historical masterpiece; Centro Habana, to the west, provides an eye-opening look at the real-life Cuba in close-up; and the more majestic Vedado is the once-notorious Mafia-run district replete with hotels, restaurants and a pulsating nightlife.

Sights

HABANA VIEJA

Studded with architectural jewels from every era, Habana Vieja offers visitors one of the finest collections of urban edifices in the Americas. At a conservative estimate, the Old Town alone contains over 900 buildings of historical importance, with myriad examples of illustrious architecture ranging from intricate baroque to glitzy art deco.

For a whistle-stop introduction to the best parts of the neighborhood, check out the suggested walking tour (p80) or stick closely to the four main squares: Plaza de Armas, Plaza Vieja, Plaza de San Francisco de Asís and Plaza de la Catedral.

PLAZA DE LA CATEDRAL & AROUND

Plaza de la Catedral SQUARE

(Map p58) Habana Vieja's most uniform square is a museum to Cuban baroque with all the surrounding buildings, including the city's magnificent cathedral, dating from the 1700s. Despite this homogeneity, it is actually the newest of the four squares in the Old Town, with its present layout dating from the 18th century.

Palacio de los Marqueses de Aguas Claras NOTABLE BUILDING

(Map p58; San Ignacio No 54) Situated on the western side of Plaza de la Catedral is this majestic one-time baroque palace completed in 1760 and widely lauded for the beauty of its shady Andalucian patio. Today it houses the Restaurante el Patio (p101).

Casa de Lombillo NOTABLE BUILDING

(Map p58; Plaza de la Catedral) Right next door to the cathedral this palacio was built in 1741 and once served as a post office (a stone-mask ornamental mailbox built into the wall is still in use). Since 2000 it has functioned as an office for the City Historian, Eusebio Leal Spengler. Next door is the equally resplendent **Palacio del Marqués de Arcos** (Map p58), which dates from the same era.

Palacio de los Condes de Casa Bayona MUSEUM

(Map p58; San Ignacio No 61) The square's southern aspect is taken up by its oldest building, constructed in 1720. Today it functions as the **Museo de Arte Colonial** (Map p58; unguided CUC$2; ⌚9am-6:30pm), a small museum displaying colonial furniture and decorative arts. Among the finer exhibits are pieces of china with scenes of colonial

HAVANA STREET NAMES

OLD NAME	NEW NAME
Av de los Presidentes	Calle G
Av de Maceo	Malecón
Av del Puerto	Av Carlos Manuel de Céspedes
Av de Rancho	Av de la Independencia Boyeros (Boyeros)
Belascoaín	Padre Varela
Cárcel	Capdevila
Carlos III (Tercera)	Av Salvador Allende
Cristina	Av de México
Egido	Av de Bélgica
Estrella	Enrique Barnet
Galiano	Av de Italia
La Rampa	Calle 23
Monserrate	Av de las Misiones
Monte	Máximo Gómez
Paseo del Prado	Paseo de Martí
Paula	Leonor Pérez
Reina	Av Simón Bolívar
San José	San Martín
Someruelos	Aponte
Teniente Rey	Brasil
Vives	Av de España
Zulueta	Agramonte

Cuba, a collection of ornamental flowers, and many colonial-era dining-room sets.

Catedral de San Cristóbal de la Habana CHURCH

(Map p58; cnr San Ignacio & Empedrado; ⏲until noon) Dominated by two unequal towers and framed by a theatrical baroque facade designed by Italian architect Francesco Borromini, Havana's incredible cathedral was once described by novelist Alejo Carpentier as 'music set in stone.' The Jesuits began construction of the church in 1748 and work continued despite their expulsion in 1767. When the building was finished in 1787, the diocese of Havana was created and the church became a cathedral – one of the oldest in the Americas. The remains of Columbus were interred here from 1795 to 1898, when they were moved to Seville. The best time to visit is during Sunday Mass (10:30am).

Centro Wilfredo Lam CULTURAL CENTER

(Map p58; cnr San Ignacio & Empedrado; admission CUC$3; ⏲10am-5pm Mon-Sat) On the corner of Plaza de Catedral (to the left of the cathedral), this cultural center contains a cafe and exhibition center named after the island's most celebrated painter but which usually displays the works of more modern painters.

Taller Experimental de Gráfica ART WORKSHOP

(Map p58; Callejón del Chorro No 6; admission free; ⏲10am-4pm Mon-Fri) Easy to miss at the end of a short cul-de-sac, but ignore it at your peril. This is Havana's most cutting-edge art workshop, which also offers the possibility of engraving classes (see p83). Come and see the masters at work.

Parque Maestranza PLAYGROUND

(Map p58; Av Carlos Manuel de Céspedes; admission CUC$1; under 4yr only) Small scale but fun kids' playground with inflatable castles and other games overlooking the harbor.

PLAZA DE ARMAS & AROUND

Plaza de Armas SQUARE

(Map p58) Havana's oldest square was laid out in the early 1520s, soon after the city's foundation, and was originally known as Plaza de Iglesia after a church – the Parroquial Mayor – that once stood on the site of the present-day Palacio de los Capitanes Generales. The name Plaza de Armas (Square of Arms) wasn't adopted until the late 16th century, when the colonial governor, then housed in the Castillo de la Real Fuerza, used the site to conduct military exercises. Today's plaza, along with most of the buildings around it, dates from the late 1700s.

In the center of the square, which is lined with royal palms and hosts a daily (except Sundays) **secondhand book market**, is a marble **statue of Carlos Manuel de Céspedes** (Map p58; 1955), the man who set Cuba on the road to independence in 1868.

Also of note on the square's eastern aspect is the late-18th-century **Palacio de los Condes de Santovenia** (Map p58), today the five-star, 27-room Hotel Santa Isabel.

Museo el Templete MUSEUM

(Map p58; Plaza de Armas; admission CUC$2; ⌚8:30am-6pm) The tiny neoclassical Doric chapel on the east side of Plaza de Armas was erected in 1828 at the point where Havana's first Mass was held beneath a ceiba tree in November 1519. A similar ceiba tree has now replaced the original. Inside the chapel are three large paintings of the event by the French painter Jean Baptiste Vermay (1786–1833).

Museo Nacional de Historia Natural MUSEUM

(Map p58; Obispo No 61; admission CUC$3; ⌚9:30am-7:30pm Tue-Sun) An average museum that contains examples of Cuba's flora and fauna, and overlooks Plaza de Armas.

Museo de la Ciudad MUSEUM

(Map p58; Tacón No 1; admission CUC$3; ⌚9:30am-6pm) Filling the whole west side of Plaza de Armas, this museum is housed in the **Palacio de los Capitanes Generales** (Map p58), dating from the 1770s. Built on the site of Havana's original church, it's a textbook example of Cuban baroque architecture hewn out of rock from the nearby San Lázaro quarries and has served many purposes over the years. From 1791 until 1898 it was the residence of the Spanish captains general. From 1899 until 1902, the US military governors were based here, and during the first two decades of the 20th century, the building briefly became the presidential palace. Since 1968 it has been home to the City Museum, one of Havana's most comprehensive and interesting. City Museum wraps its way regally around a splendid central courtyard adorned with a white marble statue of Christopher Columbus (1862). Artifacts include period furniture, military uniforms and old-fashioned 19th-century horse carriages, while old photos vividly re-create events from Havana's rollercoaster history, such as the 1898 sinking of US battleship *Maine* in the harbor. It's better to body-swerve the pushy attendants and wander around at your own pace.

A QUARTET OF SQUARES

In marked contrast to other Spanish colonial cities, Havana grew up around not *one* but *four* pivotal squares, each bequeathed with its own specific function. Plaza de la Catedral was the city's religious nexus, Plaza de Armas guarded a fort and a military parade ground, water-side Plaza San Francisco de Asís was the main shipping dock for passing Spanish galleons, and Plaza Vieja hosted an important market.

Of the contemporary four, only Plaza de Catedral retains a functioning church. Plaza de Armas' church was demolished in the 1770s to make way for the Palacio de los Capitanes Generales, Plaza San Francisco's church/convent ceased to have a religious function in the 1840s (it is now a museum and concert hall) and newer Plaza Vieja never had a church in the first place.

Interconnected by narrow cobbled streets, Habana Vieja's squares are within easy strolling distance of each other and all are wonderfully intimate, especially at night. Restoring them to their colonial glory took the City Historian's Office many years of painstaking effort, but the process is now complete. Behind their atmospheric colonial facades, the revered quartet now harbors atmospheric boutique hotels, clever museums, open-fronted cafes, a secondhand book market and even a planetarium.

Palacio del Segundo Cabo LANDMARK

(Map p58; O'Reilly No 4; admission CUC$1) Wedged into the square's northwest corner, this building was constructed in 1772 as the headquarters of the Spanish vice-governor. After several reincarnations as a post office, the palace of the Senate, the Supreme Court, the National Academy of Arts and Letters, and the seat of the Cuban Geographical Society, the building is today a well-stocked bookstore (p115). Pop-art fans should take a look at the palace's **Sala Galería Raúl Martínez** (Map p58; ⌚9am-6pm Mon-Sat). The building was being renovated at time of writing.

Castillo de la Real Fuerza MUSEUM, FORT

(Map p58) On the seaward side of Plaza de Armas is the oldest existing fort in the Americas, built between 1558 and 1577 on the site of an earlier fort destroyed by French privateers in 1555. The west tower is crowned by a copy of a famous bronze weather vane called **La Giraldilla**; the original was cast in Havana in 1632 by Jerónimo Martínez Pinzón and is popularly believed to be of Doña Inés de Bobadilla, the wife of gold explorer Hernando de Soto. The original is now kept in the Museo de la Ciudad, and the figure also appears on the Havana Club rum label. Imposing and indomitable, the castle is ringed by an impressive moat and today shelters the **Museo de Navegación** (Map p58; admission CUC$2; ⌚9am-6pm; 👪), which opened in 2008 and displays interesting exposés on the history of the fort and Old Town, and its connections with the erstwhile Spanish Empire. Look out for huge scale model of the *Santíssima Trinidad* galleon.

Museo del Automóvil MUSEUM

(Map p58; Oficios No 13; admission CUC$1; ⌚9am-7pm) Few miss the irony of this vaguely surreal museum stuffed with ancient Thunderbirds, Pontiacs and Ford Model Ts, most of which appear to be in better shape than the dinosaurs that ply the streets outside.

TOP CHOICE **Calle Mercaderes** STREET

(Map p58) Cobbled, car-free Calle Mercaderes (literally: Merchant's Street) has been extensively restored by the City Historian's Office and is an almost complete replica of its splendid 18th-century high-water mark. Interspersed with the museums, shops and restaurants are some real-life working social projects, such as a maternity home and a needlecraft cooperative. Most of the myriad museums are free, including the **Casa de Asia** (Map p58; Mercaderes No 111; ⌚10am-6pm Tue-Sat, 9am-1pm Sun), with paintings and sculpture from China and Japan; the **Museo del Tabaco** (Mercaderes No 120; ⌚10am-5pm Mon-Sat), where you can gawp at various indigenous pipes and idols; the **Armería 9 de Abril** (Map p58; Mercaderes No 157; ⌚10am-6pm Mon-Sat), an old gun shop (now museum) stormed by revolutionaries on the said date in 1958; and the **Museo de Bomberos** (Map p58; cnr Mercaderes & Lamparilla; ⌚10am-6pm Mon-Sat), which has antediluvian fire equipment dedicated to 19 Havana firemen who lost their lives in an 1890 railway fire.

Just off Mercaderes down Obrapía, it's worth slinking into the gratis **Casa de África** (Map p58; Obrapía No 157; admission free; ⌚9:30am-7:30pm), which houses sacred objects relating to Santería collected by ethnographer Fernando Ortíz.

The corner of Mercaderes and Obrapía has an international flavor, with a bronze **statue of Simón Bolívar** (Map p58), the Latin America liberator, and across the street you'll find the **Museo de Simón Bolívar** (Mercaderes No 160; donations accepted; ⌚9am-5pm Tue-Sun) dedicated to Bolívar's life. The **Casa de México Benito Juárez** (Map p58; Obrapía No 116; admission CUC$1; ⌚10:15am-5:45pm Tue-Sat, 9am-1pm Sun) exhibits Mexican folk art and plenty of books, but not a lot on Señor Juárez (Mexico's first indigenous president) himself. Just east is the **Casa Oswaldo Guayasamín** (Map p58; Obrapía No 111; donations accepted; ⌚9am-2:30pm Tue-Sun). Now a museum, this was once the studio of the great Ecuadorian artist who painted Fidel in numerous poses.

Mercaderes is also characterized by its restored **shops**, including a perfume store and a spice shop. Wander at your will.

Maqueta de La Habana Vieja MUSEUM

(Map p58; Mercaderes No 114; unguided/guided CUC$1/2; ⌚9am-6pm; 👪) Herein lies a 1:500 scale model of Habana Vieja complete with an authentic soundtrack meant to replicate a day in the life of the city. It's incredibly detailed and provides an excellent way of geographically acquainting yourself with the city's historical core.

Casa de la Obra Pía NOTABLE BUILDING

(Map p58; Obrapía No 158; admission CUC$1; ⌚9am-4:30pm Tue-Sat, 9:30am-12:30pm Sun) One of the more muscular sights on Calle Mercaderes is this typical Havana aristocratic residence

Habana Vieja

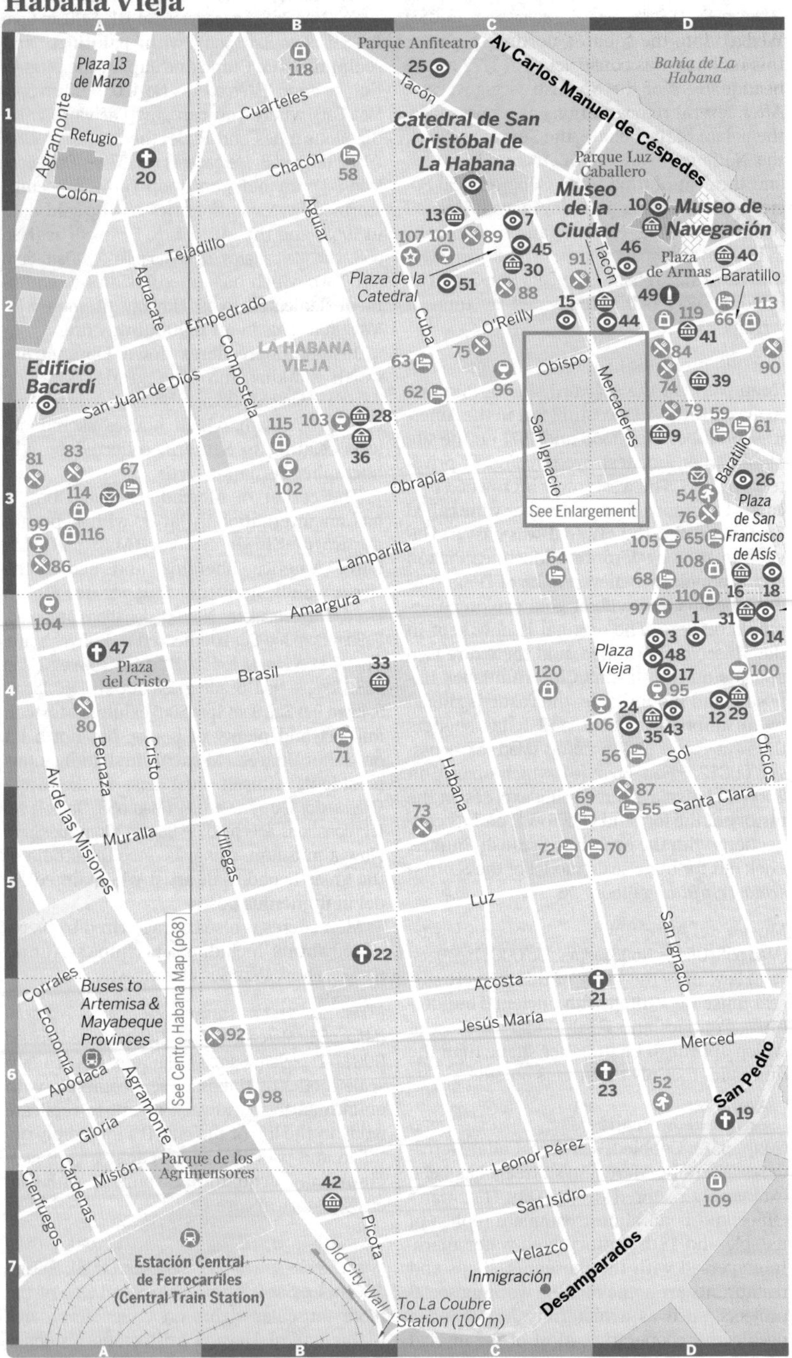

originally built in 1665 and rebuilt in 1780. Baroque decoration – including an intricate portico made in Cádiz, Spain – covers the exterior facade. In addition to its historical value, the house today contains one of the City Historian's most commendable social projects: a **sewing and needlecraft cooperative** that has a workshop inside and a small shop selling clothes and textiles on Calle Mercaderes.

PLAZA DE SAN FRANCISCO DE ASÍS & AROUND

Plaza de San Francisco de Asís — SQUARE

(Map p58) Facing Havana harbor, the breezy Plaza de San Francisco de Asís first grew up in the 16th century when Spanish galleons stopped by at the quayside on their passage through the Indies to Spain. A market took root in the 1500s, followed by a church in 1608, though when the pious monks complained of too much noise the market was moved a few blocks south to Plaza Vieja. The Plaza de San Francisco underwent a full restoration in the late 1990s and is most notable for its uneven cobblestones and the white marble **Fuente de los Leones** (Map p58; Fountain of Lions) carved by the Italian sculptor Giuseppe Gagginni in 1836. A more modern statue outside the square's famous church depicts **El Caballero de París** (Map p58), a well-known street person who roamed Havana during the 1950s, engaging passers-by with his philosophies on life, religion, politics and current events. On the eastern side of the plaza stands the **Terminal Sierra Maestra** (Map p58) cruise terminal, which dispatches shiploads of weekly tourists, while nearby the domed **Lonja del Comercio** (Map p58) is a former commodities market erected in 1909 and restored in 1996 to provide office space for foreign companies with joint ventures in Cuba.

Iglesia y Monasterio de San Francisco de Asís — MUSEUM

(Map p58) The southern side of Plaza San Francisco de Asís is taken up by an erstwhile church cum monastery. Originally constructed in 1608 and rebuilt in the baroque style from 1719 to 1738, San Francisco de Asís was taken over by the Spanish state in 1841 as part of a political move against the powerful religious orders of the day, when it ceased to be a church. Today it's both a **concert hall** (⏲from 5pm or 6pm) hosting classical music and the **Museo de Arte Religioso** (Map p58; unguided/guided CUC$2/3; ⏲9am-6pm) replete with religious paintings, silverware, woodcarvings and ceramics.

Habana Vieja

Top Sights

- Catedral de San Cristóbal de La Habana ... C1
- Edificio Bacardí ... A3
- Iglesia y Monasterio de San Francisco de Asís ... D4
- Museo de la Ciudad ... D2
- Museo de Navegación ... D2
- Museo del Ron ... E4

Sights

1 Aquarivm ... D4
2 Armería 9 de Abril ... F7
3 Cámara Oscura ... D4
4 Casa de África ... F7
5 Casa de Asia ... F6
6 Casa de la Obra Pía ... F6
7 Casa de Lombillo ... C2
8 Casa de México Benito Juárez ... F6
9 Casa Oswaldo Guayasamín ... D3
10 Castillo de la Real Fuerza ... D1
11 Catedral Ortodoxa Nuestra Señora de Kazán ... E4
12 Centro Cultural Pablo de la Torriente Brau ... D4
13 Centro Wilfredo Lam ... C2
14 Coche Mambí ... D4
15 Edificio Santo Domingo ... C2
16 El Caballero de Paris ... D3
17 Fototeca de Cuba ... D4
18 Fuente de los Leones ... D3
19 Iglesia de San Francisco de Paula ... D6
20 Iglesia del Santo Angel Custodio ... A1
21 Iglesia Parroquial del Espíritu Santo ... D6
22 Iglesia y Convento de Nuestra Señora de Belén ... B5
23 Iglesia y Convento de Nuestra Señora de la Merced ... D6
Iglesia y Convento de Santa Clara ... (see 72)
24 La Casona Centro de Arte ... D4
25 La Maestranza ... C1
26 Lonja del Comercio ... D3
27 Maqueta de La Habana Vieja ... F6
28 Museo 28 Septiembre de los CDR ... B3
29 Museo Alejandro Humboldt ... D4
30 Museo de Arte Colonial ... C2
31 Museo de Arte Religioso ... D4
32 Museo de Bomberos ... F7
33 Museo de la Farmacia Habanera ... B4
34 Museo de la Orfebrería ... F5
35 Museo de Naipes ... D4
36 Museo de Numismático ... B3
37 Museo de Pintura Mural ... F6
38 Museo de Simón Bolívar ... F7
39 Museo del Automóvil ... D2
Museo del Tabaco ... (see 117)
40 Museo el Templete ... D2
41 Museo Nacional de Historia Natural ... D2
42 Museo-Casa Natal de José Martí ... B7
43 Palacio Cueto ... D4
44 Palacio de los Capitanes Generales ... D2
Palacio de los Condes de Casa Bayona ... (see 30)
Palacio de los Condes de Santovenia ... (see 66)
Palacio de los Marqueses de Aguas Claras ... (see 89)
45 Palacio del Marqués de Arcos ... C2
46 Palacio del Segundo Cabo ... D2
47 Parroquial del Santo Cristo del Buen Viaje ... A4
48 Planetario ... D4
Sala Galería Raúl Martínez ... (see 46)
49 Statue of Carlos Manuel de Céspedes ... D2
50 Statue of Simón Bolívar ... F6
51 Taller Experimental de Gráfica ... C2

Activities, Courses & Tours

52 Gimnasio de Boxeo Rafael Trejo ... D6
53 Infotur ... E6
54 San Cristóbal Agencia de Viajes ... D3
Taller Experimental de Gráfica ... (see 51)

FREE **Museo Alejandro Humboldt** MUSEUM

(Map p58; cnr Oficios & Muralla; ⏲9am-5pm Tue-Sat) Often referred to as the 'second discoverer' of Cuba, German scientist, Alejandro Humboldt's huge Cuban legacy goes largely unnoticed by outsiders. This small museum displays a historical trajectory of his work collecting scientific and botanical data across the island in the early 1800s. Nearby is the **Coche Mambí** (Map p58), a train carriage built in the US in 1900 and brought to Cuba in 1912.

Sleeping

55 Casa de Pepe & Rafaela........D5
56 Hostal Beltrán de la Santa Cruz........D4
57 Hostal Condes de Villanueva........F7
58 Hostal Palacio O'Farrill........B1
59 Hostal Valencia........D3
60 Hotel Ambos Mundos........F6
61 Hotel el Comendador........D3
62 Hotel Florida........C2
63 Hotel Marqués de Prado Ameno........C2
64 Hotel Raquel........C3
65 Hotel San Felipe y Santiago de Bejúcal........D3
66 Hotel Santa Isabel........D2
67 Juan & Margarita........A3
68 Mesón de la Flota........D3
69 Migdalia Carraballe........C5
70 Noemi Moreno........D5
71 Pablo Rodríguez........B4
72 Residencia Académica Convento de Santa Clara........C5

Eating

73 Agropecuario Sol........C5
74 Al Medina........D2
75 Café de O'Reilly........C2
76 Café del Oriente........D3
77 Café Lamparilla........F7
78 Café Santo Domingo........E6
79 Cafetería Torre la Vega........D3
El Mecurio........(see 26)
80 Hanoi........A4
81 Harris Brothers........A3
82 La Imprenta........F7
83 La Julia........A3
84 La Mina........D2
85 La Torre de Marfil........F6
86 La Zaragozana........A3
Mesón de la Flota........(see 68)
87 Paladar la Mulata del Sabor........D5
88 Paladar Moneda Cubana........C2
89 Restaurante el Patio........C2
90 Restaurante el Templete........D2
91 Restaurante la Dominica........C2
Restaurante la Paella........(see 59)
92 Restaurante Puerto de Sagua........B6

Drinking

93 Bar Dos Hermanos........E4
94 Café de las Infusiones........F6
95 Café el Escorial........D4
96 Café París........C2
97 Café Taberna........D4
98 El Baturro........B6
99 El Floridita........A3
100 El Reloj Cuervo y Sobrinos........D4
101 La Bodeguita del Medio........C2
102 La Dichosa........B3
103 La Lluvia de Oro........B3
104 Monserrate Bar........A4
105 Museo del Chocolate........D3
106 Taberna de la Muralla........D4

Entertainment

Basílica Menor de San Francisco de Asís........(see 31)
107 Fundación Alejo Carpentier........C2

Shopping

108 Casa de Carmen Montilla........D3
109 Centro Cultural Antiguos Almacenes de Depósito San José........D7
110 Estudio Galería los Oficios........D4
111 Fundación Havana Club Shop........E4
112 Habana 1791........F6
Hostal Condes de Villanueva........(see 57)
113 La Casa de Cafe........D2
Librería Grijalbo Mondadovi........(see 46)
114 Librería la Internacional........A3
115 Longina Música........B3
116 Moderna Poesía........A3
117 Museo del Tabaco........F6
118 Palacio de la Artesanía........B1
119 Plaza de Armas Secondhand Book Market........D2
120 Taller de Serigrafía René Portocarrero........C4

Museo del Ron MUSEUM

(Map p58; San Pedro No 262; admission incl guide CUC$7; ⏲9am-5pm Mon-Fri, 10am-4pm Sat & Sun) You don't have to be an Añejo Reserva quaffer to enjoy the Museo del Ron in the Fundación Havana Club, but it probably helps. The museum, with its bilingual guided tour shows rum-making antiquities and the complex brewing process. A not over-generous measure of rum is included in the price. There's a bar and shop on site, but the savvy reconvene to Bar Dos Hermanos (p107) next door. The museum sits opposite Havana harbour and a block north from Catedral Ortodoxa Nuestra.

Aquarivm AQUARIUM
(Map p58; Brasil No 9 btwn Mercaderes & Oficios; ⌚9am-5:30pm Tue-Sun; 👪) Indoor freshwater fish in tanks make this small aquarium of interest to children.

PLAZA VIEJA & AROUND

TOP CHOICE **Plaza Vieja** SQUARE
(Map p58) Laid out in 1559, Plaza Vieja (Old Square) is Havana's most architecturally eclectic square, where Cuban baroque nestles seamlessly next to Gaudí-inspired art nouveau. Originally called Plaza Nueva (New Square), it was initially used for military exercises and later served as an open-air marketplace. During the Batista regime an ugly underground parking lot was constructed here, but this monstrosity was demolished in 1996 to make way for a massive renovation project. Sprinkled liberally with bars, restaurants and cafes, Plaza Vieja today boasts its own micro-brewery, the Angela Landa primary school and a beautiful fenced-in fountain.

Cámara Oscura LANDMARK
(Map p58; Plaza Vieja; admission CUC$2; ⌚9am-5pm Tue-Sat, 9am-1pm Sun; 👪) On the northwestern corner of Plaza Vieja is this clever optical device providing live, 360-degree views of the city from atop a 35m-tall tower. Explanations are in Spanish and English.

FREE **Fototeca de Cuba** ART GALLERY
(Map p58; Mercaderes No 307; ⌚10am-5pm Tue-Fri, 9am-noon Sat) A photo gallery with intriguing exhibits by local and international artists that also serves a more important function as the main photo archive for the City Historian's Office.

FREE **Museo de Naipes** MUSEUM
(Map p58; Muralla No 101; ⌚9am-6pm Tue-Sun) Encased in Plaza Vieja's oldest building is this quirky playing-card museum with a 2000-strong collection that includes rock stars, rum drinks and round cards.

FREE **La Casona Centro de Arte** ART GALLERY
(Map p58; Muralla No 107; ⌚10am-5pm Mon-Fri, 10am-2pm Sat) Housed in one of Plaza Vieja's most striking buildings (note the sturdy colonial overtones), this gallery/shop has great solo and group shows by up-and-coming Cuban artists.

Palacio Cueto LANDMARK
(Map p58; cnr Muralla & Mercaderes) Kissing the southeast corner of Plaza Vieja is this distinctive Gaudí-esque building, which remains Havana's finest example of art nouveau. Its outrageously ornate facade once housed a warehouse and a hat factory before it was rented by José Cueto in the 1920s as the Palacio Vienna hotel. Habaguanex, the commercial arm of the City Historian's Office, is in the process of restoring the building, which was constructed in 1906 and has lain empty and unused since the early '90s.

Planetario PLANETARIUM
(Map p58; Mercaderes; admission CUC$10; ⌚9:30am-5pm Wed-Sat, 9:30am-12:30pm Sun; 👪) One of Havana's newest sights is this planetarium built with the help of Japanese investment and opened in December 2009. At the time of writing the planetarium was only accessible by guided tours booked in advance. Tours must be booked the previous Monday. Exhibits include a scale reproduction of the solar system inside a giant orb, a simulation of the Big Bang, and a theater that allows viewing of over 6000 stars. All pretty exciting stuff.

FREE **Centro Cultural Pablo de la Torriente Brau** CULTURAL CENTER
(Map p58; www.centropablo.cult.cu; Muralla No 63; ⌚9am-5:30pm Tue-Sat) Tucked away behind Plaza Vieja, the 'Brau' is a leading cultural institution that was formed under the auspices of the Unión de Escritores y Artistas de Cuba (Uneac; Union of Cuban Writers and Artists) in 1996. The center hosts expositions, poetry readings and live acoustic music. Its Salón de Arte Digital is renowned for its groundbreaking digital art.

CALLE OBISPO & AROUND

Calle Obispo STREET
(Map p58) Narrow, car-free Calle Obispo (literally: Bishop's Street), Habana Vieja's main interconnecting artery, is packed with art galleries, shops, music bars and people. Four- and five-story buildings block out most of the sunlight, and the swaying throng of people seem to move in time to the all-pervading live music.

Museo de Numismático MUSEUM
(Map p58; Obispo btwn Aguiar & Habana; admission CUC$1; ⌚9am-4:45pm) This numismatist's heaven brings together various collections of medals, coins and banknotes from around the world, including a stash of 1000 mainly

American gold coins (1869–1928) and a full chronology of Cuban banknotes from the 19th century to the present.

Museo 28 Septiembre de los CDR MUSEUM
(Map p58; Obispo btwn Aguiar & Habana; admission CUC$2; ⏲9am-5pm) A venerable building on Obispo that dedicates two floors to a rather biased dissection of the nationwide Comités de la Defensa de la Revolución (CDR; Committees for the Defense of the Revolution). Commendable neighborhood-watch schemes, or grassroots spying agencies? Sift through the propaganda and decide.

FREE **Museo de Pintura Mural** MUSEUM
(Map p58; Obispo btwn Mercaderes & Oficios; ⏲10am-6pm) A simple museum that exhibits some beautifully restored original frescoes in the Casa del Mayorazgo de Recio, popularly considered to be Havana's oldest surviving house.

Museo de la Orfebrería MUSEUM
(Map p58; Obispo No 113; admission by donation; ⏲9am-4:30pm Tue-Sat, 9:30am-12:30pm Mon) A silverware museum set out in the house of erstwhile silversmith Gregorio Tabares, who had a workshop here from 1707.

Edificio Santo Domingo MUSEUM, ART GALLERY
(Map p58; Mercaderes btwn Obispo & O'Reilly) Across Obispo from the Hotel Ambos Mundos is the site of Havana's original university, which stood here between 1728 and 1902. It was originally part of a convent; the contemporary modern office block was built by Habaguanex in 2006 over the skeleton of an uglier 1950s office, the roof of which was used as a helicopter landing pad. It has been ingeniously refitted with the convent's original bell tower and baroque doorway – an interesting juxtaposition of old and new. Many of the university's arts faculties have now moved back here, and a small museum/art gallery displays a scale model of the original convent and various artifacts that were rescued from it.

Plaza del Cristo & Around SQUARE
(Map p58) Habana Vieja's fifth (and most overlooked) square lies at the west end of the neighborhood, a little apart from the historical core, and has yet to benefit from the City Historian's makeover. It's worth a look for the **Parroquial del Santo Cristo del Buen Viaje** (Map p58), a church dating from 1732, although there has been a Franciscan hermitage on this site since 1640. Still only partially renovated, the building is most notable for its intricate stained-glass windows and brightly painted wooden ceiling. The Plaza del Cristo also hosts a primary school (hence the noise) and a microcosmic slice of everyday Cuban life without tourists.

FREE **Museo de la Farmacia Habanera** MUSEUM
(Map p58; cnr Brasil & Compostela; ⏲9am-5pm) A few blocks up Calle Brasil from Plaza del Cristo, this museum-store founded in 1886 by Catalan José Sarrá still acts as a working pharmacy for Cubans. The small museum section displays an elegant mock-up of an old drugstore with some interesting historical explanations.

SOUTHERN HABANA VIEJA

Iglesia y Convento de Santa Clara CONVENT
(Map p58; Cuba No 610; admission CUC$2; ⏲9am-4pm Mon-Fri) South of Plaza Vieja is Havana's largest and oldest convent built between 1638 and 1643, though since 1920 it has served no religious purpose. For a while it housed the Ministry of Public Works, and today part of the Habana Vieja restoration team is based here. You can visit the large cloister and nuns' cemetery or even spend the night in cheap monastic digs (see p86).

Iglesia y Convento de Nuestra Señora de Belén CONVENT
(Map p58; Compostela btwn Luz & Acosta; admission CUC$2; ⏲9am-5pm Mon-Sat, 9am-1pm Sun) This one-time convent completed in 1718 and run by nuns from the Order of Bethlehem and (later) the Jesuits is now a convalescent home for senior citizens funded by the City Historian's Office. It is one of the city's most successful social projects and living proof of how tourist money and foresighted government planning can benefit local people.

Iglesia y Convento de Nuestra Señora de la Merced CHURCH
(Map p58; Cuba No 806; ⏲8am-noon & 3-5:30pm) Built in 1755, this hemmed-in church was reconstructed in the 19th century. Beautiful gilded altars, frescoed vaults and a number of old paintings create a sacrosanct mood; there's a quiet cloister adjacent. Two blocks away is the rather neglected **Iglesia Parroquial del Espíritu Santo** (Map p58; Acosta 161; ⏲8am-noon & 3-6pm), Havana's oldest surviving church, built in 1640 and rebuilt in 1674.

Iglesia de San Francisco de Paula CHURCH

(Map p58; cnr Leonor Pérez & Desamparados) One of Havana's most attractive churches, this building was fully restored in 2000. It is all that remains of the San Francisco de Paula women's hospital from the mid-1700s. Lit up at night for concerts, the stained glass, heavy cupola and baroque facade are romantic and inviting.

Catedral Ortodoxa Nuestra Señora de Kazán CHURCH

(Map p58; Av Carlos Manuel de Céspedes btwn Sol & Santa Clara) One of Havana's newest buildings, this beautiful gold-domed Russian Orthodox church was built in the early 2000s and consecrated at a ceremony attended by Raúl Castro in October 2008. The church was part of an attempt to reignite Russian-Cuban relations after they went sour in 1991.

Museo-Casa Natal de José Martí MUSEUM

(Map p58; Leonor Pérez No 314; admission CUC$1, camera CUC$2; ⏲9am-5pm Tue-Sat) The Museo-Casa Natal de José Martí is a humble, two-story dwelling on the edge of Habana Vieja, where the apostle of Cuban independence was born on January 28, 1853. Today it's a small museum that displays letters, manuscripts, photos, books and other mementos of his life. While not as comprehensive as the Martí museum on Plaza de la Revolución, it's a charming little abode and well worth a small detour.

Old City Wall HISTORICAL SITE

In the 17th century, anxious to defend the city from attacks by pirates and overzealous foreign armies, Cuba's paranoid colonial authorities drew up plans for the construction of a 5km-long city wall. Built between 1674 and 1740, the wall on completion was 1.5m thick and 10m high, running along a line now occupied by Av de las Misiones and Av de Bélgica. Among the wall's myriad defenses were nine bastions and 180 big guns aimed toward the sea. The only way in and out of the city was through 11 heavily guarded gates that closed every night and opened every morning to the sound of a solitary gunshot. The walls were demolished starting in 1863, but a few segments remain, the largest of which stands on Av de Bélgica close to the train station (Map p58).

AVENIDA DE LAS MISIONES

Edificio Bacardí LANDMARK

(Map p58; Bacardí building; Av de las Misiones btwn Empedrado & San Juan de Dios; ⏲hours vary) Finished in 1929, the magnificent Edificio Bacardí is a triumph of art deco architecture with a whole host of lavish finishings that somehow manage to make kitschy look cool. Hemmed in by other buildings, it's hard to get a full kaleidoscopic view of the structure from street level, though the opulent bell tower can be glimpsed from all over Havana. There's a bar in the lobby, and for CUC$1 you can travel up to the tower for an eagle's-eye view.

Iglesia del Santo Angel Custodio CHURCH

(Map p58; Compostela No 2; ⏲during Mass 7:15am Tue, Wed & Fri, 6pm Thu, Sat & Sun) Originally constructed in 1695, this church was pounded by a ferocious hurricane in 1846, after which it was entirely rebuilt in neo-Gothic style. Among the notable historical and literary figures that have passed through its handsome doors are 19th-century Cuban novelist Cirilo Villaverde, who set the main scene of his novel *Cecilia Valdés* here, and Félix Varela and José Martí, who were baptized in the church in 1788 and 1853 respectively.

PARQUE HISTÓRICO MILITAR MORRO-CABAÑA

The sweeping views of Havana from the other side of the bay are spectacular, and a trip to the two old forts of the Parque Histórico Militar Morro-Cabaña is a must. Despite their location on the opposite side of the harbor, both forts are included in the Habana Vieja Unesco World Heritage Site. Sunset is a good time to visit when you can stay over for the emblematic *cañonazo* ceremony.

To get to the forts, use the P-15, P-8 or P-11 metro buses (get off at the first stop after the tunnel), but make sure you're near an exit as very few other people get out there. Otherwise, a metered tourist taxi from Habana Vieja should cost around CUC$4. Another alternative is via the Casablanca ferry, which departs from Av Carlos Manuel de Céspedes in Habana Vieja. From the Casablanca landing follow the road up to the huge Christ statue (Estatua de Cristo), where you bear left and traverse another road across some military training fields. The entrance to La Cabaña is on your left.

Parque Histórico Militar Morro-Cabaña

Parque Histórico Militar Morro-Cabaña

Top Sights

Museo de Comandancia del Che C3

Sights

1 Batería de la Divina Pastora B2
2 Batería de los Doce Apóstoles A2
3 Batería de Velasco A1
4 Cañonazo Ceremony C3
5 Entrance B2
6 Entrance A1
7 Estatua de Cristo D3
8 Maritime Museum A1
9 Museo de Fortificaciones y Armas C2
10 Observatorio Nacional D3

Eating

11 Paladar Doña Carmela C1
12 Restaurante la Divina Pastora B2
13 Restaurante los Doce Apóstoles A2

Drinking

14 Bar el Polvorín A1

Castillo de los Tres Santos Reyes Magnos del Morro FORT, MUSEUM

(Map p65; El Morro; admission CUC$6) This imposing fort was erected between 1589 and 1630 to protect the entrance to Havana harbor from pirates and foreign invaders (French corsair Jacques de Sores had sacked the city in 1555). Perched high on a rocky bluff above the Atlantic, the fort's irregular polygonal shape, 3m-thick walls and deep protective moat offer a classic example of Renaissance military architecture. For more than a century the fort withstood numerous attacks by French, Dutch and English privateers, but in 1762, after a 44-day siege, a 14,000-strong British force captured El Morro by attacking from the landward side. The Castillo's famous **lighthouse** was added in 1844.

Aside from the fantastic views over the sea and the city, El Morro also hosts a **maritime museum** (Map p65). To climb to the top of the lighthouse is an additional CUC$2.

TOP CHOICE **Fortaleza de San Carlos de la Cabaña** FORT, MUSEUM

(Map p65; admission day/night CUC$6/8, 8am-11pm;) This 18th-century colossus was built between 1763 and 1774 on a long, exposed ridge on the east side of Havana harbor to fill a weakness in the city's defenses. In 1762 the British had taken Havana by gaining control of this strategically important ridge, and it was from here that they shelled the city mercilessly into submission. In order to prevent a repeat performance, the Spanish King Carlos III ordered the construction of a massive fort that would repel future invaders. Measuring 700m from end to end and covering a whopping 10 hectares, it is the largest Spanish colonial fortress in the Americas.

The impregnability of the fort meant that no invader ever attacked it, though during the 19th century Cuban patriots faced firing squads here. Dictators Machado and Batista used the fortress as a military prison, and immediately after the Revolution Che Guevara set up his headquarters inside the ramparts to preside over another catalog of grisly executions (this time of Batista's officers).

These days the fort has been restored for visitors, and you can spend at least half a day checking out its wealth of attractions. As well as bars, restaurants, souvenir stalls and a cigar shop (containing the world's longest cigar), La Cabaña hosts the Museo de Fortificaciones y Armas and the engrossing Museo de Comandancia del Che. The nightly 9pm **cañonazo ceremony** is a popular evening excursion in which actors dressed in full 18th-century military regalia reenact the firing of a cannon over the harbor. Until the demolition of Havana's city walls in the 1850s, the cannon shot was used to signal that the gates were about to close. You can visit the ceremony independently or as part of an organized excursion (p83).

CENTRO HABANA

Capitolio Nacional — LANDMARK

(Map p68; unguided/guided CUC$3/4; ⏲9am-8pm) The incomparable Capitolio Nacional is Havana's most ambitious and grandiose building, constructed after the 'Dance of the Millions' had gifted the Cuban government a seemingly bottomless treasure box of sugar money. Similar to the US Capitol Building in Washington, DC, but (marginally) taller and much richer in detail, the work was initiated by Cuba's US-backed dictator Gerardo Machado in 1926 and took 5000 workers three years, two months and 20 days to build at a cost of US$17 million. Formerly it was the seat of the Cuban Congress, but since 1959 it has housed the Cuban Academy of Sciences and the National Library of Science and Technology.

Constructed with white Capellanía limestone and block granite, the entrance is guarded by six rounded Doric columns atop a staircase that leads up from the Prado. Looking out over the Havana skyline is a 62m stone **cupola** topped with a replica of 16th-century Florentine sculptor Giambologna's bronze statue of Mercury in the Palazzo de Bargello. Set in the floor directly below the dome is a copy of a 24-carat diamond. Highway distances between Havana and all sites in Cuba are calculated from this point.

The entryway opens up into the **Salón de los Pasos Perdidos** (Room of the Lost Steps, so named because of its unusual acoustics), at the center of which is the **statue of the republic**, an enormous bronze woman standing 11m tall and symbolizing the mythic Guardian of Virtue and Work. In size, it's smaller than only the gold Buddha in Nara, Japan, and the Lincoln Monument in Washington, DC.

The Capitolio was closed for renovations at the time of writing, so admission prices may change.

Real Fábrica de Tabacos Partagás — CIGAR FACTORY

(Map p68; Industria No 520 btwn Barcelona & Dragones; tours CUC$10; ⏲every 15min 9-10:15am & noon-1:30pm) One of Havana's oldest and most famous cigar factories, the landmark neoclassical Real Fábrica de Tabacos Partagás was founded in 1845 by a Spaniard named Jaime Partagás. Today some 400 workers toil for up to 12 hours a day in here rolling such famous cigars as Montecristos and Cohibas. As far as tours go, Partagás is the most popular and reliable factory to visit. Tour groups check out the ground floor first, where the leaves are unbundled and sorted, before proceeding to the upper floors to watch the tobacco get rolled, pressed, adorned with a band and boxed. Though interesting in an educational sense, the tours here are often rushed and a little robotic, and some visitors find they smack of a human zoo. Still, if you have even a passing interest in tobacco and/or Cuban work environments, it's probably worth a peep.

Parque de la Fraternidad — PARK

Leafy Parque de la Fraternidad (Map p68) was established in 1892 to commemorate the fourth centenary of the Spanish landing in the Americas. A few decades later it was remodeled and renamed to mark the 1927 Pan-American Conference. The name is meant to signify American brotherhood, hence the many busts of Latin and North American leaders that embellish the green areas – including one of US president, Abraham Lincoln. Today the park is the terminus of numerous metro bus routes, and is sometimes referred to as 'Jurassic Park' because of the plethora of photogenic old American cars now used as *colectivos* (collective taxis) that congregate here.

The **Fuente de la India** (Map p68; on a traffic island opposite the Hotel Saratoga) is a white Carrara marble fountain, carved by Giuseppe Gaginni in 1837 for the Count of Villanueva. It portrays a regal Indian woman adorned with a crown of eagle's feathers and seated on a throne surrounded by four gargoyle-like dolphins. In one hand she holds a horn-shaped basket filled with fruit, in the other a shield bearing the city's coat of arms.

Asociación Cultural Yoruba de Cuba — MUSEUM

(Map p68; Paseo de Martí No 615; admission CUC$10; ⌚9am-4pm Mon-Sat) A museum that provides a worthwhile overview of the Santería religion, the saints and their powers, although some travelers have complained that the exhibits don't justify the price. There are *tambores* (Santería drum ceremonies) on alternate Fridays at 4:30pm. Note that there's a church dress code for the *tambores* (no shorts or tank tops).

Parque Central & Around — PARK

Diminutive Parque Central (Map p68) is a scenic haven from the belching buses and roaring taxis that ply their way along the Prado. The park, long a microcosm of daily Havana life, was expanded to its present size in the late 19th century after the city walls were knocked down. The marble **statue of José Martí** (Map p68; 1905) at its center was the first of thousands to be erected in Cuba. Raised on the 10th anniversary of the poet's death, the monument is ringed by 28 palm trees planted to signify Martí's birth date: January 28. Hard to miss over to one side is the group of baseball fans who linger 24/7 at the famous **Esquina Caliente**, discussing form, tactics and the Havana teams' prospects in the play-offs.

Gran Teatro de la Habana — THEATER

(Map p68; Paseo de Martí No 458; guided tours CUC$2; ⌚9am-6pm) 'A style without style that in the long run, by symbiosis, by amalgamation, becomes baroquism.' So wrote Cuban novelist and sometime architectural dabbler, Alejo Carpentier, of the ornate neobaroque **Centro Gallego** erected as a Galician social club between 1907 and 1914. The Centro was built around the existing Teatro Tacón, which opened in 1838 with five masked Carnaval dances. This connection is the basis of claims by the present 2000-seat theater that it's the oldest operating theater in the Western hemisphere. History notwithstanding, the architecture is brilliant, as are many of the weekend performances (see p108).

Hotel Inglaterra — NOTABLE BUILDING

(Map p68; Paseo de Martí No 416) Havana's oldest hotel first opened its doors in 1856 on the site of a popular bar called El Louvre (the hotel's alfresco bar still bears the name). Facing leafy Parque Central, the building exhibits the neoclassical design features in vogue at the time, although the interior decor is distinctly Moorish. At a banquet here in 1879, José Martí made a speech advocating Cuban independence, and much later US journalists covering the Spanish-Cuban-American War stayed at the hotel.

Just behind lies **Calle San Rafael**, a riot of peso stalls, 1950s department stores and local cinemas, which gives an immediate insight into everyday life in economically challenged Cuba.

TOP CHOICE Museo Nacional de Bellas Artes — MUSEUM

Cuba has a huge art culture and its dual-site art museum rivals its counterpart in San Juan, Puerto Rico, for the title of 'best art museum in the Caribbean.' You can spend a whole day here viewing everything from Greek ceramics to Cuban pop art.

Arranged inside the fabulously eclectic Centro Asturianas (a work of art in its own right), the **Colección de Arte Universal** (Map p68; cnr Agramonte & San Rafael; admission CUC$5, under 14yr free; ⌚10am-6pm Tue-Sat, 10am-2pm Sun) exhibits international art from 500 BC to the present day on three separate floors. Highlights include an extensive Spanish collection (with a canvas by El Greco), some 2000-year-old Roman mosaics, Greek pots from the 5th century BC and a suitably refined Gainsborough canvas (in the British room).

Two blocks away, the **Colección de Arte Cubano** (Map p68; Trocadero btwn Agramonte & Av de las Misiones; admission CUC$5, under 14yr

Centro Habana

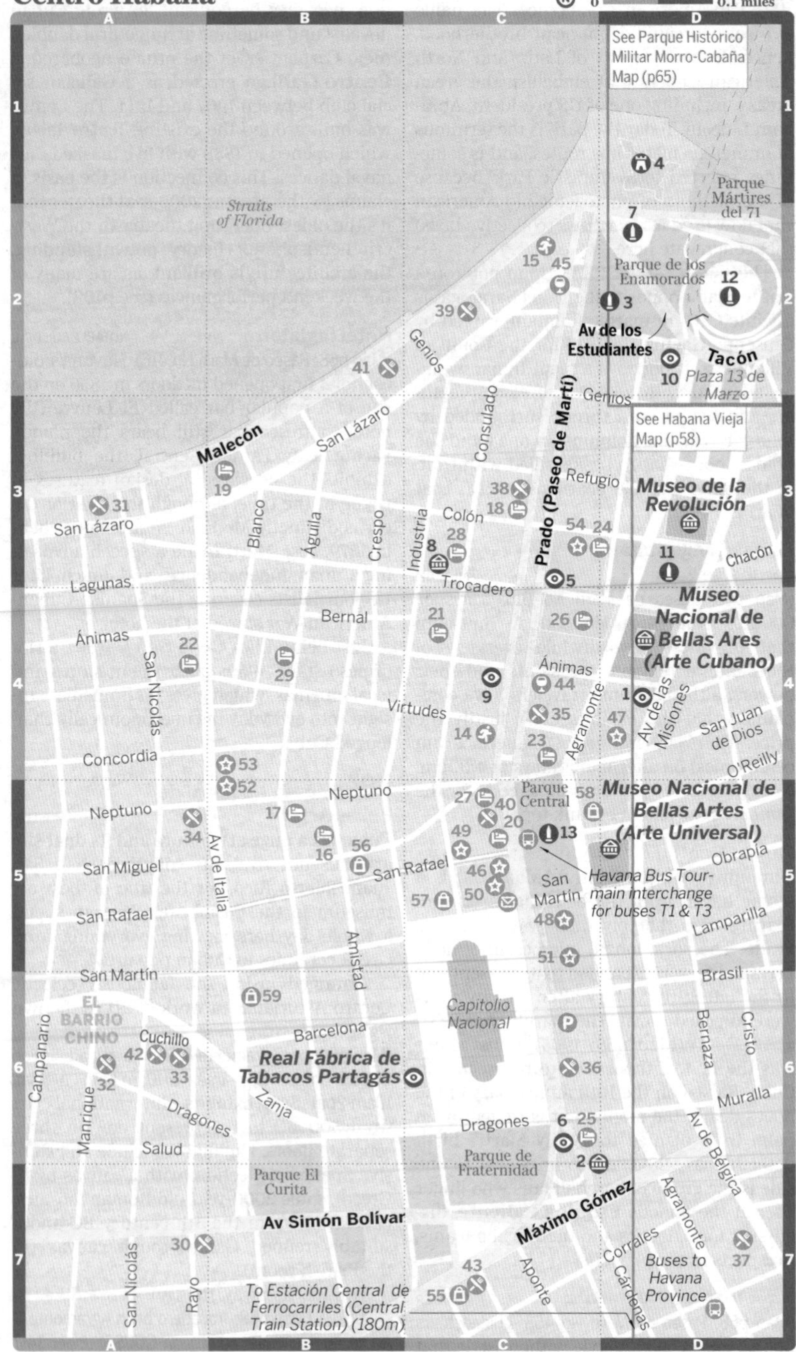

Centro Habana

free; ⌚10am-6pm Tue-Sat, 10am-2pm Sun) displays purely Cuban art and, if you're pressed for time, is the better of the duo. Works are displayed in chronological order starting on the 3rd floor and are surprisingly varied. Artists to look out for are Guillermo Collazo, considered to be the first truly great Cuban artist; Rafael Blanco with his cartoon-like paintings and sketches; Raúl Martínez, a master of 1960s Cuban pop art; and the Picasso-like Wilfredo Lam.

Museo de la Revolución MUSEUM

(Map p68; Refugio No 1; unguided/guided CUC$4/6, camera extra; ⌚10am-5pm) The Museo de la Revolución is housed in the former Presidential Palace, constructed between 1913 and 1920 and used by a string of cash-embezzling Cuban presidents, culminating in Fulgencio Batista. The world-famous Tiffany's of New York decorated the interior, and the shimmering Salón de los Espejos (Room of Mirrors) was designed to resemble the room of the same name at the Palace of Versailles. In March 1957 the palace was the target of an unsuccessful assassination attempt against Batista led by revolutionary student leader José Antonio Echeverría. The museum itself descends chronologically from the top floor starting with Cuba's pre-Columbian culture and extending to the present-day socialist regime (with *mucho* propaganda). The downstairs rooms have some interesting exhibits on the 1953 Moncada attack (see p394) and the life of Che Guevara, and highlight a Cuban penchant for displaying blood-stained military uniforms. Most of the labels are in English and Spanish. In front of the building is a fragment of the former city wall, as well as an SAU-100 tank used by Castro during the 1961 battle of the Bay of Pigs.

In the space behind you'll find the **Pavillón Granma**, a memorial to the 18m yacht that carried Fidel Castro and 81 other revolutionaries from Tuxpán, Mexico, to Cuba in December 1956. It's encased in glass and guarded 24 hours a day, presumably to stop anyone from breaking in and making off for Florida in it. The pavilion is surrounded by other vehicles associated with the Revolution and is accessible from the Museo de la Revolución.

Prado (Paseo de Martí) STREET

Construction of this stately European-style boulevard (Map p68; officially known as Paseo de Martí) – the first street outside the old city walls – began in 1770, and the work was completed in the mid-1830s during the term of Captain General Miguel Tacón (1834–38). The original idea was to create a boulevard as splendid as any found in Paris or Barcelona (Prado owes more than a passing nod to Las Ramblas). The famous bronze lions that guard the central promenade at either end were added in 1928.

Notable Prado buildings include the neo-Renaissance **Palacio de los Matrimonios** (Map p68; Paseo de Martí No 302), the streamline-modern **Teatro Fausto** (Map p68; cnr Paseo de Martí & Colón) and the neoclassical **Escuela Nacional de Ballet** (Map p68; cnr Paseo de Martí & Trocadero), Alicia Alonso's famous ballet school.

Statue of General Máximo Gómez MONUMENT

(Map p68; Malecón cnr Paseo de Martí) On a large traffic island overlooking the mouth of the harbor is a rather grand statue on the right-hand side. Gómez was a war hero from the Dominican Republic who fought tirelessly for Cuban independence in both the 1868 and 1895 conflicts against the Spanish. The impressive statue of him sitting atop a horse was created by Italian artist Aldo Gamba in 1935 and faces heroically out to sea.

Museo Lezama Lima MUSEUM

(Map p68; Trocadero No 162 cnr Industria; unguided/guided CUC$1/2; ⌚9am-5pm Tue-Sat, 9am-1pm Sun) A new museum in the old house of the late Cuban man of letters, José Lezama Lima, this place is an obligatory pit-stop for anyone attempting to understand Cuban literature beyond Hemingway. Lima's magnus opus was the rambling classic, *Paradiso,* and he wrote most of it here.

Parque de los Enamorados PARK

Preserved in Parque de los Enamorados (Map p68; Lovers' Park), surrounded by streams of speeding traffic, lies a surviving section of the colonial **Cárcel** (Map p68) or Tacón Prison, built in 1838, where many Cuban patriots including José Martí were imprisoned. A brutal place that sent unfortunate prisoners off to perform hard labor in the nearby San Lázaro quarry, the prison was finally demolished in 1939 with the park that took its place dedicated to the memory of those who had suffered so horribly within its walls. Two tiny cells and an equally minute chapel are all that remain. The beautiful wedding cake-like building (art nouveau with a dash of eclecticism) behind the park, flying the Spanish flag, is the old **Palacio Velasco** (Map p68; 1912), now the Spanish embassy.

Beyond that is the **Memorial a los Estudiantes de Medicina** (Map p68), a fragment of wall encased in marble marking the spot where eight Cuban medical students were shot by the Spanish in 1871 as a reprisal for allegedly desecrating the tomb of a Spanish journalist (in fact, they didn't do it).

Castillo de San Salvador de la Punta FORT, MUSEUM

One in a quartet of forts defending Havana harbor, La Punta (Map p68) was designed by the Italian military engineer Giovanni Bautista Antonelli and built between 1589 and 1600. During the colonial era a chain was stretched 250m to the castle of El Morro every night to close the harbor mouth to shipping. The castle's **museum** (admission CUC$6; ⏲10am-6pm Wed-Sun) displays artifacts from sunken Spanish treasure fleets, a collection of model ships and information on the slave trade.

El Barrio Chino NEIGHBORHOOD

Havana's Chinatown (Map p68) – or *Barrio Chino*, as it's more popularly known – is notable today for its almost complete lack of Chinese people. But it wasn't always so. The first Chinese arrived as contract laborers on the island in the late 1840s to fill in the gaps left by the decline of the trans-Atlantic slave trade. By the 1920s Havana's Chinatown had burgeoned into the biggest Asian neighborhood in Latin America, a booming, bustling hub of human industry that spawned its own laundries, pharmacies, theaters and grocery stores. The slide began in the early 1960s when thousands of business-minded Chinese relocated to the United States. Recognizing the tourist potential of the area in the 1990s, the Cuban government invested money and resources into rejuvenating the district's distinct historical character with bilingual street signs, a large pagoda-shaped arch at the entrance to Calle Dragones, and incentives given to local Chinese businessmen to promote restaurants. Today most of the action centers on the narrow Calle Cuchillo and its surrounding streets. Head here for cheap restaurants, plentiful food and an interesting slice of Cuban life with an Asian twist.

VEDADO

Vedado (known officially as the municipality of 'Plaza de la Revolution') is Havana's commercial hub and archetypal residential district, older than Playa but newer than Centro Habana. The first houses penetrated this formerly protected forest reserve in the 1860s, with the real growth spurt beginning in the 1920s and continuing until the 1950s.

Laid out in a near-perfect grid, Vedado has more of a North American feel than other parts of the Cuban capital, and its small clutch of *rascacielos* (skyscrapers) – which draw their inspiration from the art-deco giants of Miami and New York – are largely a product of Cuba's 50-year dance with the US.

During the 1940s and '50s, Vedado was a louche and tawdry place where Havana's pre-revolutionary gambling party reached its heady climax. The Hotel Nacional once boasted a Las Vegas-style casino, the ritzy Hotel Riviera was the former stomping ground of influential mobster Meyer Lansky, while the now empty Hotel Capri was masterfully managed by Hollywood actor (and sometime mob associate) George Raft. Everything changed in January 1959 when Fidel Castro rolled into town with his army of scruffy bearded rebels in tow and set up shop on the 24th floor of the spanking new Havana Hilton hotel (promptly renamed Hotel Habana Libre).

Today, Vedado has a population of approximately 175,000, and its leafy residential pockets are interspersed with myriad theaters, nightspots, paladares and restaurants. Bisected by two wide Parisian-style boulevards, Calle G and Paseo, its geometric grid is embellished by a liberal sprinkling of pleasant parks and the gargantuan Plaza de la Revolución laid out during the Batista era in the 1950s.

Iglesia del Sagrado Corazón de Jesús CHURCH

(Map p72; Av Simón Bolivar btwn Gervasio & Padre Varela) A little out on a limb but well worth the walk is this inspiring marble creation with a distinctive white steeple, where you can enjoy a few precious minutes of quiet and cool contemplation away from the craziness of the street. This church is rightly famous for its magnificent stained-glass windows, and the light that penetrates through the eaves first thing in the morning (when the church is deserted) gives the place an ethereal quality.

TOP CHOICE **Hotel Nacional** NOTABLE BUILDING

(Map p72; cnr Calles O & 21) Built in 1930 as a copy of the Breakers Hotel in Palm Beach, Florida, the eclectic art-deco/neoclassical Hotel Nacional is a national monument and one of Havana's 'postcard' sights.

Vedado

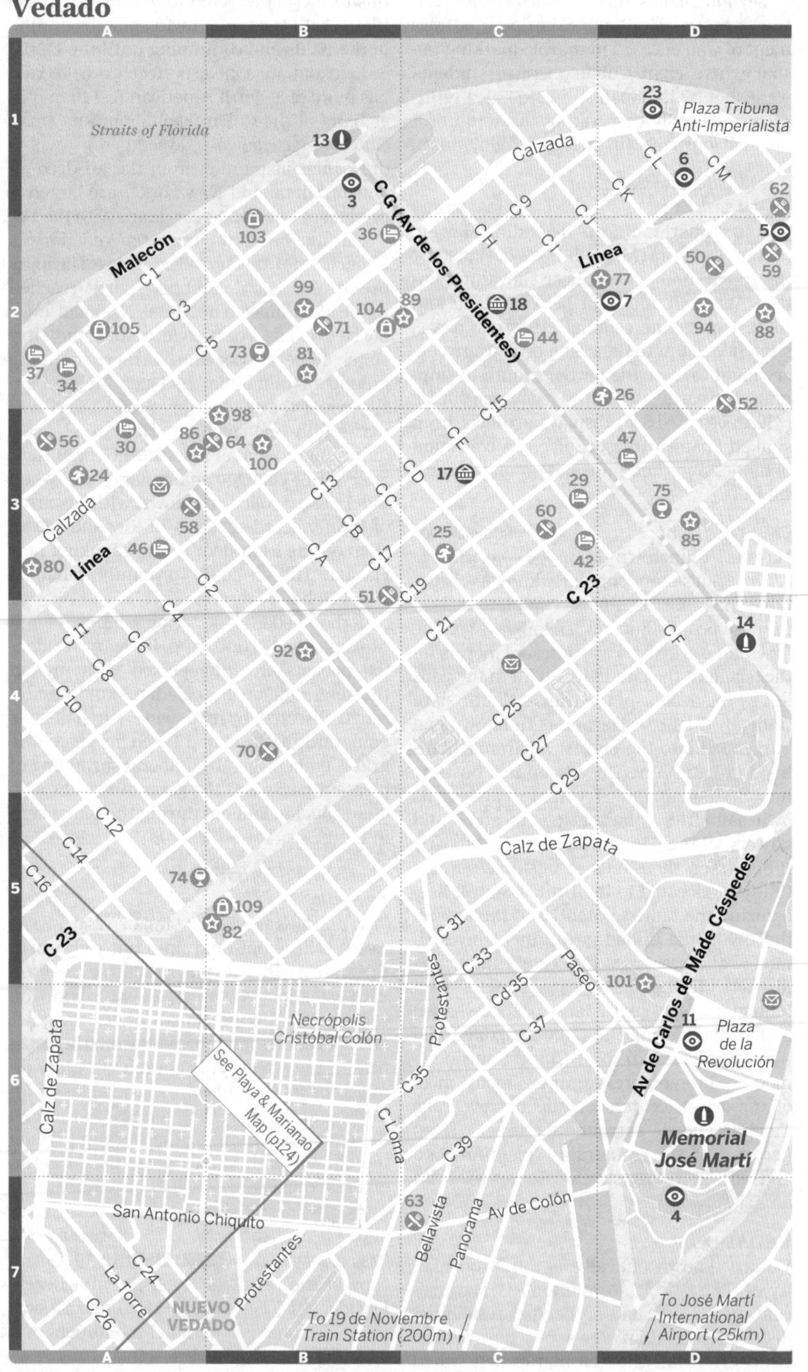
Straits of Florida
Plaza Tribuna Anti-Imperialista
Calzada
Malecón
C G (Av de los Presidentes)
Línea
Calzada
Línea
C 23
Calz de Zapata
Av de Carlos de Máde Céspedes
Paseo
Necrópolis Cristóbal Colón
Protestantes
Plaza de la Revolución
Memorial José Martí
Calz de Zapata
C 23
See Playa & Marianao Map (p124)
C Loma
San Antonio Chiquito
Av de Colón
Bellavista
Panorama
La Torre
Protestantes
NUEVO VEDADO
To 19 de Noviembre Train Station (200m)
To José Martí International Airport (25km)

0 500 m
0 0.3 miles
Malecón (Av Maceo)
Caleta de San Lázaro
Parque Maceo
San Lázaro
Universidad de La Habana
Museo Napoleónico
Plaza de la Revolución
Av Universidad
Infanta
Av Salvador Allende
Av Simón Bolívar
Av de la Independencia
Terminal de Omnibus
C 19 de Mayo
Aranguren
Arroyo (Av Manglar)
Calz de Ayestarán
Av 20 de Mayo
Calz de Infanta
Máximo Gómez
Padre Varela
Av de México
Estadio Latinoamericano
Retiro
Zanja
Pocito
Dragones
Salud
San Miguel
San Rafael
San Martín
Virtudes
Concordia
Neptuno
Lagunas
Animas
Lealtad
Escobar
Gervasio
Santiago
Oquendo
Marqués González
Lucena
Hospital
San Francisco
Aramburu
Soledad
Espada
Príncipe
Vapor
Jovellar
Enrique Barnet
Maloja
Sitio
Peñalver
Desagüe
Benjumeda
Santo Tómas
Clavel
Santa Marta
Figuras
Carmen
Rastro
San Carlos
Árbol Seco
Pozos Dulces
Bruzón
Luaces
C 27
C L
C N
C O
C P

Vedado

Top Sights
Memorial José Martí....D6
Museo Napoleónico....E3
Universidad de La Habana....E3

Sights
1 Airline Building....E2
2 Biblioteca Nacional José Martí....E6
3 Casa de las Américas....B1
4 Comité Central del Partido Comunista de Cuba....D7
5 Edificio Focsa....D2
6 Edificio López Serrano....D1
7 Gran Synagoga Bet Shalom....D2
8 Hotel Capri....E2
Hotel Habana Libre....(see 33)
Hotel Nacional....(see 35)
9 Iglesia de Sagrado Corazón de Jesús....H4
10 Mella Portraits....E3
11 Ministerio del Interior....D6
12 Monumento a Antonio Maceo....G2
13 Monumento a Calixto García....B1
14 Monumento a José Miguel Gómez....D4
15 Monumento a Julio Antonio Mella....E3
16 Monumento a las Víctimas del Maine....E1
Museo Antropológico Montané... (see 19)
17 Museo de Artes Decorativas....C3
18 Museo de Danza....C2
19 Museo de Historia Natural Felipe Poey....E3
20 Museo del Ferrocarril....H6
21 Quinta de los Molinos....E4
22 Torreón de San Lázaro....G2
23 US Interests Section....D1

Activities, Courses & Tours
24 Conjunto Folklórico Nacional de Cuba....A3
Museo de Artes Decorativas....(see 17)
25 Paradiso....C3
Teatro Nacional de Cuba....(see 101)
26 Uneac....D2
27 Universidad de La Habana....E3

Sleeping
Basilia Pérez Castro....(see 48)
28 Casa 1932....H2
Casa Particular Sandélis....(see 43)
29 Eddy Gutiérrez Bouza....C3
30 Guillermina & Roberto Abreu....A3
31 Hotel Bruzón....E5
32 Hotel Colina....E3
33 Hotel Habana Libre....E2
34 Hotel Meliá Cohiba....A2
35 Hotel Nacional....E1
36 Hotel Presidente....B2
37 Hotel Riviera....A2
38 Hotel St John's....E2
39 Hotel Vedado....E2
40 Hotel Victoria....E2
41 La Casona Colonial - José Díaz....H3
42 Luís Suávez Fiandor....C3
43 Manuel Martínez....E2
44 Marta Vitorte....C2
45 Martha Obregón....H3
46 Melba Piñada Bermudez....A3
47 Mercedes González....D3
48 Nelsy Alemán Machado....E3
49 Villa Enano Rojo....H2

Eating
50 Agropecuario 17 & K....D2
51 Agropecuario 19 & A....B3
52 Agropecuario 21 & J....D2
53 Bim Bom....F2
54 Café TV....E2
55 Cafetería Sofía....E2
56 Centro Vasco....A3
57 Coppelia....E2
58 Decameron....A3

The hotel's notoriety was cemented in October 1933 when – following a sergeant's coup by Fulgencio Batista, which toppled the regime of Gerardo Machado – 300 aggrieved army officers took refuge in the building hoping to curry favor with resident US ambassador, Sumner Wells, who was staying there. Much to the officers' chagrin, Wells promptly left, allowing Batista's troops to open fire on the hotel killing 14 of them and injuring seven. More were executed later, after they had surrendered.

In December 1946 the hotel gained notoriety of a different kind when US mobsters Meyer Lansky and Lucky Luciano used it to host the largest ever get-together of the North American Mafia, who gathered here under the guise of a Frank Sinatra concert.

These days the hotel maintains a more reputable face and the once famous casino is long gone, though the kitschy Parisién

59 El Conejito D2
60 El Gringo Viejo C3
61 Flor de Loto H4
62 La Casona & 17 .... D1
La Rampa .... (see 33)
La Torre .... (see 5)
63 Organopónico Plaza C7
64 Pain de París B3
Pain de París .... (see 107)
65 Paladar Aries E3
66 Paladar El Hurón Azul F2
67 Paladar La Guarida H3
68 Paladar Los Amigos E2
69 Peso Pizza F3
70 Peso Stalls B4
71 Restaurante Vegetariano Carmelo B2
Supermercado Meridiano .... (see 105)
72 Trattoría Maraka's E2

Drinking

73 Bar-Club Imágenes B2
74 Café Fresa y Chocolate A5
75 Café Literario del 'G' D3

Entertainment

76 Cabaret Las Vegas F2
Cabaret Parisién .... (see 35)
Cabaret Turquino .... (see 33)
Café Cantante .... (see 101)
77 Café Teatro Brecht D2
78 Callejón de Hamel F3
Casa de la Amsitad .... (see 92)
79 Casa de la Cultura Centro Habana G4
80 Casa de la Cultura de Plaza A3
Casa de las Américas .... (see 3)
81 Casa del Alba Cultural B2
Centro Cultural Cinematográfico (see 74)
82 Cine Charles Chaplín B5
83 Cine Infanta F3
84 Cine La Rampa E2
85 Cine Riviera D3
86 Cine Trianón A3
87 Cine Yara E2
Cinecito .... (see 82)
88 Club La Red D2
89 Club Tropical C2
Copa Room .... (see 37)
90 Discoteca Amanecer E1
91 El Gato Tuerto E1
El Hurón Azul .... (see 26)
Habana Café .... (see 34)
92 Instituto Cubano de Amistad con los Pueblos B4
Jazz Café .... (see 105)
93 Jazz Club La Zorra y El Cuervo E2
94 Karachi Club D2
95 La Madriguera F4
Piano Bar Delirio Habanero .... (see 101)
Pico Blanco .... (see 38)
96 Sala Polivalente Ramón Fonst E5
97 Sala Teatro El Sótano E3
98 Sala Teatro Hubert de Blanck B3
99 Teatro Amadeo Roldán B2
100 Teatro Mella B3
101 Teatro Nacional de Cuba D5
102 Teatro Nacional de Guiñol E2

Shopping

ARTex .... (see 87)
103 Feria de la Artesanía B2
Galería de Arte Latinoamericano.. (see 3)
104 Galería Habana B2
105 Galerías de Paseo A2
Instituto Cubano del Arte e Industria Cinematográficos .... (see 74)
106 La Habana Sí E2
107 Librería Centenario del Apóstol F2
Libreria Rayuela .... (see 3)
108 Plaza Carlos III G4
109 Sevando Galería del Arte B5

cabaret is still a popular draw. Nonguests are welcome to admire the Moorish lobby, stroll the breezy grounds overlooking the Malecón and examine the famous photos of past guests on the walls inside.

Hotel Habana Libre NOTABLE BUILDING

(Map p72; Calle L btwn Calles 23 & 25) This classic modernist hotel – the former Havana Hilton – was commandeered by Castro's revolutionaries in 1959 just nine months after it had opened, and promptly renamed the Habana Libre. During the first few months of the Revolution, Fidel ruled the country from a luxurious suite on the 24th floor.

A 670-sq-meter Venetian tile mural by Amelia Peláez is splashed across the front of the building, while upstairs Alfredo Sosa Bravo's *Carro de la Revolución* utilizes 525 ceramic pieces. There are some good shops here and an interesting photo gallery inside, displaying snaps of the all-conquering *barbudas* (literally 'bearded ones') lolling around with their guns in the hotel's lobby in January 1959.

Edificio Focsa LANDMARK

(Map p72; Focsa building; cnr Calles 17 & M) Unmissable on the Havana skyline, the modernist Edificio Focsa was built in 1954–56 in a record 28 months using pioneering computer technology. In 1999 it was listed as one of the seven modern engineering wonders of Cuba. With 39 floors housing 373 apartments, it was, on its completion in June 1956, the second-largest concrete structure of its type in the world, constructed entirely without the use of cranes. Falling on hard times in the early '90s, the upper floors of the Focsa became nests for vultures, and in 2000 an elevator cable snapped killing one person. Rejuvenated once more after a restoration project, this skyline-dominating Havana giant nowadays contains residential apartments and – in the shape of top-floor restaurant La Torre (p103) – one of the city's most celebrated eating establishments.

Hotel Capri RUIN

(Map p72; Calle 21 cnr Calle N) Some cities sport Roman ruins, Havana, on the other hand, has 1950s ruins. The not-so-ancient Capri was built in modernist style with mafia money in 1957. In its (brief) heyday, the hotel was owned by mobster Santo Trafficante who used American actor George Raft as his debonair front-man. When Castro's guerrillas came knocking in January 1959, Raft allegedly told them where to stick it and slammed the door in their faces. The hotel, with its rooftop pool has featured in two movies: Carol Reed's *Our Man in Havana* and Mikhael Kalatazov's *Soy Cuba*. It was also the setting for Michael Corleone's meeting with Hyman Roth in *The Godfather: Part II*, though, due to the embargo, Coppola shot the scenes in the Dominican Republic. Closed in 2003, the Capri is now a 19-story ruin awaiting its second coming.

Universidad de la Habana UNIVERSITY

(Map p72; cnr Calle L & San Lázaro) Founded by Dominican monks in 1728 and secularized in 1842, Havana University began life in Habana Vieja before moving to its present site in 1902. The existing neoclassical complex dates from the second quarter of the 20th century, and today some 30,000 students follow courses in social sciences, humanities, natural sciences, mathematics and economics here.

Perched on a Vedado hill at the top of the famous *escalinata* (stairway), near the **Alma Mater** statue, the university's central quadrangle, the Plaza Ignacio Agramonte, displays a tank captured by Castro's rebels in 1958. Directly in front is the **Librería Alma Mater** (library) and, to the left, the **Museo de Historia Natural Felipe Poey** (Map p72; admission CUC$1; ⌚9am-noon & 1-4pm Mon-Fri Sep-Jul), the oldest museum in Cuba, founded in 1874 by the Royal Academy of Medical, Physical and Natural Sciences. Many of the stuffed specimens of Cuban flora and fauna date from the 19th century. Upstairs is the **Museo Antropológico Montané** (Map p72; admission CUC$1; ⌚9am-noon & 1-4pm Mon-Fri Sep-Jul), established in 1903, with a rich collection of pre-Columbian Indian artifacts including the wooden 10th-century Ídolo del Tabaco.

Monumento a Julio Antonio Mella MONUMENT

(Map p72; cnr Neptuno & San Lázaro) At the bottom of the university steps there is a monument to the student leader who founded the first Cuban Communist Party in 1925. In 1929 the dictator Machado had Mella assassinated in Mexico City. More interesting than the monument itself are the black-and-white **Mella portraits** permanently mounted on the wall in the little park across San Lázaro.

Museo Napoleónico MUSEUM

(Map p72; San Miguel No 1159; unguided/guided CUC$3/5; ⌚9am-4:30pm Tue-Sat) An anomaly – but an interesting one – is the esoteric Museo Napoleónico situated just outside the university walls. It's a collection of 7000 objects associated with the life of Napoleon Bonaparte amassed by Cuban sugar baron Julio Lobo and politician Orestes Ferrera. Highlights include sketches of Voltaire, paintings of the battle of Waterloo, china, furniture, an interesting recreation of Napoleon's study and bedroom, and one of several bronze Napoleonic death masks made two days after the emperor's death by his personal physician, Dr Francisco Antommarchi.

Museo de Artes Decorativas MUSEUM

(Map p72; Calle 17 No 502 btwn Calles D & E; admission CUC$2; ⌚11am-7pm Tue-Sat) Worth checking out if you're in the neighborhood (it's a little out of the way) is this decorative arts museum with its fancy rococo, oriental and art deco baubles. Perhaps more interesting is the building itself, of French design, commissioned in 1924 by the wealthy Gómez family (who built the Manzana de Gómez shopping center in Centro Havana).

Museo de Danza MUSEUM
(Map p72; Línea No 365; admission CUC$2; ⌚11am-6:30pm Tue-Sat) A dance museum in Cuba – well, there's no surprise there. This long-standing place in an eclectic Vedado mansion collects objects from Cuba's rich dance history, including some personal effects of ex-ballerina, Alicia Alonso.

Plaza de la Revolución SQUARE
Conceived by French urbanist Jean Claude Forestier in the 1920s, the gigantic Plaza de la Revolución (Map p72; known as Plaza Cívica until 1959) was part of Havana's 'new city', which grew up between 1920 and 1959. As the nexus point of Forestier's ambitious plan, the square was built on a small hill (the Loma de los Catalanes) in the manner of Paris' Place de Étoile, with various avenues fanning out toward the Río Almendares, Vedado and the Parque de la Fraternidad in Centro Habana.

Surrounded by grey, utilitarian buildings constructed in the late 1950s, the square today is the base of the Cuban government and a place where large-scale political rallies are held. In January 1998, one million people (nearly one-tenth of the Cuban population) crammed into the square to hear Pope Jean Paul II say Mass.

The ugly concrete block on the northern side of the Plaza is the **Ministerio del Interior** (Map p72), well known for its huge mural of Che Guevara (a copy of Alberto Korda's famous photograph taken in 1960) with the words *Hasta la Victoria Siempre* (Always Toward Victory) emblazoned underneath. In 2009 a similarly designed image of Cuba's other heroic guerrillero, Camilo Cienfuegos was added on the adjacent telecommunications building.

On the eastern side is the 1957 **Biblioteca Nacional José Martí** (Map p72; admission free; ⌚8am-9:45pm Mon-Sat), which has a photo exhibit in the lobby, while on the west is the **Teatro Nacional de Cuba** (p110).

Tucked behind the Martí Memorial are the governmental offices housed in the heavily guarded **Comité Central del Partido Comunista de Cuba**.

Memorial a José Martí MONUMENT, MUSEUM
(Map p72; admission CUC$5; ⌚9:30am-5pm Mon-Sat) Center-stage in Plaza de la Revolución is this monument, which at 138.5m is Havana's tallest structure. Fronted by an impressive 17m marble statue of a seated Martí in a

HAVANA ECLECTIC

With its architecture – as with its music – Havana exhibits very little purity of style. Instead, what you are confronted with is a roguish mish-mash, a bastardization of various imported genres that, over time, have merged into a faintly distinguishable whole sometimes referred to as 'Havana Eclectic'.

The reasons for these deviations are manifold. In the early colonial period a lack of skilled labor in Cuba meant that the ornamentation of European architecture was often streamlined into a simpler form of 'Cuban baroque' sculpted from hard Havana limestone hewn from the nearby San Lázaro quarries. Other buildings were adapted from European architectural designs to suit local climatic needs with features such as *portales* (porches), mezzanine floors and large glassless windows added. Then there was the penetration of outside influences. Mirroring its rich ethnicity, Havana's architecture became a complicated melting pot of themes and ideas. Giuseppe Antonelli employed Italian Renaissance features in constructing his great harbor-side forts, elements of French neoclassicism seeped into early-19th-century buildings via Haiti, the influence of modernisme came with Spanish immigrants from Catalonia, and art deco arrived with forward-thinking architects from the United States.

The high point of Cuban eclecticism came during the economic boom of the early 1920s when fat-cat businessmen made rich on sugar pumped their money into ever more ostentatious mansions in the flowering suburbs of Vedado and Miramar.

Havana's greatest eclectic buildings include the Gran Teatro de La Habana (p67), the Hotel Nacional (p118), the Palacio Presidencial, which now houses the Museo de la Revolución (p70), and the Palacio Velasco (p70). For the finest concentration of eclecticism wander down Paseo de Martí (Prado) in Centro Havana, Calle 17 in Vedado, or Av Quinta in Miramar.

pensive *Thinker* pose, the memorial houses a museum – the definite word on Martí in Cuba – and a 129m lookout (reached via a small CUC$2 lift) with fantastic city views.

Quinta de los Molinos LANDMARK

(Map p72; cnr Av Salvador Allende & Luaces) The former stately residence of General Máximo Gómez, the Quinta sits amid lush botanical gardens on land that once belonged to Havana University. The residence and grounds seem to be stuck in a perennial renovation project, with promises of a new museum and touched-up botanical gardens in the ever-distant future. The potential is huge.

Necrópolis Cristóbal Colón CEMETERY

(Map p72; admission CUC$5; 8am-5pm) Once described as an 'exercise in pious excesses,' this cemetery (a national monument) is renowned for its striking religious iconography and elaborate marble statues. Far from being eerie, a walk through these 56 hallowed hectares can be an educational and emotional stroll through the annals of Cuban history. A guidebook with a detailed map (CUC$5) is for sale at the entrance. It's one of the largest cemeteries in the Americas.

After entering the neo-Romanesque **northern gateway** (1870), there's the tomb of independence leader **General Máximo Gómez** (1905) on the right (look for the bronze face in a circular medallion). Further along past the first circle, and also on the right, are the **monument to the firefighters** (1890) and the neo-Romanesque **Capilla Central** (1886) in the center of the cemetery. Just northeast of this chapel is the graveyard's most celebrated (and visited) tomb, that of **Señora Amelia Goyri** (cnr Calles 1 & F), better known as La Milagrosa (the miraculous one), who died while giving birth on May 3, 1901. The marble figure of a woman with a large cross and a baby in her arms is easy to find due to the many flowers piled on the tomb and the local devotees in attendance. For many years after her death, her heartbroken husband visited the grave several times a day. He always knocked with one of four iron rings on the burial vault and walked away backwards so he could see her for as long as possible. When the bodies were exhumed some years later, Amelia's body was uncorrupted (a sign of sanctity in the Catholic faith) and the baby, who had been buried at its mother's feet, was – allegedly – found in her arms. As a result, La Milagrosa became the focus of a huge spiritual cult in Cuba, and thousands of people come here annually with gifts in the hope of fulfilling dreams or solving problems. In keeping with tradition, pilgrims knock with the iron ring on the vault and walk away backwards when they leave.

Also worth seeking out is the tomb of Orthodox Party leader **Eduardo Chibás** (Calle 8 btwn Calles E & F). During the 1940s and early '50s Chibás was a relentless crusader against political corruption, and as a personal protest he committed suicide during a radio broadcast in 1951. At his burial ceremony a young Orthodox Party activist named Fidel Castro jumped atop Chibás' grave and made a fiery speech denouncing the old establishment – the political debut of the most influential Cuban of the 20th century.

Also worth looking out for are the graves of novelist Alejo Carpentier (1904–80), scientist Carlos Finlay (1833–1915), the Martyrs of Granma and the Veterans of the Independence Wars.

TOP CHOICE **Malecón** STREET

The Malecón (Map p72), Havana's evocative 8km-long sea drive, is one of the city's most soulful and quintessentially Cuban thoroughfares.

Long a favored meeting place for assorted lovers, philosophers, poets, traveling minstrels, fishermen and wistful Florida-gazers, the Malecón's atmosphere is most potent at sunset when the weak yellow light from creamy Vedado filters like a dim torch onto the buildings of Centro Habana, lending their dilapidated facades a distinctly ethereal quality.

Laid out in the early 1900s as a salubrious ocean-side boulevard for Havana's pleasure-seeking middle classes, the Malecón expanded rapidly eastward in the century's first decade with a mishmash of eclectic architecture that mixed sturdy neoclassicism with whimsical art nouveau. By the 1920s the road had reached the outer limits of burgeoning Vedado, and by the early 1950s it had metamorphosed into a busy six-lane highway that carried streams of wave-dodging Buicks and Chevrolets from the grey hulk of the Castillo de San Salvador de la Punta to the borders of Miramar.

Today the Malecón remains Havana's most authentic open-air theater, a real-life 'cabaret of the poor' where the whole city comes to meet, greet, date and debate.

Fighting an ongoing battle with the corrosive effects of the ocean, many of the thoroughfare's magnificent buildings now face decrepitude, demolition or irrevocable damage. To combat the problem, 14 blocks of the Malecón have been given special status by the City Historian's Office in an attempt to stop the rot.

Monumento a Antonio Maceo MONUMENT

Lying in the shadow of **Hospital Nacional Hermanos Ameijeiras** (San Lázaro No 701), a Soviet-era 24-story hospital built in 1980, is this bronze representation (Map p72) of the *mulato* general who cut a blazing trail across the entire length of Cuba during the First War of Independence. The nearby 18th-century **Torreón de San Lázaro** (Map p72) is a watchtower that quickly fell to the British during the invasion of 1762.

Monumento a las Víctimas del Maine MONUMENT

(Map p72; Malecón) West beyond Hotel Nacional is a monument to the victims of USS *Maine,* the battleship that blew up mysteriously in Havana harbor in 1898. Once crowned by an American eagle, the monument (first raised during the American-dominated period in 1926) was decapitated during the 1959 Revolution.

US Interests Section LANDMARK

(Map p72; Calzada btwn Calles L & M) The modern seven-story building with the high security fencing at the western end of this open space is the US Interests Section, first set up by the Carter administration in the late 1970s. Surrounded by hysterical graffiti, the building is the site of some of the worst tit-for-tat finger-wagging on the island. Facing the office front is the **Plaza de la Dignidad**, built during the Elián González saga to host major in-your-face protests under the nose of the Americans. Concerts, protests and marches – some one-million strong – are still held here.

Edificio López Serrano LANDMARK

(Map p72; Calle L btwn Calles 11 & 13) Tucked away behind the US Interests Section is this art deco tower, which looks like the Empire State with the bottom 70 floors chopped off. One of Havana's first *rascacielos* (skyscrapers) when it was built in 1932, the López Serrano building now houses apartments.

Av de los Presidentes STREET

Statues of illustrious Latin American leaders line the Las Ramblas style Calle G (Map p72; offically known as Av de los Presidentes), including Salvador Allende (Chile), Benito Juárez (Mexico) and Simón Bolívar. At the top of the avenue is a huge marble **Monumento a José Miguel Gómez** (Map p72), Cuba's second president. At the other end, the monument to his predecessor – Cuba's first president – Tomás Estrada Palma (long considered a US puppet) has been toppled, and all that remains are his shoes on a plinth.

Guarding the entrance to Calle G on the Malecón is the equestrian **Monumento a Calixto García** (Map p72; cnr Malecón & Calle G), paying homage to the valiant Cuban general who was prevented by US military leaders in Santiago de Cuba from attending the Spanish surrender in 1898. Twenty-four bronze plaques around the statue provide a history of García's 30-year struggle for Cuban independence.

FREE **Casa de las Américas** CULTURAL CENTER

(Map p72; www.casa.cult.cu; cnr Calles 3 & G; 10am-4:40pm Tue-Sat, 9am-1pm Sun) Just off the Malecón at the ocean-end of Calle G, this cultural institution was set up by Moncada survivor Haydee Santamaría in 1959 and awards one of Latin America's oldest and most prestigious literary prizes. Inside there's an art gallery, a bookstore and an atmosphere of erudite intellectualism.

Gran Synagoga Bet Shalom SYNAGOGUE

(Map p72; Calle I No 251 btwn Calles 13 & 15) Cuba has three synagogues servicing a Jewish population of approximately 1500. The main community center and library are located here, where the friendly staff would be happy to tell interested visitors about the fascinating and little-reported history of the Jews in Cuba.

Museo del Ferrocarril MUSEUM

(cnr Av de México & Arroyo; admission CUC$2; 9am-5pm) Two facts worth pondering: 1) Cuba was the sixth country in the world to develop a railway network; 2) it was running trains a good decade before its colonizing power, Spain. All the more reason to visit this peripheral museum housed in the old Cristina train station built in 1859. There's a big collection of signaling and communication gear here plus old locos and an overview of Cuba's pioneering railway history. Train rides are possible by prior appointment.

Walking Tour
Rehabilitated Habana Vieja Tour

The rehabilitation of Habana Vieja would be a huge achievement in any country, let alone one wracked by a devastating economic crisis. The piecing together of the Old Town began in the late 1970s and is ongoing. The plan, run by the City Historian's Office and headed up by Eusebio Leal Spengler, has restored Havana's most important historic buildings, created groundbreaking social projects for the local population, and garnered numerous international prizes for its cultural, historical and sustainable work. You can see it in all its glory on this atmospheric walk.

An ideal place to start your tour of Habana Vieja is a short block of 1 **Calle Mercaderes** holding no fewer than four separate points of interest: Maqueta de la Ciudad, Cinematógrafo Lumière, Taller de Papel Artesanal and Casa de la Obra Pía.

Start by getting orientated at the Maqueta de la Ciudad, a 1:500 scale model of Habana Vieja, with added sound effects, inaugurated by Queen Sofia of Spain in 1999. The same building houses the Cinematógrafo Lumière, a small cinema that shows nostalgia movies for senior citizens, and educational documentaries about the restoration for visitors.

Step out of the door onto Calle Mercaderes, one of the city's most complete streets, which has been undergoing piecemeal restoration since the early 1980s. The City Historian's Office employs hundreds of people to aid it in its meticulous restoration work, and specializes in everything from stone and metalwork to religious art and antique furniture.

One workshop open to the public is the Taller de Papel Artesanal, a couple of doors down from the Maqueta. This workshop has revived old manufacturing methods in order to make artisan paper for traditional art. The socio-cultural project has a small exposition room explaining its practices.

Another architectural highlight on Mercaderes is the Casa de la Obra Pía, a former Spanish nobleman's mansion dating from 1648. The house was rehabilitated in 1983 as both a museum and a community project and now produces textiles made and sold on-site by local people.

Further down the street is the 2 **Museo del Chocolate**, opened in 2003 under the auspices of a Belgian-sponsored UN project that also contributed to the rehabilitation of 64 local residences nearby. Duck inside for some sugary treats.

3 **Plaza Vieja** is the square most recently restored by the City Historian's Office, and has an impressive Carrera marble fountain in the center. On the east side is the 4 **Fototeca**, a photographic archive of Old Havana since the early 20th century that was started by former City Historian, Emilio Roig de Leuchsenring in 1937. There are an estimated 14,000 photos inside, and they have been instrumental in providing the graphic pointers for the current restoration.

Cut down Calle Brasil, turn left on Calle Oficios, and you'll come out by the 5 **Iglesia y Monasterio de San Francisco de Asís**. Built in 1739, this church/convent ceased to have a religious function in the 1840s. In the late 1980s crypts and religious objects were dug up during excavations, and many of them were later incorporated into the Museo de Arte Religioso that opened on the site in 1994. Since 2005, part of the old monastery has functioned as a children's theater for the neighborhood's young residents.

For an example of how the city has learnt to generate income from its history, take a look inside the five-star 6 **Hotel San Felipe y Santiago de Bejúcal**, overlooking the Plaza de San Francisco de Asís. Run by Habaguanex, the commercial arm of the City Historian's Office, the hotel was opened in 2010 and is one of over a dozen such establishments in the colonial core.

Following Oficios north, you'll end up in the third restored square, Plaza de Armas, dominated by the 7 **Palacio de los Capitanes Generales**, the emblematic building of Habaguanex and the first to be restored in 1968. The baroque structure was constructed between 1776 and 1791 and today houses the Museo de la Ciudad.

Diagonally across the square is the 8 **Castillo de la Real Fuerza**, one of the oldest forts in the New World, constructed in 1558 to protect Havana harbor from pirate attacks. From 1990–2005, the fort housed a ceramic museum. Freshly restored again in 2009, it has reopened as the Museo de Navegación (Naval Museum).

If you're feeling peckish at this point, divert to the Habaguanex-run 9 **Restaurant el Templete**, which overlooks the harbor. This restaurant opened in 2005 and serves fantastic seafood.

Going west from Plaza de Armas, head up Calle Obispo to the 10 **Farmacia Museo Taquechel**, an old pharmacy that was adapted from a townhouse in 1898. Restored in 1996, it functions as both a pharmaceutical museum (check out the old china pots and plush wooden counter), and a working pharmacy for the local population.

Continue up Obispo and turn left on Calle Aguiar. In one block you'll be facing the 11 **Oratorio San Felipe Neri**, a cultural center, headquartered in an old church originally built in 1693. Although it lost many of its original features when it was converted into a bank in 1952, the church was revitalized in a 2004 rehabilitation and now hosts classical-music concerts and a small exhibition of religious art.

Head two blocks west on Obrapía and several blocks south on Compostela to reach one of Havana's – and Cuba's – most commendable social projects, the little-visited 12 **Convento y Iglesia de Nuestra Señora de Belén**. This huge building was completed in 1718 and functioned first as a convalescent home and later a Jesuit convent. It was abandoned in 1925 and fell into disrepair exacerbated in 1991 by a damaging fire. The City Historian reversed the decline in the late '90s, using tourist coffers to make this splendid old building into an active community center for families, young people, the physically and mentally impaired, and the elderly (there are 18 permanent apartments for senior citizens here).

For the grand finale, follow Compostela four more blocks south and turn right on Leonor Pérez to reach the 13 **Museo Casa Natal de José Martí**, which opened in 1925 and is considered to be the oldest museum in Havana. The City Historian's Office took the house over in 1994, and its succinct stash of exhibits devoted to Cuba's national hero continues to impress.

Activities

Havana's two marinas, which offer numerous fishing, diving, and boating opportunities, lie in its outer suburbs. See p124 for more details.

Havana, with its spectacular Malecón sea drive, possesses one of the world's most scenic municipal jogging routes. The path from the Castillo de San Salvador de la Punta to the outer borders of Miramar measures 8km, though you can add on a few extra meters for holes in the pavement, splashing waves, veering *jineteros* (touts) and old men with fishing lines.

The recent upsurge in fume-belching traffic has meant that the air along the Malecón has become increasingly polluted. If you can handle it, run first thing in the morning.

Boxing enthusiasts should check out **Gimnasio de Boxeo Rafael Trejo** (Map p58; ☎862-0266; Cuba No 815 btwn Merced & Leonor Pérez, Habana Vieja). At this boxing gym you can see fights on Friday at 7pm (CUC$1), or drop by any day after 4pm to watch the training. Travelers interested in boxing can find a trainer here. Enquire within; they're very friendly.

Courses

Aside from Spanish-language courses, Havana offers a large number of learning activities for aspiring students. Private lessons can be arranged by asking around locally – try your casa particular. Your casa particular can also probably point you in the direction of dance classes. If your owner says he (or she) can't dance, he's either lying or not endowed with sufficient Cuban blood.

Universidad de la Habana LANGUAGE
(Map p72; ☎832-4245, 831-3751; www.uh.cu; Edificio Varona, 2nd fl, Calle J No 556, Vedado) Offers Spanish courses 12 months a year, beginning on the first Monday of each month. Costs start at CUC$100 for 20 hours (one week), including textbooks, and cover all levels from beginners to advanced. You must first sit a placement test to determine your level. Aspiring candidates can sign up in person at the university or reserve beforehand via email or phone.

Other places to check out Spanish courses include the following:

Uneac LANGUAGE
(Map p72; ☎832-4551; cnr Calles 17 & H, Vedado)

Paradiso LANGUAGE
(Map p72; ☎832-9538; Calle 19 No 560, Vedado)

Cubamar Viajes LANGUAGE
(Map p72; ☎830-1220; www.cubamarviajes.cu; Av 3 btwn Calle 12 & Malecón, Vedado; ⏰8:30am-5pm Mon-Sat)

Teatro América DANCE
(Map p68; ☎862-5416; Av de Italia No 253 btwn Concordia & Neptuno, Centro Habana) Next to the Casa de la Música, it can fix you up with both a class and a partner for approximately CUC$8 per hour.

Conjunto Folklórico Nacional de Cuba DANCE
(Map p72; ☎830-3060; www.folkcuba.cult.cu; Calle 4 No 103 btwn Calzada & Calle 5, Vedado) Teaches highly recommended classes in *son,* salsa, rumba, mambo and more. It also teaches percussion. Classes start on the third Monday in January and the first Monday in July, and cost in the vicinity of CUC$400 to CUC$500 for a 15-day course. An admission test places students in classes of four different levels.

Centro Hispano Americano de Cultura CULTURE
(Map p68; ☎860-6282; Malecón No 17 btwn Paseo de Martí & Capdevila, Centro Habana; ⏰9am-5pm Tue-Sat, 9am-1pm Sun) Has all kinds of facilities, including a library, cinema, internet cafe and concert venue. Pick up its excellent monthly brochure and ask about the literature courses.

Paradiso CULTURE
(Map p72; ☎832-9538; www.paradiso.cu; Calle 19 No 560, Vedado) A cultural agency that can arrange courses of between four and 12 weeks on history, architecture, music, theater, dance and more. The University of Havana also runs 60-hour courses on Cuban culture for CUC$360.

Museo de Artes Decorativas YOGA
(Map p72; ☎830-9848; Calle 17 No 502 btwn Calles D & E, Vedado) You may be able to drop in on yoga classes held in the garden here. Check at the museum for the next session.

Teatro Nacional de Cuba YOGA
(Map p72; ☎879-6011; cnr Paseo & Calle 39, Vedado) Look for the class schedule by the box office.

Centro Andaluz MUSIC
(Map p68;☎863-6745; Paseo de Martí btwn Virtudes & Neptuno, Centro Habana) Typically, Cubans perform flamenco as well as the Spanish, and you can take dance classes or even enquire about the possibility of taking guitar lessons here.

Taller Experimental de Gráfica ART
(Map p58; ☎862-0979; Callejón del Chorro No 6, Habana Vieja) Offers classes in the art of engraving. Individualized instruction lasts one month, during which the student creates an engraving with 15 copies; longer classes can be arranged. It costs around CUC$250.

Tours

Most general agencies offer the same tours, with some exceptions noted below. The regular tour diet includes a four-hour city tour (CUC$15), a specialized Hemingway tour (from CUC$20), a *cañonazo* ceremony (the shooting of the cannons at the Fortaleza de San Carlos de la Cabaña; without/with dinner CUC$15/25), a Varadero day trip (from CUC$35) and, of course, excursions to Tropicana Nightclub (starting at CUC$65). Other options include tours to Boca de Guamá crocodile farm (CUC$48), Playas del Este (CUC$20 including lunch), Viñales (CUC$44), Cayo Largo del Sur (CUC$137) and a Trinidad-Cienfuegos overnight (CUC$129). Children usually pay a fraction of the price for adults, and solo travelers get socked with a CUC$15 supplement. Note that if the minimum number of people don't sign up, the trip will be cancelled. Any of the following agencies can arrange these tours and more:

Cubatur GENERAL TOURS
(Map p72; ☎835-4155; cnr Calles 23 & M, Vedado; 8am-8pm) Below the Hotel Habana Libre.

Havanatur GENERAL TOURS
(Map p72; ☎835-3720; cnr Calles 23 & M, Vedado)

Infotur INFORMATION AGENCY
Airport (☎642-6101; Terminal 3 Aeropuerto Internacional José Martí; 24hr); Habana Vieja (Map p58; ☎863-6884; cnr Obispo & San Ignacio; 10am-1pm & 2-7pm)

Paradiso CULTURAL TOURS
(Map p72; ☎832-9538; Calle 19 No 560, Vedado) Offers tours with an emphasis on art. Tours depart from many cities and are in several languages. Check out Martí's Havana or special concert tours.

San Cristóbal Agencia de Viajes CULTURAL TOURS
(Map p58; ☎861-9171/2; www.viajessancristobal.cu; Oficios No 110 btwn Lamparilla & Amargura, Habana Vieja; 8:30am-5:30pm Mon-Fri, 8:30am-2pm Sat, 9am-noon Sun) Offers the best tours in the city including a Havana archeological tour (CUC$20 for two people) and a tour of the city's valuable social projects.

Festivals & Events

Not surprisingly, Havana has the best collection of annual festivals in Cuba. The highlights are all listed in the Month by Month chapter (see p22).

Sleeping

With nigh on 3000 private houses letting out rooms, you'll never struggle to find accommodation in Havana. Casas particulares go for anywhere between CUC$20 and CUC$40 per room, with Centro Habana offering the best bargains. Rock-bottom budget hotels can match casas for price, but not comfort. There's a dearth of decent hotels in the midrange price bracket, while Havana's top-end hotels are plentiful and offer oodles of atmosphere, even if the overall standards can't always match facilities elsewhere in the Caribbean.

Many of Havana's hotels are historic monuments in their own right. Worth a look, even if you're not staying over, are Hotel Sevilla and Hotel Saratoga (located in Centro Habana), the Raquel, Hostal Condes de Villanueva and Hotel Florida (all in Habana Vieja), and the iconic Hotel Nacional (in Vedado).

HABANA VIEJA

TOP CHOICE **Hostal Condes de Villanueva** HOTEL $$$
(Map p58; ☎862-9293; Mercaderes No 202; s/d CUC$100/160; ❄) If you are going to splash out on one night of luxury in Havana, you'd do well to check out this highly lauded colonial gem. Restored under the watchful eye of City Historian Eusebio Leal Spengler in the late '90s, the Villanueva has been converted from a grandiose city mansion into an intimate and thoughtfully decorated hotel with nine bedrooms spread spaciously around an attractive inner courtyard (complete with resident peacock). Upstairs suites contain stained-glass windows, chandeliers, arty sculptures and – in one of them – a fully workable whirlpool bathtub.

Hotel San Felipe y Santiago de Bejúcal HOTEL $$$
(Map p58; ☎864-9191; cnr Oficios & Amargura; s/d CUC$150/240; ❄@) Cuban baroque meets modern minimalist in Habaguanex's newest offering, and the results are something to behold. Spreading 27 rooms over six floors in the blustery Plaza San Francisco de Asís, this place is living proof that Habaguanex's delicate restoration work is getting better and better. If the Americans really are coming, they're going to be impressed.

START EL PRADO
FINISH MALECÓN
DISTANCE 4KM
DURATION 3 HOURS

Walking Tour
Centro Habana Architectural Tour

From the end of the 1 **Prado**, head south toward Parque Central, passing the 2 **Teatro Fausto**, an art deco classic that exhibits the sharp lines and pure cubist simplicity of Depression-era America. The theater is famous for its light plays and comedy shows.

One block further up on the right is the 3 **Casa del Científico**, an eclectic masterpiece furnished with sweeping staircases and an eye-catching rooftop lookout that was once the residence of former Cuban president, José Miguel Gómez.

Contrasting sharply with other modern architectural styles on Calle Trocadero is the neo-Moorish 4 **Hotel Sevilla**, built in 1908 but harking back to a bygone age of Spanish stucco and intricate *mudéjar* craftsmanship.

Turn right on Agramonte and detour down Ánimas for Havana's most emblematic art-deco building: the kitschy 5 **Edificio Bacardí**. It's a vivid and highly decorative incarnation of this popular interwar architectural genre, garnished with granite, Capellanía limestone and multicolored bricks.

At the southwest corner of Parque Central, eclecticism meets neobaroque at the flamboyant 6 **Centro Gallego**, erected as a Galician social club in 1915 around the existing Teatro Tacón. Facing it across leafy Parque Central is the equally eclectic 7 **Centro Asturianas**, now part of the Museo Nacional de Bellas Artes, with four separate rooftop lookouts and a richly gilded interior. Centro Havana's 8 **Capitolio Nacional**, built between 1926 and 1929, captures Latin America's neoclassical revival with sweeping stairways and Doric columns harking back to a purer and more strident Grecian ideal.

Pass beneath the Chinese pagoda on Dragones and proceed down Calle Zanja to the intersection of 9 **Calle Zanja & Av de Italia**, where you'll find one of Havana's zaniest art-deco creations, a narrow turreted townhouse with cube-like balconies and sharply defined lines. Turn right onto Av de Italia and walk north to the 10 **Malecón**, Havana's storm-lashed sea drive, a museum of brilliant eclecticism.

Hotel Florida HOTEL $$$
(Map p58; ☎862-4127; Obispo No 252; s/d incl breakfast CUC$100/160; ❄@) They don't make them like this anymore. The Florida is an architectural extravaganza built in the purest colonial style, with arches and pillars clustered around an atmospheric central courtyard. Habaguanex has restored the building (constructed in 1836) with loving attention to detail: the amply furnished rooms have retained their original high ceilings and wonderfully luxurious finishes. Anyone with even a passing interest in Cuba's architectural heritage will want to check out this colonial jewel, complemented with an elegant cafe and a popular bar-nightspot (from 8pm).

Hotel Raquel HOTEL $$$
(Map p58; ☎860-8280; cnr Amargura & San Ignacio; s/d CUC$100/160; ❄@) Encased in a dazzling 1908 palace (that was once a bank), the Hotel Raquel takes your breath away with its grandiose columns, sleek marble statues and intricate stained-glass ceiling. Painstakingly restored in 2003, the reception area in this marvelous eclectic building is a tourist sight in its own right – it's replete with priceless antiques and intricate art-nouveau flourishes. Behind its impressive architecture, the Raquel offers well-presented if noisy rooms, a small gym/sauna, friendly staff and a great central location.

Hotel Santa Isabel HOTEL $$$
(Map p58; ☎860-8201; Baratillo No 9; s/d incl breakfast CUC$150/240; ❄@) Considered one of Havana's finest hotels, as well as one of its oldest (it first began operations in 1867), the Hotel Santa Isabel is housed in the Palacio de los Condes de Santovenia, the former crash pad of a decadent Spanish count. In 1998 this three-story baroque beauty was upgraded to five-star status, but unlike other posh Cuban hotels, the Santa Isabel actually comes close to justifying the billing. The 17 regular rooms have bundles of historic charm and are all kitted out with attractive Spanish colonial furniture as well as paintings by contemporary Cuban artists. No small wonder ex-US president Jimmy Carter stayed here during his historic 2002 visit.

Hostal Valencia HOTEL $$$
(Map p58; ☎867-1037; Oficios No 53; s/d incl breakfast CUC$80/130) The Valencia is decked out like a Spanish *posada* (inn), with hanging vines, doorways big enough to ride a horse through and a popular on-site paella restaurant. With a bit of imagination, you can almost see the ghosts of Don Quixote and Sancho Panza floating through the hallways. Slap-bang in the middle of the historical core and with a price that makes it one of the cheapest offerings in the current Habaguanex stable, this hostel is an excellent old-world choice, with good service and plenty of atmosphere.

Hostal Palacio O'Farrill HOTEL $$$
(Map p58; ☎860-5080; Cuba No 102-108 btwn Chacón & Tejadillo; s/d CUC$100/160; ❄@) Not an Irish joke, but one of Havana's most impressive period hotels, the Palacio O'Farrill is a staggeringly beautiful colonial palace that once belonged to Don Ricardo O'Farrill, a Cuban sugar entrepreneur who was descended from a family of Irish nobility. Taking the Emerald Isle as its theme, there's plenty of greenery in the plant-filled 18th-century courtyard. The 2nd floor, which was added in the 19th century, provides grandiose neoclassical touches, while the 20th-century top floor merges seamlessly with the magnificent architecture below.

Casa de Pepe & Rafaela CASA PARTICULAR $
(Map p58; ☎862-9877; San Ignacio No 454 btwn Sol & Santa Clara; r CUC$30) One of Havana's best casas: antiques and Moorish tiles throughout, two rooms with balconies and gorgeous new baths, excellent location and great hosts. The son also rents a charming colonial house at San Ignacio No 656 (same price).

Juan & Margarita CASA PARTICULAR $
(Map p58; ☎867-9592; Obispo No 522 apt 8 btwn Bernaza & Villegas; r CUC$30, apt CUC$60) A two-bedroom apartment on Obispo, no less – Vieja's version of NYC's glamorous Fifth Avenue. You can bag the whole place for CUC$60: sitting room with TV and table, two clean bedrooms with baths, and a balcony. A gentleman and a scholar, Juan speaks excellent English and has a lot of local knowledge.

Hostal Beltrán de la Santa Cruz HOTEL $$$
(Map p58; ☎860-8330; San Ignacio No 411 btwn Muralla & Sol; s/d incl breakfast CUC$80/130; ❄) Excellent location, friendly staff and plenty of old-world authenticity make this compact inn just off Plaza Vieja a winning combination. Housed in a sturdy 18th-century building and offering just 11 spacious rooms, intimacy is assured and the standard of service has been regularly lauded by both travelers and reviewers.

Hotel Ambos Mundos HOTEL $$$
(Map p58; ☎860-9529; Obispo No 153; s/d CUC$100/160; ❄@) Hemingway's Havana hideout and the place where he is said to have penned his seminal guerrilla classic *For Whom the Bell Tolls* (Castro's bedtime reading during the war in the mountains), the pastel-pink Ambos Mundos is a Havana institution and an obligatory pit stop for anyone on a world tour of 'Hemingway-once-fell-over-in-here' bars. Small, sometimes windowless rooms suggest overpricing, but the lobby bar is classic enough (follow the romantic piano melody) and drinks in the rooftop restaurant one of the city's finest treats.

Mesón de la Flota HOTEL $$
(Map p58; ☎863-3838; Mercaderes No 257 btwn Amargura & Brasil; s/d incl breakfast CUC$65/100) Habana Vieja's smallest and only midrange hotel is an old Spanish tavern decked out with maritime motifs and located within spitting distance of gracious Plaza Vieja. Five individually crafted rooms contain all of the modern comforts and amenities, while downstairs a busy restaurant serves up delicious tapas.

Pablo Rodríguez CASA PARTICULAR $
(Map p58; ☎861-2111; pablo@sercomar.tele mar.cu; Compostela No 532 btwn Brasil & Muralla; r CUC$30) Another lovely old colonial classic, this place has some original frescoes partially uncovered on the walls. It would be worth millions elsewhere, but here you can rent one of venerable Pablo's two rooms with bathrooms (one ensuite, one private but separate), fan and fridge for a giveaway CUC$30 per night.

Residencia Académica Convento de Santa Clara HOSTEL $
(Map p58; ☎866-9327; Cuba No 610 btwn Luz & Sol; r per person CUC$25) Something of a novelty for Havana, this run-down but charmingly atmospheric old nunnery has been partially converted into a hostel to take in travelers. Situated a stone's throw from Plaza Vieja and priced cheaper than the surrounding casas particulares, it's a tempting budget option if you don't mind fairly spartan facilities and possible room sharing.

Hotel Marqués de Prado Ameno HOTEL $$$
(Map p58; ☎862-4127; cnr O'Reilly & Cuba; s/d incl breakfast CUC$100/160; ❄@) Connected to the Hotel Florida by a tunnel, this newish hotel offers similar facilities: thoughtful restoration, eager-to-please staff and plenty of colonial grandiosity.

Hotel el Comendador HOTEL $$$
(Map p58; ☎867-1037; cnr Obrapía & Baratillo; ❄) Situated next door to the Hostal Valencia, the El Comendador offers similar facilities and rates.

Noemi Moreno CASA PARTICULAR $
(Map p58; ☎862-3809; Cuba No 611 apt 2 btwn Luz & Santa Clara; r CUC$25-30) Offering two simple, clean rooms sharing a bathroom, Noemi's got a great location behind the Santa Clara convent. If full, apartments 1 and 4 also rent in the same building.

Migdalia Carraballe CASA PARTICULAR $
(Map p58; ☎861-7352; Santa Clara No 164 btwn Cuba & San Ignacio; r CUC$30) Located two blocks from Plaza Vieja, Migdalia rents two from a choice of three rooms. The ones with balconies overlook Santa Clara convent. Climb the staircase to the 1st floor.

CENTRO HABANA

TOP CHOICE **Hotel NH Parque Central** HOTEL $$$
(Map p68; ☎860-6627; www.nh-hotels.com; Neptuno btwn Agramonte & Paseo de Martí; s/d CUC$200/300; P❄@≋) If you have a penchant for hanging out in expensive five-star hotel lobbies sipping mojitos, the Parque Central could fill a vacuum. Reserving a room is another (more expensive) matter. Outside Havana's two Meliás, the NH is, without a doubt, Havana's best international-standard hotel, with service and business facilities on a par with top-ranking five-star facilities elsewhere in the Caribbean. Although the fancy lobby and classily furnished rooms may lack the historical riches of the Habaguanex establishments, the ambience here is far from antiseptic. Bonus facilities include a full-service business center, a rooftop swimming pool/fitness center/Jacuzzi, an elegant lobby bar, the celebrated El Paseo restaurant, plus excellent international telephone and internet links. Two of the bedrooms are wheelchair-accessible. In 2009 the Parque Central opened an even swankier new wing across Calle Virtudes, connected to the rest of the hotel by means of an underground tunnel. As well as state-of-the-art rooms, the addition includes its own luxurious restaurant, cafe and reception area.

Hotel Saratoga HOTEL $$$
(Map p68; ☎868-1000; Paseo de Martí No 603; s/d CUC$226/280; P❄@≋) One of Havana's newest, ritziest and most dramatic hotels,

the glittering Saratoga is an architectural work-of-art that stands imposingly at the intersection of Prado and Dragones with fantastic views over toward the Capitolio. Sharp, if officious, service is a feature here, as are the extra-comfortable beds, power showers and a truly decadent rooftop swimming pool. Not surprisingly, there's a price for all this luxury. The Saratoga is Havana's most expensive hotel, and while its facilities impress, its service can't quite match the marginally cheaper Meliás.

Hotel Sevilla HOTEL **$$$**
(☎860-8560; Trocadero No 55 btwn Paseo de Martí & Agramonte; s/d incl breakfast CUC$150/210; P❄@🛜≋) Al Capone once hired out the whole 6th floor, Graham Greene used it as a setting for his novel *Our Man in Havana* (room 501 to be exact) and the Mafia requisitioned it as operations centre for their prerevolutionary North American drugs racket. Now run in partnership with the French Sofitel group, the Moorish Sevilla still drips with history as countless old black-and-white photos of past guests (including Greene, Capone and Josephine Baker) will testify. Rooms are spacious and equipped with comfortable beds, and the ostentatious lobby could have been ripped straight out of the Alhambra.

Hotel Telégrafo HOTEL **$$$**
(Map p68; ☎861-1010, 861-4741; Paseo de Martí No 408; s/d CUC$100/160; ❄@🛜) A bold royal-blue charmer on the northwest corner of Parque Central, this Habaguanex beauty juxtaposes old-style architectural features (the original building hails from 1888) with futuristic design flourishes that include shiny silver sofas, a huge winding central staircase and an amazingly intricate tile mosaic emblazoned on the wall of the downstairs cafe. The rooms are equally spiffy.

Hotel Lido HOTEL **$**
(Map p68; ☎867-1102; Consulado No 210 btwn Ánimas & Trocadero; s/d CUC$28/38; ❄@) A travelers' institution, the lackluster Lido is Havana's unofficial backpacker nexus. It has been popular for years for its central location and no-frills rooms with intermittent hot water and a gritty neighborhood feel. It certainly ain't fancy (that's the point, isn't it?), but it has a handy internet terminal downstairs, breakfast on the roof and a helpful Cubanacán info desk. Then there's the price – cheaper than most of Havana's casas.

Hotel Park View HOTEL **$$**
(Map p68; Colón No 101; s/d CUC$52/86; ❄@) Built in 1928 with American money, the Park View's reputation as the poor man's 'Sevilla' isn't entirely justified. Its location alone (within baseball-pitching distance of the Museo de la Revolución) is enough to consider this mint-green city charmer a viable option. Chuck in friendly doormen, modern furnishings (it's Habaguanex-run) and a small but perfectly poised 7th-floor restaurant and you've got yourself a rare midrange bargain.

Hotel Inglaterra HOTEL **$$$**
(Map p68; ☎860-8595; Paseo de Martí No 416; s/d/tr CUC$84/120/168; P❄@) It's José Martí's one-time Havana hotel of choice and it's still playing on the fact – which says something about the current state of affairs. The Inglaterra is a better place to hang out in than stay in, with its exquisite Moorish lobby and crusty colonial interior easily outshining the lackluster and often viewless rooms. The rooftop bar is a popular watering hole, and the downstairs foyer is a hive of bustling activity where there's always live music blaring. Beware the streets outside, which are full of overzealous hustlers waiting to pounce.

Esther Cardoso CASA PARTICULAR **$**
(Map p68; ☎862-0401; esthercv2551@cubarte.cult.cu; Águila No 367 btwn Neptuno & San Miguel; r CUC$25) Esther is an actress (quite well-known in Havana), meaning that this little palace shines like an oasis in Centro Habana's dilapidated desert, with tasteful decor, funky posters, spick-and-span baths and a spectacular roof terrace. Book early, as this place is well known.

Julio & Elsa Roque CASA PARTICULAR **$**
(Map p68; ☎861-8027; julioroq@yahoo.com; Consulado No 162 btwn Colón & Trocadero; r CUC$20-30) Julio's a pediatrician and rents out two rooms in his friendly family house just a block from Prado. Taking advantage of new liberalized rental laws he has also recently opened **Hostal Peregrino** with three more rooms and an independent apartment in a building nearby (bookings through same number as the casa particular). Services include airport pickup, internet, laundry and cocktail bar. The accommodations are cozy and nicely furnished and both Julio and his wife Elsa are super-helpful and a mine of local information. English is spoken.

Hotel Deauville HOTEL $$
(Map p68; ☎866-8812; Av de Italia No 1 cnr Malecón; s/d/tr CUC$36/72/108; P ❄ ≋) The Deauville is housed in a kitschy seafront high-rise that sharp-eyed Havana-watchers will recognize from picturesque Malecón-at-sunset postcards. But while the location might be postcard-perfect, the facilities inside this former Mafia gambling den don't quite match up to the stellar views. Currently reborn in peach and red and already showing the effects of the corrosive sea water, the Deauville's handy facilities (money exchange and car rental) and reasonably priced restaurant are ever popular with the mid-priced tour-circuit crowd.

Hotel Lincoln HOTEL $
(Map p68; ☎862-8061; Av de Italia btwn Virtudes & Ánimas; s/d CUC$24/38; ❄) This peeling nine-story giant on busy Galiano (Av de Italia) was the second-tallest building in Havana when it was built in 1926. Overshadowed by taller opposition these days, it still offers 135 air-con rooms with bathroom and TV in an atmosphere that is more 1950s than 2010s. Notoriety hit in 1958 when Castro's 26th of July Movement kidnapped motor racing world champion Carlos Fangio from the lobby on the eve of the Cuban Grand Prix. A small 'museum' on the 8th floor records the event for posterity. Otherwise, the facilities are best described as timeworn.

Dulce Hostal – Dulce María González CASA PARTICULAR $
(Map p68; ☎863-2506; Amistad No 220 btwn Neptuno & San Miguel; r CUC$20) The Dulce (sweet) Hostal on Amistad (friendship) St sounds like a good combination, and sweet and friendly is what you get in this beautiful colonial house with tile floors, soaring ceilings and a quiet, helpful hostess.

Niurka O Rey CASA PARTICULAR $
(Map p68; ☎863-0278; Águila No 206 btwn Ánimas & Virtudes; r CUC$20-25) A sparkling blue house with a slightly less sparkling but adequate interior. One of the two rooms here comes with a private bathroom and there's parking close by.

Hotel Caribbean HOTEL $
(Map p68; ☎860-8233; Paseo de Martí No 164 btwn Colón & Refugio; s/d CUC$30/48; ❄) Cheap but not always so cheerful, the Caribbean offers aspiring Cuban renovators a lesson in how not to decorate. Rooms are a tad dark and pokey. Bargain-basement seekers only.

VEDADO

Casa 1932 CASA PARTICULAR $
(Map p72; ☎863-6203, 05-264-3858; www.casahabana.net; Campanario 63 btwn San Lázaro & Lagunas; r CUC$20-35; ❄) Prepare for an enchanting voyage back in time to art-deco Havana. Everything you touch in this genteel house is nigh on an antique: from the beds you'll sleep on down to the cutlery you'll use for the innovative food. That's not including, of course, the furnishings themselves, which in any other country would be in a museum – gambling chips from Cuba's last casino and an intriguing 1930s ashtray are highlights. But it's the owner that's the icing on the cake: an interior designer and local history expert who is a mine of information on everything from forgotten Cuban film to the history of pharmacy. He can arrange art-deco city tours, as well as impromptu salsa classes.

Villa Enano Rojo CASA PARTICULAR $
(Map p72; ☎863-5081; Malecón No 557 btwn Lealtad & Escobar; r CUC$25) The name translates as 'Red Dwarf House,' but you won't find any blushing short people here, just owners Lalo and Magda and a gracious upstairs apartment with two rooms, one of which has a front-row seat to that most romantic of evening cabarets – the Malecón.

Martha Obregón CASA PARTICULAR $
(Map p72; ☎870-2095; marthaobregon@yahoo.com; Gervasio No 308 Altos btwn Neptuno & San Miguel; r CUC$20-25) A pleasant family home with little balconies and small street views. You'll get a good sense of life in the crowded central quarter here, with its whistling tradesmen, snippets of music and stickball-playing kids.

(Continued on page 97)

¡Viva Cuba!

Beaches »
Havana »
Architecture »
Music & Dance »

Lady with fan and cigar, Havana

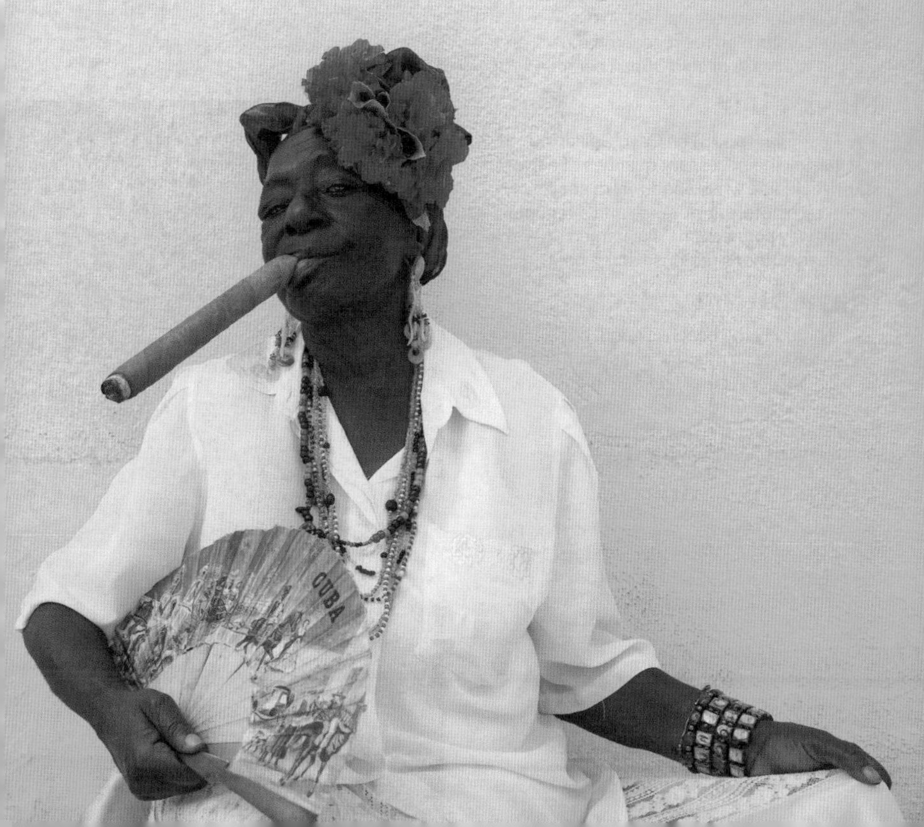

Beaches

There was a time when Cuba's beaches were points of disembarkation for US armies, or hallowed ground for revolutionaries arriving to save the nation in leaking leisure yachts. Today they're less confrontational places where you're far more likely to bump into a relaxed sunbather than a gun-toting soldier.

Playa Sirena

1 If loafing on a beach is your primary holiday occupation, you've come to the right place. Cayo Largo del Sur (p167), Cuba's sheltered 'resort island', has the widest and most impressive stretches of sand in Cuba.

Playa Maguana

2 Sandy Maguana (p441), near Baracoa, has retained its local feel. Arrive in a vintage car, turn on the *reggaetón* music, and pull out that case of cold Cuban beer.

Playa Pilar

3 Pilar Pilar (p308) on Cayo Guillermo has all the necessary qualities of a five-star beach: fine white sand, warm shallow water, zero hotel interference and a tenuous Hemingway connection – it's named after the American author's famous fishing boat.

Playa Ancón

4 Naturally the beach is good, but Ancón (p286) is as much about surroundings as sand quality. A coral reef 500m offshore, the crinkled Sierra del Escambray winking in the distance and Trinidad, the colonial jewel, less than 40 minutes away – by bike!

Playa Los Pinos

5 'Why am I the only one here?' is the first thought that strikes most visitors on seeing paradisiacal Playa Los Pinos (p324) for the first time. Don't ask; just enjoy.

BRUNO COSSA/CORBIS

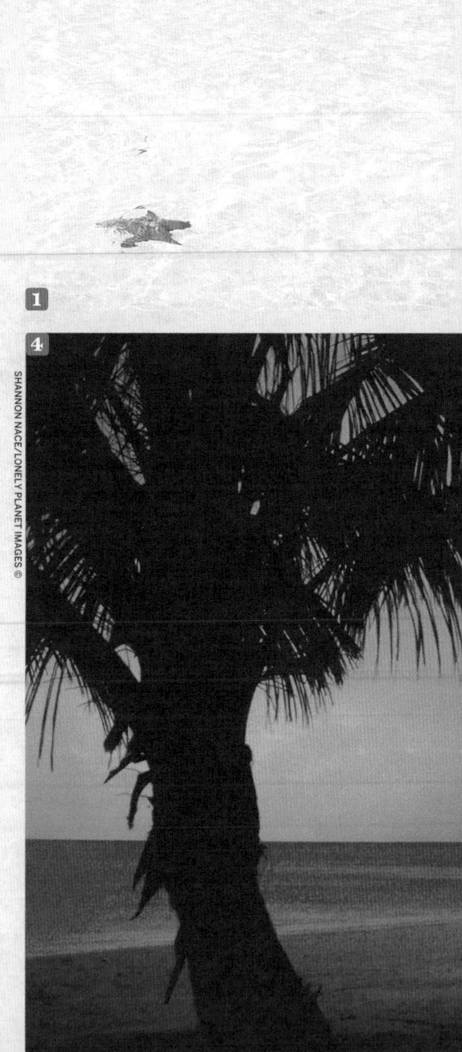

SHANNON NACE/LONELY PLANET IMAGES ©

Clockwise from top left
1. Playa Sirena, Cayo Largo del Sur **2.** Playa Maguana **3.** Playa Pilar, Cayo Guillermo **4.** Sunset at Playa Ancón.

ALEXANDER PÖSCHEL/PHOTOLIBRARY

2

IMAGEBROKER

Havana

Precious jewel of a vanquished empire, heart and soul of a struggling nation, former gambling den to the American mafia, and hallowed home to over two million people: Havana is far more than just a city. It's a spectacle, an ongoing story and a state of mind.

Restored Habana Vieja

1 It's difficult to think of anywhere else in the world where so much passion has been channeled into rehabilitating a colonial city center. Wander the streets of Habana Vieja (p80) and absorb a heady mix of time-warped history and austere modern reality.

Street Theater

2 Havana is a visceral place. The best sights can't be located on any map. To find them you'll need patience, spontaneity and a sturdy pair of legs. Walk the streets and investigate.

Capitolio Nacional

3 The most iconic sight in Havana's skyline is the dome-roofed Capitolio (p66). It's an almost exact copy of the Capitol Building in Washington DC, and a constant reminder of the often fraught relationship between Cuba and its northern neighbor.

Forts

4 Ringing Havana's harbor, the city's strong forts (p64) have served various functions through the centuries, not all of them pleasant. Today you can view them with less trepidation in their incarnations as naval museums and lofty lookouts, and at colorful cannon ceremonies.

Museums

5 Havana will educate you in subtle ways. A cache of fine museums range from the all-encompassing (the impressive Museo de la Revolución, p70), to the esoteric (a coin museum, a chocolate house, and even a playing-card museum).

1

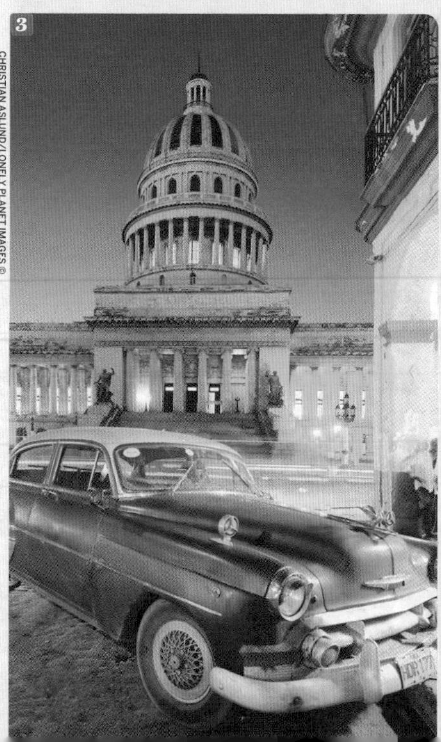

3

Clockwise from top left

1. Buildings undergoing restoration, Habana Vieja
2. Street performers, Habana Vieja **3.** Vintage car in front of the Capitolio Nacional, Habana Vieja

2

Architecture

If Cuba's soul is hidden in its music, then its architecture – in the words of novelist Alejo Carpentier – is 'its music turned to stone.' Running the gamut of styles, from baroque to art deco, the country is a museum of architectural eclecticism, fortuitously spared from developers' bulldozers.

Remedios

1 A city of legends and mysteries, Remedios (p259) is Cuba's forgotten corner, a colonial secret that glimmers subtly like an undiscovered jewel. Sit with a mojito gazing at the pretty town plaza and keep the news to yourself. Shhhh...

Havana

2 Shaped by its colonial history and embellished by myriad foreign influences from as far afield as Italy and Morocco, the Cuban capital (p77) combines *mudéjar*, baroque, neoclassical, art nouveau, art deco and modernist architectural styles to form a visually striking whole.

Trinidad

3 Soporific Trinidad (p275) went to sleep in 1850 and never really woke up. Modern-day travelers can roam through the perfectly preserved mid-19th-century sugar town like voyeurs from another era.

Cienfuegos

4 Known as the 'Pearl of the South,' Cienfuegos (p233) is Cuba's most architecturally complete city; a love letter to French neoclassicism wrapped picturesquely around one of the Caribbean's most beautiful natural bays.

Camagüey

5 Classical blends with ecclesial in Camagüey (p310) – a city of churches, spires, towers and crosses. Then there are the streets: a network of winding, sinuous thor-

Clockwise from top left

1. Old man gazing from a balcony, Remedios
2. Advertisement revealed on a restored facade, Havana
3. Museo Histórico Municipal (p277), Trinidad **4.** Classic American car outside a building in Cienfuegos

2

FRANK CARTER/LONELY PLANET IMAGES ©

3

Music & Dance

Cuba is defined by its music and dance, a complicated family tree of genres, sub-genres and rhythmic offshoots. The wider world may be familiar with mambo, salsa and the Buena Vista Social Club, but who, beyond these shores, has heard of nengon, kiribá, guanguancó, songo and danzón-chá?

Nueva Trova

1 An improbable blend of Bob Dylan, Celia Cruz, John Lennon, Víctor Jara and Joan Manuel Serrat, *nueva trova* (p478) is the Cuban Revolution's musical soundtrack. Its greatest exponents – Pablo Milanés and Carlos Puebla – came from Granma province.

Rumba

2 A hypnotizing mix of thumping drums and athletic dancing, rumba (p475) is like going back to Africa without crossing the Atlantic. Yet, the music was first played in the port cities of Havana and Matanzas still aching from the wounds of slavery.

Son

3 Take away *son* (p476) and you have no mambo, salsa, *timba* and everything thereafter. When the lilting strings of Spain were first combined with the rugged drums of Africa, the result was a Columbian moment of musical discovery.

Changüí

4 In Santiago they call it *son*. Next door in Guantánamo province they call it c*hangüí* (p430); an eastern variation on a traditional Cuban theme, born in provincial sugar refineries and influenced by slave culture.

Reggaetón

5 Love it or hate it, *reggaetón* (p478) is the sound of the moment in Cuba. A mélange of rap, hip-hop, reggae and dance, it emanates from parks, squares, schoolyards and the hard-nosed streets of its spiritual home – Alamar.

CEZARO DE LUCA/CORBIS

PETER TURNLEY/CORBIS

Right

1. Pablo Milanés, one of the founders of *nueva trova*
2. Outdoor rumba concert, Havana

(Continued from page 88)

La Casona Colonial – José Díaz CASA PARTICULAR $

(Map p72; ☎870-0489; Gervasio No 209 btwn Concordia & Virtudes; r CUC$25) A colonial house with a pleasant courtyard, this place has a shared bathroom but plenty of bed space and configurations. It's located in the thick of the Centro Habana action and has friendly owners and good access.

Hotel Victoria HOTEL $$

(Map p72; ☎833-3510; Calle 19 No 101; s/d incl breakfast CUC$80/100; P❄@≋) A well-heeled and oft-overlooked Vedado option, the Victoria is a diminutive five-story hotel situated within spitting distance of the larger and more expensive Nacional. Deluxe and compact, though (due to its size) invariably full, this venerable Gran Caribe establishment housed in an attractive neoclassical building dating from 1928 contains a swimming pool, a bar and a small shop. A sturdy midrange accommodation option (if you can get in).

Hotel Nacional HOTEL $$$

(Map p72; ☎836-3564; cnr Calles O & 21; s/d/tr CUC$120/170/238; P❄@令≋) The cherry on the cake of Cuban hotels and a flagship of the government-run Gran Caribe chain, the neoclassical/neocolonial/art deco (let's call it eclectic) Hotel Nacional is as much a city monument as it is an international accommodation option. Even if you haven't got the money to stay here, chances are you'll find yourself sipping at least one minty mojito in its exquisite ocean-side bar. Steeped in history and furnished with rooms with plaques that advertise details of illustrious past occupants, this towering Havana landmark sports two swimming pools, a sweeping manicured lawn, a couple of lavish restaurants and its own top-class nighttime cabaret, the Parisién (p111). While the rooms might lack some of the fancy gadgets of deluxe Varadero, the ostentatious communal areas and the erstwhile ghosts of Winston Churchill, Frank Sinatra, Lucky Luciano and Errol Flynn that haunt the Moorish lobby make for a fascinating and unforgettable experience.

Hotel Meliá Cohiba HOTEL $$$

(Map p72; ☎833-3636; Paseo btwn Calles 1 & 3; r CUC$150/200; P❄@令≋) Royally professional, this ocean-side concrete giant built in 1994 (it's the only building from this era on the Malecón) will satisfy the highest of international expectations with its knowledgeable, consistent staff and modern, well-polished facilities. After a few weeks in the Cuban outback, you'll feel like you're on a different planet here, although the ambience is more Houston than Havana. For workaholics there are special 'business-traveler rooms' and 59 units have Jacuzzis. On the lower levels gold-star facilities include a shopping arcade, one of Havana's plushest gyms and the ever-popular Habana Café (p111).

Hotel Habana Libre HOTEL $$$

(Map p72; ☎834-6100; Calle L btwn Calles 23 & 25; d/ste incl breakfast CUC$120/160; P❄@≋) Havana's biggest and boldest hotel opened in March 1958 on the eve of Batista's last waltz. Once part of the Hilton chain, in January 1959 it was commandeered by Castro's rebels, who put their boots over all the plush furnishings and turned it into their temporary HQ (Castro effectively ran the country from a suite on one of the upper floors). Now managed by Spain's Meliá chain as an urban Tryp Hotel, this skyline-hogging giant has all 574 rooms kitted out to international standard, though the lackluster furnishings could do with a makeover. The tour desks in the lobby are helpful for out-of-town excursions and the 25th-floor Cabaret Turquino (p112) is a city institution.

Hotel Riviera HOTEL $$$

(Map p72; ☎836-4051; cnr Paseo & Malecón; s/d incl breakfast CUC$63/106; P❄@≋) Meyer Lansky's magnificent Vegas-style palace has leapt back into fashion with its gloriously retro lobby almost unchanged since 1957 (when it was the height of modernity). It isn't hard to imagine all the old Mafia hoods congregating here with their Cohiba cigars and chauffer-driven Chevrolets parked outside. The trouble for modern-day visitors are the rooms (there are 354 of them), which, though luxurious 50 years ago, are now looking a little rough around the edges and struggle to justify their top-end price tag. You can dampen the dreariness in the fabulous '50s-style pool, the good smattering of restaurants or the legendary Copa Room cabaret (p112), which is far cheaper than Tropicana. The location on a wild and wave-lashed section of the Malecón is spectacular, although a good bus or taxi ride from the Old Town.

Hotel Presidente HOTEL $$$

(Map p72; ☎55-18-01; cnr Calzada & Calle G; s/d CUC$90/140; P❄@≋) Fully restored in 2000, this art deco influenced hotel wouldn't be out of place on a street just off Times Sq in New York. Built the same year as the Victoria (1928), the Presidente is similar but larger, with gruffer staff. Unless you're a walker or fancy getting some elbow exercise on Havana's crowded bus system, the location can be awkward.

Marta Vitorte CASA PARTICULAR $

(Map p72; ☎832-6475; martavitorte@hotmail.com; Calle G No 301 apt 14 btwn Calles 13 & 15; r CUC$35-40) Marta has lived in this sinuous apartment on Av de los Presidentes since 1960. One look at the view and you'll see why – the glass-fronted wraparound terrace that soaks up 270 degrees of Havana's stunning panorama makes it seem as if you're standing atop the Martí monument. Not surprisingly, the two rooms are deluxe with lovely furnishings, minibars and safes. Then there are the breakfasts, the laundry, the parking space, the lift attendant… Get the drift?

Eddy Gutiérrez Bouza CASA PARTICULAR $

(Map p72; ☎832-5207; Calle 21 No 408 btwn Calles F & G; r CUC$30; P❄) Eddy is a fantastic host with a great knowledge of Havana, and his huge colonial house has hosted many visitors over the years. It's an inviting abode with a well-kept garden, a grand exterior and Eddy's 1974 Argentinian-made Dodge parked in the driveway. Guests are accommodated out back in comfortable quarters, and one room comes equipped with a kitchenette.

Casa Particular Sandélis CASA PARTICULAR $

(Map p72; ☎832-4422; Calle 21 No 4 apt 61 btwn Calles N & O; r CUC$30-35) Another casa in the art-deco block overlooking the Hotel Nacional, this house on the 6th floor combines a phenomenal location with the kindness and honesty of hosts Carolina and Lenin (who is a talented painter). There is a variety of rooms to choose from, all with ensuite bathrooms.

Mercedes González CASA PARTICULAR $

(Map p72; ☎832-5840; mercylupe@hotmail.com; Calle 21 No 360 apt 2A btwn Calles G & H; r CUC$30-35) One of the most welcoming hosts in Havana, Mercedes comes highly recommended by readers, fellow travelers, other casa owners, you name it. Her lovely art deco abode is a classic Vedado apartment with two fine rooms, an airy terrace and top-notch five-star service.

Manuel Martínez CASA PARTICULAR $

(Map p72; ☎832-6713; Calle 21 No 4 apt 22 btwn Calles N & O; r CUC$30-35) There are 14 casas in this magnificent art deco building constructed in 1945 opposite the Hotel Nacional, making it like a minihotel. A *portera* (door person) guards the communal entry and can point you in the right direction. This one overlooks the hotel gardens, and is about as close as you can get to Cuba's famous five-star without having to pay the five-star rates.

Hotel St John's HOTEL $$

(Map p72; ☎833-3740; Calle O No 216 btwn Calles 23 & 25; s/d incl breakfast CUC$60/100; ❄@≋) A fair-to-middling Vedado option, the St John's has a rooftop pool, clean bathrooms, reasonable beds and the ever-popular Pico Blanco nightclub (p111) on the 14th floor. Ask for one of the western-facing rooms with killer views over the Malecón. If wall-vibrating Cuban discos aren't your thing, you might get more peace at the identically priced Hotel Vedado half a block down the road.

Hotel Vedado HOTEL $$

(Map p72; ☎836-4072; Calle O No 244 btwn Calles 23 & 25; s/d CUC$65/80; ❄@≋) Ever popular with the tour-bus crowd, the Hotel Vedado is a tough sell. Granted, there's an OK pool (rare in Havana), along with a passable restaurant and not unpleasant rooms. But the patchy service, perennially noisy lobby and almost total lack of character will leave you wondering if you wouldn't have been better off staying in a local casa particular – for half the price.

Nelsy Alemán Machado CASA PARTICULAR $

(Map p72; ☎832-8467; Calle 25 No 361 apt 1 btwn Calles K & L; r CUC$25) Nelsy is one of two renters in this house up by the university and a stone's throw from the Hotel Habana Libre. Geographically, it's one of Vedado's better options: it's safe and secure, but close to most of the action.

Guillermina & Roberto Abreu CASA PARTICULAR $

(Map p72; ☎833-6401; Paseo No 126 apt 13A btwn Calle 5 & Calzada; r CUC$30; ❄) On the 13th floor of a Vedado apartment block built in 1958, this is another 'view' property with two rooms, private bathrooms and plush china furnishings. Hold your breath as you take the clunking elevator from the ground floor up.

Hotel Colina HOTEL $
(Map p72; ☎836-4071; cnr Calles L & 27; s/d CUC$34/42; ❄@) The friendliest and least fussy of Vedado's cheaper options, the 80-room Colina is situated directly outside the university and is a good choice if you're here for a Spanish course.

Luis Suávez Fiandor CASA PARTICULAR $
(Map p72; ☎832-5213; Calle F No 510 Altos btwn Calles 21 & 23; r CUC$30) Welcome to another clean, safe Vedado option with gracious hosts and two upstairs rooms with private bathrooms and a terrace overlooking the weathered Havana rooftops.

Hotel Bruzón HOTEL $
(Map p72; ☎877-5684; Bruzón No 217 btwn Pozos Dulces & Av de la Independencia; s/d CUC$22/31; ❄) There are only two reasons to stay here: you've got an early bus to catch (the terminal's 400m away), or everywhere else is full. Otherwise, the claustrophobic rooms aren't worth it.

Basilia Pérez Castro CASA PARTICULAR $
(Map p72; ☎832-3953; bpcdt@hotmail.com; Calle 25 No 361 apt 7 Bajos btwn Calles K & L; r CUC$25) Basilia rents out two rooms with independent entrances in the same house as Nelsy. It's a mellow scene and good value.

Melba Piñada Bermudez CASA PARTICULAR $
(Map p72; ☎832-5929; lienafp@yahoo.com; Calle 11 No 802 btwn Calles 2 & 4; r CUC$30) This 100-year-old villa in a shady Vedado street would be a millionaire's pad anywhere else. But here in Havana, it's a casa particular with two large rooms and decent meals

Eating

HABANA VIEJA

Havana's Old Town has the most consistent stash of government-run restaurants in Cuba, most of them competently operated by the City Historian's agency, Habaguanex. Experimenting beyond the usual *comida criolla,* you'll find decent ethnic places here (eg Italian, Arabic and Chinese), albeit ones run primarily by Cubans. Habana Vieja's paladares have been reduced to a handful of legal places that compete enterprisingly with the heavily promoted government big-shots.

TOP CHOICE **Restaurante el Templete** SEAFOOD $$$
(Map p58; Av del Puerto No 12; meals CUC$15-20; ⏲noon-11pm) Welcome to a rare Cuban breed: a restaurant that could compete with anything in Miami – and a government-run one at that! The Templete's specialty is fish, and special it is: fresh, succulent and cooked simply without any of the pretensions so rampant in celebrity chef-obsessed America. Sure, it's a little *caro* (expensive), but it's worth every last *centivo.*

La Imprenta INTERNATIONAL $$$
(Map p58; Mercaderes No 208; ⏲noon-midnight) This new Habaguanex restaurant has raised the bar for government-run places in the Old Town, with previously unheard-of Cuban innovations such as al dente pasta, creative seafood medleys and a stash of decent wines. Service is equally impressive, bucking the trend of bored unmotivated waiters of yore, and the resplendent interior is filled with memorabilia from the building's previous incarnation as a printing works.

Restaurante la Dominica ITALIAN $$
(Map p58; O'Reilly No 108; ⏲noon-midnight) Despite a tendency to be a little overgenerous with the olive oil, La Dominica – with its wood-fired pizza oven and al dente pasta – could quite legitimately stake a claim as Havana's finest Italian restaurant. Located in an elegantly restored dining room with alfresco seating on Calle O'Reilly, the menu offers Italy's 'usual suspects,' augmented by shrimp and lobster (CUC$10 to CUC$18). Professional house bands serenade diners with a slightly more eclectic set than the obligatory Buena Vista Social Club staples.

Restaurante la Paella SPANISH $$
(Map p58; cnr Oficios & Obrapía; ⏲noon-11pm) Known for its paella (CUC$10), this place, attached to the Hostal Valencia, has an authentic ambience and tries hard to emulate its Spanish namesake (the birthplace of Spain's famous rice dish). Food can be variable, but on a good day you'll be scraping the rice off the bottom of your serving pan with relish.

Mesón de la Flota TAPAS $$
(Map p58; Mercaderes No 257 btwn Amargura & Brasil; s/d incl breakfast CUC$65/100) If Havana resembles any city, it's Cádiz in Spain, and this nautically themed tapas bar/restaurant might have been transported from Cádiz's Barrio de Santa María, so potent is the atmosphere. Old-world tapas include *garbanzos con chorizo* (chickpeas with sausage), calamari and tortilla, but there are also more substantial seafood-biased *platos principales* (main meals). For music lovers the real drawcard is the nightly *tablaos* (flamenco shows),

LOCAL KNOWLEDGE

NORBERTO HERNÁNDEZ: TOUR GUIDE, AGENCIA DE VIAJES SAN CRISTÓBAL, HAVANA

Must Hear

Callejón de Hamel (p110) Go for live street rumba and an opportunity to meet the street's original artist, Salvador González Escalona.

Must See

Museo de Bellas Artes (p67) Don't miss the Cuban displays in the building on Calle Trocadero, which is laid out chronologically and includes many of the defining pieces of Cuban art such as Gitana Tropical by Victor Manuel García Valdés.

Must do

Baseball You can go to Parque Central to hear the latest baseball chat at the Esquina Caliente, or attend an Industriales game at the Estadio Latinoamericano (p113).

Hidden Secret

Circo Trompoloco (p130) This permanent big top in Playa uses methods based on former Soviet circuses, and its animal and human performers are excellent.

After Hours

El Gato Tuerto (p110) At the end of a hard day, I like to go to the 'One-eyed Cat,' where there's a bar, some tables, soothing bolero music and a good mix of Cubans and tourists.

Jazz Café (p110) This is another good spot for late-night drinks and jazz fusion music from about 11pm onwards.

the quality of which could rival anything in Andalusia. Sit back and soak up the intangible spirit of *duende* (climactic moment in a flamenco concert inspired by the fusion of music and dance).

Al Medina ARABIC **$$**
(Map p58; Oficios No 12 btwn Obrapía & Obispo; ⏲noon-midnight; 🖉) Havana takes on the Middle East in this exotic restaurant, appropriately situated in one of the city's 17th-century *mudéjar*-style buildings. Tucked into a beautiful patio off Calle Oficios, Al Medina is where you can dine like a Moroccan sheik on lamb couscous (CUC$10), chicken tagine (CUC$5) and Lebanese sumac (CUC$8) with a spicy twist. It's especially recommended for its voluminous vegetarian platter, which comes with hummus, tabouleh, dolma, pilaf and falafel.

Café Lamparilla INTERNATIONAL **$**
(Map p58; Lamparilla btwn Mercaderes and San Ignacio; ⏲noon-midnight) In this new place on Lamparilla, you can either sit outside on the cobbled street, or enjoy the air-conditioned refinement of the sinuous art deco bar. Most people drop by for a beer or a cocktail, but the food is surprisingly good and plentiful, and the prices economical.

Café del Oriente CARIBBEAN, FRENCH **$$$**
(Map p58; Oficios 112; mains CUC$20-27; ⏲noon-11pm) Havana suddenly becomes posh when you walk through the door at this choice establishment on breezy Plaza de San Francisco de Asís. Smoked salmon, caviar (yes, caviar!), goose liver pâté, lobster thermidor, steak au poivre, cheese plate and a glass of port. Plus service in a tux, no less. There's just one small problem: the price. But what the hell?

La Zaragozana SPANISH **$$**
(Map p58; Av de Bélgica btwn Obispo & Obrapía; ⏲noon-midnight) Established in 1830, this is Havana's oldest restaurant but a long way from being its best. The Spanish-themed food – which includes the obligatory paella – would have kept Don Quixote happy, but the ambience, amid assorted Iberian flags and memorabilia, can be a little gloomy.

Paladar la Mulata del Sabor PALADAR **$$**
(Map p58; Sol No 153 btwn Cuba & San Ignacio; meals CUC$10; ⏲noon-midnight) Delicious smells emanating from the kitchen in this

hole-in-the-wall paladar have lured in many an off-track traveler disoriented after taking a wrong turn out of Plaza Vieja. Thankfully, La Mulata is an amiable hostess, and the word-of-mouth reviews from budget travelers are always good.

Restaurante el Patio CARIBBEAN **$$**
(Map p58; San Ignacio No 54; meals CUC$15-20; ⏲noon-midnight) When the hustlers stay away, El Patio is one of the most romantic settings on the planet: the mint stalks in your mojito are pressed to perfection and the band breaks spontaneously into your favorite tune. This place – in the Plaza de la Catedral – must be experienced at night alfresco, when the atmosphere is almost otherworldly. The food doesn't quite match the setting.

Cafetería Torre la Vega CARIBBEAN **$**
(Map p58; Obrapía No 114A btwn Mercaderes & Oficios; ⏲9am-9pm) This is the flop-down lunchtime place that everyone hits in the middle of a sightseeing tour. It's perfectly placed in the middle of the Old Town, with tables spilling onto the street and into a little park opposite. Diners sit with their noses in guidebooks chomping on 'spag bol,' pizza, chicken and sandwiches, none of it particularly expensive.

Hanoi INTERNATIONAL **$**
(Map p58; cnr Brasil & Bernaza; ⏲noon-11pm) The name might suggest solidarity with 'communist' Vietnam, but don't get too excited – you won't find any Saigon-flavored spring rolls here. Instead, what you get is straight-up Creole cuisine, with a couple of fried-rice dishes thrown in to justify the (rather misleading) name. One of the only fully restored buildings in untouristy Plaza del Cristo, the Hanoi is a backpacker favorite, where the foreign clientele usually has its communal nose in a guidebook.

La Mina CARIBBEAN **$$**
(Map p58; Obispo No 109 btwn Oficios & Mercaderes; ⏲24hr) A mediocre menu but a top-class location, La Mina graces a scenic corner of Plaza de Armas, meaning every tourist in Havana walks past it at some point. The food options – displayed on a stand in the street outside and backed up by an army of verbose waiters – include chicken, pork and prawns cooked in a variety of different ways, but lack culinary panache. There's a tempting Heladería (ice-cream parlor) around the corner in Calle Oficios.

La Torre de Marfil CHINESE **$$**
(Map p58; Mercaderes No 111 btwn Obispo & Obrapía; ⏲noon-10pm Mon-Thu, noon-midnight Fri-Sun) Where have all the punters gone? Chinatown, perhaps? You feel sorry for the Marfil. Perfectly placed in Calle Mercaderes with smiling wait staff and an inviting interior, it somehow always seems to be three-quarters empty. Brave the deserted interior and you'll find that the chop suey and chow mein plates – *when* they arrive – are fresh, crisp and huge.

Café Santo Domingo CAFE, BAKERY **$**
(Map p58; Obispo No 159 btwn San Ignacio & Mercaderes, Habana Vieja; ⏲9am-9pm) Tucked away above Habana Vieja's best bakery – and encased in one of its oldest buildings – this laid-back cafe is aromatic and light on the wallet. Check out the delicious fruit shakes, huge *sandwich especial,* or smuggle some cakes upstairs to enjoy over a steaming cup of *café con leche* (coffee with warm milk).

Paladar Moneda Cubana PALADAR **$$**
(Map p58; San Ignacio No 77; meals CUC$8-10; ⏲noon-midnight) There's a soccer obsession at this perfectly placed paladar just off Plaza de la Catedral that must be passed by every tourist in Cuba at some point. Underneath the sporty regalia, a quartet of tables offers chicken and pork dishes at very reasonable prices (CUC$8 to CUC$10). Go on, contribute a few convertible pesos (convertibles) to the spirit of private enterprise.

La Julia PALADAR **$$**
(Map p58; O'Reilly No 506A btwn Villegas & Av de las Misiones; meals CUC$10; ⏲noon-midnight) It's been around long enough to be called an institution and has outlasted almost all opposition. La Julia is an unfussy family-run paladar in Calle O'Reilly that serves Cuban comfort food.

Café de O'Reilly CAFE, FAST FOOD **$**
(Map p58; O'Reilly No 203 btwn Cuba & San Ignacio, Habana Vieja; ⏲11am-3am) Good old-fashioned 'spit and sawdust' cafe selling drinks and snacks. The bar is spread over two floors connected by a spiral staircase, with most of the action taking place upstairs.

El Mercurio INTERNATIONAL **$$**
(Map p58; Plaza de San Francisco de Asís; ⏲24hr) An elegant indoor-outdoor cafe/restaurant, with cappuccino machines, intimate booths and waiters in black ties, that serves cheap lunches (Cuban sandwich for CUC$5) and more substantial dinners (lobster and steak tartar).

Restaurante Puerto de Sagua SEAFOOD **$**
(Map p58; Av de Bélgica No 603; ⏲noon-midnight) This nautical-themed eating joint in Habana Vieja's grittier southern quarter is characterized by its small porthole-style windows. It serves mostly seafood at reasonable prices.

PARQUE HISTÓRICO MILITAR MORRO-CABAÑA

TOP CHOICE **Restaurante la Divina Pastora** INTERNATIONAL **$$$**
(Map p65; ⏲noon-11pm) Back below La Cabaña, just beyond the Dársena de los Franceses and another battery of huge 18th-century cannons, lies one of the big guns of Cuban cooking. Eschewing the iron rations of yore, La Divina Pastora offers homemade pasta, sun-dried tomatoes, pesto-doused vegetables and excellent seafood. To top it off, there are waiters with *savoir faire* and a credible wine list.

Paladar Doña Carmela CARIBBEAN **$$**
(Map p65; ☎863-6048; Calle B No 10; ⏲evenings only) A private eating option that offers quality chicken and pork in a very pleasant alfresco setting (when it's open). Makes for a good dinner before or after the *cañonazo,* but check ahead, as opening times are sporadic.

Restaurante los Doce Apóstoles CARIBBEAN **$$**
(Map p65; ⏲noon-11pm) Parts of the fortresses have been converted into good restaurants and atmospheric bars including this one below El Morro. The restaurant is so named (*doce* means '12') because of the battery of 12 cannons atop its ramparts. The restaurant serves *comida criolla,* and it's a better-than-average government-run kitchen with fair prices.

CENTRO HABANA

Centro offers scanter fare than Habana Vieja, with some notable exceptions. Look out for Spanish clubs run by the Centro Asturiano and dip into the restaurant strip on Calle Cuchillo in the Barrio Chino (Chinatown).

TOP CHOICE **Los Nardos** SPANISH, CARIBBEAN **$$**
(Map p68; Paseo de Martí No 563; ⏲noon-midnight) An open secret situated opposite the Capitolio, but easy to miss (look out for the queue), Los Nardos is one of a handful of semi-private Havana restaurants operated by the Spanish Asturianas society. Touted in some quarters as one of the best eateries in the city, the dilapidated exterior promises little, but the leather/mahogany décor and astoundingly delicious dishes (bank on lobster in a Catalan sauce, garlic prawns with sautéed vegetables and an authentic Spanish paella) suggest otherwise. Portions are huge and the service is attentive, and the prices, which start at around CUC$4 for chicken and pork dishes, are mind-bogglingly cheap.

Restaurante Tien-Tan CHINESE **$$**
(Map p68; Cuchillo No 17 btwn Rayo & San Nicolás; ⏲11am-11pm) One of the Barrio Chino's best authentic Chinese restaurants, Tien-Tan (the 'Temple of Heaven') is run by a Chinese-Cuban couple and serves up an incredible 130 different dishes. With such complexity, you might have thought that you would be in for a long wait and that the food would, at best, be average. Thankfully, neither is the case. Try chop suey with vegetables, or chicken with cashew nuts and sit outside in action-packed Cuchillo, one of Havana's most colorful and fastest-growing 'food streets.'

Rancho Coquito SPANISH, CARIBBEAN **$$**
(Map p68; Malecón 107 btwn Genios & Crespo; ⏲6pm-midnight) At last, a decent restaurant on the Malecón. Run by the local Spanish Asturianas society, this inconspicuous place boasts a balcony that overlooks Havana's dreamy 8km sea drive (look for the waiter posted outside) and is frequented mainly by Cubans. Upstairs, the food is tasty and unbelievably cheap. Paella goes for CUC$7, *garbanzos fritos* (fried chickpeas) CUC$5, tortilla CUC$3 and a decent portion of lobster pan-fried in butter for a giveaway CUC$8.

Los Gijones SPANISH, CARIBBEAN **$$**
(Map p68; Paseo de Martí No 309; ⏲noon-midnight) Melancholy Mozart serenades you here, causing you to weep helplessly into your *ropa vieja* (CUC$5). Dry your eyes and you'll find that you're in another Spanish mutual-aid society, this time the Centro Asturiano, whose dark mahogany dining room is frequented by a charming resident violinist.

Pastelería Francesa CAFE, PATISERRIE **$**
(Map p68; Parque Central No 411) This cafe has all the ingredients of a Champs-Élysées classic: a great location in Parque Central, waiters in waistcoats and delicate pastries displayed in glass cases. But the authentic French flavor is diminished by stroppy staff and the swarming *jineteras* who roll in with Hans from Hamburg or Marco from Milano for cigarettes and strong coffee.

Chi Tack Tong CHINESE $$

(Map p68; Dragones No 356 btwn San Nicolás & Manrique; ⏲noon-midnight) Upstairs in Calle Dragones, this place is famous for being one of the few cheap restaurants in Havana where you won't hear the words *'No hay'* (we don't have it) when you place your order. The menu is a little limited, but portion sizes are huge. Box up your leftovers.

Café Neruda INTERNATIONAL $

(Map p68; Malecón No 203 btwn Manrique & San Nicolás; ⏲11am-11pm) Barbecued Chilean ox, Nerudian skewer, Chilean turnover? Poor old Pablo Neruda would be turning in his grave if this weren't such an inviting place and a rare ray of light on the otherwise mildewed Malecón. Spend a poetic afternoon watching the waves splash over the sea wall.

Paladar Torressón PALADAR $$

(Map p68; ☎861-7476; Malecón btwn Capdevila & Genios; meals CUC$7-9; ⏲noon-midnight) Situated at the eastern end of the Malecón with views over El Morro castle, the Torressón offers complete meals of meat or fish from CUC$10 and stupendous views for free.

Paladar Doña Blanquita PALADAR $$

(Map p68; Paseo de Martí No 158 btwn Colón & Refugio; meals CUC$7-9; ⏲noon-10pm) Overlooking the Prado boulevard, this is one of Centro Habana's best-placed paladares, with a proper typewritten menu and meat-biased mains plates in the CUC$7 to CUC$9 range.

El Gran Dragón CHINESE $

(Map p68; Cuchillo No 1; ⏲11am-midnight; 🖉) First on the left as you enter Cuchillo from Calle Zanja, this place offers wonton soup, chop suey, chow mein and fried rice and is a good place for vegetarians.

VEDADO

Vedado's once-splendid paladares are fighting a losing battle against high rents and nitpicking government regulations. Although few new places open these days, there are a handful of stalwart survivors that exist alongside a handful of OK government places. The Hotel Nacional and the Hotel Habana Libre also maintain some good bars and restaurants.

TOP CHOICE **La Torre** FRENCH, CARIBBEAN $$$

(Map p72; ☎838-3088; Edificio Focsa cnr Calles 17 & M) One of Havana's tallest and most talked-about restaurants is perched high above downtown Vedado atop the skyline-hogging Focsa building. A colossus of both modernist architecture and French/Cuban haute cuisine, this lofty fine-dining extravaganza combines sweeping city views with a progressive French-inspired menu that serves everything from artichokes to foie gras to *tart almandine*. The prices at CUC$30 per main (and the rest!) are as distinctly non-Cuban as the ingredients, but with this level of service, it's probably worth it.

Paladar la Guarida INTERNATIONAL $$$

(Map p72; ☎866-9047; Concordia No 418 btwn Gervasio & Escobar; ⏲noon-3pm & 7pm-midnight) Located on the top floor of a spectacularly dilapidated Havana tenement, La Guarida's lofty reputation rests on its movie-location setting (*Fresa y chocolate* was filmed in this building) and a clutch of swashbuckling newspaper reviews (including the *New York Times* and the *Guardian*). The food, as might be expected, is up there with Havana's best, shoehorning its captivating blend of Nueva Cocina Cubana into dishes such as sea bass in a coconut reduction, and chicken with honey and lemon sauce. Reservations required.

Paladar el Hurón Azul PALADAR $$$

(Map p72; ☎879-1691; Humboldt No 153; meals CUC$15-20; ⏲noon-midnight Tue-Sun) This place is often touted as one of Havana's best private restaurants, and although the food might be tasty, the windowless interior combined with the preponderance of after-dinner smokers can leave your meal tasting more like nicotine than *comida criolla*. Nonetheless, the Hurón Azul (Blue Ferret) boasts plenty of original food and is locally famous for its adventurous smoked pork served with a pineapple salsa. That said, it's not cheap, averaging CUC$15 a pop, plus a 10% service charge added to every bill. Reserve ahead.

Pain de París CAFE, BAKERY $

(Map p72; Calle 25 No 164 btwn Infanta & Calle O; ⏲8am-midnight) With quite possibly the best cakes in Havana – including iced cinnamon buns – this small chain does box-up cakes, cappuccinos, croissants and the odd savory snack. If you've been ODing on paltry Cuban desserts, or have hit a sugar low after a super-light breakfast, get your 11am pick-me-up here. There's another **24-hour branch** on Línea, adjacent to the Trianón cinema.

DON'T MISS

HAVANA'S SPANISH CLUBS

Although largely invisible to contemporary visitors, Havana's Spanish Clubs were once powerful bastions of Iberian identity in Cuba and helped to integrate immigrant *peninsulares* (Cubans born in Spain) into daily life through the building of libraries, hospitals, theaters and social centers. In doing so, they were responsible for constructing some of the grandest buildings the city had ever seen, many of which still stand.

The first clubs took shape as mutual-aid societies in the 1870s and were nearly always organized along Spanish regional lines, with various 'Centros' formed among separate groups of immigrant Andalucians, Galicians, Canary Islanders, Catalans, Asturians and Basques. As was often the case in Latin America, the greatest number of immigrants tended to come from Spain's poorer regions, namely Galicia and Asturias (Fidel Castro's father was an expat Gallego from Galicia), and it was these people that formed what would become the largest and most powerful clubs.

The Centros were originally only open to *peninsulares*, who elected boards that promoted mutual-aid features allowing members access to libraries, medical care, education tools and – most importantly – a distinct cultural life that retained potent echoes of the old Spain (music in the form of choral societies were particularly popular in Havana). By the early 1900s Havana's Gallego (Galician) and Asturiano societies both listed more than 10,000 members, and the two clubs entered into an unofficial competition to see who could build the grandest cultural center. The 'race' bequeathed Havana's Parque Central with two magnificent buildings: the Centro Gallego (1914), now the **Gran Teatro de Habana** (p108); and the **Centro Asturiano** (1927), now part of the Museo Nacional de Bellas Artes (p67). Both buildings are riots of early-20th-century eclecticism, with tangible neobaroque and neoclassical influences.

The Revolution drastically curtailed the power of Havana's Spanish clubs, but failed to stamp them out completely. Still active today – and of interest to visitors – is the **Asociación Canaria de Cuba** (Map p68; Av de los Misiones No 258), which has a restaurant and performance space; the **Centro Andaluz** (p82), which hosts sporadic flamenco shows; and the Centro Vasco, which runs a bar and restaurant (see p105) in Vedado. Towering above all, however, is the Centro Asturiano, whose formidable restaurants have gained something of a cult following among in-the-know tourists for their atmospheric mahogany furnishings, excellent service and delicious but economical food.

Decameron PALADAR, ITALIAN **$$$**
(Map p72; ☎832-2444; Línea No 753 btwn Paseo & Calle 2; meals CUC$12-15; ⊙noon-midnight; 🖉) Ugly from the outside, but far prettier within, the Decameron is an intimate Italian-influenced restaurant where you can order from the varied menu with abandon. Veggie pizza, lasagna bolognese, steak au poivre and a divine calabaza soup – it's all good. On top of that, there's a decent wine selection and the kitchen is sympathetic to vegetarians.

El Gringo Viejo PALADAR **$$**
(Map p72; ☎831-1946; Calle 21 No 454 btwn Calles E & F; ⊙noon-11pm) The Gringo offers a good atmosphere and large portions of invariably brilliant food. Locals and visitors love it for its speedy service, fine wine list and big portions of more adventurous plates, such as smoked salmon with olives and Gouda, or crabmeat in red sauce (CUC$10 to CUC$12).

Flor de Loto CHINESE **$$**
(Map p72; Salud No 303 btwn Gervasio & Escobar) Popularly considered to be Havana's – and, by definition, Cuba's – best Chinese restaurant, as the queues outside will testify. Camouflaged beneath Centro Havana's decaying facades, it serves up extra-large portions of lobster, fried rice and sweet and sour sauce in a frigidly air-conditioned interior.

Complejo Turístico 1830 INTERNATIONAL **$$**
(Map p124; Malecón No 1252; ⊙noon-10pm) One of Havana's most elegant restaurants, this place is heavily touted, but gets mixed reviews. Try the chicken in lemon and honey sauce, and stick around until after 10pm when the kitchen closes and there's live music and salsa dancing in the garden behind the restaurant.

Paladar los Amigos PALADAR $$
(Map p72; Calle M No 253; noon-midnight) Paladar Los Amigos, situated in the back of a prerevolutionary house on the corner of Calles M and 19 near the Hotel Victoria, serves good Cuban meals for CUC$10, including side plates. It's enthusiastically recommended by locals.

Paladar Aries PALADAR $$
(Map p72; Av Universidad No 456 Bajos btwn Calles J & K; noon-midnight) Traditional Cuban fare mixed with what are generously referred to as 'international dishes,' this nicely decked-out, family-run place with occasional wandering *trovadores* (traditional singers/songwriters) is conveniently located behind the university.

Café TV FAST FOOD $
(Map p72; cnr Calles N & 19; 10am-9pm) Hidden in the bowels of Edificio Focsa, this TV-themed cafe is a funky dinner/performance venue lauded by those in the know for its cheap food and hilarious comedy nights. If you're willing to brave the frigid air-con and rather foreboding underground entry tunnel, head here for fresh burgers, healthy salad, pasta and chicken *Gordon Bleu*. Televisión Cubana is around the corner, hence the theme.

Trattoría Maraka's ITALIAN $$
(Map p72; Calle O No 260 btwn Calles 23 & 25; 10am-11pm) Don't be put off by the cheap Formica tables and the pictorial map of Italy on the wall. Real olive oil, parmesan and mozzarella cheese, plus a wood-fired oven, mean that the pizza in this Vedado Italian trattoria is among the city's best. Also on offer are Greek salad, tortellini with red sauce, and spinach-stuffed cannelloni – mostly under CUC$10.

El Conejito CARIBBEAN $$
(Map p72; Calle M No 206; noon-midnight) A red-bricked Tudor-style mansion with lederhosen-clad waiters that serves rabbit (CUC$8 and up); now that's classic! If the *conejo* (rabbit) doesn't grab you, try the chicken, beef, fish or lobster. The rather surreal ambience is lightened somewhat by a resident pianist serenading romantically in the background.

Centro Vasco SPANISH, CARIBBEAN $
(Map p72; Calle 3 cnr Calle 4; noon-10pm) This outpost of Havana's Basque society, near the Hotel Meliá Cohiba, has a decent restaurant and a 24-hour bar/cafe. The food has Spanish inflections.

La Rampa DINER $$
(Map p72; Calle L btwn Calles 23 & 25; burgers $CUC6-8; 24hr) The closest Havana gets to an American diner is in the Hotel Habana Libre. Excellent salads, burgers and milkshakes are served rather brusquely by busy waiters.

Cafetería Sofía FAST FOOD $
(Map p72; Calle 23 No 202; 24hr) Late-night hair-of-the-dog seekers meet annoyingly chirpy early risers at this 24-hour institution on La Rampa (Calle 23).

La Casona & 17 CARIBBEAN $$
(Map p72; Calle 17 btwn Calles M & N; 11am-10pm) Eclectic Vedado residence turned restaurant. Eat in the elegant dining room or outside at the barbecue grill.

Restaurante Vegetariano Carmelo VEGETARIAN $
(Map p72; Calzada btwn Calles D & E; noon-midnight Tue-Sun;) Selling itself as a vegetarian restaurant, this place, opposite the Teatro Amadeo Roldán, offers scant fare and legendary brusqueness. Prices are in Cuban pesos.

Ice-Cream Parlors

Havana has some good ice cream, available both in convertibles and pesos. Coppelia is the national chain – but its queues are long. *Paleticas* are popsicles (usually chocolate-covered), while *bocaditos* are big, ice-cream sandwiches (often handmade). Little mobile ice-cream machines selling the soft, whippy stuff can appear anyplace anytime. Cones are sold for a couple of pesos. The problem is getting them in your mouth before they melt. Here are some good parlors:

Bim Bom ICE CREAM $
(Map p72; cnr Calle 23 & Infanta, Vedado) Phenomenally creamy stuff in flavors like coffee, condensed milk (sounds gross, tastes great) and rum raisins; pay in convertibles.

Coppelia ICE CREAM $
(Map p72; cnr Calle 23 & L, Vedado) The original and best.

Takeout

There are some great peso places sprinkled about, though few have names; look for the streets. Some of the most outstanding peso pizza is at San Rafael just off Infanta (look for the lines). Av de la Italia (Galiano to anyone who lives there) also has some holes-in-the-wall. Also try around Calles H and 17, where there are clusters of peso stalls and

Calle 21 between Calles 4 and 6; this area is close to the hospital, so there's great variety and long hours.

Cajitas (take-out meals in cardboard boxes) usually cost about CUC$1. Some boxes have cutout spoons on the lid, but most don't, so you'll have to supply your own fork (or use part of the box itself as a shovel). You can usually buy *cajitas* at *agropecuarios* (vegetable markets); Chinatown is known for its *cajitas*.

Cubans haven't really caught onto the idea of coffee 'to go,' so you'll get baffled looks if you ask for a coffee *para llevar* (takeout).

Self-Catering

HABANA VIEJA

Café Santo Domingo BAKERY $
(Map p58; Obispo No 159 btwn San Ignacio & Mercaderes; 9am-9pm) Some of the best bread and pastries can be procured at this place, downstairs underneath the cafe.

Harris Brothers SUPERMARKET $
(Map p58; O'Reilly No 526; 9am-9pm Mon-Sat) The best-stocked grocery store in Habana Vieja sells everything from fresh pastries to baby's nappies. It's just off Parque Central and is open until late.

Agropecuario Sol MARKET $
(Map p58; Sol btwn Habana & Compostela) Vieja's local farmers' market.

CENTRO HABANA

Supermercado Isla de Cuba SUPERMARKET $
(Map p68; cnr Máximo Gómez & Factoría; 10am-6pm Mon-Sat, 9am-1pm Sun) On the southern side of Parque de la Fraternidad, with yogurt, cereals, pasta etc. You have to check your bag outside, to the right of the entrance.

Almacenes Ultra SUPERMARKET $
(Map p68; Av Simón Bolívar No 109; 9am-6pm Mon-Sat, 9am-1pm Sun) A decent supermarket in Centro Habana, at the corner of Rayo, near Av de Italia.

La Época SUPERMARKET $
(Map p68; cnr Av de Italia & Neptuno; 9am-9pm Mon-Sat, 9am-noon Sun) A hard-currency department store with a supermarket in the basement. Check your bags outside before entering this epic Havana emporium.

Mercado Agropecuario Egido MARKET $
(Map p68; Av de Bélgica btwn Corrales & Apodaca) For fresh produce hit this free-enterprise market.

VEDADO

Supermercado Meridiano SUPERMARKET $
(Map p72; Galerías de Paseo, cnr Calle 1 & Paseo; 10am-5pm Mon-Fri, 10am-2pm Sun) Across the street from the Hotel Meliá Cohiba, this supermarket has a good wine and liquor selection, lots of yogurt, cheese and crisps.

There are numerous *agropecuarios*:

Agropecuario 17 & K MARKET $
(Map p72; cnr Calles 17 & K) A 'capped' market with cheap prices, but limited selection.

Agropecuario 19 & A MARKET $
(Map p72; Calle 19 btwn Calles A & B) Havana's 'gourmet' market, with cauliflower, fresh herbs and rarer produce during shoulder seasons.

Agropecuario 21 & J MARKET $
(Map p72; cnr Calles 21 & J) Good selection, including potted plants.

Organopónico Plaza MARKET $
(Map p72; cnr Av de Colón & Bellavista) One of Havana's biggest organic farms with a retail market.

Drinking

HABANA VIEJA

TOP CHOICE **Taberna de la Muralla** BAR, RESTAURANT
(Map p58; cnr San Ignacio & Muralla; 11am-midnight) Havana's only microbrewery is situated on a boisterous corner of Plaza Vieja. Set up by an Austrian company in 2004, it sells smooth, cold homemade beer at sturdy wooden benches set up outside on the cobbles or indoors in an atmospheric beer hall. Get a group together and you'll get the amber nectar in a tall plastic tube drawn from a tap at the bottom. There's also an outside grill. Round the corner is the new **Factoria**, which specializes in non-alcoholic *Malta* and is popular with Cubans.

Museo del Chocolate CHOCOLATIER $
(Map p58; cnr Amargura & Mercaderes; 9am-8pm) Chocolate addicts beware, this quirky place in the heart of Habana Vieja is a lethal dose of chocolate, truffles and yet more chocolate (all made on the premises). Situated – with no irony intended – in Calle Amargura (literally: Bitterness Street), the sweet-toothed establishment is more a cafe than a museum, with a small cluster of marble tables set amid a sugary mélange of chocolate paraphernalia. Not surprisingly, everything on the menu contains one all-pervading ingredient: have it hot, cold, white, dark, rich or smooth – the stuff is divine, whichever way you choose.

Café el Escorial CAFE $

(Map p58; Mercaderes No 317 cnr Muralla; ⌚9am-9pm) Opening out onto Plaza Vieja and encased in a finely restored colonial mansion, there's something definitively European about El Escorial. Among some of the best caffeine infusions in the city served here are *café cubano, café con leche*, frappé, coffee liquor and even *daiquirí de café*. There's also a sweet selection of delicate cakes and pastries.

La Bodeguita del Medio BAR, RESTAURANT

(Map p58; Empedrado No 207; ⌚11am-midnight) Made famous thanks to the rum-swilling exploits of Ernest Hemingway (who by association instantly sends the prices soaring), this is Havana's most celebrated bar. A visit here has become de rigueur for tourists who haven't yet cottoned on to the fact that the mojitos are better and (far) cheaper elsewhere. Past visitors have included Salvador Allende, Fidel Castro, Nicolás Guillén, Harry Belafonte and Nat King Cole, all of whom have left their autographs on La Bodeguita's wall – along with thousands of others (save for the big names, the walls are repainted every few months). These days the clientele is less luminous, with package tourists from Varadero outnumbering beatnik bohemians. Purists claim the CUC$4 mojitos have lost their Hemingway-esque shine in recent years. Only one way to find out...

Bar Dos Hermanos BAR

(Map p58; San Pedro No 304; ⌚24hr) Despite its erstwhile Hemingway connections, this bar has (so far) managed to remain off the standard Havana tourist itinerary. Out of the way and a little seedy, it was a favorite watering hole of Spanish poet Federico García Lorca during a three-month stopover in 1930. With its long wooden bar and salty seafaring atmosphere, it can't have changed much since.

Café de las Infusiones CAFE

(Map p58; Mercaderes btwn Obispo & Obrapía; ⌚8am-11pm) Wedged into Calle Mercaderes, this recently restored Habaguanex coffee house is a caffeine addict's heaven; it boasts a wonderful resident pianist, too. It's fancier than your average Cuban coffee bar and more comprehensive than the Escorial. You can order more than a dozen different cuppas here, including Irish coffee, punch coffee, mocha and cappuccino.

El Floridita BAR, RESTAURANT

(Map p58; Obispo No 557; ⌚11am-midnight) Promoting itself as the 'cradle of the daiquirí,' El Floridita was a favorite of expat Americans long before Ernest Hemingway dropped by in the 1930s (hence the name, which means 'little Florida'). A bartender named Constante Ribalaigua invented the daiquirí soon after WWI, but it was Hemingway who popularized it, and ultimately the bar christened a drink in his honor: the Papa Hemingway Special (basically, a daiquirí made with grapefruit juice). His record – legend has it – was 13 doubles in one sitting. Any attempt to equal it at the current prices (CUC$7 and up for a shot) will cost you a small fortune – and a huge hangover.

La Lluvia de Oro BAR

(Map p58; Obispo No 316; ⌚24hr) It's on Obispo and there's always live music belting through the doorway – so it's always crowded. But with a higher-than-average *jinetero/jinetera* to tourist ratio, it might not be your most intimate introduction to Havana. Small snacks are available and the musician's 'hat' comes round every three songs.

La Dichosa BAR

(Map p58; cnr Obispo & Compostela; ⌚10am-midnight) It's hard to miss the rowdy La Dichosa on busy Calle Obispo. Small and cramped with at least half the space given over to the resident band, this is a good place to stop for a quick drink.

El Reloj Cuervo y Sobrinos CAFE $

(Map p58; Oficios cnr Muralla; ⌚10am-7pm Mon-Sat, 10am-1pm Sun) A new art deco coffee bar set in a restored watch shop that belonged to an erstwhile Swiss watchmaker in the 1880s. Time your air-conditioned sightseeing break over a strong café cubano.

Café Taberna BAR, RESTAURANT

(Map p58; cnr Brasil & Mercaderes) Founded in 1772 and still glowing after a recent 21st-century makeover, this drinking and eating establishment is a great place to prop up the (impressive) bar and sink a few cocktails before dinner. The music – which gets swinging around 8pm – doffs its cap, more often than not, to one-time resident mambo king Benny Moré. Skip the food.

Café París BAR

(Map p58; Obispo No 202; ⌚24hr) Things never stand still at this rough-hewn Habana Vieja dive-bar, known for its live music and gregarious tourist-heavy atmosphere. On good nights, the rum flows and spontaneous dancing erupts.

Monserrate Bar BAR

(Map p58; Obrapía No 410) A couple of doors down from El Floridita, Monserrate is a Hemingway-free zone, meaning the daiquirís are half the price.

El Baturro BAR

(Map p58; cnr Av de Bélgica & Merced; ⏲11am-11pm) In the long tradition of drinking houses situated next to train stations, El Baturro is a rough-and-ready Spanish bistro with a long wooden bar and an all-male drinking clientele.

CENTRO HABANA

Prado No 12 BAR

(Map p68; Paseo de Martí No 12; ⏲noon-11pm) A slim flat-iron building on the corner of Prado and San Lázaro that serves drinks and simple snacks, Prado 12 still resembles Havana in a 1950s time-warp. Soak up the atmosphere of this amazing city here after a sunset stroll along the Malecón.

Prado & Animas BAR

(Map p68; Paseo de Martí cnr Ánimas No 12; ⏲9am-9pm) Another good old-fashioned Prado place with a time-warped '50s feel. The cafe also serves simple food and coffee, but it's best for a beer, sitting at one of the window tables beneath the baseball memorabilia (including a picture of a *pelota*-playing Fidel).

VEDADO

Café Literario del 'G' CAFE, BAR

(Map p72; Calle 23 btwn Av de los Presidentes & Calle H) If Havana has a proverbial Left Bank, this is it: a laid-back student hangout full of arty wall scribblings and coffee-quaffing intellectuals discussing the merits of Guillén over Lorca. Relax in the airy front patio among the green plants and dusty books and magazines (available to read, lend and buy), and keep an ear out for one of the regular *trova* (traditional music), jazz and poetry presentations.

Café Fresa y Chocolate CAFE, BAR

(Map p72; Calle 23 btwn Calles 10 & 12; ⏲9am-11pm) No ice cream here, just movie memorabilia. This is the HQ of the Cuban Film Institute and a nexus for coffee-quaffing students and art-house movie addicts. You can debate the merits of Almodóvar over Scorsese on the pleasant patio before disappearing next door for a film preview.

Bar-Club Imágenes BAR

(Map p72; Calzada No 602; ⏲9pm-5am) This upscale piano bar attracts something of an older crowd with its regular diet of boleros (ballads) and *trova*, though there are sometimes comedy shows; check the schedule posted outside. Affordable meals are available (minimum CUC$5).

PARQUE HISTÓRICO MILITAR MORRO-CABAÑA

Bar el Polvorín BAR

(Map p65; ⏲10am-4am) Situated just below El Morro fort, this bar offers drinks and light snacks on a patio overlooking the bay. It's surprisingly lively after dark.

☆ Entertainment

HABANA VIEJA

Nightlife exists in the Old Town, but it's more of the live-music-in-a-bar variety. Don't forget the excellent flamenco shows in Mesón de la Flota (p99) and – occasionally – Hostal Valencia (p85).

Basílica Menor de San Francisco de Asís CLASSICAL MUSIC

(Map p58; Plaza de San Francisco de Asís, Habana Vieja; tickets CUC$3-8; ⏲from 6pm Thu-Sat) Plaza de San Francisco de Asís' glorious church, which dates from 1738, has been reincarnated as a 21st-century museum and concert hall. The old nave hosts choral and chamber music two to three times a week (check the schedule at the door) and the acoustics inside are excellent. It's best to bag your ticket at least a day in advance.

Fundación Alejo Carpentier CULTURAL CENTER

(Map p58; Empedrado No 215, Habana Vieja; ⏲8am-4pm Mon-Fri) Near the Plaza de la Catedral. Check for cultural events at this baroque former palace of the Condesa de la Reunión (1820s) where Carpentier set his famous novel *El Siglo de las Luces*.

CENTRO HAVANA

Centro's nightlife is edgier and more local than Vedado's.

TOP CHOICE **Gran Teatro de la Habana** THEATER

(Map p68; ☎861-3077; cnr Paseo de Martí & San Rafael; per person CUC$20; ⏲box office 9am-6pm Mon-Sat, to 3pm Sun) The amazing neobaroque theater across from Parque Central is the seat of the acclaimed Ballet Nacional de Cuba, founded in 1948 by Alicia Alonso. It is also the home of the Cuban National Opera.

GAY HAVANA

The Revolution had a rather ambiguous attitude toward homosexuality in its early days. While the Stonewall riots were engulfing New York City, Cuban homosexuals were still being sent to re-education camps by a government that was dominated by macho, bearded ex-guerrillas dressed in military fatigues.

But, since the 1990s, the tide has been turning, spearheaded somewhat ironically by Fidel's combative niece Mariela (the daughter of current president, Raúl Castro), the director of the Cuban National Center for Sex Education in Havana.

An important door was opened in 1993 with the release of the Oscar-nominated film *Fresa y chocolate,* a tale of homosexual love between a young communist student and a skeptical Havana artist. A decade later, gay characters hit the headlines again in a popular government-sponsored Cuban soap opera called *La cara oculta de la luna* (The Dark Side of the Moon).

The unprecedented happened in June 2008 when the Cuban government passed a law permitting free sex-change operations to qualifying citizens courtesy of the country's famously far-sighted health system.

Though Cuba still has no 'official' gay clubs, there are plenty of places where a 'gay scene' has taken root. Havana is the obvious focus, with the busy junction of Calles 23 and L in Vedado outside the Cine Yara serving as the main nighttime cruising spot. Other meeting places include the Malecón below the Hotel Nacional and the beach at Boca Ciega in Playas del Este.

Hang around at these places in the evening to get word of spontaneous gay parties in private houses, or bigger shindigs in venues such as Parque Lenin. You can now also enjoy gay film nights at the Icaic headquarters on the corner of Calles 23 and 12 and, since 2009, an annual gay parade along Calle 23 in mid-May.

A theater since 1838, the building contains the grandiose Teatro García Lorca, along with two smaller concert halls: the Sala Alejo Carpentier and the Sala Ernesto Lecuono – where art films are sometimes shown. For upcoming events enquire at the ticket office. Backstage tours of the theater leave throughout the day (CUC$2).

La Casa de la Música Centro Habana NIGHTCLUB, LIVE MUSIC

(Map p68; Av de Italia btwn Concordia & Neptuno; admission CUC$5-25) One of Cuba's best and most popular (check the queues) nightclubs and live-music venues. All the big names play here, from Bamboleo to Los Van Van – and you'll pay peanuts to see them. Of the city's two Casas de la Música, this Centro Habana version is a little edgier than its Miramar counterpart (some have complained it's too edgy), with big salsa bands and little space. Price varies depending on the band.

Cabaret Nacional CABARET

(Map p68; San Rafael No 208; per couple CUC$10; ⌚9pm-2am) Across from Parque Central, and barely noticeable below the Gran Teatro de La Habana, this subterranean dance cellar has a show nightly at 11:30pm if enough patrons are present. It's a little camper than other Havana cabarets and the noise – rather annoyingly if you're watching the opera – sometimes filters through into the Lorca auditorium next door. There's a couples-only policy and a 'no shorts/T-shirts' dress code.

Teatro América THEATER

(Map p68; Av de Italia No 253 btwn Concordia & Neptuno) Housed in a classic art deco *rascacielo* (skyscraper) on Galiano (Av de Italia), the América seems to have changed little since its theatrical heyday in the 1930s and '40s. It plays host to vaudeville variety, comedy, dance, jazz and salsa; shows are normally staged on Saturdays at 8:30pm and Sundays at 5pm. You can also enquire about dance lessons here (p109).

Teatro Fausto THEATER

(Map p68; Paseo de Martí No 201) Rightly renowned for its sidesplitting comedy shows, Fausto is a streamlined art-deco theater on Prado.

VEDADO

Although it may have lost is pre-revolutionary reputation as a ritzy casino quarter, Vedado is still *the* place for nightlife in Havana.

El Hurón Azul LIVE MUSIC
(Map p72; cnr Calles 17 & H) If you want to rub shoulders with some socialist celebrities, hang out at Hurón Azul, the social club of the Unión Nacional de Escritores y Artistas de Cuba (Uneac; Union of Cuban Writers and Artists), Cuba's leading cultural institution. Replete with priceless snippets of Cuba's under-the-radar cultural life, most performances take place outside in the garden. Wednesday is the Afro-Cuban rumba, Saturday is authentic Cuban boleros, and alternate Thursdays there's jazz and *trova*. You'll never pay more than CUC$5.

Callejón de Hamel LIVE MUSIC
(Map p72; ⊙from noon Sun) Aside from its funky street murals and psychedelic art shops, the main reason to come to Havana's high temple of Afro-Cuban culture is for the frenetic rumba music that kicks off every Sunday at around noon. For aficionados, this is about as raw and hypnotic as it gets, with interlocking drum patterns and lengthy rhythmic chants powerful enough to summon up the spirit of the *orishas* (Santería deities). Due to a liberal sprinkling of tourists these days, some argue that the Callejón has lost much of its basic charm. Don't believe them. This place can still deliver.

Jazz Café LIVE MUSIC
(Map p72; top floor, Galerías de Paseo, cnr Calle 1 & Paseo; drink minimum CUC$10; ⊙noon-late) This upscale joint located improbably in a shopping mall overlooking the Malecón is a kind of jazz supper club, with dinner tables and a decent menu. At night, the club swings into action with live jazz, *timba* and, occasionally, straight-up salsa. It attracts plenty of big-name acts.

Casa de la Amistad LIVE MUSIC
(Map p72; Paseo No 416 btwn Calles 17 & 19) Housed in a beautiful rose-colored mansion on leafy Paseo, the Casa de la Amistad mixes traditional *son* sounds with suave Benny Moré music in a classic Italian Renaissance-style garden. Buena Vista Social Club luminary, Compay Segundo, was a regular here before his death in 2003, and there is a weekly 'Chan Chan' night in his honor. Other perks include a restaurant, a bar, a cigar shop and the house itself – an Italianate masterpiece.

Teatro Nacional de Cuba THEATER
(Map p72; ☎879-6011; cnr Paseo & Calle 39; per person CUC$10; ⊙box office 9am-5pm & before performances) One of the twin pillars of Havana's cultural life, the Teatro Nacional de Cuba on Plaza de la Revolución is the modern rival to the Gran Teatro in Centro Habana. Built in the 1950s as part of Jean Forestier's grand city expansion, the complex hosts landmark concerts, foreign theater troupes, La Colmenita children's company and the Ballet Nacional de Cuba. The main hall, Sala Avellaneda, stages big events such as musical concerts or plays by Shakespeare, while the smaller Sala Covarrubias along the back side puts on a more daring program (the seating capacity of the two *salas* combined is 3300). The 9th floor is a rehearsal and performance space where the newest, most experimental stuff happens. The ticket office is at the far end of a separate single-story building beside the main theater.

El Gato Tuerto LIVE MUSIC
(Map p72; Calle O No 14 btwn Calles 17 & 19; drink minimum CUC$5; ⊙noon-6am) Once the HQ of Havana's alternative artistic and sexual scene, the 'one-eyed cat' (as Gato Tuerto translates into English) is now a nexus for karaoke-crazy baby-boomers who come here to knock out rum-fuelled renditions of traditional Cuban boleros (ballads). It's hidden just off the Malecón in a quirky two-story house with turtles swimming in a front pool. The upper floor is taken up by a restaurant, while down below late-night revelers raise the roof in a chic nightclub.

Café Cantante NIGHTCLUB
(Map p72; ☎879-0710; cnr Paseo & Calle 39; admission CUC$10; ⊙9pm-5am Tue-Sat) Below the Teatro Nacional de Cuba (side entrance), this place is a hip disco that offers live salsa music and dancing, as well as bar snacks and food. The clientele is mainly 'yummies' (young urban Marxist managers) and ageing male tourists with their youthful Cuban girlfriends. The Café tends to get feistier than the adjacent Piano Bar Delirio Habanero (p111). Musically, there are regular appearances from big-name singers such as Haila María Mompie. No shorts, T-shirts or hats may be worn, and no under-18s are allowed.

Teatro Amadeo Roldán THEATER
(Map p72; ☎832-1168; cnr Calzada & Calle D; per person CUC$10) Constructed in 1922 and burnt down by an arsonist in 1977, this wonderfully decorative neoclassical theater was rebuilt in 1999 in the exact style of the original. Named after the famous Cuban composer and the man responsible for bringing

Afro-Cuban influences into modern classical music, the theater is one of Havana's grandest with two different auditoriums. The Orquesta Sinfónica Nacional play in the 886-seat Sala Amadeo Roldán, while soloists and small groups are showcased in the 276-seat Sala García Caturla.

Cabaret Parisién CABARET
(Map p72; ☎836-3564; cnr Calles 21 & O; admission CUC$35; ⏲9pm) One rung down from the Tropicana, in both price and quality, the nightly Cabaret Parisién in the Hotel Nacional is still well worth a look, especially if you're staying in or around Vedado. It's the usual mix of frills, feathers and semi-naked women, but the choreography is first class and the whole spectacle has excellent kitsch value.

Conjunto Folklórico Nacional de Cuba LIVE MUSIC
(Map p72; Calle 4 No 103 btwn Calzada & Calle 5; admission CUC$5; ⏲3pm Sat) Founded in 1962, this high-energy ensemble specializes in Afro-Cuban dancing (all of the drummers are Santería priests). See them perform, and dance along during the regular Sábado de Rumba at El Gran Palenque. This group also performs at Teatro Mella (p112). A major festival called **FolkCuba** unfolds here biannually during the second half of January.

Casa del Alba Cultural LIVE MUSIC
(Map p72; Línea btwn Calles C & D) This new venue was designed to strengthen cultural solidarity between the ALBA nations (Cuba, Venezuela, Bolivia, Ecuador, Nicaragua), but in reality it hosts a variety of artistic and music-based shows and expos. It was opened in December 2009 with Raúl Castro, Daniel Ortega and Hugo Chávez in attendance.

Jazz Club la Zorra y El Cuervo LIVE MUSIC
(Map p72; cnr Calles 23 & O; admission CUC$5-10; ⏲10pm) Havana's most famous Jazz Club is La Zorra y El Cuervo (the vixen and the crow) on La Rampa, which opens its doors nightly at 10pm to long lines of committed music fiends. Enter through a red English phonebox and descend into a cramped, smoky basement. The freestyle jazz here is second to none, and in the past the club has hosted such big names as Chucho Valdés and George Benson.

La Madriguera LIVE MUSIC
(Map p72; cnr Salvador Allende & Luaces; admission 5-10 pesos) Locals bill it as a 'hidden place for open ideas,' while outsiders are bowled over by its musical originality and artistic innovation. Welcome to La Madriguera – home to the Hermanos Saíz organization, the youth wing of Uneac. This is where the pulse of Cuba's young musical innovators beats the strongest. Come here for arts, crafts, spontaneity and the three Rs: *reggaetón* (Cuban hip-hop), rap and rumba.

Cabaret Las Vegas NIGHTCLUB
(Map p72; Infanta No 104 btwn Calles 25 & 27; admission CUC$5; ⏲10pm-4am) Don't get duped into thinking this is another Tropicana. On the contrary, Cabaret Las Vegas is a rough and seedy local music dive (with a midnight show) where a little rum and a lot of *No moleste, por favor* will help you withstand the overzealous entreaties of the hordes of haranguing *jineteras*.

Pico Blanco NIGHTCLUB
(Map p72; Calle O btwn Calles 23 & 25; admission CUC$5-10; ⏲9pm) An insanely popular nightclub, the Pico Blanco is on the 14th floor of the Hotel St John's in Vedado and kicks off nightly at 9pm. The program can be hit or miss. Some nights it's karaoke and cheesy boleros; another it's jamming with some rather famous Cuban musicians.

Casa de la Cultura Centro LIVE MUSIC
(Map p72; Salvador Allende No 720 btwn Soledad & Oquendo) Yes, Havana has one of these venerable establishments where the music veers towards the traditional. Check the handwritten posters on the board outside.

Piano Bar Delirio Habanero NIGHTCLUB
(Map p72; cnr Paseo & Calle 39; admission CUC$5; ⏲from 6pm Tue-Sun) This suave lounge upstairs in the Teatro Nacional de Cuba hosts everything from young *trovadores* to smooth, improvised jazz. The deep red couches abut a wall of glass overlooking the Plaza de la Revolución – it's stunning at night with the Martí Memorial alluringly backlit. Come up for air here when the adjoining Café Cantante nightclub gets too hot.

Habana Café NIGHTCLUB, CABARET
(Map p72; Paseo btwn Calles 1 & 3; admission CUC$10; ⏲from 9:30pm) A hip and trendy nightclub cum cabaret show at the Hotel Meliá Cohiba laid out in 1950s American style. After 1am the tables are cleared and the place rocks to 'international music' until the cock crows.

Copa Room CABARET
(Map p72; ☎836-4051; cnr Paseo & Malecón; admission CUC$20; ⏲9pm) Doormen in tuxes and an atmosphere that's pure 1950s retro make the refurbished Copa Room in Meyer Lansky's Hotel Riviera look like a nostalgic walk through *The Godfather: Part II*.

Teatro Mella THEATER
(Map p72; Línea No 657 btwn Calles A & B) Occupying the site of the old Rodi Cinema on Línea, the Teatro Mella offers one of Havana's most comprehensive programs, including an international ballet festival, comedy shows, theater, dance and intermittent performances from the famous Conjunto Folklórico Nacional. If you have kids, come to the children's show Sunday at 11am.

Sala Teatro Hubert de Blanck THEATER
(Map p72; Calzada No 657 btwn Calles A & B) This theater is named for the founder of Havana's first conservatory of music (1885). The Teatro Estudio based here is Cuba's leading theater company. You can usually see plays in Spanish on Saturday at 8:30pm and on Sunday at 7pm. Tickets are sold just prior to the performance.

Instituto Cubano de Amistad con los Pueblos CULTURAL CENTER
(ICAP; Map p72; ☎830-3114; Paseo No 416 btwn Calles 17 & 19, Vedado; ⏲11am-11pm) Rocking cultural and musical events in an elegant mansion (1926); there's also a restaurant, bar and cigar shop.

Casa de las Américas CULTURAL CENTER
(Map p72; ☎838-2706; cnr Calles 3 & G, Vedado) Powerhouse of Cuban and Latin American culture, with conferences, exhibitions, a gallery, book launches and concerts. The Casa's annual literary award is one of the Spanish-speaking world's most prestigious. Pick up a schedule of weekly events in the library.

Sala Teatro el Sótano THEATER
(Map p72; Calle K No 514 btwn Calles 25 & 27; ⏲5-8:30pm Fri & Sat, 3-5pm Sun) If you understand Spanish, it's well worth attending some of the cutting-edge contemporary theater that's a staple of Grupo Teatro Rita Montaner at this venue near the Habana Libre.

Café Teatro Brecht THEATER
(Map p72; cnr Calles 13 & I) Varied performances take place. Your best bet is 10:30pm on a Saturday (tickets go on sale one hour before the performance).

Cabaret Turquino CABARET
(Map p72; Calle L btwn Calles 23 & 25, Vedado; admission CUC$15; ⏲from 10pm) Spectacular shows in a spectacular setting on the 25th floor of the Hotel Habana Libre.

Teatro Nacional de Guiñol THEATER
(Map p72; Calle M btwn Calles 17 & 19) This venue has quality puppet shows and children's theater.

Club la Red NIGHTCLUB
(Map p72; cnr Calles 19 & L; admission CUC$3-5) Mixed convertible peso disco in Vedado.

Karachi Club NIGHTCLUB
(Map p72; cnr Calles 17 & K; admission CUC$3-5; ⏲10pm-5am) Ferociously *caliente* (hot).

Discoteca Amanecer NIGHTCLUB
(Map p72; Calle 15 No 12 btwn Calles N & O; admission CUC$3-5; ⏲10pm-4am) Fun if your budget is blown.

DON'T MISS

ART TALK

To see a different side of Havana, home in on the **Centro Cultural Cinematográfico** (Map p72; Calle 23 btwn Calles 10 & 12) in Vedado, the HQ of the Instituto Cubano del Arte e Industria Cinematográficos (Icaic) and a hive of cutting-edge creativity. The center hosts film premieres, discussion nights, art expos and live music, and is home to Havana's best DVD movie outlet. The adjacent Café Fresa y Chocolate (p108) is a great place to get acquainted with the Icaic's movers and shakers, especially on Wednesday nights when there's an excellent live clarinet quartet. Look out in particular for El Último Jueves de Cada Mes (The Last Thursday of Each Month) an interactive debate hosted by a small panel of academics, intellectuals and experts from the arts magazine *Temas*. Respectful but enthusiastic public audiences discuss everything from politics to TV soap operas and offer a fascinating insight into the parameters of public debate in a supposedly totalitarian society. Admission is free and the debates are in Spanish.

Club Tropical NIGHTCLUB
(Map p72; cnr Línea & Calle F; ⏲9pm-2am) As with all clubs, late night Friday and Saturday are best here.

Cinemas

There are about 200 cinemas in Havana. Most have several screenings daily, and every theater posts the *Cartelera Icaic,* which lists show times for the entire city. Tickets are usually CUC$2; queue early. Hundreds of movies are screened throughout Havana during the Festival Internacional del Nuevo Cine Latinoamericano in late November/early December. Schedules are published daily in the *Diario del Festival,* available in the morning at big theaters and the Hotel Nacional. Here's a list of the best movie houses:

Cine Infanta CINEMA
(Map p72; Infanta No 357, Centro Havana) Newly renovated Infanta is possibly Havana's plushest cinema. It's an important venue during the International Film Festival.

Cine Actualidades CINEMA
(Map p68; Av de las Misiones No 262 btwn Neptuno & Virtudes, Centro Havana) Timeworn place centrally located behind the Hotel Plaza.

Cine Charles Chaplín CINEMA
(Map p72; Calle 23 No 1157 btwn Calles 10 & 12, Vedado) An art-house cinema adjacent to the Icaic HQ. Don't miss the poster gallery of great Cuban classic films next door or the movie grapevine that is the Café Fresa y Chocolate opposite.

Cine la Rampa CINEMA
(Map p72; Calle 23 No 111, Vedado) De Niro seasons, French classics, film festivals – catch them all at this Vedado staple, which houses the Cuban film archive.

Cine Payret CINEMA
(Map p68; Paseo de Martí No 505, Centro Havana) Opposite the Capitolio, this is Centro Habana's largest and most luxurious cinema, erected in 1878. Plenty of American movies play here.

Cine Riviera CINEMA
(Map p72; Calle 23 No 507 btwn Calles G & H, Vedado) Big pop, rock and sometimes rap concerts happen here. The movies are a mix of Latin American, European and North American, and the audience has a strong student demographic.

Cine Trianón CINEMA
(Map p72; Línea No 706, Vedado) Movies or live theater in a salubrious setting.

Cine Yara CINEMA
(Map p72; cnr Calles 23 & L, Vedado) One big screen and two video *salas* (cinemas) here at Havana's most famous cinema. The venue for many a hot date.

Cinecito CINEMA
(Map p68; San Rafael No 68, Centro Havana; 👪) Films for kids behind the Hotel Inglaterra. There's another one next to Cine Chaplín on Calles 23 & 12.

Sport

Estadio Latinoamericano SPORT
(Map p 70; Zequiera No 312, Vedado) From October to April, this 58,000-seat baseball stadium in Cerro is home to Los Industriales and Los Metropolitanos (they alternate home fixtures). Entry is a few pesos (but foreigners are charged CUC$2). Games are 7:30pm Tuesday, Wednesday and Thursday, and 1:30pm Saturday and Sunday. The benches are cement – painful after nine innings.

Ciudad Deportiva SPORT
(cnr Av de la Independencia & Vía Blanca, Vedado; admission 5 pesos) 'Sport City' is Cuba's premier sports training center and big basketball, volleyball, boxing and track contests happen at the coliseum here. The P-2 metro bus from the corner of Línea & Av de los Presidentes (Calle G) stops across the street.

Sala Polivalente Ramón Fonst SPORT
(Map p72; Av de la Independencia, Vedado; admission 1 peso) Basketball and volleyball games are held at this tatty-looking stadium opposite the main bus station.

Kid Chocolate SPORT
(Map p68; Paseo de Martí, Centro Habana) A boxing club directly opposite the Capitolio, which usually hosts matches on Friday at 7pm.

Shopping

Shopping isn't Havana's big draw – this, after all, is a city where disposable income is something of an oxymoron. That said, there are some decent outlets for travelers and tourists, particularly if you're after the standard Cuban shopping triumvirate of rum, cigars and coffee. Art is another lucrative field. Havana's art scene is cutting edge and ever changing, and collectors, browsers and admirers will find many galleries in which to while away hours. There are at least a dozen studios in Calle Obispo alone. For gallery events, look for the free *Arte en La Habana,* a triquarterly listings flyer (the San Cristóbal

LOS INDUSTRIALES

They may not be as globally marketable as the New York Yankees, but to thousands of *habaneros*, the all-conquering Industriales are held in equal esteem. Don't even begin to think you've understood this oxymoronic city until you've mustered at least a basic knowledge of baseball and the gigantic role played by the beloved Leones Azules (Blue Lions), as the team is known.

Enjoying premier status in the Cuban National Series (Serie Nacional de Béisbol), the country's hotly contested baseball tournament, Los Industriales have nabbed a record 12 titles since their formation in 1962. Emulating the Yankees – or soccer's Manchester United – they are Cuba's 'glory' team, retaining fans all over the country, but also attracting an equally vociferous contingent of naysayers who'd pay to see them lose.

In the face of weak local opposition (Havana's other team, the Metropolitanos, are perennial underachievers), the Industriales' traditional rivals are the combative Avispas (Wasps) from Santiago de Cuba, who they meet six times a season to replay a grudge match that has been going on ever since Havana stole the mantle of Cuban capital in 1607.

The Havana-Santiago domination was interrupted briefly in the 1990s by strong teams from Villa Clara (who won a hat trick of titles between 1993 and 1995) and Pinar del Río (who logged two straight wins in 1997 and 1998). The biggest surprise in recent years, however, was when a journeyman team from Havana Province – the Vaqueros (Cowboys) – appeared out of nowhere to steal Cuba's baseball crown in 2009.

For a no-holds-barred initiation into Havana's baseball passion, visit the **Esquina Caliente** (literally 'hot corner') in Parque Central, where an almost permanent bevy of boisterous *habaneros* loudly discuss baseball around the clock. Even better, go to a game.

agency on Plaza de San Francisco de Asís usually has them).

HABANA VIEJA

TOP CHOICE Centro Cultural Antiguos Almacenes de Deposito San José ART, SOUVENIRS

(Map p58; cnr Av Desamparados & San Ignacio; ⏲10am-6pm Mon-Sat) In November 2009 Havana's open-air handicraft market moved under the cover of this old shipping warehouse in Av del Puerto. Check your socialist ideals at the door. Herein lies a hive of free-enterprise and (unusually for Cuba) haggling. Possible souvenirs include paintings, *guayabera* shirts, woodwork, leather items, jewelry and numerous apparitions of the highly marketable El Che. There are also snacks, clean-ish toilets and a tourist information representative from the San Cristóbal agency. It's as popular with Cubans as it is with tourists.

Palacio de la Artesanía SOUVENIRS

(Map p58; Cuba No 64; ⏲9am-7pm) A former 18th-century colonial palace turned into a shopping mall! Gathered around a shaded central patio is one-stop shopping for souvenirs, cigars, crafts, musical instruments, CDs, clothing and jewelry at fixed prices. Join the gaggles of tour-bus escapees and fill your bag.

Longina Música MUSIC STORE

(Map p58; Obispo No 360 btwn Habana & Compostela; ⏲10am-7pm Mon-Sat, 10am-1pm Sun) This place on the pedestrian mall has a good selection of CDs, plus musical instruments such as bongos, guitars, maracas, *guiros* and *tumbadoras* (conga drums). It often places loudspeakers in the street outside to grab the attention of passing tourists.

Casa de Carmen Montilla ART

(Map p58; Oficios No 164; ⏲10:30am-5:30pm Tue-Sat, 9am-1pm Sun) An important art gallery named after a celebrated Venezuelan painter who maintained a studio here until her death in 2004. Spread across three floors, the house exhibits the work of Montilla and other popular Cuban and Venezuelan artists. The rear courtyard features a huge ceramic mural by Alfredo Sosabravo.

Plaza de Armas Secondhand Book Market BOOK MARKET

(Map p58; cnr Obispo & Tacón) A book market stocking old, new and rare books, including Hemingway, some weighty poetry and plenty of written pontifications from Fidel. It's all here under the leafy boughs in Plaza de Armas. Browse to your heart's content.

Habana 1791 PERFUME

(Map p58; Mercaderes No 156 btwn Obrapía & Lamparilla) A specialist shop that sells perfume made from tropical flowers, Havana 1791 retains the air of a working museum. Floral fragrances are mixed by hand – you can see the petals drying in a laboratory out the back.

Librería Grijalbo Mondadovi BOOKSTORE

(Map p58; O'Reilly No 4, Plaza de Armas) Fantastic mix of magazines, guidebooks, reference, politics and art imprints in English and Spanish encased neatly in the sublime Palacio del Segundo Cabo in Plaza de Armas.

Librería la Internacional BOOKSTORE

(Map p58; Obispo No 526; 9am-7pm Mon-Sat, 9am-3pm Sun) Good selection of guides, photography books and Cuban literature in English; next door is Librería Cervantes, an antiquarian bookseller.

Estudio Galería los Oficios ART

(Map p58; Oficios No 166; 10am-5:30pm Mon-Sat) Pop into this gallery to see the large, hectic but intriguing canvases by Nelson Domínguez, whose workshop is upstairs.

Taller de Serigrafía René Portocarrero ART

(Map p58; Cuba No 513 btwn Brasil & Muralla; 9am-4pm Mon-Fri) Paintings and prints by young Cuban artists are exhibited and sold here (from CUC$30 to CUC$150). You can also see the artists at work.

Moderna Poesía BOOKSTORE

(Map p58; Obispo 525; 10am-8pm) Perhaps Havana's best spot for Spanish-language books is this classic art deco building at the western end of Calle Obispo.

CENTRO HABANA

Galería la Acacia ART

(Map p68; San Martín No 114 btwn Industria & Consulado; 10am-3:30pm Mon-Fri, 10am-1pm Sat) This important gallery behind the Gran Teatro de La Habana has paintings by leading artists such as Zaida del Río, plus antiques. Export permits are arranged.

El Bulevar MARKET

(Map p68; San Rafael btwn Paseo de Martí & Av de Italia) This is the pedestrianized part of Calle San Rafael near the Hotel Inglaterra. Come here for peso snacks and surprises and 1950s shopping nostalgia.

La Manzana de Gómez SHOPPING CENTER

(Map p68; cnr Agramonte & San Rafael) Talk about faded glory! This once elegant European-style covered shopping arcade was built in 1910. Today it's full of shabby, half-empty stores, including El Orbe bike rentals.

Area de Vendedores por Cuenta Propia MARKET

(Map p68; Máximo Gómez No 259; 9am-5pm Mon-Sat) This is a permanent flea market where you can pick up Santería beads, old books, leather belts etc.

Librería Luis Rogelio Nogueras BOOKSTORE

(Map p68; Av de Italia No 467 btwn Barcelona & San Martín) Literary magazines and Cuban literature in Spanish at one of Centro's best bookstores.

VEDADO

Sevando Galería del Arte ART

(Map p72; cnr Calles 23 & 10; 9am-6pm Tue-Sat) This cool gallery next to the Cine Chaplín and opposite the Icaic headquarters is in an arty part of town and displays some interesting modern paintings and prints. Be sure to check out the Cuban movie-poster gallery on the other side of the cinema (two doors away).

Galería Habana ART

(Map p72; Línea No 460 btwn Calles E & F; 10am-5pm Mon-Sat) This wonderful space in the heart of Vedado shows contemporary Cuban art in big, bright galleries. Come here to see what's new and different.

Galería de Arte Latinoamericano ART

(Map p72; cnr Calles 3 & G; admission CUC$2; 10am-4:30pm Tue-Sat, 9am-1pm Sun) Situated inside the Casa de las Américas and featuring art from all over Latin America.

Instituto Cubano del Arte e Industria Cinematográficos SOUVENIRS

(Map p72; Calle 23 btwn 10 & 12; 10am-5pm) Best place in Havana for rare Cuban movie posters and DVDs. The shop is inside the Icaic (Cuban Film Institute) building and accessed through the Café Fresa y Chocolate.

Feria de la Artesanía SOUVENIRS

(Map p72; Malecón btwn Calles D & E; from 10:30am, closed Wed) This artisan market is a pale imitation of Habana Vieja's Antiguos Almacenes, with a few handmade shoes and sandals, and some old stamps and coins thrown in for good measure.

ARTex SOUVENIRS

(Map p72; cnr Calles 23 & L) A fabulous selection of old movie posters, antique postcards, T-shirts and, of course, all the greatest Cuban films on videotape are sold at this shop inside the Cine Yara.

Galerías de Paseo SHOPPING CENTER
(Map p72; cnr Calle 1 & Paseo; ⌚9am-6pm Mon-Sat, 9am-1pm Sun) Across the street from the Hotel Meliá Cohiba, this place is an upscale (for Cuba) shopping center with some designer labels and even a car dealership. It sells well-made clothes and other consumer items to tourists and affluent Cubans.

Plaza Carlos III SHOPPING CENTER
(Map p72; Av Salvador Allende btwn Arbol Seco & Retiro; ⌚10am-6pm Mon-Sat) After Plaza América in Varadero, this is probably Cuba's flashiest shopping mall – and there's barely a foreigner in sight. Step in on a Saturday and see the double economy working at a feverish pitch.

Librería Centenario del Apóstol BOOKSTORE
(Map p72; Calle 25 No 164; ⌚10am-5pm Mon-Sat, 9am-1pm Sun) Great assortment of used books with a José Martí bias in downtown Vedado.

Librería Rayuela BOOKSTORE
(Map p72; cnr Calles 3 & G; ⌚9am-4:30pm Mon-Fri) This small but respected store bivouacked in the bookish Casa de las Americas building is great for contemporary literature, compact discs and some guidebooks.

La Habana Sí SOUVENIRS
(Map p72; cnr Calles 23 & L; ⌚10am-10pm Mon-Sat, 10am-7pm Sun) This shop opposite the Hotel Habana Libre has a good selection of CDs, cassettes, books, crafts and postcards.

Information

Dangers & Annoyances

Havana is not a dangerous city, especially when compared to other metropolitan areas in North and South America. There is almost no gun crime, violent robbery, organized gang culture, teenage delinquency, drugs or dangerous no-go zones. Rather, a heavy police presence on the streets and stiff prison sentences for crimes such as assault have acted as a major deterrent for would-be criminals and kept the dirty tentacles of organized crime at bay.

But it's not all love and peace, man. Petty crime against tourists in Havana – almost nonexistent in the 1990s – is widespread and on the rise, with pickpocketing, bag-snatching by youths mounted on bicycles and the occasional face-to-face mugging all being reported.

Bring a money belt and keep it on you at all times, making sure that you wear it concealed – and tightly secured – around your waist.

In hotels use a safety deposit box (if there is one) and never leave money, passports or credit cards lying around during the day. Theft from hotel rooms is tediously common, with the temptation of earning three times your monthly salary in one fell swoop often too hard to resist.

In bars and restaurants it is wise to check your change. Purposeful overcharging, especially when someone is mildly inebriated, is a favorite (and easy) trick.

Visitors from the well-ordered European countries or litigation-obsessed North America should keep an eye out for crumbling sidewalks, manholes with no covers, inexplicable driving rules, veering cyclists, carelessly lobbed front-door keys (in Centro Habana) and enthusiastically hit baseballs (almost everywhere). Waves cascading over the Malecón sea wall might look pretty, but the resulting slime-fest has been

WHERE TO BUY RUM, CIGARS & COFFEE

Shops selling Cuba's top three homegrown products are relatively common in Havana. All are government-run. As a rule of thumb, never buy cigars off the street, as they will almost always be damaged and/or sub-standard. Havana's prime factory-outlet cigar shop is at the **Real Fábrica de Tabacos Partagás** (Map p68; Industria No 520 btwn Barcelona & Dragones; ⌚9am-7pm) and is always well stocked. Another excellent option is **La Casa del Habano** (Map p124; Av 5 cnr Calle 16) in Miramar, which has an air-conditioned smoking room and a reputable bar/restaurant. While many top hotels stock cigars, the best shop is in the **Hostal Condes de Villanueva** (Map p58; Mercaderes No 202). There's an equally good option just down the street in the **Museo del Tabaco** (Map p58; Mercaderes No 120).

For rum, look no further than the **Fundación Havana Club shop** (Map p58; San Pedro No 262; ⌚9am-9pm) at the Museo de Ron in Habana Vieja.

Coffee is sold at all of the above places, but for a bit more choice and a decent taster cup pop into **La Casa del Café** (Map p58; Baratillo cnr Obispo; ⌚9am-5pm) just off Plaza de Armas in Habana Vieja.

known to send Lonely Planet–wielding tourists flying unceremoniously onto their asses.

For other common scams, see the boxed text, p118.

Emergency

Asistur (☎886-8339, 866-8920; www.asistur.cu; Paseo de Martí No 208, Centro Habana; ⏲8:30am-5:30pm Mon-Fri, 8am-2pm Sat) Someone on staff should speak English; the alarm center here is open 24 hours.

Fire Service (☎105)

Police (☎106)

Internet Access

Havana doesn't have any private internet cafes. Your best bet outside the Etecsa Telepuntos is the posher hotels. Most Habaguanex hotels in Habana Vieja have internet terminals and sell scratch cards (CUC$6 per hour) that work throughout the chain. You don't have to be a guest to use them.

Cibercafé Capitolio (☎862-0485; cnr Paseo de Martí & Brasil, Centro Habana; per hr CUC$5; ⏲8am-8pm) Inside main entrance.

Etecsa Telepunto (Habana 406) Six terminals in a back room.

Hotel Business Centers Hotel Habana Libre (Calle L btwn Calles 23 & 25, Vedado); Hotel Inglaterra (Paseo de Martí No 416, Centro Habana); Hotel Nacional (cnr Calles O & 21, Vedado); Hotel NH Parque Central (btwn Agramonte & Paseo de Martí, Centro Habana) Costs vary at these places.

Media

Cuba has a fantastic radio culture, where you'll hear everything from salsa to Supertramp, plus live sports broadcasts and soap operas. Radio is also the best source for listings on concerts, plays, movies and dances.

Radio Ciudad de La Habana (820AM & 94.9FM) Cuban tunes by day, foreign pop at night; great '70s flashback at 8pm on Thursday and Friday.

Radio Metropolitana (910AM & 98.3FM) Jazz and traditional boleros (music in 3/4 time); excellent Sunday afternoon rock show.

Radio Musical Nacional (590AM & 99.1FM) Classical.

Radio Progreso (640AM & 90.3 FM) Soap operas and humor.

Radio Rebelde (640AM, 710AM & 96.7FM) News, interviews, good mixed music, plus baseball games.

Radio Reloj (950AM & 101.5FM) News, plus the time every minute of every day.

Radio Taíno (1290AM & 93.3FM) National tourism station with music, listings and interviews in Spanish and English. Nightly broadcasts (5pm to 7pm) list what's happening around town.

Medical Services

Most of Cuba's specialist hospitals offering services to foreigners are based in Havana; see www.cubanacan.cu for details. Consult the Playa & Marianao section of this chapter (p131) for other international clinics and pharmacies.

Centro Oftalmológico Camilo Cienfuegos (☎832-5554; cnr Calle L No 151 & Calle 13, Vedado) Head straight here with eye problems; also has an excellent pharmacy.

Farmacia Homopática (cnr Calles 23 & M, Vedado; ⏲8am-8pm Mon-Fri, 8am-4pm Sat)

Farmacia Taquechel (☎862-9286; Obispo No 155, Habana Vieja; ⏲9am-6pm) Next to the Hotel Ambos Mundos. Cuban wonder drugs such as anticholesterol medication PPG sold in pesos here.

Hospital Nacional Hermanos Ameijeiras (☎877-6053; San Lázaro No 701, Centro Habana) Special hard-currency services, general consultations and hospitalization. Enter via the lower level below the parking lot off Padre Varela (ask for CEDA in Section N).

Hotel Pharmacies Hotel Habana Libre (☎831-9538; Calle L btwn Calles 23 & 25, Vedado) Products sold in convertibles; Hotel Sevilla (☎861-5703; Prado cnr Trocadero, Habana Vieja)

Money

Banco de Crédito y Comercio Vedado (cnr Línea & Paseo); Vedado (☎870-2684; Airline Bldg, Calle 23) Expect lines.

Banco Financiero Internacional Habana Vieja (☎860-9369; cnr Oficios & Brasil); Vedado (Hotel Habana Libre, Calle L btwn Calles 23 & 25)

Banco Metropolitano Centro Habana (☎862-6523; Av de Italia No 452 cnr San Martín); Vedado (☎832-2006; cnr Línea & Calle M, Vedado)

Cadeca Centro Habana (cnr Neptuno & Agramonte; ⏲9am-noon & 1-7pm Mon-Sat); Habana Vieja (cnr Oficios & Lamparilla; ⏲8am-7pm Mon-Sat, 8am-1pm Sun); Vedado (Calle 23 btwn Calles K & L; ⏲7am-2:30pm & 3:30-10pm); Vedado (Mercado Agropecuario, Calle 19 btwn Calles A & B; ⏲7am-6pm Mon-Sat, 8am-1pm Sun); Vedado (cnr Malecón & Calle D) Cadeca gives cash advances and changes traveler's checks at 3.5% commission Monday to Friday (4% weekends).

Cambio (Obispo No 257, Habana Vieja; ⏲8am-10pm) The best opening hours in town.

Post

DHL Vedado (☎832-2112; Calzada No 818 btwn Calles 2 & 4; ⏲8am-5pm Mon-Fri); Vedado (☎836-3564; Hotel Nacional, cnr Calles O & 21)

STREET HASSLE

Well-documented *jinetero* (tout) problems aside, Havana is a relatively safe city – particularly when compared with other Latin American capitals. Stroll through the atmospheric backstreets of Centro Habana or Habana Vieja of an evening, and your biggest worry is likely to be a badly pitched baseball or a flailing line of household washing.

But innocents beware. Scams do exist, particularly in the more touristy areas, where well-practiced hustlers lurk outside the big hotels waiting to prey on unsuspecting foreign visitors.

One popular trick is for young men in the street to offer to change foreign currency into Cuban convertibles at very favorable rates. Accept this at your peril. The money that you will be given is *moneda nacional* or Cuban pesos, visually similar to convertibles, but worth one-twenty-fifth of the value when you take them into a shop.

A second scam is the illicit sale of cheap cigars usually perpetuated by hissing street salesmen around Centro Habana and Habana Vieja. It is best to politely ignore these characters. Any bartering is not worth the bother. Cigars sold on the street are almost always substandard – something akin to substituting an expensive French wine with cheap white vinegar. Instead, buy your cigars direct from the factory or visit one of the numerous Casas del Habano that are scattered throughout the city.

Post offices Centro Habana (Gran Teatro, cnr San Martín & Paseo de Martí); Habana Vieja (Plaza de San Francisco de Asís, Oficios No 102); Habana Vieja (Unidad de Filatelía, Obispo No 518; ⏲9am-7pm); Vedado (cnr Línea & Paseo; ⏲8am-8pm Mon-Sat); Vedado (cnr Calles 23 & C; ⏲8am-6pm Mon-Fri, 8am-noon Sat); Vedado (Av de la Independencia btwn Plaza de la Revolución & Terminal de Ómnibus; ⏲stamp sales 24hr) The last one has many services, including photo developing, a bank and a Cadeca. The **Museo Postal Cubano** (☎870-5581; admission CUC$1; ⏲10am-5pm Sat & Sun) here has a philatelic shop. The post office at Obispo, Habana Vieja, also has stamps for collectors.

Telephone

Etecsa Telepuntos Centro Habana (Aguilar No 565; ⏲8am-9:30pm) There's also a **Museo de las Telecomunicaciones** (⏲9am-6pm Tue-Sat) here if you get bored waiting; Habana Vieja (Habana 406)

Toilets

Havana isn't overendowed with clean and available public toilets. Most tourists slip into upscale hotels if they're caught short. Make sure you tip the lady at the door.

Hotel Ambos Mundos (Obispo No 153, Habana Vieja) Tip the attendant.

Hotel Habana Libre (Calle L btwn Calles 23 & 25, Vedado) To the left of the elevators.

Hotel Nacional (cnr Calles O & 21, Vedado) Right in the lobby and left past the elevators.

Hotel Sevilla (Trocadero No 55 btwn Paseo de Martí & Agramonte, Centro Habana) Turn right inside the lobby.

Tourist Information

Infotur Airport (☎642-6101; Terminal 3 Aeropuerto Internacional José Martí; ⏲24hr); Habana Vieja (☎863-6884; cnr Obispo & San Ignacio; ⏲10am-1pm & 2-7pm) Books tours and sells maps and phone cards.

Travel Agencies

Many of the following agencies also have offices at the airport, in the international arrivals lounge of Terminal 3.

Cubamar Viajes (☎833-2523/4; www.cubamarviajes.cu; Calle 3 btwn Calle 12 & Malecón, Vedado; ⏲8:30am-5pm Mon-Sat) Travel agency for Campismo Popular cabins countrywide. Also rents mobile homes.

Cubanacán (☎873-2686; www.cubanacan.cu; Hotel Nacional, cnr Calles O & 21, Vedado; ⏲8am-7pm) Very helpful; head here if you want to arrange fishing or diving at Marina Hemingway; also in Hotel NH Parque Central, Hotel Inglaterra and Hotel Habana Libre.

Cubatur (☎835-4155; cnr Calles 23 & M, Vedado; ⏲8am-8pm) Below Hotel Habana Libre. This agency pulls a lot of weight and finds rooms where others can't, which goes a long way toward explaining its slacker attitude. It has desks in most of the main hotels.

Ecotur (☎649-1055; www.ecoturcuba.co.cu; Av Independencia No 116 cnr Santa Catalina, Cerro) Sells all kinds of naturalistic excursions.

Havanatur (☎835-3720; www.havanatur.cu; Calle 23 cnr M, Vedado)

San Cristóbal Agencia de Viajes (☎861-9171/2; www.viajessancristobal.cu; Oficios No 110 btwn Lamparilla & Amargura, Habana Vieja; ⏲8:30am-5:30pm Mon-Fri, 8:30am-2pm Sat, 9am-noon Sun) Habaguanex agency operates

Habana Vieja's classic hotels; income helps finance restoration. It offers the best tours in Havana.

Getting There & Away

Air

Cubana Airlines (834-4446; Calle 23 No 64 cnr Infanta, Vedado; 8:30am-4pm Mon-Fri, 8:30am-noon Sat) has its head office at the Malecón end of the Airline Building on La Rampa. You can buy international or domestic tickets here. If it's packed, try the helpful **Sol y Son** (833-3647; fax 33-51-50; Calle 23 No 64 btwn Calle P & Infanta, Vedado; 8:30am-6pm Mon-Fri, 8:30am-noon Sat) travel agency a few doors down.

Aerocaribbean (832-7584; Airline Bldg, Calle 23 No 64, Vedado) is another airline with domestic services.

Boat

Buses connecting with the hydrofoil service to Isla de la Juventud leave at 9am from the **Terminal de Ómnibus** (878-1841; cnr Av de la Independencia & 19 de Mayo, Vedado), near the Plaza de la Revolución, but they're often late. You'll be told to arrive at least an hour before the bus to buy your ticket, and it's best to heed this advice. Bus/boat combo tickets are sold at the kiosk marked 'NCC' between gates 9 and 10, and we found the staff quite unhelpful. Tickets cost CUC$55. Bring your passport.

Bus

Víazul (881-1413, 881-5652; www.viazul.com; cnr Calle 26 & Zoológico, Nuevo Vedado) covers most destinations of interest to travelers, in deluxe, air-conditioned coaches. All buses are direct except those to Guantánamo and Baracoa; for these destinations you must change in Santiago de Cuba. You can board all Víazul buses at the inconveniently located terminal 3km southwest of Plaza de la Revolución, or at the Terminal de Ómnibus. Here tickets for Víazul services are sold immediately prior to departure in the Venta de Boletines office. You can get full schedules on the website or at **Infotur** (Obispo btwn Bernaza & Villegas, Habana Vieja), which also sells tickets requiring you to board at its originating station in Nuevo Vedado.

Havana-bound, you can usually get off the Víazul bus from Varadero/Matanzas in Centro Habana right after the tunnel (check with the driver beforehand), but if you arrive from most other points you'll be let out at the Nuevo Vedado terminal. From here city bus 27 will take you to Vedado or Centro Habana (ask). Alternatively a taxi will cost you a rip-off CUC$10 – unless you negotiate extra hard. Otherwise, if your bus stops at the Terminal de Ómnibus on Av de la Independencia, jump off there.

Buses to points in the Artemisa and Mayabeque provinces leave from Apodaca No 53, off Agramonte, near the main train station in Habana Vieja. They go to Güines, Jaruco, Madruga, Nueva Paz, San José, San Nicolás and Santa Cruz del Norte, but expect large crowds and come early to get a peso ticket.

Taxi

Small Lada taxis, operated by Cubataxi, park on Calle 19 de Mayo beside the Terminal de Ómnibus. They charge approximately CUC$0.50 per kilometer. This translates as CUC$70 to Varadero, CUC$80 to Pinar del Río, CUC$140 to Santa Clara, CUC$125 to Cienfuegos and CUC$165 to Trinidad. Up to four people can go for the price. It's worth considering in a pinch and is perfectly legal.

Train

Trains to most parts of Cuba depart from **Estación Central de Ferrocarriles** (862-1920, 861-8540; cnr Av de Bélgica & Arsenal, Habana Vieja), on the southwestern side of Habana Vieja. Foreigners must buy tickets in convertibles at **La Coubre station** (862-1006; cnr Av del Puerto & Desamparados, Habana Vieja; 9am-3pm Mon-Fri). If it's closed, try the Lista de Espera office adjacent, which sells tickets for trains leaving immediately. Kids under 12 travel half price.

Cuba's best train, the Tren Francés (an old French SNCF train), runs every third day between Havana and Santiago stopping in Santa Clara (CUC$17) and Camagüey (CUC$32). It leaves Havana at 7pm and arrives in Santiago the following morning at 9am. There are no sleeper cars, but carriages are comfortable and air-conditioned, and there's a snack service. Tickets cost CUC$62 for 1st class and CUC$50 for 2nd class.

Slower *coche motor* (cross-island train) services run to Santiago stopping in smaller stations, such as Matanzas (CUC$4), Sancti Spíritus (CUC$13), Ciego de Ávila (CUC$16), Las Tunas (CUC$23), Bayamo (CUC$26), Manzanillo (CUC$28) and Holguín (CUC$27). One train goes as far as Guantánamo (CUC$32). There are separate branch lines to Cienfuegos (CUC$11) and Pinar del Río (CUC$6.50).

The above information is only a rough approximation of what should happen; services are routinely delayed or canceled (including the Tren Francés, which was temporarily out of service at the time of writing). Always double-check scheduling and from which terminal your train will leave.

For information about the electric train from Casablanca to Matanzas, see p137. Suburban trains and local services to points within the Havana province are discussed under Getting Around.

Getting Around

To/From the Airport

Aeropuerto Internacional José Martí is at Rancho Boyeros, 25km southwest of Havana via Av de la Independencia. There are four terminals here. Terminal 1, on the southeastern side of the runway, handles only domestic Cubana flights. Three kilometers away, via Av de la Independencia, is Terminal 2, which receives flights and charters from Miami and New York and to and from the Cayman Islands. All other international flights use Terminal 3, a well-ordered, modern facility at Wajay, 2.5km west of Terminal 2. Charter flights on Aerocaribbean, Aerogaviota, Aerotaxi etc to Cayo Largo del Sur and elsewhere use the Caribbean Terminal (also known as Terminal 5), at the northwestern end of the runway, 2.5km west of Terminal 3. (Terminal 4 hasn't been built yet.) Check carefully which terminal you'll be using.

Public transport from the airport into central Havana is practically nonexistent. A standard taxi will cost you approximately CUC$20 (40 minutes). You can change money at the bank in the arrivals hall.

True adventurers with light luggage and a tight budget can chance their arm on the P-12 metro bus from the Capitolio or the P-15 from the Hospital Hermanos Ameijeiras on the Malecón, both of which go to Santiago de las Vegas, stopping close to the airport (about 1.5km away) on Av Boyeros. This is a lot easier for departing travelers, who will have better knowledge of local geography.

To/From the Bus Terminal

The Víazul bus terminal is in the suburb of Nuevo Vedado, and taxis will charge between CUC$5 and CUC$10 for the ride to central Havana. There are no direct metro buses from central Havana. If you take the P-14 from the Capitolio, you'll have to get off on Av 51 and walk the last 500m or so.

Bici-Taxi

Two-seater bici-taxis will take you anywhere around Centro Habana for CUC$1/2 for a short/long trip, after bargaining. It's a lot more than a Cuban would pay, but cheaper and more fun than a tourist taxi. Laws prohibit bici-taxis from taking tourists and the driver may wish to go via a roundabout route through the back streets to

VÍAZUL DEPARTURES FROM HAVANA

Check for the most up-to-date departure times on www.viazul.com.

DESTINATION	COST (CUC$)	DURATION (HR)	DEPARTURE TIMES
Bayamo	44	13	9:30am, 3:15pm, 10pm
Camagüey	33	9	8:40am, 9:30am, 3:15pm, 6:15pm, 8:30pm, 10pm
Ciego de Ávila	27	7	8:40am, 9:30am, 3:15pm, 8:30pm, 10pm
Cienfuegos	20	4	8:15am, 1pm
Holguín	44	12	8:40am, 3:15pm, 8:30pm
Las Tunas	39	11½	8:40am, 9:30am, 3:15pm, 8:30pm, 10pm
Matanzas	7	2	8am, noon, 5pm, 7pm
Pinar del Río	11	3	9am, 4pm
Sancti Spíritus	23	5¾	8:40am, 9:30am, 3:15pm, 8:30pm, 10pm
Santa Clara	18	3¾	8:40am, 9:30am, 3:15pm, 10pm
Santiago de Cuba	51	15	9:30am, 3:15pm, 6:15pm, 10pm
Trinidad	25	6	8:15am, 1pm
Varadero	10	3	8am, noon, 5pm, 7pm
Viñales	12	4	9am, 4pm

avoid police controls – a cheap tour! If a bici-taxi gets stopped, it's the driver that gets the warning/fine, not you.

Boat

Passenger **ferries** (☎867-3726; Habana Vieja) shuttle across the harbor to Regla and Casablanca, leaving every 10 or 15 minutes from Muelle Luz, at the corner of San Pedro and Santa Clara, on the southeast side of Habana Vieja. The fare is a flat 10 centavos, but foreigners often get charged CUC$1. Since the ferries were hijacked to Florida in 1994 and again in 2003 (the hijackers never made it outside Cuban waters), security has been tightened. Expect bag searches and airport-style screening.

Car

There are lots of car-rental offices in Havana, so if you're told there are no cars or there isn't one in your price range, just try another office or agency. All agencies have offices at Terminal 3 at Aeropuerto Internacional José Martí. Otherwise, there's a car-rental desk in any three-star (or higher) hotel. Prices for equivalent models are nearly always the same between the companies; it's called *socialismo*.

Cubacar (☎835-0000) have desks at most of the big hotels, including Meliá Cohiba, Meliá Habana, NH Parque Central, Habana Libre, Comodoro and Sevilla.

Rex Rent a Car (☎836-7788; cnr Línea & Malecón, Vedado) rents fancy cars for extortionate prices.

Servi-Cupet gas stations are in Vedado at Calles L and 17; Malecón and Calle 15; Malecón and Paseo, near the Riviera and Meliá Cohiba hotels; and on Av de la Independencia (northbound lane) south of Plaza de la Revolución. All are open 24 hours a day.

Guarded parking is available for approximately CUC$1 all over Havana, including in front of the Hotel Sevilla, Hotel Inglaterra and Hotel Nacional.

Public Transport

HAVANA BUS TOUR The handy new hop on/hop off **Havana Bus Tour** (☎831-7333; Calle L No 456 btwn Calles 25 & 27) runs on three routes. The main stop is in Parque Central opposite the Hotel Inglaterra. This is the pickup point for bus T1, which runs from Habana Vieja to the Plaza de la Revolución (via Centro Habana, the Malecón and Calle 23), and bus T3, which runs from Centro Habana to Playas del Este (via Parque Histórico Militar Morro-Cabaña). Bus T2 runs from the Plaza de la Revolución (where it connects with T1) to Marina Hemingway (via Necrópolis Cristóbal Colón and Playa). Bus T1 is open-top. All-day tickets are CUC$5. Services run from 9am to 9pm and routes and stops are clearly marked on all bus stops. At the time of research the T2 service was suspended and the T1 bus was running all the way to Marina Hemingway.

BUS Havana's bus service has improved immensely in recent years with the introduction of a brand new fleet of Chinese-made 'bendy' buses that replaced the famously crowded and dirty camellos (the city's former metro buses) in 2007. These buses run regularly along 14 different routes, connecting most parts of the city with the suburbs. Fares are 20 centavos (five centavos if you're using convertibles), which you deposit into a small slot in front of the driver when you enter.

Cuban buses are crowded and little used by tourists. Beware of pickpockets and guard your valuables closely.

All bus routes have the prefix P before their number:

P-1 Diezmero – Playa (via Virgen del Camino, Vedado, Línea, Av 3)

P-2 Diezmero – Línea y G (via Vibora & Ciudad Deportiva)

P-3 Alamar – Túnel de Línea (via Virgen del Camino and Vibora)

P-4 San Agustín – Terminal de Trenes (via Playa, Calle 23, La Rampa)

P-5 San Agustín – Terminal de Trenes (via Lisa, Av 31, Línea, Av de Puerto)

P-6 Calvario – La Rampa (via Vibora)

P-7 Cotorro – Capitolio (via Virgen del Camino)

P-8 Calvario – Villa Panamericano (via Vibora, Capitolio and harbor tunnel)

P-9 Vibora – Lisa (via Cuatro Caminos, La Rampa, Calle 23, Av 41)

P-10 Vibora – Playa (via Altahabana and Calle 100)

P-11 Alamar – G y 27 (via harbor tunnel)

P-12 Santiago de las Vegas – Capitolio (via Av Boyeros)

P-13 Santiago de las Vegas – Vibora (via Calabazar)

P-14 San Agustín – Capitolio (via Lisa and Av 51)

P-15 Santiago de las Vegas – Hermanos Ameijeiras (via Av Boyeros and Calle G)

P-16 Hospital Naval – Playa (via Calle 100 and Lisa)

Older buses still run along some cross-town routes (eg bus 400 to Playas del Este), but there are no printed timetables or route maps. Individual services have been mentioned in this chapter where appropriate.

Taxi

Metered tourist taxis are readily available at all of the upscale hotels, with the air-conditioned Nissan taxis charging higher tariffs than the non-air-conditioned Ladas. The cheapest official taxis are operated by **Panataxi** (☎55-55-55), with a CUC$1 starting fare, then CUC$0.50 a kilometer. Tourist taxis charge CUC$1 a kilometer and can be ordered from **Havanautos Taxi** (☎73-22-77) and **Transgaviota** (☎206-9793). **Taxi OK** (☎204-0000, 877-6666) is based in Miramar. Drivers of the tourist taxis are government employees who work for a peso salary.

The cheapest taxis are the older yellow-and-black Ladas, which are state-owned but rented out to private operators. They won't wish to use their meters, as these are set at an unrealistically low rate, but you can bargain over the fare. They're not supposed to pick up passengers within 100m of a tourist hotel.

Private pirate taxis (ie those that aren't supposed to take foreigners) with yellow license plates are a bit cheaper, but you must agree on the fare before getting into the car, and carry exact change. There are usually classic-car taxis parked in front of the Hotel Inglaterra.

Walking

Yes, walking! It's what the gas-starved *habaneros* have been doing for decades. Most parts of Habana Vieja, Centro Habana and Vedado can be easily navigated on foot if you're energetic and up for some exercise. You'll see a lot more of of the local street life in the process.

OUTER HAVANA

Splaying out on three sides from the downtown district, Havana's suburbs are full of quirky and easy-to-reach sights and activities that can make interesting day and half-day trips from the city center. Playa boasts a decent aquarium, top-class conference facilities and Cuba's best restaurants; Guanabacoa and Regla are famous for their Afro-Cuban religious culture; and the bayside forts of La Cabaña and El Morro exhibit some of the island's most impressive military architecture.

Playa & Marianao

The municipality of Playa, west of Vedado across the Río Almendares, is a paradoxical mix of prestigious residential streets and tough proletarian housing schemes.

Gracious Miramar is a leafy neighborhood of broad avenues and weeping laurel trees, where the traffic moves more sedately and diplomats' wives – clad in sun visors and Lycra leggings – go for gentle afternoon jogs along Av Quinta (Fifth Ave). Many of Havana's foreign embassies are housed here in old pre-Revolution mansions, and business travelers and conference attendees flock in from around the globe to make use of some of Cuba's grandest and most luxurious facilities. If you're interested primarily in sightseeing and entertainment, commuting to Vedado or Habana Vieja is a nuisance and an expense. However, some of the best salsa clubs, discos and restaurants are out this way and the casas particulares are positively luxurious.

Cubanacán plays host to many of Havana's business or scientific fairs and conventions, and it is also where several specialized medical institutes are situated. Despite the austerity of the *período especial* (Special Period), vast resources have been plowed into biotechnological and pharmaceutical research institutes in this area. Yachties, anglers and scuba divers will find themselves using the Marina Hemingway at Playa's west end.

Marianao is world-famous for the Tropicana Nightclub, but locally it's known as a tough, in parts rough neighborhood with a powerful Santería community and a long history of social commitment.

Sights

MIRAMAR

TOP CHOICE Fundación Naturaleza y El Hombre MUSEUM

(Map p124; ☎204-0438; Av 5B No 6611 btwn Calles 66 & 70, Playa; admission CUC$3; ⏲10am-4pm Mon-Fri) This fascinating museum displays artifacts from the 17,422km canoe trip from the Amazon source to the sea, led by Cuban intellectual and anthropologist Antonio Nuñez Jiménez in 1987. Other exhibits in an astounding collection include one of Cuba's largest photography collections, books written by the prolific Nuñez Jiménez, the famous Fidel portrait by Guayasamín, and 'the glass house' – glass cases containing all kinds of intriguing ephemera from the founder's life. The museum is a foundation and one of Havana's most rewarding.

Pabellón para la Maqueta de la Capital MUSEUM

(Map p124; Calle 28 No 113 btwn Avs 1 & 3; admission CUC$3; ⏲9:30am-5pm Tue-Sat; 👪) If you thought the Maqueta de La Habana Vieja (p57) was impressive, check out this ultramodern pavilion containing a huge 1:1000 scale model of the whole city. The model was originally created for urban-planning purposes, but is now a tourist attraction. Nearby, the two **parks** on Av 5, between Calles 24 and 26, with their immense banyan trees and dark lanes, are an atmospheric pocket.

Acuario Nacional AQUARIUM
(Map p124; cnr Av 3 & Calle 62; adult/child CUC$5/3; 10am-10pm Tue-Sun;) Founded in 1960, the national aquarium is a Havana institution that gets legions of annual visitors, particularly since its 2002 revamp. Despite its rather scruffy appearance, this place leaves all other Cuban *acuarios* (aquatic centers) and *delfinarios* (dolphin shows) in the shade (which isn't saying much). For a start, it's designed to be both educational and conservationist. Saltwater fish are the specialty, but there are also sea lions, dolphins and lots of running-around room for kids. Dolphin performances are almost hourly from 11am, with the final show at 9pm; admission price includes the show.

Russian Embassy LANDMARK
(Map p124; Av 5 No 6402 btwn Calles 62 & 66, Playa) In case you were wondering, that huge Stalinist obelisk that dominates the skyline halfway down Av Quinta is the Russian (formerly Soviet) embassy, testament to the days when Castro was best mates with Brezhnev et al.

Museo del Ministerio del Interior MUSEUM
(Av 5 cnr Calle 14; admission CUC$2; 9am-5pm Tue-Fri, to 4pm Sat) This museum showcases the work of Cuba's Interior Ministry (better known by its acronym MININT), headed up since 1989 by Abelardo Colomé Ibarra, who fought alongside Fidel and Raúl in the Sierra Maestra. You won't uncover any state secrets here, but you will find displays pertaining to MININT's role in hunting down terrorists and criminals and its role in thwarting the innumerable Cold War plots to assassinate Fidel.

Iglesia Jesús de Miramar CHURCH
(Map p124; cnr Av 5 & Calle 82, Playa) Despite its modernity, Playa cradles Cuba's second-largest church. The Jesús is an aesthetically pleasing neo-Romanesque structure topped by a giant dome. Built in 1948, it protects Cuba's largest pipe-organ and some unusual modern murals.

Parque Almendares PARK
Running along the banks of the city's Río Almendares, below the bridge on Calle 23, is this wonderful oasis of greenery and fresh air in the heart of chaotic Havana. The park was restored in 2003, and the restorers did a beautiful job: benches now line the river promenade and plants grow profusely. There are also many facilities here, including an antiquated **miniature golf course**, the **Anfiteatro Parque Almendares** (a small outdoor performance space) and a **playground**. There are several good places to eat.

MARIANAO

Museo de la Alfabetización MUSEUM
(cnr Av 29E & Calle 76; admission free; 8am-noon & 1-4:30pm Mon-Fri, 8am-noon Sat) The former Cuartel Colombia military airfield at Marianao is now a school complex called **Ciudad Libertad**. Pass through the gate to visit this inspiring museum, which describes the 1961 literacy campaign, when 100,000 youths aged 12 to 18 spread out across Cuba to teach reading and writing to farmers, workers and the aged. In the center of the traffic circle, opposite the entrance to the complex, is a tower in the form of a syringe in memory of Carlos Juan Finlay, who discovered the cause of yellow fever in 1881.

CUBANACÁN

Instituto Superior de Arte ART INSTITUTE
(Map p124; ISA; Calle 120 No 1110) The leading art academy in Cuba was established in the former Havana Country Club in 1961 and elevated to the status of institute in 1976. The cluster of buildings – some unfinished, some half-restored, but all gloriously graceful due to the arches, domes and red brick – was the brainchild of Che Guevara and a team of architects. Among them was Ricardo Porro, who designed the striking Facultad de Artes Plásticas (1961), which has long curving passageways and domed halls in the shape of a reclining woman. Some 800 students study here, and foreigners can too.

Palacio de las Convenciones NOTABLE BUILDING
(Map p124; Calle 146 btwn Avs 11 & 13) Also known as the Havana Convention Center, this is one of Cuba's most dramatic modern buildings. Built for the Nonaligned Conference in 1979, the four interconnecting halls contain a state-of-the-art auditorium with 2101 seats and 11 smaller halls. The 589-member National Assembly meets here twice a year, and the complex hosts more than 50,000 conference attendees annually. Not far from here is **Pabexpo** (cnr Av 17 & Calle 180), 20,000 sq meters of exhibition space in four interconnecting pavilions that hosts about 15 trade shows a year.

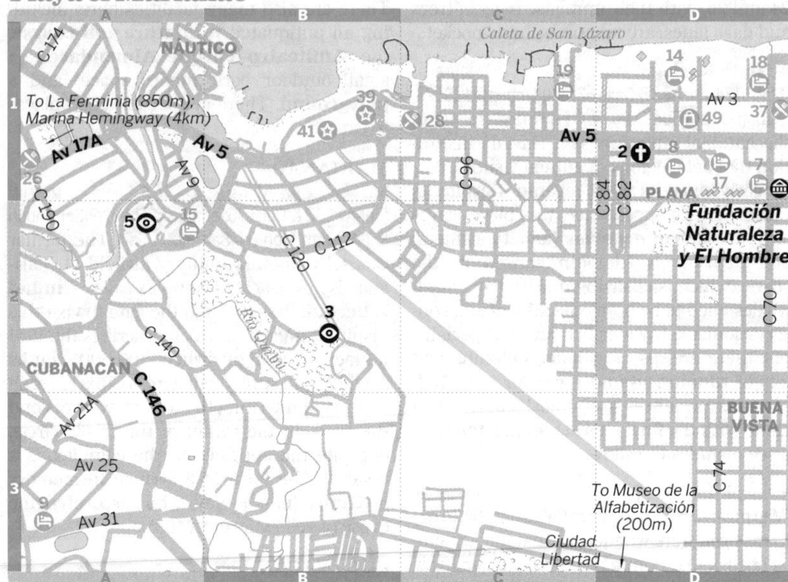

Isla del Coco AMUSEMENT PARK
(Map p124; Av 5 & Calle 112, Playa) A huge new Chinese-built amusement park in Playa with big wheels, bumper cars, rollercoasters, the works.

Activities

Marlin Náutica WATER SPORTS
(cnr Av 5 & Calle 248, Barlovento) There are many water activities available at Marina Hemingway in Barlovento, 20km west of central Havana. Fishing trips can be arranged at Marlin Náutica from CUC$150 for four anglers and four hours of bottom fishing, and CUC$280 for four anglers and four hours of deep-sea fishing. Included are a captain, a sailor, an open bar and tackle. Marlin season is June to October. Scuba packages for CUC$35 per dive and tours of Havana's littoral (CUC$60 in a catamaran) can also be arranged.

La Aguja Marlin Diving Center DIVE CENTER
(☎204-5088; cnr Av 5 & 248, Barlovento) Between Cubanacán Náutica and the shopping center, this center offers scuba diving for CUC$30 per dive, plus CUC$5 for gear. It has one morning and one afternoon departure. A diving excursion to Varadero or Playa Girón can also be arranged. Reader reviews have been favorable.

Sleeping

MIRAMAR

TOP CHOICE **Hotel Meliá Habana** HOTEL $$$
(Map p124; ☎204-8500; Av 3 btwn Calles 76 & 80; r CUC$220; P ❄ @ ≈) Ugly outside but beautiful within, Miramar's gorgeous Hotel Meliá Habana, which opened in 1998, is one of the city's best run and best-equipped accommodation options. The 409 rooms (four of which are wheelchair-accessible) are positioned around a salubrious lobby with abundant hanging vines, marble statues and gushing water features. Outside, Cuba's largest and most beautiful swimming pool stands next to a desolate, rocky shore. Throw in polite, punchy service, an excellent buffet restaurant and the occasional room discount, and you could be swayed.

Barceló Habana Ciudad HOTEL $$$
(Map p124; ☎214-1470; Av 5 btwn Calles 76 & 80, Miramar; s/d CUC$110/130; ❄ @ ≈) Playa's newest hotel is another concrete colossus opened by the government-run hotel chain Gaviota in January 2010. It completes a trio of plush accommodations set behind the Miramar Trade Center. While the facilities claim a high star-rating with expansive rooms (all with separate showers and bathtubs) and a good on-site restaurant, the place suffers

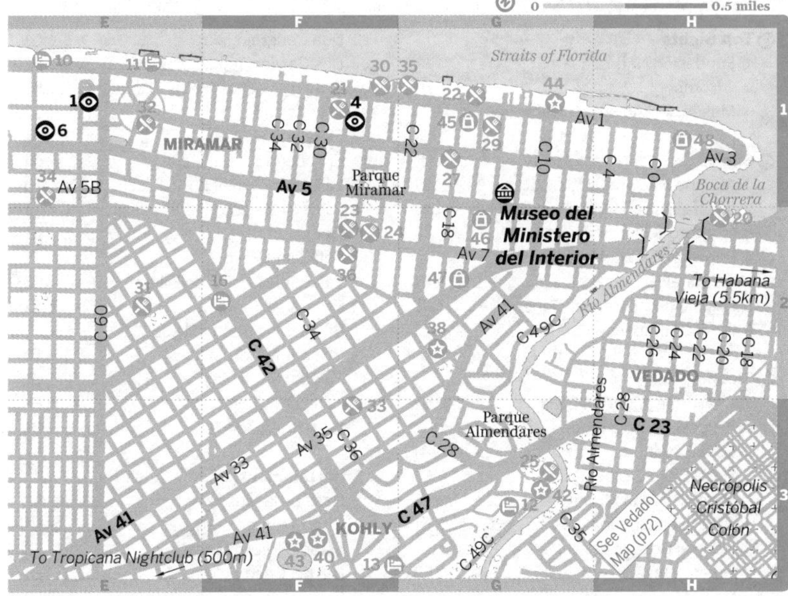

from the usual foibles of humungous chain-run establishments: a cold generic feel and a lack of personality.

Hotel el Bosque HOTEL $

(Map p124; ☎204-9232; Calle 28A btwn Calles 49A & 49B, Kohly; s/d CUC$36/48; ❄@) Economical and grossly underrated, El Bosque is the better and less costly arm of the Gaviota-run Kohly-Bosque *complejo* (complex). Clean and friendly, the hotel lies on the banks of the Río Almendares surrounded by the Bosque de La Habana– the city's green lungs – and is a good (and rare) midrange choice in this neck of the woods. The 54 rooms are small but functional, there's 24-hour internet, and out back a pleasant terrace overlooks the wooded slopes of the nearby river.

Occidental Miramar HOTEL $$$

(Map p124; ☎204-3584; fax 204-3583; cnr Av 5 & Calle 74; s/d CUC$100/130; P❄≋) Formerly the Novotel, this 427-room colossus was taken over by Gaviota a few years back and has benefited as a result. Professional staff, great business facilities and high standards of service throughout are par for the course here. There are also plenty of sporty extras if the isolated location starts to grate, including tennis courts, swimming pool, sauna, gym and games room.

Aparthotel Montehabana HOTEL $$

(Map p124; ☎206-9595; Calle 70 btwn Avs 5A & 7, Playa; s/d/tr CUC$60/80/110; P❄@) This modern Gaviota giant opened in December 2005 with the promise of something a little different. Of the rooms here, 101 are apartments with living rooms and fully equipped kitchens – a great opportunity to hit the Havana markets and find out how Cubans cook. To help you, in the kitchen there are microwaves, refrigerators, toasters and coffee machines – even your own cutlery. If you're not up to cooking, the restaurant does a CUC$8 breakfast and a CUC$15 dinner buffet. Elsewhere the facilities are shiny and new, with 24-hour internet, car rental and an on-site minimarket. Guests can use the pool at the Hotel Occidental Miramar next door.

Hotel Chateau Miramar HOTEL $$$

(Map p124; ☎204-0224; Av 1 btwn Calles 60 & 70, Playa; s/d CUC$90/125; P❄@≋) It's marketed as a 'boutique hotel,' but read between the lines – this château ain't no Loire Valley retreat. Still, techno addicts will appreciate the free internet, flat-screen TV and direct international phone service that come with the otherwise mediocre rooms.

Playa & Marianao

Top Sights

Fundación Naturaleza y El Hombre D1
Museo del Ministero del Interior G1

Sights

1 Acuario Nacional E1
2 Iglesia Jesús de Miramar D1
3 Instituto Superior de Arte (ISA) B2
4 Pabellón para la Marqueta de la Capital F1
5 Palacio de las Convenciones A2
6 Russian Embassy E1

Sleeping

7 Aparthotel Montehabana D1
8 Barceló Habana Ciudad D1
Casa Española .... (see 24)
9 Hotel Bello Caribe A3
10 Hotel Chateau Miramar E1
11 Hotel Copacabana E1
12 Hotel el Bosque G3
13 Hotel Kohly F3
14 Hotel Meliá Habana D1
15 Hotel Palco A2
16 Marta Rodríguez F2
17 Occidental Miramar D1
18 Panorama Hotel Havana D1
19 Rina & Geraldo C1

Eating

Casa Española .... (see 23)
20 Complejo Turístico 1830 .... H2
21 Doctor Cafe F1
22 Don Cangrejo G1
23 Dos Gardenias F2
24 El Aljibe F2
25 El Lugar G3
26 El Palenque A1
27 El Tocororo G1
La Casa del Habano .... (see 46)
28 La Cecilia C1
29 La Esperanza G1
30 Paladar el Palio F1
31 Paladar la Cocina de Lilliam E2
32 Paladar la Fontana E1
33 Paladar los Cactus de 33 .... F3
34 Paladar Mi Jardín E1
35 Paladar Vista Mar G1
36 Pan.com F2
37 Supermercado 70 .... D1

Entertainment

38 Casa de la Música G2
39 Circo Trompoloco B1
40 Estadio Pedro Marrero F3
41 Isla del Coco B1
42 Salón Chévere G3
43 Salón Rosado Benny Moré (El Tropical) F3
44 Teatro Karl Marx G1

Shopping

45 Egrem Tienda de Música G1
46 La Casa del Habano G2
47 La Maison G2
48 La Puntilla H1
49 Miramar Trade Center D1

Panorama Hotel Habana HOTEL **$$$**
(Map p124; 204-0100; cnr Av 3 & Calle 70; s/d CUC$95/120; P ❄ @ ≋) Gaviota's flashy 'glass cathedral' on Playa's rapidly developing hotel strip opened in 2003. The rather strange aesthetics – acres of blue-tinted glass – improve once you step inside the monumental lobby where space-age elevators whisk you promptly up to one of 317 airy rooms, which offer great views over Miramar and beyond. Extra facilities include a business center, a photo shop, numerous restaurants and a spacious and shapely swimming pool. But the Panorama is almost too big: its scale makes you feel small and gives the place a rather deserted and antiseptic feel.

Hotel Kohly HOTEL **$$**
(Map p124; 204-0240; cnr Calles 49A & 36 Kohly; s/d CUC$47/63; ❄ @ ≋) Just up the road, the Kohly is similarly priced to El Bosque and makes up for its utilitarian exterior with an inviting swimming pool and an excellent pizza restaurant.

Marta Rodríguez CASA PARTICULAR **$**
(Map p124; 203-8596; Calle 42 No 914; r CUC$40; P) There aren't many casas in Miramar, but Marta's is one that could be worth the trip, offering art-deco beds, TV, VCR, a music system and lots of space.

Hotel Copacabana HOTEL **$$**
(204-1037; Av 1 btwn Calles 44 & 46; s/d CUC$60/80; P ❄ @ ≋) Right on the beach, the Copacabana is back in business after a lengthy 2009–10 refurbishment, though there's still a dankness about the whole establishment, despite its fine ocean-side location.

Rina & Geraldo CASA PARTICULAR $
(Map p124; ☎202-4112; Av 3A No 8610 btwn Calles 86 & 88, Playa; r CUC$25-30) A venerable casa with loquacious hosts that rents two clean rooms in the vicinity of the Miramar Trade Center. If it's full there's a couple more in the same street.

CUBANACÁN

There are two hotels in this neighborhood, where you might end up if you're here for an organized activity/conference.

Hotel Bello Caribe HOTEL $$
(Map p124; ☎273-9906; cnr Av 31 & Calle 158; s/d CUC$50/67; P ❄ ≋) Next to the huge Centro de Ingenería Genética y Biotecnología, this hotel has 120 rooms often used by foreigners undergoing treatment at the nearby medical facilities.

Hotel Palco HOTEL $$$
(Map p124; ☎204-7235; Calle 146 btwn Avs 11 & 13; s/d CUC$91/111; P ❄ ≋) Two kilometers to the north and attached to the Palacio de las Convenciones, the Palco is a business hotel normally block-booked by foreigners in town to attend a conference/symposium/product launch.

MARINA HEMINGWAY

Hotel Acuario HOTEL $$
(☎204-6336; cnr Aviota & Calle 248; s/d CUC$60/90; ❄) You really shouldn't come to Marina Hemingway for the hotels. With the El Viejo y el Mar hosting medical patients from Latin America, the only real option for foreign travelers is the strung-out Acuario, splayed between two of the harbor channels and infested with cheap out-of-date furnishings. If you're booked for an early morning diving excursion, this place might just qualify; otherwise stay in Havana and commute.

Eating

Playa contains some of Havana's and Cuba's best surviving paladares, most of them situated in beautiful early-20th-century mansions with alfresco dining options. There are also some surprisingly good state-run restaurants. It's worth the CUC$5 to CUC$10 taxi fare from the city center to eat out here.

PLAYA & MARIANAO

Paladar los Cactus de 33 PALADAR $$$
(Map p124; ☎203-5139; Av 33 No 3405 btwn Calles 34 & 36, Playa; ⏰noon-midnight) Reviewed in international lifestyle magazines and used as a setting on Cuban TV, this place has impeccable service, elegant surroundings, well-prepared food and outrageous prices, once you've factored in the taxi fare (it's well out of the way). Bank on a minimum of CUC$20 for the house special: chicken breast with mushrooms, olives and cheese.

MIRAMAR

TOP CHOICE **El Aljibe** CARIBBEAN $$
(Map p124; ☎204-1583/4; Av 7 btwn Calles 24 & 26; ⏰noon-midnight) On paper a humble Palmares restaurant, but in reality a rip-roaring culinary extravaganza, El Aljibe has been delighting both Cuban and foreign diplomatic taste buds for years. The furore surrounds the gastronomic mysteries of just one dish, the obligatory *pollo asado* (roast pork), which is served up with as-much-as-you-can-eat helpings of white rice, black beans, fried plantain, French fries and salad. The accompanying bitter orange sauce is said to be a state secret.

Paladar la Cocina de Lilliam PALADAR $$$
(Map p124; ☎209-6514; Calle 48 No 1311 btwn Avs 13 & 15; ⏰noon-midnight) Slick service, secluded ambience and freshly cooked food to die for, La Cocina de Lilliam has all the ingredients of a prize-winning restaurant. Set in an illustrious villa in Miramar and surrounded by a garden with trickling fountains and lush tropical plants, diners can tuck into such Cuban rarities as chicken mousse and tuna bruschetta in an atmosphere more European than Caribbean. Not a cheese-and-ham sandwich in sight!

Paladar la Fontana PALADAR $$$
(Map p124; ☎202-8337; Av 3A No 305) Havana discovers the barbecue or, more to the point, the full-on charcoal grill. Huge portions of meat and fish are served up in this amiable villa-cum-paladar, so go easy on the starters, which include crab mixed with eggplant, quail eggs and fried chickpeas. La Fontana specializes in just about everything you'll never see elsewhere in Cuba, from lasagna to huge steaks. Big-shot reviews from the *Cigar Aficionado* and the *Chicago Tribune* testify to the burgeoning legend.

La Esperanza PALADAR $$$
(Map p124; ☎202-4361; Calle 16 No 105 btwn Avs 1 & 3; ⏰6:30-11pm, closed Thu) Few would disagree that the food, ambience and gastronomic creativity showcased at this unassuming Miramar paladar puts it among Havana's (and undoubtedly Cuba's) best eating establishments. While unspectacular from the street,

the interior of this house is a riot of quirky antiques, old portraits and refined 1940s furnishings. The food, which is produced in a standard-sized family kitchen, includes such exquisite dishes as *pollo luna de miel* (chicken flambéed in rum), fish marinated in white wine, lemon and garlic, and a lamb brochette.

Pan.com FAST FOOD **$**
(Map p124; ☎204-4232; cnr Av 7 & Calle 26; ⏲10am-midnight) Not an internet cafe but a haven of Havana comfort food with hearty sandwiches, fantastic burgers and ice-cream milkshakes to die for. Join the diplomats under the airy front canopy.

Doctor Café PALADAR **$$$**
(Map p124; ☎203-4718; Calle 28 btwn Avs 1 & 3) Ceviche, red snapper, grilled octopus and a plant-filled patio as well as an internal area for eating; this doctor is obviously getting the treatment spot on. The menu is from all over the globe, and there are numerous rarities you'll find at few other places in Cuba. Anyone for freshly baked bread?

Casa Española SPANISH **$$**
(Map p124; ☎206-9644; cnr Calle 26 & Av 7; ⏲noon-midnight) A medieval parody built in the Batista-era by the silly-rich Gustavo Guitérrez y Sánchez, this crenellated castle in Miramar has found new life as a Spanish-themed restaurant cashing in on the Don Quixote legend. The ambience is rather fine, if you don't mind suits of armor watching you as you tuck into paella, Spanish omelet or *lanja cerdo al Jerez* (Jerez-style pork fillet).

Paladar Mi Jardín PALADAR, MEXICAN **$$**
(Map p124; ☎203-4627; Calle 66 No 517; ⏲noon-midnight) The rare Cuban menu – it offers chicken mole or tacos and quesadillas – makes this Mexican place a keeper. Dining beneath the vine-covered trellis in the garden is recommended, as is the house special: fish Veracruz.

Paladar el Palio PALADAR **$$**
(Map p124; ☎202-9867; Av 1 No 2402; ⏲noon-midnight) Next door to the Vista Mar, El Palio offers a similar deal with seating options either inside in a small but tasteful dining room or outside in an equally small and tasteful garden within earshot of the Atlantic waves. The necessarily spontaneous paladar menu is anchored by seafood, but contains the odd surprise such as rabbit.

Paladar Vista Mar PALADAR **$$**
(Map p124; ☎203-8328; Av 1 btwn Calles 22 & 24; ⏲noon-midnight) The Paladar Vista Mar in Miramar is in the 2nd-floor family-room-turned-restaurant of a private residence, which faces the sea. The oceanside ambience is embellished by a beautiful swimming pool that spills its water into the sea. If enjoying delicious seafood dishes overlooking the crashing ocean sounds enticing, this could be your bag. Most mains run from CUC$8 to CUC$15 with salad.

Don Cangrejo SEAFOOD **$$**
(Map p124; Av 1 No 1606 btwn Calles 16 & 18; ⏲noon-midnight) On the seafront, this unique seafood restaurant is run by the Ministry of Fisheries and scores high points for atmosphere and service. Fresh fish dishes include red snapper, grouper and prawns (CUC$8 to CUC$12), while lobster from the pit on the terrace comes in at CUC$20 to CUC$25.

El Tocororo CARIBBEAN, JAPANESE **$$$**
(Map p124; ☎202-4530; Calle 18 No 302; meals CUC$12-35; ⏲noon-midnight) Once considered (along with El Aljibe) to be one of Havana's finest government-run restaurants, El Tocororo has lost ground to its competitors in recent years and is often criticized for being overpriced. Nonetheless, the candlelit tables and inviting garden are still worth a visit, while the unprinted menu, with such luxuries as lobster's tail and (occasionally) ostrich, still has the ability to surprise. El Tocororo also has a small attached sushi bar and restaurant called **Sakura**.

El Lugar CARIBBEAN **$**
(Map p124; cnr Calles 49C & 28A; ⏲noon-midnight) Set in Parque Almendares just across the road from the river below the bridge, this place is fantastic value, offering juicy pork filets, a Pico Turquino of *congrí* (rice flecked with black beans), salad, *tostones* (fried plantain patties), ice cream and coffee. There's music in the evenings.

La Casa del Habano CARIBBEAN **$$**
(Map p124; cnr Av 5 & Calle 16, Miramar) Most head here for its reputation as Havana's best cigar store, but repeat visitors come back for the food in the adjoining restaurant.

Dos Gardenias CARIBBEAN **$$**
(Map p124; cnr Av 7 & Calle 28; ⏲noon-midnight) You can choose from a grill or a pasta restaurant in this complex, which is famous as a bolero hot-spot. Stick around to hear the singers belting out ballads later on.

PALADARES – A UNIQUE BREED

Going to a paladar – a private Cuban restaurant – has always been about far more than just eating. Firstly, there's the pot-luck of the surroundings: a kitschy family dining room, a romantic ocean-side patio, or – if you arrive on the wrong day – a bolted, darkened room at the end of a narrow passageway. Then there's the exciting air of subterfuge, the vague notion that what goes on here occupies an unfathomable grey area between what's legal and what's not. Best of all, however, is the food. First established in 1995 during the economic chaos of the Special Period, paladares owe much of their success to the bold experimentation of local chefs, who, despite a paucity of decent ingredients, have heroically managed to keep the age-old traditions of Cuban cooking alive.

Despite international acclaim, plus a slew of famous guests (Jimmy Carter, the Queen of Spain and numerous US Congressmen) and glowing reviews (*The New York Times* and *Cigar Aficionado* to name but two), paladares felt the pinch in the early 2000s and many old stalwarts closed. Problems ranged from high taxes and more rigid inspections to greater competition from credible government-run places, particularly in the more touristy areas of Havana.

By the late 2000s, one of the last bastions of Paladar heaven was Playa, an area which still listed a good half-dozen highly reputable restaurants across its splayed suburbs. Vedado was down to scanter fare, while Centro Havana was still showcasing the shabby-chic poster child of all paladares, La Guarida. But, with a new law easing restrictions on private business passed in January 2011, paladars look set for a triumphant rebirth.

Supermercado 70 SUPERMARKET $

(Map p124; cnr Av 3 & Calle 70; ⊙9am-6pm Mon-Sat, 9am-1pm Sun) Still known as the 'Diplomercado' from the days when only diplomats came here, this place is large by Cuban standards and has a wide selection.

CUBANACÁN

La Cecilia CARIBBEAN $$

(Map p124; ☎204-1562; Av 5 No 11010 btwn Calles 110 & 112; ⊙noon-midnight) All-time Havana classic, this classy place is up there with El Aljibe in terms of food quality (check out the *ropa vieja*), but trumps all comers with its big-band music, which blasts out on weekend nights inside its large but atmospheric courtyard.

El Palenque CUBAN, ITALIAN $$

(☎208-8167; cnr Av 17A & Calle 190; Siboney; ⊙10am-10pm) A huge place, next to the Pabexpo exhibition center, that sprawls beneath a series of open-sided thatched *bohíos* (traditional Cuban huts), the Palenque offers an extensive menu at prices cheap enough to attract both Cubans and foreigners. The cuisine is Cuban/Italian, with pizzas starting at CUC$3, steak and fries coming in at CUC$9 and lobster *mariposa* maxing out at CUC$22.

La Ferminia CARIBBEAN $$$

(☎273-6786; Av 5 No 18207, Flores) Havana gets swanky at this memorable restaurant set in an elegant converted colonial mansion in the leafy neighborhood of Flores. Dine inside in one of a handful of beautifully furnished rooms, or outside on a glorious garden patio – it doesn't matter. The point is the food. Try the mixed grill, pulled straight from the fire, or lobster tails pan-fried in breadcrumbs. There's a strict dress code here: no shorts or sleeveless T-shirts (guys). It's one of the few places where Fidel Castro has dined in public.

MARINA HEMINGWAY

Restaurante la Cova ITALIAN $$

(cnr Av 5 & Calle 248; ⊙noon-midnight) In Marina Hemingway, this place vies with Paladar Piccolo in Playas del Este as Havana's best pizza joint. Part of the Pizza Nova chain, it also does fish, meat and rigatoni a la vodka (CUC$8). The pepperoni topping is purportedly flown in from Canada.

Papa's Complejo Turístico CARIBBEAN, CHINESE $$

(cnr Av 5 & Calle 248; ⊙noon-3am) There's all sorts of stuff going on here, from beer-swilling boatmen to warbling *American Idol* wannabes hogging the karaoke machine. The eating options are equally varied, with a posh Chinese place (with dress code) and an outdoor *ranchón* (rural restaurant). Good fun if there's enough people.

☆ Entertainment

MIRAMAR

Teatro Karl Marx LIVE MUSIC

(Map p124; ☎203-0801, 209-1991; cnr Av 1 & Calle 10) Size-wise the Karl Marx puts other Havana theaters in the shade with a seating capacity of 5500 in a single auditorium. The very biggest events happen here, such as the closing galas for the jazz and film festivals and rare concerts by *trovadores* like Silvio Rodríguez. In 2001 it hosted Welsh rockers the Manic Street Preachers, the first Western rock band to play live on the island (with Fidel Castro in the audience).

Casa de la Música NIGHTCLUB, LIVE MUSIC

(Map p124; ☎202-6147; Calle 20 No 3308 cnr Av 35; admission CUC$5-20; ⏲10pm Tue-Sat) Launched with a concert by renowned jazz pianist Chucho Valdés in 1994, this Miramar favorite is run by national Cuban recording company, Egrem, and the programs are generally a lot more authentic than the cabaret entertainment you see at the hotels. Platinum players such as NG la Banda, Los Van Van and Aldaberto Álvarez y Su Son play here regularly; you'll rarely pay more than CUC$20. It has a more relaxed atmosphere than its Centro Habana namesake.

MARIANAO

Tropicana Nightclub CABARET

(off Map p124; ☎267-1871; Calle 72 No 4504; ⏲10pm) A city institution since it opened in 1939, the world-famous Tropicana was one of the few bastions of Havana's Las Vegas-style nightlife to survive the clampdowns of the puritanical Castro Revolution. Immortalized in Graham Greene's 1958 classic *Our Man in Havana*, this open-air cabaret show is little changed since its '50s heyday, featuring a bevy of scantily clad *señoritas* who climb nightly down from the palm trees to dance Latin salsa amid colorful flashing lights on stage. Tickets go for a slightly less than socialistic CUC$70.

Salón Rosado Benny Moré LIVE MUSIC

(Map p124; El Tropical; ☎206-1281; cnr Avs 41 & Calle 46, Kohly; admission 10 pesos-CUC$10; ⏲9pm-late) For something completely different, check out the very *caliente* action at this outdoor venue. The Rosado (aka El Tropical) packs in hot, sexy Cuban youths dancing madly to Los Van Van, Pupi y Su Son Son or Habana Abierta. It's a fierce scene and female travelers should expect aggressive come-ons. Friday to Sunday is best. Some travelers pay pesos, others dollars – more of that Cuban randomness for you.

Circo Trompoloco CIRCUS

(Map p124; cnr Av 5 & Calle 112, Playa; admission CUC$10; ⏲7pm Thu-Sun) Havana's permanent 'Big Top' with a weekend matinee.

Estadio Pedro Marrero SPORTS

(Map p124; cnr Av 41 & Calle 46, Kohly) Football – or is it soccer in Cuba? Come over on weekends at 3pm to this 15,000-seat stadium and watch them dance down the wings.

LA LISA

Sala de Fiesta Macumba Habana NIGHTCLUB

(cnr Calle 222 & Av 37; admission CUC$10-20; ⏲10pm) Cocooned in a residential neighborhood southwest of Cubanacán is Macumba, one of Havana's biggest venues for live salsa. The outdoor setting is refreshing and the sets are long, so you'll get a lot of dancing in. This is a great place to catch jazz-salsa combos and *timba* music, a modern extension of salsa mixed with jazz and rap and championed by NG la Banda (who perform here regularly). You can also dine at La Giradilla in the same complex.

Salón Chévere NIGHTCLUB

(Map p124; Parque Almendares, cnr Calles 49C & 28A; admission CUC$6-10; ⏲from 10pm) One of Havana's most popular discos, this alfresco place in a lush park setting hosts a good mix of locals and tourists.

Shopping

La Casa del Habano CIGARS

(Map p124; Av 5 cnr Calle 16, Miramar; ⏲10am-6pm Mon-Sat, 10am-1pm Sun) Smokers and souvenir seekers will like La Casa, arguably Havana's top cigar store. You'll find a comfy smoking lounge and a decent restaurant here as well.

La Maison CLOTHING

(Map p124; Calle 16 No 701, Miramar) The Cuban fashion fascination is in high gear at this place, with a large boutique selling designer clothing, shoes, handbags, jewelry, cosmetics and souvenirs.

Egrem Tienda de Música MUSIC STORE

(Map p124; Calle 18 No 103, Miramar; ⏲9am-6pm Mon-Sat) There's a small CD-outlet here hidden in leafy Miramar at the site of Havana's most celebrated recording studios.

Casa de la Música MUSIC STORE
(Map p124; Calle 20 No 3308 cnr Av 35, Miramar; ⏲10am-10pm) A small musical outlet graces Miramar's famous music venue.

Miramar Trade Center SHOPPING CENTER
(Map p124; Av 3 btwn Calles 76 & 80) Cuba's largest and most modern shopping and business center houses myriad stores, airline offices and embassies.

La Puntilla SHOPPING CENTER
(Map p124; Calle A cnr Av 1) Decade-old shopping center spread over four floors at the Vedado end of Miramar; fairly comprehensive by Cuban standards.

Information

Internet Access

Hotel Business Centers (Hotel Meliá Habana; Av 3 btwn Calles 76 & 80, Miramar) Meliá Habana charges CUC$7 per half-hour for internet access. Also try the Aparthotel Montehabana (p125) and the Occidental Miramar (p125).

Medical Services

Clínica Central Cira García (☎204-2811; Calle 20 No 4101 cnr Av 41, Playa; ⏲9am-4pm Mon-Fri, emergencies 24hr) Emergency, dental and medical consultations for foreigners (consultations CUC$25 to CUC$35).

Farmacia Internacional Miramar (☎204-4350; cnr Calles 20 & 43, Playa; ⏲9am-5:45pm) Across the road from Clínica Central Cira García.

Pharmacy (☎204-2880; Calle 20 No 4104 cnr Calle 43, Playa; ⏲24hr) In Clínica Central Cira García; one of the city's best.

Money

Banco Financiero Internacional Miramar (Sierra Maestra Bldg, cnr Av 1 & Calle 0); Playa (cnr Av 5 & Calle 92)

Cadeca Miramar (Av 5A btwn Calles 40 & 42); Playa (☎204-9087; cnr Av 3 & Calle 70)

Post

DHL (cnr Av 1 & Calle 26, Miramar; ⏲8am-8pm)

Post office (Calle 42 No 112 btwn Avs 1 & 3, Miramar; ⏲8am-11:30am & 2-6pm Mon-Fri, 8am-11:30am Sat)

Tourist Information

Infotur (cnr Av 5 & Calle 112, Playa; ⏲8:30am-5pm Mon-Sat, 8:30am-noon Sun) Oddly located but informative office.

Travel Agencies

All of the following agencies sell the organized tours listed in the Downtown Havana section (see p118).

Cubanacán (☎204-8500) Desk in Hotel Meliá Habana.

Gaviota (☎204-4411; cnr Av 49 & Calle 36, Kohly)

Getting There & Away

The best way to get to Playa from Havana is on the Havana Bus Tour (see p121), which plies most of the neighborhoods' highlights all the way to Marina Hemingway. Coming from Habana Vieja or Centro Habana, you'll need to change buses at Plaza de la Revolución. Plenty of metro buses make the trip, though they often ply the more residential neighborhoods (see p121).

Getting Around

Cubacar (☎204-1707) has offices at the Chateau Miramar and the Meliá Habana hotels. Rental is around CUC$70 per day with insurance.

Vía Rent a Car (☎204-3606; cnr Avs 47 & 36, Kohly) has an office opposite the Hotel el Bosque.

There are Servi-Cupet gas stations at Av 31 between Calles 18 and 20 in Miramar, on the corner of Calle 72 and Av 41 in Marianao (near the Tropicana), as well as on the traffic circle at Av 5 and Calle 112 in Cubanacán. The Oro Negro gas station is at Av 5 and Calle 120 in Cubanacán. All are open 24 hours.

Parque Lenin Area

Parque Lenin, off the Calzada de Bejucal in Arroyo Naranjo, 20km south of central Havana, is the city's largest recreational area. Constructed between 1969 and 1972 on the orders of Celia Sánchez, a long-time associate of Fidel Castro, it is one of the few developments in Havana from this era. The 670 hectares of green parkland and beautiful old trees surround an artificial lake, the Embalse Paso Sequito, just west of the much larger Embalse Ejército Rebelde, which was formed by damming the Río Almendares.

Although the park itself is attractive enough, the mishmash of facilities inside has fallen on hard times since the onset of the Special Period. Taxi drivers will wax nostalgic about when 'Lenin' was an idyllic weekend getaway for scores of pleasure-seeking Havana families, though these days the place retains more of a neglected and surreal air. Fortunately, help is on the way. New management and millions of pesos of Chinese investment are currently financing a major renovation project, but it's a big job that's still a long way from completion.

Sights

Parque Lenin
PARK

The main things to see in the park are south of the lake, including the Galería de Arte Amelia Peláez (admission CUC$1). Up the hill there's a dramatic white marble **monument to Lenin** (1984) by the Soviet sculptor LE Kerbel, and west along the lake is an overgrown **amphitheater** and an aquarium (admission CUC$2; ⊙10am-5pm Tue-Sun, closed Mon) with freshwater fish and crocodiles. The 1985 bronze **monument to Celia Sánchez**, who was instrumental in having Parque Lenin built, is rather hidden beyond the aquarium. A **ceramics workshop** is nearby.

Most of these attractions are open 9am to 5pm Tuesday to Sunday, and admission to the park itself is free. You can sometimes rent a **rowboat** on the Embalse Paso Sequito from a dock behind the Rodeo Nacional, an arena where some of Cuba's best rodeos take place (the annual **Cattlemen's fair** is also held here). A 9km **narrow-gauge railway** with four stops operates inside the park from 10am to 3pm Wednesday to Sunday.

ExpoCuba
EXHIBITION HALL

(admission CUC$1; ⊙9am-5pm Wed-Sun) A visit to Parque Lenin can be combined with a trip to ExpoCuba at Calabazar on the Carretera del Rocío in Arroyo Naranjo, 3km south of Las Ruinas restaurant. Opened in 1989, this large permanent exhibition showcases Cuba's economic and scientific achievements in 25 pavilions based on themes such as sugar, farming, apiculture, animal science, fishing, construction, food, geology, sports and defense. Cubans visiting ExpoCuba flock to the **amusement park** at the center of the complex, bypassing the rather dry propaganda displays. Don Cuba (☎57-82-87), a revolving restaurant, is atop a tower. The Feria Internacional de la Habana, Cuba's largest trade fair, is held at ExpoCuba in the first week of November. Parking is available at Gate E, at the south end of the complex (CUC$1).

Jardín Botánico Nacional
BOTANICAL GARDEN

(admission CUC$1; ⊙8:30am-4:30pm Wed-Sun) Across the highway from ExpoCuba is this 600-hectare botanical garden. The **Pabellones de Exposición** (1987), near the entry gate, is a series of greenhouses with cacti and tropicals, while 2km beyond is the garden's highlight, the tranquil **Japanese Garden** (1992). Nearby is the celebrated Restaurante el Bambú (p133), where a vegetarian buffet is served (a rare treat in Cuba). The **tractor train ride** around the park departs four times a day and costs CUC$3, gardens admission included. Parking costs CUC$2.

Parque Zoológico Nacional
ZOO

(adult/child CUC$3/2; ⊙9am-3:30pm Wed-Sun) Let's face it: you don't come to Cuba to see elephants and lions, do you? The Special Period was particularly tough on the island's zoo animals, and a visit to this park on Av Zoo-Lenin in Boyeros, 2km west of the Parque Lenin riding school, only bears out this fact. Though the zoo grounds are extensive and some fauna such as rhinos and hippos roam relatively free, the park is hardly the Serengeti, and many of the animals languish in cramped cages. A trolley bus tours the grounds all day (included in admission price).

Activities

Club Hípico Iberoamericano
HORSEBACK RIDING

(Parque Lenin; ⊙9am-5pm) This is in the northwestern corner of Parque Lenin. Horseback riding through the park on a steed rented from the club costs CUC$12 an hour, but horses rented from boys at the nearby amusement park, or at the entrance to Parque Lenin proper (you'll be besieged), costs CUC$3 per hour, guide included. Watch out for undernourished or maltreated horses.

Club de Golf la Habana
GOLF CLUB

(Carretera de Venta, Km 8, Reparto Capdevila, Boyeros; ⊙8am-8pm) The club lies between Vedado and the airport. Poor signposting makes it hard to find and most taxi drivers get lost looking: ask locals for directions to the *golfito* or Dilpo Golf Club. Originally titled the Rover's Athletic Club, it was established by a group of British diplomats in the 1920s, and the diplomatic corps is largely the clientele today. There are nine holes with 18 tees to allow 18-hole rounds. Green fees start at CUC$20 for nine holes and CUC$30 for 18 holes, with extra for clubs, cart and caddie. In addition, the club has five tennis courts and a bowling alley (⊙noon-11pm). Fidel and Che Guevara played a round here once as a publicity stunt soon after the Cuban missile crisis in 1962. The photos of the event are still popular. Che won – apparently.

Sleeping & Eating

Las Ruinas CARIBBEAN $$$

(Cortina de la Presa; 11am-midnight Tue-Sun) One of Havana's most celebrated restaurants – at least in an architectural sense – is situated on the southeast side of Parque Lenin. Melding off-beat modern architecture, including some eye-catching stained glass by Cuban artist René Portocarrero, onto the ruins of an old sugar mill, this place has an arty and elegant atmosphere, though the food (which is grossly overpriced) doesn't quite live up to the lavish setting. The menu includes lobster plus a selection of Cuban and Italian dishes, and you'll be lucky to get much change out of CUC$30. Overrated.

Restaurante el Bambú VEGETARIAN $$$

(Jardín Botánico Nacional; noon-5pm, closed Mon;) This is the first and finest example of vegetarian dining in Havana, and has been a leading advocate for the benefits of a meatless diet (a tough call in the ration-card economy of Cuba). The all-you-can-eat lunch buffet is served alfresco, deep in the botanical gardens, with the natural setting paralleling the wholesome tastiness of the food. For CUC$15 you can gorge on soups and salads, root vegetables, tamales and eggplant caviar.

Getting There & Away

Your public transport choices to Parque Lenin are bus, car or taxi. The bus isn't easy. The P-13 will get you close, but to catch it you have to first get to Vibora. The best way to do this is to get on the P-9 at Calles 23 and L. Havana taxi drivers are used to this run and it should be easy to negotiate a rate with stops for CUC$25 and up.

Getting Around

There's a Servi-Cupet gas station on the corner of Av de la Independencia and Calle 271 in Boyeros, north of the airport. It's accessible only from the northbound lane and is open 24 hours a day.

Santiago de las Vegas Area

While not exactly brimming with tourist potential, downbeat and dusty Santiago de las Vegas offers a fleeting glimpse of Cuba that isn't featured in coffee-table photo spreads. Visitors, if they come here at all, usually encounter this settlement – a curious amalgamation of small town and sleepy city suburb – every December during the 5000-strong

WORTH A TRIP

MUSEO HEMINGWAY

There's only one reason to visit the mundane if tranquil Havana suburb of San Francisco de Paula – the **Museo Hemingway** (unguided/guided CUC$3/4, camera/video CUC$5/25; 9am-4:30pm Wed-Mon). In 1939 US novelist Ernest Hemingway rented a villa called Finca la Vigía on a hill at San Francisco de Paula, 15km southeast of central Havana. A year later he bought the house (1888) and property and lived there continuously until 1960, when he moved back to the US.

The villa's interior has remained unchanged since the day Hemingway left (there are lots of stuffed trophies), and the wooded estate is now a museum. Hemingway left his house and its contents to the 'Cuban people,' and his house has been the stimulus for some rare shows of US-Cuban cooperation. In 2002 Cuba agreed to a US-funded project to digitalize the documents stored in the basement of Finca la Vigía, and in May 2006 Cuba sent 11,000 of Hemingway's private documents to the JFK Presidential Library in America for digitalization. This literary treasure trove (including a previously unseen epilogue for *For Whom the Bell Tolls*) was finally made available online in January 2009.

To prevent the pilfering of objects, visitors are not allowed inside the house, but there are enough open doors and windows to allow a proper glimpse into Papa's universe. There are books everywhere (including beside the toilet), a large Victrola and record collection, and an astounding number of knickknacks. Don't come when it's raining as the house itself will be closed. A stroll through the garden is worthwhile to see the surprisingly sentimental dog cemetery, Hemingway's fishing boat *El Pilar* and the pool where actress Ava Gardner once swam naked. You can chill out on a chaise lounge below whispering palms and bamboo here.

To reach San Francisco de Paula, take metro bus P-7 (Cotorro) from the Capitolio in Centro Habana. Tell the driver you're going to the museum. You get off in San Miguel del Padrón.

devotional crawl to the Santuario de San Lázaro (named after a Christian saint known for his ministrations to lepers and the poor) in the nearby village of El Rincón.

Sights

Mausoleo de Antonio Maceo MONUMENT

On a hilltop at El Cacahual, 8km south of Aeropuerto Internacional José Martí via Santiago de las Vegas, is the little-visited mausoleum of the hero of Cuban independence, General Antonio Maceo, who was killed in the Battle of San Pedro near Bauta on December 7, 1896. An open-air pavilion next to the mausoleum shelters a historical exhibit.

Santuario de San Lázaro CHURCH

(Carretera San Antonio de los Baños) The focus of Cuba's biggest annual pilgrimage lacks ostentation and is tucked away in the rustic village of El Rincón. The saint inside the church is San Lázaro (also known as *Babalú Ayé*; an *orisha* in the Santería religion), the patron saint of healing and the sick. Without irony, the large Los Cocos sanatorium housing lepers and AIDS patients is next door.

Getting There & Away

To get here, take bus P-12 from the Capitolio or bus P-16 from outside Hospital Hermanos Ameijeiras just off the Malecón.

Regla

POP 42,390

The old town of Regla, just across the harbor from Habana Vieja, is an industrial port town known as a center of Afro-Cuban religions, including the all-male secret society Abakúa. Long before the triumph of the 1959 Revolution, Regla was known as the Sierra Chiquita (Little Sierra, after the Sierra Maestra) for its revolutionary traditions. This working-class neighborhood is also notable for a large thermoelectric power plant and shipyard. Regla is almost free of tourist trappings, and makes an easily reachable afternoon trip away from the city; the skyline views from this side of the harbor offer a different perspective.

Sights

Iglesia de Nuestra Señora de Regla CHURCH

(⏲7:30am-6pm) As important as it is diminutive, Iglesia de Nuestra Señora de Regla, which lies just behind the boat dock in the municipality of Regla, has a long and colorful history. Inside on the main altar you'll find *La Santísima Virgen de Regla,* a black Madonna venerated in the Catholic faith and associated in the Santería religion with Yemayá, the *orisha* (spirit) of the ocean and the patron of sailors (always represented in blue). Legend claims that this image was carved by St Augustine 'The African' in the 5th century, and that in the year AD 453 a disciple brought the statue to Spain to safeguard it from barbarians. The small vessel in which the image was traveling survived a storm in the Strait of Gibraltar, so the figure was recognized as the patron of sailors. These days rafters attempting to reach the US also evoke the protection of the Black Virgin.

To shelter a copy of the image, a hut was first built on this site in 1687 by a pilgrim named Manuel Antonio. But this structure was destroyed during a hurricane in 1692. A few years later a Spaniard named Juan de Conyedo built a stronger chapel, and in 1714 Nuestra Señora de Regla was proclaimed patron of the Bahía de la Habana. In 1957 the image was crowned by the Cuban Cardinal in Havana cathedral. Every year on September 8 thousands of pilgrims descend on Regla to celebrate the saint's day, and the image is taken out for a procession through the streets.

The current church dates from the early 19th century and is always busy with devotees from both religions stooping in silent prayer before the images of the saints that fill the alcoves. In Havana, there is probably no better (public) place to see the layering and transference between Catholic beliefs and African traditions.

Museo Municipal de Regla MUSEUM

(Martí No 158; admission CUC$2; ⏲9am-5pm Mon-Sat, 9am-1pm Sun) If you've come across to see the church, you should also check out this quirky museum, which is spread over two sites, one adjacent to the church and the other (better half) a couple of blocks up the main street from the ferry. Recording the history of Regla and its Afro-Cuban religions, there's an interesting, small exhibit on Remigio Herrero, first *babalawo* (priest) of Regla, and a bizarre statue of Napoleon with his nose missing. Price of admission includes both museum outposts and the Colina Lenin exhibit.

Colina Lenin MONUMENT
From the museum, head straight (south) on Martí past Parque Guaicanamar, and turn left on Albuquerque and right on 24 de Febrero, the road to Guanabacoa. About 1.5km from the ferry you'll see a high metal stairway that gives access to Colina Lenin. One of two monuments in Havana to Vladimir Ilyich Ulyanov (better known to his friends and enemies as Lenin), this monument was conceived in 1924 by the socialist mayor of Regla, Antonio Borsch, to honor Lenin's death (in the same year). Above a monolithic image of the man is an olive tree planted by Bosch, surrounded by seven lithe figures. There are fine harbor views from the hilltop.

Getting There & Away

Regla is easily accessible on the passenger ferry that departs every 15 minutes (CUC$0.25) from Muelle Luz at the intersection of San Pedro and Santa Clara, in Habana Vieja. Bicycles are readily accepted via a separate line that boards first.

Bus 29 runs to Guanabacoa from Parque Maceo between the ferry terminal and the Museo Municipal de Regla.

Guanabacoa

POP 106,374

Guanabacoa is the little village that got swallowed up by the big city. In spite of this, the settlement's main thoroughfare, diminutive Parque Martí, still retains a faintly bucolic small-town air. Locals call it *el pueblo embrujado* (the bewitched town) for its strong Santería traditions, though there are indigenous associations too. In the 1540s the Spanish conquerors concentrated the few surviving Taínos at Guanabacoa, 5km east of central Havana, making it one of Cuba's first official *pueblos Indios* (Indian towns). A formal settlement was founded in 1607, and this later became a center of the slave trade. In 1762 the British occupied Guanabacoa, but not without a fight from its mayor, José Antonio Gómez Bulones (better known as Pepe Antonio), who attained almost legendary status by conducting a guerrilla campaign behind the lines of the victorious British. José Martí supposedly gave his first public speech here, and it was also the birthplace of the versatile Cuba singer Rita Montaner (1900–58), after whom the Casa de la Cultura is named.

Today, Guanabacoa is a sleepy yet colorful place that can be tied in with an excursion to nearby Regla (easily accessible by ferry).

Sights

Iglesia de Guanabacoa CHURCH
(cnr Pepe Antonio & Adolfo del Castillo Cadenas) The church on Parque Martí in the center of town, is also known as the Iglesia de Nuestra Señora de la Asunción, and was designed by Lorenzo Camacho and built between 1721 and 1748 with a Moorish-influenced wooden ceiling. The gilded main altar and nine lateral altars are worth a look, and there is a painting of the *Assumption of the Virgin* at the back. In typical Cuban fashion, the main doors are usually locked; knock at the **parochial office** (8-11am & 2-5pm Mon-Fri) out back if you're keen.

Museo Municipal de Guanabacoa MUSEUM
(Martí No 108; admission CUC$2; 10am-6pm Mon & Wed-Sat, 9am-1pm Sun) The town's main sight is the renovated museum two blocks west of Parque Martí. Founded in 1964, it tracks the development of the neighborhood throughout the 18th and 19th centuries and is famous for its rooms on Afro-Cuban culture, slavery and the Santería religion, with a particular focus on the *orisha* Elegguá. The museum has another arm further west along Calle Martí in the **Museo de Mártires** (Martí No 320; admission free; 10am-6pm Tue-Sat, 9am-1pm Sun), which displays material relevant to the Cuban Revolution.

Eating

TOP CHOICE **Centro Cultural Recreativo los Orishas** CARIBBEAN $$
(cnr Martí & Lamas; admission CUC$3; 10am-midnight) Situated in the hotbed of Havana's Santería community, this funky bar-restaurant hosts live rumba music at weekends, including regular visits from the Conjunto Folklórico Nacional. The pleasant garden bar is surrounded by colorful Afro-Cuban sculptures that depict various Santería deities such as Babalou Aye, Yemayá and Changó. Well off the beaten track and hard to get to at night, this quirky music venue is usually visited by foreigners in groups. It also does a good selection of food from a CUC$1 pizza to CUC$20 lobster.

Los Ibelly Heladería ICE CREAM $
(Adolfo del Castillo Cadenas No 5a; 10am-10pm) As close as Guanabacoa gets to the Coppelia, with quick-serve ice cream.

Getting There & Away

Bus P-15 from the Capitolio in Centro Habana goes to Guanabacoa via Av del Puerto. Alternatively, you can walk uphill from Regla, at which the Havana ferry docks, to Guanabacoa (or vice versa) in about 45 minutes, passing Colina Lenin on the way.

Cojímar Area

Situated 10km east of Havana is the little port town of Cojímar, famous for harboring Ernest Hemingway's fishing boat *El Pilar* in the 1940s and '50s. This picturesque, if slightly run-down, harbor community served as the prototype for the fishing village in Hemingway's novel *The Old Man and the Sea,* which won him the Nobel Prize for Literature in 1954. It was founded in the 17th century at the mouth of the Río Cojímar. In 1762 an invading British army landed here on its way through to take Havana; in 1994 thousands of 'rafters' split from the sheltered but rocky bay, lured to Florida by US radio broadcasts and promises of political asylum.

To the southwest of Cojímar just off the Vía Blanca is the rather ugly sporting complex and athletes' village built when Cuba staged the 1991 Pan-American Games.

Sights

Estadio Panamericano — SPORTS STADIUM

The huge 55,000-seat stadium on the Vía Monumental between Havana and Cojímar, was built for the 1991 Pan-American Games and is already looking prematurely dilapidated. There are also tennis courts, Olympic-sized swimming pools and other sporting facilities nearby.

Torreón de Cojímar — FORT

Overlooking the harbor is an old Spanish fort (1649) presently occupied by the Cuban Coast Guard. It was the first fortification taken by the British when they attacked Havana from the rear in 1762. Next to this tower and framed by a neoclassical archway is a gilded **bust of Ernest Hemingway**, erected by the residents of Cojímar in 1962.

Alamar — NEIGHBORHOOD

East across the river from Cojímar is a large housing estate of prefabricated apartment blocks built by *micro brigadas* (small armies of workers responsible for building much of the postrevolutionary housing), beginning in 1971. This is the birthplace of Cuban rap and the annual hip-hop festival is still centered here.

Sleeping

Hotel Panamericano — HOTEL $

(☎95-10-00/10; s/d incl breakfast CUC$28/44; P❄≋) This four-story ugly duckling was used as the accommodations for the 1991 Pan-American Games (thank God Havana isn't hosting the Olympics). Inconveniently located and rough around the edges, the Panamericano establishment was due to reopen at the time of writing after a spell housing Operación Milagros (whereby Cuba's medical system offered free eye operations for tens of thousands of nationals). Call ahead to check the status.

WORTH A TRIP

SANTA MARÍA DEL ROSARIO

Santa María del Rosario, 19km southeast of central Havana, is an old colonial town founded in 1732. Unlike most other towns from that period, it has not become engulfed in modern suburbs, but stands alone in the countryside. The charms of this area were recognized by one of Cuba's greatest living painters, Manuel Mendive, who selected it for his personal residence. You can also see the local countryside in Tomás Gutiérrez Alea's film *La última cena,* a metaphorical critique of slavery.

Also called the Catedral de los Campos de Cuba the **Iglesia de Nuestra Señora del Rosario** (⏰5:30-7:30pm), on Santa María del Rosario's old town square, was built in 1720 by the Conde de Casa Bayona near the Quiebra Hacha sugar mill, of which nothing remains today. Inside are a gilded mahogany altar and a painting by Veronese. It is one of suburban Havana's most attractive secrets.

From the Capitolio in Centro Habana take the metro bus P-7 to Cotorro and then bus 97, which runs from Guanabacoa to Santa María del Rosario.

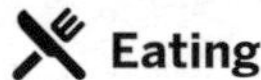

Eating

Restaurante la Terraza SEAFOOD $$$
(Calle 152 No 161; ⊙noon-11pm) Another photo-adorned shrine to the ghost of Ernest Hemingway, La Terraza specializes in seafood and does a roaring trade from the hordes of Papa fans who pour in daily. The terrace dining room overlooking the bay is pleasant. More atmospheric, however, is the old bar out front, where mojitos haven't yet reached El Floridita rates. The food is surprisingly mediocre.

Just down from the Hotel Panamericano is a **bakery** (⊙8am-8pm). Across the Paseo Panamericano is a grocery store, the **Mini-Super Caracol** (⊙9am-8pm), and a clean and reasonably priced Italian restaurant **Allegro** (⊙noon-11pm), which offers lasagna, risotto, spaghetti and pizza, all for under CUC$5.

Information

Bandec (⊙8:30am-3pm Mon-Fri, 8:30-11am Sat), which is just down the Paseo Panamericano, changes traveler's checks and gives cash advances.

Getting There & Away

Metro bus P-8 goes to the Villa Panamericano from the Capitolio in Centro Habana. From the hotel it's around 2km downhill through the village to the Hemingway bust.

Casablanca

Casablanca, just across the harbor from Habana Vieja and in the shadow of La Cabaña fort, is a small village surrounded by urbanization. It's dominated by a white marble **statue of Christ** (Estatua de Cristo; Map p65), created in 1958 by Jilma Madera. It was promised to President Batista by his wife after the US-backed dictator survived an attempt on his life in the Presidential Palace in March 1957, but was (ironically) unveiled on Christmas Day 1958 one week before the dictator fled the country. As you disembark the Casablanca ferry, follow the road uphill for about 10 minutes until you reach the statue. The views from up here are stupendous and it is a favorite nighttime hangout for locals. Behind the statue is the **Observatorio Nacional** (Map p65; closed to tourists).

Passenger ferries to Casablanca depart Muelle Luz, on the corner of San Pedro and Santa Clara in Habana Vieja, about every 15 minutes (CUC$0.25). Bicycles are welcome. The **Casablanca train station**, next to the ferry wharf, is the western terminus of the only electric railway in Cuba. In 1917 the Hershey Chocolate Company of the US state of Pennsylvania built this line to Matanzas. Trains still depart for Matanzas three times a day (at 6:11am, 12:27pm, 5:51pm). You'll travel via Guanabo (CUC$0.75, 25km), Hershey (CUC$1.40, 46km), Jibacoa (CUC$1.65, 54km) and Canasí (CUC$1.95, 65km) to Matanzas (CUC$2.80, 90km) and dozens of smaller stations. No one on a tight schedule should use this train; it usually leaves Casablanca on time but often arrives an hour late. Bikes aren't officially allowed. It's a scenic four-hour trip (on a good day), and tickets are easily obtainable at the station.

Playas del Este

In Cuba you're never far from an idyllic beach. Havana's very own pine-fringed Riviera, Playas del Este, begins just 18km to the east of the capital at the small resort of Bacuranao, before continuing east through Tarará, El Mégano, Santa María del Mar and Boca Ciega to the town of Guanabo. Although none of these places has so far witnessed the kind of megadevelopment redolent of Cancún or Varadero, Playas del Este is still a popular tourist drawcard. During the summer months of July and August, all of Havana comes to play and relax on the soft white sands and clear aquamarine waters of the beautiful Atlantic coastline.

While the beaches might be postcard-perfect, Playas del Este can't yet boast the all-round tourist facilities of other Cuban resorts such as Varadero and Cayo Coco, much less the all-out luxury of celebrated Caribbean getaways. Come here in the winter and the place often has a timeworn and slightly abandoned air, and even in the summer, seasoned beach bums might find the tatty restaurants and ugly Soviet-style hotel piles more than a little incongruous.

But for those who dislike modern tourist development or are keen to see how the Cubans get out and enjoy themselves at weekends, Playas del Este is a breath of fresh air.

Each of the six beaches that dot this 9km stretch of attractive coastline has its own distinctive flavor. Tarará is a yacht and diving haven, Santa María del Mar is where the largest concentration of resorts (and foreigners)

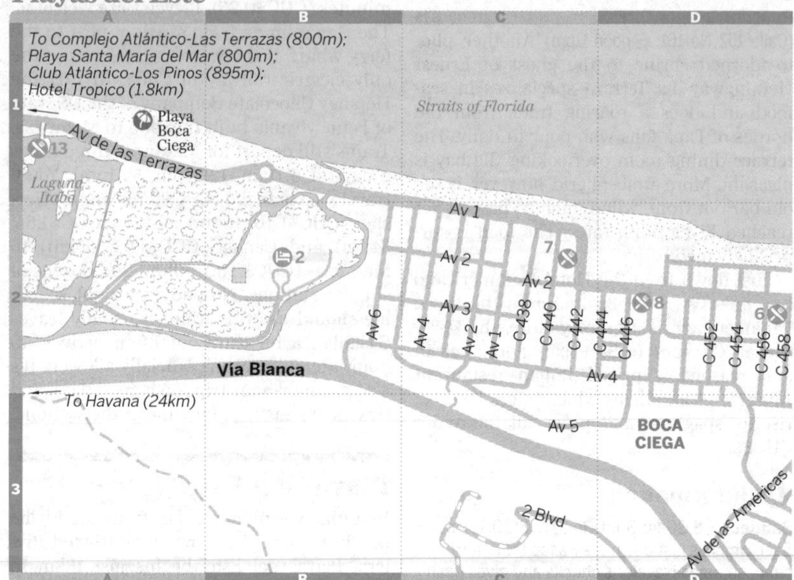

can be found, Boca Ciega is popular with gay couples, while Guanabo is the rustic Cuban end of the strip, with shops, a nightclub and plenty of cheap casas particulares.

Activities

Yacht charters, deep-sea fishing and scuba diving are offered by **Cubanacán Náutica Tarará** (☎96-15-08/9; VHF channels 16 & 77; cnr Av 8 & Calle 17, Tarará), 22km east of Havana. Ask about this at your hotel tour desk.

There are a number of **Club Náutica** points spaced along the beaches. The most central is outside Club Atlántico in the middle of Playa Santa María del Mar. Here you can rent pedal boats (CUC$6 per hour; four to six people), banana boats (CUC$5 per five minutes; maximum five people), one-/two-person kayaks (CUC$2/4 per hour), snorkel gear (CUC$4) and catamarans (CUC$12 per hour; maximum four people plus lifeguard). A paddle around the coast exploring the mangrove-choked canals is a pleasure.

Beach toys such as sailboards, water bikes and badminton gear may also be available; ask. Many people rent similar equipment all along the beach to Guanabo, but check any water vessels and gear carefully, as we've received complaints about faulty equipment. Consider leaving a deposit instead of prepaying in full, should anything go awry.

Sleeping

GUANABO

Guanabo has dozens of casas particulares and one passable hotel.

Elena Morina CASA PARTICULAR $
(Map p138; ☎796-7975; Calle 472 No 7B11 btwn Avs 7B & 9; r CUC$25-30; ❄) *Hay Perro* reads the sign, but don't worry, the pit bull that lives here is friendly (really), as is the hostess Elena, who once lived in Italy. The chatty host makes great coffee and rents two decent rooms with a leafy patio a few blocks back from the beach.

Pablo M Durán Jubiel & Rosario Redonda CASA PARTICULAR $
(Map p138; ☎796-5281; Calle 476 No 905 btwn Avs 9 & 9B; r CUC$25-30; P❄) A little house near the beach with a kitchen and patio; there are also rooms at Nos 906 and 9B01 nearby.

Villa Playa Hermosa HOTEL $
(Map p138; ☎796-2774; Av 5D btwn Calles 472 & 474; s/d with shared bathroom CUC$20/25; P❄@≋) This unpretentious villa has 47 rooms in small bungalows with shared bath-

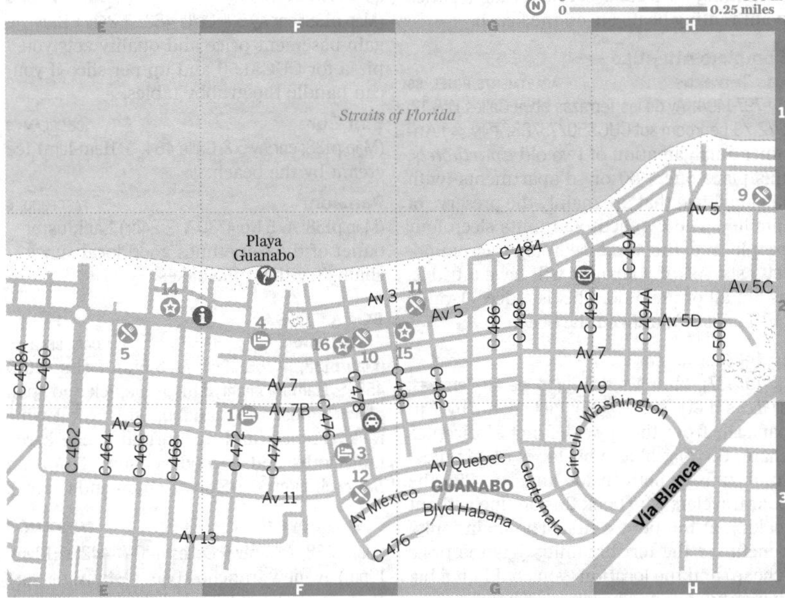

room and TV. It's a popular spot, so expect music, dancing and drinking to all hours; Playa Hermosa is 300m away.

SANTA MARÍA DEL MAR

None of Santa María's hotels is a knockout and some are downright ugly. The Blau Club Arenal is the closest the strip gets to Varadero levels of comfort.

Hotel Blau Club Arenal RESORT **$$$**
(Map p138; ☎797-1272; all-incl s/d CUC$95/150; P ❄ ≈) Playas del Este's most stylish option, this modern hotel is on the Laguna Itabo, between Boca Ciega and Santa María del Mar. It has 166 rooms set around a translucent pool. Ground-floor rooms have patios, but suites are much larger and cost about 20% more. The beach is just 150m away via a wooden footbridge suspended over the lagoon (which you can explore by rowboat).

Club Atlántico – Los Pinos APARTMENTS, HOTEL **$$$**
(☎797-1085; Av de las Terrazas btwn Calles 11 & 12; all-incl s/d/2-bed house CUC$105/150/160; P ❄ @ ≈) An amalgamation of two of Playas del Este's better resorts, the Atlántico is a 92-room hotel right on the beach, while Los Pinos is a collection of little houses (two to four bedrooms) with kitchens and TVs that were holiday homes before the Revolution. Collectively, they're one of the resort's best bets. Extra facilities include tennis courts, a

Playas del Este

Sleeping

Eating

Entertainment

swimming pool, cabaret and a Club Náutica point renting boats etc on the beach.

Complejo Atlántico – Las Terrazas APARTMENTS, HOTEL **$$**
(☎797-1494; Av de las Terrazas btwn Calles 11 & 12; 1-/2-/3-bedroom apt CUC$50/75/88; P ❄ ≋) Another amalgamation of two old *aparthotels*, this place offers 60 or so apartments (with kitchenettes) that are mainly the preserve of families. The two-bedroom units sleep four people and the three-bedrooms accommodate six. Ask if your unit will have a fridge, as not all of them do. This is a decent-value choice just 100m from the beach.

Hotel Tropicoco RESORT **$$**
(☎797-1371; btwn Avs del Sur & de las Terrazas; all-incl s/d CUC$69/99; ≋) Picked up by Cubanacán from the now defunct Horizontes chain, this big blue monster is an architectural disaster both inside and out. Pity the poor travelers who book this on-line without looking at the photos first. The main (only) benefit for the terribly unfussy is the price (cheap) and the location (you could hit a big home run onto the beach from here).

BACURANAO

Villa Bacuranao HOTEL **$**
(☎65-76-45; s/d CUC$38/44) On the Vía Blanca, 18km east of Havana, this is the closest beach resort to Havana. There's a long sandy beach between the resort and mouth of the Río Bacuranao, across which is the old Torreón de Bacuranao (inside the compound of the military academy and inaccessible). The beach here isn't as attractive as its more easterly counterparts, but the price is nice.

Eating

Surprise! Playas del Este does some good pizza.

GUANABO

Paladar el Piccolo PALADAR, ITALIAN **$$**
(Map p138; ☎796-4300; cnr Av 5 & Calle 502; ⊙noon-11pm) This paladar is a bit of an open secret among *habaneros*, some of whom consider it to be the best pizza restaurant in Cuba. Out of the way and a little more expensive than Playas del Este's other numerous pizza joints, it's well worth the walk.

Restaurante Maeda PALADAR **$$**
(Map p138; Av Quebec; ⊙noon-midnight) Guanabo's other paladar is still going strong hidden away on the hill (near Calle 476). It's enthusiastically recommended by locals.

Pizzería al Mare PIZZA **$**
(Map p138; cnr Av 5 & Calle 482; ⊙24hr) Bargain-basement price and quality gets you pizza for CUC$1.50 and up per slice if you can handle the grubby tables.

Bim Bom ICE CREAM **$**
(Map p138; cnr Av 5 & Calle 464; ⊙11am-1am) Ice cream by the beach.

Pan.com FAST FOOD **$**
(Map p138; Av 5 No 47802; ⊙24hr) Lackluster outlet of the sometimes good local snack chain. Try the milkshakes.

BOCA CIEGA

El Cubano CARIBBEAN **$$**
(Map p138; ☎796-4061; Av 5 btwn Calles 456 & 458; ⊙11am-midnight) This is a spick and span place almost in Guanabo, with a full wine rack (French and Californian), checkered tablecloths and a good version of *Gordon Bleu* (chicken stuffed with ham and cheese).

Los Caneyes CARIBBEAN **$**
(Map p138; Av 1 btwn Calles 440 & 442; ⊙10am-10pm) A new rancho-style restaurant just steps from the east end of Boca Ciega beach with a thatched roof and open sides. The food is pretty traditional, but the fish dishes taste better with the sea breeze lapping round your nostrils.

SANTA MARÍA DEL MAR

Restaurante Mi Cayito CARIBBEAN **$$**
(Map p138; ☎797-1339; ⊙10am-6pm) On a tiny island in the Laguna Itabo, this place serves lobster, shrimp and grilled fish in an open-air locale. There's a live show here every Saturday and Sunday at 3pm that you can enjoy for the price of a drink.

Restaurante Mi Casita de Coral SEAFOOD **$$**
(cnr Av del Sur & Calle 8; ⊙10am-11pm) Tucked just off the roundabout by the international clinic. This secluded little place is surprisingly upscale for this neck of the woods. Serves good seafood at reasonable prices.

Don Pepe SEAFOOD **$**
(Av de las Terrazas; ⊙10am-11pm) When the Guanabo pizza gets too much, head to this thatched-roof, beach-style restaurant about 50m from the sand. It specializes in seafood.

Self-Catering

Among the many small grocery stores in and around Santa María del Mar are **Minisuper la Barca** (cnr Av 5 & Calle 446; ⊙9:15am-6:45pm Mon-Sat, 9:15am-2:45pm Sun); **Mini-Super**

Santa María (cnr Av de las Terrazas & Calle 7; ⏲9am-6:45pm), located opposite Hotel Tropicoco; and Tienda Villa los Pinos (Av del Sur btwn Calles 5 & 7; ⏲9am-6:45pm).

EL MÉGANO

Pizzería Mi Rinconcito ITALIAN $

(cnr Av de las Terrazas & Calle 4; ⏲noon-9:45pm) Located near Villa los Pinos, this place contains a surprisingly delicious pizza-fest (CUC$2 to CUC$3), plus cannelloni, lasagna, salads and spaghetti (CUC$2 to CUC$3.50).

☆ Entertainment

GUANABO

Cabaret Guanimar CABARET

(Map p138; cnr Av 5 & Calle 468; per couple CUC$10; ⏲9pm-3am Tue-Sat) An outdoor club with a show at 11pm; if you want to be in the front rows, it's CUC$16 for a couple.

Teatro Avenida THEATER

(Map p138; Av 5 No 47612 btwn Calles 476 & 478; 👪) General theater with children's matinees at 3pm Saturday and Sunday.

Cine Guanabo CINEMA

(Map p138; Calle 480; ⏲5:30pm except Wed) Just off Av 5, this movie house shows mainly action flicks.

SANTA MARÍA DEL MAR

Playas del Este's gay scene revolves around a beach bar called La Paté (Calle 1), near Restaurante Mi Cayito, at the east end of Santa María del Mar. You might also check all the way west on Playa el Mégano for cruising opportunities.

ℹ Information

Medical Services

Clínica Internacional Habana del Este (☎96-18-19; Av de las Terrazas No 36, Santa María del Mar) Open 24 hours; doctors can make hotel visits. There's also a well-stocked pharmacy on-site. This clinic was being renovated at the time of writing.

Farmacia (cnr Av 5 & Calle 466, Guanabo)

Money

Banco Popular de Ahorro (Av 5 No 47810 btwn Calles 478 & 480, Guanabo) Changes traveler's checks.

Cadeca Guanabo (Av 5 No 47612 btwn Calles 476 & 478); Santa María del Mar (Edificio los Corales, Av de las Terrazas btwn Calles 10 & 11)

Post

Post office (Av 5 btwn Calles 490 & 492, Guanabo)

Internet Access & Telephone

Etecsa Telepunto (Edificio los Corales, Av de las Terrazas btwn Calles 10 & 11, Santa María del Mar)

Tourist Information

Infotur Guanabo (Av 5 btwn Calles 468 & 470); Santa María del Mar (Edificio los Corales, Av de las Terrazas btwn Calles 10 & 11)

Travel Agencies

Cubatur and Havanatur both have desks at Hotel Tropicoco, between Av del Sur and Av de las Terrazas in Santa María del Mar. Their main business is booking bus tours, though they might be willing to help with hotel reservations.

ℹ Getting There & Away

Bus & Taxi

The Havana Bus Tour (see p121) runs a regular (hourly) service from Parque Central out to Playa Santa María, stopping at Villa Bacuranao, Tarará, Club Mégano, Hotel Tropicoco and Club Atlántico. It doesn't go as far as Guanabo. All-day tickets cost CUC$3.

Bus 400 to Guanabo leaves every hour or so from Calle Agramonte in Centro Habana and stops near the central train station in Habana Vieja. Going the other way, it stops all along Av 5, but it's best to catch it as far east as possible. Bus 405 runs between Guanabacoa and Guanabo.

A **Taxis OK** (☎796-6666) tourist taxi from Playas del Este to Havana will cost around CUC$20.

Train

One of the most novel ways to get to Guanabo is on the Hershey Train (p154), which leaves five times a day from either Casablanca train station or Matanzas. The train will drop you at Guanabo station, approximately 2km from the far eastern end of Guanabo. It's a pleasant walk along a quiet road to the town and beaches.

ℹ Getting Around

A large guarded parking area is off Calle 7, between Av de las Terrazas and Av del Sur, near Hotel Tropicoco (CUC$1 a day from 8am to 7pm). Several other paid parking areas are along Playa Santa María del Mar.

Cubacar Club Atlántico (☎797-1650); Hotel Blau Club Arenal (☎797-1272); Guanabo (☎796-6997; cnr Calle 478 & Av 9) Rents average-sized cars for far from average prices – bank on CUC$70 a day with insurance.

Servi-Cupet Guanabo (cnr Av 5 & Calle 464); west of Bacuranao (Vía Blanca) Both gas stations have snack bars and are open 24 hours. The gas station west of Bacuranao is opposite the military academy.

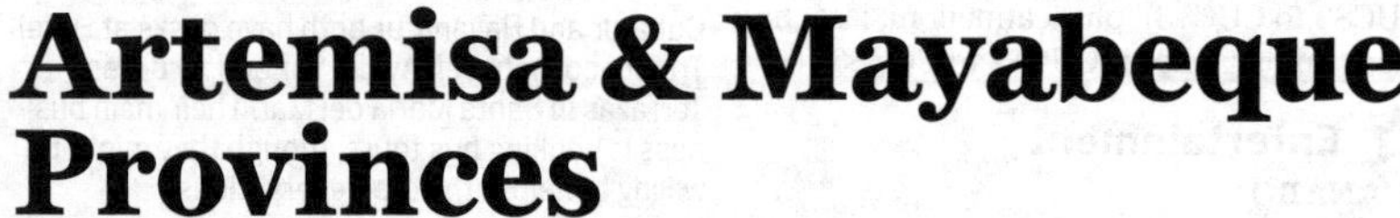

Artemisa & Mayabeque Provinces

047 / POP 883,838

Includes »

Best Places to Eat

» El Romero (p150)

» Patio de María (p151)

» El Criollo (p155)

Best Places to Stay

» Hotel Moka (p150)

» Hospedaje los Sauces (p147)

» Hotel & Villas Soroa (p147)

» Campismo los Cocos (p153)

» Hotel las Yagrumas (p145)

Why Go?

Glancing from your window as you leave Havana, you will see a flat, fertile plain stretching away from the capital. As far as the eye can see – west to the mountainous Sierra de Rosario and east to Matanzas province's wildlife-rich swamps – spreads a patchwork of dusty farmland and cheerful one-horse towns and hamlets. Travel-wise this has been bypassed by tourists, and has instead long been the bastion of weekending *habaneros* (Havana folk).

This could – possibly – be changing. Formerly Havana province, this region was has been redefined in 2011 as the all-new dual provinces of Artemisa and Mayabeque.

Artemisa's big draw is Cuba's gorgeously situated eco-capital, Las Terrazas. Mayabeque beckons with beaches of Varadero-quality sand (without the crowds), and one of Cuba's greatest train journeys: the delightful Hershey train, which traverses the gentle, lolling countryside to Matanzas.

Time, maybe, to step back and live Cuban-style: in the slow, infinitely more intriguing lane.

When to Go

The provinces' big attractions vary considerably climate-wise. Because of their unique geographical situation, Soroa and Las Terrazas have a microclimate: more rain and minimum monthly temperatures 2°C to 3°C colder than Havana. As it gets hotter later here than elsewhere in the region, February through May is the optimum time to visit, being warm without being significantly wet. April sees the provinces' premier festival, the International Humor Festival in San Antonio de los Baños; December through April is best for the beaches at Playa Jibacoa.

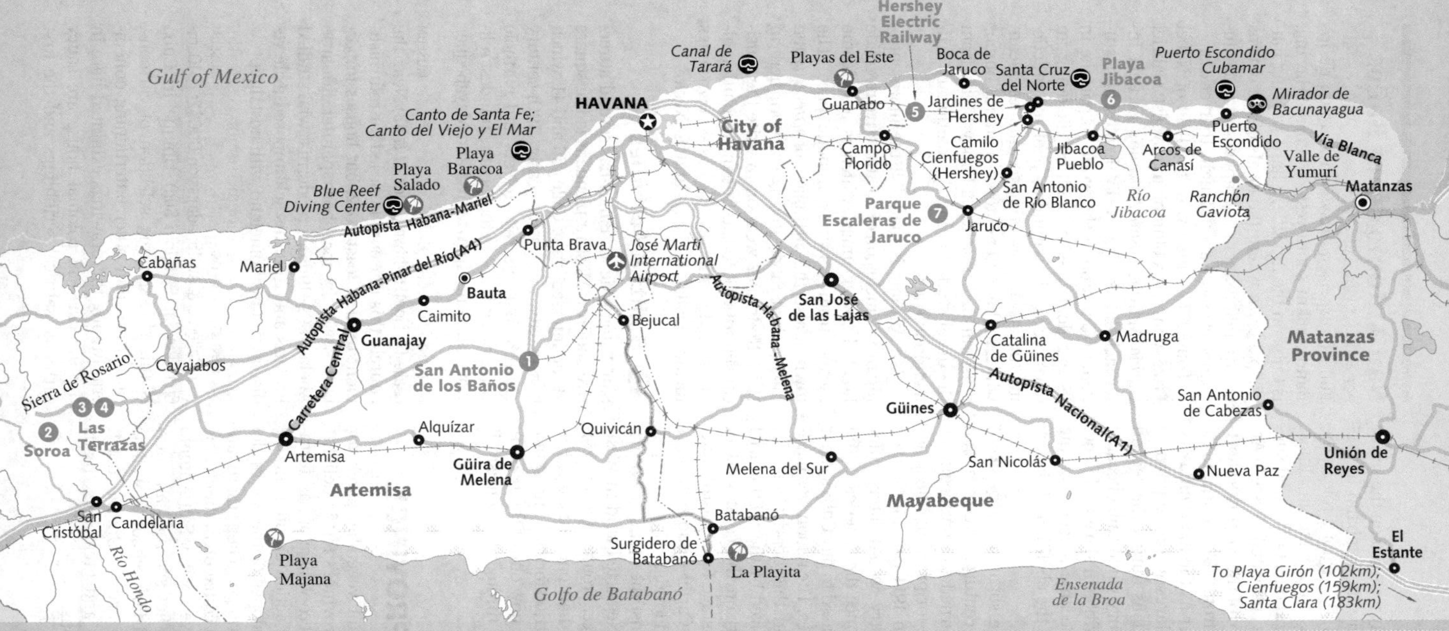

Artemisa & Mayabeque Provinces Highlights

1. Split your sides at San Antonio de los Baños' **Museo del Humor** (p144)
2. Hike the hills above verdant **Soroa** (p147)
3. Go green at **Las Terrazas** (p149), Cuba's primary eco-village where the slopes have been replanted with trees, orchids, painters and poets
4. Luxuriate at the **Hotel Moka** (p150) at Las Terrazas, the country's first and best eco-hotel
5. Escape the tourist trails on the historic **Hershey Electric Railway** (p154)
6. Bag a beach retreat with a cabin at **Campismo los Cocos** (p153) beside alluring Playa Jibacoa
7. Feast with a view and with weekending Havana folk at scenic **Parque Escaleras de Jaruco** (p155)

History

Havana was originally founded on the site of modern-day Surgidero de Batabanó in 1515 but rapidly relocated; the region's role in the shaping of Cuba was to become an almost exclusively agricultural one. Coffee and sugar were the key crops cultivated. Western Artemisa was the centre of the country's short-lived coffee boom from 1820 until 1840, when sugar took over as the main industry. Large numbers of slaves were recruited to work on the plantations during the second half of the 19th century when Cuba became the centre of the Caribbean slave trade and, as such, the area became a focus for the events leading up to the abolition of slavery in the 1880s.

The success of the sugar industry swept over into the 20th century: sweets mogul Milton S Hershey turned to Mayabeque as a dependable source for providing sugar for his milk chocolate in 1914 (see p154). Even this lucrative industry would later suffer under Fidel Castro, once the Americans and then the Russians ceased to buy Cuba's sugar at over-the-odds prices. The region was hard-hit economically, and this deprivation was perhaps best epitomized by the 1980 Mariel Boatlift, when a port on the coast west of Havana became the stage for a Castro-sanctioned (and Jimmy Carter–endorsed) mass exodus of Cubans to Florida.

A major step against the area's downturn was taken in 1968. Neglected land in Western Artemisa province, around the very coffee plantations that had once sustained it, was reforested and transformed into a pioneering eco-village – now one of the region's economic mainstays through the tourism it has generated.

ARTEMISA PROVINCE

In many ways a giant vegetable patch for Havana, Artemisa province's fertile delights include the verdant eco-village of Las Terrazas and the outdoor action on offer among the scenic forested slopes of the Sierra del Rosario mountain range. Then there are myriad mystery-clad coffee plantation ruins and the ever-inventive town of San Antonio de los Baños, which has spawned an internationally renowned film school as well as some of Cuba's top artists. On the north coast, good beaches and great back roads entice the adventurous.

San Antonio de los Baños

POP 49,942

Full of surprises, artsy San Antonio de los Baños, 35km southwest of central Havana, is Cuba on the flip side, a hard-working municipal town where the local college churns out wannabe cinematographers and the museums are more about laughs than crafts.

Founded in 1986 with the help of Nobel Prize–winning Columbian novelist Gabriel García Márquez, San Antonio's Escuela Internacional de Cine y TV invites film students from around the world to partake in its excellent on-site facilities, including an Olympic-sized swimming pool for practicing underwater shooting techniques. Meanwhile, in the center of town, a unique humor museum makes a ha-ha-happy break from the usual stuffed animal/revolutionary artifact double act.

San Antonio is made all the more enticing by the inclusion of an attractive riverside hotel, Las Yagrumas, which is a welcome escape from Havana's frenetic pace. The town is also the birthplace of *nueva trova* music giant Silvio Rodríguez, born here in 1946. Rodríguez went on to write the musical soundtrack to the Cuban Revolution almost single-handedly. His best-known songs include 'Ojalá,' 'La Maza' and 'El Necio.'

Sights & Activities

San Antonio de los Baños has several attractive squares. Most resplendent is the square at the intersection of Calles 66 and 41, which boasts an impressive early 19th-century **church**. With its twin towers and porthole windows, it is one of the largest, grandest religious buildings in Artemisa and Mayabeque.

Museo Municipal MUSEUM
(Calle 66 No 4113 btwn Calles 41 & 43) Near the church, this museum is closed for refurbishment until at least 2012, but houses important works by local-born painter Eduardo Abela (1899–1965), a modernist who studied in Paris and from his self-imposed exile rediscovered his homeland with nostalgia.

Museo del Humor MUSEUM
(cnr Calle 60 & Av 45; admission CUC$2; ⌚10am-6pm Tue-Sat, 9am-1pm Sun) Unique in Cuba is this side-splitting selection of cartoons, caricatures and other entertaining ephemera. Among the drawings exhibited here in this neoclassical colonial house are saucy cartoons, satirical scribblings and the first

LOCAL KNOWLEDGE

ALBERTO LLORENS: MUSEUM CURATOR, SAN ANTONIO DE LOS BAÑOS

Art in San Antonio de los Baños is not just confined to the film school. The annual humor show has exhibited works by artists from 80 countries, including Cuban cartoonist and famous painter Eduardo Abela and René de la Nuez. Abela was born in San Antonio and his character El Bobo (the fool) was one of the first cartoons to publically criticize the Cuban government. The cartoons of de la Nuez spoke out against the Batista regime. That association between the town and pioneering art continues today: there are 115 professional artists practicing here. If you're not around for the humor festival in April, drop in to the Galeria Provincial Eduardo Abela to see which artists are currently being exhibited.

known Cuban caricature, dating from 1848. Look out for the work of Cuba's foremost caricaturist, Carlos Julio Villar Alemán, a member of Unión de Escritores y Artistas de Cuba (Uneac) and a one-time judge at the **International Humor Festival**, which is still held here every April (entries remain on display for several weeks during this period).

More local artwork is displayed at **Galería Provincial Eduardo Abela** (Calle 58 No 3708 cnr Calles 37; admission free; ⌚noon-8pm Mon-Sat, 8am-noon Sun).

Hiking

A footbridge across the river next to La Quintica restaurant leads to a couple of **hiking trails** around the leafy banks.

Sleeping & Eating

The main shopping strip is Av 41, and there are numerous places to snack on peso treats along this street. The pizzeria in the rose-pink building opposite **Banco de Crédito y Comercio** (Av 41 No 6004 btwn 60 & 62) is popular.

TOP CHOICE **Hotel las Yagrumas** HOTEL $
(☎38-44-60/-61/-62; s/d from CUC$15/25; P❄🏊👪) Good enough to be listed as a town highlight, Las Yagrumas is situated 3km north of San Antonio de los Baños, overlooking the picturesque but polluted Río Ariguanabo. With its 120 rooms with balcony and terrace (some of which face the river), it is generally considered to be one of the better Islazul hotels and is, as a consequence, popular with peso-paying Cubans. Buffet meals are surprisingly good and table tennis, a gigantic pool and hilarious karaoke add to a pleasant family atmosphere. The cover charge for pool use is CUC$6.

La Quintica CARIBBEAN $
(⌚Tue-Sun) A local peso restaurant, situated just past the baseball stadium alongside the river 2km north of town. There's live music Friday and Saturday nights.

☆ Entertainment

Taberna del Tío Cabrera NIGHTCLUB
(Calle 56 No 3910 btwn Calles 39 & 41; ⌚2-5pm Mon-Fri, 2pm-1am Sat & Sun) An attractive garden nightclub that puts on occasional humor shows (organized in conjunction with the museum). The clientele is a mix of townies, folk from surrounding villages and film-school students.

Getting There & Away

Hard to get to without a car, San Antonio is supposedly connected to Havana's Estación 19 de Noviembre (four trains a day), but check well ahead. Otherwise, a taxi should cost CUC$30 one way from central Havana.

Artemisa

POP 82,917

Becoming the capital of Artemisa province is unlikely to ever transform Artemisa into a tourist mecca: this farming town's days of affluence and appeal lie firmly embedded in the past. Having once attracted notables such as Ernest Hemingway and the famed Cuban poet Nicolás Guillén, and having grown wealthy on the back of 19th-century sugar and coffee booms, Artemisa declined when the importance of its main crops did. It's known now as the Villa Roja (Red Town), or the Jardín de Cuba (Garden of Cuba) for the famous fertility of its soil, which still yields a rich annual harvest of sugarcane, tobacco and bananas. If you're passing, Artemisa contains two national monuments, along with a restored section

PROVINCE SHAKE-UP

The latest shuffle-around in Cuba's territorial divides has seen the former Havana province, which ringed the capital, divided into two: Artemisa province to the west and Mayabeque province to the east. The split has seen Artemisa province gain the old Pinar del Río municipalities of San Cristóbal, Candelaria and Bahía Honda (which most significantly for the visitor includes Soroa and Las Terrazas). The split between Artemisa and Mayabeque provinces is along the line of Bejucal and Surgidero de Batabanó, both of which now fall into Mayabeque territory.

of the Trocha Mariel-Majana, a defensive wall erected by the Spanish during the Wars of Independence.

Revolution buffs may want to doff a cap to the **Mausoleo a los Mártires de Artemisa** (☎36-32-76; Av 28 de Enero; admission CUC$1; ⏲9am-5pm Tue-Sun). Of the 119 revolutionaries who accompanied Fidel Castro in the 1953 assault on the Moncada Barracks, 28 were from Artemisa or this region. Fourteen of the men presently buried below the cube-shaped bronze mausoleum died in the actual assault or were killed soon after by Batista's troops. The other Moncada veterans buried here died later in the Sierra Maestra. There's a small adjacent museum containing photos and personal effects of the combatants.

The **Antiguo Cafetal Angerona**, 5km west of Artemisa on the road to Cayajabos and the Autopista Habana–Pinar del Río (A4), was one of Cuba's earliest *cafetales* (coffee farms). It is now a national monument. Erected between 1813 and 1820 by Cornelio Sauchay, Angerona once employed 450 slaves tending 750,000 coffee plants. Behind the ruined mansion lie the slave barracks and an old watchtower, from which the slaves were monitored. The estate is mentioned in novels by Cirilo Villaverde and Alejo Carpentier, and James A Michener devotes several pages to it in *Six Days in Havana*. It's a quiet and atmospheric place that has the feel of a latter-day Roman ruin. Look for the stone-pillared gateway on the right as you leave Artemisa.

Artemisa has no accommodation for foreigners: Soroa is the nearest option. As if in compensation, several stalls at the town end of the road to Antigua Cafetal Angerona do mean peso pizza.

The **Artemisa train station** (Av Héroes del Moncada) is four blocks east of the bus station. There are supposed to be two trains a day from Havana at noon and midnight, but don't bank on it.

The bus station is on the Carretera Central in the center of town.

North of Artemisa

The coastline north of Artemisa is visited, though rarely, for its beaches and the little-used back road from Havana to Bahía Honda and the northern coast of Pinar del Río province. Beaches are stony more often than sandy and pollution is rife in places. The monstrous main settlement here, Mariel, is Cuba's second-most polluted town after Moa in Holguín province. Mariel, 45km west of Havana, is best known for the 125,000 Cubans who left here for Florida in April 1980. Once you see it, you'll want to flee, too, but Mariel has a redeeming feature: namely its proximity to a couple of good (and nonpolluted) beaches.

Twenty-two kilometers east on the Autopista is **Playa Salado**, a largely deserted beach with some 15 dive sites lying offshore, mostly accessed via excursion groups from Havana. The more developed **Playa Baracoa** is a few kilometers further east. Big dudes near the shoreline lean on old American cars supping beer while fishers throw lines from the rocky shore. A couple of basic beach shacks sell food.

Soroa

Soroa, 95km west of Havana, is the closest mountain-resort area to the capital and makes a popular day trip. It's above Candelaria in the Sierra del Rosario, the easternmost and highest section of the Cordillera de Guaniguanico. Soroa is nicknamed the 'rainbow of Cuba,' and the region's heavy rainfall (more than 1300mm annually) promotes the growth of tall trees and orchids. The area gets its name from Jean-Pierre Soroa, a Frenchman who owned a 19th-century coffee plantation in these hills. One of his descendants, Ignacio Soroa, created the park as a personal retreat in the 1920s, and only since the Revolution has this luxuriant region been developed for tourism. This is a great area to explore by bike (see p150).

Sights & Activities

All Soroa's sights are conveniently near Hotel & Villas Soroa, where you can also organize horseback riding and a couple of hikes into the surrounding forest. For an average hourly rate of CUC$6, you can arrange several guided hikes through the Hotel & Villas Soroa.

Orquideario Soroa GARDEN
(admission CUC$3, camera CUC$2; 8:30am-4:30pm) Tumbling down a landscaped hillside garden next door to the hotel is a labor of love built by Spanish lawyer Tomás Felipe Camacho in the late 1940s in memory of his wife and daughter. Camacho traveled round the world to amass his collection of 700 orchid species (the largest in Cuba), including many endemic plants. Though he died in the 1960s, the Orquideario, connected to the University of Pinar del Río, lives on with guided tours in Spanish or English.

La Rosita ECO-VILLAGE, HIKE
The most exciting trail here is to the village of La Rosita, perched in the hills beyond the Hotel. Besides great bird-watching en route, the focus is on spending time at this pioneering eco-community established in 1997, meeting the people, finding out about their way of life and tasting the coffee cultivated on the plantations here. It's one of the all too rare, hands-on opportunities to experience rural life as Cubans do – without the gimmicks and the 'acting up' to tourists. La Rosita is accessed via the El Brujito path; the route is 5km or 17km, depending on your preference.

Castillo de las Nubes CASTLE
A romantic castle with a circular tower on a hilltop above the Orquideario, the Castillo de las Nubes (Castle of the Clouds) makes for a good leg stretch. There are good views of the Valle de Soroa and the coastal plain from the ridge beyond the bar, but the interior – formerly a restaurant – is currently closed to visitors.

Other trails lead to a rock formation known as **Labyrinth de la Sierra Derrumbada** and an idyllic bathing pool, the **Poza del Amor** (Pond of Love). Ask at the hotel.

Swimming

Salto del Arco Iris WATERFALL
(admission CUC$3) This is a 22m waterfall on the Arroyo Manantiales. The entrance to the park encompassing it is to the right just before the hotel. The falls are at their most impressive in the May-to-October rainy season; otherwise it's a trickle. You can swim here. Entry is free for Hotel & Villas Soroa guests.

Baños Romanos THERMAL BATHS
(per hr CUC$5) On the opposite side of the stream from the waterfall car park is a stone bathhouse with a pool of cold sulfurous water. Ask at the hotel about the baths and massage treatments. It's a half-hour steep scramble up the hill from the bathhouse to the **Mirador**, a rocky crag with a sweeping view of all Soroa.

Bird-Watching

This part of the Sierra del Rosario boasts one of the best bird-watching sites in western Cuba after the Cienaga de Zapata. You don't have to venture far from the Hotel & Villas Soroa to see species such as the Cuban Trogan and the entertaining Cuban Tody. Guided tours, arranged through the hotel, are CUC$6 per hour.

Sleeping & Eating

Several signposted houses on the road from Candelaria to Soroa, 3km below the Hotel & Villas Soroa, rent rooms and concoct meals. These are also worth considering as bases for visiting Las Terrazas.

TOP CHOICE **Hospedaje los Sauces** CASA PARTICULAR $
(527-38277; Carretera a Soroa Km 3; r CUC$20-25; P ❄) Even Soroa's *orquideario* (orchid farm) might seem underwhelming after a stay at this vibrant bungalow, 5km south of the hotel and hiding inside a garden lined with fruit trees and flowers. Rooms are cozy and homely, and dinner is served on a delightful sheltered patio behind the house.

Hotel & Villas Soroa RESORT $
(52-35-34; all-incl s/d CUC$46/66; P ❄ ≋) You can't knock the setting of this place: nestled in a narrow valley amid stately trees and verdant hills. But if you've just drifted over from ecofriendly Hotel Moka (p150), you might wonder what the architect was thinking when he juxtaposed these scattered blocklike cabins against such a breathtaking natural backdrop. Isolated and tranquil, there are 80 rooms in this spacious complex, along with an inviting pool, a small shop and an OK restaurant. The forest is just shouting distance from your front door.

Maité Delgado CASA PARTICULAR $
(☎522-70069; Carretera a Soroa Km 7; r CUC$20-25; P❄) This accommodation is within easy walking distance of the Soroa sights, the family is pleasant and there are kitchen privileges. If it's full, the owners will point you down the road in the direction of a few other houses.

Restaurante el Salto CARIBBEAN $
(⏰9am-4pm) This simple place next to the Baños Romanos is your only eating option outside the hotel.

Getting There & Away

The Havana–Viñales Víazul bus stops in Las Terrazas, but not Soroa; you can cover the last 16km in a taxi for approximately CUC$8. If staying at a casa particular, ask about lifts. Transfer buses (not to be depended upon) sometimes pass through Soroa between Viñales and Havana. Inquire at Hotel & Villas Soroa, or at Havanatur in Viñales (p188) or Havana (p118).

The only other access to Soroa and the surrounding area is with your own wheels: car, bicycle or moped. The Servi-Cupet gas station is on the Autopista at the turn-off to Candelaria, 8km below Villas Soroa.

Las Terrazas

POP 1200

The pioneering eco-village of Las Terrazas dates back to a reforestation project in 1968. Today it's a Unesco Biosphere Reserve, a burgeoning activity center (with Cuba's only canopy tour) and the site of the earliest surviving coffee plantations in Cuba. Not surprisingly, it attracts day-trippers from Havana by the busload.

Overnighters can stay in the community's sole hotel, the mold-breaking Hotel Moka, an upmarket eco-resort built between 1992 and 1994 by workers drawn from Las Terrazas to attract foreign tourists. Close by, in the picturesque whitewashed village that overlooks a small lake, there's a vibrant art community with open studios, woodwork and pottery workshops. But the region's biggest attraction is its verdant natural surroundings, which are ideal for hiking, relaxing and bird-watching.

Sights

The Las Terrazas area supported 54 coffee estates at the height of the Cuban coffee boom in the 1820s and '30s. Today, coffee is barely grown at all, but you can discover the jungle-immersed ruins of at least half a dozen old *cafetales* in the area.

Cafetal Buenavista HISTORICAL SITE
About 1.5km up the hill from the Puerta las Delicias (eastern) gate, and accessible by road, are the restored ruins of Cuba's oldest coffee plantation, built in 1801 by French refugees from Haiti. The huge *tajona* (grindstone) out the back once extracted the coffee beans from their shells. Next the beans were sun-dried on huge platforms. Ruins of the quarters of some of the 126 slaves held here can be seen alongside the driers. The attic of the master's house (now a restaurant) was used to store the beans until they could be carried down to the port of Mariel by mule. There are decent views from here.

Hacienda Unión HISTORICAL SITE
About 3.5km west of the Hotel Moka access road, the Hacienda Unión is another partially reconstructed coffee-estate ruin that features a country-style restaurant, a small flower garden known as the **Jardín Unión** and horseback riding (CUC$6 per hour).

San Pedro & Santa Catalina HISTORICAL SITE
These 19th-century coffee-estate ruins are down a branch road at **La Cañada del Infierno** (Trail to Hell), midway between the Hotel Moka access road and the Soroa side entrance gate. A kilometer off the main road, and just before the ruins of the San Pedro coffee estate, a bar overlooks a popular swimming spot. After this it's another kilometer to Santa Catalina. A trail does lead on from here to Soroa (p150).

Looming elsewhere in the fecund forest and only accessible by hiking trails are the **Santa Serafina**, the **San Idelfonso** and **El Contento** coffee-estate ruins.

FREE **Peña de Polo Montañez** MUSEUM
(⏰Tue-Sun) The former lakeside house of local *guajiro* musician Polo Montañez is now a small museum containing various gold records and assorted memorabilia. It's right in the village overlooking the lake. Polo's most famous songs include 'Guajiro Natural' and 'Un Monton de Estrellas'; they captured the heart of the nation between 2000 and 2002 with simple lyrics about love and nature, during which time Montañez came to be regarded as one of Cuba's finest-ever folk sing-

NEW MODEL VILLAGE

Back in 1968, when Al Gore was still cramming at Harvard and the nascent environmental movement was a prickly protest group for renegades with names like 'Swampy,' the forward-thinking Cubans – concerned about the ecological cost of island-wide deforestation – came up with an idea.

The plan involved taking a 5000-hectare tract of degraded land in Cuba's mountainous west around the remains of some old French *cafetales* (coffee farms) and reforesting it on terraced, erosion-resistant slopes. In 1971, with the first phase of the plan completed, the workers on the project created a reservoir and on its shores constructed a groundbreaking new model village to provide much-needed housing for the area's disparate inhabitants.

The result was Las Terrazas, Cuba's first eco-village, a thriving community of 1200 inhabitants whose self-supporting, sustainable settlement includes a hotel, myriad artisan shops, a vegetarian restaurant and small-scale organic farming techniques.

The project was so successful that, in 1985, the land around Las Terrazas was incorporated into Cuba's first Unesco Biosphere Reserve, the Sierra del Rosario.

In 1994, as the tourist industry was expanded to counteract the economic effects of the Special Period, Las Terrazas opened Hotel Moka, an environmentally congruous hotel designed by minister of tourism and green architect Osmani Cienfuegos, brother of the late revolutionary hero Camilo.

Now established as Cuba's most authentic eco-resort, Las Terrazas operates on guiding principles that include energy efficiency, sustainable agriculture, environmental education and a sense of harmony between buildings and landscape.

The area is also home to an important ecological research center.

ers. His stardom was short-lived, however: he died in a car accident in 2002.

FREE Galleria de Lester Campa ART GALLERY

(⏲24hr) Several well-known Cuban artists are based at Las Terrazas, including Lester Campa, whose work has been exhibited internationally. Pop into his lakeside studio-gallery, on the right-hand side a few houses after Peña de Polo Montañez.

La Plaza PLAZA

(⏲24h) In the village, the area just above Hotel Moka encompasses a cinema, a library and an absorbing museum. All are generally open throughout the day, or can become so if you ask.

Activities

Hiking

First the good news: the Sierra del Rosario boasts some of the best hikes in Cuba. Now the bad: they're all guided, ie you can't officially do any of them on your own (and nonexistent signposting deters all but the hardiest from trying). On the upside, most of the area's guides are highly trained, which means you'll emerge from the experience both a fitter *and* wiser person. The cost of the hikes varies depending on the number of people and the length of the walk. Bank on anything between CUC$15 and CUC$25 per person. Book at the Oficinas del Complejo (p151) or Hotel Moka.

San Claudio HIKE

The biosphere's toughest hike is a 13km trail traversing the hills to the northwest of the community, and culminating in the 20m-high San Claudio waterfall. It is sometimes offered as an overnighter with opportunities to camp out in the forest (equipment provided).

El Contento HIKE

This 8km ramble takes you through the reserve's foothills between the Campismo el Taburete (for Cubans only) and the Baños del San Juan, taking in two coffee-estate ruins: San Idelfonso and El Contento.

El Taburete HIKE

This hike (6.5km) has the same start and finish point as El Contento, but follows a more direct route over the 452m Loma el Taburete where a poignant **monument** is dedicated to the 38 Cuban guerrillas who trained in these hills for Che Guevara's ill-fated Bolivian adventure.

Sendero la Serafina HIKE

Easier on the legs is the 4km La Serafina loop, starting and finishing near the Rancho Curujey. It's a well-known paradise for bird-watchers (there are more than 70 species on show).

Sendero las Delicias HIKE

This 3km route runs from Rancho Curujey to the Cafetal Buenavista, incorporating some fantastic views.

Valle del Bayate trail HIKE

A 7km trail beginning near the San Pedro *cafetal* and tracking downriver to the Santa Catalina *cafetal*. It's possible to continue to Soroa along this path. Ask when booking.

Swimming

Baños del San Juan WATERFALL, POOLS

(admission with/without lunch CUC$10/4) It's hard to envisage more idyllic natural swimming pools than those situated 3km to the south of Hotel Moka down an undulating paved road. These *baños* (baths) are surrounded by naturally terraced rocks, where the clean, bracing waters cascade into a series of pools. Riverside, there are a handful of open-air eating places, along with changing rooms, showers and overnight cabins, though the spot still manages to retain a sense of rustic isolation.

Baños del Bayate POOLS

(admission CUC$4) More natural baths; these offer a similar idyll on the Río Bayate near the San Pedro coffee-estate ruins.

Cycling

A 30km guided cycling tour takes in most of the area's highlights for CUC$22 (CUC$20 with your own bike). Inquire at Hotel Moka, which hires bicycles out for CUC$2 per hour.

Canopy Tour

Cuba's only **canopy tour** (per person CUC$25) maintains three zip lines that catapult you over Las Terrazas village and the Lago del San Juan like an eagle in flight. The total 'flying' distance is 800m. Professional instructors maintain high safety standards.

Sleeping & Eating

TOP CHOICE **Hotel Moka** ECO-RESORT $$

(57-86-00; Las Terrazas; all-incl s/d CUC$80/110; P ❄ ≋) Cuba's only *real* eco-hotel might not qualify for the four stars it advertises, but who's arguing? With its trickling fountains, blooming flower garden and resident tree growing through the lobby, Moka would be a catch in any country. The 26 bright, spacious rooms have fridges, satellite TV and bathtubs with a stupendous view (there are blinds for the shy). Equipped with a bar, restaurant, shop, pool and tennis court, the hotel also acts as an information center for the reserve and can organize everything from hiking to fishing.

Villa Duque CASA PARTICULAR $

(532-21431; Finca San Andres, Carretera a Cayajabos Km 2; r CUC$20 P ❄) Eco-tourism doesn't have to come at a cost. Those on a budget might wish to check out this farmhouse 2km before the eastern entrance of Las Terrazas, which has one spick-and-span room, a fridge full of beer, a wrap-around balcony and breakfast included in the price. The fresh country smells come free of charge, too.

TOP CHOICE **El Romero** VEGETARIAN $

(Las Terrazas; 9am-10pm) The most interesting place to grab a bite, this full-blown eco-restaurant (unique in Cuba) specializes in vegetarian fare. El Romero uses solar energy and home-grown organic vegetables and

CYCLING IN ARTEMISA & MAYABEQUE

Within touching distance of Havana is one of Cuba's best bicycling regions (see also, p514). With cars in the minority and bicycles the bona fide transport, drivers are both courteous and relatively rare, while roads branching off from the capital are tire-friendly and become virtually traffic-free very quickly. The routes from Havana along the verdant valleys and coast to Matanzas and the trip to Soroa are the two classics. Most of the 120-odd kilometer route to Matanzas is through Mayabeque province's sleepy rural hinterland, with ample opportunities to get off the main (but still pretty uncrowded) Vía Blanca. The most scenic way wends through the Playas del Este, Campo Florido, Jaruco, Jibacoa Pueblo, Arcos de Canasí and Mena. Heading southwest to Soroa, the Carretera Central is probably the best route, with more rural roads (and the only real climbs) after Artemisa.

herbs, and keeps its own bees. You'll think you've woken up in San Francisco when you browse the menu replete with hummus, bean pancake, pumpkin and onion soup, and extra-virgin olive oil.

Patio de María CAFE $
(Las Terrazas; 9am-11pm) A couple of doors down is the Patio de María, a small, brightly painted coffee bar, which might just qualify as the best brew in Cuba. The secret comes in the expert confection (María lives upstairs) and the fact that the beans are grown about 20m away from your cup in front of the airy terrace.

Casa del Campesino CARIBBEAN $
(Las Terrazas; 9am-9pm) Of the *ranchón*-style restaurants dotted around, this one adjacent to the Hacienda Unión is a visitor favorite.

Rancho Curujey CARIBBEAN $
Undergoing refurbishment at the time of writing, this *ranchón*-style set-up offers beer and snacks under a small thatched canopy overlooking a small lake.

Through the Moka you can also book five rustic cabins 3km away in Río San Juan (single/double CUC$15/25) or arrange tent camping (own tent/rented tent CUC$5/12). There are also three villas (single/double CUC$60/85) available for rent in the village.

You'll find other *ranchones* at Cafetal Buenavista, Baños del Bayate and Baños de San Juan.

Information

Las Terrazas is 20km northeast of Hotel & Villas Soroa and 13km west of the Havana-Pinar del Río Autopista at Cayajabos. There are toll gates at both entrances to the reserve (CUC$3 per person). The eastern toll gate, **Puerta las Delicias**, is a good source of information on the park, while the best place to get information and arrange excursions is at the **Oficinas del Complejo** (57-87-00, 57-85-55), adjacent to Rancho Curujey, or on the other side of the road at Hotel Moka; both places act as nexus points for the reserve. None of these information points should be confused with the **Centro de Investigaciones Ecológicas**, a research station approached via a separate driveway east of Rancho Curujey.

Getting There & Away

Two Víazul buses a day currently stop at the Rancho Curujey next door to Las Terrazas; one at around 10am from Havana to Pinar del Río and Viñales, the other at 4pm heading in the opposite direction. Occasional transfer buses pass through bound for Havana or Viñales. Inquire at Hotel Moka or contact the Viñales office of **Havanatur** (p188).

Getting Around

The 1950s-style Esso station, 1.5km west of the Hotel Moka access road, is one of Cuba's quirkiest gas stations. Fill up here before heading east to Havana or west to Pinar del Río. Most excursions organize transport. Otherwise, you'll have to rely on hire car, taxi or your own two feet to get around.

Bahía Honda & Around

The wild, whirling road north from Soroa along the coast to either Bahía Honda and the north of Pinar del Río province (west) or Havana (east) is surprisingly low-key and bucolic. You'll feel as if you're 1000 miles from the busy capital here. Forested hills give way to rice paddies in the shaded river valleys as you breeze past a picturesque succession of thatched farmhouses, craning royal palms and machete-wielding *guajiros* (rural workers). It makes a tough but highly rewarding cycling route.

Bahía Honda itself is a small bustling town with a pretty church. Despite its relative proximity to Havana, you'll feel strangely isolated here, particularly as the road deteriorates after Soroa.

Your nearest accommodation options are Soroa to the southeast and Playa Mulata (see p193) to the west.

MAYABEQUE PROVINCE

Tiny Mayabeque, now the country's smallest province, is a productive little place, cultivating citrus fruit, tobacco, grapes for wine and the sugar cane for Havana Club rum, the main distillery of which is also here. Tourists, predominantly Cubans, come here principally for the sandy coast in the northeast, drawn by the good-value resorts that back onto beautiful beaches for a fraction of the price of a Varadero vacation. Inland amid the workaday agricultural atmosphere lie some luxuriant scenic treats: landscaped gardens, the picturesque protected area of Jaruco, Cuba's best bridge (yes, really) and a classic Cuban train journey transecting the lot.

Playa Jibacoa Area

Playa Jibacoa is the Varadero that never was, or the Varadero yet to come – depending on your hunch. For the time being it's a mainly Cuban getaway with an all-inclusive resort, a hotel-standard campismo (national network of camping installations) and several other scenic sleeping options thrown in for good measure. Punctuated by a series of small but splendid beaches and blessed with good offshore snorkeling, Jibacoa is backed by a lofty limestone terrace overlooking the ocean. The terrace offers excellent views and some short DIY hikes. Travelers with children will find interesting things to do in the surrounding area, and the popularity of the region with Cuban families means fast friends are made wherever you go. The Vía Blanca, running between Havana and Matanzas, is the main transport artery in the area, although few buses make scheduled stops

SUGAR – A BITTER-SWEET HISTORY

As synonymous with Cuba as Che Guevara or Havana Club rum, sugarcane was first introduced onto the island by the Spanish in the early 1500s. With its flat rolling plains and fertile limestone soil, the colony quickly proved ideal for the new crop, and within decades sugar had become Cuba's leading export.

During the 17th and 18th centuries Cuba played second fiddle to French Haiti as a sugar producer. But following Toussaint L'Ouverture's 1791 slave rebellion, the pendulum swung inexorably west as thousands of exiled French planters arrived on the island, bringing business know-how and pioneering agro-industrial techniques.

Over the next two centuries, Cuba metamorphosed from a nascent regional sugar economy into the world's biggest exporter, with a huge influx of African slaves pushing production through the roof and making vast fortunes for a new class of wealthy landowners.

But the boom didn't last. Devastated by the two independence wars in the late 19th century, when huge swathes of cane fields were summarily razed, the industry faced ruin as production fell into a seemingly terminal decline.

However, it was only a temporary blip. Pulled out of the mire in the early 1900s by profit-hungry American businessmen who bought struggling Cuban mills and land on the cheap, sugar's comeback was as dramatic as it was sweet.

Cuba's second big sugar high took place between 1915 and 1920, when the world sugar price hit $0.22 per pound and annual production peaked out at more than four million tonnes. Enormous amounts of money were made, and Havana reaped the economic benefits with a lavish public works program that saw the construction of such landmark buildings as the US$17 million Capitolio Nacional (p66).

But Cuba's over-reliance on its sweet-tasting mono-crop would again come back to haunt it. Following the 1959 Revolution, one of the US government's first retaliatory acts was to cancel Cuba's preferential sugar quota in response to Castro's nationalization campaign. But the 'punishment' soon backfired. The next day the Soviet Union stepped in and bought up the US quota, and a 30-year Soviet-Cuban alliance was sealed right under Washington's nose.

Sugar production in Cuba peaked in 1970 when a bumper harvest hit nearly 10 million tonnes. But thanks to foreign competition, antiquated production techniques and the massive growth of the tourist economy, it's been declining ever since.

In 2002 the government shut down 70 of its 150 sugar mills. One notable casualty was the Camilo Cienfuegos (formerly Hershey) mill in Havana province (p153). Here, as in other sugar towns, laid-off workers were offered graduate study programs and continued to draw their full state salaries (around 400 pesos a month). The aim was to raise the basic level of schooling among ex-sugar workers from ninth to 12th grade and enable them to find new employment elsewhere.

These days Cuba produces a more modest 2.5 million tonnes of sugar a year, and skeletal factories such as Camilo Cienfuegos stand as soot-stained reminders of another era.

HAVANA CLUB'S HUB

Some 30km west of the province-spanning bridge, Santa Cruz del Norte is a quiet town that's home to a famous rum factory: the Ronera Santa Cruz, producer of Havana Club rum and one of the biggest plants of its kind in Cuba. Havana Club, founded in 1878 by the Arrechabala family of Cárdenas, opened its first distillery at Santa Cruz del Norte in 1919, and in 1973 a new factory was built with the capacity to produce 30 million liters of rum annually. No tours are currently available.

here, making Playa Jibacoa a more challenging pit stop than it should be. Just inland are picturesque farming communities and tiny time-warped hamlets linked by the Hershey Electric Railway.

Sights

Puente de Bacunayagua LANDMARK

Marking the border between Havana and Matanzas provinces, this is Cuba's longest (314m) and highest (103m) bridge. Begun in 1957 and finally opened by Fidel Castro in September 1959, the bridge carries the busy Vía Blanca across a densely wooded canyon that separates the Valle de Yumurí from the sea. There is a restaurant and observation deck on the Havana side of the bridge where you can sink some drinks in front of one of Cuba's most awe-inspiring views. Imagine dark, bulbous hills, splashes of blue ocean and hundreds upon hundreds of royal palm trees standing like ghostly sentries in the valley haze. The bridge restaurant is a favorite stopping-off point for tour buses and taxis.

Central Camilo Cienfuegos LANDMARK

Five kilometers south of Santa Cruz del Norte is this former sugar mill, once one of Cuba's largest and a testimony to the country's previous production clout. Known as Central Hershey until 1959, the mill, which opened in 1916, once belonged to the Philadelphia-based Hershey Chocolate Company, which used the sugar to sweeten its world-famous chocolate. An electric train track known as the **Hershey Electric Railway** (p154) used to transport produce and workers between Havana, Matanzas and the small town that grew up around the mill. While the train still runs three times a day, the mill was closed in July 2002. It now stands disused on a hilltop like a huge rusting iron skeleton.

Jardines de Hershey GARDEN

(☎20-26-85) The gardens here are on a tract of land formerly owned by the famous American chocolate tycoon, Milton Hershey, who ran the nearby sugar mill. They're pretty wild these days, with attractive paths, plenty of green foliage and a beautiful river, and this essentially is its charm. There are a couple of thatched-roof restaurants on-site. It's a serene spot for lunch and a stroll. The gardens are approximately 1km north of Camilo Cienfuegos train station on the Hershey train line. Alternatively, if you're staying in Playa Jibacoa, it's approximately 4km south of Santa Cruz del Norte. The road is quiet and it makes a nice hike if you're up to it.

Activities

There is good snorkeling from the beach facing Campismo los Cocos; heading westward along the coast you'll find unpopulated pockets where you can don a mask or relax under a palm.

Ranchón Gaviota HORSEBACK RIDING, KAYAKING

(☎61-47-02; admission incl meal CUC$8; ⏲9am-6pm; 👪) This activities center, 12km inland from Puerto Escondido, is usually incorporated into day trips from Matanzas and Varadero. It's approached via a pretty drive through the palm-sprinkled countryside of the Valle de Yumurí. The hilltop ranch itself overlooks a reservoir and offers such delights as horseback riding, kayaking and cycling, plus a massive feast of *ajiaco* (meat stew), roasted pork, *congrí* (rice with beans), salad, dessert and coffee. To get to the Ranchón, take the inland road for 2km to Arcos de Canasí and turn left at the fork for another 10km to the signpost.

Sleeping & Eating

TOP CHOICE **Campismo los Cocos** CABINS $

(☎29-52-31/32; s/d CUC$12/16; P❄📶🏊👪) The newest and, arguably, the plushest of Cubarmar's 80 or more campismo sites, Los Cocos has facilities to match a midrange hotel and a beachside setting that emulates the big shots in Varadero. Ninety self-contained,

THE HERSHEY TRAIN

'Cow on the line,' drawls the bored-looking ticket seller. 'Train shut for cleaning' reads a scruffy hand-scrawled notice. To *habaneros*, the catalog of daily transport delays is tediously familiar. While the name of the antediluvian Hershey Electric Railway might suggest a sweet treat to most visitors, in Cuba it signifies a more bitter mix of bumpy journeys, hard seats and interminable waits.

Built in 1921 by US chocolate 'czar' Milton S Hershey (1857–1945), the electric-powered railway line was originally designed to link the American mogul's humungous sugar mill in eastern Havana province with stations in Matanzas and the capital. Running along a trailblazing rural route, it soon became a lifeline for isolated communities cut off from the provincial transport network.

In 1959 the Hershey factory was nationalized and renamed Central Camilo Cienfuegos after Cuba's celebrated rebel commander. But the train continued to operate, clinging unofficially to its chocolate-inspired nickname. In the true tradition of the postrevolutionary 'waste not, want not' economy, it also clung to the same tracks, locomotives, carriages, signals and stations.

While a long way from Orient Express–style luxury, an excursion on today's Hershey train is a captivating journey back in time to the days when cars were for rich people and sugar was king. For outsiders, this is Cuba as the Cubans see it. It's a microcosm of rural life at the sharp end, with all its daily frustrations, conversations, foibles and – er – fun.

The train seemingly stops at every house, hut, horse stable and hillock between Havana and Matanzas. Getting off is something of a toss-up. Beach bums can disembark at Guanabo and wander 2km north for a taste of Havana's rustic eastern resorts. History buffs can get off at Camilo Cienfuegos and stroll around the old Hershey sugar mill ruins. The rest can choose between Playa Jibacoa, Arcos de Canasí and the beautiful Valley of Yumurí.

For more information on train times, stations and prices, see p137 and p205.

supermodern cabins are clustered around a pool set in the crook of the province's low step-like cliffs. Facilities here include a small library, a medical post, an à la carte restaurant, a games room, rooms for disabled travelers and plenty of walking trails. The downsides? Amenities were showing their age on our last visit and there's always the blaring poolside music – seemingly par for the course in Cuban campismos – to contend with. The campismo is also a fully equipped campervan site. As always, it's best to book ahead with Cubamar Viajes (see p118).

SuperClub Breezes RESORT **$$**
(☎29-51-22; all-incl s/d CUC$98/156; P ❄ @ ≋) Just east of Cameleón Villas Jibacoa, SuperClub Breezes is Jibacoa's only swanky choice (this author was even searched before being admitted!). It's a beachfront place that exhibits more panache than Playas del Este, but less pretension than Varadero. Laid out in front of a choice nook of sandy beach, guests are accommodated in attractive two-story bungalows that sit amid a tranquil mélange of blooming flowers, leafy gardens and trickling fountains. SuperClub also has a reputation for good food, entertainment and activities. Ocean view rooms (single/double CUC$110/176) are available for a price. Children under 16 are not accepted. Coming from Matanzas, the turn-off is 13km west of the Bacunayagua Bridge.

Villa Loma de Jibacoa CABINS **$**
(☎29-53-16; 1-/2-/3-/4-bed apt with shared bathroom CUC$15/30/40/45; P ≋) This popular place stands on a hill overlooking a small beach near the mouth of the Río Jibacoa, just off the Vía Blanca. The perfect spot for a family or group beach vacation, it is actually 13 individual houses of one to four rooms each sharing a TV, fridge and bathroom. As each one is different, and several rooms are a tad run-down these days, look at a few before deciding.

Eating is a grim prospect over this way unless you're in a hotel. You could try the Bacunayagua Bridge restaurant; otherwise there are a couple of bars around selling microwave pizza. Striking up a friendly conversation with the locals pulling in their fishing nets and arranging a meal might yield better results.

Getting There & Away

The best – some would say the *only* – way to get to Playa Jibacoa is on the Hershey Electric Railway from Casablanca train station in Havana to Jibacoa Pueblo (see p137 for times). There's no bus to the beach from the station and traffic is sporadic, so bank on hiking the last 5km – a not unpleasant walk if you don't have too much gear. The electric train also stops at Arcos de Canasí, but that's still 6km from the beach and it's not a good walking road.

One other option is to take crowded thrice-daily bus 669 from outside **Estación la Coubre** (Desamparados), just south of Havana's Estación Central, to Santa Cruz del Norte, still 9km from Jibacoa. Another alternative: go to the Havana bus station and take any bus headed for Matanzas along the Vía Blanca. Talk to the driver to arrange a drop-off at Playa Jibacoa, just across a long bridge from Villa Loma de Jibacoa.

Jaruco

POP 25,135

Jaruco, set back from the coast between Havana and Matanzas, is a good day trip for travelers with a car, moped or bike who want to give the beaches a body-swerve and instead sample quintessential rural Cuba.

Jaruco village is a wash of pastel-hued houses bunched along steeply pitching streets that wouldn't look amiss in the Peruvian Andes. The Parque Escaleras de Jaruco, 6km west via hushed unmarked lanes, is a protected area featuring forests, caves and strangely shaped limestone cliffs similar to the *mogotes* of the Viñales valley. Habaneros (residents of Havana) come here for bucolic weekend breaks, but otherwise the park is a forgotten oasis with outstanding *miradors* (viewpoints) over Mayabeque province. A handful of restaurants open up from Thursday to Sunday and blare out cheesy music, which can disrupt the serenity. The best of these is the pleasant *ranchón*-style El Criollo (11:30am-5pm), where you'll pay in pesos for various pork and fish-focused offerings. It's 32km to Jaruco from Guanabo in a southeasterly direction via Campo Florido, and you can make it a loop by returning through Santa Cruz del Norte, 18km northeast of Jaruco via Central Camilo Cienfuegos. A taxi from Havana costs CUC$30 one-way.

Surgidero de Batabanó

POP 26,994

Spanish colonizers founded the original settlement of Havana on the site of Surgidero de Batabanó on August 25, 1515, but quickly abandoned it in favor of the north coast. Looking around the decrepit town today, with its ugly apartment blocks and grubby beachless seafront, it's not difficult to see why. The only reason you're likely to visit this fly-blown port is to catch the daily boat to the Isla de la Juventud. Should there be unforeseen delays, either staying within the port confines or cabbing it back to Havana, however depressing, are preferable to spending any time in the town itself.

Fidel Castro and the other Moncada prisoners disembarked here on May 15, 1955, after Fulgencio Batista granted them amnesty.

Getting There & Away

The ferry from Surgidero de Batabanó to Isla de la Juventud (p163) is supposed to leave daily at noon with an additional sailing at 3:30pm on Wednesday, Friday and Sunday (CUC$55, two hours). It is advisable to buy your bus-boat combo ticket in Havana from the office at the main Astro bus station (p119) rather than turning up and doing it here. More often than not convertible tickets are sold out to bus passengers.

There's a **Servi-Cupet gas station** (Calle 64 No 7110 btwn Calles 71 & 73) in Batabanó town. The next Servi-Cupet station east is in Güines.

Isla de la Juventud (Special Municipality)

☎046 / POP 86,256

Includes »

Best Beaches

» Playa Sirena (p167)
» Cayo Rico (p167)
» Playa Larga (p166)
» Punta Francés (p159)

Best Places to Stay

» Sol Cayo Largo (p168)
» Playa Blanca Beach Resort (p168)
» Villa Choli – Ramberto Pena Silva (p161)
» Hotel Colony (p165)

Why Go?

Fabulous dive sites (Cuba's best) and phenomenal beaches seduce travelers to the country's quirkiest island these days, but Isla de la Juventud has in its past lives been a pirate's hideaway, a prison and even a giant school.

The history of La Isla – as locals call it – is as colorful as the shoals of fish off its idyllic shores. Prior inhabitants include the Siboney Indians (who left behind some of the Caribbean's most important prehistoric art), a young José Martí, countless crocodiles and prisoner number RN3859, better known as Fidel Castro.

Today life on La Isla is so laid-back it's almost becalmed. Few visit, but adventures far from the tourist loop beckon for the intrepid: reefs, sun-kissed sands and overwhelmingly hospitable locals.

At the other end of the Archipiélago de los Canarreos from La Isla is Cayo Largo del Sur, a tourist paradise famous for its turtles and large white (nudist) beaches.

When to Go

The highlights of a holiday to La Isla, Cayo Largo or any of the other mini-paradises in the Archipiélago de los Canarreos are the beach life, diving and snorkeling. The hottest times are therefore the best: July to August along with the cooler-but-balmy high season months of December to April. Anglers may wish to flock to Cayo Largo's September fishing tournaments.

Isla de la Juventud Highlights

1. Meditate on revolutionary days gone by at the hacienda home of José Martí, **Museo Finca el Abra** (p159)
2. Dance the night away in petite but party-mad **Nueva Gerona** (p162)
3. Explore the ominous prison where Fidel Castro was once incarcerated at **Presidio Modelo** (p164)
4. Investigate an important crocodile conservation project at the Isla's **Criadero Cocodrilo** (p165)
5. Dive amid wrecks, walls, coral gardens and caves at **Punta Francés** (p159), *the* best place to dive in Cuba
6. Watch turtles nesting on the moonlit beaches of **Cayo Largo del Sur** (p167)
7. Trek along the wide, white (sometimes nudist) beaches to Cayo Largo del Sur's **Playa Sirena** (p167)

History

La Isla's first settlers were the Siboney Indians, a pre-ceramic civilization who came to the island around 1000 BC via the Lesser Antilles and settled down as hunters and fishermen. They named their new-found homeland Siguanea and created a fascinating set of cave paintings, which still survive in Cueva de Punta del Este (p166).

By the time Columbus arrived on these shores in June 1494, the Siboney had long departed (either dying out or returning to the mainland). The intrepid navigator promptly renamed the island Juan el Evangelista, claiming it for the Spanish crown. But the Spanish did little to develop their new possession, which was knotted with mangroves and surrounded by a circle of shallow reefs.

Instead La Isla became a hideout for pirates (see p164), including Francis Drake and Henry Morgan. They called it Parrot Island, and their exploits are said to have inspired Robert Louis Stevenson's novel *Treasure Island*.

In December 1830 the Colonia Reina Amalia (now Nueva Gerona) was founded, and throughout the 19th century the island served as a place of imposed exile for independence advocates and rebels, including José Martí. Twentieth-century dictators Gerardo Machado and Fulgencio Batista followed this Spanish example by sending political prisoners – Fidel Castro included – to the island, which had by then been renamed a fourth time and was known as Isla de Pinos (Isle of Pines).

Aside from its Spanish heritage, La Isla has had its dose of English and American influences. In the 19th century families from the British colony of the Cayman Islands settled on the south coast. The infamous 1901 Platt Amendment included a proviso placing Isla de Pinos outside the boundaries of the 'mainland' part of the archipelago), and subsequently some 300 US colonists established themselves here.

The Americans stayed, worked the citrus plantations and built the efficient infrastructure that survives today. During WWII, the Presidio Modelo was used by the US to inter Axis prisoners, and by the 1950s La Isla had become a favored vacation spot for rich Americans, who flew in daily from Miami. Fidel Castro abruptly ended the decadent party in 1959.

Before the Revolution, Isla de Pinos was sparsely populated. In the 1960s and 1970s, however, thousands of young people from across the developing world volunteered to study here at specially built 'secondary schools' (see p166). In 1978 their role in developing the island was officially recognized when the name was changed for the fifth time to Isla de la Juventud (Isle of Youth).

ISLA DE LA JUVENTUD

The Caribbean's sixth-largest land mass, welcoming La Isla is a world apart from anywhere else on the archipelago. The laid-back pace and opportunities for getting (way) off the beaten track here will appeal to escape artists and adventure types alike. The social opportunities for mixing with locals around capital Nueva Gerona are excellent, while the island's southern half, with its preserved ecosystems and rich natural wildlife, is largely wilderness. The southwestern part of the island around Punta Francés is famed for magnificent scuba diving.

Nueva Gerona

☎46 / POP 47,038

Flanked by the Sierra de las Casas to the west and the Sierra de Caballos to the east, Nueva Gerona is a small, unhurried town that hugs the left bank of the Río las Casas, the island's only large river. It's a little-visited, cheap and incredibly friendly place with a cracking entertainment scene, and you could easily find that you're the only foreign face around.

Sights

This is a good area to discover on bicycle, with beaches, Museo Finca el Abra and the Presidio Modelo all only a few kilometers from Nueva Gerona. The folk at Villa Choli organize bike rental.

Museo de Historia Natural MUSEUM

(cnr Calles 41 & 52; admission CUC$2; ⊙8am-5pm Tue-Sat, to noon Sun) Want to feast your eyes on the natural history, geology and archaeology of the island, of Cuba, and of Latin America generally? Even if the answer's 'hmm...,' it's worth checking out this bright and friendly (if not mind-blowing) museum. There used to be a planetarium here, but questions about reopening this were invariably met

INTO THE BLUE

Protected from sea currents off the Gulf of Mexico and blessed with remarkable coral and marine life, Isla de la Juventud offers some of the Caribbean's best diving: 56 buoyed dive sites here include everything from caves and passages to vertical walls and coral hillocks. Wreck diving is also possible further east where the remains of 70 ships have been found in an area known as **Bajo de Zambo**.

International Diving Center (☎39-81-81, 39-82-82), run from the Marina Siguanea just south of Hotel Colony on the island's west coast, is the center of diving operations. The establishment has a modern on-site recompression chamber along with the services of a dive doctor. It's from here that you can be transported out to the National Maritime Park at **Punta Francés**.

Boat transfers to Punta Francés take an hour and deliver you to a gorgeous stretch of white-sand beach (there's a restaurant, but it was closed at the time of research), from which most main dive sites are easily accessible. Cream of the crop are **Cueva Azul** (advanced) and **Pared de Coral Negro** (intermediate), where you'll see lots of fish, including tarpon, barracuda, groupers, snooks and angelfish – along with the odd sea turtle.

Diving costs start at CUC$30. Nondivers can get to the wonderful Punta Francés beach for CUC$8. Enquire at **Hotel Colony** (☎39-81-81) about diving and other nautical activities on offer first.

with sighs and shakes of the head from staff. It's just before the distinctive tower of the Archivo Histórico on the Hotel Colony road.

El Pinero MONUMENT

(Calle 28 btwn Calle 33 & river) Two blocks east of Parque Central, you'll see a huge black-and-white ferry set up as a memorial next to the river. This is El Pinero, the original boat used to transport passengers between La Isla and the main island. On May 15, 1955, Fidel and Raul Castro, along with the other prisoners released from Moncada, returned to the main island on this vessel.

Museo de la Lucha Clandestina NOTABLE BUILDING

(Calle 24 btwn Calles 43 & 45) This former museum was recently flattened by a cyclone; rebuilding work when we visited looked very far from completion. A pity: this was formerly stuffed with fascinating Revolutionary artifacts, including reams of letters written by a then-imprisoned Castro.

Nuestra Señora de los Dolores CHURCH

(Calle 28 cnr Calle 39) On the northwest side of Parque Central, this dinky, Mexican colonial-style church was built in 1926, after the original was destroyed by a hurricane. In 1957 the parish priest, Guillermo Sardiñas, left Nueva Gerona to join Fidel Castro in the Sierra Maestra, the only Cuban priest to do so.

Museo Finca el Abra MUSEUM

(Carretera Siguanea Km 2; ⏲9am-5pm Tue-Sun) The teenage José Martí arrived at Finca el Abra on October 17, 1870, to spend nine weeks of exile on this farm, prior to his deportation to Spain. Legend has it that the revolutionary's mother forged the shackles he wore here into a ring, which Martí wore to his death. The old hacienda is directly below the Sierra de las Casas, and it's worth coming as much for the surroundings as for the museum. Cuban oaks and eucalyptus trees line the access road, and a huge ceiba tree stands next to the museum. The adjacent house is still occupied by descendents of Giuseppe Girondella, who hosted Martí here.

This museum is 3km southwest of Nueva Gerona, off the road to La Demajagua (the continuation of Calle 41). Coming from Motel el Rancho el Tesoro, go southwest a few hundred meters on a dirt road to another highway. Turn right and cross a bridge over the Río las Casas. At the next junction, turn right again and you'll soon come to a sign indicating the access road to Finca el Abra.

A dirt road just before the museum leads north to the island's former **marble quarry**, clearly visible in the distance. The quarry is moderately interesting (if you like big holes in the ground), but the real attraction is the climb up the hill, from where there are lovely views. After descending, continue north between a garbage dump and several rows of pig pens (not very attractive, but any loop has got to be better than

Nueva Gerona

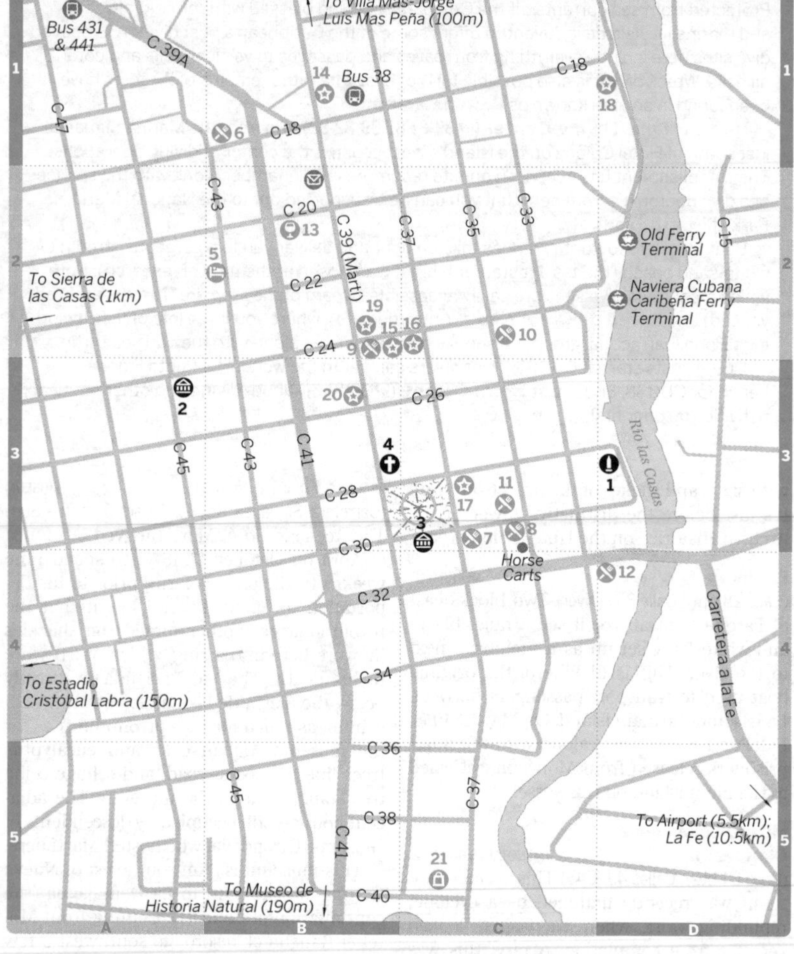

backtracking, right?) to Calle 54 on the right. This street will bring you back into town via the Museo de Historia Natural, six blocks to the east.

Museo Municipal MUSEUM

(Calle 30 btwn Calles 37 & 39; ⏲8am-1pm & 2-5pm Mon-Fri, to 4pm Sat, to noon Sun) In the former Casa de Gobierno (1853), the Museo Municipal houses a small historical collection that combines assorted pirate tidbits with the usual bones and birds.

Activities

Sierra de las Casas HIKING

It's possible to climb to this distinctively shaped hill from the west end of Calle 22. A few hundred meters along a dirt track, you will see a trail on the left toward the hills. At the very foot of the hill is a deep cave with a concrete stairway leading down to the local swimming hole. A trail beyond this leads to the mountaintop, from where you can see most of the north of the island.

Nueva Gerona

Sights

1 El Pinero ... D3
2 Museo de la Lucha Clandestina ... A3
3 Museo Municipal ... C3
4 Nuestra Señora de los Dolores ... B3

Sleeping

5 Elda Cespero ... B2

Eating

6 Cafetería la Cocinita ... B1
7 Coppelia ... C3
8 Cubalse Supermarket ... C3
9 El Cochinito ... B2
10 Mercado Agropecuario ... C2
11 Pizzería la Gondóla ... C3
12 Restaurante Río ... D4

Drinking

13 Casa de los Vinos ... B2

Entertainment

14 Bar Piano de Cuba ... B1
15 Cabaret el Patio ... B2
16 Casa de la Cultura ... C2
17 Cine Caribe ... C3
18 Disco la Movida ... D1
El Pinero ... (see 1)
19 La Rumba ... B2
20 Sucu Sucu ... B3

Shopping

21 Centro Experimental de Artes Aplicadas ... C5

Festivals & Events

Fiesta de la Toronja (Grapefruit Festival) is held on La Isla every March. Pucker up for this one.

Sleeping

Casas are your only town-centre options and will provide meals; the owners will invariably meet arriving ferries. Nueva Gerona's state-run hotels are south of town.

TOP CHOICE Villa Choli – Ramberto Pena Silva CASA PARTICULAR $
(32-31-47; Calle C No 4001A btwn Calles 6 & 8; r CUC$20-25; P✻@) Two large, modern 1st-floor rooms with TV, internet access, secure parking space, delicious food and – possibly the highlight – a gorgeous terrace with a hammock. You'll receive attentive treatment at this reader-recommended place. There are bicycles for rent, and port/airport pick-up can be arranged.

Motel el Rancho el Tesoro HOTEL $
(32-30-35; Autopista Nueva Gerona-La Fe Km 2; s/d CUC$25/36; P✻) This welcoming motel with its castellated front lies in a wooded area near the Río las Casas, 3km south of town, just off the Autopista Nueva Gerona-La Fe. There are 34 sizeable rooms here, with cable TV and a cozy restaurant (as good as Nueva Gerona's state-run eating scene gets).

Villa Isla de Juventud HOTEL $
(32-32-90; Autopista Nueva Gerona-La Fe Km 1; s/d incl breakfast CUC$29/33; P✻≋) About 5km from the airport and 2.5km from Nueva Gerona, this hotel has 20 rooms with fridges in two-story, four-unit blocks. Benefitting from great views (it's framed by the island's twin marble mountains), the hotel has a surprising amount of atmosphere, despite a somewhat desultory external appearance. It's only open in high season.

Villa Mas – Jorge Luis Mas Peña CASA PARTICULAR $
(32-35-44; Calle 41 No 4108 apt 7 btwn Calles 8 & 10; r CUC$20-25; ✻) Forget the rather ugly apartment-block setting; there are two above-average rooms here with recently refurbished full marble bathrooms. Jorge and his partner are formidable cooks and will serve you dinner on their refreshing rooftop terrace. It's just outside the town behind the hospital.

Elda Cepero CASA PARTICULAR $
(32-27-74; Calle 43 No 2004 btwn Calles 20 & 22; r 20-25; ✻) One of the most centrally located casas in town, and one of the best: large rooms, a self-catering pantry and a garden/terrace out back.

Eating

Casas particulares (most of which are licensed to serve food) serve better-value meals than any of the state-run restaurants.

Restaurante Río SEAFOOD $
(Calle 32 btwn Calle 33 & river; noon-10pm; ✻) Head here for fresh river and sea fish (one of the few places in Cuba where you can eat both). It's where the locals gather for good grub. You'll pay in pesos whether you opt for the *langosta* (lobster) or the signature paella dish. It has an outside terrace with a stereo

blasting out the latest Cuban pop and an air-conditioned interior.

El Cochinito CARIBBEAN $
(cnr Calles 39 & 24; ⏲noon-10pm Thu-Tue) Get your pork steaks, yucca, rice and beans here in one of the town's better restaurants. It has local art on the walls and even tablecloths on the tables.

Pizzería la Góndola ITALIAN $
(cnr Calles 30 & 35; ⏲noon-10pm) Offering a break from the pork-chicken-*congrí* (rice flecked with beans) staples, the pizza here is on par with other Cuban pizza places.

Cafetería la Cocinita FAST FOOD $
(cnr Calles 18 & 41; ⏲24hr) This is a good place for peso sandwiches and juice, or more substantial meals in the nicer sit-down section in the back.

Coppelia ICE-CREAM PARLOR $
(Calle 37 btwn Calles 30 & 32; ⏲noon-10pm Tue-Sun) Just to remind you you're still in Cuba, there's a Coppelia. Head here to satisfy all ice-cream cravings.

Self-Catering

Mercado agropecuario MARKET $
(cnr Calles 24 & 35) Try this large market for fresh vegetables and meat.

Cubalse supermarket SUPERMARKET $
(Calle 35 btwn Calles 30 & 32; ⏲9:30am-6pm Mon-Sat) Sells groceries and sundries.

Drinking

Casa de los Vinos BAR
(cnr Calles 20 & 41; ⏲1-10pm Mon-Thu, 1pm-midnight Fri-Sun) A nice local drinking hole with 'ahoy matey!' nautical decor. You can get weird and wonderful wine made from grapefruit, grapes and melon by the glass and mingle with the equally bizarre assortment of local characters.

Entertainment

Nueva Gerona's options are incredibly varied given this is a small town miles from anywhere. Live music is sometimes staged outside the Cine Caribe.

El Pinero BAR, NIGHTCLUB
(Calle 28 btwn Calle 33 & river) Loud music along with most of the town's teenagers and 20-somethings converge by the boat for alfresco dancing. Drink and snack stalls also set up shop.

Casa de la Cultura CULTURAL CENTER, LIVE MUSIC
(cnr Calles 37 & 24) Various forms of evening entertainment are held here. Ask about the famous local *sucu-sucu* (a variation of *son,* Cuba's popular music) group led by Mongo Rives.

Sucu Sucu BAR, LIVE MUSIC
(Calle 39 btwn Calles 24 & 26) A joint with live music and theatre: there's a board out front with upcoming events. When nothing else is on, it serves as an intimate drinking spot.

Bar Piano de Cuba LIVE MUSIC
(Calle 39 btwn Calles 16 & 18) Locals swear by this dark venue with an attached, half-decent restaurant and good La Isla music acts live at weekends (at other times it is missable).

Cabaret el Patio CABARET
(Calle 24 btwn Calles 37 & 39; per couple CUC$3; ⏲10pm-2am Thu-Sun) Next door to the Casa de la Cultura, this venue has an entertaining floorshow at 11pm. Show up early to get in; official policy is couples only.

La Rumba NIGHTCLUB
(Calle 24 btwn Calles 37 & 39; ⏲10pm-2am) Buy your drinks in the cagelike bar next door then head to the courtyard and hectic disco round the corner. If you don't dance hard, you'll stand out here.

Disco la Movida NIGHTCLUB
(Calle 18; ⏲from 11pm) For a little atmospheric booty shaking, join the throngs of locals dancing in an open-air locale hidden among the trees near the river.

Super Disco NIGHTCLUB
(admission CUC$1; ⏲from 10pm Thu-Sun) You've got to love a place with a name like this. The locals do: this club next to Villa Isla de la Juventud is always packed.

Cinemas

Cine Caribe CINEMA
(cnr Calles 37 & 28) For a film or video, check out this cinema on Parque Central.

Sport

Estadio Cristóbal Labra SPORTS
(cnr Calles 32 & 53) Nueva Gerona's baseball stadium, Estadio Cristóbal Labra is seven blocks west of Calle 39. Ask at your local casa particular for details of upcoming games (staged from October to April).

Shopping

Calle 39, also known as Calle Martí, is a pleasant pedestrian mall interspersed with small parks.

Centro Experimental de Artes Aplicadas (Calle 40 btwn 39 & 37; ⏲8am-4pm Mon-Fri, 8am-noon Sat), near the Museo de Historia Natural, makes artistic ceramics.

Information

Banco de Crédito y Comercio (Calle 39 No 1802; ⏲8am-3pm Mon-Fri) Has an ATM.

Cadeca (Calle 39 No 2022; ⏲8:30am-6pm Mon-Sat, to 1pm Sun) Also has an ATM.

Ecotur (☎32-71-01; Calle 24 btwn Calle 33 & river; ⏲8am-4pm Mon-Fri) Organizes trips into the militarized zone and to Punta Francés.

Etecsa Telepunto (Calle 41 No 2802 btwn Calles 28 & 30; ⏲8:30am-7:30pm)

Farmacia Nueva Gerona (☎32-60-84; cnr Calles 39 & 24; ⏲8am-11pm Mon-Sat)

Hospital General Héroes de Baire (☎32-30-12; Calle 39A) This one has a recompression chamber.

Photo Service (Calle 39 No 2010 btwn Calles 20 & 22)

Post office (Calle 39 No 1810 btwn Calles 18 & 20; ⏲8am-6pm Mon-Sat)

Radio Caribe Broadcasts varied music programs on 1270AM.

Victoria Local paper published on Saturday.

Getting There & Away

Air

The most hassle-free and (often) the cheapest way to get to La Isla is to fly. Unfortunately, most people have cottoned onto this. so flights are usually booked out at least a week in advance.

Rafael Cabrera Mustelier Airport (airport code GER) is 5km southeast of Nueva Gerona. **Cubana** Havana (☎834-4446; Calle 23 No 64 cnr Infanta, Vedado); Nueva Gerona (☎32-25-31; Calle 39 No 1415 btwn Calles 16 & 18) flies here from Havana three times daily for CUC$35 one-way. There are no international flights.

There are no regular flights from Isla de la Juventud to Cayo Largo del Sur.

Boat

Getting to La Isla by boat isn't easy. First book your bus transfer (CUC$5) at the **Naviera Cubana Caribeña (NCC) kiosk** (☎878-1841; ⏲7am-noon) in Havana's main Terminal de Ómnibus for the Astro bus (8am) to the ferry port; a second departure usually runs at noon (Wednesday, Friday and Sunday). Arrive at least half an hour before departure to beat the crowds.

The bus gets you as far as the port in Surgidero de Batabanó where lengthy, disorderly queues congregate at the office to pay for the boat (CUC$50) to Nueva Gerona. You'll then be ushered through airport-style security into a waiting room for a likely period of one to two hours before the boat departs. The crossing by catamaran takes about two hours 30 minutes; there are no printed schedules. If you take the early bus/boat and all goes well you'll be on La Isla at 4pm (total journey time eight hours, total ticket cost CUC$55).

Refreshments on this trip are either basic or not available and, as it's mostly Cubans traveling, often purchasable only in pesos. Due to limited space and perennial popularity, it is wise to make reservations a day early at the NCC kiosk.

Do not show up independently in Batabanó with the intention of buying a ferry ticket direct from the dock. Although technically possible, a number of travelers have come unstuck here, being told that the tickets have been sold out through the NCC kiosk in Havana. Furthermore, bedding down overnight in Batabanó holds little appeal for travelers.

The return leg is equally problematic. Procure your ticket the day before you wish to travel in Nueva Gerona's **NCC ferry terminal** (☎32-49-77, 32-44-15; cnr Calles 31 & 24), beside the Río las Casas. The **ticket office** (⏲Mon-Fri) is across the road. The ferry leaves for Surgidero de Batabanó daily at 8am (CUC$50), but you'll need to get there at least two hours beforehand to tackle the infamous queues. A second boat is supposed to leave at noon (with a check-in time of 9:30am).

Before reserving tickets, ask if there are sufficient bus connections from Surgidero de Batabanó to Havana and, importantly, that you have a reservation. A connecting bus should cost CUC$5.

Don't take anything as a given until you have booked your ticket. Isla boat crossings, rather like Cuban trains, have a tendency of being late, breaking down or getting cancelled altogether.

Traveling in either direction you'll need to show your passport. See Surgidero de Batabanó (p155) and Havana (p119) for more information.

There are three monthly boats from the Naviera Cubana Caribeña (NCC) ferry terminal in Nueva Gerona to Cayo Largo del Sur (6am, departing on the 5th, 15th, 25th of each month). These boats are primarily for workers and you may or may not be allowed to board.

Getting Around

To/From the Airport

From the airport, look for the bus marked 'Servicio Aéreo,' which will take you into town for one peso. To get to the airport, catch this bus in front of Cine Caribe (cnr Calles 28 & 37). A taxi to town will cost about CUC$6, or CUC$35 to the Hotel Colony.

PIRATES OF THE CARIBBEAN

In the mid-1590s, English sea captain and privateer Sir Francis Drake was trying to salvage his reputation after disastrous defeats at Lisbon (1588) and Las Palmas (1595). When Spain issued a moratorium on international debts pending the arrival of treasure-laden ships from their Latin American colonies, Drake seized his chance and persuaded Queen Elizabeth I to send him on one final voyage to the Caribbean.

The chance of intercepting some of Spain's returning ships was high but Drake, second-in-command John Hawkins and the English fleet endured several terrible months. They suffered a humiliating defeat in Puerto Rico at the Battle of San Juan, where Drake, instead of capturing the Spanish treasure ship there, had his vessel cannoned and was forced to retreat. A fruitless ransacking campaign along the Central American coast followed in which Drake tried desperately to seize the treasure he had promised his queen. Despondency and disease set in among the crew, and first Hawkins and then Drake perished.

The remnants of the English fleet turned for home under command of Drake's old friend Thomas Baskerville, but the Spanish, pressing for a prestigious victory, gave chase. Most of Baskerville's ships were caught while watering in a cove off the Isla de Pinos by Spanish ships under Don Bernardino de Avellaneda. By now the English fleet was in no position or mindset to engage in combat. The ships jettisoned what little treasure they had obtained in order to escape, and returned to England in tatters. The Spanish, meanwhile, arrived home that year with some 20 million silver dollars, one of the greatest shipments they ever landed from the New World.

Bus

Ecotur (☎32-71-01; Calle 24 btwn Calle 33 & river; ⏲8am-4pm Mon-Fri) can organize trips/transfers from Nueva Gerona to the diving areas and into the militarized zone. A taxi (easily arranged through your casa or hotel) from Nueva Gerona to Hotel Colony should cost approximately CUC$25. There are less reliable local buses: buses 431 to La Fe (26km) and 441 to the Hotel Colony (45km) leave from a stop opposite the cemetery on Calle 39A, just northwest of the hospital.

Bus 38 leaves from the corner of Calles 18 and 37, departing for Chacón (Presidio Modelo), Playa Paraíso and Playa Bibijagua, about four times a day.

Car

Cubacar (☎32-44-32; cnr Calles 32 & 39; ⏲7am-7pm) rents cars (from a steep CUC$105 per day) and can arrange transport into the military zone.

The Servi-Cupet gas station is at the corner of Calles 30 and 39 in the center of town.

Horse Carts

Horse *coches* (carts) often park next to the Cubalse supermarket on Calle 35. You can easily rent one at CUC$10 per day for excursions to the Presidio Modelo, Museo Finca el Abra, Playa Bibijagua and other nearby destinations. If you've got the time, you can be sure the driver will.

East of Nueva Gerona

Presidio Modelo NOTABLE BUILDING

Welcome to the island's most impressive yet depressing sight. Located near Reparto Chacón, 5km east of Nueva Gerona, this striking prison was built between 1926 and 1931, during the repressive regime of Gerardo Machado. The four striking six-story, yellow circular blocks were modeled after those of a notorious penitentiary in Joliet, Illinois, and could hold 5000 prisoners at a time. During WWII, assorted enemy nationals who happened to find themselves in Cuba (including 350 Japanese, 50 Germans and 25 Italians) were interned in the two rectangular blocks at the north end of the complex.

The Presidio's most famous inmates, however, were Fidel Castro and the other Moncada rebels, who were imprisoned here from October 1953 to May 1955. They were held separately from the other prisoners, in the hospital building at the south end of the complex.

In 1967 the prison was closed and the section where Castro stayed was converted into a **museum** (☎32-51-12; admission CUC$2; ⏲8am-4pm Mon-Sat, to noon Sun). There is one room dedicated to the history of the prison and another focusing on the lives of the Moncada prisoners. Admission includes a tour, but cameras/videos are CUC$3/25 extra. Bring exact change. Admission to the circular blocks (the most moving part of the experience) is free.

Cementerio Colombia CEMETERY

The cemetery here contains the graves of Americans who lived and died on the island during the 1920s and 1930s. It's about 7km east of Nueva Gerona and 2km east of Presidio Modelo. Bus 38 passes by.

Playa Paraíso, about 2km north of Chacón (about 6km northeast of Nueva Gerona), is a dirty brown beach with good currents for water sports. The wharf was originally used to unload prisoners heading to the Presidio Modelo. There is a small bar here. A better beach, **Playa Bibijagua** lies 4km to the east of Chacón. Here there are pine trees, a peso restaurant and plenty of low-key Cuban ambience. Nondrivers can catch bus 38 from Nueva Gerona.

South of Nueva Gerona

Sights & Activities

The main reason to come here is for the diving at Punta Francés (see p159), but there are a couple of other diversions for those who have time.

La Jungla de Jones GARDEN

(admission CUC$3; 24hr) Situated 6km west of La Fe in the direction of Hotel Colony, this is a botanical garden containing more than 80 tree varieties. Bisected by shaded trails and punctuated by a cornucopia of cacti and mangoes, this expansive garden was established by two American botanists, Helen and Harris Jones, in 1902. The highlight is the aptly named Bamboo Cathedral, an enclosed space surrounded by huge clumps of craning bamboo that only a few strands of sunlight manage to penetrate.

Criadero Cocodrilo CROCODILE FARM

(admission CUC$3; 7am-5pm) This farm has played an important part in crocodile conservation in Cuba over the last few years and the results are interesting to see. Harboring more than 500 crocodiles of all shapes and sizes, the *criadero* (hatchery) acts as a breeding center, similar to the one in Guamá in Matanzas (p226), although the setting here is infinitely wilder. Taken care of until they are seven years old, the center releases groups of crocs back into the wild when they reach a length of about 1m. To get to the *criadero* turn left 12km south of La Fe just past Julio Antonio Mella.

Sleeping & Eating

Hotel Colony HOTEL, RESORT $$

(39-81-81; all-incl s/d CUC$74/84; P) This hotel 46km southwest of Nueva Gerona originated in 1958 as part of the Hilton chain, but was confiscated by the revolutionary government before it began operating. Today the main building is a bit run down, but the newer bungalows are clean, bright and airy. You might save a few cents by taking a package that includes three meals and scuba diving. The water off the hotel's white-sand beach is shallow, with sea urchins littering the bottom. Take care if you decide to swim. A safer bet is the Colony's convivial pool. A long wharf (with a bar perfect for sunset mojitos) stretches out over the bay, but the snorkeling in the immediate vicinity of the hotel is mediocre. The diving, however, is to die for. A Havanautos car-rental office is at the hotel.

Getting There & Away

Transport is tough on La Isla, and bus schedules make even the rest of Cuba seem efficient. Try bus 441 from Nueva Gerona. Otherwise, your best bet to get to the hotel is by taxi (approximately CUC$35 from the airport), moped or rental car (p164).

The Southern Military Zone

The entire area south of Cayo Piedra is a military zone, and to enter you must first procure a one-day pass (CUC$12) from **Ecotur** (32-71-01; Calle 24 btwn Calle 33 & river; 8am-4pm Mon-Fri) in Nueva Gerona. The company will provide you with a Spanish-/English-/German-/French-/Italian-speaking guide, but it is up to you to find your own 4WD transport for within the zone itself. This can be organized with Cubacar in Nueva Gerona (p164). Traveling in the military zone is not possible without a guide or an official pass, so don't arrive at the Cayo Piedra checkpoint without either. As the whole excursion can wind up rather expensive, it helps to split the transport costs with other travelers. Good places to fish around for other people are Hotel Colony and Villa Isla de la Juventud. Both of these places also have tourist information offices that can give you more up-to-date advice on the region.

CUEVA DE PUNTA DEL ESTE

The Cueva de Punta del Este, a national monument 59km southeast of Nueva Gerona, has been called the 'Sistine Chapel' of Caribbean Indian art. Long before the Spanish conquest (experts estimate around AD 800), Indians painted some 235 pictographs on the walls and ceiling of the cave. The largest has 28 concentric circles of red and black, and the paintings have been interpreted as a solar calendar. Discovered in 1910, they're considered the most important of their kind in the Caribbean. The long, shadeless white beach nearby is another draw (for you and the mosquitoes – bring repellent).

COCODRILO

A potholed road runs south from Cayo Piedra to the gorgeous white-sand beach of Playa Larga, then west 50km to the friendly village of Cocodrilo. Barely touched by tourism, and with a population of just 750, Cocodrilo was formerly known as Jacksonville, and was colonized in the 19th century by families from the Cayman Islands. You still occasionally meet people here who can converse in English. Through the lush vegetation beside the potholed road one catches glimpses of cattle, birds, lizards and bee hives. The rocky coastline, sporadically gouged by small, white sandy beaches lapped by crystal-blue water, is magnificent.

Sea Turtle Breeding Center TURTLE FARM

(admission CUC$1; 8am-6pm) One kilometer west of Cocodrilo, the breeding center does an excellent job in conserving one of Cuba's rarest and most endangered species. Rows of green-stained glass tanks teem with all sizes of turtles.

CAYO LARGO DEL SUR

45

If you came to Cuba to witness historic colonial cities, exotic dancers, asthmatic Plymouths and peeling images of Che Guevara, then Cayo Largo del Sur, second-largest (38 sq km) and easternmost island of the Archipiélago de los Canarreos, will hugely disappoint. If, instead, you booked tickets while dreaming of glittering white beaches, teeming coral reefs, fabulous all-inclusive resorts and lots of fleshy Canadians and Italians wandering around naked, then this small mangrove-covered tropical paradise is undeniably the place for you.

No permanent Cuban settlement has ever existed on the Cayo. Instead, the is-

OPEN UNIVERSITY

The Isla de la Juventud's record as an international educator is, arguably, one of the Revolution's greatest triumphs. Starting as a government initiative to stamp out illiteracy and provide free, fair education for all Cubans, the first school opened here in 1961, and by the 1970s over 40 junior high schools and eight fully fledged high schools had been built on La Isla, along with technical institutes and teacher-training colleges.

Castro's long-term aim had always been to share Cuba's successful literacy campaign with other developing countries, and in 1977 the first overseas scholarships were awarded to 2000 seventh-graders from the war-torn African state of Angola. This initial intake was quickly followed by other groups from Angola and Mozambique, and within a few years there were close to 150,000 students on La Isla studying everything from art to zoology.

Encouraged to give back as much as they took, the overseas students were expected to learn Spanish and socialistically contribute to the annual fruit harvest in the island's famous citrus plantations. In return, they were given free tuition and board, a monthly stipend and – most importantly – a quality of education that, in their own countries, would have been little more than a pipe dream.

Buoyed by its new role as the unofficial mentor of the world's developing nations, Cuba hosted the 11th World Youth Festival in 1978 in Havana, during which a headmaster-like Fidel stood up and announced to the world that he was renaming Cuba's giant offshore classroom, La Isla de la Juventud. No one argued.

Changes to the world order along with the economic chaos that accompanied the Special Period put a dent in Cuba's international education campaign, and today there are far fewer students on La Isla.

land was developed in the early 1980s purely as a tourism enterprise. Cayo Largo del Sur (Cayo Largo for short) is largely frequented by Italian tourists – one resort caters exclusively for them. The other all-inclusives are less picky. The heavenly beaches (26km of 'em) surpass most visitors' expectations of Caribbean paradise and are renowned for their size, emptiness and – during summer – nesting turtles. There's also a profusion of iguanas and birdlife, including cranes, *zunzuncitos* (bee hummingbirds) and flamingos.

The island can be done as an expensive day trip from Havana, but most people come here on prebooked packages for a week or two. It's a paradisiacal hideaway, even though it neither looks nor feels like Cuba.

Cayo Largo del Sur lies between the Golfo de Batabanó and the Caribbean Sea, 114km east of Isla de la Juventud and 300km due north of Grand Cayman Island.

Sights

Playa Sirena BEACH

Cayo Largo's (and, perhaps, Cuba's) finest beach is the broad westward-facing Playa Sirena, where 2km of powdery white sand is wide enough to accommodate a couple of football pitches. Tourists on day trips from Havana and Varadero are often brought here, and the usual nautical activities (kayaks, catamarans) are available. Set back from the beach there's a *ranchón*-style bar and restaurant along with showers and toilets.

Just southeast is **Playa Paraíso**, a narrower and less shady but nonetheless wonderful strip of sand, serviced by a small bar.

Granja de las Tortugas TURTLE FARM

(Combinado; CUC$1; ⏲7am-noon & 1-6pm) A small, often-closed complex on the northwest end of the island beyond the airstrip in the settlement of Combinado. From May to September guides here can organize nighttime turtle-watching on the Cayo's beaches.

Playa los Cocos BEACH

You can head up the island's east coast via this beach, where there is good snorkeling (the paved road gives out after Playa Blanca).

Playa Tortuga BEACH

Beyond Playa los Cocos at the far end of the island is this beach, where sea turtles lay their eggs in the sand.

Cayo del Rosario & Cayo Rico ISLANDS

The other big day-trip destinations are these islands between Cayo Largo and Isla de la Juventud. Boat excursions to these beaches from the hotels cost around CUC$56 per person.

Cayo Iguana ISLAND

Off the northwest tip of Cayo Largo, Cayo Iguana is home to, that's right, hundreds of iguanas. A yacht trip here will cost you CUC$69 with lunch.

Activities

The island's best (and only) hike is from Playa Sirena round to Sol Cayo Largo along the beach (7km) or vice versa. A broken path follows the dune ridge for much of the way if the tide is high. You can also procure a bicycle if you're staying in one of the resorts and head east beyond the Playa Blanca Beach Resort to some of the island's remoter beaches.

Other activities available on the island include snorkeling, windsurfing, sailing, kayaking, tennis and volleyball. Ask at the hotels.

Marina Internacional Cayo Largo DIVING, FISHING

(☎24-81-33; Combinado) Just beyond the turtle farm in Combinado, this is the departure point for deep-sea fishing trips (CUC$325 for four hours and eight people) and diving (CUC$37 for one immersion including hotel transfer). Prices are more expensive here because you can't shop around. The marina also organizes two international fishing tournaments held here in September.

Horseback Riding Center HORSEBACK RIDING

(CUC$6 per hour) Coming from the airport, beyond the branch-off to the Sol resorts near the *torre de jardin* (garden tower; probably the island's most interesting building), there is a *ranchón*-style horseback-riding center where you can head out on Cayo Largo's limited selection of trails. Cantering along a gorgeous beach can make a pleasant change from lying on it.

Sleeping

All of Cayo Largo del Sur's hotels face the 4km beach on the south side of the island. Though largely shadeless, the beach here is gorgeous and rarely crowded (as no one lives here). If you're on a day trip, a day pass to the Sol resorts is CUC$35 including lunch.

Cayo Largo del Sur

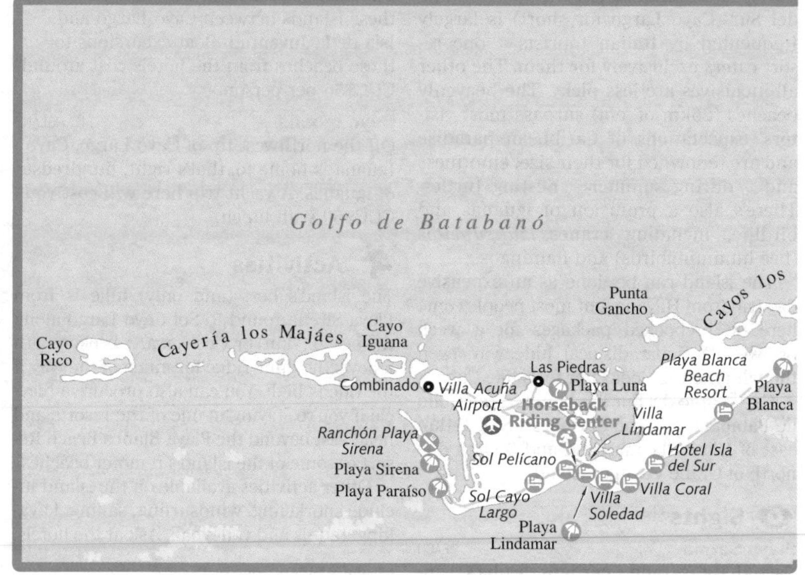

TOP CHOICE Sol Cayo Largo RESORT **$$$**
(☎24-82-60; all-incl s/d CUC$160/270; P❄@≋) Sol Meliá's best property is the five-star Sol Cayo Largo, with its Greek-temple-like lobby and trickling Italianate fountains. The beach out here is fantastic (and nudist) and the brightly painted (but not luxurious) rooms all have terraces with sea views. To date, it's Cayo Largo's most exclusive resort and great if you want to escape the families and poolside bingo further east. Check out the on-site spa and gym – a trip to Shangri-La.

Playa Blanca Beach Resort RESORT **$$$**
(☎24-80-80; all-incl s/d CUC$102/170; P❄@≋👪) Cayo Largo's newest resort is set apart from the rest on an expansive stretch of Playa Blanca. Rather drab architecture is augmented by three different dining options and an impressive array of sporting activities. There's an individual touch, too. Artworks by leading Cuban artist Carlos Guzmán decorate the public areas, and the suites in the upper echelons with their mezzanine sleeping areas could hold their own in Greenwich Village. Well, nearly. Some shade wouldn't go amiss, though.

Hotel Isla del Sur & Eden Village Complex RESORT **$$$**
(☎34-81-11; all-incl s/d CUC$80/120; P❄≋) The Isla del Sur, the first hotel on Cayo Largo, is now the hub of the Eden Village complex, known as Eden Viaggi to its predominantly Italian guests, or El Pueblito due to the fact it does indeed resemble a small town (one with nightmarish architecture). Most resort facilities are concentrated around 59-room Isla del Sur, a long two-story building close to the slightly tacky nightly poolside entertainment. Heading back west there are also 55-room Villa Coral, with 10 two-story, faux-colonial buildings and a swimming pool, and finally the drabber 24-room Villa Soledad, looking more like a displaced retirement village than a dream Caribbean getaway. All the above are owned by Gran Caribe and charge identical prices. The other hotel here, Villa Lindamar, is actually the best, but it caters exclusively for Italian tourists who book through agencies back home.

Sol Pelícano RESORT **$$$**
(☎24-82-33; all-incl s/d CUC$112/180; P❄@≋👪) This Spanish-style resort, flush on the beach 5km southeast of the airport, has 203 rooms in a series of three-story buildings and two-story duplex *cabañas* (cabins) built in 1993. This is the island's largest resort but it's open

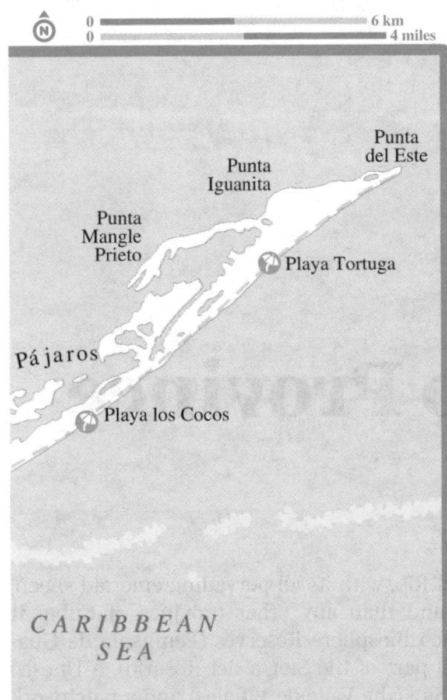

only in high season. Facilities include a nightclub and plenty of family-friendly concessions.

Eating

Of the all-inclusives, the Sol Cayo Largo serves the best food.

TOP CHOICE Ranchón Playa Sirena SEAFOOD, CARIBBEAN $$$
(⌚9am-5pm) A rather fetching beach bar amid the Playa Sirena palm trees, with Latino Tom Cruises tossing around the cocktail glasses. Good food is also served here and a buffet (CUC$20) happens if enough tourists are around. It offers no-nonsense, salt-of-the-earth *comida criolla* (Creole food) and good grilled *pargo* (red snapper) for CUC$12.

Restaurante el Torreón CARIBBEAN, SPANISH $$
(⌚noon-midnight) In Cayo Largo's Combinado settlement, and encased in a stone fortlike building by the marina, El Torreón serves Cuban food with a glint of imagination, along with several Spanish surprises (and wine).

Entertainment

Taberna el Pirata NIGHTCLUB
(⌚24hr) About the only non-all-inclusive option, Taberna el Pirata is primarily a haunt for boat-hands, resort workers and the odd escaped tourist alongside Marina Internacional Cayo Largo.

Fiesta Marán NIGHTCLUB
(admission CUC$15; ⌚11pm-2:30am) A night disco held on a yacht/catamaran off Playa Sirena.

Information

There's a **Cubatur** (☎24-82-58) in the Sol Pelícano and further information offices in the Sol Cayo Largo and Playa Blanca Resorts. You can change money at the hotels; otherwise Combinado houses the island's main bank, **Bandec** (⌚8:30am-noon & 2-3:30pm Mon-Fri, 9am-noon Sat & Sun). Adjacent is a **Casa del Tabaco** (☎24-82-11; ⌚8am-8pm) cigar shop and a **Clínica Internacional** (☎24-82-38; ⌚24hr) medical clinic. Euros are accepted at tourist installations here.

Due to dangerous currents, swimming is occasionally forbidden. This will be indicated by red flags on the beach. Mosquitoes can be a nuisance, too.

Getting There & Away

Several charter flights arrive directly from Canada weekly, and Cubana has weekly flights from Montreal and Milan.

For pop-by visitors, daily flights from Havana to Cayo Largo del Sur with **Aerogaviota** (☎20 3-8686; Av 47 No 2814 btwn Calles 28 & 34, Kohly, Havana) or Cubana (p119) cost CUC$129 for a return trip. The island makes a viable day trip from Havana, although you'll have to get up early for the airport transfer (all Cayo Largo flights depart between 7am and 8am from the airport at Playa Baracoa, a few miles west of Marina Hemingway).

Organized day trips from Havana or Varadero to Cayo Largo del Sur cost about CUC$137, including airport transfers, return flights and lunch, plus trips to Playa Sirena and Cayo Iguana. The Havana airport transfer starts its rounds of the hotels about 5am; check to make sure it's stopping at your hotel. All the Havana travel agencies (p118) offer this.

Getting Around

Getting around Cayo Largo shouldn't present too many challenges. A taxi or transfer bus can transport you the 5km from the airport to the hotel strip. From here a mini bus-train (the *trencito*) carts tourists out to Playa Paraíso (6km) and Playa Sirena (7km). The train returns in the afternoon, or you can hike back along the beach. The tiny settlement of Combinado is 1km north of the airport and 6km from the nearest resort. Ever-popular **Miguel Taxi** (☎529-03-282) has wheels to ferry you around. Otherwise hang around outside the hotels and airport.

Pinar del Río Province

☎048 / POP 594,279

Includes »

Best Places to Eat

» Restaurante la Casa de Don Tomás (p186)

» Restaurante Mural de la Prehistoria (p191)

» Rumayor (p175)

Best Places to Stay

» Hotel los Jazmines (p185)

» Villa Pitín & Juana (p185)

» La Ermita (p185)

» Villa los Reyes (p185)

» Hotel Vueltabajo (p175)

» Hotel Mirador (p193)

Why Go?

Bucolic Pinar del Río, with its all-pervading emerald sheen, protects more land than any other province of Cuba. It sports two Unesco Biosphere Reserves (Península de Guanahacabibes and part of the Sierra del Rosario), a Unesco World Heritage Site (the Valle de Viñales) and a patchwork of carefully managed flora and fauna zones. This is also the world's best place to grow tobacco, a blessing that fosters one of Cuba's most quintessential landscapes: fertile, rust-red, oxen-furrowed fields and rustic tobacco-drying houses guarded by sombrero-wearing *guajiros*.

One of Cuba's classic regional stereotypes, the *guajiro* is Pinar del Río personified: an amiable rural hick whose spiritual home is venerable Viñales, a serene visitor-friendly settlement ringed by craggy *mogotes* (flat-topped hills).

Beyond the countryside, Pinar's beach highlights are the idyllic sandy carpets of Cayo Jutías and Cayo Levisa, and María la Gorda on the island's remote tip, where over 50 dazzling dive sites await offshore.

When to Go

Come from May through August to see prized wildlife, such as the Guanahacabibes turtles, October through March for bird-watching, and December through March for the best beach weather. August to early October – hurricane season in a region renowned for its devastating hurricanes – might be best avoided.

History

The pre-Columbian history of western Cuba is synonymous with the Guanahatabeys, a group of nomadic Indians who lived in caves and procured their livelihood largely from the sea. Less advanced than the other indigenous peoples who lived on the island, the Guanahatabeys were a peaceful and passive race whose culture had developed more or less independently of the Taíno and Siboney cultures further east. Extinct by the time the Spanish arrived in 1492, little firsthand documentation remains on how the archaic Guanahatabey society was structured, although some archaeological sites have been found on the Península de Guanahacabibes.

Post-Columbus the Spanish left rugged Pinar del Río largely to its own devices, and the area developed lackadaisically only after Canary Islanders began arriving in the late 1500s. Originally called Nueva Filipina (New Philippines) for the large number of Filipinos who came to the area to work the burgeoning tobacco plantations, the region was renamed Pinar del Río in 1778, supposedly for the pine forests crowded along the Río Guamá. By this time the western end of Cuba was renowned for its tobacco, already home to what is now the world's oldest tobacco company, Tabacalera, dating from 1636. Cattle ranching also propped up the economy. The fastidious farmers who made a living from the delicate and well-tended crops here became colloquially christened *guajiros,* a native word that means – literally – 'one of us.' By the mid-1800s, Europeans were hooked on the fragrant weed and the region flourished. Sea routes opened up and the railway was extended to facilitate the shipping of the perishable product.

These days tobacco, along with tourism, keep Pinar del Río both profitable and popular. The region has more or less fully recovered from the two catastrophic hurricanes that hit during 2008, and continues to fly the flag as Cuba's eco-epicenter.

PINAR DEL RÍO AREA

Pinar del Río

POP 191,660

You might well smell Pinar del Río before you see it: Cuba's tobacco capital, plunked in the middle of the fertile Vuelta Abajo, has prospered from its proximity to the plantations from which the best cigars on the planet are made. Not surprisingly, the place boasts its own tobacco factory (open for visits) plus an affable population of leather-faced cigar-imbibing locals keen to show visitors there is more to their sleepy city than smoking *puros* (cigars) and the *jineteros* (tourist touts) for which the otherwise tranquil Pinar used to have an unfortunate reputation.

Pinar del Río was one of the last provincial capitals on the island to take root, and still seems a tad stuck in the slow lane. Overlooked by successive central governments who preferred sugarcane to tobacco, the city became an urban backwater and the butt of countless jokes about the supposedly easy-to-fool *guajiros* who were popularly portrayed as simple-minded rural hicks. But the city fought back. It's overcome neglect, derision and most recently a category 4 hurricane, and is busily overturning its negative connotations. A truly inspirational art scene is now alive and kicking, and there is a glut of

PINAR DEL RÍO STREET NAMES

Locals stick to the old street names; this chart should help.

OLD NAME	NEW NAME
Calzada de la Coloma	Rafael Ferro
Caubada	Comandante Pinares
Recreo	Isabel Rubio
Rosario	Ormani Arenado
San Juan	Rafael Morales
Vélez Caviedes	Gerardo Medina
Virtudes	Ceferino Fernández

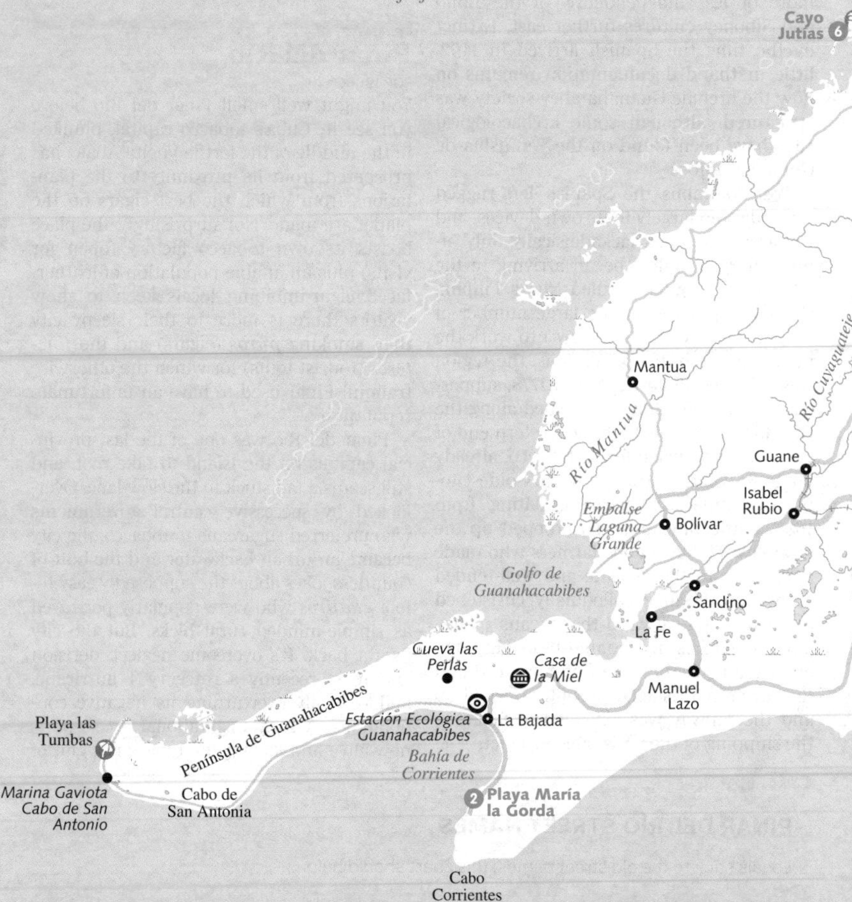

Pinar del Río Province Highlights

1 Get in touch with the region's cosmopolitan side with a walk around **Pinar del Río** (p174)

2 Experience scuba diving at translucent **Playa María la Gorda** (p181)

3 Get out of the tour bus and see, smell and taste the agricultural beauty of **Valle de Viñales** (p183)

4 Mount a horse and take a ride with the *guajiros* into the Palmarito Valley in **Parque Nacional Viñales** (p189)

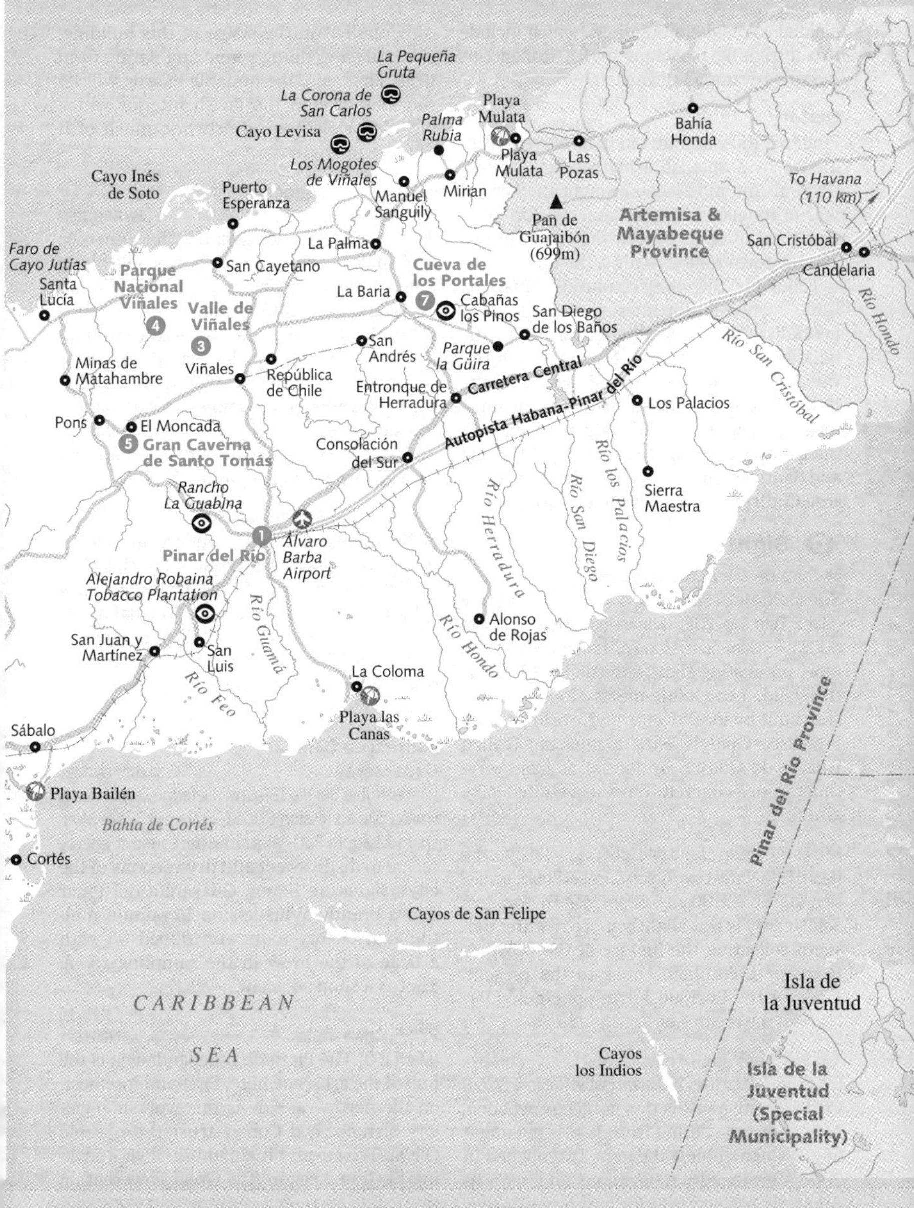

5 Get gobsmacked by the grottos and caves of **Gran Caverna de Santo Tomás** (p189), one of Latin America's largest subterranean systems.

6 Recharge your batteries on dreamy **Cayo Jutías** (p191)

7 See where Che Guevara played chess during the Cuban Missile Crisis in **Cueva de los Portales** (p194)

palatial colonial-era buildings, which include two intriguing museums and a stupendous recently revamped theater.

History

Pinar del Río was founded in its current form in 1774 by a Spanish army captain. In 1896 General Antonio Maceo brought the Second War of Independence to Pinar del Río in an ambitious attempt to split the island in two and the town rallied to his wake-up call.

Following the 1959 revolution Pinar del Río's economic fortunes improved exponentially; this was facilitated further by the building of the Autopista Nacional from Havana and the development of tourism in the 1980s. The city baseball team has also historically reared some of the best players in the country after the big boys from Havana and Santiago: many, like Alexi Ramíerez and José Contreras, have defected to the US.

Sights

Museo de Ciencias Naturales Sandalio de Noda MUSEUM

(Martí Este No 202; admission CUC$1, camera CUC$1; 9am-5pm Mon-Fri, to 1pm Sun) The most interesting sight, externally at least, is this wild, neo-Gothic-meets-Moorish mansion built by local doctor and world traveler Francisco Guasch. Now a museum (called Palacio de Guasch by locals), it has everything from a concrete T. rex to a stuffed baby giraffe.

Museo Provincial de Historia MUSEUM

(Martí Este No 58 btwn Colón & Isabel Rubio; admission CUC$1; 8:30am-6:30pm Mon-Fri, 9am-1pm Sat) Nearby is this slightly more riveting museum collecting the history of the province from pre-Columbian times to the present. Look for the Enrique Jorrín ephemera (Jorrín was the creator of the *chachachá*).

Teatro José Jacinto Milanés THEATER

(75-38-71; Martí No 160 btwn Isabel Rubio & Colón) On the same block is this gorgeous, wooden, 540-seat venue dating from 1845 – making it one of Cuba's oldest theaters. It reopened in 2006 after lengthy renovations and, with its colorfully painted interior and Spanish-style patio and cafe, is well worth a look.

FREE **Palacio de los Matrimonios** NOTABLE BUILDING

(Martí btwn Rafael Morales & Plaza de la Independencia) Heading west up Martí, the grand neoclassical facades give way to the outlandishly opulent in the shape of this building, primarily a wedding venue and dating from 1924. That said, the amiable guards will let you look around the lavish interior which includes a plethora of artwork, much of it Chinese in origin.

Fábrica de Tabacos Francisco Donatien CIGAR FACTORY

(Maceo Oeste No 157; admission CUC$5; 9am-noon & 1-4pm Mon-Fri) You can observe people busily rolling some of Pinar's (read: the world's) finest cigars here at this building, which was a jail until 1961 but is now tobacco central on the tourist circuit. Smaller than the Partagás factory in Havana, it gives a more intimate insight here, though the foibles are the same – robotic guides, rushed tours and the nagging notion that it's all a bit voyeuristic. There's an excellent cigar shop opposite.

Catedral de San Rosendo CHURCH

(Maceo Este No 3) The city's understated cathedral is four blocks southeast of the cigar factory. It dates from 1883 and its pastel-yellow exterior seems to get a more regular paint job than the rest of the city's buildings. As with most Cuban churches, the interior is often closed. Slip inside for a peek during Sunday morning service.

Fábrica de Bebidas Casa Garay BRANDY FACTORY

(Isabel Rubio Sur No 189 btwn Ceferino Fernández & Frank País; admission CUC$1; 9am-3:30pm Mon-Fri, to 12:30pm Sat) Workers here use a secret recipe to distill sweet and dry versions of the city's signature liquor, Guayabita del Pinar guava brandy. Whistle-stop 15-minute multilingual factory tours are topped off with a taste of the brew in the sampling room. There's a shop adjacent.

FREE **Casa Taller** ART GALLERY

(Martí 160) The Plaza de Independencia is the hub of the art scene here. First and foremost, on the northwest side is this workshop-gallery of renowned Cuban artist Pedro Pablo Olivia. The current highlight is Olivia's striking El Gran Apagón (the Great Powercut), a satirical (and therefore brave) artwork said to represent the country's current problems and political predicament better than any other. The key point of the gallery though is to promote and encourage artistic talent in Pinar del Río; several local artists also have work displayed. Stop by most days for a browse.

FREE **Centro Provincial de Artes Plásticas Galería** ART GALLERY
(Antonio Guiteras; 8am-9pm Mon-Sat) Across the plaza, this is another top-notch Pinar gallery, housing many local works.

Activities

Estadio Capitán San Luis Sports BASEBALL
(75-38-95; admission 1 peso; matches 7pm Tue-Thu & Sat, 4pm Sun) From October to April, exciting baseball games happen at this stadium on the north side of town. Pinar del Río is one of the country's best teams, often challenging the Havana–Santiago monopoly. Pop by in the evening to see the players going through a training session.

Festivals & Events

Carnaval in early July features a procession of *carrozas* (carriages) through the streets with couples dancing between the floats. It's a big, drunken dance party.

Sleeping

TOP CHOICE **Casa Colonial – José Antonio Mesa** CASA PARTICULAR $
(75-31-73; Gerardo Medina Norte No 67 btwn Adela Azcuy & Isidro de Armas; r CUC$25; P) Loads of space and an improvised Jacuzzi in the backyard. Not surprisingly José is a Pinar stalwart and his two rooms and lovely communal living spaces are perennially popular.

Hotel Vueltabajo HOTEL $
(75-93-81; cnr Martí & Rafael Morales; s/d CUC$35/55;) Stylishly colonial with high ceilings and striped Parisian window awnings, the rooms at this fabulous hotel are so spacious you almost think they must have run out of furniture. Old-fashioned shutters open onto the street and downstairs there's an OK bar-restaurant; a reasonable breakfast is included in the price.

Gladys Cruz Hernández CASA PARTICULAR $
(77-96-98; Av Comandante Pinares Sur No 15 btwn Martí & Máximo Gómez; r CUC$20;) A splendid house with tasteful colonial furnishings situated near the train station; there are two rooms with baths and fridges, a TV and a vast rear patio.

La Mesón CASA PARTICULAR $
(75-28-67; Martí Este 205; r CUC$20;) This former paladar is now trying its hand at hospitality of the overnight kind. Extensive public areas prepare you for rooms rather grander than what's on offer, but they're decent, clean, quiet and with balconies overlooking a colorful courtyard.

Villa Aguas Claras CABINS $
(77-84-27; s/d incl breakfast CUC$36/40; P) This plush campismo lies 8km north of town on the Carretera a Viñales (off Rafael Morales) and has the facilities of a midrange hotel. The 50 bungalows with hot showers sleep two (10 have air-con). The rooms are adequate, the landscaping lush and the staff congenial. Besides an OK restaurant, the Villa Aguas Claras also offers horseback riding and day trips. Insect repellent is essential here. Aguas Claras is accessible from Pinar del Río by bus several times a day.

Eating

Rumayor CARIBBEAN $$
(76-80-07; Carretera a Viñales Km 1; noon-midnight; P) The best food in Pinar del Río is probably found here at Rumayor, located 2km north of the town center, off the Carretera a Viñales. Justly famous for its succulent *pollo ahumado* (smoked chicken), you'll pay a little extra here (around CUC$10), but it is definitely worth it. This is one of Pinar's premier cabaret spots in the evening.

La Casona CARIBBEAN $
(cnr Martí & Colón; mains CUC$5; 8am-3pm & 4pm-11pm) Hard to believe, but this is Pinar's best government-run restaurant outside Rumayor. Encouragingly there are tablecloths and wine glasses here, along with steak, chicken and pasta on the menu, but positioned unstrategically on the town's busiest nexus the hissing hustlers are never far away. Get a seat away from the door.

Restaurante Criollo CARIBBEAN $
(Carretera Central Km 1 btwn Av Aeropuerto & Carretera a Viñales; mains from CUC$2; noon-9.45pm; P) Out near the hospital, this is an atmospheric restaurant with standard pork and chicken dishes in above-par surrounds. It abuts a vast patio which transforms into another top cabaret venue aftern the sun goes down.

El Marino SEAFOOD $
(Martí cnr Isabel Rubio; noon-3pm & 6pm-9.15pm) Pay in pesos for tasty paella and other fish dishes, and let the pleasant nautical decor enhance the experience.

Pinar del Río

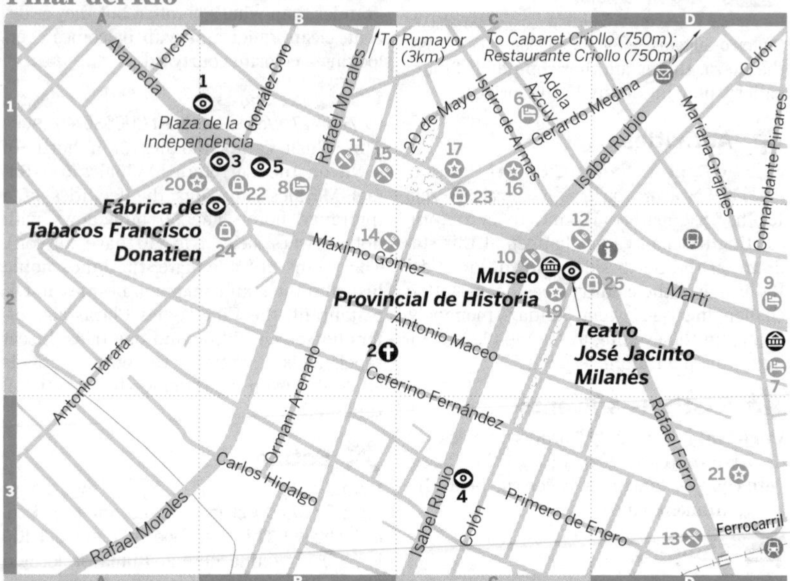

Heladería ICE-CREAM PARLOR $
(cnr Martí & Rafael Morales; 9am-9pm) A substantial *tres gracias* (three scoops) at this clean, cheerful place is the price of half a teaspoon's worth of Haagen Daas.

Self-Catering

Mercado agropecuario MARKET $
(Rafael Ferro; 8am-6pm Mon-Sat, to 1pm Sun) Pinar del Río's colorful open-air market is almost on top of the tracks near the train station. You'll see the odd tour group tramping through here getting a grip on Special Period economics.

Panadería Doña Neli BAKERY $
(cnr Gerardo Medina Sur & Máximo Gómez; 7am-7pm) Gives you each day your daily bread.

Supermercado el Comercio SUPERMARKET $
(cnr Martí Oeste & Arenado; 9am-5pm Mon-Sat, to noon Sun) One of the best supermarkets in town.

☆ Entertainment

Rumayor CABARET
(76-30-51; Carretera a Viñales Km 1; cover charge CUC$5; noon-midnight) Besides serving very good food, this place undergoes a metamorphosis at night from Tuesday through Sunday to a kitschy cabaret with a fantastic floor show that starts at 11pm. It's not the Tropicana, but it ain't half bad.

Cabaret Criollo CABARET
(Carretera Central Km 1 btwn Av Aeropuerto & Carretera a Viñales; 9pm-2am Mon-Sat;) The musical half of the homonymous restaurant, locals rate this nightly cabaret in an enormous (often ebrious) open-air patio rather highly.

Café Pinar LIVE MUSIC
(Gerardo Medina Norte No 34; admission CUC$3; 10am-2am) This spot gets the local youth vote and is also the best place to meet other travelers. Situated on a lively stretch of Calle Gerardo Medina there are live bands at night on the open patio, and light menu items such as pasta, chicken and sandwiches during the day.

Casa de la Música LIVE MUSIC
(Gerardo Medina Norte No 21; admission CUC$1; concerts start at 9pm nightly) After warming up at Café Pinar, many revelers cross the street for more live music here.

Disco Azul NIGHTCLUB
(cnr Gonzales Alcorta & Autopista; admission CUC$5; from 10pm Tue-Sun) A drab hotel,

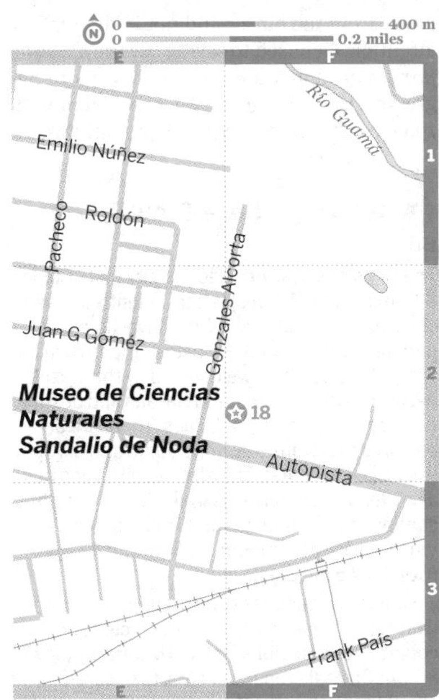

but a kicking disco – this glittery nightclub in Hotel Pinar del Río, on the edge of town coming from the Autopista, is the city's most popular.

La Piscuala CULTURAL CENTER
(cnr Martí & Colón) With the Milanés back in business you'd be foolish to miss this theatrical patio alongside the real deal. Check the schedule posted outside for nightly cultural activities.

Teatro Lírico Ernesto Lecuona THEATER
(Antonio Maceo Oeste No 163) Near the cigar factory, this theater is best for classical music and opera.

Uneac CINEMA
(Antonio Maceo 178) In addition to the venues listed above, try Unión de Escritores y Artistas de Cuba (Uneac) near the train station for nightly film screenings and occasional live music.

Shopping

Fondo Cubano de Bienes Cultural CRAFTS
(cnr Martí & Gerardo Medina; 9am-5pm) The most interesting selection of regional handicrafts, although revenue goes almost exclusively to the government rather than the makers themselves.

Pinar del Río

Top Sights
Fábrica de Tabacos Francisco Donatien ... B2
Museo de Ciencias Naturales Sandalio de Noda ... D2
Museo Provincial de Historia ... C2
Teatro José Jacinto Milanés ... C2

Sights
1 Casa Taller ... B1
2 Catedral de San Rosendo ... B2
3 Centro Provincial de Artes Plásticas Galería ... B1
4 Fábrica de Bebidas Casa Garay ... C3
5 Palacio de los Matrimonios ... B1

Sleeping
6 Casa Colonial — José Antonio Mesa ... C1
7 Gladys Cruz Hernández ... D2
8 Hotel Vueltabajo ... B1
9 La Mesón ... D2

Eating
10 El Marino ... C2
11 Heladería ... B1
12 La Casona ... C2
13 Mercado Agropecuario ... D3
14 Panadería Doña Neli ... B2
15 Supermercado el Comercio ... B1

Entertainment
16 Cafe Pinar ... C1
17 Casa de la Música ... C1
18 Disco Azul ... F2
19 La Piscuala ... C2
20 Teatro Lírico Ernesto Lecuona ... A1
21 Uneac ... D3

Shopping
22 Casa del Habano ... B1
23 Fondo Cubano de Bienes Cultural ... C1
24 La Casa del Ron ... B2
25 Todo Libro Internacional ... D2

Casa del Habano CIGARS
(Antonio Maceo No 162) Opposite the tobacco factory, this store is one of the better outlets of this popular government cigar chain, with a patio bar, air-conditioned shop, smoking room and Infotur desk.

La Casa del Ron CRAFTS, RUM
(Antonio Maceo Oeste No 151; 9am-4:30pm Mon-Fri, to 1pm Sat & Sun) Near the cigar

factory, sells souvenirs, CDs and T-shirts, plus plenty of the strong stuff.

Todo Libro Internacional BOOKS
(cnr Martí & Colón; ⏰8am-noon & 1:30-6pm Mon-Fri, 8am-noon & 1-4pm Sat) Selection of maps, books and office supplies in same building as Cubanacán office.

Information

Internet Access & Telephone

Etecsa Telepunto (cnr Gerardo Medina & Juan Gómez; per hr CUC$6; ⏰8:30am-7:30pm)

Media

Guerrillero is published on Friday. Radio Guamá airs on 1080AM or 90.2FM.

Medical Services

Farmacia Martí (Martí Este No 50; ⏰8am-11pm)

Hospital Provincial León Cuervo Rubio (☎75-44-43; Carretera Central) Two kilometers north of town.

Money

Banco Financiero Internacional (Gerardo Medina Norte No 46; ⏰8:30am-3:30pm Mon-Fri) Opposite Casa de la Música.

Cadeca (Martí No 46; ⏰8:30am-5:30pm Mon-Sat)

Post

DHL (Gerardo Medina Norte No 160 btwn Juan Gualberto Gómez & Isabel Rubio)

Post office (Martí Este No 49; ⏰8am-8pm Mon-Sat)

Travel Agencies

Cubanacán (☎77-01-04, 75-01078; Martí No 109) Has moped rental.

Havanatur (☎77-84-94; Ormani Arenado cnr Martí; ⏰8am-8pm)

Infotur (☎72-86-16; ⏰9am-5.30pm Mon-Fri) At the Hotel Vueltabajo, one of the city's most helpful sources of information.

Dangers & Annoyances

For a relatively untouristed city Pinar del Río has had its fair share of unsolicited touts or *jineteros*. The majority are young men who hang around on Calle Martí offering everything from paladar meals to 'guided tours' of tobacco plantations. Most will back off at your first or second 'no' but bolder ones have been known to mount bicycles and accost tourist cars (identifiable by their purple/brown number plates) when they stop at traffic lights. Although they're generally nonaggressive, it's best to be firmly polite from the outset and not invite further attention. Get used to saying *'no me moleste, por favor'* and watch out for the more aggressive touts on bicycles. The problem with *jineteros* has improved lately but still worth being aware of.

Getting There & Away

Bus

The city's **bus station** (Adela Azcuy btwn Colón & Comandante Pinares) is conveniently located close to the center. Tickets in convertibles are purchased at the window upstairs (open 8am to 7pm). Pinar del Río is well-served by the Víazul network, with all services to Havana and destinations east originating in Viñales. There are departures to Havana at 9am, 2:50pm and 6:50pm (CUC$11, 2½ hours). The afternoon Havana bus also stops in Las Terrazas while the morning bus continues to Cienfuegos and Trinidad. Buses to Viñales leave at 12:05pm, 3:25pm and 4:40pm (CUC$6, 45 minutes).

Numerous tour buses and excursions leave daily for Havana – a trip that may include a couple of tourist stops. Ask at **Havanatur** (☎77-84-94; Ormani Arenado cnr Martí; ⏰8am-8pm) about these and other transfers to Cayo Levisa, Cayo Jutías and María la Gorda.

Beyond the main hubs, transport can be scant. There are sporadic transfer buses from Havana and Viñales to María la Gorda; hiring a taxi or car allows more flexibility.

Taxi

Private taxis hanging around outside the bus station will offer prices all the way to Havana. Sometimes these are worth considering. A fare to José Martí International Airport, for example, will cost around CUC$60 compared to the standard CUC$25 just from Havana.

Colectivo taxis congregate at the start of the Carretera a Viñales outside the hospital north of town, offering the scenic Viñales jaunt for CUC$1.

Train

Before planning any train travel, check the station blackboards for canceled/suspended/rescheduled services. From the **train station** (☎75-57-34; cnr Ferrocarril & Comandante Pinares Sur; ⏰ticket window 6:30am-noon & 1-6:30pm) there's a painfully slow train to Havana (CUC$7, 5½ hours, 9:45am) every other day. You can buy your ticket for this train the day of departure; be at the station between 7am and 8pm. Local trains go southwest to Guane via Sábalo (CUC$2, two hours, 7:18am and 6:30pm). This is the closest you can get by train to the Península de Guanahacabibes.

Getting Around

Cubacar (☎75-93-81) has a car-rental office at Hotel Vueltabajo and **Havanautos** (☎77-80-15) has one at Hotel Pinar del Río. Mopeds can be rented from **Cubanacán** (p178).

Servicentro Oro Negro is two blocks north of the Hospital Provincial on the Carretera Central. The Servi-Cupet gas station is 1.5km further north on the Carretera Central toward Havana; another is on Rafael Morales Sur at the south entrance to town.

Horse carts (one peso) on Isabel Rubio near Adela Azcuy go to the Hospital Provincial and out onto the Carretera Central. Bici-taxis cost five pesos around town.

If you are up for cadging a ride to Viñales Cuban-style, trudge north to the junction of the Carretera a Viñales with the Carretera Central and get talking to the *amarillo* (traffic organizer).

La Coloma

A quiet fishing village 25km south of Pinar del Río through exquisite countryside, La Coloma has the best beach on the province's south coast in delightful Las Canas. You can arrange boat trips from here to the still-lovelier Cayos de San Felipe. Public transport: you're joking, right? Visit strictly under your own steam/wheels.

Southwest of Pinar del Río

If Cuba is the world's greatest tobacco producer and Pinar del Río its proverbial jewel box, then the verdant San Luis region southwest of the provincial capital is the diamond in the stash. Few deny that the pancake-flat farming terrain around the smart town of **San Juan y Martínez** churns out the crème de la crème of the world's best tobacco and the rural scenery is typically picturesque. Further on, there are a couple of little-visited southern beaches and the freshwater **Embalse Laguna Grande**, stocked with largemouth bass.

Sights

Alejandro Robaina Tobacco Plantation TOBACCO PLANTATION
(☎79-74-70; CUC$5; ⏲10am-5pm Mon-Sat) Admittedly not quite the same since its charismatic former owner died, the plantation here is nevertheless as fascinating as tobacco tourism gets. Robaina's famous *vegas* (fields), in the rich Vuelta Abajo region southwest of Pinar del Río, have been growing quality tobacco since 1845, but it wasn't until 1997 that a new brand of cigars known as Vegas Robaina was first launched to wide international acclaim. This made Señor Robaina the only contemporary Cuban with a brand of cigars named after him, and when the 'Godfather' of Cuban tobacco passed away in April 2010 there is little doubt in most minds that a chapter in the history of the country's cigar-making industry did too. Still, the show must go on, and does at the plantation today: it's been unofficially open to outside visitors for some years. With a little effort and some deft navigational skills, you can roll up at the farm and, for a small fee, get the lowdown on the tobacco-making process from delicate plant to aromatic wrapper.

To get there, take the Carretera Central southwest out of Pinar del Río for 18km, turn left onto another straight road and then left again (after approximately 4km) onto the rougher track that leads to the farm. Tours are generally available every day bar Sunday, but call ahead to check for the latest situation, or ask in Pinar del Río/Viñales at the tourist agencies. The tobacco-growing season runs from October to February and this is obviously the best time to visit.

Rancho la Guabina ACTIVITIES RANCH
(☎75-76-16; Carretera de Luis Lazo Km 9.5) A former Spanish farm spread over 1000 hectares of pasture, forest and wetlands, the Rancho la Guabina is a jack of all trades and a master of at least one. You can partake in horseback riding here, go boating on a lake, enjoy a scrumptious Cuban barbecue, or even see a cockfight. The big drawcard for most, though, is the fantastic horse shows. The Rancho is a long-standing horse-breeding center that raises fine Pinto Cubano and Apaloosa horses, and mini-rodeo-style shows run on Monday, Wednesday and Friday from 10am to noon and from 4pm to 6pm. Agencies in Viñales and Pinar del Río run excursions here starting at CUC$29, or you can arrive on your own. It's a great place to enjoy the peaceful *guajiro* life. Limited accommodation is available.

Playa Bailén BEACH
The beach life here can't match the alluring north coast; still, this makes a pleasant, sandy deviation on the way out west.

Sleeping & Eating

The best places to try for casas particulares are bright San Juan y Martínez and Sandino, 6km from the Laguna Grande turn-off. There are rough cabins for rent around Playa Bailén.

Rancho la Guabina CABINS, HOSTEL **$$**
(☎75-76-16; Carretera de Luis Lazo Km 9.5; r CUC$65; P❄) Just outside Pinar del Río, this expansive farm offers eight rooms, five in a cottage-style house and three in separate cabins. It's a charming and unhurried place with excellent food and friendly staff.

Villa Laguna Grande CABINS **$**
(☎84-34-53; Carretera a Ciudad Bolívar; r from CUC$23) Something of an anomaly, this rough-around-the-edges fishing resort, 29km southwest of Guane and 18km off the highway to María la Gorda, is Islazul's most isolated outpost. The 12 rather scruffy thatched cabins sit in woodland directly below the Embalse Laguna Grande, a reservoir stocked with bass where locals come to fish.

Getting There & Away

Two trains a day travel between Pinar del Río and Guane stopping at San Luis, San Juan y Martínez,

ROLLING, ROLLING, ROLLING...

Cuban *puros* (cigars) have had famous fans from Che Guevara to Arnold Schwarzenegger. John F Kennedy even purportedly told his press secretary Pierre Salinger to order in a thousand of his favorite Petit Upmanns the night before signing the US trade embargo on Cuba into law.

This is hardly surprising. Reared in the rust-red fields of Pinar del Río province in the island's luscious west, all genuine Cuban cigars are hand-rolled by trained experts, before being packed in tightly sealed cedar boxes and classified into 42 different types and sizes. The unsurpassed quality of the country's cigars in the world market stems from a combination of geography, terrain and fine local workmanship, and the production process is complex enough to make smokers savour the end result.

Cuba's flagship brand is Cohiba, popularized by Fidel Castro who used to puff on Cohiba Espléndidos before he gave up smoking for health reasons in 1985. Other international favorites include the Partagás brand, rolled in Havana since 1845; the classic Montecristo No 2, another *fuerte* (strong) smoke much admired by Cubans; and the milder Romeo y Julieta brand, invented in 1903 by a Cuban who had traveled widely in Europe. The uniquely Pinar del Río–produced tobacco stuffed into Vegas Robainos, meanwhile, is the world's very finest, and the brand is thus more exclusive. Then there are the so-called locally smoked peso cigars – not branded, perhaps – but Cubans are said to save the best for themselves.

Most of the manufacturing story unfolds before your eyes in Pinar del Río's countryside. Given rich soil and the right humidity, seeds typically take around 80 days to grow into plants prime for harvesting. Tobacco planting is generally staggered, so the harvest lasts several months. Upon maturing, the leaf selection process is conducted by a team of highly skilled workers, who will have needed years of experience to be given this responsibility. Each plant carries three types of leaves: the *ligero*, the strongest leaves located at the top of the plant, the *seco*, which provides the cigar's taste, and the *volado* (light-flavoured leaf, used for combustibility).

Leaves are subsequently transferred to one of the province's numerous *casas de tobacos* (drying houses) and, depending on their size, placed at different heights within these long thatched huts to dry. Then begins the fermentation of the leaves, which can last 40 to 50 days, followed by the aging process, which often runs to two or three years. Afterward, leaves are sorted according to their attributes (such as size and color), stemmed and left to cure – again for up to several years. The next stage is the first typically seen in a cigar factory: a second categorizing of the leaves followed by the filler leaves being positioned, bound and pressed in a mold. An experienced master roller then hand-finishes the cigar by adding a wrapping leaf and a head.

Ever-obliging, Pinar del Río has several places to learn more about cigar-making. Casa del Veguero (p184) gives an insight into tobacco drying and maturing but, for a full-blown cigar factory where the magical weed gets sculpted into smokable sticks, try Pinar del Río's Francisco Donatien factory (p174).

Sábalo and Isabel Rubio (two hours). Passenger trucks run periodically between Guane and Sandino but, southwest of there, public transport is sparse bar the sporadic Havanatur transfer (p178). Fill your tank up at the Servi-Cupet gas station in Isabel Rubio if you intend to drive to Cabo de San Antonio, as this is the last gasp for gas.

PENÍNSULA DE GUANAHACABIBES

As the island narrows at its western end, you fall upon the low-lying and ecologically rich Península de Guanahacabibes. One of Cuba's most isolated enclaves, it once provided shelter for its earliest inhabitants, the Guanahatabeys. A two-hour drive from Pinar del Río, this region lacks major tourist infrastructure, meaning it feels far more isolated than it is. The Guanahacabibes is famous for its national park (also a Unesco Biosphere Reserve) and an international-standard diving center at María la Gorda.

Parque Nacional Península de Guanahacabibes

Flat and deceptively narrow, the elongated Península de Guanahacabibes begins at La Fe, 94km southwest of Pinar del Río. In 1987, 1015 sq km of this uninhabited sliver of idyllic coastline was declared a Biosphere Reserve by Unesco – one of only six in Cuba. The reasons for the protection measures were manifold. Firstly, the reserve's submerged coastline features a wide variety of different landscapes including broad mangrove swamps, low-scrub-thicket vegetation and an uplifted shelf of alternating white sand and coral rock. Secondly, the area's distinctive limestone karst formations are home to a plethora of unique flora and fauna including 172 species of bird, 700 species of plant, 18 types of mammal, 35 types of reptiles, 19 types of amphibian, 86 types of butterfly and 16 orchid species. Sea turtles, including loggerhead and green turtles, come ashore at night in summer to lay their eggs – the park is the only part of mainland Cuba where this happens. If you're here between May and October, night tours can be arranged to watch the turtles nest. Another curiosity is the swarms of *cangrejos colorados* (red and yellow crabs) that crawl across the peninsula's rough central road only to be unceremoniously crushed under the tires of passing cars. The stench of the smashed shells is memorable.

To date, Guanahacabibes' value as an archaeological goldmine is in the discovery stage. Suffice to say the area is thought to shelter at least 100 important archaeological sites relating to the Guanahatabey people.

Sights

Casa de la Miel MUSEUM

(8:30am-3:30pm Mon-Sat) About to open at the time of research, the latest attraction in the reserve is just before the park entrance, an eco-museum telling the tale of the area's agriculture and selling honey straight from the on-site hives. Enquire at the visitor center.

Activities

Península de Guanahacabibes is a paradise for divers, eco-travelers, conservationists and bird-watchers – or, at least, it ought to be. Feathered species on display here include parrots, *tocororos,* woodpeckers, owls, tody flycatchers, and *zunzuncitos* (bee hummingbirds) and, with no official settlements, the peninsula is one of Cuba's most untouched. However, thanks to strict park rules (you can't go anywhere without a guide), some travelers have complained that the experience is too limiting.

The visitor center can arrange guides, specialized visits and a five-hour tour to the park's (and Cuba's) western tip at Cabo de San Antonio. The responsibility is yours to supply transport, sufficient gas, water, sunscreen, insect repellent and food, which makes the task a little more difficult for travelers without their own wheels. During most of the 120km round-trip you'll have dark, rough *diente de perro* (dog's teeth) rock on one side and the brilliant blue sea on the other. Iguanas will lumber for cover as you approach and you might see small deer, *jutías* (tree rats) and lots of birds. Beyond the lighthouse is deserted Playa las Tumbas where you'll be given 30 minutes for a swim. Any hire car can make this trip though a 4WD is preferable. The five-hour excursion costs CUC$10 per person, plus the CUC$80 or so you'll need to hire a car (there's car rental at Hotel María la Gorda). Besides the diving, the beaches and the chance to see turtles, the wealth of lesser-known activities (such as exploring caves and viewing rare wildlife like the fish eagle) at Cabo San Antonio makes staying out here worthwhile.

There's the possibility of other excursions from the visitor center to local communities in the area and some new hikes in the works; call ahead to check developments.

Centro Internacional de Buceo DIVING
(☎77-13-06; María la Gorda) Diving is María la Gorda's raison d'être and the prime reason people come here. The nerve center is this well-run base next to the eponymous hotel at the Marina Gaviota. Good visibility and sheltered offshore reefs are highlights, plus the proximity of the 50-plus dive sites to the shore. Couple this with the largest formation of black coral in the archipelago and you've got a recipe for arguably Cuba's best diving reefs outside the Isla de la Juventud.

A dive here costs a reasonable CUC$35 (night diving CUC$40), plus CUC$7.50 for equipment. The center offers a full CMAS (Confédération Mondiale des Activités Subaquatiques; World Underwater Activities Federation) scuba certification course (CUC$365; four days) and snorkelers can hop on the dive boat for CUC$12. The dive center also offers four hours of deep-sea fishing for CUC$200 for up to four people and line fishing/trolling at CUC$30 per person, four maximum.

Among the 50 identified dive sites in the vicinity, divers are shown El Valle de Coral Negro, a 100m-long black-coral wall, and El Salón de María, a cave 20m deep containing feather stars and brilliantly colored corals. The concentrations of migratory fish can be incredible. The furthest entry is only 30 minutes by boat from shore.

Marina Gaviota Cabo de San Antonio DIVING
(☎75-01-18) Another option is Cuba's most westerly located boat dock, on Playa las Tumbas at the end of the Península Guanahacabibes. The marina here has fuel, boat mooring, a small restaurant, shop and easy access to 27 diving sites. The Villa Cabo San Antonio is nearby.

Cueva las Perlas HIKING, CAVE
(3km; CUC$8) The three-hour trek to the 'pearl cave' traverses deciduous woodland replete with a wide variety of birds, including *tocororos, zunzuncitos* and woodpeckers. After 1.5km you come to the cave itself, where you can spy (and hear) screech owls: it's a multi-gallery cavern with a lake of which 300m is accessible to hikers.

Del Bosque al Mar HIKING
(1.5km; CUC$6) Leaving from near the eco-station, this trail passes a lagoon where you can view resident birdlife, and takes in some interesting flora including orchids, as well as a *cenote* (a kind of water-submerged cave) for swimming. At 90 minutes it's rather short for such an immense park, but the guides are highly trained and informed, and tours can be conducted in Spanish, English or Italian. Ask about other new trails at the visitor center.

Sleeping & Eating

Hotel María la Gorda HOTEL $$
(☎77-81-31, 77-30-67; s/d incl breakfast CUC$54/76; P❄) This is the most remote hotel on the main island of Cuba and the isolation has its advantages. But, while the adjoining palm-fringed beach is pretty, most people come here to dive; reefs and vertical drop-offs beckon just 200m from the hotel. María la Gorda (literally 'Maria the Fatso') is on the Bahía de Corrientes, 150km southwest of Pinar del Río. Room-wise you get a choice of three pink-concrete, motel-type buildings or 20 newer cabins set back from the beach. The latter are more comfortable and private. Far from being a posh resort, María la Gorda is an easygoing place where hammocks are strung between palm trees, cold beers are sipped at sunset and dive talk continues into the small hours.

Buffet meals cost CUC$15 for lunch or dinner; reports on the food vary. Water in the hotel shop is expensive, so bring your own or purify the tap water.

Villa Cabo San Antonio CABINS $$
(☎75-01-18, 75-76-76; Playa las Tumbas; r CUC$65-120; ❄) A 16-villa complex on the almost-virgin Península de Guanahacabibes, set 3km from the Roncali Lighthouse and 4km from the new Gaviota Marina, this environmentally friendly and surprisingly well-appointed place has satellite TV, car rental, bike hire and a small cafe.

Information

Although the park border straddles the tiny community of La Fe, the reserve entrance is at La Bajada. Some 25km before the reserve proper, Manuel Lazo has the last accommodation for budget-conscious travelers.

Just before Manuel Lazo is the **Oficina de Guardaparque** (☎75-03-66) or park ranger's office which at this remote end of Cuba is a useful information source. It's advisable to phone here or the **visitor center** (☎75-03-66; osmanibf@yahoo.es; ⊙8:30am-3pm) at La Bajada to arrange park activities before showing up at the park entrance, as with limited resources there are often not the staff to arrange impromptu guided tours.

The visitor center, adjacent to the **Estación Ecológica Guanahacabibes**, has interpretive displays on the local flora and fauna. English is spoken. You can arrange to meet guides here for all activities except the diving, which is organized from Hotel María la Gorda. Just beyond the center the road splits with the left-hand branch going south to María la Gorda (14km along a deteriorating coastal road) and the right fork heading west toward the end of the peninsula.

It's a 120km round-trip to Cuba's westernmost point from here. The lonesome Cabo de San Antonio is populated by a solitary lighthouse, the Faro Roncali, inaugurated by the Spanish in 1849, and Gaviota Marina and villa. Four kilometers northwest is Playa las Tumbas, an idyllic beach where visitors to the park are permitted to swim.

There's a CUC$5 charge to visit Hotel María la Gorda and its adjoining 5km beach. Divers are unanimous about the quality of the reefs here and it's also one of Cuba's prime yachting venues.

Getting There & Away

Without a hire car or a prearranged transfer, getting to Cuba's extreme west is difficult.

A transfer bus (return CUC$35) operates between Viñales and María la Gorda, usually only with a 10-passenger minimum and therefore on average once weekly at best. It is scheduled to leave Viñales at 7am and arrive at the peninsula at 9:30am. The return leg leaves María la Gorda at 5pm and arrives in Viñales at 7pm. A single fare costs CUC$25 (only feasible if you are staying at Hotel María la Gorda). You can inquire at **Cubanacán** (☎79-63-93) in Viñales or **Havanatur** (☎77-84-94) and **Infotur** (☎72-86-16) in Pinar del Río.

Via Gaviota (☎77-81-31) has an office at Hotel María la Gorda, offering a jeep taxi service with driver to Cabo de San Antonio at CUC$50 for up to four people. Via Gaviota and other companies also offer transfers to/from Pinar del Río at CUC$50 one way for the whole car (or CUC$120 to/from Havana).

VALLE DE VIÑALES

Embellished by soaring pine trees and scattered with bulbous limestone cliffs that teeter like giant haystacks above placid tobacco plantations, Parque Nacional Viñales is one of Cuba's most magnificent natural settings. Wedged spectacularly into the Sierra de los Órganos mountain range, this 11km-by-5km valley was declared a Unesco World Heritage Site in 1999 for its dramatic rocky outcrops (known as *mogotes*), coupled with the vernacular architecture of its traditional farms and villages.

Once upon a time the whole region was several hundred meters higher. Then, during the Cretaceous period 100 million years ago, underground rivers ate away at the limestone bedrock, creating vast caverns. Eventually the roofs collapsed leaving only the eroded walls we see today. It is the finest example of a limestone karst valley in Cuba and contains the Caverna Santo Tomás, the island's largest cave system.

Rock studies aside, Viñales also offers opportunities for fine hiking, history, rock climbing and horseback trekking. On the accommodation front it boasts first-class hotels and some of the best casas particulares in Cuba. Despite drawing in day-trippers by the busload, the area's well-protected and spread-out natural attractions have somehow managed to escape the frenzied tourist circus of other less well-managed resorts, while the atmosphere in and around the town remains refreshingly hassle-free.

LOCAL KNOWLEDGE

TRACY COOPER: CLIMBER, VIÑALES

Climbing in Viñales is really taking off as a sport, especially since the website www.cubaclimbing.com has been operating and the book *Cuba Climbing* by Anibal Fernandez and Armando Menocal (2009) has been out. It's a great way to see some of the countryside around town. Finca Raúl Reyes, owned by the family of Yoan and Yarelis Reyes, has access to some great routes. One of my favorite climbs here is The Wasp Factory, which takes you to the big overhanging stalactite visible from some distance on the rockface. The One-Inch Punch route nearby is technically the toughest in Cuba. There is always a good, knowledgeable group of climbers at the base of the rocks to turn to for help and advice.

Viñales

POP 27,806

Sombrero-wearing *guajiros* saunter home on horseback after a tough day in the tobacco fields; rocking chairs creak on well-swept porches; cigar-sucking farmers navigate oxen through tilling the rich, red fields that roll around town; climbers tackle the sheer, forest-fringed *mogotes* that shoot up beyond: you have arrived at Viñales, hub of what many reckon on being Cuba's most mesmerizing spot of scenery. Despite a double pummeling by Hurricanes Gustav and Ike in 2008, this most unhurried and friendly of Cuban towns has lost none of its picturesque charm. Well established on the standard tourist circuit, this is where travelers come to relax, ruminate and revel in the great outdoors.

Sights

Founded in 1875, Viñales is more about setting than sights with most of its activities of a lung-stretching outdoor nature. Nevertheless the town has some engaging architecture and a lively main square backed by the sturdy colonial **Casa de la Cultura**, one of the oldest structures in the valley. Next door is a tiny art gallery while to the right is an equally diminutive (and dilapidated) **church**.

Museo Municipal MUSEUM
(Salvador Cisneros No 115; ⏲8am-10pm Mon-Sat, to 4pm Sun) Positioned halfway down Cisneros, Viñales' pine-lined main street, the Museo Municipal occupies the former home of independence heroine Adela Azcuy (1861–1914) and tracks the local history. Four different hikes leave from here daily.

El Jardín de Caridad GARDEN
(donations accepted; ⏲8am-5pm) Just opposite the Servi-Cupet gas station as the road swings north out of town, you'll spot an outlandish, vine-choked gate beckoning you in. This is the entrance to a sprawling garden almost a century in the making. Cascades of orchids bloom alongside plastic doll heads, thickets of orange lilies grow in soft groves and turkeys run amok. Knock on the door of the Little-Red-Riding-Hood cottage and one of the elderly owners will probably show you around.

La Casa del Veguero TOBACCO PLANTATION
(Carretera a Pinar del Río Km 24; ⏲10am-5pm) To learn about the local tobacco-growing process, stop by just outside Viñales on the road to Los Jazmines and see a fully operating *secadero* (drying house) in which tobacco leaves are cured from February to May. The staff gives brief explanations and you can buy loose cigars here at discount prices. There's a restaurant here too.

Activities

While most of the activities in Viñales are located outside town, there's a handful – including some climbing routes – within easy walking distance. Even if you're staying in a casa, it's worth strolling the 2km uphill to the lovely La Ermita where you can **swim** (CUC$7, including bar cover) in the gorgeous pool or book a **massage** (CUC$20-35). Los Jazmines has an equally amazing pool (CUC$7, including bar cover) though the ubiquitous tour buses can sometimes kill the tranquility.

Yoan & Yarelis Reyes HIKE, CLIMBING
(☎69-52-25; Rafael Trejo No 134) Casa owners in Viñales are particularly adept at being able to rustle up all number of activities, and this couple are particularly resourceful. Not only do they rent out rooms in their engaging casa, they also organize walks, cycling tours, horseback riding, massage, salsa lessons and visits to a nearby farm and tobacco plantation. The services are enhanced by the fact that Yarelis is a qualified national park biologist and Yoan's father owns the Garden of Eden-like **Finca Raúl Reyes**, 1km out of town, nestled beneath the *mogotes*. For a small fee Yoan will take you there (and onto the **Cueva de la Vaca**) to sample fruit, coffee and a dose of throat-warming rum. The area's best climbing kicks off nearby. It's sublime.

Tours

Cubanacán (☎79-63-93; Salvador Cisneros No 63C; ⏲9am-7pm Mon-Sat) organizes perennially popular day trips to Cayo Levisa (CUC$29), Cayo Jutías (CUC$22), San Tomás Cave (CUC$10) and María la Gorda (CUC$35). There's an organized valley bike tour for CUC$20 and horseback riding from CUC$5. Official park hikes leave from here daily (CUC$8).

Sleeping

Almost every house rents rooms in Viñales, giving you well over one hundred to choose from (you'll always find space somewhere). Most are good, but the below stand out from the crowd. The two hotels within walking distance of Viñales village are both spectacularly located gems.

TOP CHOICE 'Villa los Reyes' – Yoan & Yarelis Reyes CASA PARTICULAR $
(69-52-25; joanmanuel2008@yahoo.es; Rafael Trejo No 134; r CUC$20-25; P ❄ @) A great modern house with all amenities and a secluded patio for dining; the young owners can organize everything from salsa dancing to Spanish lessons. Yarelis is a biologist at the national park and Yoan has Viñales running through his veins. Given the number of sights nearby not served by public transport, it's a blessing that Yoan also offers a taxi service.

TOP CHOICE Hotel los Jazmines HOTEL $$
(79-64-11; Carretera a Pinar del Río; s/d/ste incl breakfast CUC$66/72/90; P ❄ ≋) Prepare yourself: the vista from this pastel-pink colonial-style hotel is one of the best and most quintessential in Cuba. Open the shutters of your classic valley-facing room and drink in the shimmering sight of magnificent *mogotes,* oxen-ploughed red fields and palm-frond-covered tobacco drying houses. While no five-star palace, Los Jazmines benefits from its unrivaled location, gloriously inviting swimming pool and a host of handy extras such as international clinic, massage room and small shop/market. The setting comes at a cost: bus tours stop off here every hour or two eroding some of the ethereal ambience. The hotel is walkable from Viñales: 4km south on the Pinar del Río road. The Viñales tour bus stops here (p188).

Hostal Doña Hilda CASA PARTICULAR $
(79-60-53; Carretera a Pinar del Río Km 25 No 4; r CUC$20-25; ❄) One of the first houses in town on the road from Pinar del Río, Hilda's house is small, unpretentious, and classic Viñales – just like the perennially smiling hostess – with truly wonderful food. The *mojitos* are among Cuba's very best. Ask here about dance classes.

Villa Pitín & Juana CASA PARTICULAR $
(79-33-38; Carretera a Pinar del Río Km 25 No 2; r CUC$25; P ❄) With two wonderful rooms on separate floors (the top floor with the private double patio is the classic traveler retreat) and a fantastic family atmosphere, this place also benefits from scrumptious home cooking. No wonder this is one of the longest-running casas in town.

La Ermita HOTEL $$
(79-62-50; Carretera de La Ermita Km 1.5; s/d incl breakfast CUC$46/54; P ❄ ≋) While Los Jazmines might edge the prize for best view, La Ermita takes top honors for architecture, interior furnishings and all-round services and quality. It's also a lot less frenetic, thanks to the absence of any tour buses. Among a plethora of extracurricular attractions are an excellent pool, skillfully mixed cocktails, tennis courts, a shop, horseback riding and massage. Rooms with views are housed in handsome two-story colonial edifices and the restaurant is an ideal perch for breakfast. You can walk the 2km downhill to the village or take the Viñales tour bus (p188).

Villa Cafetal CASA PARTICULAR $
(533-11752; Adela Ascuy Final; r CUC$15-20; ❄) The owners of this reader-recommended house are experts on climbing and have a shed stacked with equipment: appropriately, since the best climbs in Viñales are on their doorstep. Ensconced in a resplendant garden which cultivates its own coffee (yes, you get it for breakfast) you can practically taste the mountain air here as you swing on the hammock. There's only one room, though.

El Balcón & Casa Josefína & Esther CASA PARTICULAR $
(69-67-25, 79-31-65, Rafael Trejo No 48; r CUC$25; ❄ ≋) Really two places rolled into one, these houses, owned by the same family, lie above each other a block south of the plaza. On top, El Balcón boasts two rooms and a mini swimming pool, and the owners speak English, while Casa Josefína y Esther with its haughty antique furnishings and spacious rear patio has one room available.

Villa Nelson CASA PARTICULAR $
(79-61-94; Camilo Cienfuegos No 4; r CUC$20-25; ❄) Loquacious Nelson has been around for ages surviving Gustav, Ike, high taxes and more. He still offers a prized local cocktail known as Ochún (rum, honey and orange juice) in his homely backyard along with two recently renovated rooms with baths.

Señor Tito Crespo CASA PARTICULAR $
(79-33-83; Las Maravillas No 58; r CUC$20; ❄) Last but not least, on the way out of Viñales towards the northern part of Parque Na-

Valle de Viñales

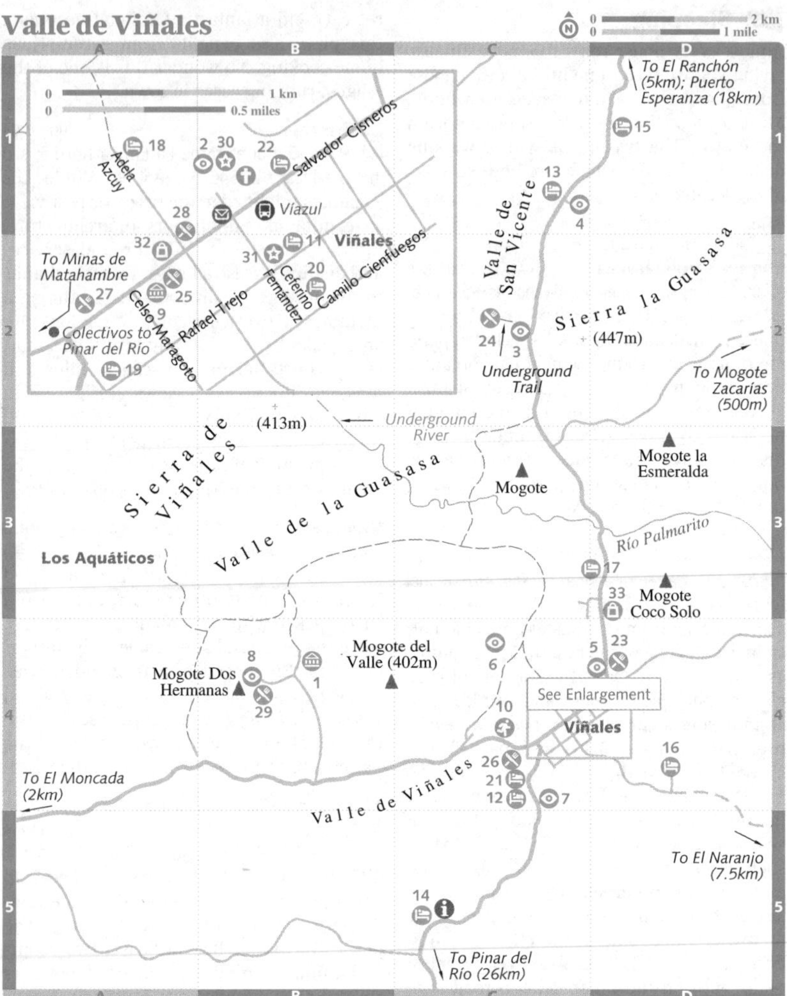

cional Viñales, is this house with two large rooms. A patio and an impressive bar are out back. On the edge of town, you feel immersed in the countryside here. The owner is a fount of knowledge on folk music.

Villa Purry & Isis CASA PARTICULAR $
(☎69-69-21; Salvador Cisneros No 64; r CUC$20) This expansive colonial casa with one room on offer has a column-bedecked front terrace with rocking chairs to watch the world trundle by, and a rear patio too. It's a stone's throw from the plaza.

Eating & Drinking

Viñales home-cooking is some of the best in Cuba – eat at your casa particular! Hostal Doña Hilda and Villa los Reyes are particularly recommended: they'll rustle something tasty up even if you're not staying there. The following places are OK if you're stuck for lunch.

Restaurante la Casa de Don Tomás CARIBBEAN, INTERNATIONAL $$
(Salvador Cisneros No 140; ⏲10am-11pm) The oldest house in Viñales is also its best restaurant – by default (there's no real opposition). The

Valle de Viñales

Sights

1 Archaeological Museum B4
2 Casa de la Cultura B1
3 Cueva de San Miguel C2
4 Cueva del Indio C1
5 El Jardín de Caridad D4
6 Finca Raúl Reyes C4
7 La Casa del Veguero C4
8 Mural de la Prehistoria B4
9 Museo Municipal A2

Activities, Courses & Tours

10 Carlos Millo C4
Villa los Reyes .... (see 19)
Yoan & Yarelis Reyes .... (see 19)

Sleeping

11 El Balcón/Casa Josefina & Esther B2
12 Hostal Doña Hilda C4
13 Hostal las Magnolias C1
14 Hotel los Jazmines C5
15 Hotel Rancho San Vicente D1
16 La Ermita D4
17 Señor Tito Crespo D3
18 Villa Cafetal A1
19 Villa los Reyes A2
20 Villa Nelson B2
21 Villa Pitín & Juana C4
22 Villa Purry & Isis B1

Eating

23 El Estanco II D4
24 El Palenque de los Cimarrones C2
25 El Viñaiero A2
La Casa del Veguero .... (see 7)
26 Mercado Agropecuario C4
27 Restaurante la Casa de Don Tomás A2
28 Restaurante Las Brisas A1
29 Restaurante Mural de la Prehistoria B4

Entertainment

30 Centro Cultural Polo Montañez B1
31 Cine Viñales B2
Patio del Decimista .... (see 32)

Shopping

32 ARTex A2
33 Casa del Habano D3

casa, with its terra-cotta roof and exuberant flowering vines, is suitably salubrious and the house special, *las delicias de Don Tomás,* a rich mélange of rice, lobster, fish, pork, chicken and sausage with an egg on top (CUC$10), is divine. There's a good wine selection too. If live music sessions get too much for your eardrums, the balcony above provides respite.

El Estanco II ITALIAN $
(Carretera a Esperanza; ⏰10am-11pm) A simple pizza and beer place 1km out of town on the road north, and a decent pit stop. A pizza costs a couple of convertibles, a plate of spaghetti slightly more.

Restaurante las Brisas CARIBBEAN $
(Salvador Cisneros No 96; ⏰11:30am-10pm) This place serves deep-fried chicken and *congrí* (rice) for peanuts, otherwise pick up a lunchtime grilled-cheese sandwich at either the Patio del Decimista or the Centro Cultural Polo Montañez.

La Casa del Veguero CARIBBEAN $
(☎79-60-80; Carretera a Pinar del Río Km 24; ⏰10am-5pm) Just outside Viñales toward Pinar del Río, this *ranchón* (rural restaurant) serves mediocre à la carte items (from CUC$5). It's a Viñales bus tour stop; there's a *secadero* (drying house) adjacent.

El Viñaiero BAR
(Salvador Cisneros btwn Celso Mararagoto & Adela Azcuy; ⏰11am-midnight Sun-Fri, 8am-midnight Sat) Delectable juices and cocktails, Creole food and run-of-the-mill pizza. If Patio del Decimista is too full or frantic, travelers amicably congregate here.

Mercado Agropecuario MARKET
(Carretera a Dos Hermanas Km 1) Viñales' agricultural market is about 100m from town at the west end of Salvador Cisneros down the road toward Dos Hermanas. Get your peso rum and Convertible bread here.

☆ Entertainment

Centro Cultural Polo Montañez LIVE MUSIC
(cnr Salvador Cisneros & Joaquin Pérez; admission after 9pm CUC$2) Named for the late Pinar del Río resident-turned-*guajiro* hero, Polo Montañez, this open-to-the-elements patio off the main plaza is a bar-restaurant with a full-blown stage and lighting rig that comes alive after 9pm.

Patio del Decimista LIVE MUSIC
(Salvador Cisneros No 102; admission free; ⏲music at 9pm) Smaller but equally ebullient is this long-standing place that serves live music, cold beers, snacks and great cocktails.

Cine Viñales CINEMA
(cnr Ceferino Fernández & Rafael Trejo) The settlement's only cinema is a block south of the main square.

Shopping

ARTex SOUVENIRS
(Salvador Cisneros No 102) You can get postcards, T-shirts and CDs here. It's attached to the Patio del Decimista.

La Casa del Veguero CIGARS, BOOKS
(☎79-60-80; Carretera a Pinar del Río km 24; ⏲10am-5pm) A hot selection of cigars – many made right on-site – and books on Cuba

Information

Internet Access & Telephone

Etecsa Telepunto (Ceferino Fernández No 3; internet per hr CUC$6; ⏲8:30am-4:30pm) One of Cuba's tiniest Telepunto offices where two computers are squeezed into an office that accommodates three Etecsa clerks.

Medical Services

Farmacia Internacional (☎79-64-11) In Hotel los Jazmines.

Money

Banco de Crédito y Comercio (Salvador Cisneros No 58; ⏲8am-noon & 1:30-3pm Mon-Fri, 8-11am Sat)

Cadeca (cnr Salvador Cisneros & Adela Azcuy; ⏲8:30am-4pm Mon-Sat)

Post

Post office (cnr Salvador Cisneros & Ceferino Fernández; ⏲9am-6pm Mon-Sat) Relocated to a small booth near the park post Hurricane Gustav.

Travel agencies

Cubanacán (☎79-63-93; Salvador Cisneros No 63C; ⏲9am-7pm Mon-Sat) Arranges tours, excursions and transfer buses.

Havanatur (☎79-62-62; Salvador Cisneros No 65; ⏲9am-7pm Mon-Sat) Similar to Cubanacán next door but with a few different offers.

Getting There & Around

Bus

The well-ordered **Víazul ticket office** (Salvador Cisneros No 63A; ⏲8am-noon & 1-3pm) is opposite the main square in the same building as Cubataxi. The daily Víazul bus for Havana via Pinar del Río departs at 8am, 2pm and 6pm (CUC$12). The morning bus continues to Cienfuegos (CUC$32; eight hours) and Trinidad (nine hours 30 minutes). At the time of research only the second bus stopped in Las Terrazas.

There are also daily transfer buses to Havana (CUC$15), Soroa (CUC$12) and Las Terrazas (CUC$12); and a daily – except Tuesday – service to Cienfuegos (CUC$25) and Trinidad (CUC$40). The transfers to Cayo Levisa (CUC$29; two person minimum), Cayo Jutías (CUC$22; six minimum) and María la Gorda (CUC$35; six minimum) run if enough people book. Cayo Levisa departs most days while María la Gorda runs approximately once a week. Transfers can be booked through Havanatur or Cubanacán (p184).

Car & Moped

To reach Viñales from the south, take the long and winding road from Pinar del Río; the roads from the north coast are not as sinuous, but are pretty drives. The remote mountain road from the Península de Guanahacabibes through Guane and Pons is one of Cuba's most spectacular routes. Allow a lot of travel time.

Car hire can be arranged at **Cubacar** (☎79-60-60; Salvador Cisneros No 63C; ⏲9am-7pm) in the Cubanacán office and **Havanautos** (☎76-63-30; Salvador Cisneros final) opposite the Servi-Cupet gas station at the northeast end of Viñales town.

Mopeds can be rented for CUC$24 a day at Restaurante la Casa de Don Tomás.

Taxi

Cubataxi (☎79-31-95; Salvador Cisneros No 63A) shares an office with Víazul. Drivers hanging around outside will take you to Pinar del Río for approximately CUC$15, Palma Rubia (for the boat to Cayo Levisa) for CUC$28 or Gran Caverna de Santo Tomás for CUC$13. Good value at around CUC$60 are the cabs to José Martí International Airport: the ride from Havana to the airport alone costs CUC$25.

For cheaper travel to Pinar, head to the intersection of the Carretera a Pinar del Río and Salvador Cisneros, just down from Restaurante la Casa de Don Tomás: old 1950s *colectivo* taxis splutter the route for CUC$1 per seat.

Viñales Bus Tour

The Viñales Bus Tour is a hop-on/hop-off minibus that runs nine times a day between the valley's spread-out sites. Starting and finishing in the town plaza, the whole circuit takes an hour and five minutes with the first bus leaving at 9am and the last at 4:50pm. There are 18 stops along the route, which runs from Hotel los Jazmines to Hotel Rancho San Vincente, and all are clearly marked with route maps and timetables. All-day tickets cost CUC$5 and can be purchased on the bus.

Parque Nacional Viñales

Parque Nacional Viñales' extraordinary cultural landscape covers 150 sq km and supports a population of 25,000 people. A mosaic of *mogote*-studded settlements grow coffee, tobacco, sugarcane, oranges, avocados and bananas on some of the oldest landscapes in Cuba.

Sights

Mural de la Prehistoria RUINS

(admission incl drink CUC$3) Four kilometers west of Viñales village on the side of Mogote Dos Hermanas is a 120m-long painting designed in 1961 by Leovigildo González Morillo, a follower of Mexican artist Diego Rivera (the idea was hatched by Celia Sánchez, Alicia Alonso and Antonio Núñez Jiménez). On a cliff at the foot of the 617m-high Sierra de Viñales, the highest portion of the Sierra de los Órganos, this massive mural took 18 people four years to complete. The huge snail, dinosaurs, sea monsters and humans on the cliff symbolize the theory of evolution and are either impressively psychedelic or monumentally horrific, depending on your point of view. You don't really have to get up close to appreciate the artwork, but the admission fee is waived if you take the delicious, if a little overpriced, CUC$15 lunch at the site restaurant. Horses are usually available here (CUC$5 per hour) for various excursions.

Campismo Dos Hermanas MUSEUM

(☎79-32-23) Just before the Mural de la Prehistoria entrance is a small yet riveting **archaeological museum** in the grounds of Campismo Dos Hermanas, which gives you far better an insight into prehistory than the mural. Another restaurant (open to foreigners although the campismo is not) is here too.

Los Aquáticos HIKE, TRADITIONAL VILLAGE

(3-hour tour per person incl Spanish-speaking guide CUC$10)A kilometer beyond the turn-off to Dos Hermanas, a dirt road leads toward the mountain community of Los Aquáticos, founded in 1943 by followers of visionary Antoñica Izquierdo, who discovered the healing power of water when the *campesinos* of this area had no access to conventional medicine. They colonized the mountain slopes and several families still live there. Unfortunately, the last patriarch practicing the water cure died in 2002, taking the tradition with him, but you can still visit. Los Aquáticos is accessible only by horse or on foot. Ask at your casa for guide contacts; horses can be hired from farmers living near the trailhead. From the main road it's 1km inland to the trailhead (just across the stream) of La Ruta de las Aguas. After your visit, you can make this a loop by continuing on this road (fork left at the same stream, recrossing it a few hundred meters to the east) another 3km to Campismo Dos Hermanas and the cliff paintings; it's a wonderfully scenic route (the complete Los Aquáticos–Dos Hermanas circuit totals 6km from the main highway).

CLIMBING IN VIÑALES

You don't need to be Reinhold Messner to recognize the unique climbing potential of Viñales, Cuba's mini-Yosemite. Sprinkled with steep-sided *mogotes* (limestone monoliths) and blessed with whole photo-albums' worth of stunning natural vistas, climbers from around the world have been coming here for over a decade to indulge in a sport that has yet to be officially sanctioned by the Cuban government.

Thanks to the numerous gray areas, Viñales climbing remains very much a word-of-mouth affair. There are no printed route maps and no official on-the-ground information (indeed, most state-employed tourist reps will deny all knowledge of it). If you are keen to get up onto the rock-face, your first point of reference should be the comprehensive website of **Cuba Climbing** (www.cubaclimbing.com). Once on the ground, the best nexus for climbers is Casa de Oscar (Adela Azcuy No 43) and the Villa Cafetal (p185).

Viñales has numerous well-known climbing routes and a handful of skillful Cuban guides, but there's no reliable equipment hire (bring your own) and no adequate safety procedures in place. Everything you do is at your own risk, and this includes any sticky situations you may encounter with the authorities (although they generally tend to turn a blind eye). Also bear in mind that unregulated climbing in a national park area has the potential to damage endangered flora and ecosystems. Proceed with caution and care.

Cueva del Indio CAVE
(admission CUC$5; ⏲9am-5:30pm) North of here is the prettiest part of Viñales, although the cave itself, 5.5km north of Viñales village, is very popular with tourists. An ancient indigenous dwelling, it was rediscovered in 1920. Motor boats now ply the underground river through the electrically lit cave.

Cueva de San Miguel CAVE
(admission CUC$1; ⏲9am-5:30pm) This is a smaller cave at the jaws of the Valle de San Vicente. Your entrance fee gets you into a gaping cave that engulfs you for five minutes or so before dumping you a tad cynically in the El Palenque de los Cimarrones restaurant.

Activities

Cycling

Despite the hilly terrain, Viñales is one of the best places in Cuba to cycle (note: there are no off-road routes). Restaurante la Casa de Don Tomás usually rents bikes (p186). You can also inquire at your casa particular. Viñales residents have a habit of making marvelous two-wheeled cycling machines appear out of thin air. Agencies in town offer valley cycling tours.

Hiking

The Parque Nacional Viñales has three official hikes (four if you count the Gran Caverna de Santo Tomás) and others continually under 'consideration.' All of them can be arranged directly at the visitor center, the Museo Municipal, or the town's tour agencies. The cost is CUC$6 to CUC$8 per person.

Below are just the official hikes. There are many more unofficial treks available and asking around at your casa particular will elicit further suggestions. Try the hike to Los Aquáticos with its incredible vistas, the Cueva de la Vaca, a cave that forms a tunnel through the *mogotes* and is easily accessible (1.5km) from Viñales village, and the **Palmerito Valley**, infamous among in-the-know locals for its high-stakes cockfights.

Cocosolo Palmarito HIKE
This walk starts on a spur road just before La Ermita hotel and progresses for 8km past the Coco Solo and Palmarito *mogotes* and the Mural de la Prehistoria. There are good views here and plenty of opportunities to discover the local flora and fauna including a visit to a tobacco *finca* (farmhouse; ask about lunch with one of the families there). It returns you to the main road back to Viñales.

Maravillas de Viñales HIKE
A 5km loop beginning 1km before El Moncada and 13km from the Dos Hermanas turn-off, this hike takes in endemic plants, orchids and the biggest ant-cutter hive in Cuba (so they say).

San Vicente/Ancón HIKE
The trail around the more remote Valle Ancón enables you to check out still-functioning coffee communities in a valley surrounded by *mogotes*: it's an 8km loop.

Horseback Riding

The lush hills and valleys (and the *guajiros*, indeed) around town lend themselves to horseback riding, particularly the Palmarito Valley and the route to Los Aquáticos. Ask at Villa los Reyes (p185) or the Mural de la Prehistoria.

Carlos Millo HORSEBACK RIDING
(☎522-39071) A recommended guide is Señor Millo, based at the southwestern end of town down a track off the Minas de Matahambre road.

Swimming

It is possible to swim in a natural pool at **La Cueva de Palmerito** in the Palmerito Valley. This place is a doable hike/horseback ride from Viñales. Ask the locals for directions.

Sleeping

Now the Campismo Dos Hermanas is closed to foreigners, options are limited.

Hotel Rancho San Vicente HOTEL $$
(☎79-62-01; Carretera a Esperanza Km 33; s/d CUC$42/60; P❄≋) After Viñales' two spectacularly located hotels, you probably thought it couldn't get any better, but Rancho San Vicente does a good job trying. Situated 7km north of the village, this highly attractive hotel nestled in a grove with two dozen or more wooden cabins is lush and – for once – the interior furnishings match the magnificent setting. There's a restaurant, pool, massage facility and short bird-watching hike on-site.

Hostal las Magnolias HOSTEL $
(☎79-62-80; Carretera a Esperanza Km 38; CUC$25; P❄) This small, lackluster build-

ing with three rooms (restaurant attached) opposite the Cueva del Indio offers a cheap alternative to Hotel Rancho San Vicente. Self-caterers will appreciate the shared kitchen.

Eating & Drinking

TOP CHOICE **El Ranchón** CARIBBEAN $$
(Carretera a Esperanza Km 38; ⊙8am-5pm) Eat here! You won't forget the experience. The set meal, which is (judging by the crowds) a proverbial rite of passage on the tour bus circuit, is melt-in-your-mouth delicious. You pay CUC$11 for a huge traditional spread of roast pork and all the trimmings.

Restaurante Mural de la Prehistoria CARIBBEAN, INTERNATIONAL $$
(⊙8am-7pm) Steep but almost worth it, the Mural's humungous CUC$15 set lunch – tasty pork roasted and smoked over natural charcoal – ought to keep you going at least until tomorrow's breakfast.

El Palenque de los Cimarrones CARIBBEAN $
(⊙noon-4pm) If you're exploring the murky Cueva de San Miguel, you'll be unsubtly ushered through this restaurant as you grope for the exit. It's an odd combination of folklore show, eating joint and plantation slavery museum, but the young Cubans dressed as *cimarrones* (runaway slaves) don't really stimulate the appetite.

Information

The park is administered through the highly informative **Parque Nacional Viñales Visitors Center** (☎79-61-44; Carretera a Pinar del Río Km 22; ⊙8am-6pm) on the hill just before you reach Hotel los Jazmines. Inside, colorful displays (in Spanish and English) map out the park's main features. Hiking information and guides are also on hand.

Getting Around

Bike, car, moped or the Viñales Bus Tour (p188); take your pick.

West of Viñales

El Moncada, a pioneering postrevolutionary workers' settlement 14km west of Dos Hermanas and 1.5km off the road to Minas de Matahambre, is also the site of the **Gran Caverna de Santo Tomás** (admission CUC$8; ⊙8:30am-3pm), Cuba's most extensive cave system and the second-largest on the American continent. There are over 46km of galleries on eight levels, with a 1km section accessible to visitors. There's no artificial lighting, but headlamps are provided for the 90-minute guided tour. Expect bats, stalagmites and stalactites, underground pools, interesting rock formations and a replica of an ancient native Indian mural. Specialists should contact the **Escuela de Espeleología** (☎79-31-45) for more information.

The visitor center contains a small **museum** (admission CUC$1; ⊙10am-10pm) with ephemera relating to Cuban scientist Antonio Núñez Jiménez. Most people visit the cave on an organized trip from Viñales. Further north on the Cayo Jutías road, the scattered old mining community of Minas de Matahambre has a **Museo Municipal** (admission CUC$1; ⊙Mon-Sat) dedicated to the harrowing history of mining hereabouts.

THE NORTHERN COAST

Considering their relative proximity to Havana, Pinar del Río province's northern shores are remote and largely unexplored. Facilities are sparse and roads are rutted on the isolated Gulf of Mexico coast, though visitors who take the time to make the journey out have reported memorable DIY adventures and famously hospitable locals.

Cayo Jutías

Pinar del Río's most discovered 'undiscovered' beach is the 3km-long blanket of sand that adorns the northern coast of Cayo Jutías, a tiny mangrove-covered key situated approximately 65km northwest of Viñales and attached to the mainland by a short *pedraplén* (causeway). Jutías – named for its indigenous tree rats – vies with Cayo Levisa to the east for the title of the province's most picturesque beach and, while the latter might be prettier, the former has less crowds and more tranquility.

The serenity is thanks to the lack of any permanent accommodation (unlike Levisa). The only facilities on the island are the airy oceanside **Restaurante Cayo Jutías** (⊙11am-5pm), specializing in local seafood, and a small beach hut that rents out kayaks for CUC$1 per hour and runs snorkeling trips to an offshore reef for CUC$12. Beyond the initial arc of sand the beach continues for 3km; you can hike barefoot through the mangroves. The Cayo's access road starts about 4km west of Santa Lucía. Four kilometers further on you'll come to a control post at the beginning of the causeway where you'll need to pay a CUC$5 per person entry fee. Ten minutes later the **Faro de Cayo Jutías** appears, a metal lighthouse built by the US in 1902. The route ends at the white Jutías beach caressed by crystal-clear water, 12.5km from the coastal highway.

Tours from Viñales (basically just transport and a snack lunch) cost CUC$22 and will give you an adequate six hours' beach time. Otherwise you will have to make your own transport arrangements. The fastest, and by far the prettiest, route is Minas de Matahambre, through rolling pine-clad hills.

Puerto Esperanza

Puerto Esperanza (Port of Hope), 6km north of San Cayetano and 25km north of Viñales, is a sleepy fishing village visited sometimes by yachts sailing around the country and, mostly, by absolutely no one. According to town lore, the giant mango trees lining the entry road were planted by slaves in the 1800s. A long pier pointing out into the bay is decent for a jump in the ocean. Otherwise the clocks haven't worked here since… oh…1951.

Sights & Activities

Puerto Esperanza's sights are not the domain of guidebook listings. Rather, this is the kind of low-key, put-down-the-Lonely-Planet sort of place where it's more fun to unravel the social life on your own. Discover some weirdly transcendental Santería ritual or take a spontaneous tour around your neighbor's tobacco plantation in search of pungent peso cigars.

Sleeping & Eating

Villa Leonila Blanco CASA PARTICULAR $

(☎79-36-48; Hermanos Caballeros No 41; r CUC$15; ❄) The town has six legal casas including this one. There are two big rooms with bath, garage and meals, and the option of an independent house out back with a bath.

Getting There & Away

There's a handy Servi-Cupet gas station at San Cayetano. The road to Santa Lucía and Cayo Jutías deteriorates to dirt outside of San Cayetano: expect a throbbing backside if you're on a bike or moped.

Cayo Levisa

More frequented than Cayo Jutías but equally splendid, Cayo Levisa sports a beach-bungalow-style hotel, basic restaurant and fully equipped diving center, yet still manages to feel relatively isolated. Separation from the mainland obviously helps. Unlike other Cuban keys, there's no causeway here, and visitors must make the 35-minute journey by boat from Palma Rubia. It's a well worthwhile trip: three kilometers of sugar-white sand and sapphire waters earmark Cayo Levisa as Pinar del Río's best beach. American writer Ernest Hemingway first 'discovered' the area, part of the Archipiélago de los Colorados, in the early 1940s after he set up a fishing camp on Cayo Paraíso, a smaller coral island 10km to the east. These days Levisa attracts up to 100 visitors daily as well as the 50-plus hotel guests. While you won't feel like an errant Robinson Crusoe here, you should find time (and space) for plenty of rest and relaxation.

Sights & Activities

Levisa has a small marina offering scuba diving for CUC$40 per immersion, including gear and transport to the dive site. fourteen dive sites are peppered off the coast, including towering coral *mogotes* and the popular **Corona de San Carlos** (San Carlos' Crown), the formation of which allows divers to get close to turtles and the like unobserved. Snorkeling plus gear costs CUC$12 and a sunset cruise goes for the same price. Kayaking and aqua biking are also possible.

Sleeping & Eating

Hotel Cayo Levisa HOTEL $$$

(☎75-65-03; s/d CUC$109/136; ❄) With an idyllic tropical beach just outside your front door, you won't worry about the slightly outdated *cabañas* (cabins) and dull food choices here. Expanded to a 40-room capacity in 2006, the Levisa's newer wooden cabins (all with bath) are an improvement on the old concrete blocks and the service has pulled its socks up too. Book ahead as this place is understandably popular.

Mario & Antonia CASA PARTICULAR $

(☎523-01983, 533-56310; Carretera Palma Rubia; r CUC$20; P) A clean, respectable house

700m back from the Palma Rubia dock. One room is for rent.

Getting There & Away

The landing for Cayo Levisa is around 21km northeast of La Palma or 40km west of Bahía Honda. Take the turnoff to Mirian and proceed 4km through a large banana plantation to reach the coast-guard station at Palma Rubia, where there is a **snack bar** (10am-6pm) and the departure dock for the island. The Cayo Levisa boat leaves at 10am and returns at 5pm, and costs CUC$25 per person round-trip (CUC$10 one-way) including lunch. From the Cayo Levisa dock you cross the mangroves on a wooden walkway to the resort and gorgeous beach along the island's north side. If you are without a car, the easiest way to get here is via a day excursion from Viñales, good value at CUC$29 including the boat and lunch.

Playa Mulata Area

Squeezed into the edge of the province on road to Bahia Honda, the countryside around Playa Mulata is the domain of *guajiros*, meditative cattle and the occasional fisherman. Away beyond the isolated beaches rears the ridge of the **Pan de Guajaibón**, one of Western Cuba's highest peaks. There is a bust of independence leader Antonio Maceo at the top. By the turnoff to Playa Mulata, **Villa José Otaño Pimentel** (525-49810; r CUC$15; P) is the only accommodation around, in a serene fruit-tree-festooned garden. José can organize horseback rides (CUC$5 per hour) up Pan de Guajaibón. The decent strip of beach 200 meters down the road has a basic restaurant. The nearest public transport terminates 16km west at the Cayo Levisa turn-off. If terrible tarmac isn't an issue, you can continue along this secluded coast road to Bahia Honda, Soroa and even Havana.

SAN DIEGO DE LOS BAÑOS & AROUND

Halfway between Viñales and Soroa, San Diego de los Baños is a famous spa town but there's more to this area than mud baths and massages. Stop by for some memorable wildlife-watching and to discover one of Che Guevara's old hideaways.

San Diego de los Baños

Sitting 130km southwest of Havana, this nondescript town just north of the Carretera Central is popularly considered the country's best spa location. As with other Cuban spas, its medicinal waters were supposedly 'discovered' in the early colonial period when a sick slave stumbled upon a sulfurous spring, took a revitalizing bath and was miraculously cured. Thanks to its proximity to Havana, San Diego's fame spread quickly and a permanent spa was established here in 1891. During the early 20th century American tourists flocked here, leading to the development of the current hotel-bathhouse complex in the early 1950s.

Sitting beside the Río San Diego, the village enjoys an attractive natural setting, with the Sierra del Rosario to the east, the Sierra de Güira to the west, and a nature reserve with pine, mahogany and cedar forests. It's a favorite spot for bird-watchers. The town, despite numerous possibilities for tourism, has been long due an overhaul by the authorities, who have let it slump into an amiable, leafy lethargy.

Sights & Activities

Balneario San Diego THERMAL BATHS
(8am-5pm) Undergoing refurbishment until late 2011, the Balneario is a decrepit-looking bathing complex where thermal waters of 30°C to 40°C are used to treat all manner of muscular and skin afflictions. The sulfurous waters of these mineral springs are potent and immersions of only 20 minutes per day are allowed (CUC$4/6 for collective/private pools). Mud from the Río San Diego is also used here for revitalizing mud baths (CUC$20). Other health services include massage (CUC$25) and a 15-day course of acupuncture; don't expect fluffy towels and complimentary cups of coffee. The Balneario San Diego is more like a Moroccan hammam than a five-star hotel facility, though it's perennially popular with Cubans undergoing courses of medical treatment, plus the odd curious tourist.

If you're looking for cold water, you can swim at the Hotel Mirador **pool** (admission CUC$1; 9am-6pm).

Sleeping & Eating

Hotel Mirador HOTEL, GRILL $
(77-83-38, 54-88-66; s/d CUC$23/36; P) The Mirador is a low-key gem. Predating the Revolution by five years, the hotel was

built in 1954 to accommodate spa-seekers headed for the adjacent Balneario San Diego. Well-tended terraced gardens slope up to rooms which match the pretty exterior: crisp, cozy and looking for the most part onto balconies with garden and *balneario* views. Downstairs there's a pleasant swimming pool and an outdoor **grill** (meals under CUC$8) that does whole roast pig on a spit. There's also a proper **restaurant** *con una vista* (with a view) inside serving Cuban cuisine. Inquire with the helpful front desk staff (they outnumber guests on most days) about bird-watching trips to the Parque la Güira.

Carlos Alberto González CASA PARTICULAR $
(☎54-89-98; Calle 21A No 3003 btwn 30 & 32; r CUC$20) For a decent casa particular, this house can oblige. If this is full, the owners can point you toward others.

Around San Diego de los Baños

With rough roads and precious little accommodation, the untamed Sierra de Güira, a medley of limestone karst cliffs and swooping pockets of forest west of San Diego de los Baños, is off the tourist radar. This didn't prevent it becoming a retreat for the Revolution's most renowned figures in the past and, to this day, a host of rare birdlife.

Sights

Parque la Güira PARK
Five kilometers west of San Diego de los Baños sprawls surreal Parque la Güira, an abandoned – and vaguely spooky – country mansion surrounded by 219 sq km of protected parkland. Known formerly as the Hacienda Cortina, this rich-man's-fantasy-made-reality was built in the style of a giant urban park during the 1920s and '30s by wealthy lawyer José Manuel Cortina who plunked a stately home in its midst. Various remnants of the estate remain – most notably the grand crenellated entry gate, along with a gatehouse, the ruins of a Chinese pavilion and huge clusters of bamboo – but there's little structure to the surrealism. Wander around to soak up the atmosphere; the complex behind the unimpressive state-operated restaurant (1km beyond the gate and closed at the time of research) is reserved for vacationing military personnel. You'll need your own wheels to get here. Isolation has allowed the park to become an important refuge for birds like the olive-capped warbler and Cuban solitaire: the Hotel Mirador in San Diego de los Baños runs tours.

Cabañas los Pinos RETREAT
Twelve kilometers west of San Diego de los Baños via Parque la Güira is the Cabañas los Pinos, an abandoned mountain retreat used by Castro's secretary Celia Sánchez in the 1960s. The cabins are built like tree houses above the ground with Sánchez' circular abode standing in the center of the eerie complex. It's another rather surreal curiosity that gets few visitors but is worth a spare hour or two of silent contemplation. Ask at Hotel Mirador for directions.

Cueva de los Portales CAVES
(admission CUC$1) During the October 1962 Cuban Missile Crisis, Ernesto 'Che' Guevara transferred the headquarters of the Western Army to this rather spectacular cave, 11km west of Parque la Güira and 16km north of Entronque de Herradura on the Carretera Central. The cave is set in a beautiful remote area among steep-sided vine-covered *mogotes* and was declared a national monument in the 1980s. A small outdoor museum contains a few of Che's roughshod artifacts including his bed and the table where he played chess (while the rest of the world stood at the brink of nuclear Armageddon). Three other caves called **El Espejo**, **El Salvador** and **Cueva Oscura** are up on the hillside. Again, this area is brilliant bird-watching turf: trips can be arranged at the Hotel Mirador, or you can ask the staff at the cave entrance. There's a campismo and small restaurant outside the cave. Both have been closed since Hurricanes Gustav and Ike.

Getting Around

Ask the Havana–Pinar del Río Víazul drivers nicely and they may stop at the Carretera Central turnoff 10km from town. The walk isn't too bad. There's a Servi-Cupet gas station at the entrance to San Diego de los Baños from Havana. The road across the mountains from Cabañas los Pinos and Che Guevara's cave is beautiful, but precariously narrow and full of potholes. That said; a brave driver or super fit (and careful) cyclist should make it.

Matanzas Province

045 / POP 690,223

Includes »

Best Places to Eat

» Restaurante Teni (p202)
» Dante (p213)
» Restaurante Mallorca (p213)
» Casa del Queso Cubano (p213)

Best Places to Stay

» Mansión Xanadú (212)
» Hostal Azul (p202)
» Hotel Varadero Internacional (p211)
» Hostal Alma (p202)
» Finca Confidencia (p223)

Why Go?

With a name translating as 'massacres,' Matanzas province conceals an appropriately tumultuous past beneath its salubrious reputation for glam all-inclusive holidays. Once pillaging pirates ravaged the region's prized north coast; two centuries later, in April 1961, another group of mercenaries grappled ashore in the Bay of Pigs under the dreamy notion that they had arrived to liberate the nation.

The province's modern-day drawcard is Varadero, the vastest Caribbean beach resort and tropical mecca for international mass-tourism, stretching 20km along the sandy Península de Hicacos.

But Matanzas' Cuban soul lies west in its scruffy-yet-pulsating port capital. While glitzy Varadero has spawned high-rise hotels, music-rich Matanzas city has given the world rumba, *danzón* and countless grand neoclassical buildings.

Southward, wild Península de Zapata is the Caribbean's largest swamp, a protected area guarding Cuba's widest variety of ecosystems. Nearby, the Bay of Pigs now attracts more divers than invaders with fantastical offshore coral walls.

When to Go

December through to April is when the all-inclusive hotels in the province's tourist set-piece, Varadero, hike prices for the *temporada alta* (high season). This is the best time for beach-basking: the hurricane season is over and the weather is hot without being unbearable. Hit Matanzas city around October 10th for the annual rumba festival.

NORTHERN MATANZAS

Home to Cuba's largest resort area (Varadero) and one of its biggest ports (Matanzas), the northern coastline is also the province's main population center and a hub for industry and commerce. Despite this, however, the over-riding feel is distinctly green, and most of the region is undulating farmland – think a cross between the North American Prairie and the UK's Norfolk Broads – occasionally rupturing into lush, dramatic valleys like the Valle del Yumurí.

Matanzas

POP 151,354

Sprawled around a vast bay of the same name, visually arresting Matanzas is one of Cuba's cultural giants, awaking slowly from

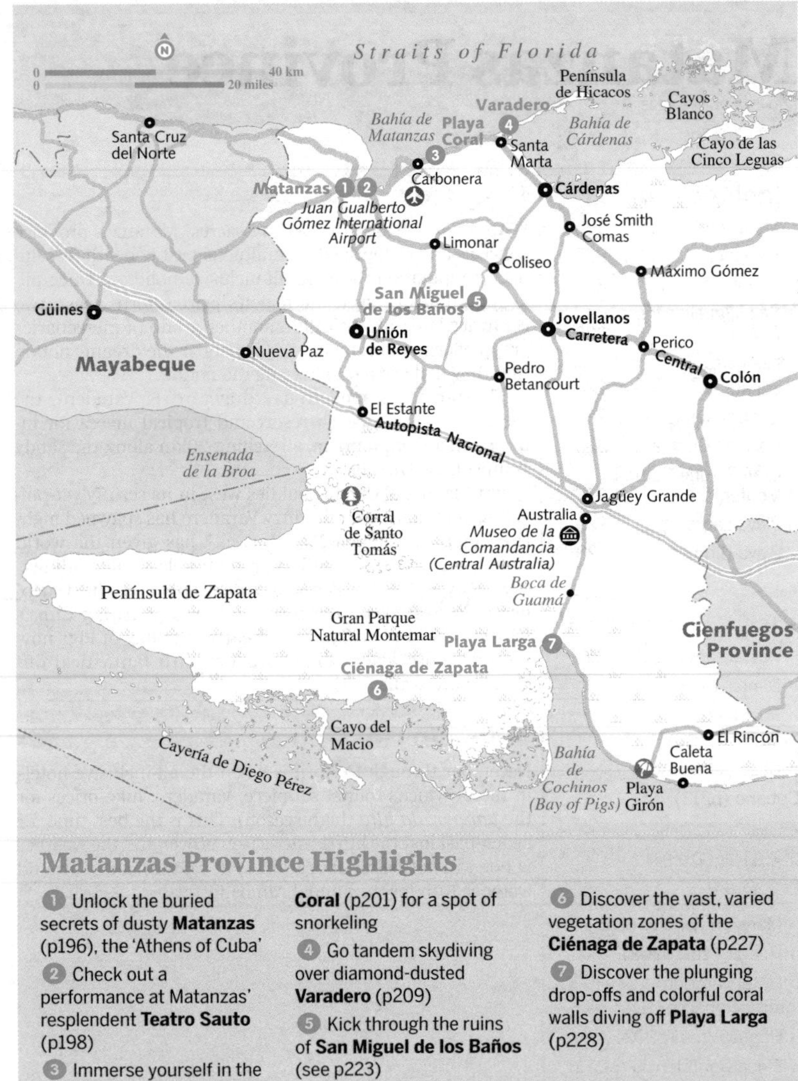

Matanzas Province Highlights

1. Unlock the buried secrets of dusty **Matanzas** (p196), the 'Athens of Cuba'
2. Check out a performance at Matanzas' resplendent **Teatro Sauto** (p198)
3. Immerse yourself in the crystalline waters of **Playa Coral** (p201) for a spot of snorkeling
4. Go tandem skydiving over diamond-dusted **Varadero** (p209)
5. Kick through the ruins of **San Miguel de los Baños** (see p223)
6. Discover the vast, varied vegetation zones of the **Ciénaga de Zapata** (p227)
7. Discover the plunging drop-offs and colorful coral walls diving off **Playa Larga** (p228)

MATANZAS STREET NAMES

The numbering system of Matanzas' streets is confusing. Even-numbered north–south streets bear even numbers, beginning at Calle 268 near the bay. Odd-numbered east–west streets increase from Calle 75 at the Yumurí bridge (Puente de la Concordia) to Calle 97 along the banks of the San Juan.

Matanzas residents ignore the numbering system of their streets and continue using the old colonial street names. However, here we have used the numbers because that's what you'll see on street corners.

OLD NAME	NEW NAME
Contreras	Calle 79
Daoíz	Calle 75
Maceo	Calle 77
Medio/Independencia	Calle 85
Milanés	Calle 83
San Luis	Calle 298
Santa Teresa	Calle 290
Zaragoza	Calle 292

a long slumber. Split by two rivers and surrounded by coast to make even nearby Varadero's touts give a concerned backward glance, the *Ciudad de los puentes* (city of bridges) has two key reasons to visit, stationed either side of the Río Yumurí. Amid the bright but sleepy streets to the south, the city's principal plazas harbor vestiges of its 19th-century heyday – when influential white residents concocted great works of literature, and architectural jewels to trump even Havana shot up. Simultaneously, north of the river in the dynamic *barrio* (neighborhood) of Versalles, freed slaves, united in secret brotherhoods or *cabildos*, began to measure out the drum patterns that gave birth to what the world now knows as rumba.

Sadly for Matanzas, it lies on the main route between Havana and Varadero 32km to the east: since the Revolution the city's grand buildings have been overlooked by the former and its coastal appeal by the latter. Fifty years of dust is only now being wiped away, but with Varadero funds poised to infiltrate city coffers and some of western Cuba's most atmospheric casas particulares having established themselves, things are looking up.

Spanning cave-riddled valleys and a yawning swath of beach with offshore reefs yielding top-notch diving, Matanzas municipality and its striking amalgam of bridges hide plenty of places from which to appreciate the unhurried pace of life local.

If it's five-star comforts you're after, hop on a Víazul bus to Planet Varadero. But if any combination of ritualistic drum beats, battered colonial charm, cutting-edge theatre and underground (or underwater) adventures appeals, stay awhile: this gritty port is starting to gleam. Particularly, that is, if you bring that duster.

History

In 1508 Sebastián de Ocampo sighted a bay that the indigenous population called Guanima. Now known as the Bahía de Matanzas, it's said the name recalls the *matanza* (massacre) of a group of Spaniards during an early indigenous uprising. In 1628 the Dutch pirate Piet Heyn captured a Spanish treasure fleet carrying 12 million gold florins, ushering in a lengthy era of smuggling and piracy. Undeterred by the pirate threat, 30 families from the Canary Islands arrived in 1693, on the orders of King Carlos III of Spain, to found the town of San Carlos y Severino de Matanzas; the first fort went up in 1734. More conflict would arrive here too: in 1898 the bay saw the first engagement of the Spanish-American War.

In the late 18th and 19th centuries Matanzas flourished economically, through the building of numerous sugar mills and coffee exporting. In 1843, with the laying of the first railway to Havana, the floodgates for prosperity were opened.

The second half of the 19th century became a golden age in Matanzas' history: the city set new cultural benchmarks with the development of a newspaper, a public library, a high school, a theater and a philharmonic society. Due to the large number of writers and intellectuals living in the area, Matanzas became known as the 'Athens of Cuba' with a cultural scene that dwarfed even Havana.

It was then that African slaves, imported to meet burgeoning labor demands, began to foster another reputation for Matanzas as the spiritual home of rumba. In tandem, and from the same roots, spread a network of Santería *cabildos* (associations) – brotherhoods of those from slave descent who came together to celebrate the traditions and rituals of their African ancestors. Both rumba and *cabildos* flourish here to this day.

Other landmarks in Matanzas' history include staging Cuba's first *danzón* performance (1879); later the city produced nationally important poets Cintio Vitier and Carilda Oliver Labra.

Sights & Activities

CITY CENTER

Teatro Sauto THEATER

(Plaza de la Vigía; ☎24-27-21) The defining symbol of the city according to Diego Rivera, the Teatro Sauto (1863) on the plaza's south side is one of Cuba's finest theaters and famous for its superb acoustics. The lobby is graced by marble Greek goddesses and the main-hall ceiling bears paintings of the muses. Three balconies enclose this 775-seat theater, which features a floor that can be raised to convert the auditorium into a ballroom. The original theater curtain is a painting of Matanzas' very own **Puente de la Concordia**, and notables like Soviet dancer Anna Pavlova have performed here. Much-needed restoration work should have been completed by the end of 2011. Performances are generally Friday and Saturday nights and Sunday afternoons.

Puente Calixto García LANDMARK

If you've only got time to see *one* bridge (there are 21 in total) in Cuba's celebrated 'city of bridges,' get an eyeful of this impressive steel structure built in 1899, spanning the Río San Juan with its kayaks floating lazily by. Just south is an eye-catching **Che Mural** while the northern side leads directly into Plaza de la Vigía.

Plaza de la Vigía SQUARE

The original Plaza de Armas still remains as Plaza de la Vigía (literally 'lookout place'), a reference to the threat from piracy and smuggling that the first settlers here faced. This diminutive square was where Matanzas was founded in the late 17th century and numerous historical buildings still stand guard.

Ediciones Vigía BOOK WORKSHOP

(Plaza de la Vigía cnr Calle 91; ⏰9am-6pm) To the southwest of the plaza is this unique book publisher, founded in 1985. It produces high-quality handmade paper and 1st-edition books on a variety of topics. The books are typed, stenciled and pasted in editions of 200 copies. Visitors are welcome in the workshop and can purchase numbered and signed copies (CUC$5 to CUC$15).

Museo Histórico Provincial MUSEUM

(cnr Calles 83 & 272; admission CUC$2; ⏰10am-6pm Tue-Fri, 1-7pm Sat, 9am-noon Sun) Aka Palacio del Junco (1840), this double-arched edifice on the Plaza de la Vigía showcases the full sweep of Matanzas' history from 1693 to the present. Cultural events are also held here.

Museo Farmaceútico MUSEUM

(Calle 83 No 4951; admission CUC$3; ⏰10am-6pm Mon-Sat, 8am-noon Sun) On Parque Libertad, Matanzas' modern nexus with a bronze statue (1909) of José Martí in its center, you'll find one of the city's showcase sights, the Museo Farmaceútico. Founded in 1882 by the Triolett family, this antique pharmacy was the first of its type in Latin America. The fine displays include all the odd bottles, instruments and suchlike used in the trade.

Biblioteca Gener y Del Monte NOTABLE BUILDING

(cnr Calles 79 & 290) Staying on Parque Libertad, this library, formerly the Casino Español, is on the northern side beside the just-renovated, grandiose peach facade of Hotel Velazco. The library was where the first performance of the *danzonete* (ballroom dance) Rompiendo la Rutina, by Anceto Díaz, took place.

Catedral de San Carlos Borromeo CHURCH

(Calle 282 btwn Calles 83 & 85; donation welcome; ⏰8am-noon & 3-5pm Mon-Sat, 9am-noon Sun) Standing back from the meleé of Calle 83 behind shady Plaza de la Iglesia, this once-great, perennially shut, neoclassical cathedral was constructed in 1693 and contains some of Cuba's most famous frescoes, suffering terribly after years of neglect.

Archivo Histórico NOTABLE BUILDING
(Calle 83 No 28013 btwn Calles 280 & 282) The city archives are housed in the former residence of local poet José Jacinto Milanés (1814–63). A bronze statue of Milanés stands on the nearby Plaza de la Iglesia in front of the cathedral.

Palacio de Gobierno NOTABLE BUILDING
(Calle 288 btwn Calles 79 & 83) Dating from 1853, this muscular building dominates the east side of Parque Libertad; these days it's the seat of the Poder Popular (Popular Power), the local government.

Palacio de Justicia NOTABLE BUILDING
(Plaza de la Vigía & Calle 85) This is another impressive construction on the Plaza de la Vigía opposite the Teatro Sauto, first erected in 1826 and rebuilt between 1908 and 1911.

Palmar del Junco SPORTS VENUE
(Calle 171) Baseball fans can make the pilgrimage to the south of the city, the site of Cuba's first baseball field (1904) and a source of much civic pride.

VERSALLES & THE NORTH

North of the Río Yumurí, Versalles is the birthplace of rumba. From the Plaza de la Vigía you enter the *barrio* by taking Calle 272 across graceful **Puente de la Concordia**.

Castillo de San Severino FORT
(☎28-32-59; Av del Muelle; admission CUC$2, camera CUC$1; ⏲10am-7pm Tue-Sat, 9am-noon Sun) Northeast of Versalles lies this formidable crenellation built by the Spanish in 1735 as part of Cuba's defensive ring. Slaves were offloaded here in the 18th century and, later, Cuban patriots were imprisoned within the walls – and sometimes executed. San Severino remained a prison until the 1970s and in more recent times became the scantly populated slavery-themed **Museo de la Ruta de los Esclavos** (admission CUC$2; ⏲10am-6pm). The castle itself with its well-preserved central square has great views of the Bahía de Matanzas. A taxi from the city center costs CUC$2.

Iglesia de Monserrate CHURCH
For an excellent view of Matanzas and the picturesque Valle del Yumurí, climb 1.5km northeast of the center up Calle 306 to the recently renovated church dating from 1875. The lofty bastion perched high above the city was built by colonists from Catalonia in Spain as a symbol of their regional power. The lookout near here has a couple of *ranchón*-style restaurants good for skull-splitting music and basic refreshments.

Iglesia de San Pedro Apóstol CHURCH
(cnr Calles 57 & 270) In the heart of Versalles, this neoclassical church is another Matanzas jewel in need of a makeover.

OUTSIDE TOWN

Cuevas de Bellamar CAVES
(☎26-16-83, 25-35-38; admission CUC$8, camera CUC$5; ⏲9am-5pm; 👪) The Cuevas de Bellamar, 5km southeast of Matanzas, are 300,000 years old and locally promoted as Cuba's oldest tourist attraction. There are 2500m of caves here, discovered in 1861 by a Chinese workman in the employ of Don Manual Santos Parga. A 45-minute Cuevas de Bellamar visit leaves almost hourly starting at 9:30am; well-maintained, well-lit paths mean it's easy for kids to imbibe the stupendous geology, too. The caves on show include a vast 12m stalagmite and an underground stream; cave walls glitter eerily with crystals. The entrance is through a small museum. Outside the Cuevas de Bellamar are two restaurants and a playground. To get there, take bus 16, 17 or 20 east toward Canímar and ask the driver to let you out near Calle 226. From there it's a 30-minute walk uphill to the caves.

Río Canímar & Around NATURE RESERVE
Boat trips on the Río Canímar, 8km east of Matanzas, are a truly magical experience. Gnarly mangroves dip their jungle-like branches into the ebbing water and a warm haze caresses the regal palm trees as your boat slides silently 12km upstream from an insalubrious start beneath the Vía Blanca bridge. Cubamar (p218) in Varadero offers this wonderful excursion with lunch, horseback riding, fishing and snorkeling for CUC$25, or you can chance it by showing up at the landing below the bridge on the east side. Rowboats (CUC$2 per hour) are also available here for rent anytime from **Bar Cubamar**.

Castillo del Morrillo CASTLE
(admission CUC$1; ⏲9am-5pm Tue-Sun) On the Matanzas side of the Río Canímar bridge, a road runs 1km down to a cove presided over by the four guns of this yellow-painted castle (1720). The castle is now a museum dedicated to the student leader Antonio Guiteras Holmes (1906–35), who founded

Matanzas

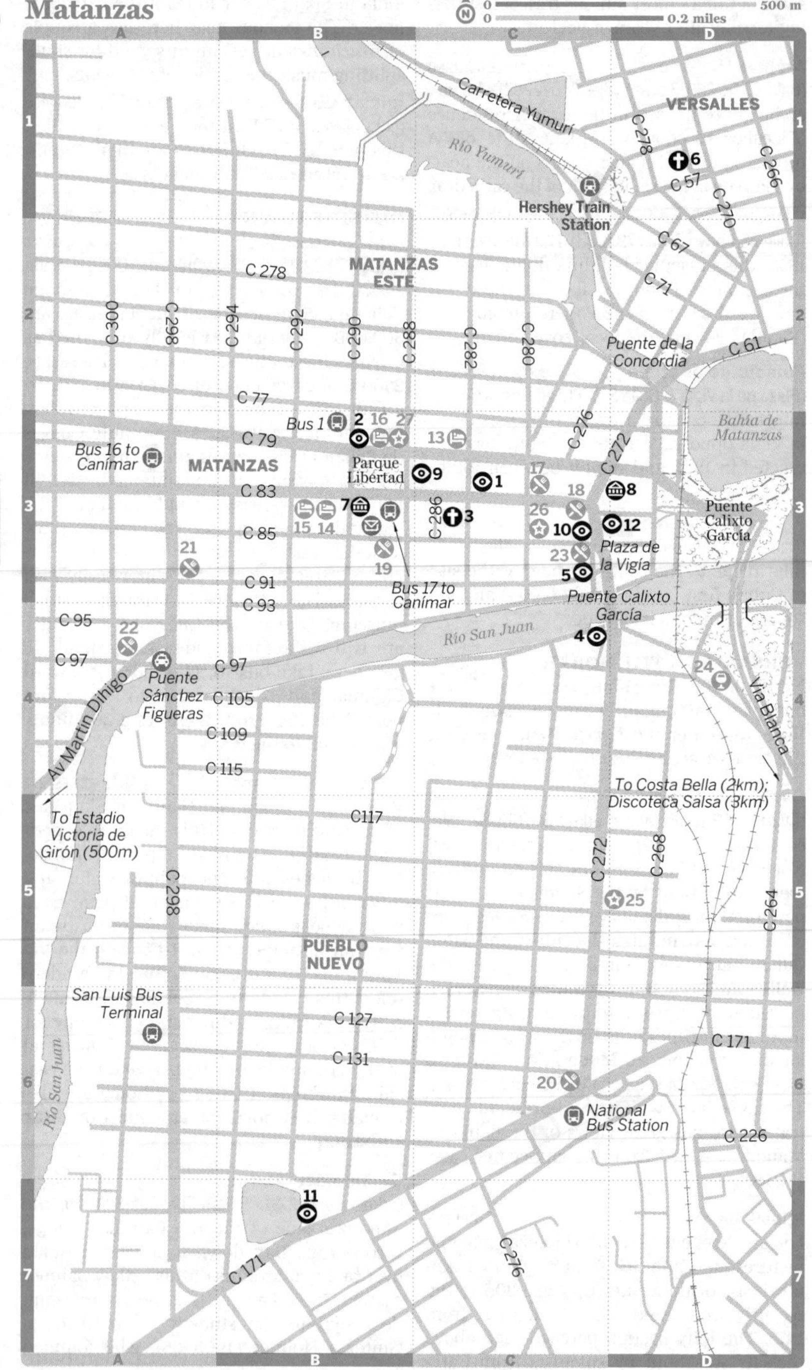

0 500 m
0 0.2 miles
Carretera Yumurí
Río Yumurí
VERSALLES
Hershey Train Station
C 278
C 57
C 266
C 270
C 67
C 71
MATANZAS ESTE
C 300
C 298
C 294
C 292
C 290
C 288
C 282
C 280
Puente de la Concordia
C 61
Bahía de Matanzas
C 77
Bus 1
C 79
Bus 16 to Canímar
MATANZAS
Parque Libertad
C 83
C 276
C 272
C 286
C 85
Puente Calixto García
Plaza de la Vigía
C 91
C 93
Bus 17 to Canímar
Puente Calixto García
Río San Juan
C 95
C 97
Puente Sánchez Figueras
C 97
C 105
C 109
C 115
Av Martín Dihigo
Vía Blanca
To Costa Bella (2km); Discoteca Salsa (3km)
To Estadio Victoria de Girón (500m)
C117
C 272
C 268
C 298
C 264
PUEBLO NUEVO
San Luis Bus Terminal
C 127
C 131
C 171
Río San Juan
National Bus Station
C 226
C 171
C 276

Matanzas

Sights

1	Archivo Histórico	C3
2	Biblioteca Gener y Del Monte	B3
3	Catedral de San Carlos Borromeo	C3
4	Che Mural	C4
5	Ediciones Vigía	C3
6	Iglesia de San Pedro Apóstol	D1
7	Museo Farmaceútico	B3
8	Museo Histórico Provincial	D3
9	Palacio de Gobierno	C3
10	Palacio de Justicia	C3
11	Palmar del Junco	B7
12	Teatro Sauto	D3

Sleeping

13	Evelio & Isel	C3
14	Hostal Alma	B3
15	Hostal Azul – Joel Báez & Aylín Hernández	B3
16	Hotel Velazco	B3

Eating

17	Cadena Cubana del Pan	C3
18	Café Atenas	C3
19	Centro Variedades Commercial	B3
20	Coppelia	C6
21	En Familia	A3
22	Mercado La Plaza	A4
23	Plaza la Vigía	C3

Drinking

24	Ruinas de Matasiete	D4

Entertainment

25	Casa de la Cultura Municipal Bonifacio Bryne	D5
26	Casa del Danzón	C3
	Teatro Sauto	(see 12)
27	Teatro Velazco	B3

Shopping

	Ediciones Vigía	(see 5)

the revolutionary group Joven Cuba (Young Cuba) in 1934. After serving briefly in the post-Machado government, Guiteras was forced out by army chief Fulgencio Batista and shot on May 8, 1935. A bronze bust marks the spot where he was executed.

Playa Coral SNORKELING

With no reefs accessible from the coast in Varadero, your closest bet for a bit of shore snorkeling is the aptly named Playa Coral on the old coastal road (about 3km off the Vía Blanca) halfway between Matanzas and Varadero. Although you can snorkel solo from the beach itself, it's far better (and safer) to enter via the **Laguna de Maya** (8am-5pm). The **Flora and Fauna Reserve** 400m to the east is where professional **Ecotur guides** can rent you snorkeling gear and guide you out to the reef at a bargain CUC$10 for one hour. There are a reported 300 species of fish here and visibility is a decent 15m to 20m. Decent diving is on offer too. The Laguna de Maya also incorporates a snack bar-restaurant by a small lake with boat rental and horseback-riding opportunities. A package including all the activities is offered for CUC$25. You can hike 2.5km to the Cueva Saturno from here. Most of the coast hereabouts is a gray-white coral shelf but there are beaches just west of Playa Coral.

Cuevas de Santa Catalina CAVES

(combined admission with Cuevas de Bellamar CUC$15; 9am-5pm) You'll also need to show up at the Cuevas de Bellamar for trips to this less-visited cave system off the Matanzas–Varadero highway near Boca de Camarioca, where highlights include Amerindian cave paintings.

Cueva Saturno CAVES, DIVING

(25-32-72; admission incl snorkel gear CUC$5; 8am-6pm) One kilometer south of the Vía Blanca, near the airport turn-off, is the Cueva Saturno. While it's widely billed as a snorkeling spot, it's really just a ho-hum cave with limited snorkeling access, unless you're an experienced cave diver with all the equipment. It's popular with locals looking to cool off at their local water hole, and the snack bar sells good coffee.

Festivals & Events

During the 10 days following October 10, Matanzas rediscovers its rumba roots with talented local musicians at the **Festival del Bailador Rumbero** in the Teatro Sauto. This coincides with the anniversary of the city's founding (October 12th), a multiday party which includes celebrations of luminaries who have made the city what it is (or was). **Carnaval** in Matanzas every August doesn't quite reach the dizzying heights of Santiago but it's still a lively affair.

Sleeping

CITY CENTER

Matanzas boasts the recently reopened Hotel Velazco and some cracking casas particulares.

TOP CHOICE **Hostal Azul** CASA PARTICULAR $
(☎24-78-10; hostalazul.cu@gmail.com; Calle 83 No 29012 btwn Calles 290 & 292; r CUC$20-25; ❄) This is the type of fine colonial house that once made Matanzas a cultural tour de force, with three vast, *muy azul* (very blue) rooms. Throw in a tranquil internal courtyard, scintillating cuisine cooked by a Varadero-trained chef and its location (just off Parque Libertad) and voilà: you have one of the province's premium casas particulares. The enterprising hosts, Joel and Aylín, also offer a taxi service to guests.

Hostal Alma CASA PARTICULAR $
(☎24-24-49; Calle 83 No 29008 btwn Calles 290 & 292; r CUC$20-25; ❄) Vying with the 'Azul' next door for the title of best city digs, this mid-19th-century colonial house has baths, sun loungers, balconies and two huge terraces (the higher one has stunning 360-degree views of Matanzas). Vast portions of food along with oodles of *alma* (soul) are most definitely on the menu.

Costa Bella CASA PARTICULAR $
(☎28-56-57; Calle 127 No 20615 btwn Calles 206 & 208; r CUC$25; P❄) Out in Playa, 3km from the center with the sweeping bayside views that go hand in hand, this place has two large rooms (try to bag the top one) with private entrances in a block at the end of a garden studded with coconut trees.

Hotel Velazco HOTEL $$
(☎25-38-80; Calle 79 btwn Calles 290 & 288; d CUC$90; ❄) Finally! After over a decade in the pipeline, painstaking renovation is complete and the splendid colonial Hotel Velazco has reopened. There are 17 rooms here right on Parque Libertad, the first step perhaps of the much-talked-about city center revamp.

Evelio & Isel CASA PARTICULAR $
(☎24-30-90; Calle 79 No 28201 btwn 282 & 288; r CUC$20-25; P❄) Rooms at this 2nd-floor apartment have TV, security boxes, balconies and underground parking. The owner is a font of knowledge on the Matanzas music scene.

OUTSIDE TOWN

Hotel Canimao HOTEL $
(☎26-10-14; s/d CUC$21/25; P❄≋) Perched above the Río Canímar 8km east of Matanzas, the Canimao has 160 comfortable rooms with little balconies. It's handy for Río Canímar excursions, the Cuevas de Bellamar, or to visit the Tropicana Matanzas, but otherwise you're isolated here. There are two restaurants: one Cuban and one Italian. Bus 16 from the corner of Calles 300 and 83 in Matanzas will drop you by the driveway.

Eating

CITY CENTER

The best cheap peso take-out windows are on Calle 272 just over Puente de la Concordia in Versalles.

TOP CHOICE **En Familia** CARIBBEAN, ITALIAN $
(cnr Calles 298 & 91; ⏰10am-11pm) This jack-of-all-trades restaurant with its tables splayed around a leafy terrace does a bit of everything very well – pizza, pasta and *comida criolla* (Creole food). The house specialty, however, is a freshly landed fish fillet with chorizo for CUC$2.50. It's heartening to see lots of local families feasting here: a sure sign something good is going on in the kitchen.

Plaza la Vigía CAFE $
(cnr Plaza de la Vigía & Calle 85; ⏰10am-midnight) Bar with food or restaurant with bar? It's hard to tell with this place but who cares when there's more ambience here than in most of the city center's food stops put together? The ornate interior is reminiscent of a Vienna coffeehouse: with its stained glass and intriguing old pictures of Matanzas together with its buzzing, plaza-fronting terrace, the ambience will absorb you far more than the hamburgers on offer. Cocktails aren't bad though and European beers are sometimes served. What next: coffee machines and table service?

Restaurante Teni CARIBBEAN $
(cnr Calles 129 & 224; ⏰noon-10:45pm) A large, thatched-roof affair alongside the beach in Reparto Playa, this ambient place offers substantial set *comida criolla* meals, with rice, root vegetables, salad and meat, for just CUC$5. There's live music on weekends.

Café Atenas CARIBBEAN $
(Calle 83 No 8301; ⏰10am-11pm) Settle down here in the clean, bland, interior or out on the *terraza* (terrace) with the local students, taxi drivers and hotel workers on a day off, and contemplate everyday life on Plaza de

la Vigía outside. Decent sandwiches, grilled meats and fish fillets are available.

Coppelia ICE-CREAM PARLOR
(cnr Calles 272 & 171; ⏲10am-10pm) This lackluster place is near the bus station.

Self-Catering

Cadena Cubana del Pan BAKERY
(Calle 83 btwn Calles 278 & 280; ⏲24hr) Best for bread.

Centro Variedades Commercial SUPERMARKET
(Calle 85 btwn Calles 288 & 290; ⏲9am-6pm) For groceries and (upstairs) great cakes.

Mercado la Plaza MARKET
(cnr Calles 97 & 298) Near the Puente Sánchez Figueras; for produce/peso stalls.

OUTSIDE TOWN

El Ranchón Bellamar CARIBBEAN $$
(⏲noon-8:30pm) If you're visiting the Cuevas de Bellamar, you'd do well to grab a *comida criolla* lunch at this *ranchón*-style restaurant before heading back into town. Good pork or chicken meals with the trimmings go for between CUC$7 and CUC$8.

El Marino SEAFOOD $
(⏲noon-9pm; ❄) On the main Varadero road next to the Hotel Canimao turn-off, El Marino specializes in seafood, namely lobster and shrimp.

Drinking

Ruinas de Matasiete BAR
(cnr Vía Blanca & Calle 101; ⏲24hr) One of the best drinking holes, this engaging bar is housed in the ruins of a 19th-century, bay-facing warehouse. Drinks and grilled meats are served on an open-air terrace, but a better reason to come here is to hear live music (9pm Friday to Sunday; cover charge CUC$3).

☆ Entertainment

TOP CHOICE **Teatro Sauto** THEATER
(☎24-27-21) Across Plaza de la Vigía, Teatro Sauto is a national landmark and one of Cuba's premier theaters. Performances have been held here since 1863 and you might catch the Ballet Nacional de Cuba or the Conjunto Folklórico Nacional de Cuba. Performances are at 8:30pm with Sunday matinees at 3pm.

Tropicana Matanzas
(☎26-53-80; admission CU… Tue-Sat) Capitalizing on its su… and Santiago de Cuba, the fam… cabaret has a branch 8km east o… next to the Hotel Canimao. You ca… with the Varadero bus crowds and e… same entertaining formula of lights, … …ers, flesh and frivolity in the open air. Rain stops play if the weather cracks.

Museo Histórico Provincial LIVE MUSIC
(Map p200; cnr Calles 83 & 272; admission CUC$2; ⏲10am-6pm Tue-Fri, 1-7pm Sat & 9am-noon Sun) Check the board outside this building (also known as the Palacio del Junco) for events ranging from theater to *danzón* performances to rumba, with listings for the month ahead.

Estadio Victoria de Girón SPORTS
(Av Martin Dihigo) From October to April, baseball games take place at this stadium 1km southwest of the market. Once one of the country's leading teams, the local Los Cocodrilos (Crocodiles) struggle to beat La Isla de la Juventud these days.

Teatro Velazco CINEMA
(cnr Calles 79 & 288) On Parque Libertad, this is Matanzas' main movie house.

Discoteca Salsa NIGHTCLUB
(Carretera Varadero Km 1; admission CUC$1; ⏲10pm-2am Tue-Sun) For straight-up riotous dancing to recorded music, this is the place. There's a leafy terrace outside if things get too heated. Heading toward Varadero, it's on the bay side of the Vía Blanca, 4km from the center.

Las Palmas LIVE MUSIC
(cnr Calles 254 & 127; admission CUC$1; ⏲noon-midnight Mon-Wed, to 2am Fri-Sun) A good starlit night out for a fraction of the price of the Tropicana shindig can be had at this ARTex place.

Casa de la Cultura Municipal Bonifacio Bryne LIVE MUSIC
(Calle 272 No 11916 btwn Calles 119 & 121) A font of all things cultural: always good for a musical romp.

Casa del Danzón DANCING
(Calle 85 btwn Calle 280 & Plaza de la Vigía) If you fancy learning some local dance steps, enquire here as it offers weekend *danzón* classes.

A IN MATANZAS

'Without rumba there is no Cuba, and without Cuba there is no rumba,' runs a Cuban saying. Matanzas certainly gave birth to one of the Cuba's defining musical forms and occupies a pivotal place both in the history and in the future development of music in the country.

Rumba originated here in the city's African *cabildos*, secret brotherhoods formed among the slaves brought over from West Central Africa during the 19th century, to work Cuba's plantations, and their descendents. These brotherhoods came together in the port backstreets to worship their *orishas* (deities) and keep their traditions alive. So rumba in Matanzas began, and rapidly spread: the music of a repressed but, most importantly, displaced people whose driving force was not so much speaking out against their treatment as remembering their roots through music. It was the outlet through which initially Afro-Cubans, but later other subjugated groups from deprived backgrounds, expressed fears and hopes about their position in society.

Matanzas is responsible for most of the main forms of rumba. The most ancient variety, Rumba Yambú, stems from Versalles district in the late 19th century, and has a slower, smoother place. Rumba Guaguancó is more modern and sensual, emulating the mating ritual between a rooster and a hen, and using conga drums. Then there is Rumba Columbia, named after an old bus stop outside Matanzas, performed only by men because of its dangerous moves. Only recently recognized as a sub-genre, there is also Bata Rumba, invented and best exemplified by contemporary group AfroCuba de Matanzas. Percussion here is provided by hourglass-shaped Batá drums, a ritual instrument of Nigeria's Yoruba people.

Masters of the first three of these forms are Los Muñequitos de Matanzas, formed almost 60 years ago after an inspired impromptu jamming session on bottles in a bar in the city's Barrio Marina persuaded various locals they could gel as a group. And gel they did. Originally named Guaguancó Mattancero, their first A-side 'Los Muñequitos' (little comics) was so popular that was how the group became known.

Los Muñequitos de Matanzas and AfroCuba de Matanzas are descended from the early days of *cabildos*, with Lucumí and Kongo origins. But the music they are making now is as much about re-evaluating the roots of music as remembering the roots of their ancestors. A great example is AfroCuba's groundbreaking collection of songs, *The Sign and the Seal*, which uses a focus on traditional *orishas* to seemingly push the boundaries of music itself. Songs are dedicated to such deities as Agayú – in Yoruba culture, an uninhabited space or wilderness – while another explores Oshún, the source of rivers, water and life. In returning to the building blocks of a culture the album revisits the building blocks of music and reassembles sound as the universe (the relationship with which is the cornerstone of Yoruba beliefs) reassembles sound.

Better than reading about the city's rumba is listening to some and both of the groups mentioned here perform in Matanzas. An incredible ingredient to the city is that, in the home of rumba, its two most renowned exponents can still be found indulging in a spot of low-key jamming here. The best bet to catch rumba is the great alfresco performances that take place at 4pm on the third Friday of every month outside the Museo Histórico Provincial (p198).

Shopping

Bad luck, shopaholics: checking out the stores (what stores?) in Matanzas makes a car boot sale look like Hollywood Boulevard.

Ediciones Vigía BOOKS
(Plaza de la Vigía; ⏲8am-4pm Mon-Fri) Browse here for original handmade books.

Information

Banco Financiero Internacional (cnr Calles 85 & 298) ATM.

Cadeca (Calle 286 btwn Calles 83 & 85; ⏲8am-6pm Mon-Sat, 8am-noon Sun) Two portable money-exchange kiosks behind the cathedral.

Etecsa Telepunto (cnr Calles 83 & 282; per hr CUC$6; ⏲8:30am-7:30pm) Phone services.

Servimed (☎25-31-70; Hospital Faustino Pérez, Carretera Central Km 101) Clinic just southwest of town.

Post office (Calle 85 No 28813) On the corner of Calle 290.

Getting There & Away

Air

Matanzas is connected to the outside world through Juan Gualberto Gómez International Airport, located 20km east of town.

Bicycle

Matanzas is easy to reach by bike from Varadero. The 32km road is well-paved and completely flat, bar the last 3km into the city starting at the Río Canímar bridge (a relatively easy uphill climb if you're heading east). Bike hire is available at most Varadero all-inclusive hotels.

Bus

All buses, long distance and provincial, use the **National Bus Station** (☎91-64-45) in the old train station on the corner of Calles 131 and 272 in Pueblo Nuevo south of the Río San Juan. Matanzas has decent connections to the rest of the country, although for destinations like Cienfuegos and Trinidad you need to change at Varadero. Practically this means taking the first Varadero bus of the day then waiting for the afternoon Varadero–Trinidad bus. **Víazul** (www.viazul.com) has three daily departures to Havana (CUC$7, two hours, 8:55am, 12:20pm, 6:55pm) and Varadero (CUC$6, one hour, 10:05am, 2:05pm, 8:05pm). The first two Varadero departures also call at the airport (CUC$3, 25 minutes) while the 8:05pm bus continues to Santa Clara, Camagüey and Santiago de Cuba.

For bus services to Cárdenas, ask at the bus station.

Train

The **train station** (☎29-16-45; Calle 181) is in Miret, at the southern edge of the city. Foreigners usually pay the peso price in convertibles to the *jefe de turno* (shift manager). Most trains between Havana and Santiago de Cuba stop here (except the fast Tren Francés). In theory, there are eight daily trains to Havana beginning at 3:25am (CUC$3, 1½ hours). Travel to the capital is a more secure bet: in the other direction (eastbound) trains have a habit of abruptly terminating. The daily Santiago de Cuba train (CUC$27) should leave early evening at around 10:50pm (but check), stopping at Santa Clara, Ciego de Ávila, Camagüey and Las Tunas. Other eastbound trains reach Sancti Spíritus. At the time of research the Cienfuegos departure, formerly 8:05pm on alternate days (CUC$6, three hours), was not running.

Latest train information is plastered on pieces of paper stuck to a billboard on the far wall of the waiting room. Get here well in advance to beat the bedlam.

The **Hershey Train Station** (☎24-48-05; cnr Calles 55 & 67) is in Versalles, an easy 10-minute walk from Parque Libertad. There are three trains a day to Casablanca station in Havana (CUC$2.80, four hours) via Canasí (CUC$0.85), Jibacoa (CUC$1.10, 1½ hours, for Playa Jibacoa), Hershey (CUC$1.40, two hours, for Jardines de Hershey) and Guanabo (CUC$2). Departure times from Matanzas are 6:16am, 11:30am (an express service that should take three hours) and 4:54pm.

Ticket sales begin an hour before the scheduled departure time and, except on weekends and holidays, there's no problem getting aboard. Bicycles may not be allowed (ask). The train usually leaves on time, but often arrives in Havana's Casablanca station (just below La Cabaña fort on the east side of the harbor) one hour late. This is the only electric railway in Cuba, and during thunderstorms the train doesn't run. It's a scenic trip if you're not in a hurry, and a great way of reaching the little-visited attractions of Mayabeque province.

Getting Around

To get to the train station from the center, bus 1 leaves from Calle 79 between Calles 290 and 292. Buses 16 (from Calle 300) and 17 (leaving more conveniently from Parque Libertad) run from the city center to Río Canímar via Calle 226 (for the Cuevas del Bellamar). Municipal buses cost one peso per journey.

The Oro Negro gas station is on the corner of Calles 129 and 210, 4km outside the city of Matanzas on the Varadero road. The **Servi-Cupet gas station** and **Havanautos** (☎25-32-94; cnr Calles 129 & 210) are a block further on. If you're driving to Varadero, you will pay a CUC$2 highway toll between Boca de Camarioca and Santa Marta (no toll between Matanzas and the airport).

Bici-taxis congregate next to the Mercado la Plaza (cnr Calles 97 & 298) and can take you to most of the city's destinations for one to two Cuban pesos. A taxi to Varadero town should cost around CUC$25.

Varadero

POP 27,170

Wrapped up for tourist consumption and packaged as a cheap alternative to Cancún, the seaside sprawl of Varadero greets you with an ambience more akin to coastal California or Florida than the archetypal tropical paradise you might have been expecting. Much of esoteric Cuba is indeed mainly noticeable by its absence, from

Varadero

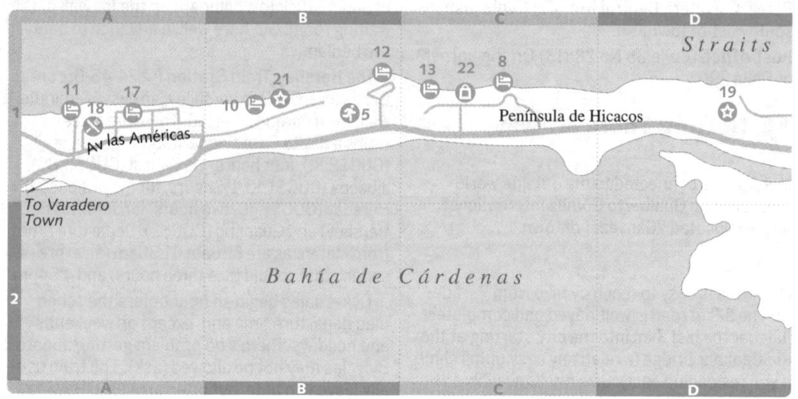

the lack of history and, frequently, lack of Cuban people themselves. But, kissed by gentle Caribbean breezes and lapped by the iridescent waters of the ebbing Atlantic, it has its pluses, including great beaches and vast hotels. And the resort's popularity is waxing not waning – Varadero's hallowed beach is one of the best in the archipelago and the weighty cache of 50 or more three- to five-star hotels acts as a tantalizing magnet to the hordes of midrange vacationers who descend here annually from the frozen north. For those on a more serendipitous voyage of discovery, Varadero lacks one vital ingredient: magic. The sort of magic, that is, that can't be replicated in fancy air-conditioned cocktail lounges or grandiose faux-Greek hotel lobbies, however many mojitos you sink.

At least one third of the peninsula is given over to Varadeo town, which, while lacking the atmosphere of Havana or Santiago, still retains a rough semblance of everyday Cuban life.

Sights

For art and history, you're in the wrong place; nevertheless, there are a few sights worth checking out if the beach life starts to bore you.

Parque Central & Parque de las 8000 Taquillas PARK

(Map p214; btwn Calles 44 & 46) Standing together between Avs 44 and 46, these parks were once the center of the town's social life, but became neglected during the 1990s as bigger resorts sprouted up further east. Recently redeveloped, Parque de las 8000 Taquillas now boasts a brand-new shopping center beneath the ever-popular Coppelia ice-cream parlor.

Museo Municipal de Varadero MUSEUM

(Map p214; Calle 57; admission CUC$1; ⏲10am-7pm) Working up the beach from Hotel Acuazul Varazul, you'll see many typical wooden beach houses with elegant wrap-around porches. The most attractive of the bunch, Varadero's Museo Municipal, has been turned into a balconied chalet displaying period furniture and a snapshot of the resort's history.

Parque Josone PARK

(Map p214; cnr Av 1 & Calle 58; ⏲9am-midnight) This green oasis is more enclosed and much prettier than Parque Central. The gardens date back to 1940, taking their name from the former owners, José Fermín Iturrioz y Llaguno and his wife Onelia, who owned the Arechabala rum distillery in nearby Cárdenas and built a neoclassical mansion here: the Retiro Josone. Expropriated after the Revolution, the mansion became a guesthouse for visiting foreign dignitaries. The park is now a public space for the enjoyment of all – you may see Cuban girls celebrate their *quinceñeras* (15th-birthday celebrations) here. Josone's expansive, shady grounds feature a lake with rowboats (CUC$0.50 per person per hour), atmospheric eateries, resident geese, myriad tree species and a minitrain. There's a public swimming pool (admission CUC$2) in the south of the park and the odd ostrich lurking nearby. Good music can be heard nightly.

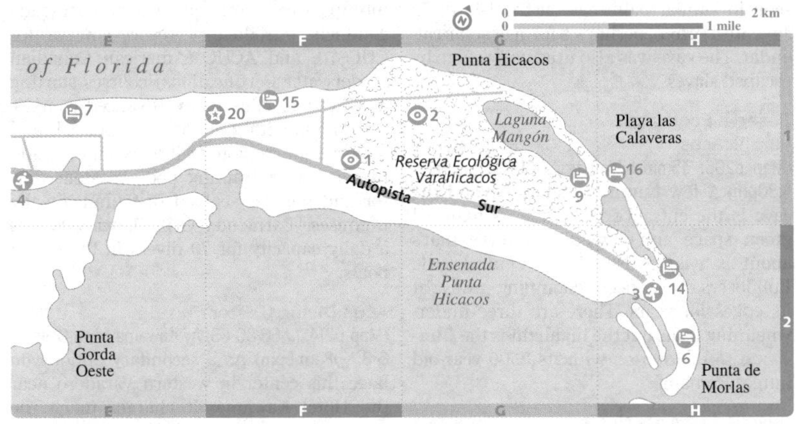

Varadero

Mansión Xanadú NOTABLE BUILDING

(Map p206) Everything east of the small stone water tower (it looks like an old Spanish fort, but was built in the 1930s), next to the Restaurant Mesón del Quijote, once belonged to the Du Pont family. Here the millionaire American entrepreneur Irenée built the three-story Mansión Xanadu, now an upscale hotel atop Varadero's 18-hole golf course, with a top-floor bar conducive to sipping sunset cocktails in.

Cueva de Ambrosio CAVE

(Map p206; admission CUC$3; ⏲9am-4:30pm) Beyond Marina Chapelín, Varadero sprawls east like a displaced North American suburb with scrubby mangroves interspersed with megahotel complexes, the odd iron crane and a *delfinario*. Pass all this and 500m beyond the Club Amigo Varadero on the Autopista Sur, you'll find this cave, which is an incredibly interesting sight due to some 47 pre-Columbian drawings, discovered in this 300m recess in 1961. The black-and-red drawings feature the same concentric circles seen in similar paintings on the Isla de la Juventud (p165), perhaps a form of solar calendar. The cave was also used as a refuge by escaped slaves.

Reserva Ecológica Varahicacos NATURE RESERVE
(Map p206; 45min hiking trails CUC$3; ⏲9am-4:30pm) A few hundred meters beyond the cave is the entrance to Varadero's nominal green space and a wildlife reserve that's about as 'wild' as New York's Central Park. Bulldozers have been chomping away at its edges for years. There are three underwhelming trails but the highlight is the **Cueva de Musalmanes** with its 2500-year-old human remains.

Cayo Piedras del Norte MARINE PARK
Five kilometers north of Playa las Calaveras (one hour by boat), Cayo Piedras del Norte has been made into a 'marine park' through the deliberate sinking of an assortment of vessels and aircraft in 15m to 30m of water during the late 1990s. Scuttled for the benefit of divers and glass-bottom boat passengers are a towboat, a missile-launching gunboat (with missiles intact), an AN-24 airplane and the yacht Coral Negro.

Iglesia de Santa Elvira CHURCH
(Map p214; cnr Av 1 & Calle 47) Just east of Parque Central is this tiny colonial-style building resembling a displaced alpine chapel.

Activities

Diving & Snorkeling

Varadero has four excellent dive centers offering competitively priced immersions and courses. All of the 21 dive sites around the Península de Hicacos require a boat transfer of approximately one hour. Highlights include reefs, caverns, pitchers and a Russian patrol boat sunk for diving purposes in 1997. The nearest shore diving is at Playa Coral 20km west (p201). The centers also offer day excursions to superior sites at the Bahía de Cochinos (Bay of Pigs) in the south of the province (one/two immersions CUC$50/70, with transfer).

Barracuda Diving Center DIVING
(Map p214; ☎61-34-81; cnr Av 1 & Calle 59; ⏲8am-6pm) Varadero's top scuba facility is the mega-friendly, multilingual Barracuda Diving Center. Diving costs CUC$50 per dive with equipment, cave diving is CUC$60 and night diving costs CUC$55. Packages of multiple dives work out cheaper. Barracuda conducts introductory resort courses for CUC$70, and ACUC (American Canadian Underwater Certifications) courses starting at CUC$220, plus many advanced courses. Snorkeling with guide is CUC$30. A brand new recompression facility is on site and there's also a training pool, resident doctor and popular seafood restaurant on the premises, Barracuda Grill. Barracuda has a daily capacity for 70 divers in three 12m boats.

Acua Diving Center DIVING
(Map p214; ☎66-80-63; Av Kawama btwn Calles 2 & 3; ⏲8am-5pm) As a secondary option you have this center in western Varadero near the Hotel Kawama. It charges much the same prices as Barracuda, but doesn't have quite the facilities, or volume. When a north wind is blowing and diving isn't possible in the Atlantic, you can be transferred to the Caribbean coast in a minibus (90-minute drive); this costs a total of CUC$55/75 for one/two dives. Popular trips include Cueva Saturno for diving and Playa Coral for snorkeling and diving.

Marina Gaviota DIVING
(Map p206; ☎66-47-22; Autopista Sur y Final) Another professional outfit at the eastern end of Autopista Sur, this has slightly cheaper scuba diving/snorkeling excursions both locally and at the Bahía de Cochinos (Bay of Pigs).

Aquaworld Diving Center DIVING
(Map p206; ☎66-75- 50; Autopista Sur Km 12) At the Marlin Marina Chapelín, Aquaworld also organizes diving/snorkeling trips.

Fishing

Varadero has three marinas, all of which offer a similar variety of nautical activities and facilities.

Marlin Marina Chapelín FISHING
(Map p206; ☎66-75-50) Situated close to the entrance to Hotel Riu Turquesa, five hours of deep-sea fishing here costs CUC$290 for four people (price includes hotel transfers, open bar and licenses; nonfishing companions pay CUC$30).

Marina Gaviota FISHING
(Map p206; ☎66-47-22) At the eastern end of Autopista Sur; has similar packages to Marlin Marina Chapelín.

Skydiving

Centro Internacional de Paracaidismo SKYDIVING

(Map p206; ☎66-72-56, 66-72-60) For those with a head for heights, Varadero's greatest thrill has to be skydiving at this base at the old airport just west of Varadero. The terminal is 1km up a dirt road, opposite Marina Acua. Skydivers take off in an Antonov AN-2 biplane of WWII design (don't worry, it's a replica) and jump from 3000m using a two-harness parachute with an instructor strapped in tandem on your back. After 35 seconds of free fall the parachute opens and you float tranquilly for 10 minutes down onto Varadero's white sandy beach. The center also offers less spectacular (but equally thrilling) ultralight flights at various points on the beach. Prices for skydiving are CUC$150 per person with an extra CUC$45 for photos and CUC$50 for video. Ultralight flights start at CUC$30 and go up to CUC$300 depending on the length of time. If you are already a qualified skydiver, solo jumps are also available on production of the relevant certification.

A day's notice is usually required for skydiving (which many hotels can book on your behalf), and jumps are (obviously) weather dependent. Since opening in 1993 the center has reported no fatalities.

Golf

Varadero Golf Club GOLF

(Map p206; ☎66-77-88; www.varaderogolfclub.com; Mansión Xanadu; green fees 9/18 holes CUC$48/70; 7am-7pm) While it's no Pebble Beach, golfers can have a swinging session at this uncrowded and well-landscaped club: Cuba's first 18-hole course. The original nine holes created by the Du Ponts are between Hotel Bella Costa and Dupont's Mansión Xanadú; another nine holes added in 1998 flank the southern side of the three Meliá resorts. Bookings for the course (par 72) are made through the pro shop next to the Mansión Xanadú (now a cozy hotel with free, unlimited tee time). A 50-minute lesson costs CUC$30.

El Golfito MINIGOLF

(Map p214; cnr Av 1 & Calle 42; per person CUC$3; 24hr) Golf neophytes can play the miniature version here.

Other Activities

Sailboards are available for rent at various points along the public beach (CUC$10 per hour), as are small catamarans, banana boats, sea kayaks etc. The upmarket resorts usually include these water toys in the all-inclusive price.

Centro Todo En Uno BOWLING

(Map p214; cnr Calle 54 & Autopista Sur; per game CUC$2.50; 24hr) Bowling alleys are popular in Cuba and the *bolera* here, including a small shopping/games complex on Autopista Sur, is usually full of Cuban families who also come to enjoy the adjacent kids' playground and fast-food joints.

Courses

Many of Varadero's all-inclusive hotels lay on free Spanish lessons for guests. If you're staying in cheaper digs, ask at the reception of one of these larger hotels and see if you can find your way onto an in-house language course by offering to pay a small fee.

Tours

Tour desks at the main hotels book most of the nautical or sporting activities mentioned earlier and arrange organized sightseeing excursions from Varadero. You'll pay a surcharge (usually CUC$5 per person) if you book at these desks instead of going directly to the tour operator.

Among the many off-peninsula tours offered are a half-day trip to the Cuevas de Bellamar (see p199) near Matanzas, a bus tour to the Bahía de Cochinos and a whole range of other bus tours to places as far away as Santa Clara, Trinidad, Viñales and, of course, Havana.

Gaviota HELICOPTER TOUR

(Map p214; ☎61-18-44; cnr Calle 56 & Av de la Playa) This operator features a variety of helicopter tours in Russian M1-8 choppers; the Trinidad trip (CUC$229) is popular. The Tour de Azúcar (sugarcane tour) visits a disused sugar mill and takes a steam train ride to Cárdenas station. Prices are CUC$39/30 per adult/child. It also organizes 4WD safaris to the scenic Valle del Yumurí. The excursion (adult/child CUC$45/34) includes a visit to a *campesino* family and a huge, delicious meal at Ranchón Gaviota (p153).

Varasub SCENIC TOUR

(90-min tour adult/child CUC$35/20) If you want to enjoy snorkeling without getting wet, book an excursion on the *Varasub*, a 48-berth glass-bottomed boat that allows you to peer out at the fantastic marine life from windows set below the waterline. This underwater adventure leaves approximately six times a day, and includes unlimited alcoholic or nonalcoholic beverages and transfers. Book through any information desk or office.

Aquaworld Marina Chapelín BOAT TRIPS, WATERSPORTS
(Map p206; ☎66-75-50; Autopista Sur Km 12) Aquaworld Marina Chapelín organizes Varadero's nautical highlight in the popularity stakes: the **Seafari Cayo Blanco**, a seven-hour sojourn (CUC$75) from Marina Chapelín to nearby Cayo Blanco and its idyllic beach. The trip includes an open bar, lobster lunch, two snorkeling stops, live music and hotel transfers. There's also a shorter CUC$45 catamaran tour with snorkeling, open bar and a chicken lunch. The **Fiesta en el Cayo** is a sunset cruise (CUC$41) to Cayo Blanco with dinner, music and more free-flowing rum at the key.

Boat Adventure Boat Trip BOAT TRIPS
(Map p206; ☎66-84-40; per person CUC$39; ⌚9am-4pm) This two-hour guided trip, also leaving from the Marina Chapelín, is a speedy sortie through the adjacent mangroves on two-person jet skis or motorboats to view myriad wildlife including friendly crocs. Bookings for all these watery excursions can also be made at most of the big hotels.

Festivals & Events

Golf tournaments are held at the Varadero Golf Club in June and October and the annual regatta is in May. Varadero also hosts the annual tourism convention in the first week in May when accommodation is tight and some places are reserved solely for conference participants.

Sleeping

Varadero is huge – there are at least 50 hotels. For budget travelers turning up impromptu, hunting down bargain rooms is a sport akin to marathon running. Book ahead or concentrate your efforts on the peninsula's southwest end where hotels are cheaper and the town retains a semblance of Cuban life.

It is illegal to rent private rooms in Varadero and the law is strictly enforced.

All-inclusive hotel packages booked through travel agents in your home country may have differing (cheaper) rates to those given here.

TOP CHOICE **Sandals Royal Hicacos** RESORT $$$
(Map p206; ☎66-88-44/51; Punta Hicacos; all-incl r CUC$160-190; P❄@≋) Having a more understated look (and more personable service) than many of its neighbors has helped Sandals Royal Hicacos immeasurably: it just might be the most appealing resort on this part of the peninsula with vast *ranchón*-style public areas and babbling water features lending a mellifluous air. Bedrooms, done up in sunny yellows and oranges, have their own reception areas and huge bathrooms. English and German are spoken.

Hotel Kawama RESORT $$
(Map p214; ☎61-44-16; Av 1 & Calle 1; all-incl s/d CUC$84/128; P❄@≋) A venerable old hacienda-style building from the 1930s, the Kawama is a piece of Varadero history. It was the first of the 50-plus hotels to inhabit this once-deserted peninsula more than 70 years ago and, as far as character and architectural ingenuity go, it's still one of the best. The property is huge, with some 235 colorful rooms blended artfully into the thin sliver of beach that makes up Varadero's western extremity. All-inclusive prices include everything from tennis to aquabike usage.

Villa la Mar HOTEL $
(Map p214; ☎61-45-15; Av 3 btwn Calles 28 & 30; s/d CUC$28/36; ❄) At no-frills, no-pretensions Villa la Mar you'll dine on fried chicken, mingle with peso-paying Cuban tourists and fall asleep to the not-so-romantic sound of the in-house disco belting out the Cuban version of Britney Spears.

Hotel Turquino HOTEL $
(Map p214; ☎61-37-96; Av 3 btwn Calles 33 & 34; s/d low season CUC$15/30, high season CUC$20/39; ❄) This hotel is a training ground for Cuban students vying to work in the tourist industry and is the best bargain in town, barring a night on the beach. Conveniently positioned just two blocks from the Víazul bus station, furnishings are a tad drab but everything is clean, functional and spacious.

Club Herradura HOTEL $
(Map p214; ☎61-37-03; Av de la Playa btwn Calles 35 & 36; low season s/d incl breakfast CUC$30/44; ❄≋) Plain from the front, but infinitely more attractive on the oceanside, this four-story, crescent-shaped hotel is right on a recently replenished section of the beach. Accommodation is ample, if a little dog-eared, with timeless wicker furniture and good bal-

cony view rooms facing the beach. A pleasant all-round unpretentious vibe.

Hotel Dos Mares & Hotel Pullman HOTEL **$**
(Map p214; ☎61-27-02; s/d incl breakfast CUC$28/40) This complex is actually made up of two hotels situated three blocks apart. Hotel Pullman (Av 1 btwn Calles 49 & 50) is the more striking building, a turreted castle-like abode with heavy wooden furniture and rocking chairs on the front porch overlooking the street. Old-fashioned but comfortable rooms include a quadruple. Hotel Dos Mares (cnr Av 1 & Calle 53) is a more modern three-story building, 70m from a cracking niche of beach. Rooms are cozy, if dark.

Hotel Acuazul Varazul RESORT **$$**
(Map p214; ☎66-71-32; Av 1 btwn Calles 13 & 14; s/d incl breakfast CUC$67/94;) This old stalwart stands like a royal blue sentinel at the entrance to Varadero. With its 78 rooms having benefited from a recent face-lift and the food buffet looking like it's had a *Hell's Kitchen* revamp, things are looking up at this once-austere prerevolutionary concrete pile, which also offers all-inclusive options. Other features are 24-hour internet, a fantastic Infotur office on-site and an unashamedly tacky nightly show. Next door Aparthotel Varazul has one-bedroom apartments with kitchenettes and small balconies.

Apartamentos Mar del Sur APARTMENT, HOTEL **$$**
(Map p214; ☎61-22-46; cnr Av 3 & Calle 30; s/d CUC$43/68;) Affording some semblance of independence, the one- and two-bedroom apartments in this scattered complex have cooking facilities and living rooms. It's all several hundred meters from the beach (a long way in Varadero), but decent value. Night time here is all about raucous bingo and recorded music.

Hotel los Delfines RESORT **$$**
(Map p214; ☎66-77-20; cnr Av de la Playa & Calle 38; all-incl s/d from CUC$75/100;) Hotel chain Islazul goes (almost) all-inclusive in this friendlier, cozier copy of the big resorts further northeast. The 100 rooms come packed with additional extras such as satellite TV, minibar and safe deposit box, and there's a lovely scoop of wide protected beach.

Hotel Barlovento RESORT **$$$**
(Map p214; ☎66-71-40; Av 1 btwn Calles 10 & 12; all-incl s/d CUC$88/140;) The first hotel you encounter when driving into Varadero is an attractive enough place with a lovely palm-fringed pool, integrated colonial-style architecture, and a choice stretch of beach. The food here is good, though points get deducted for the nighttime entertainment – water ballet and magic shows – which are not a patch on the standard Cuban knees-up. For an ocean-view room you'll pay more, despite the portion of sea visible being tame by peninsula standards.

Hotel Cuatro Palmas RESORT **$$$**
(Map p214; ☎66-70-40; Av 1 btwn Calles 60 & 62; all-incl s/d CUC$127/187;) This large resort right on the beach now run by the French Accor chain was once a personal residence of dictator Fulgencio Batista. Jammed together across the street are a series of shared two-story villas with another 122 rooms with fridges and toilet only (shower is shared). This is the first of the real 'posh' all-inclusive resorts as you head east, though it's still close enough to town for getting around on foot.

Hotel Tuxpán RESORT **$$**
(Map p206; ☎66-75-60; Av las Américas Km 2; all-incl s/d from CUC$70/120;) The 1960s concrete-block architecture make this all-inclusive one of Varadero's ugliest tourist shrines, but the Tuxpán is famous for other reasons, such as its disco, La Bamba, purportedly one of the resort's hottest. For those not enamored with Soviet architectonics, the beautiful beach is never far away.

Hotel Varadero Internacional RESORT **$$$**
(Map p206; ☎66-70-38; Av las Américas Km 1; all-incl s/d CUC$115/162;) Opened in December 1950 as a sister hotel to Miami's Fontainebleau, the four-story Internacional is Varadero's most famous and fabulously retro resort. While retaining its '50s charm, the rooms have been regularly upgraded and the extensive facilities include tennis courts, massages and Varadero's best cabaret (p216). Unlike some of Varadero's more featureless options it's also right on the beach. Bonuses at the Internacional include cool art (there's a large René Portocarrero mural in the lobby) and super-friendly staff.

Villa Cuba RESORT **$$$**
(Map p206; ☎66-82-80; Av las Américas Km 2; all-incl s/d low season CUC$75/120, high season CUC$132/189;) Admittedly, this 1970s Legoland structure is never going to win any architectural prizes. Up against Varadero's other all-inclusive giants, it seems

a bit like a dated dinosaur, but a variety of accommodation options and activities here along with a bright splash of paint and plenty of plants make it a popular family choice. The one- to two-bedroom villas (singles/doubles in low season CUC$199/249) feature communal living areas, fridge, TV and a patio. There are four rooms designed for disabled guests.

Mansión Xanadu RESORT **$$$**
(Map p206; ☎66-84-82; Av las Américas Km 3; all-incl s/d CUC$160/210; P❄@) Varadero's most intriguing, intimate lodging is in the grand former residence of US chemical entrepreneur Irenée Du Pont, where eight lavish rooms tempt guests. The first large-scale building to go up at the Península de Hicacos's eastern end and an outstanding jewel in a bland architectural desert, Mansión Xanadu is still decked with the millions of dollars' worth of Cuban marble and furnishings commissioned by Du Pont in the 1930s. Rates here include unlimited tee time at the adjoining golf club (Cuba's first), also a Du Pont innovation. The Kublai Khan–inspired building alights on a small bluff, with beach access just alongside.

Hotel Meliá Varadero RESORT **$$$**
(Map p206; ☎66-70-13; Autopista Sur Km 7; all-incl d to $510; P❄@≋♿) This stunning resort wins the prize for Varadero's most impressive lobby (and there's some pretty ostentatious competition), with its seven-story domed vine-dripping atrium ensuring that reception area's wow factor. Rooms overlook the golf course or the beach and it's a popular honeymoon spot. The Meliá Varadero sits on a rocky headland, so you have to walk a bit to reach the beach, but what the hey! Kids aged 12 and under stay here for 50%.

Meliá las Américas RESORT **$$$**
(Map p206; ☎66-76-00; Autopista Sur Km 7; all-incl s/d CUC$200/340; P❄@≋) You've arrived at the luxury end of the peninsula. Everything that went before was small-fry compared to these proverbial giants. Parked on the eastern side of the golf course, this upscale resort is on a choice stretch of beach with plush decor and swanky fittings. The rooms are big, the pool has a cracking sea view and meals are lavish. Golfers, especially, will have fun here.

Blau Varadero RESORT **$$$**
(Map p206; ☎66-75-45; Carretera las Morlas Km 15; all-incl s/d CUC$120/170; P❄@≋) Built in the shape of a pre-Columbian Mexican pyramid, the Blau might have taken the Cancún comparisons too far, especially as the vast vine-draped reception evokes more a retro space station than a Mayan monument. Room quality and service here are unquestionable, and one of Varadero's more well-appointed spa complexes is on hand.

Hotel Sirenis la Salina RESORT **$$$**
(Map p206; ☎66-70-09; Autopista Sur Km 8; all-incl standard s/d CUC$195/242; P❄@≋) The monstrously sized 1025-room Sirenis, opened in 2007, is Cuba's biggest hotel (you'd need a book to list half the facilities). The temple-like lobby is beautiful and the grounds pleasantly manicured. There are 27 suites, a 900-seat theater, umpteen restaurants and it's a 1km walk just to get from one end of the resort to the other (golf cars can help out!).

Tryp Península Varadero RESORT **$$$**
(Map p206; ☎66-88-00; Reserva Ecológica Varahicacos; all-incl r from CUC$180; P❄@≋) Some may revel in Tryp's four-star luxuries. The facilities here are admittedly plush, but there's not much cross-fertilizing with the real Cuba.

Barceló Marina Palace & Cayo Libertad Resort RESORT **$$$**
(Map p206; ☎66-99-66; Autopista Sur Final; s CUC$160-240, all-incl d CUC$260-380; P❄@≋) Apparently this garden suburb of cream bungalows sits on the most coveted part of the peninsula judging by the prices of the Barceló. There are thoughtful elements to the resort architecture, such as the mock lighthouse and stilted bar perched above the ocean, but at this end of the peninsula it's a long way from central Varadero and a million cultural miles from Cuba. Higher prices listed are for the adjoining Cayo Libertad resort, on an island connected by bridge to the rest of the complex.

Paradisus Princesa del Mar RESORT **$$$**
(Map p206; ☎66-72-00; Carretera las Morlas Km 19; r from CUC$260; P❄@≋) Ever had the feeling of déjà vu? You will here at this other large end-of-peninsula complex, where children are banned and the atmosphere is that of a retirement village: tranquil but flat. If you successfully distinguish the entrance among the clutch of lookalike holiday bungalows hereabouts, you'll come upon a resort with engaging staff, a variety of innovative eating options (including a Japanese restaurant) and the special 'Royal Service' – a section of the hotel with its own private restaurant/heated pool/extra-lavish suites – as highlights.

Eating

You can eat well for under CUC$10 in Varadero in a variety of state restaurants (paladares are banned). As 95% of the hotels on the eastern end of the peninsula are all-inclusive, you'll find the bulk of the independent eating joints west of Calle 64.

TOP CHOICE Dante ITALIAN $$
(Map p214; ☎66-77-38; Parque Josone; meals CUC$5-10; ⊙noon-10:45pm) Going strong since 1993, Dante takes its name from its entrepreneurial chef who has been rustling up delectable Italian fare to complement the lakeside setting since the place started up. Antipasto starts at CUC$6; Varadero's most impressive wine stash also awaits. Spoil your tastebuds in Cuba while you have the chance. As one of the best restaurants in town, it's often full.

Kiki's Club ITALIAN $
(Map p214; cnr Av Kawama & Calle 6; meals CUC$3-6; ⊙noon-10.30pm) Delicious pizzas served with innovative toppings like shrimp are the hallmarks of this place, which sports a terrace and a good cocktail menu: a haven from the overriding blandness of the peninsula's western edge.

TOP CHOICE Restaurante Esquina Cuba CARIBBEAN $
(Map p214; cnr Av 1 & Calle 36; ⊙noon-11pm) This place was one-time favorite of Buena Vista Social Club luminary Compay Segundo, and the man obviously had taste. Salivate over the lashings of beans, rice, plantain chips and chicken under the gaze of the great Cuban ephemera that line the walls.

Castel Nuovo ITALIAN $
(Map p214; cnr Av 1 & Calle 11; pizzas CUC$5-10; ⊙noon-11pm) At the gateway to the peninsula stands one of the town's best pizza and pasta restaurants, a cheap, no-nonsense place where atmosphere is lively and the food comes fast. Skip the chicken, beef and fish dishes and go with the Italian fare.

Ranchón Bellamar CARIBBEAN $
(Map p214; Av 1 btwn Calles 16 & 17; meals CUC$2-5; ⊙10am-10pm) Wedged between the main avenue and the beach, this open-sided thatched *ranchón* is part of the Hotel Sunbeach across the road. With its cheap lunches and maracas-shaking musicians, it's a good bet for an unhurried bite, despite the infamously dire service.

Restaurante el Criollo CARIBBEAN $
(Map p214; cnr Av 1 & Calle 18; ⊙noon-midnight) This is one of the more enjoyable state-run places serving what its name suggests, typical *comida criolla* for a few convertibles.

Lai-Lai CHINESE $$
(Map p214; cnr Av 1 & Calle 18; meals CUC$6-10; ⊙noon-11pm) An old stalwart set in a two-storey mansion on the beach, Lai Lai has traditional Chinese set menus with several courses. If you've been craving some wonton soup, crave no more.

La Vicaria CARIBBEAN $
(Map p214; Av 1 btwn Calles 37 & 38; meals from CUC$4; ⊙noon-10:30pm) Munch with the locals under outside tables with *ranchón*-style canopies: portions are generous, especially if you go for the whopping house special, lobster with chicken and pork (CUC$12.95).

Coppelia ICE-CREAM PARLOR $
(Map p214; Av 1 btwn Calles 44 & 46; ⊙3-11pm) What, a Coppelia with no queues? Set above the new shopping complex in Parque de las 8000 Taquillas, Varadero's ice-cream cathedral is bright, airy and surprisingly uncrowded.

Ranchón el Compay SEAFOOD $
(Map p214; cnr Av de la Playa & Calle 54; ⊙10:30am-10pm) There are not so many Varadero restaurants facing the beach, which makes this chirpy thatched-roof affair all the more alluring. Set just off the Parque Central, it serves lobster, shrimp and a mean filet mignon.

Barracuda Grill SEAFOOD $$
(Map p214; cnr Av 1 & Calle 58; meals CUC$7; ⊙11am-7pm) In a thatched pavilion overlooking the beach on the grounds of the Barracuda Diving Center, this popular place has tasty fish and shellfish and it has satisfied many a post-dive appetite.

Restaurante Mallorca SPANISH $$
(Map p214; ☎66-77-46; Av 1 btwn Calles 61 & 62; meals CUC$5-10; ⊙noon-midnight; ❄) This is a fine, intimate venue renowned for its tasty paella. It's surprisingly spacious inside, with a well-stocked bar (a good South American wine selection) and generous servings/service.

Casa del Queso Cubano FRENCH $$
(Map p214; Av 1 cnr Calle 62; ⊙noon-midnight) Locals rate this fondue-focused restaurant next to the Mallorca as one of the best in town and it's a welcome change for the palate, too. Beef fillet fondue, the signature dish, is CUC$10.

Varadero Town

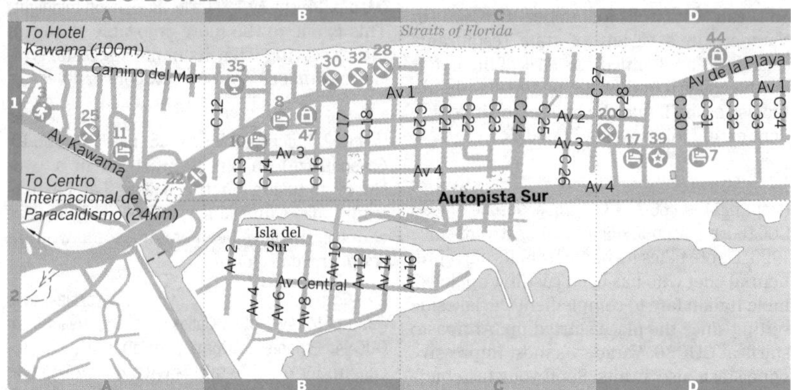

Restaurante Mesón del Quijote SPANISH $$
(Map p206; Reparto la Torre; mains CUC$8-15; ⊙noon-midnight) Next to a statue of Cervantes' famous Don who seems to be making off rather keenly toward the all-inclusive resorts, this restaurant is one of the eastern peninsula's only non-resort options. Perched on a grassy knoll above the Av las Américas, its Spanish-tinged menu makes a refreshing change from the all-you-can-eat buffet.

Restaurante la Campana CARIBBEAN $$
(Map p214; ☎66-72-24; Parque Josone; mains CUC$10; ⊙noon-10:30pm) With its rustic stonework, terracotta roof and bell tower, La Campana transports a little bit of the Greek countryside to Parque Josone. It throws some novel takes on Cuban dishes.

La Casa de Antigüedades INTERNATIONAL
(☎66-73-29; cnr Av 1 & Calle 59) On the edge of Parque Josone, this is an old mansion crammed with antiques where beef, fish and shellfish dishes are served beneath chandeliers. It's the former home of Irenée Du Pont's butler, an example of how the other half lived.

El Retiro INTERNATIONAL
(Map p214; ☎66-73-16; ⊙noon-10pm) International cuisine in neoclassical surrounds in Parque Josone.

Panadería Doña Neli BAKERY
(Map p214; cnr Av 1 & Calle 43; ⊙24hr) Dependable for bread and pastries.

Self-Catering

There's a handy grocery store beside **Aparthotel Varazul** (Map p214; Calle 15; ⊙9am-7pm), with others at **Caracol Pelicano** (Map p214; cnr Calle 27 & Av 3; ⊙9am-7:45pm) and **Club Herradura** (Map p214; Av de la Playa btwn Calles 35 & 36; ⊙9am-7pm).

Drinking

Bar Benny BAR
(Map p214; Camino del Mar btwn Calles 12 & 13; ⊙noon-midnight) A tribute to Benny Moré, this place has a jazz-den energy, with black-and-white photos of the legendary musician lining the walls and his velvety voice oozing from the sound system. Post-beach cocktails and olives are recommended.

Calle 62 BAR, CAFE
(Map p214; cnr Av 1 & Calle 62; ⊙8am-2am) Set in the transition zone between old and new Varadero, this simple snack bar attracts clientele from both ends. It's good for a cheese sandwich during the day, and the ambience becomes feistier after dark with live music going on until midnight.

Bar Mirador BAR
(Map p206; Av las Américas; admission CUC$2) On the top floor of the Mansión Xanadu, Bar Mirador is Varadero's ultimate romantic hangout where happy hour conveniently coincides with sunset cocktails.

☆ Entertainment

While Varadero's nightlife might look enticing on paper, there's no real entertainment 'scene' as such, and the concept of bar-hopping à la Cancún or Miami Beach is almost nonexistent, unless you're prepared to incorporate some long-distance hiking into your drinking schedule. Most happening spots – the good and, more often than not, the bad – are attached to the hotels.

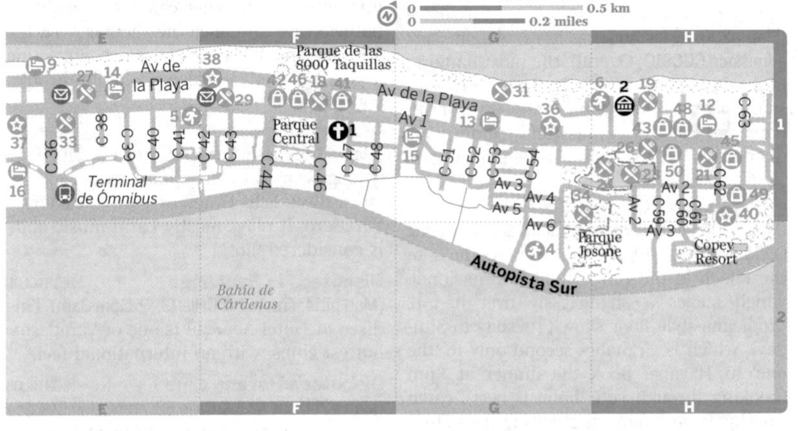

Varadero Town

Sights

1 Iglesia de Santa Elvira ... F1
2 Museo Municipal de Varadero ... H1

Activities, Courses & Tours

3 Acua Diving Center ... A1
Barracuda Diving Center ... (see 19)
4 Centro Todo En Uno ... G2
5 El Golfito ... E1
6 Gaviota ... H1

Sleeping

7 Apartamentos Mar del Sur ... D1
8 Aparthotel Varazul ... B1
9 Club Herradura ... E1
10 Hotel Acuazul Varazul ... B1
11 Hotel Barlovento ... A1
12 Hotel Cuatro Palmas ... H1
13 Hotel Dos Mares ... G1
14 Hotel los Delfines ... E1
15 Hotel Pullman ... G1
16 Hotel Turquino ... E1
17 Villa la Mar ... D1

Eating

18 Coppelia ... F1
19 Barracuda Grill ... H1
20 Caracol Pelicano ... D1
21 Casa del Queso Cubano ... H1
22 Castel Nuovo ... A1
23 Dante ... H1
24 El Retiro ... H1
Grocery Store ... (see 9)
Grocery Store ... (see 8)
25 Kiki's Club ... A1
26 La Casa de Antigüedades ... H1
27 La Vicaria ... E1
28 Lai-Lai ... B1
29 Panadería Doña Neli ... F1
30 Ranchón Bellamar ... B1
31 Ranchón el Compay ... G1
32 Restaurante el Criollo ... B1
33 Restaurante Esquina Cuba ... E1
34 Restaurante la Campana ... G1
Restaurante Mallorca ... (see 21)

Drinking

35 Bar Benny ... B1
Calle 62 ... (see 45)

Entertainment

36 Cabaret Mediterráneo ... G1
37 Casa de la Cultura Los Corales ... E1
38 Casa de la Música ... F1
39 Disco la Red ... D1
40 Discoteca Havana Club ... H1
Discoteca la Pachanga ... (see 10)

Shopping

41 ARTex Store ... F1
42 Bazar Varadero Publicigraf ... F1
43 Casa de las Américas ... H1
44 Casa del Habano ... D1
45 Casa del Habano ... H1
46 Centro Comercial Hicacos ... F1
Galería de Arte Varadero ... (see 43)
47 Gran Parque de la Artesanía ... B1
48 Kawama Sport ... H1
Librería Hanoi ... (see 42)
49 Photo Service ... H1
50 Taller de Cerámica Artística ... H1

TOP CHOICE **Palacio de la Rumba** NIGHTCLUB
(Map p206; Av las Américas Km 2; ⏰10pm-3am; admission CUC$10) Overall, the most banging night out on the peninsula. There's live salsa music at weekends and a good mix of Cubans and tourists. Admission includes your drinks. It's located by the Hotel Bella Costa.

TOP CHOICE **Cabaret Continental** CABARET
(Map p206; Av las Américas; admission incl drink CUC$25; ⏰show 10pm) There's a coolness to the kitsch at the retro Hotel Internacional, which stages a shamelessly over-the-top, Tropicana-style floor show (Tuesday to Sunday), which is, arguably, second only to 'the one' in Havana. Book the dinner at 8pm (booking through your hotel is best), catch the singers and dancers strutting their stuff, and stay after midnight for the tie-loosening disco.

Casa de la Cultura los Corales CULTURAL CENTER
(Map p214; cnr Av 1 & Calle 34) A place where the locals still hold sway. You can catch *filin* (feeling) matinees here, where singers pour their heart into Neil Sedaka–style crooning. There are also instructors available for Cuban music, or take dance lessons for around CUC$2 an hour.

Casa de la Música LIVE MUSIC
(Map p214; cnr Av de la Playa & Calle 42; admission CUC$10; ⏰10:30pm-3am Wed-Sun) Aping its two popular Havana namesakes, this place has some quality live acts and a definitive Cuban feel. It's in town and attracts a local crowd who pay in pesos.

Club Mambo LIVE MUSIC
(Map p206; Av las Américas; open bar, admission CUC$10; ⏰10pm-2am Mon-Fri, to 3am Sat & Sun) Cuba's 1950s mambo craze lives on at this quality live music venue – arguably one of Varadero's hippest and best. Situated next to Club Amigo Varadero in the eastern part of town, the CUC$10 entry includes all your drinks. A DJ spins when the band takes a break, but this place is all about live music. There's a pool table if you don't feel like dancing.

Cabaret Cueva del Pirata CABARET
(Map p206; ☎66-77-51; Autopista Sur; open bar CUC$10; ⏰10pm-3am Mon-Sat) A kilometer east of the Hotel Sol Elite Palmeras, Cabaret Cueva del Pirata presents scantily clad dancers in a Cuban-style floor show with a buccaneer twist (eye patches, swashbuckling moves etc). This cabaret is inside a natural cave and once the show is over, the disco begins. It's a popular place, attracting a young crowd. It's also bookable through your hotel.

Discoteca la Bamba NIGHTCLUB
(Map p206; guests/nonguests free/CUC$10; ⏰10pm-4am) Varadero's most modern video disco is at Hotel Tuxpán, in eastern Varadero. It plays mostly Latin music and is considered 'hot.'

Discoteca la Pachanga NIGHTCLUB
(Map p214; cnr Av 1 & Calle 13; ⏰11pm-3am) This disco at Hotel Acuazul is one of Varadero's hottest clubs, with an international feel.

Discoteca Havana Club NIGHTCLUB
(Map p214; cnr Av 3 & Calle 62; admission CUC$5) Near the Centro Comercial Copey. Expect big, boisterous crowds and plenty of male posturing.

Disco la Red NIGHTCLUB
(Map p214; Av 3 btwn Calles 29 & 30; admission CUC$1; ⏰from 11pm) A good, local atmosphere can be found here.

Cabaret Mediterráneo CABARET
(Map p214; cnr Av 1 & Calle 54; admission CUC$10; ⏰doors 8:30pm, show 10pm) Cabaret Mediterráneo has a professional two-hour show in an open-air location beneath thatched roofs nightly.

Shopping

Caracol shops in the main hotels sell souvenirs, postcards, T-shirts, clothes, alcohol and snack foods. Prices are usually equivalent to those elsewhere.

Centro Comercial Hicacos SHOPPING MALL
(Map p214; ⏰10am-10pm) Parque de las 8000 Taquillas has undergone extensive remodeling with a new mall tucked under a reborn (and plusher) Coppelia. Now called the Centro Comercial Hicacos there are a variety of shops here including souvenirs, cigars and photo developing, and an Infotur office.

Casa de las Américas BOOKS, MUSIC
(Map p214; cnr Av 1 & Calle 59) A retail outlet of the famous Havana cultural institution, this place sells CDs, books and art.

Casa del Habano CIGARS
Av de la Playa btwn Calles 31 & 32(Map p214; ⏰9am-6pm); cnr Av 1 & Calle 63 (Map p214; ☎66-78-43; ⏰9am-9pm) The place for cigars: it has top-quality merchandise from humi-

dors to perfume and helpful service. The latter branch serves a wicked cup of coffee in the upstairs cafe.

Galería de Arte Varadero ART
(Map p214; Av 1 btwn Calles 59 & 60; ⏲9am-7pm) Antique jewelry, museum-quality silver and glass, paintings and other heirlooms from Varadero's bygone bourgeois days are sold here. As most items are of patrimonial importance, everything is already conveniently tagged with export permission.

Plaza América SHOPPING MALL
(Map p206; Autopista Sur Km 7) For a hint of American-style consumerism and the shape of things to come, head here: Varadero's and Cuba's largest shopping complex. There's fancy boutiques, music shops, a cigar store, bars, restaurants, a bank, a post office, a **minimarket** (⏲10am-8:30pm) – oh, and the Varadero Convention Center.

Taller de Cerámica Artística CRAFTS
(Map p214; Av 1 btwn Calles 59 & 60; ⏲9am-7pm) Next door to Galería de Arte Varadero and Casa de las Américas, you can buy fine artistic pottery that's made on the premises. Most items are in the CUC$200 to CUC$250 range.

Gran Parque de la Artesanía MARKET
(Map p214; Av 1 btwn Calles 15 & 16) The open-air artisans' market that once stood on the site of the Centro Comercial Hicacos has been reborn further down Av 1.

Librería Hanoi BOOKS
(Map p214; cnr Av 1 & Calle 44; ⏲9am-9pm) A good selection of books in English, from poetry to politics.

Bazar Varadero Publicigraf SOUVENIRS
(Map p214; cnr Av 1 & Calle 44; ⏲9am-7pm) In Parque Central; ceramics, T-shirts, books and more.

Kawama Sport OUTDOOR GEAR
(Map p214; cnr Av 1 & Calle 60; ⏲9am-8pm) Sells swimming trunks, running shoes and the like.

Photo Service ACCESSORIES
(Map p214; Calle 63 btwn Avs 2 & 3; ⏲9am-10pm) Your photo needs fulfilled.

ARTex Store MUSIC, SOUVENIRS
(Map p214; Av 1 btwn Calles 46 & 47) Showcases CDs, T-shirts, musical instruments and more.

ℹ Information

Dangers & Annoyances

Crime-wise, Varadero's dangers are minimal. Aside from getting drunk at the all-inclusive bar and tripping over your bath mat on the way to the toilet, you haven't got too much to worry about. Watch out for mismatched electrical outlets in hotels. In some rooms, a 110V socket might sit right next to a 220V one. They should be labeled, but aren't always.

Out on the beach, a red flag means no swimming allowed due to the undertow or some other danger. A blue jellyfish known as the Portuguese man-of-war can produce a bad reaction if you come in contact with its long tentacles. Wash the stung area with sea water and seek medical help if the pain becomes intense or you have difficulty breathing. They're most common in summer when you'll see them washed up on the beach; tread carefully. Theft of unguarded shoes, sunglasses and towels is routine along this beach.

Emergency

Asistur (☎66-72-77; Av 1 No 4201 btwn Calles 42 & 43; ⏲9am-4:30pm Mon-Fri)

Internet Access & Telephone

Most hotels have internet access for CUC$6 an hour. Buy a scratch card from the reception. If you're in a cheaper place, use the public **Etecsa Telepunto** cnr Av 1 & Calle 30).

Medical Services

Many large hotels have infirmaries that can provide free basic first aid.

Clínica Internacional Servimed (☎66-77-11; cnr Av 1 & Calle 60; ⏲24hr) Medical or dental consultations (CUC$25 to CUC$70) and hotel calls (CUC$50 to CUC$60). There's also a good pharmacy (open 24 hours) here with items in convertibles.

Farmacia Internacional Marina Chapelín (☎61-85-56; Autopista Sur Km 11; ⏲9am-9pm); Kawama (☎61-44-70; Av Kawama; ⏲9am-9pm); Plaza América (☎66-80-42; Av las Américas Km 6; ⏲9am-9pm)

Money

In Varadero, European visitors can pay for hotels and meals in euros. If you change money at your hotel front desk, you'll sacrifice 1% more than at a bank.

Banco de Ahorro Popular (Calle 36 btwn Av 1 & Autopista Sur; ⏲8:30am-4pm Mon-Fri) Probably the slowest option.

Banco Financiero Internacional Av 1 (cnr Av 1 & Calle 32; ⏲9am-3pm Mon-Fri, 9am-5pm Sat & Sun); Plaza América (cnr Av las Américas & Calle 61; ⏲9am-noon & 1-6pm Mon-Fri, 9am-6pm Sat & Sun) Traveler's checks and cash advances on Visa and MasterCard.

Cadeca (cnr Av de la Playa & Calle 41; ⌚8:30am-6pm Mon-Sat, 8:30am-noon Sun)

Post

Many of the larger hotels have branch post offices.

DHL (Av 1 btwn Calles 39 & 40; ⌚8am-noon & 1-5pm Mon-Fri, 8am-noon Sat)

Post office (cnr Av 1 & Calle 36; ⌚8am-6pm Mon-Sat)

Travel Agencies

Almost every hotel has a tourism desk where staff will book adventure tours, skydiving, scuba diving, whatever. It's almost always cheaper, however, to go directly to the tour agency.

Cubamar (☎66-88-55; Av 1 btwn Calles 14 & 15) Office on ground floor of Aparthotel Varazul. Arranges trips to Río Canímar.

Cubatur (☎66-72-16; cnr Av 1 & Calle 33; ⌚8:30am-6pm) Reserves hotel rooms nationally; organizes bus transfers to Havana hotels and excursions to Península Zapata and other destinations.

Gaviota (Map p214; ☎61-18-44; cnr Calle 56 & Playa)

Havanatur (☎66-70-27; Av 3 btwn Calles 33 & 34; ⌚8am-6pm)

Infotur (☎66-29-61; cnr Av 1 & Calle 13) Next to Hotel Acuazul.

Getting There & Away

Air

Juan Gualberto Gómez International Airport (Map p200; ☎61-30-16) is 20km from central Varadero toward Matanzas and another 6km off the main highway. Airlines here include Thomas Cook from London and Manchester; Cubana from Buenos Aires and Toronto; LTU International Airways from Düsseldorf and four other German cities; Martinair from Amsterdam; and Air Transat and Skyservice from various Canadian cities. The check-in time at Varadero is 90 minutes before flight time.

Aerogaviota also flies to Cayo Largo from Varadero; there are no other domestic flights.

Bus

Terminal de Ómnibus (Map p214; cnr Calle 36 & Autopista Sur) has daily air-con **Víazul** (☎61-48-86; ⌚7am-noon & 1-7pm) buses to a few destinations.

All four daily Havana buses (CUC$10, three hours) stop at Matanzas (CUC$6, one hour); all bar the second of these also call at Juan Gualberto Gómez International Airport (CUC$6, 25 minutes). Buses depart from Varadero at 8am, 11:25am, 3:30pm and 6pm.

Two buses run to Trinidad (CUC$20, six hours) via Cienfuegos (CUC$16, 4½ hours) at 8:15am and 2:55pm. The morning departure also stops at Santa Clara (CUC$11, three hours 20 minutes).

The Santiago bus (CUC$49, 12 hours) leaves nightly at 9:25pm stopping in Cárdenas (CUC$6, 20 minutes), Colón (CUC$6, 1½ hours), Santa Clara (CUC$11, three hours 20 minutes), Sancti Spíritus (CUC$17, five hours), Ciego de Ávila (CUC$19, 6¼ hours), Camagüey (CUC$25), Las Tunas (CUC$33), Holguín (CUC$38) and Bayamo (CUC$41).

If you have the time, you can get to Havana by catching the Víazul bus to Matanzas and taking the Hershey Railway from there.

Aside from the new 9:25pm Víazul bus to Cárdenas, you can go local on bus 236, which departs every hour or so from next to a small tunnel marked 'Ómnibus de Cárdenas' outside the main bus station. You can also catch this bus at the corner of Av 1 and Calle 13 (CUC$1). Don't rely on being able to buy tickets for non-Víazul buses from Varadero to destinations in Matanzas province and beyond: the official line is tourists can't take them, and tourists in Varadero are generally recognizable from Cubans. With decent Spanish you could get lucky.

Another easy way to get to Havana is on one of the regular tour buses booked through the tour desk at your hotel or at any Havanatur/Cubanacán office. It's possible to buy just transport between Varadero and Havana for CUC$25/30 per one way/round-trip. These buses collect passengers right at the hotel door, so you'll save money on taxi links.

Car

You can hire a car from practically every hotel in town and prices are pretty generic between different makes and models. Once you've factored in fuel and insurance, a standard car will cost you approximately CUC$80 a day.

Aside from the hotel reps, you can try **Havanautos** (☎61-44-09; cnr Av 1 & Calle 31) or **Cubacar** (☎66-73-26; cnr Av 1 & Calle 21).

Havanautos (☎25-36-30), **Transtur** (☎25-36-21), **Vía** (☎61-47-83) and **Cubacar** (☎61-44-10) all have car-rental offices in the airport car park. Expect to pay at least CUC$75 a day for the smallest car (or CUC$50 daily on a two-week basis).

Luxury cars are available at **Rex** (Meliá las Américas ☎66-77-39; Autopista Sur Km 7; Juan Gualberto Gómez International Airport ☎66-75-39). It rents Audi and automatic-transmission (rare in Cuba) cars starting from CUC$100 per day.

There's a **Servi-Cupet gas station** (cnr Autopista Sur & Calle 17; ⌚24hr) on the Vía Blanca at the entrance to Marina Acua near Hotel Sunbeach, and one at **Centro Todo En Uno** cnr Calle 54 & Autopista Sur).

If heading to Havana, you'll have to pay the CUC$2 toll at the booth on the Vía Blanca upon leaving.

Train

The nearest train stations are 18km southeast in Cárdenas (p220) and 42km west in Matanzas (p196).

Getting Around

To/From the Airport

Varadero and Matanzas are each about 20km from the spur road to Juan Gualberto Gómez International Airport; it's another 6km from the highway to the airport terminal. A tourist taxi costs CUC$20 to Matanzas and around CUC$25 for the ride from the airport to Varadero. Convince the driver to use the meter and it should work out cheaper. Unlicensed private taxis are prohibited from picking up or delivering passengers to the airport. Three of the Víazul buses bound for Havana call at the airport, leaving at 8am, 3:30pm and 6pm and arriving 25 minutes later. Tickets cost CUC$6.

Bus

Varadero Beach Tour (all-day ticket CUC$5; ⌚9:30am-9pm) is a handy open-top double-decker tourist bus with 45 hop-on/hop-off stops linking all the resorts and shopping malls along the entire length of the peninsula. It passes every half-hour at well-marked stops with route and distance information. You can buy tickets on the bus itself. Meanwhile a gimmicky toy train connects the three large Meliá resorts.

Local buses 47 and 48 run from Calle 64 to Santa Marta, south of Varadero on the Autopista Sur; bus 220 runs from Santa Marta to the far eastern end of the peninsula. There are no fixed schedules. Fares are a giveaway at 20 centavos. You can also utilize bus 236 to and from Cárdenas, which runs the length of the peninsula.

Horse Carts

A state-owned horse and cart around Varadero costs CUC$5 per person for a 45-minute tour or CUC$10 for a full two-hour tour – plenty of time to see the sights.

Moped & Bicycle

Mopeds and bikes are an excellent way of getting off the peninsula and discovering a little of the Cuba outside. Rentals are available at most of the all-inclusive resorts, and bikes are usually lent as part of the package. The generic price is CUC$9 per hour and CUC$24 per day, with gas included in hourly rates (though a levy of CUC$6 may be charged on a 24-hour basis, so ask). There's one **Palmares rental post** (Map p214; cnr Av 1 & Calle 38) in the center of town with mopeds for those not staying at an all-inclusive. This guy also has a couple of rickety bikes with no gears

WORTH A TRIP

COLÓN

Matanzas is a big province, right, so there must be something in that vast tract of agricultural land in the middle? The answer is no, not really. Just a glimpse of towns like Jagüey Grande on the Autopista Nacíonal or Jovellanos on the Carretera Central will make you appreciative of the fuel in your tank but Colón, tucked away in the east of the province 40km beyond Jovellanos, makes an appealing journey-breaker. With its striking colonnaded buildings and one of Cuba's prettiest, greenest central plazas, this town is more about ambience than attractions. What you will be seeing in Colón is an example (and there are many across the country) of what Cuba is like for Cubans untouched by the tourism industry and the money it generates.

Stroll up the main thoroughfare Calle Marti to soak up local life on leafy **Parque de la Libertad** (aka Parque de Colón) with its statue of Christopher Columbus among the numerous other busts, and then marvel at the forgotten delights nearby like the **Iglesia Catholica** (catholic church), **Escuela de Artes y Oficios** (School of Arts and Works) with its striking colonial revivalist architecture and the optimistically named **Hotel Nuevo Continental** dating from 1937. There is also a museum, an art gallery and an old fort to see. Despite its grandiose buildings, Colón is far from the reach of holidaymakers' resuscitating coffers and desperately poor. With one of the province's main orphanages, **Hogar Por Ninos Sin Amparo y Filial** (Mario Muñoz No 260 cnr Martha Abreu y Clotilde Garcías) located here, the town also presents the ideal opportunity to ensure your trip through Cuba directly improves the lives of Cubans themselves (as opposed to funding the government, which is all the money you spend at state-run hotels and restaurants will do). Visits and donations (anything from clothes to medicines) are welcome. See p510 for more information on volunteering.

and 'pedal-backwards' brakes: pay no more than CUC$2 per hour or CUC$15 per day.

Taxi

Metered tourist taxis charge a CUC$1 starting fee plus CUC$1 per kilometer (same tariff day and night). Coco-taxis (*coquitos* or *huevitos* in Spanish) charge less with no starting fee. A taxi to Cárdenas/Havana will be about CUC$20/85 one way. Taxis hang around all the main hotels or you can phone **Cuba Taxi** (☎61-05-55) or **Transgaviota** (☎61-97-62). The latter uses large cars if you're traveling with big luggage. Tourists are not supposed to use the older Lada taxis. It can be worth haggling.

Cárdenas

POP 109, 552

It's hard to imagine a more jarring juxtaposition. Twenty kilometers east of the bright lights of Varadero lies shabby Cárdenas, home to countless resort-based waiters, front-desk clerks and taxi drivers; but with barely a restaurant, hotel or motorized cab to serve it.

Threadbare after 50 years of austerity, Cárdenas is the Miss Havisham of Cuba: an ageing dowager, once beautiful, but now looking more like a sepia-toned photo from another era. Streets once filled with illustrious buildings have suffered irrevocably since the Revolution, leaving this former sugar port a shadow of its former self.

Spurned these days by most modern travelers, Cárdenas has nevertheless played an episodic role in Cuban history. In 1850 Venezuelan adventurer Narciso López and a ragtag army of American mercenaries raised the Cuban flag here for the first time in a vain attempt to free the colony from its Spanish colonizers. Other history-making inhabitants followed, including revolutionary student leader Antonio Echeverría, shot during an abortive raid to assassinate President Batista in 1957. This rich past is showcased in three fabulous museums stationed around Parque Echeverría, the city's main plaza, which today constitute the key reason to visit.

Museums aside, the dilapidated facades of Cárdenas can be a shock to travelers coming from Varadero. If you want to see a picture of real Cuban life, it doesn't get more eye-opening; if it's minty mojitos and all-day volleyball you're after, stick to the tourist beaches.

When asking for directions, beware that Cárdenas residents often use the old street names rather than the new street-naming system (numbers). Double-check if uncertain.

⊙ Sights

In among the battered buildings and dingy peso restaurants of central Cárdenas, three excellent museums, all situated on pretty Parque Echeverría, stand out as city highlights.

TOP CHOICE Museo de Batalla de Ideas MUSEUM

(Av 6 btwn Calles 11 & 12; admission CUC$2; camera CUC$5; ⏲9am-5pm Tue-Sat, 9am-1pm Sun) Across the park from the other museums is this newer attraction, with a well-designed and organized overview of the history of US-Cuban relations, replete with sophisticated graphics. Inspired by the case of Elián Gonzalez, a boy from Cardeñas whose mother, stepfather and 11 others drowned attempting to enter the United States by boat in 1999, the museum is the solid form of Castro's resulting *batalla de ideas* (battle of ideas) with the US Government. The museum's collection has grown ever since, with the displays' theme naturally centering round the eight months during which Cuba and the US debated the custody of Elián – but it extends also to displays on the quality of the Cuban education system and a courtyard containing busts of anti-imperialists that died for the revolutionary cause. The exhibit that most epitomizes the purpose of the museum, however, is possibly the sculpture of a child in the act of disparagingly throwing away a Superman toy.

Museo Casa Natal de José Antonio Echeverría MUSEUM

(Av 4 Este No 560; admission CUC$1 incl guide; ⏲10am-5pm Tue-Sat, 9am-1pm Sun) This museum has a macabre historical collection including the original garrote used to execute Narciso López by strangulation in 1851. Objects relating to the 19th-century independence wars are downstairs, while the 20th-century Revolution is covered upstairs, reached via a beautiful spiral staircase. In 1932 José Echeverría was born here, a student leader slain by Batista's police in 1957 after a botched assassination attempt in Havana's Presidential Palace. There's a statue of him in the eponymous square outside.

Museo Oscar María de Rojas MUSEUM
(cnr Av 4 & Calle 13; admission CUC$5; 9am-6pm Tue-Sat, 9am-1pm Sun) Here you can come and check out Cuba's second-oldest museum (after the Museo Bacardí in Santiago). Its extensive, if rather incongruous, collection of artifacts include a strangulation chair from 1830, a face mask of Napoleon, the tail of Antonio Maceo's horse, Cuba's largest collection of snails and, last but by no means least, some preserved fleas – yes fleas – from 1912. The museum is set in a lovely colonial building and staffed with knowledgeable official guides.

Catedral de la Inmaculada Concepción CHURCH
(Av Céspedes btwn Calles 8 & 9) Parque Colón is the city's other interesting square and here stands the main ecclesiastical building of Cárdenas. Built in 1846, it's noted for its stained glass and purportedly the oldest statue of Christopher Columbus in the western hemisphere. Dating from 1862, Colón, as he's known in Cuba, stands rather authoritatively with his face fixed in a thoughtful frown and a globe resting at his feet. It's Cárdenas' best photo op.

Flagpole Monument MONUMENT
(cnr Av Céspedes & Calle 2) This is not just any flagpole. At the northern end of Av Cespedes, this is a flagpole attached to a monument and commemorates the first raising of the Cuban flag on May 19, 1850.

Arrechabala Rum Factory RUM FACTORY
(cnr Calle 2 & Av 13) To the northwest of the city center in the industrial zone is where Varadero rum is distilled: the Havana Club rum company was founded here in 1878. The company (and its international partner Bacardi) has recently been entangled in a trademark dispute with the Cuban government and partner Pernod Ricard over the rights to sell Havana Club in the US. There are no tours officially available.

Sleeping

Down the road Varadero flaunts more than 50 hotels. Here in humble Cárdenas there are precisely zero now that the once-grand Hotel Dominica (next to the cathedral) has closed indefinitely. Fortunately Cárdenas sports several good (if notoriously hard-to-find) casas particulares.

TOP CHOICE **Hostal Angelo's** CASA PARTICULAR $
(528-491-8; Av 12 btwn Calles 14 & 15; CUC$25;) A veritable oasis from the dusty streets and careening horse carts, this is easily the best option in town: a gay-friendly house abutting a serene, secure courtyard and boasting a Jacuzzi too. English, French and Italian are spoken and, there being a Varadero guide in charge, you can get invaluable information on the local area.

Ricardo Domínguez CASA PARTICULAR $
(528-944-31; cnr Avs 31 & Calle 12; r CUC$35; P) If Angelo's is full, make the trek 1.5km northwest of Parque Echeverría to this spick-and-span bungalow with its leafy garden seemingly just plucked from one of Miami's more tasteful suburbs. The price, though, is steep for a casa this far from the center.

Eating

Half the chefs in Varadero probably come from Cárdenas, which adds irony to the city's dire restaurant scene.

Espriu SEAFOOD $
(Calle 12 btwn Avs 4 & 6; mains CUC$1-3; 9.30am-10pm) The best in town and handily located on Parque Echeverría, Espriu is an OK, if dark, restaurant among uninspired choices. Choose from espresso, shrimp cocktails, fish fillets, burgers and rather tasty paella.

La Barra 1470 PIZZERIA $
(Calle 13 btwn Avs 5 & 7) Tablecloths and wine glasses and a nice inner decor raise expectations that probably won't be met when it comes to the food.

Self-Catering

There are many convertible supermarkets and stores near the cast-iron 19th-century market hall **Plaza Molocoff** (cnr Av 3 Oeste & Calle 12). You can get cheap peso snacks in the market itself and the surrounding area, where merchants peddle everything from fake hair to plastic Buddhas.

Vegetable Market MARKET
(Plaza Molocoff; 8am-5pm Mon-Sat, 8am-2pm Sun) Inside Plaza Molocoff.

El Dandy (Av 3 on Plaza Molocoff; 9am-5pm Mon-Sat, 9am-noon Sun) Sells drinks and groceries.

Entertainment

Casa de la Cultura CULTURAL CENTER
(Av Céspedes No 706 btwn Calles 15 & 16) Housed in a beautiful but faded colonial building

Cárdenas

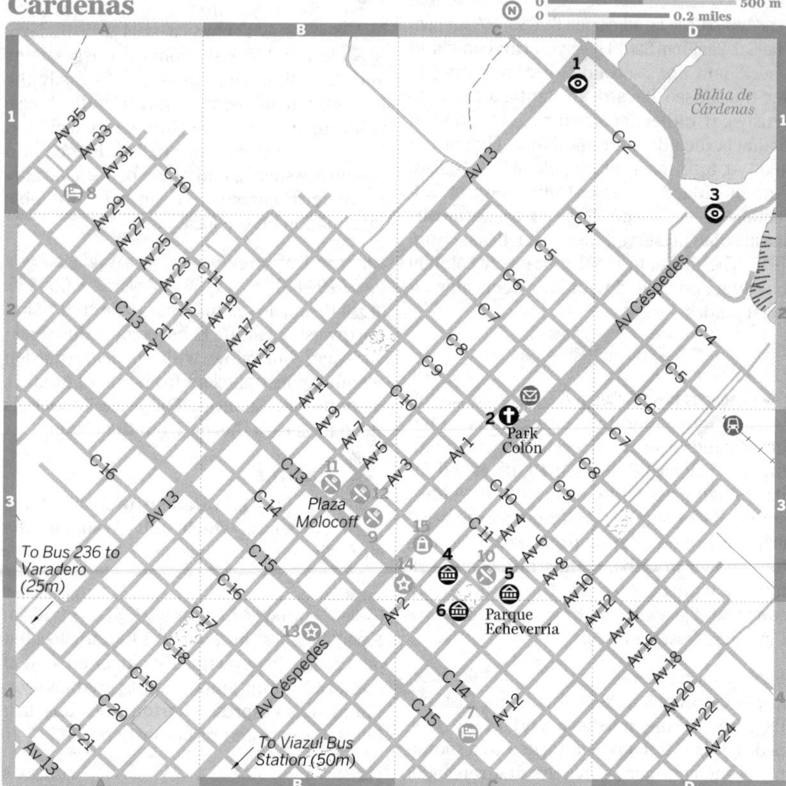

with stained glass and an interior patio with rockers. Search the handwritten advertising posters for rap *peñas* (performances), theater and literature events.

Cine Cárdenas CINEMA
(cnr Av Céspedes & Calle 14) Has daily movie screenings.

Shopping

Librería la Concha de Venus BOOKS
(Av Céspedes No 551 cnr Calle 12; ⏲9am-5pm Mon-Fri, 8am-noon Sat) Books in Spanish.

Information

Banco de Crédito y Comercio (cnr Calle 9 & Av 3)

Cadeca (cnr Av 1 Oeste & Calle 12)

Centro Médico Sub Acuática (☎52-21-14; channel 16 VHF; Calle 13; per hr CUC$80; ⏲8am-4pm Mon-Sat, doctors on-call 24hr) Two kilometers northwest on the road to Varadero at Hospital Julio M Aristegui; has a Soviet recompression chamber dating from 1981.

Etecsa Telepunto (cnr Av Céspedes & Calle 12; ⏲8:30am-7:30pm) Telephone and internet services.

Pharmacy (Calle 12 No 60; ⏲24hr)

Post office (cnr Av Céspedes & Calle 8; ⏲8am-6pm Mon-Sat)

Getting There & Away

The Varadero–Santiago **Víazul** (www.viazul.com) bus stops at the **bus station** (cnr Av Céspedes & Calle 22) once daily in either direction. The eastbound service leaves Varadero at 9:25pm and arrives in Cárdenas at 9:45pm. It then heads east via Colón (CUC$6, one hour), Santa Clara (CUC$11, three hours), Sancti Spíritus (CUC$16, 4½ hours), Ciego de Ávila (CUC$17, five hours 50 minutes), Camagüey (CUC$23, 7¾ hours), Las Tunas (CUC$31, 10 hours), Holguín (CUC$35, 11 hours 10 minutes) and Bayamo (CUC$41, 12½ hours) to Santiago (CUC$48,

Cárdenas

Sights

1 Arrechabala Rum Factory C1
2 Catedral de la Inmaculada Concepción C3
3 Flagpole Monument D1
4 Museo Casa Natal de José Antonio Echeverría C3
5 Museo de Batalla de Ideas C3
6 Museo Oscar María de Rojas C4

Sleeping

7 Hostal Angelo's C4
8 Ricardo Domínguez A1

Eating

9 El Dandy B3
10 Espriu C3
11 La Barra 1470 .... B3
12 Plaza Molocoff B3

Entertainment

13 Casa de la Cultura B4
14 Cine Cárdenas C3

Shopping

15 Librería La Concha de Venus C3

1½ hours). The return bus leaves Cárdenas at 10:40am and arrives in Varadero at 11am.

Local buses leave from the bus station to Havana and Santa Clara daily, but they're often full upon reaching Cárdenas. There are also trucks to Jovellanos/Perico, which puts you 12km from Colón and onto possible onward transport to the east. The ticket office is at the rear of the station.

Bus 236 to/from Varadero leaves hourly from the corner of Av 13 Oeste and Calle 13 (50 centavos, but they like to charge tourists CUC$1).

Getting Around

The main horse-carriage (one peso) route through Cárdenas is northeast on Av Céspedes from the bus station and then northwest on Calle 13 to the hospital, passing the stop of bus 236 (to Varadero) on the way.

The **Servi-Cupet gas station** (cnr Calle 13 & Av 31 Oeste) is opposite an old Spanish fort on the northwest side of town, on the road to Varadero.

San Miguel de los Baños & Around

Nestled away in the interior of Matanzas province amid rolling hills punctuated by vivid splashes of bougainvillea, San Miguel de los Baños is an atmospheric old spa town that once rivaled Havana for elegant opulence. Once, that is. Flourishing briefly as a destination for wealthy spa seekers seeking the soothing medicinal waters that were 'discovered' here in the early 20th century, San Miguel saw a smattering of lavish neoclassical villas shoot up that still line the town's arterial Avenida de Abril today. But the boom times didn't last. Just prior to the Revolution pollution from a local sugar mill infiltrated the water supply and the resort quickly faded from prominence. Now, it's a curious mix between an architectural time capsule from a bygone era and something out of a post-apocalyptic John Wyndham novel.

Sights & Activities

Passing visitors will be shocked at the architectural contrasts here: the smaller houses of the current population juxtaposed with the surreally ostentatious buildings of the glory days, such as the ornate multi-domed **Gran Hotel y Balneario**, on the north side of town, a replica of the Grand Casino at Monte Carlo. Plans to reopen the hotel haven't yet materialized but it's relatively easy to wander the eerie grounds down to the still-standing red-brick Romanesque bath houses. You'll sometimes have to negotiate a guard at the main entrance; a small tip usually suffices. It's probably best to give bathing a miss, though.

Looming above town are the steep slopes of **Loma de Jacán**, a glowering hill with 448 steps embellished by faded murals of the Stations of the Cross. When you reach the small chapel on top you can drink in the town's best views with the added satisfaction that you are standing at the highest point in the province.

Sleeping & Eating

Finca Confidencia CASA PARTICULAR $
(☎81-39-23; Carretera Central btwn Colesio & Jovellanos; r CUC$20; P) Here is your chance to enhance your taste for bucolic provincial life away from the razzmatazz of the province's north coast at this idyllic farm 14km northeast of San Miguel de los Baños and 6km east of the town of Colesio on the Carretera Central. Here you can chill in grounds replete with mango and guava trees, participate in ceramics classes and help out on a farm where some 83 types of plants are cultivated. The food you'll eat is

almost exclusively from the smallholding; the owner also produces his own delicious coffee. The downside? There's currently only one room available. Plans to add a second are afoot.

Getting There & Away

To get to San Miguel de los Baños, follow Rte 101 from Cárdenas to Colesio where you cross the Carretera Central; the town is situated a further 8km to the southwest of Colesio. A taxi from Cárdenas should cost CUC$20 to CUC$25 – bargain hard. You may be able to catch a ride on a truck/local bus from Cárdenas bus station.

PENÍNSULA DE ZAPATA

POP 9334

A vast, virtually uninhabited swampy wilderness spanning the entirety of southern Matanzas, the 4520-sq-km Península de Zapata quickens the pulses of wildlife-watchers and divers alike with the country's most important bird species and some of the most magical off-shore reef diving secreted in its humid embrace. Most of the peninsula, a protected zone now part of Gran Parque Natural Montemar, was formerly known as Parque Nacional Ciénaga de Zapata: in 2001, it was declared a Unesco Biosphere Reserve.

The sugar-mill town of Australia in the northeast of the peninsula marks the main access point to the park. Near here is one of the region's big tourist money-spinners, the cheesy yet oddly compelling Boca de Guamá, a reconstructed Taíno village.

The road hits the coast at Playa Larga, home to the peninsula's best beaches, at the head of the Bahía de Cochinos (Bay of Pigs) where propaganda billboards still laud Cuba's historic victory over the *Yanqui* imperialists in 1961.

Ornithologists and nature lovers will want to veer southwest from here, where the sugarcane plantations fade fast into sticky swamp. This is one of the remotest regions of Cuba, rarely penetrated by tourists. Yet intrepid visitors will reap the benefits: an incredible diversity of birds, as well endemic reptile and plant species, can be glimpsed on the mangrove-flecked waterways here.

Aside from its reputation as a proverbial banana-skin for US imperialism, the east coast of the Bay of Pigs also boasts some of the best cave diving in the Caribbean (see boxed text, p228) and southeast of Playa Larga the dive sites fan out temptingly, accompanied by less-inviting, moth-eaten resort hotels.

Accommodation outside of the resorts, however, is thankfully abundant. You can check out excellent options in Central Australia, Playa Larga and Playa Girón.

The peninsula is too isolated to receive public transport links – buses get no closer than just north of Australia – but a shuttle service (see boxed text p226) now runs between Boca de Guamá and Caleta Buena.

Information

La Finquita (☎91-32-24; Autopista Nacional Km 142; ⊙9am-5pm Mon-Sat, 8am-noon Sun), a highly useful information center-cum-snack bar run by Cubanacán just by the turn-off toward Playa Larga from the Autopista Nacional, arranges trips into the Península de Zapata (see p227) and books rooms at the Villa Guamá. This is the only information center proper on the peninsula.

Etecsa, the post office and convertible stores are across the Autopista in Jagüey Grande. Insect repellent is absolutely essential on the peninsula and while Cuban repellent is available locally, it's like wasabi on sushi for the ravenous buggers here.

Central Australia & Around

No, you haven't just arrived Down Under. About 1.5km south of the Autopista Nacional on the way to Boca de Guamá, is the large Central Australia sugar mill, built in 1904.

Sights

Museo de la Comandancia MUSEUM
(admission CUC$1; ⊙9am-5pm Tue-Sat, 8am-noon Sun) During the 1961 Bay of Pigs invasion, Fidel Castro had his headquarters in the former office of the sugar mill, but today the building is devoted to this revolutionary museum. You can see the desk and phone from where Fidel commanded his forces, along with other associated memorabilia. Outside is the wreck of an invading aircraft shot down by Fidel's troops. The concrete memorials lining the road to the Bahía de Cochinos mark the spots where defenders were killed in 1961. A more moving testimony to the Bay of Pigs episode is the Museo de Playa Girón (p229).

Bahía de Cochinos

Finca Fiesta Campesina WILDLIFE PARK
(admission CUC$1; ⌚9am-6pm) Approximately 400m on your right after the Central Australia exit is a kind of wildlife-park-meets-country fair with labeled examples of Cuba's typical flora and fauna. The highlights of this strangely engaging place are the coffee (some of the best in Cuba and served with a sweet wedge of sugarcane), the bull-riding and the hilarious if slightly infantile games of guinea-pig roulette overseen with much pizzazz by the gentleman at the gate. It's the only place in Cuba – outside the cockfighting – where you encounter any form of open gambling.

Sleeping & Eating

There are more casas in Playa Larga (32km) and Playa Girón (48km).

Motel Batey Don Pedro CABINS $
(☎91-28-25; Carretera a Península de Zapata; s/d CUC$26/31; P) The best bet for accommodations in the area, this sleepy motel is down a track just south of the turn-off to the Península de Zapata, from Km 142 on the Autopista Nacional at Jagüey Grande. There are 12 rooms here in thatched double units with ceiling fans, crackling TVs and patios – and a random frog or two in the bathroom. Two cabins have air-con. The motel is designed to resemble a peasant settlement. For food there is an on-site restaurant serving just-OK and, a far better option, the Finca Fiesta Campesina at the beginning of the track. English is spoken here and energy-boosting *guarapo* (sugarcane juice) along with some of Zapata's best coffee is served.

Pío Cuá CARIBBEAN $$
(Carretera de Playa Larga Km 8; meals CUC$8-20; ⌚11am-5pm) A favorite with Guamá-bound tour buses, this huge place is set up for big groups, but retains fancy decor with lots of stained glass. Shrimp, lobster or chicken meals are pretty good. It's 8km from the Autopista turn-off, heading south from Australia.

Getting There & Away

Víazul buses between Havana and Cienfuegos will stop on the Autopista Nacíonal 1.5km north of Australia; as this isn't an official stop negotiating a pick-up is complicated. Ring the bus stations in Havana (see p119) or Cienfuegos (see p242).

Boca de Guamá

Boca de Guamá may be a tourist creation, but as resorts around here go it's among the more imaginative. Situated about halfway between the Autopista Nacional at Jagüey Grande and the famous Bahía de Cochinos, it takes its name from native Taíno chief Guamá, who made a last stand against the Spanish in 1532 (in Baracoa). The big attraction here is the boat trip through mangrove-lined waterways and across Laguna del Tesoro (Treasure Lake) to a 're-creation' of a Taíno village. Fidel used to holiday here and had a hand in developing the Taíno theme. You'll soon be struggling to draw parallels with pre-Columbian Cuba however: raucous tour groups and even louder rap music welcome your voyage back in time. Arranged around the dock the boats depart from a

PENINSULA SHUTTLE SERVICE

In the continuing absence of a Víazul connection, the Península de Zapata has improvised and those lacking wheels can now negotiate key sights on a twice-daily shuttle bus. The service starts at Hotel Playa Girón at 8:30am, heads out to Caleta Buena and then back past Punta Perdiz, Cueva los Peces and Hotel Playa Larga to Boca de Guamá at 10am. The shuttle then leaves Boca de Guamá at 11am for the reverse journey. The service is repeated in the afternoon with departure times being 1:30pm from Hotel Playa Girón and 3:30pm from Boca de Guamá. A ticket for the day costs CUC$3 per person.

cluster of restaurants, expensive snack bars, knickknack shops and a crocodile farm. Palm-dotted grounds here make a pleasant break from the surrounding swampy heat.

Sights

Laguna del Tesoro LAKE

This lake is 5km east of Boca de Guamá via the Canal de la Laguna, accessible only by boat. On the far (east) side of this 92-sq-km body of water is a tourist resort named Villa Guamá, built to resemble a Taíno village, on a dozen small islands. A sculpture park next to the mock village has 32 life-size figures of Taíno villagers in a variety of idealized poses. The lake is called 'Treasure Lake' due to a legend about some treasure the Taíno supposedly threw into the water just prior to the Spanish conquest (not dissimilar to South American El Dorado legends). The lake is stocked with largemouth bass, so fishers frequently convene.

Criadero de Cocodrilos CROCODILE FARM

(adult/child incl drink CUC$5/3; 9am-5pm) Inside the Guamá complex near the Villa Guamá departure dock, the Criadero de Cocodrilos farm breeds crocodiles – although the fenced-off lake seems barely more authentic than the Taíno village. Lots of crocs languish about; there are other caged animals here. It used to be possible to visit the nucleus of this breeding program just across the road from the crocodile farm, run by the Ministerio de Industrias Pesqueras. Two species of crocodiles are raised here: the native *Crocodylus rhombifer* (*cocodrilo* in Spanish), and the *Crocodylus acutus* (*caimán* in Spanish), which is found throughout the tropical Americas. Tourism is not encouraged however, and security guards will point you back across the road to Boca de Guamás faux farm. On your right as you come from the Autopista, the Criadero de Cocodrilos is a breeding facility, run by the zoo, but try your luck and you could get a guided tour here (in Spanish), taking you through each stage of the breeding program. Prior to the establishment of this program in 1962 (considered the first environmental protection act undertaken by the revolutionary government), these two species of marsh-dwelling crocodiles were almost extinct.

The breeding has been so successful that across the road in the Boca de Guamá complex you can buy stuffed baby crocodiles or dine, legally, on crocodile steak.

If you buy anything made from crocodile leather at Boca de Guamá, be sure to ask for an invoice (for the customs authorities) proving that the material came from a crocodile farm and not wild crocodiles. A less controversial purchase would be one of the attractive ceramic bracelets sold at the nearby **Taller de Cerámica** (9am-6pm Mon-Sat) where you can see five kilns in operation.

Sleeping & Eating

Villa Guamá CABINS $

(91-55-51; s/d CUC$29/42) This place was built in 1963 on the east side of the Laguna del Tesoro, about 8km from Boca de Guamá by boat (cars can be left at the crocodile farm; CUC$1). The 50 thatched *cabañas* (cabins) with bath and TV are on piles over the shallow waters. The six small islands bearing the units are connected by wooden footbridges to other islands with a bar, cafetería, overpriced restaurant and a swimming pool containing chlorinated lake water. Rowboats are available for rent, and the bird-watching at sunrise is reputedly fantastic. You'll need insect repellent if you decide to stay. The ferry transfer is not included in the room price.

At the boat dock you'll find **Bar la Rionda** (9:30am-5pm) and **Restaurante la Boca** (set meals CUC$12).

Getting There & Away

Your own transport is best. The nearest public buses stop 18km north just beyond Australia.

There are regular tours from Varadero to Boca de Guamá.

Getting Around

A passenger ferry (adult/child CUC$12/6, 20 minutes) departs Boca de Guamá for Villa Guamá across Laguna del Tesoro four times a day. Speedboats depart more frequently and whisk you across to the pseudo-Indian village in just 10 minutes any time during the day for CUC$12 per person round-trip (with 40 minutes waiting time at Villa Guamá, two-person minimum). In the morning you can allow yourself more time on the island by going one way by launch and returning by ferry.

You can travel on shuttle bus between Boca de Guamá and Caleta Buena (see boxed text p226).

Gran Parque Natural Montemar

The largest *ciénaga* (swamp) in the Caribbean, **Ciénaga de Zapata** is also one of Cuba's most diverse ecosystems. Crowded into this vast wetland (essentially two swamps divided by a rocky central tract) are 14 different vegetation formations including mangroves, wood, dry wood, cactus, savannah, selva and semideciduous. There are also extensive salt pans. The marshes support more than 190 bird species, 31 types of reptiles, 12 species of mammals, plus countless amphibians, fish and insects (including the insatiable mosquito). There are more than 900 plant species here, some 115 of them endemic. It is also an important habitat for the endangered *manatí* (manatee), the Cuban *cocodrilo* (crocodile; *Crocodylus rhombifer*), and the *manjuarí* (alligator gar; *Atractosteus tristoechus*), Cuba's most primitive fish with an alligator's head but a fish-like body. The almost-extinct dwarf hutia (a kind of wild guinea pig) has the swamp as its only refuge.

The Zapata is the best bird-watching spot in Cuba: the place to come to see *zunzuncitos* (bee hummingbirds; the world's smallest bird), cormorants, cranes, ducks, flamingos, hawks, herons, ibis, owls, parrots, partridges and *tocororos* (Cuba's national bird). There are 18 birds endemic to the region. Numerous migratory birds from North America winter here, making November to April prime bird-watching season. It's also the nation's number-one nexus for catch-and-release sportfishing and fly-fishing, where the *palometa, sábalo* and *robalo,* as well as bonefish, thrive.

Communications in Zapata, unsuitable for agriculture, were almost nonexistent before the Revolution when poverty was the rule. Charcoal makers burn wood from the region's semideciduous forests, and *turba* (peat) dug from the swamps is an important source of fuel. The main industry today is tourism and ecotourists are arriving in increasing numbers. Public transport only runs as far as Playa Larga: to see anything of the *ciénaga* proper you'll need to come here as part of a tour.

Activities

There are four main excursions into the park, with an understandable focus on bird-watching. Itineraries are flexible. Transport is not usually laid on; it's best to arrange beforehand. Cars (including chauffeur-driven jeeps) can be rented from **Havanautos** (☎98-41-23) in Playa Girón; Cienfuegos has the next-nearest car rental.

Aspiring fishers can arrange **fly-fishing** from canoes or (due to the shallowness of the water) on foot at either Las Salinas or Hatiguanico. Ask at Cubanacán's La Finquita office or just turn up if you have your own gear. Between them the two locations offer Cuba's best angling: Las Salinas has excellent fishing; Hatiguanico is great for Tarpon.

Laguna de las Salinas BIRD-WATCHING

(per person CUC$10) One of the most popular excursions is to this *laguna* where large numbers of migratory waterfowl can be seen from November to April: we're talking 10,000 pink flamingos at a time, plus 190 other feathered species. The first half of the road to Las Salinas is through the forest, while the second half passes swamps and lagoons. Here, aquatic birds can be observed. Guides are mandatory to explore the refuge. The 22km visit lasts over four hours but you may be able to negotiate for a longer visit.

Observación de Aves BIRD-WATCHING

(per person CUC$19) This trip offers an extremely flexible itinerary and the right to roam (with a qualified park ornithologist) around a number of different sites, including the **Reserva de Bermejas**. Among 18 species of endemic bird found here you can see prized *ferminins, cabreritos* and *gallinuelas de Santo Tomás* – found only on the Península de Zapata.

DIVING IN THE BAHÍA DE COCHINOS

While the Isla de la Juventud and María la Gorda lead most Cuban divers' wish lists, the Bahía de Cochinos has some equally impressive underwater treats. There's a huge drop-off running 30m to 40m offshore for over 30km from Playa Larga down to Playa Girón, a fantastic natural feature that has created a 300m-high coral-encrusted wall with amazing swim-throughs, caves, gorgonians and marine life. Even better, the proximity of this wall to the coastline means that the region's 30-plus dive sites can be easily accessed without a boat – you just glide out from the shore. Good south coast visibility stretches from 30m to 40m and there are a handful of wrecks scattered around.

Organizationally, Playa Girón is well set up with highly professional instructors bivouacked at five different locations along the coast. Generic dive prices (CUC$25 per immersion, CUC$100 for five or CUC$365 for an open-water course) are some of the cheapest in Cuba. Snorkeling is CUC$5 per hour.

The **International Scuba Center** (☎98-41-18), at Villa Playa Girón, is the main diving headquarters. It is complemented by the **Club Octopus International Diving Center** (☎98-72-94, 98-72-25), 200m west of Villa Playa Larga.

Eight kilometers southeast of Playa Girón is **Caleta Buena** (10am-6pm), a lovely sheltered cove perfect for snorkeling and kitted out with another diving office. Black coral ridges protect several sinkholes and underwater caves teaming with the oddly-shaped sponges for which the area is renowned: a great opportunity for speleo-scuba diving! Because saltwater meets freshwater the fish here are different to other sites. Admission to the beach is CUC$12 and includes an all-you-can-eat lunch buffet and open bar. Beach chairs and thatched umbrellas spread along the rocky shoreline. Snorkel gear is CUC$3.

More underwater treasures can be seen at the **Cueva de los Peces** (admission CUC$1; 9am-6pm), a flooded tectonic fault (or *cenote*), about 70m deep on the inland side of the road, almost exactly midway between Playa Larga and Playa Girón. There are lots of bright, tropical fish, plus you can explore back into the darker, spookier parts of the *cenote* with snorkel or dive gear (bring torches). The beach facing has good snorkeling too off a black coral shelf. There's a handy restaurant and an on-site dive outfit.

Just beyond the Cueva is **Punta Perdiz**, another phenomenal snorkeling/scuba-diving spot with the wreck of a US landing craft scuppered during the Bay of Pigs invasion to explore. The shallow water is gemstone-blue here and there's good snorkeling right from the shore. There's a smaller on-site diving concession. It costs CUC$1 to use the thatched umbrellas, beach chairs and showers, and there's another decent restaurant. Non-water based activities include volleyball and chances to play the amiable custodians at dominoes. Beware the swarms of mosquitoes and *libélulas* (enormous dragonflies).

Río Hatiguanico BIRD-WATCHING

(per person CUC$19) Switching from land to boat, this excursion takes you on a three-hour 12km river trip through the densely forested northwestern part of the peninsula. You'll have to duck to avoid the branches at some points, while at others the river opens out into a wide delta-like estuary. Birdlife is abundant and you may also see turtles and crocodiles.

Señor Orestes Martínez Garcías BIRD-WATCHING

(☎98-75-45, 525-39004; chino.zapata@gmail.com; excursions per person CUC$10-20) Garnering a reputation as the area's most knowledgeable resident bird-watcher, 'el Chino' as he is otherwise known can take you on more personalized, and reportedly highly rewarding ornithological forays into the *ciénaga*.

Santo Tomás OUTDOOR ACTIVITIES

(per person CUC$10) It's also worth asking about this trip, an excursion that begins 30km west of Playa Larga in the park's only real settlement (Santo Tomás) and proceeds along a tributary of the Hatiguanico – walking or boating, depending on the season. It's another good option for bird-watchers.

 Information

Cubanacán's La Finquita on the Autopista near Central Australia is the park information point, and a good place to book your chosen excursion. The Playa Larga or Girón hotels can also arrange tours, as can Hostal Enrique in the village of Caletón by Playa Larga.

Playa Larga

Continuing south from Boca de Guamá you reach Playa Larga, on the Bahía de Cochinos (Bay of Pigs) after 13km. Larga was one of two beaches invaded by US-backed exiles on April 17, 1961 (although Playa Girón, 35km further south, saw far bigger landings). It's now a diver's paradise. There's a cheapish resort here, a scuba-diving center, and a smattering of casas particulares in the adjacent beachside village of Caletón. With the nearest accommodations for access to Gran Parque Natural Montemar, it is a good base for environmental excursions around the area.

Sleeping & Eating

Hostal Enrique CASA PARTICULAR $
(98-74-25; Caletón; r CUC$20-25;) Five hundred meters down the road to Las Salinas is the best of the casas in this area, with two rooms, both with private bathrooms, a large dining area (serving large portions of food) and a path from the back garden leading to the often-deserted Caletón beach. Enrique can help arrange diving and bird-watching at distinctly cheaper prices than the hotels hereabouts.

Villa Playa Larga HOTEL $
(98-72-94; s/d low season incl breakfast CUC$34/48; P) On a small scimitar of white-sand beach by the road, just east of the village of Caletón, this hotel has huge rooms with bath, sitting room, fridge and TV. There are also eight two-bedroom family bungalows. A recent overhaul has spruced the place up slightly, though the restaurant is still pretty forlorn.

Villa Marieta CASA PARTICULAR $
(98-71-24; Caletón; r CUC$20-25;) Behind the one room on offer, this hospitable house has a lovely eating area/bar/terrace right by the sea.

Palmares restaurant CARIBBEAN
(meals CUC$2-7) Outside of your chosen accommodation, this pleasant-enough place across the road from Villa Playa Larga is the sole dining option.

Getting There & Away

A taxi from Cienfuegos will cost around CUC$60; to the Autopista Nacional at Australia around CUC$20. Otherwise, tours to the peninsula from Varadero usually stop at Playa Larga.

Getting Around

Taxi, car/moped hire at Playa Girón or the peninsula shuttle service: your choice.

Playa Girón

The sandy arc of Playa Girón nestles peacefully on the eastern side of the infamous Bahía de Cochinos, 48km south of Boca de Guamá. Notorious as the place where the Cold War almost got hot, the beach is actually named for a French pirate, Gilbert Girón, who met his end here by decapitation in the early 1600s at the hands of embittered locals. In April 1961 it was the scene of another botched raid, the ill-fated, CIA-sponsored invasion that tried to land on these remote sandy beaches in one of modern history's classic David and Goliath struggles. Lest we forget, there are still plenty of propaganda-spouting billboards dotted around rehashing past glories, though these days Girón, with its clear Caribbean waters and precipitous off-shore drop-off, is a favorite destination for scuba divers and snorkelers.

Besides some decent private houses, Playa Girón's one and only resort is the modest Villa Playa Girón, a low-key all-inclusive that is perennially popular among the diving fraternity. Long, shady Playa los Cocos, where the snorkeling is good, is just a five-minute walk south along the shore. In common with many of Cuba's southern coastal areas, there's often more *diente de perro* (dog's tooth) than soft white sand.

On the main entry road to the hotel there's a pharmacy, a post office and a Caracol shop selling groceries. The settlement of Playa Girón is a tiny one-horse town, so the hotel is the best pit-stop if you need any goods or services.

Sights

Museo de Playa Girón MUSEUM
(admission CUC$2, camera CUC$1; 8am-5pm) Perhaps unsurprisingly, this museum with its gleaming glass display cases evokes a tangible sense of the history of Bahía de Cochinos (the Bay of Pigs) episode that unfolded on this spot in 1961. Housed across the street from Villa Playa Girón, it offers two rooms of artifacts from Bahía de Cochinos plus numerous photos with (some)

THE BAY OF PIGS

What the Cubans call Playa Girón, the rest of the world has come to know as the Bay of Pigs 'fiasco,' a disastrous attempt by the Kennedy administration to invade Cuba and overthrow Fidel Castro.

Conceived in 1959 by the Eisenhower administration and headed up by deputy director of the CIA, Richard Bissell, the plan to initiate a program of covert action against the Castro regime was given official sanction on March 17, 1960. There was but one proviso: no US troops were to be used in combat.

The CIA modeled their operation on the 1954 overthrow of the left-leaning government of Jacobo Arbenz in Guatemala. However, by the time President Kennedy was briefed on the proceedings in November 1960, the project had mushroomed into a full-scale invasion backed by a 1400-strong force of CIA-trained Cuban exiles and financed with a military budget of US$13 million.

Activated on April 15, 1961, the invasion was an unmitigated disaster from start to finish. Intending to wipe out the Cuban Air Force on the ground, US planes painted in Cuban Air Force colors (and flown by Cuban exile pilots) missed most of their intended targets. Castro, who had been forewarned of the plans, had scrambled his air force the previous week. Hence when the invaders landed at Playa Girón two days later, Cuban sea furies were able to promptly sink two of their supply ships and leave a force of 1400 men stranded on the beach.

To add insult to injury, a countrywide Cuban rebellion that had been much touted by the CIA never materialized. Meanwhile a vacillating Kennedy told a furious Bissell that he would not provide the marooned exile soldiers with US air cover.

Abandoned on the beaches, without supplies or military back up, the disconsolate invaders were doomed. There were 114 killed in skirmishes and a further 1189 captured. The prisoners were returned to the US a year later in return for US$53 million worth of food and medicine.

The Bay of Pigs failed due to a multitude of factors. Firstly, the CIA had overestimated the depth of Kennedy's personal commitment and had made similarly inaccurate assumptions about the strength of the fragmented anti-Castro movement inside Cuba. Secondly, Kennedy himself, adamant all along to make a low-key landing, had chosen a site on an exposed strip of beach close to the Zapata swamps. Thirdly, no one had given enough credit to the political and military know-how of Fidel Castro or to the extent to which the Cuban Intelligence Service had infiltrated the CIA's supposedly covert operation.

The consequences for the US were far reaching. 'Socialism or death!' a defiant Castro proclaimed at a funeral service for seven Cuban 'martyrs' on April 16, 1961. The Revolution had swung irrevocably toward the Soviet Union.

bilingual captions. The mural of victims and their personal items is harrowing and the tactical genius of the Cuban forces comes through in the graphic depictions of how the battle unfolded. The 15-minute film about the 'first defeat of US imperialism in the Americas' is CUC$1 extra. A British Hawker Sea Fury aircraft used by the Cuban Air Force is parked outside the museum; round the back are other vessels used in the battle.

Sleeping & Eating

Aside from Villa Playa Girón, the small settlement of Playa Girón has some decent private houses, with most serving food.

Hostal Luis CASA PARTICULAR $
(99-42-58; r incl breakfast CUC$25; P ❄) The first house on the road to Cienfuegos is also the village's premier casa. Instantly recognizable by the blue facade and the two stone lions guarding the gate, youthful Luis and his wife offer two spotless rooms on a large lot with plenty of room for parking.

KS Abella CASA PARTICULAR $
(98-43-83; r CUC$20-25; ❄) The *señor* is a former chef at Villa Playa Girón now trying out his seafood specialties on his casa guests. The casa is situated on the corner of the main road in the set-back red-and-cream

bungalow, and the already charming terrace is currently being extended.

Villa Playa Girón RESORT $
(☎98-41-10; all-incl s/d CUC$46/65; P ❄ ≋) On a beach imbued with historical significance lies this rather ordinary hotel – although an all-inclusive, with its spartan bungalows and spatially challenged dining room, it rarely feels like one. Always busy with divers, the villa is an unpretentious place with clean, basic rooms that are often a long walk from the main block. The beach is a 50m dash away, though its allure has been spoiled somewhat by the construction of a giant wave-breaking wall. Ask about low season discounts.

Getting There & Away

A taxi should cost approximately CUC$40 to/from Cienfuegos; from Playa Girón to Playa Larga, the fare will be closer to CUC$20.

Getting Around

Havanautos (☎98-41-23) has a car-rental office at Villa Playa Girón or you can hire a moto for CUC$24 per day. There is also the twice-daily shuttle service (see boxed text p226)

Servi-Cupet gas stations are located on the Carretera Central at Jovellanos and on Colón at Jagüey Grande, as well as on the Autopista Nacional at Aguada de Pasajeros in Cienfuegos province.

East of Caleta Buena the coastal road toward Cienfuegos is not passable in a normal car; backtrack and take the inland road via Rodas.

Cienfuegos Province

☎043 / POP 405,545

Includes »

Best Places to Eat

» Paladar Aché (p240)
» Hacienda la Vega (p245)
» Palacio de Valle (p240)
» Club Cienfuegos (p243)

Best Places to Stay

» Villa Lagarto Maylin & Tony (p238)
» Hotel la Unión (p242)
» Hostal Palacio Azul (p239)
» Bella Perla Marina (p238)
» Villa Guajimico (p246)

Why Go?

Bienvenue (welcome) to Cienfuegos province. If Cuba has a Gallic heart, it's hidden beneath the crinkled Sierra del Escambray; if it has a Paris, it is the finely-sculpted provincial capital, glistening pearl-like beside the island's best natural bay.

The original French colonizers arrived here in 1819. They brought with them the ideas of the European Enlightenment, which they industriously incorporated into their fledgling neoclassical city.

Cienfuegos sits on a coast curling like a mini-rainbow of emerald greens and iridescent blues, flecked with coves, caves and sublime coral reefs. The province's apex is just inland at El Nicho, a lush outpost of Topes de Collantes Natural Park.

Though ostensibly white, Cienfuegos' once-muted African 'soul' gained a mouthpiece in the 1940s in perhaps Cuba's most versatile musician, Benny Moré. Nor was he Cienfuegos' only Afro-Cuban improviser: in nearby Palmira, Santería brotherhoods still preserve the traditions of Cuba's hybrid Catholic-Yoruba religious culture.

When to Go

Cienfuegos' high season, such as it is, doesn't really get going until January and runs through to April. Beach-lovers and divers should hit the Caribbean coast then but party-goers will prefer August and September, when despite the imminent hurricane season, the Cienfuegos carnival and the bi-annual Benny Moré festival respectively can be enjoyed. Up at El Nicho in the Sierra del Escambray, travel in the wet season (August to October) is tougher at this time due to difficult road conditions.

History

The first settlers in the Cienfuegos area were Taínos, who called their fledgling principality, Cacicazgo de Jagua – a native word for 'beauty.' In 1494 Columbus 'discovered' the Bahía de Cienfuegos (Cuba's third-largest bay, with a surface area of 88 sq km) on his second voyage to the New World and 14 years later Sebastián de Ocampo stopped by during his pioneering circumnavigation of the island. He liked the bay so much he built a house there. The pirates followed the explorers: during the 16th and 17th centuries buccaneering raids got so bad the Spanish built a bayside fort, the imposing Castillo de Jagua (p244), one of the most important military structures in Cuba.

Cienfuegos

POP 143,894

La ciudad que más me gusta a mí (the city I like the best), reads a billboard on the Bahía de Cienfuegos, quoting the words of native singer Benny Moré. He wasn't the settlement's only cheerleader. Cuba's so-called Perla del Sur (Pearl of the South) has long seduced travelers from around the island with its elegance, enlightened French spirit and feisty Caribbean panache. If Cuba has a Paris, this is most definitely it.

Arranged around the country's most spectacular natural bay, Cienfuegos is a nautical city with an enviable waterside setting. Founded in 1819, it's one of Cuba's newest settlements, but also one of its most architecturally homogeneous, a factor that earned it a Unesco World Heritage Site listing in 2005. Geographically, the city is split into two distinct parts: the colonnaded central zone with its elegant Prado and Parque Martí; and Punta Gorda, a thin knife of land slicing into the bay with a clutch of eclectic early 20th-century palaces, including Cuba's prettiest palatial buildings.

While much of Cuba is visibly reeling in the current economic crisis, Cienfuegos seems to positively glitter. It's not

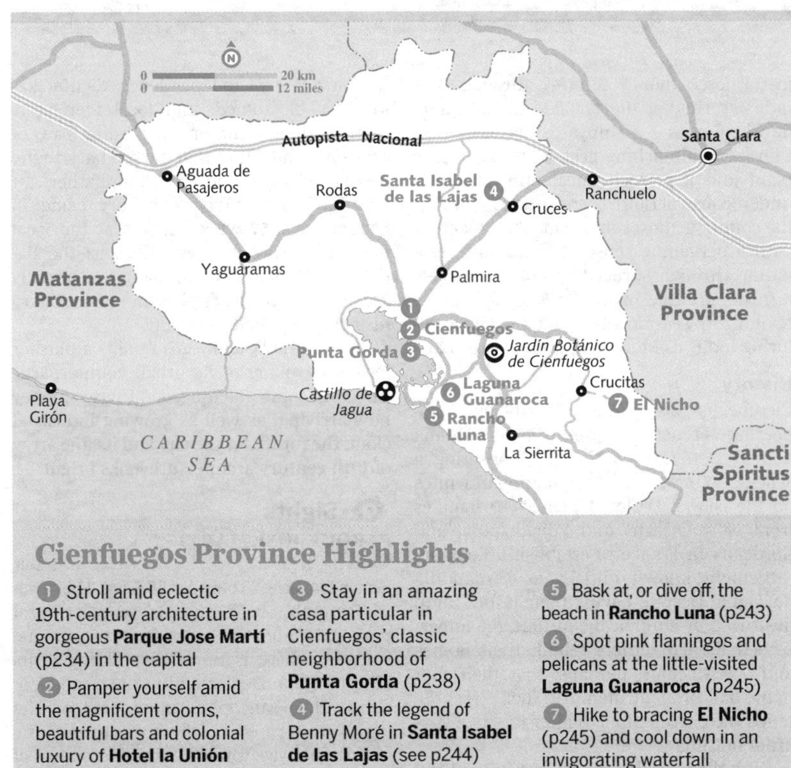

Cienfuegos Province Highlights

1. Stroll amid eclectic 19th-century architecture in gorgeous **Parque Jose Martí** (p234) in the capital
2. Pamper yourself amid the magnificent rooms, beautiful bars and colonial luxury of **Hotel la Unión** (p242) in Cienfuegos
3. Stay in an amazing casa particular in Cienfuegos' classic neighborhood of **Punta Gorda** (p238)
4. Track the legend of Benny Moré in **Santa Isabel de las Lajas** (see p244)
5. Bask at, or dive off, the beach in **Rancho Luna** (p243)
6. Spot pink flamingos and pelicans at the little-visited **Laguna Guanaroca** (p245)
7. Hike to bracing **El Nicho** (p245) and cool down in an invigorating waterfall

Central Cienfuegos

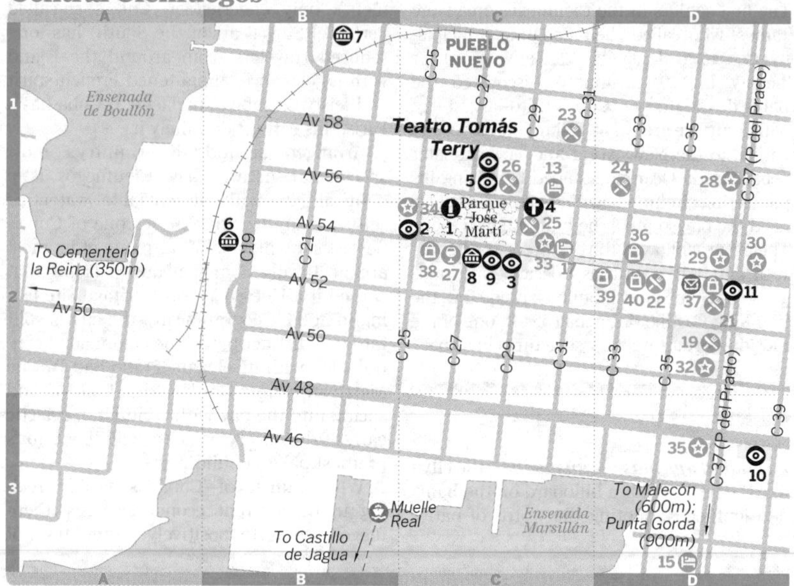

just Unesco money filtering through. The industry ringing the far side of the Bahía de Cienfuegos – a shipyard, the bastion of Cuba's shrimp-fishing fleet, a thermoelectric plant and a petrochemical hub (currently under construction) – constitutes some of the country's most important. This, together with a pervading sense of tranquility resonating through spruced-up colonial streets refreshingly free of *jineteros* (touts) and a revitalizing seaside vibe make the city as alluring today as Moré found it 60 years ago.

History

Cienfuegos was founded in 1819 by a pioneering French émigré from Louisiana named Don Louis D'Clouet. Sponsoring a scheme to increase the population of whites on the island, D'Clouet invited 40 families from New Orleans and Philadelphia, and Bordeaux in France to establish a fledgling settlement known initially as Fernandina de Jagua. Despite having their initial camp destroyed by a hurricane in 1821, the unperturbed French settlers rebuilt their homes and – suspicious, perhaps, that their first name had brought them bad luck – rechristened the city Cienfuegos after the then governor of Cuba.

With the arrival of the railway in 1850 and the drift west of Cuban sugar growers after the First War of Independence, Cienfuegos' fortunes blossomed, and local merchants pumped their wealth into a dazzling array of eclectic architecture that harked back to the neoclassicism of their French forefathers.

D-Day in Cienfuegos' history came in September 1957 when officers at the local naval base staged a revolt against the Batista dictatorship. The uprising was brutally crushed, but the city's place in revolutionary history was sealed in infamy.

Modern-day Cienfuegos retains a plusher look than many of its urban counterparts. And with some much-needed Unesco money now arriving, as well as growing industrial clout, the future for the city and its fine array of 19th-century architecture looks bright.

Sights

PARQUE JOSÉ MARTÍ

Arco de Triunfo LANDMARK

(Map p234; Calle 25 btwn Avs 56 & 54) The 'Arch of Triumph' on Cienfuegos' serene central park catapults the plaza into the unique category: there is no other building of its kind in Cuba. Dedicated to Cuban independence, the Francophile monument on the park's western edge ushers you through its gilded gateway toward a marble statue of José Martí.

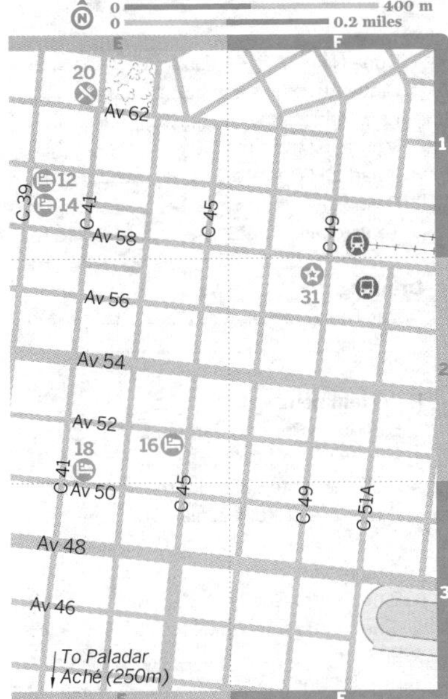

Catedral de la Purísima Concepción CHURCH
(Map p234; Av 56 No 2902; donations accepted; ⌚7am-noon Mon-Fri) Opposite the park, the cathedral dates from 1869 and is distinguished by its wonderful French stained-glass windows. Chinese writing discovered on columns during recent restoration is thought to date from the 1870s. The cathedral is nearly always open; you can also join the faithful for a service (7:30am weekdays, 10am Sundays).

Teatro Tomás Terry THEATER
(Map p234; ☎51-33-61; Av 56 No 270 btwn Calle 27 & 29; tours CUC$2; ⌚10am-6pm) Swapping French influences for Italian, this theater on the northern side of the Parque is grand from the outside, but even grander within. Built between 1887 and 1889 to honor Venezuelan industrialist Tomás Terry, the 950-seat auditorium is embellished with Carrara marble, hand-carved Cuban hardwoods and whimsical ceiling frescoes. In 1895 the theater opened with a performance of Verdi's Aïda and it has witnessed numerous landmarks in Cuban music, as well as performances by the likes of Enrico Caruso and Anna Pavlova.

Colegio San Lorenzo NOTABLE BUILDING
(Map p234; Av 56 cnr Calle 29) On the other side of Teatro Café Tomás, this building with its striking colonnaded facade was constructed during the 1920s with funds left by wealthy city patron Nicholas Acea Salvador, whose name also graces one of the city's cemeteries. Admire from the outside only.

Casa de la Cultura Benjamin Duarte NOTABLE BUILDING
(Map p234; Calle 25 No 5401; admission free; ⌚8:30am-midnight) On the western side of Parque Martí, this is the former Palacio de Ferrer (1918), now a riveting neoclassical building with Italian marble floors and – most noticeably – a domed rooftop cupola equipped with a wrought-iron staircase. View-seekers should still be able to clamber up to see spectacular city-wide vistas once the building reopens following refurbishment in 2011.

Museo Provincial MUSEUM
(Map p234; cnr Av 54 & Calle 27; admission CUC$2; ⌚10am-6pm Tue-Sat, 10am-noon Sun) The main attraction on the south side of Parque Martí, the museum offers a microcosm of Cienfuegos' history and displays the frilly furnishings of refined 19th-century French-Cuban society, as well as other assorted knickknacks.

Palacio de Gobierno NOTABLE BUILDING
(Map p234; Av 54 btwn Calles 27 & 29) Most of Parque Martí's south side is dominated by the grandiose, silvery-grey building where the provincial government (Poder Popular Provincial) holds forth. The Palacio de Gobierno doesn't allow visitors, but you can steal a look at the palatial main staircase through the front door.

Casa del Fundador NOTABLE BUILDING
(Map p234; cnr Calle 29 & Av 54) On the park's southeastern corner stands the city's oldest building, once the residence of city founder Louis D'Clouet. **El Bulevar** (Av 54), Cienfuegos' quintessential shopping street, heads east from here to link up with the Paseo del Prado.

CAYO LOCO & REINA

A few attractions lie west of Parque José Marti.

Museo Histórico Naval Nacional MUSEUM
(Map p234; cnr Av 60 & Calle 21; admission CUC$2; ⌚9am-6:30pm Tue-Sat, 9am-1pm Sun) The small promontory of Cayo Loco five blocks northwest of the Parque Martí is the eye-catching location of this rose-pink museum, dating from 1933. It's housed in the former head-

Central Cienfuegos

Top Sights
Teatro Tomás Terry ... C1

Sights
1 Arco de Triunfo ... C2
2 Casa de la Cultura Benjamin Duarte ... C2
3 Casa del Fundador ... C2
4 Catedral de la Purísima Concepción ... C2
5 Colegio San Lorenzo ... C1
6 Museo de Locomotivas ... B2
7 Museo Histórico Naval Nacional ... B1
8 Museo Provincial ... C2
9 Palacio de Gobierno ... C2
10 Sports Museum ... D3
11 Statue of Benny Moré ... D2

Activities, Courses & Tours
Hotel la Unión Swimming Pool ... (see 17)
La Bolera ... (see 35)

Sleeping
12 Bella Perla Marina ... E1
13 Casa de la Amistad ... C1
14 Casa las Golondrinas ... E1
15 Casa Prado ... D3
16 Hostal Colonial Pepe & Isabel ... E2
17 Hotel la Unión ... C2
18 Olga & Eugenio ... E2

Eating
1869 Restaurant ... (see 17)
19 Coppelia ... D2
20 Doña Neli ... E1
21 Gioventu ... D2
22 La Verja ... D2
23 Mercado Municipal ... C1
24 Paladar El Criollito ... D1
25 Polineso ... C2
26 Teatro Café Tomás ... C1

Drinking
Bar Terrazas ... (see 17)
27 El Palatino ... C2

Entertainment
28 Biblioteca Roberto García Valdés ... D1
29 Café Cantante Benny Moré ... D2
Casa de la Cultura Benjamin Duarte ... (see 2)
30 Cine Prado ... D2
31 Cine-Teatro Guanaroca ... F2
32 Cine-Teatro Luisa ... D2
33 El Benny ... C2
Hotel la Unión ... (see 17)
34 Jardines de Uneac ... C2
35 Tropisur ... D3

Shopping
36 Casa del Habano 'El Embajador' ... D2
37 Librería Dionisio San Román ... D2
38 Maroya Gallery ... C2
39 Photo Service Jagua ... D2
Tienda Terry ... (see 5)
40 Variedades Cienfuegos ... D2

quarters of the Distrito Naval del Sur, and approached by a wide drive flanked with armaments dating from different eras. It was here in September 1957 that a group of sailors and civilians staged an unsuccessful uprising against the Batista government. The revolt is the central theme of the museum. The ramparts offer great bay views.

Cementerio la Reina CEMETERY
(off Map p234; cnr Av 50 & Calle 7) The city's oldest cemetery was founded in 1837, and is lined with the graves of Spanish soldiers who died in the Wars of Independence. La Reina is the only cemetery in Cuba where bodies are interred above ground (in the walls) due to the high groundwater levels. A listed national monument, the cemetery also has a marble statue called *Bella Durmiente*: a tribute to a 24-year-old woman who died in 1907 of a broken heart. It's an evocative place if you're into graveyards, but foreigners aren't generally permitted to enter. Tipping the guard might work. Approach is via Av 50: a long, hot walk or horse-cart ride via the sorry-looking collection of trains passing as the **Museo de Locomotivas** (Map p234; Calle 19).

PASEO DEL PRADO & THE MALECÓN

Stately Paseo del Prado (Calle 37), stretching from the Río el Inglés in the north to Punta Gorda in the south, is the longest street of its kind in Cuba and a great place to see *cienfuegueños* going about their daily business. The boulevard is a veritable smorgasbord of fine neoclassical buildings and pastel-painted columns.

Malecón STREET

(Map p239) Continuing south on the Prado, the street becomes the Malecón as it cuts alongside one of the world's finest natural bays, offering exquisite vistas. Like all sea drives (Havana's being the archetype), this area comes alive in the evening when poets come to muse and couples to canoodle.

Statue of Benny Moré MONUMENT

(Map p234) Before you hit the Malecón, at the intersection of Av 54 and the Paseo del Prado, you can pay your respects to this life-sized likeness of the musician.

FREE **Sports Museum** MUSEUM

(Map p234; cnr Calle 37 & Av 48) South of the Moré statue, this little museum is largely devoted to local boxing hero, Julio González Valladores, who brought back a gold medal from the 1996 Atlanta Olympics.

PUNTA GORDA

When the Malecón sea wall runs out, you will know you have landed in Punta Gorda, Cienfuegos' old upper-class neighborhood characterized by its bright clapboard homes and turreted palaces. Highlighting a 1920s penchant for grandiosity are the cupola-topped **Palacio Azul** (now the Hostal Palacio Azul; p239) and the **Club Cienfuegos** (p243), once an exclusive yacht club and still offering nautical excursions aplenty. Nearby, an inventive **Parque de Esculturas** throws some innovative modern sculpture into the mix.

Palacio de Valle NOTABLE BUILDING

(Map p239; cnr Calle 37 btwn Avs 0 & 2; ⌚9:30am-11pm) The ultimate in kitsch is yet to come. Continue south on Calle 37, and with a sharp intake of breath, you'll stumble upon the *Arabian Nights*-like Palacio de Valle. Built in 1917 by Alcisclo Valle Blanco, a Spaniard from Asturias, the structure resembles an outrageously ornate Moroccan casbah. Batista planned to convert this colorful riot of tiles, turrets and stucco into a casino, but today it's an (aspiring) upscale restaurant with an inviting terrace bar.

Centro Recreativo la Punta PARK

(Map p239; ⌚10am-10pm) Lovers come to watch the sunset amid sea-framed greenery at the gazebo on the extreme southern tip of this park. The **bar** is also oddly popular with local policemen.

EAST OF CITY CENTER

Necrópolis Tomás Acea CEMETERY

(Carretera de Rancho Luna Km 2; admission CUC$1; ⌚8am-6pm) The city's other national monument-listed resting place is classed as a 'garden cemetery' and is entered through a huge neoclassical pavilion (1926) flanked by 64 Doric columns modeled on the Parthenon in Greece. This cemetery contains a monument to the marine martyrs who died during the abortive 1957 Cienfuegos naval uprising. It's easier to get into than Cementerio la Reina.

Activities

Marlin Marina Cienfuegos FISHING, SAILING

(Base Náutica; Map p239; ☎55-12-41; Calle 35 btwn Avs 6 & 8; ⌚11am-8:45pm) Hook up with this 36-berth marina a few blocks north of Hotel Jagua to arrange deep-sea fishing trips. Prices start at CUC$200 for four people for four hours. Multiday trips start at CUC$400/3900 for one night/one week (gear and crew included), depending on the boat used. A classic bay cruise costs CUC$16 for the day or CUC$10 for a two-hour sunset cruise (stopping briefly at Castillo de Jagua). Book through Cubatur or Cubanacán (p242).

Base de Charter Blue Sails WATERSPORTS

(Map p239; ☎52-65-10; Calle 35 btwn Avs 10 & 12; ⌚10am-6pm) At this nautical base at the Club Cienfuegos you can organize water sports including kayaking and windsurfing. It also has a tennis court and an amusement center with bumper cars, go-carts and video games.

La Bolera BOWLING

(Map p234; Calle 37 btwn Avs 46 & 48; per hr CUC$1-2; ⌚11am-2am) If you're into billiards or bowling, come here. It also has an ice-cream parlor and occasional live music.

Hotel la Unión Swimming Pool SWIMMING

Even if you're a nonguest, you can use the beautiful Italianate pool at Hotel la Unión (p242) for CUC$10.

Courses

Universidad de Cienfuegos (☎52-15-21; www.ucf.edu.cu; Carretera las Rodas Km 4, Cuatro Caminos) Offers Spanish courses ranging from beginner to advanced. The courses last one month and incorporate 64 hours of study (CUC$340). It also offers courses in 'Cuban Culture' (CUC$340). Language courses run monthly; culture courses every other month. Check the website for details.

Tours

Cubanacán (Map p234; ☎55-16-80; Av 54 btwn Calles 29 & 31) organizes some interesting local tours, including the three-hour Along the Paths of the Orishas (CUC$12) and the ever-popular El Nicho excursion (p245, CUC$30). Onward trips to Trinidad in Sancti Spíritus province can be added on to tours. Cienfuegos is also the most convenient base from which to explore the Península de Zapata in Matanzas province (p224) and tours to Playa Giron (CUC$30) are also organized.

Festivals & Events

Local festivals in Cienfuegos include the cultural events marking the foundation of the city on April 22, 1819, the **Carnaval** in August, and the **Benny Moré International Music Festival** in September on odd-numbered years, held in town and in nearby Santa Isabel de las Lajas.

Sleeping

Cienfuegos has some quality private rooms – your best bet for budget accommodation. Those at Punta Gorda are more removed, more atmospheric and generally pricier. There are excellent hotels in Cienfuegos proper and in Punta Gorda.

CENTRAL CIENFUEGOS

Hotel la Unión BOUTIQUE HOTEL $$
(Map p234; ☎55-10-20; www.hotellaunion-cuba.com; Calle 31 cnr Av 54; s/d CUC$70/100; ❄≋) Barcelona, Naples, Paris? There are echoes of all of them in this plush colonial-style hotel with its European aspirations and splendid Italianate pool, fit for a Roman emperor. Tucked away in a maze of marble pillars, antique furnishings and two tranquil inner courtyards are 46 well-furnished rooms with balconies either overlooking the street or a mosaic-lined patio. You'll also find a gym, Jacuzzi and local art gallery. Service is refreshingly efficient: there's an airy roof terrace that showcases live salsa and a well-regarded restaurant.

Casa Prado CASA PARTICULAR $
(☎528-96613; Calle 37 4235 btwn Avs 42 & 44; r CUC$20-25; ❄) This has established itself as one of the very best casas in the city center. The two high-ceilinged rooms are ensconced with period furniture and a twisting staircase leads to a terrace with phenomenal city views. The location is great too: poised on Prado half-way between the city center and the Malecón. Summon forth all your visions of haughty colonial elegance and you'll arrive prepared.

TOP CHOICE **Bella Perla Marina** CASA PARTICULAR $
(Map p234; ☎51-89-91; bellaperlamarina@yahoo.es; Calle 39 No 5818 cnr Av 60; r CUC$20-25; P❄@) Gracious hosts Amileidis and Waldo must have almost as many plants on their lush roof terrace as the local botanical gardens. The food here is legendary, the traveler vibe resonates and there is also (rarely for Cuba) a garage for those with wheels. Waldo is a databank of Cienfuegos information, too. A paladar is on the cards for 2011.

Casa de la Amistad CASA PARTICULAR $
(Map p234; ☎51-61-43; Av 56 No 2927 btwn Calles 29 & 31; r CUC$20-25; P❄) Friendship's the word in this venerable colonial house stuffed full of family heirlooms just off Parque Martí. Legendary food includes the exotic Cola chicken (yes, *pollo* cooked in the 'real thing'). Chatty hosts Armando and Leonor offer two wonderful, well-kept rooms and a lovely roof terrace.

Hostal Colonial Pepe & Isabel CASA PARTICULAR $
(Map p234; ☎51-82-76; Av 52 No 4318 btwn Calles 43 & 45; r CUC$20-25; ❄) This colonial house must stretch the best part of a block. The friendly hosts offer two large, clean rooms with ornate bathrooms, hunger-trouncing meals and a tantalizing, two-level roof terrace. Plans to add three more rooms were afoot at the time of writing.

Casa las Golondrinas CASA PARTICULAR $
(Map p234; ☎51-57-88; Calle 39 btwn Avs 58 & 60; r CUC$20-25; ❄) Another gorgeous recently renovated colonial house with two rooms available.

Olga & Eugenio CASA PARTICULAR $
(Map p234; ☎51-77-56; Av 50 no 4109 btwn Calles 41 & 43; r CUC$15; ❄) One of the best-value options in Cienfuegos. Two large rooms, clean bathrooms and an attractively tiled roof terrace.

PUNTA GORDA

TOP CHOICE **Villa Lagarto – Maylin & Tony** CASA PARTICULAR $
(Map p239; ☎51-99-66; Calle 35 No 4B btwn Avs 0 & Litoral; r CUC$30- 35; ❄≋) When your casa comes with a luxurious Italianate swimming pool, you know you're onto something. Toss in welcome mojitos, swinging hammocks, king-

sized beds, fine food and a beautiful bayside setting and you'll be hard pushed to find better accommodation for your money in Cuba.

Hostal Palacio Azul HOTEL $$
(Map p239; ☎58-28-28; Calle 37 No 201 btwn Avs 12 & 14; s/d/tr CUC$42/60/71; P❄) This striking blue palace was built in 1921 and reopened as a seven-room (16-person capacity) hotel in 2004. One of the first big buildings to grace Punta Gorda, the hotel's huge recently renovated rooms are named after flowers and sparkle with plenty of prerevolutionary character. You'll find an intimate on-site restaurant called **El Chelo** and an eye-catching rooftop cupola with splendid views.

Hotel Jagua HOTEL $$
(Map p239; ☎55-10-03; Calle 37 No 1; s/d CUC$61/98; P❄@≈) It's not clear what Batista's brother had in mind when he erected this modern concrete giant on Punta Gorda in the 1950s, though making money was probably the prime motivation. Still, the Jagua is a jolly good hotel – airy and surprisingly plush. Upper rooms (there are seven floors) are best. Any lack of historical credentials is compensated for by inviting amenities: namely the fine restaurant, appealing pool, attractive public areas, large bright rooms, in-house cabaret show and beautiful bayside setting. There's always at least one tour group staying here.

Casa Verde HOTEL $$
(Map p239; ☎55-10-03 ext 889; Calle 37 btwn Avs 0 & 2; s/d CUC$61/98; P❄) More architecturally pleasing than Hotel Jagua is this colonial mansion owned by the same people. It boasts eight vast rooms (one is a suite), mixing tiled floors and period furniture with flat-screen cable TV. Out back is a waterfront bar with occasional live music.

Vista Al Mar CASA PARTICULAR $
(Map p239; ☎51-83-78; www.vistaalmarcuba.com; Calle 37 No 210 btwn 2 & 4; r CUC$25; P❄) It really is a *vista al mar* (sea view) – in fact, this highly professional casa has even got its own private scoop of beach out back with hammocks.

Villa Nelly CASA PARTICULAR $
(Map p239; ☎51-15-19; Av 37 btwn Calles 6 & 8; r CUC$20-25; ❄) Well located, with a self-catering kitchen for guests, a well-stocked bar and an extensive garden.

Punta Gorda

0 — 200 m
0 — 0.1 miles

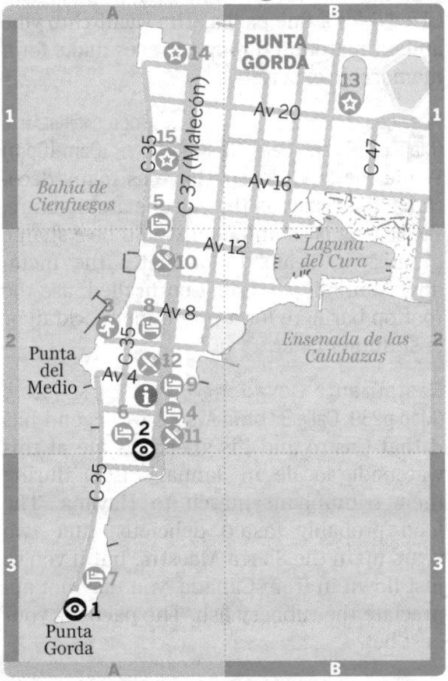

Punta Gorda

Sights

- Club Cienfuegos (see 10)
- 1 Centro Recreativo la Punta A3
- 2 Palacio de Valle A2
- Parque de Esculturas (see 3)

Activities, Courses & Tours

- Base de Charter Blue Sails (see 10)
- 3 Marlin Marina Cienfuegos A2

Sleeping

- 4 Casa Verde A2
- 5 Hostal Palacio Azul A1
- 6 Hotel Jagua A2
- 7 Villa Lagarto – Maylin & Tony A3
- 8 Villa Nelly A2
- 9 Vista al Mar A2

Eating

- 10 Club Cienfuegos A2
- Palacio de Valle (see 2)
- 11 Restaurante Covadonga A2
- 12 Restaurante el Cochinito A2

Entertainment

- Cabaret Guanaroca (see 6)
- 13 Estadio 5 de Septiembre B1
- 14 Los Pinitos A1
- 15 Palacio de la Música (Patio de ARTex) A1

Eating

IN TOWN

Teatro Café Tomás CAFE $
(Map p234; Av 56 No 2703 btwn Calles 27 & 29; ⏲10am-10pm) Cafe, souvenir stall and nightly music venue, this delightful place wedged between the Teatro Tomás Terry and the neoclassical Colegio San Lorenzo is the most atmospheric place to flop down and observe the morning exercisers in Parque Martí. The flower canopy-covered patio to the side comes alive in the evenings with great live music ranging from *trova* to jazz.

TOP CHOICE **Paladar Aché** PALADAR $$
(off Map p234; Av 38 btwn Calles 41 & 43; mains CUC$8; ⏲noon-4pm & 6pm-10:30pm) The city's – and the province's – best paladar veers between nautical and African tribal decor, but the quality of the food is unswerving, with a good choice of grilled meats and service many times better than most of the city restaurants. A nice relief map of Cienfuegos welcomes guests.

Paladar el Criollito PALADAR $
(Map p234; Calle 33 btwn Avs 56 & 58; mains CUC$7) This is a salt-of-the-earth, old-school paladar: a no-frills family-run restaurant business that makes do with limited ingredients and little encouragement from the government. Standard fish and meat dishes are plentiful, if not memorable.

1869 Restaurant INTERNATIONAL $$
(Map p234; cnr Av 54 & Calle 31; mains CUC$10; ⏲breakfast, lunch & dinner) Cienfuegos' most upmarket city-center dining experience can be found in this elegant restaurant in the La Unión hotel (p242). Although the food doesn't quite match the lush furnishings, a varied international menu makes a welcome change from rice/beans/pork staples elsewhere.

La Verja CARIBBEAN $
(Map p234; Av 54 No 3306 btwn Calles 33 & 35; mains CUC$5-7; ⏲noon-3pm & 6:30-9:30pm) Another place where food rarely achieves the standards of the fancy décor, but you won't eat your pork or fish fillet in plusher surroundings: decidedly convenient if hunger strikes on El Bulevar.

Gioventu ITALIAN, ICE-CREAM PARLOR $
(Map p234; Calle 37 btwn Avs 52 & 54; ⏲to 9pm) A popular pizzeria with the standard Cuban-Italian offerings. The spacious terrace means you can also feast on the Benny Moré statue and general Prado life.

Coppelia ICE-CREAM PARLOR $
(Map p234; cnr Calle 37 & Av 52) At two pesos a scoop, this place practically gives away ice cream.

Polineso SANDWICH SHOP $
(Map p234; Calle 29 btwn Calles 54 & 56) Right under the portals in Parque Jose Martí, this is a salubrious setting for snacks.

Self-Catering

Mercado Municipal MARKET $
(Map p234; Calle 31 No 5805 btwn Avs 58 & 60) Groceries in pesos for picnickers and self-caterers.

Doña Neli BAKERY $
(Map p234; cnr Calle 41 & Av 62; ⏲9am-10:15pm) Provides breakfast goodies (pastries, bread, cakes) in convertibles.

PUNTA GORDA

Club Cienfuegos SEAFOOD, INTERNATIONAL $$
(Map p239; ☎51-28-91; Calle 37 btwn Avs 10 & 12; ⏲noon-10:30pm) With a setting as good as this grand old sports-club-cum-restaurant, it's easy for the food to fall short, which it often does. But there are plenty of options here, with the **Bar Terraza** (⏲noon-2:30am) for cocktails and chicken sandwiches; **El Marinero** (⏲noon-10pm), a 1st-floor seafood establishment; and **Restaurante Café Cienfuegos** (⏲4pm-10:30pm), a more refined adventurous place on the top floor, where you'll pay CUC$10 for a steak and CUC$6 for a fine paella. The yacht-club vibe and wraparound dining terraces make for a memorable experience.

Palacio de Valle SEAFOOD, CARIBBEAN $
(Map p239; cnr Calle 37 & Av 2; ⏲10am-10pm) While the food doesn't have as many decorative flourishes as the eclectic architecture, the setting is so unique it would be a shame to miss it. Seafood dominates the menu downstairs; if you aren't enthralled, use the rooftop bar here for a pre-dinner cocktail or post-dinner cigar.

Restaurante Covadonga SEAFOOD $
(Map p239; Calle 37 btwn Avs 2 & 0) Legend has it that Castro and his guerrillas ate at this waterside locale in January 1959 during their triumphant march to Havana. The food probably tasted delicious after two years up in the Sierra Maestra, but if you've just flown in from Canada, you may not appreciate the rubbery fish. The paella is your best bet.

Restaurante el Cochinito FAST FOOD $
(Map p239; cnr Calle 37 & Av 4; ⌚noon-3pm & 7-10pm Wed-Mon) Cheap pork for tight budgets.

Drinking

Bar Terrazas BAR
(Map p234; ☎55-10-20; cnr Av 54 & Calle 31) Recreate the dignified days of old with a mojito upstairs at the Hotel la Unión; live music starts at 10pm. Other excellent drinking perches (especially at sunset) can be found at Club Cienfuegos (p243) and the upstairs bar of the Palacio de Valle (p237).

El Palatino BAR
(Map p234; Av 54 No 2514) Liquid lunches were invented with El Palatino in mind – a darkwood bar set in one of the city's oldest buildings on the southern side of Parque Martí. Impromptu jazz sets sometimes erupt, but prepare to be hit up for payment at the end of song number three.

☆ Entertainment

El Benny NIGHTCLUB
(Map p234; Av 54 No 2907 btwn Calles 29 & 31; admission per couple CUC$8; ⌚10pm-3am Tue-Sun) It's difficult to say what the 'Barbarian of Rhythm' would have made of this disco/club named in his honor. Bring your dancing shoes, stock up on the rum and Cokes, and come prepared for music that's more techno than Benny Moré.

TOP CHOICE **Patio de ARTex** NIGHTCLUB, LIVE MUSIC
(Map p239; cnr Calle 35 & Av 16) A highly recommendable and positively heaving patio in Punta Gorda where you can catch *son* (Cuba's popular music), salsa, *trova* and a touch of Benny Moré nostalgia live in the evenings as you mingle with true *cienfuegueños*. Do El Benny on Thursday and this on Friday night.

Teatro Tomás Terry LIVE MUSIC, THEATER
(Map p234; ☎51-33-61; Av 56 No 270 btwn Calles 27 & 29; ⌚10pm-late) As important as any of the above live-music venues is the versatile music program in the atmospheric courtyard of the theater. The theater building itself is worth a visit in its own right, but you'll really get to appreciate this architectural showpiece if you come for a concert or play; the box office is open 11am to 3pm daily and 90 minutes before show time.

LOCAL KNOWLEDGE

WALDO RODRIGUEZ DEL REY: CASA PARTICULAR OWNER

Cienfuegos has a great music scene. Most people don't realize that a lot of it takes place at Teatro Tomás Terry. On Fridays Nelson Valdés and his group, who are quite famous, perform *trova*. On Saturdays lots of new, local bands can be seen, and Sundays are for jazz: there's usually a concert on this day. The other place for live music is Jardines de Uneac on the other side of Parque Jose Martí. The best disco is Patio de ARTex in Punta Gorda.

Jardines de Uneac LIVE MUSIC, CULTURAL CENTER
(Map p234; Calle 25 No 5413 btwn Avs 54 & 56; admission CUC$2) Uneac's a good bet in any Cuban city for live music in laid-back environs. Here it's quite possibly Cienfuegos' best venue with an outdoor patio hosting Afro-Cuban *peñas* (musical performances), *trova* and top local bands such as the perennially popular Los Novos.

Café Cantante Benny Moré LIVE MUSIC
(Map p234; cnr Av 54 & Calle 37) This is where you might get some suave Benny tunes, especially after hours. A restaurant by day, this place metamorphoses in the evenings when it mixes up mean cocktails and tunes into live traditional music.

Tropisur NIGHTCLUB, CABARET
(Map p234; cnr Calle 37 & Av 48; admission CUC$1; ⌚Fri-Sun) An open-air venue with a more traditional Cuban vibe is this feisty place on the Prado.

Cabaret Guanaroca CABARET
(Map p239; Calle 37 No 1; admission CUC$5; ⌚9:30pm Tue-Fri, 10pm Sat) In Hotel Jagua, the Guanaroca offers a more professional tourist-orientated cabaret extravaganza.

Hotel la Unión DANCE HALL
(Map p234; ☎55-10-20; cnr Av 54 & Calle 31) The rooftop bar here puts on a good salsa show.

Los Pinitos LIVE MUSIC
(Map p239; Calle 37 & Av 22) A playground for kids during the day, Los Pinitos matures tenfold by nightfall, hosting decent weekend music shows with a Benny Moré bias.

Casa de la Cultura Benjamin Duarte LIVE MUSIC, THEATER
(Map p234; Calle 25 No 5403) On Parque Martí, this cultural center offers various events to match its grandiose setting.

Biblioteca Roberto García Valdés LIVE MUSIC
(Map p234; Calle 37 No 5615) This library holds classical-music concerts, discussions on Martí and flamenco-inspired searches for *duende* (an inspired physical response to music, drawing upon elements of traditional folklore).

Estadio 5 de Septiembre SPORTS
(Map p239; ☎51-36-44; Av 20 btwn Calles 45 & 55) From October to April, the provincial baseball team – nicknamed Los Elefantes – plays matches here. Its best-ever national series finish was fourth in 1979.

Cine Prado CINEMA
(Map p234; Calle 37 No 5402) The most central cinema.

Cine-Teatro Luisa CINEMA
(Map p234; Calle 37 No 5001) Another cinematic option close to the center.

Cine-Teatro Guanaroca CINEMA
(Map p234; cnr Calle 49 & Av 58) Opposite the bus station.

Shopping

Cienfuegos' main drag – known officially as Av 54, but colloquially as El Bulevar – is an archetypal Cuban shopping street with not a chain store in sight. The best traffic-free stretch runs from Calle 37 (Prado) to Parque Martí, full of shops of all shapes and sizes.

Check out the **Maroya Gallery** (Map p234; Av 54 btwn Calles 25 & 27) for folk art, **Variedades Cienfuegos** (Map p234; cnr Av 54 & Calle 33) for peso paraphernalia or **Casa del Habano 'El Embajador'** (Map p234; cnr Av 54 & Calle 33) for cigars.

Tienda Terry (Map p234; Av 56 No 270 btwn Calle 27 & 29) in Teatro Tomás Terry is a good bet for books and souvenirs; another well-stocked bookstore is **Librería Dionisio San Román** (Map p234; Av 54 No 3526 cnr Calle 37).

Photo Service Jagua (Map p234; Av 54 No 3118 btwn Calles 31 & 33; ⏲9am-9pm) will attend to your camera requirements.

Information

Emergency

Asistur (☎51-16-24; Av 54 No 3111 btwn Calles 32 & 34) Tourist police.

Internet Access & Telephone

Etecsa Telepunto (Calle 31 No 5402 btwn Avs 54 & 56; per hr CUC$6; ⏲8:30am-7:30pm)

Media

5 de Septiembre The local newspaper comes out on Fridays.

Radio Ciudad del Mar 1350AM and 98.9FM.

Medical Services

Clínica Internacional (☎55-16-22; Av 10 btwn Calles 37 & 39, Punta Gorda) This all-new center catering to foreigners and handling dental emergencies was about to open as this book was going to press, moving from its old location across the road from Hotel Jagua. It has a 24-hour pharmacy.

Hotel la Unión (☎55-10-20; Calle 31 cnr Av 54; ⏲24hr) The pharmacy here is aimed at international tourists.

Money

Banco de Credito y Comercio (Bandec) (cnr Av 56 & Calle 31) The best exchange rates.

Cadeca (Av 56 No 3316 btwn Calles 33 & 35)

Post

Post office (Av 54 No 3514 btwn Calles 35 & 37)

Tourist Information

Alfonso Menéndez (☎527-10120; alfonsodmp@yahoo.com; Calle 37 No 209 btwn Avs 2 & 4) Responsible, unbiased regional travel advice from this former travel-agency manager with 10 years' industry experience. Fluent English spoken.

Travel Agencies

Cubanacán (☎55-16-80; Av 54 btwn Calles 29 & 31) Friendly, efficient service; variety of province-wide tours offered.

Cubatur (☎55-12-42; Calle 37 No 5399 btwn Avs 54 & 56)

Paradiso (Av 54 No 3301 btwn Calles 33 & 35) Specializes in historical tourism.

Getting There & Away

Air

Jaime González Airport, 5km northeast of Cienfuegos, receives weekly international flights from Miami and Canada (November to March only). There are no connections to Havana.

Bus

From the **bus station** (☎51-8114, 51-57-20; Calle 49 btwn Avs 56 & 58) there are Víazul buses to Havana four times daily (CUC$18, four hours) at 9:10am, 9:40am, 4:50pm and 8:50pm, and to Trinidad six times a day (CUC$6, one hour 35 minutes) at 12:35pm, 12:50pm, 3:20pm, 5:10pm, 6:10pm and 6:50pm.

There are also two daily buses to Varadero (CUC$17, 4½ hours) at 10:30am and 4:30pm, with the afternoon departure also calling at Santa Clara (CUC$6, 1½ hours). The one Viñales (CUC$32, seven hours 45 minutes) departure of the day is at 9:40am and calls at Havana and Pinar del Río (CUC$31, seven hours). To reach other destinations, you have to connect in Trinidad or Havana. Note that when heading to Trinidad from Cienfuegos, buses originate further west and may be full.

Cienfuegos' bus station is clean and well organized. It also offers cheap and safe luggage storage (CUC$1 per item). A Víazul office on the upper level issues tickets; for local buses to Rancho Luna (CUC$1), Pasacaballo (CUC$1) or Santa Isabel de las Lajas (CUC$3) check the blackboard on the lower level; tickets must be purchased from the *jefe de turno* (shift manager) downstairs.

Train

The **train station** (☎52-54-95; cnr Av 58 & Calle 49; ⏲ticket window 8am-3:30pm Mon-Fri, 8-11:30am Sat) is across from the bus station. Trains are often canceled. When they do run, trains travel to Havana (CUC$11, 10 hours, every three days), Santa Clara (CUC$2.10, two hours, 4:10am daily) and Sancti Spíritus (CUC$5.20, five hours, Friday and Sunday).

Getting Around

Boat

A 120-passenger ferry runs to the Castillo de Jagua (CUC$1, 40 minutes) from the **Muelle Real** (Map p234; cnr Av 46 & Calle 25). Take note – this is a Cuban commuter boat, not a sunset cruise. Check at the port for current schedules. It's supposed to run three times a day in each direction. A smaller ferry (CUC$0.50, 15 minutes) also makes frequent runs between the Castillo and the Hotel Pasacaballo (p243). Last departure from the Castillo is 8pm.

Car & Moped

The Servi-Cupet gas station is on Calle 37 at the corner of Av 16 in Punta Gorda. There's another station 5km northeast of Hotel Rancho Luna.

Club Cienfuegos (Map p239; ☎52-65-10; Calle 37 btwn Avs 10 & 12) Hires mopeds for CUC$24 per day.

Cubacar Hotel Rancho Luna (☎54-80-26; Carretera de Rancho Luna Km 16); Hotel Unión (Map p234; ☎55-16-45; cnr Av 51 & Calle 31); Hotel Jagua (Map p239; ☎55-20-14; Calle 37 No 1) Hires cars.

Horse Carts

Horse carts and bici-taxis ply Calle 37 charging Cubans one peso a ride and foreigners CUC$1 (Spanish speakers might be able to 'pass' and pay a peso). It's a pleasant way to travel between town and Punta Gorda and the cemeteries.

Taxi

There are plenty of cabs in Cienfuegos. Most hang around outside Hotel Jagua and Hotel la Unión, or linger around the bus station. If you have no luck at these spots, phone **Cubacar** (☎51-84-54) or **Taxi OK** (☎55-11-72). A taxi to the airport from downtown should cost CUC$6.

Rancho Luna

Rancho Luna is a diminutive, picturesque beach resort 18km south of Cienfuegos close to the jaws of Bahía de Cienfuegos. It has two hotel complexes, but it's also possible to stay in rooms in a privately owned home here, one of the few resort areas in Cuba where this is allowed. Protected by a coral reef, the coast has good snorkeling. The small village on the Faro Luna road is where the handful of casas particulares are situated.

Sights & Activities

Besides sun-bathing or viewing the *faro* (lighthouse), the main activity here is diving organized through the dive center at Hotel Club Amigo Rancho Luna, which visits 30 sites within a 20-minute boat ride. Caves, profuse marine life and dazzling coral gardens as well as six sunken ships are among the attractions. From November to February harmless whale sharks frequent these waters. For more details check out the **Dive Center** (☎54-80-87; commercial@marlin.cfg.tur.cu; Carretera Pasacaballos Km 18; dives from CUC$35, open-water certification CUC$365). There's another center at Faro Luna, too.

Sleeping

Hotel Pasacaballo HOTEL $

(☎54-80-13; Carretera Pasacaballos Km 22; s/d CUC$34/45; P❄≋) Once popular with Venezuelan medical students, the Pasacaballo is architecturally repulsive but offers clean, perfectly decent accommodation at rock-bottom prices in a cracking location. Downstairs by the horse statue you'll find a spacious bar, a restaurant, a pool and pool tables – although given that there's nothing else around for miles, even this array of entertainment may prove insufficient. The best strip of beach is a 4km hike away.

DAY-TRIPPER

The settlement of **Santa Isabel de las Lajas**, a few kilometers west of Cruces on the Cienfuegos–Santa Clara road, was where Bartolomé (Benny) Moré was born on August 24, 1919 (see p246). Easily accessible in a half-day trip from Cienfuegos, this pleasant village hosts the biannual **Benny Moré International Music Festival** every other September. Curiosities include a **Municipal Museum** with assorted Moré memorabilia and the **Casino de los Congos**, a music venue where you can view *tambores* (drums) and Santería rituals, and where the self-styled Bárbaro del Ritmo (Barbarian of Rhythm) allegedly banged his first drum.

On the way back you may want to stop off briefly in the town of **Cruces** on the Santa Clara road. This settlement was the site of one of the most important battles of the Independence Wars in 1895 – the historic Battle of Mal Tiempo – in which Mambí generals Antonio Maceo and Máximo Gómez inflicted a crushing defeat on the Spanish forces. A needlelike **obelisk** in the middle of a pleasant colonial park commemorates the great battle. The park was declared a national monument in 1981.

Also worth a visit is **Palmira**, 8km north of Cienfuegos, a town famous for its Santería brotherhoods, including the societies of Cristo, San Roque and Santa Barbara. Further information can be found at the centrally located **Museo Municipal de Palmira** (☎54-45-33; admission CUC$1; ⌚10am-6pm Tue-Sat). The interesting African traditions of this town can be better observed during the Along the Paths of the Orishas tour (p238).

Hotel Club Amigo Rancho Luna-Faro Luna RESORT $$
(☎54-80-30; Carretera Pasacaballos Km 18; s/d low season CUC$45/68; P❄≋) This large yet lackluster 222-room resort has a massive pool, a private beach and the usual Cuban all-inclusive features such as cable TV, currency exchange and cheesy poolside entertainment along with decent sports facilities. The mustard color scheme in the rooms won't attract praise from interior designers, though. All-inclusive deals are almost always available. Part of the same complex, and open only during high season, is nearby **Hotel Club Amigo Faro Luna**, offering more of the same with further run-down facilities but a better location on a bluff overlooking the sea. Watch for the tumbleweed blowing by.

Casa de Julio CASA PARTICULAR
(☎524-52195; Carretera de Faro Luna; r CUC$25; ❄) Just before Hotel Club Amigo Faro Luna.

Finca los Colorados CASA PARTICULAR
(☎51-38-08; Carretera de Faro Luna; r CUC$25) Just past the lighthouse; another sound option with sea views.

Eating

Aside from the hotels, your dining options are limited. Try Hotel Club Amigo Faro Luna's beach snack bar or one of the private houses that rent rooms. The Servi-Cupet gas station 5km north of town serves microwave pizza 24 hours a day.

Getting There & Away

Theoretically, there are local buses from Cienfuegos seven times a day. The Jagua ferry runs from the dock directly below Hotel Pasacaballo several times throughout the day; more sporadic is the boat from Castillo de Jagua back to Cienfuegos, which was running only three times daily at the time of research. Most reliable is a taxi; a one-way fare to Cienfuegos should cost around CUC$$10 – bargain hard.

An even better way to get here is zipping along from Cienfuegos on a rented moped (see p243).

Castillo de Jagua

Predating the city of Cienfuegos by nearly a century, the **Castillo de Nuestra Señora de los Ángeles de Jagua** (admission CUC$3; ⌚8am-6pm), to the west of the mouth of Bahía de Cienfuegos, was designed by José Tantete in 1738 and completed in 1745. Built to keep pirates (and the British) out, it was at the time the third most important fortress in Cuba, after those of Havana and Santiago de Cuba.

Extensive renovation in 2010 has finally given the castle the makeover it was crying out for. In addition to a cracking view of the bay and a basic museum, the castle also has a reasonably atmospheric restaurant down below, due to open following refurbishment in mid-2011.

Passenger ferries from the castle ply the waters to Cienfuegos (CUC$1, 40 minutes) a few times daily and frequently to a landing just below the Hotel Pasacaballo (CUC$0.50, 15 minutes). Cubans pay the equivalent in pesos.

Some distance away on this side of the bay, you might glimpse the infamous **Juragua nuclear power plant**, a planned joint venture between Cuba and the Soviet Union that was conceived in 1976 and incorporated the ominous disused apartment blocks of the adjacent Ciudad Nuclear. Only 288km from Florida Keys, construction met with strong opposition from the US and was abandoned following the collapse of communism. Foreigners can't visit.

Laguna Guanaroca

The representation of the moon on earth according to local Siboney legend, the shimmering **Laguna Guanaroca** (admission incl tour CUC$7; ⌚8am-noon) is a mangrove-rimmed saline lake southeast of Cienfuegos. It's second only to Las Salinas on the Zapata Peninsula in terms of Cuba's bird magnets, and is the province's only *area protegida* (natural protected area). Trails lead to a viewing platform where flamingos, pelicans and *tocororos* (trogons; Cuba's national bird) are regular visitors. Plant life includes pear, lemon and avocado trees, as well as the güira, the fruit used to make maracas. Tours take two to three hours and include a boat trip to the far side of the lake. Arrive early to maximize your chances of seeing a variety of birds.

The reserve entrance (accessible only by hire car or taxi) is 12km from Cienfuegos, off the Rancho Luna road on the cut-through to Pepito Tey. Cubanacán (p242) in Cienfuegos run excursions here for a bargain CUC$10.

Jardín Botánico de Cienfuegos

The 94-hectare **botanic garden** (admission CUC$2.50; ⌚8am-5pm), near the Pepito Tey sugar mill, 17km east of Cienfuegos, is one of Cuba's biggest gardens. It houses 2000 species of plants, including 23 types of bamboo, 65 types of fig and 280 different palms (purportedly the greatest variety in one place anywhere in the world). The botanic garden was founded in 1901 by US sugar baron Edwin F Atkins, who initially intended to use it to study different varieties of sugarcane, but instead began planting exotic tropical trees from around the globe.

To reach the gardens you'll need your own wheels. The cheapest method is to go with an organized excursion; Cubanacán (p242) in Cienfuegos runs trips for CUC$10. Drivers coming from Cienfuegos should turn right (south) at the junction to Pepito Tey.

El Nicho

While Cienfuegos province's share of the verdant Sierra del Escambray is extensive (and includes the range's highest summit, 1156m Pico de San Juan), access is limited to a small protected area around **El Nicho** (admission CUC$5; ⌚8:30am-6:30pm), an outpost of the Topes de Collantes Natural Park.

El Nicho is actually the name of a beautiful waterfall on the Río Hanabanilla, but the area also offers a 1.5km nature trail (Reino de las Aguas), swimming in natural pools, caves, excellent bird-watching opportunities and a *ranchón*-style restaurant.

The beautiful road to El Nicho via Cumanayagua is legendary for its twists and turns: *tienes mas curvas de la carretera por Cumanayagua* (you have more curves than the road to Cumanayagua) is reportedly a compliment to *chicas* (girls) hereabouts. That said, recent improvements mean the trip from Cienfuegos to El Nicho now takes two hours. The daily truck that serves the small local community leaves at very inconvenient times; hiring a car or a taxi (about CUC$70) is far better. Half-day tours can be organized through the excellent Cubanacán (p242), which also offers an El Nicho trip with onward transportation to Trinidad.

The Caribbean Coast

Heading east toward Trinidad in Sancti Spíritus province, postcard views of the Sierra del Escambray loom ever closer until their ruffled foothills almost engulf the coast road, while offshore hidden coral reefs offer excellent diving.

Sights & Activities

Hacienda la Vega HORSEBACK RIDING, SNORKELING
(Carretera de Trinidad Km 52) On the main road approximately 9km east of Villa Guajimico, this bucolic cattle farm is surrounded by fruit trees and has an attached **restaurant**, serving the usual Cuban staples (CUC$5 to

BENNY MORÉ

No one singer encapsulates the full gamut of Cuban music more eloquently than Bartolomé 'Benny' Moré. A great-great-grandson of a king of the Congo, Moré was born in the small village of Santa Isabel de las Lajas in Cienfuegos province in 1919. He later gravitated to Havana in 1936 where he earned a precarious living selling damaged fruit on the streets. He graduated to playing and singing in the smoky bars and restaurants of Habana Vieja's tough dockside neighborhood, where he made just enough money to get by.

His first big break came in 1943 when his velvety voice and pitch-perfect delivery won him first prize in a local radio singing competition and landed him a regular job as lead vocalist for a Havana-based mariachi band called the Cauto Quartet.

His meteoric rise was confirmed two years later when, while singing at a regular gig in Havana's El Temple bar, he was spotted by Siro Rodríguez of the famed Trío Matamoros, then Cuba's biggest *son*-bolero band. Rodríguez was so impressed by what he heard and saw that he asked Moré to join the band as lead vocalist for an imminent tour of Mexico.

In the late 1940s, Mexico City was a proverbial Hollywood for young Spanish-speaking Cuban performers. Moré was signed up by RCA records and his fame rapidly spread.

Moré returned to Cuba in 1950 a star, and was quickly baptized the Prince of Mambo and the Barbarian of Rhythm. In the ensuring years, he inventing a brand new hybrid sound called *batanga* and put together his own 40-piece backing orchestra, the Banda Gigante. With the Banda, Moré toured Venezuela, Jamaica, Mexico and the US, culminating with a performance at the 1957 Oscars ceremony. But the singer's real passion was always Cuba. Legend has it that whenever Benny performed in Havana's Centro Gallego hundreds of people would fill the parks and streets to hear him sing.

With his multitextured voice and signature scale-sliding glissando, Moré's real talent lay in his ability to adapt and seemingly switch genres at will. As comfortable with a tear-jerking bolero as he was with a hip-gyrating rumba, Moré could convey tenderness, exuberance, emotion and soul, all in the space of five tantalizing minutes. Although he couldn't read music, Moré composed many of his most famous numbers, including 'Bonito y Sabroso' and the big hit 'Que Bueno Baila Usted.' When he died in 1963, more than 100,000 people attended his funeral. No one in Cuba has yet been able to fill his shoes.

CUC$10). After the city, it's a good place to relax over a shady lunch. Unhurried travelers can hire horses and canter down to a nearby beach called Caleta de Castro, where the snorkeling is excellent.

Cueva Martín Infierno CAVE

(north of Caleta de Muñoz) In the Valle de Yaganabo, 56km from Cienfuegos via the shore hamlet of Caleta de Muñoz, this cave contains a 67m stalagmite said to be the world's tallest. The cave is not always open for general tourism. Check with Cubanacán (p242) in Cienfuegos first. The valley is also a good bird-watching area.

Villa Guajimico DIVING

(☎54-09-46; Carretera de Trinidad Km 42) Unusually for a campismo, Villa Guajimico has its own dive center situated atop an offshore coral ridge. The center serves 16 dive sites, and packages with five immersions go for CUC$125.

Sleeping & Eating

Villa Yaguanabo CABINS $

(☎54-19-05, 54-00-99; Carretera de Trinidad Km 55; d CUC$30) Twenty-six kilometers west of Trinidad and 52km east of Cienfuegos, the Yaguanabo has 30 nicely situated cabins and offers horseback riding, boating on the Río Yaguanabo and short walks along the Villa Yaguanabo trail.

TOP CHOICE **Villa Guajimico** CABINS $

(☎54-09-46; Carretera de Trinidad Km 42; s/d CUC$22/36; P❄≋) This is one of Cubamar's most luxurious campismos. The 51 attractive cabins with their idyllic seaside setting have facilities matching most three-star hotels, acting as a nexus for scuba divers. Also offered are bike hire, car rental, various catamaran/kayaking options and short hiking trails. It's a fully equipped Campertour site too. Cienfuegos–Trinidad buses pass by.

Villa Clara Province

☎042 / POP 803,690

Includes »

Best Places to Eat

» La Concha (p255)
» El Alba (p255)
» El Louvre (p260)

Best Places to Stay

» Villa las Brujas (p264)
» Hostal Florida Center (p253)
» 'Villa Colonial' – Frank & Arelys (p260)
» La Paloma (p260)
» Hotel & Spa Elguea (p264)

Why Go?

He wasn't born here, never lived here and died in the distant Bolivian mountains, yet Che Guevara is synonymous with Villa Clara, for liberating its capital Santa Clara from the Batista dictatorship. Yet the land wedged between the Sierra del Escambray (Escambray Mountains) and Cuba's northern keys, a pastiche of misty tobacco fields and placid lakes, has reasons aplenty to drop by.

Cool Santa Clara, an important junction for cross-country travelers, hides a cutting-edge nightlife behind its Che monuments, while nearby the Escambray peaks glimmer with adventure possibilities, including mirror-like Embalse de Hanabanilla, Cuba's largest upland lake.

Picturesque Remedios is the region's oldest settlement, and its somnolence is annually shattered by a frenzied firework party, Las Parrandas. Northeastward, on Villa Clara's coveted coast, beach life revolves around the archipelago of the Cayerías del Norte, Cuba's fastest-growing resort. The presence of an adjacent Unesco Biosphere Reserve has meant development has been relatively sustainable – so far.

When to Go

It's hard to conceive of a better time to take a trip to Villa Clara than December. The 24th, specifically. That's right. Swap your cold Christmas for one of the Caribbean's hottest street parties in Remedios and then head over to the Cayerías del Norte for the start of the high season, when the chances of the skies raining on your beach parade are as low as they get.

Villa Clara Province Highlights

1. Trace the Che legend at Santa Clara's **Monumento Ernesto Che Guevara** (p252) and **Monumento a la Toma del Tren Blindado** (p252)
2. Get your tobacco and caffeine fix at Santa Clara's cigar factory, **Fábrica de Tabacos Constantino Pérez Carrodegua** (p250), and the neighboring, coffee-concocting **La Veguita** (p251)
3. Plug into the electric (sometimes downright shocking!) nightlife in Santa Clara's **Club Mejunje** (p256)
4. Hike the trails, bathe in the pools and soak up the solitude of **Embalse Hanabanilla** (p258)
5. People-watch from the plaza's cafes in the unspoiled colonial pocket of **Remedios** (p259)
6. See the Villa Clara the tourist board forgot at ramshackle yet heart-warming **Caibarién** (p261)
7. Bask on the balmy beaches of the **Cayo Santa María** (p262)

History

The Taíno people were the first known inhabitants of the region, but a re-creation of a settlement at a cheesy hotel outside Santa Clara is their only surviving legacy. Located strategically in the island's geographical center, Villa Clara has historically been a focal point for corsairs, colonizers and revolutionaries vying for material gains. Pirates were a perennial headache in the early colonial years, with the province's first town, Remedios, being moved twice and then abandoned altogether in the late 1600s by a group of families who escaped inland to what is now Santa Clara. Later the area's demographics were shaken up further by Canary Islanders, who brought their agricultural know-how and distinctive lilting Spanish accents to the tobacco fields of the picturesque Vuelta Arriba region. In December 1958 Ernesto 'Che' Guevara – aided by a motley crew of scruffy *barbudas* (bearded ones) – orchestrated the fall of the city of Santa Clara by derailing an armored train carrying more than 350 government troops and weaponry to the east. The victory rang the death knell for Fulgencio Batista's dictatorship and signaled the triumph of the Cuban Revolution.

Santa Clara

POP 239,091

Che city has long been hallowed turf for hero-worshipping, beret-wearing Guevara buffs, but away from the bombastic monuments the city pulsates with a vitality that includes some of the country's most eclectic nighttime entertainment outside Havana. Think a mix of music, theater and dance made in Cuba for Cubans – none of your touristy cabaret shows here. The celebrated cultural scene is thanks to the city boasting the country's second-most prestigious university, a feature that lends it academic airs and a brash youthfulness. Santa Clara might not be pretty like Trinidad, but Cuba's self-styled 'liberal city' with its impromptu concerts, drag shows and heavy-metal festival is certainly full of life, even if it isn't exactly the kind you envisaged experiencing when you booked your trip to Cuba.

Santa Clara is a great springboard, too, for almost anywhere else you want to get to in Cuba: it's no wonder that once Guevara had wrested this city from Batista's grasp the revolution was all but nailed.

History

Christopher Columbus believed that Cubanacán (or Cubana Khan; an Indian name that meant 'the middle of Cuba'), an Indian village once located near Santa Clara, was the seat of the khans of Mongolia; hence his misguided notion that he was exploring the Asian coast. Santa Clara proper was founded in 1689 by 13 families from Remedios, who were tired of the unwanted attention of passing pirates. The town grew quickly after a fire emptied Remedios in 1692, and in 1867 it became the capital of Las Villas province. A notable industrial center, Santa Clara was famous for its prerevolutionary Coca-Cola factory and its pivotal role in Cuba's island-wide communications network (see boxed text, p254). Today it continues to support a textile mill, a marble quarry and the Constantino Pérez Carrodegua tobacco factory. Santa Clara was the first major city to be liberated from Batista's army in December 1958.

Sights

Santa Clara's sights are liberally distributed to the north, east and west of Parque Vidal. All are within walking distance, with the big Che sight, Monumento Ernesto Che Guevara, only 2km from the center.

SANTA CLARA STREET NAMES

OLD NAME	NEW NAME
Candelaria	Maestra Nicolasa
Caridad	General Roloff
Nazareno	Serafín García
San Miguel	Calle 9 de Abril
Sindico	Morales

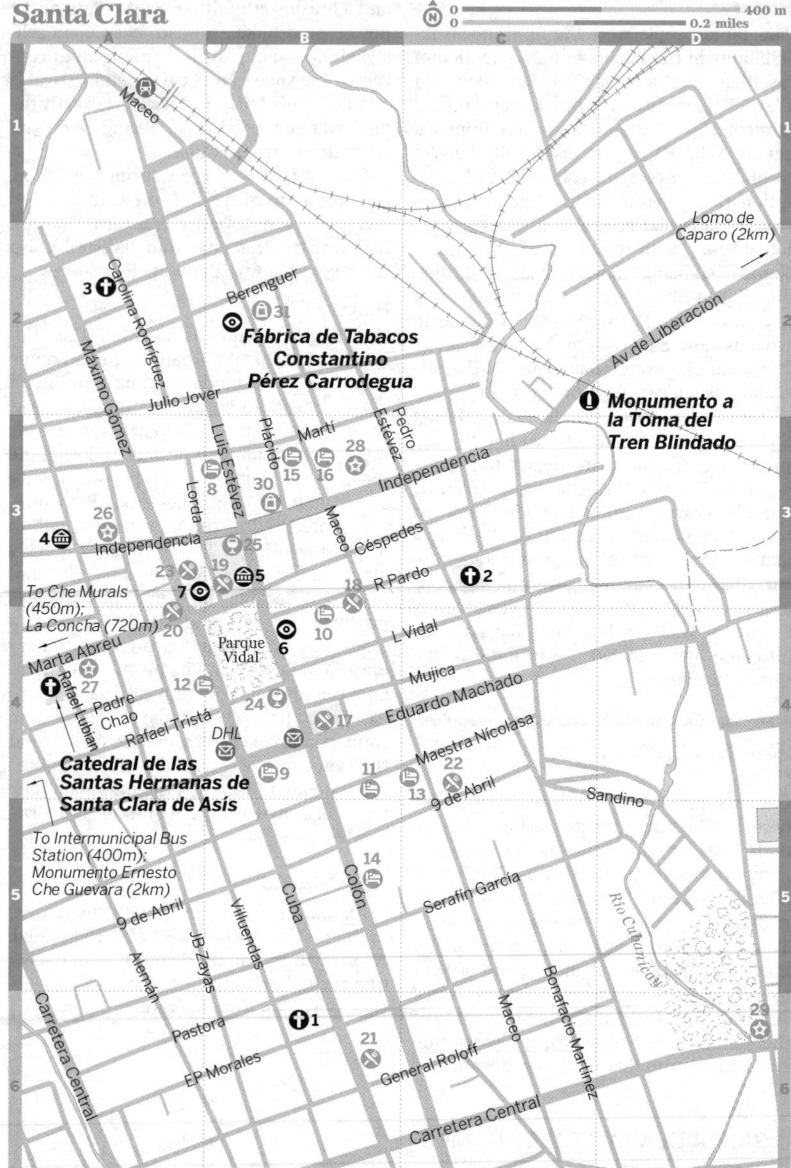

NORTH OF PARQUE VIDAL

Fábrica de Tabacos Constantino Pérez Carrodegua CIGAR FACTORY

(Maceo No 181 btwn Julio Jover & Berenguer; admission CUC$4; ⏲9-11am & 1-3pm) Santa Clara's tobacco factory, one of Cuba's best, makes a quality range of Montecristos, Partagás and Romeo y Julieta cigars. Tours here are lo-fi compared to those in Havana, and so the experience is a lot more interesting and less rushed. Book tickets through the Cubanacán office (p257).

Santa Clara

Top Sights
Catedral de las Santas Hermanas de Santa Clara de Asís ... A4
Fábrica de Tabacos Constantino Pérez Carrodegua ... B2
Monumento a la Toma del Tren Blindado ... C2

Sights
1 Iglesia de la Santísima Madre del Buen Pastor ... B6
2 Iglesia de Nuestra Señora del Buen Viaje ... C3
3 Iglesia de Nuestra Señora del Carmen ... A2
4 La Casa de la Ciudad ... A3
5 Museo de Artes Decorativas ... B3
6 Palacio Provincial ... B4
7 Teatro La Caridad ... A3

Sleeping
8 Authentica Pérgola ... B3
9 Casa de Mercy ... B4
10 Hector Martínez ... B4
11 Hostal Florida Center ... B4
12 Hotel Santa Clara Libre ... A4
13 Isidoro & Marta ... C4
14 La Casona Jover ... B5
15 Mary & Raicort ... B3
16 Vivian & José Rivero ... B3

Eating
17 Coppelia ... B4
18 El Alba ... B3
19 El Recreo ... B3
20 La Toscana ... A4
21 Mercado Agropecuario ... B6
22 Panadería Doña Neli ... C4
23 Restaurante Colonial 1878 ... A3

Drinking
24 Café Literario ... B4
25 Europa ... B3
La Marquesina ... (see 7)
La Veguita ... (see 31)

Entertainment
Biblioteca José Martí ... (see 6)
Cine Camilo Cienfuegos ... (see 12)
26 Cine Cubanacán ... A3
27 Club Mejunje ... A4
28 El Bar Club Boulevard ... B3
29 El Bosque ... D6
La Casa de la Ciudad ... (see 4)
Museo de Artes Decorativas ... (see 5)

Shopping
30 ARTex ... B3
31 La Veguita ... B2

Across the street you'll find **La Veguita** (☎20-89-52; ⌚8:30am-5:30pm), the factory's diminutive but comprehensively stocked sales outlet, staffed by a friendly ultraprofessional team of cigar experts. You can buy cheap rum here, and the bar out back brews exquisite coffee.

La Casa de la Ciudad CULTURAL CENTER
(cnr Independencia & JB Zayas; admission CUC$1; ⌚8am-5pm) The pulse of the city's progressive cultural life is inside this building northwest of Parque Vidal. If you want to see another side to Santa Clara aside from the obligatory Che memorabilia, get chatting to the young artists here. The historic center hosts art expositions (including an original Wilfredo Lam sketch), Noches del Danzón and a film museum, as well as impromptu music events. The real buzz of this place, however, is mingling with the local culture-vultures and finding out what makes this most unprepossessing of Cuban cities tick.

Iglesia de Nuestra Señora del Carmen CHURCH
(Carolina Rodríguez) The city's oldest church is five blocks north of Parque Vidal. It was built in 1748, with a tower added in 1846. During the War of Independence, it was used as a jail for Cuban patriots. A modern cylindrical monument facing the church commemorates the spot where Santa Clara was founded in 1689 by 13 refugee families from Remedios.

Museo Provincial Abel Santamaría MUSEUM
(☎20-30-41; admission CUC$1; ⌚9am-5pm Mon-Fri, to 1pm Sat) Not actually a memorial to Señor Santamaría (Fidel's right-hand man at Moncada), but rather a small provincial museum quartered in former military barracks where Batista's troops surrendered to Che Guevara on January 1, 1959. It contains a room on natural history and a room dedicated to Cuban women throughout history.

The museum is situated on a hilltop at the north end of Esquerra across the Río Bélico. Look for the large cream-colored building behind the horse field.

EAST OF PARQUE VIDAL

Monumento a la Toma del Tren Blindado MONUMENT

History was made here on December 29, 1958, when Ernesto 'Che' Guevara and a band of 18 rifle-wielding revolutionaries barely out of their teens derailed an armored train using a borrowed bulldozer and homemade Molotov cocktails. The battle lasted 90 minutes and effectively sealed the fate of the Batista dictatorship, ushering in 50 years of Fidel Castro. The event is remembered with a **boxcar museum** (admission CUC$1; ⏲9am-5:30pm Mon-Sat) east on Independencia, just over the river, which marks the spot where the train derailed and ejected its 350 heavily armed government troops. The celebrated bulldozer is mounted on its own plinth at the entrance.

Estatua Che y Nino MONUMENT

Far more intimate and intricate a monument than its big brother on the other side of town, this statue in front of the Officina de la Provincia (PCC) four blocks east of Tren Blindado shows El Che with a baby (symbolizing the next generation) on his shoulder. Looking closer you'll see smaller sculptures incorporated into the revolutionary's uniform depicting junctures in his life, including likenesses of the 38 men killed with Guevara in Bolivia concealed within the belt buckle.

Lomo de Caparo LANDMARK

Continuing two blocks further east from the Estatua Che y Nino, a road to the right leads to Santa Clara's best lookout, the distinctive Lomo de Caparo. The crest is marked by a flag and a series of stakes supporting the metallic but recognizable face of, you've guessed it, Che Guevara. The hill was a crucial vantage point for his forces during the 1958 liberation of Santa Clara.

Iglesia de Nuestra Señora del Buen Viaje CHURCH

(cnr Pedro Estévez & R Pardo) East of center is this riotous mix of Gothic, Romanesque and neoclassical architecture.

Iglesia de la Santísima Madre del Buen Pastor CHURCH

(EP Morales No 4 btwn Cuba & Villuendas) A singular colonial-style church located south of the center.

WEST OF PARQUE VIDAL

FREE **Monumento Ernesto Che Guevara** MONUMENT

The site of many a Che pilgrimage, this monument, mausoleum and museum complex is 2km west of Parque Vidal via Rafael Tristá

DOWNTIME IN PARQUE VIDAL

The old man in the starched-white *guayabera* (pleated, buttoned men's shirt) inhales deeply on his well-chewed cigar and lazily contemplates the weekend theater of Parque Vidal. It's Saturday evening and the whole town has come out to celebrate. An enterprising ice-cream vendor dispatches cheap peso cones from a patched-together machine, and an overworked goat pulls a cart of giggling children around leafy walkways while, sheltered under a splendid gazebo, members from the local philharmonic band tune up their instruments for an impromptu early-evening concert.

This quintessentially Cuban park is named for Colonel Leoncio Vidal y Caro, who was killed here on March 23, 1896. Shaded by palm trees, Parque Vidal is embellished by monuments to noted city luminaries including Vidal, local philanthropist Marta Abreu (see p254) and the emblematic El Niño de la Bota (Boy with a Boot), a long-standing city symbol.

Plenty of iconic buildings rim the periphery. You'll see the 1885 **Teatro la Caridad** (Máximo Gómez), one of the three great rural theaters of the colonial era with frescoes inside by Camilo Zalaya; the **Museo de Artes Decorativas** (Parque Vidal No 27; admission CUC$3; ⏲9am-6pm Mon-Thu, 1-10pm Fri & Sat, 6-10pm Sun), an 18th-century museum packed with period furniture; and the **Palacio Provincial**, a neoclassical beauty, built between 1902 and 1912, housing the Martí library (with a rare-book collection).

But the real treat is the inherent Cuban-ness of the setting – no cars, no stressed-out shoppers and no hurrying crowds. Sit down next to the *guayabera*-clad gent and enjoy the moment.

on Av de los Desfiles, near the Víazul bus station. It's in a vast square spanning both sides of the *carretera*, guarded by a bronze statue of El Che. The statue was erected in 1987 to mark the 20th anniversary of Guevara's murder in Bolivia, and can be viewed any time. Accessed from the statue's rear, the sublime **mausoleum** (Av de los Desfiles; ⏲9am-5pm Tue-Sun) contains 38 stone-carved niches dedicated to the other guerrillas killed in the failed Bolivian revolution. In 1997 the remains of 17 of them, including Guevara, were recovered from a secret mass grave in Bolivia and reburied in this memorial. Fidel Castro lit the eternal flame on October 17, 1997. The adjacent museum collects the details and ephemera of Che's life and death.

The best way to get to the monument is a 30-minute walk, or by hopping on a horse carriage in Calle Marta Abreu outside the cathedral for a couple of pesos.

Catedral de las Santas Hermanas de Santa Clara de Asís CHURCH

(Marta Abreu) Two blocks west of the square, the cathedral was constructed amid huge controversy in 1923 after the demolition of Santa Clara's original church in Parque Vidal. It contains a fantastic collection of stained-glass windows and a mythical white statue of Mother Mary known (unofficially) as La Virgen de la Charca (Virgin of the Pond). The statue was discovered in a ditch in the 1980s, having mysteriously disappeared shortly after the cathedral's consecration in 1954. It returned to grace the cathedral in 1995.

Murals LANDMARK

(Carretera Central btwn Vidaurreta & Carlos Pichado) Heading west on Carretera Central (the extension of Marta Abreu), you'll reach a fascinating series of comic book–style murals with a tongue-in-cheek look at Cuban-American relations as the predominant theme. Glimpse such scenes as the Statue of Liberty being made off with by Cuban helicopters and an unsavory-looking man draped in the stars-and-stripes shouting '*terroristas!*' (terrorists) at Cuban guerillas while himself concealing a bomb. Easily incorporated into a walk to the Che monument, the pictures are just before the intermunicipal bus station.

Jardin Zoologico Camilo Cienfuegos PARK

(admission CUC$1; ⏲Tue-Sun; 👪) From the murals, it's a 500m walk northwest to this leafy local recreation area. It's the best place to escape the midday heat, with its animal-themed playground for kids and cafeterias serving ice cream and snacks. There's a sorry selection of live animals here, too. The park is adjacent to the city cemetery.

Courses

Santa Clara boasts Cuba's second-most prestigious university, **Universidad Central Marta Abreu de las Villas** (☎28-14-10; www.uclv.edu.cu; Carretera de Camajuaní Km 5.5). Many international students study here, although most arrange everything through universities back home. Non-Cubans have, however, been able to turn up and study Spanish almost impromptu on occasion. Check the website for current details.

You might be able to pick up dancing and percussion lessons at the ever-adaptable **Club Mejunje** (Marta Abreu No 107; ⏲4pm-1am Tue-Sun) if you ask.

Festivals

Santa Clara's renegade annual offerings include **Miss Trasvesti**, a Miss World–type event with transvestite contestants in March, and October's **Metal Festival**, when headbanging to the country's leading heavy-metal acts happens at various venues across the city.

Sleeping

TOP CHOICE **Hostal Florida Center** CASA PARTICULAR $

(☎20-81-61; Maestra Nicolasa Este No 56 btwn Colón & Maceo; r CUC$20-25; ❄) The Florida is a national treasure. It boasts more antiques than the local decorative-arts museum and serves better food than most Havana restaurants (in a jaw-dropping central patio replete with plants). Your main dilemma is which room to choose: the grandiose colonial suite, or the gloriously retro art deco digs? The charismatic owner is opening an on-site paladar in 2011, thus cementing its place as one of the city's very best eating options. There's a fabulous wine selection here.

Casa de Mercy CASA PARTICULAR $

(☎21-69-41; Eduardo Machado No 4 btwn Cuba & Colón; r CUC$20-25; ❄) There are two rooms with private bathrooms available in this beautiful family house with no fewer than two terraces, a dining room, a book exchange and a tempting cocktail menu. English, French and Italian are spoken by the engaging hosts.

MARTA ABREU

You won't find many places in Cuba without a street dedicated to Marta Abreu, the country's most famed philanthropist, but in her home city of Santa Clara her name and legacy is everywhere, including the university (Cuba's second-most important). Before Che exploded onto the scene, Abreu had already established herself as the city's best-loved figure, and no wonder: the lady was responsible for the construction of most of Santa Clara's significant buildings, and was an important contributor to the demise of Spanish colonialism in the 1890s. At one time the city was known as the Ciudad de Marta and was renowned for its revelatory social services, installed by Abreu.

Born into a wealthy family, Abreu soon came to realize the contrasts in living standards between Cuba and comparatively luxurious Europe, and brought about many changes in Santa Clara to help the city rise to greater heights. Her most outstanding contribution remains the Teatro la Caridad, the building of which she oversaw, but the Biblioteca José Martí, Santa Clara's train station, four schools, a weather station, an old people's home and the provincial gas factory also exist because of funds she donated.

It isn't just her public works for which she is remembered, however. A humanitarian who stood for causes small and large, Abreu championed a campaign against homelessness in Santa Clara, funded construction of the power station that gave the city street lighting, and improved sanitation with the creation of public laundry stations. Perhaps most significantly, she raised the vast sum of 240,000 pesos (the equivalent of millions of dollars today) toward the liberation of Cuba from the Spanish in the 1890s.

Authentica Pérgola CASA PARTICULAR $
(%20-86-86; Luis Estévez No 61 btwn Independencia & Martí; r CUC$20-25; a) Delivering precisely what its name suggests, the plant-packed Pérgola is celebrating four years in the business, although judging by the service you'll receive you'd think the hosts had been catering far longer. A vast, leafy central *terraza* (terrace) with a fountain is the focal point: the rooms with their wonderfully hot showers lead off from that.

Isidoro & Marta CASA PARTICULAR $
(☎20-38-13; Maestra Nicolasa No 74 btwn Colón & Maceo; r CUC$20-25; ❄) This couple's more modern house is kept *muy limpia* (very clean). A long thin patio leads to two fine bedrooms sporting Santa Clara's best showers. Breakfast and dinner are served.

Villa la Granjita HOTEL $
(☎21-81-90; Carretera de Maleza Km 21.5; s/d CUC$22/41; P❄@≋) Situated approximately 3km north of town, La Granjita poses as a native Taíno village and does well with its *bohío*-style (thatched) huts, equipped with all the mod cons, but loses authenticity at nighttime when a cheesy poolside show and blaring disco remind you that you're still very much in 21st-century Cuba. Nevertheless, the hotel is better than the usual out-of-town rustic affair, with a good on-site restaurant, a massage therapist and even horseback riding available.

Hotel Santa Clara Libre HOTEL $
(☎20-75-48; Parque Vidal No 6; s/d CUC$17/24; ❄) The only tourist hotel is accommodated in Santa Clara's tallest building, a minty-green 168-room eyesore that played a key role in the December 1958 battle for the city between Guevara and Batista's government troops (you can still see the bullet holes on the building's facade). Inside, the poky rooms and tired furnishings appear worn, but there are cracking views from the 10th-floor restaurant.

Mary & Raicort CASA PARTICULAR $
(☎20-70-69; Placído No 54 btwn Independencia & Martí; r CUC$20-25; ❄) A charming 2nd-floor house with two rooms (one with a balcony) for rent and possibly Santa Clara's fruitiest *desayuno* (breakfast); steep stairs ascend to a roof terrace.

Vivian & José Rivero CASA PARTICULAR $
(☎20-37-81; Maceo No 64 btwn Martí & Independencia; r CUC$20; P❄) Two rooms with TV, fridge and private bathrooms are available in this lovely house dating from 1908. A terrace overlooks a colorful oasis of an inner garden. Secure motorcycle parking.

Héctor Martínez CASA PARTICULAR $
(☎21-74-63; R Pardo No 8 btwn Maceo & Parque Vidal; r CUC$20-25; ❄) A quiet haven just off Parque Vidal with a fern-and-flower-filled

patio and two huge rooms with two beds (one double) and a writing/domino table.

La Casona Jover CASA PARTICULAR $
(☎20-44-58; Colón No 167 btwn Calle 9 de Abril & Serafín García; r CUC$20-25; ❄) Two large rooms set well back from the road and a small terrace for contemplation.

Eating

Casas particulares trump the state-run joints. Guests and nonguests can stop by Hostal Florida Center for a scrumptious paladar-style meal (arrange in advance).

 **El Alba** PALADAR $
(R Pardo cnr Maceo; ⏲noon-4pm & 6-9:30pm Tue-Sun) The town's best peso restaurant is a block east of Parque Vidal. It's a deservedly popular joint. Seating is limited, but comfy sofas and cozy decor eases the wait for a table and the food comes in copious quantities. Go for the fish if it's available.

La Concha CARIBBEAN, ITALIAN $
(cnr Carretera Central & Danielito; mains CUC$3-8) Easily top of the state-run eateries is this posh (well, relatively) spot on the outskirts of town. It does a good trade in capturing the coach parties on their way to and from the Che memorial. There are some classy lunchtime bands here, though the highlight is generally considered to be the cheap but tasty pizza (from CUC$4).

Restaurante Colonial 1878 RESTAURANT $
(Máximo Gómez btwn Marta Abreu & Independencia; ⏲noon-2pm & 7-10:30pm) Hold on to the table when you cut your steak here, or you might lose it on the floor. Tough meat aside, 1878 is amiable enough, though the food struggles to emulate the dusty colonial setting. Pop in for a cocktail or a light lunch.

La Toscana ITALIAN $
(Máximo Gómez cnr Marta Abreu; ⏲10am-3:15pm & 6-11:15pm) Interior designers are, apparently, rarely recruited to lend Santa Clara's eateries any va-va-voom. La Toscana seems to aspire to an American Midwest out-of-town-retail-park look: soulless, in a word. The pizza's all right, though.

El Recreo BURGERS $
(Parque Vidal btwn Lorda & Luis Estévez; ⏲to 8:30pm) Looking more like a day centre than an eatery, El Recreo nevertheless attracts the crowds and delivers the goods (burgers) – without a smile.

Coppelia ICE-CREAM PARLOR $
(cnr Colón & Mujica; ⏲10:30am-10pm Tue-Sun) Stock up on peso ice cream at this architecturally hideous, but massive, construction.

Several peso cafeterías are near the corner of Independencia Oeste and Zayas, around Cine Cubanacán. Your ever-faithful ice-cream man sometimes operates out of a window on Abreu.

Self-Catering

Panadería Doña Neli BAKERY $
(cnr Maceo Sur & Calle 9 de Abril; ⏲7am-6pm) This joyous bakery amid the austere shopfronts on Calle Maceo will have your stomach rumbling with its aromatic fruit cakes, bread and pastries. Arrive early and celebrate breakfast.

Mercado Agropecuario MARKET $
(Cuba No 269 btwn EP Morales & General Roloff) Small, but centrally located and amply stocked.

Drinking

La Veguita (p250) serves Santa Clara's best coffee; the peso bars around the corner of Independencia Oeste and Zayas might not look glam, but can rustle up good cocktails. Casas particulares also make for atmospheric evening drinks.

Café Literario CAFE
(cnr Rafael Tristá & Colón; ⏲9am-9pm) What, a student coffee bar with no laptops? Revisit the pre-Microsoft years with strong espresso, piles of books and plenty of pent-up undergraduate idealism.

La Marquesina BAR
(Parque Vidal bwtn Máximo Gómez & Lorda; ⏲9am-1am) Glued onto the corner of the wondrous Teatro la Caridad, this lively bar is where the young intelligentsia go to down cocktails and listen to local bands.

Europa BAR
(cnr Independencia & Luis Estévez; ⏲noon-midnight) Everyone likes to drink at the Europa: that's because it's in prime people-watching territory on the boulevard, and locals and tourists alike feel welcomed on its laid-back street-facing terrace.

Entertainment

Aside from the places listed here, don't discount the **Biblioteca José Martí** (Colón on Parque Vidal), inside the Palacio Provincial, for

CHE COMANDANTE, AMIGO

Few 20th-century figures have successfully divided public opinion as deeply as Ernesto Guevara de la Serna, better known to his friends (and enemies) as El Che. He has been revered as an enduring symbol of Third World freedom and celebrated as the hero of the Sierra Maestra, and yet Che was also the most wanted man on the CIA hit list. The image of this handsome and often misunderstood Argentine physician-turned-*guerrillero* is still plastered over posters and tourist merchandise across Cuba. But what would the man himself have made of such rampant commercialization?

Born in Rosario, Argentina, in June 1928 to a bourgeois family of Irish-Spanish descent, Guevara was a delicate and sickly child who developed asthma at the age of two. It was an early desire to overcome this debilitating illness that instilled in the young Ernesto a willpower that would dramatically set him apart from other men.

A pugnacious competitor in his youth, Ernesto earned the name 'Fuser' at school for his combative nature on the rugby field. Graduating from the University of Buenos Aires in 1953 with a medical degree, he shunned a conventional medical career in favor of a cross-continental motorcycling odyssey, accompanied by his old friend and colleague Alberto Granado. Their nomadic wanderings – well documented in a series of posthumously published diaries – would open Ernesto's eyes to the grinding poverty and stark political injustices all too common in 1950s Latin America.

By the time Guevara arrived in Guatemala in 1954 on the eve of a US-backed coup against Jacobo Arbenz' leftist government, he was enthusiastically devouring the works of Marx and nurturing a deep-rooted hatred of the US. Deported to Mexico for his pro-Arbenz activities in 1955, Guevara fell in with a group of Cubans that included Moncada veteran Raúl Castro. Impressed by the Argentine's sharp intellect and never-failing political convictions, Raúl – a long-standing Communist Party member himself – decided to introduce Che to his charismatic brother, Fidel.

refined classical music, **La Casa de la Ciudad** (p251) for boleros and *trova* (verse), and vibrant **Parque Vidal** (see boxed text, p252), which presents everything from mime artists to full-scale orchestras.

TOP CHOICE Club Mejunje LIVE MUSIC, NIGHTCLUB
(Marta Abreu No 107; ⏲4pm-1am Tue-Sun; 👪) Set in the ruins of a roofless building given over to sprouting greenery, Club Mejunje is Havana-hip and more. Among its plethora of nighttime attractions is Cuba's only official drag show every Saturday night – a must-see! Other items on an eclectic entertainment menu include regular *trova*, bolero and *son* concerts, children's theater and disco nights. If you've only got one night, this is the place. On weekday afternoons there is some form of dancing, usually salsa.

Museo de Artes Decorativas LIVE MUSIC
(Parque Vidal No 27) In the atmospheric museum courtyard there is live music (mostly sit-down concerts) several times weekly, which makes for a relaxing evening. Expect everything from rock to *chachachá*.

Estadio Sandino SPORTS
(Calle 9 de Abril Final) You can catch baseball games east of the center via Calle 9 de Abril, from October to April. Villa Clara, nicknamed Las Naranjas (the Oranges) for their team strip, won a trio of championships from 1993 to 1995 and were losing finalists to their nemesis, Los Industriales (Havana), in 1996, 2003 and 2004. They are Cuba's third-biggest baseball team, after the Havana and Santiago heavyweights.

El Bar Club Boulevard NIGHTCLUB
(Independencia No 2 btwn Maceo & Pedro Estévez; admission CUC$2; ⏲10pm-2am Mon-Sat) This much-talked-about cocktail lounge has live bands and dancing, plus the odd humor show. It generally gets swinging about 11pm.

El Bosque CABARET, NIGHTCLUB
(Cnr Carretera Central & Calle 1; ⏲9pm-1am Wed-Sun) Santa Clara's cabaret hot spot.

Cine Camilo Cienfuegos CINEMA
(Parque Vidal) This is below Hotel Santa Clara Libre; large-screen English-language films are shown.

The meeting between the two men at Maria Antonia's house in Mexico City in June 1955 lasted 10 hours and ultimately changed the course of history. Rarely had two characters needed each other as much as the hot-headed Castro and the calmer, more ideologically polished Che. Both were favored children from large families, and both shunned the quiet life to fight courageously for a revolutionary cause. Similarly, both men had little to gain and much to throw away by abandoning professional careers for what most would have regarded as narrow-minded folly. 'In a revolution one either wins or dies,' wrote Guevara prophetically years later, 'if it is a *real* one.'

In December 1956 Che left for Cuba on the *Granma* yacht, joining the rebels as the group medic. One of only 12 or so of the original 82 rebel soldiers to survive the catastrophic landing at Las Coloradas, he proved himself to be a brave and intrepid fighter who led by example and quickly won the trust of his less reckless Cuban comrades. As a result Castro rewarded him with the rank of Comandante in July 1957, and in December 1958 Che repaid Fidel's faith when he masterminded the battle of Santa Clara, an action that effectively sealed a historic revolutionary victory.

Guevara was granted Cuban citizenship in February 1959 and soon assumed a leading role in Cuba's economic reforms as president of the National Bank and minister of industry. His insatiable work ethic and regular appearance at enthusiastically organized volunteer worker weekends quickly saw him cast as the living embodiment of Cuba's New Man.

But the honeymoon wasn't to last. Disappearing from the Cuban political scene in 1965, Guevara eventually materialized again in Bolivia in late 1966 at the head of a small band of Cuban *guerrilleros*. After the successful ambush of a Bolivian detachment in March 1967, he issued a call for 'two, three, many Vietnams in the Americas.' Such bold proclamations could only prove his undoing. On October 8, 1967, Guevara was captured by the Bolivian army. After consultation with military leaders in La Paz and Washington DC, he was shot the next day in front of US advisors. His remains were eventually returned to Cuba in 1997 and reburied in Santa Clara.

Cine Cubanacán CINEMA
(Independencia Oeste No 60) A picture house showing large-screen films in English.

Shopping

Independencia, between Maceo and JB Zayas, is the pedestrian shopping street called the Boulevard by locals. It's littered with all kinds of shops and restaurants and is the bustling hub of city life. An outlet of **ARTex** (Independencia btwn Luis Estévez & Plácido) sells handicrafts here. Don't forget **La Veguita** (p250) for some of the best cigars outside Havana.

Information

Internet Access & Telephone

Etecsa Telepunto (Marta Abreu No 55 btwn Máximo Gómez & Villuendas; internet access per hr CUC$6; 8:30am-7pm) Three internet terminals and three phone cabins.

Media

Radio CMHW broadcasts on 840AM and 93.5FM. The *Vanguardia Santa Clara* newspaper is published Saturday.

Medical Services

Farmacia Internacional (Colón No 106 btwn Maestra Nicolasa & Calle 9 de Abril; 9am-6pm)

Hospital Arnaldo Milián Castro (27-00-69; btwn Circumvalacion & Av 26 de Julio) Southeast of the city center, just northwest of the intersection with Calle 3. It's the best all-round option for foreigners, often called just Hospital Nuevo.

Money

Banco Financiero Internacional (Cuba No 6 cnr Rafael Tristá)

Cadeca (cnr Rafael Tristá & Cuba; 8:30am-4:30pm Mon-Sat, to 11:30am Sun) On Parque Vidal.

Post

DHL (Cuba No 7 btwn Rafael Tristá & Eduardo Machado; 8am-6pm Mon-Sat, 8am-noon Sun)

Post office (Colón No 10; 8am-6pm Mon-Sat, to noon Sun)

Travel Agencies

Cubanacán (20-51-89; Colon btwn Calle 9 de Abril & Serafin García; 8am-8pm Mon-Sat) Book tobacco factory tours and Villa la Granjita at this professional outfit.

Havanatur (☎20-40-01; Máximo Gómez No 9B; ⌚8:30am-noon & 1-5:30pm Mon-Fri, 8:30am-12:30pm Sat) Near Independencia.

Getting There & Away

Santa Clara's Abel Santamaría Airport receives weekly flights from Montreal and Toronto. There are no flights to Havana. Located in the center of the island, Santa Clara has excellent transport connections heading east or west.

Bus

The **Terminal de Ómnibus Nacionales** (☎20-34-70) is 2.5km out on the Carretera Central toward Matanzas, 500m north of the Che monument.

Tickets for air-conditioned **Víazul** (www.viazul.com) buses are sold at a special ticket window for foreigners at the station entrance.

Three buses leave for Havana (CUC$18, 3¾ hours) at 3:20am, 8:35am and 5:50pm via Entronque de Jagüey (CUC$6, 1½ hours), the nearest public transport stop to Península de Zapata. Buses to Varadero (CUC$11, three hours 20 minutes) are at 7:55am and 5:50pm.

The Santiago de Cuba–bound bus departs four times daily at 12:30am, 2:05am, 2:20pm and 8pm, travelling via Sancti Spíritus (CUC$6, 1¼ hours), Ciego de Ávila (CUC$9, two hours 35 minutes), Camagüey (CUC$15, four hours 25 minutes), Holguín (CUC$26, seven hours 50 minutes) and Bayamo (CUC$26, nine hours 10 minutes).

The **intermunicipal bus station** (Carretera Central), west of the center via Calle Marta Abreu, has daily buses to Remedios (CUC$1.45) and Caibarién, from where you can catch cheaper taxis to the Cayos. The 10am Remedios bus is most dependable. Other destinations served from here include Corralillo daily at 12:45pm and Manicaragua (for Embalse de Hanabanilla) three times daily. Transport could be by bus or truck, often gets overcrowded and isn't 100% reliable.

Colectivo Taxi

Colectivo drivers hang around the Víazul terminal to drum up custom for the journey to Havana. The best time to catch them is just before the scheduled Víazul departures. They'll whisk you to addresses in Central Havana in three hours for CUC$15 (less if you bargain hard), but they only leave when full (three person minimum).

Train

The **train station** (☎20-28-95) is straight up Luis Estévez from Parque Vidal on the north side of town. The **ticket office** (Luis Estévez Norte No 323) is across the park from the train station.

The comparatively luxurious Tren Francés passes through the city on odd-numbered days heading for Santiago de Cuba (12¾ hours) via Camagüey (CUC$13, 4¼ hours). The Havana-bound train leaves on even-numbered days.

There's an additional long-distance service to Santiago (CUC$33, 12¼ hours) stopping in Ciego de Ávila, Camagüey and Las Tunas; some trains run on to Guantánamo. In the opposite direction, there are approximately five daily trains to Havana (CUC$14, five hours), most of which stop in Matanzas (CUC$8, 3½ hours).

The train to Cienfuegos (CUC$3, 2½ hours) runs Fridays and Sundays only, departing at 5:40pm, while Sancti Spíritus trains run on alternate days (CUC$4, three hours). Trains to Remedios and Caibarién are not currently running. In the fickle world of Cuban trains, information can change weekly and we strongly advise you to double-check all this information at the station a day or two before departing.

Getting Around

Horse carriages congregate outside the cathedral on Marta Abreu (two pesos per ride). Bici-taxis (from the northwest of the park) cost CUC$1 a ride.

Car & Moped

Agencies renting wheels:

Cubacar (☎20-20-40; Hotel Santa Clara Libre, Parque Vidal No 6)

Havanautos (☎21-81-77; Marta Abreu; ⌚8am-noon & 1pm-9:15pm) By the cathedral.

Servicentro Oro Negro (cnr Carretera Central & Calle 9 de Abril) Just southwest of the center.

Taxi

Private cabs hang around in front of the national bus station and will offer you lifts to Remedios and Caibarién. A state taxi to the same destinations will cost approximately CUC$25 and CUC$30 respectively. To get to Cayo las Brujas, bank on CUC$50/$80 return including waiting time; drivers generally congregate in Parque Vidal outside Hotel Santa Clara Libre, or you can call **Cubataxi** (☎20-25-55, 20-03-63).

Embalse Hanabanilla

Embalse Hanabanilla, Villa Clara's main gateway to the Sierra del Escambray, is a 36-sq-km reservoir nestled picturesquely amid traditional farms and broccoli-green hills. The glittering lake is fjord-like and comes stocked with a famed supply of record-breaking bass. Besides fishers, boaters and nature-lovers are also well catered for, with several excursions and short but rewarding hikes available. The area is best accessed via the Hotel Hanabanilla on the reservoir's northwestern shore, some 80km south of Santa Clara. Cuba's largest hydroelectric generating station is also headquartered here.

Activities

Whopping 9kg largemouth bass have been caught on the lake, and **fishing trips** can be organized at the hotel: prices start at CUC$20 for one hour for two people. Boats ferry passengers over to Casa del Campesino, offering coffee, fresh fruit and a taste of bucolic Cuban life. A trail from the hotel heads here too. Another popular **boat trip** is to the Río Negro Restaurant, perched atop a steep stone staircase overlooking the lake shore 7km away. You can enjoy *comida criolla* (Creole food) here surrounded by nature, and hike up to a **mirador**. Both these boat trips cost CUC$6 per person. Another 2km by boat from Río Negro Restaurant is a tiny quay; disembark for the 1km hike to the **Arroyo Trinitario waterfall**, where you can swim. A couple of other trails lead off from here. You can organize these activities at Hotel Hanabanilla or book a day excursion (CUC$33 from Santa Clara; CUC$69 from Cayo Santa María).

Sleeping & Eating

Hotel Hanabanilla HOTEL $

(☎20-84-61; s/d CUC$14/22; P❄≋) Incongruous and lacking any subtlety, this four-story, 125-room hotel merits closer inspection. Despite an unsightly exterior, well-kept facilities inside include an à la carte restaurant, a swimming pool, a vista-laden bar and lake-facing rooms with small balconies. Peaceful during the week but packed with mainly Cuban guests at weekends, it's your only accommodation for miles and the best base for lakeside activities. Forty-nine new rooms should be ready in 2011.

Getting There & Away

Three daily buses run from Santa Clara to Manicaragua at 7:40am, 1:30pm and 9:30pm. Theoretically, there are buses from Manicaragua to Embalse Hanabanilla, but the only practical access is by car, bike or moped. Taxi drivers will energetically offer the trip. Bank on CUC$25 one way in a state cab. Negotiate hard if you want the driver to wait over while you participate in excursions.

Remedios

POP 45,836

One of Cuba's oldest settlements, sedate Remedios erupts each December for one of the wildest street parties in the Caribbean, the legendary **Las Parrandas**, in which exuberant citizens take sides and face off against each other with floats, fireworks and dancing competitions.

Founded sometime between 1513 and 1524, the city (when it isn't *parrandas*-ing) is a relaxed, resplendent place used as both a cheap base for the Cayerías del Norte and a colonial getaway in its own right. Despite losing half its citizens to Santa Clara in the 1689 exodus (see p249), Remedios has managed to maintain its unique cultural charisma – an atmosphere best savored in a couple of phenomenal casas particulares and in its striking but somnolent central square, which is a treasure trove of grand 18th- and 19th-century buildings.

Sights

Remedios is the only city in Cuba with two churches in its main square, Plaza Martí.

Parroquia de San Juan Bautista de Remedios CHURCH

(Camilo Cienfuegos No 20; ⏲9am-noon & 2-5pm Mon-Thu) One of the island's finest ecclesiastical buildings, this church dates from the late 18th century, although a church was founded on this site as early as 1545. The campanile was erected between 1848 and 1858, and its famous gilded high altar and mahogany ceiling are thanks to a restoration project (1944–46) financed by millionaire philanthropist Eutimio Falla Bonet. The pregnant Inmaculada Concepción to the left of the entrance is said to be the only one of its kind (ie expectant) in Cuba. If the front doors are closed, go around to the rear or attend 7:30pm Mass.

Also on Parque Martí is the 18th-century **Iglesia de Nuestra Señora del Buen Viaje** (Alejandro del Río No 66), which is awaiting a long-overdue restoration and is currently closed.

Museo de Música Alejandro García Caturla MUSEUM

(Parque Martí No 5; admission CUC$1; ⏲9am-noon & 1-6pm Mon-Thu, 7-11pm Fri, 2pm-midnight Sat) Between the churches is a museum commemorating García Caturla, a Cuban composer and musician who lived here from 1920 until his murder in 1940. Look for occasional impromptu concerts.

Museo de las Parrandas Remedianas MUSUEM

(Máximo Gómez No 71; admission CUC$1; ⏲9am-6pm) Visiting this lively museum (and you

PARRANDAS

Sometime during the 18th century, the priest at Remedios cathedral, Francisco Vigil de Quiñones, had the bright idea of providing local children with cutlery and crockery and getting them to run about the city making noise in a bid to increase mass attendance in the lead-up to Christmas. He could not have imagined what he was starting. Three centuries later and *parrandas*, as these cacophonous rituals became known, have developed into some of the best-known Caribbean street parties. Peculiar to the former Las Villas region of Cuba, *parrandas* take place only in towns in Villa Clara, Ciego de Ávila and Sancti Spíritus provinces, and the biggest party erupts annually in Remedios on December 24th.

Festivities kick off at 10pm with the city's two traditional neighborhoods (El Carmen and El Salvador) grouping together to outdo the other with displays of fireworks and dance, from rumba to polka. The second part of the party is a parade of vast floats, elaborate carnival-like structures only with the fancifully dressed people in the displays standing stock still as the tractor-towed artworks traverse the streets. Further fireworks round off the revelry.

The success of *parrandas* has morphed over the years and neighboring towns from Camajuani to Caibarién have (almost) equivalently raucous celebrations.

don't often hear those two words together in provincial Cuba) two blocks off Parque Martí is probably a poor substitute for partying here on December 24, but what the hell? The downstairs photo gallery usually recaps the previous year's *parrandas*, while the upstairs rooms outline the history of this tradition, including scale models of floats and depictions of how the fireworks are made. Another room is jammed with revelry gear from celebrations past.

FREE Galería del Arte Carlos Enríquez ART GALLERY
(Parque Martí No 2; ⏲9am-noon & 1-5pm) Back on the main plaza, this is named after the gifted painter who hailed from the small Villa Clara town of Zulueta. It displays some interesting local art and occasional exhibitions by touring artists.

Sleeping

TOP CHOICE 'Villa Colonial' – Frank & Arelys CASA PARTICULAR $
(☎39-62-74; Maceo No 43 cnr Av General Carrillo; r CUC$20-25; ❄) A truly elegant villa with high ceilings and huge wrought-iron window guards, this place has been restored with a meticulous eye for history. You can enjoy your own private entrance and lobby, an antique-stuffed sitting room, a gorgeous patio and spacious bedrooms with modern bathrooms. The young hosts are charming and passionate about their town and its history.

La Paloma CASA PARTICULAR $
(☎39-54-90; Balmaseda No 4 btwn Capablanca & Máximo Gómez; r CUC$20-25; P❄) Another grand Remedios casa with tilework and furnishings that would be worth zillions anywhere else, La Paloma dates from 1875 and is right on the main square. The two rooms have massive shower units, art deco beds, and doors big enough to ride a horse through.

Hotel Mascotte BOUTIQUE HOTEL $$
(☎39-53-41; Parque Martí; s/d CUC$45/60; ❄) Remedios makes up for its lack of tourist hotels by the quality of this one, housed in a beautiful rose-pink colonial building dating from 1869. Run by the Cubanacán chain as a boutique hotel, the Mascotte has 10 spacious rooms, five of which have balconies overlooking the main square.

Hostal San Carlos CASA PARTICULAR $
(☎39-56-24; José A Peña No 75 btwn Maceo & La Pastora; r CUC$20; ❄) Another solid option: two rooms, sparkling bathrooms and a roof terrace.

Eating

El Louvre CAFE $
(Máximo Gómez No 122; ⏲7:30am-midnight) With a gravitational pull on Remedios' scattering of tourists, El Louvre is, so locals will tell you, the oldest bar in the country in continuous service (since 1866). Longevity awards aside, the fried-chicken-and-sandwiches menu can't quite match the quaint park-side location. The bar was good enough for Spanish

poet Federico García Lorca, who heads the list of famous former patrons (one suspects the culinary offerings might have been better back then, though). If you're looking for a room/paladar/taxi, park yourself here and wait for offers.

Portales a la Plaza CARIBBEAN **$**
(Parque Martí btwn Av del Rio & Montaiván) On the opposite side of the Plaza to El Louvre, this restaurant is sequestered in a colonial courtyard, which lends atmosphere as you tuck in to staples of the pork, banana and rice variety. Pay in pesos.

Restaurante el Curujey CARIBBEAN **$**
(36-33-05; Carretera Remedios–Caibarién Km 3.5; 10am-5pm) If you're Cayo-bound from Remedios, this rustic ARTex place 3km out on the Caibarién road is a good bet. It's signposted 'Finca la Cabana' from the highway.

✩ Entertainment

Additional cultural activities can be found in **Uneac** (Maceo No 25), and outside in the parks and squares.

Bar Juvenil NIGHTCLUB
(Adel Río No 47; 9pm-1am Sat & Sun) Dancers head here, a courtyard disco near Máximo Gómez (enter via park), with palms, pillars and Moorish tiles. During the day there's table tennis and dominoes; at night it's an alcohol-free party.

El Güije NIGHTCLUB
(cnr Independencia & Maceo; 2pm-2am) This is a newish open-air venue; ask about dancing classes during the day.

Centro Cultural las Leyendas CULTURAL CENTER
(Máximo Gómez btwn Margali & Independencia) Next door to El Louvre is an ARTex cultural center with music till 1am Wednesday to Saturday.

Teatro Rubén M Villena THEATER
(Cienfuegos No 30) A block east of the park is an elegant old theater with dance performances, plays and Theater Guiñol for kids. The schedule is posted in the window and tickets are in pesos.

Getting There & Away

The bus station is on the southern side of town at the beginning of the 45km road to Santa Clara. There are six daily buses to Santa Clara (one hour), three daily services to Caibarién (20 minutes) and two departures Monday, Wednesday and Friday to Zulueta (30 minutes). Fares are negligible. Remedios is not on the Víazul network; the closest you can get is Santa Clara.

No trains currently serve Remedios. A state taxi from the bus station to Caibarién will cost roughly CUC$5 one way, and CUC$25 to Santa Clara. A bici-taxi from the bus station to Parque Martí costs two pesos.

Caibarién

POP 37,902

After smart Santa Clara and the colonial splendor of Remedios, this once-busy shipping port on Cuba's Atlantic coast will come as a shock with its crumbling old buildings and decrepit feel. Since the piers slumped into the sea and the provincial sugar mills closed down, Caibarién's economic foundations have been whipped from under it, and it's never really recovered. Just talking too loudly here seems enough to bring whole houses tumbling down, so fragile do they look.

But give this place a chance. Travelers report that some of their best experiences in Cuba came at ultrafriendly Caibarién, which is colorfully framed by its restored *malecón*

LOCAL KNOWLEDGE

ANGEL GONZALEZ: GUIDE, CAIBARIÉN

The cayos are beautiful, but they're also expensive. One way to save money is to stay in Caibarién, Remedios or even Santa Clara and visit for the day. A taxi from Caibarién to Villa las Brujas, for example, costs CUC$50 there and back, including waiting time while you enjoy the beach. Many beaches are private, however: either the property of the hotels or protected flora and fauna reserves. Two of the best beaches – Perla Blanca, at the far end of Cayo Santa María, and Playa las Salinas, near Villa las Brujas and easiest to access – can still be visited for free. To avoid paying an entry fee to Playa las Salinas, take the left turn just after the gas station on Cayo las Brujas and follow the track to the public entry point. Bring a packed lunch to avoid paying for the pricey, and limited, eating options.

sea wall and bustling fishing fleet. Nine kilometers east of Remedios and 40km from the alluring Cayerías del Norte, it's a 'real' corner of Cuba that the authorities forgot to dress up for tourists. Catch a taste of the former commercial bustle by trying a just-landed *cangrejo* (crab) or taking a sweet trip back to the sugar heyday at a restored sugar mill museum. Then there are the December *parrandas,* allegedly second only to Remedios in their explosiveness.

The town also makes a cheap base for those keen to catch a glimpse of the pristine cayos without shelling out the expensive all-inclusive prices. **Havanatur** (☎35-11-71; Av 9 btwn Calles 8 & 10) can arrange accommodation on Cayo Santa María. There's a **Cadeca** (Calle 10 No 907 btwn Avs 9 & 11) nearby.

Sights

FREE Museo de Agroindustria Azucarero Marcelo Salado MUSEUM
(☎36-32-86; ⏲8am-4pm Mon-Fri) Three kilometers past the crab statue on the Remedios road you'll see this museum, which is especially interesting because it is housed in the old regional sugar mill. There's a video of Cuba's sugar industry, models of figures toiling to harvest the product and lots of original machinery, which, while appearing Industrial Revolution-esque to most Western eyes, was imperative in Cuba right up until Castro's clampdown on the industry in the 1990s. An added bonus is the extensive collection of locomotives (the place is also known as the Museo de Vapor or Museum of Steam); top billing here goes to Latin America's largest steam engine.

Crab Statue MONUMENT
The entrance to Caibarién is guarded by a giant crustacean designed by Florencio Gelabert Pérez and erected in 1983.

Museo Municipal María Escobar Laredo MUSEUM
(cnr Av 9 & Calle 10) This is the best of the town center attractions and is conveniently placed on the main plaza. It's worth a once-over, if only to marvel at the fact that even humble Caibarién had a heyday.

Sleeping & Eating

Caibarién is the most economical launchpad for the resort-strewn, casa particular–free zone of the Cayerías del Norte; many travelers alight here for this very reason.

Virginia's Pension CASA PARTICULAR $
(☎36-33-03; Ciudad Pesquera No 73; r CUC$20-25; P ❄) Among Caibarién's handful of sleeping options, this reputable professional place run by Virginia Rodríguez is the most popular. Food here is delicious and gives you a great chance to sample local *mariscos* (seafood).

Complejo Brisas del Mar HOTEL $
(☎35-16-99; Reparto Mar Azul; d CUC$22; P ❄ 🏊) Also known as Villa Blanca, this 17-room Islazul hotel is located 4km east of the town right by Caibarién beach (seven rooms face the sea). Facilities include bar, restaurant, swimming pool and satellite TV.

Restaurante la Vicaria SEAFOOD $
(Calle 10 & Av 9; ⏲10am-10:30pm) Whooshing in at number one for eating choices is this establishment on the main square, specializing in fish.

Entertainment

Piste de Baile NIGHTCLUB
(Calle 4; admission 2 pesos) Surprisingly, Caibarién has a hot, happening disco near the train station. It's known by a generic name (*piste de baile* means dance floor) and jumps with hundreds of young locals on weekends.

Getting There & Away

Four buses a day go to Remedios (CUC$1, 20 minutes), two carry on to Santa Clara (CUC$2, 1½ hours) and three go to Yaguajay (CUC$1.50, 45 minutes) from Caibarién's old blue-and-white **bus & train station** (Calle 6) on the western side of town. No trains run to Caibarién, however.

The Servi-Cupet gas station is at the entrance to town from Remedios, behind the crab statue. **Cubacar** (☎35-19-60; Av 11 btwn Calles 6 & 8) rents cars at the standard rates and mopeds for CUC$22.

Cayerías del Norte

The hundreds of small keys off the province's north coast – known collectively as the Cayerías del Norte – are Cuba's next big tourism project. There are currently five resorts splayed out here (including one of the archipelago's newest), scattered over three of the largest keys, **Cayo las Brujas**, **Cayo Ensenachos** and **Cayo Santa María**, but plans are on the table for several more. The existing hotels are all linked by an impressive 48km causeway called **El**

Cayo Santa María Area

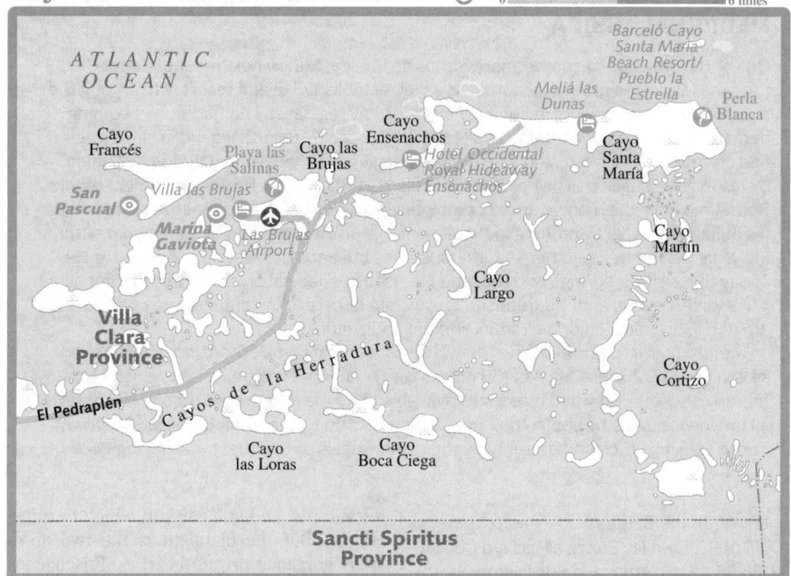

Pedraplén, which runs across the shallow Bahía de Buenavista from Caibarién crossing 45 bridges en route. The bridges were incorporated in the mid-1990s to allow the exchange of tidal waters after studies on an older bridgeless *pedraplén* (causeway) in Cayo Coco revealed significant environmental damage.

In keeping with its elitist aspirations (Tom Cruise has reportedly holidayed here), tourist development on the Cayerías del Norte has, to date, been carefully managed. Protecting 248 species of flora and incorporating parts of the Unesco-listed Buenavista Biosphere Reserve, the government has wisely earmarked large tracts of land as protected flora and fauna reserves. These measures have ensured that the area's fine white beaches have (so far) retained a pristine and detached feel noticeably absent in other resort complexes such as Cayo Coco and Varadero.

Sights & Activities

Marina Gaviota WATERSPORTS
(☎35-00-13; Cayo las Brujas) Most water-based activities can be arranged at this marina next to Villa las Brujas. Highlights include a one-hour catamaran excursion with snorkeling (CUC$35), a day-long catamaran cruise (CUC$72), a sunset cruise (CUC$49) and deep-sea fishing (CUC$260 for four people). Diving to one of 24 offshore sites is also offered (CUC$65 for two immersions). Most water activities are cancelled if there is a cold weather front.

San Pascual HISTORICAL SITE
One of the area's oldest and oddest curiosities is the San Pascual, a San Diego tanker built in 1920 that got wrecked in 1933 on the opposite side of nearby Cayo Francés. Later the ship was used to store molasses, and later still it was opened up as a rather surreal hotel-restaurant (now closed). The journey out to see the ship is included in snorkeling excursions and sunset cruises.

Pueblo la Estrella SPA, BOWLING
(⏲9am-7:30pm) On a more modern note, this is a vast shopping mall similar to Varadero's Plaza América. It has souvenir stands, restaurants, bars, spas and bowling. It's located in the middle of the Barceló complex between the Santa Maria Beach and Tropical hotels, and with the exception of the gym is open to all.

Sleeping

There are five hotels here. The following run the gamut of price ranges.

WORTH A TRIP

MEDICINAL MECCA

Out-of-the-way, out-of-the-ordinary Baños de Elguea, 136km northwest of Santa Clara near the Matanzas provincial border, is a well-established health resort with among the most rejuvenating powers in Latin America (so say regulars). The tradition of coming here to be cleansed of ills dates back to 1860. According to local legend, a slave who had contracted a serious skin disease was banished to modern-day Baños de Elguea by his master, sugar-mill owner Don Francisco Elguea, so that he wouldn't infect others. Sometime later the man returned completely cured. He explained that he had relieved his affliction merely by bathing in the region's natural mineral spring. Somewhat surprisingly, his master believed him. A bathhouse was built and the first hotel opened in 1917. Today these sulfur springs and the mud are used by medical professionals to treat skin irritations, arthritis and rheumatism. The waters here reach a temperature of 50°C and are rich in bromide, chlorine, radon, sodium and sulfur.

Situated north of Coralillo, **Hotel & Spa Elguea** (68-62-90; s/d incl breakfast low season CUC$13/20; P) has 139 rooms with numerous spa treatments, such as mud therapy, hydrotherapy and massages available at the nearby thermal pools. The hotel is all but inaccessible by public transport, which gets no further than Coralillo 9km away. Those seeking cures had better have their own wheels or their best walking legs.

TOP CHOICE **Villa las Brujas** HOTEL, RESORT **$$**
(35-01-99; Cayo las Brujas; all-incl s/d CUC$76-89/86-98; P) Atop a small, relatively untamed headland crowned by a statue of a *bruja* (witch), Villa las Brujas has the air of a tropical *Wuthering Heights* when a cold front blows in. It all adds to the unique atmosphere of this comfortable but affordable small resort situated among the mangroves on one of Cuba's prettiest northern keys. The 24 spacious *cabañas* are equipped with coffee machines, cable TV and massive beds (higher prices given are for rooms with premium views), while the Farallón restaurant overlooks a magnificent scoop of private beach (part of paradisiacal Playa las Salinas). The nearest resort to the mainland, Villa las Brujas lies by the marina, 3km from the airport.

Hotel Occidental Royal Hideaway Ensenachos RESORT **$$$**
(35-03-00; Cayo Ensenachos; all-incl s/d CUC$300/400; P@) Noticeably superior to the other offerings in the Cayerías del Norte, this top-end paradise is on a par with some of the five-star resorts in Puerto Rico and Cancún (with a Canadian rather than an American demographic). It's refined and tranquil with Alhambra-esque fountains and attractive natural foliage. Guests here are accommodated in pretty 20-unit blocks, each with their own private concierge. Among the all-inclusive luxuries: king-sized beds, bathrobes, water toys, tennis coaching, myriad restaurants, and golf carts in which to travel around. But the highlight is the two absolutely gorgeous private beaches, Ensenachos and Mégano.

Barceló Cayo Santa María Beach Resort RESORT **$$$**
(35-04-00; jefeventas.barcelo@cayosantamaria.co.cu; Cayo Santa María; all-incl s/d from CUC$101/162; P@) The vast new Barceló Cayo Santa María Resort is actually four hotels divided into two complexes: the Caribe, the Tropical, the Santa Maria Beach and the Colonial. Between them they sport 2694 rooms, most of which are suite standard. Shelling out for top-end digs here will get you a balcony, a room with a king-sized bed and two satellite TVs plus your own Jacuzzi.

Meliá las Dunas RESORT **$$$**
(35-01-00; Cayo Santa María; all-incl d CUC$243; P@) The mind-boggling 925-room Meliá is one of Cuba's newest and biggest resorts – it opened to rave reviews in 2007. The size of an English village, Meliá has golf carts to get around the extensive grounds. Stays here are in a classic Caribbean beach-paradise bubble, light-years away from any inkling of authentic, everyday Cuba.

Eating

For non-hotel-guests the best bet for a decent meal is in the Farallón restaurant, perched like a bird's nest overlooking blissful Las Salinas beach. Access is via Villa las

Brujas. Lunch with use of beach, bathrooms and parking costs CUC$20 (CUC$16 will be your food and drink credit). Pueblo la Estrella (p263) has several new restaurants. Otherwise your only option is the airport cafetería (mean coffee but precious little else) or an expensive day pass to the big all-inclusive resorts.

Getting There & Away

A typical all-inclusive zone, Cayo Santa María was not developed with public transport in mind. **Las Brujas airport** (☎35-00-09) has mainly charter flights to Havana. There's a Servicentro gas station opposite. For those not fortunate enough to be shepherded around in the air-conditioned buses laid on by the big hotels for their guests, access is by rental car/moped or taxi from Caibarién (56km), Remedios (65km) or Santa Clara (110km). A taxi from Caibarién/Remedios/Santa Clara costs approximately CUC$50/60/80 return, including waiting time, to Villa las Brujas. Cyclists: head winds on the causeway make pedaling problematic. The causeway is accessed from Caibarién and there's a toll booth (CUC$2 each way), where you'll need to show your passport/visa.

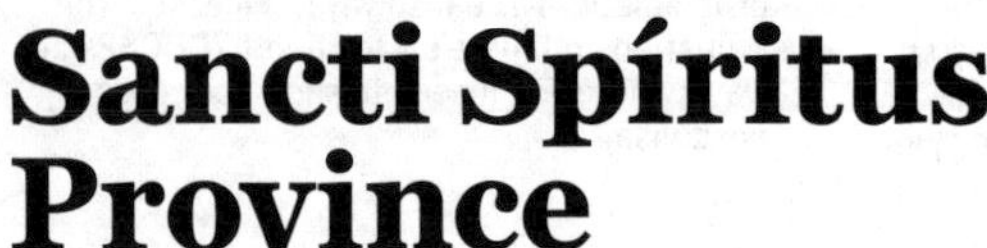

Sancti Spíritus Province

☎041 / POP 465,468

Includes »

Best Places to Eat

- Paladar Sol y Son (p282)
- Mesón de la Plaza (p272)
- Restaurante Hostal del Rijo (p273)
- Paladar Estela (p282)

Best Places to Stay

- Hostal del Rijo (p271)
- Casa Muñoz – Julio & Rosa (p280)
- Iberostar Grand Hotel (p280)
- Hotel Plaza (p271)
- 'Hospedaje Yolanda' – Yolanda María Alvarez (p281)

Why Go?

Sancti Spíritus is the province of good fortune; there's more of everything here, and it's all squeezed into an area half the size of Camagüe-y or Pinar del Río.

The cities are a perennial highlight. In the east is the understated provincial capital, a soporific mix of weather-beaten buildings and bruised Ladas. South, and within sight of the coast, is ethereal Trinidad, Cuba's time-warped colonial jewel.

Unlike other colonial belles, Trinidad has beaches – nearby Ancón is a stunner, easily the best on Cuba's southern coast – and mountains. Within mirror-glinting distance of the city's colonial core lies the haunting Escambray, which, with a network of decent trails, is Cuba's best hiking area.

The rest of the province hides a surprisingly varied cache of oft-overlooked curiosities, including fishing at Lake Zaza, a seminal museum to Cuba's guerrilla icon Camilo Cienfuegos in Yaguajay, and the beautiful Bahía de Buenavista.

When to Go

Trinidadians don't wait long after Christmas to rediscover their celebratory style. The Semana de la Cultura Trinitaria (Trinidad Culture Week) takes place during the second week of January and coincides with the city's anniversary. The quiet month of May is a good time to visit this province, as you can avoid both crowds and bad weather during the off-season. Stick around until June and you'll witness Trinidad's second big annual shindig, the Fiestas Sanjuaneras, a local Carnaval where rum-fueled horsemen gallop through the streets. Take cover!

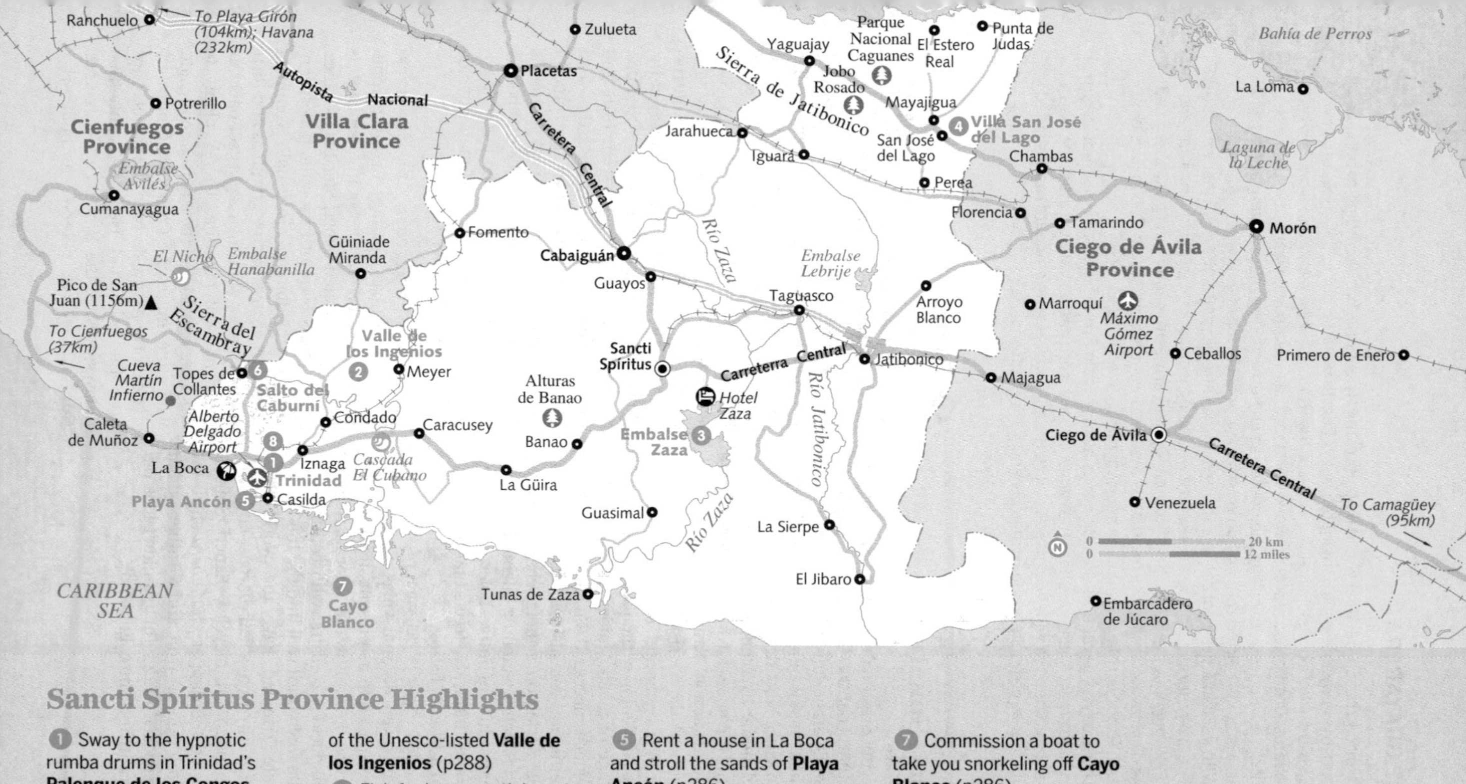

Sancti Spíritus Province Highlights

1 Sway to the hypnotic rumba drums in Trinidad's **Palenque de los Congos Reales** (p283)

2 Climb the tower at the Manaca Iznaga for a killer view of the Unesco-listed **Valle de los Ingenios** (p288)

3 Fish for largemouth bass in **Embalse Zaza** (p272)

4 Soak in the mineral springs at **Villa San José del Lago** (p292)

5 Rent a house in La Boca and stroll the sands of **Playa Ancón** (p286)

6 Hike down to the **Salto del Caburní** (p289) and jump into a frigid natural bathing pool

7 Commission a boat to take you snorkeling off **Cayo Blanco** (p286)

8 Visit one of half-a-dozen museums in time-warped **Trinidad** (p277)

THE GUAYABERA

No Mexican beach wedding would be complete without one, but according to popular legend, the *guayabera* shirt originated not in Puerto Vallarta, but in Sancti Spíritus in the late 1800s, where people who lived close to the Río Yayabo were known colloquially as Yayaberos. Crafting comfortable work-shirts for their menfolk to wear out in the fields, the local women took to calling their deftly sewn homemade garments *guayaberas* when their husbands started coming home with their pockets full of *guayabas* (guavas).

With its distinctive *alforzas* (pleats) and rustic retro elegance, the *guayabera's* popularity quickly spread, and by the 1880s it was being worn at official events in towns and cities throughout the Sancti Spíritus area. By the early 20th century the *guayabera* had arrived in Havana, and in the mid-1940s the trend went national when Cuban President Ramón Grau San Martín was seen sporting one.

These days, *guayaberas* are ubiquitous all over Latin America, from backstreet bars in Mexico to smart Miami business meetings. Usually worn casually untucked at the waist, the shirt comes in a variety of pastel colors (though white is the standard) and is noted for its four large pockets and numerous decorative buttons.

Sancti Spíritus

POP 105,815

Don't underestimate Sancti Spíritus. In any other country this attractive colonial city would be a cultural tour de force. But cocooned inside illustrious Sancti Spíritus province and destined to always play second fiddle to Trinidad, it barely gets a look-in. Of course, for many visitors therein lies the attraction. Sancti Spíritus is Trinidad without the tourist hassle. You can get served in a restaurant here and search for a casa particular without an uninvited assemblage of pushy 'guides' telling you that the owner is deceased, on vacation or living in Miami. You can also get decidedly comfortable sitting on a metal chair in Parque Serafín Sánchez watching talented kids play stickball while plaintive boleros (romantic love songs) infiltrate streets that never quite earned a Unesco listing.

Founded in 1514 as one of Diego Velázquez' seven original villas, Sancti Spíritus was moved to its present site on the Río Yayabo in 1522. But the relocation didn't stop audacious corsairs, who continued to loot the town until well into the 1660s.

While Trinidad gave the world Playa Ancón, filthy-rich sugar barons and *jineteros* (touts) on bicycles, Sancti Spíritus concocted the dapper *guayabera* shirt, the *guayaba* (guava) fruit and a rather quaint hump-backed bridge that wouldn't look out of place in Yorkshire, England.

Sights

The main streets north and south of the Av de los Mártires and Calle M Solano axis get an appropriate north/south suffix.

Puente Yayabo & Around LANDMARK

Looking like something out of an English country village, this quadruple-arched bridge is Sancti Spíritus' signature sight. Built by the Spanish in 1815, it carries traffic across the Río Yayabo and is now a national monument. For the best view (and a mirror-like reflection) hit the outdoor terrace at the Quinta Santa Elena. The **Teatro Principal**, alongside the bridge, dates from 1876, and the sun-bleached cobbled streets that lead uphill toward the city center are some of the settlement's oldest. The most sinuous is narrow **Calle Llano**, where old ladies peddle live chickens door to door, and feisty neighbors gossip noisily in front of their sky-blue or lemon-yellow houses.

Parque Serafín Sánchez SQUARE

While not Cuba's shadiest or most atmospheric square, pretty Serafín Sánchez is full of understated Sancti Spíritus elegance. Metal chairs laid out inside the pedestrianized central domain are usually commandeered by cigar-smoking grandpas and flirty young couples with their sights set on some ebullient local nightlife. There's plenty to whet the appetite on the square's south side, where the impressive Casa de la Cultura often exports its music onto the street. Next door the columned Hellenic beauty that today serves as the **Biblioteca Provincial Rubén Martínez Villena** was built originally in 1929 by the Progress Society. Sport and coins make improbable bedfellows in the obligatory **Museo Provincial** (Máximo Gómez Norte No 3; admission CUC$1; ⏲9am-6pm Mon-Thu, 9am-6pm & 8-10pm Sat, 8am-noon Sun), making it a must-see for numismatically minded baseball fanatics. Others can reserve 15 minutes for the full show.

The magnolia-colored grand dame on the square's northern side is the former **La Perla** hotel, which lay rotting and unused for years before being turned into a three-level government-run shopping center.

Fundación de la Naturaleza y El Hombre MUSEUM

(Cruz Pérez No 1; admission CUC$1; ⏲10am-5pm Mon-Fri, to noon Sat) Replicating its equally diminutive namesake in Miramar, Havana, this museum on Parque Maceo chronicles the 17,422km canoe odyssey from the Amazon to the Caribbean in 1987 led by Cuban writer and Renaissance man Antonio Nuñez Jiménez (1923–98). Some 432 explorers made the journey through 10 countries, from Ecuador to the Bahamas, in the twin dugout canoes *Simón Bolívar* and *Hatuey*. The latter measures over 13m and is the collection's central, prized piece. Beware of sporadic opening hours.

Museo de Arte Colonial MUSEUM

(Plácido Sur No 74; admission CUC$2; ⏲9am-5pm Tue-Sat, 8am-noon Sun) This small museum displays 19th-century furniture and decorations in an imposing 17th-century building that once belonged to the sugar-rich Iznaga family, who owned half of Trinidad's Valle de los Ingenios.

Iglesia Parroquial Mayor del Espíritu Santo CHURCH

(Agramonte Oeste No 58; ⏲9-11am & 2-5pm Tue-Sat) Overlooking Plaza Honorato is this verging-on-decrepit church. Originally constructed of wood in 1522 and rebuilt in stone in 1680, it's said to be the oldest church in Cuba still standing on its original foundations (although the clock seems to have given out in recent years). While the interior is crying out for some care and attention, locals are proud of this place. The best time to take a peek is during Sunday morning Mass. A small donation will go a long way.

Plaza Honorato SQUARE

Formerly known as Plaza de Jesús, this tiny square was where the Spanish authorities once conducted grisly public hangings. Later on, it hosted a produce market, and scruffy peso stalls still line the small connecting lane to the east. The north side of the square is now occupied by the boutique hotel, Hostal del Rijo.

Calle Independencia Sur STREET

The city's revived shopping street is traffic-free and lined with statues, sculptures and myriad curiosity shops. Check out the the opulent **Colonia Española Building**, once a whites-only gentlemen's club, now a mini–department store. The **Galería de Arte** (Céspedes Sur No 26; admission free; ⏲8am-noon & 2-5pm Tue-Sat, 8am-noon Sun), next to the *agropecuario* (vegetable market; enter via Independencia Sur), houses numerous works by local painter Oscar Fernández Morera (1890–1946).

Museo de Ciencias Naturales MUSEUM

(Máximo Gómez Sur No 2; admission CUC$1; ⏲8:30am-5pm Mon-Sat, to noon Sun) Not much of a natural history museum, this colonial house just off Parque Serafín Sánchez has a stuffed crocodile (which will scare the wits out of your three-year-old) and some shiny rock collections.

Museo Casa Natal de Serafín Sánchez MUSEUM

(Céspedes Norte No 112; admission CUC$0.50; ⏲8am-5pm) Serafín Sánchez was a local patriot who took part in both Wars of Independence and went down fighting in November 1896. This museum cataloguing his heroics deserves a cursory glance. Be prepared to be followed from room to room by the ever-vigilant staff.

Iglesia de Nuestra Señora de la Caridad CHURCH

(Céspedes Norte No 207) Across from the Fundación de la Naturaleza y El Hombre is this once-handsome building, the city's second church. Its internal arches are a favored nesting spot for Cuban sparrows, who seem unfazed by the church's shocking state of disrepair.

Sleeping

IN TOWN

Trinidad's Iberostar aside, Sancti Spíritus' hotels are better than those of its more famous neighbor. The city is blessed with two excellent boutique establishments, branded as Encanto hotels belonging to the Cubanacán chain. Both occupy attractive restored colonial buildings and are blissful nooks to spend a night or two.

Sancti Spíritus

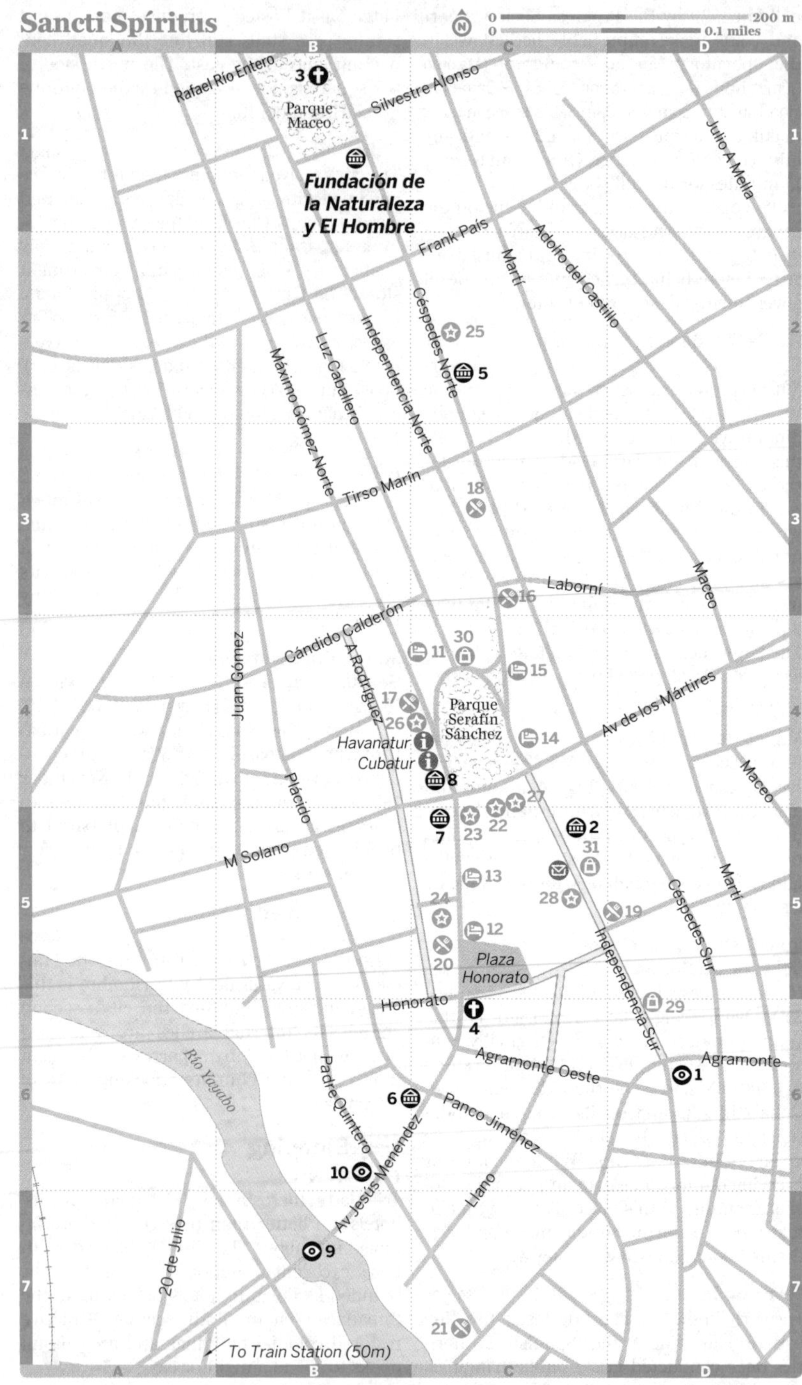

Sancti Spíritus

Top Sights

Fundación de la Naturaleza y El Hombre....B1

Sights

Biblioteca Provincial Rubén Martínez Villena....(see 8)
1 Colonia Española Building....D6
2 Galería de Arte....C5
3 Iglesia de Nuestra Señora de la Caridad....B1
4 Iglesia Parroquial Mayor del Espíritu Santo....C6
La Perla....(see 30)
5 Museo Casa Natal de Serafín Sánchez....C2
6 Museo de Arte Colonial....B6
7 Museo de Ciencias Naturales....C5
8 Museo Provincial....C4
9 Puente Yayabo....B7
10 Teatro Principal....B6

Sleeping

11 Estrella González Obregón....C4
12 Hostal del Rijo....C5
13 Hostal Paraíso....C5
14 Hotel Plaza....C4
15 'Los Richards' – Ricardo Rodríguez....C4

Eating

16 Cremería el Kikiri....C3
17 D'Prisa....B4
18 La Época....C3
Las Arcadas....(see 14)
19 Mercado Agropecuario....D5
20 Mesón de la Plaza....C5
21 Quinta Santa Elena....C7
Restaurante Hostal del Rijo....(see 12)

Entertainment

22 Cafe ARTex....C5
23 Casa de la Cultura....C5
24 Casa de la Trova Miguel Companioni....C5
25 Casa del Joven Creador....C2
26 Cine Conrado Benítez....C4
27 Cine Serafín Sánchez....C4
Teatro Principal....(see 10)
28 Uneac....C5

Shopping

Colonia....(see 1)
29 Galería la Arcada....D6
30 La Perla....C4
31 Librería Julio Antonio Mella....C5

TOP CHOICE **Hostal del Rijo** BOUTIQUE HOTEL $$
(32-85-88; Honorato No 12; s/d CUC$42/60;) Even committed casa particular fans will have trouble resisting this meticulously restored 1818 mansion situated on quiet (until the Casa de la Trova opens) Plaza Honorato. Sixteen huge, plush rooms – many with plaza-facing balconies – are equipped with everything a romance-seeking Cuba-phile could wish for, including satellite TV, complimentary shampoos and chunky colonial furnishings. Downstairs in the elegant courtyard restaurant you'll be served the kind of sumptuous, unhurried breakfast that'll have you lingering until 11am. Oh, what the hell, might as well stay another night.

Hotel Plaza BOUTIQUE HOTEL $$
(32-71-02; Independencia Norte No 1; s/d CUC$38/54;) The Rijo's sibling, the Plaza is a block north on Parque Serafín Sánchez. Spreading 28 rooms over two stories, the recently refurbished hotel has pulled itself up to boutique standard with fluffy bathrobes, chunky furnishings, a romantic patio bar and prime viewing windows overlooking the ever-busy square. It also has a *mirador* (lookout) on the roof and great service throughout. It once lived in the Rijo's shadow, but no longer!

'Los Richards' – Ricardo Rodríguez CASA PARTICULAR $
(32-30-29; Independencia Norte No 28 Altos; r CUC$25;) The small stairway off the main square belies the size of this place. The front room is enormous, dwarfing the two beds, rocking chairs, full bar area and fridge. There's a smaller room out back.

Hostal Paraíso CASA PARTICULAR $
(52-71-1257; Máximo Gómez Sur No 11 btwn Honorato & M Solano; r CUC$25;) Hang out amid the hanging plants with this new kid on the block. The house itself dates from 1838, and although the rooms are a little dark, the bathrooms are huge and the surrounding greenery is spirit-lifting.

WORTH A TRIP

EMBALSE ZAZA

Freshwater fishing is not a pastime traditionally associated with Cuba, where visiting fishers tend to sport beards and take to the high seas in pursuit of the Hemingway legend. But, evading standard tourist stereotypes, lake angling is still widely practiced in a handful of constructed reservoirs, including the country's largest, Embalse Zaza, 11km outside Sancti Spíritus.

Created in the early '70s by damming several local rivers, the Zaza covers an area of 113 sq km. Currently nearly 50% of the reservoir is given over to fishing, with abundant stocks of largemouth bass (weighing up to 8kg) providing rich pickings for anglers. Excursions are run out of the adjacent **Hotel Zaza** (☎32-85-12; s/d incl breakfast CUC$11/18; P❄≋), an ugly blemish on the landscape even by the cheap and cheerful standards of 1970s Soviet architectonics. Stay in Sancti Spíritus and get a taxi out. A fishing trip costs CUC$30 for four hours. There are also trips to the Río Agabama, situated on the way to Trinidad, starting at CUC$70.

Hostal los Pinos CASA PARTICULAR $
(☎32-93-14; Carretera Central Norte No 157 btwn Mirto Milián & Coronel Lagón; r CUC$20-25; ❄) Good for travelers in transit, this museum to art deco is on Carretera Central and has a garage, delicious dinners and two comfy rooms.

Estrella González Obregón CASA PARTICULAR $
(☎32-79-27; Maximo Gomez Norte No 26; r CUC$25) Two rooms with plenty of space and some cooking facilities make this place ideal for families. There's a roof terrace with good views of the Escambray Mountains.

NORTH OF TOWN

There are two very agreeable hotels along Carretera Central as you head north; either one is a good choice if the city center is full or you're merely passing through.

Villa los Laureles HOTEL $
(☎32-73-45; Carretera Central Km 383; s/d CUC$23/36; P❄≋) Not content to rest on them, Los Laureles lines its laurel trees up along a shady entrance drive that beckons visitors into a surprisingly classy Islazul out-of-towner. There's no dodgy Soviet architectonics here. In fact, even those with in-the-clouds expectations might fill out a favorable comments card here. Supplementing big, bright rooms with fridges, satellite TV and patio/balcony are an attractive pool, leafy flower-studded gardens and a colorful in-house cabaret, the Tropi, with a nightly show at 9pm.

Villa Rancho Hatuey HOTEL $
(☎32-83-15; Carretera Central Km 384; s/d CUC$26/42; P❄@≋) Here's the dilemma. Not 1km from Los Laureles' row of gnarly laurel trees lies another veritable Islazul gem, accessible from the southbound lane of Carretera Central. Probably the more peaceful of the two options, Rancho Hatuey spreads 76 rooms in two-story cabins across expansive landscaped grounds set back a good 500m from the road. While catching some rays around the swimming pool or grabbing a bite in the serviceable on-site restaurant, you'll see bus groups from Canada and Communist Party officials from Havana mingling in awkward juxtaposition.

Eating

You could burn vital calories searching for a square meal in Sancti Spíritus. Cut to the chase: aside from the casas particulares and hotels, there are just two places to seriously test your taste buds, the Mesón de la Plaza and the Quinta Santa Elena, both of which are operated by state-run restaurant group Palmares.

Mesón de la Plaza CARIBBEAN, SPANISH $$
(Máximo Gómez Sur No 34; ⊙noon-2:30pm & 6-10pm) The best food in town and the best location after the Quinta Santa Elena. Encased in a 19th-century mansion that once belonged to a rich Spanish tycoon, you can tuck in to classic Spanish staples such as *potaje de garbanzos* (chickpeas with pork) and some chewable beef while appetizing music drifts in from the Casa de la Trova next door.

Quinta Santa Elena CARIBBEAN $
(Padre Quintero No 60; dishes CUC$4-8; ⊙10am-midnight) 'Old clothes' is a name that has never really done justice to Cuba's famous shredded-beef dinner *(ropa vieja)*. There's certainly nothing old or clothes-like about the dish here, or the equally tasty shrimp in red sauce for that matter. While the Mesón has the edge on food, the Santa Elena wins the Oscar for location, as it's set on a charming riverside patio in front of the city's famous packhorse bridge.

Restaurante Hostal del Rijo INTERNATIONAL $$
(Honorato No 12) You could come here on a first date, so alluring is the quiet colonial ambience in this hotel's impressive central courtyard. Service is equally good, and there is a fine selection of desserts and coffee.

Cremería el Kikiri ICE-CREAM PARLOR $
(cnr Independencia Norte & Laborni) What, no Coppelia? Kikiri is Sancti Spíritus' long-standing provincial stand-in and is actually – ahem – better. Alternatively, hang around long enough in Parque Serafín Sánchez and a DIY ice-cream man will turn up with his ice-cream maker powered by a washing-machine motor.

Las Arcadas CARIBBEAN $
(Independencia Norte No 1) The refined colonial surroundings of the Hotel Plaza add extra flavor to the all-too-familiar *comida criolla* (Creole food).

D'Prisa FAST FOOD $
(Máximo Gómez Norte No 15) A park-side government-run staple that has pulled its socks up in recent years; it serves 'pizza' (note: inverted commas) and fried chicken et al, all in convertibles.

Self-Catering

Mercado Agropecuario MARKET $
(cnr Independencia Sur & Honorato) This centrally located *agropecuario* is situated just off the main shopping boulevard. Stick your head in and see how Cubans shop.

La Época SUPERMARKET $
(Independencia Norte No 50C) Good for groceries and assorted knickknacks.

☆ Entertainment

Sancti Spíritus has a wonderful evening ambience: cool, inclusive and unpretentious. You can sample it in any of the following places.

TOP CHOICE **Uneac** LIVE MUSIC
(Unión Nacional de Escritores y Artistas de Cuba, National Union of Cuban Writers & Artists; Independencia Sur No 10) There are friendly nods as you enter, handshakes offered by people you've never even met, and a starry-eyed crooner on stage blowing kisses to his girlfriend(s) in the audience. Uneac concerts always feel more like family gatherings than organized cultural events, and Sancti Spíritus' is one of the nicest 'families' you'll meet.

Casa de la Trova Miguel Companioni LIVE MUSIC
(Máximo Gómez Sur No 26) Another of Cuba's famous *trova* houses, this kicking folk-music venue in a colonial building off Plaza Honorato is on a par with anything in Trinidad. But here the crowds are 90% local and 10% tourist.

Café ARTex NIGHTCLUB
(M Solano; admission CUC$1; ⊙10pm-2am Tue-Sun) On an upper floor on Parque Serafín Sánchez, this place has more of a nightclub feel than the usual ARTex patio. It offers dancing, live music and karaoke nightly and a Sunday matinee at 2pm (admission CUC$3). Thursday is *reggaetón* (Cuban hip-hop) night, and the cafe also hosts comedy. Good groups to look out for in Sancti Spíritus are the Septeto Espirituanao and the Septeto de Son del Yayabo.

Casa del Joven Creador LIVE MUSIC
(Céspedes Norte No 118) Instead of hanging around on street corners with their hands in their pockets, Sancti Spíritus' youth head to this happening cultural venue near the Museo Casa Natal de Serafín Sánchez for rock and rap concerts.

FREE **Casa de la Cultura** CULTURAL CENTER
(☎32-37-72; M Solano No 11) Hosts numerous cultural events that, at weekends, spill into the street and render the pavement impassable.

Estadio José A Huelga SPORTS
(Circunvalación) From October to April, baseball games are held at this stadium, 1km north of the bus station. The provincial team Los Gallos (the Roosters) last tasted glory in 1979.

Teatro Principal THEATER
(☎232-5755; Av Jesús Menéndez No 102) This landmark architectural icon next to the Puente Yayabo has weekend matinees (at 10am) with kids' theater.

Cine Conrado Benítez CINEMA
(☎32-53-27; Máximo Gómez Norte No 13) Of the city's two main cinemas, this is your best bet for a decent movie.

Shopping

Anything you might need – from batteries to frying pans – is sold at stalls along the pedestrian street on Independencia Sur, which recently benefited from a handsome refurbishment.

Colonia ACCESSORIES
(Independencia Sur cnr Agramonte; ⏲9am-4pm) Mini-department store housed in one of the city's finest colonial buildings.

La Perla ACCESSORIES
(Parque Serafín Sánchez; ⏲9am-4pm) Three levels of austerity-busting shopping behind a beautifully restored colonial edifice on Parque Serafín Sánchez.

Galería la Arcada ART, CRAFTS
(Independencia Sur) This place has Cuban crafts and paintings.

Librería Julio Antonio Mella BOOKSTORE
(Independencia Sur No 29; ⏲8am-5pm Mon-Sat) Revolutionary reading material for erudite travelers in a store opposite the post office.

Information

Internet Access & Telephone

Etecsa Telepunto (Independencia Sur; internet access per hr CUC$6; ⏲8:30am-7:30pm) Two rarely busy computer terminals.

Media

Radio Sancti Spíritus CMHT Airing on 1200AM and 97.3FM.

Medical Services

Farmacia Especial (Independencia Norte No 123; ⏲24hr) Pharmacy on Parque Maceo.

Hospital Provincial Camilo Cienfuegos (☎32-40-17; Bartolomé Masó) Five hundred meters north of Plaza de la Revolución.

Policlínico los Olivos (☎32-63-62; Circunvalación Olivos No 1) Near the bus station. Will treat foreigners in an emergency.

Money

Banco Financiero Internacional (Independencia Sur No 2) On Parque Serafín Sánchez.

Cadeca (Independencia Sur No 31) Lose your youth in this line.

Post

Post office (⏲9am-6pm Mon-Sat) There are two branches: one at Independencia Sur No 8; the other at the Etecsa building, Bartolomé Masó No 167.

Travel Agencies

Cubatur (Máximo Gómez Norte No 7; ⏲9am-5pm Mon-Sat) On Parque Serafín Sánchez.

Havanatur (Máximo Gómez Norte) Office next door to Cubatur that opens somewhat sporadically.

Getting There & Away

Bus

The provincial **bus station** (Carretera Central) is 2km east of town. Punctual and air-conditioned **Víazul** (www.viazul.com) buses serve numerous destinations.

Five daily Santiago de Cuba departures (CUC$29, eight hours) also stop in Ciego de Ávila (CUC$6, 1¼ hours), Camagüey (CUC$10, three hours), Las Tunas (CUC$17, five hours 40 minutes) and Bayamo (CUC$21, seven hours). Four daily Havana (CUC$24, five hours) buses stop at Santa Clara (CUC$6, 1¼ hours) and Entronque de Jagüey (CUC$10, three hours). The link to Trinidad (CUC$6, one hour 20 minutes) leaves at a sleep-reducing 5:35am.

Train

There are two train stations serving Sancti Spíritus. For Havana (CUC$14, eight hours, 9pm alternate days) via Santa Clara (CUC$4, two hours), and to Cienfuegos (CUC$5.50, five hours, 4am Monday) use the main **train station** (Av Jesús Menéndez al final; ⏲ticket window 7am-2pm Mon-Sat), southwest of the Puente Yayabo, an easy 10-minute walk from the city center.

Points east are served out of Guayos, 15km north of Sancti Spíritus, including Holguín (CUC$14, 8½ hours, 9:30am), Santiago de Cuba (CUC$21, 10¼ hours, 8:45am) and Bayamo (CUC$13, 8¼ hours). If you're on the Havana–Santiago de Cuba cross-country express and going to Sancti Spíritus or Trinidad, get off at Guayos.

The ticket office at the Sancti Spíritus train station can sell you tickets for Guayos trains, but you must find your own way there (CUC$8 to CUC$10 in a taxi, but bargain hard).

Trucks & Taxis

Trucks to Trinidad, Jatibonico and elsewhere depart from the bus station. A state taxi to Trinidad will cost you around CUC$35.

Getting Around

Horse carts on Carretera Central, opposite the bus station, run to Parque Serafín Sánchez when full (1 peso). Bici-taxis gather at the corner of

Laborni and Céspedes Norte. There is a **Cubacar** (☎32-85-33) booth on the northeast corner of Parque Serafín Sánchez; prices for daily car hire start at around CUC$70. The **Servi-Cupet gas station** (Carretera Central) is 1.5km north of Villa los Laureles, on the Carretera Central toward Santa Clara. Parking in Parque Serafín Sánchez is relatively safe. Ask in hotels Rijo and Plaza, and they will often find a man to stand guard overnight for CUC$1.

Alturas de Banao

Still well off the antennae of most guidebooks, which push tourists toward Topes de Collantes, this ecological reserve, situated off the main road between Sancti Spíritus and Trinidad, hides a little-explored stash of mountains, waterfalls, forest and *mogotes* (steep limestone cliffs). The reserve's highest peak – part of the Guamuhaya mountain range – is 842m, while its foothills are replete with rivers, abundant plant life, including epiphyte cacti, and the ruins of a handful of pioneering 19th-century farmhouses. The park HQ is at Jarico just off the Sancti Spíritus–Trinidad road and incorporates a restaurant and visitors' center next to an old cock-fighting ring. From here the 5.4km **La Sabina trail** leads to an eponymous bio-station, where the recently constructed **La Sabina Chalet** (r CUC$56) offers overnight accommodation and food in four double rooms. **Ecotur** (☎54-74-19; www.ecoturcuba.co.cu) is the best local point of contact. It's best to check ahead regarding trail access and room availability.

Trinidad

POP 52,896

Trinidad is one-of-a-kind, a perfectly preserved Spanish colonial settlement where the clocks stopped ticking in 1850 and – bar the odd gaggle of tourists – have yet to restart. Built on huge sugar fortunes amassed in the adjacent Valle de Ingenios during the early 19th century, the riches of the town's pre–War of Independence heyday are still very much in evidence in illustrious colonial-style mansions bedecked with Italian frescoes, Wedgewood china, Spanish furniture and French chandeliers.

Declared a World Heritage Site by Unesco in 1988, Trinidad's secrets quickly became public property, and it wasn't long before busloads of visitors started arriving to sample the beauty of Cuba's oldest and most enchanting 'outdoor museum.' Yet tourism has done little to deaden Trinidad's gentle southern sheen. The town retains a quiet, almost soporific air in its rambling cobbled streets replete with leather-faced *guajiros* (country folk), snorting donkeys and melodic guitar-wielding troubadours.

Ringed by sparkling natural attractions, Trinidad is more than just a potential PhD thesis for history buffs. Twelve kilometers to the south lies platinum-blond Playa Ancón, the south coast's best beach, while looming 18km to the north the purple-hued shadows of the Sierra del Escambray (Escambray Mountains) offer a lush adventure playground.

With its Unesco price tag and a steady stream of overseas visitors, Trinidad, not surprisingly, has an above-average quota of prowling *jineteros* (tourist hustlers), though mostly they're more annoying than aggressive. If you get worn down by the constant unwanted attention, head for a friendly casa particular in the small town of La Boca, 5km to the south, and bike or hike back in for the daytime and evening attractions.

History

In 1514 pioneering conquistador Diego Velázquez de Cuéllar founded La Villa de la Santísima Trinidad on Cuba's south coast, the island's third settlement after Baracoa and Bayamo. Legend has it that erstwhile 'Apostle of the Indians' Fray Bartolomé de las Casas held Trinidad's first Mass under a calabash tree in present-day Plazuela Real del Jigúe. In 1518 Velázquez' former secretary, Hernán Cortés, passed through the town recruiting mercenaries for his all-conquering expedition to Mexico, and the settlement was all but emptied of its original inhabitants. Over the ensuing 60 years it was left to a smattering of the local Taíno people to keep the ailing economy alive through a mixture of farming, cattle-rearing and a little outside trade.

Reduced to a small rural backwater by the 17th century and cut off from the colonial authorities in Havana by dire communications, Trinidad became a haven for pirates and smugglers who controlled a lucrative illegal slave trade with British-controlled Jamaica.

Things began to change in the early 19th century when the town became the capital of the Departamento Central, and hundreds of French refugees fleeing a slave rebellion in Haiti arrived, setting up more than 50 small sugar mills in the nearby Valle de los Ingenios. Sugar soon replaced leather in

Trinidad

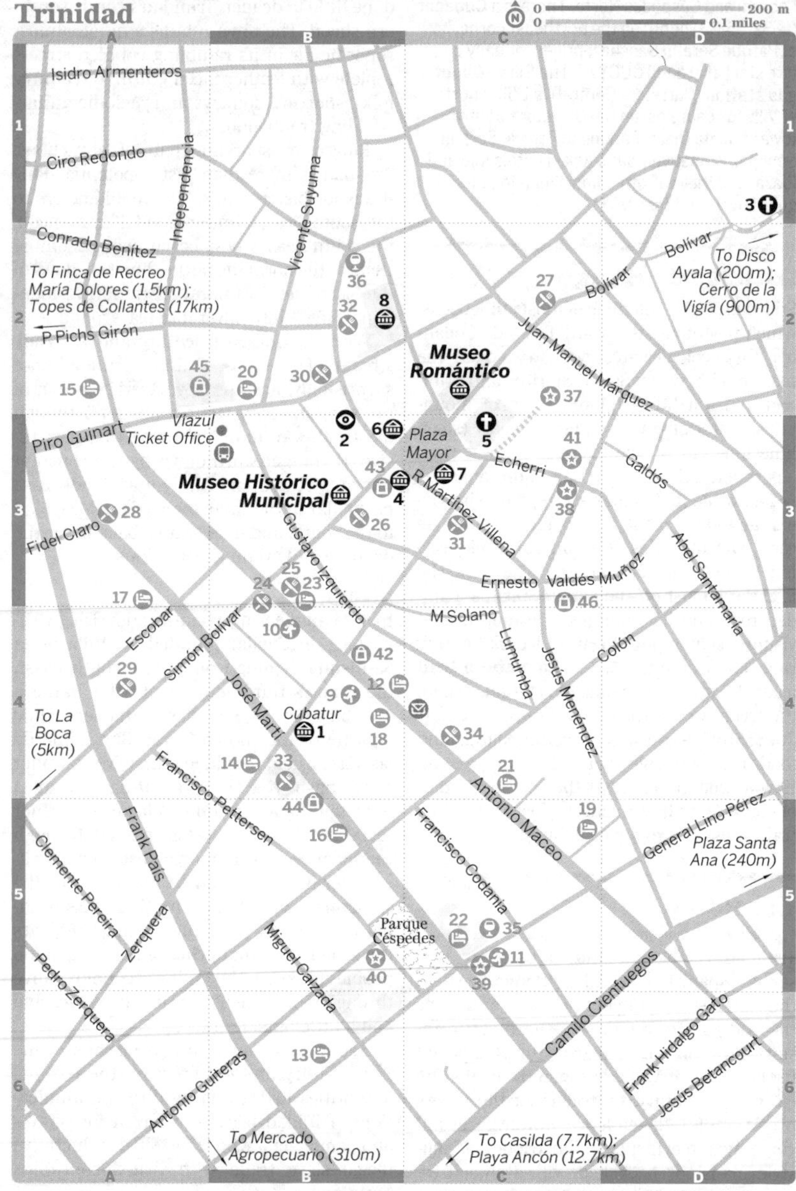

salted beef as the region's most important product. By the mid 19th century the area around Trinidad was producing a third of Cuba's sugar, generating enough wealth to finance the rich cluster of opulent buildings that characterize the town today.

The boom ended rather abruptly during the Independence Wars, when the surrounding sugar plantations were devastated by fire and fighting. The industry never fully recovered. By the late 19th century the focus of the sugar trade had shifted to

Trinidad

Top Sights

- Museo Histórico Municipal B3
- Museo Romántico C2

Sights

1. Casa de los Mártires de Trinidad B4
2. Casa Templo de Santería Yemayá B3
3. Ermita de Nuestra Señora de la Candelaria de la Popa D1
4. Galería de Arte B3
5. Iglesia Parroquial de la Santísima Trinidad C3
6. Museo de Arqueología Guamuhaya B3
7. Museo de Arquitectura Trinitaria C3
8. Museo Nacional de la Lucha Contra Bandidos B2

Activities, Courses & Tours

9 Cubatur B4
10 Las Ruinas del Teatro Brunet B4
Mireya Medina Rodríguez .... (see 23)
11 Paradiso C5

Sleeping

12 Casa Arandia B4
13 Casa de Araceli B6
14 Casa de la Amistad B4
15 Casa de Victor A2
16 Casa Gil Lemes B5
17 Casa Muñoz - Julio & Rosa A3
18 Casa Santana B4
19 Casa Smith C5
20 'Hospedaje Yolanda' - Yolanda María Alvarez B2
21 Hostal Colina C4
22 Iberostar Grand Hotel C5
23 Mireya Medina Rodríguez B3

Eating

24 Cafeteria Las Begonias B3
25 Cremería las Begonias B3
26 Mesón del Regidor B3
27 Paladar Estela C2
28 Paladar la Coruña A3
29 Paladar Sol y Son A4
30 Restaurante el Jigüe B2
31 Restaurante Plaza Mayor C3
32 Restorante Vía Reale B2
33 Tienda Universo B4
34 Trinidad Colonial C4

Drinking

35 Bar Daiquirí C5
36 Taberna la Canchánchara B2

Entertainment

37 Casa de la Música C2
38 Casa de la Trova C3
39 Casa Fischer C5
40 Cine Romelio Cornelio B5
Las Ruinas del Teatro Brunet .... (see 10)
41 Palenque de los Congos Reales C3

Shopping

Arts & Crafts Market .... (see 38)
42 Casa del Habano B4
43 Fondo Cubano de Bienes Culturales B3
44 Librería Ángel Guerra B5
45 Palacio de la Artesanía A2
46 Taller Instrumentos Musicales C3

Cienfuegos and Matanzas provinces, and Trinidad slipped into a somnolent and life-threatening economic coma. Trinidad's tourist renaissance began in the 1950s when President Batista passed a preservation law that recognized the town's historical value. In 1965 the town was declared a national monument, and in 1988 it became a Unesco World Heritage Site.

Sights

In Trinidad, all roads lead to **Plaza Mayor**, the town's remarkably peaceful main square, located at the heart of the *casco histórico* (historic city center) and ringed by a quartet of impressive buildings.

TOP CHOICE **Museo Histórico Municipal** MUSEUM

(Simón Bolívar No 423; admission CUC$2; ⏲9am-5pm Sat-Thu) For Trinidad's showpiece museum look no further than this grandiose structure just off Plaza Mayor, a mansion that belonged to the Borrell family from 1827 to 1830. Later the building passed to a German planter named Kanter or Cantero, and it's still called Casa Cantero. Reputedly Dr Justo Cantero acquired vast sugar estates by poisoning an old slave trader and marrying his widow, who also suffered an untimely death. Cantero's ill-gotten wealth is well displayed in the stylish neoclassical decoration of the rooms. The view of Trinidad from the top of the tower alone is worth the price of admission. Visit before 11am, when the tour buses start rolling in.

Iglesia Parroquial de la Santísima Trinidad CHURCH
(11am-12:30pm Mon-Sat) Despite its rather unremarkable outer facade, this church on the northeastern side of Plaza Mayor graces countless Trinidad postcard views. Rebuilt in 1892 on the site of an earlier church destroyed in a storm, the church mixes 20th-century touch-ups with artifacts from as far back as the 18th century, such as the venerated Christ of the True Cross (1713), which occupies the second altar from the front to the left. Your best chance of seeing it is during Mass at 8pm weekdays, 4pm Saturday, and 9am and 5pm Sunday.

Museo Romántico MUSEUM
(Echerri No 52; admission CUC$2; 9am-5pm Tue-Sun) Across Calle Simón Bolívar is the glittering Palacio Brunet. The ground floor was built in 1740, and the upstairs was added in 1808. In 1974 the mansion was converted into a museum with 19th-century furnishings, a fine collection of china and various other period pieces. Pushy museum staff may materialize out of the shadows for a tip. The shop adjacent has a good selection of photos and books in English.

Museo de Arquitectura Trinitaria MUSEUM
(Ripalda No 83; admission CUC$1; 9am-5pm Sat-Thu) Another public display of wealth sits on the southeastern side of Plaza Mayor in a museum showcasing upper-class domestic architecture of the 18th and 19th centuries. The museum is housed in buildings that were erected in 1738 and 1785 and joined in 1819. It was once the residence of the wealthy Iznaga family.

Museo de Arqueología Guamuhaya MUSEUM
(Simón Bolívar No 457; admission CUC$1; 9am-5pm Tue-Sat) On the northwestern side of Plaza Mayor is this odd mix of stuffed animals, native bones and vaguely incongruous 19th-century kitchen furniture. Don't make it your first priority.

FREE **Galería de Arte** ART GALLERY
(cnr Rubén Martínez Villena & Simón Bolívar; 9am-5pm) Admission is completely free at the 19th-century Palacio Ortiz, which today houses an art gallery on the southwestern side of Plaza Mayor. Worth a look for its quality local art, particularly the embroidery, pottery and jewelry. There's also a pleasant courtyard.

Casa Templo de Santería Yemayá MUSEUM, LANDMARK
(Rubén Martínez Villena No 59 btwn Simón Bolívar & Piro Guinart) No Santería museum can replicate the ethereal spiritual experience of Regla de Ocha (Cuba's main religion of African origin), though this house has a try. Containing a Santería altar to Yemayá, Goddess of the Sea, with myriad offerings of fruit, water and stones, the house is presided over by *santeros* (priests of the Afro-Cuban religion Santería), who'll emerge from the back patio and surprise you with some well-rehearsed tourist spiel. On the godddess's anniversary, March 19, ceremonies are performed day and night.

Museo Nacional de la Lucha Contra Bandidos MUSEUM
(Echerri No 59; admission CUC$1; 9am-5pm Tue-Sun) Perhaps the most recognizable building in Trinidad is the withered pastel-yellow bell tower of the former convent of San Francisco de Asís. Since 1986 the building has housed a museum. The displays are mostly photos, maps, weapons and other objects relating to the struggle against the various counterrevolutionary bands that took a leaf out of Fidel's book and operated illicitly out of the Sierra del Escambray between 1960 and 1965. The fuselage of a US U-2 spy plane shot down over Cuba is also on display. You can climb the tower for good views.

FREE **Casa de los Mártires de Trinidad** MUSEUM
(Zerquera No 254 btwn Antonio Maceo & José Martí; 9am-5pm) It's easy to miss this small museum dedicated to the 72 Trinidad residents who died in the struggle against Fulgencio Batista, the campaign against the counterrevolutionaries, and the little-mentioned war in Angola.

Iglesia de Santa Ana CHURCH
Grass grows around the domed bell tower and the arched doorways were bricked up long ago, but the shell of this ruined church (1812) defiantly remains. Looming like a time-worn ecclesiastical stencil, it looks ghostly after dark. Across the eponymous square, which delineates Trinidad's northeastern reaches, is a former Spanish prison (1844) that has been converted into the

Plaza Santa Ana (Camilo Cienfuegos; ⊙11am-10pm) tourist center. The complex includes an art gallery, handicraft market, ceramics shop, bar and restaurant.

FREE Taller Alfarero POTTERY
(Andrés Berro; ⊙8am-noon & 2-5pm Mon-Fri) Trinidad is known for its pottery. In this large factory, teams of workers make trademark Trinidad ceramics from local clay using a traditional potter's wheel. You can watch them at work and buy the finished product.

Activities

Ride a bike to one of Cuba's outstanding beaches, work up a sweat on a couple of DIY hikes, or get a different perspective astride a horse.

Playa Ancón CYCLING
(Map p287) The bicycle ride to Playa Ancón is a great outdoor adventure, and once there you can snorkel, catch some rays or use the swimming pool or ping-pong table. The best route by far is via the small seaside village of La Boca (18km one-way). See p285 for information about bicycle rental.

Cerro de la Vigía HIKING
For views and a workout, walk straight up the street between the Iglesia Parroquial and the Museo Romántico (Calle Simón Bolívar) to the destroyed 18th-century Ermita de Nuestra Señora de la Candelaria de la Popa, part of a former Spanish military hospital situated on a hill to the north of the town (use insect repellent). From here it's a 30-minute hike further up the hill to the radio transmitter atop 180m-high Cerro de la Vigía, which delivers broad vistas of Trinidad, Playa Ancón and the entire littoral.

Parque el Cubano HIKING
(Map p287; admission CUC$6.50) Another option is to hike west out of town on the (quiet) road to Cienfuegos. Pass the 'Welcome to Trinidad' sign and cross a bridge over the Río Guaurabo. A track on your left now leads back under the bridge and up a narrow, poorly paved road for 5km to Parque el Cubano. This pleasant spot within a protected park consists of a *ranchón*-style restaurant that specializes in *pez gato* (catfish), a fish farm and a 2km trail, known as **Huellas de la História**, to the refreshing **Javira Waterfall**. There are also stables and opportunities for horseback riding. If you hike to El Cubano from Trinidad, you'll clock up a total of approximately 16km. With a stop for lunch in the *ranchón*, it can make an excellent day trip. Alternatively, for CUC$15 you can organize a day excursion with Cubatur (p284) including motor transport.

Closer to town is the Finca Ma Dolores (Map p287; ☎99-64-81; Carretera de Cienfuegos Km 1.5), a rustic Cubanacán hotel that hosts sporadic *fiestas campesinas* (country fairs).

LOCAL KNOWLEDGE

JULIO MUÑOZ: PHOTOGRAPHER & CASA PARTICULAR OWNER, TRINIDAD

» **What makes Trinidad ideal for photography?** Its location on the side of a south-facing slope brings a fantastic soft light at sunset. Add in beautiful colonial architecture, photogenic people, and the long shadows in the morning and you've got a perfect setting for photography.

» **What's your favorite type of photography here?** Documentary photography of people going about their everyday lives.

» **How do you approach your photography in Trinidad?** You have to be quick and ready, and make the camera a part of your body. Position yourself as a spectator to a game of dominoes, a baseball match, or a religious festival, and wait for that split-second opportunity to freeze time and tell a story.

» **What are your other photography tips?** Be like a ghost with an eagle eye. Find a good background, choose your main characters, and then try to predict what is going to happen. It's your job to capture that brief moment of magic.

» **Do people in Trinidad mind being photographed?** Not if you smile at your subjects and ask questions – remember, the Cubans love to talk! Also, be quick and make people feel relaxed. If you're slow, people are more likely to get nervous.

Centro Ecuestre Diana HORSEBACK RIDING
(☎99-36-73; www.trinidadphoto.com) This new center is run out of a *finca* (farm) on the edge of town, but aspiring riders should enquire first with owner Julio at Casa Muñoz in the *casco histórico* (old town). The *finca* is also a rescue centre for maltreated and ill horses, and the owners promise good conditions and safety standards (helmets can be rented). Various horse-related activities are offered, including nature excursions, riding lessons, horse-whispering techniques and traditional *campesino* food. At the time of writing, owner Julio was also hoping to offer some form of cattle-herding activities. Prices are between CUC$15 and CUC$30, depending on the activity.

Courses

At **Las Ruinas del Teatro Brunet** (Map p276; Antonio Maceo No 461 btwn Simón Bolívar & Zerquera) you can take drumming lessons (9am to 11am Saturday) and dance lessons (1pm to 4pm Saturday). Dance lessons are also available with popular local teacher **Mireya Medina Rodríguez** (☎99-39-94; Antonio Maceo No 472 btwn Simon Bolivar & Zerquera), who teaches everything from *chachachá* to rumba in her front room. Another option is the travel agent **Paradiso** (paradisotr@sctd.artex.cu; Casa ARTex, General Lino Pérez No 306), which offers salsa lessons from CUC$5 for 90 minutes.

Paradiso has incorporated a number of interesting courses into its cultural program, including Cuban architecture (CUC$20), Afro-Cuban culture (CUC$30), *artes plásticas* (visual arts; CUC$30) and popular music (CUC$30). These courses last four hours and are taught by cultural specialists. The courses require a minimum number of six to 10 people, but you can always negotiate. At the same venue there are guitar lessons for CUC$5 an hour and courses in Spanish language/Cuban culture for CUC$8 an hour.

Tours

With its sketchy public transport and steep road gradients (making cycling arduous), it's easiest to visit Topes de Collantes (p289) via a day tour. A tour to Topes de Collantes by state taxi shouldn't cost more than CUC$25 including wait time; bargain hard. **Cubatur** (Antonio Maceo No 447; ⏲9am-8pm), just outside the *casco histórico*, organizes a variety of hiking and nature trips for between CUC$23 and CUC$43 per person.

Paradiso (paradisotr@sctd.artex.cu; Casa ARTex, General Lino Pérez No 306) offers the best-value day tour to the Valle de los Ingenios (CUC$9 per person), and an artist-studio tour in Trinidad (CUC$10 per person).

For diving, fishing, sailing and snorkeling tours, see Playa Ancón (p286); any of Trinidad's travel agencies (p284) can organize the same excursions.

Festivals & Events

Semana Santa is important in Trinidad, and on Good Friday thousands of people form a procession.

Sleeping

Trinidad has, at a guestimate, 400 casas particulares, meaning competition is hot. Arriving by bus or walking the streets with luggage, you'll be besieged by hustlers working for commissions, or by the casa owners themselves. With so many beautiful homes and hospitable families renting, there's no reason to be rushed. Take your time and shop around.

IN TOWN

TOP CHOICE **Casa Muñoz – Julio & Rosa** CASA PARTICULAR $
(☎99-36-73; www.trinidadphoto.com; José Martí No 401; r CUC$35; P❄) Julio is an accomplished published photographer (see p279) who runs workshops and courses out of his stunning colonial home (which has been featured in *National Geographic*). He's also a horse whisperer – his beautiful mare lives out back next to a slightly less attractive Russian Moskvich car. There are three huge rooms here, delicious food and highly professional service. Book early – it's insanely popular.

Iberostar Grand Hotel BOUTIQUE HOTEL $$$
(☎99-60-70; cnr José Martí & General Lino Pérez; s/d CUC$118/148; ❄@) Look out, Habaguanex! One of a trio of Spanish-run Iberostar's Cuban hotels, the five-star Grand oozes luxury the moment you arrive in its fern-filled, tile-embellished lobby. Maintaining 36 classy rooms in a remodeled 19th-century building, the Grand shies away from the standard all-inclusive tourist formula, preferring to press privacy, refinement and an appreciation of history (you are, after all, in Trinidad). The service is as sleek as the fittings are flash.

'Hospedaje Yolanda' – Yolanda María Alvarez CASA PARTICULAR $
(☎99-30-51; yolimar56@yahoo.com; Piro Guinart No 227; r CUC$25-30) This isn't a casa; it's a palace! There are eight rooms for starters, though only two can be rented at one time. Dating from the 1700s, its dazzling interior makes the Museo Romántico look like a jumble sale. There are Italian tiles, French frescoes, a rare Mexican spiral staircase, fabulous terrace views; the list goes on...

Mireya Medina Rodríguez CASA PARTICULAR $
(☎99-39-94; miretrini@yahoo.es; Antonio Maceo No 472 btwn Simón Bolívar & Zerquera; r CUC$20-25; ❄) Right in the center of things. Mireya is a popular dance teacher who rents out one room with private bathroom in her well-kept colonial house. Expect excellent dinners, hospitable service and plenty of salsa in the front room.

Casa de Victor CASA PARTICULAR $
(☎99-64-44; Maceo btwn Piro Guinart & P Pichs Girón; r CUC$20-25; ❄) If Casa Muñoz is full, you can stay with other members of the family here at Victor's place just down the road, where two self-contained upstairs rooms share a couple of spacious *salas,* a balcony overlooking the street, and a fine *terraza* decorated rather ingeniously with recycled ceramic pots.

Motel las Cuevas HOTEL $$
(☎99-61-33; s/d incl breakfast CUC$60/86; P❄≋) Perched on a hill above town, Las Cuevas is more hotel than motel, with bus tours being the main drive-by clientele. While the setting is lush, the rooms – which are arranged in scattered two-storied units – are a little less memorable, as is the breakfast. Value is added with a swimming pool, well-maintained gardens, panoramic views and the murky Cueva la Maravillosa, accessible down a stairway, where you'll see a huge tree growing out of a cavern (entry CUC$1).

Hostal Colina CASA PARTICULAR $
(☎99-23-19; Antonio Maceo No 374 btwn General Lino Pérez & Colón; r CUC$25-35; ❄) Another place that leaves you struggling for superlatives. Although the house dates from the 1830s, it's got a definitive modern touch, giving you the feeling of being in a plush Mexican hacienda. Two pastel-yellow rooms give out onto a patio where you can sit at the plush wooden bar and catch mangos and avocados as they fall from the trees.

TALL STORIES

Trinidad's *jineteros* (hustlers) are becoming increasingly sophisticated and meddlesome for locals and tourists alike. Touts on bikes besiege travelers fresh off the buses, or divert rental cars entering the city, with tall stories about how the traveler's chosen casa particular is full or out of business. They have even been known to assume the identities of real casa owners in order to lure travelers elsewhere. If you have pre-booked your casa particular, make sure you agree to meet the casa owner *inside* the house in question. If you haven't, feel free to stroll the streets unmolested and make your own choice. Arriving with a *jinetero* in tow will not only add at least CUC$5 to your room rate, but will also exacerbate a problem that has left many of Trinidad's honest casa owners unfairly out of pocket.

Casa Gil Lemes CASA PARTICULAR $
(☎99-31-42; José Martí No 263 btwn Colón & Zerquera; r CUC$25) More museum-standard digs on Calle Martí, the street that hides a thousand priceless antiques. There's too much to take in on first viewing. Cast an eye over the noble arches in the front room and the religious statues, and save some breath (yes, you'll gasp) for the patio and fountain, a unique array of pots and sea serpents. Get in early for this one – there's only one room.

Casa de la Amistad HOSTEL $
(Zerquera btwn José Martí & Francisco Pettersen; r CUC$25) This hostel, run by the Instituto Cubano de la Amistad, is popular among visitors who are politically sympathetic to Cuba. It has six clean and well-equipped rooms with brand-new showers and TVs, plus a small eating area and patio out the back. It's a decent budget option in the center of town.

Casa de Araceli CASA PARTICULAR $
(☎99-35-58; General Lino Pérez No 207 btwn Frank País & Miguel Calzada; r CUC$20-25; ❄) Had enough of the colonial splendor? Head away from the tourist frenzy to General Lino Pérez, where Araceli rents two upstairs rooms with a private entrance and a very quiet flower-bedecked terrace.

Casa Smith CASA PARTICULAR $
(☎99-40-60; www.casasmith.trinidadhostales.com; Callejón Smith No 3 btwn Antonio Maceo &

Av Jesús Menéndez; r CUC$20-25; ❄) With two independent rooms off a back patio this place is clean and relaxing with welcoming hosts. Check out the website for photos and more details.

Casa Santana CASA PARTICULAR $
(☎99-43-72; Antonio Maceo No 425 btwn Zerquera & Colón; r CUC$20-25; ❄) Another venerable colonial institution on arterial Calle Maceo. It's run by a dentist and his wife, with all the Trinidadian trimmings (huge rooms, weighty antiques, attractive patio).

Casa Arandia CASA PARTICULAR $
(☎99-32-40; Antonio Maceo No 438 btwn Colón & Zerquera; r CUC$20-25; ❄) Another Trinidad dream home. It comes with a loft room, a terrace and views.

OUTSIDE TOWN

Finca Ma Dolores HOTEL $$
(Map p287; ☎99-64-10; Carretera de Cienfuegos Km 1.5; s/d CUC$41/58; P❄≋) Trinidad goes rustic with the out-of-town Finca Ma Dolores, situated 1.5km west on the road to Cienfuegos and Topes de Collantes. It's equipped with hotel-style rooms and cabins – the latter are the better option (try for one with a porch overlooking the Río Guaurabo). On nights when groups are present, there's a *fiesta campesina* (country fair) with country-style Cuban folk dancing at 9:30pm (free/CUC$5 for guests/nonguests, including one drink). It also has a swimming pool, a *ranchón* restaurant, and boat and horseback-riding tours. One kilometer west of the Finca Ma Dolores is a **monument to Alberto Delgado**, a teacher murdered by counterrevolutionaries.

✖ Eating

Housed in an attractive array of colonial mansions, Trinidad's government restaurants are full of the standard state-run foibles: average food, bored staff, and menus where most of the dishes have gone AWOL. These places are OK for an unfancy lunch, but for a filling dinner you might want to stick to the home cooking in your casa particular.

Paladar Sol y Son PALADAR $$
(☎99-29-26; Simón Bolívar No 283 btwn Frank País & José Martí; mains CUC$8-10; ⏲noon-2pm & 7:30-11pm) All the ingredients of a fine Trinidad evening – think antiques, an elegant patio and the dulcet strains of an eloquent *trovador* – plus good food. Even the waiting room (yes, it gets busy) is a veritable museum piece. The house special is roast chicken, and it's worth the wait. English is spoken.

Paladar Estela PALADAR $$
(☎99-43-29; Simón Bolívar No 557; ⏲2-11:30pm) You can choose the dining room or pretty rear garden at this popular place located above the Plaza Mayor (the owner also rents rooms). *Cordero* (lamb) served shredded is the house specialty, and the portions are large.

Restaurante Plaza Mayor CARIBBEAN $$
(cnr Rubén Martínez Villena & Zerquera; dishes from CUC$4; ⏲11am-10pm) The best government-run bet courtesy of its on-off lunchtime buffet, which, for around CUC$10, ought to fill you up until dinnertime. Nighttime offerings aren't bad either if you stick to the chicken and beef, though the atmosphere can be a little flat.

Trinidad Colonial CARIBBEAN $
(Antonio Maceo No 402; ⏲11:30am-10pm) Here you'll dine on good portions of Cuban cuisine in the elegant 19th-century Casa Bidegaray. The service is a bit frosty, but the meals are reasonable, with smoked pork topping out at CUC$6. The store attached has a good selection of books.

Mesón del Regidor FAST FOOD $
(Simón Bolívar No 424; ⏲10am-10pm) A cafe-cum-restaurant with a friendly ambience and a revolving lineup of local musicians, including the town's best *trovador,* Israel Moreno, who'll drop by during the day and serenade you with a song over grilled cheese sandwiches and *café con leche* (coffee with milk). Savor the surprise.

Cafetería las Begonias CAFE $
(cnr Antonio Maceo & Simón Bolívar; ⏲9am-10pm; @) The daytime nexus for Trinidad's transient backpacker crowd, meaning it's a good source of local information and the best place in town to meet other travelers over sandwiches, espresso and ice cream. It has a bar behind a partition wall, cleanish toilets in a rear courtyard, and five or six cheap – but always crowded – internet terminals.

Paladar la Coruña PALADAR $$
(José Martí No 428; ⏲11am-11pm) A battling third in Trinidad's paladar scene, Coruña's eager-to-please and friendly staff offer chicken, pork and occasional fish in a house they've worked hard to renovate.

Restaurante Vía Reale ITALIAN $
(Rubén Martínez Villena No 74 btwn Piro Guinart & Pablo Pichs Girón; lunch CUC$4; ⌚noon-4pm;) Break the chicken-and-pork grind at this Italian place, which has good pizza and spaghetti lunches. This is a viable vegetarian option.

Restaurante el Jigüe CARIBBEAN $$
(cnr Rubén Martínez Villena & Piro Guinart; ⌚11am-10pm) Stunning setting with less-than-stunning food. Bank on the house specialty, the aptly named *pollo al Jigüe;* it's baked at least, offering savory flavors distinct from the usual *frito* (fried).

Cremería las Begonias ICE-CREAM PARLOR $
(Antonio Maceo) Just across the street from the eponymous cafetería is another cafe that doubles as a Cubatur office and offers the best ice cream in town.

Self-Catering

Mercado Agropecuario MARKET $
(cnr Pedro Zerquera & Manuel Fajardo; ⌚8am-6pm Mon-Sat, to noon Sun) Trinidad's *agropecuario* (vegetable market) isn't Covent Garden, but you should still be able to get basic fruits and vegetables.

Tienda Universo SUPERMARKET $
(José Martí) This shop, near Zerquera in the Galería Comercial Universo, is Trinidad's best (and most expensive) grocery store. Head here for yogurt, nuts and those lifesaving biscuits.

Drinking

Bar Daiquirí BAR
(General Lino Pérez No 313; ⌚24hr) Presumably Papa Hemingway never dropped by this cozy joint named after the drink he so famously popularized, because the prices are extremely reasonable. Shoehorned into lively Lino Pérez, this is where locals and backpackers warm up on their way to an all-night salsa binge. There are snacks, if you've got the stomach.

Taberna la Canchánchara BAR
(cnr Rubén Martínez Villena & Ciro Redondo) This place is famous for its eponymous house cocktail made from rum, honey, lemon and water. Local musicians regularly drop by for off-the-cuff jam sessions, and it's not unusual for the Canchánchara-inebriated crowd to break into spontaneous dancing.

Entertainment

Get ready for the best nightlife you'll find outside Havana.

TOP CHOICE **Palenque de los Congos Reales** RUMBA
(cnr Echerri & Av Jesús Menéndez; admission free) A must for rumba fans, this open patio on Trinidad's music alley has an eclectic menu incorporating salsa, *son* (Cuban popular music) and *trova* (traditional poetic singing). The highlight, however, is the 10pm rumba drums with soulful African rhythms and energetic fire-eating dancers.

FREE **Casa de la Música** NIGHTCLUB
One of Trinidad's and Cuba's classic venues, this casa is an alfresco affair that congregates on the sweeping staircase beside the Iglesia Parroquial off Plaza Mayor. A good mix of tourists and locals take in the 10pm salsa show here. Alternatively, full-on salsa concerts are held in the casa's rear courtyard (also accessible from Juan Manuel Márquez; cover CUC$2).

Casa Fischer CULTURAL CENTER
(General Lino Pérez No 312 btwn José Martí & Francisco Codania; admission CUC$1) This is the local ARTex patio, which cranks up at 10pm with a salsa orchestra (on Tuesday, Wednesday, Thursday, Saturday and Sunday) or a folklore show (Friday). If you're early, kill time at the art gallery (free) and chat to the staff at the on-site Paradiso office about salsa lessons and other courses (p280).

Casa de la Trova LIVE MUSIC
(Echerri No 29; admission CUC$1; ⌚9pm-2am) Trinidad's spirited casa retains its earthy essence despite the high package-tourist-to-Cuban ratio. Local musicians to look out for here are Semillas del Son, Santa Palabra and the town's best *trovador,* Israel Moreno.

Disco Ayala NIGHTCLUB
(admission CUC$10; ⌚10pm-3am) It might not be the first time you've gone jiving in a cave, but this surreal place up by the Ermita Popa church beats all others for atmosphere. While it's mainly a place to go dancing in the semi-darkness after as many mojitos as you care to sink, this disco also puts on a decent cabaret show. To get there follow Calle Simón Bolívar from Plaza Mayor up to the Ermita de Nuestra Señora de la Candelaria de la Popa. The disco is 100m further along on your left.

Las Ruinas del Teatro Brunet LIVE MUSIC
(Antonio Maceo No 461 btwn Simón Bolívar & Zerquera; admission CUC$1) This jazzed-up ruin has an athletic Afro-Cuban show on its pleasant patio at 9:30pm nightly.

Las Ruinas de Sagarte LIVE MUSIC
(Av Jesús Menéndez; admission free; ⌚24hr) Another ruin (Trinidad's full of them) with a good house band and a high-energy, low-pressure dance scene.

Cine Romelio Cornelio CINEMA
(Parque Céspedes; ⌚8pm Tue-Sun) This cinema, on the southwestern side of Parque Céspedes, shows films nightly.

Estadio Rolando Rodríguez SPORTS
(Eliope Paz; ⌚Oct-Apr) This stadium, at the southeastern end of Frank País, hosts baseball games.

Shopping

You can shop until you drop in Trinidad, at least at the open-air markets, which are set up all over town. You can see local painters at work – and buy their paintings too – at various points along Calles Francisco Toro, Valdés and Muñoz.

Arts & Crafts Market CRAFTS, SOUVENIRS
(Av Jesús Menéndez) This excellent open-air market situated in front of the Casa de la Trova is the place to buy souvenirs, especially textiles and crochet work. Note: should you see any black coral or turtle-shell items, don't buy them. They're made from endangered species and are forbidden entry into many countries.

Fondo Cubano de Bienes Culturales CRAFTS, SOUVENIRS
(Simón Bolívar No 418; ⌚9am-5pm Mon-Fri, to 3pm Sat & Sun) Just down from Plaza Mayor, this store has a good selection of Cuban handicrafts.

Palacio de la Artesanía CRAFTS
(Piro Guinart No 221) This store, located opposite the bus station, also sells handicrafts.

Taller Instrumentos Musicales MUSICAL INSTRUMENTS
(cnr Av Jesús Menéndez & Valdés Muñoz) Musical instruments are made here and sold in the adjacent shop.

Librería Ángel Guerra BOOKS
(José Martí No 273 btwn Colón & Zerquera; ⌚8am-3pm Mon-Sat) Restock your traveling library.

Casa del Habano CIGARS
(Maceo cnr Zerquera; ⌚9am-7pm) Dodge the street hustlers and satisfy your alcoholic (rum) and tobacco vices here.

Information

Internet Access

Café Internet las Begonias (Antonio Maceo No 473; internet access per half hr CUC$3; ⌚9am-9pm) On the corner of Simón Bolívar. Crowded.

Etecsa Telepunto (cnr General Lino Pérez & Francisco Pettersen; internet access per hr CUC$6; ⌚8:30am-7:30pm) Freshly refurbished Telepunto with modern, if slow, computer terminals. Less crowded.

Media

Radio Trinidad Broadcasts over 1200AM.

Medical Services

General Hospital (☎99-32-01; Antonio Maceo No 6) Southeast of the city center.

Servimed Clínica Internacional Cubanacán (☎99-62-40; General Lino Pérez No 103; ⌚24hr) On the corner of Anastasio Cárdenas. There is an on-site pharmacy selling products in convertibles.

Money

Banco de Crédito y Comercio (José Martí No 264)

Cadeca (José Martí No 164) Between Parque Céspedes and Camilo Cienfuegos.

Post

Post office (Antonio Maceo No 418) Between Colón and Zerquera.

Travel Agencies

Cubatur (Antonio Maceo No 447; ⌚9am-8pm) On the corner of Zerquera. Good for general tourist information, plus hotel bookings, car rentals, excursions etc. State taxis congregate outside.

Infotur (Plaza Santa Ana, Camilo Cienfuegos)

Paradiso (General Lino Pérez No 306) Cultural and general tours in English, Spanish and French.

Dangers & Annoyances

Thefts, though still relatively uncommon, are on the rise in Trinidad. Incidents usually occur late at night and the victims are, more often than not, inebriated. To avoid being a potential target for thieves, make sure that you are alert and on your guard, particularly when returning to your hotel or casa after a night out on the drink. A little bit of caution can go a long way.

VÍAZUL BUS DEPARTURES FROM TRINIDAD

DESTINATION	COST (CUC$)	DURATION	DEPARTURE
Cienfuegos	6	1½hr	7:30am, 8:40am, 3pm
Havana	25	6hr 20min	7:30am, 8:40am
Santa Clara	8	3hr	3pm
Santiago de Cuba	33	12hr	8am
Varadero	20	6hr	3pm

Getting There & Away

Air

Alberto Delgado Airport is 1km south of Trinidad, off the road to Casilda. Only Aerotaxi charters fly here.

Bus

The **bus station** (Piro Guinart No 224) runs provincial buses to Sancti Spíritus and Cienfuegos, though most foreigners use the more reliable Víazul service. Tickets are sold at a small window marked Taquilla Campo near the station entrance. Check the blackboard for the current schedule.

The **Víazul ticket office** (⏲8-11:30am & 1-5pm) is further back in the station. This office is well organized and you can usually book tickets a couple of days in advance. See the boxed text for details regarding the tickets, prices and destination.

The Varadero departures can deposit you in Jagüey Grande (CUC$15, three hours) with stops on request in Jovellanos, Colesio and Cárdenas. The Santiago de Cuba departure goes through Sancti Spíritus (CUC$6, 1½ hours), Ciego de Ávila (CUC$9, two hours 40 minutes), Camagüey (CUC$15, five hours 20 minutes), Las Tunas (CUC$22, 7½ hours), Holguín (CUC$26, eight hours) and Bayamo (CUC$26, 10 hours). There are stops on request in Jatibonico, Florida, Sibanicú, Guáimaro and Palma Soriano.

Train

Train transport out of Trinidad is awful even by Cuban standards. The town hasn't been connected to the main rail network since a hurricane in the early 1990s, meaning the only functioning line runs up the Valle de Ingenios, stopping in Iznaga (35 minutes) and terminating at Meyer (one hour 10 minutes). There are supposedly four trains a day, the most reliable leaving Trinidad at 9am and 1pm, but they often don't run; always check ahead at the **terminal** (Lino Pérez final) in a pink house across the train tracks on the western side of the station.

For information on train tours, see p288.

Getting Around

Bicycle

You can hire gearless bikes at **Las Ruinas del Teatro Brunet** (Antonio Maceo No 461 btwn Simón Bolívar & Zerquera; per day CUC$3) or you can ask around at your casa particular. These are fine for getting to Playa Ancón, but nowhere near adequate for the steep climbs up to Topes de Collantes.

Car & Taxi

The rental agencies at the Playa Ancón hotels rent mopeds (CUC$27 per day), or you can try the **Las Ruinas del Teatro Brunet** (Antonio Maceo No 461 btwn Simón Bolívar & Zerquera).

Cubacar (cnr Antonio Maceo & Zerquera) rents cars for approximately CUC$70 per day. They also have an office in Hotel Club Amigo Ancón.

The **Servi-Cupet gas station** (⏲24hr), 500m south of town on the road to Casilda, has an El Rápido snack bar attached. The Oro Negro gas station is at the entrance to Trinidad from Sancti Spíritus, 1km east of Plaza Santa Ana.

Guarded parking is available in certain areas around the *casco histórico*. Ask at your hotel or casa particular, where staff can arrange it.

Trinidad has Havana-style coco-taxis; they cost approximately CUC$5 to Playa Ancón. A car costs from CUC$6 to CUC$8 both ways. State-owned taxis tend to congregate outside the Cubatur office on Antonio Maceo. A cab to Sancti Spíritus should cost approximately CUC$35.

Horse Carts

Horse carts (costing 2 pesos) leave for Casilda from Paseo Agramonte at the southern end of town.

Trinidad Tour Bus

Trinidad now has a handy hop-on/hop-off **minibus** (all-day ticket CUC$5), similar to Havana's and Viñales', linking its outlying sights. It plies a route from outside the Cubatur office on Antonio Maceo to Finca Ma Dolores, Playa la Boca, Bar las Caletas, and the three Playa Ancón hotels. It runs approximately five times a day in both directions starting at 9am and terminating at 6pm.

Playa Ancón & Around

Playa Ancón, a precious ribbon of white beach on Sancti Spíritus' iridescent Caribbean shoreline, is usually touted – with good reason – to be the finest arc of sand on Cuba's south coast.

While not comparable in all-round quality to the north-coast giants of Varadero, Cayo Coco and Guardalavaca, Ancón has one important trump card: Trinidad, Latin America's sparkling colonial diamond, shimmering just 12km to the north. You can get here in less than 15 minutes in a car or in a leisurely 40 on a bike. Alternatively, Ancón has three all-inclusive hotels and a well-equipped marina that runs catamaran trips to a couple of nearby coral keys.

Beach bums who want to be near the water, but don't have the money or inclination to stay at one of the resorts, might consider a private home in the seaside village of La Boca.

There's no doubting Ancón's beauty, but what gushing tourist brochures fail to mention are the sand fleas: they're famously ferocious at sunrise and sunset. Be warned.

The old fishing port of **Casilda**, 6km due south of Trinidad, is a friendly village with one paved road that was devastated during the 2005 hurricane season. On August 17 the **Fiesta de Santa Elena** engulfs little Casilda, with feasting, competitions, horse races and loads of rum. The road from Ancón to Casilda crosses a tidal flat, meaning abundant birdlife is visible in the early morning.

Activities

From Hotel Club Amigo Ancón, it's 18km to Trinidad via Casilda, or 16km on the much nicer coastal road via La Boca. The hotel pool is also open to nonguests and you can usually nab the ping-pong table undetected.

Marina Trinidad FISHING, DIVING
(☎99-62-05; www.nauticamarlin.com) This is a few hundred meters north of Hotel Club Amigo Ancón. Eight hours of deep-sea fishing, including transport, gear and guide, costs CUC$400 per boat (maximum four people), or CUC$300 for four hours of troll fishing. Fly-fishing is also possible around the rich mangrove forests of Península de Ancón (CUC$250 for six hours, maximum two people).

Diving with the **Cayo Blanco International Dive Center**, located at the marina, costs CUC$35 a dive and CUC$320 for an open-water course. **Cayo Blanco**, a reef islet 25km southeast of Playa Ancón, has 22 marked scuba sites where you'll see black coral and bountiful marine life. The marina also runs a seven-hour snorkeling-and-beach tour to Cayo Blanco for CUC$45 per person with lunch. There are similar trips to the equally pristine **Cayo Macho**.

Sunset Catamaran Cruise BOAT TRIPS
(cruise with/without dinner CUC$35/20) Romantic types might want to check out this cruise, which has been enthusiastically recommended by readers. There is a minimum of eight passengers. Inquire at the Marina Trinidad or ask at the Cubatur office in Trinidad.

Windward Islands Cruising Company BOAT TRIPS
(www.caribbean-adventure.com) This company charters crewed and bareboat monohulls and catamarans out of the Marina Trinidad to the Jardines de la Reina (p307). You can sail with or without guides, on a partial package or an all-inclusive tour. Interested parties should inquire using contact details on the website.

Sleeping

LA BOCA

The small village of La Boca, a few clicks up the coast from Ancón, has about a dozen lovely casas.

'Villa Sonia' – Sonia Santos Barrera CASA PARTICULAR $
(☎99-29-23; Av del Mar No 11, La Boca; r CUC$25-30; P❄) If you need an excuse to stay in La Boca, here it is. A beautiful house with a wraparound porch all to yourself, complete with polished-wood dining area, private kitchen, hammocks, rocking chairs and a thatched gazebo. Situated right opposite the (rocky) beach.

'Villa Río Mar' – Nestor Manresa CASA PARTICULAR $
(☎99-31-08; San José No 65, La Boca; r with shared bathroom CUC$20-25; P❄) There are further treats at Río Mar, where two rooms give out onto a lovely tiled veranda. If it's full, there's more next door.

PENÍNSULA DE ANCÓN

Ancón's three hotels offer all-inclusive rates.

Hotel Club Amigo Costasur RESORT $$
(☎99-61-74; all-incl s/d CUC$64/92; P❄≋) Playa Ancón's oldest and humblest resort, this hotel is at the base of the peninsula,

Trinidad Area

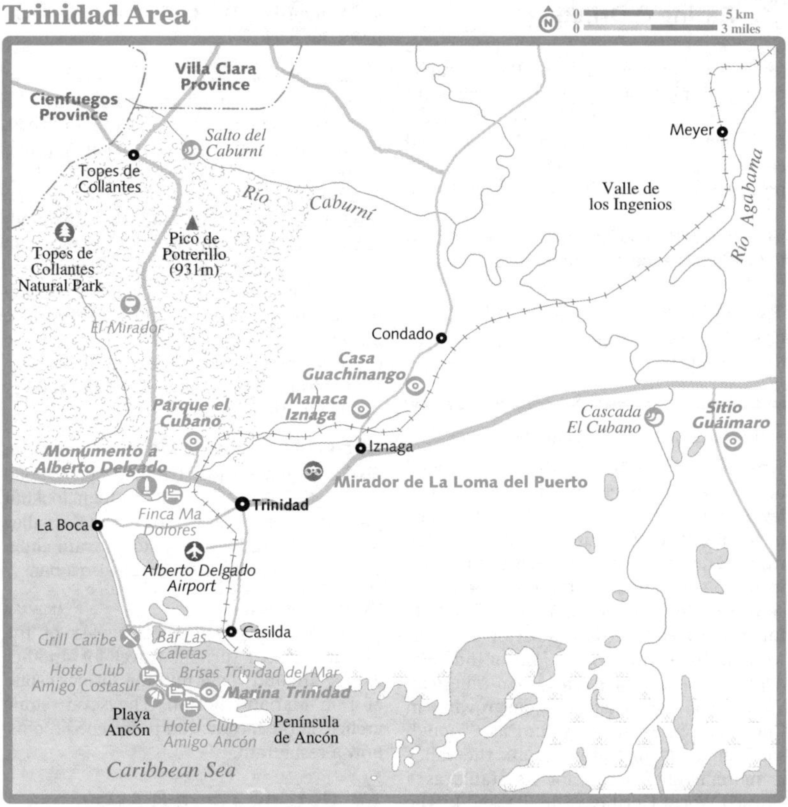

9km from Casilda. For about CUC$10 more you can upgrade to a superior room, which gives you better location and views (but not decor unfortunately). There are also 20 rooms in duplex bungalows that are better still. From here you can scuba dive and ride horses. The hotel faces a rocky shore, but a white, sandy beach is just to the right. Swimming is difficult on the shallow reef. This place is popular with Canadian package tourists.

Hotel Club Amigo Ancón RESORT **$$$**
(☎99-61-23, 99-61-27; all-incl s/d CUC$73/104; P❄@≋) Built during Cuba's 30-year flirtation with Soviet architectonics, the Ancón wouldn't win any beauty contests. Indeed, this steamship-shaped seven-story concrete pile looks more than a little incongruous next to the natural beauty of Ancón beach. But if it's location you're after (especially given its proximity to the historic delights of Trinidad), this deal could cut ice. Even better, you're just a short walk from Marina Trinidad, where you can fish, learn to scuba dive or enjoy a sunset cruise. Additionally, nonguests can use the facilities, which is exceptional for a resort.

Brisas Trinidad del Mar RESORT **$$$**
(☎99-65-00; all-incl s/d CUC$101/134; P❄@≋) Although it's a kitschy attempt to re-create Trinidad in an all-inclusive resort environment, Brisas wins kudos for rejecting the monolithic architecture of Hotel Club Amigo Ancón in favor of low-rise colonial-style villas. But after barely half a decade in operation, the quality of this place has begun to suffer from poor maintenance and decidedly iffy service. Though the swath of beach is stunning and the massage, sauna, gym and tennis courts handy for the sports-minded, you might be better off saving a few dollars and opting for one of the Club Amigos.

Eating & Drinking

Grill Caribe CARIBBEAN $$

(24hr) Other than the hotel restaurants, there's this place on a quiet beach 2km north of Club Amigo Costasur. It specializes in seafood, such as fish and shrimp or lobster, and charges a pretty price. Strict vegetarians will be disappointed here. It's a great sunset spot.

Bar las Caletas, at the junction of the road to Casilda, is a local drinking place.

Getting There & Away

Bike, bus, coco-taxi or taxi – take your pick. See p285 for details.

Valle de los Ingenios

Trinidad's immense wealth was garnered not in the town itself, but in a verdant valley 8km to the east. The Valle de los Ingenios (or Valle de San Luis) still contains the ruins of dozens of 19th-century sugar mills, including warehouses, milling machinery, slave quarters, manor houses and a fully functioning steam train. Most of the mills were destroyed during the War of Independence and the Spanish-Cuban-American War, when the focus of sugar-growing in Cuba shifted west to Matanzas. Though some sugar is still grown here, the valley is more famous today for its status as a Unesco World Heritage Site. Backed by the shadowy sentinels of the Sierra del Escambray, the pastoral fields, royal palms and peeling colonial ruins are timelessly beautiful. A horseback-riding tour from Trinidad should take in most (if not all) of the following sites.

Sights

Manaca Iznaga MUSEUM, LANDMARK

(admission CUC$1;) The valley's main focal point is 16km northeast of Trinidad. Founded in 1750, the estate was purchased in 1795 by the dastardly Pedro Iznaga, who became one of the wealthiest men in Cuba through the unscrupulous business of slave trafficking. The 44m-high tower next to the hacienda was used to watch the slaves, and the bell in front of the house served to summon them. Today you can climb to the top of the tower for pretty views, followed by a reasonable lunch (from noon to 2:30pm) in the restaurant-bar in Iznaga's former colonial mansion. Don't miss the huge sugar press out back.

Casa Guachinango LANDMARK, RESTAURANT

(9am-5pm) Three kilometers beyond the Manaca Iznaga, on the valley's inland road, is an old hacienda built by Don Mariano Borrell toward the end of the 18th century. The building now houses a restaurant. The Río Ay is just below, and the surrounding landscape is truly wonderful. To get to Casa Guachinango, take the paved road to the right, just beyond the second bridge you pass as you come from Manaca Iznaga. The Meyer train stops right beside the house every morning, and you can walk back to Iznaga from Guachinango along the railway line in less than an hour.

Mirador de la Loma del Puerto VIEWPOINT

Six kilometers east of Trinidad on the road to Sancti Spíritus, this 192m-high lookout provides the best eagle-eye view of the valley with – if you're lucky – a steam train chugging through its midst. There's also a bar.

Sitio Guáimaro LANDMARK

(7am-7pm) Seven kilometers east of the Manaca Iznaga turnoff, travel for another 2km south and you'll find the former estate of Don Mariano Borrell. The seven stone arches on the facade lead to frescoed rooms, now a restaurant.

Getting There & Away

There are two train options for getting to and from Valle de los Ingenios – both are equally unreliable. The tourist steam train goes at the speed of Thomas the Tank Engine, but it's a sublime journey when it's running through an impossibly green valley full of munching cows and slender bridges. The train is pulled by the indomitable and classic engine No 52204, built by the Baldwin Locomotive Company of Philadelphia in August 1919. Organized as an excursion (CUC$10), passengers pay for their own lunch separately at the Manaca Iznaga, where they can visit the famous bell tower. **Cubatur** (Antonio Maceo No 447; 9am-8pm) in Trinidad will know when the next tourist-train trip is scheduled and if it's working. Tour desks at the Ancón hotels sell the same train tour for CUC$17, including bus transfers to Trinidad. For details of the daily local train from Trinidad, see p285.

Horseback riding tours can be arranged at the travel agencies in Trinidad or Playa Ancón. Alternatively, you can contract a horse and guide privately in Trinidad for CUC$15 per six hours.

Topes de Collantes

ELEV 771M

The crenellated, 90km-long Sierra del Escambray is Cuba's second-largest mountain range, and it straddles the borders of three provinces: Sancti Spíritus, Cienfuegos and Villa Clara. Though not particularly high (the loftiest point, Pico de San Juan, measures just 1156m), the mountain slopes are rich in flora and surprisingly isolated. In late 1958 Che Guevara set up camp in these hills on his way to Santa Clara and, less than three years later, CIA-sponsored counter-revolutionary groups operated their own cat-and-mouse guerrilla campaign from the same vantage point.

Though not strictly a national park, Topes is, nonetheless, a heavily protected area. The umbrella park, comprising 200 sq km, overlays four smaller parks – Parque Altiplano, Parque Codina, Parque Guanayara and Parque el Cubano (see p279) – while a fifth enclave, El Nicho (p245) in Cienfuegos province, is also administered by park authority Gaviota.

The park takes its name from its largest settlement, an ugly health resort founded in 1937 by dictator Fulgencio Batista to placate his sick wife, for whom he built a quaint rural cottage. The architecture went downhill thereafter with the construction of an architecturally grotesque tuberculosis sanatorium (now the Kurhotel) begun in the late '30s but not opened until 1954.

Topes de Collantes has three hotels open to foreigners, plus excellent guided and unguided hiking. Its jungle-like forests harboring vines, lichens, mosses, ferns and eye-catching epiphytes are akin to a giant outdoor biology classroom.

The **Carpeta Central information office** (8am-5pm), near the sundial at the entrance to the hotel complexes, is the best place to procure maps, guides and trail info.

Sights

Museo de Arte Cubano Contemporáneo MUSEUM

(admission CUC$3) Believe it or not, Topes de Collantes' monstrous sanitarium once harbored a treasure trove of Cuban art, boasting works by Cuban masters such as Tomás Sánchez and Rubén Torres Llorca. Raiding the old collection in 2008 inspired provincial officials to open this infinitely more attractive museum, which displays over 70 works in six *salas* (rooms) spread over three floors.

Casa Museo del Café CAFE, MUSEUM

(7am-7pm) Coffee has been grown in these mountains for over two centuries, and in this small rustic cafe you can fill in the gaps on its boom-bust history while sipping the aromatic local brew (called Cristal Mountain). Just up the road there is the **Jardín de Variedades de Café**, a short hike around 25 different varieties of coffee plant.

Plaza de las Memorias MUSEUM

(8am-5pm) Topes' newest museum is this quaint little display housed in three small wooden abodes just down from the Casa Museo del Café. It tells the history of the settlement and its resident hotels.

Activities

Topes is the only place in Cuba where you can participate in the burgeoning sport of **canyoning**, but there are limitations and you'd be wise to do your homework first. The up-and-coming scene focuses on four main rivers, the Calburni, Vegas Grandes, Cabagan and Gruta Nengoa, where canyoners travel spectacularly downstream equipped with ropes, wetsuits, helmets and harnesses. The highlight of the trip is a 200m series of vertical cascades over Salto Vegas Grandes. One experienced Canadian outfit offering excursions is **Canyoning Quebec** (www.canyoning-quebec.com), which runs eight-day trips into the Sierra del Escambray.

There are currently no organized tours in-country and no equipment available for hire. At the time of writing there was at least one Gaviota parks guide who was a qualified canyon guide. Ask at the Carpeta Central information office (p289) for more up-to-date information.

TOP CHOICE **Salto del Caburní** HIKE

(entry CUC$6.50) The Blue Riband hike, and the one most easily accessed on foot from the hotels, is to this 62m waterfall that cascades over rocks into cool swimming holes before plunging into a chasm where macho locals dare each other to jump. At the height of the dry season (March to May) you may be disappointed by these falls. The entry fee is collected at the toll gate to Villa Caburní, just down the hill from the Kurhotel near the Carpeta Central (it's a long approach on foot). Allow an hour down and an hour and a half back up for this 5km (round trip) hike. Some slopes are steep and can be slippery after rain.

Sendero los Helechos HIKE
A 1km trail billed rather ambitiously as an eco-walk, it's basically just a shortcut between the Kurhotel and the Hotel los Helechos. Look out for snow-white mariposas and multiple species of fern along the route.

Sendero Jardín del Gigante HIKE
(entry CUC$7) Parque la Represa on the Río Vega Grande, just downhill from La Batata trail entry, contains 300 species of trees and ferns, including the largest *caoba* (mahogany) tree in Cuba. You can take it all in on this 1km trail. The small restaurant at the entrance to the garden is in a villa built by Fulgencio Batista's wife, whose love for the area inspired her husband to build the Topes resort.

Sendero la Batata HIKE
(entry CUC$3) This 6km out-and-back trail to a large cave containing an underground river starts at a parking sign just downhill from Casa Museo del Café. When you reach another highway, go around the right side of the concrete embankment and down the hill. Keep straight or right after this point (avoid trails to the left). Allow an hour each way. It's possible to swim in the cave's pools.

Vegas Grandes HIKE
(entry CUC$5) The Vegas Grandes trail begins at the apartment blocks known as Reparto el Chorrito on the southern side of Topes de Collantes, near the entrance to the resort as you arrive from Trinidad. Allow a bit less than an hour each way to cover the 2km to the waterfall. It's possible to continue to the Salto del Caburní, though consider hiring a guide.

Hacienda Codina HIKING
(entry CUC$5) The hacienda is another possible destination. The 3.5km jeep track begins on a hilltop 2.5km down the road toward Cienfuegos and Manicaragua, 1km before the point at which these roads divide. There's a shorter trail to the hacienda from below Hotel los Helechos that links for part of the way with La Batata, but you'll need a guide to use it. At the hacienda itself is the 1.2km circular **Sendero de Alfombra Mágica** through orchid and bamboo gardens and past the Cueva del Altar. Also here are mud baths, a restaurant and a scenic viewpoint.

Sendero 'Centinelas del Río Melodioso' HIKE
(entry CUC$7) The least accessible but by far the most rewarding hike from Topes de Collantes is the 2.5km (5km return) hike in the Parque Guanayara, situated 15km from the Carpeta Central along a series of rough and heavily rutted tracks. For logistical reasons this excursion is best organized with a guide from the Carpeta, or as part of an organized tour from Trinidad with Cubatur (CUC$43 with lunch). The trail itself begins in cool, moist coffee plantations and descends steeply to **El Rocio** waterfall, where you can strip off and have a bracing shower. Following the course of the Río Melodioso (Melodic River), you pass another inviting waterfall and swimming pool before emerging into the salubrious gardens of the riverside **Casa la Gallega**, a traditional rural hacienda where a light lunch can be organized and camping is sometimes permitted in the lush grounds.

Sleeping & Eating

Hotel los Helechos HOTEL $
(☎54-02-31; s/d CUC$34/44; P ❄ ≋) For years the Achilles heel of the Gaviota chain, Los Helechos has recently undergone extensive refurbishments to pull it out of its 1970s stupor. Never 100% at home in its verdant natural surroundings, the clumsy chocolate-box building with its wicker furnishings and holiday-camp-style villas still looks a bit awkward. Not helping matters is the unattractive indoor pool, poky steam baths (if they're working), journeyman restaurant and kitschy local disco (in a natural park of all places!). The saving grace is the restaurant's delicious homebaked bread – surely the best in Cuba.

Villa Caburní CABINS $
(☎54-01-80; s/d CUC$40/50; ❄ P) This place is a veritable rural gem that offers, in a small park next to the Kurhotel, one- or two-story Swiss-style chalets with kitchenettes and private bathrooms.

Kurhotel Escambray HOTEL $
(☎54-02-31; s/d CUC$40/50) Doing a good impersonation of the mental institution in *One Flew Over the Cuckoo's Nest,* this eight-story architectural monster dreamt up by Batista in the 1930s would be an eyesore anywhere, let alone in a jaw-droppingly beautiful natural park. Judging by the grotesque Stalinist design of the exterior, the wily Cuban dictator must have sensed that the Russians were already on the way. Conceived originally as

WORTH A TRIP

NORTH COAST NIRVANA

Northern Sancti Spíritus province is one of Cuba's most heavily protected areas. It's dominated by the 313-sq-km **Buenavista Unesco Biosphere Reserve** and also boasts a Ramsar Convention Site (important wetlands area).

The nucleus of this reserve is the rarely mentioned (in tourist literature) **Parque Nacional Caguanes**, made up of the sinuous Caguanes Peninsula, the Guayabera swamps and 10 tiny islets known collectively as Cayos de Piedra.

The park is unique for its unusual karst formations; there are over 75 caves here and a pristine ecosystem that guards manatees, flamingos and the world's only freshwater cave sponge.

Indigenous people once frequented this area; so far 263 pictographs have been discovered in 40 different archaeological sites. In the late 19th and early 20th centuries hunters and charcoal burners made sporadic incursions, but they showed little long-term interest, and these days the human population is minimal.

Strict conservation measures mean public access is limited, but not impossible. There is a basic visito' center and eco-station on the coast due north of Yaguajay, but rather than just turn up, your best bet is to check details first at the Villa San José del Lago (p292).

The one advertised excursion is Las Maravillas que Atesora Caguanes, which incorporates a path to the Humboldt and Los Chivos caves and a boat trip around the Cayos de Piedra.

Refreshingly, the park has logged some landmark successes in environmental regeneration in recent years. Pollution in the Bahía de Buenavista bay from inefficient sugar mills had driven numerous bird species away from Caguanes by the late 1990s, but the closure of the mills in 2002, coupled with sustained environmental efforts on the part of park authorities, has seen many species start to return.

a sanitarium, the complex still serves as a therapeutic treatment center; you can book in for a session if you're up to donning the obligatory tracksuit. The rest of the building acts as a very spooky-looking hotel.

Restaurante Mi Retiro CARIBBEAN $$
(Carretera de Trinidad) Situated 3km back down the road to Trinidad, Restaurante Mi Retiro does fair-to-middling *comida criolla* to the sound of the occasional traveling minstrel.

Three other eating options exist on the trails: the **Hacienda Codina**, **Restaurante la Represa** and **Casa la Gallega** (in Parque Guanayara). **El Mirador** (Carretera de Trinidad) is a simple bar with a stunning view halfway up the ascent road from Trinidad.

Getting There & Away

Without a car, it's very difficult to get here and harder still to get around to the various trailheads. Your best bet is a taxi (CUC$25 return with a two- to three-hour wait), an excursion from Trinidad (p280) or a hire car.

The road between Trinidad and Topes de Collantes is paved, but it's very steep. When wet, it becomes slippery and should be driven with caution. There's also a spectacular 44km road that continues right over the mountains from Topes de Collantes to Manicaragua via Jibacoa (occasionally closed, so check in Trinidad before setting out). It's also possible to drive to and from Cienfuegos via San Blas on a partly paved, partly gravel road (4WD only).

Northern Sancti Spíritus

For every 1000 tourists that visit Trinidad, a small handful gets to see the province's narrow northern corridor, which runs between Remedios, in Villa Clara, and Morón, in Ciego de Ávila. For the minority who do pass through, there's a trio of worthwhile stop-offs plus a modest Islazul hotel.

Sights & Activities

TOP CHOICE **Museo Nacional Camilo Cienfuegos** MUSEUM
(admission CUC$1; 8am-4pm Tue-Sat, 9am-1pm Sun) This excellent museum at Yaguajay, 36km southeast of Caibarién, was opened in 1989 and is eerily reminiscent of the Che Guevara monument in Santa Clara. Camilo fought a crucial battle in this town on the eve

of the Revolution's triumph, taking control of a local military barracks (now the Hospital Docente General opposite the museum). The museum is directly below a modernist plaza embellished with a 5m-high statue of *El Señor de la Vanguardia* (The Man at the Vanguard). It contains an interesting display of Cienfuegos' life intermingled with facts and mementos from the revolutionary struggle. A replica of the small tank 'Dragon I,' converted from a tractor for use in the battle, stands in front of the hospital.

Jobo Rosado NATURE RESERVE

This region, protected as an area of 'managed resources', is still little-explored by most travelers, although organized groups are increasingly being let in. Measuring just over 40 sq km, it includes the **Sierra de Jatibonico**, a range of hills that runs across the entire north of the province and acts as a kind of buffer zone for the heavily protected Bahía de Buenavista. As in the Sierra Maestra, history is intertwined with the ecology here: General Máximo Gomez battled through these hills during the Spanish-Cuban-American War and in 1958 Camilo Cienfuegos' rebel army (column No 2) pitched their final command post here. An imaginative monument by sculptor José Delarra marks the spot.

Guided hikes can be organized either through Ecotur (p292) or at Villa San José del Lago. Highlights include a three-hour excursion along the **Río Jatibonico**, the 1km **La Solapa de Genaro** hike through tropical savannah to the ruins of a slave wall, and the 800m **Cueva de Valdés** walk through semideciduous woodland to the cave.

Sleeping

Villa San José del Lago HOTEL $

(☎55-61-08; Antonio Guiteras, Mayajigua; s/d CUC$14/22; P❄≋) This novel spa, once popular with vacationing Americans, is situated just outside Mayajigua in northern Sancti Spíritus province. The tiny rooms set in a variety of two-story villas nestle beside a small palm-fringed lake (with pedal boats and resident flamingos). The complex is famous for its thermal waters, which were first used by injured slaves in the 19th century but are now mainly the preserve of holidaying Cubans. The 67 rooms are no-frills, but the setting, wedged between the Sierra de Jatibonico and Parque Nacional Caguanes, is magnificent and makes a good base for some of Cuba's lesser-known excursions. There's a restaurant and snack bar on-site.

Information

Ecotur (☎54-74-19; Carretera Yaguajay Km 1.5) The best information portal for the region, located just south of Yaguajay on the road to Meneses.

Ciego de Ávila Province

☎033 / POP 422,576

Includes »

Best Places to Eat

» Ranchón Playa Pilar (p308)

» La Atarraya (p302)

» Don Ávila (p297)

» Restaurante Maité la Qbana (p300)

Best Places to Stay

» Meliá Cayo Coco (p305)

» Alojamiento Vista al Parque (p300)

» Alojamiento Maité (p300)

» Iberostar Daiquirí (p307)

Why Go?

For centuries Ciego de Ávila was little more than an overnight stop on Cuba's arterial east–west highway. Then came Cuba's ambitious post–Special Period tourist project and the resort development of Cayo Coco and Cayo Guillermo, the bright tropical pearls that had once seduced Hemingway, laced with glorious beaches and bedizened with nearly a dozen exclusive tourist resorts. Within 10 years, the boring former drive-by had become a potentially exciting drive-*in*.

Chopped off the western flank of Camagüey province in 1975, Ciego de Ávila has – in reality – been harboring intriguing secrets for over a century. Various non-Spanish immigrants first arrived here in the 19th century from Haiti, Jamaica, the Dominican Republic and Barbados, bringing with them myriad cultural quirks, including cricket in Baraguá, voodoo in Venezuela, country dancing in Majagua and explosive fireworks in Chambas. Thanks to their traditions and cultural ambiguities, they have made Ciego one of the most offbeat provinces in the nation.

When to Go

The weather is pretty constant in Ciego de Ávila. Take to the field on August 1st in Baraguá, where people celebrate Slave Emancipation Day with music, dancing and a game of cricket. In September there's Morón's Aquatic Carnival, which kicks off in the channel leading to the Laguna de Leche. Finally in November the citizens of Majagua dance in the streets during the Fiesta de los Bandas Rojo y Azul.

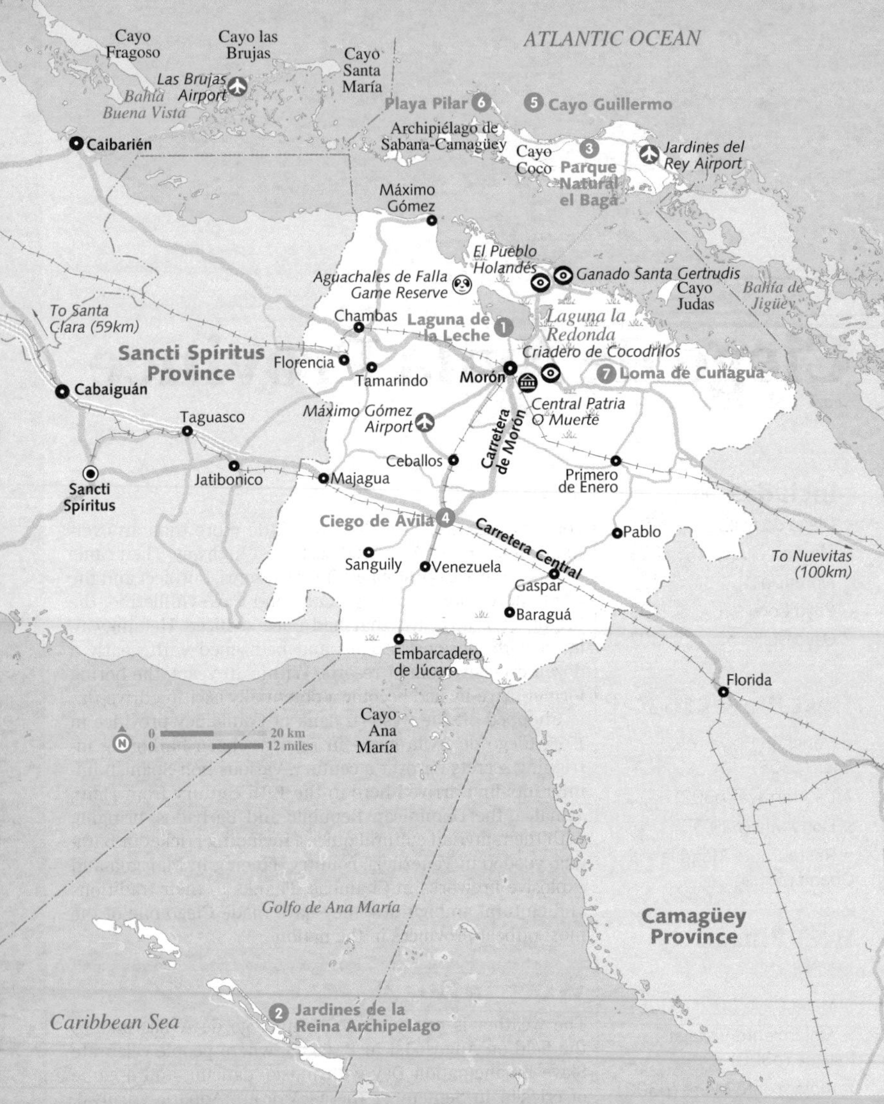

Ciego de Ávila Province Highlights

1. Eat fresh fish for ridiculously cheap prices at the **Laguna de la Leche** (p305)
2. Dive from a liveaboard in the almost-virgin waters of the secluded **Jardines de la Reina archipelago** (p307)
3. See how an old airport has been made into a successful nature reserve at **Parque Natural el Bagá** (p303) on Cayo Coco
4. Browse through the best municipal museum in Cuba, **Museo Provincial Simón Reyes** (p295) in Ciego de Ávila
5. Follow in the wake of Papa Hemingway while deep-sea fishing off **Cayo Guillermo** (p307)
6. Dig your toes in the sand at the beach paradise of **Playa Pilar** (p306)
7. Escape the resorts and immerse yourself in the rustic simplicity of the **Loma de Cunagua** (p302)

History

The area now known as Ciego de Ávila province was first prospected in 1513 by Spanish adventurer Pánfilo de Narváez, who set out to explore the expansive forests and plains of the north coast, then presided over by a local Taíno chief called Ornofay. Integrating itself into the new Spanish colony of Cuba in the early 1500s, the province got its present name from a local merchant, Jacomé de Ávila, who was granted an *encomienda* (indigenous workforce) in San Antonio de la Palma in 1538. A small *ciego* (clearing) on Ávila's estate was put aside as a resting place for tired travelers heading east or west, and it quickly became a burgeoning settlement.

Throughout the 16th and 17th centuries the northern keys provided a valuable refuge for buccaneering pirates fresh from their lucrative raids on cities such as Havana and Puerto Príncipe. Two hundred years later a buccaneer of a different kind arrived, in the shape of American writer Ernest Hemingway, who played his own game of cat-and-mouse tracking German submarines in the waters off Cayo Guillermo.

During the wars of independence in the latter half of the 19th century, the area was infamous for its 67km-long Morón–Júcaro defensive line, better known to historians as La Trocha. Characterized by its sturdy military installations and manned by a force of up to 20,000 men, the defense system was built up by the ruling Spanish administrators in the 1870s and was designed to stop the marauding Mambís (19th-century rebels) from forging a passage west.

Ciego de Ávila

POP 104,850

A small city of shady colonnaded shopfronts, Ciego de Ávila is the most modern of Cuba's provincial capitals, founded in 1840. Growing up originally in the 1860s and '70s as a military town behind the defensive Morón–Júcaro (Trocha) line, it later became an important processing center for the region's lucrative sugarcane and pineapple crops (the pineapple is the city mascot). Although a minor-league attraction compared to Trinidad and Camagüey, Ciego's inhabitants are proud of their modest city (which they refer to affectionately as 'the city of porches') and their understated enthusiasm is infectious.

Famous *avileñas* include Cuban pop-art exponent Raúl Martínez and local socialite Ángela Hernández Viuda de Jiménez, a rich widow who helped finance many of the city's early-20th-century neoclassical buildings, including the 500-seat Teatro Principal.

Sights

Manageable and friendly, Ciego de Ávila engenders a leisurely pace. The city has worked hard to make its relatively low-key history appear interesting and relevant and deserves at least an afternoon of your time!

TOP CHOICE Museo Provincial Simón Reyes MUSEUM

(cnr Honorato del Castillo & Máximo Gómez; admission CUC$1; 8am-10pm) Quite possibly the best-presented municipal museum in Cuba, this mustard-yellow building with a typical *avileña* porch is one convertible well spent. Fascinating exhibits include a scale model of La Trocha (p303), detailed information on Afro-Cuban culture and religion, and explanations on the province's rich collection of traditional festivals. Afterwards it's worth wandering down to the **Plano-Mural de Ciego de Ávila** (cnr Marcial Gómez & Joaquín de Agüero), where a bronze map of the city in the late 19th century marks the site of its founding in 1840.

Parque Martí SQUARE

All Ciego roads lead to this textbook colonial park laid out in 1877 in honor of the then king of Spain, Alfonso XII, but renamed in the early 20th century for the newly martyred Cuban national hero, José Martí. The inevitable white monument of the apostle was raised in 1925. It is overlooked by the 1911 **Ayuntamiento** (City Hall; no visitors), now the provincial government headquarters; the 1947 vintage **Iglesia Católico** (Independencia btwn Marcial Gómez & Honorato del Castillo), emblazoned with the city's patron saint, San Eugenio de la Palma; and – one block away – the grand **Teatro Principal** (cnr Joaquín Agüero & Honorato del Castillo), built in 1927 with the help of local financier Angela Jiménez.

Museo de Artes Decorativas MUSEUM

(cnr Independencia & Marcial Gómez; admission CUC$1; 8am-5pm Mon & Tue, 8am-10pm Wed-Sat, 8am-noon & 6-10pm Sun) This thoughtful collection contains quirky items from a bygone age, such as a working Victrola (Benny Moré serenades your visit), antique pocket watches

Ciego de Ávila

and ornate canopy beds with mother-of-pearl inlays. A CUC$1 tip gets you a typically enthusiastic local guide (in English or Spanish).

Centro Raúl Martínez Galería de Arte Provincial ART GALLERY
(Independencia No 65 btwn Honorato del Castillo & Antonio Maceo; ⌚8am-noon & 1-5pm Mon & Wed, 1-9pm Thu & Fri, 2-10pm Sat, 8am-noon Sun) Duck under the signature Ciego porches along Calle Independencia to reach this gallery where works by Cuba's king of pop art are on permanent display, along with many new works by other local artists.

Fábrica de Tabacos el Sucro CIGAR FACTORY
(cnr Libertad & Antonio Maceo) The cigar factory right in the center of town is a post-revolution addition to the local economy. Tours are normally group-only. Ask at the Havanatur office (p299) and you may be able to tag along.

Parque de la Ciudad PARK
The once scrubby wasteland between Hotel Ciego de Ávila and the rest of the city on the northwestern edge of town has recently been spruced up to pass as a proper park surrounding the artificial Lago la Turbina. Paths have been marked out, *ranchón*-style eating shelters constructed, kids' playgrounds erected and a couple of old steam trains dusted off in memory of Ciego's transport history. The result is another pleasant reflection of the city's blushing civic pride.

El Boulevard STREET
Ciego's newest feature is the three-block stretch of Calle Independencia between Parque Martí and Calle Agramonte that has been pedestrianized and beautified with streetlights, benches, outdoor art and green areas. Come and view Cuba's confusing dual economy working at full throttle.

Sleeping

Ciego's casas aren't Trinidad-spectacular, but they can act as a worthwhile pit stop on the long journey east or west. The city's two hotels could garner a star between them.

Hotel Ciego de Ávila HOTEL $
(☎22-80-13; Carretera a de Ceballos Km 1.5; s/d CUC$20/28; P❄≋) Where have all the tourists gone? Cayo Coco probably, leaving this Islazul staple, 2km from the city center, overlooking the Parque de la Ciudad, the domain of Cuban sports teams and workers on government-sponsored vacation time. Nothing unusual here except for, perhaps, the solar panels on the roof, which deflect from the monotony of the bog-standard rooms, noisy

Ciego de Ávila

Top Sights

Museo Provincial Simón Reyes C1

Sights

1 Ayuntamiento C2
2 Centro Raúl Martínez Galería de Arte Provincial C2
3 Fábrica de Tabacos el Sucro B2
4 Iglesia Católico C2
5 Museo de Artes Decorativas D2
6 Plano-Mural de Ciego de Ávila D3
7 Teatro Principal C3

Sleeping

8 Casa Hospedaje la Villa D3
9 Hotel Santiago-Habana C3
10 María Luisa Muñoz Álvarez C1

Eating

11 Don Ávila D2
12 Fonda la Estrella C1
13 Mercado Agropecuario A3
Panadería Doña Neli .... (see 15)
14 Restaurante Don Pepe B2
15 Solaris C2
16 Supermercado Cruz Verde D2

Drinking

17 La Confronta C3
18 La Fontana C2

Entertainment

19 Casa de la Cultura C2
20 Casa de la Trova Miguel Angel Luna B2
21 Cine Carmen B2
22 Cine Iriondo C3
23 Discoteca Colibrí C1
24 La Macarena C2
25 Patio de ARTex C2

Shopping

26 La Época C2

swimming-pool area and boring breakfasts. Friendly staff and regular paint-jobs add much-needed color.

Hotel Santiago-Habana HOTEL $
(☎22-57-03; cnr Chicho Valdés & Honorato del Castillo; s/d CUC$11/16; ❄) Your one-and-only town-center option is notable only for being the cheapest hotel on the island. The 76 musty but serviceable rooms are 1970s motel style, and there's a restaurant along with the Disco Centro Nocturno la Cima on the top floor. Bring ear plugs.

Casa Hospedaje la Villa CASA PARTICULAR $
(☎22-58-54; cnr Chico Valdés & Abraham Delgado; r CUC$15-20; ❄P) A bright-pink detached place on the Carretera Central that's easy to find. Tired cyclists and drivers look no further. Rooms are clean, if unspectacular, and there's a carport.

María Luisa Muñoz Álvarez CASA PARTICULAR $
(☎20-86-49; Máximo Gómez No 74 btwn Honorato del Castillo & Antonio Maceo; r CUC$20-25; P❄) Two rooms off a sinuous outdoor corridor are textbook private-rental standard, with no real quirks. But you're a block from the center and the owners are keen to please.

Eating

TOP CHOICE **Don Ávila** CARIBBEAN $$
(Marcial Gómez cnr Libertad) Debuting at number one in Ciego's culinary greatest hits, the newly opened Don Ávila impresses with its regal ambience, on-site cigar outlet, old-gents-style bar and typically friendly *avileña* service. Oh yeah, and don't forget the generous portions of *comida criolla* food.

Fonda la Estrella CARIBBEAN $
(Honorato del Castillo No 34 cnr Máximo Gómez; ⏰10am-midnight) Quite possibly the cheapest quality food in Cuba. This small, airy place serves four set dishes for just CUC$1.50. But it's far tastier than your standard fried-chicken ration. For a few convertibles more, you can bag paella and a delicious *ropa vieja* (shredded beef cooked in a tomato-based sauce).

La Vicaria CARIBBEAN $
(Carretera Central; ⏰24hr) A dependable national chain with affordable food and efficient service. The open-fronted sitting area on the Carretera Central is less than salubrious, but the food's adequate for a pre-bus-journey snack.

Restaurante Don Pepe CARIBBEAN $
(Independencia No 103 btwn Antonio Maceo & Simón Reyes; ⏰8-11:45pm Wed-Mon) A bartender named Eladio invented the Coctel Don Pepe here (two shots of orange juice, 1.5 shots of white rum and half a shot of crème de menthe, stirred) back in the day. The restaurant is still serving them, along with the good old pork and chicken dishes, in this pleasant colonial building. There's occasional live music.

Solaris FUSION $
(Doce Plantas Bldg, cnr Honorato del Castillo & Libertad) Enthusiastically recommended by the locals, this city-center joint, on the 12th floor of the rather ugly Doce Plantas building, offers excellent city views and has a menu that includes a special cordon bleu (chicken stuffed with ham and cheese). Ask to try the unique Solaris cocktail.

Self-Catering

Mercado Agropecuario MARKET $
(Chicho Valdés btwn Agramonte & Fernando Callejas) There is a vegetable market located in a blemished part of town below the overpass.

Supermercado Cruz Verde SUPERMARKET $
(cnr Independencia & Marcial Gómez; ⌚9am-6pm Mon-Sat, to noon Sun) Sells groceries in one of Ciego's grandest fin de siècle buildings.

Panadería Doña Neli BAKERY $
(Doce Plantas Bldg, cnr Honorato del Castillo & Libertad) For bread, look no further than this old stalwart, which also displays tempting sweet pastries.

Drinking

La Confronta BAR
(cnr Marcial Gómez & Joaquín Agüero) Amid the well-worn bar stools and Benny Moré paraphernalia you can sample a range of 25 different cocktails. Prices are in Cuban pesos, a tempting (potentially dangerous) proposition for a convertible-loaded traveler. There's also a limited food menu.

La Fontana CAFE
(cnr Independencia & Antonio Maceo; ⌚6am-2pm & 3-11pm) Ciego's famous coffee institution has lost its shine since a 2008 renovation failed to evoke the atmosphere of yore. For the caffeine-starved, it's OK – if you don't mind drinking your coffee in a thick fog of cigarette smoke.

Entertainment

For total spontaneity hit the streets on a Saturday night for the wonderful Noches Avileñas, when music and temporary food stands set up in the street around various venues, including the main park and Museo de Artes Decorativas. Every Sunday morning at 10am a brass band plays in Parque Martí.

Cine Carmen CINEMA
(Antonio Maceo No 51) If you're in the mood to catch a film, try Cine Carmen on the corner of Calle Libertad. It provides big-screen and video offerings daily. Don't miss the big movie projector spilling film on the Libertad side of the building.

Casa de la Trova Miguel Angel Luna LVIE MUSIC
(Libertad No 130) In the dice-roll of traditional musical entertainment, Ciego's *trova* (song) house scores a magic six with polished Thursday night regional *trovadores* in a pleasant colonial setting.

FREE **Casa de la Cultura** CULTURAL CENTER
(Independencia No 76 btwn Antonio Maceo & Honorato del Castillo) All sorts of stuff goes on here, including a Wednesday *danzón* club.

Patio de ARTex LIVE MUSIC
(Libertad btwn Antonio Maceo & Honorato del Castillo; admission 5 pesos) This trusty alfresco patio has a bit of everything; check the *cartelera* (culture calendar) out front.

La Macarena NIGHTCLUB
(Independencia No 57 btwn Antonio Maceo & Honorato del Castillo) Slightly tacky discos haunt Ciego's hotels, including this one at the Cuban-only Hotel Sevilla.

El Batanga NIGHTCLUB
(Carretera a de Ceballos Km 1.5; admission per couple CUC$3; ⌚10pm-2am) Youthful disco fever in the Hotel Ciego de Ávila that the people actually sleeping there probably won't appreciate.

Discoteca Colibrí NIGHTCLUB
(cnr Máximo Gómez & Honorato del Castillo; admission CUC$1; ⌚10pm-3am) Delusions of Saturday-night stardom? Look no further than the karaoke machine here.

Estadio José R Cepero SPORTS
(Máximo Gómez) October to April, baseball games take place to the northwest of the center. Ciego's Tigres (Tigers) aren't as fierce as their name suggests and rarely qualify for the play-offs.

Shopping

Stroll El Boulevard for typical Cuban fodder. The only place that may have you reaching inside your money belt is the ARTex souvenir store **La Época** (Independencia btwn Antonio Maceo & Honorato del Castillo).

Information

Internet Access & Telephone

Etecsa Telepunto (Joaquín Agüero No 62; internet access per hr CUC$6; ⌚8:30am-7:30pm) Three terminals.

Media

Radio Surco Broadcasting over 1440AM and 98.1FM.

Medical Services

General Hospital (☎22-24-29; Máximo Gómez No 257) Not far from the bus station.

Money

Banco Financiero Internacional (cnr Honorato del Castillo & Joaquín Agüero Oeste)

Bandec (cnr Independencia Oeste & Antonio Maceo)

Cadeca (Independencia Oeste No 118 btwn Antonio Maceo & Simón Reyes)

Post

Post office (cnr Chicho Valdés & Marcial Gómez)

Tourist Information

Havanatur (Libertad btwn Antonio Maceo & Honorato del Castillo; ⌚9am-5pm Mon-Fri, to noon Sat)

Infotur (Doce Plantas Bldg, cnr Honorato del Castillo & Libertad; ⌚9am-noon & 1-6pm Mon-Sun) Quite possibly Cuba's friendliest and most informative Infotur office. In the same building as Solaris restaurant.

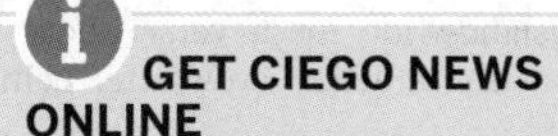

GET CIEGO NEWS ONLINE

Ciego de Ávila has its own newspaper, **Invasor** (www.invasor.cu), available in English and Spanish online. It's a useful source of both current Cuba news and deeper cultural content on the city and the province.

Getting There & Away

Air

Ciego de Ávila's **Máximo Gómez Airport** (airport code AVI; Carretera a Virginia) is 10km northwest of Ceballos, 23km north of Ciego de Ávila and 23km south of Morón. **Cubana** (Chicho Valdés No 83 btwn Honorato del Castillo & Antonio Maceo) has weekly flights to Havana (CUC$78 one way, 1½ hours).

International flights arrive daily from Canada, Argentina, France, the UK and Italy, and visitors are bused off to Cayo Coco.

Bus

The **bus station** (Carretera Central), situated about 1.5km east of the center, has daily Víazul services.

Five daily Santiago de Cuba (CUC$24, 8¾ hours) departures also stop at Camagüey (CUC$6, one hour 35 minutes), Las Tunas (CUC$13, four hours 25 minutes), Holguín (CUC$17, five hours 40 minutes) and Bayamo (CUC$17, seven hours). Four daily Havana (CUC$27, seven hours) buses also stop at Sancti Spíritus (CUC$6, two hours) and Santa Clara (CUC$9, three hours 20 minutes). There are also daily buses to Trinidad (CUC$9, two hours 40 mins) and Varadero (CUC$19, six hours 20 minutes).

Train

The **train station** (☎22-33-13) is located six blocks southwest of the center. Ciego de Ávila is on the main Havana–Santiago railway line. There are nightly trains to Bayamo (CUC$11, seven hours), Camagüey (CUC$3, two hours 10 minutes), Guantánamo (CUC$17, 9½ hours), Havana (CUC$16, 7½ hours), Holguín (CUC$11, seven hours), Manzanillo (CUC$12, 8½ hours) and Santiago de Cuba (CUC$15, 9¼ hours). Different train numbers run on alternate nights, so make sure you check the latest timetable before you leave. There are four trains daily to Morón (CUC$1, one hour).

Truck

Private passenger trucks leave from the Ferro Ómnibus bus station adjacent to the train station heading in the direction of Morón and Camagüey. Check the blackboards for current details.

Getting Around

Car & Moped

The **Carretera a Morón gas station** (Carretera de Morón) is just before the bypass road, northeast of the town center. The **Oro Negro gas station** (Carretera Central) is near the bus station.

You can park safely in front of the Hotel Santiago-Habana overnight.

Cubacar (Hotel Ciego de Ávila, Carretera a Ceballos) can help with vehicle rental for around CUC$70 per day. It also rents out mopeds for CUC$24 a day.

Taxi

A taxi ride to the airport will cost around CUC$12; bargain if they're asking more. You can book a cab at Hotel Ciego de Ávila or find one in Parque Martí. A one-way ride to Cayo Coco should cost in the vicinity of CUC$60.

Morón

POP 59,194

Despite its slightly removed position 35km north of Cuba's arterial Carretera Central, Morón remains an important travel nexus (thanks to its railway) and acts as a viable base camp for people not enamored with the resort-heavy Cayo Coco.

Founded in 1643, two centuries before provincial capital Ciego de Ávila, Morón is known as the Ciudad del Gallo (City of the

Cockerel) island-wide for a verse about a cockerel that continued to crow after being de-feathered.

Compact and easygoing, Morón has some excellent casas particulares and offers a surprisingly varied list of things to do in the surrounding countryside.

Sights

Morón is famous for its emblematic cockerel, which stands guard on a roundabout opposite the Hotel Morón on the southern edge of town. It crows (electronically) at 6am every morning.

Terminal de Ferrocarriles LANDMARK
(Av de Tarafa) Morón has long been central Cuba's main railway crossroads and, not surprisingly, it exhibits the most elegant railway station outside Havana. Built in 1923, the building's edifice is neocolonial, though inside the busy ticket hall hides a more streamlined art deco look. Equally eye-catching is the colorful stained glass skylight.

Museo de Arqueología e Historia MUSEUM
(Martí; admission CUC$1; ⌚9am-noon & 6-10pm) Shoehorned in among the busy sidewalks and peeling colonnades, this well-laid-out museum is spread over two floors, the upper of which is given over to the city's history. There is a mirador (lookout) on the roof with a good view out over the town.

Sleeping

Morón's best casas are far superior to its lone 1960s-era hotel.

TOP CHOICE **Alojamiento Maité** CASA PARTICULAR $
(☎50-41-81; maite68@enet.cu; Luz Caballero No 40B btwn Libertad & Agramonte; r CUC$20-25; P❄@) Plush facilities and sharp service are par for the course in what must be one of Cuba's most comfortable and professionally run casas particulares. Cast your eye over the wall-mounted TV, starched white sheets (changed daily), complimentary bottles of shampoo, and wine in the fridge.

Alojamiento Vista al Parque CASA PARTICULAR $
(☎50-41-81; yio@moron.cav.sid.cu; Luz Caballero No 49D Altos btwn Libertad & Agramonte; r CUC$20-25; P❄@) There's more of the same comfort and slick service across the street in this lovely pale-blue house with two upstairs rooms run by Maité's friend Idolka.

'Hospedaje Liberluz' – Carlos Manuel Baez CASA PARTICULAR $
(☎50-50-54; Libertad No 148 btwn Luz Caballero & Padre Cabo; r CUC$20-25; ❄) Blooming bougainvillea, comfortable rockers, a patio and two well-equipped rooms spread over two floors. Morón has its pleasant escapes and this is one of them.

Hotel Morón HOTEL $
(☎50-22-30; Av de Tarafa; s/d CUC$18/22; P❄≋) Morón might be known for its cockerel, but it's the in-house disco that's more likely to keep you awake at this modern-ish, four-story hotel at the south entrance to town. Package tourists are the main clientele, with the odd stray fisher thrown in for good measure. The pool is a rare highlight; nonguests can ask about day passes. Maintain low expectations for the restaurant and you might be pleasantly surprised.

Eating

Restaurante Maité la Qbana PALADAR $$
(☎50-41-81; Luz Caballero No 40 btwn Libertad & Agramonte) Maité is a highly creative cook whose international dishes, prepared with *mucho amor*, will leave you wondering why insipid all-inclusive buffets ever got so popular. Cuba travel veterans will score numerous 'firsts' here, including al dente pasta, fine wine, homemade desserts and paella that has visiting Valencianos reminiscing about their homeland.

Paraíso Palmares CARIBBEAN $
(Martí No 382; ⌚noon-2pm & 7-9pm) This restaurant has standard chicken fare with the obligatory *arroz congrí* (rice and beans). Since the closure of Las Fuentes it has ruled the roost among the government-run restaurants in Morón.

Coppelia ICE-CREAM PARLOR $
(cnr Callejas & Martí) While the Coppelia chain invariably offers good ice cream, the setting is often dire, and never more so than in this hollowed-out shell of a building. Get a takeout and head to the park.

Self-Catering

On the self-catering front there's the dependable **Doña Neli Dulcería** (Serafín Sánchez No 86 btwn Narciso López & Martí) for bread and pastries and **Supermercado los Balcones** (Martí) for groceries.

Entertainment

Casa de la Trova Pablo Bernal LIVE MUSIC
(Libertad No 74 btwn Martí & Narciso López) A good night out in Morón usually decamps at some point to this alfresco music house. So hefty is its reputation that advance bookings are sometimes required, especially for the Wednesday night comedy.

Cabaret Cueva CABARET, NIGHTCLUB
(Laguna de la Leche) Locals willingly hitch, walk or carpool to make the 6km trip to this cabaret in a cave on the southern shores of the Laguna de la Leche.

Discoteca Morón NIGHTCLUB
(Hotel Morón, Av de Tarafa; ⏲10pm) Young, raucous entertainment-seekers test the patience of sleep-deprived paying guests at the Hotel Morón.

Information

You'll find internet at **Etecsa** (Martí cnr Céspedes; ⏲8:30am-7:30pm) and there are money-changing facilities at the **Cadeca** (Martí cnr Gonzalo Arena) in the same street. Information on the Laguna la Redonda and Laguna de la Leche can be procured at **Cubatur** (⏲9am-5pm), which has a desk in the Casa de la Trova.

Getting There & Away

Five buses a day leave from the hectic **train station** (cnr Martí & JF Poey) for Ciego de Ávila. There are also four daily trains to Ciego de Ávila (CUC$1), one to Jucaro and one to Camagüey (CUC$4). The line from Santa Clara to Nuevitas passes through Morón via Chambas. A *coche motor* (cross-island) railcar to Havana (CUC$24, 6½ hours) operates daily.

Getting Around

The roads from Morón northwest to Caibarién (112km) and southeast to Nuevitas (168km) are both good. **Cubacar** (Hotel Morón, Av de Tarafa) rents cars and mopeds, and the **Servi-Cupet gas station** (⏲24hr) is near Hotel Morón.

Around Morón

Just as interesting as Morón itself is the grab bag of attractions to the north.

LAGUNA DE LA LECHE & LAGUNA LA REDONDA

These two large natural lakes lie to the north of Morón. Redonda is best accessed via the road to Cayo Coco. The 5km entry road for Laguna de la Leche starts just north of Morón's Parque Agramonte. Buses ply the route from the train station.

Sights & Activities

Laguna de la Leche LAKE
Measuring 66 sq km, the Laguna de la Leche (Milk Lake) is named for its reflective underwater lime deposits and is the largest natural lake in Cuba. Even weirder is its water content, an unusual mixture of fresh and salt water. Accessed from the south via a link road from Morón (5km), the lake is popular among budding anglers who flock here to take advantage of its abundant stocks of carp, tarpon, snook and tilapia. Guided fishing trips can be arranged from the on-site Flora y Fauna office and start at CUC$50 for four hours (the more people, the cheaper per person). For a little more you can keep your catch and cook it on a mobile BBQ aboard the boat. Explanatory nonfishing boat excursions ($25 for 45 minutes) are also available.

Every year Laguna de la Leche is the venue for the **Morón Aquatic Carnival**. The area has also twice hosted the Jardines del Rey **F-1 speedboat competition**.

Laguna la Redonda LAKE
The next world-record largemouth bass will come from Cuba, if fishing around this lake is anything to go by. The lake has already yielded a humongous 9.5kg specimen. Situated 18km north of Morón, off the road to Cayo Coco, the mangroves surrounding this 4-sq-km lake have the best square-kilometer density of bass and trout on the island. Four/eight hours of fishing costs CUC$35/70, or a 45-minute boat trip without rods costs CUC$4 per person (four person minimum). There's a decent, rustic bar-restaurant combo here if you only want to stop for a drink with a lake view. Try the house specialty, a fillet of fish called *calentico* – great with ketchup and Tabasco.

Aguachales de Falla Game Reserve HUNTING RESERVE
This is the main attraction of the area for Morón's small but dedicated hunting crowd. The area contains seven natural lakes and abundant flocks of pigeons, ducks and doves. If you really feel the urge, you can take the Hemingway tour to its natural conclusion (Papa loved firing guns at feathered targets).

Eating

TOP CHOICE La Atarraya SEAFOOD $
(mains CUC$2-5; noon-10pm) Raised on stilts in a clapboard building just off the southern shoreline of Laguna de la Leche, you'll find one of Cuba's best local fish restaurants. The insanely cheap menu is headlined by Paella Valenciana and Pescado Monteroro (fish fillet with ham and cheese), while the ambience is ebulliently local.

Pescado Frito SEAFOOD $
(mains CUC$2-5; noon-6pm) It's almost too much of a good thing. Recently opened just along from La Atarraya is this open-air rustic beauty (the sign says 'Ranchón la Boca,' but everyone calls it 'Pescado Frito'). Access the pleasant grounds via a humpbacked wooden bridge and follow the smell (and crackle) of frying catfish, tilapia and carp.

CENTRAL PATRIA O MUERTE

(admission CUC$3; 8am-4pm) Cuba's sugar industry is in the process of being preserved at this huge rusting ex-sugar mill in the village of Patria 3km south of Morón. First opened in 1914, the mill and its 263-strong workforce were passed over to the Americans in 1919, and it remained in Yanqui hands until it was nationalized in 1960. A 1920 Baldwin steam train made in Philadelphia takes pre-booked tour groups on a 5km jaunt through the cane fields to **Rancho Palma** (Carretera a Bolivia Km 7), a bucolic *finca* (farmhouse) with a bar-restaurant and country airs where you can sample *guarapo* (pressed cane juice). Independent visitors can ask for a tour here, but to get the full train treatment you'll need to tag onto a group. Check schedules with Cubatur (p301) in Morón.

LOMA DE CUNAGUA & AROUND

Loma de Cunagua (admission CUC$5; 9am-4pm), 18km east of Morón on the Carretera de Bolivia, rises like a huge termite mound above the surrounding flatlands. It's a protected flora and fauna reserve that harbors a *ranchón*-style restaurant, a small network of trails and excellent bird-watching opportunities. At the time of writing, visits had to be pre-arranged through **Ecotur** (30-81-63; Hotel Sol Coco, Cayo Coco). At 364m above sea level, the Loma is the province's highest point and the views over land and ocean are formidable. You can arrange horseback riding here or stroll along the 1.3km Palmar de las Cotottas trail in search of *tocororos*, *zunzúns* and panoramas of the Jardines del Rey archipelago. The restaurant whips up a decent all-in pork lunch and a trio of **cabins** (r CUC$30) offer rustic overnight accommodation for those in search of rural tranquility.

CRIADERO DE COCODRILOS

(Carretera de Bolivia Km 9; admission CUC$2; 7am-7pm) Cuba has a good half-dozen of these crocodile farms, which, at best, act as glorified zoos. This one is primarily designed for day-trippers bused in from Cayo Coco, but you can roll up independently if you so desire. Hit the right hour and you'll get a feeding display and some basic info on Cuba's only dangerous land animal. There's an OK restaurant on site.

ISLA TURIGUANÓ

Hold your horses (and cows). You're not in the keys quite yet; Turiguanó isn't a real island. Rather it is a drained swamp that today plays host to a cattle-breeding ranch, a model revolutionary community and one of Cuba's three pioneering wind farms.

Ganado Santa Gertrudis RANCH, RODEO
Santa Gertrudis cattle are bred at this large farm on the Isla Turiguanó right on the main road just before you enter the causeway to Cayo Coco. The adjoining stadium is evidence that in rodeo-land Cuba is right up there with the Calgary Stampede. Cowboys, bulls, horses and lassos are out most weekends at around 2pm for exciting 90-minute *espectáculos* (shows). Alternatively, you can drop by for a look at the animals any time. There's a small bar out front.

El Pueblo Holandés VILLAGE
A small community with 49 red-roofed, Dutch-style dwellings, El Pueblo Holandés is on a hill next to the highway, 4km north of La Redonda. It was built by Celia Sánchez in 1960 as a home for cattle workers. It's an interesting blip on the landscape and worth a short detour.

Florencia

Ringed by gentle hills, the town of Florencia, 40km west of Morón, was named after Florence in Italy by early settlers who claimed that the surrounding countryside reminded them of Tuscany. The town itself grew up around the Santa Clara–Nuevitas railway in the 1920s, when local farmers began transporting their products to more lucrative markets in the west. In the early 1990s the Cuban government constructed a hydroelectric dam, the **Liberación de Florencia**, on the Río Chambas and the resulting lake has become a recreational magnet for nature lovers. There are a number of activities available here, including horseback riding through the Florencia hills, kayaking, aqua-biking, and a boat ride on the lake to a tiny key called La Presa with a restaurant and small 'zoo.' The area's main focal point is a ranch called **La Presa de Florencia** (9am-5pm) by the side of the lake in Florencia. You can get more details at Infotur in Ciego de Ávila (p299) or at **Palmares** (50-21-12; Martí No 306) in Morón. For a place to stay you may get lucky in the lovely Campismo Boquerón, 5km west of Florencia, normally only available to Cubans, but sometimes able to take in foreigners. Enquire at La Presa de Florencia.

Cayo Coco

Situated in the Archipiélago de Sabana-Camagüey, or the Jardines del Rey as travel brochures prefer to call it, Cayo Coco is Cuba's fourth-largest island and the main tourist destination after Varadero. The area north of the Bahía de Perros (Bay of Dogs) was uninhabited before 1992, when the first hotel – the Cojímar – went up on adjoining Cayo Guillermo. The bulldozers haven't stopped buzzing since.

While the beauty of the beaches on these islands is world famous, Cayo Coco pre-1990 was little more than a mosquito-infested mangrove swamp. French corsair Jacques de Sores was one of the earliest visitors, fresh from successful raids on Havana and Puerto Príncipe, and he was followed in 1752 by the island's first landowner, an opportunistic Spaniard named Santiago Abuero Castañeda. Between 1927 and 1955 a community of 600 people scraped a living by producing charcoal for use as domestic fuel on the island, but with the rise of electrical power after the Revolution this too died.

Since 1988 Cayo Coco has been connected to the mainland by a 27km causeway slicing across the Bahía de Perros. There are also causeways from Cayo Coco to Cayo Guillermo in the west and to Cayo Romano in the east.

Sights

Parque Natural el Bagá NATURE RESERVE
(9.30am-5.30pm) Bagá is a commendable eco-project where the Cuban government has juxtaposed environmental reclamation with lucrative but controlled tourist development. Sited on what was Cayo Coco's original airport, this 769-hectare natural park is a sublime mix of dense mangroves, small

TROCHA DE JÚCARO A MORÓN

Shaped by a volatile history, many of Ciego de Ávila's provincial towns grew up in the mid-19th century around the formidable Trocha, a line of fortifications that stretched 68km from Morón in the north to Júcaro in the south, splitting the island in two.

Constructed by the Spanish in the early 1870s using a mixture of black slaves and poorly paid Chinese laborers, the gargantuan Trocha was designed to contain the rebellious armies of the Oriente and stop the seeds of anarchy from spreading west during the First War of Independence.

By the time it was completed in 1872, La Trocha was the most sophisticated military defense system in the colonies, a seemingly unbreakable bastion that included 17 forts, 5000 full-time military guards and a parallel railway line.

Armed to the hilt, it held firm during the First War of Independence, preventing the rebel armies of Antonio Maceo and Máximo Gómez from causing widespread destruction in the richer western provinces of Matanzas and Pinar del Río, where more conservative sugar planters held sway.

Despite renovations that doubled the number of forts and tripled the number of armed guards by 1895, La Trocha proved to be more porous during the Spanish-Cuban-American War, enabling the audacious Maceo to break through and march his army as far west as Pinar del Río.

A handful of old military towers that once acted as lookouts and guardhouses on La Trocha are still scattered throughout the countryside between Ciego de Ávila and Morón. While none are, as yet, official museums, they stand as timeworn testaments to a more divisive and violent era.

Cayo Coco & Cayo Guillermo

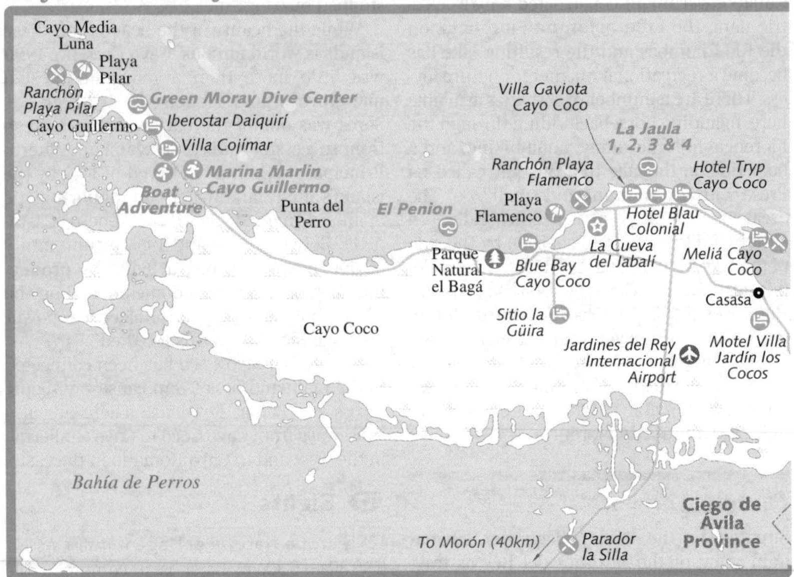

lakes, idyllic coastline and winding trails. A three-hour tour with a guide costs CUC$25 (no minimum group size), but these guys are flexible, knowledgeable and passionate about their subject. You can see *jutías* (tree rats) and iguanas here and handle a live croc (mouth taped of course), but the real highlight is the 130 species of bird that frequent the area. Slightly lower in the authenticity stakes are a reconstructed native village (including shows) and the on-site restaurant, which specializes in rabbit.

Cayo Paredón Grande ISLAND

East of Cayo Coco, a road crosses Cayo Romano and turns north to Cayo Paredón Grande and **Faro Diego Velázquez**, a 52m working lighthouse that dates from 1859. This area has a couple of beaches – including the lauded Playa los Pinos – and is good for fishing.

Activities

The **Marina Marlin Aguas Tranquilas** (www.nauticamarlin.com), near the Meliá Cayo Coco, offers deep-sea fishing outings (CUC$270 per four hours).

The **Centro Internacional de Buceo Coco Diving** (www.nauticamarlin.com), on the west side of Hotel Tryp Cayo Coco, is accessible via a dirt road to the beach. Scuba diving costs CUC$40, plus CUC$10 for gear. The open-water certification course costs CUC$365, less in low season. The diving area stretches for over 10km mainly to the east, and there are six certified instructors with the capacity for 30 divers per day. **Centro Internacional de Buceo Blue Diving** (www.nauticamarlin.com) in Hotel Meliá Cayo Coco offers similar services. Dive masters are multilingual, and there are liveaboard options.

Tours

There's no lack of day excursions available from the main hotel information desks, which are usually staffed by Cubatur or Cubanacán representatives. Highlights include Por la Ruta de Hemingway, a journey through the keys mentioned in Hemingway's novel *Islands in the Stream,* a motorboat cruise around Cayo Paredón Grande, as well as a flamingo-spotting tour. Prices are in the CUC$25 to CUC$30 range.

Sleeping

Cayo Coco's all-inclusive resorts are policed pretty diligently. Unless you're wearing the 'access all areas' plastic wristband, think twice about sneaking in to use the toilets. Room rates are all-inclusive.

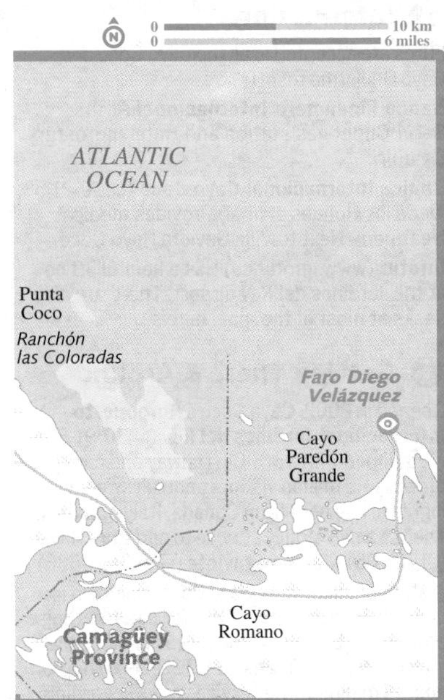

Meliá Cayo Coco RESORT $$$
(☎30-11-80; all-incl s/d CUC$132/208; P❄@≋) The romantic choice. This intimate resort on Playa las Coloradas, at the eastern end of the hotel strip is everything you'd expect from the Spanish Meliá chain. For a luxury twist try staying in one of the elegant white bungalows that perch on stilts in the middle of a lagoon. Yes, the prices are high, but the Meliá is unashamedly classy and a 'no kids' policy enhances the tranquility.

Hotel Tryp Cayo Coco RESORT $$$
(☎30-13-00; all-incl s/d CUC$140/230; P❄@≋👪) The family choice. Tryp is a quintessential all-inclusive resort with a meandering pool, myriad bars, nightly tourist show and the obligatory plastic wristband. While the facilities are good, overzealous poolside 'entertainers' lend the place a holiday-camp feel at times. The 500-plus rooms – housed in sunny three-story apartment blocks – are big, with balconies and huge beds, although the finishes are sometimes a little worn considering the room price. The hotel is immensely popular with families and European travelers.

Hotel Blau Colonial RESORT $$$
(☎30-13-11; all-incl r from CUC$130; P❄@≋) Formerly known as the Guitart Cayo Coco, this well-designed resort was the island's first hotel when it opened in 1993 (ancient history by Cayo Coco standards). The hotel gained notoriety in 1994 when, according to Cuban media, gunmen from the right-wing Cuban exile movement Alpha 66 opened fire on the building. Fortunately, no one was hurt. Refurbished under new management in 2003, the Blau boasts attractive Spanish colonial-style villas that lend it a more cloistered and refined air than the Tryp next door.

Sitio la Güira CABINS $
(☎30-12-08; cabaña CUC$25; ❄) A simple abode situated on a small farm 8km west of the Servi-Cupet gas station (which is itself some 8km southwest of Villa Gaviota Cayo Coco), La Güira rents four pseudo-rustic *bohíos* (thatched huts) with private bathrooms and – get this – air-con (to dissuade the mosquitoes apparently). There's a *ranchón*-style restaurant and bar on-site.

Motel Villa Jardín los Cocos HOTEL $
(☎30-21-80; s/d/tr CUC$20/30/40) This is one of Cayo Coco's few cheap options. Don't expect much – it was originally designed for Cuban workers and is a fair walk from the beach – but if budget is your main consideration, one of the cheap musty rooms here could work.

Blue Bay Cayo Coco RESORT $$$
(☎30-23-50; all-incl s/d CUC$123/216; P❄@≋) Cayo Coco's newest resort (opened 2008) is another Gaviota giant that offers no real surprises. Expect lined-up sun-loungers, plentiful buffet food and kitschy pink flamingos.

Villa Gaviota Cayo Coco RESORT $$$
(☎30-21-80; all-incl d/tr CUC$130/185; P❄@≋) An amiable low-key place, Villa Gaviota has friendly service and a degree of intimacy missing from most of the larger resorts. It's right on the beach.

Eating

Amid the ubiquitous as-much-as-you-can-eat hotel buffets, there are some rather good independent restaurants – mainly thatched roof, *ranchón*-style places on or near the beaches.

Restaurant Sitio la Güira CARIBBEAN $$
(🕗8am-11pm) Set in the old reconstructed charcoal burners' camp, La Güira's food is fresh, plentiful and not too charcoaly. Try

the big, fresh sandwiches for CUC$2 or the shrimp plates for CUC$12. Strumming music trios do the rounds.

Parador la Silla CARIBBEAN **$$**
(⏲9am-6pm) A thatched-roof snack bar halfway along the causeway into Cayo Coco that seems to almost float on the shallow Bahía de Perros. After a full plate of *comida criolla*, you can climb up an adjacent lookout tower and try to spot distant specks of pink (flamingos).

Ranchón Playa Flamenco CARIBBEAN **$$**
(⏲9am-4pm) Eat exquisite seafood, drink cold beer, swim, snorkel, sunbathe, eat more seafood, drink more beer...you get the picture.

Ranchón las Coloradas CARIBBEAN **$$**
(⏲9am-4pm) Seafood again, in an even more paradisiacal setting – can it be possible?

☆ Entertainment

All the *ranchónes* reviewed have attached bars and the all-inclusive hotels have a full nightly entertainment program (usually only available to hotel guests).

La Cueva del Jabalí NIGHTCLUB
(admission CUC$5; ⏲Tue-Sat) For those bored with the all-inclusive floor show, this is the only independent entertainment venue in Cayo Coco. It's 5km west of the Tryp complex, in a natural cave. The place features a cabaret show and it's free all day to visit the bar.

ℹ Information

Euros are accepted in all the Cayo Coco and Cayo Guillermo resorts.

Banco Financiero Internacional At the Servi-Cupet gas station and Hotel Iberostar Daiquirí.

Clínica Internacional Cayo Coco (☎30-21-58; Av de los Hoteles al final) Provides medical treatment. Next to Villa Gaviota Cayo Coco.

Infotur (www.infotur.cu) Has a helpful office at the Jardines del Rey airport. There are also desks at most of the main hotels.

ℹ Getting There & Around

Opened in 2002, Cayo Coco's **Aeropuerto Internacional Jardines del Rey** (☎30-91-65) is equipped with a 3000m runway and can process 1.2 million visitors annually. Weekly flights arrive here from Canada, Italy and the UK. There's a twice-daily service to and from Havana (CUC$105) with **Aerogaviota** (☎7-203-0686).

Although getting to Cayo Coco is nigh on impossible without a car or taxi (or bike), getting around has become infinitely easier since the introduction of a **Transtur** (☎30-11-75) hop-on/hop-off minibus. The service varies according to season, but expect a minimum service of two buses per day in either direction. The bus runs east to west between Meliá Cayo Coco and Playa Pilar, stopping at all Cayo Coco and Cayo Guillermo hotels as well as Parque Natural el Bagá. An all-day pass costs CUC$5.

A taxi to Cayo Coco from Morón will cost about CUC$30, from Ciego de Ávila closer to CUC$55. You pay a CUC$2 fee to enter the causeway.

You can rent a car or moped at **Cubacar** (☎30-12-75) on the second roundabout between the Meliá and Tryp complexes. Cubacar

PLAYA PILAR

Sometimes travel can be anticlimactic; the exalted sight, when you finally get there, doesn't quite live up to the hype. No such letdown applies to Playa Pilar, a sublime strip of sand on Cayo Guillermo that's regularly touted as Cuba's – and the Caribbean's – greatest beach. Pilar's claim rests on two lofty pillars. First, there's the diamond-dust white sand, so fine that if you drop a handful, it will blow away rather than hit the ground (or so say the locals). Second, there are the rugged 15m-high sand dunes (the largest of their kind in the Caribbean) strafed by rough trails that incite piratical exploration. You can hike along the beach back to Guillermo's nearest hotel, a breathtaking 7km, or pitch north to the cayo's tip.

The sea at Pilar is warm, shallow and loaded with excellent snorkeling possibilities. One kilometer away across a calm channel lies the shimmering sands of **Cayo Media Luna**, a one-time beach escape of Fulgencio Batista. Regular boats provide passage to the key (CUC$11), or you can partake in a day-long catamaran excursion (CUC$49) including snorkeling and lobster lunch. The hop-on/hop-off bus from Cayo Coco stops at Playa Pilar three to four times daily in either direction. There's an excellent bar-restaurant nestled in the dunes.

WORTH A TRIP

JARDINES DE LA REINA

Jardines de la Reina are a 120km-long mangrove and coral-island system situated 80km off the south coast of Ciego de Ávila province and 120km north of the Cayman Islands. The local marine park measures 3800 sq km, with virgin territory left more or less untouched since the time of Columbus. Commercial fishing in the area has been banned, and with a permanent local population of precisely zero inhabitants, visitors must stay on board a two-story, seven-bedroom houseboat called **Hotel Flotante Tortuga**, refurbished in 2008, or venture in from the port of Embarcadero de Júcaro on the mainland aboard one of two yachts, the six-cabin *Halcon* or the four-cabin *La Reina*.

The flora consists of palm trees, pines, sea grapes and mangroves, while the fauna – aside from tree rats and iguanas – contains an interesting variety of resident birds, including ospreys, pelicans, spoonbills and egrets. Below the waves the main attraction is sharks (both whale and hammerhead), and this, along with the pristine coral and the unequaled clarity of the water, is what draws divers from all over the world.

Getting to the Jardines is not easy – or cheap. The only company currently offering excursions is the Italian-run **Avalon** (www.cubanfishingcenters.com). One-week dive packages, which include equipment, six nights of accommodation, guide, park license, 12 dives and transfer from Embarcadero de Júcaro, cost in the vicinity of CUC$1500. Ask for a quote via the website. Another option is to sail with the Windward Islands Cruising Company (p286) departing from Trinidad.

also has a desk at all the major hotels. Bicycles are in short supply at Cayo Coco's hotels. Ask around.

Cayo Guillermo

Ah, Cayo Guillermo: haunt of pink flamingos, stunning blond beaches and Cuba's second-most famous Ernesto after Mr Guevara – Señor Hemingway. It was Hemingway who initiated Guillermo's early publicity drive, describing it radiantly in his posthumously published Cuban novel *Islands in the Stream* (1970). Development of the northern cayos began here in 1988 with the opening of a small floating hotel, and was anchored in 1993 when the first land-based all-inclusive resort on the cayos – Villa Cojímar – received its formative guests. Long a prized deep-sea fishing spot, 13-sq-km Guillermo retains a more exotic feel than its larger eastern cousin to which it is connected by a causeway. The mangroves off the south coast are home to pink flamingos and pelicans, and there's a tremendous diversity of tropical fish and crustaceans on the Atlantic reef.

Activities

Marina Marlin Cayo Guillermo FISHING
On the right of the causeway as you arrive from Cayo Coco, this 36-berth marina is one of Cuba's seven certified international entry ports. You can organize deep-sea fishing for mackerel, pike, barracuda, red snapper and marlin here on large boats that troll 5km to 13km offshore. Prices start at CUC$290 per half day (four persons).

Green Moray Dive Center DIVING
The dive center is in Hotel Meliá Cayo Guillermo. It charges CUC$45 for one dive with equipment.

Boat Adventure BOAT TRIPS
This popular activity has its own separate dock on the left-hand side of the causeway as you enter Guillermo. For CUC$41 you are treated to a two-hour motorboat trip (with a chance to operate the controls) through the key's natural mangrove channels. Trips leave four times daily starting from 9am.

Sleeping & Eating

Guillermo has four hotels at present, lined up on its northern shore; there are plans for two more. As well as the Daiquirí and Cojímar, you'll find the familiar luxury Sol/Meliá combo.

Iberostar Daiquirí HOTEL $$$
(30-16-50; s/d CUC$105/150; P ❄ @ ≋) Plenty of shade, a lily pond, and a curtain of water cascading in front of the pool bar add up to make the Daiquirí the pick of the bunch in Guillermo. The 312 rooms are encased in

attractive colonial-style apartment blocks, and the thin slice of paradisiacal beach is straight out of the brochure. Extensive gardens are a bonus.

Villa Cojímar HOTEL **$$$**
(☎30-17-12; s/d CUC$102/145; P ❄ @ ≋) The oldest hotel on the Sabana-Camagüey archipelago opened back in 1993, and it comprises a rather low-key collection of bungalows in a quiet beachside location. The advertising blurb refers to it as a 'Cuban-style hotel,' but the only Cubans you're likely to meet are the people who make up your room.

TOP CHOICE **Ranchón Playa Pilar** CARIBBEAN **$$**
(⏲9am-4pm) Not staying here? Worry not – Cuba's greatest beach also has an excellent bar and restaurant with fresh lobster and boneless chicken fillets as spectacular as the view.

ℹ Getting There & Around

Access information is the same as for Cayo Coco (see p306). The twice-daily hop-on, hop-off bus carries people to and from Cayo Coco, stopping at all four Cayo Guillermo hotels and terminating at Playa Pilar. An all-day ticket costs CUC$5.

Cars can be hired from **Cubacar** (☎30-17-43; Villa Cojímar).

Camagüey Province

☎032 / POP 782,458

Includes »

Best Places to Eat

- Café Ciudad (p317)
- Restaurante la Isabella (p317)
- El Bucanero (p326)
- Paladar la Terraza (p317)

Best Places to Stay

- Gran Hotel (p315)
- Hotel Colón (p315)
- Los Vitrales (p315)
- Motel la Belén (p322)

Why Go?

Neither Occidente nor Oriente, Camagüey is Cuba's provincial contrarian, a region that likes to go its own way in political and cultural matters – and usually does – much to the chagrin of its neighbors in Havana and Santiago.

The seeds were sown in the colonial era, when Camagüey's preference for cattle ranching over sugarcane meant less reliance on slave labor and more enthusiasm to get rid of a system that bred misery.

Today Cuba's largest province is a pastoral mix of grazing cattle and disused sugar mills. Devoid of any mountains of note, it is flanked by Cuba's two largest archipelagos: the Sabana-Camagüey in the north and the Jardines de la Reina in the south, both underdeveloped and almost virgin in places.

Staunchly Catholic Camagüey is the province as a microcosm, a city that nurtured revolutionary poet Nicolás Guillén, groundbreaking scientist Carlos J Finlay and an internationally famous ballet company.

When to Go

There's debate about the actual year of Camagüey's founding, but that doesn't stop everyone taking to the streets in early February to celebrate the Jornada de la Cultura Camagüeyana (Days of Camagüeyan Culture). For outdoor enthusiasts, March is prime time for viewing migratory birds on the northern keys. To the east, in Playa Santa Lucía, the amazing underwater shark-feeding show is held when the sharks are in the area between June and January.

Camagüey

POP 324,921

Welcome to the maze. Caught inadvertently in the tide of history, Camagüey is a Latin American city without precedent. The oddities lie in its unique urban layout. Two centuries spent fighting off musket-toting pirates such as Henry Morgan led the fledgling settlement to develop a peculiar labyrinthine street pattern designed to confuse pillaging invaders and provide cover for its long-suffering residents (or so legend has it). As a result, Camagüey's sinuous streets and narrow winding alleys are more reminiscent of a Moroccan medina than the geometric grids of Lima or Mexico City.

Sandwiched on Carretera Central halfway between Ciego de Ávila and Las Tunas, the city of *tinajones* (clay pots), as Camagüey is sometimes known, is Cuba's third-largest city and the bastion of the Catholic Church on the island. Well known for going their own way in times of crisis, the resilient citizens are popularly called 'Agramontinos' by other Cubans, after local First War of Independence hero Ignacio Agramonte, coauthor of the Guáimaro constitution and courageous leader of Cuba's finest cavalry brigade. In 2008 its well-preserved historical center was made Cuba's ninth Unesco World Heritage Site.

Some travelers love Camagüey with its secret nooks and crannies. Others are not so enamored, with its unsavory reputation for bike thieves and *jineteros* (touts). Take to the maze and find out for yourself.

History

Founded in February 1514 as one of Diego Velázquez' hallowed seven 'villas', Santa María del Puerto Príncipe was originally established on the coast near the site of present-day Nuevitas. Due to a series of bloody rebellions by the local Taíno people, the site of the city was moved twice in the early 16th century, finally taking up its present location in 1528. Its name was changed to Camagüey in 1903.

Camagüey developed quickly in the 1600s – despite continued attacks by corsairs – with an economy based on sugar production and cattle-rearing. Due to acute water shortages in the area, the townsfolk were forced to make *tinajones* in order to collect rainwater and even today Camagüey is known as the city of *tinajones* – although the pots now serve a strictly ornamental purpose.

Aside from swashbuckling independence hero Ignacio Agramonte, Camagüey has produced several local personalities of note, including poet and patriot Nicolás Guillén and eminent doctor Carlos J Finlay, the man who was largely responsible for discovering the causes of yellow fever. In 1959 the prosperous citizens quickly fell foul of the Castro revolutionaries when local military commander Huber Matos (Fidel's one-time ally) accused El Líder Máximo of burying the Revolution. He was duly arrested and later thrown in prison for his pains.

Loyally Catholic, Camagüey welcomed Pope John Paul II in 1998 and in 2008 it beatified Cuba's first saint, 'Father of the Poor' Fray José Olallo, a member of the Order of Saint John who aided the wounded of both sides in the 1868–78 War of Independence. Raúl Castro attended the ceremony.

Sights

Plaza San Juan de Dios SQUARE

(cnr Hurtado & Paco Recio) Wide-open Plaza San Juan de Dios is Camagüey's most picturesque corner and the only town plaza to retain its original layout and buildings. Its eastern aspect is dominated by the **Museo de San Juan de Dios** (admission CUC$1; ⌚9am-5pm Tue-Sat, to 1pm Sun), housed in what was once a hospital administered by Father José Olallo, the Cuban friar who became Cuba's first saint. The hospital has a front cloister dating from 1728 and a unique triangular rear patio with Moorish touches, built in 1840. Since ceasing to function as a hospital in 1902, the building has served as a teachers college, a refuge during the 1932 cyclone, and the Centro Provincial de Patrimonio directing the restoration of Camagüey's monuments. The museum chronicles Camagüey's history and exhibits some local paintings.

Museo Casa Natal de Ignacio Agramonte MUSEUM

(Av Agramonte No 459; admission CUC$2; ⌚10am-5:45pm Tue-Thu, 8am-noon Sun) Opposite Iglesia de Nuestra Señora de la Merced, on the corner of Independencia, is the birthplace of the independence hero Ignacio Agramonte (1841–73), the cattle rancher who led the revolt against Spain in this area in 1868. In July 1869 rebel forces under Agramonte bombarded Camagüey, and four years later he was killed in action (aged only 32) fighting bravely against the Spanish. You can hear Cuban folk singer Silvio Rodríguez' anthem to this hero, who was nicknamed 'El Mayor' (Major),

Camagüey Province Highlights

1 Get lost in the wickedly twisted streets of **Camagüey** (p310)

2 Watch dive instructors fearlessly feed sharks off **Playa Santa Lucía** (p325)

3 Discover huge flamingo nesting sites on the **Refugio de Fauna Silvestre Río Máximo** (p323)

4 Say your penance in Camagüey and sally forth to find Cuba's Catholic soul in a stash of colonial **churches** (p316)

5 Stop in **Guáimaro** (p322), where Cuba's first constitution was signed

6 Go fly-fishing for tarpon and bonefish in the shallow flats off **Cayo Cruz** (p323)

7 Take a bici-taxi through Cuba's largest urban park, the **Casino Campestre** (p314) in Camagüey

8 Go shopping for fresh produce with the locals at Camagüey's **Mercado Agropecuario Hatibonico** (p314)

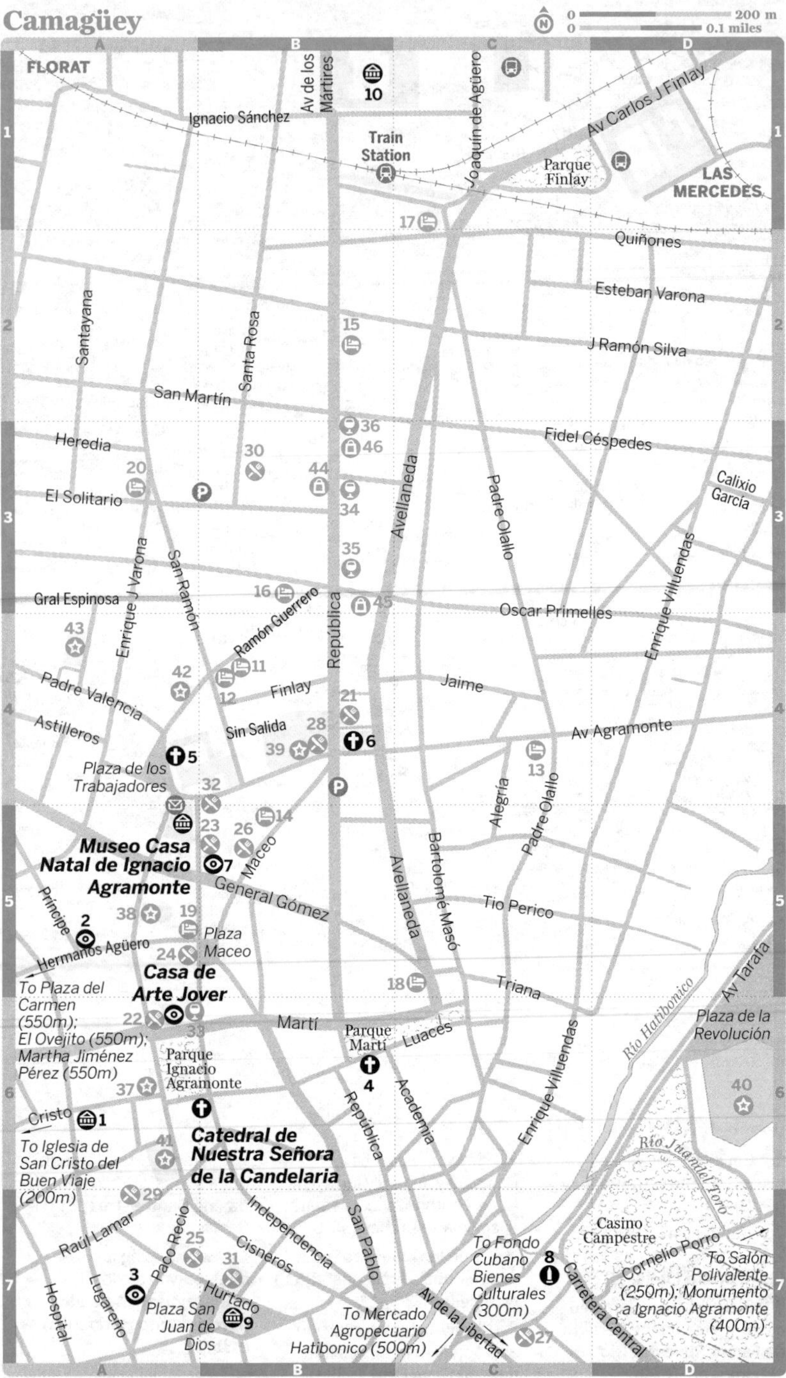

FLORAT
Av de los Mártires
10
Joaquín de Agüero
Av Carlos J Finlay
Ignacio Sánchez
Train Station
Parque Finlay
LAS MERCEDES
17
Quiñones
Esteban Varona
J Ramón Silva
Santayana
Santa Rosa
15
San Martín
36
46
Heredia
Fidel Céspedes
30
44
20
El Solitario
34
Calixio García
Padre Olallo
Avellaneda
35
Enrique J Varona
San Ramón
16
Ramón Guerrero
45
Gral Espinosa
Oscar Primelles
República
Enrique Villuendas
43
42
11
12
Finlay
Jaime
Padre Valencia
21
Astilleros
Sin Salida
28
Av Agramonte
39
6
5
13
Plaza de los Trabajadores
32
Alegría
Padre Olallo
14
23
26
Museo Casa Natal de Ignacio Agramonte
7
Maceo
Bartolomé Masó
Avellaneda
General Gómez
Tío Perico
Príncipe
38
19
2
Plaza Maceo
Hermanos Agüero
24
Casa de Arte Jover
18
Triana
Av Tarafa
To Plaza del Carmen (550m); El Ovejito (550m); Martha Jiménez Pérez (550m)
22
33
Martí
Parque Martí
Luaces
Plaza de la Revolución
Río Hatibonico
Parque Ignacio Agramonte
4
Academia
37
Enrique Villuendas
40
Cristo
1
To Iglesia de San Cristo del Buen Viaje (200m)
41
Catedral de Nuestra Señora de la Candelaria
República
Río Juan del Toro
29
Independencia
San Pablo
Casino Campestre
Raúl Lamar
Paco Recio
25
To Fondo Cubano Bienes Culturales (300m)
Cornelio Porro
31
Cisneros
8
To Salón Polivalente (250m); Monumento a Ignacio Agramonte (400m)
3
Hospital
Lugareño
Hurtado
Plaza San Juan de Dios
9
To Mercado Agropecuario Hatibonico (500m)
Av de la Libertad
Carretera Central
27

Camagüey

on his album *Días y flores*. The house – an elegant colonial building in its own right – tells the oft-overlooked role of Camagüey and Agramonte in the First War of Independence.

Museo Provincial Ignacio Agramonte MUSEUM
(Av de los Mártires No 2; admission CUC$2; ⏲10am-6pm Tue-Thu & Sat, 2:30-10pm Fri, 9am-1pm Sun) Named – like half the city – after the exalted local War of Independence hero, this museum, just north of the train station, is housed in a building erected in 1848 as a Spanish cavalry barracks. In 1902 the structure became a hotel and in 1948 it changed to its present function. Large and full of minute detail, the museum, like many in Cuba, has plenty of interesting artifacts but no thematic glue. Consequently, you'll find yourself wandering listlessly through a hazy mishmash of local history, natural history, fine arts, antique furniture, family heirlooms; the list goes on.

TOP CHOICE **Casa de Arte Jover** ART GALLERY
(Martí No 154 btwn Independencia & Cisneros) Camagüey is home to two of Cuba's most creative and prodigious contemporary painters, Joel Jover and his wife Ileana Sánchez. Their magnificent home in Plaza Agramonte functions both as a gallery and a piece of art in its

own right. Check out the vintage toys, family heirlooms, plant-filled patio and slew of original art; even the kitchen is a collection of kitschy antiques. You're welcome to browse the house and, if you like high-quality original art, buy a painting. The artists also keep a studio and showroom, the **Estudio-Galería Jover** (Paco Recio; ⌚9am-noon & 3-5pm Mon-Sat) in Plaza San Juan de Dios.

Plaza del Carmen SQUARE

(Hermanos Agüero btwn Honda & Carmen) Six hundred meters west of the frenzy of República, is Camagüey's prettiest (and least visited) square. Little more than 10 years ago this whole place was a ruin, but local foresight and some canny restoration work has restored it to a state better than the original. The eastern half of the square is dominated by the Iglesia de Nuestra Señora del Carmen (see boxed text, p316) but, juxtaposing new against old, the cobbled central space has been infused with giant *tinajones,* atmospheric street lamps and unique life-sized sculptures of *camagüeyanos* going about their daily business.

Mercado Agropecuario Hatibonico MARKET

(Matadero; ⌚7am- 6pm) If you visit just one market in Cuba, make sure it's this one. Glued (by mud) beside the murky Río Hatibonico just off the Carretera Central, and characterized by its *pregones* (singsong, often comic, offering of wares) ringing through the stalls, this open-air piece of Camagüeyan theater is a classic example of Cuban-style free enterprise juxtaposed with cheaper but lower quality government stalls. Check out the *herberos* (purveyors of herbs, potions and secret elixirs), huge avocados (in season) and bundles of garlic. Be sure to also visit the plant nursery where Cubans can buy dwarf mango trees and various ornamental plants. Be sure to keep a tight hold on your money belt.

Parque Ignacio Agramonte SQUARE

(cnr Martí & Independencia) This dazzling square in the heart of the city lures visitors with rings of marble benches and an equestrian statue (from 1950) of Camagüey's precocious War of Independence hero.

Casa Finlay MUSEUM

(Cristo btwn Cisneros & Lugareño; ⌚10am-6pm Tue-Thu & Sat) Camagüey's other hero, Dr Carlos J Finlay, was more concerned with saving lives than taking them. This small museum at the site of his birth documents his life and scientific feats, most notably his medical breakthrough in discovering how mosquitoes transmit yellow fever. There's a splendid indoor patio and cafetería.

FREE Casa Natal de Nicolás Guillén CULTURAL CENTER

(Hermanos Agüero No 58; ⌚8:30am-4:30pm) This modest house gives visitors a small insight into Cuba's late national poet and his books, and today doubles as the Instituto Superior de Arte, where local students come to study music.

Casino Campestre PARK

(Carretera Central) Across the bridge over the Río Hatibonico from the *casco histórico* (old town) is Cuba's largest urban park, laid out in 1860, with lots of shaded benches, a baseball stadium, concerts and activities.

CAMAGÜEY STREET NAMES

To make things even more confusing, locals doggedly stick to using the old names of streets, even though signs and maps (including those in this book) carry the new names. Here's a cheat sheet.

OLD NAME	NEW NAME
Estrada Palma	Agramonte
Francisquito	Quiñones
Pobre	Padre Olallo
Rosario	Enrique Villuendas
San Estéban	Oscar Primelles
San Fernando	Bartolomé Masó
San José	José Ramón Silva
Santa Rita	El Solitario

Get one of the ubiquitous bici-taxis to pedal you around. On a traffic island near the entrance to the park is a **monument** dedicated to Mariano Barberán and Joaquín Collar, two Spaniards who made the first nonstop flight between Spain (Seville) and Cuba (Camagüey) in June 1933 in their plane *Cuatro Vientos*. Tragically the plane disappeared when flying to Mexico a week later and both men were presumed dead.

Maqueta de la Ciudad MUSEUM
(cnr Independencia & General Gómez; admission CUC$1; ⏲9am-8pm) Cuban cities No 1 (Havana) and No 2 (Santiago) have got them, so why not No 3? Relishing its new Unesco status, Camagüey has built this fine scale model of itself in a pleasant air-conditioned colonial building with a wraparound mezzanine gallery for better viewing. Interesting displays (in Spanish) explain the architecture and urban design.

Festivals & Events

The annual carnival, known as the **San Juan Camagüeyano**, runs from June 24 to 29 and includes dancers, floats and African roots music. On September 8, there's also a religious festival, the **Nuestra Señora de la Caridad**, to honor the city's – and Cuba's – patron saint. The **Jornada de la Cultura Camagüeyana** celebrates the anniversary of the city's founding in February.

Sleeping

TOP CHOICE **Gran Hotel** HOTEL $$
(☎29-20-93; Maceo No 67 btwn Av Agramonte & General Gómez; s/d incl breakfast CUC$44/70; P❄@≋) You'll swear you've been reincarnated as your father (or grandfather) in this time-warped city center hotel dating from 1939. A potent pre-revolutionary atmosphere stalks the 72 clean rooms reached by a worn marble staircase or ancient lift replete with cap-doffing attendants and antique gate. There are bird's-eye citywide views from the 5th-floor restaurant or you can brave the frenzy in the downstairs street-side snack bar. A *jinetera*-friendly piano bar is accessed through the lobby and an elegant renaissance-style swimming pool shimmers out back.

'Los Vitrales' – Emma Barreto & Rafael Requejo CASA PARTICULAR $
(☎29-58-66; requejobarreto@gmail.com; Avellaneda No 3 btwn General Gómez & Martí; r CUC$20-25; P❄) This painstakingly restored colonial house was once a convent and sports broad arches, high ceilings and dozens of antiques. Three rooms are arranged around a shady patio embellished with 50 different types of plants and a fantastic tile mural. Owner Rafael is an architect and it shows.

Hotel Colón HOTEL $
(☎28-11-85; República No 472 btwn José Ramón Silva & San Martín; s/d incl breakfast CUC$30/44; ❄) A classic long mahogany bar, colorful tile-flanked walls, and a stained-glass portrait of Christopher Columbus over the lobby door give this place a mixed colonial/fin-de-siècle feel. Sandwiched between shops on busy República, the Colón is both a good base for exploring and a good place to relax; there are rocking chairs on the upstairs balcony and a sheltered colonial patio out back.

Manolo Banegas CASA PARTICULAR $
(☎29-46-06; Independencia No 251 altos, btwn Hermanos Agüero & General Gómez; r CUC$20-25) Great expectations spring to mind with this place (think Miss Havisham's house) and, mostly, they're fulfilled. There are some seriously valuable antiques, including the bed you'll be sleeping in, plus an amazing roof terrace overlooking intimate Plaza Maceo. If it's full, try the house of **Dalgis Fernández Hernández** (☎28-57-32) next door, which shares the same stairway and roof terrace.

Yamilet & Edgar CASA PARTICULAR $
(☎25-29-91; San Ramón No 209 btwn El Solitario & Heredia; r CUC$20-25) Edgar is a *maletero* (porter) in the Gran Hotel by day, and a casa owner by night, running this inviting place just northwest of the center with his wife Yamilet. There's one pleasant room with private bath, plus meals and access to a comfortable sitting area.

Carmen González Fonseca CASA PARTICULAR $
(☎29-69-30; Av Agramonte No 229 btwn Padre Olallo & Alegría; r CUC$20-25; P❄) A well-equipped, self-contained room on the top floor with its own terrace and fridge. Daredevil drivers who have already negotiated the confusing Camagüeyan maze ought to have no problem reversing into the tight-fitting garage (a rarity here).

Hotel Isla de Cuba HOTEL $
(☎28-15-14; Oscar Primelles No 453 cnr Ramón Guerrero; s/d incl breakfast CUC$18/26; P❄) An often-overlooked bargain bang in the center of town, the Isla de Cuba is cheap,

CUBA'S CATHOLIC SOUL

If Cuba has a Catholic soul, it undoubtedly resides in Camagüey, a city of baroque churches and gilded altars, where haunting ecclesial spires rise like minarets above the narrow, labyrinthine streets.

Any exploration of Camagüey's religious history should begin at its most important church, the **Catedral de Nuestra Señora de la Candelaria** (Cisneros No 168), rebuilt in the 19th century on the site of an earlier chapel dating from 1530. The cathedral, which is named for the city's patron saint, was fully restored with funds raised from Pope John Paul II's 1998 visit. While not Camagüey's most eye-catching church, it is noted for its noble Christ statue that sits atop a craning bell tower.

The **Iglesia de Nuestra Señora de la Merced** (Plaza de los Trabajadores), dating from 1748, is arguably Camagüey's most impressive colonial church. Local myth tells of a miraculous figure that floated from the watery depths here in 1601 and it has been a place of worship ever since. The active convent in the attached cloister is distinguished by its two-level arched interior, spooky catacombs (where church faithful were buried until 1814) and the dazzling Santo Sepulcro, a solid-silver coffin.

Gleaming after a much-lauded 2007 renovation, the **Iglesia de Nuestra Señora de la Soledad** (cnr República & Av Agramonte) is a massive brick structure dating from 1779. Its picturesque cream-and-terracotta tower actually predates the rest of the structure and is an eye-catching landmark on the city skyline. Inside there are ornate baroque frescoes and the hallowed font where patriotic hero Ignacio Agramonte was baptized in 1841.

Baroque becomes Gothic in rectangular Parque Martí, a few blocks east of Parque Ignacio Agramonte, where the triple-spired **Iglesia de Nuestra Corazón de Sagrado Jesús** (cnr República & Luaces) dazzles with its ornate stained glass, ironwork and updated interpretation of Europe's favorite medieval architectural style (a rarity in Cuba).

The **Iglesia de Nuestra Señora del Carmen** (Plaza del Carmen), a twin-towered baroque beauty dating from 1825, is another church that shares digs with a former convent. The Monasterio de las Ursalinas is a sturdy arched colonial building with a pretty, cloistered courtyard that once provided shelter for victims of the furious 1932 hurricane. Today it is the offices of the City Historian.

The **Iglesia de San Cristo del Buen Viaje** (Plaza del Cristo), next door to the necropolis and overlooking a quiet square, is probably the least visited of Camagüey's ecclesial sextet, but it is worth a peek if you're visiting the graveyard. An original chapel was raised here in 1723, but the current structure is of mainly 19th-century vintage.

friendly and keen to please – and because tour groups tend to shun it in favor of the Gran or Colón, it's usually half-empty. Budget backpackers, look no further.

Hotel Plaza HOTEL $
(☎28-24-13; Van Horne No 1; s/d/tr incl breakfast CUC$27/38/42; P ❄) No two rooms are alike in this rough-around-the-edges colonial hotel built in the dying days of the Spanish era, so peek inside a few to see what's on offer. All have sitting areas, TVs and big fridges – and you can't argue with the price. Its location opposite the station makes it a logical spot for brutally early train departures (the 5:07am to Santiago, for instance).

Hotel Camagüey HOTEL $
(☎28-72-67; Carretera Central Este Km 4.5; s/d incl buffet breakfast CUC$21/30; P ❄ ≋) A built-to-spec Soviet-era out-of-towner 5km southeast of the center, Hotel Camagüey presents that all-too-familiar mix of dodgy architecture, noisy disco and dated 1970s furnishings. On the plus side, it's cheap, clean and relatively friendly.

Alba Ferraz CASA PARTICULAR $
(☎28-30-30; misleydis2000@yahoo.com; Ramón Guerrero No 106 btwn San Ramón & Oscar Primelles; r CUC$20-25; ❄) Two rooms sharing a bath open onto a rather grand colonial courtyard bedecked with plants. There's a roof terrace and your host, Alba, can arrange dance and guitar lessons for guests.

Alex & Yanitze CASA PARTICULAR $
(☎29-78-97; Ramón Guerrero No 104 btwn San Ramón & Oscar Primelles; r CUC$20-25) A huge bath, along with a TV and a comfortable bed. The room might be small, but the welcome's huge.

Eating

With restaurants specializing in Italian and Spanish fare, and a couple more offering a Cuban rarity, lamb, Camagüey has an up-and-coming selection of eating establishments. The bars are equally eclectic.

TOP CHOICE Café Ciudad CAFE $
(cnr Martí & Cisneros; snacks CUC$2-5; ⏲10am-10pm) What a difference a Unesco billing makes. Following its 2008 listing, Camagüey has made Agramonte-like efforts to carve some modern quality into its historical inheritance. This lovely 'new' colonial cafe on Plaza Agramonte melds grandiosity with great service and comes out emulating anything in Havana Vieja. Try the *jamón serrano* (cured ham) or the ice cream and enjoy a *café con leche* under the louvers.

Restaurante la Isabella ITALIAN $$
(cnr Av Agramonte & Independencia; pizzas CUC$5-8; ⏲11am-4pm & 6:30-10pm) Cool, cinematic and perennially crowded, Camagüey's funkiest restaurant was opened during a visit by delegates from Gibara's iconic film festival, the Festival Internacional del Cine Pobre, in April 2008. Blending Italian food with a maverick movie-themed decor (each of the 32 director-style seats is emblazoned with the name of a different Cuban star), the restaurant occupies the site of Camagüey's first ever cinema and is named after local actor Isabella Santos. Hungry gastronomes won't be disappointed by the ample plates of pizza, lasagna and fettuccine.

Paladar la Terraza PALADAR $$
(Santa Rosa No 8 btwn San Martín & El Solitario; dishes CUC$7-10) This old Camagüey standby is popular for a reason: seriously good *comida criolla* (Creole food) and lots of it. Try the pull-off-the-bone lamb served in an upstairs terrace by polite, efficient wait staff.

Bodegón Don Cayetano TAPAS $$
(☎26-19-61; República No 79; tapas CUC$3-5) Of Camagüey's handful of Spanish-style taverns, this is undoubtedly the best – and the only one that serves food. Nestled in the shadow of the Iglesia de Nuestra Señora de la Soledad, the restaurant has tables spilling into the adjacent alley. The food is primarily Spanish with quality tapas, such as tortilla, chorizo and garbanzos (chickpeas), but for something more substantial, try the chef's special: beefsteak in red wine and mushroom sauce (CUC$7.50).

Restaurante de los Tres Reyes CARIBBEAN $$
(Plaza San Juan de Dios No 18; meals CUC$7; ⏲10am-10pm) A handsome state-run place set in beautiful colonial digs on Plaza San Juan de Dios that sells mainly chicken dishes. Ruminate over life in Cuba's third-largest city by one of the giant iron-grilled windows out front or enjoy greater privacy on a plant-bedecked patio behind. The equally romantic **Campana de Toledo** is next door.

Don Ronquillo CARIBBEAN $$
(cnr Av Agramonte & República; meals CUC$7-10) A rather inviting restaurant hidden in the pretty Galería el Colonial with polished wine glasses and OK *comida criolla*. Stick around for the cabaret.

Paladar el Califa PALADAR $$
(Raúl Lamar No 49a btwn Cisneros & Lugareño; meals CUC$8; ⏲noon-midnight) Boy, the food here is fantastic – and such big portions. Hard to pick out in old-fashioned Calle Raúl Lamar, El Califa has been around for donkey's years and is rightly renowned for its huge plates of *uruguayano* (a type of pork fillet) and cordon bleu.

El Ovejito CARIBBEAN $
(Hermanos Agüero btwn Honda & Carmen; ⏲noon-10pm Wed-Mon) No, the name isn't a joke, El Ovejito does actually serve 'little sheep' (as the name translates). Even better, it's situated on sublime Plaza del Carmen with nary a hustler to bother you. There are lamb chops and lamb fricassee, but this is a state-run place and the menu's often more a wish list than a rundown of what's actually available.

Dinos Pizza ITALIAN $
(☎29-06-93; Humboldt No 3 btwn Av de la Libertad & Aurelio Batista; pizzas CUC$2-3; ⏲24hr) Truly revolutionary! This Dinos is one of the only restaurants in Cuba to offer a home-delivery service in a cute little electric van. The pizza, pasta and lasagna have all garnered praise from passing Italians.

Gran Hotel INTERNATIONAL $$
(Maceo No 67 btwn Av Agramonte & General Gómez; dinner buffet CUC$12) The 5th-floor restaurant here has superb city views and a rather nice buffet; get here early and watch the sun set over the church towers.

Gran Hotel Snack Bar FAST FOOD $
(Maceo No 67 btwn Av Agramonte & General Gómez; ⏲9am-11pm) This generally lively snack bar accessible off Maceo has coffee, sandwiches, chicken and ice cream. The

hamburgers (when available) are good and the atmosphere is 1950s retro.

Cafetería las Ruinas FAST FOOD $
(Plaza Maceo) A fern-filled colonial patio with a bargain-basement menu of fried chicken and pizza. Order a margarita and strike up a conversation with local street hawkers through the iron railings.

Coppelia ICE-CREAM PARLOR $
(Maceo btwn Av Agramonte & General Gómez) Ice cream wasn't meant to be eaten in dark, cavernous canteens, but sometimes you've got to integrate. Join the queue and toss a coin – *fresa* (strawberry) or chocolate?

Café Cubanitas CAFE $
(cnr Independencia & Av Agramonte) Another new Camagüeyan coffee bar just off the Plaza de los Trabajadores, Cubanitas is alfresco and lively. Most importantly it sells good coffee, as well as snacks and beer.

Self-Catering

Mercado Agropecuario Hatibonico MARKET $
(Matadero; ⌚7am-6pm) Recently relocated further along the fetid Río Hatibonico, this place is a classic example of a Cuban market where government (lower quality, but cheaper price) and private (vice-versa) produce is sold side by side. Chew heartily on peso sandwiches and fresh *batidos* (fruit shakes, sold in jam jars) and buy fruit and vegetables grown less than 500m from where you stand. There's a good herb section and the market also sells an excellent selection of fruit and vegetables. Watch out for pickpockets.

Drinking

Maybe it's the pirate past, but Camagüey has some great tavern-style drinking houses.

Bar el Cambio BAR
(cnr Independencia & Martí; ⌚7am until late) The Hunter S Thompson choice. A dive bar with graffiti-splattered walls and interestingly named cocktails, this place consists of one room, four tables and bags of atmosphere.

La Terraza BAR
(República No 352; ⌚8am-midnight) The local choice. An open-air peso place full of carefree *camagüeyanos* getting smashed on cheap beer and rum.

Taberna Bucanero BAR
(cnr República & Fidel Céspedes; ⌚2-11pm) The buccaneer's choice. Fake pirate figures and Bucanero beer on tap characterize this swashbuckling tavern, which is more reminiscent of an English pub.

La Bigornia BAR
(República btwn El Solitario & Oscar Primelles) The young person's choice. This lurid-purple boutique bar-restaurant, with a sports store on its mezzanine level, is where the city's well-dressed (read scantily dressed) 18 to 25s come for date nights and Noche Camagüeyana warm-ups.

Gran Hotel Piano Bar BAR
(Maceo No 67 btwn Av Agramonte & General Gómez; ⌚1pm-2am) The *jinetera's* choice. An atmospheric hotel bar in the stately 'Gran', with a long wooden bar, vintage jukebox and grand piano, that allows cross-cultural fertilization between Cubans and tourists. Live music happens nightly after 9pm.

Entertainment

Every Saturday night, the raucous **Noche Camagüeyana** spreads up República from La Soledad to the train station with food and alcohol stalls, music and crowds. Often a rock or *reggaetón* (Cuban hip-hop) concert takes place in the square next to La Soledad.

TOP CHOICE **Teatro Principal** THEATER
(☎29-30-48; Padre Valencia No 64; tickets CUC$5-10; ⌚8:30pm Fri & Sat, 5pm Sun) If a show's on – GO! Second only to Havana in its ballet credentials, the Camagüey Ballet Company, founded in 1971 by Fernando Alonso (ex-husband of number-one Cuban dancing diva Alicia Alonso), is internationally renowned and performances are the talk of the town. Also of interest is the wonderful theater building of 1850 vintage, bedizened with majestic chandeliers and stained glass.

Casa de la Trova Patricio Ballagas LIVE MUSIC
(Cisneros No 171 btwn Martí & Cristo; cover CUC$3; ⌚Tue-Sun) An ornate entrance hall gives way to an atmospheric patio where old crooners sing and young couples *chachachá*. One of Cuba's best *trova* houses, where the regular tourist traffic takes nothing away from the old-world authenticity.

Centro de Promoción Cultural Ibero Americano CULTURAL CENTER
(Cisneros btwn General Gómez & Hermanos Agüero) Check out what's happening at this under-the-tourist-radar cultural center housed in the former Spanish Club, which hosts tango nights and the like.

LOCAL KNOWLEDGE

RAFAEL REQUEJO: ARCHITECT & CASA PARTICULAR OWNER, CAMAGÜEY

Why is Camagüey's architecture different from other Cuban cities?

There are various theories, aside from the pirate idea. It could have been Camagüey's former isolation in the center of the island, its opposition to traditional Spanish design laws, its unique location at the confluence of two rivers and close to good cattle-grazing ground, or its plethora of influential churches, each developing separately around their own neighborhoods and plazas.

What are its main architectural features?

Intimate Andalucian-style patios characterized by large *tinajones* (clay pots), pointed *mudéjar* arches, protective wooden and metal window balustrades, *aljibes* (storage wells), stained glass, Greek columns and decorative ceilings.

What are the city's typical buildings?

The Iglesia de Nuestra Señora de la Soledad, the Casa Natal de Ignacio Agramonte, and the Casa de la Trova Patricio Ballagas. There are also less obvious buildings, such as the Banco de Crédito y Comercio in Plaza de los Trabajadores and the birthplace of Cuban author Gertrudis Gómez de Avellaneda on Calle Avellaneda No 67.

Where can you find out more about Camagüey's architecture?

Good sources include the City Historian's Office in Plaza del Carmen, or the Centro Provincial de Patrimonio in Plaza San Juan de Dios.

Centro Cultural Caribe CABARET
(cnr Calle 1 & Freyre; tickets CUC$3-6; ⏲from 10pm) Some say it's the best cabaret outside Havana and, at this price, who's arguing. Book your seat (from the box office on the same day) and pull up a pew *sin* tourists for an eyeful of feathers and a few frocks. There's a trousers-and-shirt dress code.

Sala Teatro José Luis Tasende THEATER
(☎29-21-64; Ramón Guerrero No 51; ⏲8:30pm Sat & Sun) For serious live theater, head to this venue, which has quality Spanish-language performances.

FREE **Galería Uneac** CULTURAL CENTER
(Cisneros No 159; ⏲5pm & 9pm Sat) Folk singing and Afro-Cuban dancing happen at this place, just south of the cathedral.

Cine Encanto CINEMA
(Av Agramonte) Big-screen showings take place at the city's one reliable movie house.

Estadio Cándido González SPORTS
(Av Tarafa) From October to April, baseball games are held here alongside Casino Campestre. Team Camagüey, known as the Alfareros (the Ceramicists), have an empty trophy cabinet despite representing Cuba's largest province.

Salón Polivalente SPORTS
(Plaza de la Revolución) This place is near Estadio Cándido González, behind the huge Monumento a Ignacio Agramonte, and hosts other athletic matches.

Shopping

Calle Maceo is Camagüey's top shopping street, with a number of souvenir shops, bookstores and department stores. The whole street was being dug up and renovated at last visit.

Casa de los Santos CRAFTS
(Oscar Primelles No 406; ⏲9am-5pm) Interesting primarily as an insight into Camagüey's staunch Catholicism is this small religious outlet (literally a 'hole in the wall') that sells homemade statues of the saints.

ARTex Souvenir SOUVENIRS
(República No 381; ⏲9am-5pm) Che T-shirts, mini-*tinajones*, Che key-rings, CDs, Che mugs. Get the picture?

Fondo Cubano Bienes Culturales CRAFTS
(Av de la Libertad No 112; ⏲8am-6pm Mon-Sat) Sells all kinds of artifacts in a pleasantly

non-touristy setting, just north of the train station.

Martha Jiménez Pérez CRAFTS
(Martí No 282 btwn Carmen & Onda; ⌚9am-5pm Mon-Sat) You're in Cuba's ceramics capital so why not gravitate to the studio of Martha Jiménez Pérez, one of its best living artists, to buy work direct from the source?

Librería Ateneo BOOKSTORE
(República No 418 btwn El Solitario & San Martín) Carries a large selection of books in Spanish.

Information

Dangers & Annoyances

Camagüey invites more hassle than other cities. Thefts have been reported in its narrow, winding streets, mainly from bag-snatchers who then jump onto the back of a waiting bicycle for a quick getaway. Keep your money belt tied firmly around your waist and don't invite attention.

Internet Access & Telephone

Etecsa Telepunto (República btwn San Martín & José Ramón Silva; internet access per hr CUC$6)

Media

The local newspaper *Adelante* is published every Saturday. Radio Cadena Agramonte broadcasts in the city over frequencies 910AM and 93.5FM; it's located south of the city by tuning to 1340AM, and north by tuning your radio to 1380AM.

Medical Services

Farmacia Internacional (Av Agramonte No 449 btwn Independencia & República)

Policlínico Integral Rodolfo Ramirez Esquival (☎28-14-81; cnr Ignacio Sánchez & Joaquín de Agüero) North of the level crossing from the Hotel Plaza; it will treat foreigners in an emergency.

Money

Banco de Crédito y Comercio (cnr Av Agramonte & Cisneros)

Banco Financiero Internacional (Independencia btwn Hermanos Agüero & Martí)

Cadeca (República No 353 btwn Oscar Primelles & El Solitario)

Post

Post office (Av Agramonte No 461 btwn Independencia & Cisneros)

Travel Agencies

Cubanacán (Gran Hotel, Maceo No 67) The best place for information on Playa Santa Lucía.

Cubatur (Av Agramonte No 421 btwn República & Independencia) Can book hotels in Playa Santa Lucía.

Ecotur (☎27-49-51; Av Céspedes btwn Calle C & Carretera Central) Can arrange excursions to the Hacienda la Belén.

Getting There & Away

Air

Ignacio Agramonte International Airport (Carretera Nuevitas Km 7) is 9km northeast of town on the road to Nuevitas and Playa Santa Lucía.

Cubana (República No 400) has daily flights to Havana (CUC$93 one-way, 1½ hours). **Air Transat** (www.airtransat.com) and **Sunwing** (www.sunwing.ca) fly in the all-inclusive crowd from Toronto, who are hastily bussed off to Playa Santa Lucía.

Bus & Truck

The **regional bus station** (Av Carlos J Finlay), near the train station, has trucks to Nuevitas (87km, twice daily) and Santa Cruz del Sur (82km, three daily). You pay in Cuban pesos. Trucks for Playa Santa Lucía (109km, three daily) leave from here as well: ask for *el último* (last in the queue) inside the station and you'll be given a paper with a number; line up at the appropriate door and wait for your number to come up.

Long-distance **Víazul** (www.viazul.com) buses depart **Álvaro Barba Bus Station** (Carretera Central), 3km southeast of the center.

The Santiago de Cuba departure also stops at Las Tunas (CUC$7, two hours), Holguín (CUC$11, 3¼ hours) and Bayamo (CUC$11, 4½ hours). The Havana bus stops at Ciego de Ávila (CUC$6, 1¾ hours), Sancti Spíritus (CUC$10, four hours), Santa Clara (CUC$15, 4½ hours) and Entronque de Jagüey (CUC$25, 6¼ hours). For Víazul tickets, see the *jefe de turno* (shift manager).

Passenger trucks to nearby towns, including Las Tunas and Ciego de Ávila, also leave from this station. Arriving before 9am will greatly increase your chances of getting on one of these trucks.

Public transport to Playa Santa Lucía is scant unless you're on a prearranged package tour. Expect to pay CUC$70 for a taxi one-way from Camagüey.

Train

The **train station** (cnr Avellaneda & Av Carlos J Finlay) is more conveniently located than the bus station – though its service isn't as convenient. Foreigners buy tickets in convertibles from an unmarked office across the street from the entrance to Hotel Plaza. The Tren Francés leaves for Santiago at around 4:42am every third day and for Havana (stopping in Santa Clara) at around 2:25a, also every third day. Slower *coche motor* (cross-island) trains also serve the

VÍAZUL BUS DEPARTURES FROM CAMAGÜEY

DESTINATION	COST (CUC$)	DURATION (HR)	DAILY DEPARTURES
Havana	33	7¾	3:45am, 12:30pm, 4:30pm, 10:45pm, 11:30pm, 12:10am
Holguín	11	3	12:35am, 4:35am, 5:30am, 1:20pm, 5:35pm
Santiago de Cuba	18	6	12:35am, 1:45am, 5:30am, 6:40am, 1:20pm, 6:55pm
Trinidad	15	4½	2:15am
Varadero	24	8¼	2:50am

Havana–Santiago route, stopping at places such as Matanzas, Sancti Spíritus and Ciego de Ávila. Going east there are daily services to Las Tunas, Manzanillo and Bayamo. Heading north there are (theoretically) four daily trains to Nuevitas and four to Morón.

Getting Around

To/From the Airport

A taxi to the airport should cost CUC$5 from town, or you can hang around for the local bus (No 22) from Parque Finlay (opposite the regional bus station) that runs every 30 minutes on weekdays and hourly on weekends.

Bici-Taxis

Bicycle taxis are found on the square beside La Soledad or in Plaza Maceo. Technically bici-taxis aren't permitted to carry tourists, but they do (including organized tour groups); they should cost five pesos, but drivers will probably ask for payment in convertibles.

Car

Car-hire prices start at around CUC$70 a day plus gas, depending on the make of car and hire duration. Companies include **Havanautos** (Hotel Camagüey; Carretera Central Este Km 4.5).

Guarded parking (CUC$2 for 24 hours) is available for those brave enough to attempt Camagüey's maze in a car. Ask at your hotel or casa particular for details.

There are two **Servi-Cupet gas stations** (Carretera Central; 24hr) near Av de la Libertad. Driving in Camagüey's narrow one-way streets is a sport akin to base-jumping. Experts only!

Horse Carts

Horse carts shuttle along a fixed route (CUC$1) between the regional bus station and the train station, though you may have to change carts at Casino Campestre, near the river.

Florida

POP 53,441

A million metaphoric miles from Miami, the hard-working sugar-mill town of Florida, 46km northwest of Camagüey on the way to Ciego de Ávila, is a viable overnighter if you're driving around central Cuba and are too tired to negotiate the labyrinthine streets of Camagüey after dark (a bad idea, whatever your physical or mental state). There's a working rodeo, a hospital and an Etecsa telephone office.

The two-story **Hotel Florida** (51-30-11; Carretera Central Km 534; s/d CUC$13/20; P) is located 2km west of the center of town and has 74 adequate rooms. The entry drive is potholed, which sort of sets the tone for the place, but the staff are friendly and the price no more than a local casa particular. Next door is Cafetería Caney, a thatched restaurant that's better value than the flyblown hotel restaurant.

Passenger trucks run from Florida to Camagüey, where you can connect with Víazul long-distance buses. If you're driving there's a Servi-Cupet gas station in the center of town on Carretera Central.

Sierra del Chorrillo

This protected area 36km southeast of Camagüey contains three low-hill ranges: the Sierra del Chorrillo, the Sierra del Najasa and the Guaicanámar (highest point 324m).

Nestled in their grassy uplands is **La Hacienda la Belén** (27-49-95; admission CUC$6), a handsome country ranch that was built by a Peruvian architect during WWII, and is now run as a nature reserve by travel agency **Ecotur** (☎27-49-95). As well as boasting an interesting display of non-indigenous animals, such as zebras, deer, cattle and horses, the park functions as a **bird reserve**, and is one of the best places in Cuba to view rare species, such as the Cuban parakeet, the giant kingbird and the Antillean palm swift. Another curiosity is a three-million-year-old **petrified forest** of fossilized tree stumps spread over 1 hectare. Treks can be arranged around the reserve by jeep or on horseback and there are two guided walks: the **Sendero Santa Gertrudis** (4.5km) covering flora, fauna and a cave, and the **Sendero de las Aves** (1.8km), which reveals a cornucopia of birdlife.

The countrified but comfortable **Motel la Belén** (☎86-43-49; r with bath CUC$40; ❄☒) is set in a wonderfully rustic hacienda and boasts a swimming pool, an on-site restaurant, a TV room, and 10 clean, air-conditioned rooms that can accommodate up to 16 people. Glorious landscapes are within stone-chucking distance.

You'll need your own wheels to get to Sierra del Chorrillo. Drive 24km east of Camagüey on Carretera Central, then 12km southeast toward Najasa. Alternatively, you can negotiate a rate with a taxi in Camagüey.

Guáimaro

POP 35,813

Guáimaro would be just another nameless Cuban town if it wasn't for the famous Guáimaro Assembly of April 1869, which approved the first Cuban constitution and called for emancipation of slaves. The assembly elected Carlos Manuel de Céspedes as president. Guáimaro is also famous for its sculpture culture.

Sights

Parque Constitución PARK

The events of 1869 are commemorated by a large **monument** erected in 1940 in this park in the center of town. Around the base of the monument are bronze plaques with the likenesses of José Martí, Máximo Gómez, Carlos Manuel de Céspedes, Ignacio Agramonte, Calixto García and Antonio Maceo, the stars of Cuban independence.

The park also contains the **mausoleum** of Cuba's first – and possibly greatest – heroine, Ana Betancourt (1832–1901) from Camagüey, who fought for women's emancipation alongside the abolition of slavery during the First War of Independence.

Museo Histórico MUSEUM

(Constitución No 83 btwn Libertad & Máximo Gómez; admission CUC$1; ⌚9am-5pm Mon-Fri) If you're making a pit stop, this small museum has a couple of rooms given over to art and history.

Sleeping & Eating

Casa de Magalis CASA PARTICULAR $

(☎81-28-91; Olimpo No 5 btwn Benito Morell & Carretera Central; r CUC$20-25) Of the half dozen or so legal casas in town, this is one of the better ones; a super upper-floor apartment with, quite possibly, the largest bathroom in Cuba.

There is a Servi-Cupet gas station on your entry into town from Camagüey with an El Rápido **snack bar** attached.

Minas

POP 21,708

Minas, 60km northeast of Camagüey en route to Nuevitas, is notable only for the musical-instrument factory that opened here in 1976. The **Fábrica de Violines** (Camilo Cienfuegos; admission CUC$2; ⌚Mon-Sat), at the eastern entrance to town, carves beautiful instruments out of local hardwoods. Ten kilometers north of Minas, near the village of Senado, is a **Criadero de Cocodrilos** (admission CUC$2; ⌚7am-4pm), a crocodile zoo, frequented mainly by the Playa Santa Lucía 'all-inclusive' crowd.

Nuevitas

POP 40,607

Nuevitas, 87km northeast of Camagüey, is a 27km jaunt north off the Camagüey–Playa Santa Lucía road. It's an industrial town and sugar-exporting port with friendly locals and easy shore access, but not worth a major detour. In 1978 Cuban movie director Manual Octavio Gómez filmed his revolutionary classic *Una mujer, un hombre, una ciudad* here, giving the city its first, and to date only, brush with fame.

Sights

Museo Histórico Municipal MUSEUM

(Máximo Gómez No 66; admission CUC$1; ⌚Tue-Sun) The only specific sight in Nuevitas, near Parque del Cañón, is this museum in the center of town. It has the standard, semi-interesting mix of stuffed animals and sepia-toned photographs; you can hike up the steps in the town center for a sweeping view of the bay and industry in ironic juxtaposition.

Playa Cuatro Vientos BEACH

Below the Hotel Caonaba there's a shaggy amusement park/playground, which you may or may not want your kids to negotiate. A bit further along the coast is a local beach, from which you can see two of the three small islands, called Los Tres Ballenatos, in the Bahía de Nuevitas. If you snake along the coast for 2km, you'll come to **Santa Rita** at the end of the road – a friendly place with a pier jutting into the bay.

King Ranch RANCH

(Carretera de Santa Lucía Km 35; ⏲10am-10pm) Texans will be flummoxed by such a familiar-sounding name in the wilds of northern Camagüey, but this Wild West apparition is no phony. King Ranch, en route to Playa Santa Lucía, 4km beyond the crossroads where you join the main highway from Camagüey, was once an off-shoot of its legendary Texan namesake (the largest ranch in the US). The ranch was expropriated after the Revolution, but the Cubans kept the name and have broadened its appeal to include a restaurant, a rodeo show and horses for rent. It mostly caters for tour groups from Playa Santa Lucía, but you can turn up unannounced.

Sleeping & Eating

Hotel Caonaba HOTEL $

(☎24-48-03; cnr Martí & Albisa; s/d CUC$11/18; ❄) This friendly, three-story hotel is on a rise overlooking the sea. It's at the entrance to town as you arrive from Camagüey, near a favorite local swimming spot. The rooms have fridges and some have views; but don't expect the Ritz – or even the Rex. In summer you can eat at the **restaurant**, 200m along the coast from the amusement park. The hotel also has a terrace **bar** (open from noon till late).

Getting There & Away

Nuevitas is the terminus of railway lines from Camagüey via Minas and Santa Clara via Chambas and Morón. The station is near the waterfront on the northern side of town. There should be up to four trains a day to Camagüey (CUC$2), and a service on alternate days to Santa Clara, but they are often canceled. Trucks are more reliable than buses. Trucks to Camagüey leave around 4:30am and 9am.

A Servi-Cupet gas station is at the entrance to town, a block from Hotel Caonaba. There's a Transtur taxi office nearby.

Brasil & Around

A once vibrant, now sleepy, former sugar town situated halfway between Morón and Nuevitas, Brasil is the gateway to the still-virgin Cayo Romano, the archipelago's third-largest island. The area has recently been rediscovered by in-the-know fisherfolk who ply the waters out as far as Cayo Cruz. The flats, lagoons and estuaries off Camagüey's north coast are fly-fishing heaven. Bank on catching bonefish, permit and tarpon in a designated fishing area measuring more than 350 sq km that's nearly always deserted. The fishing season runs from November to August and no commercial fishing is allowed. **Ecotur** (☎27-49-95) runs trips.

For something completely different, you can stay at **Hotel Casona de Romano** (Calle 6 btwn Calles B & C; r from CUC$50; ❄), a beautiful, quasi-stately home, originally built for a local sugar merchant in 1919 and renovated in 2008. Its eight rooms

WORTH A TRIP

REFUGIO DE FAUNA SILVESTRE RÍO MÁXIMO

Few know about it, and still fewer come here. The wetlands between the Ríos Máximo and Cagüey on the northern coast of Camagüey province are the largest flamingo nesting ground in the world. Add in migratory water fowl, American crocodiles and a healthy population of West Indian manatees and you're talking special – very special. Protected since 1998 as a Refugio de Fauna Silvestre (Wild Fauna Refuge) and, more recently, as a **Ramsar Convention Site**, the Río Máximo delta faces a precarious future due to human and agricultural contamination coupled with occasional droughts. The area is roadless and hard to reach, but trips in can sometimes be organized courtesy of **Ecotur** (☎27-49-95).

(six doubles, two singles) are furnished with TVs, fridges and air-con and there's an on-site restaurant (upstairs) and bar (downstairs). The place caters mainly for fishers in organized groups. Contact Ecotur for more details.

Cayo Sabinal

Cayo Sabinal, 22km to the north of Nuevitas, is virgin territory, a 30km-long coral key with marshes favored by flamingos and iguanas. The land cover is mainly flat and characterized by marshland and lagoons. The fauna consists of tree rats, wild boar and a large variety of butterflies. It's astoundingly beautiful.

Sights & Activities

Fuerte San Hilario FORT

Cayo Sabinal has quite some history for a wilderness area. Due to repeated pirate attacks in the 17th and 18th centuries, the Spanish built a fort here in 1831 to restore order and keep the marauding corsairs at bay. Some years later the fort became a prison and, in 1875, it was witness to the only Carlist uprising (a counterrevolutionary movement in Spain that opposed the reigning monarchy) in Cuba.

Faro Colón LIGHTHOUSE

(Punta Maternillo) Erected in 1848, Faro Colón is one of the oldest lighthouses still in operation on the Cuban archipelago. As a result of various naval battles fought in the area during the colonial era, a couple of Spanish shipwrecks – *Nuestra Señora de Alta Gracia* and the *Pizarro* – rest in shallow waters nearby, providing great fodder for divers.

Playas Bonita & Los Pinos BEACHES

Of Cayo Sabinal's 30km of beaches, these two compete for top billing. The former has been commandeered for use by daily boat excursions from Playa Santa Lucía and has a rustic *ranchón* (rural farm) serving food. The latter once had five overnight cabins, but these blew away in a hurricane. Activities today are hence of the do-it-yourself variety. Try hiking, strolling, swimming, stretching, writing, thinking, philosophizing or meditating. Everything seems to be more accentuated here.

CAYOS & CAUSEWAYS

In any other country, the necklace of beach-embellished *cayos* (keys) that lies between Cayo Coco and Playa Santa Lucía would have been requisitioned by the biggest, richest hotel chains, but in Cuba, due to a mix of economic austerity and nit-picking government bureaucracy, they remain refreshingly untouched – for now!

Rough causeways and roads were built across Camagüey's *cayos* in the late 1980s in preparation for Cuba's next big tourist project – a plan that, due to the economic meltdown of the Special Period, never got off the ground. Instead, the islands and their unblemished waters have remained the preserve of in-the-know fisherfolk, resolute bird-watchers and those in search of splendid solitude. Running west to east are **Cayo Paredón Grande**, home to checkered lighthouse Faro Diego Velázquez, a sultry beach and bevies of enamored day-trippers from Cayo Coco; **Cayo Romano**, Cuba's third-largest island and a haven for flamingos, mangroves and blood-thirsty mosquitoes; **Cayo Cruz**, a long, sinuous key that lies beyond Romano (a causeway links the two) and is legendary for its pristine fishing waters (trips are run out of a fishing lodge in the mainland village of Brasil); **Cayo Guajaba**, an untouched roadless wilderness; and **Cayo Sabinal**, which has a rough road and a trio of unblemished beaches, plus an old Spanish fort and lighthouse. Tucked away to the north is 800m-long **Cayo Confites**, where a 21-year-old Fidel Castro hid out in 1947 in preparation for an abortive plot to overthrow the dictatorial regime of Rafael Trujillo in the Dominican Republic (Fidel jumped ship in the Bay of Nipe and swam 15km to shore carrying his weapon).

You'll need a sturdy car or a bike to penetrate these potholed northern wildernesses. Entry points to Cayo Romano are from Cayo Coco, or Brasil in northwestern Camagüey province. Cayo Cruz is accessed via a causeway from Cayo Romano. Cayo Sabinal is linked to the mainland by a small causeway northwest of Nuevitas. There are police checkpoints, so you'll need your passport.

Getting There & Away

There are three options: private car, taxi or boat. The dirt road to Cayo Sabinal begins 6km south of Nuevitas, off the road to Camagüey. You must show your passport at the bridge to the key and pay CUC$5. The 2km causeway linking the key to the mainland was the first of its kind constructed in Cuba and the most environmentally destructive. The Playa Santa Lucía tour agencies all offer day trips to Cayo Sabinal: by boat from around CUC$69 including transfers and lunch, or by jeep for CUC$75. Book through the hotels.

Playa Santa Lucía

Playa Santa Lucía is an isolated resort 112km northeast of Camagüey, situated on an unbroken 20km-long stretch of pale-yellow beach that competes with Varadero as Cuba's longest. The bulk of travelers come here to scuba dive on one of the island's best and most accessible coral reefs that lies just a few kilometers offshore. Another highlight is the beach itself – a tropical gem, most of it still deserted – though it narrows and collects more seaweed the further you wander from the hotels.

The area around Playa Santa Lucía is flat and featureless, the preserve of flamingos, scrubby bushes and the odd grazing cow. Aside from the micro-village of Santa Lucía that serves as lodging for itinerant hotel workers and the half-forgotten apostrophe of La Boca, there are no large Cuban settlements of note. History seekers will be disappointed – Trinidad this is not! The swimming, snorkeling and diving are a different story, however, and the large hotels lay on plenty of activities for those with the time and inclination to explore. Packages to Playa Santa Lucía are usually cheaper than those to Cayo Coco (which it predates) though the resorts themselves are less luxuriant and have more of a holiday camp feel. The clientele is primarily Canadian.

Sights

Playa los Cocos BEACH

This arched comma of beach at the end of 20km-long Playa Santa Lucía, 7km from the hotels at the mouth of the Bahía de Nuevitas, is another stunner, with yellow-white sand and iridescent jade water. Sometimes flocks of pink flamingos are visible in Laguna el Real, behind this beach. A horse and carriage from the Santa Lucía hotels to Playa los Cocos is CUC$20 return plus the wait, or you can walk it, jog it, bike it (free gearless but adequate bikes are available at all the resorts), or jump in a taxi. This is a fine swimming spot, with views of the Faro Colón (lighthouse) on Cayo Sabinal, but beware of tidal currents further out.

The small Cuban settlement here is known as **La Boca**. There's a snack bar and a good restaurant. Sometimes the locals roast a pig on a spit and will invite you across.

Activities

Playa Santa Lucía is a diving destination extraordinaire that sits alongside what is, purportedly, the world's second-longest coral reef (after Australia's Great Barrier Reef). The 35 scuba sites take in six Poseidon ridges, the Cueva Honda dive site, shipwrecks, several types of rays and the abundant marine life at the entrance to the Bahía de Nuevitas. A much-promoted highlight is the hand-feeding of bull sharks, sized between 3m and 4m long (June to January). The hotels can organize other water activities, including a full-day catamaran cruise along the shoreline (CUC$57 with lunch and snorkeling), a flamingo tour (CUC$59) and deep-sea fishing (CUC$200 for the boat for 3½ hours).

Centro Internacional de Buceo Shark's Friends DIVING

(www.nauticamarlin.com, in Spanish; Av Tararaco) Shark's Friends is a professional outfit with dive masters who speak English, Italian and German. The center, on the beach between Brisas Santa Lucía and Gran Club Santa Lucía, offers dives for CUC$30, plus night dives (CUC$40) and the famous shark feeds (CUC$65), where cool-as-a-cucumber dive guides chuck food into the mouths of 3m-long bull sharks. It has boats going out every two hours between 9am and 3pm daily, though the last dive is contingent on demand. The open-water course costs CUC$360; a resort course is CUC$60. It also has snorkeling excursions.

Sleeping

The small hotel strip begins 6km northwest of the roundabout at the entrance to Santa Lucía. The four big ones are Cubanacán resorts whose star ratings and quality decrease as you head northwest. Due to Playa Santa Lucía's size and isolation, it's a good idea to book a room beforehand.

Playa Santa Lucía

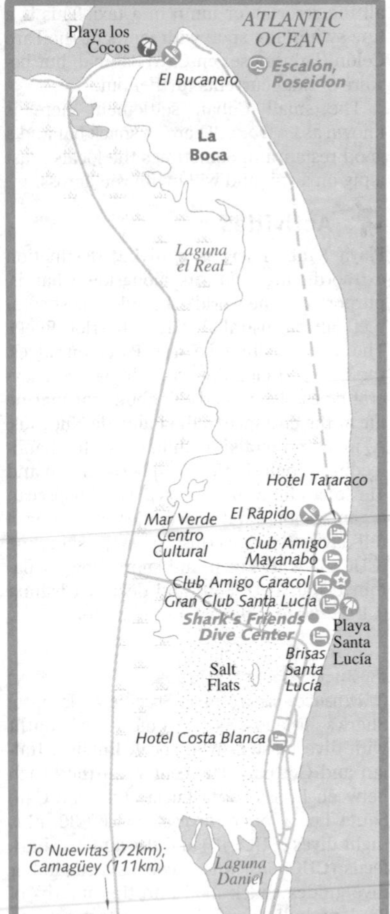

Gran Club Santa Lucía RESORT $$$
(☎33-61-09; all-incl s/d CUC$71/102; P ❄ @ ≋ ♿) Though claiming only three stars to Brisas' four, Gran Club comes out top on the strip for its 249 colorfully painted rooms (in well-maintained two-story blocks), prettily landscaped grounds and slightly less deafening poolside action. **Discoteca la Jungla** is the not overly inspiring nightclub that offers an evening music/comedy show with *mucho* audience participation.

Brisas Santa Lucía RESORT $$$
(☎33-63-02; all-incl s/d CUC$75/120; P ❄ @ ≋ ♿) This resort has 412 rooms in several three-story buildings. Covering a monstrous 11 hectares, it gets the strip's top rating: four stars, though with its over-jaunty holiday camp atmosphere (think mic-happy pool entertainers and a show where everything is repeated in three languages), it rarely justifies the billing. There is special kids' programming and Shark's Friends dive center is handily placed next door.

Hotel Tararaco HOTEL $
(☎33-63-10; s/d CUC$20/26; ❄) There are no casas particulares in Playa Santa Lucía, so thank Changó for the Tararaco, the strip's oldest hotel (it actually predates the Revolution) where the staff are keen enough and every room has a TV and a little patio, and is within stone-chucking distance of the beach.

Hotel Costa Blanca HOTEL $
(☎33-63-73; Playa Residencial; s/d CUC$14/20; ❄) The exception to the rule, Costa Blanca is a small but engaging low-rise Cuban cheapie situated in the micro-village. There's an on-site restaurant and the ocean is within earshot.

Club Amigo Mayanabo RESORT $
(☎36-51-68; all-incl s/d/tr CUC$35/58/79; P ❄ @ ≋) You are the weakest link here – goodbye! Doing a good impersonation of a tacky postwar British holiday camp, the Mayanabo has seen better days – a long time ago. But if budget's your prime consideration, it's cheap and right on the beach.

Club Amigo Caracol RESORT $$
(☎36-51-58; all-incl s/d CUC$45/55; P ❄ @ ≋ ♿) A newer version of the Mayanabo, the Caracol has the edge on its more worn partner and, with its large kids program, is usually promoted as the beach's family favorite.

✕ Eating

Aside from the hotel buffets and the two gold nuggets following, your choices are limited. There's an El Rápido opposite Hotel Tararaco that serves cheap (for a reason) fast food, and a peso place called La Concha in Santa Lucía village.

TOP CHOICE **El Bucanero** SEAFOOD $$
(Playa los Cocos; ⏲10am-10pm) Located on Playa los Cocos at the Santa Lucía end of the beach, this place is in a different class, serving seafood – lobster and prawns (CUC$12) is the house special – which is enhanced by the setting.

Restaurante Luna Mar SEAFOOD **$$**
(Playa Santa Lucía; ⌚10am-10pm) This place, flush up against the beach and wedged between Gran Club Santa Lucía and Club Amigo Caracol, offers exactly the same menu as El Bucanero, but in an easier-to-reach setting.

Entertainment

Outside of the resort entertainment, nothing much happens here.

The **Mar Verde Centro Cultural** (admission CUC$1) has a pleasant patio bar and a cabaret with live music nightly.

Shopping

The Mar Verde Centro Comercial in between the Gran Club Santa Lucía and Club Amigo Caracol has an ARTex store, a bookstore and a couple of government-run Caracol outlets selling Che Guevara T-shirts and the like.

Information

The **BANDEC** (Banco de Crédito y Comercio) where you can change money is in the Cuban residential area between the Servi-Cupet gas station at the southeastern entrance to Playa Santa Lucía and the hotel strip. Nearby is **Clínica Internacional de Santa Lucía** (☎36-53-00; Residencia 4), a well-equipped Cubanacán clinic for emergencies and medical issues. The best **pharmacy** is in Brisas Santa Lucía. Etecsa, 1.5km further along near the entrance to the hotel zone, has internet access for CUC$6 per hour and international phone capabilities. For tour agencies, Cubanacán, which owns four of the five hotels here, is well represented. There's a good **Cubatur** office just outside Gran Club Santa Lucía.

Getting There & Around

Anything is possible in Cuba, even getting to Playa Santa Lucía without your own transport. The only regular **bus** heads out from Camagüey every Friday at noon, arriving at Playa Santa Lucía at 1.30pm. A return bus leaves the resorts at 2pm on Sunday and arrives in Camagüey at 3.30pm. This bus is run by **Transtur** and costs CUC$18 one-way. Reserve one day in advance with **Cubatur**. Another option for independent travelers is to jump on one of the charter bus links with spare seats. The prices are: Camagüey airport (CUC$20, Thursday); Holguín airport (CUC$28, Wednesday & Friday). A **taxi** from Camagüey to Playa Santa Lucía will cost you CUC$70 one-way. Alternatively you can get a **train** to Nuevitas from Morón or Camagüey and taxi it from there.

The **Servi-Cupet gas station** is at the southeastern end of the strip, near the access road from Camagüey. Another large Servi-Cupet station, with a Servi-Soda snack bar, is just south of Brisas Santa Lucía.

You can rent cars or mopeds (CUC$24 per day, including a tank of gas) at **Cubacar** (Hotel Tararaco) or at any of the other hotels.

Las Tunas Province

031 / POP 536,027

Includes »

Best Places to Eat

- El Baturro (p332)
- Restaurante la Bodeguita (p332)
- Cremería las Copas (p332)

Best Places to Stay

- Hotel Cadillac (p331)
- Caballo Blanco – Pepe (p331)
- Brisas Covarrubias (p336)
- Roberto Lío Montes de Oca (p336)

Why Go?

Las Tunas is the province that's famous for not being famous. Wedged between uppity Camagüey to the west and the cultural powerhouse of the Oriente to the east, it's usually only experienced by people in transit. Sleepy and unspectacular, its historical legacy rests on the mastery of Victória de Las Tunas, an 1897 War of Independence battle won by Mambí general Calixto García.

With such a lackluster role of honor, it would be easy to forgive the unassuming *tuneros* a little pique – but they aren't the wallowing sort. Doubters should check out the provincial capital on Saturday night when there's a rodeo in town, or drive by Puerto Padre on any given Sunday to shoot the breeze with the locals.

Marshy in the south, Las Tunas' north coast is a largely undiscovered nirvana of colorful coral reefs and deserted eco-beaches that, to date, hosts just one all-inclusive resort. Long may it continue!

When to Go

Las Tunas has many festivals for a small town and the best one is the Jornada Cucalambeana in June, Cuba's biggest celebration of country music where local lyricists impress each other with their 10-line *décima* verses. Other highlights are the Festival Internacional de Magia (Magic Festival) held in the provincial capital in November and the National Sculpture Exhibition, an event befitting the so-called 'City of Sculptures', that takes place in February.

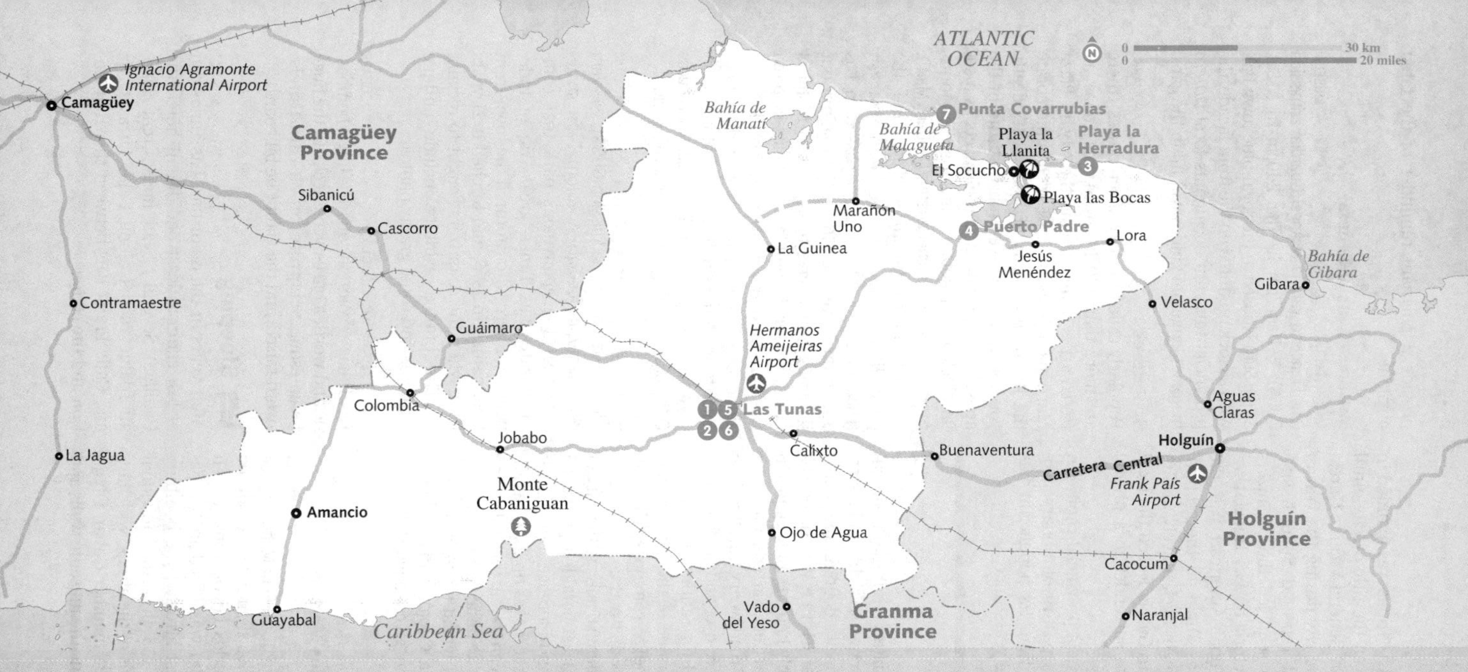

Las Tunas Province Highlights

1 Stroll the streets of sleepy **Las Tunas** (p330), where imaginative sculptures embellish the cityscape

2 Check out the dudes with lassos in **Parque 26 de Julio** (p334), Las Tunas' celebrated traveling rodeo

3 Enjoy the unkempt beaches of **Playa la Herradura** (p336), before resort developers shatter the tranquility

4 Linger awhile in friendly **Puerto Padre** (p335), where the locals have always got time to talk

5 Roll into Las Tunas in June to experience some country crooning at the **Jornada Cucalambeana** (p328) music festival

6 Enjoy the confines of some slick new provincial accommodation at **Hotel Cadillac** (p331) in Las Tunas

7 Go diving in the largely undiscovered reefs off **Punta Covarrubias** (p336)

History

The settlement of Las Tunas was founded in 1759 but wasn't given the title of 'city' until 1853. In 1876 Cuban General Vicente García briefly captured the city during the War of Independence, but repeated Spanish successes in the area soon led the colonizers to rename it La Victória de Las Tunas. During the Spanish-Cuban-American War the Spanish burned Las Tunas to the ground, but the Mambís fought back bravely, and in 1897 General Calixto García forced the local Spanish garrison to surrender in a pivotal Cuban victory.

Las Tunas became a provincial capital in 1975 during Cuba's post-revolutionary geographic reorganization. Its population has mushroomed in the years since.

Las Tunas

POP 139,637

First impressions matter – but they're not always right. If it was down to sights and historical attractions alone, it's doubtful that many people would bother with La Victória de Las Tunas (as it's officially known). But, thanks to its handy location on Cuba's arterial Carretera Central, handfuls of road-weary travelers drop by. Some give it a once-over and quickly rejoin the highway, bound for Santiago or Havana; others, swept up in one of the city's riotous Saturday-night shindigs, come over all affectionate and book another night.

Referred to euphemistically as the 'city of sculptures,' Cuba's least-heralded provincial capital is certainly no Florence. But what it lacks in grandiosity it makes up for in small-town quirks. You can see a thigh-slapping rodeo here, admire a statue of a two-headed Taíno chief, or wax lyrical at the weird and witty Cucalambeana, Cuba's leading country-music festival. Go on, give it a whirl!

Sights

FREE Memorial a los Mártires de Barbados MUSEUM

(Lucas Ortíz No 344; ⏲10am-6pm Mon-Sat) Las Tunas' most evocative sight is located in the former home of Carlos Leyva González, an Olympic fencer who was killed in the nation's worst terrorist atrocity: the bombing of Cubana Flight 455 in 1976. Individual photos of the victims of the attack, which included the entire 24-member Cuban Olympic fencing team, line the museum walls and provide a poignant reminder of the fated airplane.

Museo Provincial General Vicente García MUSEUM

(cnr Francisco Varona & Ángel Guardia; admission CUC$1; ⏲11am-7pm Tue-Thu, 2-10pm Fri & Sat, 3-7pm Sun) Housed in the royal-blue town hall with a clock mounted on the front facade, the provincial museum documents local *tunero* history. Congenial guides will fill in the gaps.

Sculptures LANDMARKS

Popularly called the 'city of sculptures' (there are more than 100 in town), Las Tunas' alfresco art is dotted around the city. In Plaza Martiana, opened in 1995 to commemorate the 100th anniversary of José Martí's death, you'll see an inventive bronze **statue** of the apostle by Rita Longa that also acts as a solar clock. Other notables include the **Monumento al Trabajo** (cnr Carretera Central & Martí), commemorating Cuban workers, and the pencil-like **Monumento a Alfabetización** (Lucas Ortiz), marking the act passed in Las Tunas on November 16, 1961 to stamp out illiteracy. You'll have to get out to Motel el Cornito to see the emblematic Janus-inspired **Cacique Maniabo y Jibacoa**, a two-headed Taíno chief looking in opposite directions. Back in town the small **Galería Taller Escultura Rita Longa** (cnr Av 2 de Diciembre & Lucas Ortiz) pulls together some fine local work.

Memorial Vicente García MUSEUM

(Vicente García No 7; admission CUC$1; ⏲3-7pm Mon, 11am-7pm Tue-Sat) A colonial-era structure near the eponymous park that commemorates Las Tunas' great War of Independence hero who captured the town from the Spanish in 1876, and torched it 21 years later when the colonizers sought to reclaim it. The limited exhibits include antique weapons and some grainy photos.

Plaza de la Revolución SQUARE

Las Tunas' revolution square is huge, bombastic and worth a once-over. Check out the huge Lenin-esque **sculpture of Vicente García**, sword raised, and the giant Che billboard.

Sleeping

After years in the doldrums, Las Tunas can at last claim at least one decent hotel (the Cadillac). Several private houses rent clean, affordable rooms along Calle Lucas Ortíz and Calle Frank País between the train station and the center.

FLIGHT 455

Blink and you'll miss it. The tiny bronze monument beside the Río Hormiguero in unfashionable Las Tunas is Cuba's sole memorial to one of the country's darkest hours.

On October 6, 1976, Cubana de Aviación Flight 455, on its way back to Havana from Guyana, took off after a stopover in Barbados' Seawell airport. Nine minutes after clearing the runway, two bombs went off in the cabin's rear toilet causing the plane to crash into the Atlantic Ocean. All 73 people on board – 57 of whom were Cuban – were killed. The toll included the entire Cuban fencing team fresh from a clean sweep of gold medals at the Central American Championships. At the time, the tragedy of Flight 455 was the worst ever terrorist attack in the Western hemisphere.

Hours after the bombing, two Venezuelan men were arrested in Barbados and a line was quickly traced back to Luis Posada Carriles and Orlando Bosch, two Cuban-born anti-Castro activists with histories as CIA operatives.

Arrested in Venezuela in 1977, the men were tried by both civilian and military courts and spent the best part of 10 years in Venezuelan prisons. Bosch was released in 1987 and went to live in the US. Carriles, meanwhile, broke out of jail in 1985 in a daring escape in which he dressed up as a priest. A year later he re-emerged in Nicaragua coordinating military supply drops for Contra rebels.

Despite worsening relations with the CIA and a failed attempt on his life in Guatemala City in 1990, Carriles remained active. In 1997 he was implicated in a series of bombings directed against tourist sites in Havana, and in 2000 he was arrested in Panama City for allegedly attempting to assassinate Fidel Castro.

Pardoned in 2004 by outgoing Panamanian president Mireya Moscoso, Carriles sought asylum in the US after the Venezuelan Supreme Court filed an extradition request for him. The US has so far refused to hand him over claiming that he faces the threat of torture in Venezuela.

As of 2011 Carriles was still living in the US, aged 83. Bosch died in April 2011, aged 84, also in the US. Among some anti-Castro extremists they are hailed as freedom fighters, while to most Cubans they are unrepentant terrorists.

TOP CHOICE Hotel Cadillac HOTEL $$
(☎37-27-91; cnr Angel de la Guardia & Francisco Vega; s/d/ste CUC$40/50/60; ❄) At last Las Tunas gets a hotel that doesn't give you flashbacks to the Khrushchev and Brezhnev years. Opened in 2009, this rehabilitated 1940s beauty bang in the city center is verging on boutique standard with just eight rooms including a lovely corner suite. There are flat-screen TVs, up-to-the-minute bathrooms and a dash of old-fashioned prerevolutionary class. A true Cadillac!

Caballo Blanco – Pepe CASA PARTICULAR $
(☎37-36-58; Frank País No 85 Altos; r CUC$20-25; ❄) Once you've gotten over the Gaudiesque, stone-dashed facade and colorful tiled stairway and realized you're in Las Tunas not Barcelona, take a peep inside at the dazzling tiled floors, hotel-standard bathrooms, wall-mounted TVs and operating-room all-round cleanliness (no surprise that Pepe is a doctor). Welcome to the best private digs in Las Tunas. If they're full the neighbors at Frank País Nos 79, 82 and 82A also rent out rooms.

Motel el Cornito CABINS $
(☎34-50-14; Carretera Central Km 8; r CUC$20) A Cuban-oriented place located outside of town near the site of El Cucalambé's old farm. The annual country music festival takes place here. You might get lucky with one of the basic bungalows. Phone ahead.

Carlos A Patiño Alvarez CASA PARTICULAR $
(☎34-22-88; Lucas Ortíz No 120; r CUC$20-25; ❄) There are two apartments here, each with their own bathroom, sitting room and kitchen equipped with pots and pans. The upstairs one is brighter and has a terrace.

Hotel Las Tunas HOTEL $
(☎34-50-14; Av 2 de Diciembre; s/d CUC$18/28; P❄≋) What you see is what you get: unimaginative architecture, austere interiors, out-of-the-way location, dodgy restaurant and a wake-you-up-at-2am disco. Room TVs pick up HBO – a small consolation.

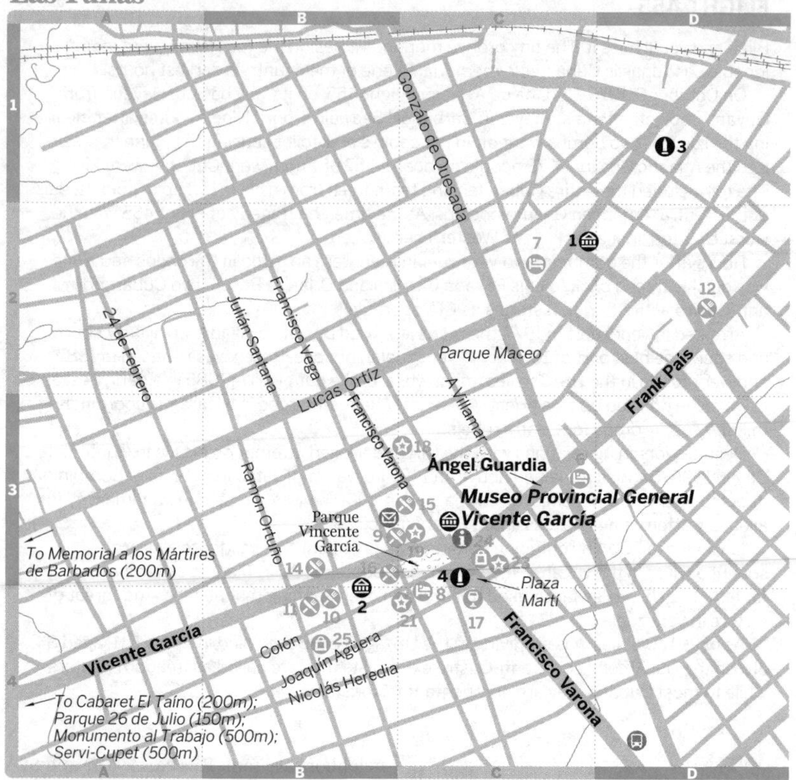

Eating

Las Tunas has two decent government-run restaurants in the city center serving *comida criolla* (Creole food) with a couple of surprises. Elsewhere the menus are fairly scant.

TOP CHOICE El Baturro CARIBBEAN $
(Av Vicente García btwn Julián Santana & Ramón Ortuño; 11am-11pm) The walls are covered in scribbled prose – love notes and eulogies to murdered Chilean troubadour Victor Jara – and the plates are stuffed with better-than-average Cuban cooking, including a surprise rabbit dish, making this the best restaurant in Las Tunas.

Restaurante la Bodeguita CARIBBEAN $
(Francisco Varona No 293; 11am-11pm) A Palmares joint, meaning that it's a better bet than the usual peso parlors. You'll get checkered tablecloths here, a limited wine list and what the Cuban government calls 'international cuisine' – read spaghetti and pizza. Try the chicken breast with mushroom sauce for around CUC$5.

Cremería las Copas ICE-CREAM PARLOR $
(cnr Francisco Vega & Vicente García; 10am-4pm & 5-11pm;) Las Tunas' substitute Coppelia; queue up with your pesos for sundaes or *tres gracias* (three scoops) in flavors such as coconut, and *café con leche* (espresso with milk). Not surprisingly, it's insanely popular.

Restaurante 2007 CARIBBEAN $
(Vicente García btwn Julián Santana & Ramón Ortuño; noon-2:45pm & 6-10:45pm) A new-ish attempt at fine dining in Las Tunas (albeit in pesos), this place claims to be 'reservations only' and doesn't exactly encourage non-Cubans. The plush interior and suited waiters look promising, but you'll get a friendlier welcome at El Baturro across the road.

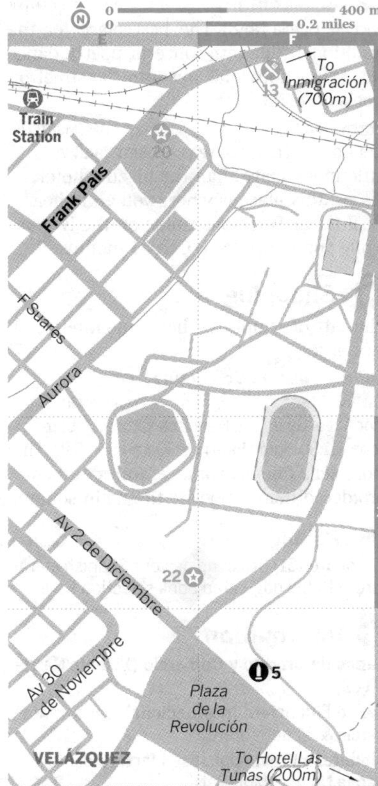

Las Tunas

Top Sights
Museo Provincial General Vicente García....C3

Sights
1 Galería Taller Escultura Rita Longa....C2
2 Memorial Vicente García....B4
3 Monumento a Alfabetización....D1
4 Statue of Jose Martí....C3
5 Vicente García Monument....F4

Sleeping
6 Caballo Blanco - Pepe....C3
7 Carlos A Patiño Alvarez....C2
8 Hotel Cadillac....C4

Eating
9 Cremería las Copas....B3
10 El Baturro....B4
11 En Familla....B4
12 La Bamba....D2
13 Mercado Agropecuario....F1
14 Restaurante 2007....B3
15 Restaurante la Bodeguita....C3
16 Supermercado Casa Azul....B3

Drinking
Cadillac Snack bar....(see 8)
17 Casa del Vino Don Juan....C4

Entertainment
18 Cabildo San Pedro Lucumí....C3
19 Casa de la Cultura....C3
20 Estadio Julio Antonio Mella....E1
21 Piano Bar....C4
22 Sala Polivalente....E3
23 Teatro Tunas....C3

Shopping
24 Fondo Cubano de Bienes Culturales....C3
25 Librería Fulgencio Oroz....B4

La Bamba PALADAR $$
(☎34-43-15; Frank País No 52; dishes CUC$5-8) An old-school, rough-around-the-edges Tunero paladar with big portions of *comida criolla*, including the reliable (lobster) and the rare (rabbit).

En Familla FAST FOOD $
(Vicente García btwn Ramon Ortuño & Julián Santana; ⏰11am-11pm) Promising sign, morbid surroundings, scant menu; but if you can rouse the pizza man from his catatonic slumber you might just get lucky.

Self-Catering

To stock up on groceries (or to break bigger bills), try **Supermercado Casa Azul** (cnr Vicente García & Francisco Vega; ⏰9am-6pm Mon-Sat, to noon Sun). **Mercado Agropecuario** (Av Camilo Cienfuegos) is a small market not far from the train station.

Drinking

Casa del Vino Don Juan BAR
(cnr Francisco Varona & Joaquín Agüero; ⏰9am-midnight) Wine-tasting in Las Tunas probably sounds about as credible as food rationing in Beverley Hills, yet here it is; and only seven pesos for a shot of Cuba's – er – finest wine, the slightly vinegary Soroa (red or white). The Don Juan is a down-to-earth corner bar with large open doors and just a handful of tables. Go just to say you've been there.

Cadillac Snack Bar CAFE
(cnr Angel de la Guardia & Francisco Vega; ⏲9am-11pm) This offshoot of the Hotel Cadillac has four pleasant tables on a terrace overlooking the Plaza Martiana action and serves decent *café con leche.*

☆ Entertainment

Las Tunas comes alive on Saturday nights when packed streets and fun-seeking locals defy the city's 'boring' image. The main hubs are: **Parque Vicente García**, where alfresco *son* music competes with more modern *reggaetón* (Cuban hip-hop); and Parque 26 de Julio.

TOP CHOICE **Parque 26 de Julio** FAIRGROUND
(Av Vicente García; admission free; ⏲9am-6pm Sat & Sun; 👪) Located in Parque Julio 26 where Vicente García bends into Av 1 de Mayo, it kicks off every weekend with a market, music, food stalls, kids' activities and, if you're lucky, a full-scale rodeo (you'll see the large permanent arena as you walk in).

Estadio Julio Antonio Mella SPORTS
(1ra de Enero) From October to April is baseball season. Las Tunas plays at this stadium near the train station. Los Magos (the Wizards) haven't produced much magic of late and usually compete with the likes of Ciego de Ávila for bottom place in the East League. Other sports happen at the **Sala Polivalente**, an indoor arena near Hotel Las Tunas.

FREE **Cabildo San Pedro Lucumí** CULTURAL CENTER
(Francisco Varona btwn Vicente García & Lucas Ortíz; ⏲from 9pm Sun) Cultural activities happen at this friendly Afro-Caribbean association, HQ of the Compañía Folklórica Onilé. Drop in on Sunday for some dancing and drumming.

Teatro Tunas THEATER, CINEMA
(cnr Francisco Varona & Joaquín Agüera) A recently revitalized theater that shows quality movies and some of Cuba's best touring entertainment including flamenco, ballet and plays.

Cabaret el Taíno THEATER
(cnr Vicente García & A Cabrera; admission per couple CUC$10; ⏲9pm-2am Tue-Sun) This large thatched venue at the west entrance to town has the standard feathers, salsa and pasties show. Cover charge includes a bottle of rum and cola.

Casa de la Cultura CULTURAL CENTER
(Vicente García No 8) The best place for the traditional stuff with concerts, poetry, dance etc. The action spills out into the street on weekend nights.

Piano Bar BAR, NIGHTCLUB
(cnr Colón & Francisco Vega; ⏲9pm-2am) A little more suave than the blazing hotel discos, this place is where you go to hear local Oscar Petersons tinkle on the ivories while you knock back CUC$1 mojitos.

Shopping

The 'city of sculptures' has some interesting local art.

Fondo Cubano de Bienes Culturales ART, CRAFTS
(cnr Angel Guardia & Francisco Varona; ⏲9am-noon & 1:30-5pm Mon-Fri, 8:30am-noon Sat) This store sells fine artwork, ceramics and embroidered items opposite the main square.

Librería Fulgencio Oroz BOOKSTORE
(Colón No 151) Brush up on your Spanish literature with the dog-eared book selection here.

Information

Banco de Crédito y Comercio (Vicente García No 69)

Banco Financiero Internacional (cnr Vicente García & 24 de Febrero)

Biblioteca Provincial José Martí (Vicente García No 4; ⏲Mon-Sat)

Cadeca (Colón No 41) Money changing.

Cubana (cnr Lucas Ortíz & 24 de Febrero) Travel agent.

Etecsa Telepunto (Francisco Vega btwn Vicente García & Lucas Ortiz; ⏲8:30am-7:30pm) Spanking modern air-conditioned haven on the shopping boulevard.

Hospital Che Guevara (☎34-50-12; cnr Avs CJ Finlay & 2 de Diciembre) One kilometer from the highway exit toward Holguín.

Infotur (cnr Ángel Guardia & Francisco Varona) Travel agent.

Post office (Vicente García No 6; ⏲8am-8pm) There are internet terminals here too.

Getting There & Away

Bus

The main **bus station** (Francisco Varona) is 1km southeast of the main square. **Víazul** (www.viazul.com) buses have daily departures; tickets are sold by the *jefe de turno* (shift manager).

There are five daily buses to Havana (CUC$39, 11 hours) leaving at 1:45am, 10:35am, 2:30pm, 8:45pm and 9:35pm; four to Holguín (CUC$6,

Holguín

Sights

Sleeping

Eating

Entertainment

Casa Natal de Calixto García MUSEUM

(Map p348; Miró No 147; admission CUC$1; ⌚9am-9pm Tue-Sat) To learn more about the militaristic deeds of Holguín's local hero, head to this house situated two blocks east of the namesake park. The hugely underestimated García – who stole the cities of Las Tunas, Holguín and Bayamo from Spanish control between 1896 and 1898 – was born here in 1839 and this small collection gives a reasonable overview of his life.

Museo de Historia Natural MUSEUM

(Map p348; Maceo No 129 btwn Parques Calixto García & Peralta; admission CUC$1; ⌚9am-10pm Tue-Sat) You'll find more stuffed animals here than in a New York toy store – everything from the world's smallest frog to the world's smallest hummingbird. The museum was undergoing renovations at the time of writing.

Plaza de la Marqueta SQUARE

(Map p348) Long earmarked for a major renovation, hopelessly ruined Plaza de la Marqueta is a plaza of possibilities that have, so far, remained unfulfilled. Laid out in 1848 and rebuilt in 1918, the square is dominated by an impressive covered marketplace that is supposed to be undergoing a transformation into a top-notch concert hall (after nearly a decade of rumors, however, the work has yet to start). Running along the north and south sides of the plaza are myriad shops that are meant to provide quality shopping but, at the time of writing, only a couple of music and cigar outlets were open and even these few stores were poorly stocked. For the time being, the most interesting sights are the telephone poles turned into totems, which anchor the plaza's corners, as well as the numerous bronze statues of well-known *holguiñeros* that decorate the sidewalks.

Plaza de la Revolución SQUARE

(Map p342) Holguín is a city most *fiel* (faithful), and its bombastic revolutionary plaza, east of the center, is a huge monument to the heroes of Cuban independence, bearing quotations from José Martí and Fidel Castro. Massive rallies are held here every May 1 (Labor Day). The **tomb of Calixto García** (Map p342), containing his ashes, is also here, as well as a smaller monument to García's mother.

WILL HISTORY ABSOLVE HIM?

Has the world misunderstood Fidel Castro? Is this rugged survivor of the Cold War and the catastrophic economic meltdown that followed just a Machiavellian dictator responsible for driving an immovable wedge into US–Cuban relations? Or is he the de facto leader of an unofficial Third World alliance pioneering the fight for equal rights and social justice on the world stage? To get closer to the personality that lies behind the public mask we must (as every good Freudian knows) delve into his childhood.

Born near the village of Birán in Holguín province on August 13, 1926, the illegitimate product of a relationship between Spanish-born landowner Ángel Castro and his cook and housemaid Lina Ruz (they later married), Fidel grew up as a favored child in a large and relatively wealthy family of sugar farmers. Educated at a Jesuit school and sent away to study in the city of Santiago at the age of seven, the young Castro was an exceptional student whose prodigious talents included a photographic memory and an extraordinary aptitude for sport. Indeed, legend has it that at the age of 21, Fidel – by then a skilled left-arm pitcher – was offered a professional baseball contract with the Washington Senators.

At the age of 13 Fidel staged his first insurrection, a strike organized among his father's sugarcane workers against their exploitative boss, a gesture that did little to endear him to the fraternal fold.

One year later the still-teenage Castro penned a letter to US president FD Roosevelt congratulating him on his re-election and asking the American leader for a US$10 bill 'because I have not seen a US$10 bill and I would like to have one of them.' Rather ominously for future US–Cuban relations, the request was politely turned down.

Undeterred, Fidel marched on. On the completion of his high school certificate in 1945, his teacher and mentor Father Francisco Barbeito predicted sagely that his bullish star pupil would 'fill with brilliant pages the book of his life.' With the benefit of hindsight, he wasn't far wrong. Armed with tremendous personal charisma, a wrought-iron will and a

OUTSIDE TOWN

La Loma de la Cruz LANDMARK

At the northern end of Maceo you'll find a stairway built in 1950, with 465 steps ascending a 275m-high hill with panoramic views. A cross was raised here in 1790 in hope of relieving a drought, and every May 3 during Romerías de Mayo devotees climb to the summit where a special Mass is held. It's a 20-minute walk from town or you can flag a bici-taxi to the foot of the hill for around 10 Cuban pesos. This walk is best tackled early in the morning when the light is pristine and the heat not too debilitating.

Fábrica de Órganos ORGAN FACTORY

(Carretera de Gibara No 301; ⌚8am-4pm Mon-Fri) This is the only mechanical music-organ factory in Cuba. This small factory produces about six organs a year, as well as guitars and other instruments. A good organ costs between the equivalent of US$10,000 and US$25,000. Eight professional organ groups exist in Holguín (including the Familia Cuayo, based at the factory), and, if you're lucky, you can hear one playing on Parque Céspedes on Thursday afternoons or Sunday mornings.

Mirador de Mayabe FARM, LOOKOUT

The Mirador de Mayabe is a motel cum restaurant cum traditional farm high on a hill 10km from Holguín city. It gained fame for a beer-drinking donkey named Pancho, who hung out near the bar in the 1980s. The original Pancho died in 1992 and they're now onto his grandson, Pancho III who also drinks beer but is, apparently, fussier about the brand. Typical Cuban lunches are served at the Finca Mayabe (p347), just above the motel, where there's also a cockfighting ring. Traditional country shows occur here most weeks. A bus runs to Holguín from the bottom of the hill, 1.5km from the motel, three times a day.

Festivals & Events

Carnaval OUTDOOR FESTIVAL

Holguín's annual shindig happens in the third week of August with outdoor concerts and copious amounts of dancing, roast pork and potent potables.

natural ability to pontificate interminably for hours on end, Fidel made tracks for Havana University where his forthright and unyielding personality quickly ensured he excelled at everything he did.

Training ostensibly as a lawyer, Castro spent the next three years embroiled in political activity amid an academic forum that was riddled with gang violence and petty corruption. 'My impetuosity, my desire to excel, fed and inspired the character of my struggle,' he recalled candidly years later.

Blessed with more lives than a cat, Castro has survived a failed putsch, 15 months in prison, exile in Mexico, a two-year guerrilla war in the mountains and a reported 617 attempts on his life. His sense of optimism in the face of defeat is nothing short of astounding. With his rebel army reduced to a ragged band of 12 men after the Granma landing, he astonished his beleaguered colleagues with a fiery victory speech. 'We will win this war,' he trumpeted confidently, 'We are just beginning the fight!'

As an international personality who has outlasted 11 American presidents, the 21st-century incarnation of Fidel Castro that emerged following the Special Period was no less enigmatic than the revolutionary leader of yore. Fostering his own peculiar brand of Caribbean socialism with an unflinching desire to 'defend the Revolution at all costs,' the ever-changing ideology that Castro so famously preached is perhaps best summarized by biographer Volker Skierka as 'a pragmatic mixture of a little Marx, Engels and Lenin, slightly more of Che Guevara, a lot of José Martí, and a great deal indeed of Fidel Castro.'

Castro stepped out of public life in July 2006 after a serious bout of diverticulitis and handed the reins of power to his younger brother Raúl. Despite penning regular articles for national newspaper *Granma* and making the odd jarring public statement on world affairs, he looks destined to see out his final years like a Caribbean Napoleon wistfully pondering his historical legacy from his lonely island prison. Whether history will absolve him is still anybody's guess.

Sleeping

IN TOWN

Motel el Bosque HOTEL $

(☎48-11-40; Av Jorge Dimitrov; s/d incl breakfast CUC$20/30; P ❄ ≋) One kilometer beyond Hotel Pernik and at least one notch up on the quality ratings, the 69 duplex bungalows here are set among extensive green grounds, making it feel more removed than it is. There's a relaxing bar beside the swimming pool (non-guests can use it for a small fee) and the late-night music decibels aren't as ear-shattering as its noisy neighbor (the Pernik).

'La Palma' – Enrique R Interián Salermo CASA PARTICULAR $

(Map p342; ☎42-46-83; Maceo No 52A btwn Calles 16 & 18, El Llano; r CUC$25; ❄) Enrique's detached neocolonial house dates from 1945 and is situated in the shadow of the Loma de la Cruz. The slightly removed location is worth the minor inconvenience. Enrique is a fantastic host and his spacious house has a pleasant garden. Furthermore, his son is a talented painter and sculptor and you can check out the terra-cotta bust of Che Guevara in the living room next to an unusual 3m-long canvas copy of Da Vinci's *TheLast Supper* (with St John as a woman).

Raciel Laffita Rodríguez CASA PARTICULAR $

(Map p342; ☎42-59-30; cnr Cables & Manduley; r CUC$25) A friendly *holguiñero* who rents two small upstairs rooms with terraces slap-bang in the middle of town. The TVs here can (unusually) pick up a couple of English-language channels. If they're full, there's another option two doors down at Calle Cables No 105.

Hotel Pernik HOTEL $

(Map p342; ☎48-10-11; cnr Avs Jorge Dimitrov & XX Aniversario; s/d/tr incl breakfast CUC$24/34/46; P ❄ @ ≋) The nearest hotel to the city center is another dose of Soviet-inspired '70s nostalgia, though it has attempted to counter its dour reputation in recent years with some quirky improvements. A handful of the rooms were given over to a group of local artists who covered every available space (including the sinks and toilets) with colorful art. As for the basics, the breakfast buffet is plentiful and there's an information office, Cadeca and internet cafe; but the hotel suffers from the usual foibles of interminable renovations and blaring late-night music.

Maricela García Martínez CASA PARTICULAR $
(Map p348; ☎47-10-49; Miró No 110 btwn Martí & Luz Caballero; r CUC$20-25) If you can negotiate your way around the motorbike in the front room, the place is yours. The downstairs bedroom is a little on the dark side, but it has an en suite bath and is a block from the central parks.

Milagro López Felipe CASA PARTICULAR $
(Map p348; Miró No 207; r CUC$25) The blue-and-white sign outside makes this place difficult to miss. One upstairs room with all mod cons and terrace is shielded from the street by a pretty curtain of begonias.

OUTSIDE TOWN

Villa Mirador de Mayabe HOTEL $
(☎42-54-98; Alturas de Mayabe; s/d CUC$30/40; P❄🏊) This motel, high up on the Loma de Mayabe 10km southeast of Holguín, has 24 rooms tucked into lush grounds. The views, taking in vast mango plantations, are especially good from the pool.

Eating

Holguín is what you might call 'gastronomically challenged'; there's only one restaurant that'll stick in your memory for the right reasons – the dusty colonial Salón 1720. On the brighter side there are some good streetside bars and cafes where you can slump down with a beer or coffee and watch half the city troop by.

IN TOWN

TOP CHOICE **Salón 1720** CARIBBEAN $$
(Map p348; Frexes No 190 cnr Miró; ⌚12:30-10:30pm) Holguín's finest dining by a mile is in this painstakingly restored wedding cake mansion where you can tuck into paella (CUC$6) or chicken stuffed with vegetables and cheese (CUC$8); there's even complimentary crackers. In the same colonial-style complex there's a cigar shop, a bar, a boutique, car rental and a terrace with nighttime music. Check out the wall plaques that give interesting insights into Holguín's history.

Taberna Pancho CARIBBEAN $
(Map p342; Av Jorge Dimitrov; ⌚noon-10pm) This bar between Hotel Pernik and Motel el Bosque inspired by the Finca Mayabe's famous beer-drinking donkey has echoes of a Spanish *taberna*. While a long way from being memorable, the menu includes a sausage special of chorizo (unusual in Cuba). The draft Mayabe beer comes in proper frosted glasses. Nothing on the menu is more than CUC$3.

Colonial 1545 CARIBBEAN $
(Map p348; cnr Calle Maceo & Luz y Caballero; dishes CUC$1-2; ⌚noon-10.45pm Mon-Thu, to 2am Fri-Sun) This slightly flyblown colonial building on Parque Peralta looks like it might have potential, but this is a Cuban peso place (though they'll accept convertibles). Arrive with low expectations.

Cafetería Cristal FAST FOOD $
(Map p348; ground fl, Edificio Pico de Cristal, cnr Manduley & Martí; ⌚24hr) Reliable, affordable chicken meals are served at the chilly Cristal, where the air-con does its best to replicate a frigid day in Vancouver. A more upscale restaurant – the Isla Cristal – is upstairs (open noon to 10pm).

Cafetería Tocororo FAST FOOD $
(Map p348; Manduley No 189; ⌚24hr) The lackluster menu may give survivors of post-WWII rationing a sneaking sense of déjà vu (count on the terrible trio of pizza, chicken and cheese-and-ham sandwiches), but to enjoy Parque Calixto García in all its glory you've got to get in on the act. Pull up a seat at this park-side cafe and get down to some serious square-spotting with the local barflies and the odd Guardalavaca escapee.

Pizzería Roma PIZZA $
(Map p348; cnr Maceo & Agramonte) It's a long way from Rome, let alone Naples. You don't need to cross the threshold of this popular local place by Parque Céspedes; just get the guy on the stall by the door to hand you over a slice of thick dough smeared with cheese and tomatoes for six pesos.

Cremería Guamá ICE-CREAM PARLOR $
(Map p348; cnr Luz Caballero & Manduley; ⌚10am-10:45pm) A Coppelia in all but name. Lose an hour underneath the striped red-and-white awning overlooking pedestrianized Calle Manduley and enjoy peso ice-cream alfresco.

Self-Catering

There are two *agropecuarios* (vegetable markets; Map p342): one is off Calle 19, the continuation of Morales Lemus near the train station, the other on Calle 3 in Dagoberto Sanfield. There are plenty of peso stalls beside the baseball stadium.

La Luz de Yara SUPERMARKET $
(Map p348; cnr Frexes & Maceo; ⌚8:30am-7pm Mon-Sat, to noon Sun) Relatively well-stocked Cuban department store and supermarket with a bakery section on Parque Calixto García.

La Epoca SUPERMARKET $

(Map p348; Frexes No 194) Another supermarket option on Parque Calixto García.

OUTSIDE TOWN

Finca Mayabe CARIBBEAN $$

(Alturas de Mayabe) This *finca* (farm) set on the Mirador de Mayabe, a hill 8km southeast of Holguín, is a destination in its own right, and not just for the famous beer-drinking donkey. The food is good too, augmented by the broad views, rustic setting, and cooking that is reminiscent of the delicious spit-roasted simplicity that the country-dwelling Cubans do so well.

Drinking

Stand down all other claimants: Holguín brews the best beer in Cuba. The large Fábrica de Cerveza on the outskirts of the city produces the nation's two most popular beers, Cristal and Bucanero, as well as local favorites Mayabe and Cacique. None of the local bars are fancy, but you can cobble together a decent pub crawl here. In no specific order, hit on some of the following...

Taberna Mayabe BAR

(Map p348; Manduley btwn Aguilera & Frexes; ⌚3-6pm & 8pm-midnight Tue-Sun) Not the famous *finca*, but a good local bar on pedestrian-only Manduley with wooden tables, ceramic mugs and a hearty pub atmosphere that serves the eponymous local brew. Doormen ensure the action remains courteous.

La Cubita CAFE

(Map p348; Manduley btwn Frexes & Aguilera; ⌚24hr) Formica tables, some local gossip and cheap shots of strong coffee slammed down on the bar for two Cuban pesos. It should give you enough rocket fuel to last the rest of the day.

Bar Terraza BAR

(Map p348; Frexes btwn Manduley & Miró; ⌚9pm-2am) Perched above Salón 1720, this is the poshest spot to sip a mojito with views over Parque Calixto García and regular musical interludes.

La Caverna BAR, LIVE MUSIC

(Map p348; cnr Aguilera & Maceo; ⌚4pm-2am) Not a cave, but a bar named in honor of The Beatles whose songs are reproduced by local bands such as Los Beltas and Retorno. Graffiti adorns walls decorated with familiar Fab Four album covers.

☆ Entertainment

TOP CHOICE **Uneac** CULTURAL CENTER

(Map p348; Manduley btwn Luz Caballero & Martí) If you only visit one Uneac (Unión Nacional de Escritores y Artistas de Cuba; National Union of Cuban Writers and Artists) center in Cuba – there are 14 of them in all (one in each province) – make sure it's this one. Situated in a lovingly restored house on car-free Calle Manduley, this friendly establishment offers everything from literary evenings (with famous authors) and music nights, to patio theater (including Lorca) and cultural reviews. There's an intermittent bar on a gorgeous central patio.

Teatro Comandante Eddy Suñol THEATER

(Map p348; Martí No 111) Holguín's premier theater is an art deco treat from 1939 on Parque Calixto García. It hosts both the Teatro Lírico Rodrigo Prats and the Ballet Nacional de Cuba and is renowned both nationally and internationally for its operettas, dance performances and Spanish musicals. Check here for details of performances by the famous children's theater Alas Buenas and the Orquesta Sinfónica de Holguín (Holguín Symphony Orchestra).

Biblioteca Alex Urquiola THEATER, LIVE MUSIC

(Map p348; Maceo No 180) Culture vultures steam the creases out of their evening dresses to come here to see live theater, and performances by the Orquesta Sinfónica de Holguín.

Casa de la Trova LIVE MUSIC

(Map p348; Maceo No 174; ⌚Tue-Sun) Old guys in Panama hats croon under the rafters, musicians in *guayaberas* (pleated, buttoned shirts) blast on trumpets, while ancient couples in their Sunday best map out a perfect *danzón* (traditional Cuban ballroom dance colored with African influences). So timeless, so Holguín.

Casa de la Música NIGHTCLUB

(Map p348; cnr Frexes & Manduley; ⌚Tue-Sun) There's a young, trendy vibe at this place on Parque Calixto García. If you can't dance, stay static sinking beers on the adjacent Terraza Bucanero (entry via Calle Manduley).

Disco Cristal NIGHTCLUB

(Map p348; 3rd fl, Edificio Pico de Cristal, Manduley No 199; admission CUC$2; ⌚9pm-2am Tue-Thu) A nexus for Holguín's dexterous dancers (most of whom are young, cool and determined to have a good time), this place is insanely popular at weekends when you'll find lots of

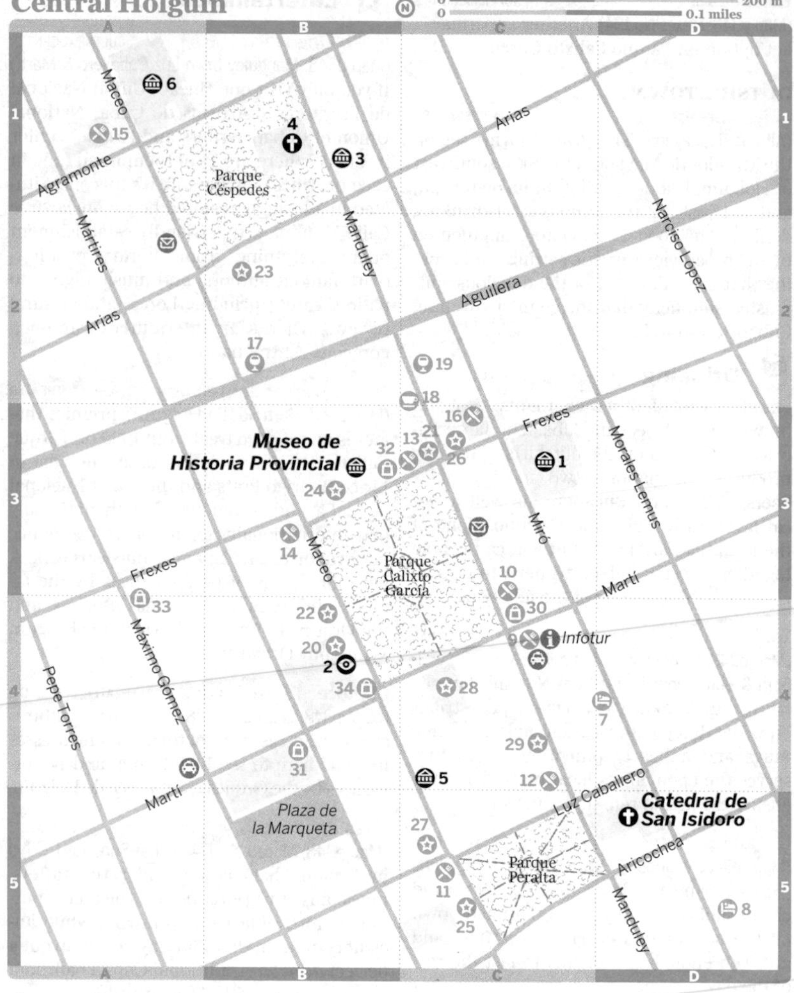

inspiration for the salsa/rap/*reggaetón* (Cuban hip-hop) repertoire.

Cabaret Nuevo Nocturno NIGHTCLUB
(admission CUC$10; ⏲10pm-2am) This is a Tropicana-style cabaret club beyond the Servi-Cupet gas station 3km out on the road to Las Tunas. Rather like a cricket match, there's no show if it's raining.

Salón Benny Moré LIVE MUSIC, DANCE HALL
(Map p348; cnr Luz Caballero & Maceo; ⏲show 10.30pm) Holguín's impressive new outdoor music venue is the best place to round off a bar crawl with some live music and dancing.

Jazz Club JAZZ
(Map p348; cnr Frexes & Manduley; ⏲11am-3am) The jazz jams get moving around 8pm-ish and continue weaving their magic until 11pm. Then there's taped music until 3am. During the daytime, hit the cafe or restaurant downstairs.

Casa Iberoamericana CULTURAL CENTER
(Map p348; Arias No 161) Situated on quieter Parque Céspedes, this paint-peeled place

Central Holguín

Top Sights
- Catedral de San Isidoro D5
- Museo de Historia Provincial B3

Sights
- Biblioteca Alex Urquiola .... (see 20)
- 1 Casa Natal de Calixto García C3
- 2 Centro de Arte B4
- 3 Galería Holguín B1
- 4 Iglesia de San José B1
- 5 Museo de Historia Natural C4
- 6 Museo Eduardo García Feria y José García Castañeda A1

Sleeping
- 7 Maricela García Martínez D4
- 8 Milagro López Felipe D5

Eating
- 9 Cafetería Cristal C4
- 10 Cafetería Tocororo C3
- 11 Colonial 1545 .... C5
- 12 Cremería Guamá C4
- 13 La Epoca C3
- 14 La Luz de Yara B3
- 15 Pizzería Roma A1
- 16 Salón 1720 .... C3

Drinking
- Bar Terraza .... (see 16)
- 17 La Caverna B2
- 18 La Cubita C2
- 19 Taberna Mayabe C2

Entertainment
- 20 Biblioteca Alex Urquiola B4
- 21 Casa de la Música C3
- 22 Casa de la Trova B4
- 23 Casa Iberoamericana B2
- 24 Cine Martí B3
- 25 Cominado Deportivo Henry García Suárez C5
- Disco Cristal .... (see 9)
- 26 Jazz Club C3
- 27 Salón Benny Moré C5
- 28 Teatro Comandante Eddy Suñol C4
- 29 Uneac C4

Shopping
- 30 ARTex C4
- 31 El Jigue B4
- 32 Fondo de Bienes Culturales B3
- 33 Librería Villena Botev A4
- 34 Pentagrama B4

frequently hosts *peñas* (musical performances) and cultural activities.

Cine Martí CINEMA
(Map p348; Frexes No 204; tickets 1-2 pesos) The best of a quintet of city-center cinemas, head here for big-screen movies. It's on Parque Calixto García.

Disco Havana Club NIGHTCLUB
(Map p342; Hotel Pernik, cnr Avs Jorge Dimitrov & XX Aniversario; guest/nonguest CUC$2/4; ⏲10pm-2am Tue-Sun) Holguín's premier disco. If you're staying at Hotel Pernik the music will visit you – in your room – like it or not, until 1am.

Sports

Estadio General Calixto García SPORTS
(Map p342; admission CUC$1-2) The excitement (disbelief?) has died down somewhat since Holguín's feisty Perros came out of nowhere to snatch the national baseball championship from under the noses of the 'big two' in 2002. But they're still a team to be watched. Mosey on down to this stadium, just off Av de los Libertadores near the Hotel Pernik, to see the giant-killers confidently swing their bats at pitchers from across the island. The stadium also houses a small but interesting **sport museum**.

Cominado Deportivo Henry García Suárez SPORTS
(Map p348; Maceo; admission 1 peso; ⏲8pm Wed, 2pm Sat) You can catch boxing matches at this spit-and-sawdust gym on the western side of Parque Peralta, where three Olympic medalists have trained. You can also pluck up the courage to ask about some (noncontact) training sessions. They're very friendly.

Shopping

Fondo de Bienes Culturales CRAFTS, SOUVENIRS
(Map p348; Frexes No 196; ⏲10am-3pm Mon-Fri, 9am-noon Sat) This shop on Parque Calixto García has one of the best selections of Cuban handicrafts.

ARTex BOOKS, SOUVENIRS
(Map p348; Manduley No 193A) Sells books, CDs, posters and Che T-shirts on Parque Calixto García.

Pentagrama MUSIC STORE
(Map p348; cnr Maceo & Martí; 9am-9pm) Official outlet of the Cuban state record company Egrem, selling a wide-ranging stash of CDs.

Librería Villena Botev BOOKSTORE
(Map p348; cnr Frexes & Máximo Gómez) Some good magazines here, including cultural Cuban monthly *Temas* along with a popular 'book of the week' nomination.

El Jigue BOOKS, SOUVENIRS
(Map p348; cnr Martí & Mártires) Book and souvenir outlet adjacent to Plaza de la Maqueta – the first of many, one hopes, in the rehabilitation of the square.

Information

The local newspaper *Ahora* is published on Saturday. Radio Angulo CMKO can be heard on 1110AM and 97.9FM.

Banco de Crédito y Comercio (Arias) Bank on Parque Céspedes.

Banco Financiero Internacional (Manduley No 167 btwn Frexes & Aguilera)

Cadeca (Manduley No 205 btwn Martí & Luz Caballero) Money changing.

Cubatur (ground fl, Edificio Pico de Cristal, cnr Manduley & Martí) Travel agent bivouacked inside the Cafetería Cristal.

Etecsa Telepunto Parque Calixto García (cnr Martí & Maceo; per hr CUC$6; 8:30am-7:30pm) Calle Martí (Martí btwn Martires & Máximo Gómez; per hr CUC$6; 8:30am-7:30pm) There are only telephones at the Parque Calixto García branch, while Calle Martí has three rarely busy computer terminals.

Farmacia Turno Especial (Maceo No 170; 8am-10pm Mon-Sat) Pharmacy on Parque Calixto García.

Hospital Lenin (☎42-53-02; Av VI Lenin) Will treat foreigners in an emergency.

Infotur (1st fl Edificio Pico de Cristal, cnr Manduley & Martí) Tourist information.

Paradiso (cnr Avs Jorge Dimitrov & XX Aniversario) Agent organizing mainly cultural trips from office in Hotel Pernik.

Post office Manduley No 183 (10am-noon & 1-6pm Mon-Fri); Parque Céspedes (Maceo No 114) There's a DHL office at the first branch, on Parque Calixto García.

Getting There & Away

Air

There are up to 16 international flights a week into Holguín's well-organized **Frank País Airport**, 13km south of the city, including from Amsterdam, Düsseldorf, London, Montreal and Toronto. Almost all arrivals get bused directly off to Guardalavaca and see little of Holguín city.

Domestic destinations are served by **Cubana** (Edificio Pico de Cristal, cnr Manduley & Martí), which flies daily to Havana (CUC$103 one-way, 1¼ hours).

Bus

The **Interprovincial Bus Station** (cnr Carretera Central & Independencia), west of the center near Hospital Lenin, has air-conditioned **Víazul** (www.viazul.com) buses leaving daily.

The fours-times-daily Havana bus (CUC$44, 12¾ hours) stops in Las Tunas, Camagüey, Ciego de Ávila, Sancti Spíritus and Santa Clara. The thrice-daily Santiago departure (CUC$11, four hours) also stops in Bayamo. There are also daily buses to Trinidad (CUC$26, 7¾ hours) and Varadero (CUC$38, 11¼ hours).

Train

The **train station** (Map p342; Calle V Pita) is on the southern side of town. Foreigners must purchase tickets in convertibles at the special **Ladis ticket office** (7:30am-3pm). The ticket office is marked 'U/B Ferrocuba Provincial Holguín' on the corner of Manduley, opposite the train station.

Theoretically, there's one daily morning train to Las Tunas (CUC$4, two hours), a daily afternoon train to Santiago de Cuba (CUC$5, 3½ hours), and a daily 6:15pm train to Havana (CUC$31, 15 hours). This train stops in Camagüey (CUC$9), Ciego de Ávila (CUC$13), Guayos (CUC$17), Santa Clara (CUC$20) and Matanzas (CUC$20). You may have to change trains at the Santiago–Havana mainline junction in Cacocum, 17km south of Holguín.

The only service that operates with any regularity is the train to Havana. The service to Santiago de Cuba is rather irregular. Research beforehand.

Truck

The **Terminal Dagoberto Sanfield Guillén** (Map p342; Av de los Libertadores), opposite Estadio General Calixto García, has at least two daily trucks to Gibara, Banes and Moa. To reach Guardalavaca, take a truck to Rafael Freyre (aka Santa Lucía) and look for something else there.

Getting Around

To/From the Airport

The public bus to the airport leaves daily around 2pm from the **airport bus stop** (Map p342; General Rodríguez No 84) on Parque Martí near the train station. A tourist taxi to the airport costs from CUC$8 to CUC$10. It's also possible to spend your last night in Bayamo, then catch a taxi (CUC$18 to CUC$20) to Holguín airport.

Bici-taxi

Holguín's bici-taxis are ubiquitous. They charge 5 pesos for a short trip, 10 pesos for a long one.

Car

You can rent or return a car at these places: **Cubacar** Hotel Pernik (Av Jorge Dimitrov); Aeropuerto Frank País (☎46-84-14); Cafetería Cristal (cnr Manduley & Martí)

A **Servi-Cupet gas station** (Carretera Central; ⏰24hr) is 3km out toward Las Tunas; another station is just outside town on the road to Gibara. An **Oro Negro gas station** (Carretera Central) is on the southern edge of town. The road to Gibara is north on Av Cajígal; also take this road and fork left after 5km to reach Playa la Herradura.

Taxi

A **Cubataxi** (Máximo Gómez No 302 cnr Martí) to Guardalavaca (54km) costs around CUC$35. To Gibara one-way should cost no more than CUC$20.

Gibara

POP 28,826

Matched only by Baracoa for its wild coastal setting, Gibara is one of those special places where geography, meteorology and culture have conspired to create something tempestuous and unique. Though your first impression might not be open-mouthed incredulity (Hurricane Ike almost wiped the town off the map in 2008), suspend your judgment; Gibara casts a more subtle spell.

Columbus first arrived in the area in 1492 and called it Río de Mares (River of Seas) for the Ríos Cacoyugüín and Yabazón that drain into the Bahía de Gibara. The current name comes from *jiba,* the indigenous word for a bush that still grows along the shore.

Refounded in 1817, Gibara prospered in the 19th century as the sugar industry expanded and the trade rolled in. To protect the settlement from pirates, barracks and a 2km wall were constructed around the town in the early 1800s, making Gibara Cuba's second walled city (after Havana). The once sparkling-white facades earned Gibara its nickname, La Villa Blanca.

Holguín's outlet to the sea was once an important sugar-export town that was linked to the provincial capital via a railway. With the construction of the Carretera Central in the 1920s, Gibara lost its mercantile importance and after the last train service was axed in 1958, the town fell into a sleepy slumber from which it has yet to awaken.

Situated 33km from Holguín via a scenic road that undulates through friendly, eye-catching villages, Gibara is a small, intimate place characterized by pretty plazas, crumbling Spanish ruins and a postcard view of the saddle-shaped Silla de Gibara that so captivated Columbus.

Each year in April Gibara hosts the **Festival Internacional de Cine Pobre** (International Low-Budget Film Festival) which draws films and filmmakers from all over the world.

Sights

Having swept up after the devastation of Hurricane Ike in 2008, Gibara has regained some of its color and vibe. Though the specific sights are few, rather like Baracoa, this is more a town to troll the streets and absorb the local flavor.

IN TOWN

Spanish Forts FORTS

At the top of Calle Cabada is **El Cuartelón**, a crumbling-brick Spanish fort with graceful arches that provides stunning town and bay views. Continue on this street for 200m to **Restaurante el Mirador** for an even better vantage point. You'll see remnants of the old fortresses here and at the **Fuerte Fernando VII**, on the point beyond Parque de las Madres, a block over from Parque Calixto García. There's also a sentinel tower at the entrance to the town, coming in from Holguín.

Parque Calixto García SQUARE

The centerpiece of this park lined with weird *robles africanos* – African oaks with large penis-shaped pods – is **Iglesia de San Fulgencio** (1850). The Statue of Liberty in front commemorates the Spanish-Cuban-American War. On the western side of the square, in a beautiful colonial palace (more interesting than the stuffed stuff it collects), is the **Museo de Historia Natural** (Luz Caballero No 23; admission CUC$1; ⏰8am-noon & 1-5pm Mon-Sat). Through barred windows you can watch women rolling cheroots in the **cigar factory** across the square.

Museo de Historia Municipal MUSEUM

(admission CUC$1; ⏰8am-noon & 1-5pm Mon-Wed, 8am-noon, 1-5pm & 8-10pm Thu-Sun) Two museums share the colonial mansion (1872) at Independencia No 19: this history museum downstairs, and the **Museo de Artes Decorativas** (admission CUC$2) upstairs. The latter is more interesting, with nearly 800 pieces collected from Gibara's colonial heyday. Across the street is **Galería Cosme Proenza** (Independencia No 32), with wall-to-wall works by one of Cuba's foremost painters.

OUTSIDE TOWN

There are three decent beaches within striking distance of Gibara.

Playa los Bajos BEACH

Los Bajos, to the east, is accessible by a local *lancha* (ferry) that leaves at least twice daily from the fishing pier on La Enramada, the waterfront road leading out of town. It costs CUC$1 either way. These boats cross the Bahía de Gibara to **Playa Blanca**, from where it's 3km east to Playa los Bajos. Should the ferry be out of action, Los Bajos is a rough 30km drive via Floro Pérez and Fray Benito.

Playa Caletones BEACH

You'll need some sort of transport (bike, taxi, rental car) to get to this lovely little beach, 17km to the west of Gibara. The apostrophe-shaped stretch of white sand and azure sea here is a favorite of vacationers from Holguín. The town is ramshackle, with no services except the thatched place guarded by a palm tree that serves as a bar in summer.

Caverna de Panaderos CAVES

This complex cave system with 19 galleries and a lengthy underground trail is close to town at the top end of Calle Independencia. There are no official tourist facilities, but you can look inside with a local guide and some torches. Ask in your casa particular re current details.

Sleeping

Hostal Buena Vista HOTEL $

(☎84-45-96; Plaza del Fuerte; s/d CUC$15/25; ❄P) After years without a hotel, Gibara has finally acquired a corker, and one that honorably puts quality over quantity. Despite the bargain-basement price, this diminutive four-room abode above Restaurante el Faro is a modest masterpiece with the magnificent ocean within spitting distance outside the window.

Hostal los Hermanos CASA PARTICULAR $

(☎84-45-42; Céspedes No 13 btwn Luz Caballero & J Peralta; r CUC$20; ❄) Bedizened with colonial splendor, you can relax here, with big bedrooms, a salubrious patio and fountain, signature Gibara stained glass and delicious meals, all located a block and a half from Parque Calixto García. The house also doubles up as a paladar for nonguests.

Villa Caney CASA PARTICULAR $

(☎84-45-52; Sartorio No 36 btwn J Peralta & Luz Caballero; r CUC$20-25; ❄) There's more stunning Gibara beauty here, captured in a sturdy stone colonial house that withstood the category 4 force of Hurricane Ike. Two rooms off an impressive courtyard are large and have private baths. The food – all kinds of seafood specialties – helps the place qualify for paladar status. Expect plenty of dinnertime company.

Eating

Gibara is still in the Special Period as far as government restaurants go, though some enterprising casas particulares have recently starting operating as paladares.

Paladar Villa Caney PALADAR $

(☎84-45-52; Sartorio No 36 btwn J Peralta & Luz Caballero) Encased in the Villa Caney paladar, the surroundings are suitably stunning and the food – especially the seafood – isn't far behind.

Restaurante el Faro CARIBBEAN $

(Plaza del Fuerte; ⏰10am-10pm) This place, on Parque de las Madres, serves chicken and fish meals overlooking the bay. It's a simple, potentially romantic spot that was damaged by Hurricane Ike.

Restaurante el Mirador FAST FOOD $

(⏰24hr) Perched high above town near El Cuartelón, this place has a view to die for but not much in the way of good food.

Entertainment

For theater and dance, it's the historic **Casino Español** (1889). **Patio Colonial**, wedged between the Museo de Historia Natural and Casino Español, is an atmospheric outdoor cafetería that hosts regular musical performances.

Cine Jiba CINEMA

(Parque Calixto García) Cuba's improbable poor man's film festival hosts most of its cutting-edge movies in this small but quirky cinema covered with colorful art house movie posters. If you're going to go to the cinema anywhere in Cuba, it should be in Gibara – it's a local rite of passage.

Centro Cultural Batería Fernando VII CULTURAL CENTER
(Plaza del Fuerte) The diminutive Spanish fort hovering above the choppy ocean is today an atmospheric cultural center run by ARTex that puts on weekend shows and serves food and drink from a sinuous bar-restaurant.

Casa de Cultura CULTURAL CENTER
(Parque Colón) You might catch a salsa night here, or gain an appreciation of the poetry of Nicolas Guillén in the pleasant inner courtyard.

Information

Most services line Calle Independencia.

Bandec (cnr Independencia & J Peralta) Also changes traveler's checks.

Post office (Independencia No 15) There are few public phones here.

Getting There & Away

There are no Víazul buses to Gibara. Travelers can tackle the route with Cuban transport on a truck or bus from Holguín. The **bus station** is 1km out on the road to Holguín. There are two daily buses in each direction. A taxi (to Holguín) should cost no more than CUC$20.

For drivers heading toward Guardalavaca, the link road from the junction at Floro Pérez is hell at first, but improves just outside Rafael Freyre. There's an **Oro Negro gas station** at the entrance to town.

Playa Pesquero & Around

Of Holguín's three northern resort areas, Playa Pesquero (Fishermen's Beach) is the most high-end. There are four tourist colossi here, including the five-star Hotel Playa Pesquero, and the strip has a luxury Caribbean sheen missing elsewhere on the island. Not surprisingly, the adjacent beach is sublime, with golden sand, shallow, warm water and great opportunities for snorkeling. The resorts and beaches are accessible off the main Holguín–Guardalavaca road via a spur road just before the Cuatro Palmas junction.

Sights & Activities

Both of the sights below as well as Las Guanas (p356) at Playa Esmeralda are part of the **Parque Natural Cristóbal Colón**.

Parque Nacional Monumento Bariay HISTORICAL SITE
(admission CUC$8; 9am-5pm;) Ten kilometers west of Playa Pesquero and 3km west of Villa Don Lino is **Playa Blanca**; Columbus is thought to have landed somewhere near here in 1492, and this great meeting of two cultures is commemorated in a varied mix of sights and memorabilia, the centerpiece of which is an impressive Hellenic-style monument designed by Holguín artist Caridad Ramos for the 500th anniversary of the landing in 1992. Other points of interest here include an **information center**, the remains of a 19th-century **Spanish fort**, three reconstructed **Taíno Indian huts**, an **archaeological museum** and the reasonable Restaurante 'Columbo.' It makes a pleasant afternoon's sojourn.

TOP CHOICE **Bioparque Rocazul** NATURE RESERVE
(9am-5pm) Located just off the link road that joins Playa Turquesa with the other Pesquero resorts, this protected bio-park offers the usual hand-holding array of outdoor activities under the supervision of a nonnegotiable government guide. It's a commendable

THE POOR MAN'S FILM FESTIVAL

There's no red carpet, no paparazzi and no Brangelina, but what the **Festival Internacional de Cine Pobre** (International Low-Budget Film Festival) lacks in glitz it makes up for in raw, undiscovered talent. Then there's the setting – ethereal Gibara, Cuba's crumbling Villa Blanca, a perfect antidote to the opulence of Hollywood and Cannes.

Inaugurated in 2003, the Cine Pobre was the brainchild of late Cuban director Humberto Solás, who fell in love with this quintessential fisherman's town after shooting his seminal movie *Lucía* here in 1968.

Open to independent filmmakers of limited means, the festival takes place in April and, despite limited advertising, attracts up to US$100,000 in prize money. Lasting for seven days, proceedings kick off with a gala in the Cine Jiba followed by film showings, art expositions and nightly music concerts. The competition is friendly but hotly contested, with prizes used to reward and recognize an eclectic cache of digital movie guerrillas drawn from countries as varied as Iran and the US.

environmental effort in a major resort area, but the limitations on your right to roam can be a little stifling (and costly). Leisurely walking excursions go for CUC$8/10/12 for one/two/three hours. You can go horseback riding for CUC$16 an hour or fishing for CUC$29. An all-inclusive package costs CUC$40. The park is extensive with hills, trails, ocean access and the **Casa de Compay Kike**, a working farm where you can sample Cuban food and coffee. There's a friendly bar at the entrance to the park where you weigh can up the financial pros and cons.

Sleeping

PLAYA PESQUERO

TOP CHOICE **Hotel Playa Pesquero** RESORT $$$
(☎43-35-30; all-incl s/d CUC$175/300; P ❄ @ ≋ ♿) Once Cuba's biggest hotel, Playa Pesquero had its mantle stolen in 2007 by the precocious Sirenis la Salina in Varadero, but who cares? With 933 rooms, the Pesquero is no slouch and no ugly duckling either. Beautifully landscaped grounds spread over 30 hectares include Italianate fountains, fancy shops, seven restaurants, a classy spa, floodlit tennis courts, and enough swimming pool space to accommodate a school of whales. And then there's the beach...in a word, beautiful. Opened in 2003 by Fidel Castro, the loquacious leader's speech is reprinted on a wall in the reception area. Fortunately, it was one of his shorter efforts.

Occidental Grand Playa Turquesa RESORT $$$
(☎43-35-40; all-incl s/d CUC$150/200; P ❄ @ ≋) Slightly apart from the other three resorts on its own clean scoop of beach (known confusingly as Playa Yuraguanal), Turquesa writes the word 'privacy' into its four stars. Otherwise you're looking at all the usual high-end, all-inclusive givens – meaning most punters are happy to never leave the complex.

Hotel Playa Costa Verde RESORT $$$
(☎43-35-20; all-incl s/d/tr CUC$150/230/327; P ❄ @ ≋ ♿) Stuck somewhere between the elegance of Hotel Playa Pesquero and the simplicity of Villa Don Lino, the Costa Verde feels a bit faux – not that top-notch facilities are lacking. There's a Japanese restaurant, a gym, colorful gardens and a lagoon you cross to get to the beach. Good diving trips are run out of the confusingly named Blau Costa Verde next door.

Casa de Compay Kike CABINS $$
(☎43-33-10 ext 115; s/d CUC$49/84) A rustic *finca* in the Parque Rocazul where you can sidle up to nature in one of two cabins and pretend you're a million miles from all-inclusive-land.

WEST OF PLAYA PESQUERO

TOP CHOICE **Villa Don Lino** CABINS $$
(☎43-03-08; s/d CUC$39/50; ≋) The cheap alternative to Playa Pesquero's 'big four,' Don Lino's 36 single-story *cabañas* (bungalows) are planted right on its own diminutive white beach, and make for a romantic retreat. There's a small pool, nighttime entertainment and an element of Cuban-ness missing in the bigger resorts. Villa Don Lino is 8.5km north of Rafael Freyre along a spur road.

Campismo Silla de Gibara CABINS $
(☎42-15-86; s/d CUC$11.50/17; ≋) This rustic campismo (camping installation) sits on sloping ground beneath Gibara's signature saddle-shaped hill. Reached via a rough road between Floro Pérez and Rafael Freyre, it's 35km southeast of Gibara itself and 1.5km off the main road. There are 42 rooms sleeping two, four or six people, but come for the views, not the comfort. There's also a cave you can hike to, 1.5km up the hill, and horses for rent. It's best to make reservations with **Cubamar** (www.cubamarviajes.cu) in Havana rather than just turn up.

Guardalavaca

Guardalavaca is a string of megaresorts draped along a succession of idyllic beaches 54km northeast of Holguín. But glimmering in the background, the landscape of rough green fields and haystack-shaped hills remind you that rural Cuba is never far away.

In the days before towel-covered sun loungers and poolside bingo, Columbus described this stretch of coast as the most beautiful place he had ever laid eyes on. Few modern-day visitors would disagree. Love it or hate it, Guardalavaca's enduring popularity has its raison d'être: enviable tropical beaches, verdant green hills and sheltered turquoise coral reefs that teem with aquatic action. More spread out than Varadero and less isolated than Cayo Coco, for many discerning travelers Guardalavaca gets the bal-

Guardalavaca

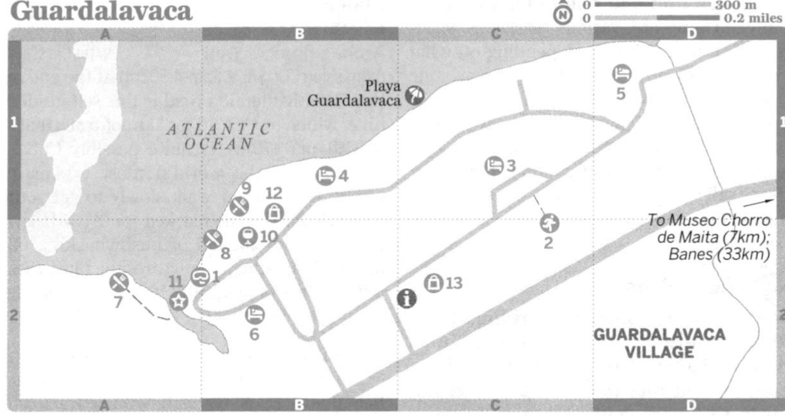

ance just right – R and R (read: relaxation and realism).

In the early 20th century this region was an important cattle-rearing area and the site of a small rural village (Guardalavaca means, quite literally, 'guard the cow'). The tourism boom moved into first gear in the late 1970s when local *holguiñero* Fidel Castro inaugurated Guardalavaca's first resort – the sprawling Atlántico – by going for a quick dip in the hotel pool. The local economy hasn't looked back since.

The resort area is split into three separate enclaves: Playa Pesquero (see p353), Playa Esmeralda and, 7km to the east, Guardalavaca proper, the original hotel strip that is already starting to peel around the edges. Guardalavaca has long allowed beach access to Cubans, meaning it is less snooty and flecked with a dash of local color.

Sights

Museo Chorro de Maita MUSEUM
(admission CUC$2; 9am-5pm Tue-Sat, to 1pm Sun) This archaeological-site-based museum protects the remains of an excavated Indian village and cemetery, including the well-preserved remains of 62 human skeletons and the bones of a barkless dog. The village dates from the early 16th century and is one of nearly 100 archaeological sites in the area. Across from the museum is a reconstructed **Aldea Taína** (Taíno village; admission CUC$3) that features life-sized models of native dwellings and figures in a replicated indigenous village. Shows of native dance rituals are staged here and there's also a restaurant.

Guardalavaca

Activities, Courses & Tours
1 Eagle Ray Marlin Dive Center A2
2 Horseback Riding Center C2

Sleeping
3 Club Amigo Atlántico – Guardalavaca C1
4 Club Amigo Atlántico – Guardalavaca B1
5 Hotel Brisas D1
6 Villa Cabañas B2

Eating
7 El Ancla A2
8 Los Amigos B2
9 Vicaria Guardalavaca B1

Drinking
10 La Rueda B2

Entertainment
11 Disco Club la Roca A2

Shopping
12 Boulevard B1
13 Centro Comercial los Flamboyanes C2

Parque Natural Bahía de Naranjo NATURE RESERVE
The Parque Natural Bahía de Naranjo, 4km southwest of Playa Esmeralda and about 8km from the main Guardalavaca strip, is an island complex designed to keep the resort crowds entertained. An **aquarium** (9am-9pm) is on a tiny island in the bay and your entry fee includes a zippy boat tour of the islands included in the complex,

and a **sea lion and dolphin show** (noon daily). There are various packages starting at around CUC$40, depending on what you want to do – yacht trips, seafaris etc – so check around before you embark. For an extra CUC$50 or so, you can swim with the dolphins for 20 minutes. All of Guardalavaca's (and Playa Esmeralda's) hotel tour desks sell aquarium excursions. Boats to the aquarium leave from the Marina Bahía de Naranjo.

Activities

You can arrange **horseback riding** at the **horseback-riding center** opposite Club Amigo Atlántico starting at CUC$8 per hour. You can rent **mopeds** at all the hotels for up to CUC$30 per day. Most all-inclusive packages include bicycle use, but the bikes are fairly basic (no gears). The road between Guardalavaca and Playa Esmeralda, and on to Playa Pesquero, is flat and quiet and makes an excellent day excursion. For a bit more sweat you can make it to Banes and back (66km round-trip).

Diving

Guardalavaca has some excellent diving (better than Varadero and up there with Cayo Coco). The reef is 200m out and there are 32 dive sites, most of which are accessed by boat. Highlights include caves, wrecks, walls and La Corona, a giant coral formation said to resemble a crown. Guardalavaca beach's one dive center, **Eagle Ray Marlin Dive Center**, is on the beach behind Disco Club la Roca. There's another outlet in Playa Esmeralda (ask at the hotels) that serves the same reefs. All the outfits offer generic prices and facilities. There are open-water certification courses for CUC$365, resort courses for CUC$40 and dives for CUC$35, with discounts for multiple dives.

Boat Trips

Many other water-based excursions leave from the **Marina Gaviota Puerto de Vita** and can be booked through the hotels. There's the ubiquitous sunset cruise (CUC$69), deep-sea fishing (CUC$270 for up to six people), and a catamaran trip across Bahía de Vita with snorkeling and open bar to the Parque Nacional Monumento Bariay, where you can disembark where Columbus did and visit the park that stands in memoriam (CUC$59).

Hiking

Las Guanas Eco-Archaeological Trail NATURE RESERVE
(admission CUC$6; ⌚8am-4:30pm) At the end of the Playa Esmeralda road is this self-guided hike, which at CUC$6 for 1km of trail (that's CUC$1 per 170m), is quite possibly Cuba's (and one of the world's) most expensive walks. You'd better walk slowly to get your money's worth! The marked route (with several more kilometers of bushwhacking on fire trails leading to a picturesque bluff with a lighthouse) apparently boasts 14 endemic plant species.

Eco-Parque Cristóbal Colón NATURE RESERVE
Cheaper, but pretty barren post-Hurricane Ike, this area is reachable via a track off the hotel access road. There's a small animal 'zoo' here and a rustic *finca* restaurant called Conuco de Mongo Viña where you can grab a bite.

Tours

The Cubanacán travel desk in the lobby of the Club Amigo Atlántico – Guardalavaca offers an interesting 'beer tour' of Holguín city leaving at 6.30pm every Sunday (CUC$20).

Sleeping

There are no casas particulares here, as renting rooms is banned. Banes, 33km to the southeast, is the closest town with private rooms.

GUARDALAVACA

Villa Cabañas CABINS **$**
(☎43-01-64; s/d CUC$19/31; ❄) Despite the lack of private rooms, you can still shoestring it in Guardalavaca by decamping to one of these comfortable cabins at the end of Guardalavaca's main resort strip. The 20 rooms have double beds, TVs, hot water, kitchenettes and the odd resident frog (provided free of charge). Also onsite is the **Cubanacán Clínica Internacional**. A lively stretch of beach with a couple of passable snack-bar restaurants is two minutes' walk away.

Club Amigo Atlántico – Guardalavaca RESORT **$$**
(☎43-01-21, all-incl s/d CUC$69/99; P ❄ @ ≋ 👪) This hard-to-fathom resort is a fusion of the former Guardalavaca and Atlántico hotels, the latter of which is the resort's oldest, completed in 1976 and christened by Fidel Castro, who went for a quick dip in the pool.

The architecture in this small 'village' (there are an astounding 600 rooms here in total) is a mishmash of villas, bungalows and standard rooms, and is ever-popular with families for its extensive kids' activities program. Expect bingo around the pool and microphone-happy 'entertainers.' The hotel has two locations. The rooms associated with the former Hotel Guardalavaca are further from the beach but also less noisy.

Hotel Brisas RESORT $$$
(☎43-02-18; all-incl s/d CUC$129/178; P❄@🏊👪) This über-resort made up of the Villa las Brisas and Hotel las Brisas at the eastern end of the beach is a package-tour paradise that stirs memories of 1970s British holiday camps. Bonuses are the huge comfortable rooms, floodlit tennis courts and general lack of pretension. But with its fake pink flamingos and cheesy violinist serenading the buffet crowd with old Abba hits, the kitsch is never far from the surface.

PLAYA ESMERALDA

Two megaresorts line this superior stretch of beach, 6km to the west of Guardalavaca and accessed by a spur just east of the Cayo Naranjo boat launch. Esmeralda occupies the middle ground between Guardalavaca's economy and Playa Pesquero's opulence.

TOP CHOICE **Paradisus Río de Oro** RESORT $$$
(☎43-00-90; all-incl s/d CUC$185/311; P❄@🏊) Elegant and environmentally conscious (a tough combination), this 292-room resort has five-star written all over it, and is often touted as the best resort in Cuba. There's massage available in a cliffside hut, a Japanese restaurant floating on a koi pond, and garden villas with private pools. Paradise is the word. It's adults only.

Sol Río Luna Mares Resort RESORT $$$
(☎43-00-60; all-incl s/d CUC$104/170; P❄@🏊👪) This two-in-one hotel is an amalgamation of the former Sol Club Río de Luna and the Meliá Río de Mares. Rooms are large and come with a few extras (such as coffee machines), but the main advantages for luxury seekers over Guardalavaca is the superior food (Mexican and Italian restaurants) and the better beach (beach toys are included in the price).

Rooms are also available in cabins at **Villa Cayo Naranjo**. Enquire at the hotel desks for details.

Eating

There are a handful of options outside of the all-inclusive resorts, mainly in Guardalavaca itself.

El Ancla SEAFOOD $$
(⏰9am-10:30pm) Somehow El Ancla, which is situated on a rocky promontory of land at the far western end of Guardalavaca beach, didn't get blown away by Hurricane Ike and has survived to serve its excellent lobster in front of magnificent sea views.

Los Amigos FAST FOOD $
(⏰9am-9pm) At the epicenter of Guardalavaca's liveliest strip of beach (accessed via the flea market just west of Club Amigo Atlántico), Los Amigos is a bog-standard beach shack with beer, music and enough ingredients to muster up a sand-free fish and rice lunch.

Vicaria Guardalavaca FAST FOOD $
(⏰9am-9:45pm) You'll feel like an outcast eating at this place beside Centro Comercial Guardalavaca, while everyone else tucks into the all-you-can-eat buffets a couple of hundred meters away. Nevertheless, pizzas are big and service is quick and amiable. A good meal for two won't break CUC$10.

Cayo Naranjo SEAFOOD $$
(Cayo Naranjo) On Gaviota's theme park of a *cayo* (key), this will be your only lunch option. Fortunately it's pretty good, with a signature plate of Marinera Especial pushing the fish theme.

Drinking & Entertainment

Disco Club la Roca CABARET
(admission CUC$1; ⏰1-5pm & 9:30pm-3am) This establishment just west of the Centro Comercial Guardalavaca has a pleasant open-air locale overlooking the beach. It's a bar-restaurant by day with video games and karaoke. On weekend evenings it hosts cabaret shows good enough to lure clientele from the posh resorts.

La Rueda BAR
(⏰7am-11pm) A Palmares bar (next to the Boulevard) that provides a welcome haven from the resorts. Small snacks and ice cream are also available.

Shopping

Boulevard SOUVENIRS
There's a touristy handicraft market next to Club Amigo Atlántico – Guardalavaca that caters to resort clients from the surround-

ing area. It's art, crafts, postcards and cheap clothing – there's nothing much outside the knickknack box.

Centro Comerical los Flamboyanes SHOPPING CENTER
Guardalavaca's small shopping mall has a limited cache of stores, including a handy Casa del Habano which has all the smoke you need and then some.

Information

Euros are accepted in all the Guardalavaca, Playa Esmeralda and Pesquero resorts. Additionally, all the big hotels have money-changing facilities.

Asistur (43-01-48; Centro Comercial Guardalavaca; 8:30am-5pm Mon-Fri, to noon Sat) Traveler emergency assistance.

Banco Financiero Internacional (Centro Comercial Guardalavaca) In the complex just west of Club Amigo Atlántico – Guardalavaca.

Canadian Consulate (43-03-20; Club Amigo Atlántico – Guardalavaca, ste 1)

Clínica Internacional (43-02-91) A 24-hour pharmacy on the same site as Villa Cabañas.

Cubatur (8am-4pm) Travel agent just behind the Centro Comercial los Flamboyanes.

Ecotur (Centro Comercial Guardalavaca) Runs nature-themed trips to places such as Cayo Saetía, Baracoa and Gran Piedra.

Getting There & Away

Club Amigo Atlántico – Guardalavaca can sometimes arrange transfers to Holguín for CUC$10; ask around. A taxi from Guardalavaca to Holguín will cost a heftier CUC$35 one-way for the car. For radio taxis, call **Cubataxi** (43-01-39) or **Transgaviota** (43-49-66).

Marina Gaviota Puerto de Vita (43-04-45) is an international entry port for yachts and boats and has 38 berths. There's a hardware store, restaurant, electricity and customs authorities on-site.

Getting Around

A hop-on/hop-off double-decker bus in Guardalavaca links the three beach areas and the Aldea Taína (p355). The red-and-blue bus is operated by Transtur. Theoretically it runs three times a day in either direction, but check at your hotel to see if there are any glitches. Drop-offs include Parque Rocazul, Playa Pesquero, Playa Costa Verde, Playa Esmeralda hotels, Club Amigo Atlántico – Guardalavaca and the Aldea Taína. Tickets cost CUC$5 for an all-day pass.

Coches de caballo (horse carriages) run between Playas Esmeralda and Guardalavaca, or you can rent a moped (CUC$24 per day) or bicycle (free if you're staying at an all-inclusive) at all of the resort hotels. All the rental agencies have offices in Guardalavaca and can also rent mopeds.

A **Servi-Cupet gas station** (24hr) is situated between Guardalavaca and Playa Esmeralda.

Cubacar (Club Amigo Atlántico – Guardalavaca)

Banes

POP 44,983

The former sugar town of Banes, just north of the Bahía de Banes, is the site of one of Cuba's biggest oxymorons. Cuban president Fulgencio Batista was born here in 1901. Then, 47 years later, in the local clapboard church of Nuestra Señora de la Caridad, another fiery leader-in-waiting, Fidel Castro, tied the knot with the blushing Birta Díaz Balart. A generous Batista gave them a US$500 gift for their honeymoon. Ah, how history could have been so different.

Founded in 1887, this effervescent company town was a virtual fiefdom of the US-run United Fruit Company until the 1950s and many of the old American company houses still remain. These days in the sun-streaked streets and squares you're more likely to encounter cigar-smoking cronies slamming dominoes and mums carrying meter-long loaves of bread; in short, everything Cuban that is missing from the all-inclusive resorts.

In September 2008 Banes was pummeled by Hurricane Ike, which damaged or destroyed 70% of its buildings. True to Cuba's survivalist spirit, the town has recovered remarkably quickly.

Sights & Activities

If you're coming from the resorts, Banes' biggest attraction may be enjoying the street life provided by a stroll through town. Don't miss the fine old company houses that once provided homes for the fat cats of United Fruit. If you're fit and adventurous, getting here by bicycle is a rare treat through undulating bucolic terrain.

Iglesia de Nuestra Señora de la Caridad CHURCH
On October 12, 1948, Fidel Castro Ruz and Birta Díaz Balart were married in this unusual art deco church on Parque Martí in the center of Banes. After their divorce in 1954, Birta remarried and moved to Spain.

Through their only child, Fidelito, Fidel has several grandchildren.

Museo Indocubano Bani MUSEUM
(General Marrero No 305; admission CUC$1; ⏲9am-5pm Tue-Sat, 8am-noon Sun) This museum's small but rich collection of indigenous artifacts is one of the best on the island. Don't miss the tiny golden fertility idol unearthed near Banes (one of only 20 gold artifacts ever found in Cuba). The museum was being renovated at the time of writing.

Steam Locomotive 964 TRAIN
(El Panchito; Calle Tráfico) Railway enthusiasts shouldn't miss this old steamer built at the HK Porter Locomotive Works in Pittsburgh, Pennsylvania, in 1888, now on display 400m east of the bus station.

Playa de Morales BEACH
One day in the not-too-distant future (after its been Cancun-ized) we'll all wax nostalgic about this precious strip of sand situated 13km east of Banes along the paved continuation of Tráfico. For the time being enjoy this fishing village while you can, whiling away an afternoon dining with locals and watching the men mend their nets. A few kilometers to the north is the even quieter Playa Puerto Rico.

Sleeping

There are no hotels in the town proper, but Banes has some super-friendly private renters.

Campismo Puerto Rico Libre CABINS $
(per person CUC$5) A mainly Cuban enclave near deserted Playa de Morales, 13km east from Banes, the Puerto Rico has basic cabins that line the rocky shore. There's a restaurant, and people in the nearby fishing villages will happily cook seafood meals for you. Ask about the caves (about 1km from the campismo), and bring insect repellent. It's best to enquire with Cubamar (see p118) before arriving.

Casa 'Las Delicias' CASA PARTICULAR $
(☎80-37-18; Augusto Blanca No 1107 btwn Bruno Merino & Bayamo; r CUC$20-25; ❄) Spick-and-span rooms, a private entrance, friendly owners and decent food; what more could you ask from tranquil Banes?

Sergio Aguilera CASA PARTICULAR $
(☎80-24-12; Iglesias No 4089, Reparto Nicaragua; r CUC$20; ❄) A lovely detached villa with a great family atmosphere and tasty meals served.

Casa Evelin Feria CASA PARTICULAR $
(☎80-31-50; Bruno Meriño No 3401A btwn Delfin Pupo & JMH, Reparto Cárdenas; r CUC$20-25; ❄) A town-center location, bright modern baths and an attentive hostess/cook make any stay in Evelin's house a pleasure.

Eating

Restaurant el Latino CARIBBEAN $$
(General Marrero No 710; ⏲11am-11pm) A top Banes choice is this Palmares place with all the usual Creole dishes delivered with a little extra flair and charm. Service is good, and the accompanying musicians unusually talented and discreet.

La Vicaria FAST FOOD $
(⏲24hr) Across the street from El Latino is yet another reliable La Vicaria, with pasta, burgers and cordon bleu (chicken stuffed with ham and cheese), plus eggs and coffee for breakfast (everything is less than CUC$4).

Coctelera FAST FOOD $
(General Marrero No 327A) Several peso bars dotted around town are jumping with atmosphere and cheap hooch, including this one, as well as the super-popular **Doña Yulla** next door.

DIYers can find groceries in a couple of supermarkets, **La Epoca** and **Isla de Cuba** on the main nexus of General Marrero.

Entertainment

Cafe Cantante LIVE MUSIC
(General Marrero No 320) This gregarious, music-filled patio is the top spot in Banes, with honking municipal band rehearsals, discos, *son* (Cuba's basic form of popular music) septets and zen-inducing jazz jams.

FREE **Casa de Cultura** CULTURAL CENTER
(General Marrero No 320) Next door to Cafe Cantante this venue, housed in the former Casino Español (1926), has a regular Sunday *trova* (traditional poetic song) matinee at 3pm and Saturday *peña del rap* (rap music session) at 9pm.

Information

Banes is one of those towns with no street signs and locals who don't know street names, so prepare to get lost.

Getting There & Away

From the **bus station** (cnr Tráfico & Los Ángeles), one morning bus goes to Holguín (72km) daily (supposedly). An afternoon bus connects with the train to Havana. Trucks leave Banes for Holguín more frequently. A taxi from Guardalavaca (33km) will cost around CUC$20 one-way, or you can tackle it with a moped (easy) or bicycle (not so easy) in a fantastic DIY day trip.

Birán

Fidel Castro Ruz was born on August 13, 1926, at the **Finca las Manacas** (aka Casa de Fidel) near the village of Birán, south of Cueto. The farm, which was bought by Fidel's father Ángel in 1915, is huge, and includes its own workers' village (a cluster of small thatched huts for the mainly Haitian laborers), a cockfighting ring, a post office, a store and a telegraph. The several large yellow wooden houses that can be glimpsed through the cedar trees are where the Castro family lived.

Sitio Histórico de Birán MUSEUM
(admission/camera/video CUC$10/20/40; 9am-noon & 1:30-4pm Tue-Sat, to noon Sun)
Finca las Manacas opened as a museum in 2002 under this unassuming name, supposedly to downplay any Castro 'per-

BRUISED FRUIT

United Fruit is a name riddled with historical contradictions. On one hand, the company gave the world the Big Mike, the first mass-produced imported banana; on the other, it developed a reputation for meddling covertly in the internal affairs of successive Latin American 'banana republics' – including Cuba.

Formed back in 1899 when Minor C Keith's Costa Rican–based banana-growing company merged with Andrew Preston's Boston fruit import business, United Fruit quickly morphed into a huge global monolith that went on to become one of the world's first multinational corporations.

zin the early 1900s, the company invested in 36 hectares of sugar plantations in eastern Cuba, where they constructed 544km of railroad and two large sugar mills – the Boston and the Preston – in what is now Holguín province. One of the company's early laborers was Ángel Castro (father of Fidel), who helped clear land for the company's burgeoning plantations before setting up on his own in Birán in 1915. Encased in an expansive new rural estate, Castro Senior began hiring out labor to United Fruit for a tidy profit and quickly became a wealthy man.

Holguín was soon the darling scion of United Fruit in Cuba, with provincial towns such as Banes and Mayarí sporting prosperous Americanized enclaves that owed both their existence and wealth to the omnipresent US-owned conglomerate. But dissatisfaction among Cubans was quietly growing.

Like many nationalistically minded leftists, Fidel Castro was incensed with the clandestine role United Fruit played in the 1954 overthrow of Jacobo Arbenz' socialist government in Guatemala and, spurred on by other radicals such as Che Guevara, was determined to make amends.

The payback began during the revolutionary war when Fidel's rebel army famously burned the fields of his late father's Birán estate in a portentous taste of things to come.

On taking power in 1959, Castro nationalized all United Fruit land and property in Cuba and sent its owners back to the US. Unable to gain financial compensation from the Cuban government, the company attempted to get even two years later by lending two ships from its Great White Fleet (the largest private navy in the world) to Cuban mercenaries taking part in the abortive Bay of Pigs landings (see p230). But the invasion was unsuccessful.

United Fruit's demise was exacerbated in 1975 when CEO Eli Black committed suicide by jumping from the 44th floor of New York's PanAm building, after it was alleged he had bribed the Honduran president US$1.2 million to pull out of a banana cartel hostile to United Fruit's interests.

The company rebranded in 1984 and was reincarnated as Chiquita Brands. Meanwhile, in Cuba, the legacy of United Fruit can still be seen in the peeling colonial houses of Banes and – more ironically – at the former Castro farm in Birán.

sonality cult.' The modesty extends to the signage, which is nonexistent. Nonetheless, the museum is an interesting excursion containing more than a hundred photos, assorted clothes, Fidel's childhood bed and his father's 1918 Ford motorcar. With 27 installations, the place constitutes a *pueblito* (small town) and, if nothing else, shows the extent of the inheritance that this hot-headed ex-lawyer gave up when he lived in the Sierra Maestra for two years surviving on a diet of crushed crabs and raw horse meat.

You'll find the **graves of Fidel's parents**, Ángel Castro and Lina Ruz, to the right of the entrance gate.

To get here, take the southern turnoff 7km west of Cueto, and drive 7km south to the Central Loynaz Hechevarría sugar mill at Marcané. From there a road runs 8km east to Birán, from which it's another 3km northeast to Finca las Manacas.

Sierra del Cristal

Cuba's own 'Little Switzerland' is a rugged amalgam of the Sierra del Cristal and the Altiplanicie de Nipe that contains two important national parks. **Parque Nacional Sierra Cristal**, Cuba's oldest, was founded in 1930 and harbors 1213m Pico de Cristal, the province's highest summit. Of more interest to travelers is the 5300-hectare **Parque Nacional la Mensura**, 30km south of Mayarí, which protects the island's highest waterfall, yields copious Caribbean pines and hosts a mountain research center run by the Academia de Ciencias de Cuba (Cuban Academy of Sciences). Notable for its cool alpine microclimate and 100 or more species of endemic plants, La Mensura offers hiking and horseback-riding activities and accommodation in a Gaviota-run eco-lodge.

Sights & Activities

Most activities can be organized at Villa Pinares del Mayarí or via excursions from Guardalavaca's hotels (CUC$78 by jeep or CUC$110 by helicopter; see p356).

Salto del Guayabo WATERFALL

At just over 100m in height, Guayabo (15km from the Villa Pinares de Mayarí) is considered the highest waterfall in Cuba. There's a spectacular overlook and the guided 1.2km hike to its base through fecund tropical forest costs CUC$5 and includes swimming in a natural pool.

La Plancha FARM

(admission free) On the access road a few kilometers before the hotel, on the right, is a small flower and crop garden containing everything from mariposas to sugarcane. There have been coffee plantations growing here since the 1940s and you can peer into a still-functioning coffee drying shed.

Sendero la Sabina TRAIL

More flora can be observed on the, a short interpretive trail at the Centro Investigaciones para la Montaña (1km from the hotel), which exhibits the vegetation of eight different ecosystems, a 150-year-old tree – the 'Ocuje Colorado' – and some rare orchids.

Hacienda la Mensura FARM

Eight kilometers from the hotel is this breeding center for exotic animals such as antelope and *guapeti*. Horseback riding can be arranged here.

Farallones de Seboruco CAVES

Speleologists may want to ask about trips to these ghostly caves, designated a national monument, which contain aboriginal cave paintings.

Sleeping

TOP CHOICE **Villa Pinares del Mayarí** HOTEL $

(☎50-33 08; s/d CUC$30/35, cabins CUC$35/40; P ❄ 🏊) One in a duo of classic Gaviota Holguín hideaways – Cayo Saetía is the other – Pinares del Mayarí stands at 600m elevation between the Altiplanicie de Nipe and Sierra del Cristal, 30km south of Mayarí on a rough dirt road. Part chalet resort, part mountain retreat, this isolated rural gem is situated in one of Cuba's largest pine forests and the two- and three-bedroom cabins, with hot showers and comfortable beds, make it seem almost alpine-esque. There's also a large restaurant, bar, sports court, gym, and a small natural lake (El Cupey) 300m away which is great for an early morning dip.

Los Exóticos CABINS $

(r from CUC$37) A rustic Ecotur-run chalet with eight double rooms with shared bath, set amid the lushness of the Parque Nacional la Mensura a few kilometers below the Villa Pinares del Mayarí. For those wishing to wake up surrounded by orchids, dewy mountains and roaming deer, look no further.

Getting There & Away

The only way to get to Villa Pinares del Mayarí and Parque Nacional la Mensura outside an organized tour is via car, taxi or bicycle (if you're adventurous and it's not a Cuban one). The access road is rough and in a poor state of repair, but it's passable in a hire car if driven with care. If arriving from Santiago the best route is via the small settlement of Mella.

Cayo Saetía

East of Mayarí the road becomes increasingly potholed and the surroundings, while never losing their dusty rural charm, progressively more remote. The culmination of this rustic drive is lovely Cayo Saetía, a small, flat wooded island in the Bahía de Nipe that's connected to the mainland by a small bridge. During the 1970s and '80s this was a favored hunting ground for communist apparatchiks who enjoyed spraying lead into the local wildlife. Fortunately those days are now gone. Indeed, ironic as it may sound, Cayo Saetía is now a protected wildlife park with 19 species of exotic animals, including camels, zebras, antelopes, ostriches and deer. Bisected by grassy meadows and adorned by hidden coves and beaches, it's the closet Cuba gets to an African wildlife reserve. Well worth a visit.

Sleeping

TOP CHOICE Villa Cayo Saetía CABINS $$
(☎42-53-20; s/d CUC$58/70; ❄) This wonderfully rustic but comfortable resort on a 42-sq-km island at the entrance to the Bahía de Nipe is small, remote and more upmarket than the price suggests. The 12 rooms are split into rustic and standard *cabañas* with a minimal price differential, while the in-house restaurant La Güira – decked out Hemingway-style with hunting trophies mounted on the wall like gory art – serves exotic meats such as antelope. You'll feel as if you're a thousand miles from anywhere.

Campismo Río Cabonico CABINS $
(☎59-41-18; r per person from CUC$5) This place is at Pueblo Nuevo, 9km east of Levisa and 73km west of Moa, about 900m south of the main road. The 23 cabins with baths and fans on a low terrace beside the Río Cabonico (decent swimming) have four or six beds. It may accept foreigners, if there's space; check ahead or contact Cubamar in Havana.

Getting There & Around

There are three ways to explore Cayo Saetía, aside from the obvious two-legged sorties from the villa itself. A one-hour jeep safari costs CUC$9, while excursions by horse and boat are CUC$6 and CUC$5 respectively. Though isolated you can secure passage on a twice-weekly Gaviota helicopter from Guardalavaca (CUC$124, Saturday and Monday) or a bus-boat combo from the town of Antilles. If arriving by car, the control post is 15km off the main road. Then it's another 8km along a rough, unpaved road to the resort. A hire car will make it – with care.

Granma Province

☎023 / POP 835,675

Includes »

Best Places to Eat

- » La Bodega (p369)
- » Paladar la Roca (p377)
- » Restaurante el Cabo (p381)
- » Restaurante Plaza (p369)

Best Places to Stay

- » Hotel Royalton (p368)
- » Villa Santo Domingo (p374)
- » Adrián & Tonia (p377)
- » Hotel Marea del Portillo (p383)
- » La Bodega (p369)
- » Paladar la Roca (p377)

Why Go?

Barring some of the more obscure parts of Guantánamo, Granma is Cuba's most remote province with a road network reminiscent of the African bush and a jungle of lofty tropical mountains dense enough to have harbored a fugitive Fidel Castro for more than two years in the 1950s. Yet, despite its out-on-a-limb apartness, Granma is where Cuban patriotism burns the brightest. This is the land where José Martí died, where Fidel Castro clambered ashore with his bedraggled band of shipwrecked revolutionaries, and where Granma native Carlos Manuel de Céspedes freed his slaves and formally declared Cuban independence for the first time in 1868.

The isolation has bred a special kind of Cuban identity. Granma's towns and villages are esoteric places enlivened with weekly street parties characterized by their outdoor barbecues and archaic hand-operated street organs. Its two cities – Bayamo and Manzanillo – are among the most tranquil and cleanest settlements in the archipelago.

When to Go

Parts of Granma have a balmy climate and during January and February Marea del Portillo is the warmest place in Cuba. The mountains are traditionally wetter. If you're planning on hiking in the Sierra Maestra, March and April are the driest months when nighttime temperatures are bearable. December 2 is the anniversary of the Granma landing and it is celebrated with a ceremony at Los Coloradas.

Granma Province Highlights

1 Enjoy one of Cuba's balmiest microclimates in secluded **Marea del Portillo** (p382)

2 Trek up to Fidel's wartime headquarters at **Comandancia de la Plata** (p373) in Gran Parque Nacional Sierra Maestra

3 Investigate marine terraces and archaeological remains in **Parque Nacional Desembarco del Granma** (p380)

4 Stand atop Cuba's highest mountain, **Pico Turquino** (p376), next to the bust of José Martí, and admire the view

5 Make time for pork roast, street organs and a game of chess in Bayamo's **Fiesta de la Cubanía** (p370)

6 Relax by the river with the *bayameses* (people from Bayamo) in **Parque Chapuzón** (p368)

7 Visit the site where the Cubans uttered their first cry of independence in **Museo Histórico la Demajagua** (p377)

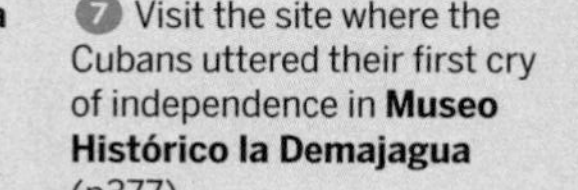

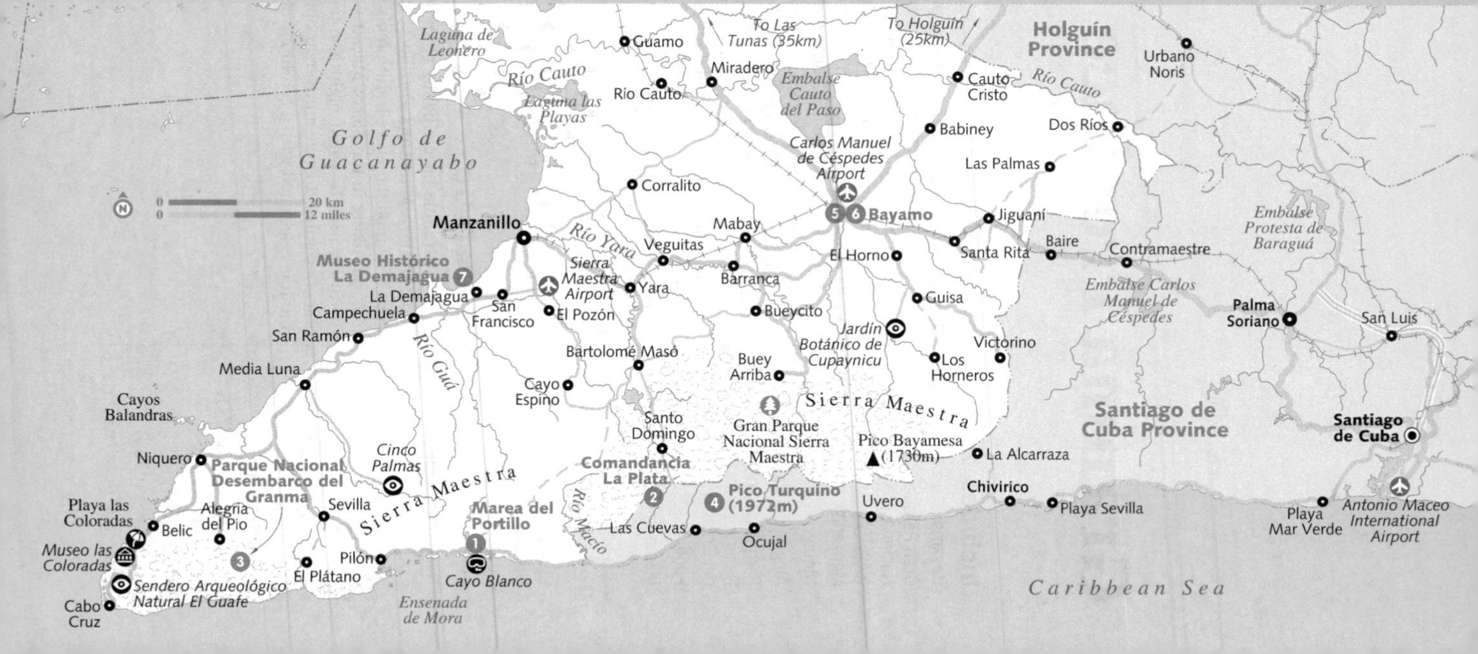

History

Stone petroglyphs and remnants of Taíno pottery unearthed in the Parque Nacional Desembarco del Granma suggest the existence of native cultures in the Granma region long before the arrival of the Spanish.

Columbus, during his second voyage, was the first European to explore the area, tracking past the Cabo Cruz Peninsula in 1494, before taking shelter from a storm in the Golfo de Guanacayabo. All other early development schemes came to nothing and by the 17th century Granma's untamed and largely unsettled coast had become the preserve of pirates and corsairs.

Granma's real nemesis didn't come until October 10, 1868, when sugar-plantation owner Carlos Manuel de Céspedes called for the abolition of slavery from his Demajagua sugar mill near Manzanillo and freed his own slaves by example, thus inciting the First War of Independence.

Drama unfolded again in 1895 when the founder of the Cuban Revolutionary Party, José Martí, was killed in Dos Ríos just a month and a half after landing with Máximo Gómez off the coast of Guantánamo to ignite the Spanish-Cuban-American War.

Sixty-one years later, on December 2, 1956, Fidel Castro and 81 rebel soldiers disembarked from the yacht *Granma* off the coast of Granma province at Playa las Coloradas. Routed by Batista's troops while resting in a sugarcane field at Alegría del Pío, 12 or so survivors managed to escape into the Sierra Maestra, establishing headquarters at Comandancia la Plata. From there they fought and coordinated the armed struggle, broadcasting their progress from Radio Rebelde and consolidating their support among sympathizers nationwide. After two years of harsh conditions and unprecedented beard growth, the forces of the M-26-7 Movement triumphed in 1959.

Bayamo

POP 143,844

Predating both Havana and Santiago, and cast for time immemorial as the city that kick-started Cuban independence, Bayamo has every right to feel self-important. Yet somehow it doesn't. Instead, bucking standard categorization, Granma's easygoing and understated provincial capital is one of the most peaceful and hassle-free places on the island.

That's not to say that *bayameses* aren't aware of their history. *Como España quemó a Sagunto, así Cuba quemó a Bayamo* ('as the Spanish burnt Sagunto, the Cubans burnt Bayamo'), wrote José Martí in the 1890s, highlighting the sacrificial role that Bayamo has played in Cuba's convoluted historical development. But, while the self-inflicted 1869 fire might have destroyed most of the city's classic colonial buildings, it didn't destroy its underlying spirit or its long-standing traditions.

Today, Bayamo is known for its cerebral chess players (Céspedes was the Kasparov of his day), Saturday night street parties and antiquated street organs (imported via Manzanillo). All three are on show at the weekly Fiesta de la Cubanía, one of the island's most authentic street shows and *bayamés* (from Bayamo) to the core.

History

Founded in November 1513 as the second of Diego Velázquez de Cuellar's seven original villas (after Baracoa), Bayamo's early history was marred by Indian uprisings and bristling native unrest. But with the indigenous Taíno decimated by deadly European diseases such as smallpox, the short-lived insurgency soon fizzled out. By the end of the 16th century, Bayamo had grown rich and was established as the region's most important cattle-ranching and sugarcane-growing center. Frequented by pirates, the town filled its coffers further in the 17th and 18th centuries via a clandestine smuggling ring run out of the nearby port town of Manzanillo. Zealously counting up the profits, Bayamo's new class of merchants and landowners lavishly invested their money in fine houses and an expensive overseas education for their offspring.

One such protégé was local lawyer-turned-revolutionary Carlos Manuel de Céspedes, who, defying the traditional colonial will, led an army against his hometown in 1868 in an attempt to wrest control from the conservative Spanish authorities. But the liberation proved to be short-lived. After the defeat of an ill-prepared rebel army by 3000 regular Spanish troops near the Río Cauto on January 12, 1869, the townspeople – sensing an imminent Spanish reoccupation – set their town on fire rather than see it fall into the hands of the enemy.

Bayamo was also the birthplace of Perucho Figueredo, composer of the Cuban national anthem, which begins, rather patriotically,

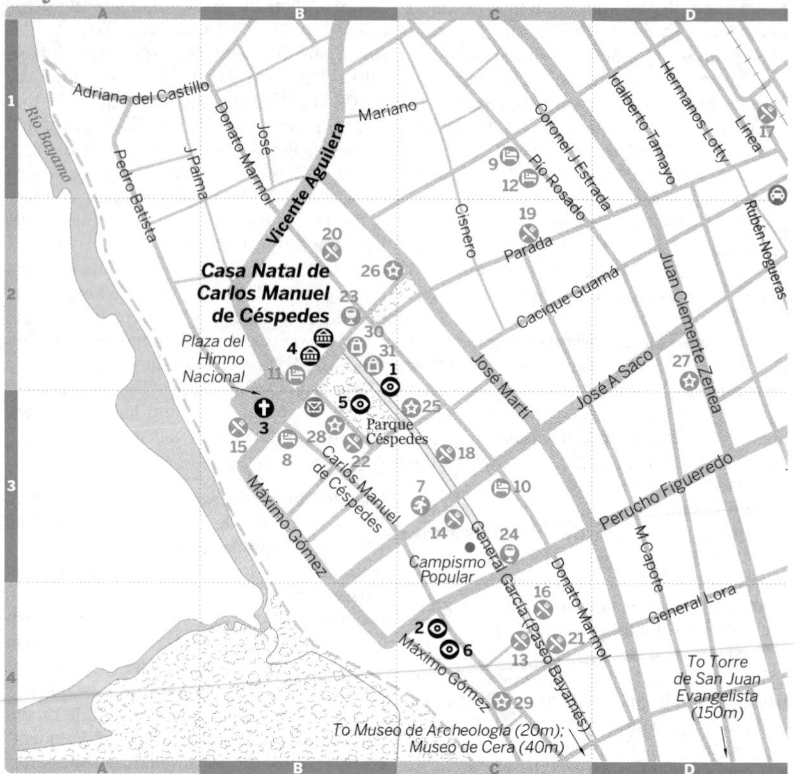

with the words *Al combate corred, bayameses* (Run to battle, people of Bayamo).

Sights

Casa Natal de Carlos Manuel de Céspedes MUSEUM
(Maceo No 57; admission CUC$1; 9am-5pm Tue-Fri, 9am-2pm & 8-10pm Sat, 10am-1pm Sun) The birthplace of the 'father of the motherland,' this significant museum is on the north side of the square. Born here on April 18, 1819, Céspedes spent the first 12 years of his life in this residence, and the Céspedes memorabilia inside is complemented by a collection of period furniture. It's notable architecturally as the only two-story colonial house remaining in Bayamo and was one of the few buildings to survive the 1869 fire.

Parque Céspedes SQUARE
One of Cuba's leafiest and friendliest squares, and the birthplace of the man (Céspedes) himself, Bayamo's central meeting point is officially known as Plaza de la Revolución. Despite its easygoing airs and secondary role as the city's best outdoor music venue (orchestras regularly play here), the square is loaded with historical significance. In 1868 Céspedes proclaimed Cuba's independence for the first time in front of the columned **Ayuntamiento** (city hall). Clean and atmospheric, the square is surrounded by a smorgasbord of grand monuments and beautified further by big, shady trees. Facing each other in the center are a bronze statue of **Carlos Manuel de Céspedes**, hero of the First War of Independence, and a marble bust of **Perucho Figueredo**, with the words of the Cuban national anthem carved upon it. Marble benches and friendly *bayameses* make this a pleasant place to linger.

Museo Provincial MUSEUM
(Maceo No 55; admission CUC$1) Directly next door to Céspedes ex-home, the provincial

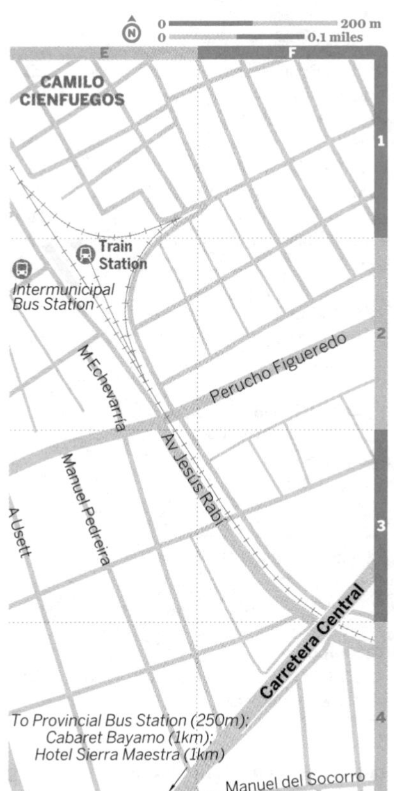

museum completes Bayamo's historical trajectory with a yellowing city document dating from 1567 and a rare photo of Bayamo immediately after the fire.

Iglesia Parroquial Mayor de San Salvador CHURCH

There's been a church on this site since 1514. The current edifice dates from 1740 and the section known as the **Capilla de la Dolorosa** (donations accepted; 9am-noon & 3-5pm Mon-Fri, 9am-noon Sat) was another building to survive the 1869 fire. A highlight of the main church is the central arch, which exhibits a mural depicting the blessing of the Cuban flag in front of the revolutionary army on October 20, 1868. Outside, **Plaza del Himno Nacional** is where the Cuban national anthem, 'La Bayamesa,' was sung for the first time in 1868.

Paseo Bayamés NEIGHBORHOOD

Bayamo's main shopping street is officially known as Calle General García, but no one calls it that. In the late 1990s it was pedestrianized and reconfigured with funky murals and lampposts posing as trees and paint tubes. It's a great place to observe the nuances of everyday Bayamo life. Halfway along its course you'll find the tiny **Museo de Cera** (42-65-25; General García No 261; admission CUC$1; 9am-noon & 1-5pm Mon-Fri, 2-9pm Sat, 9am-noon Sun), Bayamo's version of Madame Tussaud's, with convincing waxworks of personalities such as Polo Montañez, Benny Moré and local hero Carlos Puebla. Next door the equally tiny **Museo de Arqueología** (admission CUC$1) is worth a 10 minute once-over.

Ventana de Luz Vázquez LANDMARK

(Céspedes btwn Figueredo & Luz Vázquez) A forerunner of the national anthem, co-written by Céspedes (and also, confusingly, called 'La Bayamesa') was first sung from here on March 27, 1851. A memorial plaque has been emblazoned onto the wall next to the wood-barred colonial window.

Casa de Estrada Palma CULTURAL CENTER

(Céspedes No 158) Welcome to the house where Cuba's first post-independence president, Tomás Estrada Palma, was born in 1835. A one-time friend of José Martí, Estrada Palma was disgraced after the Revolution for his perceived complicity with the US over the Platt Amendment. His birth house is now the seat of Uneac (Unión Nacional de Escritores y Artistas de Cuba; National Union of Cuban Writers and Artists), but you'll find little about the famous former occupant inside.

Torre de San Juan Evangelista LANDMARK

(cnr José Martí & Amado Estévez) A church dating from Bayamo's earliest years stood at this busy intersection until it was destroyed in the great fire of 1869. Later, the church's tower served as the entrance to the first cemetery in Cuba, which closed in 1919. The cemetery was demolished in 1940, but the tower survived. A **monument** to local poet José Joaquín Palma (1844–1911) stands in the park diagonally across the street from the tower, and beside the tower is a bronze **statue of Francisco Vicente Aguilera** (1821–77), who led the independence struggle in Bayamo.

Bayamo

Top Sights

Casa Natal de Carlos Manuel de Céspedes B2

Sights

1 Ayuntamiento B2
2 Casa de Estrada Palma C4
3 Iglesia Parroquial Mayor de San Salvador B3
4 Museo Provincial B2
5 Parque Céspedes B3
6 Ventana de Luz Vázquez C4

Activities, Courses & Tours

7 Academia de Ajedrez C3

Sleeping

8 Ana Martí Vázquez B3
9 Casa de la Amistad C1
10 Hotel Escuela Telégrafo C3
11 Hotel Royalton B2
12 Juan Valdés C1

Eating

13 Cuadro Gastronómica de Luz Vázquez C4
14 El Siglo C3
15 La Bodega B3
16 La Sevillana C4
17 Mercado Agropecuario D1
18 Mercado Cabalgata C3
19 Paladar el Polinesio C2
20 Paladar Sagitario B2
Restaurante Plaza .... (see 11)
21 Restaurante Vegetariano C4
22 Tropi Crema B3

Drinking

23 Bar la Esquina B2
24 La Taberna C3

Entertainment

25 Casa de la Cultura C3
26 Casa de la Trova La Bayamesa B2
27 Centro Cultural Los Beatles D2
28 Cine Céspedes B3
29 Sala Teatro José Joaquín Palma C4
Uneac .... (see 2)

Shopping

30 ARTex B2
31 Librería Ateneo B2

FREE **Museo Ñico López** MUSEUM
(Abihail González; 8am-noon & 2-5:30pm Tue-Sat, 9am-noon Sun) This interesting museum is in the former officers' club of the Carlos Manuel de Céspedes military barracks, 1km southeast of Parque Céspedes. On July 26, 1953, this garrison was attacked by 25 revolutionaries in tandem with the assault on Moncada Barracks in Santiago de Cuba in order to prevent reinforcements from being sent. Though a failure, Ñico López, who led the Bayamo attack, escaped to Guatemala, and he was the first Cuban to befriend Ernesto 'Che' Guevara in 1954. López was killed shortly after the *Granma* landed in 1956.

Parque Chapuzón PARK
(Av Amado Éstevez;) Greenery beckons not a kilometer from Bayamo's main square where the Bayamo River has carved a lush belt through the urban grid. Locals come to this blissful spot to wash their bikes, water their horses or swim. You can cross the river by taking off your shoes and walking over a weir. Footpaths and gazebo-shaped stalls selling food and drink embellish the banks, but never detract from the all-pervading mood of tranquility.

Activities

The Cubans love chess, and nowhere more so than in Bayamo. Check out the street-side chess aficionados who set up on Saturday nights during the Fiesta de la Cubanía. The **Academia de Ajedrez** (José A Saco No 63 btwn General García & Céspedes) is the place to go to improve your pawn-king-four technique. Emblazoned on the wall of this cerebral institution, pictures of Che, Fidel and Carlos Manuel de Céspedes offer plenty of inspiration.

Forty-five-minute **horse-and-cart tours** can be arranged at the **Cubanacán desk** (Hotel Telegrafo, Maceo No 53) for CUC$4 per person.

Sleeping

TOP CHOICE **Hotel Royalton** HOTEL $$
(42-22-90; Maceo No 53; s/d CUC$39/50;) Melting in with the colonial ambience of Parque Céspedes, the Royalton is Bayamo's best hotel – and best bargain. The 33 rooms

have recently been upgraded to boutique standard with power showers and flat-screen TVs, while downstairs an attractive bar has been added to the main reception area with seats spilling out onto the sidewalk terrace overlooking leafy Parque Céspedes. The on-site **Plaza restaurant** is one of Bayamo's better eating options and you can sunbathe in private on the roof terrace.

Casa de la Amistad CASA PARTICULAR $
(☎42-57-69; Pío Rosado No 60 btwn Ramíriez & N López; r CUC$25; P❄@) Gabriel and Rosa let out most of the upper floor of their pastel-shaded house as a separate apartment with its own entrance, kitchen, sitting area, bedroom and bathroom. They are fine hosts who speak excellent English and can cook up some delicious local dishes. There's even an internet connection.

Ana Martí Vázquez CASA PARTICULAR $
(☎42-53-23; Céspedes No 4; r CUC$25; P❄) As close as you can get to Parque Céspedes without actually being in it, Ana's rooms score highly for size, cleanliness and decent food. The darker front room is accessed by stairs so steep they almost constitute a ladder. The brighter back room has a double and single bed plus windows that open onto a light-filled inner courtyard.

Juan Valdés CASA PARTICULAR $
(☎42-33-24; Pío Rosado No 64 btwn Ramírez & N López; r CUC$25; P❄) Two doors down from Casa de la Amistad, Juan rents one room, but it's effectively an apartment on the upper floor with its own bedroom, bathroom, kitchen, sitting area and balcony overlooking rambling Pío Rosado.

Hotel Escuela Telégrafo HOTEL $
(☎42-55-10; Saco No 108; s/d CUC$15/20; ❄) Always a good bet for budget travelers, the Telégrafo is one of Cuba's best *hotel escuelas* (hotel schools) staffed by students learning the ropes in the tourist trade. This one is housed in a beautiful old colonial building on busy Calle Saco where big shuttered windows open out onto the street. Rooms are basic but clean, service is suitably perky, and there's a decent restaurant adjacent to the bustling lobby downstairs.

Villa Bayamo HOTEL $
(☎42-31-02; s/d/cabin CUC$15/24/32; P❄≋) This out-of-town option (it's 3km southwest of the center on the road to Manzanillo) has a definitive rural feel and a rather pleasant swimming pool overlooking fields at the back. Well-appointed rooms are in a larger main block or detached cabins off to the side. There's a reasonable restaurant on-site.

Hotel Sierra Maestra HOTEL $
(☎42-79-70; Carretera Central; s/d CUC$19/30; P❄≋) Check before you jump in the pool here – there may be no water in it. With a ring of the Soviet '70s about it, the Sierra Maestra hardly merits the three stars it professes, although the rooms have had some much-needed attention in the last three years and the coffee and TV reception have improved. Three kilometers from the town center, it's OK for an overnighter.

Eating

There's some unique street food in Bayamo, sold from the stores along Calle Saco and in Parque Céspedes. Otherwise you're dealing with mainly local restaurants with prices in Cuban pesos. Aside from the places reviewed here, you'll find decent *comida criolla* (Creole food) in the two city-center hotels, the Royalton and the Telégrafo, both of which have atmospheric restaurants.

TOP CHOICE **La Bodega** CARIBBEAN $$
(Plaza del Himno Nacional No 34; cover after 9pm CUC$3; ⏱11am-1am) The best of both worlds. The front door opens out onto Bayamo's main square; the rear terrace overlooks Río Bayamo and is fringed by a bucolic backdrop that will leave you wondering if you've been transported to an isolated country villa. La Bodega is Bayamo's best restaurant and not only for its urban-rural juxtapositions. Try the beef and taste the coffee, or relax on the open terrace before the traveling troubadours arrive at 9pm.

Restaurante Plaza INTERNATIONAL $$
(☎42-22-90; Hotel Royalton, Maceo No 53) Bayamo's finest hotel (the Royalton) also hosts one of its best restaurants; nothing legendary mind you, but with an excellent setting including options to sit outside overlooking one of Cuba's most pleasant squares. Food is generously labeled 'international' with a strong meat, rice and beans bias. Service is officious on a bad day, quietly polite on a good one.

Paladar el Polinesio PALADAR $$
(☎42-24-49; Parada No 125 btwn Pío Rosado & Cisnero) Bayamo's two paladares are old school; ie you'll feel as if you're eating in someone's hastily converted front room in

DON'T MISS

FIESTA DE LA CUBANÍA

Bayamo's quintessential nighttime attraction is an ebullient and unique street party, the like of which you'll find nowhere else in Cuba. Set up willy-nilly along Calle Saco, it includes the locally famous pipe organs, whole roast pig, an eye-watering oyster drink called *ostiones* and – incongruously in the middle of it all – rows of tables laid out diligently with chess sets. Dancing is, of course, de rigueur. The action kicks off at 8pm-ish every Saturday.

an atmosphere of quiet subterfuge. The Polinesio's meals are served upstairs in an open-fronted family dining room with four or five tables. There's an improvised bar and a 'waiter' trying hard to look officious in a bow-tie. The menu depends on what ingredients are available, though there's usually a bottle of Spanish wine hiding somewhere.

Paladar Sagitario PALADAR $$
(Donato Marmol No 107 btwn Maceo & Vicente Aguilera; meals CUC$7-9; ⏲noon-midnight) Sagitario has been in the game for 13 years, knocking out such delicacies as chicken cordon bleu and pork chops topped with cheese on an attractive back patio with occasional musical accompaniment. The daily specials are usually taped to the front door.

La Sevillana SPANISH $
(☎42-14-95; General García btwn General Lora & Perucho Figueredo; ⏲noon-2pm & 6-10:30pm) Come and see Cuban chefs have a go at Spanish cuisine – paella and *garbanzos* (chickpeas). This is a new kind of peso restaurant, with a dress code (no shorts), a doorman in a suit, and a reservations policy. Press your trousers, brush up on your Spanish, but don't expect *sevillano* creativity.

Restaurante Vegetariano VEGETARIAN $
(General García No 173; ⏲7-9am, noon-2:30pm & 6-9pm; ✍) Manage your expectations before you check out this peso place. This is Cuba where *vegetarianismo* is still in its infancy. Don't expect nut roast, but you should be able to order something other than the ubiquitous omelet.

Fiesta de la Cubanía CARIBBEAN $
(Saco btwn Donato Mármol & Céspedes) Every Saturday night your eating options improve tenfold when impromptu restaurants pop up along Calle Saco after 8pm serving delicious *comida criolla* washed down with cacique beer.

Cuadro Gastronómica de Luz Vázquez FAST FOOD $
(off General García btwn Figueredo & General Lora) Along this short lane are parked at least a dozen clean-looking food carts selling *bayamés* street snacks in Cuban pesos. Bank on hot dogs, croquettes, ice cream, sardines and empanadas.

Tropi Crema ICE-CREAM PARLOR $
(⏲9am-9:45pm) In the absence of a Coppelia, the Tropi, on the southwest corner of Parque Céspedes, does its best – in pesos.

Self-Catering

El Siglo BAKERY $
(cnr General García & Saco; ⏲9am-8pm) Fresh warm cakes sold in pesos have saved the taste buds of many a hungry Bayamo visitor. They're well worth smuggling back to your hotel room for a midnight feast.

Mercado agropecuario MARKET $
(Línea) The vegetable market is in front of the train station. There are many peso food stalls along here also.

Mercado Cabalgata SUPERMARKET $
(General García No 65; ⏲9am-9pm Mon-Sat, to noon Sun) This store on the main pedestrian street sells basic groceries.

Drinking

Bar la Esquina BAR
(cnr Donato Marmol & Maceo; ⏲11am-1am) International cocktails are served in this tiny corner bar replete with plenty of local atmosphere.

La Taberna BAR
(General García btwn Saco & Figueredo; ⏲10am-10pm) This busy new local place on the main shopping street has beer on tap in proper pint glasses and a constant buzz of conversation. Pay in Cuban pesos.

Entertainment

The two main hotels, the Royalton and the Sierra Maestra, have decent bars; the latter also has a loud but popular disco that's better at weekends.

Cine Céspedes CINEMA
(admission CUC$2) This cinema is on the western side of Parque Céspedes, next to the post

office. It offers everything from Gutiérrez Alea to the latest Hollywood blockbuster.

Centro Cultural Los Beatles LIVE MUSIC
(Zenea btwn Figueredo & Saco; admission 10 pesos; ⏲6am-midnight) Just as the West fell for the exoticism of the Buena Vista Social Club, the Cubans fell for the downright brilliance of the Fab Four. Guarded by life-size statues of John, Paul, George and Ringo, this quirky place hosts Beatles tribute bands (in Spanish) every weekend. Unmissable!

FREE **Uneac** CULTURAL CENTER
(Céspedes No 158; ⏲4pm) You can catch heartfelt boleros on the flowery patio here in the former home of disgraced first president Tomás Estrada Palma, the man invariably blamed for handing Guantánamo to the *Yanquis*.

Sala Teatro José Joaquín Palma THEATER
(Céspedes No 164) In a stylish old church, this venue presents theater on Friday, Saturday and Sunday nights, while the Teatro Guiñol, also here, hosts children's theater on Saturday and Sunday mornings.

Cabaret Bayamo CABARET
(Carretera Central Km 2; ⏲9pm Fri-Sun) Bayamo's glittery nightclub/cabaret opposite the Hotel Sierra Maestra draws out the locals on weekends in their equally glittery attire.

Casa de la Trova la Bayamesa TRADITIONAL MUSIC
(cnr Maceo & Martí; admission CUC$1; ⏲9pm, Tue-Sun) One of Cuba's best *trova* houses lies in a lovely colonial building on Maceo. Pictures on the wall display the famous '70s afro of Bayamo-born *trova* king Pablo Milanés.

Casa de la Cultura CULTURAL CENTER
(General García No 15) Wide-ranging cultural events, including art expos, on the east side of Parque Céspedes.

Estadio Mártires de Barbados SPORTS
(Av Granma) From October to April, there are baseball games at this stadium, approximately 1km northeast of the Hotel Sierra Maestra.

Shopping

The Paseo Bayamés is the main pedestrian shopping street but, with few tourists, the stores are mainly aimed at Cubans.

ARTex SOUVENIRS
(General García No 7) The usual mix of Che Guevara T-shirts and bogus Santería dolls in Parque Céspedes.

Librería Ateneo BOOKS
(General García No 9) Follow the smell of musty books to the east side of Parque Céspedes.

Information

Banco de Crédito y Comercio (cnr General García & Saco) Bank.

Banco Financiero Internacional (Carretera Central Km 1) In a big white building near the bus terminal.

Cadeca (Saco No 101) Money changing.

Campismo Popular (General García No 112) You can make bookings for La Sierrita and Las Colorados campismos here.

Cubanacán (Hotel Telegrafo, Maceo No 53) Arranges hikes to Pico Turquino (two/three/four days per person CUC$45/65/99), El Yarey (CUC$19) and Parque Nacional Desembarco del Granma (CUC$45), among other places.

Ecotur (☎42-79-70; Hotel Sierra Maestra) Travel agency.

Etecsa Telepunto (General García btwn Saco & Figueredo; per hr CUC$6; ⏲8:30am-7:30pm) Two internet terminals; rarely busy.

Farmacia Internacional (General García btwn Figueredo & Lora; ⏲8am-noon & 1-5pm Mon-Fri, 8am-noon Sat & Sun) Pharmacy.

Hospital Carlos Manuel de Céspedes (☎42-50-12; Carretera Central Km 1)

Post office (cnr Maceo & Parque Céspedes; ⏲8am-8pm Mon-Sat)

Getting There & Away

Air

Bayamo's **Carlos Manuel de Céspedes Airport** (airport code BYM) is about 4km northeast of town, on the road to Holguín. **Cubana** (Martí No 52) flies to Bayamo from Havana twice a week (CUC$103 one way, two hours). There are no international flights to or from Bayamo.

Bus & Truck

The **provincial bus station** (cnr Carretera Central & Av Jesús Rabí) has **Víazul** (www.viazul.com) buses to several destinations.

There are three buses a day to Havana (CUC$44, 13½ hours); one to Varadero (CUC$41, 12½ hours); one to Trinidad (CUC$27, nine hours); and five to Santiago (CUC$6, two hours). Buses heading west also stop at Holguín, Las Tunas, Camagüey, Ciego de Ávila, Sancti Spíritus, and Santa Clara.

Passenger trucks leave from an adjacent terminal for Santiago de Cuba, Holguín, Manzanillo and Pilón. You can get a truck to Bartolomé Masó, as close as you can get on public transport to the Sierra Maestra trailhead. The trucks leave when full and you pay as you board.

The **intermunicipal bus station** (cnr Saco & Línea), opposite the train station, receives mostly local buses of little use to travelers. However, trucks to Las Tunas and Guisa leave from here.

Taxis

State taxis can be procured for hard-to-reach destinations such as Manzanillo (CUC$30), Pilón (CUC$70) and Niquero (CUC$65). Prices are estimates and will depend on the current price of petrol. Nonetheless, at the time of writing it was cheaper to reach all these places by taxi than by hired car.

Train

The **train station** (cnr Saco & Línea) is 1km east of the center. There are three local trains a day to Manzanillo (via Yara). Other daily trains serve Santiago and Camagüey. The long-distance Havana–Manzanillo train passes through Bayamo every third day (CUC$28).

Getting Around

Cubataxi (☎42-43-13) can supply a taxi to Bayamo airport for CUC$5, or to Aeropuerto Frank País in Holguín for CUC$35. A taxi to Villa Santo Domingo (setting-off point for the Alto del Naranjo trailhead for Sierra Maestra hikes) or Comandancia la Plata will cost approximately CUC$35 one way. There's a taxi stand in the south of town near Museo Ñico López.

Via Transgaviota (Saco No 108) rents cars from the Hotel EscuelaTelégrafo while **Cubacar** (Carretera Central) is at the Hotel Sierra Maestra.

The **Servi-Cupet gas station** (Carretera Central) is between Hotel Sierra Maestra and the bus terminal as you arrive from Santiago de Cuba.

The main horse-cart route (one peso) runs between the train station and the hospital, via the bus station. Bici-taxis (a few pesos a ride) are also useful for getting around town. There's a stand near the train station.

Around Bayamo

Most are lured towards the so-close-you-can-almost-touch-them mountains, but Bayamo's hinterland hides some less obvious haunts.

Sights & Activities

Jardín Botánico de Cupaynicu GARDEN

(Carretera de Guisa Km 10; admission with/without guide CUC$2/1) For a floral appreciation of Bayamo's evergreen hinterland, head to this botanical garden about 16km outside the city off the Guisa road. It's on very few itineraries, so you can have the 104 hectares of the tranquil botanic gardens to yourself. There are 74 types of palms, scores of cacti, blooming orchids and sections for endangered and medicinal plants. The guided tour (Spanish only) gains you access to greenhouses, notable for the showy ornamentals.

To get here, take the road to Santiago de Cuba for 6km and turn left at the signposted junction for Guisa. After 10km you'll see the botanic gardens sign on the right. Trucks in this direction leave from the intermunicipal bus station in front of the train station.

Laguna de Leonero LAKE

This algae-filled natural lake in the Cauto River delta, 40km northwest of Bayamo near the provincial border with Las Tunas, is loaded with memorable fly fishing possibilities. Black bass are the prized catch here especially during the November to March fishing season. Ecotur runs yacht excursions from CUC$250 for a maximum of six people. For more details contact their office (p371) in Bayamo's Hotel Sierra Maestra.

Dos Ríos MONUMENT

At Dos Ríos, 52km northeast of Bayamo, almost in Holguín, a white obelisk overlooking the Río Cauto marks the spot where José Martí was shot and killed on May 19, 1895. In contrast to other Martí memorials, it's surprisingly simple and low-key. Go 22km northeast of Jiguaní on the road to San Germán and take the unmarked road to the right after crossing the Cauto.

Sleeping

Villa el Yarey HOTEL $

(☎42-76-84; s/d CUC$31/46) Back toward Jiguaní, 23km southwest of Dos Ríos, is this relaxed, attractive hotel with 16 rooms on a ridge with an excellent view of the Sierra Maestra. This accommodation is perfect for those who want tranquility in verdant natural surroundings. Ecotur or Cubanacán organizes bird-watching trips here. Book through their offices in Bayamo (p371).

To get to Villa el Yarey from Jiguaní, go 4km east of town on the Carretera Central and then 6km north on a side road. From Dos Ríos proceed southwest on the road toward Jiguaní and turn left 2km the other side of Las Palmas. It makes an ideal stop for anyone caught between Bayamo and Santiago de Cuba, or for those taking the backdoor Bayamo–Holguín route. Note that public transport here is scant.

WORTH A TRIP

YARA

A small town with a big history, Yara (population 29,237) – sandwiched halfway between Bayamo and Manzanillo amid vast fields of sugarcane – is barely mentioned in most travel literature. While ostensibly agricultural, the town's soul is defiantly Indian. The early Spanish colonizers earmarked it as one of their *pueblos Indios* (Indian towns) and a **statue** of rebel *cacique* (chief) Hatuey in the main square supports claims that the Spanish burned the dissenting Taíno chief here rather than in Baracoa. Chapter two of Yara's history began on October 11, 1868, when it became the first town to be wrested from Spanish control by rebel forces led by Carlos Manuel de Céspedes. A second **monument** in the main square recalls this important event and the famous *Grito de Yara* (Yara Declaration) that followed, in which Céspedes proclaimed Cuba's independence for the first time.

Just off the square, the **Museo Municipal** (Grito de Yara No 107; admission CUC$1; ⌚8am-noon & 2-6pm Mon-Sat, 9am-noon Sun) chronicles Yara's historical legacy along with the town's role as a key supply center during the revolutionary war in the 1950s.

There's a Servi-Cupet here if you need a gas top-up. The Bayamo–Manzanillo train stops here three times a day.

Gran Parque Nacional Sierra Maestra

Comprising a sublime mountainscape of broccoli-green peaks and humid cloud forest, and home to honest, hardworking *campesinos* (country folk), the Gran Parque Nacional Sierra Maestra is an alluring natural sanctuary that still echoes with the gunshots of Castro's guerrilla campaign of the late 1950s. Situated 40km south of Yara, up a very steep 24km concrete road from Bartolomé Masó, this precipitous and untamed region contains the country's highest peak, Pico Turquino (just over the border in Santiago de Cuba province), unlimited birdlife and flora, and the rebels' one-time wartime headquarters, Comandancia la Plata.

History

History resonates throughout these mountains, the bulk of it linked indelibly to the guerrilla war that raged throughout this region between December 1956 and December 1958. For the first year of the conflict Fidel and his growing band of supporters remained on the move, never staying in one place for more than a few days. It was only in mid-1958 that the rebels established a permanent base on a ridge in the shadow of Pico Turquino. This headquarters became known as La Plata and it was from here that Castro drafted many of the early revolutionary laws while he orchestrated the military strikes that finally brought about the ultimate demise of the Batista government.

Sights & Activities

TOP CHOICE Comandancia de la Plata LANDMARK

Situated atop a crenellated mountain ridge amid thick cloud forest this pioneering camp was first established by Fidel Castro in 1958 after a year on the run in the Sierra Maestra. Well camouflaged and remote, the rebel HQ was chosen for its inaccessibility and it served its purpose well – Batista's soldiers never found it. Today it remains much as it was left in the '50s, with 16 simple wooden buildings (including a small museum) providing an evocative reminder of one of the most successful guerrilla campaigns in history.

Comandancia de la Plata is controlled by the Centro de Información de Flora y Fauna in the village of Santo Domingo. Aspiring guerrilla-watchers must first hire a guide at the park headquarters, get transport (or walk) 5km up to Alto del Naranjo, and then proceed on foot along a muddy track for the final 3km. These days you're looking at a price of CUC$20; CUC$5 if you want to use a camera (photos of the site were banned until 2009). For further information, contact Villa Santo Domingo (p374) or Cubanacán in Bayamo (p371).

Santo Domingo VILLAGE

This tiny village nestles in a deep green valley beside the gushing Río Yara. Communally it provides a wonderful slice of peaceful Cuban *campesino* life that has carried on pretty much unchanged since Fidel and Che prowled these shadowy mountains in

Gran Parque Nacional Sierra Maestra

the late 1950s. If you decide to stick around, you can get a taste of rural socialism at the local school and medical clinic, or ask at Villa Santo Domingo about the tiny village **museum** (admission CUC$1; ⏲varies). The locals have also been known to offer horseback riding, pedicure treatments, hikes to natural swimming pools and some classic old first-hand tales from the annals of revolutionary history.

The park closes at 4pm but rangers won't let you pass after mid-morning, so set off early to maximize your visit.

Alto del Naranjo LANDMARK

All trips into the park begin at the end of the near-vertical, corrugated-concrete access road at Alto del Naranjo (after Villa Santo Domingo the road gains 750 vertical meters in 5km). To get there, it's an arduous two-hour walk, or zippy ride in a jeep (the bone-rattling Russian trucks seem to have been phased out). There's a wondrous view of the plains of Granma from this 950m-high lookout, otherwise it's just a launching pad for La Plata (3km) and Pico Turquino (13km).

Sleeping & Eating

There are three accommodation options for park-bound visitors.

TOP CHOICE **Villa Santo Domingo** HOTEL $

(☎56-53-68; s/d incl breakfast CUC$24/37; ❄) This villa, 24km south of Bartolomé Masó, sits at the gateway to Gran Parque Nacional Sierra Maestra. There are 20 separate cabins next to the Río Yara and the setting, among cascading mountains and *campesino* huts, is idyllic. From a geographical aspect, this is the best jumping-off point for the La Plata and Turquino hikes. You can also test your lungs going for a challenging early morning hike up a painfully steep road to Alto del Naranjo (5km; 750m of ascent). Other attractions include horseback riding, river swimming and traditional music in the villa's restaurant. If you're lucky, you might even catch the wizened old Rebel Quintet, a group of musicians who serenaded the revolutionary army in the late 1950s. Fidel stayed here on various occasions (in hut 6) and Raúl Castro dropped by briefly in 2001 after scaling Pico Turquino at the ripe old age of 70.

Campismo la Sierrita CAMPISMO $

(☎59-33-26; r CUC$20) Situated 8km south of Bartolomé Masó you first start to feel the slanting shadow of the mountains here. The campismo (rustic cabins) is 1km off the main highway on a very rough road and boasts 27 cabins with bunks, baths and electricity. There's a restaurant, and a river for swimming. Ask at the desk about trips to the national park. To ensure it's open and has space, reserve in advance with **Cubamar** (☎7-833-2523/4) in Havana or at the **Campismo Popular** (☎42-42-00; General García No 112) office in Bayamo.

Motel Balcón de la Sierra HOTEL $
(☎59-51-80; s/d CUC$14/18; P❄≋) One kilometer south of Bartolomé Masó and 16km north of Santo Domingo, this attractively located place nestled in the mountain foothills is a little distant for easy access to the park. A swimming pool and restaurant are perched on a small hill with killer mountain views, while 20 air-conditioned cabins are scattered below. A lovely natural ambience is juxtaposed with the usual basic but functional Islazul furnishings.

Information

Aspiring visitors should check the current situation before arriving in the national park. Tropical storms and/or government bureaucracy have been known to put the place temporarily out of action.

The best source of information is **Cubamar** (☎7-833-2523/4) in Havana, or you can go straight to the horse's mouth by directly contacting **Villa Santo Domingo** (☎56-53-02). These guys can put you in touch with the Centro de Información de Flora y Fauna next door (see p374). Additional information can be gleaned at the Ecotur office in the Hotel Sierra Maestra in Bayamo (see p371).

Getting There & Around

There's no public transport from Bartolomé Masó to Alto del Naranjo. A taxi from Bayamo to Villa Santo Domingo should cost from CUC$30 to CUC$35 one-way. Ensure it can take you all the way; the last 7km before Villa Santo Domingo is extremely steep but passable in a normal car. Returning, the hotel should be able to arrange onward transport for you to Bartolomé Masó, Bayamo or Manzanillo.

A 4WD vehicle with good brakes is necessary to drive the last 5km from Santo Domingo to Alto del Naranjo; it's the steepest road in Cuba with 45% gradients near the top. Powerful 4WDs pass regularly, usually for adventurous tour groups, and you may be able to find a space on board for approximately CUC$7 (ask at Villa Santo Domingo). Alternatively, it's a tough but rewarding 5km hike.

Manzanillo

POP 114,789

Bayside Manzanillo might not be pretty but – like most low-key Granma towns – it has an infectious feel to it. Sit for 10 minutes in the semi-ruined central park with its old-fashioned street organs and distinctive neo-Moorish architecture and you'll quickly make a friend or three. With bare-bones transport links and only one grim state-run hotel, not many travelers make it out this far. As a result, Manzanillo is a good place to get off the standard guidebook trail and see how Cubans have learned to live with 50 years of rationing, austerity and school playground-style politics with their big neighbor in the north.

Founded in 1784 as a small fishing port, Manzanillo's early history was dominated by smugglers and pirates trading in contraband goods. The subterfuge continued into the late 1950s, when the city's proximity to the Sierra Maestra made it an important supply center for arms and men heading up to Castro's revolutionaries in their secret mountaintop headquarters.

Manzanillo is famous for its hand-operated street organs, which were first imported into Cuba from France by the local Fornaris and Borbolla families in the early 20th century (and are still widely in use). The city's musical legacy was solidified further in 1972 when it hosted a government-sponsored *nueva trova* festival that culminated in a solidarity march to Playa las Coloradas.

Sights

IN TOWN

Though it may look a little dingy to first-time visitors, Manzanillo has been undergoing a gradual facelift. The town is well known for its striking architecture, a psychedelic mélange of wooden beach shacks, Andalusian-style townhouses and intricate neo-Moorish facades. Check out the old **City Bank of NY building** (cnr Merchán & Dr Codina), dating from 1913, or the ramshackle wooden abodes around Perucho Figueredo, between Merchán and JM Gómez.

Parque Céspedes PARK
Manzanillo's central square is notable for its priceless **glorieta** (gazebo/bandstand), where Moorish mosaics, a scalloped cupola and arabesque columns set off a theme that's replicated elsewhere. Completely restored a decade ago, the bandstand – an imitation

DON'T MISS

PICO TURQUINO

Towering 1972m above the azure Caribbean, Pico Turquino – so named for the turquoise hue that colors its steep upper slopes – is Cuba's highest and most regularly climbed mountain.

Carpeted in lush cloud forest and protected in a 140-sq-km national park, the peak's lofty summit is embellished by a bronze bust of national hero José Martí, the work of Cuban sculptor Jilma Madera. In a patriotic test of endurance, the statue was dragged to the top in 1953 by a young Celia Sánchez and her father, Manuel Sánchez Silveira, to mark the centennial of the apostle's birth.

Four years later, Sánchez visited the summit again, this time with a rifle-wielding Fidel Castro in tow to record an interview with American news network, CBS. Not long afterwards, the rebel army pitched their permanent headquarters in the mountain's imposing shadow, atop a tree-protected ridge near La Plata.

Best tackled as a through trek from the Santo Domingo side, the rugged, two- to three-day grind up Turquino starts from Alto del Naranjo near La Plata and ends at Las Cuevas on the Caribbean coast. Guides are mandatory and can be arranged through Flora y Fauna employees at Villa Santo Domingo (p374) or at the small hut at Las Cuevas. The cost varies, depending on how many days you take. If you organize it through Cubanacán in Bayamo (p371), bank on CUC$45/65/99 per person for two/three/four days. You'll also need to stock up on food, warm clothing, candles and some kind of sleeping roll or sheet. Even in August it gets cold at the shelters, so be prepared. Sufficient water is available along the trail.

The trail through the mountains from Alto del Naranjo passes the village of La Platica (water), Palma Mocha (campsite), Lima (campsite), Pico Joachín (shelter and water), El Cojo (shelter), Pico Joachín, Regino, Paso de los Monos, Loma Redonda, Pico Turquino (1972m), Pico Cuba (1872m; with a shelter and water at 1650m), Pico Cardero (1265m) and La Esmajagua (600m) before dropping down to Las Cuevas on the coast. The first two days are spent on the 13km section to Pico Turquino (overnighting at the Pico Joachín and/or Pico Cuba shelters), where a prearranged guide takes over and leads you down to Las Cuevas. As with all guide services, tips are in order. Prearranging the second leg from Pico Cuba to Las Cuevas is straightforward and handled by park staff.

These hikes are well coordinated and the guides efficient. The sanest way to begin is by spending the night at Villa Santo Domingo and setting out in the morning (you should enter the park gate by 10am). Transport from Las Cuevas along the coast is sparse with one scheduled truck on alternate days. Arrange a taxi in advance.

See p422 for a description of the Las Cuevas–Pico Turquino leg.

of the Patio de los Leones in Spain's Alhambra – shines brightly amid the urban decay. Nearby, a permanent **statue of Carlos Puebla,** Manzanillo's famous homegrown troubadour, sits contemplatively on a bench admiring the surrounding cityscape.

FREE Museo Histórico Municipal MUSEUM
(Martí No 226; ⌚8am-noon & 2-6pm Tue-Fri, 8am-noon & 6-10pm Sat & Sun) On the eastern side of Parque Céspedes, Manzanillo's municipal museum gives the usual local history lesson with a revolutionary twist. The **Galería de Arte Carlos Enriquez**, displaying revolving local collections, is next door.

Iglesia de la Purísima Concepción CHURCH
The city's neoclassical church was initiated in 1805, but the twin bell towers were added in 1918. The church, named after Manzanillo's patron saint, is notable for its impressive gilded altarpiece.

Celia Sánchez Monument MONUMENT
About eight blocks southwest of the park lies Manzanillo's most evocative sight. Built in 1990, this terracotta tiled staircase embellished with colorful ceramic murals runs up Calle Caridad between Martí and Luz Caballero. The birds and flowers on the reliefs represent Sánchez, lynchpin of the M-26-7 Movement and longtime aid to Castro, whose visage appears on the central mural

near the top of the stairs. It's a moving memorial with excellent views out over the city and bay.

OUTSIDE TOWN

TOP CHOICE Museo Histórico la Demajagua MUSEUM

(admission CUC$1; ⏲8am-6pm Mon-Fri, 8am-noon Sun) It started with a cry. Ten kilometers south of Manzanillo across the grassy expanses of western Granma lies La Demajagua, the site of the sugar estate of Carlos Manuel de Céspedes whose *Grito de Yara* and subsequent freeing of his slaves on October 10, 1868, marked the opening shot of Cuba's independence wars. There's a small museum here along with the remains of Céspedes' *ingenio* (sugar mill), a poignant monument (with a quote from Castro) and the famous Demajagua bell that Céspedes tolled to announce Cuba's (then unofficial) independence. In 1947 an as yet unknown Fidel Castro 'kidnapped' the bell and took it to Havana in a publicity stunt to protest against the corrupt Cuban government. To get to La Demajagua, travel south 10km from the Servi-Cupet gas station in Manzanillo, in the direction of Media Luna, and then another 2.5km off the main road, toward the sea.

Criadero de Cocodrilos CROCODILE FARM

(admission CUC$5; ⏲7am-6pm Mon-Fri, 7-11am Sat) The nearby Cauto River delta is home to a growing number of wild crocodiles, so it's no surprise to encounter one of Cuba's half dozen or so crocodile farms here. There are close of 1000 crocs at this breeding farm, although they're all of the less-endangered 'American' variety. The farm is 5km south of Manzanillo on the road to Media Luna.

Sleeping

Manzanillo – thank heavens – has a smattering of private rooms, as there's not much happening on the hotel scene.

TOP CHOICE Adrián & Tonia CASA PARTICULAR $

(☎57-30-28; Mártires de Vietnam No 49; r CUC$20-25; ❄P) This attractive casa, full of clever workmanship (double-glazed windows) and weeping plants, would stand out in any city, let alone Manzanillo. The position, on the terracotta staircase that leads to the Celia Sánchez monument, obviously helps. But youthful Adrián and Tonia have gone beyond the call of duty with a vista-laden terrace, Jacuzzi-sized cool-off pool and dinner provided in a paladar (privately owned restaurant) next door.

Villa Luisa CASA PARTICULAR $

(☎57-27-38; Rabena No 172 btwn Maceo & Masó; r CUC$20-25; P❄) Two newly renovated rooms in a clean, open house with coco palms and a small pool in the garden.

Hotel Guacanayabo HOTEL $

(☎57-40-12; Circunvalación Camilo Cienfuegos; s/d low season CUC$15/20, high season CUC$18/24; ❄≈) The cheapest and most austere of Islazul's Cuban hotels, the Guacanayabo looks like a tropical reincarnation of a Gulag camp. The fake flamingos in the lobby fail to lighten the mood, although the affable staff tries its best. Rooms are badly lit, if relatively clean, and the restaurant is reminiscent of a scene from *Fawlty Towers*.

Eating

Manzanillo is known for its fish, though strangely not a lot of the fresh seafood seems to find its way onto the plates in the restaurants. In common with many less touristy Cuban cities, the culinary scene here is grim. If in doubt, eat in your casa particular, or drop in on the weekend Sábado en la Calle (p378) where the locals cook up traditional whole roast pig.

Paladar la Roca PALADAR $$

(Mártires de Vietnam No 68) Halfway up the Célia Sánchez steps is the best spot to sample Manzanillo's seafood in a modest clapboard house with ever-smiling hosts. Fish is the dish and comes with some pleasant sauces.

Cafetería la Fuente ICE-CREAM PARLOR $

(cnr Avs Jesús Menéndez & Masó; ⏲8am-midnight) The Cubans are as stalwart about their ice cream as the British are about their tea. Come what may, the scooper's always in the tub. Join the line here to sweeten up your views of surrounding Parque Céspedes.

Restaurante Licetera SEAFOOD $

(Av Masó btwn Calles 9 & 10; ⏲noon-9:45pm) A decent indoor-outdoor place down near the seafront that specializes in local fish served with the head and bones on but still rather tasty. Prices are in *moneda nacional* (Cuban pesos).

Restaurante Yang Tsé CHINESE $

(Merchán btwn Masó & Saco; ⏲7am-10pm) *Comida China* is served for *moneda nacional* in this centrally located place with delusions of grandeur (there's a dress code!). It overlooks

Parque Céspedes and gets good reports from locals.

Dinos Pizza la Glorieta PIZZA $
(Merchán No 221 btwn Maceo & Masó; ⌚8am-midnight) This small Cuba pizza chain could come in handy here. Perched on the main square, it's run by the government restaurant group, Palmares, and accepts convertibles.

Cafetería Piropo Kikiri FAST FOOD $
(Martí btwn Maceo & Saco; ⌚10am-10pm) This place has everything from ice-cream sandwiches to sundaes, available for convertibles.

☆ Entertainment

As in most Cuban cities, Manzanillo's best 'gig' takes place on Saturday evenings in the famed **Sábado en la Calle**, a riot of piping organs, roasted pigs, throat-burning rum and, of course, dancing locals. Don't miss it!

Teatro Manzanillo THEATER
(Villuendas btwn Maceo & Saco; admission 5 pesos; ⌚shows 8pm Fri-Sun) Touring companies such as the Ballet de Camagüey and Danza Contemporánea de Cuba perform at this lovingly restored venue. Built in 1856 and restored in 1926 and again in 2002, this 430-seat beauty is packed with oil paintings, red flocking and original detail.

Casa de la Trova TRADITIONAL MUSIC
(Merchán No 213; admission 1 peso) In the spiritual home of *nueva trova*, a renovation of the local *trova* house was long overdue. Pay a visit to this hallowed and freshly painted musical shrine where Carlos Puebla once plucked his strings.

FREE **Uneac** CULTURAL CENTER
(cnr Merchán & Concession) For traditional music you can head for this dependable option, which has Saturday and Sunday night *peñas* (musical performances) and painting expos.

Complejo Costa Azul CABARET
(⌚8pm-midnight Tue-Sat, 8pm-1am Sun) Manzanillo's nightly cabaret by the bay is kitschier than most making it all the more watchable.

Cine Popular CINEMA
(Av 1 de Mayo; ⌚Tue-Sun) This is the town's top movie house.

ℹ Information

Banco de Crédito y Comercio (cnr Merchán & Saco)

Cadeca (Martí No 188) Two blocks from the main square. With few places accepting convertibles here, you'll need some Cuban pesos.

Post office (cnr Martí & Codina) One block from Parque Céspedes.

Etecsa (cnr Martí & Codina; ⌚8:30am-7:30pm) After years of waiting, Manzanillo finally has a posh new phone office with internet terminals.

ℹ Getting There & Away

Air

Manzanillo's **Sierra Maestra Airport** (airport code MZO) is on the road to Cayo Espino, 8km south of the Servi-Cupet gas station in Manzanillo. **Cubana** (www.cubana.cu) has a nonstop flight from Havana once a week on Saturday (CUC$103, two hours). **Sunwing** (www.sunwing.ca) flies directly from Toronto and Montreal in winter and transfers people directly to the Marea del Portillo hotels.

A taxi between the airport and the center of town should cost approximately CUC$6.

Bus & Truck

The **bus station** (Av Rosales) is 2km northeast of the city center. There are no Víazul services to or from Manzanillo. This narrows your options down to *guaguas* (local Cuban buses) or trucks (no reliable schedules and long queues). Services run several times a day to Yara and Bayamo in the east and Pilón and Niquero in the south. For the latter destinations you can also board at the crossroads near the Servi-Cupet gas station and the hospital, which is also where you'll find the *amarillos* (transport officials).

Car

Cubacar (☎57-77-36) has an office at the Hotel Guacanayabo (p377). There's a sturdy road running through Corralito up into Holguín, making this the quickest exit from Manzanillo toward points north and east.

Train

All services from the train station on the north side of town are via Yara and Bayamo. Every third day there's a link to Havana. Trains go to several destinations but they are painfully slow.

ℹ Getting Around

Horse carts (one peso) to the bus station leave from Dr Codina between Plácido and Luz Caballero. Horse carts along the Malecón to the shipyard leave from the bottom of Saco.

WORTH A TRIP

MEDIA LUNA

One of a handful of small towns that punctuate the swaying sugar fields between Manzanillo and Cabo Cruz, Media Luna (population 15,493) is worth a pit stop on the basis of its Celia Sánchez connections. The Revolution's 'first lady' was born here in 1920 in a small clapboard house that is now the **Celia Sánchez Museum** (Paúl Podio No 111; admission CUC$1; ⏲9am-noon & 2-5pm Tue-Sat, 9am-1pm Sun).

If you have time, take a stroll around this quintessential Cuban sugar town dominated by a tall soot-stained mill (now disused) and characteristic clapboard houses decorated with gingerbread embellishments. Aside from the Sánchez museum, Media Luna showcases a lovely **glorieta**, almost as outlandish as the one in Manzanillo. The main park is the place to get a take on the local street theater while supping on peso fruit shakes and quick-melting ice cream.

A signposted road from Media Luna leads 28km to **Cinco Palmas** where a monument marks the spot where Castro's depleted rebel army regrouped after the debacle of the *Granma* landing in December 1956.

Niquero

POP 20,273

Niquero, a small fishing port and sugar town in the isolated southwest corner of Granma, is dominated by the local Roberto Ramírez Delgado sugar mill, built in 1905 and nationalized in 1960. It is one of the few mills in the area still in operation after the 2002 closedowns. Like many Granma settlements, Niquero is characterized by its distinctive clapboard houses and has a lively *Noche de Cubanilla,* when the streets are closed off and dining is at sidewalk tables. Live bands replete with organ grinders entertain the locals.

Ostensibly, there isn't much to do in Niquero, but you can explore the park, where there's a **cinema**, and visit the town's small **museum**. Look out for a **monument** commemorating the oft-forgotten victims of the *Granma* landing, who were hunted down and killed by Batista's troops in December 1956.

Niquero makes a good base from which to visit the Parque Nacional Desembarco del Granma. There are two Servi-Cupet petrol stations, a bank, a nightclub and plenty of spontaneous street-side action.

Sleeping

Hotel Niquero HOTEL $

(☎59-24-98; Esquina Martí; s/d CUC$14/18; P ❄) Nestled in the middle of the small town, this low-key, out-on-a-limb hotel situated opposite the local sugar factory has dark, slightly tatty rooms with little balconies that overlook the street. The service here is variable, though the affordable on-site restaurant has been known to rustle up a reasonable beef steak with sauce. Better hunker down because it's the only accommodation in town.

Alegria del Pio

Pause for a moment. You're on hallowed revolutionary ground. Accessed via 28km of potholed purgatory from a turn-off in Niquero, this is the spot where Castro's shipwrecked rebels were intercepted by Bastista's army in 1956 and forced to split up and flee. A monument went up in 2009 to mark the event and from the end of the road there are a couple of little-used trails which can be undertaken independently or with a guide; enquire with Ecotur (p371) in Bayamo or at the Parque Nacional Desembarco del Granma (p380).

Morlotte-Fustete is a 2km trail that traverses the spectacular marine terraces (sometimes using wooden ladders) and takes in the **Cueva del Fustete** – a 5km-long cavern replete with stalagmites and stalactites – and the **Hoyo de Morlotte**, a 77m deep dolina caused by water corrosion. **El Samuel** is a 1.3km trail to the **Cueva Espelunca**, another cave thought to have been used by aboriginals for religious ceremonies.

Alegria del Pio is also the finish point for the 30km hike from Las Coloradas that replicates the path of the shipwrecked rebels in December 1956. As there are no facilities here you'll need to bring all your own food and water.

Parque Nacional Desembarco del Granma

Mixing unique environmental diversity with heavy historical significance, the **Parque Nacional Desembarco del Granma** (admission CUC$5) consists of 275 sq km of teeming forests, peculiar karst topography and uplifted marine terraces. It is also a spiritual shrine to the Cuban Revolution – the spot where Castro's stricken leisure yacht *Granma* limped ashore in December 1956.

Named a Unesco World Heritage Site in 1999, the park protects some of the most pristine coastal cliffs in the Americas. Of the 512 plant species identified thus far, about 60% are endemic and a dozen of them are found only here. The fauna is equally rich, with 25 species of mollusk, seven species of amphibian, 44 types of reptile, 110 bird species and 13 types of mammal.

In El Guafe, archaeologists have uncovered the second-most important community of ancient agriculturists and ceramic-makers discovered in Cuba. Approximately 1000 years old, the artifacts discovered include altars, carved stones and earthen vessels along with six idols guarding a water goddess inside a ceremonial cave. As far as archaeologists are concerned, it's probably just the tip of the iceberg.

Sights

The area is famous as the landing place of the yacht *Granma,* which brought Fidel and Revolution to Cuba in 1956.

Museo las Colorados MUSEUM
(admission CUC$2; 8am-6pm Tue-Sat, 8am-noon Sun) A large monument just beyond the park gate marks the *Granma's* landing spot. A small museum outlines the routes taken by Castro, Guevara and the others into the Sierra Maestra, and there's a full-scale replica of the *Granma* which – if you're lucky – a machete-wielding guard will let you climb inside to wonder how 82 men ever made it. The entry ticket includes a visit to the simple reconstructed hut of the first *campesino* (a poor charcoal-burner) to help Fidel after the landing. An enthusiastic guide will also accompany you along a 1.3km path through dense mangroves to the ocean and the spot where the *Granma* ran aground, 70m off-shore.

Sendero Arqueológico Natural el Guafe TRAIL
(admission CUC$3) About eight kilometers southwest of Las Coloradas is this well-signposted 2km-long trail, the park's headline nature/archaeological hike. An underground river here has created 20 large caverns, one of which contains the famous Ídolo del Agua, carved from stalagmites by pre-Columbian Indians. You should allow two hours for the stroll in order to take in the butterflies, 170 different species of birds (including the tiny *colibrí*), and multiple orchids. There's also a 500-year-old cactus. A park guide can guide you through the more interesting features for an extra CUC$2. There are hundreds of flies here. Bring repellent.

The park is flecked with other trails, the best of which is the 30km trek to Alegria del Pio replicating the journey of the 82 rebels who landed here in 1956. Due to its length and lack of suitable signage, this rarely-tackled trail is best done with a guide. Enquire at Ecotur in Bayamo (p371) beforehand and reserve approximately seven to eight hours to complete it. You'll need to arrange for transport to meet you at Alegria del Pio.

Comunidad Cabo Cruz LANDMARK
Three kilometers beyond the El Guafe trailhead is a tiny fishing community with skiffs bobbing offshore and sinewy men gutting their catch on the golden beach. There's not much to see here except the 33m-tall Vargas lighthouse, which was erected in 1871 and now belongs to the Cuban military. In its shadow lies Restaurante el Cabo, source of the cheapest fresh seafood you'll find anywhere.

There's good swimming and shore snorkeling east of the lighthouse; bring your own gear as there are no facilities.

Sleeping & Eating

Campismo las Colorados CAMPISMO $
(Carretera de Niquero Km 17; s/d CUC$8/12; ❄) A Category 3 campismo with 28 duplex cabins standing on 500m of murky beach, 5km southwest of Belic, just outside the park. All cabins have air-con and baths and there's a restaurant, a games hall and watersport rental on-site. Las Coloradas underwent a lengthy reconstruction following damage inflicted by Hurricane Dennis

in 2005. You can book through Cubamar (p118) in Havana.

TOP CHOICE **Restaurante el Cabo** SEAFOOD $
(⏲7am-9pm Tue-Sun) The cheapest seafood in Cuba comes straight out of the Caribbean behind this restaurant that lies in the shadow of the Vargas lighthouse. Expect fresh fillets of snapper and swordfish, and prices in Cuban pesos that top out at the equivalent of CUC$2 a meal. You'll be laughing all the way back to Bayamo.

Ranchón las Colorados CARIBBEAN $
(⏲noon-7pm) A traditional thatched-roof restaurant selling fairly basic *comida criolla* just before the park gates, this place does the business if you're hungry after a long drive.

Getting There & Away

Ten kilometers southwest of Media Luna the road divides, with Pilón 30km to the southeast and Niquero 10km to the southwest. Belic is 16km southwest of Niquero. It's another 6km from Belic to the national park entry gate on a badly potholed road.

If you don't have your own transport, getting here can be tough. Irregular buses go as far as the Campismo las Coloradas daily and there are equally infrequent trucks from Belic. As a last resort, you can try the *amarillos* in Niquero. The closest gas stations are in Niquero.

Pilón

POP 11,904

Pilón is a small, isolated settlement wedged between the Marea del Portillo resorts and the Parque Nacional Desembarco del Gran-

AND THEN THERE WERE THREE...

It seemed like an ignominious defeat. Three days after landing in a crippled leisure yacht on Cuba's southeastern coast, Castro's expeditionary force of 82 soldiers had been decimated by Batista's superior army. Some of the rebels had fled, others had been captured and killed. Escaping from the ambush, Castro found himself cowering in a sugarcane field along with two ragged companions; his 'bodyguard,' Universo Sánchez, and diminutive Havana doctor, Faustino Pérez. 'There was a moment when I was commander-in-chief of myself and two others,' said the man who would one day go on to overthrow the Cuban government, thwart a US-sponsored invasion, incite a nuclear standoff and become one of the most enduring political figures of the 20th century.

Hunted by ground troops and bombed from the air by military planes, the trio lay trapped in the cane field for four days and three nights. The hapless Pérez had inadvertently discarded his weapon; Sánchez, meanwhile, had lost his shoes. Wracked by fatigue and plagued by hunger, Fidel continued to do what he always did best. He whispered incessantly to his beleaguered colleagues – about the Revolution, about the philosophies of José Martí. Buoyantly he pontificated about how 'all the glory of the world would fit inside a grain of maize.' Sánchez, not unwisely, concluded that his delirious leader had gone crazy and that their grisly fate was sealed – it was just a matter of time.

At night, Fidel – determined not to be caught alive – slept with his rifle cocked against his throat, the safety catch released. One squeeze of the finger and it would have been over. No Cuban Revolution, no Bay of Pigs, no Cuban Missile Crisis, no Battle of Cuito Cuanavale.

Fatefully, the moment didn't arrive. With the army concluding that the rebels had been wiped out, the search was called off. Choosing their moment, Fidel and his two companions crept stealthily northeast toward the safety of the Sierra Maestra, sucking on stalks of sugarcane for nutrition.

It was a desperate fight for survival. For a further eight days the rebel army remained a bedraggled trio as the three fugitive soldiers dodged army patrols, crawled through sewers and drank their own urine. It wasn't until December 13 that they met up with Guillermo García, a *campesino* sympathetic to the rebel cause, and a corner was turned.

On December 15 at a safe meeting house Fidel's brother, Raúl, materialized out of the jungle with three men and four weapons. Castro was ecstatic. Three days later a third exhausted band of eight soldiers – including Che Guevara and Camilo Cienfuegos – turned up, swelling the rebel army to an abject 15.

'We can win this war,' proclaimed an ebullient Fidel to his small band of not-so-merry men, 'We have just begun the fight.'

ma. It is the last coastal town of any note before Chivirico over 150km to the east. Since its sugar mill shut down nearly a decade ago, Pilón has lost much of its raison d'être, though the people still eke out a living despite almost nonexistent transport links and a merciless bludgeoning from Hurricane Dennis in 2005.

Sights

Casa Museo Celia Sánchez Manduley MUSEUM
(admission CUC$1; 9am-5pm Mon-Sat, 9am-1pm Sun) Inspired by Fidel's revolutionary call, the town's inhabitants were quick to provide aid to the disparate rebel army after the *Granma* yacht landed nearby in 1956, and Castro muse Celia Sánchez briefly based herself here. This tiny museum has been named in her honor – though it functions mainly as a local history museum.

Festivals & Events

Sábado de Rumba STREET PARTY
(8pm Sat) There's a popular dance in Cuba called the *pilón* (named after the town), which imitates the rhythms of pounding sugar. Your best chance of seeing it is to attend Pilón's weekly street party – similar to those in Manzanillo and Bayamo – with whole roast pig, shots of rum and plenty of live music. The hotels at Marea del Portillo run a weekly Saturday evening transfer bus to Pilón for CUC$5 return.

Sleeping

Villa Turística Punta Piedra HOTEL $
(59-70-62; s/d CUC$28/40; P) On the main road 11km east of Pilón and 5km west of Marea del Portillo, this small low-key resort, comprising 13 rooms in two single-story blocks, makes an interesting alternative to the larger hotel complexes to the east. There's a restaurant here and an intermittent disco located on a secluded saber of sandy beach. The staff, once they've recovered from the surprise of seeing you, will be mighty pleased with your custom.

Getting There & Around

Public transport in and out of Pilón is dire in both directions. The only regular bus is the Astro to Santiago de Cuba via Bayamo on alternate days – but this is no longer available to non-Cubans. Otherwise it's car, long-distance bike, or winging it with the *amarillos*.

The Servi-Cupet gas station is by the highway at the entrance to Pilón and sells snacks and drinks. Drivers should be sure to fill up here; the next gas station is in Santiago de Cuba nearly 200km away.

Marea del Portillo

There's something infectious about Marea del Portillo, a tiny south-coast village bordered by two low-key all-inclusive resorts. Wedged into a narrow strip of dry land between the glistening Caribbean and the cascading Sierra Maestra, it occupies a spot of great natural beauty – and great history.

The problem for independent travelers is getting here. There is no regular public transport, which means that you may, for the first time, have to go local and travel with the *amarillos*. Another issue for beach lovers is the sand, which is of a light gray color and may disappoint those more attuned to the brilliant whites of Cayo Coco.

The resorts themselves are affordable and well maintained places but they are isolated; the nearest town of any size is lackluster Manzanillo 100km to the north. Real rustic Cuba, however, is a gunshot outside the hotel gates.

Activities

There's plenty to do here, despite the area's apparent isolation. Both hotels operate horseback riding for CUC$5 per hour (usually to El Salto; see p383) or a horse-and-carriage sojourn along the deserted coast road for CUC$4. A jeep tour to Las Yaguas waterfall is CUC$49 and trips to Parque Nacional Desembarco del Granma start at about the same price. Trips can be booked at Cubanacán desks in either hotel.

Diving & Fishing

Centro Internacional de Buceo Marea de Portillo DIVING
Adjacent to Hotel Marea del Portillo, this Cubanacán-run dive center offers scuba diving for a giveaway CUC$25/49 per one/two immersions. A more exciting dive to the *Cristóbal Colón* wreck (sunk in the 1898 Spanish-Cuban-American War) costs CUC$70 for two immersions. Deep-sea fishing starts at CUC$200 for a boat (four anglers) plus crew and gear.

Other water excursions include a seafari (with snorkeling) for CUC$35, a sunset cruise for CUC$15 and a trip to uninhabited Cayo Blanco for CUC$25.

Hiking

El Salto HIKING

This wondrous 20km out-and-back hike starts right outside the hotel complex. Turn right onto the coast road and then, after approximately 400m, hang left onto an unpaved track just before a bridge. The track winds through some fields, joins a road and traverses a dusty, scattered settlement. On the far side of the village a dam rises above you. Rather than take the paved road up the embankment to the left, branch right and, after 200m, pick up a clear path that rises steeply up above the dam and into view of the lake behind. This beautiful path tracks alongside the lake before crossing one of its river feeds on a wooden bridge. Go straight on and uphill here and, when the path forks on the crest, bear right. Heading down into a verdant tranquil valley, pass at a **casa de campesino** (the friendly owners keep bees and will give you honey, coffee, and a geographical reorientation), cross the river (Río Cilantro) and then follow it upstream to **El Salto** where there's a small waterfall, a shady thatched shelter and an inviting swimming hole.

Salto de Guayabito HIKING

Starting in the village of Mata Dos about 20km east of Marea, this hike is normally done as part of an organized trip from the hotels. Groups – who often embark on horseback – follow the Río Motas 7km upstream to an enchanting waterfall surrounded by rocky cliffs, ferns, cacti and orchids.

Sleeping

TOP CHOICE **Hotel Marea del Portillo** HOTEL $$

(☎59-70-08; all-incl s/d CUC$55/78; P❄@≋) It's not Cayo Coco, but it barely seems to matter here. In fact, Marea's all-round functionalism and lack of big-resort pretension seem to work well in this traditional corner of Cuba. The 74 rooms are perfectly adequate, the food buffet does a good job, and the dark sandy arc of beach set in the warm rain shadow of the Sierra Maestra is within baseball-pitching of your balcony/patio. Servicing older Canadians and some Cuban families means there is a mix of people here; plus plenty of interesting excursions to some of the island's lesser heralded sights.

Hotel Farallón del Caribe HOTEL $$$

(☎59-70-09; all-incl s/d CUC$95/120; P❄@≋) Perched on a low hill with the Caribbean on one side and the Sierra Maestra on the other, the Farallón is Marea's bigger and richer sibling. Three-star all-inclusive facilities are complemented by five-star surroundings and truly magical views across Granma's hilly hinterland. Exciting excursions can be organized at the Cubanacán desk here into the Parque Nacional Desembarco del Granma, or you can simply sit by the pool/beach and do absolutely nothing. The resort is popular with package-tour Canadians bussed in from Manzanillo and is only open April through October.

Getting There & Away

The journey east to Santiago is one of Cuba's most spectacular, but also one of its most difficult (there aren't even any *amarillos* here). Public transport is sporadic to say the least and you'll undoubtedly have to undertake the trip in stages. The occasional Cuban buses do pass; ask around in Pilón or Marea del Portillo. **Cubacar** (☎59-70-05) has a desk at Hotel Marea del Portillo.

Getting Around

The hotels rent out scooters for approximately CUC$24 a day. Cars are available from Cubacar, or you can join in an excursion with Cubanacán at the hotels. The route to El Salto can be covered on foot.

Santiago de Cuba Province

☎022 / POP 1,047,015

Includes »

Best Places to Eat

- El Barracón (p405)
- Finca el Porvenir (p418)
- Paladar Salón Tropical (p405)
- Ristorante Italiano la Fontana (p405)
- Restaurante Zunzún (p405)

Best Places to Stay

- Hostal San Basilio (p402)
- Hotel Horizontes el Saltón (p420)
- Casa Colonial 'Maruchi' (p402)
- Brisas Sierra Mar (p420)

Why Go?

Stuck out in Cuba's mountainous 'Oriente' region, and long a hotbed of rebellion and sedition, Santiago's cultural influences have often come from the east, imported via Haiti, Jamaica, Barbados and Africa. For this reason the province is often cited as being Cuba's most 'Caribbean' enclave, with a raucous West Indian–style carnival and a cache of *folklórico* dance groups that owe as much to French-Haitian culture as they do to Spanish.

As the focus of Spain's new colony in the 16th and early 17th centuries, Santiago de Cuba enjoyed a brief spell as Cuba's capital until it was usurped by Havana in 1607. The subsequent slower pace of development has some distinct advantages. Drive 20km or so along the coast in either direction from the provincial capital and you're on a different planet, a land full of rugged coves, crashing surf, historical coffee plantations and hills replete with riotous endemism.

When to Go

July is the key month in Santiago de Cuba's cultural calendar when the city is *caliente* (hot) in more ways than one. The month begins with the vibrant Festival del Caribe and ends with the justifiably famous Carnaval. More music is on offer in March at the Festival Internacional de Trova when the city rediscovers its musical roots. The period between these two events (March through June) is renowned for its high water clarity, ensuring excellent diving conditions off the south coast.

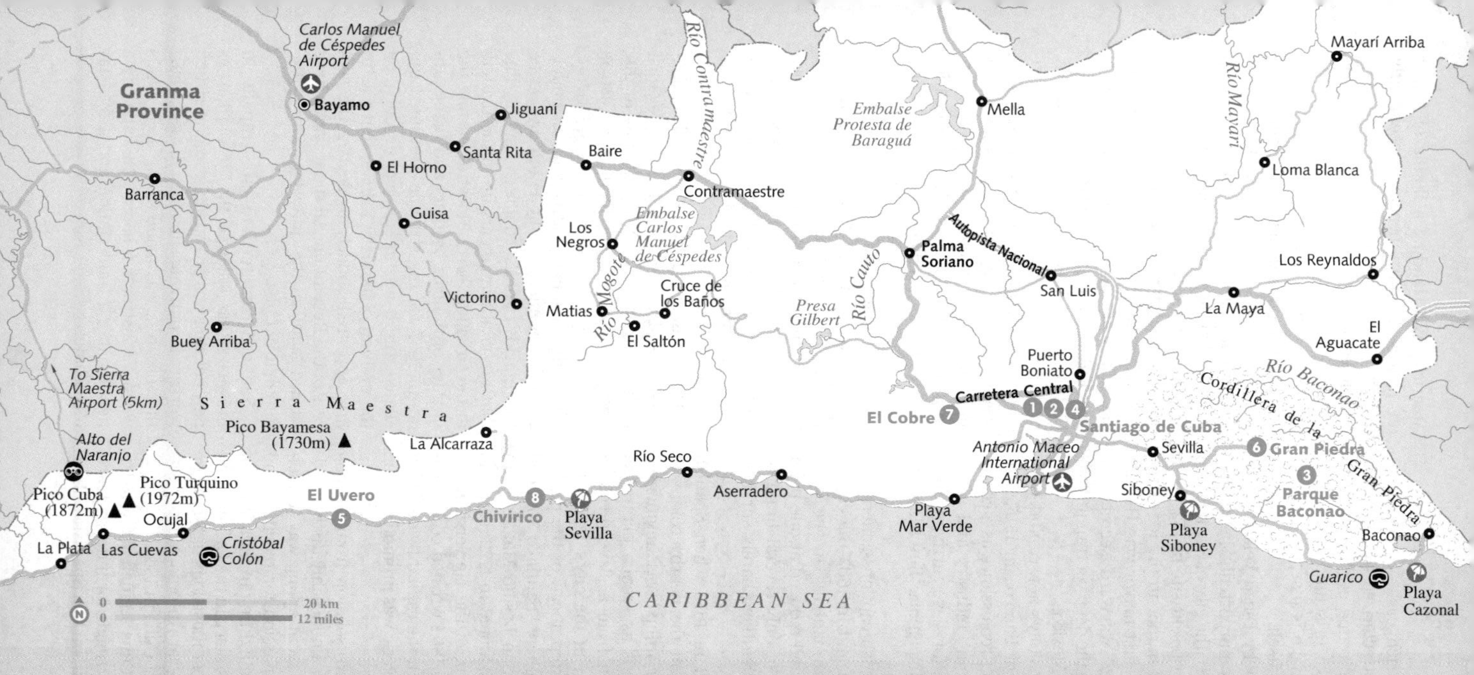

Santiago de Cuba Province Highlights

1. Round off a musical evening in Santiago de Cuba's legendary **Casa de la Trova** (p408)
2. Visit the **Cuartel Moncada** (p395) in Santiago de Cuba and evaluate the audacity (or folly) of Castro's 1953 insurrection
3. Enjoy traditional food and a rodeo in Parque Baconao's **Fiesta Guajira** (p416)
4. Explore Cuba's numerous Afro-Cuban dance genres at a **folklórico show** (p407) in Santiago de Cuba
5. Take the coast road west toward **El Uvero** (p421) amid rolling mountains and crashing surf
6. Trace the history of Cuba's French-inspired coffee culture at **Cafetal la Isabelica** (p415) in Gran Piedra
7. Make a pilgrimage to **El Cobre** (p419) to visit the shrine of Cuba's patron saint, La Virgen de la Caridad
8. Dive down to the wreck of Spanish warship *Cristóbal Colón* off the coast near **Chivirico** (p421)

History

Illuminated by a rich cast of revolutionary heroes and characterized by a cultural legacy that has infiltrated everything from music and language to sculpture and art, the history of Santiago is inseparable from the history of Cuba itself.

Founded in 1514 by Diego Velázquez de Cuéllar (his bones purportedly lie underneath the cathedral), the city of Santiago de Cuba moved to its present site in 1522 on a sharp horseshoe of harbor in the lee of the Sierra Maestra. Its first mayor was Hernán Cortés – Velázquez' wayward secretary – who departed from the deep yet tranquil bay in 1518 en route to Mexico.

Installed as the colony's new capital, after the abandonment of Baracoa in 1515, Santiago enjoyed a brief renaissance as a center for the copper-mining industry and a disembarkation point for slaves arriving from West Africa via Hispaniola. But the glory wasn't to last.

In 1556 the Spanish captains-general departed for Havana and in 1607 the capital was transferred permanently to the west. Raided by pirates and reduced at one point to a small village of only several hundred people, embattled Santiago barely survived the ignominy.

The tide turned in 1655 when Spanish settlers arrived from the nearby colony of Jamaica, and this influx was augmented further in the 1790s as French plantation owners on the run from a slave revolt in Haiti settled down in the city's Tivolí district. Always one step ahead of the capital in the cultural sphere, Santiago founded the Seminario de San Basilio Magno as an educational establishment in 1722 (six years before the founding of the Universidad de La Habana) and in 1804 wrested ecclesiastical dominance from the capital by ensuring that the city's top cleric was promoted to the post of archbishop.

Individuality and isolation from Havana soon gave Santiago a noticeably distinct cultural heritage and went a long way in fuelling its insatiable passion for rebellion and revolt. Much of the fighting in both Wars of Independence took place in the Oriente, and one of the era's most illustrious fighters, the great *mulato* general Antonio Maceo, was born in Santiago de Cuba in 1845.

In 1898, just as Cuba seemed about to triumph in its long struggle for independence, the US intervened in the Spanish-Cuban-American War, landing a flotilla of troops on nearby Daiquirí beach. Subsequently, decisive land and sea battles of both Wars of Independence were fought in and around Santiago. The first was played out on July 1 when a victorious cavalry charge led by Teddy Roosevelt on outlying Loma de San Juan (San Juan Hill) sealed a famous victory. The second ended in a highly one-sided naval battle in Santiago harbor between US and Spanish ships, which led to the almost total destruction of the Spanish fleet.

A construction boom characterized the first few years of the new, quasi-independent Cuban state, but after three successive US military interventions (the last of which, in 1917, saw US troops stationed in the Oriente until 1923), things started to turn sour. Despite its ongoing influence as a cultural and musical powerhouse, Santiago began to earn a slightly less respectable reputation as a center for rebellion and strife, and it was here on July 26, 1953, that Fidel Castro and his companions launched an assault on the Cuartel Moncada (Moncada Barracks, see p394). This was the start of a number of events that changed the course of Cuban history. At his trial in Santiago, Castro made his famous *History Will Absolve Me* speech, which became the basic platform of the Cuban Revolution.

On November 30, 1956, the people of Santiago de Cuba rose up in rebellion against Batista's troops in a futile attempt to distract attention from the landing of Castro's guerrillas on the western shores of Oriente. Although not initially successful, an underground movement led by Frank and Josué País quickly established a secret supply line that ran vital armaments up to the fighters in the Oriente's Sierra Maestra. Despite the murder of the País brothers and many others in 1957–58, the struggle continued unabated, and it was in Santiago de Cuba, on the evening of January 1, 1959, that Castro first appeared publicly to declare the success of the Revolution. All these events have earned Santiago the title 'Hero City of the Republic of Cuba.'

Santiago continued to grow rapidly in the years that followed the Revolution, as new housing was provided for impoverished workers in outlying suburban districts. Further progress was made in the early 1990s when a construction boom gifted the city a new theater, a train station and a five-star Meliá hotel.

Santiago de Cuba

POP 493,623

You can take Santiago de Cuba in one of two ways: a hot, aggravating city full of hustlers and hassle that'll have you gagging to get on the first bus back to Havana; or a glittering cultural capital that has played an instrumental part in the evolution of Cuban literature, music, architecture, politics and ethnology. Yes, Santiago divides opinions among Cubans and foreigners almost as much as one of its most famous former scholars, Fidel Castro. Some love it, others hate it; few are indifferent.

Enlivened by a cosmopolitan mix of Afro-Caribbean culture and situated closer to Haiti and the Dominican Republic than to Havana, Santiago's influences tend to come as much from the east as from the west, a factor that has been crucial in shaping the city's distinct identity. Nowhere else in Cuba will you find such a colorful combination of people or such a resounding sense of historical destiny. Diego Velázquez de Cuéllar made the city his second capital, Fidel Castro used it to launch his embryonic nationalist Revolution, Don Facundo Bacardí based his first-ever rum factory here, and just about every Cuban music genre from salsa to *son* first emanated from somewhere in these dusty, rhythmic and sensuous streets.

Setting-wise Santiago could rival any of the world's great urban centers. Caught dramatically between the indomitable Sierra Maestra and the azure Caribbean, the city's *casco histórico* (historical center) retains a time-worn and slightly neglected air that's vaguely reminiscent of Barbados, Salvador in Brazil, or the seedier parts of New Orleans.

Santiago is also hot, in more ways than one. While the temperature rises into the 30s out on the street, *jineteros* (touts) go about their business in the shadows with a level of ferocity unmatched elsewhere in Cuba. Then there's the pollution, particularly bad in the central district, where cacophonous motor-

Greater Santiago de Cuba

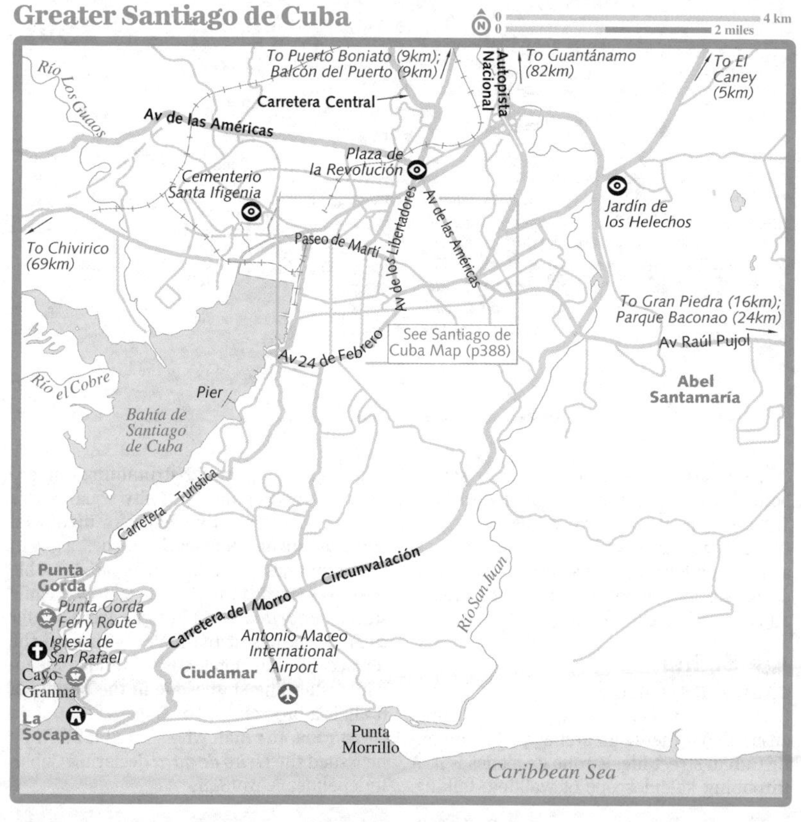

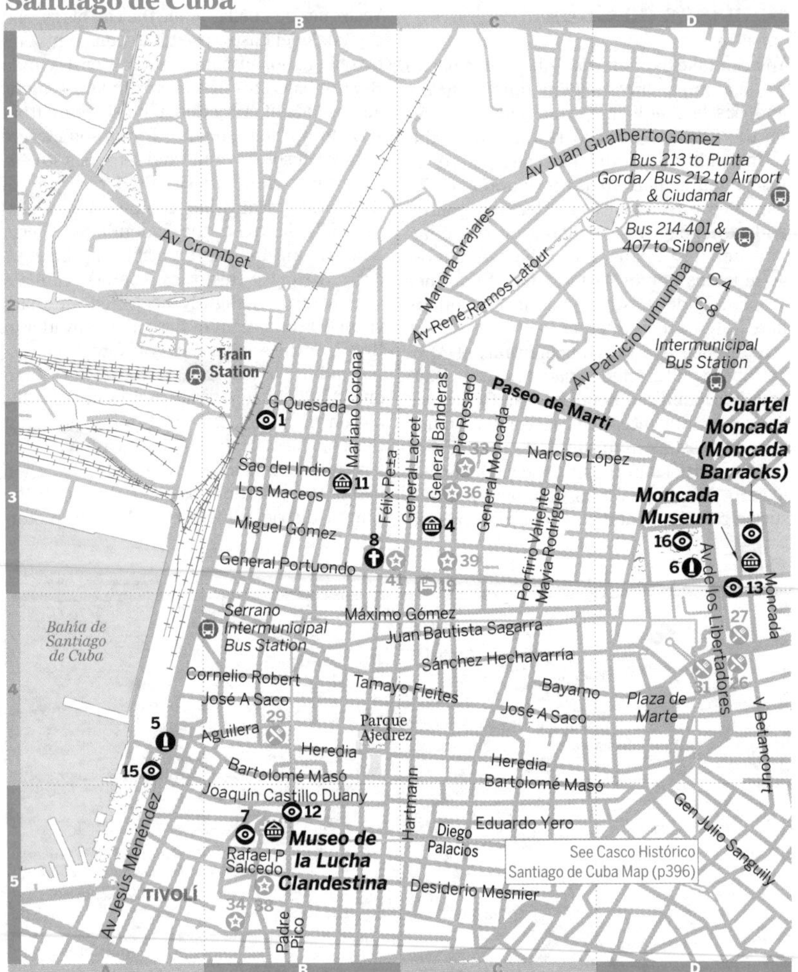

cycles swarm up and down narrow streets better designed for horses or pedestrians. Travelers should beware. While never particularly unsafe, everything in Santiago feels a little madder, more frenetic, a tad more desperate, and visitors should be prepared to adjust their pace accordingly.

Sights

CASCO HISTÓRICO

Parque Céspedes PARK

(Map p396) If there's an archetype for romantic Cuban street life, Parque Céspedes is it. A throbbing kaleidoscope of walking, talking, hustling, flirting, guitar-strumming humanity, this most ebullient of city squares is a sight to behold any time of day or night. Old ladies gossip on shady park benches, a guy in a panama hat drags his dilapidated double bass over toward the Casa de la Trova, while sultry *señoritas* in skin-tight lycra flutter their eye-lashes at the male tourists on the terrace of the Hotel Casa Granda. Meanwhile, standing statuesque in the middle of it all, is a bronze **bust of Carlos Manuel de Céspedes**, the man who started it all when he issued the *Grito de yara* declaring Cuban independence in 1868.

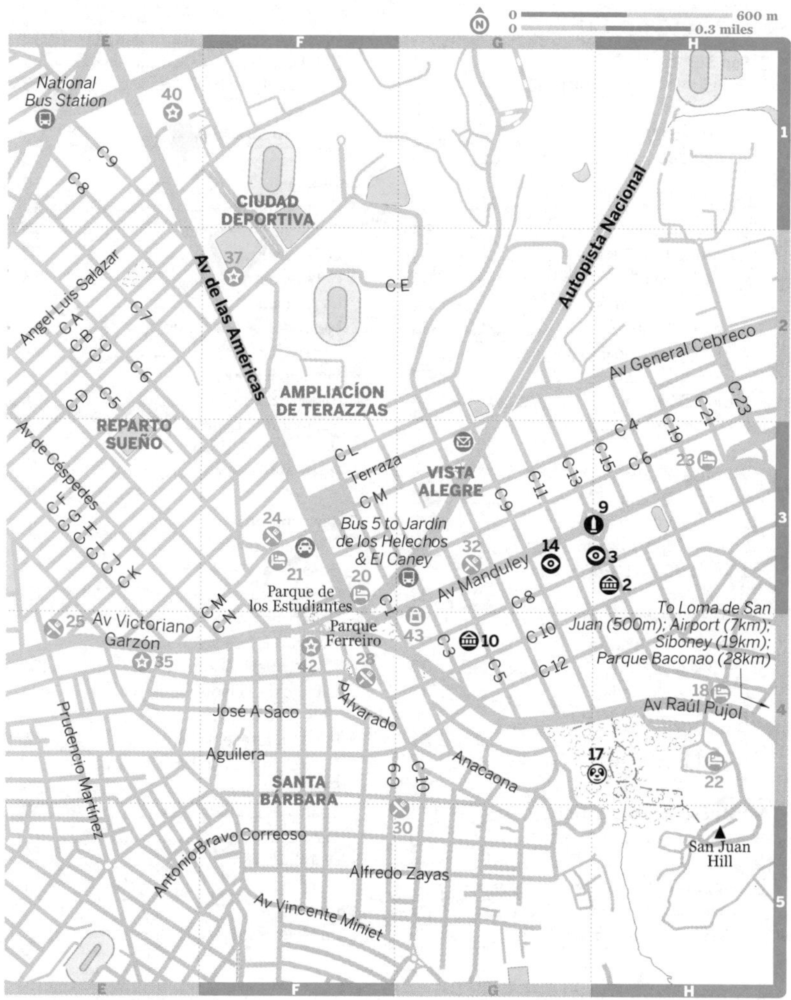

Aside from a jarring modernist bank on its west side, Parque Céspedes is a treasure trove of colonial architecture. The **Casa de la Cultura Miguel Matamoros** (General Lacret 651), on the square's eastern aspect, is the former San Carlos Club, a social center for wealthy *santiagüeros* until the Revolution. Next door British novelist Graham Greene once sought literary inspiration in the Parisian terrace bar of the **Hotel Casa Granda** (1914). The neoclassical **Ayuntamiento** (cnr General Lacret & Aguilera), on the northern side of the square, was erected in the 1950s using a design from 1783 and was once the site of Hernán Cortés' mayoral office. Fidel Castro appeared on the balcony of the present building on the night of January 2, 1959, trumpeting the Revolution's triumph.

Casa de Diego Velázquez MUSEUM

(Map p396; Felix Peña No 602) The oldest house still standing in Cuba, this early colonial abode dating from 1522 was the official residence of the island's first governor. Restored in the late 1960s, the Andalusian-style facade with fine, wooden lattice windows was inaugurated in 1970 as the **Museo de Ambiente Histórico Cubano** (admission CUC$2;

Santiago de Cuba

Top Sights

Cuartel Moncada (Moncada Barracks) ... D3
Moncada Museum ... D3
Museo de la Lucha Clandestina ... B5

Sights

1 Bacardí Rum Factory ... B3
Barrita de Ron Caney ... (see 1)
2 Casa de las Religiones Populares ... H3
Casa de las Tradiciones ... (see 34)
3 Casa del Caribe ... H3
4 Casa Museo de Frank y Josue País ... C3
5 Clock Tower ... A4
6 Fountain of Martí and Abel Santamaría ... D3
7 House Where Castro Lived ... B5
8 Iglesia de Santo Tomás ... B3
9 José María Heredia Statue ... H3
10 Museo de la Imagen ... G4
11 Museo-Casa Natal de Antonio Maceo ... B3
12 Padre Pico Steps ... B5
13 Palacio de Justicia ... D3
14 Palacio de Pioneros ... G3
15 Parque Alameda ... A4
16 Parque Histórico Abel Santamaría ... D3
17 Parque Zoológico ... H4

Activities, Courses & Tours

Casa del Caribe ... (see 3)

Sleeping

18 Caridad Leyna Martínez ... H4
19 Casa Colonial 'Maruchi' ... C3
20 Hotel Las Américas ... F3
21 Meliá Santiago de Cuba ... F3
22 Motel San Juan ... H4
23 Villa Gaviota ... H3

Eating

24 Cafe Palmares ... F3
Cafetería Las Arecas ... (see 43)
25 El Barracón ... E4
26 Heladería Km 969 ... D4
27 La Arboleda ... D4
28 Mercado Agropecuario Ferreiro ... F4
29 Municipal Market ... B4
30 Paladar Salón Tropical ... G5
31 Restaurante España ... D4
32 Restaurante Zunzun ... G3
Ristorante Italiano la Fontana ... (see 21)

Entertainment

33 Carabalí Izuama ... C3
34 Casa de las Tradiciones ... B5
35 Cine Capitolio ... E4
36 Departmento de Focos Culturales de la Dirección Municipal de Cuba ... C3
37 Estadio de Beisbol Guillermón Moncada ... F2
38 Foco Cultural el Tivolí ... B5
39 Foco Cultural Tumba Francesa ... C3
Santiago Cafe ... (see 21)
40 Teatro José María Heredia ... E1
41 Teatro Martí ... B3
42 Wamby Bolera ... F4

Shopping

43 La Maison ... G4

9am-1pm & 2-4:45pm Mon-Thu, 2-4:45pm Fri, 9am-9pm Sat & Sun). The ground floor was originally a trading house and gold foundry, while the upstairs was where Velázquez lived. Today, rooms display period furnishings and decoration from the 16th to 19th centuries. Visitors are also taken through an adjacent 19th-century neoclassical house.

Catedral de Nuestra Señora de la Asunción CHURCH

(Map p396; Mass 6:30pm Mon & Wed-Fri, 5pm Sat, 9am & 6:30pm Sun) It might not be particularly old, but Santiago's most important church is stunning both inside and out. There has been a cathedral on this site since the city's inception in the 1520s, though a series of pirate raids, earthquakes and dodgy architects put paid to at least three previous incarnations. The present cathedral, characterized by its two neoclassical towers and open-winged trumpeting archangel, was completed in 1922 and it is believed that the remains of first colonial governor, Diego Velázquez, are still buried underneath. Meticulously restored, the cathedral's interior is a magnificent mélange of intricate ceiling frescoes, hand-carved choir stalls and an altar honoring the venerated Virgen de la Caridad. The adjacent **Museo Arquidiocesano** (9am-5pm Mon-Fri, 9am-2pm Sat, 9am-noon Sun) is rather a disappointment by comparison, housing a dullish collection of furniture, liturgical objects and paintings including the *Ecce homo,* believed to be Cuba's oldest painting. Behind the cathedral and two blocks downhill from the park is the open-air **Balcón de Velázquez** (cnr Bartolomé Masó & Mariano Corona), the site of an old Spanish fort which offers ethereal views over the terracotta-tiled roofs of the Tivolí neighborhood toward the harbor.

Calle Heredia STREET

(Map p396) The music never stops on Calle Heredia, Santiago's most sensuous street, and also one of its oldest. The melodies start in the paint-peeled **Casa del Estudiante** (Heredia No 204), where *danzón*-strutting pensioners mix with svelte rap artists barely out of their teens. One door up is Cuba's original **Casa de la Trova** (Heredia No 208), a beautiful balconied townhouse redolent of New Orleans' French quarter that is dedicated to pioneering Cuban *trovador*, José 'Pepe' Sánchez (1856–1928). It first opened as a *trova* (traditional poetic singing/songwriting) house in March 1968.

Museo Municipal Emilio Bacardí Moreau MUSEUM

(Map p396; admission CUC$2; ⌚10am-6pm) Narrow Pío Rosado links Calle Heredia to Calle Aguilera and the fabulous Grecian facade of the Bacardí Museum. Founded in 1899 by the rum magnate war hero and city mayor, Emilio Bacardí y Moreau (the palatial building was built to spec), the museum is one of Cuba's oldest and most eclectic. Artifacts amassed from Bacardí's travels include an extensive weapons collection, paintings from the Spanish *costumbrismo* (19th-century artistic movement that predated Romanticism) school and the only Egyptian mummy on the island.

Casa Natal de José María de Heredia MUSEUM

(Map p396; Heredia No 260; admission CUC$1; ⌚9am-6pm Tue-Sat, 9am-9pm Sun) A small museum illustrating the life of one of Cuba's greatest Romantic poets (1803–39) and the man after whom the street is named. Heredia's most notable work, *Ode to Niagara,* is inscribed on the wall outside, and attempts to parallel the beauty of Canada's Niagara Falls with his personal feelings of loss about his homeland. In common with many Cuban independence advocates, Heredia was forced into exile, dying in Mexico in 1839.

Museo del Carnaval MUSEUM

(Map p396; Heredia No 303; admission CUC$1; ⌚9am-5pm Tue-Sun) A colorful museum displaying the history of Santiago's carnaval tradition, the oldest and biggest between Río and Mardi Gras. Drop in to see floats, effigies and the occasional *folklórico* dance show on the patio.

Maqueta de la Ciudad MUSEUM

(Map p396; Mariano Corona No 704; admission CUC$1) Aping Havana's two impressive scale models of the city, Santiago has come up with its own incredibly detailed 'Maqueta'. Interesting historical and architectural information is displayed on illustrated wall panels and you can climb up to a mezzanine gallery for a true vulture's-eye city view. There's a small cafe on site.

Museo del Ron MUSEUM

(Map p396; Bartolomé Masó 358; admission CUC$2; ⌚9am-5pm Mon-Sat) While nowhere near as informative as its Havana equivalent, this diminutive museum offers a rough outline of the history of Cuban rum along with a potent shot of the hard stuff *(añejo).* Encased in a handsome townhouse on Calle Masó, it was undergoing extensive renovations at the time of writing.

Plaza de Dolores SQUARE

(Map p396; cnr Aguilera & Porfirio Valiente) East of Parque Céspedes is the pleasant and shady Plaza de Dolores, a former marketplace now dominated by the 18th-century **Iglesia de Nuestra Señora de los Dolores**. After a fire in the 1970s, the church was rebuilt as a concert hall (Sala de Conciertos Dolores; p409). Many restaurants and cafes flank this square. It's also Santiago's most popular gay cruising spot.

Plaza de Marte SQUARE

(Map p396) Guarding the entrance to the *casco histórico,* the motorcycle-infested Plaza de Marte was formerly a macabre 19th-century Spanish parade ground, where prisoners were executed publicly by firing squad for revolutionary activities. Today, the plaza is the site of Santiago de Cuba's *esquina caliente* (hot corner), where local baseball fans plot the imminent downfall of Havana's glory-hunting Industriales. Among the flowering plants rises a tall column with a red cap perched on top, symbolizing liberty.

START PARQUE ALAMEDA
FINISH CUARTEL MONCADA
DISTANCE 2KM
DURATION 3 TO 4 HOURS

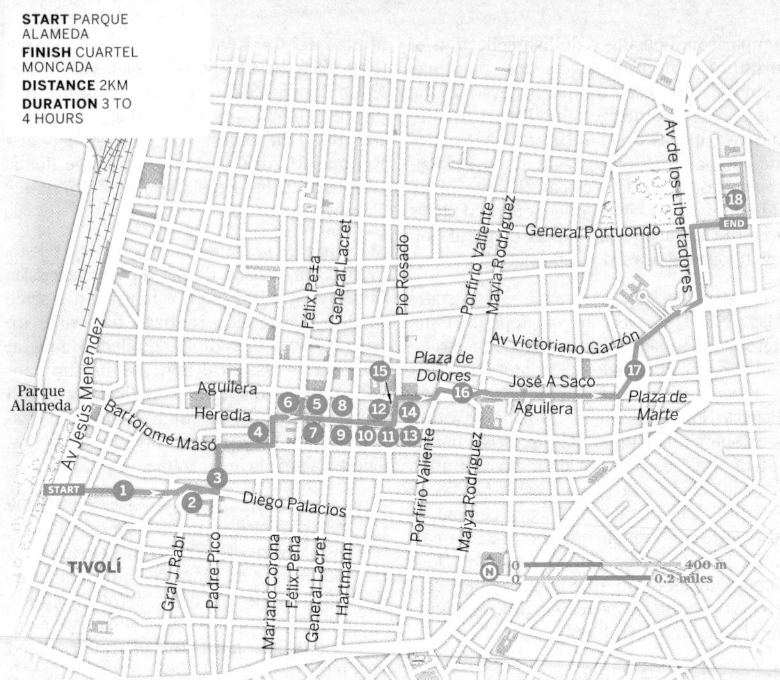

Walking Tour
Santiago: A Walk Through History

Against a backdrop of spinach-green mountains and a steely blue bay, a walking tour of Santiago's *casco histórico* (old town) is an obligatory rite of passage for first-time visitors keen to uncover the steamy tropical sensations that make this city tick. Listen out for buzzing motorbikes, pounding drums and slam-bang games of dominoes in among the urban action, and see how many new '*frens*' you can make between the start point in Tivoli and the final chapter in Moncada.

Start beside the bay with your sights set uphill. Parque Alameda inhabits the rundown thoroughfare facing Santiago's not-so-busy port. Most of the excitement lies to the east in a hilly neighborhood colonized by French-Haitians in the early 1800s and baptized 1 **El Tivolí**. Tivolí is one of Santiago's most picturesque and traffic-lite quarters where red-roofed houses and steep streets retain a time-warped Cuban atmosphere. Absorb it at your leisure. The neighborhood's only real 'sight' is the 2 **Museo de la Lucha Clandestina** reached by following Calle Diego Palacios uphill from the port. This museum, encased in a former police station with striking bay views, gives a lucid insight into Santiago's favorite topic: rebellion; more specifically the trajectory of the urban underground led by Frank País in the 1950s that provided invaluable support to Fidel in the nearby mountains. From the museum take the famous 3 **Padre Pico steps** – a terracotta staircase built into the hillside – downhill to Calle Bartolomé Masó where a right turn will deposit you on the breeze-lapped 4 **Balcón de Velázquez**, site of an ancient fort. This stupendous view once inspired less calming contemplations; early Spanish colonists used it to look out for meddlesome pirates. Head east next, avoiding the angry roar of the motorbikes that swarm like wasps in the surrounding streets, until you resurface in 5 **Parque Céspedes**, Santiago's pulsating heart with its resident *jineteras* (female touts) and craggy-faced men in Panama hats who strum their way through old Carlos Puebla favorites with the exuberance of 18 year olds. The 6 **Casa de Diego Velázquez**, with its Moorish fringes and intricate wooden arcades, is believed to be the oldest house still standing in Cuba and anchors the square on its west side. Contrasting impressively on the south side is the mighty, mustard facade of the 7 **Catedral de Nuestra Señora de la Asunción**. This building has been ransacked, burned, rocked by earthquakes and rebuilt, then remodeled and restored and ransacked again. Statues of Christopher Columbus and Fray Bartolomé de las Casas flank the entrance in ironic juxtaposition.

If you're tired already, you can step out onto the lazy terrace bar at the 8 **Hotel Casa Granda** on the southeastern corner of the park, for mojitos or Montecristo cigars, or both. Graham Greene came here in the 1950s on a clandestine mission to interview Fidel Castro. The interview never came off, but he managed instead to smuggle a suitcase of clothes up to the rebels in the mountains.

Follow the music as you exit and plunge into the paint-peeled romance of Calle Heredia, Santiago's – and one of Cuba's – most atmospheric streets that rocks like New Orleans at the height of the jazz era. Its centerpiece is the infamous 9 **Casa de la Trova**, Cuba's first *trova* house, where, come 10pm, everything starts to get a shade more *caliente* (hot) with people winking at you lewdly from the overcrowded upstairs balcony.

Heading upstream on Heredia, you'll pass street stalls, cigar peddlers, a guy dragging a double bass, and countless motorbikes. That yellowish house on the right with the poem emblazoned on the wall is 10 **Casa Natal de José María de Heredia**, birthplace of one of Cuba's greatest poets. You might find a living scribe in 11 **Uneac**, the famous national writers' union a few doors down. Stick your head inside and check out the *cartelera* (culture calendar) advertising the coming week's offerings. Plenty more dead legends are offered up in print in funky 12 **Librería la Escalera**, an unkempt but roguish bookstore across the street where busking musicians often crowd the stairway. Down the street is the 13 **Patio ARTex**, where boleros are de rigueur and tourists browse through the CDs. Cross the street next (mind that motorbike) and stick your nose into the 14 **Museo del Carnaval**, which aims to demonstrate how Santiago de Cuba lets its hair down (more than usual) every July in the best carnival between here and – oh – anywhere.

Divert along Pío Rosado one block to Aguilera where you'll be confronted by the sturdy Grecian columns of the 15 **Museo Municipal Emilio Bacardí Moreau**, Santiago's – as well as Cuba's – oldest functioning museum set up by the city's first mayor, Emilio, of worldwide rum fame. The gathered ephemera is all over the map, from old muskets to ancient mummies. Back outside, narrow Aguilera winds uphill to the shady 16 **Plaza de Dolores** which remains amazingly tranquil, considering the ongoing motorcycle mania. There are benches to relax on underneath the trees while you weigh up if you've got enough energy to keep going or abort into one of the nearby bars or restaurants.

Stalwarts should continue east to 17 **Plaza de Marte**, the third of the *casco histórico*'s pivotal squares and far more manic than the other two with its traffic, shops and vociferous baseball fanatics discussing current form under the pretty trellises.

The walk ends in what is perhaps Santiago's most politically significant site, the art-deco 18 **Cuartel Moncada**, a one-time military barracks where the first shots of Cuba's Castro-led revolution were fired in 1953. Today it functions more innocuously as a school, but a preserved section at the rear where the short skirmishes between the soldiers and the rebels took place is now one of Cuba's most interesting and poignant museums.

Memorial de Vilma Espín Guillois MUSEUM
(Map p396; Sánchez Hechavarría No 473; admission CUC$1) This erstwhile home of Cuba's former 'first lady,' Vilma Espín, the wife of Raúl Castro, and instrumental force in the success of the Cuban Revolution, opened in 2010, three years after her death. The daughter of a lawyer to the Bacardí clan, Vilma was first radicalized after a meeting with Frank País in Santiago in 1956. Joining the rebels in the mountains she went on to marry Raúl Castro and founded the influential Federation of Cuban Women in 1960. This house, where she lived from 1939 to 1959, is packed with photos, exhibits and lucid snippets of her life.

Iglesia de Nuestra Señora del Carmen CHURCH
(Map p396; Félix Peña No 505) You can dig deeper into Santiago's ecclesiastical history in this tumbledown construction, a hall church dating from the 1700s that is the final resting place of Christmas-carol composer Esteban Salas (1725–1803), choir master of Santiago de Cuba's cathedral from 1764 until his death.

Museo Tomás Romay MUSEUM
(Map p396; cnr José A Saco & Monseñor Barnada; admission CUC$1; ⌚8:30am-5:30pm Tue-Fri, 9am-2pm Sat) A block west of Plaza de Marte is this natural-science museum collecting natural history and archaeology artifacts, with some modern art thrown in.

Iglesia de San Francisco CHURCH
(Map p396; Juan Bautista Sagarra No 121) This three-nave church is another understated 18th-century ecclesial gem situated three blocks north of Parque Céspedes.

Gobierno Provincial NOTABLE BUILDING
(Map p396; Poder Popular; cnr Pío Rosado & Aguilera) Situated opposite the Bacardí Museum, the equally Hellenic provincial government seat is another building from Cuba's 20th-century neoclassical revival.

SOUTH OF THE CASCO HISTÓRICO

Tivolí NEIGHBORHOOD
(Map p388) Santiago's old French quarter was first settled by colonists from Haiti in the late 18th and early 19th centuries. Set on a south-facing hillside overlooking the shimmering harbor, its red-tiled roofs and hidden patios are a tranquil haven these days, with old men pushing around dominoes and ebullient kids playing stickball amid pink splashes of bougainvillea. The century-old **Padre Pico steps**, cut into the steepest part of Calle Padre Pico, stand at the neighborhood's gateway.

MONCADA – 26/7

Glorious call to arms or poorly enacted putsch – the 1953 attack on Santiago's Moncada Barracks, while big on bravado, came to within a hair's breadth of destroying Castro's nascent revolutionary movement before the ink was even dry on the manifesto.

With his political ambitions decimated by Batista's 1952 coup, Castro – who had been due to represent the Orthodox Party in the canceled elections – quickly decided to pursue a more direct path to power by swapping the ballot box for a rifle.

Handpicking and training 116 men and two women from Havana and its environs, the combative Fidel, along with his trusty lieutenant, Abel Santamaría, began to put together a plan so secret that even his younger brother Raúl was initially kept in the dark.

The aim was to storm the Cuartel Moncada, a sprawling military barracks in Santiago in Cuba's seditious Oriente region with a shabby history as a Spanish prison. Rather than make an immediate grab for power, Castro's more savvy plan was to capture enough ammunition to escape up into the Sierra Maestra from where he and Santamaría planned to spearhead a wider popular uprising against Batista's malignant Mafia-backed government.

Castro chose Moncada because it was the second-biggest army barracks in the country, yet distant enough from Havana to ensure it was poorly defended. With equal sagacity, the date was set for July 26, the day after Santiago's annual carnival when both police and soldiers would be tired and hungover from the boisterous revelries.

But as the day of attack dawned, things quickly started to go wrong. The plan's underlying secrecy didn't help. Meeting in a quiet rural farmhouse near the village of Siboney, many recruits arrived with no idea that they were expected to fire guns at armed soldiers and they nervously baulked. Secondly, with all but one of the Moncadistas drawn from the Havana region (the only native *santiagüero* was an 18-year-old local fixer named Renato

TOP CHOICE **Museo de la Lucha Clandestina** MUSEUM

(Map p388; admission CUC$1; General Jesús Rabí No 1; ⌚9am-5pm Tue-Sun) Up the slope and to the right is a former police station attacked by M-26-7 activists on November 30, 1956, to divert attention from the arrival of the tardy yacht *Granma*, carrying Fidel Castro and 81 others. The gorgeous colonial-style building now houses this museum detailing the underground struggle against Batista in the 1950s. It's a fascinating, if macabre, story enhanced by far-reaching views from the balcony. Across the street is the **house** (General Jesús Rabí No 6) where Fidel Castro lived from 1931 to 1933, while a student in Santiago de Cuba (not open for visits).

Casa de las Tradiciones CULTURAL CENTER

(Map p388; Rabí No 154) Downhill from the Padre Pico steps, on General Jesús Rabí, is this legendary music house known as 'La Casona' to locals. There's some colorful art and a gritty bar but, to get a real taste, come back after dark. One block west, via José de Diego, the street opens out onto another superb Tivolí view over Bahía de Santiago de Cuba.

Parque Alameda PARK

(Map p388; Av Jesús Menéndez) At the foot of this Tivoli quarter, this narrow park embellishes a dockside promenade that opened in 1840 and was redesigned in 1893. At the north end you'll see the old **clock tower**, *aduana* (customs house) and cigar factory.

NORTH OF CASCO HISTÓRICO

North of the historic center, Santiago de Cuba turns residential

TOP CHOICE **Cuartel Moncada** MUSEUM

(Map p388; Moncada Barracks; Av Moncada) Santiago's famous Moncada Barracks is named after Guillermón Moncada, a War of Independence fighter who was held prisoner here in 1874, though these days the name is more synonymous with one of history's greatest failed putsches.

The first barracks on this site was constructed by the Spanish in 1859, and in 1938 the present crenellated building was completed. Moncada earned immortality on the morning of July 26, 1953, when more than 100 revolutionaries led by then little known Fidel Castro stormed Batista's troops at what was then Cuba's second-most important military garrison.

Guitart), few were familiar with Santiago's complex street layout and, after setting out at 5am in convoy from the Siboney farm, at least two cars became temporarily lost.

The attack, when it finally began, lasted approximately 10 minutes from start to finish and was little short of a debacle. Splitting into three groups, a small contingent led by Raúl Castro took the adjacent Palacio de Justicia, another headed up by Abel Santamaría stormed a nearby military hospital, while the largest group led by Fidel attempted to enter the barracks itself.

Though the first two groups were initially successful, Fidel's convoy, poorly disguised in stolen military uniforms, was spotted by an outlying guard patrol and only one of the cars made it into the compound before the alarm was raised.

In the ensuing chaos, five rebels were killed in an exchange of gunfire before Castro, seeing the attack was futile, beat a disorganized retreat. Raúl's group also managed to escape, but the group in the hospital (including Abel Santamaría) were captured and later tortured and executed.

Fidel escaped briefly into the surrounding mountains and was captured a few days later; but, due to public revulsion surrounding the other brutal executions, his life was spared and the path of history radically altered.

Had it not been for the Revolution's ultimate success, this shambolic attempt at an insurrection would have gone down in history as a military nonevent. But viewed through the prism of the 1959 Revolution, it has been depicted as the first glorious shot on the road to power.

It also provided Fidel with the political pulpit he so badly needed. 'History will absolve me,' he trumpeted confidently at his subsequent trial. Within six years it effectively had.

Casco Histórico Santiago de Cuba

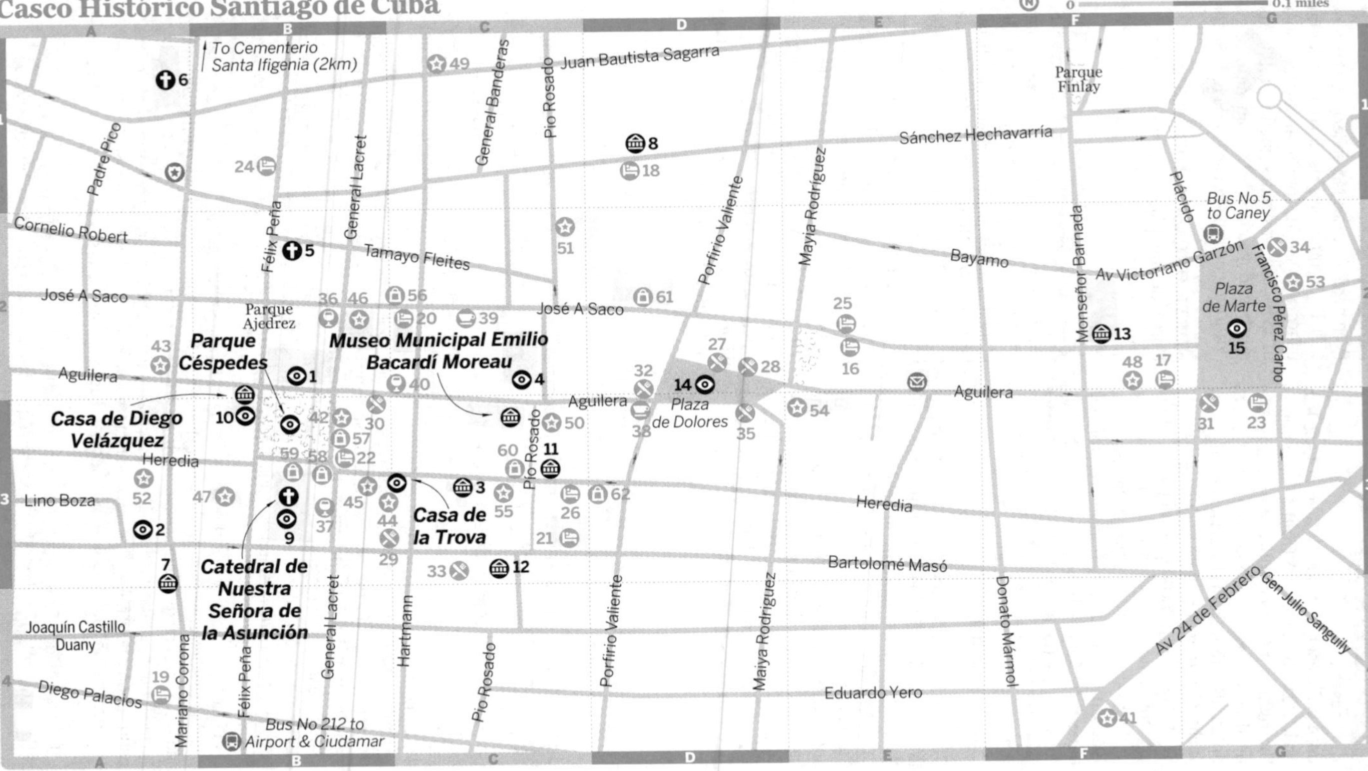

Casco Histórico Santiago de Cuba

After the Revolution, the barracks, like all others in Cuba, was converted into a school called Ciudad Escolar 26 de Julio, and in 1967 a **museum** (admission CUC$2; ⏲9am-5pm Mon-Sat, 9am-1pm Sun) was installed near gate 3, where the main attack took place. As Batista's soldiers had cemented over the original bullet holes from the attack, the Castro government remade them (this time without guns) years later as a poignant reminder. The museum contains a scale model of the barracks plus interesting and sometimes grisly artifacts of the attack, its planning and its aftermath. It's one of Cuba's best.

Museo-Casa Natal de Antonio Maceo MUSEUM
(Map p388; Los Maceos No 207; admission CUC$1; ⏲9am-5pm Mon-Sat) This important but little-visited museum is where the *mulato* general and hero of both Wars of Independence was born on June 14, 1845. Known as the Bronze Titan in Cuba for his bravery in battle, Maceo was the definitive 'man of action' to Martí's 'man of ideas.' In his 1878 *Protest of Baraguá,* he rejected any compromise with the colonial authorities and went into exile rather than sell out to the Spanish. Landing at Playa Duaba in 1895, he marched his army as far west as Pinar del Río before being killed in action near Havana in 1896. This simple museum exhibits highlights of Maceo's life with photos, letters and a tattered flag that was flown in battle.

Casa Museo de Frank y Josué País MUSEUM
(Map p388; General Banderas No 226; admission CUC$1; ⏲9am-5pm Mon-Sat) Integral to the success of the Revolution, the young País brothers organized the underground section of the M-26-7 in Santiago de Cuba until Frank's murder by the police on July 30, 1957. The exhibits in this home-turned-museum tell the story. It's located about five blocks southeast of Museo-Casa Natal de Antonio Maceo.

Plaza de la Revolución SQUARE
(Map p388) As with all Cuban cities, Santiago has its bombastic revolution square. This one placed strategically at the junction of two sweeping avenues and anchored by an eye-catching statue of the city's dedicated hero (and native son), Antonio Maceo. The modernist rendition of Maceo atop his horse, hand cupped regally outwards is surrounded by a series of dagger-like bronze statuettes. Underneath the giant mound/plinth is a small **museum** (admission free; ⏲8am-4pm Mon-Sat) documenting his life. Other notable buildings bordering the square include the modern Teatro Heredia and the National bus station.

Bacardí Rum Factory LANDMARK
(Map p388; Fábrica de Ron; Av Jesús Menéndez) While it's not as swanky as its modern Bahamas HQ, the original Bacardí factory which opened in 1868, oozes history. Spanish-born founder Don Facundo dreamt up the world-famous Bacardí bat symbol after finding a colony of the winged mammals living in the factory's rafters. Although the family fled the island after the Revolution, the Cuban government has continued to make traditional rum here – the signature Ron Caney brand coupled with smaller amounts of Ron Santiago and Ron Varadero. In total, the factory knocks out nine million liters a year, 70% of which is exported. There are currently no factory tours, but the **Barrita de Ron Caney** (Av Jesús Menéndez No 703; ⏲9am-6pm), a tourist bar attached to the factory, offers rum sales and tastings. A great billboard opposite the station announces Santiago's modern battle cry: *Rebelde ayer, hospitalaria hoy, heroica siempre* (Rebellious yesterday, hospitable today, heroic always).

Parque Histórico Abel Santamaría PARK
(Map p388; cnr General Portuondo & Av de los Libertadores) This is the site of the former Saturnino Lora Civil Hospital, stormed by Abel Santamaría and 60 others on that fateful July day (see p394). On October 16, 1953, Fidel Castro was tried in the Escuela de Enfermeras for leading the Moncada attack. It was here that he made his famous *History Will Absolve Me* speech. The park contains a giant cubist fountain engraved with the countenances of Abel Santamaría and José Martí that gushes out a veritable Niagara Falls of water.

Palacio de Justicia LANDMARK
(Map p388; cnr Av de los Libertadores & General Portuondo) On the opposite side of the street to the park, this court building was taken by fighters led by Raúl Castro during the Moncada attack. They were supposed to provide cover fire to Fidel's group from the rooftop but were never needed. Many of them came back two months later to be tried and sentenced in the court.

Iglesia de Santo Tomás CHURCH
(Map p388; Félix Peña No 308) Tracking up Calle Felix Peña, you can orientate yourself by the baroque bell tower of this ecclesial building, one in a trio of notable, if dilapidated, 18th-century churches in this neighborhood.

VISTA ALEGRE

In any other city, Vista Alegre would be a leafy upper-middle-class neighborhood (indeed, it once was); but in revolutionary Cuba the dappled avenues and whimsical early-20th-century architecture are the domain of clinics, cultural centers, government offices and state-run restaurants. With most of their former owners either underground or drawing their pensions in Miami, the rough triangle of properties that fans out from Parque Ferreiro between Av Raúl Pujol and Av General Cebreco today hides a handful of esoteric points of interest.

Loma de San Juan MONUMENT
(San Juan Hill; off Map p388) Future American president Teddy Roosevelt forged his reputation on Loma de San Juan where, flanked by the immortal rough-riders, he supposedly led a fearless cavalry charge against the Spanish to seal a famous US victory. In reality, it is doubtful that Roosevelt even mounted his horse in Santiago, while the purportedly clueless Spanish garrison – outnumbered 10 to one – managed to hold off more than 6000 American troops for 24 hours. Protected on pleasantly manicured grounds adjacent to the modern-day Motel San Juan, the Loma de San Juan marks the spot of the Spanish-Cuban-American War's only land battle, which took place on July 1, 1898. Cannons, trenches and numerous US monuments, including a bronze figure of a rough rider, enhance the classy gardening, while the only acknowledgement of a Cuban presence is the rather understated monument to the unknown Mambí soldier.

FREE **Casa del Caribe** CULTURAL CENTER
(Map p388; Calle 13 No 154; ⏲9am-5pm Mon-Fri) Founded in 1982 to study Caribbean life, this cultural institution organizes the Festival del Caribe and the Fiesta del Fuego every July, and also hosts various concert nights. Interested parties can organize percussion courses here or studies in Afro-Cuban culture (p401). A block south is the affiliated **Casa de las Religiones Populares** (Calle 13 No 206; admission CUC$1; ⏲9am-6pm Mon-Sat), with a large, if haphazard, collection of all things Santería.

Museo de la Imagen MUSEUM
(Map p388; Calle 8 No 106; admission CUC$1; ⏲9am-5pm Mon-Sat) A short but fascinating journey through the history of Cuban photography from Kodak to Korda, with little CIA spy cameras and lots of old and contemporary photos. The museum also guards a library of rare films and documentaries.

Palacio de Pioneros LANDMARK
(Map p388; cnr Av Manduley & Calle 11) This large eclectic mansion built between 1906 and 1910 was once the largest and most opulent in Santiago. Since 1974 it has been a developmental center for kids *(pioneros)*. Parked in a corner patch of grass outside, you can spy an old MiG fighter plane on which the younger pioneers play. The traffic circle at the corner of Av Manduley and Calle 13 contains an impressive marble **statue** of poet José María de Heredia.

Parque Zoológico ZOO
(Map p388; Av Raúl Pujol; admission CUC$1; ⏲10am-5pm Tue-Sun) Just west of the Loma de San Juan is Santiago's doleful zoo, good only if you're hopelessly bored or have seriously hyperactive children.

AROUND SANTIAGO DE CUBA

Cementerio Santa Ifigenia CEMETERY
(Map p387; Av Crombet; admission CUC$1, ⏲8am-6pm) Nestled peacefully on the western edge of the city, the Cementerio Santa Ifigenia is second only to Havana's Necrópolis Cristóbal Colón in its importance and grandiosity. Created in 1868 to accommodate the victims of the War of Independence and a simultaneous yellow-fever outbreak, the Santa Ifigenia includes many great historical figures among its 8000-plus tombs. Names to look out for include Tomás Estrada Palma (1835–1908), Cuba's now disgraced first president; Emilio Bacardí y Moreau (1844–1922) of the famous rum dynasty; María Grajales, the widow of independence hero Antonio Maceo, and Mariana Grajales, Maceo's mother; 11 of the 31 generals of the independence struggles; the Spanish soldiers who died in the battles of San Juan Hill and Caney; the 'martyrs' of the 1953 Moncada Barracks attack; M-26-7 activists, Frank and Josué País; father of Cuban independence, Carlos Manuel de Céspedes (1819–74); and international celebrity-cum-popular-musical-rake, Compay Segundo (1907–2003), of Buena Vista Social Club fame.

The highlight of the cemetery, for most, is the quasi-religious mausoleum to national hero, José Martí (1853–95). Erected in 1951 during the Batista era, the imposing hexagonal structure is positioned so that Martí's wooden casket (draped solemnly in a Cuban flag) receives daily shafts of sunlight. This is in response to a comment Martí made in one of his poems that he would like to die not as a traitor in darkness, but with his visage facing the sun. A round-the-clock guard of the mausoleum is changed, amid much pomp and ceremony, every 30 minutes.

Horse carts go along Av Jesús Menéndez, from Parque Alameda to Cementerio Santa Ifigenia (one peso); otherwise it's a good leg-stretching walk.

TOP CHOICE Castillo de San Pedro de la Roca del Morro FORT, MUSEUM

(Map p387; admission CUC$4; ⌚9am-5pm Mon-Fri, 8am-4pm Sat & Sun; 👪) A Unesco World Heritage Site since 1997, the San Pedro fort sits like an impregnable citadel atop a 60m-high promontory at the entrance to Santiago harbor, 10km southwest of the city. The fort was designed in 1587 by famous Italian military engineer Giovanni Bautista Antonelli (who also designed La Punta and El Morro forts in Havana) to protect Santiago from pillaging pirates who had successfully sacked the city in 1554. Due to financial constraints, the building work didn't start until 1633 (17 years after Antonelli's death) and it carried on sporadically for the next 60 years. In the interim British privateer, Henry Morgan sacked and partially destroyed it.

Finally finished in the early 1700s, El Morro's massive batteries, bastions, magazines and walls got little opportunity to serve their true purpose. With the era of piracy in decline, the fort was converted into a prison in the 1800s and it stayed that way – bar a brief interlude during the 1898 Spanish-Cuban-American War – until Cuban architect Francisco Prat Puig mustered up a restoration plan in the late 1960s.

Today, the fort hosts the swashbuckling **Museo de Piratería**, with another room given over to the US-Spanish naval battle that took place in the bay in 1898. The stupendous views from the upper terrace take in the wild western ribbon of Santiago's coastline backed by the velvety Sierra Maestra.

To get to El Morro from the city center, you can take bus 212 to Ciudamar and cover the final 20 minutes on foot. Alternatively, a round-trip taxi ride from Parque Céspedes with wait should cost CUC$12 to CUC$15.

Cayo Granma ISLAND

(Map p387) A small, populated key near the jaws of the bay, Cayo Granma (formerly known as Cayo Smith) is a little fantasy island of red-roofed wooden houses – many of them on stilts above the water – that guard a traditional fishing community. Come here to enjoy a slower, more hassle-free Santiago. You can hike the short route up to the small whitewashed **Iglesia de San Rafael** at the key's highest point, or walk around the whole island in 15 minutes, but the best thing about this place is just hanging out, soaking up a bit of the real Cuba.

The only official eating establishment is the seafood-biased Restaurante el Cayo (p406), but local families often offer to cook up excellent fish dinners.

To get to the key, take the regular ferry (leaving every 30 minutes or so) ferry from Punta Gorda just below El Morro fort.

Jardín de los Helechos GARDEN

(Map p387; Carretera de El Caney No 129; admission CUC$1; ⌚9am-5pm Mon-Fri) Two kilometers from downtown Santiago de Cuba on the road to El Caney, the peaceful Jardín de los Helechos is a lush haven of 350 types of ferns and 90 types of orchids that started life in 1976 as the private collection of *santiagüero* Manuel Caluff. In 1984 Caluff donated his collection of 1000-plus plants to the Academia de Ciencias de Cuba (Cuban Academy of Science), which continues to keep the 3000-sq-meter garden in psychedelic bloom (the best time for orchids is November to January). The center of the garden has an inviting dense copse-cum-sanctuary dotted with benches.

Bus 5 (20 centavos) from Plaza de Marte (Map p396) in central Santiago passes this way, or you can hire a taxi.

Courses

Opportunities for courses abound in Santiago; everything from architecture to music, either official or unofficial. You can sign up for something beforehand, or jump on the bandwagon when you arrive.

UniversiTUR LANGUAGE

(☎64-31-86; www.uo.edu.cu; Universidad de Oriente, cnr Calle L & Ampliación de Terrazas) Arranges Spanish courses. Monthly rates for 60-hour courses (three hours a day, five days a week) start at CUC$250.

Ballet Folklórico Cutumba MUSIC, DANCE

(Map p396; Teatro Galaxia, cnr Avs 24 de Febrero & Valeriano Hierrezuelo) Santiago's Folklorico groups are highly inclusive and can organize dance and percussion lessons either in groups or individually. Start with the Cutumba who often perform at Hotel las Américas. Also helpful are Conjunto Folklórico de Oriente (p407).

SANTIAGO DE CUBA STREET NAMES

Welcome to another city where the streets have two names.

OLD NAME	NEW NAME
Calvario	Porfirio Valiente
Carniceria	Pío Rosado
Enramada	José A Saco
José Miguel Gómez	Havana
Paraíso	Plácido
Reloj	Mayía Rodríguez
Rey Pelayo	Joaquín Castillo Duany
San Félix	Hartmann
San Francisco	Sagarra
San Gerónimo	Sánchez Hechavarría
San Mateo	Sao del Indio
Santa Rita	Diego Palacios
Santo Tómas	Felix Peña
Trinidad	General Portuondo

Casa del Estudiante MUSIC, DANCE

(Map p396; ☎62-78-04; Heredia No 204) Another central option where you can organize singing, dancing or percussion lessons under the auspices of renowned performers. There are 11 or so teachers here and classes start at CUC$8 per hour.

Casa del Caribe MUSIC, DANCE

(Map p388; ☎64-22-85; Calle 13 No 154) The portal of all things Santería organizes dance lessons in conga, *son* and salsa; it's CUC$10 for two hours or CUC$5 for one. Resident staff member Juan Eduardo Castillo can also organize lessons in percussion. Real aficionados can inquire about in-depth courses on Afro-Cuban religions and culture. These guys are experts and they're very flexible.

Cuban Rhythm MUSIC, DANCE

(www.cubanrhythm.com) This organization offers dance lessons and percussion lessons for CUC$12 an hour. Take a look at their excellent website and make arrangements beforehand.

Tours

Cubatur (p410) sells all manner of excursions, for everything from La Gran Piedra to El Cobre. Cubanacán (p410) in Hotel Casa Granda offers an interesting trip to a Cuban baseball game including a signed shirt and an opportunity to meet the players afterwards. There's also a chance to visit a cigar factory just outside of town (CUC$5). Ecotur (p410) based in the Santiago Aquarium are the best bets for summit attempts on Pico Turquino to the west.

Alternatively, you can arrange your own tour to some of the out-of-town sights with one of the ubiquitous taxis that park in Parque Céspedes in front of the cathedral. Cubataxi cabs should charge approximately CUC$0.50 per kilometer for longer trips. Tot up your expected mileage, factor in some waiting time, and get ready to bargain.

Festivals & Events

Few cities can match the variety and vivacity of Santiago de Cuba's annual festivals.

The summer season begins with the **Fiesta de San Juan** (June 24), celebrated with processions and conga dancing by cultural associations called *focos culturales*. This is followed by the 'big two' the **Festival del Caribe, Fiesta del Fuego** (Festival of Caribbean Culture, Fire Celebration) in early July followed by Santiago de Cuba's **Carnaval**, held in the last week of July.

Other celebrations include the following.

Boleros de Oro MUSIC

Arrive in mid to late June for this crooner's extravaganza that is replicated in various cities throughout the country.

Festival Internacional Matamoros Son MUSIC
A tribute to one of Santiago de Cuba's musical greats, Miguel Matamoros kicks off in late October with dances, lectures, concerts and workshops. Main venues include the Casa de la Trova and the Teatro Heredia.

Festival Internacional de Coros MUSIC
The international choir festival in late November brings in some strong international singing groups for some cultural cross-fertilization and spirit-lifting music.

Sleeping

TOP CHOICE **Hostal San Basilio** BOUTIQUE HOTEL $$
(Map p396; ☎65-17-02; Bartolomé Masó No 403 btwn Pío Rosado & Porfirio Valiente; r CUC$60; ❄) The lovely eight-room San Basilio (named for the original name of the street in which it lies) is another of Cubanacán's Encanto brand. Think intimate, comfortable and refreshingly contemporary within a romantic colonial setting. Rooms come with clever little frills such as DVD players, umbrellas, bathroom scales and mini bottles of rum, and the communal patio is a riot of dripping ferns. There's a small restaurant serving breakfast and lunch.

Meliá Santiago de Cuba HOTEL $$$
(Map p388; ☎68-70-70; cnr Av de las Américas & Calle M; s/d CUC$110/140; P❄@≋) A blue-mirrored monster (or marvel, depending on your taste) dreamt up by respected Cuban architect José A Choy in the early '90s, the Meliá is Santiago's only 'international' hotel. Raising its game for the business crowd, there are real bathtubs (in every room), three pools, four restaurants, various shopping facilities, a fancy bar on the 15th floor, and rooms for nonsmokers. The downsides are its out-of-center location and lack of genuine Cuban charm.

Hotel Casa Granda HOTEL $$$
(Map p396; ☎65-30-24; Heredia No 201; s/d CUC$78/112; ❄) This elegant hotel (1914), artfully described by Graham Greene in his book *Our Man in Havana*, has 58 rooms and a classic red-and-white-striped front awning. Greene used to stay here in the late 1950s where he enjoyed relaxing on the streetside terrace, while his famous pen captured the nocturnal essence of the city as it wafted up from the bustling square below. Half a century later and – aside from the Che Guevara posters and some seriously erratic service on reception – not much has changed. The hotel's 5th-floor **Roof Garden Bar** (⊙11am-1am) is well worth the CUC$2 minimum consumption charge and the upstairs terrace is an obligatory photo stop for foreign tourists on the lookout for bird's-eye city views. There's music here most nights and an occasional buffet on the roof.

Casa Colonial 'Maruchi' CASA PARTICULAR $
(Map p388; ☎62-07-67; maruchib@yahoo.es; Hartmann No 357 btwn General Portuondo & Máximo Gómez; r CUC$25; ❄) Maruchi is quintessential Santiago and is the best advert the city could give. For a start it's a hive of all things Santería. You'll meet all types here: *santeros* (priests of Santería), backpackers and foreign students studying for PhDs on the Regla de Ocha. The food's legendary and the fecund courtyard equally sublime. Book early as it's no secret.

Hotel Libertad HOTEL $
(Map p396; ☎62-77-10; Aguilera No 658; s/d CUC$24/36; ❄@) Cheap Cuban hotel chain Islazul breaks out of its ugly Soviet-themed concrete block obsession and goes colonial in this venerable sky-blue beauty on Plaza de Marte. Eighteen clean (if sometimes dark) high-ceilinged rooms and a pleasant street-side restaurant are a bonus. The belting (until 1am) rooftop disco isn't.

Motel San Juan HOTEL $$
(Map p388; ☎68-72-00; San Juan Hill; s/d CUC$32/50; P❄≋) Surrounded by beautiful grounds on historic Loma de San Juan, with lots of lawn and a children's pool, this place is great if you don't mind some long walks (or taxi rides) into the city center. The rooms are laid out in small blocks and have good amenities with welcome little extras such as radios. Service is friendly. Drive 1km east of Hotel las Américas via Av Raúl Pujol to get here.

Casa Yisel CASA PARTICULAR $
(Map p396; ☎62-05-22; martingisel78@yahoo.es; Diego Palacios No 177 btwn Padre Pico & Mariano Corona; r CUC$20-25; P❄) The young hosts run a surgically clean house three blocks from Céspedes and one from the Padre Pico steps. It's an apartment of sorts with a living room, bedroom and super-big bath. There's a little patio and they make great coffee. Guarded parking is nearby.

Nelson Aguilar Ferreiro & Deysi Ruíz Chaveco CASA PARTICULAR $
(Map p396; ☎65-63-72; José A Saco No 513; r CUC$20-25) Slap-bang in the center but with a quieter more suburban feel, this is one of Santiago's best casas with a secluded plant-filled patio from which lead two spick-and-span double rooms. The dinner menu is huge with nearly 100 items and offers welcome relief for vegetarians sick of omelets.

Hotel Versalles HOTEL $$
(☎68-70-70; Alturas de Versalles; s/d with breakfast CUC$43/62; P ❄ ≋) Not to be confused with the namesake rumba district of Matanzas, or the resplendent home of Louis XIV, this modest hotel is on the outskirts of town off the road to El Morro and the airport. Formerly one of Cubanacán's tattier hotel choices it's had a recent upgrade that has injected some style into its inviting pool and its comfortable rooms with small terraces.

Caridad Leyna Martínez CASA PARTICULAR $
(☎64-29-55; Calle 14 No 352, Reparto Vista Alegre; r CUC$20-25) For a break from the motorbike noise you may want to consider this tranquil place out in once-posh Vista Alegre where Caridad's pleasant house has one room up for grabs with en-suite bathroom not far from the Loma de San Juan.

Raimundo Ocana & Bertha Pena CASA PARTICULAR $
(Map p396; ☎62-40-97; Heredia No 308 btwn Pío Rosado & Porfirio Valiente; r CUC$20-25; ❄) A classic 200-year-old house right in the thick of the action on Calle Heredia meaning you can literally shimmy out of your front door and be inside one of half a dozen legendary music houses within seconds.

Arelis González CASA PARTICULAR $
(Map p396; ☎65-29-88; Aguilera No 615; r CUC$20-25) This striking blue classical facade on Aguilera is just off Plaza de Marte. It's a noisy street, but the house has a nice ambience. There are two rooms and a three-level terrace, the top of which constitutes a tower-like *mirador* (lookout) that provides great views over the rooftops to the mountains beyond. The gnarly vines on level two are used to make grape juice.

Aida & Ali CASA PARTICULAR $
(Map p396; ☎62-27-47; Saco No 516 btwn Mayía Rodríguez & Donato Mármol; r CUC$20-25; ❄) A thick-in-the-action house on Saco (Enramadas) with two rooms perched on a terrace high above the street. The one at the front is the spiffiest.

Casa Nenita CASA PARTICULAR $
(Map p396; ☎65-41-10; Sánchez Hechavarría No 472 btwn Pío Rosado & Porfirio Valiente; r CUC$20-25) Santiago throws up another *palacio* of colonial splendor that gives away little from its street-side appearance. Dating from 1850, Nenita's house has soaring ceilings, original floor tiles and a truly amazing back patio. Sit back beneath the louvers and soak up the history.

Lourdes de la Caridad Gómez Beaton CASA PARTICULAR $
(Map p396; ☎65-44-68; Félix Peña No 454 btwn Sagarra & Sánchez Hechavarría; r CUC$20-25) Another colonial gem that has huge bedrooms with baths and typical Santiago features. There are three levels of terrace and fine harbor views.

Gran Hotel Escuela HOTEL $
(Map p396; ☎65-30-20; Saco No 310; s/d/tr CUC$19/28/35; ❄) Shoehorned like a 1950s relic into the retro-fest that is Calle Saco, this old four-story establishment has huge rough-edged rooms that fairly dwarf the single beds and wall-mounted small-screen TVs. Despite its bargain-basement apparel, the Gran is an Escuela hotel, meaning service is keen and welcomes are generally warm. And at these prices you're almost undercutting the casas particulares.

Hotel Balcón del Caribe HOTEL $
(☎69-10-11; Carretera del Morro Km 7.5; s/d incl breakfast CUC$18/28; ❄ ≋) The tremendous setting next to El Morro castle is countered by all the usual Islazul hotel-chain foibles: flowery curtains, ancient mattresses and furnishings salvaged from a 1970s garage sale. But you'll feel better after a dip in the pool and some time contemplating the stunning Caribbean view. Situated 10km from the city center you'll need your own wheels if you're staying here.

Hotel las Américas HOTEL $$
(Map p388; ☎64-20-11; cnr Avs de las Américas & General Cebreco; s/d CUC$32/50; P ❄ @ ≋) Cheap and normally pretty cheerful, Las Américas sits opposite the Meliá but is a long way from it in price and quality. The 70 rooms offer the usual Islazul interiors though the general facilities – restaurant, 24-hour cafetería, small pool, nightly entertainment, and car rental – are comprehensive for the price. The downside is the distance to the historical center (20 to 30 minutes on foot).

Villa Gaviota HOTEL $$

(Map p388; ☎64-13-70; Av Manduley No 502 btwn Calles 19 & 21, Vista Alegre; s/d CUC$49/59; P❄≋) Sitting pretty in an oasis of calm in Santiago's salubrious Vista Alegre district, Villa Gaviota has been upgraded from the tacky holiday camp of yore to embrace a sharper, edgier look. Features include a swimming pool, restaurant, three bars, a billiards room and laundry. It's a good bet if you want to escape the motorcycle madness of the city center.

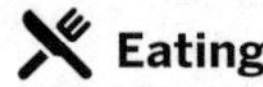

Eating

For a city of such fine cultural traditions, Santiago's restaurant scene is surprisingly lean. You'll find no hidden Havana-style experimentation here. Instead, the outlook is generally mediocre with the odd get-out-of-jail card. Paladares are rare in Santiago – high taxes and draconian regulations have done their work – though there has been a recent blossoming of new state-run seafood restaurants where you pay in Cuban pesos.

CITY OF HEROES

When it comes to heroic icons Santiago de Cuba shows little modesty. Indeed, the city is known nationally by the moniker 'City of Heroes.' Here's a rundown of four of them – one a poet, one a warrior, one an underground resistance fighter, and one a rum baron turned revered patriot.

Antonio Maceo

Known as the 'Bronze Titan' for his wartime heroics, Maceo was a *mulato* general during the slave era who led from the front in both Independence Wars and was revered as one of the few Mambises (Cuban rebels) who never sold out to the Spanish. The definitive 'man of action' to José Martí's intellectual 'man of ideas,' Maceo was injured 22 times on the battlefield until his luck ran out in a skirmish outside Havana in December 1896. You can see him re-created in bronze in Plaza de la Revolución, or visit his birth-house/museum in the city center.

Frank País

Dead by the age of 22, Frank País' short life left a long legacy. In the mid-50s he began forming revolutionary cells in Santiago in resistance to the Batista regime, and his role in organizing and coordinating the urban underground was vital in cementing supply routes from the city up to Fidel Castro's rebels in the mountains. País was murdered by Batista's police in July 1957, but he had already created the bedrock for Castro's future success. Today, he is honored all over Cuba in streets, squares, monuments and even an airport (Holguín). You can visit his birth-house in Calle General Banderas.

Emilio Bacardí

Today, the relationship between Bacardí and the Cuban Government is famously fraught but, back in the 1890s, under the auspices of Bacardí-clan scion, Emilio, it was far less caustic. Emilio led a dual life as the head of a lucrative rum dynasty, and as a plotting *independista*, unbending in his opposition to the Spanish during the Spanish-Cuban-American War. He was imprisoned more than once for his 'transgressions' but returned heroically to Santiago in 1898 where he became the city's first mayor and a beacon of tolerance and sanity in the fledgling nation. He was also responsible for founding Cuba's first museum.

José María Heredia

A man of words rather than action, Heredia expressed his revolutionary thoughts through poetry instead of politics. But such nuanced observations were still enough to provoke the ire of the heavy-handed Spanish authorities and, in 1823, he was arrested on a trumped-up conspiracy charge and banished from Cuba for life. Most of his later work was written from exile and is heavy with nostalgia for the homeland he missed. Heredia's birth-house in the street that bears his name is now a museum with the words of his poem *Niagara* emblazoned on the wall outside.

In the heart of the *casco histórico*, Calle José A Saco is now designated traffic-free daily until at least 9pm. It offers all manner of mobile food units selling *comida ligera* (light food).

TOP CHOICE **El Barracón** CARIBBEAN $
(Map p388; Av Victoriano Garzón; ⌚noon-midnight) Santiago's finest food house – no contest! El Barracón opened its doors amid much publicity in August 2008 to reignite the roots of Afro-Cuban culture and cuisine. The fanfare was justified. The restaurant's interior, a mix of atmospheric Santería shrine and *cimarrón* (runaway slave), is intriguing and the creative food is even better. Try the delicious *tostones* (fried plantain patties) filled with chorizo and cheese, or opt for the lamb special.

Paladar Salón Tropical PALADAR $$$
(Map p388; ☎64-11-61; Fernández Marcané No 310, Reparto Santa Bárbara; ⌚5pm-midnight Mon-Sat, noon-midnight Sun) The city's best paladar is a few blocks south of Hotel las Américas on a pleasant rooftop terrace with fairy lights and city views. The food is plentiful and tasty with a varying menu of succulent smoked pork, chicken and sometimes lamb, served with *congrí* (rice flecked with black beans), salad and plantains (green bananas) and delicious *yuca con mojo* (starchy root vegetables with garlic lime sauce). Reservations are a good idea as this is a favorite spot for young Cuban women and their older foreign escorts.

Ristorante Italiano la Fontana ITALIAN $$
(Map p388; Meliá Santiago de Cuba, cnr Av de las Américas & Calle M; ⌚11am-11pm) Pizza *deliciosa* (from CUC$5) and lasagna *formidable* (CUC$8), ravioli and garlic bread (CUC$1); *mamma mía,* this has to be the number-one option for breaking away from all that chicken and pork!

Hotel Casa Granda CAFE $$
(Map p396; Casa Granda, Heredia No 201; ⌚9am-midnight) Positioned like a whitewashed theater box overlooking the colorful cabaret of Parque Céspedes, the Casa Granda's Parisian-style terrace cafe has to be one of the best people-watching locations in Cuba. Food-wise, you're talking snacks (burgers, hot dogs, sandwiches etc) and service-wise you're talking impassive, verging on the grumpy; but with this setting, who cares?

Restaurante Zunzún CARIBBEAN $$$
(Map p388; Av Manduley No 159; ⌚noon-10pm Mon-Sat, noon-3pm Sun) Dine in bygone bourgeois style in this urban mansion-turned-restaurant. Zunzún, in the once upscale Vista Alegre neighborhood, has always been one of Santiago's best restaurants when it comes to food and ambience. Exotic dishes include chicken curry, paella or a formidable cheese plate and cognac. Expect professional, attentive service and entertaining troubadours.

Restaurante el Morro CARIBBEAN $$
(Castillo del Morro; ⌚noon-9pm) A gleaming white plate mounted in a glass case on the wall announces that Paul McCartney once ate here during a whistle-stop 2000 visit (he flew in for four hours from the Turks and Caicos). According to the waiters, the world's most famous vegetarian made do with an omelet. For meat-eaters, the complete *comida criolla* lunch (CUC$12) is a better bet, a filling spread that includes soup, roast pork, a small dessert and one drink. The spectacular cliff-side location offers occasional views of breaching whales. Take bus 212 to Ciudamar and walk the last 20 minutes, or take a taxi.

Restaurante Matamoros CARIBBEAN $$
(Map p396; cnr Aguilera & Porfirio Valiente) Some interesting wall art, a couple of bolero-singing *muchachas* and a decent menu (if you're happy with chicken and pork) have breathed new life into this once-dingy joint on Plaza Dolores that celebrates the life and career of Cuba's greatest *son* exponents, the Trio Matamoros.

Restaurante España SEAFOOD $
(Map p388; Victoriano Garzón) Readjust your Cuban food preconceptions before you walk into España, one of three new Moneda Nacional eating houses on the same street that specializes in seafood cooked with panache and – on occasion – fresh herbs. Try the lobster or tangy prawns, but bypass the Cuban wine which is almost undrinkable.

Cafetería las Arecas CARIBBEAN $$
(Map p388; Av Manduley No 52; dishes around CUC$3; ⌚10am-1am) Nestled in the garden patio of La Maison, the mansion-turned-boutique-shopping-experience, this cafetería has an inexpensive menu with spaghetti, pizzas and chicken dishes. Fish filets start at CUC$5.50. The fancier dining-room **restaurant** (called '1912') in the rear part of the main building is open until 10pm.

Santiago 1900 CARIBBEAN **$**
(Map p396; Bartolomé Masó No 354; ⏲noon-midnight) In the former Bacardí residence you can dine on the standard chicken, fish or pork for Cuban pesos in a plush dining room that recently recovered its fin de siècle colonial airs. Beware the draconian dress code. No shorts or T-shirts.

Pan.com FAST FOOD **$**
(Map p396; Aguilera btwn General Lacret & Hartmann; snacks CUC$3; ⏲11am-11pm) Havana's refreshingly efficient fast(ish)-food chain has a smaller Santiago branch, but the staff has yet to cotton onto the capital's slicker service. Arrive with low expectations and see what's available on the ostensibly long menu.

La Teresina CARIBBEAN **$$**
(Map p396; Aguilera btwn Porfirio Valiente & Mayía Rodríguez; ⏲11am-11pm) One in a triumvirate of inviting-looking restaurants along the north side of Plaza de Dolores, La Teresina doesn't quite live up to its splendid colonial setting. But the terrace is shady, the beers affordable and the food – a familiar mix of spaghetti, pizza and chicken – enough to take the edge off a hungry appetite.

Café Ven CAFE **$**
(Map p396; José A Saco btwn Hartmann & Pío Rosado; ⏲9am-9pm) Valuable new cafe tucked into busy Saco (Enramadas) with lung-enriching air-con, interesting coffee *cafetal* (plantation) paraphernalia and life-saving sandwiches and cakes.

La Arboleda ICE-CREAM PARLOR **$**
(Map p388; cnr Avs de los Libertadores & Victoriano Garzón; ⏲10am-11:40pm Tue-Sun) Santiago's ice-cream cathedral is a little out of the center, not that this lessens the queue length. Yell out *¿Quién es último?* (who is last?) and take your place on the Av de los Libertadores side of the parlor. Milkshakes are sometimes sold from the outside window.

Heladería Km 969 ICE-CREAM PARLOR **$**
(Map p388; cnr Av Victoriano Garzón & Av 24 de Febrero; ⏲8:30am-11pm) Got bored waiting in the queues at Coppelia? Cross Victoriano Garzón to this less-frenetic pit stop where you should be enjoying your *copa de helado* (ice-cream sundae) within minutes.

Café Palmares FAST FOOD **$**
(Map p388; Calle M cnr Calle 6; ⏲24hrs) Yards from the relative opulence and inflated prices of the Meliá Santiago de Cuba is this alfresco place where they practically give away substantial snacks and hearty plates of rice and meat.

Taberna de Dolores CARIBBEAN **$$**
(Map p396; Mayia Rodríguez cnr Aguilera) Atmospheric two-level, tavern-like restaurant on Plaza Dolores that trumps all local opposition with slick service, table-side troubadours and no-pretension Cuban food.

Restaurante el Cayo SEAFOOD **$$**
(lunch CUC$6-20) If the congenial fishers on Cayo Granma don't corner you beforehand, this is the island's only state-run place, serving seafood in a classic clapboard house suspended over the water on El Cayo island south of the center.

Paladar las Gallegas PALADAR **$$**
(Map p396; Bartolomé Masó No 305; meals CUC$8-10; ⏲1-11pm) Around the corner from the cathedral, this place has been here for donkey's years in Santiago-paladar terms, bashing out unremarkable potions of pork, chicken and sometimes *carnero* (lamb).

La Perla del Dragón CHINESE **$**
(Map p396; Aguilera btwn Porfirio Valiente & Mayía Rodríguez; ⏲11am-11pm) Santiago's token Chinese restaurant doesn't quite match up to the diversity of Havana's Barrio Chino, though it enjoys a pleasant setting on shady Plaza de Dolores.

Self-Catering

Supermercado Plaza de Marte SUPERMARKET **$**
(Map p396; Av Garzón; ⏲9am-6pm Mon-Sat, 9am-noon Sun) One of the better-stocked supermarkets in town, with a great ice-cream selection and cheap bottled water. It's in the northeastern corner of Plaza de Marte.

Panadería Doña Neli BAKERY **$**
(Map p396; cnr Aguilera & Sánchez; ⏲7:30am-8pm) Nice early morning aromas will send you in the direction off this hard-currency bakery on Plaza de Marte.

Municipal market MARKET
(Map p388; cnr Aguilera & Padre Pico) The main market, two blocks west of Parque Céspedes, has a poor selection considering the size of the city.

Mercado Agropecuario Ferreiro MARKET
(Map p388; Nuñez de Balboa) Across the traffic circle from Hotel las Américas and up the side street beside the gas station, this is another market option.

Drinking

Bar la Fontana di Trevi BAR

(Map p396; General Lacret; ⏲noon-2am) Could it be that the lounge trend has hit Santiago de Cuba? You might think so walking into this cocoon off José A Saco with low stools grouped around individual tables lining the wall. Just don't order any apple martinis; it's strictly peso beer and rum at this cool saloon.

Café de la Catedral CAFE

(Map p396; General Lacret btwn Heredia & Bartolomé Masó; ⏲8am-9pm) A frigidly air-conditioned cafe sheltered beneath the cathedral that offers 24 different types of coffee – with a biscuit, if you're lucky. There are some coffee-farming artifacts scattered around the interior and a colorful *cafetal* mural emblazoned on the wall.

El Baturro BAR

(Map p396; cnr Aguilera & Hartmann) A slavishly local downtown joint that looks like a leftover from the city's pirate days. Slightly seedy and very Santiago.

Café la Isabelica CAFE

(Map p396; cnr Aguilera & Porfirio Valiente; ⏲9am-9pm) Stronger, smokier, darker cantina-type equivalent of Café de la Catedral, with the prices in pesos.

☆ Entertainment

'Spoilt for choice' would be an understatement in Santiago. For what's happening, look for the bi-weekly *Cartelera Cultural*. The reception desk at Hotel Casa Granda (p402) usually has copies. Every Saturday night Calle José A Saco becomes a happening place called **Noche Santiagüera**, where street food, music and crowds make an all-

DON'T MISS

FOLKLÓRICO DANCE GROUPS

Santiago de Cuba is home to more than a dozen *folklórico* dance groups, which exist to teach and perform traditional Afro-Cuban *bailes* (dances) and pass their traditions on to future generations. Most of the groups date from the early 1960s and all enjoy strong patronage from the Cuban government.

A good place to find out about upcoming *folklórico* events is at the **Departamento de Focos Culturales de la Dirección Municipal de Cuba** (Map p388; ☎65-69-82; Los Maceos No 501 btwn General Bandera & Pío Rosado), which acts as a kind of HQ for the various *cabildos* (Afro-Cuban brotherhoods) and dance groups, most of which are bivouacked nearby. Another good nexus is the Casa del Caribe (p399) in Vista Alegre.

Ballet Folklórico Cutumba FOLKLÓRICO

(Map p396; Teatro Galaxia, cnr Avs 24 de Febrero & Valeriano Hierrezuelo; admission CUC$2) This internationally known Afro-Cuban-Franco-Haitian *folklórico* dance group was founded in 1960 and currently appears at Teatro Galaxia (while its home base, the Teatro Oriente, is being renovated). You can pop in to see the group practice between 9am and 1pm Tuesday to Friday or attend an electrifying *café teatro* at 10pm every Saturday. The 55-strong troupe perform such dances as the *tumba francesa, columbia, gagá, guaguancó, yagüetó, tajona* and *conga oriental*. It's one of the finest programs of its kind in Cuba and has toured the world from New York to New Zealand.

Foco Cultural el Tivolí AFRO-CUBAN

(Map p388; Desiderio Mesnier No 208; ⏲8pm Mon-Fri) Carnaval practice for the Sarabanda Mayombe happens weekly at this Tivolí *foco* (a show that takes place in Tivolí). Saturdays at 5pm it performs a *mágica religiosa* program of *orishas* (Afro-Cuban religious deities), *bembé* (Afro-Cuban drumming ritual) and *palo monte* (Bantu-derived Afro-Cuban religion) at the nearby Casa de las Tradiciones (p408).

Also worth seeking out are the **Conjunto Folklórico de Oriente** (Map p396; Hartmann No 407), the **Carabalí Izuama** (Map p388; Pío Rosado No 107) and the **Foco Cultural Tumba Francesa** (Map p388; Pio Rosado No 268), a colorful group of French-Haitian drumming masters who can be seen in their rehearsal rooms on Tuesdays and Thursdays at 8pm.

night outdoor party. Calle Heredia, meanwhile, is Santiago's Bourbon Street, a musical cacophony of stabbing trumpets, multilayered bongos and lilting guitars. For the more secretive corners, prowl the streets with your ears open and let the sounds lure you in.

TOP CHOICE **Casa de las Tradiciones** LIVE MUSIC

(Map p388; Rabí No 154; admission CUC$1; ⏲from 8:30pm) The most discovered 'undiscovered' spot in Santiago still retains its smoke-filled, foot-stomping, front-room feel. Hidden in the gentile Tivolí district, some of Santiago de Cuba's most exciting ensembles, singers and soloists take turns improvising. Friday nights are reserved for straight-up, classic *trova,* à la Ñico Saquito and the like.

Casa de la Trova LIVE MUSIC

(Map p396; Heredia No 208; admission from CUC$2; ⏲11am-3pm & 8:30-11pm Tue-Sun) Nearly 40 years after its initial incarnation, Santiago's shrine to the power of traditional music is still going strong and continuing to attract big names such as Buena Vista Social Club singer Eliades Ochoa. Warming up on the ground floor in the late afternoon, the action slowly gravitates upstairs where, come 10pm, everything starts to get a shade more *caliente.* Arrive with a good pair of shoes and prepare to be – quite literally – whisked off your feet.

Casa del Estudiante LIVE MUSIC

(Map p396; Heredia No 204; admission CUC$1; ⏲9pm Wed, Fri & Sat, 1pm Sun) Grab a seat (or stand in the street) and settle down for whatever this spontaneous place can throw at you. Orchestral *danzón,* folkloric rumba, lovelorn *trovadores* or rhythmic *reggaetón* (Cuban hip-hop): you never know what you're going to get. See also Courses, p401.

FREE **Patio ARTex** LIVE MUSIC

(Map p396; Heredia No 304; ⏲11am-11pm) Art lines the walls of this shop-and-club combo that hosts live music both day and night in a quaint inner courtyard; a good bet if the Casa de la Trova is full, or too frenetic.

Patio los Dos Abuelos LIVE MUSIC

(Map p396; Francisco Pérez Carbo No 5; admission CUC$2; ⏲10pm-1am Mon-Sat) The old-timers label (*abuelos* means grandparents) carries a certain amount of truth. This relaxed live-music house is a bastion for traditional *son* sung the old-fashioned way. The musicians are seasoned pros and most of the patrons are perfect ladies and gentlemen.

Tropicana Santiago CABARET

(Map p387; entry from CUC$35; ⏲10pm Wed-Sun) Anything Havana can do, Santiago can do better – or at least cheaper. Styled on the Tropicana original, this 'feathers and baubles' Las Vegas–style floor show is heavily hyped by all the city's tour agencies who offer it for CUC$35 plus transport (Havana's show is twice the price, but no way twice as good). Located out of town, 3km north of the Hotel las Américas, a taxi or rental car is the only independent transport option, making the tour-agency deals a good bet. The Saturday night show is superior.

Teatro José María Heredia THEATER

(Map p388; ☎64-31-90; cnr Avs de las Américas & de los Desfiles; ⏲box office 9am-noon & 1-4:30pm) Santiago's huge, modern theater and convention center went up during the city refurbishment in the early 1990s. Rock and folk concerts often take place in the 2459-seat Sala Principal, while the 120-seat Café Cantante Niagara hosts more esoteric events. Ask about performances by the Compañía Teatro Danza del Caribe.

Club el Iris BAR, NIGHTCLUB

(Map p396; Aguilera No 617; admission CUC$3; ⏲10pm-2am) Just off Plaza de Marte, with an old-fashioned neon sign (which rarely works), the Iris is Santiago de Cuba's loudest, hottest and most 'happening' disco. The cover includes one drink, but at night it's couples only. Things generally get moving around midnight.

Casa de la Cultura Miguel Matamoros LIVE MUSIC

(Map p396; General Lacret btwn Aguilera & Heredia; admission CUC$1) This cultural stalwart in historic digs on Parque Céspedes hosts many crowded musical events, including rumba and *son;* check the *cartelera* (calendar) posted at the door. It also presents some good art expos.

Santiago Café CABARET

(Map p388; cnr Av de las Américas & Calle M; admission CUC$5; ⏲10pm-2am) This is the Hotel Meliá Santiago de Cuba's slightly less spectacular version of the Tropicana, though the setting is appropriately upscale. Cabarets take place on Saturdays with a disco afterwards. It's on the hotel's 1st floor. Head up to the 15th floor for the exciting **Bello Bar**.

Teatro Martí THEATER
(Map p388; Félix Peña No 313;) Children's shows are staged at 5pm on Saturday and Sunday at this theater near General Portuondo, opposite the Iglesia de Santo Tomás.

Sala de Conciertos Dolores LIVE MUSIC
(Map p396; cnr Aguilera & Mayía Rodríguez; 8:30pm) Housed in a former church on Plaza de Dolores, you can catch the Sinfónica del Oriente here, plus the impressive children's choir (at 5pm). The *cartelera* is posted outside.

Orfeón Santiago LIVE MUSIC
(Map p396; Heredia No 68) This classical choir sometimes allows visitors to attend its practice sessions from 9am to 11:30am Monday to Friday.

Coro Madrigalista LIVE MUSIC
(Map p396; Pio Rosado No 555) Across from the Museo Bacardí, this choir is similar to Orfeón Santiago.

Cine Rialto CINEMA
(Map p396; Félix Peña No 654) This cinema, next to the cathedral, is one of Santiago de Cuba's favorites, showing large-screen films and video.

Casa de la Música NIGHTCLUB
(Map p396; Corona No 564; admission CUC$3-10; 10pm-4am) Similar to the venues in Havana, this Casa de la Música features a mix of live salsa and taped disco and is usually a cracking night out.

Cine Cuba CINEMA
(Map p396; cnr Saco & General Lacret) Recipient of a recent refurbishment, this place is the best in town with an inviting lobby, a decent array of movies and plenty of crowds.

Uneac CULTURAL CENTER
(Map p396; Unión Nacional de Escritores y Artistas de Cuba; Union of Cuban Writers & Artists; Heredia No 266) First stop for art fiends seeking intellectual solace in talks, workshops, encounters and performances in a gorgeous colonial courtyard.

Wamby Bolera BOWLING
(Map p388; cnr Victoriano Garzón & Calle 7) Anyone for indoor bowling? Stick CUC$0.25 in one of the two machines and roll the balls. There's also an on-site cafe.

Cine Capitolio CINEMA
(Map p388; Av Victoriano Garzón No 256) Videos are the usual fare here.

Sport

Estadio de Béisbol Guillermón Moncada SPORT
(Map p388; Av de las Américas) This stadium is on the northeastern side of town within walking distance of the main hotels. During the baseball season, from October to April, there are games at 7:30pm Tuesday, Wednesday, Thursday and Saturday, and 1:30pm Sunday (one peso). The Avispas (Wasps) are the main rivals of Havana's Industriales with National Series victories in 2005, 2007 and 2008. Cubanacán runs trips to Avispa games with a visit to the dressing room afterwards to meet the players.

Gimnasio Cultura Física GYM
(Map p396; Pio Rosado No 455 btwn Saco & Hechavarría; 6am-6:45pm Mon-Fri, 8am-4pm Sat, 8am-noon Sun) No manicures here! For a wicked workout drop into this gym with its well-pummeled punching bags, rusty old weights and cold showers.

Shopping

Innovative creativity is inscribed into the louvers in colonial Santiago, and a brief sortie around the *casco histórico* will reveal exciting snippets of eye-catching art. Decent craft stalls are set up in Calle Heredia most days.

ARTex SOUVENIRS
(Map p396) General Lacret (General Lacret btwn Aguilera & Heredia); Heredia (Heredia No 304; 11am-11pm); Patio ARTex (Heredia No 208; 11am-7pm Tue-Sun) From mouse pads to Che trinkets, the branch of ARTex below Hotel Casa Granda collects any type of Cuban souvenir imaginable. The other branches – in the Casa de la Trova and at Patio ARTex one block further up Calle Heredia – focus more on music, with a respectable selection of CDs and cassettes.

Discoteca Egrem MUSIC
(Map p396; Saco No 309; 9am-6pm Mon-Sat, 9am-2pm Sun) The definitive Cuban specialist music store; this retail outlet of Egrem Studios has a good selection of local musicians.

La Maison CLOTHING
(Map p388; 64-11-17; Av Manduley No 52; 10am-6pm Mon-Sat) The Santiago version of the famous Havana fashion house located in an appropriately grand Vista Alegre *maison* (house). There are regular weekly fashion shows.

Galería de Arte de Oriente ART
(Map p396; General Lacret No 656) Probably the best gallery in Santiago de Cuba, the art here is consistently good.

Galería Santiago ART
(Map p396; Heredia) This gallery, below the cathedral on the southern side of Parque Céspedes, is another one with quality art. There are several more galleries along Heredia, east of here.

Librería Internacional BOOKS
(Map p396; ☎68-71-47; Heredia btwn General Lacret & Félix Peña) On the southern side of Parque Céspedes. Decent selection of political titles in English; sells postcards and stamps.

Librería la Escalera BOOKS
(Map p396; Heredia No 265; ⊙10am-11pm) A veritable museum of old and rare books stacked ceiling high. Sombrero-clad *trovadores* (traditional singers) often sit on the stairway and strum.

Librería Manolito del Toro BOOKS
(Map p396; Saco No 411; ⊙8am-4:30pm Mon-Fri, 8am-4pm Sat) Good for political literature.

Information

Dangers & Annoyances

Santiago is well known, even among Cubans, for its overzealous *jineteros* (hustlers), all working their particular angle – be it cigars, paladares, *chicas* (girls) or unofficial 'tours'. Sometimes it can seem nigh on impossible to shake off the money-with-legs feeling, but a firm 'no' coupled with a little light humor ought to keep the worst of the touts at bay.

Santiago's traffic is second only to Havana's in its environmental fallout. Making things worse for pedestrians is the plethora of noisy motorcyclists bobbing and weaving for position along the city's sinuous 1950s streets. Narrow or nonexistent sidewalks throw further obstacles into an already hazardous brew.

Emergency

Asistur (☎68-61-28; www.asistur.cu; Heredia No 201) Situated under the Casa Granda Hotel, this office specializes in offering assistance to foreigners, mainly in the insurance and financial fields.

Police (☎116; cnr Corona & Sánchez Hechavarría)

Internet Access & Telephone

Etecsa Multiservicios (cnr Heredia & Félix Peña; per hr CUC$6; ⊙8:30am-7:30pm) Three internet terminals in a small office on Plaza Céspedes.

Etecsa Telepunto (cnr Hartmann & Tamayo Fleites; per hr CUC$6; ⊙8:30am-7:30pm)

Media

Radio Mambí CMKW At 1240AM and 93.7FM.

Radio Revolución CMKC Broadcasting over 840AM and 101.4FM.

Radio Siboney CMDV Available at 1180AM and 95.1FM.

Sierra Maestra Local paper published Saturday.

Medical Services

Clínica Internacional Cubanacán Servimed (☎64-25-89; cnr Av Raúl Pujol & Calle 10, Vista Alegre; ⊙24hr) Capable staff speak some English. A dentist is also present.

Farmacia Clínica Internacional (☎64-25-89; cnr Av Raúl Pujol & Calle 10; ⊙24hr) Best pharmacy in town, selling products in convertibles.

Farmacia Internacional (☎68-70-70; Meliá Santiago de Cuba, cnr Av de las Américas & Calle M; ⊙8am-6pm) In the lobby of the Meliá Santiago de Cuba, it sells products in convertibles.

Hospital Provincial Saturnino Lora (☎64-56-51; Av de los Libertadores) With recompression chamber.

Money

Banco de Crédito y Comercio (Felix Peña No 614) Housed in the jarring modern building in Plaza Céspedes.

Banco Financiero Internacional (cnr Av de las Américas & Calle I)

Bandec General Lacret (cnr General Lacret & Aguilera); Saco (cnr Saco & Mariano Corona)

Cadeca Aguilera (Aguilera No 508); Hotel las Américas (cnr Avs de las Américas & General Cebreco); Meliá Santiago de Cuba (cnr Av de las Américas & Calle M)

Post

DHL (Aguilera No 310)

Post office Aguilera (Aguilera No 519); Calle 9 (Calle 9, Ampliación de Terrazas) Near Av General Cebreco; telephones are here too.

Travel Agencies

Cubatur Garzón (Av Victoriano Garzón No 364 btwn Calles 3 & 4; ⊙8am-8pm); Heredia (Heredia No 701 cnr General Lacret) Also has desks in the main hotels.

Ecotur (Bartolemé Masó cnr Hartmann) Offices in Santiago's otherwise forgettable 'Acuario' (Aquarium) building.

Cubanacán (Heredia No 201) This very helpful desk is in the Hotel Casa Granda.

Oficina Reservaciones de Campismo (Cornelio Robert No 163; ⊙8:30am-noon & 1-4:30pm

Mon-Fri, 8am-1pm Sat) For information on the Caletón Blanco and La Mula campismos.

Getting There & Away

Air

Antonio Maceo International Airport (Map p387; airport code SCU) is 7km south of Santiago de Cuba, off the Carretera del Morro. International flights arrive from Paris-Orly, Madrid, Toronto and Montreal on **Cubana** (cnr Saco & General Lacret). Toronto and Montreal are also served by **Sunwing** (www.sunwing.ca) and **Canjet** (www.canjet.com). **AeroCaribbean** (General Lacret btwn Bartolomé Masó & Heredia) flies weekly between here and Port Au Prince, Haiti and twice weekly to Santo Domingo. **American Eagle** (www.aa.com) run regular charters to and from Miami serving the Cuban-American community.

Internally, Cubana flies nonstop from Havana to Santiago de Cuba two or three times a day (CUC$114 one-way, 1½ hours). There are also services to Varadero and Holguín.

Bus

The **National Bus Station** (Map p388; cnr Av de los Libertadores & Calle 9), opposite the Heredia Monument, is 3km northeast of Parque Céspedes. **Víazul** (www.viazul.cu) buses leave from the same station.

The Havana bus stops at Bayamo (CUC$7, two hours), Holguín (CUC$11, 4¼ hours), Las Tunas (CUC$11, 5½ hours), Camagüey (CUC$18, 7½ hours), Ciego de Ávila (CUC$24, 9½ hours), Sancti Spíritus (CUC$28, 11½ hours) and Santa Clara (CUC$33, 13 hours). The Trinidad bus can drop you at Bayamo, Las Tunas, Camagüey, Ciego de Ávila and Sancti Spíritus. The Baracoa bus stops in Guantánamo.

Train

The modern French-style **train station** (Map p388; cnr Av Jesús Menéndez & Martí) is situated near the rum factory northwest of the center. The *Tren Francés* leaves at 9pm every third day for Havana (CUC$62, 16 hours) stopping at Camagüey (CUC$11) and Santa Clara (CUC$20) en route.

Another slower *coche motor* (cross-island) train also plies the route to Havana every third day when a *Tren Francés* isn't running, stopping at Las Tunas, Camagüey, Ciego de Ávila, Guayos, Santa Clara and Matanzas.

Cuban train schedules are fickle, so you should always verify beforehand what train leaves when and get your ticket as soon as possible thereafter.

Truck

Intermittent passenger trucks leave **Serrano Intermunicipal Bus Station** (Map p388; cnr Av Jesús Menéndez & Sánchez Hechavarría) near the train station to Guantánamo and Bayamo throughout the day. Prices are a few pesos, and early mornings are the best time to board. For these destinations, don't fuss with the ticket window; just find the truck parked out front going your way. Trucks for Caletón Blanco and Chivirico also leave from here.

The **Intermunicipal Bus Station** (Terminal Cuatro; Map p388; cnr Av de los Libertadores & Calle 4), 2km northeast of Parque Céspedes, has two buses a day to El Cobre. Two daily buses also leave for Baconao from here.

Getting Around

To/From the Airport

A taxi to or from the airport should cost around CUC$7, but drivers will often try to charge you more. Haggle hard before you get in. You can also get to the airport on bus 212, which leaves from Av de los Libertadores opposite the Hospital de Maternidad (Map p388). Bus 213 also goes to the airport from the same stop, but visits Punta Gorda first. Both buses stop just beyond the west end of the airport car park to the left of the entrances.

To/From the Train Station

To get into town from the train station, catch a southbound horse cart (one peso) to the clock tower at the north end of Parque Alameda (Map p388), from which Aguilera (to the left) climbs straight up to Parque Céspedes. Horse carts between the National Bus Station (they'll shout 'Alameda') and train station (one peso) run along Av Juan Gualberto Gómez and Av Jesús Menéndez (Map p388).

VÍAZUL BUS DEPARTURES FROM SANTIAGO DE CUBA

DESTINATION	COST (CUC$)	DURATION (HR)	DAILY DEPARTURES
Baracoa	15	4¾	7:45am
Havana	51	15½	9am, 3:15pm, 6:50pm, 10pm
Trinidad	34	12	7:30pm
Varadero	49	16	8pm

Bus & Truck

Useful city buses include bus 212 to the airport and Ciudamar, bus 213 to Punta Gorda (both of these buses start from Av de los Libertadores, opposite the Hospital de Maternidad, Map p388, and head south on Felix Peña in the *casco histórico*), and bus 214 or 407 to Siboney (from near Av de los Libertadores No 425; Map p388). Bus 5 to El Caney stops on the northwestern corner of Plaza de Marte (Map p396) and at Gral Cebreco and Calle 3 in Vista Alegre (Map p388). These buses (20 centavos) run every hour or so; more frequent trucks (one peso) serve the same routes.

Trucks to El Cobre and points north leave from Av de las Américas near Calle M (Map p388). On trucks and buses you should be aware of pickpockets and wear your backpack in front.

Car & Moped

Santiago de Cuba suffers from a chronic shortage of rental cars (especially in peak season) and you might find there are none available; though the locals have an indefatigable Cuban ability to *conseguir* (to manage or get) and *resolver* (to resolve or work out). The airport offices usually have better availability than those in town. If you're completely stuck, you can usually rent one at the Hotel Guantánamo, two hours to the east.

Cubacar (Hotel las Américas; cnr Avs de las Américas & General Cebreco; ⏲8am-10pm) rents out mopeds for CUC$24 per day. There is also an office at Antonio Maceo International Airport.

Guarded parking is available in Parque Céspedes, directly below the Hotel Casa Granda. Official attendants, complete with small badges, charge CUC$1 a day and CUC$1 a night.

The **Servi-Cupet gas station** (cnr Avs de los Libertadores & de Céspedes) is open 24 hours. There's an **Oro Negro gas station** (cnr Av 24 de Febrero & Carretera del Morro) on the Carretera del Morro and another Oro Negro on the Carretera Central at the northern entrance to Santiago de Cuba.

Taxi

There's a Turistaxi stand in front of Meliá Santiago de Cuba. Taxis also wait on Parque Céspedes in front of the cathedral and hiss at you expectantly as you walk past. Always insist the driver uses the *taxímetro* (meter) or hammer out a price beforehand. To the airport, it will be between CUC$5 and CUC$7 depending on the state of the car.

Bici-taxis charge about five pesos per person per ride, but it's illegal to carry tourists, so they'll drop you a couple of blocks from Parque Céspedes.

Siboney

Playa Siboney is Santiago's Playas del Este, an exuberant seaside town 19km to the east that's more rustic village than deluxe resort. Guarded by precipitous cliffs and dotted with a mixture of craning palms and weather-beaten clapboard houses, the setting here is laid-back and charming, with a beach scene that mixes fun-seeking Cuban families and young, nubile *santiagüeras* with their older, balder foreign partners.

In terms of quality, Siboney's small crescent of grayish sand isn't in Varadero's league and the hotel choice (there *is* no choice, just one rock-bottom villa) is none too inspiring either. But what Siboney lacks in facilities it makes up for in price, location (it's on the doorstep of Parque Baconao) and all-embracing Cuban atmosphere. There's a plethora of legal casas particulares here (more than 30, which in a settlement of this size constitutes half the village) and a decent sit-down restaurant on a hill overlooking the beach. For those in need of a break from the culture-jamming and street hassle of sweltering Santiago, it makes a good little hideaway.

⊙ Sights

Granjita Siboney MUSEUM

(admission CUC$1; ⏲9am-5pm) Had the Revolution been unsuccessful, this insignificant red-and-white farmhouse 2km inland from Playa Siboney on the road to Santiago de Cuba, would be the forgotten site of a rather futile putsch. As it is, it's another shrine to the glorious national episode that is Moncada. It was from this place, at 5:15am on July 26, 1953, that 26 cars under the command of Fidel Castro left to attack the military barracks in Santiago de Cuba. The house retains many of its original details, including the dainty room used by the two *compañeras* (female revolutionaries) who saw action, Haydee Santamaría and Melba Hernández. There are also displays of weapons, interesting documents, photos and personal effects related to the attack. Notice the well beside the building, where weapons were hidden prior to the attack. In 1973, 26 monuments were erected along the highway between the Granjita Siboney and Santiago de Cuba to commemorate the assault.

Museo de la Guerra Hispano-Cubano-Norteamericano MUSEUM
(admission CUC$1; ⏲9am-5pm) Adjacent to the Granjita, this museum displays objects related to the 1898 American military intervention at Santiago de Cuba. Several scale models of both the land and sea battles are provided.

Overlooking the stony shoreline is an American **war memorial** dated 1907, which recalls the US landing here on June 24, 1898.

Sleeping

There's an abundance of casas particulares (at least a dozen) in this small seaside settlement.

Ángel Figuredo Zolórzano CASA PARTICULAR $
(☎39-91-81; dgarrido1961@yahoo.es; Av Serrano No 63; r CUC$15-20) Nicely outfitted little pad, with a patio, at the end of the street.

Marlene Pérez CASA PARTICULAR $
(☎39-92-19; r CUC$15-20) A seaside apartment with a balcony perched on the coast a block south of the post office. This place has a modern sheen and easy parking.

Ovidio González Salgado CASA PARTICULAR $
(☎39-93-40; Av Serrano; r CUC$20-25) A reader-recommended place above the local pharmacy, serving great meals.

Villa Siboney CABINS $
(☎39-93-21; bungalows CUC$23) You're wiser heading for the casas particulares first in this neck of the woods, but if for some reason they're all full there's always the bog-standard Villa Siboney; seven independent rustic cabins on the beach that sleep up to four people. Ask at the *carpeta* (reception desk), below the apartment building beside the commercial center.

Eating

Restaurante la Rueda CARIBBEAN $
(Calle Montenegro) Take note, dear diner, you are sitting in the former house of musical sage-turned-international icon, Francisco Repilado the man responsible for writing the immortal song 'Chan Chan,' which you've probably already heard at least a dozen times since your plane landed. Born in a small shack on this site in 1907, Compay Segundo, as he was more commonly known, shot to superstardom at the advanced age of 90 as the guitarist and winking joker in Ry Cooder's *Buena Vista Social Club*. Despite predictions that he would make 115, Segundo died in 2003 aged 95. La Rueda is Siboney's only real dining option and would have kept old Francisco happy with its no-frills *comida criolla*, friendly service and good beach views.

A number of cheap peso **food stalls** overlook the beach. There is also an open-air **bar** selling drinks in convertibles on the beach itself.

Getting There & Away

Bus 214 runs from Santiago de Cuba to Siboney from near Av de los Libertadores 425, opposite Empresa Universal, with a second stop at Av de Céspedes 110. It leaves about once an hour, and bus 407 carries on to Juraguá three times a day. Passenger trucks also shuttle between Santiago de Cuba and Siboney.

A taxi to Playa Siboney will cost in the vicinity of CUC$20 to CUC$25, depending on whether it's state or private.

La Gran Piedra

Crowned by a 63,000-ton boulder that sits perched like a grounded asteroid high above the Caribbean, the Cordillera de la Gran Piedra forms part of Cuba's greenest and most bio-diverse mountain range. Not only do the mountains have a refreshingly cool microclimate, they also exhibit a unique historical heritage based on the legacy of some 60 or more coffee plantations set up by French farmers in the latter part of the 18th century. On the run from a bloody slave rebellion in Haiti in 1791, enterprising Gallic immigrants overcame arduous living conditions and difficult terrain to turn Cuba into the world's number-one coffee producer in the early 19th century. Their workmanship and ingenuity have been preserved for posterity in a Unesco World Heritage Site that is centered on the Cafetal la Isabelica. The area is also included in the Baconao Unesco Biosphere Reserve, instituted in 1987.

Sights

The steep 12km road up the mountain range becomes increasingly beautiful as the foliage closes in and the valley opens up below. Mango trees are ubiquitous here.

Prado de las Esculturas PARK
(admission CUC$1; ⏲8am-4pm) Near the beginning of the access road to La Gran Piedra, 16km southeast of Santiago de Cuba, is this sculpture park. Strewn along a 1km loop

La Gran Piedra & Parque Baconao

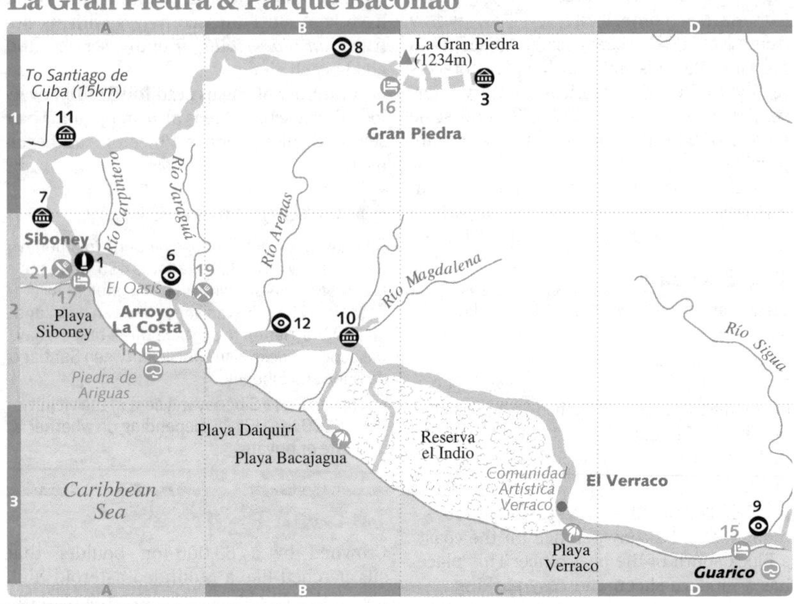

La Gran Piedra & Parque Baconao

Sights

1 American War Memorial A2
2 Aquario Baconao E3
3 Cafetal la Isabelica C1
4 Criadero de Cocodrilos F3
5 Exposición Mesoamericana E3
6 Fiesta Guajira A2
7 Granjita Siboney A2
8 Jardín Botánico B1
9 Jardín de Cactus D3
Museo de Historia Natural (see 12)
Museo de la Guerra Hispano Cubano Norteamericano (see 7)
10 Museo Nacional de Transportes Terrestre B2
11 Prado de las Esculturas A1
12 Valle de la Prehistoria B2

Activities, Courses & Tours

Centro Internacional de Buceo Carisol de Corales (see 13)
Centro Internacional de Buceo de Bucanero (see 14)

Sleeping

13 Club Amgio Carisol – Los Corales E3
14 Club Bucanero A2
15 Hotel Costa Morena D3
16 Villa la Gran Piedra. B1
17 Villa Siboney A2

Eating

18 Casa del Piedra el Cojo E3
Fiesta Guajira (see 6)
19 Finca el Porveni A2
20 Restaurante Casa de Rolando E3
21 Restaurante la Rueda. A2

road, here are 20 monumental sculptures of metal, wood, concrete, brick and stone by the artists of 10 countries. It's the first of this region's numerous artistic oddities.

Jardín Botánico GARDEN
(admission CUC$3; ⌚8am-4:30pm Tue-Sun) One kilometer before Villa la Gran Piedra and 800m down a muddy road is a botanical garden with orchids (best November to January) and other flowers. Look for the showy

yellow, orange and violet blooms of the *ave de paraíso* (bird of paradise).

La Gran Piedra MOUNTAIN SUMMIT
(admission CUC$1) You don't need to be Tenzing Norgay to climb the 459 stone steps to the summit of La Gran Piedra at 1234m. The huge rock on top measures 51m in length and 25m in height and weighs…a lot. On a clear day there are excellent views out across the Caribbean and on a dark night you are supposedly able to see the lights of Jamaica.

Cafetal la Isabelica MUSEUM
(admission CUC$2; 8am-4pm) The nexus of the Unesco World Heritage Site bestowed in 2000 upon the First Coffee Plantations in the Southeast of Cuba. It's a 2km hike beyond La Gran Piedra on a rough road to the impressive two-story stone mansion, with its three large coffee-drying platforms, built in the early 19th century by French émigrés from Haiti, and once one of more than 60 in the area. There's a workshop, furniture and some slave artifacts, and you can stroll around the pine-covered plantation grounds at will. It's worth using a guide (for a tip) to show you round as there are no explanatory notices.

Activities

Hiking

You can visit the ruins of many of the 100-plus coffee plantations on foot. Trails lead out from Cafetal la Isabelica, but there are no signs. Enquire at La Isabelica about the possibility of hiring a local farmer to show you around for a prearranged fee.

Sleeping & Eating

Villa la Gran Piedra HOTEL $
(65-12-05; s/d CUC$13/20; P) It might not be the biggest or the best, but Villa la Gran Piedra has at least one claim to fame – it is the highest hotel in Cuba. Situated at 1225m, near the mountain's summit, there are 17 cabins and five bungalows here with red-tiled roofs and local stone walls. Rooms are basic but perfectly adequate and the verdant setting surrounded by ferns, orchids and wondrous vistas makes up for a lot. There's an on-site restaurant and various short hiking trips are available.

Getting There & Away

A steep, winding paved road climbs 1.2 vertical kilometers from the junction with the coast road near Siboney (on the 214 bus route) through *muchos* potholes. A taxi from Santiago de Cuba will cost approximately CUC$40-50 (bargain hard) for the round trip. Sturdy Cubans and the odd ambitious foreigner hike up 12km from the bus stop at the road junction in Las Guásimas.

Parque Baconao

Parque Baconao, covering 800 sq km between Santiago de Cuba and the Río Baconao, is as wondrous as it is weird. A Unesco Biosphere Reserve that is also home to an outdoor car museum, a run-down aquarium and a rather odd collection of 240 life-size dinosaur sculptures, it looks like a historically displaced Jurassic Park, yet in reality acts as an important haven for a whole ecosystem of flora and fauna.

Not surprisingly, the Unesco tag wasn't earned for a museum full of old cars (or for a field full of concrete dinosaurs, for that matter). According to biological experts, Baconao boasts more than 1800 endemic species of flora and numerous types of endangered bats and spiders. Encased in a shallow chasm with the imposing Sierra Maestra on one side and the placid Caribbean on the other, the biodiversity of the area (which includes everything from craning royal palms

CAFETALES

The Cubans have always been enthusiastic coffee drinkers. But, while the shade-loving national coffee crop thrives in the cool tree-covered glades of the Sierra del Escambray and Sierra Maestra, it's not indigenous to the island.

Coffee was first introduced to Cuba in 1748 from the neighboring colony of Santo Domingo, yet it wasn't until the arrival of French planters from Haiti in the early 1800s that the crop was grown commercially.

On the run from Toussaint Louverture's slave revolution, the displaced French found solace in the mountains of Pinar del Río and the Sierra Maestra, where they switched from sugarcane production to the more profitable and durable coffee plant.

Constructed in 1801 in what is now the Sierra del Rosario Reserve in Artemisa province, the Cafetal Buenavista (p148) was the first major coffee plantation in the New World. Not long afterward, planters living in the heavily forested hills around La Gran Piedra began constructing a network of more than 60 *cafetales* (coffee farms) using pioneering agricultural techniques to overcome the difficult terrain. Their stoic efforts paid off and, by the second decade of the 19th century, Cuba's nascent coffee industry was thriving.

Buoyed by high world coffee prices and aided by sophisticated new growing techniques, the coffee boom lasted from 1800 to about 1820, when the crop consumed more land than sugarcane. At its peak, there were more than 2000 *cafetales* in Cuba, concentrated primarily in the Sierra de Rosario region and the Sierra Maestra to the east of Santiago de Cuba.

Production began to slump in the 1840s with competition from vigorous new economies (most notably Brazil) and a string of devastating hurricanes. The industry took another hit during the War of Independence, though the crop survived and is still harvested today on a smaller scale using mainly traditional methods.

The legacy of Cuba's pioneering coffee industry is best evidenced in the Archaeological Landscape of the First Coffee Plantations in the Southeast of Cuba, a Unesco World Heritage Site dedicated in 2000 that sits in the foothills of the Sierra Maestra close to La Gran Piedra (p413).

to prickly cliffside cacti) is nothing short of remarkable.

The beaches are smaller here than those on the northern coast and not quite as white, but the fishing is good and there are 73 scuba-diving sites to choose from nearby, including the *Guarico,* a small steel wreck just south of Playa Sigua.

Baconao is also famous for its crabs. From mid-March to early May, tens of thousands of large land crabs congregate along the coast beyond Playa Verraco, getting unceremoniously squashed under the tires of passing cars and sending up a rare stench as they bake in the sun.

Sights

El Oasis ART STUDIOS

Three kilometers east of the Playa Siboney road at the Club Bucanero turn-off is this small artistic community where a dozen painters have studios displaying and selling their works.

Fiesta Guajira RANCH, RODEO

(admission CUC$5; 9am & 2pm Wed & Sun) Situated in the El Oasis community, opposite the turn-off to Club Bucanero, this Ecotur-run *finca* (farm) stages rodeos with *vaqueros* (Cuban cowboys) four times a week. There's a cockpit, restaurant and horseback riding is available for CUC$5 for the first hour.

Valle de la Prehistoria AMUSEMENT PARK

(admission CUC$1; 8am-6pm) One of the oddest in a plethora of odd attractions is this Cuban Jurassic Park cast in stone that materializes rather serendipitously beside the meandering coastal road. Here giant brontosauruses mix with concrete cavemen, seemingly oblivious to the fact that 57 million years separated the two species' colonization of planet Earth. With your tongue planted firmly in your cheek, you can take in the full 11 hectares of this surreal kitsch park with its 200 life-size concrete dinosaurs built by inmates from a nearby prison. The **Museo de Historia Natural** (admission CUC$1; 8am-

4pm Tue-Sun) is also here, but something of an anticlimax after the surrealism of the prehistoric beasts.

Museo Nacional de Transporte Terrestre MUSEUM
(admission CUC$1; ⌚8am-5pm) What's the point, is the question that springs to mind when you stumble upon this alfresco museum 2km east of the Valle de la Prehistoria. All very impressive that they've nabbed Benny Moré's 1958 Cadillac and the Chevrolet Raúl Castro got lost in on the way to the Moncada Barracks; but in Cuba where '50s car relics are as common as cheap cigars, it's the equivalent of a Toyota Yaris museum in Kyoto.

Playa Daiquirí BEACH
The main US landings during the Spanish-Cuban-American War took place on June 24, 1898 at this beach, 2km down a side road from the museum. They might have named a cocktail after it, but the area is now a holiday camp for military personnel and entry is prohibited.

Comunidad Artística Verraco ART STUDIOS
(⌚9am-6pm) Ten kilometers past the Playa Daiquirí turn-off lies another village of painters, ceramicists and sculptors who maintain open studios. Here you can visit the artists and buy original works of art.

Jardín de Cactus GARDEN
(admission CUC$5; ⌚8am-3pm) Soon after passing the Verraco you burst onto the coast, where the hotels begin. This garden, 600m east of Hotel Costa Morena, has 200 kinds of cactus beautifully arrayed along the rocky hillside, with a large cave at the rear of the garden. Keep your eyes peeled for tiny green *colibrí* (hummingbird) suckling nectar from flowering cacti.

Aquario Baconao AQUARIUM
(admission CUC$7; ⌚9am-5pm) Situated between the Costa Morena and Hotel Carisol, this aquarium has dolphin shows (with sultry narration) a couple of times a day. Some travelers love the spectacle; others aren't so enamored. You can swim with the animals – if you so desire – for approximately CUC$50.

Exposición Mesoamericana PARK
(admission CUC$1) Every Cuban resort area seems to have an attraction replicating indigenous scenes. Here it's the Exposición Mesoamericana, just east of Club Amigo Carisol – Los Corales. Indigenous cave art from Central and South America is arranged in caves along the coastal cliffs.

Laguna Baconao LAKE
At the Laguna Baconao, 2km northeast of Los Corales, you'll find a **Criadero de Cocodrilos** (admission CUC$1; ⌚8am-5pm) where a dozen crocodiles are kept in pens below a restaurant, plus other caged animals such as lizards and *jutías* (tree rats). Horses are (supposedly) for hire here, as well as boats to ply the lake (CUC$2) where there are resident wild dolphins. A road from the hamlet of Baconao follows the lake's north shore to the decent Restaurante Casa de Rolando.

From **Playa Baconao** at the eastern corner of the lake, the paved road continues 3.5km up beautiful **Valle de Río Baconao** before turning into a dirt track. A dam up the Río Baconao burst in 1994, inundating Baconao village. Soldiers at a **checkpoint** at the village turn back people trying to use the direct coastal road to Guantánamo because it passes alongside the US Naval Base. To continue east, you must backtrack 50km to Santiago de Cuba and take the inland road.

Playa Cazonal BEACH
Generally considered to be the best public beach in the area, this strip offers lots of tawny sand, natural shade and a big sandy swimming hole (much of the coast here is clogged with seaweed forests). Turn into the Club Amigo Carisol – Los Corales and then it's a quick left to the beach access road.

Activities

Horseback Riding

Available at Fiesta Guajira, Finca la Porvenir and the Laguna Baconao.

Diving

Centro Internacional de Buceo Carisol los Corales DIVING
(www.nauticamarlin.com; Club Amgio Carisol – Los Corales) Situated in the hotel of the same name 45km east of Santiago, this center is run by government company Marlin. It picks divers up at the other hotels daily. Scuba diving costs CUC$30 with gear, and two boats can take up to 20 people to any of 24 local dive sites. Marlin's open-water certification course is CUC$300. There are shipwrecks close to shore here and you can feed black groupers by hand. **Centro Internacional de Buceo Bucanero** (Hotel Club Bucanero) offers similar services at Club Bucanero. The water off this bit of coast is some of Cuba's warm-

est (25°C to 28°C); best visibility is between February and June.

Sleeping

Hotel Costa Morena HOTEL $$
(☎35-61-35; s/d CUC$31/50; P❄≋) This place is at Sigua, 44km southeast of Santiago de Cuba and 17km east of the Complejo la Punta Servi-Cupet gas station. It has attractive architecture, a large terrace right on the cliffs, but no direct beach access. A shuttle will bus you to the beach at Club Amigo Carisol – Los Corales instead.

Club Amigo Carisol – Los Corales RESORT $$
(☎35-61-21; all-incl s/d CUC$55/78; P❄@≋) There's the swim-up bar, umbrellas in the piña coladas, and the government-sponsored band knocking out their 65th rendition of 'Guantanamera' as you tuck into your lukewarm buffet dinner. You must be back in all-inclusive land, or the Parque Baconao version of it to be more precise. The Carisol – Los Corales is a two-piece Cubanacán resort situated 44km east of Santiago on the coast's best section of beach (though parts of it have been damaged by successive hurricanes). Bonuses are a tennis court, a disco, multiple day trips on offer, and bright spacious clean rooms. Nonguests can purchase a day pass for CUC$15 including lunch.

Club Bucanero RESORT $$$
(☎68-63-63; Carretera de Baconao Km 4; all-incl s/d CUC$84/120; P❄≋) Tucked beneath low limestone cliffs with a small scratch of beach, this resort at Arroyo la Costa, 25km southeast of Santiago de Cuba, is a beautiful little haven away from the bustle of the city. The rooms are set in a series of attractive gray stone villas and are within earshot of the ocean. A lovely pool area boasts El Morro–like *garitas* (lookout posts) and the lush mountains beckon invitingly behind. Beware, facilities and food are limited in the off-season.

Eating

Finca el Porvenir CARIBBEAN $$
(62-90-64; Carretera de Baconao Km 18; ⊙noon-7pm) Situated on the left of the main Carretera about 4km east of El Oasis, this Palmares-run *finca* is probably the best place to eat out in this neck of the woods, knocking out no-frills *comida criolla* and specializing in *puerco asado en púa* (pork roasted Oriente-style on a skewer). It's finger-licking good. There's a natural swimming pool and horse-riding available on site.

Fiesta Guajira CARIBBEAN $$
(El Oasis, Carretera Baconao) The popular rodeo's restaurant serves typical Cuban food from noon to 2pm daily.

Casa del Piedra el Cojo SEAFOOD $
(Carretera Baconao) The most reliable year-round restaurant aside from the Fiesta Guajira rodeo is this peso place just beyond Sigua on the coast. Try the prawn cocktail for about eight pesos.

Restaurante Casa de Rolando SEAFOOD $$
(Carretera Baconao Km 53; ⊙10:30am-5pm) This scenic joint on the north shore of Laguna Baconao serves mainly seafood.

Getting There & Away

Most people access Baconao's spread-out sights by private car, taxi or as part as an organized trip from Santiago de Cuba. Cubataxi usually charges approximately CUC$0.50 per kilometer out this way or you can hire a moped from **Cubacar** (Club Bucanero) for CUC$24 per day.

Bus 415 from the municipal bus terminal in Santiago's Av de la Libertad plies this route three times a day, but the bus timetables are not set in stone. Check ahead.

When planning your visit to this area, remember that the coastal road from Baconao to Guantánamo is closed to nonresidents.

Getting Around

Cubacar (Club Bucanero) has cars and mopeds. There's also a branch at Los Corales.

The **Servi-Cupet gas station** (Complejo la Punta; ⊙24hr) is 28km southeast of Santiago de Cuba.

El Cobre

The Basílica de Nuestra Señora del Cobre, high on a hill 20km northwest of Santiago de Cuba on the old road to Bayamo, is Cuba's most sacred pilgrimage site and shrine of the nation's patron saint: La Virgen de la Caridad (Our Lady of Charity), or Cachita, as she is also known. In Santería, the Virgin is syncretized with the beautiful *orisha* Ochún, Yoruba goddess of love and dancing, and a religious icon to almost all Cuban women. Ochún is represented by the color yellow, mirrors, honey, peacock feathers and the number five. In the minds of many worshipers, devotion to the two religious figures is intertwined.

Legend dictates that the Virgin was first discovered floating on a board in the Bay of Nipe in 1612 by three fishermen called the 'three Juans' caught up in a violent storm. Assuming their lives were in danger they pulled the figurine from the water and found the words 'I am the Virgin of Charity' inscribed on the board. As the storm subsided and their lives were spared, they assumed a miracle had been granted and a legend was born.

The copper mine at El Cobre has been active since pre-Columbian times and was once the oldest European-operated mine in the Western hemisphere (by 1530 the Spanish had a mine here). However, it was shut in 2000. Many young villagers, who previously worked in the mine, now work over tourists in the car park of the basilica, offering to 'give' you shiny but worthless chalcopyrite stones from the mine. You'll find that a firm but polite *'No, gracias!'* usually does the trick. The road to the basilica is lined with sellers of elaborate flower wreaths, intended as offerings to La Virgen, and hawkers of miniature 'Cachitas,' the popular name for the Virgin.

⊙ Sights

Basílica de Nuestra Señora del Cobre CHURCH

(⌚6:30am-6pm) Stunning as it materializes above the village of El Cobre, Cuba's most revered religious site shimmers against the verdant hills behind. Apart from during Mass (8am except on Wednesday, with additional Sunday services at 10am and 4:30pm), La Virgen lives in a small chapel above the visitors center on the side of the basilica. To see her, take the stairs on either side of the entry door. For such a powerful entity, she's amazingly diminutive, some 40cm from crown to the hem of her golden robe. Check out the fine Cuban coat of arms in the center; it's an amazing work of embroidery. During Mass, Nuestra Señora de la Caridad faces the congregation from atop the altar inside the basilica.

The 'room of miracles' downstairs in the visitors center contains thousands of offerings giving thanks for favors bestowed by the virgin. Clumps of hair, a TV, a thesis, a tangle of stethoscopes, a raft and inner-tube sculpture (suggesting they made it across the Florida Straits safely) and floor-to-ceiling clusters of teeny metal body parts crowd the room.

Follow the signs through the town of El Cobre to the **Monumento al Cimarrón**. A 10-minute hike up a stone staircase brings you to this anthropomorphic sculpture commemorating the 17th-century copper-mine slave revolt. The views are superb from up here; walk to the far side of the sculpture for a vista of copper-colored cliffs hanging over the aqua-green reservoir.

Sleeping & Eating

Hospedaría el Cobre HOSTEL $

(☎34-62-46; s/d CUC$25/40) This large two-story building behind the basilica has 15 basic rooms with one, two or three beds, all with bath. Meals are served punctually at 7am, 11am and 6pm, and there's a pleasant large sitting room with comfortable chairs. The nuns here are very hospitable. House rules include no drinking and no unmarried couples. A convertible donation to the sanctuary is appreciated. Foreigners should reserve up to 15 days in advance.

FAMOUS GIFTS TO CACHITA

Many have offered gifts and keepsakes to the Virgin of El Cobre – some of them famous. The most celebrated donor was Ernest Hemingway who elected to leave the 23-karat gold medal he won for the Nobel Prize for Literature in 1954 to the 'Cuban people'. Rather than hand it over to the Batista regime, Hemingway donated the medal to the Catholic Church who subsequently placed it in the *sanctuario*. The medal was stolen temporarily in the 1980s but, despite being retrieved a few days later, it has since been kept under lock and key and out of public view.

In 1957 Lina Ruz left a small guerilla figurine at the feet of the Virgin to pray for the safety of her two sons – Fidel and Raúl Castro – then fighting in the Sierra Maestra. Fate – or was it the spirit of El Cobre? – shone brightly. Both sons are now into their 80s and still going strong!

More recently, dissident Cuban blogger, Yoani Sánchez visited the Virgin and left her Ortega and Gasset journalistic award in the sanctuary where – in her own words – 'the long arm of censor does not enter.'

There are several peso stalls in town where you can get *batidos* (fruit shakes), pizza and smoked-pork sandwiches.

 Getting There & Away

Bus 2 goes to El Cobre twice a day from the **Intermunicipal Bus Station** (Map p388; cnr Av de los Libertadores & Calle 4), in Santiago de Cuba. Trucks are more frequent on this route.

A Cubataxi from Santiago de Cuba costs around CUC$20 for a round-trip.

If you're driving toward Santiago de Cuba from the west, you can join the Autopista Nacional near Palma Soriano, but unless you're in a big hurry, it's better to continue on the Carretera Central via El Cobre, which winds through picturesque hilly countryside.

El Saltón

Basking in its well-earned eco-credentials, El Saltón is a tranquil mountain escape in the Tercer Frente municipality, where hills that once echoed with the sound of crackling rifle fire now reverberate to the twitter of tropical birds. Secluded and hard to reach (that's the point), it consists of a lodge, a hilltop *mirador* and a 30m cascading waterfall with an adjacent natural pool ideal for swimming. Eco-guides can offer horseback riding or hiking into the nearby cocoa plantations at Delicias del Saltón. Alternatively, you can just wander off on your own through myriad mountain villages with alluring names like Filé and Cruce de los Baños.

Sleeping

Hotel Horizontes el Saltón HOTEL **$$**
(56-63-23; Carretera Puerto Rico a Filé; s/d with breakfast CUC$43/62; P) The 22-room lodge is spread over three separate blocks that nestle like hidden tree houses amid the thick foliage. Spirit-lifting extras include a sauna, hot tub, massage facilities, and the hotel's defining feature, a refreshing natural waterfall and pool. The hotel has an OK restaurant and bar with a popular pool table, both of which reside just meters from a gushing mountain river.

Getting There & Away

To get to El Saltón, continue west from El Cobre to Cruce de los Baños, 4km east of Filé village. El Saltón is 3km south of Filé. With some tough negotiating in Santiago de Cuba, a sturdy taxi will take you here for CUC$40. Money well spent.

Chivirico & Around

POP 4000

Chivirico, 75km southwest of Santiago de Cuba and 106km east of Marea del Portillo, is the only town of any significance on the south-coast highway. Transport links are relatively good up until this point but, heading west, they quickly deteriorate.

In terms of atmosphere, Chivirico feels like a town from another era, even by Cuban standards, and, while there's not much to do here in the traditional tourist sense, it's a good place to pick up on the nuances of everyday Cuban life. The deep, clear waters of the Cayman Trench just offshore wash the many beaches along this portion of the south coast.

There's a challenging trek that begins at Calentura, 4km west of Chivirico, and passes through La Alcarraza (12km), crossing the Sierra Maestra to Los Horneros (20km), from where truck transport to Guisa is usually available. Whether skittish local authorities will let you loose in the area is another matter. Don't just turn up – do your homework in Santiago or Chivirico first. Try asking at Cubatur in Santiago or at one of the two Cubanacán Brisas hotels.

Sleeping

Brisas Sierra Mar RESORT **$$$**
(32-91-10; all-incl s/d CUC$70/100; P) This isolated and rather inviting place is at Playa Sevilla, 63km west of Santiago de Cuba and a two-hour drive from the airport. The big, pyramid-shaped hotel is built into a terraced hillside with a novel elevator to take you down to a brown-sand beach famous for its sand fleas. Get into the water quickly and discover a remarkable coral wall great for snorkeling just 50m offshore (dolphins sometimes frequent these waters too). Horseback riding is available, there's a **Marlin Dive Center** on the premises, and plenty of special kids' programs (kids under 13 stay free). The hotel is popular with Canadians and gets a lot of repeat visits. Nonguests can buy a CUC$35 day pass that includes lunch, drinks and sport until 5pm. If you're doing the south coast by bike, it's a nice indulgence.

Brisas Sierra Mar los Galeones HOTEL **$$$**
(32-61-60; Carretera Chivirico Km 72; all-incl high season s/d CUC$82/118; P) This is a small hotel with big surprises; the setting for instance – high on a bluff with shadowy mountains behind and bucolic life mooing

and crowing all around. Then there's the steep 296-step stairway that takes you down 100m to the tiny beach. Compared with its sister hotel, the Sierra Mar, Los Galeones is quiet (no kids under 16 here) and secluded, but not posh. All in all, a nice place to relax.

Campismo Caletón Blanco CABINS $
(☎62-57-97; Caletón Blanco Km 30, Guamá; s/d CUC$16/26; Ⓟ❄) One of two handy campismos situated along this route (the other is La Mula; see p422), Caletón Blanco is the closest to Santiago (30km) and the newest. Open to both international visitors and Cubans are 22 bungalows sleeping two to four people. There's also a restaurant, snack bar and bike rental available. Campervans are accommodated at this site, which is one of Cubamar's top picks. Make your reservations with Cubamar's Havana office (p118) before arrival.

Getting There & Away

Trucks run to Chivirico throughout the day from the Serrano Intermunicipal Bus Station opposite the train station in Santiago de Cuba. There are also three buses a day.

Theoretically, buses and private trucks operate along the south coast from Chivirico to Campismo la Mula, Río Macío (on the border with Granma province) and Pilón, but they are sporadic. Ask around at Chivirico's bus and truck station 700m up, off the coastal road from Cine Guamá.

El Uvero

A major turning point in the revolutionary war took place in this nondescript settlement, situated 23km west of Chivirico, on May 28, 1957, when Castro's rebel army – still numbering less than 50 – audaciously took out a government position guarded by 53 of Batista's soldiers. By the main road are two red trucks taken by the rebels and nearby a double row of royal palms leads to a large **monument** commemorating the brief but incisive battle. It's a poignant but little-visited spot.

Pico Turquino Area

Not far before the border of Granma and Santiago de Cuba provinces you'll reach the pinprick settlement of Las Cuevas, embarkation point for quick ascents of Cuba's highest mountain.

WORTH A TRIP

CUBA'S MOST SPECTACULAR ROAD

Existing as a vital transport artery between the escarpment and the sea, the rutted road west out of Santiago toward Marea de Portillo, 181km away, is a roller coaster of crinkled mountains, hidden bays and crashing surf. This is, without doubt, one of the most breathtaking routes in Cuba, if not the Caribbean. There are countless remote beaches where you can stop along the way, all of them spectacular, and most without a soul within loud-hailing distance. The main problem in this region is that public transport barely exists; a headache for convenience freaks but a blessing in disguise for DIY adventurers.

Sights

Museo de la Plata MUSEUM
(admission CUC$1; ⏲Tue-Sat) Five kilometers west of Las Cuevas (which is 40km west of El Uvero) at La Plata is this small museum next to the river just below the highway. The first successful skirmish of the Cuban Revolution took place here on January 17, 1957. The museum has three rooms with photos and artifacts from the campaign, including a piece of paper signed by the 15 *Granma* survivors who met up at Cinco Palmas in late 1956. Marea del Portillo is 46km to the west (see p382). Don't confuse this La Plata with the Comandancia La Plata, Fidel Castro's revolutionary headquarters high up in the Sierra Maestra (p373).

Activities

Cristóbal Colón DIVING
The well-preserved wreck of the Spanish cruiser *Cristóbal Colón* lies where it sank in 1898, about 15m down and only 30m offshore near La Mula. This is Cuba's greatest wreck dive; no scuttled fishing boat, but a casualty of the Spanish-Cuban-American War. Dive centers from Sierra Mar and Club Amigo Carisol–Los Corales (in Parque Baconao) come here. No scuba gear is available, but you can see the wreck with a mask and snorkel.

If you have the time, hike up the Río Turquino to Las Posas de los Morones, which has a few nice pools where you can swim (allow four hours round-trip). You must wade across the river at least three times unless it's dry.

Pico Turquino HIKING

This emblematic hike is often tackled from Las Cuevas on the remote coast road 130km west of Santiago de Cuba. If summiting the mountain is your main aim, this is probably the quickest and easiest route. If you also want to immerse yourself in the area's history and hike from Comandancia la Plata through and/or across the Sierra Maestra, you should set out from Alto del Naranjo in adjacent Granma province (see p376). Bear in mind that both options can be linked in a spectacular through trek (note that onward transport is better from the Alto del Naranjo side).

The hike from Las Cuevas can be organized at relatively short notice at the trailhead. A good option is to book through **Ecotur** (☎65-38-59) in Santiago de Cuba. See p374 for the map of this hike.

Camps & Shelters

The trail from Las Cuevas begins on the south-coast highway, 7km west of Ocujal and 51km east of Marea del Portillo. This trek also passes Cuba's second-highest peak, **Pico Cuba** (1872m). Allow at least six hours to go up and another four hours to come down, more if it has been raining, as the trail floods in parts and becomes a mud slick in others. Most climbers set out at 4am (but if you're on the trail by 6:30am, you'll be OK), having slept at the Campismo la Mula, 12km east; self-sufficient hikers also have the option of pitching **camp** at Las Cuevas visitors center. The CUC$15 per person fee (camera CUC$5 extra) that you pay at the visitors center/trailhead includes a compulsory Cuban guide. You can overnight at the **shelter** (2 days/1 night CUC$30) on Pico Cuba if you don't want to descend the same day. Alternatively, you can do the entire Las Cuevas–Alto del Naranjo three-day hike by arranging to be met by a new team of guides at Pico Turquino (three days/two nights CUC$48). Add an extra CUC$5 onto the latter two options if you wish to include a side trip to Castro's former headquarters at Comandancia la Plata (p373).

The Route

This hike is grueling because you're gaining almost 2km in elevation across only 9.6km of trail. But shade and peek-a-boo views provide plenty of respite. Fill up on water before setting out. The well-marked route leads from Las Cuevas to La Esmajagua (600m; 3km; there's water here and a hospitable country family), Pico Cardero (1265m; quickly followed by a series of nearly vertical steps called Saca la Lengua, literally 'flops your tongue out'), Pico Cuba (1872m; 2km; water and shelter here) and Pico Turquino (1972m; 1.7km). When the fog parts and you catch your breath, you'll behold a bronze bust of José Martí that stands on the summit of Cuba's highest mountain. You can overnight at either Pico Cuba on the ascent or La Esmajagua on the descent. The Pico Cuba shelter has a rudimentary kitchen and a wood-fire stove, plank beds (no mattresses) or, if those are taken, floor space. For the Alto del Naranjo–Santo Domingo continuation, see p376.

Alternatively, walkers with less lofty ambitions can arrange a short four-hour, 6km trek from Las Cuevas to La Esmajagua and back for CUC$13 (camera CUC$5 extra).

What to Bring

Trekkers should bring sufficient food, warm clothing, a sleeping bag and a poncho – precipitation is common up here (some 2200mm annually), from a soft drizzle to pelting hail. Except for water, you'll have to carry everything you'll need, including extra food to share if you can carry it and a little something for the *compañeros* (comrades) who take 15-day shifts up on Pico Cuba.

Ask ahead if you would like an English-speaking guide (park officials claim they now have at least one). Also ask about food provision at Pico Cuba. Drinks are available for purchase at the trailhead in Las Cuevas. Tipping the guides is mandatory – CUC$3 to CUC$5 is sufficient. For competitive types, the (unofficial) summit record by a guide is two hours, 45 minutes. So if you're feeling energetic…

Sleeping

Campismo la Mula CABINS $

(Carretera Granma Km 120; s/d CUC$7/10) On a remote pebble beach at the mouth of Río la Mula, 12km east of the Pico Turquino trailhead, La Mula has 50 small cabins popular with holidaying Cubans, hikers destined for Turquino and the odd hitchhiking south-coast adventurer short on lifts.

It's pretty much the only option on this isolated stretch of coast. It's wise to check with Cubamar or the Oficina Reservaciones de Campismo (see p410) in Santiago de Cuba before turning up. If it's full, you *may* be able to pitch a tent.

There's also a rustic **cafe** and **restaurant** on site.

Getting There & Away

Private trucks and the odd rickety bus connect La Mula to Chivirico, but they are sporadic and don't run on any fixed schedules. A taxi from Santiago should cost CUC$50 to CUC$60. Traffic is almost nonexistent in this neck of the woods and even the *amarillos* are sparse.

Guantánamo Province

021 / POP 510,863

Includes »

Best Places to Eat

- » Restaurante la Punta (p438)
- » Finca Duaba (p440)
- » Rancho Toa (p440)
- » Paladar el Colonial (p438)

Best Places to Stay

- » Hotel El Castillo (p436)
- » Hostal la Habanera (p437)
- » Villa Maguana (p441)
- » Villa la Lupe (p427)

Why Go?

To most of the world Guantánamo conjures up pictures of nameless prisoners in orange jumpsuits. But Cuba's wettest, driest, hottest, oldest and most mountainous province is far more than an anachronistic US Naval Base. Cuba in the modern sense started here in 1511, when Diego Velázquez and his band of colonizers landed uninvited on the rain-lashed eastern coastline. Today it lives on in Baracoa, the city Velázquez founded, one of the country's most isolated settlements and beautifully unique as a consequence.

The province's rugged transport artery is La Farola, one of the seven engineering marvels of modern Cuba, a weaving roller-coaster that travels from the dry cacti-littered southern coast up into the humid Cuchillas de Toa Mountains. Overlaid by the fecund Parque Nacional Alejandro de Humboldt, this heavily protected zone is one of the last few swaths of virgin rainforest left in the Caribbean and guards an incredible array of endemic species.

When to Go

Baracoa's biggest festival is in April when locals hit the streets to celebrate the 1895 landing of Antonio Maceo. The city of Guantánamo gets equally animated in mid-December when it lifts the cloak on its indigenous music in the Festival Nacional de Changüí. Guantánamo's climate varies hugely, but it's dependent more on geography than season. Baracoa is prone to some heavy storms. To avoid the worst of them, don't come during September and October.

Guantánamo Province Highlights

1. Search for the world's smallest frog in **Parque Nacional Alejandro de Humboldt** (p442)
2. Sample the culinary smorgasbord of exotic **Baracoa** (p438)
3. Cycle **La Farola** (p441), the lighthouse road from Cajababo to Baracoa
4. Get an eye-full of the stony statues at the **Zoológico de Piedras** (p433)
5. Hike through the tropical jungle to the top of Baracoa's mysterious flat-topped mountain, **El Yunque** (p440)
6. Uncover the mysteries of *changüí* music during a stopover in the City of **Guantánamo** (p430)
7. Imagine Taíno life pre-Columbus at Baracoa's **Museo Arqueológico 'La Cueva del Paraíso'** (p434)
8. Take a local boat upstream from the **Boca de Yumurí** (p433) through the jaws of a mysterious river gorge.

History

Long before the arrival of the Spanish, the Taíno populated the mountains and forests around Guantánamo forging a living as fishermen, hunters and small-scale farmers. Columbus first arrived in the region in November 1492, a month or so after his initial landfall near Gibara, and planted a small wooden cross in a beautiful bay he ceremoniously christened Porto Santo – after an idyllic island off Portugal where he had enjoyed his honeymoon. The Spanish returned again in 1511 under the auspices of Columbus' son Diego in a flotilla of four ships and 400 men that included the island's first governor Diego Velázquez de Cuéllar. Building a makeshift fort constructed from wood, the conquistadors consecrated the island's first colonial settlement, Villa de Nuestra Señora de la Asunción de Baracoa, and watched helplessly as the town was subjected to repeated attacks from hostile local Indians led by a rebellious *cacique* (chief) known as Hatuey.

Declining in importance after the capital moved to Santiago in 1515, the Guantánamo region became Cuba's Siberia – a mountainous and barely penetrable rural backwater where prisoners were exiled and old traditions survived. In the late 18th century the area was recolonized by French immigrants from Haiti who tamed the difficult terrain in order to cultivate coffee, cotton and sugarcane on the backs of African slaves. Following the Spanish-Cuban-American War, a brand new foe took up residence in Guantánamo Bay – the all-powerful Americans – intent on protecting their economic interests in the strategically important Panama Canal region. Despite repeated bouts of mudslinging in the years since, the not-so-welcome *Yanquis*, as they are popularly known, have repeatedly refused to budge.

Guantánamo

POP 216,834

There's nothing visually remarkable about Guantánamo – which accounts, in part, for its low profile on the tourist 'circuit.' But, amid the ugly grey buildings and hopelessly decaying infrastructure a buoyant culture has been putting up a brave rearguard action. Between them, the feisty *guantanameros* have produced 11 Olympic gold medals, blasted a man into orbit (Cuban cosmonaut, Arnaldo Méndez) and spawned their own unique brand of traditional *son* music known as *son-changüí*. Then there's the small matter of *that* song – 'Guantanamera' (if you've made it this far, you'll have already heard it 25 times).

'Discovered' by Columbus in 1494 and given the once-over by the ever curious British 250 years later, a settlement wasn't built here until 1819, when French plantation owners evicted from Haiti founded the town of Santa Catalina del Saltadero del Guaso between the Jaibo, Bano and Guaso Rivers. In 1843 the burgeoning city changed its name to Guantánamo and in 1903 the bullish US Navy took up residence in the bay next door. The sparks have been flying ever since.

Sights

Ostensibly unexciting, Guantánamo's geometric city grid has a certain rhythm. The tree-lined Av Camilo Cienfuegos with its morning exercisers, bizarre sculptures and central Ramblas-style walkway is the best place to get into the groove.

Palacio Salcines MUSEUM

(cnr Pedro A Pérez & Prado; admission CUC$1; 8am-noon & 2-6pm Mon-Fri) Local architect Leticio Salcines (1888–1973) left a number of impressive works around Guantánamo including his personal residence built in 1916, a triumph of eclecticism and a monument said to be the building most representative of the city. The *palacio* is now a small museum exhibiting colorful frescoes, Japanese porcelain and a rusty old music box that pipes out rather disappointing Mozart. A guided tour (CUC$1) makes the dull exhibits infinitely more interesting. On the palace's turret is **La Fama**, a sculpture designed by Italian artist Americo Chine that serves as the symbol of Guantánamo, her trumpet announcing good and evil.

Museo Municipal MUSEUM

(cnr José Martí & Prado; admission CUC$1; 2-6pm Mon, 8am-noon & 3-7pm Tue-Sat) Though it's no Louvre, this esoteric museum contains some interesting US Naval Base ephemera including prerevolutionary day passes and some revealing photos.

Parque Martí SQUARE

Anchored by its church, Parque Martí has benefited from a substantial facelift in the last couple of years: a lick of paint, some information boards and a handful of interesting new shops and entertainment nooks.

Sitting timelessly amid the action is a seated **statue** of 'El Maestro' from whom the square – like so many others – takes its name.

Parroquia de Santa Catalina de Riccis CHURCH
(Parque Martí) This unspectacular but noble church dates from 1863. In front is a **statue** of local hero, Mayor General Pedro A Pérez, erected in 1928, opposite a tulip fountain and diminutive **glorieta** (bandstand).

Biblioteca Policarpo Pineda Rustán LIBRARY
(cnr Los Maceos & Emilio Giro) Another Salcines creation was this beautiful provincial library which was once the city hall (1934–51). Trials of Fulgencio Batista's thugs were held here in 1959, and a number were killed when they snatched a rifle and tried to escape.

Plaza Mariana Grajales SQUARE
The huge, bombastic **Monument to the Heroes**, glorifying the Brigada Fronteriza 'that defends the forward trench of socialism on this continent,' dominates Plaza Mariana Grajales (opposite the Hotel Guantánamo), one of the more impressive 'Revolution squares' on the island.

Festivals & Events

Noches Guantanameras STREET PARTY
(8pm Sat) Saturday nights are reserved for this local coming together, when Calle Pedro A Pérez is closed to traffic and stalls are set up in the street. Locals enjoy whole roast pig, belting music and copious amounts of rum. Watch out for the *borrachos* (drunks)!

Sleeping

Villa la Lupe HOTEL $
(38-26-12; Carretera de El Salvador Km 3.5; s/d CUC$23/30; P) Located 5km north of the city on the road to El Salvador, Villa la Lupe – named after a song by Moncada and Granma survivor, Juan Almeida – is Guantánamo's best lodging option, despite its out-of-town location. Attractive, spacious cabins are arranged around a clean central swimming pool and the adjacent restaurant, which serves the usual staples of pork and rice, overlooks a leafy river where young girls celebrate their *quinciñeras* (15th birthday). For music geeks the words of Almeida's famous song are emblazoned onto a granite wall.

Lissett Foster Lara CASA PARTICULAR $
(32-59-70; Pedro A Pérez No 761 btwn Prado & Jesús del Sol; r CUC$20-25;) Like many *guantanameras,* Lissett speaks perfect English and her house is polished, comfortable and decked out with the kind of plush fittings that wouldn't be out of place in a North American suburb. The highlight here, in more ways than one, is the roof terrace where you can recline above the car honks and street hassle for an hour or three.

Osmaida Blanco Castillo CASA PARTICULAR $
(32-51-93; Pedro A Pérez No 664 btwn Paseo & Narciso López; r CUC$20-25;) Another well-appointed place with a superb roof terrace (with bar!), two spacious rooms, a shady patio (with fish tank) and excellent meals available (you'll need them in this town). If it's full, try house 670A in the same street.

Hotel Guantánamo HOTEL $
(38-10-15; Calle 13 Norte btwn Ahogados & 2 de Octubre; s/d CUC$23/30; P) A lick of paint, a quick cleanup around the lobby and some newly planted flowers in the garden, and hey presto – the Hotel Guantánamo's back in business after a couple of years serving as a convalescent home for Operación Milagros. It's still a long way from the Ritz, but at least the generic rooms are clean, the pool has water in it, and there's a good reception bar-cafe mixing up tempting mojitos and serving coffee. It's located 1km northwest of the train station.

Eating

Newly pedestrianized Parque Martí has some passable peso restaurants that during the evenings pull their tables out onto the street. At weekends the square is a smorgasbord of mobile food stalls selling cheap fried *comida ligera* (light food).

TOP CHOICE **Restaurante Girasoles** CARIBBEAN $$
(Calle 15 Norte; noon-9.30pm) A nude statue, not a *girasol* (sunflower), marks the entrance to what is, by process of elimination, one of Guantánamo's best restaurants. Housed in a diminutive modern house tucked away behind the Hotel Guantánamo, the Palmares-run Girasoles serves up chicken and fish, occasionally in some interesting sauces. Your *agua con gas* (mineral water) will probably go flat waiting for the meal to emerge from the kitchen, but who cares; for once it's worth the wait.

Bar-Restaurante Olimpia BURGERS $
(cnr Calixto García & Aguilera; 9am-midnight) In part a celebration of Guantánamo's

Guantánamo

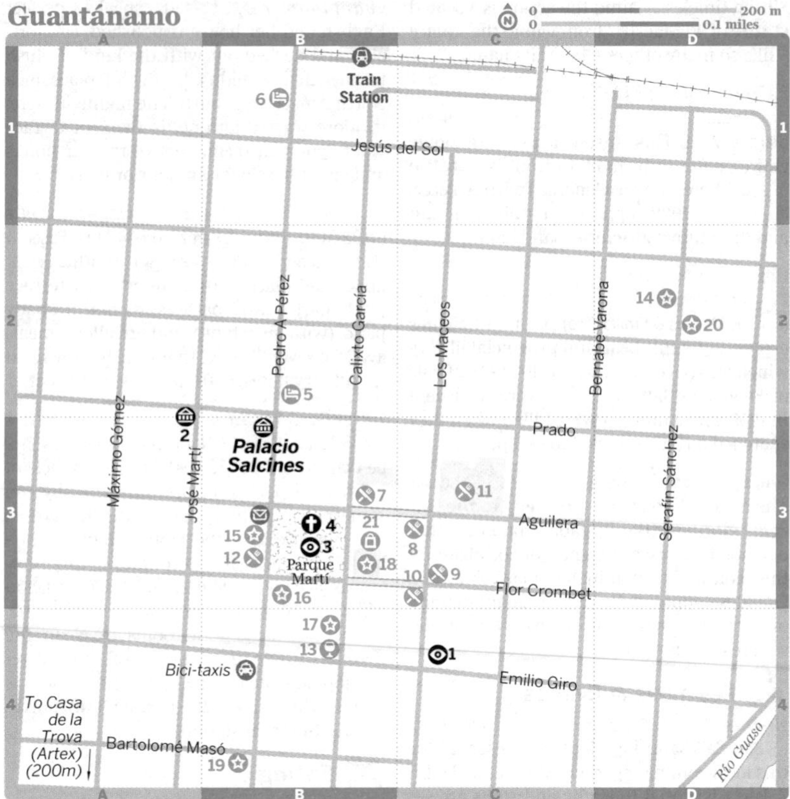

remarkable record in the Olympic Games, this new bar-restaurant displays framed baseball shirts, boxing vests and athletics memorabilia. There are a variety of nooks inside including a small open patio and a mezzanine bar where you can enjoy beers, relatively substantial burgers, and the usual Cuban suspects. The nocturnal essence of adjacent Parque Martí drifts through the open doors.

Dinos Oroazul FAST FOOD $
(cnr Los Maceos & Aguilera) A good place to catch a breather, feel the cool ceiling fan on your face and grab a revitalizing plate of spaghetti cooked a good 10 minutes past al dente. There are cleanish toilets inside.

Restaurante la Criolla CARIBBEAN $
(Pedro A Pérez; ⏲noon-2:30pm & 5-10:30pm) This is a slightly scruffy-looking local peso place situated by the main square, though it could help you jump off the daily cheese sandwich and tortilla treadmill.

El Rápido FAST FOOD $
(cnr Flor Crombet & Los Maceos; ⏲10am-10pm) It's a testament to Guantánamo's dire dining scene that you may have to resort to Cuba's gastronomically challenged fast-food chain with its microwaved cheese sandwiches. Rapid it ain't.

Self-Catering

Plaza del Mercado Agro Industrial MARKET $
(cnr Los Maceos & Prado; ⏲7am-7pm Mon-Sat, 7am-2pm Sun) The town's public vegetable market is a red-domed Leticio Salcines creation and rather striking – both inside and out.

Agropecuario MARKET $
(Calle 13) The city's other outdoor market is opposite Plaza Mariana Grajales, just west

Guantánamo

Top Sights
Palacio Salcines B3

Sights
1 Biblioteca Policarpo Pineda Rustán C4
2 Museo Municipal A2
3 Parque Martí B3
4 Parroquia de Santa Catalina de Riccis B3
Plaza del Mercado Agro Industrial ..... (see 11)

Sleeping
5 Lissett Foster Lara B2
6 Osmaida Blanco Castillo B1

Eating
7 Bar-Restaurante Olimpia B3
8 Dinos Oroazul C3
9 El Rápido C3
10 Panadería la Palmita C3
11 Plaza del Mercado Agro Industrial C3
12 Restaurante la Criolla B3

Drinking
13 La Ruina B4

Entertainment
14 Casa de Changüí D2
15 Casa de la Cultura B3
16 Casa de la Trova (Parque Martí) B3
17 Casa de las Promociones Musicales 'La Guantanamera' B4
18 Cine Huambo B3
19 Club Nevada B4
20 Tumba Francesa Pompadour D2

Shopping
21 Fondo de Bienes Culturales B3

of the Hotel Guantánamo; it sells bananas, yucca and onions by the truckload, plus plenty of peso snacks.

Panadería la Palmita BAKERY $
(Flor Crombet No 305 btwn Calixto García & Los Maceos; ⏲7:30am-5pm Mon-Sat) Welcome fresh bread.

Drinking

Two newly pedestrianized streets – Aguilera and Flor Crombet – leading a block east of Parque Martí are embellished by a handful of lively bars where preened *guantanameros* like to flaunt their fake designer clothing.

La Ruina BAR
(cnr Calixto García & Emilio Giro; ⏲10am-1am) This shell of a ruined colonial building has 9m ceilings and a crusty feet-on-the-table kind of ambience. There are plenty of benches to prop you up after you've downed yet another bottle of beer and a popular karaoke scene for those with reality-TV ambitions. The bar menu's good for a snack lunch.

Entertainment

Guantánamo has its own distinctive musical culture, a subgenre of *son* known as *changüí* (see p430). You can get a taste at the following venues.

TOP CHOICE **Tumba Francesa Pompadour** LIVE MUSIC
(Serafín Sánchez No 715) This peculiarly Guantánamo nightspot situated four blocks east of the train station specializes in a unique form of Haitian-style dancing. Programs (generally listed on the door) include *mi tumba baile* (*tumba* dance), *encuentro tradicional* (traditional get-together) and *peña campesina* (country music).

Casa de la Trova (Parque Martí) LIVE MUSIC
(cnr Pedro Pérez & Flor Crombet; admission CUC$1) The only Cuban city with two *trova* (traditional music) houses, Guantánamo offers options galore. This one of the corner of Parque Martí is the more traditional haunt with *viejos* (old men) in Panama hats casting aside their arthritis to dance athletically.

Casa de la Trova (Artex) LIVE MUSIC
(Máximo Gómez No 1062; admission CUC$1; ⏲8pm-1am Tue-Sun) Housed in a royal-blue building on a quiet urban street, Casa de la Trova Mk 2 is openly referred to as 'the Artex place.' It offers the local blend of traditional sounds with a *son-changüí* bias.

Casa de las Promociones Musicales 'La Guantanamera' NIGHTCLUB
(Calixto García btwn Flor Crombet & Emilio Giro) Another well-maintained concert-orientated venue, with Thursday rap *peñas* (performances)

CHANGÜÍ

Before you write off Guantánamo as a glorified bus stop between Santiago and Baracoa, lend an ear to the syncopated strains of *changüí*, the city's native music genre that predates Cuban *son* and is widely considered to be the first authentic melding of African drums and Spanish guitars in a Caribbean setting.

Changüí's origins are sketchy and complex. Its roots lie in the fusion of two antiquated musical rites known as *nengon* and *kiribá* both concocted in the mountains of the Oriente during the late 19th century. The former was the staple of black sugar workers living in the vicinity of Guantánamo City; the latter was a product of the Baracoa region where it had absorbed myriad French slave and indigenous Taíno influences. Both *nengon* and *kiribá* were highly percussive sounds that used simple instrumentation (sometimes a tree stump was hit to keep rhythm). But, as the music became more complex and syncopated, incorporating guitars and melodies, it split into two new genres. Pure *nengon* played in Santiago de Cuba province developed into *son*, while *nengon* mixed with *kiribá* in Guantánamo province evolved into what is today known as *changüí*.

Definitive *changüí* music is nearly always played by a four-piece band consisting of bongos, *tres* (guitar), *güiro* and *marimbula* overlaid by a vocalist. Rhythmically, it is more syncopated and layered than *son*, lacking the distinctive son *clave* (beat), which instead is provided by the *tres*. In the early 20th century when *son* was 'dressed up' and taken to Havana where it metamorphosed into salsa, *changüí* stayed close to home finding its most famous exponent in local *guantanamero*, Elio Revé whose Orquestra Revé nurtured the likes of jazz giant, Chucho Valdés and salsa-songo-king Juan Formell (of Los Van Van). As a result *changüí* is considered to be a much purer musical style than *son* that has remained true to its Oriente roots.

and Sunday *trova* matinees, this casa is perhaps the town's most revered music house.

Estadio Van Troi SPORTS
Baseball games are played from October to April at this stadium in Reparto San Justo, 1.5km south of the Servi-Cupet gas station. Despite a strong sporting tradition, Guantánamo – nicknamed Los Indios – are perennial underachievers who haven't made the play-offs since 1999.

FREE **Casa de la Cultura** CULTURAL CENTER
(Pedro A Pérez) In the former Casino Español, on the west side of Parque Martí, this venue holds classical concerts and Afro-Cuban dance performances.

Club Nevada NIGHTCLUB
(Pedro A Pérez No 1008 Altos cnr Bartolomé Masó; admission CUC$1) For the city's funkiest disco, head to this tiled-terrace rooftop, which blasts out salsa mixed with disco standards.

Casa de Changüí LIVE MUSIC
(Serafín Sánchez No 710 btwn N López & Jesús del Sol) As the primary pulpit for Guantánamo's indigenous music, this is *the* place to experience *changüí* and a shrine to its main exponent, local *timbalero* (percussionist), Elio Revé.

Cine Huambo CINEMA
(Parque Martí) Revamped cinema in the heart of the Parque Martí action exhibiting everything from Spielberg to Almodóvar.

Shopping

Fondo de Bienes Culturales SOUVENIRS
(1st fl, Calixto García No 855) No one comes to Guantánamo to shop but, if you want a local souvenir that doesn't have a US flag emblazoned on it, try this place on the east side of Parque Martí.

Information

Banco de Crédito y Comercio (Calixto García btwn Emilio Giro & Bartolomé Masó)

Cadeca (cnr Calixto García & Prado) Money changing.

Clínica Internacional (Flor Crombet No 305 btwn Calixto García & Los Maceos; 9am-5pm) On the northeast corner of Parque Martí.

Etecsa Telepunto (cnr Aguilera & Los Maceos; per hr CUC$6; 8:30am-7:30pm) Four computers plus hardly any tourists equals no queues.

Havanatur (Aguilera btwn Calixto García & Los Maceos; 9am-noon & 1-4pm Mon-Fri) Travel agency.

Hospital Agostinho Neto (35-54-50; Carretera de El Salvador Km 1; 24hr) At the west end of Plaza Mariana Grajales near Hotel Guantánamo. It will help foreigners in an emergency.

Oficina de Monumentos y Sitios Históricos (Los Maceos btwn Emilio Giro & Flor Crombet) For a fuller exposé of Guantánamo's interesting architectural heritage you might want to stop by here and ask about a map of city walking trails.

Post office (Pedro A Pérez; 8am-1pm & 2-6pm Mon-Sat) On the west side of Parque Martí. There's also a DHL office here.

Radio Trinchera Antimperialista CMKS Trumpets the word over 1070AM.

Venceremos & Lomería Two local newspapers published on Saturday.

 Getting There & Away

Air

Cubana (Calixto García No 817) flies five times a week (CUC$124 one-way, 2½ hours) from Havana to **Mariana Grajales Airport**. There are no international flights to this airport.

Bus

The rather inconveniently placed Terminal de Ómnibus (bus station) is 5km west of the center on the old road to Santiago (a continuation of Av Camilo Cienfuegos). A taxi from the Hotel Guantánamo should cost CUC$3.

There are daily **Víazul** (www.viazul.com) buses to Baracoa (CUC$10, 9:30am) and Santiago de Cuba (CUC$6, 5:25pm).

Car

The Autopista Nacional to Santiago de Cuba ends near Embalse la Yaya, 25km west of Guantánamo, where the road joins the Carretera Central (at the time of writing work had begun to extend this road). At El Cristo, 12km outside Santiago de Cuba, you rejoin the Autopista. To drive to Guantánamo from Santiago de Cuba, follow the Autopista Nacional north about 12km to the top of the grade, then take the first turn to the right. Signposts are sporadic and vague, so take a good map and keep alert.

Train

The **train station** (Pedro A Pérez), several blocks north of Parque Martí, has one departure for Havana (CUC$32, 11.40pm) every third day. This train also stops at Camagüey (CUC$13), Ciego de Ávila (CUC$16), Guayos (CUC$20; you should disembark here for Sancti Spíritus), Santa Clara (CUC$22) and Matanzas (CUC$29). There was no service to Santiago de Cuba at the time of writing. Purchase tickets in the morning of the day the train departs at the office on Pedro A Pérez.

Truck

Trucks to Santiago de Cuba and Baracoa leave from the Terminal de Ómnibus. These will allow you to disembark in the smaller towns in between.

Trucks for Moa park on the road to El Salvador north of town near the entrance to the Autopista.

 Getting Around

Havanautos (Cupet Guantánamo) is by the Servi-Cupet gas station on the way out of town toward Baracoa. If you couldn't get a car in Santiago, you should be able to pick one up here.

The **Oro Negro gas station** (cnr Los Maceos & Jesús del Sol) is another option to fill up on gas before the 150km trek east to Baracoa.

Taxis hang out around Parque Martí or you can call **CubaTaxi** (32-36-36). The bus 48 (20 centavos) runs between the center and the Hotel Guantánamo every 40 minutes or so. There are also plenty of bici-taxis.

Around Guantánamo US Naval Base

MIRADOR DE MALONES

Traditionally, it has been possible to enjoy a distant view of the base from the isolated Mirador de Malones, a Gaviota-run restaurant perched on a 320m-high hill just east of the complex. At the time of writing, visits here had been suspended indefinitely. Check the current status beforehand at Hotel Guantánamo (p427) or one of the Gaviota-run hotels in Baracoa (p436).

Should you get lucky, the entrance to the *mirador* (lookout) is at a Cuban military checkpoint on the main Baracoa highway, 27km southeast of Guantánamo.

CAIMANERA

Contrary to popular belief, Caimanera not Guantánamo, is the nearest Cuban town to the American Naval Base. Situated on the west shore of Guantánamo Bay just north of the US military checkpoint, this seaport/fishing settlement of 10,000 people (many of them first or second generation Jamaicans) was a boomtown before the revolution when local workers were employed in the naval station. According to old-timers, the most popular profession was prostitution. Since 1959, Caimanera has struggled economically. A sole hotel (p432) acted as a lookout spot for curious 'Bay-watchers' before the era of Bush Jnr and Camp Delta. It reopened for pre-organized visits in 2009.

GITMO – A SHORT HISTORY

Procured via the infamous Platt Amendment in 1903 in the aftermath of the Spanish-American War, the US' initial reason for annexing Guantánamo Bay (or Gitmo, as generations of homesick US marines have unsentimentally dubbed it) was primarily to protect the eastern approach to the strategically important Panama Canal.

In 1934 an upgrade of the original treaty reaffirmed the lease terms and agreed to honor them indefinitely unless both governments accorded otherwise. It also set an annual rent of approximately US$4000, a sum that the US generously continues to cough up but which the Cubans defiantly won't bank on the grounds that the occupation is illegal (Castro allegedly stored the checks in the top drawer of his office desk).

Until 1958, when motorized traffic was officially cut off between Guantánamo and the outside world, hundreds of Cubans used to travel daily into the base for work, and there were still a handful of workers making the commute up until the turn of the 21st century. Expanded post-WWII, the oldest US military base on foreign soil has gone through many metamorphoses in the last 50 years, from tense Cold War battleground to the most virulent surviving political anachronism in the Western hemisphere.

Castro was quick to demand the unconditional return of Guantánamo to Cuban sovereignty in 1959 but, locked in a Cold War deadlock with the Soviet Union and fearing the Cuban leader's imminent flight to Moscow, the US steadfastly refused. As relations between the countries deteriorated, Cuba cut off water and electricity to the base while the Americans surrounded it with the biggest minefield in the Western hemisphere (the mines were removed in 1996).

The recent history of the facility has been equally notorious. In January 1992, 11,000 Haitian migrants were temporarily held here, and in August 1994 the base was used as a dumping ground for 32,000 Cubans picked up by the US Coast Guard while trying to reach Florida. In May 1995 the Cuban and US governments signed an agreement allowing these refugees to enter the US but, since then, illegal Cuban immigrants picked up by the US Coast Guard at sea have been returned to Cuba under the 'wet foot, dry foot' policy.

Since 2002 the US has held more than 750 prisoners with suspected Al-Qaeda or Taliban links at the infamous Camp Delta in Guantánamo Bay without pressing criminal charges. Denied legal counsel and family contact while facing rigorous interrogations, the detainees mounted hunger strikes and at least four are known to have committed suicide. Following calls from Amnesty International and the UN in 2004 to close the base down and reports from the Red Cross that certain aspects of the camp regime were tantamount to torture, the US released 420 prisoners and charged just three of them. Of the remaining 170 or so prisoners (as of early 2011), the US government intended to repatriate some to other countries for rehab or release, and transfer the rest to prisons in the US.

On taking office in January 2009, President Barack Obama promised to shut down Guantánamo's detention camps and thus end what he termed 'a sad chapter in US history.' However, due to bipartisan opposition in Congress, Obama failed to meet his one year deadline on this issue. At the time of research it was still unclear how and when the closure would be completed.

To the west of Caimanera the dry cacti-covered hills are characterized by **Monitongos**, rocky wind-eroded plateaus redolent of a desert landscape. The region has a high level of endemism and is protected as a fauna reserve. There are trails here, but you'll need to be on an organized trip to access them.

Sleeping

Hotel Caimanera HOTEL $

(☎49-94-14; s/d incl breakfast CUC$23/30; P❄≋) This oddly attractive (considering its position) hotel is on a hilltop at Caimanera, near the perimeter of the US Naval Base, 21km south of Guantánamo. It has peculiar rules which permit only groups of seven or more on prearranged tours with an official

Cuban guide to stay and enjoy the lookout. Ask at the Havanatur office (p430) in Guantánamo about joining a trip.

Getting There & Away

Caimanera is the eastern terminus of the Cuban railway network (which doesn't extend to Baracoa). There are supposedly four trains a day to Guantánamo City.

South Coast

Leaving Guantánamo in a cloud of dust, you quickly hit the long, dry coastal road to the island's eastern extremity, Punta de Maisí. This is Cuba's spectacular semi-desert region where cacti nestle on rocky ocean terraces and prickly aloe vera poke out from the dry scrub. Several little stone beaches between Playa Yacabo and Cajobabo make refreshing pit stops for those with time to linger, while the diverse roadside scenery – punctuated at intervals by rugged purple mountains and impossibly verdant riverside oases – impresses throughout.

Playita de Cajobabo BEACH

At the far end of this usually deserted beach, just before the main road bends inland, there is a **monument** commemorating José Martí's 1895 landing here to launch the Second War of Independence. A colorful billboard depicts the bobbing rowboat making for shore with Martí sitting calmly inside, dressed rather improbably in trademark dinner suit, not a hair out of place. It's a good snorkeling spot, flanked by dramatic cliffs. The famous **La Farola** (the lighthouse road) starts here (see p441). Cyclists, take a deep breath...

Sleeping

Campismo Yacabo CABINS $

(s/d CUC$7.5/11) This place, by the highway 10km west of Imías, has 18 well-maintained cabins overlooking the sea near the mouth of the river. The cabins sleep four to six people and make a great beach getaway for groups on a budget. It's supposed to accept foreigners, but check ahead.

Cabañas Playa Imías CABINS $

(1-2 people CUC$10; ❄) This place, 2km east of Imías midway between Guantánamo and Baracoa, is near a long dark beach that drops off quickly into deep water. The 15 cement cabins have baths, fridges and TVs. It doesn't guarantee foreign admission but, as ever in Cuba, the rules are flexible.

WORTH A TRIP

ZOOLÓGICO DE PIEDRAS

A surreal spectacle even by Cuban standards, the **Zoológico de Piedras** (admission CUC$1; ⏲9am-6pm Mon-Sat) is an animal sculpture park set amid thick foliage in the grounds of a mountain coffee farm, 20km northeast of Guantánamo. Carved quite literally out of the existing rock by sculptor Angel Iñigo Blanco starting in the late '70s, the animal sculptures now number more than 300 and range from hippos to giant serpents. A 1km path covers the highlights. To get here you'll need your own wheels or a taxi. Head east out of town and fork left toward Jamaica and Honduras. The 'zoo' is in the settlement of Boquerón.

Punta de Maisí

From Cajobabo, the coastal road continues 51km northeast to La Máquina. As far as Jauco, the road is good; thereafter it's not so good. Coming from Baracoa to La Máquina (55km), it's a good road as far as Sabana, then rough in places from Sabana to La Máquina. Either way, La Máquina is the starting point of the very rough 13km track down to Punta de Maisí; it's best covered in a 4WD.

This is Cuba's easternmost point and there's a **lighthouse** (1862) and a small fine white-sand beach. You can see Haiti 70km away on a clear day.

At the time of writing the Maisí area was designated a military zone and not open to travelers.

Boca de Yumurí

Five kilometers south of Baracoa a road branches left off La Farola and travels 28km along the coast to Boca de Yumurí at the mouth of Río Yumurí. Near the bridge over the river is the **Túnel de los Alemanes** (German Tunnel), an amazing natural arch of trees and foliage. Though lovely, the dark-sand beach here has become *the* day trip from Baracoa. Hustlers hard-sell fried fish meals, while other people peddle colorful land snails called *polymitas*. They have become rare as a result of being harvested wholesale for tourists, so refuse all offers. From the end of the beach a boat taxi (CUC$2) heads upstream to where the steep river banks narrow into a haunting natural gorge.

Boca de Yumurí makes a superb bike jaunt from Baracoa (56km round-trip): hot, but smooth and flat with great views and many potential stopovers (try Playa Bariguá at Km 25). You can arrange bikes in Baracoa – ask at your casa particular. Taxis will also take you here from Baracoa, or you can organize an excursion with Cubatur (CUC$22; see p439).

Playa Cajuajo BEACH

Halfway between Baracoa and Boca de Yumurí is this little-visited sandy beach close to the Bahía de Mata. Ecotur (p439) in Baracoa runs hiking trips here. The 5km trail runs from the Río Mata through biologically diverse woodland to the bay and, ultimately, the beach.

Baracoa

POP 42,285

Take a pinch of Tolkien, a dash of Gabriel García Márquez, mix in a large cup of 1960s psychedelia and temper with a tranquilizing dose of Cold War–era socialism. Leave to stand for 400 years in a geographically isolated tropical wilderness with little or no contact with the outside world. The result: Baracoa – Cuba's weirdest, wildest, zaniest and most unique settlement that materializes like a surreal apparition after the long dry plod along Guantánamo's southern coast.

Cut off by land and sea for nearly half a millennium, Cuba's oldest city is, for most visitors, one of its most interesting. Founded in 1511 by Diego Velázquez de Cuéllar, Baracoa is a visceral place of fickle weather and haunting legends. After being semi-abandoned in the mid-16th century, the town became a Cuban Siberia where rebellious revolutionaries were sent as prisoners. In the early 19th century French planters crossed the 70km-wide Windward Passage from Haiti and began farming the local staples of coconut, cocoa and coffee in the mountains and the economic wheels began to turn.

Baracoa developed in relative isolation from the rest of Cuba until the opening of La Farola in 1964, a factor that has strongly influenced its singular culture and traditions. Today its premier attractions include trekking up mysterious El Yunque, the region's signature flat-topped mountain, or indulging in some inspired local cooking using ingredients and flavors found nowhere else in Cuba.

Sights & Activities

IN TOWN

TOP CHOICE Museo Arqueológico 'La Cueva del Paraíso' MUSEUM

(Moncada; admission CUC$3; 8am-5pm) Baracoa's newest and most impressive museum is situated in Las Cuevas del Paraíso 800m southeast of the Hotel El Castillo. The exhibits here are showcased in a series of caves that once acted as Taíno burial chambers. Among nearly 2000 authentic Taíno pieces are unearthed skeletons, ceramics, 3000-year-old petroglyphs and a replica of the *Ídolo de Tabaco*, a sculpture found in Maisí in 1903 that is considered to be one of the most important Taíno finds in the Caribbean. One of the staff will enthusiastically show you around.

Fuerte Matachín FORT, MUSEUM

(cnr José Martí & Malecón; admission CUC$1; 8am-noon & 2-6pm) Baracoa is protected by a trio of muscular Spanish forts. This one built in 1802 at the southern entrance to town, now houses the **Museo Municipal**. Though small, this museum showcases an engaging chronology of Cuba's oldest settlement including *polymita* snail shells, the story of Che Guevara and the chocolate factory, and exhibits relating to pouty Magdalena Menasse (née Rovieskuya, 'La Rusa') after whom Alejo Carpentier based his famous book, *La Consagración de la Primavera* (The Rite of Spring).

Catedral de Nuestra Señora de la Asunción CHURCH

(Antonio Maceo No 152) Crying out for a major renovation, this rapidly disintegrating church was constructed in 1833 on the site of a much older ecclesial building. Its most famous artifact is the priceless **Cruz de la Parra**, a wooden cross said to have been erected by Columbus near Baracoa in 1492. Carbon dating has authenticated the cross' age (it dates from the late 1400s), but has indicated that it was originally made out of indigenous Cuban wood, thus disproving the legend that Columbus brought the cross from Europe. The church was closed at the time of writing and the cross was being displayed in the last house on Calle Antonio Maceo, behind the church to the right.

Baracoa

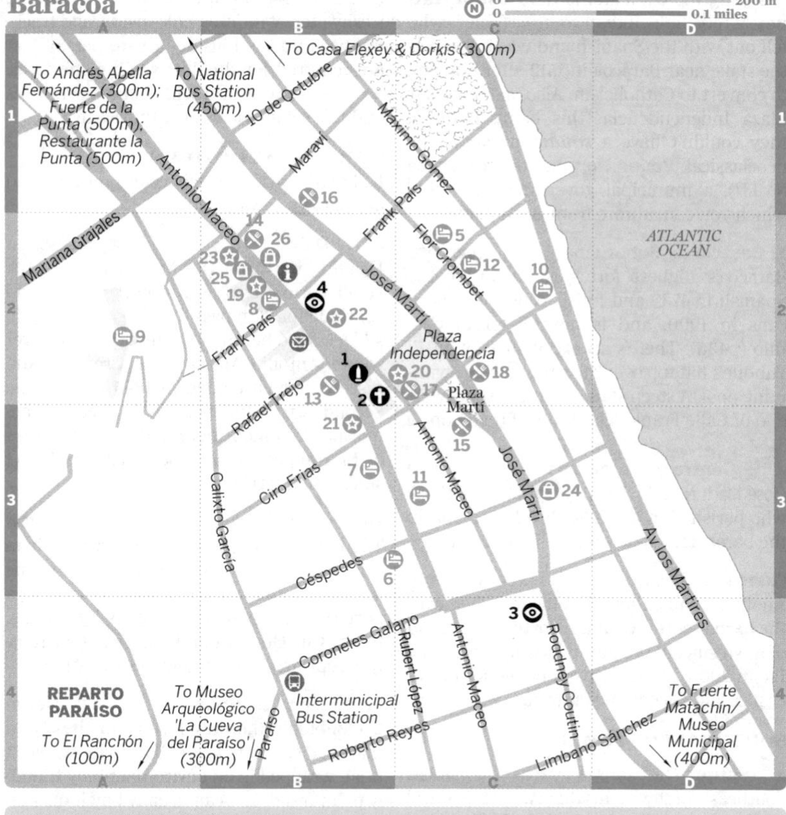

Baracoa

Sights

1 Bust of Hatuey B2
2 Catedral de Nuestra Señora de la Asunción B2
3 Centro de Veteranos C4
El Castillo de Seboruco .... (see 9)
4 Poder Popular B2

Sleeping

5 Casa Colonial – Gustavo & Yalina C2
6 Casa Colonial Lucy B3
7 Casa Colonial Ykira Mahiquez B3
8 Hostal la Habernera B2
9 Hotel El Castillo A2
10 Hotel la Rusa C2
11 Nelsy Borges Teran C3
12 Nilson Abad Guilaré C2

Eating

13 Cafetería el Parque B2
14 Casa del Chocolate B2
15 Dulcería la Criolla C3
16 Paladar el Colonial B1
17 Pizzería Baracoesa C2
18 Tienda la Primada C2

Entertainment

19 Casa de la Cultura B2
20 Casa de la Trova Victorino Rodríguez C2
21 Cine-Teatro Encanto B3
22 Disco Karaoke B2
23 La Terraza B2

Shopping

24 ARTex C3
25 Fondo Cubano de Bienes Culturales B2
26 Taller la Musa B2

Facing the cathedral is the **Bust of Hatuey**, a rebellious Indian *cacique* (chief) who fell out with the Spanish and was burned at the stake near Baracoa in 1512 after refusing to convert to Catholicism. Also on triangular Plaza Independencia (this being Baracoa, they couldn't have a *square* plaza) is the neoclassical Poder Popular (Antonio Maceo No 137), a municipal government building which you can admire from the outside.

El Castillo de Seboruco FORT, HOTEL

Baracoa's highest fort was begun by the Spanish in 1739 and finished by the Americans in 1900, and is now Hotel El Castillo (p436). There's an excellent view of El Yunque's flat top over the shimmering swimming pool. A steep stairway at the southwest end of Calle Frank País climbs directly up.

FREE **Centro de Veteranos** MUSEUM

(José Martí No 216) Displays photos of those who perished in the 1959 Revolution and in the barely talked-about conflict in Angola.

Fuerte de la Punta FORT, RESTAURANT

Another Spanish fort that has watched over the harbor entrance at the northwestern end of town since 1803. Pummeled by Hurricane Ike in 2008, it's recently reopened as a rather pleasant Gaviota restaurant.

SOUTHEAST OF TOWN

Parque Natural Majayara HIKING

Southeast of town in the Parque Natural Majayara are a couple of magical **hikes** that can only be done on foot. Passing the Fuerte Matachín, hike southeast past the baseball stadium and along the dark-sand beach for about 20 minutes to a rickety wooden bridge over the Río Miel. After crossing the bridge turn left, and follow a track up through a cluster of rustic houses to another junction. A guard-post here is sometimes staffed by a park official who will collect CUC$1. Turn left again and continue along the vehicle track until the houses clear and you see a fainter single-track path leading off left to Playa Blanca, an idyllic spot for a picnic.

Staying straight on the track, you'll come to a trio of wooden homesteads. The third of these houses belongs to the Fuentes family. Do not continue alone past this point as you are entering a military zone. For a donation (CUC$3 to CUC$5 per person), Señor Fuentes will lead you on a hike to his family finca, where you can stop for coffee, coconuts and tropical fruit. Further on he'll show you the Cueva de Aguas, a cave with a sparkling, freshwater swimming hole inside, and tracking back up the hillside (a sure pair of feet are required for this bit) you'll come to an archaeological trail with some more caves and marvelous views over the ocean.

NORTHWEST OF TOWN

Follow the aroma of chocolate on the road out of town toward Moa.

Playa Duaba BEACH, MONUMENT

Heading north on the Moa road, take the Hotel Porto Santo and airport turnoff and continue for 2km past the airport runway to a black-sand beach at the mouth of the river where Antonio Maceo, Flor Crombet and a score of men landed in 1895 to start the Second War of Independence. There's a memorial monument here and close-up views of El Yunque, though the beach itself isn't sunbathing territory.

Fábrica de Chocolate FACTORY

The delicious sweet smells filling the air in this neck of the woods are concocted in the famous chocolate factory, 1km past the airport turnoff opened, not by Willy Wonka, but by Che Guevara in 1963. It's not currently accepting visits (or golden tickets!).

Fábrica de Cucuruchu FACTORY

Undoubtedly the only factory in the world that makes *cucurucho*, Baracoa's sweetest treat, wrapped in an environmentally friendly palm frond. You can usually buy it on-site.

Tours

Organized tours are a good way to view Baracoa's hard-to-reach outlying sights, and the Cubatur and Ecotur offices (p439) on Plaza Independencia can book most of them. Highlights include: El Yunque (CUC$18), Playa Maguana (CUC$18), Parque Nacional Alejandro de Humboldt (CUC$28), Río Toa (CUC$11) and Boca de Yumurí (CUC$22).

Sleeping

TOP CHOICE **Hotel El Castillo** HOTEL $$

(☎64-51-64; Loma del Paraíso; s/d CUC$44/60; ❄🏊) You could recline like a colonial-era conquistador in this historic place housed in the hilltop Castillo de Seboruco, except that conquistadors didn't have access to swimming pools, satellite TV or a room maid who folds towels into ships, swans and other advanced forms of origami. This fine Gaviota-run hotel has just added 28 rooms in a new cleverly-integrated block, an addition that adds kudos to the jaw-dropping El Yunque views and all-pervading Baracoan friendliness.

Hostal la Habanera HOTEL $
(☎64-52-73; Antonio Maceo No 126; s/d CUC$35/40; ❄) Atmospheric and inviting in a way only Baracoa can muster, La Habanera sits in a restored pastel-pink colonial mansion where the cries of passing street hawkers compete with an effusive mix of hip-gyrating music emanating from the Casa de la Cultura next door. The four front bedrooms share a street-facing balcony replete with tiled floor and rocking chairs, while the downstairs lobby boasts a bar, a restaurant, and an interesting selection of local books.

Nilson Abad Guilaré CASA PARTICULAR $
(☎64-31-23; abadcub@gmail.com; Flor Crombet No 143 btwn Ciro Frías & Pelayo Cuervo; r CUC$25; ❄) Nilson's a real gent who keeps what must be one of the cleanest houses in Cuba. This fantastic self-contained apartment has a huge bathroom, kitchen access and roof terrace with sea views. Nilson has also recently opened his house as a paladar called La Terraza. The fish dinners with coconut sauce are to die for.

Casa Colonial – Gustavo & Yalina CASA PARTICULAR $
(☎64-25-36; Flor Crombet No 125 btwn Frank País & Pelayo Cuervo; r CUC$15-20; ❄) This grand house was built in 1898 by a French sugar baron from Marseille, an esteemed ancestor of the current residents. The big rooms lack natural light but have antique furnishings, and culinary treats include local freshwater prawns and hot (Baracoan) chocolate for breakfast.

Hotel Porto Santo HOTEL $$
(☎64-51-06; Carretera del Aeropuerto; s/d CUC$44/60; P❄≋) On the bay where Columbus, allegedly, planted his first cross, this well-integrated low-rise hotel has the feel of a small resort. Situated 4km from the town center and 200m from the airport, there are 36 more-than-adequate rooms all within earshot of the sea. Lie awake with the windows open and let the ethereal essence of Baracoa transport you. A steep stairway leads down to a tiny, wave-lashed beach.

Casa Colonial Lucy CASA PARTICULAR $
(☎64-35-48; Céspedes No 29 btwn Rubert López & Antonio Maceo; r CUC$20; ❄) A perennial favorite, Casa Lucy – which dates from 1840 – has a lovely local character with patios, porches and flowering begonias. There are two rooms as well as terraces here on different levels and the atmosphere is quiet and secluded. Lucy's son is trilingual and offers salsa lessons and massage.

Casa Colonial Ykira Mahiquez CASA PARTICULAR $
(☎64-38-81; Antonio Maceo No 168A btwn Ciro Frías & Céspedes; r CUC$20; ❄) Welcoming and hospitable, Ykira is Baracoa's hostess with the mostess and serves a mean dinner made with homegrown herbs. Her cozy house is one block from the cathedral and has a full terrace and *mirador* with sea views.

Nelsy Borges Teran CASA PARTICULAR $
(☎64-35-69; Antonio Maceo No 171 btwn Ciro Frías & Céspedes; r CUC$20; ❄) The food is better than the room – and the room ain't half bad. You'll have no culinary worries at Nelsy's with plenty of vegetarian options and adventurous desserts. The rooms have TV and stocked fridge (including chocolate) and there's a great terrace upstairs with rocking chairs overlooking the street.

Hotel la Rusa HOTEL $
(☎64-30-11; Máximo Gómez No 161; s/d CUC$25/30; ❄) Khrushchev wasn't the first Russian to hedge his bets with Fidel Castro. Long before the Bay of Pigs sent the Cubans running into the arms of the Soviets, Russian émigré Magdalena Rovieskuya was posting aid to Castro's rebels up in the Sierra Maestra. Rovieskuya – known affectionately as 'La Rusa' – first came to Baracoa in the 1930s where she built a 12-room hotel and quickly became a local celebrity receiving such esteemed guests as Errol Flynn, Che Guevara and Fidel Castro. After her death in 1978, La Rusa became a more modest government-run joint that was all but washed away in 2008's Hurricane Ike. Right on the seafront it continues to fight the paint-peeling effects of the salty ocean air.

Andrés Abella Fernánadez CASA PARTICULAR $
(☎64-32-98; Maceo No 56; r CUC$20-25; ❄) Comfort reigns in Andrés' proud home, with two large clean-as-a-whistle rooms and a lovely intimate patio (unusual in Baracoa) with relaxing rockers.

Casa Elexey & Dorkis CASA PARTICULAR $
(☎64-34-51; Flor Crombet No 58 Altos; r CUC$20-25; ❄) Upstairs at Elexey and Dorkis' place you'll find a clean nicely furnished room

BARACOAN CUISINE

Unlike Italy or France, Cuba doesn't really have a *regional* cuisine, at least not until you arrive in Baracoa where everything, including the food, is different. Home to the country's most fickle weather, Baracoa has used its wet microclimate and geographic isolation to jazz up notoriously unambitious Cuban cuisine with spices, sugar, exotic fruits and coconuts. Fish anchors most menus yet even the seafood can pull out some surprises. Count on tasting freshwater prawns the size of mini-lobsters or tiny tadpole-like *teti* fish drawn from the Río Toa between July to January during a waning moon.

The biggest taste explosion is a locally concocted coconut sauce known as *lechita*, a mixture of coconut milk, tomato sauce, garlic and a medley of spices best served over prawns, *aguja* (swordfish) or dorado. Other main course accompaniments include *bacán*, raw green plantain melded with crabmeat and wrapped in a banana leaf; or *frangollo*, a similar concoction but where the ground bananas are mixed with sugar.

Sweets are another Baracoa tour de force thanks largely to the ubiquity of the cocoa plant and the presence of the famous Che Guevara chocolate factory. Baracoan chocolate is sold all over the island though you're more likely to get it for breakfast in your casa particular, stirred into a local hot-chocolate drink known as *chorote*. Baracoa's most unique culinary invention is undoubtedly *cucurucho*, a delicate mix of dried coconut, sugar, honey, papaya, guayaba, mandarin and nuts (no concoction is ever quite alike) that is wrapped in an ecologically friendly palm frond. There's a *cucurucho* factory on the coast road to Moa just past the chocolate factory (p436) but, by popular consensus, the best stuff is sold by the *campesinos* on La Farola coming into town from Guantánamo.

flooded with natural light. There's a pleasant terrace with Atlantic views – ideal for a couple of days of lazy relaxation.

Eating

After the dull monotony of just about everywhere else, eating in Baracoa is a full-on sensory experience. Cooking here is creative, tasty and – above all – different. To experience the real deal, eat in your casa particular.

TOP CHOICE Restaurante la Punta CARIBBEAN $$
(Fuerte de la Punta; ⏲10am-11pm) At last! The La Punta fort gets a facelift and Baracoa gets a decent government-run restaurant befitting a city that broadcasts its own distinctive cuisine. Cooled by Atlantic breezes, the Gaviota-run La Punta aims to impress with well-prepared, garnished food in lovely historical surroundings. Try the chicken and go on a Saturday night when there's accompanying music.

Paladar el Colonial PALADAR $$
(José Martí No 123; mains CUC$10; ⏲lunch & dinner) The town's only surviving paladar has been knocking out good food for years with an exotic Baracoan twist. Still run out of a handsome wooden clapboard house on Calle José Martí, the menu has become a bit more limited in recent times (less octopus and more chicken), though you still get the down-to-earth service and the delicious coconut sauce.

Casa del Chocolate CHOCOLATERY $
(Antonio Maceo No 123; ⏲7:20am-11pm) It's enough to make even Willy Wonka wonder. You're sitting next to a chocolate factory but, more often than not, there's none to be had in this bizarre little casa just off the main square. The quickest way to check out Baracoa's on-off supply situation is to stick your head around the door and question one of the bored-looking waitresses. *No hay* equals 'no,' a faint nod equals 'yes.' On a good day it sells chocolate ice cream and the hot stuff in mugs. For all its foibles, it's a Baracoa rite of passage.

Cafetería el Parque FAST FOOD $
(Antonio Maceo No 142; ⏲24hr) This open terrace gets regularly drenched in those familiar Baracoa rain showers, but that doesn't seem to detract from its popularity. The favored meeting place of just about everyone in town, you're bound to end up here at some point tucking into spaghetti and pizza as you watch the world go by.

Pizzería Baracoesa PIZZA $
(Antonio Maceo No 155) A recent renovation (ie new tablecloths) have upped the ante a little at this peso place, but it's still got a long way to go to tempt you out of your casa particular.

Self-Catering

Tienda la Primada SUPERMARKET $
(Plaza Martí cnr Ciro Frías; ⏲8:30am-4:30pm Mon-Sat, 8:30am-noon Sun) Get in line for the good selection of groceries here.

Dulcerito la Criolla BAKERY $
(José Martí No 178) This place sells bread, pastries and – when it feels like it – the famous Baracoan chocolate.

☆ Entertainment

TOP CHOICE **Casa de la Trova Victorino Rodríguez** TRADITIONAL MUSIC
(Antonio Maceo No 149A) Cuba's smallest, zaniest, wildest and most atmospheric *casa de la trova* (*trova* house) rocks nightly to the voodoo-like rhythms of *changüí-son*. Order a mojito in a jam jar and sit back and enjoy the show.

El Ranchón NIGHTCLUB
(admission CUC$1; ⏲from 9pm) Atop a long flight of stairs at the western end of Coroneles Galano, El Ranchón mixes an exhilarating hilltop setting with taped disco and salsa music and legions of resident *jineteras* (women who attach themselves to male foreigners). Maybe that's why it's so insanely popular. Watch your step on the way down – it's a scary 146-step drunken tumble.

Casa de la Cultura CULTURAL CENTER
(Antonio Maceo No 124 btwn Frank País & Maraví) This venue does a wide variety of shows including some good rumba incorporating the textbook Cuban styles of *guaguancó, yambú* and *columbia* (subgenres of rumba). Go prepared for *mucho* audience participation.

Estadio Manuel Fuentes Borges SPORTS
From October to April, baseball games are held at this stadium situated, literally, on the beach and quite possibly the only ground in Cuba where players come into bat with the taste of fresh sea spray on their lips. It's just southeast of the Museo Municipal.

La Terraza CABARET
(Antonio Maceo btwn Maraví & Frank País; admission CUC$1; ⏲9pm-2am Mon-Thu, 9pm-4am Fri-Sun) A casual rooftop cabaret/variety show that kicks off most nights at 11pm; expect rumba, Benny Moré, and the local hairdresser singing Omara Portuondo.

Cine-Teatro Encanto CINEMA
(Antonio Maceo No 148) The town's only cinema is in front of the cathedral. It looks disused but you'll probably find it's open.

Disco Karaoke NIGHTCLUB
(Antonio Maceo No 141; ⏲6pm-2am) More a packed, throbbing disco than a karaoke joint (thank heavens!), this place is notable for its strict 'no smoking' policy – almost unheard of in Cuba.

Shopping

Good art is easy to find in Baracoa and, like most things in this whimsical seaside town, it has its own distinctive flavor.

Fondo Cubano de Bienes Culturales SOUVENIRS
(Antonio Maceo No 120; ⏲9am-5pm Mon-Fri, 9am-noon Sat & Sun) This shop sells Hatuey woodcarvings and T-shirts with indigenous designs.

ARTex SOUVENIRS
(José Martí btwn Céspedes & Coroneles Galano) For the usual tourist fare check out this place.

Taller la Musa ART GALLERY
(Antonio Maceo No 124) Call by this place for typically imaginative Baracoan art. There's another studio in the Casa de Cultura opposite.

ℹ Information

Banco de Crédito y Comercio (Antonio Maceo No 99; ⏲8am-2:30pm Mon-Fri)

Banco Popular de Ahorro (José Martí No 166; ⏲8-11:30am & 2-4:30pm Mon-Fri) Cashes traveler's checks.

Cadeca (José Martí No 241) Money changer.

Clínica Internacional (☎64-10-37; cnr José Martí & Roberto Reyes; ☎24hr) A newish place that treats foreigners; there's also a hospital 2km out of town on the road to Guantánamo.

Cubatur (Antonio Maceo; ⏲8am-noon & 2-5pm Mon-Fri) Helpful office that organizes tours to El Yunque and Parque Nacional Alejandro de Humboldt.

Ecotur (☎64-36-65; Coronel Cardoso No 24; ⏲9am-5pm) Organizes more specialized nature tours to Duaba, Toa and Yumurí Rivers.

Etecsa Telepunto (cnr Antonio Maceo & Rafael Trejo; per hr CUC$6; ⏲8:30am-7:30pm) Internet and international calls.

Infotur (Antonio Maceo btwn Frank País & Maraví; ⏲8am-6pm) Very helpful.

Post office (Antonio Maceo No 136; ⏲8am-8pm)

Radio CMDX 'La Voz del Toa' Broadcasts over 650AM.

ℹ Getting There & Away

The closest train station is in Guantánamo, 150km southwest.

Air

Gustavo Rizo Airport (airport code: BCA) is 4km northwest of the town, just behind the Hotel Porto Santo. **Cubana** (José Martí No 181; ⌚8am-noon & 2-4pm Mon-Fri) has two weekly flights from Havana to Baracoa (CUC$135 one-way, Thursday and Sunday).

Be aware that the planes and buses out of Baracoa are sometimes fully booked, so don't come here on a tight schedule without outbound reservations.

Bus

The **national bus station** (cnr Av Los Mártires & José Martí) has **Víazul** (www.viazul.com) buses to Guantánamo (CUC$10, three hours), continuing to Santiago de Cuba (CUC$16, five hours) daily at 2:15pm. Bus tickets can be reserved in advance through **Cubatur** (Antonio Maceo No 181) for a CUC$5 commission, or you can usually stick your name on the list a day or so beforehand.

Truck

The **intermunicipal bus station** (cnr Coroneles Galano & Calixto García) has two or three trucks a day to Moa (90 minutes, departures from 6am) and Guantánamo (four hours, departures from 2am). Bank on big crowds and bad roads. Prices are a few Cuban pesos.

Getting Around

The best way to get to and from the airport is by taxi (CUC$2) or bici-taxi (CUC$1), if you're traveling light.

There's a helpful **Havanautos** (☎64-53-44) car-rental office at the airport. **Cubacar** (☎64-51-55) is at the Hotel Porto Santo. The **Servi-Cupet gas station** (José Martí; ⌚24hr) is at the entrance to town and also 4km from the center, on the road to Guantánamo. If you're driving to Havana, note that the northern route through Moa and Holguín is fastest but the road disintegrates rapidly after Playa Maguana. Most locals prefer the La Farola route.

Bici-taxis around Baracoa should charge five pesos a ride, but they often ask 10 to 15 pesos from foreigners.

Most casas particulares will be able to procure you a bicycle for CUC$3 per day. The ultimate bike ride is the 20km ramble down to Playa Maguana, one of the most scenic roads in Cuba. Lazy daisies can rent mopeds for CUC$24 either at Cafetería el Parque (p438) or Hotel El Castillo (p436).

Northwest of Baracoa

The rutted road heading out of town toward Moa is a green paradise flecked with palm groves, rustic farmsteads and serendipitous glimpses of the ocean.

Sights & Activities

Finca Duaba FARM, MUSEUM

(admission free; ⌚8am-7pm) Five kilometers out of Baracoa on the road to Moa and then 1km inland, Finca Duaba offers a fleeting taste of the Baracoan countryside. It's a verdant farm surrounded with profuse tropical plants and embellished with a short *cacao* (cocoa) **trail** that explains the history and characteristics of the plant with some interactive displays. There's also a good *ranchón*-style restaurant and the opportunity to swim in the Río Duaba. A bici-taxi can drop you at the road junction.

Río Toa RIVER, FARM

Ten kilometers northwest of Baracoa is the third-longest river on the north coast of Cuba and the country's most voluminous. The Toa is also an important bird and plant habitat. Cocoa trees and the ubiquitous coconut palm are grown in the Valle de Toa. A vast hydroelectric project on the Río Toa was abandoned after a persuasive campaign led by the Fundación de la Naturaleza y El Hombre convinced authorities it would do irreparable ecological damage; engineering and economic reasons also played a part. **Rancho Toa** is a Palmares restaurant reached via a right-hand turnoff just before the Toa Bridge. You can organize boat or kayak trips here for CUC$3 to CUC$10 and watch acrobatic Baracoans scale *cocotero* (coconut palm). A traditional Cuban feast of whole roast pig is available if you can rustle up enough people (eight usually).

Most of this region lies within the **Cuchillas de Toa Unesco Biosphere Reserve**, an area of 2083 sq km that incorporates the Alejandro de Humboldt World Heritage Site. This region contains the largest rainforest in Cuba, with trees exhibiting many precious woods, and has a high number of endemic species.

El Yunque NATURE RESERVE

Baracoa's rite of passage is the 8km (up and down) hike to the top of this moody, mysterious mountain. At 575m, El Yunque (the anvil) isn't Kilimanjaro, but the views from the summit and the flora and birdlife along the way are stupendous. Cubatur (p439) offers this tour almost daily (CUC$18 per person, minimum two people). The fee covers admission, guide, transport and a sandwich. The hike is hot (bring up to 2L of

LA FAROLA

Cut from the rest of the island by the velvety peaks of the Cuchillas de Toa, the only way in or out of Baracoa before the 1960s was by sea.

Four hundred and fifty years of solitude finally came to an end in 1964 with the opening of La Farola (the lighthouse road), a present from a grateful Fidel Castro to Baracoa's loyal revolutionaries who had supported him during the war in the mountains.

Fifty-five kilometers in length, La Farola traverses the steep-sided Sierra del Puril before snaking its way precipitously down through a landscape of grey granite cliffs and pine-scented cloud forest and falling, with eerie suddenness, upon the lush tropical paradise of the Atlantic coastline.

Giant ferns sprout from lichen-covered rocks; small wooden *campesino* (country) huts cling to sharp bends; and local hawkers appear, seemingly out of nowhere, holding up bananas, oranges and a sweet-tasting local delicacy wrapped in a palm frond known as *cucuruchu*.

Construction of La Farola actually began during the Batista era, but the project was indefinitely shelved when it ran into problems with engineering and funds (workers weren't paid). Reignited after the Revolution, the ambitious highway ultimately took 500 workers more than four years to build and consumed 300kg of concrete per square meter.

Today, La Farola remains the only fully paved route into Baracoa and is responsible for 75% of the town's supplies. Listed as one of the seven civil-engineering wonders of modern Cuba (and the only one outside Havana), it crosses from the island's driest zone to its wettest and deposits travelers in what, for many, is its most magical and serendipitous destination.

water) and usually muddy. It starts from the campismo 3km past the Finca Duaba (4km from the Baracoa–Moa road). Bank on seeing *tocororo* (Cuba's national bird), *zunzún* (the world's smallest bird), butterflies and *polymitas*.

If you're not up to bagging the peak itself ask about the shorter, flatter **Sendero el Jutiero** that starts at the same point as the El Yunque trek, or the 7km **Sendero Juncal-Rencontra** that bisects fruit plantations and rainforest between the Duaba and Toa Rivers. Ecotur (p439) has details.

Playa Maguana BEACH

Not quite the tranquil getaway it once was, Maguana is still nonetheless magical, a relatively undone Caribbean beach with a rustic food-shack that is populated primarily by fun-seeking Cubans who roll up in their vintage American cars and haul their prized music boxes out of the boot. Aside from the fenced-off Villa Maguana and a couple of basic food concessions, there's no infrastructure here – all part of the attraction. Watch your valuables!

Sleeping & Eating

TOP CHOICE **Villa Maguana** HOTEL $$

(☎64-53-72; Carretera a Moa Km 20; s/d CUC$66/83; P ❄) Knocking the socks off any Cuban all-inclusive is this delightful place, 22km north of Baracoa, consisting of four rustic wooden villas housing 16 rooms in total. Environmental foresight has meant that it clings precariously to Maguana's famously dreamy setting above a bite-sized scoop of sand guarded by two rocky promontories. There's a restaurant and some less rustic luxuries in the rooms such as satellite TV, fridge and air-con.

Campismo el Yunque CABINS $

(☎64-52-62; r CUC$10) Simple Cuban-style campismo offering very basic cabins at the end of the Finca Duaba road, 9km outside of town. The El Yunque hike starts here.

Finca la Esperanza HOTEL $

(☎64-36-65; Carretera a Moa Km 9; r from CUC$30) Rustic accommodation in a thatched *finca* (farm) in one of Baracoa's verdant coconut/cocoa plantations next the Toa River; there are four rooms with electricity, shared baths and a restaurant.

Playa Maguana snack bar CARIBBEAN $

(⏲9am-5pm) Right on the beach this open-sided snack bar is good for cheese sandwiches, beer and rum. There's a more substantial *parrillada*/grill about 150m further down the beach.

Parque Nacional Alejandro de Humboldt

'Unmatched in the Caribbean' is a phrase often used to describe this most dramatic and diverse of Cuban national parks, named after German naturalist and explorer Alexander von Humboldt who first came here in 1801. The accolade is largely true. Designated a Unesco World Heritage Site in 2001, Humboldt's steep pine-clad mountains and creeping morning mists protect an unmatched ecosystem that is, according to Unesco, 'one of the most biologically diverse tropical island sites on earth.' Perched above the Bahía de Taco, 40km northwest of Baracoa, lie 594 sq km of pristine forest and 2641 hectares of lagoon and mangroves. With 1000 flowering plant species and 145 types of fern, it is far and away the most diverse plant habitat in the entire Caribbean. Due to the toxic nature of the underlying rocks in the area, plants have been forced to adapt in order to survive. As a result, endemism in the area is high – 70% of the plants found here are endemic, as are many vertebrates and invertebrates. Several endangered species also survive, including Cuban Amazon parrots, hook-billed kites and – arguably – the ivory-billed woodpecker. Lauded for its unique evolutionary processes, the park is heavily protected and acts as a paradigm for Cuba's environmental protection efforts elsewhere.

Activities

The park contains a small **visitors center** (☎38-14-31; Carretera a Moa) staffed with biologists plus a network of trails leading to waterfalls, a *mirador* and a massive karst system with caves around the Farallones de Moa. Three trails are currently open to the public and take in only a tiny segment of the park's 594 sq km. Typically, you can't just wander around on your own. The available hikes are: **Balcón de Iberia**, at 7km the park's most challenging loop which bisects both agricultural land and pristine rainforest and includes a swim in a natural pool near the Salto de Agua Maya waterfall; **El Recreo**, a 2km stroll around the bay; and the **Bahía de Taco circuit**, which incorporates a boat trip (with a manatee-friendly motor developed by scientists here) through the mangroves and the bay, plus a 2km hike. Each option is accompanied by a highly professional guide. Prices range from CUC$5 to CUC$10, depending on the hike, but most people organize an excursion through Cubatur (p439) in Baracoa which includes transport and a pit-stop on Playa Maguana on the way back (CUC$24).

Getting There & Away

The park visitor's center is situated approximately halfway between Baracoa and Moa. You can arrange a tour through an agency in Baracoa or get here independently. The gorgeously scenic road is a collection of holes but passable in a hire car if driven with care.

Understand Cuba

population per sq km

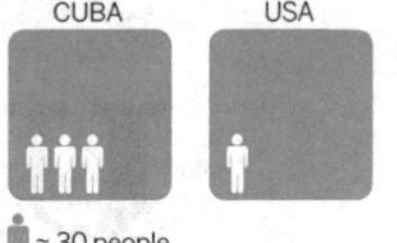

Cuba Today

» **Population** 11.47 million

» **Percentage over 60 yrs** 17%

» **Life expectancy** 77.6

» **Infant mortality** 5.72 per 1000

» **Doctor/ patient ratio** 1/170

» **Population growth rate** 0.22%

» **Literacy rate** 99.8%

For almost a decade now, foreign news stories about Cuba have been replaying the same cliffhanger: Fidel Castro falls ill, thousands of exiles go wild in Miami, and a generation of patient Americans dig out their *guayaberas* (Cuban shirts) and get ready to reacquaint themselves with mambo dancing, *Guantanameras* and *real* cigars. Unless you've been on the moon since 2001, you'll know that this speculative scenario has yet to transpire. Life in Cuba remains suspended in 'pause' mode, the economy – buoyed by record tourist numbers in 2010 – has staggered on for another year and, most surprising of all, the octogenarian Fidel carries on defying his doctors like he once defied Kennedy and Khrushchev.

But not even Fidel can roll back the ageing process. In February 2008, after suffering for 18 months with diverticulitis disease, the old warhorse handed the leadership reins over to his younger brother, Raúl. A charisma-free zone in the eyes of many Cubans, Raúl chanced his arm with some mediocre early reforms, allowing Cubans access to tourist hotels (they had previously been barred from all but the cheapest), permitting ownership of cell phones and opening up larger tracts of land to private farmers. It wasn't radical, but it was a start.

Guarded Optimism

The Cubans greeted the inauguration of Barack Obama in January 2009 with guarded optimism. Cautiously they envisaged, if not an immediate end to the embargo, then at least the start of some long-overdue dialogue. The caution was justified. Though Obama rolled back some of the Bush administration's more controversial laws, allowing Cuban-Americans to visit their families and send financial remittances without hindrance, the anachronistic trade and travel embargo remains in place.

History Books

Cuba: The Pursuit of Freedom (Hugh Thomas; 1971) Ten years in the making, this is the definitive take on Cuban history from a British academic.

Cuba: A New History (Richard Gott; 2004) Gott offers new insights into old topics.

My Life by Fidel Castro (with Ignacio Ramonet; 2006) History straight from the horse's mouth.

Che Guevara: A Revolutionary Life (John Lee Anderson) Anderson's meticulous research led to the unearthing of Che's remains and their return to Cuba.

Greeting People

» *Que bolá? Que tal? Dime? Como estas?* and *Como van las cosas?* all mean: how are you?

» Address people as *Señor/a* (formal), *compañero/a, socio/a, amigo/a, asere* (informal), *compay* (in the Oriente only), or *hermano/a* (very friendly)

belief systems
(% of population)

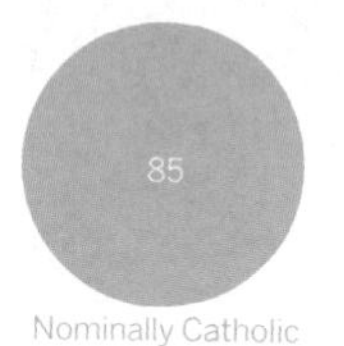

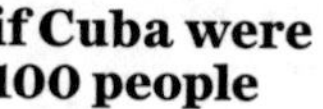

if Cuba were 100 people

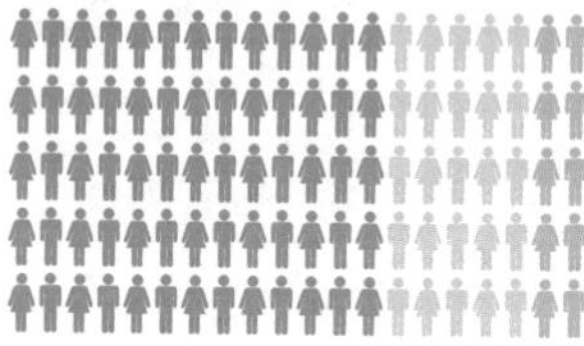

With the archipelago battered by three hurricanes inside two months in 2008, and badly bloodied by the global recession, the long-awaited celebrations to mark the 50th anniversary of the Revolution in January 2009 turned out to be low-key. The silence didn't last. Raúl showed his steely side the following March, firing two of his top government ministers (and possible successors), vice president Carlos Lage and foreign minister Felipe Pérez Roque. They both later 'confessed' to grave errors. In response to prolonged international pressure, he also freed 52 dissidents – Cuba's biggest prisoner release in decades.

Economic Adjustments

The Cuban economy successfully weaned itself off sugar in the early 2000s and has since spun inexorably toward Latin America through the signing of new trade agreements, including the 2004 Bolívarian Alternative for the Americas (ALBA) accords, which have exchanged Cuban medical know-how for Venezuelan oil. Other modern economic mainstays include nickel mining (Cuba is the world's second-largest producer) and tourism, which overtook sugar as the main money-bagger in 1995. As the economy began to improve, the government reined in some of the market reforms of the Special Period, and sidled up to China with joint ventures in transportation, nickel processing, oil and biotechnology. Everything was going swimmingly until Cuba's fragile economy was hit by the 2008–09 worldwide recession.

The government's response was slow but – when it came – unprecedented. In September 2010, an unusually candid Fidel was reported to have told an American journalist that the Cuban economy wasn't working (he later claimed he had been quoted out of context). Misconstrued or not, a couple of weeks later Raúl announced some shocking news. The

Top Films

Che: The Argentine (Steven Soderbergh; 2008)

Before Night Falls (Julian Schnabel; 2000)

Our Man in Havana (Carol Reed; 1959)

The Lost City (Andy García; 2005)

Top Blogs

Generación Y (www.desdecuba.com/generaciony) Award-winning blog of Yoani Sánchez, outspoken critic of the Cuban government.

Along the Malecón (www.alongthemaleconblogspot.com) Entertaining blogspot by *Dallas Morning News*' ex-Havana bureau chief.

El Yuma (www.elyumablogspot.com) Blog by highly respected Cubanologist Ted Henken, professor of Black and Hispanic Studies at Baruch College in New York City.

government was going to lay off over half a million of its workforce and loosen its hold on the tight rules guiding private enterprise.

Help to Haiti & Beyond

Cuba, as ever, is a two-sided equation. While political writers struggle to make themselves heard, and the economy has never fully divorced itself from its post-Cold War Special Period, the nation's doctors have continued to spin their lifesaving magic. Unreported in the international media was Cuba's response to the 2010 Haitian earthquake. A well-trained Cuban medical team had been operating in the impoverished country years before anyone else (since 1998, in fact) and stayed long after most other aid agencies had gone home. Indeed, when a cholera epidemic broke out in Haiti in October 2010, over 40% of the 30,000 victims were treated by 1200 Cuban doctors, who helped avert a catastrophe.

The actions were nothing new. Between 2004 and 2009, Cuban medics restored the sight of approximately 1.8 million people, from as far apart as Bolivia and Honduras, in a campaign code-named Operación Milagros. On top of this, the government continues to send Cuban doctors to over 70 developing countries and is currently training another 8000 foreigners in medicine at home. All services are provided free of charge.

2011 & On...

2011 broke with Cubans digesting complicated new privatization laws and pondering over life without ration books for first time in 49 years. The word on the street was cagey, guarded and, at times, a little confused. As to what was round the corner? No one was placing any bets.

Top Tips

» Carry tissues and antiseptic handwash for public toilets.

» Use a concealable money belt.

» Keep small change for tips.

» Don't buy cigars or change money in the street.

» Bring a torch in case of power outages.

Cuba Journals

Temas (www.temas.cult.cu) Cuba's top cultural magazine; a ray of journalistic light.

Bohemia (www.bohemia.cu) In print since 1908, Bohemia was the only periodical to survive the post-revolutionary censorship clampdown.

Granma (www.granma.cu) Daily Cuban newspaper available online in English, Spanish, French, Portuguese, German and Italian.

History

Embellished by extraordinary feats of revolutionary derring-do, and plagued routinely by the meddling armies of foreign invaders, Cuba has achieved a historical importance far greater than its size would suggest. The underlying and – until the 1960s – ongoing historical themes have been external interference and internal strife, and the results of both have often been bloody. Since the arrival of Columbus in 1492, the archipelago has suffered genocide, slavery, two bitter independence wars, a period of corrupt and violent quasi-independence, and, finally, a populist revolution that, despite early promise, hit a metaphoric pause button. The fallout has led to the emigration of almost one-fifth of the Cuban population, mostly to the United States.

For the sake of simplicity, Cuba's historical eras can be divided into three broad categories: pre-colonial, colonial and post-colonial. Before 1492, Cuba was inhabited by a trio of migratory civilizations that originated in the Orinoco Basin of South America before island-hopping north. Their cultures have been only partially evaluated to date, primarily because they left very little behind in the way of documentary evidence.

Cuba's colonial period was dominated by the Spanish and the divisive issue of slavery, which spanned the whole era from the 1520s until abolition in 1886. Slavery left deep wounds on Cuba's collective psyche, but its existence and final quashing was integral to the evolution of the country's highly distinctive culture, music, dance, and religion. Understand this and you're halfway to understanding the complexities of the contemporary nation.

Post-colonial Cuba has had two distinctive sub-eras, the second of which can be further subdivided in two. The period from the defeat of Spain in 1898 to the Castro coup of 1959 is usually seen as an age of quasi-independence with a strong American influence. It was also a time characterized by violence, corruption and frequent insurrection on the part of opposition groups intent on toppling the government.

Best Historical Sites

- » Museo de la Revolución, Havana
- » Cuartel Moncada, Santiago de Cuba
- » Comandancia de la Plata, Granma
- » Fortaleza de San Carlos de la Cabaña, Havana

TIMELINE

BC 2000

The Guanahatabeys, Cuba's earliest known Stone Age civilization, is known to be living in the caves along the coast of present-day Pinar del Río province.

AD 1100

Taíno people start arriving in Cuba after leapfrogging their way across the islands of the Lesser Antilles from the Orinoco Basin in present-day Venezuela.

1492

Christopher Columbus lands in Cuba in modern-day Holguín province. He sails for a month along the coast, as far as Baracoa, planting religious crosses and meeting with the indigenous Taínos.

The post-1959 Castro era breaks conveniently into two stages: the age of Soviet domination from 1961 to 1991, and the historical trajectory from the Special Period till the present day, when Cuba, despite its devastating economic difficulties, became a truly independent power for the first time.

Pre-colonial Cuba

In most historical texts, Cuba's pre-Columbian human history (all 3500 years of it) is designated a couple of pages, while the subsequent 500 years is allotted the rest of the book. The imbalance is understandable given the facts – or lack of them. None of Cuba's early cultures possessed a written language. What little we know about them has been garnered almost exclusively from archaeological finds and, to a lesser extent, the testimonies of early Spanish colonizers.

According to carbon dating, Cuba has been inhabited by humans for over 4000 years. In the period up until Columbus' arrival in 1492, the archipelago was successively colonized by three separate anthropological groups, all of which are thought to have originated in the Orinoco Basin in present-day Venezuela.

José Martí Sites

» Museo-Casa Natal de José Natal, Havana

» Memorial a José Martí, Havana

» Cemeterio Santa Ifigenia, Santiago de Cuba

» Dos Rios, Granma

Guanahatabey & Siboney Cultures

The first known civilization in Cuba was that of the Guanahatabeys, a primitive Stone Age people who lived in caves and eked out a meager existence as hunter-gatherers. At some point over a 2000-year trajectory, the Guanahatabeys were gradually pushed west into what is now Pinar del Río province, displaced by the arrival of another pre-ceramic culture known as the Siboneys. The Siboneys were a slightly more developed group of fishermen and small-scale farmers, who settled down comparatively peacefully on the archipelago's sheltered southern coast. By the second millennium AD, they were also gradually displaced by the more sophisticated Taíno, who liked to use Siboneys as domestic servants.

Evidence of Guanahatabey and, to a lesser extent, Siboney culture has been found in caves around Viñales and on the Guanahacabibes Peninsula in Pinar del Río, and it is believed that their descendents were still living there at the time of Columbus' arrival. During his second voyage in 1494, the explorer noted how his Taíno translator couldn't communicate with the natives in the far west, and later historians have confirmed that the Guanahatabey language was not related to the Arawak language of the Taínos. Other testimonies from Cuba's first governor, Diego Velázquez, describe the people of western Cuba as 'savages' who lived in caves and were archaic compared to their more developed eastern brethren. Whatever the case, the Guanahatabeys were completely extinct

1511

Diego Velázquez lands at Baracoa with 400 colonizers, including Hernán Cortés (the future colonizer of Mexico). The new arrivals construct a fort and quickly make enemies of the local Taínos.

1522

The first slaves arrive in Cuba from Africa, ushering in an era that was to last for 350 years and have a profound effect on the development of Cuban culture.

1555

The age of piracy is inaugurated. French buccaneer, Jaques de Sores, attacks Havana and burns it to the ground. In response, the Spanish start building a huge network of forts.

1607

Havana is declared capital of Cuba and becomes the annual congregation point for Spain's Caribbean treasure fleet, loaded up with silver from Peru and gold from Mexico.

within a decade or so of Columbus' arrival, and their archaic culture has had no noticeable impact on the Cuba of today.

The Taínos

The island's third and most important pre-Columbian civilization, the Taínos, first started arriving in Cuba around 1100AD in a series of waves, concluding a migration process that had begun on mainland South America several centuries earlier. Related to the Greater Antilles Arawaks, the new peace-loving natives were escaping the barbarism of the cannibalistic Caribs who had colonized the Lesser Antibes pushing the Taínos northwest into Puerto Rico, Hispaniola and Cuba.

Taíno culture was more developed and sophisticated than that of its predecessors; the adults practiced a form of cranial transformation by flattening the soft skulls of their young children, and groups lived together in villages characterized by their thatched *bohios* (rustic huts) and *bateys* (communal 'plazas').

The Taínos were skillful farmers, weavers, ceramicists and boat-builders, and their complex society exhibited an organized system of participatory government that was overseen by series of local *caciques* (chiefs). Sixty percent of the crops still grown in Cuba today were pioneered by Taíno farmers, who even planted cotton for use in hammocks, fishing nets and bags. They were also the first of the world's pre-Columbian cultures to nurture the delicate tobacco plant into a form that could easily be processed for smoking.

Columbus described the Taíno with terms such as 'gentle', 'sweet', 'always laughing' and 'without knowledge of what is evil', which makes the genocide to come even harder to comprehend. Estimates vary wildly as to how many indigenous people populated Cuba pre-Columbus, though 100,000 is a good consensus figure. Within 30 years 90% of the Taínos had been wiped out.

Though Cuban culture retains echoes of the Taíno, the independence leaders of later years rarely invoked their erstwhile civilization in the way other Latin Americans celebrated the Aztecs and the Maya, preferring instead to identify with Cuba's African and Spanish roots. Nonetheless, Taíno influences seeped into Cuba's language (for instance, the words for hammock and hurricane), eating habits (root vegetables), music (*kiriká* and *changüí*), living space (Taíno-style *bohios* are still used by Cuban campesinos), smoking habits and the spirit of resistance.

PUEBLOS INDIOS

In the 17th century the Spanish herded the remaining indigenous population into towns known as *Pueblos Indios*. Old and New World cultures cross-fertilized, allowing Indian practices and words to seep into everyday Cuban life.

1741

A British Navy contingent under the command of Admiral Edward Vernon briefly captures Guantánamo Bay during the War of Jenkin's Ear, but is sent packing after a yellow fever epidemic.

1762

Spain joins France in the Seven Years' War, provoking the British to attack and take Havana. They occupy Cuba for 11 months before exchanging it for Florida in 1763.

1791

A bloody slave rebellion in Haiti causes thousands of white French planters to flee west to Cuba, where they set up the earliest coffee plantations in the New World.

1808

Pre-empting the Monroe Doctrine, US president Thomas Jefferson proclaims Cuba 'the most interesting addition which could be made to our system of states,' thus beginning a 200-year US fixation.

Colonial Cuba

Columbus & Colonization

When Columbus neared Cuba on October 27, 1492, he described it as 'the most beautiful land human eyes had ever seen,' naming it 'Juana' in honor of a Spanish heiress. But deluded in his search for the kingdom of the Great Khan, and finding little gold in Cuba's lush and heavily forested interior, Columbus quickly abandoned the territory in favor of Hispaniola (modern-day Haiti and the Dominican Republic).

The colonization of Cuba didn't begin until nearly 20 years later in 1511, when Diego Velázquez de Cuéllar led a flotilla of four ships and 400 men from Hispaniola to conquer the island for the Spanish Crown. Docking near present-day Baracoa, the conquistadors promptly set about establishing seven pioneering settlements throughout their new colony (see p451). Watching nervously from the safety of their *bohíos* (thatched huts), a scattered population of Taínos looked on with a mixture of fascination and fear.

Despite Velázquez's attempts to protect the local Indians from the gross excesses of the Spanish swordsmen, things quickly got out of hand and the invaders soon found that they had a full-scale rebellion on their hands. Leader of the embittered and short-lived insurgency was the feisty Hatuey, an influential Taíno *cacique* and archetype of the Cuban resistance, who was eventually captured and burned at the stake, Inquisition-style, for daring to challenge the iron fist of Spanish rule.

With the resistance decapitated, the Spaniards set about emptying Cuba of its relatively meager gold and mineral reserves, using the beleaguered natives as forced labor. As slavery was nominally banned under a papal edict, the Spanish got around the various legal loopholes by introducing a ruthless *encomienda* system, whereby thousands of natives were rounded up and forced to work for Spanish landowners on the pretext that they were receiving free 'lessons' in Christianity. The brutal system lasted 20 years before the 'Apostle of the Indians,' Fray Bartolomé de Las Casas, appealed to the Spanish Crown for more humane treatment, and in 1542 the *encomiendas* were abolished for the indigenous people. For the unfortunate Taínos, the call came too late. Those who had not already been worked to death in the gold mines quickly succumbed to fatal European diseases such as smallpox, and by 1550 only about 5000 scattered survivors remained.

The Independence Wars

With Cuba's landowners worried about a repetition of Haiti's 1791 slave rebellion, Cuba's independence wars came more than half a century after

1850

Venezuelan filibuster Narciso López raises the Cuban flag for the first time in Cárdenas during an abortive attempt to 'liberate' the colony from Spain.

1868

Céspedes frees his slaves in Manzanillo and proclaims the *Grito de Yara,* Cuba's first independence cry and the beginning of a 10-year war against the Spanish.

1878

The Pact of El Zanjón ends the First War of Independence. Cuban general Antonio Maceo issues the Protest of Baraguá and resumes hostilities the following year before disappearing into exile.

1886

After more than 350 years of exploitation and cross-Atlantic transportation, Cuba becomes the second-last country in the Americas to abolish slavery.

the rest of Latin America had broken away from Spain. But when they arrived, they were no less impassioned – or bloody.

The First Independence War

Fed up with Spain's reactionary policies and enviously eyeing Lincoln's new American dream to the north, *criollo* (Spaniards born in the Americas) landowners around Bayamo began plotting rebellion in the late 1860s. The spark was auspiciously lit on October 10, 1868, when Carlos Manuel de Céspedes, a budding poet, lawyer and sugar-plantation owner, launched an uprising from his Demajagua sugar mill near Manzanillo in the Oriente. Calling for the abolition of slavery and freeing his own slaves in an act of solidarity, Céspedes proclaimed the famous *Grito de Yara*, a cry of liberty for an independent Cuba, encouraging other disillusioned separatists to join him. For the colonial administrators in Havana, such an audacious bid to wrest control was an act tantamount to treason. The furious Spanish reacted accordingly.

Fortunately for the loosely organized rebels, the cagey Céspedes had done his military homework. Within weeks of the historic *Grito de Yara*,

THE MAGNIFICENT SEVEN

Soon after landing in Cuba in 1511, the new Spanish authorities under the auspices of Diego Velázquez founded seven *villas* (towns) on the main island in a bid to bring their new colony under strong central rule. Here are the details of the towns and the dates they were founded.

CONTEMPORARY NAME	ORIGINAL NAME	PROVINCE	DATE OF FOUNDING
Baracoa	Nuestra Señora de la Asunción	Guantánamo	Aug 1511
Bayamo	San Salvador de Bayamo	Granma	Nov 1513
Camagüey	Santa María del Puerto de Príncipe	Camagüey	Feb 1514
Santiago de Cuba	Santiago de Cuba	Santiago de Cuba	Jun 1514
Sancti Spíritus	Espíritu Santo	Sancti Spíritus	Aug 1514
Trinidad	Santísima Trinidad	Sancti Spíritus	Dec 1514
Havana	San Cristóbal de la Habana	La Habana (former province; now Artemisa and Mayabeque)	Aug 1515

1892

From exile in the US, José Martí galvanizes popular support and forms the Cuban Revolutionary Party, starting to lay the groundwork for the resumption of hostilities against Spain.

1895

José Martí and Antonio Maceo arrive in Cuba to ignite the Second Independence War. Martí is killed at Dos Ríos in May and is quickly elevated to a martyr.

MARTIN ENGELMANN/PHOTOLIBRARY

» José Martí memorial, Plaza de la Revolución, Havana

Independence War Heroes

» Carlos Manuel de Céspedes (1819–74)

» Máximo Gómez (1836–1905)

» Calixto García (1839–98)

» Ignacio Agramonte (1841–73)

» Antonio Maceo (1845–96)

the diminutive lawyer-turned-general had raised an army of more than 1500 men and marched defiantly on Bayamo, taking the city in a matter of days. But initial successes soon turned to lengthy deadlock. A tactical decision not to invade western Cuba, along with an alliance between *peninsulares* (Spaniards born in Spain but living in Cuba) and the Spanish, soon put Céspedes on the back foot. Temporary help arrived in the shape of *mulato* general Antonio Maceo, a tough and uncompromising Santiagüero, nicknamed the 'Bronze Titan' for his ability to defy death on countless occasions, and the equally formidable Dominican Máximo Gómez. But despite economic disruption and the periodic destruction of the sugar crop, the rebels lacked a dynamic political leader capable of uniting them behind a singular ideological cause.

With the loss of Céspedes in battle in 1874, the war dragged on for another four years, reducing the Cuban economy to tatters and leaving an astronomical 200,000 Cubans and 80,000 Spanish dead. Finally, in February 1878 a lackluster pact was signed at El Zanjón between the uncompromising Spanish and the exhausted separatists, a rambling and largely worthless agreement that solved nothing and acceded little to the rebel cause. Maceo, disgusted and disillusioned, made his feelings known in the antidotal 'Protest of Baraguá,' but after an abortive attempt to restart the war in 1879, both he and Gómez disappeared into a prolonged exile.

A BRITISH INTERLUDE

In 1762 Spain, by now a European power in serious decline, joined in the Seven Years' War on the side of France against Britain. For their important colony, Cuba, it quickly turned out to be a fatal decision. Unperturbed by their new Spanish foes and sensing an opportunity to disrupt trade in Spain's economically lucrative Caribbean empire, 20,000 British troops honed in on Havana, landing in the village of Cojímar on June 6 and attacking and capturing the seemingly impregnable castle of El Morro from the rear. Worn down and under siege, the Spanish reluctantly surrendered Havana two months later, leaving the British to become the city's (and Cuba's) rather unlikely new overlords.

The British occupation turned out to be brief but incisive. Bivouacking themselves inside Havana's formidable city walls for 11 months, the enterprising English flung open the doors to free trade and sparked a new rush of foreign imports in the form of manufacturing parts and consumer goods. Not surprisingly, it was the sugar industry that benefited most from this economic deregulation, and in the years that followed the British handover, the production of sugarcane boomed like never before.

The Spanish didn't 'win' Cuba back from the British. Instead, they swapped it for Florida at the Treaty of Paris, which ended the Seven Years' War in 1763.

1896

After sustaining more than 20 injuries in a four-decade military career, Antonio Maceo meets his end at Cacahual, Havana, where he is killed in an ambush.

1898

Following the loss of the battleship USS *Maine*, the US declares war on Spain and defeats its forces near Santiago. A four-year US occupation begins.

SPL/PHOTOLIBRARY

» USS *Maine* entering Havana Harbour

1902

Cuba gains nominal independence from the US and elects Tomás Estrada Palma as its president. US troops are called back three times within the first 15 years of the republic.

The Second Independence War

Cometh the hour, cometh the man. José Martí – poet, patriot, visionary and intellectual – had grown rapidly into a patriotic figure of Bolívarian proportions in the years following his ignominious exile in 1871, not just in Cuba but in the whole of Latin America. After his arrest at the age of 16 during the First War of Independence for a minor indiscretion, Martí had spent 20 years formulating his revolutionary ideas abroad in places as diverse as Guatemala, Mexico and the US. Although impressed by American business savvy and industriousness, he was equally repelled by the country's all-consuming materialism and was determined to present a workable Cuban alternative.

Dedicating himself passionately to the cause of the resistance, Martí wrote, spoke, petitioned and organized tirelessly for independence for well over a decade and by 1892 had enough momentum to coax Maceo and Gómez out of exile under the umbrella of the Partido Revolucionario Cubano (PRC; Cuban Revolutionary Party). At last, Cuba had found its Bolívar.

Predicting that the time was right for another revolution, Martí and his compatriots set sail for Cuba in April 1895, landing near Baracoa two months after PRC-sponsored insurrections had tied down Spanish forces in Havana. Raising an army of 40,000 men, the rebels promptly regrouped and headed west, engaging the Spanish for the first time on May 19 in a place called Dos Ríos. It was on this bullet-strafed and strangely anonymous battlefield that Martí, conspicuous on his white horse and dressed in his trademark black dinner suit, was shot and killed as he charged suicidally toward the Spanish lines. Had he lived he would certainly have become Cuba's first president; instead, he became a hero and a martyr whose life and legacy would inspire generations of Cubans in years to come.

Conscious of mistakes made during the First War of Independence, Gómez and Maceo stormed west with a scorched-earth policy that left everything from the Oriente to Matanzas in flames. Early victories quickly led to a sustained offensive and, by January 1896, Maceo had broken through to Pinar del Río, while Gómez was tying down Spanish forces near Havana. The Spaniards responded with an equally ruthless general named Valeriano Weyler, who built countrywide north-south fortifications to restrict the rebels' movements. In order to break the underground resistance, *guajiros* (country people) were forced into camps in a process called *reconcentración,* and anyone supporting the rebellion became liable for execution. The brutal tactics started to show results, and on December 7, 1896, the Mambís (the name for the 19th-century

In the 1880s there were over 100,000 Chinese people living in Cuba, mainly as cheap labor on sugar plantations in and around the Havana region.

IMMIGRANTS

1920

Sharp increases in world sugar prices after WWI spearhead the so-called 'Dance of the Millions' in Cuba. Huge fortunes are made overnight. A heavy economic crash quickly follows.

1933

The 1933 revolution is sparked by an Army Officers' Coup that deposes the Machado dictatorship and installs Fulgencio Batista in power.

1952

Batista stages a bloodless military coup, cancelling the upcoming Cuban elections in which an ambitious young lawyer named Fidel Castro was due to stand.

1953

Castro leads a band of rebels in a disastrous attack on the Moncada army barracks in Santiago. He uses his subsequent trial as a platform to expound his political plans.

rebels fighting Spain) suffered a major military blow when Antonio Maceo was killed south of Havana trying to break out to the east.

Enter the Americans

By this time Cuba was a mess: thousands were dead, the country was in flames, and William Randolph Hearst and the US tabloid press were leading a hysterical war campaign characterized by sensationalized, often inaccurate reports about Spanish atrocities.

Preparing perhaps for the worst, the US battleship *Maine* was sent to Havana in January 1898, on the pretext of 'protecting US citizens.' Its touted task never saw fruition. On February 15, 1898, the *Maine* exploded out of the blue in Havana Harbor, killing 266 US sailors. The Spanish claimed it was an accident, the Americans blamed the Spanish, and some Cubans accused the US, saying it provided a convenient pretext for intervention. Despite several investigations conducted over the following years, the real cause of the explosion may remain one of history's great mysteries, as the hulk of the ship was scuttled in deep waters in 1911.

After the *Maine* debacle, the US scrambled to take control. They offered Spain US$300 million for Cuba and, when this deal was rejected, demanded a full withdrawal of the Spanish from the island. The long-awaited US-Spanish showdown that had been simmering imperceptibly beneath the surface for decades had finally resulted in war.

The only important land battle of the conflict was on July 1, when the US Army attacked Spanish positions on San Juan Hill just east of Santiago de Cuba. Despite vastly inferior numbers and limited, antiquated weaponry, the under-siege Spanish held out bravely for over 24 hours before future US President Theodore Roosevelt broke the deadlock by leading a celebrated cavalry charge of the Rough Riders up San Juan Hill. It was the beginning of the end for the Spaniards, and an unconditional surrender was offered to the Americans on July 17, 1898.

Cuba's first three presidents

» Tomás Estrada Palma (1902–06)

» José Miguel Gómez (1906–13)

» Mario García Menocal (1913–21)

A 1976 book entitled *How the Battleship Maine Was Destroyed* concluded that the explosion of the *Maine* in Havana Harbor in 1898 was caused by the spontaneous combustion of coal in the ship's bunker.

Post-Colonial Cuba

The Batista Era

Fulgencio Batista, a *holguiñero* of mixed race from the town of Banes, was a wily and shrewd negotiator who presided over Cuba's best and worst attempts to establish an embryonic democracy in the 1940s and '50s. After an army officers' coup in 1933, he had taken power almost by default, gradually worming his way into the power vacuum it left amid the corrupt factions of a dying government. From 1934 onwards Batista served as the army's chief of staff and, in 1940 in a relatively free and fair election, he was duly elected president. Given an official mandate, Batista began to enact a wide variety of social reforms and set about drafting

1956

The *Granma* yacht lands in eastern Cuba with Castro and 81 rebels aboard. Decimated by the Cuban Army, only about a dozen survive to regroup in the Sierra Maestra.

1958

Che Guevara masterminds an attack against an armored train in Santa Clara, a military victory that finally forces Batista to concede power. The rebels march triumphantly on Havana.

1959

Castro is welcomed ecstatically in Havana. The new government passes the historic First Agrarian Reform Act. Camilo Cienfuegos' plane goes missing over the Cuban coast off Camagüey.

1960

Castro nationalizes US assets on the island, provoking the US to cancel its Cuban sugar quota. Castro immediately sells the sugar to the Soviet Union.

Cuba's most liberal and democratic constitution to date. But neither the liberal honeymoon nor Batista's good humor were to last. Stepping down after the 1944 election, the former army sergeant handed power over to the politically inept President Ramón Grau San Martín, and corruption and inefficiency soon reigned like never before.

The Revolutionary Spark is Lit

Aware of his underlying popularity and sensing an easy opportunity to line his pockets with one last big paycheck, Batista cut a deal with the American Mafia, promising to give them carte blanche in Cuba in return for a cut of their gambling profits, and positioned himself for a comeback. On March 10, 1952, three months before scheduled elections that he looked like losing, Batista staged a military coup. Wildly condemned by opposition politicians inside Cuba, but recognized by the US government two weeks later, Batista quickly let it be known, when he suspended various constitutional guarantees including the right to strike, that his second incarnation wouldn't be as enlightened as his first.

After Batista's coup, a revolutionary circle formed in Havana around the charismatic figure of Fidel Castro, a lawyer by profession and a gifted orator who had been due to stand in the cancelled 1952 elections. Supported by his younger brother Raúl and aided intellectually by his trusty lieutenant Abel Santamaría (later tortured to death by Batista's thugs), Castro saw no alternative to the use of force in ridding Cuba of its detestable dictator. Low on numbers but determined to make a political statement, Castro led 119 rebels in an attack on the strategically important Moncada army barracks in Santiago de Cuba on July 26, 1953 (see p394). The audacious and poorly planned assault failed dramatically when the

MAFIA

In December 1946 the Mafia convened the biggest ever get-together of North American mobsters in Havana's Hotel Nacional, under the pretence that they were going to see a Frank Sinatra concert.

INDEPENDENCE OR DEPENDENCE?

On May 20, 1902, Cuba became an independent republic – or did it? Despite three years of blood, sweat and sacrifice during the Spanish-Cuban-American War, no Cuban representatives were invited to the historic peace treaty held in Paris in 1898 that had promised Cuban independence *with conditions*. The conditions were contained in the infamous Platt Amendment, a sly addition to the US 1901 Army Appropriations Bill that gave the US the right to intervene militarily in Cuba whenever it saw fit. The US also used its significant leverage to secure itself a naval base in Guantánamo Bay in order to protect its strategic interests in the Panama Canal region. Despite some opposition in the US and a great deal more in Cuba, the Platt Amendment was passed by Congress and was written into Cuba's 1902 constitution. In Cuba, Spain had been replaced by the USA. The repercussions were to continue for over a century.

1961

Cuban mercenaries with US backing stage an unsuccessful invasion at the Bay of Pigs. The US declares a full trade embargo. Cuba embarks on a highly successful literacy campaign.

» Bay of Pigs Musem, Playa Girón

1962

The discovery of medium-range nuclear missiles in Cuba, installed by the Soviet Union, brings the world to the brink of nuclear war in the so-called Cuban Missile Crisis.

rebels' driver (who was from Havana) took the wrong turning in Santiago's badly signposted streets and the alarm was raised.

Fooled, flailing and hopelessly outnumbered, 64 of the Moncada conspirators were rounded up by Batista's army and brutally tortured and executed. Castro and a handful of others managed to escape into the nearby mountains, where they were found a few days later by a sympathetic army lieutenant named Sarría, who had been given instructions to kill them. 'Don't shoot, you can't kill ideas!' Sarría is alleged to have shouted on finding Castro and his exhausted colleagues. By taking Castro to jail instead of doing away with him, Sarría ruined his military career, but saved Fidel's life. (One of Fidel's first acts after the Revolution triumphed was to release Sarría from prison and give him a commission in the revolutionary army.) Castro's capture soon became national news, and he was put on trial in the full glare of the media spotlight. Fidel defended himself in court, writing an eloquent and masterfully executed speech that he later transcribed into a comprehensive political manifesto entitled *History Will Absolve Me.* Basking in his newfound legitimacy and backed by a growing sense of dissatisfaction with the old regime in the country at large, Castro was sentenced to 15 years imprisonment on Isla de Pinos (a former name for Isla de la Juventud). Cuba was well on the way to gaining a new national hero.

Of the 12 or so men that survived the disastrous *Granma* landing in December 1956, only three were still alive in 2011: Fidel Castro, Raúl Castro and Ramiro Valdés.

In February 1955 Batista won the presidency in what were widely considered to be fraudulent elections and, in an attempt to curry favor with growing internal opposition, agreed to an amnesty for all political prisoners, including Castro. Believing that Batista's real intention was to assassinate him once out of jail, Castro fled to Mexico, leaving Baptist schoolteacher Frank País in charge of a fledgling underground resistance campaign that the vengeful Moncada veterans had christened the 26th of July Movement (M-26-7).

The Revolution

In Mexico City, Castro and his compatriots plotted and planned afresh, drawing in key new figures such as Camilo Cienfuegos and the Argentine doctor Ernesto 'Che' Guevara, both of whom added strength and panache to the nascent army of disaffected rebel soldiers. On the run from the Mexican police and determined to arrive in Cuba in time for an uprising that Frank País had planned for late November 1956 in Santiago de Cuba, Castro and 81 companions set sail for the island on November 25 in an old and overcrowded leisure yacht named *Granma*. After seven dire days at sea they arrived at Playa Las Coloradas near Niquero in Oriente on December 2 (two days late). Following a catastrophic landing – 'It wasn't a disembarkation; it was a shipwreck,' a wry Guevara later

Che Guevara – whose father's family name was Guevara Lynch – can trace his Celtic roots back to a Patrick Lynch, born in Galway in Ireland in 1715, who emigrated to Buenos Aires via Bilbao in 1749.

1967

Che Guevara is hunted down and executed in Bolivia in front of CIA observers after a 10-month abortive guerrilla war in the mountains.

KARL BLACKWELL/LONELYPLANETIMAGES©

» Che Guevara monument, Santa Clara

1968

The Cuban government nationalizes 58,000 small businesses in a sweeping socialist reform package. Everything falls under strict government control.

commented – they were spotted and routed by Batista's soldiers in a sugarcane field at Alegría de Pío three days later.

Of the 82 rebel soldiers who had left Mexico, little more than a dozen managed to escape. Splitting into three tiny groups, the survivors wandered around hopelessly for days half-starved, wounded and assuming that the rest of their compatriots had been killed in the initial skirmish. 'At one point I was Commander in Chief of myself and two other people,' Fidel commented sagely years later (see p381). However, with the help of the local peasantry, the dozen or so hapless soldiers finally managed to reassemble two weeks later in Cinco Palmas, a clearing in the shadows of the Sierra Maestra, where a half-delirious Fidel gave a rousing and premature victory speech. 'We will win this war,' he proclaimed confidently. 'We are just beginning the fight!'

Castro's government passed over 1000 laws in its first year (1959), including rent and electricity cost reductions, the abolition of racial discrimination, and the First Agrarian Reform Act.

The comeback began on January 17, 1957, when the guerrillas scored an important victory by sacking a small army outpost on the south coast in Granma province called La Plata (p421). This was followed in February by a devastating propaganda coup when Fidel persuaded *New York Times* journalist Herbert Matthews to come up into the Sierra Maestra to interview him. The resulting article made Castro internationally famous and gained him much sympathy among liberal Americans. Suffice to say, by this point he wasn't the only anti-Batista agitator. On March 13, 1957, university students led by José Antonio Echeverría attacked the Presidential Palace in Havana in an unsuccessful attempt to assassinate Batista. Thirty-two of the 35 attackers were shot dead as they fled, and reprisals were meted out on the streets of Havana with a new vengeance. Cuba was rapidly disintegrating into a police state run by military-trained thugs.

Elsewhere passions were running equally high. In September 1957 naval officers in the normally tranquil city of Cienfuegos staged an armed revolt and set about distributing weapons among the disaffected populace. After some bitter door-to-door fighting, the insurrection was brutally crushed and the ringleaders rounded up and killed, but for the revolutionaries the point had been made. Batista's days were numbered.

Back in the Sierra Maestra, Fidel's rebels overwhelmed 53 Batista soldiers at an army post in El Uvero in May and captured more badly needed supplies. The movement seemed to be gaining momentum and despite losing Frank País to a government assassination squad in Santiago de Cuba in July, support and sympathy around the country was starting to mushroom. By the beginning of 1958 Castro had established a fixed headquarters at La Plata (not to be confused with the La Plata in Granma province) in a cloud forest high up in the Sierra Maestra, and was broadcasting propaganda messages from Radio Rebelde (710AM and 96.7FM) all across Cuba. The tide was starting to turn.

In 1991, Castro declared a five-year *período especial* (Special Period) austerity program that sent living standards plummeting.

1970

Castro attempts to achieve a 10-million-ton sugar harvest. The plan fails and Cuba begins to wean itself off its unhealthy dependence on its mono-crop.

1976

Terrorists bomb a Cuban jet in Barbados, killing all 73 people aboard. A line is traced back to anti-Castro activists with histories as CIA operatives working out of Venezuela.

1980

Following an incident at the Peruvian embassy, Castro opens the Cuban port of Mariel. Within six months 125,000 have fled the island for the US in the so-called Mariel Boatlift.

1988

Cuban forces play a crucial role in the Battle of Cuito Cuanavale in Angola, a serious defeat for the white South African army and its system of apartheid.

Sensing his popularity waning, Batista sent an army of 10,000 men into the Sierra Maestra in May 1958, on a mission known as Plan FF (*Fin de Fidel* or End of Fidel). The intention was to liquidate Castro and his merry band of loyal guerrillas who had now burgeoned into a solid fighting force of 300 men. The offensive became something of a turning point as the rebels – with the help of the local *campesinos* (country people) – gradually halted the onslaught of Batista's young and ill-disciplined conscript army. With the Americans increasingly embarrassed by the no-holds-barred terror tactics of their one-time Cuban ally, Castro sensed an opportunity to turn defense into offense and signed the groundbreaking Caracas Pact with eight leading opposition groups calling on the US to stop all aid to Batista. Che Guevara and Camilo Cienfuegos were promptly dispatched to the Escambray Mountains to open up new fronts in the west, and by December, with Cienfuegos holding down troops in Yaguajay (the garrison finally surrendered after an 11-day siege) and Guevara closing in on Santa Clara, the end was in sight. It was left to Che Guevara to seal the final victory, employing classic guerrilla tactics to derail an

EXILES

It is easy to forget that more than one-fifth of Cuba's population lives overseas, the vast majority in the US where many have become naturalized US citizens. Displaced Cuban-Americans include the actor Andy García, the singer Gloria Estefan (both born in Havana), recording artist Chirino (from Pinar del Río province), and former CNN news anchor Rick Sánchez (from Guanabacoa). All arrived as young children, sent or accompanied by middle-class parents who were at odds with Castro's creeping socialist reforms.

The first wave of Cuban exiles in the 1960s was made up primarily of rich, politically motivated professionals. They formed the powerful Cuban American Federation in South Florida and retreated to the political right where their intransigence has been matched only by Castro's. They were followed in the 1980s and '90s by a new wave of migrants, who left Cuba for mainly economic reasons; their vitriol for Fidel has generally been less heated.

Fatefully, it is the 'old guard' who retain the political power in the US. Between them, they have formed a strong Cuban-American lobby allied to the Republican Party in Florida, which wields an inflated influence in Washington and remains one of the main reasons why the US travel and trade embargo is still in place.

Life as a Cuban exile is most marked in Miami's 'Little Havana' neighborhood (though there are enclaves all over the US, most notably in New Jersey). It is characterized by a number of well-known 'Cubanisms' that have endured for decades, irrespective of political ideology: cigars, rum, strong sweet coffee, religious superstition, Santería, the Virgin of El Cobre, Benny Moré, a penchant for dance, rice and beans, dynamic street festivals and – towering above it all – the icon of everyone from Fidel to Lionel Diaz-Balart: José Martí.

1991

The Soviet Union collapses and Cuba heads toward its worst economic collapse of modern times, entering what Castro calls a 'Special Period in a Time of Peace.'

1993

Attempting to revive itself from its economic coma, Cuba legalizes the US dollar, opens up the country to tourism and allows limited forms of private enterprise.

1996

Miami 'Brothers to the Rescue' planes are shot down by Cuban jets, provoking Bill Clinton to sign the Helms-Burton Act, further tightening the terms of the US embargo.

1998

Pope John Paul II visits Cuba and is watched by more than one million people in Havana. Despite conversing politely with Castro, he diplomatically questions Cuba's human-rights record.

armored train in Santa Clara and split the country's battered communications system in two. By New Year's Eve 1958, the game was up: a sense of jubilation filled the country, and Che and Camilo were on their way to Havana unopposed.

In the small hours of January 1, 1959, Batista fled by private plane to the Dominican Republic. Meanwhile, materializing in Santiago de Cuba the same day, Fidel made a rousing victory speech from the town hall in Parque Céspedes before jumping into a jeep and traveling across the breadth of the country to Havana in a Caesar-like cavalcade. The triumph of the Revolution was seemingly complete.

Cuba's history since the revolution has been a David and Goliath tale of confrontation, rhetoric, Cold War stand-offs and an omnipresent US trade embargo that has featured 11 US presidents and two infamous Cuban leaders – both called Castro. For the first 30 years, Cuba allied itself with the Soviet Union as the US used various retaliatory tactics (all unsuccessful) to bring Fidel Castro to heel, including a botched invasion, 600-plus assassination attempts, and one of the longest economic blockades in modern history. When the Soviet bloc fell in 1989–91, Cuba stood alone behind an increasingly defiant and stubborn leader surviving, against all odds, through a decade of severe economic austerity known as the Special Period. GDP fell by more than half, luxuries went out the window, and a wartime spirit of rationing and sacrifice took hold among a populace that, ironically, had prised itself free from foreign (neo)colonial influences for the first time in its history.

The 'wet foot dry foot' law (Cuban Adjustment Act) signed by Bill Clinton in 1995 means that only Cubans who make it onto US soil can apply for citizenship. Those picked up at sea are sent home.

2002

Half of Cuba's sugar refineries are closed, signaling the end of a three-century-long addiction to the boom-bust monocrop. Laid-off sugar workers continue to draw salaries and are offered free education.

2003

The Bush administration tightens the noose for US citizens traveling to Cuba. Many political dissidents are arrested by Cuban authorities in an island-wide crackdown.

2006

Castro is taken ill just before his 80th birthday with divertilitus disease and steps down from the day-to-day running of the country. He is replaced by his brother Raúl.

2009

The inauguration of Barack Obama signifies a long-awaited thaw in Cuban-US relations. In an early act of rapprochement, Obama loosens restrictions for Cuban-Americans, returning to the island to visit relatives.

The Cuban Way of Life

Take a dose of WWII rationing, and a pinch of Soviet-era austerity; add in the family values of South America, the educational virtues of the US, and the loquaciousness of the Irish. Mix with the tropical pace of Jamaica and innate musicality of pastoral Africa before dispersing liberally around the sultry streets of Havana, Santiago de Cuba, Camagüey and Pinar del Río.

Life in Cuba is an open and interactive brew. Spend time in a local home and you'll quickly start to piece together an archetype. There's the pot of coffee brewing on the stove, and the rusty Chinese bike leant languidly against the wall of the front room, the faded photo of José Martí above the TV, and the statue of the venerated Virgin of El Cobre lurking in the shadows. Aside from the house-owner and their mother, brother, sister and niece, every Cuban home has a seemingly endless queue of 'visitors' traipsing through. A shirtless neighbor who's come over to borrow a wrench, the local busybody from the CDR (Committee for the Defense of the Revolution), a priest popping by for a glass of rum *sin hielo* (no ice); plus the cousin, the second cousin, the long-lost friend, the third cousin twice removed ... you get the picture. Then there are the sounds. A cock crowing, a saxophonist practicing his scales, dogs barking, car engines exploding, a salsa beat far off, and those all-too-familiar shouts from the street. *Dime, hermano! Que pasa, mi amor? Ah, mi vida – no es fácil!*

Habana Vieja is one of the most crowded quarters in Latin America with over 70,000 people living in an area of just 4.5 sq km.

Yes. *No es fácil* – it ain't easy. Life in Cuba is anything but easy but, defying all logic, it's perennially colorful and rarely dull.

Lifestyle

Survivors by nature and necessity, Cubans have long displayed an almost inexhaustible ability to bend the rules and 'work things out' when it matters. The two most overused verbs in the national phrasebook are *conseguir* (to get, manage) and *resolver* (to resolve, work out), and Cubans are experts at doing both. Their intuitive ability to bend the rules and make something out of nothing is borne out of economic necessity. In a small nation bucking modern sociopolitical realities, where monthly salaries top out at around the equivalent of US$25, survival can often mean getting innovative as a means of supplementing personal income. Cruise the crumbling streets of Centro Habana and you'll see people *conseguir*-ing and *resolver*-ing wherever you go. There's the casa particular owner offering guided tours using his car as a taxi, or the lady selling lobsters in defiance of government regulations. Other schemes may be ill-gotten or garnered through trickery, such as the *compañero* (comrade) who pockets the odd blemished cigar from the day job to sell to unsuspecting Canadians. Old Cuba hands know one of the most popular ways to make extra cash is working with (or over) tourists.

Havana city Historian Eusebio Leal Spengler was born in the city in 1942. He has a degree in history and archaeological sciences, and a masters in Latin American, Caribbean and Cuban studies.

In Cuba, hard currency (ie convertible pesos) rules, primarily because it is the only way of procuring the modest luxuries that make living in this austere socialist republic more comfortable. Paradoxically, the post-1993 double economy has reinvigorated the class system the Revolution worked so hard to neutralize, and it's no longer rare to see Cubans with access to convertibles touting designer clothing while others hassle tourists mercilessly for bars of soap. This stark re-emergence of 'haves' and 'have nots' is among the most ticklish issues facing Cuba today.

Other social traits absorbed since the Revolution are more altruistic and less divisive. In Cuba sharing is second nature and helping out your *compañero* with a lift, a square meal or a few convertibles when they're in trouble is considered a national duty. Check the way that strangers interact in queues or at transport intersections and log how in Cuban houses neighbors share everything from tools, to food, to babysitting time without a second thought.

Cubans are informal. The *tú* form of Spanish address is much more common that the formal *usted*, and people greet each other with a variety of friendly addresses. Don't be surprised if a complete stranger calls you *mi amor* (my love) or *mi vida* (my life), and expect casa particular owners to regularly open the front door shirtless (men), or with their hair in rollers (women). To confuse matters further, Cuban Spanish is rich in colloquialisms, irony, sarcasm and swear words.

DOCTORS

Cuba has 70,000 qualified doctors. The whole of Africa has only 50,000.

Sport

Considered a right of the masses, professional sport was abolished by the government after the Revolution. Performance-wise it was the best thing the new administration could have done. Since 1959 Cuba's Olympic medal haul has rocketed into the stratosphere. The crowning moment came in 1992 when Cuba – a country of 11 million people languishing low on the world's rich list – brought home 14 gold medals and ended fifth on the overall medals table. It's a testament to Cuba's high sporting standards that their 11th-place finish in Athens in 2004 was considered something of a national failure.

Characteristically, the sporting obsession starts at the top. Fidel Castro was once renowned for his baseball-hitting prowess, but what is lesser known was his personal commitment to the establishment of a widely accessible national sporting curriculum at all levels. In 1961 the National Institute of Sport, Physical Education and Recreation (Inder) founded a system of sport for the masses that eradicated discrimination and integrated children from a young age. By offering paid leisure-time to workers and dropping entrance fees to major sports events, the organization caused participation in popular sports to multiply tenfold by the 1970s and the knock-on effect to performance was tangible.

Cuba high-jumper, Javier Sotomayor has held the world record (2.45m) for the event since 1993, and has recorded 17 of the 24 highest jumps ever.

Cuban *pelota* (baseball) is legendary and the country is riveted during the October–March regular season, turning rabid for the play-offs in April. You'll see passions running high in the main square of provincial capitals, where fans debate minute details of the game with lots of finger-wagging in what is known as a *peña deportiva* (fan club) or *esquina caliente* (hot corner).

Cuba is also a giant in amateur boxing, as indicated by champions Teófilo Stevenson, who brought home Olympic gold in 1972, 1976 and 1980, and Félix Savón, another triple medal winner, most recently in 2000. Every sizable town has an arena called *sala polivalente,* where big boxing events take place, while training and smaller matches happen at gyms, many of which train Olympic athletes.

Multiculturalism

A convergence of three different races and numerous nationalities, Cuba is a multicultural society that, despite difficult challenges, has been relatively successful in forging racial equality.

Elements of French culture imported via Haiti in the 1790s are still visible in Cuba today, particularly in the French-founded settlements of Guantánamo and Cienfuegos.

The annihilation of the indigenous Taíno by the Spanish and the brutality of the slave system left a bloody mark in the early years of colonization, but the situation had improved significantly by the second half of the 20th century. The Revolution guarantees racial freedom by law, though black Cubans are still far more likely to be stopped by the police for questioning, and over 90% of Cuban exiles in the US are of white descent. Black people are also under-represented in politics; of the victorious rebel army officers that took control of the government in 1959 only a handful (Juan Almeida being the most obvious example) were black or mixed race.

According to the most recent census, Cuba's racial breakdown is 24% *mulato* (mixed race), 65% white, 10% black and 1% Chinese. Aside from the obvious Spanish legacy, many of the so-called 'white' population are the descendants of French immigrants who arrived on the island in various waves during the early part of the 19th century. Indeed, the cities of Guantánamo, Cienfuegos and Santiago de Cuba were all either pioneered or heavily influenced by French *émigrés*, and much of Cuba's coffee and sugar industries owes their development to French entrepreneurship.

The black population is also an eclectic mix. Numerous Haitians and Jamaicans came to Cuba to work in the sugar fields in the 1920s and they brought many of their customs and traditions with them. Their descendants can be found in Guantánamo and Santiago in the Oriente or places

GENERACIÓN Y – THE BLOGGING REVOLUTION

In November 2009, Yoani Sánchez, a Cuban blogger and rare voice of online dissent in internet-gagged Cuba, wrote seven questions to US president, Barack Obama. Surprising Sánchez, the blogosphere and just about everybody else, Obama quickly wrote back, not just with seven answers, but with an unqualified message of support for Yoani – a vociferous critic of the Cuban government – applauding her 'courageous' efforts to provide the world 'with a unique window into the realities of daily life in Cuba.'

In truth, Sánchez's gritty blog, 'Generación Y' had been testing the mettle of Cuba's censorship police since April 2007. Despite being blithely ignored by the authorities at first, the site had garnered numerous awards by 2009, including the Ortega & Gasset prize for digital journalism plus a plug from *Time* Magazine hailing Yoani as one of the 100 most influential people on the planet.

Packed with candid insights from daily Cuban life and covering topics as diverse as gay rights to the workings of a Cuban car, Sánchez's blog is no unbending political polemic, through her penchant for exercising the right of free speech has increasingly brought her to the attention of Cuba's prickly authorities (she was once allegedly beaten by government officials). Having lived abroad in Switzerland for two years, Sánchez is aware that life on the 'other side' is no unblemished paradise and her worldliness enhances her objectivity. Not that this makes writing her blog any easier. In a country with an internet usage rate lower than Haiti, she frequently has to circumnavigate petty bureaucracy in order to update her blog entries, which are sent to friends in Germany to be posted online. Ironically, the Generación Y site is blocked in Cuba, rendering Sánchez a blind blogger unable to read her work along with the thousands of comments it inspires.

Sánchez has another avid reader – Fidel Castro. In June 2008 the convalescing Cuban leader paid her a veiled compliment when he quoted text from her blog (albeit disparagingly) in the prologue to one of his reissued books.

To read Yoani Sánchez's blog (available in 21 languages) hit www.desdecuba.com/generaciony.

such as Venezuela in Ciego de Ávila province where Haitian voodoo liturgies are still practiced.

Religion

Religion is among the most misunderstood and complex aspects of Cuban culture. Before the Revolution 85% of Cubans were nominal Roman Catholics, though only 10% attended church regularly. Protestants made up most of the remaining church-going public, though a smattering of Jews and Muslims have always practiced in Cuba and still do. When the Revolution triumphed, 140 Catholic priests were expelled for reactionary political activities and another 400 left voluntarily, while the majority of Protestants, who represented society's poorer sector, had less to lose and stayed.

In June 2008 the Cuban government legalized sex-change operations and agreed to provide them free to qualifying parties.

When the government declared itself Marxist-Leninist and therefore atheist, life for *creyentes* (literally 'believers') took on new difficulties. Though church services were never banned and freedom of religion never revoked, Christians were sent to Unidades Militares de Ayuda a la Producción (UMAPs; Military Production Aid Units), where it was hoped hard labor might reform their religious ways; homosexuals and vagrants were also sent to the fields to work. This was a short-lived experiment, however. More trying for believers were the hard-line Soviet days of the '70s and '80s, when they were prohibited from joining the Communist Party and few, if any, believers held political posts. Certain university careers, notably in the humanities, were off-limits as well.

Things have changed dramatically since then, particularly in 1992 when the constitution was revised, removing all references to the Cuban state as Marxist-Leninist and recapturing the laical nature of the government. This led to an aperture in civil and political spheres of society for religious adherents, and to other reforms (eg believers are now eligible for party membership). Since Cuban Catholicism gained the papal seal of approval with Pope John Paul II's visit in 1998, church attendance has surged and posters welcoming him are still displayed with pride. It's worth noting that church services have a strong youth presence. There are currently 400,000 Catholics regularly attending Mass and 300,000 Protestants from 54 denominations. Other denominations such as the Seventh Day Adventists and Pentecostals are rapidly growing in popularity.

For details on Cuba's religions of African origin see p480.

Literary Cuba

Spend an evening conversing with the Cubans and you'll quickly realize that they *love* to talk. This loquaciousness extends to books. Maybe it's something they put in the rum, but since time immemorial, writers in this highly literate Caribbean archipelago have barely paused for breath, telling and retelling their stories with passionate zeal and, in the process, producing some of most ground-breaking and influential literature in Latin America. Nineteenth-century Cuban authors were some of the first to question the ethics of slavery, while 20th-century innovators such as Alejo Carpentier planted the seeds of magic realism, a writing style later adopted by Gabriel García Márquez and Salman Rushdie.

The Classicists

Any literary journey should begin in Havana in the 1830s. Cuban literature found its earliest voice in *Cecilia valdés*, a novel by Cirilo Villaverde (1812–94), published in 1882, but set 50 years earlier in a Havana divided by class, slavery and prejudice. It's widely considered to be the greatest Cuban novel of the 19th century

Preceding Villaverde, in publication if not historical setting, was romantic poet and novelist, Gertrudis Gómez Avellaneda. Born to a rich Camagüeyan family of privileged Spanish gentry in 1814, Avellaneda was a rare female writer in a rigidly masculine domain. Eleven years before *Uncle Tom's Cabin* woke up America to the same themes, her novel *Sab,* published in 1841, tackled the prickly issues of race and slavery. It was banned in Cuba until 1914 due to its abolitionist rhetoric. What contemporary critics chose not to see was Avellaneda's subtle feminism, which depicted marriage as just another form of slavery.

CALVINO

Postmodern author Italo Calvino was born in the Havana suburb of Santiago de Las Vegas in 1923. He moved back to San Remo, Italy, in 1925, aged two.

Further east, neoclassical poet and native Santiaguero, José María de Heredia, lived and wrote mainly from exile in Mexico, after being banished for allegedly conspiring against the Spanish authorities. His poetry, including the seminal *Himno del desterrado*, is tinged with a nostalgic romanticism for his homeland. He died like so many 19th century poets – young, unfulfilled and in exile.

Martí – A Category of His Own

Rarely does an author step out of normal categorization and stand alone, but José Julián Martí Pérez was no ordinary human being. A pioneering philosopher, revolutionary and modernist writer, Martí broadened the political debate in Cuba beyond slavery (which was abolished in 1886) to issues such as independence and – above all – freedom. His instantly quotable prose remains a rare unifying force among Cubans around the world, whatever their political affiliations, and he is similarly revered by Spanish speakers globally for his internationalism, which has put him on a par with Simón Bolívar.

Martí's writing covered a huge range of genres: essays, novels, poetry, political commentaries, letters and even a hugely popular children's magazine called *La Edad de Oro*. He was an accomplished master of aphorisms, and his powerful one-liners still crop up in everyday Cuban speech. His two most famous works, published in 1891, are the political essay *Nuestra América* and his collected poems, *Versos sencillos,* both of which laid bare his hopes and dreams for Cuba and Latin America.

Heberto Padilla (1932–2000) was a Cuban poet whose dissident writings in the 1960s led to his imprisonment, inspiring the 'Padilla Affair.'

The Experimentalists

Cuban literature grew up in the early 1900s. Inspired by a mixture of Martí's modernism and new surrealistic influences wafting over from Europe, the first half of the 20th century was an age of experimentation for Cuban writers. The era's literary legacy rests on three giant pillars: Alejo Carpentier, a baroque wordsmith who invented the much copied style of *lo real maravilloso* (magic realism); Guillermo Cabrera Infante, a Joycean master of colloquial language, who pushed the parameters of Spanish to barely comprehensible boundaries; and José Lezama Lima, a gay poet of Proustian ambition, whose weighty novels were rich in layers, themes and anecdotes. None were easy to read, but all broke new ground inspiring erudite writers far beyond Cuban shores (Márquez and Rushdie among them). Swiss-born Carpentier's magnum opus was *El siglo de las luces* (Explosion in a Cathedral), which explores the impact of the French revolution in Cuba through a veiled love story. Many consider it to be the finest novel ever written by a Cuban author. Infante, from Gibara, rewrote the rules of language in *Tres tristes tigres* (Three Trapped Tigers), a complex study of street life in pre-Castro Havana. Lezama, meanwhile, took an anecdotal approach to novel writing in *Paradiso* (Paradise), a multi-layered, widely interpreted evocation of Havana in the 1950s with homoerotic undertones.

Grasping at the coattails of this verbose trio was Miguel Barnet, an anthropologist from Havana, whose *Biografía de un cimarrón* (Biography of a Runaway Slave), published in 1963, gathered testimonies from 103-year-old former slave Esteban Montejo, and crafted them into a fascinating written documentary of the brutal slave system nearly 80 years after its demise.

Enter Guillén

Born in Camagüey in 1902, mulatto poet Nicolás Guillén was far more than just a writer: he was a passionate and lifelong champion of Afro-Cuban rights. Rocked by the assassination of his father in his youth and inspired by the drum-influenced music of former black slaves, Guillén set about articulating the hopes and fears of dispossessed black laborers with the rhythmic Afro-Cuban verses that would ultimately become his

LITERARY PIT-STOPS

» Casa Natal de Nicolás Guillén (p314)

» Museo-Casa Natal de José Martí (p64)

» Casa Natal de José María de Heredia (p391)

» Museo Lezama Lima (p70)

» Museo Hemingway (p133)

» Fundación Alejo Carpentier (p108)

trademark. Famous poems in a prolific career included the evocative *Tengo* and the patriotic *Che comandante, amigo*.

Working in self-imposed exile during the Batista era, Guillén returned to Cuba after the revolution whereupon he was given the task of formulating a new cultural policy and setting up the Writer's Union, Uneac (Unión de Escritores y Artistas de Cuba).

The Dirty Realists

In the 1990s and 2000s, baby boomers that had come of age in the era of censorship and Soviet domination began to respond to radically different influences in their writing. Some fled the country, others remained; all tested the boundaries of artistic expression in a system weighed down by censorship and creative asphyxiation.

Stepping out from the shadow of Lezama Lima was Reinaldo Arenas, a gay writer from Holguín province, who, like Guillermo Cabrera Infante, fell out with the revolution in the late '60s and was imprisoned for his efforts. Arenas finally escaped to the US in 1980 during the Mariel boatlift. He went on to write his hyperbolic memoir, *Antes que anochezca* (Before Night Falls), about his imprisonment and homosexuality. Published in the US in the 1993, it met with huge critical acclaim.

The so-called 'dirty realist' authors of the late '90s and early 2000s took a more subtle approach to challenging contemporary mores. Pedro Juan Gutiérrez earned his moniker as the 'tropical Bukowski' for the *Dirty Havana Trilogy*, a sexy, sultry study of Centro Habana during the Special Period. The trilogy held a mirror up to the desperate economic situation, but steered clear of direct political polemics. Zoé Valdés, born the year Castro took power, has been more direct in her criticism of the regime, particularly since leaving Cuba for Paris in 1995. Her most readily available novels in English translation are *I Gave You All I Had* and *Dear First Love*.

Graham Greene originally set his comic take on British espionage in Soviet-occupied Tallinn, Estonia. But a chance visit to Havana changed his mind. The novel ultimately became *Our Man in Havana*.

The Outsiders

Adorned with color, life and unfathomable contradictions, Cuba's cultural palette has cast a powerful spell over expat authors, inspiring them to compose some vividly memorable novels. In the 1940s and '50s, Cuba played a part in the fiction of two of the greatest English-language writers of the 20th century: Graham Greene and Ernest Hemingway. Greene crammed his lucid Cuban musings into one legendary book, *Our Man in Havana,* a fitting ode to the greedy, gaudy, gambling-obsessed Havana of the 1950s. Hemingway, meanwhile, penned a trio of Caribbean classics: *To Have and Have Not,* the tale of a grizzled sailor running contraband between Florida and Cuba;

LITERARY DEPICTIONS OF HAVANA

- *Cecilia valdés*, Cirilo Villaverde, 1830s
- *Cuba Libre*, Elmore Leonard, 1890s
- *Our Man in Havana*, Graham Greene, 1950s
- *Tres tristes tigres*, Guillermo Cabrera Infante, 1950s
- *Cuba and the Night*, Pico Iyer, 1980s-'90s
- *Dirty Havana Trilogy*, Pedro Juan Gutiérrez, 1990s
- *Havana Quartet*, Leonardo Padura, 2000s

Islands in the Stream followed a stoic American on the lookout for German U-boats off Cuba during WWII, and the Nobel/Pulitzer prize-winning *The Old Man and the Sea*, an allegorical story about an old fisherman's battle to catch a huge marlin off the north coast of Cuba.

The closest any writer has come to emulating Greene and Hemingway since the 1950s is Pico Iyer, an Anglo-American of Indian parentage whose wonderfully evocative *Cuba and the Night* sums up the ambivalence of the Special Period through the eyes of a foreign photo-journalist seduced by the country's passion, yet flummoxed by its politics.

Relying less on personal experience and more on historical fact, *Cuba Libre*, by American pulp-fiction writer, Elmore Leonard is a racy, plot-driven story set in Cuba during the Second Independence War. The action takes place against the backdrop of the explosion of the USS *Maine* in Havana Harbor and the storming of San Juan Hill by Teddy Roosevelt's Rough Riders. Equally accessible, though set 80 years later during the Soviet era, is the gritty crime novel *Havana Bay* by another American writer, Martin Cruz Smith.

Contemporary writer Leonardo Padura Fuentes is well known for his quartet of Havana-based detective novels *Los cuatro estaciones* (The Four Seasons).

Arts & Architecture

The Arts

Leave your preconceptions about 'art in a totalitarian state' at home. The breadth of Cuban cinema, painting and sculpture could put many far more politically libertarian nations to shame. The roll call starts at grassroots level. Every provincial town in Cuba, no matter how small, has a Casa de Cultura that acts as a nexus for the country's bubbling cultural life. Casas de Cultura stage everything from traditional salsa music to innovative comedy nights, with upcoming events penned onto a *cartelera* outside. On top of this, countless other theaters, organizations and institutions bring highbrow art to the masses completely free – yes, *free* – of charge.

Best Uneac Cultural Venues

- » Huron Azul, Havana
- » Holguín
- » Sancti Spíritus
- » Santiago de Cuba
- » Cienfuegos
- » Puerto Padre

The quality of what's on offer is equally impressive. The Cubans seem to have made a habit out of taking almost any artistic genre and reinventing it for the better. You'll pick up first-class flamenco, ballet, classical music and Shakespearean theater here in the most mundane of places, not to mention Lorca plays, alternative cinema and illuminating, sometimes heated, deconstructions of novels by the likes of Gabriel García Márquez and Alejo Carpentier.

Cinema

Cuban cinema has always been closer to the European art-house tradition than to the formula movies of Hollywood, especially since the revolution, when cultural life veered away from American influences. Few notable movies were made until 1959, when the new government formed the Instituto Cubano del Arte e Industria Cinematográficos (Icaic), headed up by longtime film sage and former Havana University student, Alfredo Guevara, who held the position on and off until 2000. The 1960s were Icaic's *Década de oro* (golden decade) when, behind an artistic veneer, successive directors were able to test the boundaries of state-imposed censorship and, in some cases, gain greater creative license. Innovative movies of this era poked fun at bureaucracy, made pertinent comments on economic matters, questioned the role of intellectualism in a socialist state and, later on, tackled previously taboo gay issues. The giants behind the camera were Humberto Solás, Tomás Gutiérrez Alea, and Juan Carlos Tabío, who, working under Guevara's guidance, put cutting-edge Cuban cinema on the international map.

Cuba's first notable postrevolutionary movie, the joint Cuban-Soviet *Soy Cuba* (I am Cuba; 1964) was directed by a Russian, Mikhail Kalatozov, who dramatized the events leading up to the 1959 Revolution in four interconnecting stories. Largely forgotten by the early '70s, the movie was resurrected in the mid-1990s by American director Martin Scorsese, who, upon seeing the film for the first time, was astounded by the cinematography, atmospheric camera-work and, above all, technically amazing tracking shots. The film gets a rare 100% rating on the 'Rotten Tomatoes' website and has been described by one American film critic as 'a unique, insane, exhilarating spectacle.'

Serving his apprenticeship in the 1960s, Cuba's most celebrated director, Tomás Gutiérrez Alea, cut his teeth directing art-house movies such as *La muerte de un burócrata* (Death of a Bureaucrat; 1966), a satire on excessive socialist bureaucratization; and *Memorias de subdesarrollo* (Memories of Underdevelopment; 1968), the story of a Cuban intellectual too idealistic for Miami, yet too decadent for the austere life of Havana. Teaming up with fellow director Juan Carlos Tabío in 1993, Gutiérrez went on to make another movie classic, the Oscar-nominated *Fresa y chocolate* (Strawberry and Chocolate) – the tale of Diego, a skeptical homosexual who falls in love with a heterosexual communist militant. It remains Cuba's cinematic pinnacle. Humberto Solás, a master of low budget (*cine pobre*) movies, first made his mark in 1968 with the seminal *Lucía*. It explored the lives of three Cuban women at key moments in the country's history: 1895, 1932 and the early 1960s. Solás made his late-career masterpiece, *Barrio Cuba,* in 2005. It's the tale of a family torn apart by the historical upheavals of the revolution.

In 2010, Cuban film director Fernando Pérez brought the early life of José Martí to the screen in a film called *El ojo del canario* (The Eye of the Canary).

Since the death of Gutiérrez Alea in 1996 and Solás in 2008, Cuban cinema has passed the baton to a new, equally talented, stash of movie guerrillas. Their uncrowned king is Fernanado Pérez, who leapt onto the scene in 1994 with the Special Period classic *Madagascar,* focusing on an inter-generational struggle between a mother and daughter. Pérez's peak to date is 2003's *Suite Habana,* a moody documentary about a day in the life of 13 real people in the capital that uses zero dialogue. Pérez's closest 'rival' is Juan Carlos Cremata, whose 2005 road movie *Viva Cuba,* a study of class and ideology as seen through the eyes of two children, garnered much international praise.

Havana's growing influence in the film culture of the American hemisphere is highlighted each year in the Festival Internacional del Nuevo Cine Latinoamericano held every December in Havana. Described as the ultimate word in Latin American cinema, this annual get-together of critics, sages and filmmakers has been fundamental in showcasing recent Cuban classics to the world.

ARTISTIC BOUNDARIES

In June 1961, during a speech in Havana's Biblioteca Nacional, Fidel Castro laid down the cultural parameters that have guided Cuban art for the last 50 years with the words: 'Within the revolution anything, against the revolution nothing'.

Although art and culture are actively encouraged in Cuban society, there's an imaginary line in the sand outside of which writers of all genres are set strict limits. Conformists enjoy prestige, patronage and a certain amount of artistic freedom, while dissidents face oppression, incarceration and the knowledge that their hard-won literary reputation will be quickly airbrushed out of Cuban history. The decision artists must make is whether or not they can work within these limits. Some, such as national poet Nicolás Guillén, filmmaker Tomás Gutiérrez Alea and musician Silvio Rodríguez, have used subtlety, black humor and veiled poetry to push the boundaries of Cuban censorship and get formerly taboo subjects thrust into the mainstream. Others, such as Guillermo Cabrera Infante, Herberto Padilla and Reinaldo Arenas, have taken their criticism abroad, where they have continued to write, create and debate away from the interfering arm of censors.

Painting & Sculpture

Thought-provoking and visceral, modern Cuban art combines lurid Afro-Latin American colors with the harsh reality of the 52-year-old Revolution. For foreign art lovers visiting Cuba it's a unique and intoxicating brew. Forced into a corner by the constrictions of the culture-redefining Cuban Revolution, modern artists have invariably found that, by co-opting (as opposed to confronting) the socialist regime, opportunities for academic training and artistic encouragement are almost unlimited. Encased in such a volatile, creative climate, abstract art in Cuba – well established in its own right before the Revolution – has flourished.

The first flowering of Cuban art took place in the 1920s when painters belonging to the so-called *Vanguardia* movement relocated temporarily to Paris to learn the ropes from the avant-garde European school then dominated by the likes of Pablo Picasso. One of the Vanguardia's earliest exponents was Victor Manuel García (1897–1969), the genius behind one of Cuba's most famous paintings, *La gitana tropical* (1929), a portrait of an archetypal Cuban woman with her luminous gaze staring into the middle distance. The canvas, displayed in Havana's Museo Nacional de Bellas Artes, is often referred to as the Latin Mona Lisa. Victor Manuel's contemporary, Amelia Peléaz (1896–1968), was another Francophile who studied in Paris, where she melded avant-gardism with more primitive Cuban themes. Though Peléaz worked with many different materials, her most celebrated work was in murals, including the 670-sq-m tile mural on the side of the Hotel Habana Libre.

Top Contemporary Artists

- » José Villa
- » Joel Jover
- » Flora Fong
- » José Rodríguez Fúster
- » Tomás Sánchez

In the international context, art in Cuba is dominated by the prolific figure of Wilfredo Lam (1902–82), painter, sculptor and ceramicist of mixed Chinese, African and Spanish ancestry. Born in Sagua La Grande, Villa Clara province, in 1902, Lam studied art and law in Havana before departing for Madrid in 1923 to pursue his artistic ambitions in the fertile fields of post-WWI Europe. Displaced by the Spanish Civil War in 1937, he gravitated toward France, where he became friends with Pablo Picasso and swapped ideas with the pioneering surrealist André Breton. Having absorbed various cubist and surrealist influences, Lam returned to Cuba in 1941, where he produced his own seminal masterpiece *La jungla* (The Jungle), considered by critics to be one of the developing world's most representative paintings.

Post-Lam, Cuban art was organized around a group of abstract painters known as the *Grupo de los once* (Group of Eleven). One of its lead-

BEST PLACES TO SEE CUBAN ART

» **Museo Nacional de Bellas Artes** (p67) Havana's dual-sited art museum vies for 'best-in-the-Caribbean' status.

» **Museo de Arte Cubano Contemporáneo** (p289) An improbably situated contemporary art museum in Topes de Collantes natural park.

» **Comunidad Artística Verraco** (p417) An artistic community that inhabits Parque Baconao in Santiago de Cuba Province.

» **Camagüey** Strong art and ceramic tradition spearheaded by the studio of Joel Jover (p313).

» **Las Terrazas** (p148) Numerous artistic workshops are scattered throughout Artemisa province's eco-village.

» **Baracoa** (p439) Colorful Gauguin-style art is sold by private vendors in their home studios.

» **Las Tunas** (p330) The city of sculptures has over 100 pieces of public art to admire.

ers was Raúl Martínez from Ciego de Ávila, a pioneer of pop art, poster art and revolutionary iconography. His famous portrait studies have featured personalities such as Camilo Cienfuegos, José Martí and Che Guevara, while his film posters (including for the Humberto Solás movie, *Lucía*) have become classics of 1960s pop art.

Art has enjoyed strong government patronage since the revolution (albeit within the confines of strict censorship), exemplified with the opening of the Instituto Superior de Arte in the outlying Havana neighborhood of Cubanacán in 1976.

Architecture

There's nothing *pure* about Cuban architecture. Rather like its music, cityscapes exhibit an unashamed hybrid of styles, ideas and background influences. It's not all pretty. Cuba's brief flirtation with Soviet architectonics in the 1960s and '70s threw up plenty of breeze-block apartments and ugly hotels that sit rather jarringly alongside the beautiful relics of the colonial era. Emerging relatively unscathed from the turmoil of three revolutionary wars, well-preserved cities like Camagüey, Santiago de Cuba and Havana have survived into the 21st century with the bulk of their original colonial features intact. The preservation has been aided further by the nomination of Havana Vieja, Trinidad, Cienfuegos and Camagüey as Unesco World Heritage Sites.

Top Havana Buildings

- » **Art deco** Edifico Bacardí
- » **Art nouveau** Palacio Cueto
- » **Baroque** Catedral de San Cristóbal de La Habana
- » **Eclectic** Palacio Presidencial
- » **Modernist** Edifico Focsa
- » **Neoclassical** Capitolio

Cuba's oldest architectural creation is the network of Spanish fortresses erected around the country during the 16th and 17th centuries to deter attacks from pirates and corsairs on the archipelago's coastal cities. Notable examples include Havana's Castillo de la Real Fuerza (p57), the second-oldest fort in the Americas; the labyrinthine Castillo de San Pedro de la Roca del Morro (p400) in Santiago, designed by Italian military architect Giovanni Bautista Antonelli; and the massive Cabaña (p65) overlooking Havana Bay, the largest fort in the Americas.

Cuba's earliest townscapes were dominated by ecclesiastical architecture, reflected initially in the noble cloisters of Havana's Convento de Santa Clara (p63), built in 1632, and culminating a century or so later in the magnificent Catedral de San Cristóbal (p55), considered by many to be the country's most outstanding baroque monument. Some of the best architecture from this period can be viewed in Habana Vieja, whose peculiar layout around *four* main squares – each with its own specific social or religious function – sets it apart from other Spanish colonial capitals.

Cuban Baroque

Baroque architecture arrived in Cuba in the early 1700s via Spain a good 50 years after its European high-water mark. Fuelled by the rapid growth of the island's nascent sugar industry, *nouveau riche* slave-owners and sugar merchants ploughed their juicy profits into grandiose urban buildings. The finest examples of baroque in Cuba adorn the homes and public buildings of Habana Vieja, although the style didn't reach its zenith until the mid-1700s with the construction of the Catedral de San Cristóbal de la Habana and the surrounding Plaza de la Catedral (p54).

Due to climate and vernacular, traditional baroque (the word is taken from the Portuguese noun *barroco,* which means an 'elaborately-shaped pearl') was quickly 'tropicalized' in Cuba, with local architects adding their own personal flourishes to the new municipal structures that were springing up in various provincial cities. Indigenous features included *rejas* (wooden window grilles), *vitrales* (colorful stained glass), *entresuelos* (mezzanine floors) and elegantly arched *portales* (galleried exterior walkways that provided pedestrians with shelter from the sun and the rain). Signature baroque buildings, such as the Palacio de los Capitanes Generales (p56) in Plaza de Armas in Havana were made from hard local limestone dug from the nearby San Lázaro quarries and constructed using slave labor. As a result, the intricate exterior decoration that characterized baroque architecture in Italy and Spain was noticeably toned down in Cuba, where local workers lacked the advanced stonemasonry skills of their more accomplished European cousins.

Some of the most exquisite baroque buildings in Cuba are found in Trinidad and date from the city's sugar boom in the early decades of the 19th century when designs and furnishings were heavily influenced by the haute couture furnishings of Italy, France and Georgian England. Now protected by law as part of a Unesco World Heritage Site, the settlement's cobbled streets form part of one of Latin America's most intact colonial cities.

Neoclassical

Neoclassicism first evolved in the mid-18th century in Europe as a reaction to the lavish ornamentation and gaudy ostentation of baroque. Conceived in the progressive academies of London and Paris, the movement's early adherents advocated sharp primary colors and bold symmetrical lines, coupled with a desire to return to the perceived architectural 'purity' of ancient Greece and Rome. The style eventually reached Cuba at the beginning of the 19th century via groups of French émigrés who had fled west from Haiti following a violent slave rebellion in 1791. Within a couple of decades, neoclassicism had established itself as the nation's dominant architectural style.

By the mid-19th century sturdy neoclassical buildings were the norm among Cuba's bourgeoisie in cities such as Cienfuegos and Matanzas, with bold symmetrical lines, grandiose frontages and rows of imposing columns replacing the decorative baroque flourishes of the early colonial period.

Havana's first true neoclassical building was El Templete (p56), a diminutive Doric temple constructed in Habana Vieja in 1828 next to the spot where Fr Bartolomé de las Casas is said to have conducted the city's first Mass. As the city gradually spread westward in the mid-1800s, outgrowing its 17th-century walls, the style was adopted in the construction of more ambitious buildings, such as the the famous Hotel Inglaterra (p67) overlooking Parque Central. Havana grew in both size and beauty during this period, bringing into vogue new residential design features such as spacious classical courtyards and rows of imposing street-facing colonnades, leading seminal Cuban novelist Alejo Carpentier to christen it the 'city of columns.'

A second neoclassical revival swept Cuba at the beginning of the 20th century, spearheaded by the growing influence of the US on the island. Prompted by the ideas and design ethics of the American Renaissance (1876–1914), Havana underwent a full-on building explosion, sponsoring such gigantic municipal buildings as the Capitolio Nacional (p66) and the Universidad de la Habana (p76). In the provinces, the style reached its high-water mark in a trio of glittering theaters: the Caridad in Santa Clara (see p252), the Sauto in Matanzas (p203) and the Tomás Terry in Cienfuegos (p241).

Cuba's Modern Engineering Wonders

- » Albear Aqueduct (1893)
- » Havana's sewers (1912)
- » Carretera Central (1931)
- » Edificio Focsa (1956)
- » Havana Harbor Tunnel (1958)
- » Bacunayagua Bridge (1959)
- » La Farola (1964)

Art Deco

Art deco was an elegant, functional and modern architectural movement that originated in France at the beginning of the 20th century and reached its apex in America in the 1920s and '30s. Drawing from a vibrant mix of Cubism, futurism and primitive African art, the genre promoted lavish yet streamlined buildings with sweeping curves and exuberant sun-burst motifs such as the Chrysler building in New York and the architecture of the South Beach neighborhood in Miami.

Brought to Cuba via the United States, the nation quickly acquired its own clutch of signature art-deco buildings with the lion's share residing in Havana. One of Latin America's finest examples of early art deco is the Edifico Bacardí (p64) in Habana Vieja, built in 1930 to provide a Havana headquarters for Santiago de Cuba's world-famous rum-making family. Another striking creation was the 14-story Edificio López Serrano (p79) in Vedado, constructed as the city's first real *rascacielo* (skyscraper) in 1932, using New York's Rockefeller Center as its inspiration. Other more functional art-deco skyscrapers followed, including the Teatro América on Av de la Italia, the Teatro Fausto on Paseo de Martí and the Casa de las Américas on Calle G (see p84). A more diluted and eclectic interpretation of the genre can be seen in the famous Hotel Nacional (p118), whose sharp symmetrical lines and decorative twin Moorish turrets dominate the view over the Malecón.

TOUR

Havana-based travel agency Habaguanex runs a great architectural tour of the city. It's tailored toward small groups or individuals and led by experts.

Eclecticism

Eclecticism is the term often applied to the non-conformist and highly experimental architectural zeitgeist that grew up in the United States during the 1880s. Rejecting 19th-century ideas of 'style' and categorization, the architects behind this revolutionary new genre promoted flexibility and an open-minded 'anything goes' ethos, drawing their inspiration from a wide range of historical precedents.

Thanks to the strong US presence in the decades before 1959, Cuba quickly became a riot of modern eclecticism, with rich American and Cuban landowners constructing huge Xanadu-like mansions in burgeoning upper-class residential districts. Expansive, ostentatious and, at times, outlandishly kitschy, these fancy new homes were garnished with crenellated walls, oddly shaped lookout towers, rooftop cupolas and leering gargoyles. For a wild tour of Cuban eclecticism, head to Miramar in Havana, Alegre Vista in Santiago de Cuba and the Punta Gorda neighborhood in Cienfuegos.

Music & Dance

Juxtapose two ancient cultures from two very different continents (Africa and Europe). Relocate them to a slave society in a far-off tropical land. Give them some drums, a maraca and a couple of improvised guitars. See what happens.

Rich, vibrant, layered and soulful, Cuban music has long acted as a standard-bearer for the sounds and rhythms emanating out of Latin America. This is the land where salsa has its roots, where elegant white dances adopted edgy black rhythms, and where the African drum first fell in love with the Spanish guitar. From the down-at-heel docks of Matanzas to the bucolic villages of the Sierra Maestra, the amorous musical fusion went on to fuel everything from *son,* rumba, mambo*, chachachá, charanga changüí, danzón* and more.

Aside from the obvious Spanish and African roots, Cuban music has drawn upon a number of other influences. Mixed into an already exotic melting pot are genres from France, the US, Haiti and Jamaica. Conversely, Cuban music has also played a key role in developing various melodic styles and movements in other parts of the world. In Spain they called this process *ida y vuelta* (return trip) and it is most clearly evident in a style of flamenco called *guajira.* Elsewhere the 'Cuban effect' can be traced back to forms as diverse as New Orleans jazz, New York salsa and West African Afrobeat.

Described by aficionados as 'a vertical representation of a horizontal act,' Cuban dancing is famous for its libidinous rhythms and sensuous close-ups. Inheriting a love for dancing from childbirth and able to replicate perfect salsa steps by the age of two or three, most Cubans are natural performers who approach dance with a complete lack of self-consciousness – a notion that can leave visitors from Europe or North America feeling as if they've got two left feet.

Types of Cuban Dances

» Chachachá
» Guaguancó
» Mambo
» Danzón
» Columbia
» Yambú

Danzón Days

In the mid-19th century, Cuba's first hybrid musical genre, the *habanera,* a traditional European-style dance with a syncopated drumbeat, had risen to the fore. It lasted until the 1870s when the Cubans, always hungry for innovation, began to adapt it, injecting *habanera* rhythms with ever more complex African influences and ultimately creating what became known as the *danzón.*

The invention of the *danzón* is usually credited to innovative Matanzas band leader, Miguel Failde, who first showcased it with his catchy dance composition *Las Alturas de Simpson* in Matanzas in 1879. Elegant and purely instrumental in its early days, the *danzón* was slower in pace than the *habanera,* and its intricate dance patterns required dancers to circulate in couples rather than groups, a move that scandalized polite society at the time. From the 1880s onward, the genre exploded, expanding its peculiar syncopated rhythm, and adding such improbable extras as conga drums and vocalists. By the early 20th century, the *danzón* had evolved from a stately ballroom dance played by an *orchestra típica* into a more jazzed-up free-for-all known alternatively as *charanga, danzonete* or *danzón-chá*. Not surprisingly, it became Cuba's national dance, though since it was primarily a bastion of moneyed white society, it was never considered a true hybrid.

Africa Calling

While drumming in the North American colonies was ostensibly prohibited, Cuban slaves were able to preserve and pass on many of their musical traditions via influential Santería *cabildos,* religious brotherhoods that re-enacted ancient African percussive music on simple *batá* drums or *chequeré* rattles. Performed at annual festivals or on special Catholic saint's days, this rhythmic yet highly textured dance music was offered up as a form of religious worship to the *orishas* (deities).

Over time the ritualistic drumming of Santería evolved into a more complex genre known as rumba. Rumba was first concocted in the docks of Havana and Matanzas during the 1890s when ex-slaves, exposed to a revolving series of outside influences, began to knock out soulful rhythms on old packing cases in imitation of various African religious rites. As the drumming patterns grew more complex, vocals were added, dances emerged and, before long, the music had grown into a collective form of social expression for all black Cubans.

The *danzón* was originally an instrumental piece. Words were added in the late 1920s and the new form became known as the *danzónete*.

Spreading in popularity throughout the 1920s and '30s, rumba gradually spawned three different but interrelated dance formats: *guaguancó,* an overtly sexual dance; *yambú,* a slow couples' dance; and *columbia,* a fast, aggressive dance often involving fire torches and machetes. The latter originated as a devil dance of the Náñigo rite, and today it's performed only by solo males.

Pitched into Cuba's cultural melting pot, these rootsy yet highly addictive musical variants slowly gained acceptance among a new audience of middle-class whites, and by the 1940s the music had fused with *son* in a new subgenre called *son montuno,* which, in turn, provided the building blocks for salsa.

Indeed, so influential was Cuban rumba by the end of WWII that it was transposed back to Africa with experimental Congolese artists, such as Sam Mangwana and Franco Luambo (of OK Jazz fame), using ebullient Cuban influences to pioneer their own variation on the rumba theme – a genre popularly known as *soukous*.

Raw, expressive and exciting to watch, Cuban rumba is a spontaneous and often informal affair performed by groups of up to a dozen musicians. Conga drums, claves, *palitos* (sticks), *marugas* (iron shakers) and *cajones* (packing cases) lay out the interlocking rhythms, while the vocals alternate between a wildly improvising lead singer and an answering *coro* (chorus).

BEST PLACES TO SEE CUBAN MUSIC

» **Son** Casa de la Trova (p408), Santiago de Cuba
» **Nueva Trova** Casa de la Trova (p283), Trinidad
» **Salsa/Timba** Casa de la Música (p109), Centro Havana
» **Reggaetón** Noche Camagüeyana (p318), Camagüey
» **Rumba** Callejón de Hamel (p110), Havana
» **Jazz** Jazz Club La Zorra y El Cuervo (p111), Havana
» **Classical Music** Basílica Menor de San Francisco de Asís (p108), Havana
» **Changüí** Casa de Changüí (p430), Guantánamo

Rising Son

Cuba's two most celebrated 19th-century sounds, rumba and *danzón,* came from the west – specifically the cities of Havana and Matanzas. But as the genres remained largely compartmentalized between separate black and white societies, neither can be considered true hybrids. The country's first real musical fusion came from the next great sound revolution, *son*.

Filin' is a term derived from the English word 'feeling.' It was a style of music showcased by jazz crooners in the 1940s and '50s. In Cuba *filin'* grew out of bolero and *trova*.

Son emerged from the mountains of the Oriente region in the second half of the 19th century, though the earliest known testimonies go back as far as 1570. It was one of two genres to arise at around the same time (the other was *changüí*), both of which blended the melodies and lyricism of Spanish folk music with the drum patterns of recently freed African slaves. *Son's* precursor was *nengon*, an invention of black sugar-plantation workers who had evolved their percussive religious chants into a form of music and song. The leap from *nengon* to *son* is unclear and poorly documented, but at some point in the 1880s or '90s the *guajiros* (country folk) in the mountains of present-day Santiago de Cuba and Guantánamo provinces began blending *nengon* drums with the Cuban *tres* guitar while over the top a singer improvised words from a traditional 10-line Spanish poem known as a *décima*.

In its pure form, *son* was played by a sextet consisting of guitar, *tres* (guitar with three sets of double strings), double bass, bongo and two singers who played maracas and claves (sticks that tap out the beat). Coming down from the mountains and into the cities, the genre's earliest exponents were the legendary Trio Oriental, who stabilized the sextet format in 1912 when they were reborn as the Sexteto Habanero. Another early *sonero* was singer Miguel Matamoros, whose self-penned *son* classics such as *'Son de la Loma'* and *'Lágrimas Negras'* are de rigueur among Cuba's ubiquitous musical entertainers, even today.

In the early 1910s *son* arrived in Havana, where it adopted its distinctive rumba clave (rhythmic pattern), which later went on to form the basis of salsa. Within a decade it had become Cuba's signature music, gaining wide acceptance among white society and destroying the myth that black music was vulgar, unsophisticated and subversive.

By the 1930s the sextet had become a septet with the addition of a trumpet, and exciting new musicians such as blind *tres* player Arsenio Rodríguez – a songwriter who Harry Belafonte once called the 'father of salsa' – were paving the way for mambo and *chachachá*.

Barbarians of Rhythm

CHARANGAS

Charangas were Cuban musical ensembles that showcased popular *danzón*-influenced pieces.

In the 1940s and '50s the *son* bands grew from seven pieces to eight and beyond, until they became big bands boasting full horn and percussion sections that played rumba, *chachachá* and mambo. The reigning mambo king was Benny Moré (p246), who with his sumptuous voice and rocking 40-piece all-black band was known as El Bárbaro del Ritmo (The Barbarian of Rhythm).

Mambo grew out of *charanga* music, which itself was a derivative of *danzón*. Bolder, brassier and altogether more exciting than its two earlier incarnations, the music was characterized by exuberant trumpet riffs, belting saxophones and regular enthusiastic interjections by the singer (usually in the form of the word *dilo!* or 'say it!'). The style's origins are mired in controversy. Some argue that it was invented by native Habanero Orestes López after he penned a new rhythmically dextrous number called 'Mambo' in 1938. Others give the credit to Matanzas band leader Pérez Prado, who was the first musician to market his songs under the increasingly lucrative mambo umbrella in the early '40s. Whatever the case, mambo had soon spawned the world's first universal dance craze, and from New York to Buenos Aires, people couldn't get enough of its infectious rhythms.

A variation on the mambo theme, the *chachachá*, was first showcased by Havana-based composer and violinist Enrique Jorrín in 1951 while playing with the Orquesta América. Originally known as 'mambo-rumba,' the music was intended to promote a more basic kind of Cuban dance that less coordinated North Americans would be able to master, but it was quickly mambo-ized by overenthusiastic dance competitors, who kept adding complicated new steps.

Described as 'a vertical representation of a horizontal act,' Cuban dancing is famous for its libidinous rhythms.

Salsa & Its Off-Shoots

Salsa is an umbrella term used to describe a variety of musical genres that emerged out of the fertile Latin New York scene in the 1960s and '70s, when jazz, *son* and rumba blended to create a new, brassier sound. While not strictly a product of Cubans living in Cuba, salsa's roots and key influences are descended directly from *son montuno* and owe an enormous debt to innovators such as Pérez Prado, Benny Moré and Miguel Matamoros.

The self-styled Queen of Salsa was Grammy-winning singer and performer Celia Cruz. Born in Havana in 1925, Cruz served the bulk of her musical apprenticeship in Cuba before leaving for self-imposed exile in the US in 1960. But due to her longstanding opposition to the Castro regime, Cruz' records and music have remained largely unknown on the island despite her enduring legacy elsewhere. Far more influential on their home turf are the legendary salsa outfit Los Van Van, a band formed by Juan Formell in 1969 and one that still performs regularly at venues across Cuba. With Formell at the helm as the group's great improviser, poet, lyricist and social commentator, Los Van Van are one of the few contemporary Cuban groups to have created their own unique musical genre – that of songo-salsa. The band also won top honors in 2000 when they memorably took home a Grammy for their classic album, *Llego Van Van*.

Modern salsa mixed and merged further in the '80s and '90s, allying itself with new cutting-edge musical genres such as hip-hop, *reggaetón* and rap, before coming up with some hot new alternatives, most notably *timba* and songo-salsa.

Timba is, in many ways, Cuba's own experimental and fiery take on traditional salsa. Mixing New York sounds with Latin jazz, *nueva trova*, American funk, disco, hip-hop and even some classical influences, the music is more flexible and aggressive than standard salsa, incorporating greater elements of the island's potent Afro-Cuban culture. Many *timba* bands such as Bambaleo and La Charanga Habanera use funk riffs and rely on less-conventional Cuban instruments such as synthesizers and kick drums. Others – such as NG La Banda, formed in 1988 (and often credited as being the inventors of *timba*) – have infused their music with a more jazzy dynamic.

'Guajira Guantanamera' means 'country girl from Guantánamo.' Written by *trovador* Joseito Fernández, most of the original lyrics have been replaced with words from José Martí's *Versos sencillos*.

Traditional jazz, considered the music of the enemy in the Revolution's most dogmatic days, has always seeped into Cuban sounds. Jesús 'Chucho' Valdés' band Irakere, formed in 1973, broke the Cuban music scene wide open with its heavy Afro-Cuban drumming laced with jazz and *son*, and the Cuban capital boasts a number of decent jazz clubs. Other musicians associated with the Cuban jazz set include pianist Gonzalo Rubalcaba, Isaac Delgado and Adalberto Álvarez y Su Son.

The Trovadores

The original *trovadores* were like wandering medieval minstrels, itinerant songsmiths who plied their musical trade across the Oriente region in the early 20th century, moving from village to village and city to city with the carefree spirit of gypsies. Equipped with simple acoustic guitars and armed with a seemingly limitless repertoire of soft, lilting rural ballads, early Cuban *trovadores* included Sindo Garay, Nico Saquito and Joseíto Fernández, the man responsible for composing the overplayed Cuban *trova* classic, 'Guantanamera.' As the style developed into the 1960s, new advocates such as Carlos Puebla from Bayamo gave the genre a grittier and more political edge, penning classic songs such as 'Hasta Siempre Comandante,' his romantic if slightly sycophantic ode to Che Guevara.

Traditional *trova* is still popular in Cuba today, though its mantle has been challenged since the '60s and '70s by its more philosophical modern offshoot, *nueva trova*.

Rap, Reggaetón & Beyond

The contemporary Cuban music scene is an interesting mix of enduring traditions, modern sounds, old hands and new blood. With low production costs, solid urban themes and lots of US-inspired crossover styles, hip-hop and rap are taking the younger generation by storm.

Born in the ugly concrete housing projects of Alamar, Havana, Cuban hip-hop, rather like its US counterpart, has gritty and impoverished roots.

NUEVA TROVA – THE SOUNDTRACK OF A REVOLUTION

The 1960s were heady days for radical new forms of musical expression. In the US Dylan released *Highway 61 Revisited,* in Britain the Beatles concocted *Sgt Pepper* while, in the Spanish-speaking world, musical activists such as Chilean Víctor Jara and Catalan Joan Manuel Serrat were turning their politically charged poems into passionate protest songs.

Determined to develop their own revolutionary music apart from the capitalist West, the innovative Cubans under the stewardship of Haydee Santamaría, director at the influential Casa de las Américas, came up with *nueva trova*.

A caustic mix of probing philosophical lyrics and folksy melodic tunes, *nueva trova* was a direct descendent of pure *trova*, a bohemian form of guitar music that had originated in the Oriente in the late 19th century.

Post-1959 the genre became increasingly politicized and was taken up by more sophisticated artists such as Manzanillo-born Carlos Puebla, who provided an important bridge between old and new styles with his politically tinged ode to Che Guevara, 'Hasta Siempre Comandante' (1965).

Nueva trova came of age in February 1968 at the Primer Encuentro de la Canción Protesta, a concert organized at the Casa de las Américas in Havana and headlined by such rising stars as Silvio Rodríguez and Pablo Milanés. In a cultural context, it was Cuba's mini-Woodstock, an event that resounded forcefully among leftists worldwide as a revolutionary alternative to American rock 'n' roll.

In December 1972 the nascent *nueva trova* movement gained official sanction from the Cuban government during a music festival held in the city of Manzanillo to commemorate the 16th anniversary of the *Granma* landing.

Highly influential throughout the Spanish-speaking world during the '60s and '70s, *nueva trova* has often acted as an inspirational source of protest music for the impoverished and downtrodden populations of Latin America, many of whom looked to Cuba for spiritual leadership in an era of corrupt dictatorships and US cultural hegemony. This solidarity was reciprocated by the likes of Rodríguez, who penned numerous internationally lauded classics such as 'Canción Urgente para Nicaragua' (in support of the Sandinistas), 'La Maza' (in support of Salvador Allende in Chile) and 'Canción para mi Soldado' (in support of Cuban soldiers in Angola).

First beamed across the nation in the early 1980s when American rap was picked up on homemade rooftop antennae from Miami-based radio stations, the new music quickly gained ground among a population of young urban blacks culturally redefining themselves during the inquietude of the Special Period. By the '90s groups such as Public Enemy and NWA were de rigueur on the streets of Alamar and by 1995 there was enough hip-hop to throw a festival.

Tempered by Latin influences and censored by the parameters of strict revolutionary thought, Cuban hip-hop – or *reggaetón* as locals prefer to call it – has shied away from US stereotypes, instead taking on a progressive flavor all of its own. Instrumentally the music uses *batá* drums, congas and electric bass, while lyrically the songs tackle important national issues such as sex tourism and the difficulties of the stagnant Cuban economy.

Despite being viewed early on as subversive and antirevolutionary, Cuban hip-hop has gained unlikely support from inside the Cuban government, whose art-conscious legislators consider the music to have played a constructive social role in shaping the future of Cuban youth. Fidel Castro has gone one step further, describing hip-hop as 'the vanguard of the Revolution' and – allegedly – trying his hand at rapping at a Havana baseball game.

Today there are upwards of 800 hip-hop groups in Cuba, and the Cuban Rap Festival is well into its second decade. The event even has a sponsor, the fledgling Cuban Rap Agency, a government body formed in 2002 to give official sanction to the country's burgeoning alternative music scene. Groups to look out for include Obsession, 100% Original, Freehole Negro (co-fronted by a woman) and Anónimo Consejo, while the best venues are usually the most spontaneous ones.

It's hard to categorize Interactivo, a collaboration of young, talented musicians led by pianist Robertico Carcassés. Part funk, jazz and rock, and very 'in the groove,' this band jams to the rafters – a guaranteed good time. Interactivo's bassist is Yusa, a young black woman whose eponymous debut album made it clear she's one of the most innovative musicians on the Cuban scene today. Other difficult-to-categorize modern innovators include X Alfonso, an ex-student of the Conservatorio Amadeo Roldán; and dynamic nueva *trova*-rock duo Buena Fe, whose guitar-based riffs and eloquent lyrics push the boundaries of art and expression within the confines of the Cuban Revolution.

Best Casas de la Trova

» Baracoa

» Santiago de Cuba

» Trinidad

» Camagüey

» Sancti Spíritus

Son Revisited

In the late 1990s, US guitar virtuoso Ry Cooder famously breathed new life into Cuban *son* music with his remarkable *Buena Vista Social Club* album and its accompanying movie directed by Wim Wenders. Linking together half a dozen or so long-retired musical sages from the 1940s and '50s, including 90-year-old Compay Segundo (writer of Cuba's second-most played song, *Chan Chan*), dulcet singer Ibrahim Ferrer and the pianist Rúben González (ranked by Cooder as the greatest piano player he had ever heard), the unprepossessing American producer sat back in the studio and let his ragged clutch of old-age pensioners work their erstwhile magic.

The album sold five million copies worldwide, won a Grammy and launched a world tour that included gigs in Amsterdam and New York. It also led to a noticeable increase in Cuban tourism, and the songs from the album – *Chan Chan, Cuarto de Tula, Dos Gardenias* et al – have since become staples for musical groups performing in tourist areas. Unruffled by the acclaim, most Cubans are happy to sit back and listen to the more modern sounds of timba, reggaetón and songo-salsa.

Sindo Garay was one of Cuba's original *trovadores*. Born in Santiago de Cuba, he lived until the age of 99 and claimed to have shaken hands with both José Martí and Fidel Castro.

Santería

Of all Cuba's cultural mysteries (and there are many), Santería is the most complex, cloaking an inherent 'African-ness' and leading you down an unmapped road that is at once foggy and fascinating.

A syncretistic religion that hides African roots beneath a symbolic Catholic veneer, Santería is a product of the slave era, but remains deeply embedded in contemporary Cuban culture where it has had a major impact on the evolution of the country's music, dance and rituals. Today, over three million Cubans claim to be believers, including numerous writers, artists and politicians.

Santería's misrepresentations start with its name; the word is a historical misnomer first coined by Spanish colonizers to describe the 'saint worship' practiced by 19th-century African slaves. A more accurate moniker is Regla de Ocha (way of the *orishas*), or Lucumí named for the original adherents who hailed from the Yoruba ethno-linguistic group in southwestern Nigeria, a prime looting ground for brutal slave-traders.

Strong Santería Locales

- » Regla, Havana
- » Marianao, Havana
- » Matanzas
- » Palmira, Cienfuegos
- » Santiago de Cuba

The Basics

Adherents of Santería (called *santeros*) believe in one God known as Oludomare, the creator of the universe and the source of Ashe (all life forces on earth). Rather than interact with the world directly, Oludomare communicates through a pantheon of *orishas*, various imperfect deities similar to Catholic saints or Greek gods, who are blessed with different natural (water, weather, metals) and human (love, intellect, virility) qualities. *Orishas* have their own feast days, demand their own food offerings, and are given numbers and colors to represent their personalities.

Unlike Christianity or Islam, Santería has no equivalent to the Bible or Koran. Instead, religious rites are transmitted orally and, over time, have evolved to fit the realities of modern Cuba. Another departure from popular world religions is the abiding focus on 'life on earth' as opposed to the afterlife, although Santería adherents believe strongly in the powers of dead ancestors, known as *egun*, whose spirits are invoked during initiation ceremonies.

Santería's syncretism with Catholicism occurred surreptitiously during the colonial era when African animist traditions were banned. In order to hide their faith from the Spanish authorities, African slaves secretly twinned their *orishas* with Catholic saints. Thus, Changó the male *orisha* of thunder and lightning was hidden somewhat bizarrely behind the feminine form of Santa Bárbara, while Elegguá, the *orisha* of travel and roads became St Anthony de Padua. In this way an erstwhile slave praying before a statue of Santa Bárbara was clandestinely offering his/her respects to Changó, while Afro-Cubans ostensibly celebrating the feast day of Our Lady of Regla (September 7) were, in reality, honoring Yemayá. This syncretization, though no longer strictly necessary, is still followed today.

Santería is also practiced in Puerto Rico, the Dominican Republic, Panama, Columbia, Venezuela and in some parts of the US.

The Orishas

The *orishas* (deities) are central to the understanding of Santería. There are over 400 of them in the traditional Yoruba religion, though only about a dozen are significant in contemporary Cuba. The most important are known as the Siete Potencias (seven powers) which, between them, control all aspects of daily life. They comprise of: Changó, the Zeus-like king of the gods; Yemayá, mother of the gods; Elegguá god of destiny and travelers; Oggún god of war; Ochún god of love and sensuality; Oyá guardian of cemeteries; and Obalatá the white-clad god of peace and intellect. Two additional *orishas* important in Cuba are Babalú Ayé, god of healing; and Orula, god of fortune and wisdom, through whom the high priests of Santería *(babalawos)* interpret the oracles (Ifá).

The most popular *orishas* in Cuba are combative Changó, represented by Santa Bárbara; loving Ochún syncretized with Cuba's patron saint, the black Virgen de la Caridad; and motherly Yemayá, the patron saint of sailors and fishermen twinned with Our Lady of Regla. The *orisha* Babalú Ayé or San Lázaro, is also widely venerated by the sick for his healing powers. Every December 17th thousands of pilgrims make a procession to El Rincón, a church near Havana, in the hope of achieving better health.

Santeros believe that the *orishas* control every aspect of daily life and can bring both good and bad fortune. To garner their favor, people build altars, offer food or animal sacrifices, and summon up their spirits during drumming and initiation ceremonies. It is believed that by successfully harnessing the power of the *orishas*, a person can achieve a healthy balance between the forces of nature and the conflicting tugs on their personality. The ultimate goal is to determine your personal destiny.

Every practicing *santero* has an *orisha* special to them. The choice is usually determined by one's personal attributes; a strong man is a son of Changó, a bright child the offspring of Obalatá, and a sensuous woman a daughter of Ochún.

REGLA DE OCHA

Regla de Ocha stems from Yorubaland, a cultural region in West Africa that encompasses parts of southern Togo and Benin, and a large swath of southwestern Nigeria.

Babalawos & Ifá

Babalawos are the high priests of Santería, religious sages who interpret the Ifá oracles (wise predictions) by 'communicating' with Orula, *orisha*

KEY CUBAN ORISHAS & THEIR ATTRIBUTES

ORISHA	CATHOLIC SAINT	QUALITIES/MANIFESTATIONS	COLORS	FEAST DAY
Ochún	Virgen de la Caridad	love, marriage, money	yellow, aquamarine	Sep 8
Changó	Santa Bárbara	drums, dance, passion, virility	red, white	Dec 4
Yemayá	Virgen de Regla	water, children, motherhood	blue, white	Sep 7
Elegguá	St Anthony de Padua	travelers, roads	red, black	Jun 13
Oggún	San Pedro	war, energy, metals	green, black	Jun 29
Oyá	Santa Teresa	wind, storms, death, magic	purple, brown	Oct 15
Obalatá	Virgen de la Merced	peace, spirituality, intelligence	white	Sep 24
Babalú Ayé	San Lázaro	healing	white, pale blue	Dec 17
Orula	St Francis de Asís	fortune, wisdom	green, yellow	Oct 4

of wisdom and fortune. Oracles are interpreted by a complicated process of throwing down 16 cowry shells onto a board and watching how they land. Since there are hundreds of ways in which the shells can configure, only an experienced *babalawo* is qualified to read them.

In a societal context, the role of the *babalawo* is to use his spiritual knowledge to assist people – *santeros* or otherwise – to grow spiritually and achieve peace and balance in their lives. They thus act as a go-betweens through which ordinary people can communicate with the *orishas*, fulfilling a similar role to fortune tellers, but backing it up with years of training, countless initiations, and the learning of 250 plus verses of the Ifá. A female *babalawo* is called an *iyanifa* (mother with the knowledge of Ifá).

Initiation as a Santero

To become a *santero*, a person must go through an elaborate initiation ceremony or *ebbó* lasting up to seven days and involving ritualized drumming, animal sacrifice and invocation of the *orishas*. Subsequently, the aspiring *santero* (known as an *iyawó*) has to live a rigorous monastic existence for one year during which time they must wear white, refrain from consuming alcohol, eat food from a mat on the floor, and not go out after dark.

Ebbós are potent and lengthy affairs where trance-like states are induced by hours of sung verses, ritual dances and beating on *batá* drums – the sacred drums of Regla de Ocha. Ceremonies involve the whole Santería community and are presided over by an Oba Oriate, the highest of the high priests. Initiates have their heads washed, and are dressed in a satin robe displaying the colors of their *orishas*. The aim of all Santería ceremonies is to invoke the spiritual presence of the *orishas* and *egun* (ancestors) in order to verify that the offered prayers have reached God.

Other Cuban Religions of African Origin

Contrary to popular belief, Regla de Ocha is not the only religion of African origin in Cuba, though it is by far the most widespread. Alongside it exist other syncretistic religions that emerged during the 19th century

THE CABILDOS OF MATANZAS

Santería has many hotbeds, but none are more powerful than the port city of Matanzas. Dubbed the 'Athens of Cuba' in the mid-19th century for its abundance of poets and writers, the city's erudite white intellectuals obscured an underlying 'African-ness,' a cultural force that found expression in the roots music of rumba and the mysterious *cabildos* that helped shape it.

Afro-Cuban *cabildos* trace their origins back to the start of the colonial period when African slaves of similar ethnic backgrounds formed 'brotherhoods', coming together on feast days to worship the *orishas* (deities) and keep their ancient traditions alive.

By the mid-19th century there were an estimated 100 different *cabildos* in Cuba incorporating enslaved and freed blacks from the same African 'nations.' In the 1920s, Cuban scholar Fernando Ortiz identified four broad 'nations' on the island: the Lucumí, from Nigeria's Yoruba tribe; the Arará, from Dahomey in present-day Benin; the Abakuá, from southwestern Cameroon; and the Kongo, from Angola.

A number of *cabildos* are still active in Matanzas today. The Iyesá Cabildo of San Juan de Bautista, a branch of Lucumí dating from 1854, is known for its distinctive ritualistic drumming. The Cabildo Arará Sabalú Nonjó, founded in 1880, is a small Arará offshoot that originated with slaves transported from the Dahomean city of Savalu. The Cabildo Santa Teresa Lucumí is an arm of the influential Villamil family whose members have played in numerous musical groups including the legendary Muñequitos de Matanzas.

representing other African 'nations' such as the Arará, from Dahomey in present-day Benin; the Abakuá, from Nigeria and Cameroon; and the Bantu from the Congo River Basin.

Arará

Just as Regla de Ocha was brought to Cuba by the Yoruba people of Nigeria, Arará has its origins within the Fon and Mahi ethno-linguistic groups of present-day Benin. Geographic factors place it closer to Haitian vodou than other Afro-Cuban religions and many of its traditions, such as the worship of vodun deities and use of body percussion in music, were imported to Cuba by resettled Haitian slaves in the early 1800s. Arará strongholds in Cuba include Havana, Matanzas and the nearby towns of Jovellanos and Máximo Gómez, but overall observance is on the wane and the sect is in danger of being assimilated into Regla de Ocha.

Abakuá

Abakuá is perhaps the most intriguing of Cuba's African religions – if indeed it is a religion at all. An all-male society with a secret language known only to initiates, Abakuá's traditions were brought to Cuba by the Efik people of southeastern Nigeria. The group is best known for its masked dances still showcased in various annual carnivals and they were instrumental in the development of the *guanguancó* style of rumba. Outside this, information is scant. The first Abakuá *cabildos* (brotherhoods) were formed in Matanzas in the 1830s, but never penetrated into east or central Cuba. In the west they reached as far as Havana, where Abakuá brotherhoods remain strong in the neighborhoods of Regla and Guanabacoa. Initiates of the group are known as *ñáñigos* and intensely secret ceremonies take place in a temple or *famba*. Cuban anthropologist, Fernando Órtiz once referred to Abakuá societies as a form of 'African masonry' and research suggests that they function like mutual aid societies and once played a key role in buying their brethren out of slavery. During Cuba's Independence Wars Abakuá cabildos linked up with other Masonic lodges to thwart a common enemy – the Spanish. The symbol of their power is an African leopard.

Find out More at...

» Asociación Cultural Yoruba de Cuba (Havana)

» Casa Templo de Santería Yemayá (Trinidad)

» Museo Municipal de Palmira (Cienfuegos)

» Museo Municipal de Regla (Havana)

Palo Monte

Palo Monte or Las Reglas de Congo is a semi-syncretized Bantu belief system that originated in what is now present-day Congo and Angola. While sharing a similar blueprint to Regla de Ocha, there are key differences. Palo focuses more on the dead (through ancestor worship) and less on the *orishas*. *Paleros* venerate natural objects (called *nganga*), in particular sticks *(palos)* which are said to retain spiritual powers. Special sticks are used to decorate altars with sacred religious vessels known as *nkisi*, believed to be inhabited by dead spirits.

In Palo Monte the creator god is known as Nzambi and divination methods are similar to Regla de Ocha. However, although some of the religious groupings (organized in the structure of 'families') have syncretized their beliefs with Catholicism, others haven't. The syncretized groups – called Palo Cristiano – differ from Santería in that they were syncretized in Africa before undertaking the journey to Cuba in order to hide their religion from the original European colonizers. The un-syncretized strand is known as Palo Judio.

The Church of Lukumí Babalú Ayé, established in 1974, was the first Santería church in the US.

The Cuban Landscape

The Land

Measuring 1250km from east to west and between 31km and 193km from north to south, Cuba is the Caribbean's largest island with a total land area of 110,860 sq km. Shaped like an alligator and situated just south of the Tropic of Cancer, the country is actually an archipelago made up of 4195 smaller islets and coral reefs, though the bulk of the territory is concentrated on the expansive Isla Grande and its 2200-sq-km smaller cousin, Isla de la Juventud.

Cuba's Highest Mountains

» **Pico Turquino** 1972m, Santiago de Cuba Province

» **Pico Cuba** 1872m, Santiago de Cuba Province

» **Pico Bayamesa** 1730m, Granma Province

Formed by a volatile mixture of volcanic activity, plate tectonics and erosion, the landscape of Cuba is a lush and varied concoction of caves, mountains, plains and *mogotes* (strange flat-topped hills). The highest point, Pico Turquino (1972m), is situated in the east among the lofty triangular peaks of the Sierra Maestra. Further west, in the no less majestic Sierra del Escambray, ruffled hilltops and gushing waterfalls straddle the borders of Cienfuegos, Villa Clara and Sancti Spíritus provinces. Rising like purple shadows in the far west, the 175km-long Cordillera de Guanguanico is a more diminutive range that includes the protected Sierra del Rosario Biosphere Reserve and the distinctive pincushion hills of the Valle de Viñales.

Lapped by the warm turquoise waters of the Caribbean Sea in the south, and the foamy white chop of the Atlantic Ocean in the north, Cuba's 5746km of coastline shelters more than 300 natural beaches and features one of the largest tracts of coral reef in the world. Home to approximately 900 reported species of fish and more than 410 varieties of sponge and coral, the country's unspoiled coastline is a marine wonderland and a major reason why Cuba has become renowned as a diving destination extraordinaire.

Cuba's Isla Grande (main island) is the 17th-largest island in the world by area; slightly smaller than Newfoundland, but marginally bigger than Iceland.

The 7200m-deep Cayman Trench between Cuba and Jamaica forms the boundary of the North American and Caribbean plates. Tectonic movements have tilted the island over time, creating uplifted limestone cliffs along parts of the north coast and low mangrove swamps on the south. Over millions of years Cuba's limestone bedrock has been eroded by underground rivers, creating interesting geological features including the 'haystack' hills of Viñales and more than 20,000 caves countrywide.

As a sprawling archipelago, Cuba contains thousands of islands and keys (most uninhabited) in four major offshore groups: the Archipiélago de los Colorados, off northern Pinar del Río; the Archipiélago de Sabana-Camagüey (or Jardines del Rey), off northern Villa Clara and Ciego de Ávila; the Archipiélago de los Jardines de la Reina, off southern Ciego de Ávila; and the Archipiélago de los Canarreos, around Isla de la Juventud. Most visitors will experience one or more of these island idylls, as the majority of resorts, scuba diving and virgin beaches are found in these regions.

Being a narrow island, never measuring more than 200km north to south, Cuba's capacity for large lakes and rivers is severely limited (preventing hydroelectricity). Cuba's longest river, the 343km-long Río Cauto that flows from the Sierra Maestra in a rough loop north of Bayamo, is only navigable by small boats for 110km. To compensate, 632 *embalses* (reservoirs) or *presas* (dams), covering an area of larger than 5km altogether, have been created for irrigation and water supply; these supplement the almost unlimited groundwater held in Cuba's limestone bedrock.

Lying in the Caribbean's main hurricane region, Cuba has been hit by some blinders in recent years, including three devastating storms in 2008 – its worst year for more than a century.

Cuba's Longest River

» **Name** Río Cauto

» **Length** 343km

» **Navigable length** 110km

» **Basin area** 8928 sq km

» **Source** Sierra Maestra Mountains

» **Mouth** Caribbean Sea

Protected Areas

Cuba protects its land in multiple ways: at a local level it has set up fauna reserves, bio-parks and areas of managed resources; at a national level it sponsors national and natural parks; and international protection is provided in Unesco Biosphere Reserves, Unesco World Heritage Sites and Ramsar Convention Sites. The most ecologically important and vulnerable zones (eg the Ciénaga de Zapata and the rainforest around Baracoa) are protected at more than one level. For example, Parque Nacional Alejandro de Humboldt is a national park, a Unesco World Heritage Site *and* part of the Cuchillos de Toa Unesco Biosphere Reserve. Lower down the pecking order, the smaller parks suffer from less watertight restrictions and are more open to rule-bending.

Unesco & Ramsar Sites

The highest level of environmental protection in Cuba is provided by Unesco, which has created six Biosphere Reserves over the last 25 years. Biosphere reserves are areas of high biodiversity that rigorously promote conservation and sustainable practices. After a decade and a half of successful reforestation the Sierra del Rosario became Cuba's first Unesco Biosphere Reserve in 1985. It was followed by Cuchillos del Toa (1987), Península de Guanahacabibes (1987), Bacanao (1987), Ciénaga de Zapata (2000) and the Bahía de Buenavista (2000). Additionally, two of Cuba's nine Unesco World Heritage Sites are considered 'natural'

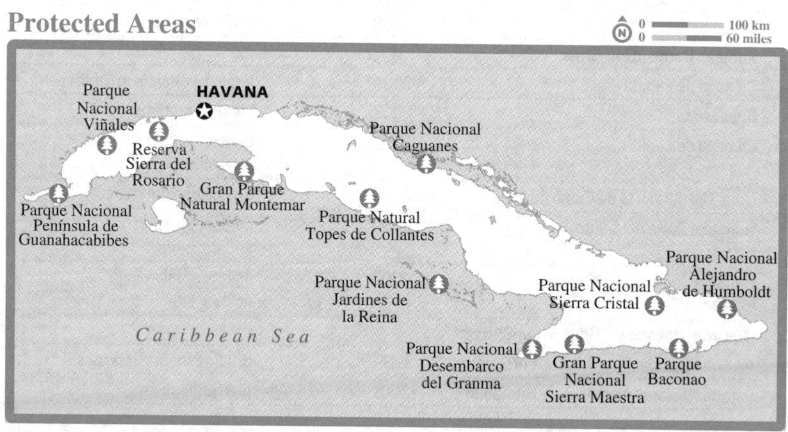

sites, ie nominated primarily for their ecological attributes. They are: Parque Nacional Desembarco del Granma (1999), hailed for its uplifted marine terraces, and Parque Nacional Alejandro de Humboldt (2001), well known for its extraordinary endemism. Complementing the Unesco sites are half a dozen Ramsar Convention Sites earmarked in 2001–02 to conserve Cuba's vulnerable wetlands. The Ramsar Convention gives added protection to the Ciénaga de Zapata and Bahía de Buenavista, and also throws a lifeline to previously unprotected regions such as the Lanier Swamp on the Isla de la Juventud (prime crocodile territory), the expansive Cauto River delta in Granma/Las Tunas, and the vital flamingo nesting sites on the north coasts of Camagüey and Ciego de Ávila provinces.

National Parks

The definition of a national park is fluid in Cuba (some are often referred to as natural parks or flora reserves) and there's no umbrella organization as in Canada or the US. A handful of the dozen listed parks – most notably Ciénaga de Zapata – now lie within Unesco Biosphere Reserves or Ramsar Convention Sites, meaning their conservation policies are better monitored. The country's first national park was Sierra del Cristal, established in 1930 (home to Cuba's largest pine forest), though it was 50 years before the authorities created another, Gran Parque Nacional Sierra Maestra (also known as Turquino), which safeguards Cuba's highest mountain. Other important parks include Viñales, with its mogotes, caves and tobacco plantations; Caguanes, an amalgam of cayos (keys) and caves surrounded by the Bahía de Buenavista; and Gran Piedra, near Santiago de Cuba, which is overlaid by the Baconao Unesco Biosphere

CUBA'S PROTECTED AREAS

AREA NAME	YEAR DESIGNATED	OUTSTANDING FEATURES
Unesco Biosphere Reserves		
Sierra del Rosario	1985	eco-practices
Cuchillos del Toa	1987	primary rainforest
Península de Guanahacabibes	1987	turtle nesting site
Bacanao	1987	coffee culture
Ciénaga de Zapata	2000	largest wetlands in Caribbean
Buenavista	2000	karst formations
Ramsar Convention Sites		
Ciénaga de Zapata	2001	largest wetlands in Caribbean
Buenavista	2002	karst formations
Ciénaga de Lanier	2002	unusual mosaic of ecosystems
Humedal del Norte de Ciego de Ávila	2002	unique coastal lakes
Humedal Delta del Cauto	2002	large population of aquatic birds
Humedal Río Máximo-Cagüey	2002	significant flamingo nesting site
'Natural' Unesco World Heritage Sites		
Parque Nacional Desembarco del Granma	1999	pristine marine terraces
Parque Nacional Alejandro de Humboldt	2001	high endemism

ECO-RESORTS

Cuba's most lauded eco-resort, Hotel La Moka in the Sierra del Rosario reserve, first opened in 1994 and its clever design features quickly set a new precedent for environmental tourism in Cuba. Other resorts that have attempted to emulate La Moka's eco-credentials are El Saltón near Santiago de Cuba and Pinares de Mayarí in the soaring pine forests southeast of Holguín.

More recently, government-run environmental body Ecotur has opened a network of rustic chalets situated in idyllic natural areas. Highlights include the Finca Esperanze near Baracoa, La Guabina near Pinar del Río, and the Hacienda del Belén in the Sierra del Chorrillo. Some chalets have shared baths and no air-con, while the more luxurious abodes enjoy swimming pools and on-site guides. All, to date, are equipped with restaurants, electricity and a variety of eco-oriented activities starting just outside the front door.

Reserve. Two important offshore national parks off the south coast are the Jardines de la Reina, an archipelago and legendary diving haven off the coast of Ciego de Ávila province; and the rarely visited Cayos de San Felipe off the coast of Pinar del Río province.

Other Reserves

On top of its national parks and Unesco sites, Cuba protects land in flora and fauna reserves, eco-reserves and areas of managed resources. Examples include the Sierra del Chorrillo in Camagüey and the Reserva Ecológica Varahicacos in Varadero. Some smaller reserves, such as Jobo Rosado in northern Sancti Spíritus province, act as buffer zones to larger parks such as the Bahía de Buenavista Unesco Biosphere Reserve.

Although Cuba's interconnecting network of protected areas is often confusing (many parks have two interchangeable names) – and sometimes overlapping – the sentiment's the same: environmental stewardship with a solid governmental backing.

Environmental Issues

Most of Cuba's environmental threats are of human origin and relate either to pollution or habitat loss, often through deforestation. Efforts to conserve the archipelago's diverse ecology were almost nonexistent until 1978, when Cuba established the National Committee for the Protection and Conservation of Natural Resources and the Environment (Comarna). Attempting to reverse 400 years of deforestation and habitat destruction, the body set about designating green belts and initiating ambitious reforestation campaigns. The conservation policies are directed by Comarna, which acts as a coordinating body, overseeing 15 ministries and ensuring that current national and international environmental legislation is being carried out efficiently. This includes adherence to the important international treaties that govern Cuba's six Unesco Biosphere Reserves and nine Unesco World Heritage Sites.

Cuba's greatest environmental problems are aggravated by an economy struggling to survive. As the country pins its hopes on tourism to save the financial day, a contradictory environmental policy has evolved. Therein lies the dilemma: how can a developing nation provide for its people *and* maintain high (or at least minimal) ecological standards?

Cayos with a Hotel Infrastructure

- Largo del Sur
- Santa María
- Las Brujas
- Coco
- Guillermo
- Levisa
- Ensenachos
- Saetia

Deforestation

It is estimated that at the time of Columbus' arrival in 1492, 95% of Cuba was covered in virgin forest. By 1959, thanks to unregulated land-clearing for sugarcane and citrus plantations, this area had been reduced to a paltry 16%. The implementation of large-scale tree-planting and the organization of significant tracts of land into protected parks has seen this figure creep back up to 24% (making it the leader in Latin America), but there is still a lot of work to be done. Las Terrazas in Pinar del Río province provided a blueprint for reforestation efforts in the late 1960s, when it saved hectares of denuded woodland from ecological disaster. More recent efforts have focused on safeguarding the Caribbean's last virgin rainforest in Parque Nacional Alejandro de Humboldt and adding protective forest fringes to wetlands in the Cauto River delta.

Cuban tobacco and cigar exports net approximately CUC$200 million annually, but every year 6000 Cubans die from smoking-related illnesses.

TOBACCO

Causeways

An early blip in Cuba's economic–ecological struggle was the 2km-long stone *pedraplén* (causeway) constructed to link offshore Cayo Sabinal with mainland Camagüey in the late 1980s. This massive project, which involved piling boulders in the sea and laying a road on top (without any bridges), interrupted water currents and caused irreparable damage to bird and marine habitats. And to what end; no resorts, as yet, inhabit deserted Cayo Sabinel. Other longer causeways were later built connecting Jardines del Rey to Ciego de Ávila (27km long) and Cayo Santa María to Villa Clara (a 48km-long monster). This time more ecofriendly bridges have enabled a healthier water flow, though the full extent of the ecological damage won't be known for another decade at least.

Wildlife & Habitat Loss

Maintaining healthy animal habitats is crucial in Cuba, a country with high levels of endemism and hence a higher threat of species extinction. The problem is exacerbated by the narrow range of endemic animals, such as the Cuban crocodile that lives almost exclusively in the Ciénaga de Zapata, or the equally rare *Eleutherodactylus iberia* (the world's smallest frog). The latter has a range of just 100 sq km and exists only in the Parque Nacional Alejandro de Humboldt, whose formation in 2001 undoubtedly saved it from extinction. Other areas under threat include the giant flamingo nesting sites on the Sabana-Camagüey archipelago, and Moa, where contaminated water runoff has played havoc with the coastal mangrove ecosystems favored by manatees.

Building new roads and airports, and the frenzied construction of giant resorts on virgin beaches, exacerbate the clash between human activity and environmental protection. The grossly shrunken extent of the Reserva Ecológica Varahicacos in Varadero due to encroaching resorts is one example. Cayo Coco – part of an important Ramsar-listed wetland that sits adjacent to a fast-developing hotel strip – is another.

Parque Nacional Alejandro de Humboldt is named for the German naturalist Alexander von Humboldt (1769–1859) who visited the island between 1801 and 1804.

Rounding up wild dolphins as entertainers in tourist-oriented *delfinarios* has rankled many activists (performing dolphins are supposed to be bred in captivity). Cockfighting, a cruel sport deeply enshrined in Cuban machismo culture, is another hot potato. Though not strictly legal it is still widely practiced. Overfishing (including turtles and lobster for tourist consumption), agricultural runoff, industrial pollution and inadequate sewage treatment have contributed to the decay of coral reefs. Diseases such as yellow band, black band and nuisance algae have begun to appear.

Pollution

As soon as you arrive in Havana or Santiago de Cuba, the air pollution hits you like a sharp slap on the face. Airborne particles, old trucks belching black smoke and by-products from burning garbage are just some of the culprits. Cement factories, sugar refineries and other heavy industries have also made their (dirty) mark. The nickel mines engulfing Moa serve as stark examples of industrial concerns taking precedence: this is

THE WORLD'S MOST SUSTAINABLE COUNTRY?

With its antiquated infrastructure and fume-belching city traffic, Cuba might not always seem like a font of innovative environmentalism. But in 2006, in an environmental report entitled *The Living Planet*, the World Wildlife Foundation (WWF) named Castro's struggling island nation as the only country in the world with sustainable development.

The WWF based its study on two key criteria: a human welfare index (life expectancy, literacy and GDP) and the ecological footprint (the amount of land needed to fulfill a person's food and energy needs). Most countries failed to meet their sustainability requirements either because their ecological footprint was too high (the mega-consuming West), or their human welfare index was too low (the poverty-stricken countries of Africa and Asia). Cuba, with its excellent health and education indices and low rates of consumption, proved to be the only exception.

It would be naive to suggest that Cuba achieved its sustainability record through foresight alone. On the contrary, the Cubans are largely ecologists by necessity. The country's sustainability credentials were first laid out in the Special Period when, shorn of Soviet subsidies and marginalized from the world economy by a US trade embargo, rationing and recycling measures were necessary to survive.

To their credit, the Cubans haven't wavered since. Despite a car-ownership ratio of 28 per 1000 (the US is closer to 850 per 1000) and an almost total absence of chemical fertilizers, the country refused to take the easy route toward greater prosperity post–Special Period and, instead, quickly fell in with the new global environmental zeitgeist.

Before his much-publicized health relapse, Fidel Castro named 2006 as the 'Year of the Energy Revolution' and gave out free energy-efficient appliances to millions of Cuban households. Visit a Cuban casa particular these days and you'll find that dinner is made in a pressure cooker, all the light bulbs are LEDs and the old inefficient 1950s fridge has, more often than not, been replaced by a more ecofriendly (and quieter) model.

some of the prettiest landscape in Cuba, turned into a barren wasteland of lunar proportions. Unfortunately there are no easy solutions; nickel is one of Cuba's largest exports, a raw material the economy couldn't do without. And while old American cars in Havana might paint a romantic picture to tourists, they're hardly fuel efficient or clean. Then there's the public transport – even Fidel has gone on the record to lament the adverse health effects of Cuba's filthy buses.

Environmental Successes

On the bright side of the environmental equation is the enthusiasm the Cuban government has shown for reforestation and protecting natural areas – especially since the mid-1980s – along with its willingness to confront mistakes from the past. Havana Harbor, once Latin America's most polluted, has been undergoing a massive cleanup project, as has the Río Almendares, which cuts through the heart of the city. Both programs are beginning to show positive results. Sulfur emissions from oil wells near Varadero have been reduced, and environmental regulations for developments are now enforced by the Ministry of Science, Technology and the Environment. Fishing regulations, as local fishers will tell you, have become increasingly strict. Striking the balance between Cuba's immediate needs and the future of its environment is one of the Revolution's increasingly pressing challenges.

Approximately 2% of Cuba's arable land is given over to coffee production and the industry supports a workforce of 265,000.

Las Terrazas is the nation's most obvious eco-success, though there have been others. Visitors to Cayo Coco can check out Parque El Bagá, a former airport that is now an eco-park, while on the Isla de la Juventud, Cuban crocodiles have been successfully reintroduced into the wild in the expansive Lanier Swamp.

Wildlife

Animals

While it isn't exactly the Serengeti, Cuba has an unusual share of indigenous fauna and serious animal-watchers won't be disappointed. Birds are probably the biggest draw and Cuba is home to more than 350 different varieties, two dozen of them endemic. Head to the mangroves of Ciénaga de Zapata near the Bahía de Cochinos (Bay of Pigs) or to the Península de Guanahacabibes in Pinar del Río for the best sightings of the blink-and-you'll-miss-it *zunzuncito* (bee hummingbird), the world's smallest bird and, at 6.5cm, not much longer than a toothpick. These areas are also home to the *tocororo* (Cuban trogon; see p491), Cuba's national bird, which sports the red, white and blue colors of the Cuban flag. Other popular bird species include *cartacubas* (a type of bird indigenous to Cuba), herons, spoonbills, parakeets and rarely seen Cuban pygmy owls.

Endemic Fauna

- » Cuban crocodile
- » Bee hummingbird
- » *Tocororo* (bird)
- » *Jutía* (tree rat)
- » Cuban gar (fish)
- » *Eleutherodactylus Iberia* (frog)
- » Cuban boa (snake)
- » Cuban red bat

Flamingos are abundant in Cuba's northern keys where they have established the largest nesting ground in the western hemisphere in the Río Máximo delta in Camagüey province, with numbers in the tens of thousands.

Land mammals have been hunted almost to extinction with the largest indigenous survivor the friendly *jutía* (tree rat), a 4kg edible rodent that scavenges on isolated keys living in relative harmony with armies of inquisitive iguanas. The vast majority of Cuba's other 38 species of mammal are from the bat family.

Cuba harbors a species of frog so small and elusive that it wasn't discovered until 1996 in what is now Parque Nacional Alejandro de Humboldt near Baracoa. Still lacking a common name the endemic amphibian is known as *Eleutherodactylus iberia*; it measures less than 1cm in length, and has a range of only 100 sq km.

Other odd species include the *mariposa de cristal* (Cuban clear-winged butterfly), one of only two clear-winged butterflies in the world; the rare *manjuarí* (Cuban alligator gar), an ancient fish considered a living fossil; and the *polimita*, a unique land snail distinguished by its festive yellow, red and brown bands.

The Caribbean manatee can grow 4.5m long and weigh up to 600kg. They can consume up to 50kg of plant life a day.

Reptiles are well represented in Cuba. Aside from iguanas and lizards, there are 15 species of snake, none of them poisonous. Cuba's largest snake is the *majá*, a constrictor related to the anaconda that grows up to 4m in length; it's nocturnal and doesn't usually mess with humans. The endemic Cuban crocodile *(Crocodylus rhombifer)* is relatively small but agile on land and in water. Its 68 sharp teeth are specially adapted for crushing turtle shells. Crocs have suffered from major habitat loss in the last century though greater protection since the 1990s has seen numbers increase. Cuba has established a number of successful crocodile breeding farms *(criaderos)*, the largest of which is at Guamá near the Bay of Pigs. Living in tandem with the Cuban croc is the larger American crocodile

(*Cacutus*) found in the Zapata Swamps and in various marshy territories on Cuba's southern coast.

Cuba's marine life makes up for what the island lacks in land fauna. The manatee, the world's only herbivorous aquatic mammal, is found in the Bahía de Taco and the Península de Zapata, and whale sharks frequent the María la Gorda area at Cuba's eastern tip from August to November. Four turtle species (leatherback, loggerhead, green and hawksbill) are found in Cuban waters and they nest annually in isolated keys or on the protected western beaches of the Península de Guanahacabibes.

Endangered Species

Due to habitat loss and persistent hunting by humans, many of Cuba's animals and birds are listed as endangered species. These include the critically endangered Cuban crocodile, which has the smallest habitat range of any crocodile, existing only in 300 sq km of the Cíenega de Zapata (Zapata Swamp) and in the Lanier Swamp on Isla de la Juventud. Protected since 1996, wild numbers now hover at around 6000. Other vulnerable species include the *jutía,* which was hunted mercilessly during the Special Period, when hungry Cubans tracked them for their meat (they still do – in fact, it is considered something of a delicacy); the tree boa, a native snake that lives in rapidly diminishing woodland areas; and the elusive *carpintero real* (ivory-billed woodpecker; see p492) spotted after a 40-year gap in the Parque Nacional Alejandro de Humboldt near Baracoa in the late 1980s, but not seen since.

It is estimated that Cuba harbors between 6500 and 7000 different species of plant, almost half of which are endemic.

The seriously endangered West Indian manatee, while protected from illegal hunting, continues to suffer from a variety of human threats, most notably from contact with boat propellers, suffocation caused by fishing nets and poisoning from residues pumped into rivers from sugar factories.

Cuba has an ambiguous attitude toward the hunting of turtles. Hawksbill turtles are protected under the law, though a clause allows for up to 500 of them to be captured per year in certain areas (Camagüey and Isla de la Juventud). Travelers will occasionally encounter *tortuga* (turtle) on the menu in places such as Baracoa. You are advised not to partake as these turtles may have been caught illegally.

Plants

Cuba is synonymous with the palm tree; through songs, symbols, landscapes and legends the two are inextricably linked. The national tree is the *palma real* (royal palm), and it's central to the country's coat of

TOCORORO

In the forested mountains of rural Cuba, there are few birds as striking or emblematic as the *tocororo*.

Endemic to the island, the *tocororo* – or Cuban trogon, to give it its scientific name – is a medium-sized black-and-white bird with a bright red belly and a bluish-green patch between the wings. Other distinctive features include a sharp serrated bill and a sweeping concave tail.

Easy to spot if you know where to look, the bird is widely distributed throughout Cuba in heavily forested areas, especially near rivers and streams. The unusual name is derived from its distinctive call which sounds out: *to-co-ro-ro*.

Long venerated for its striking plumage, the *tocororo* was chosen as Cuba's national bird due to its coloring (which replicates the red, white and blue of the Cuban flag) and its apparent resistance to captivity. Nationalistically minded Cubans will tell you that *tocororos* are instinctively libertarian, and if you cage one, it will quickly die.

THE IVORY-BILLED WOODPECKER

Considered the Holy Grail for binocular-wielding ornithologists, sightings of the *carpintero real* (ivory-billed woodpecker) are so rare that US-based twitchers have been known to break the travel embargo in an attempt to see it.

Native to both eastern Cuba and parts of the American South, the last verified sighting of this striking black-and-white bird was by Cuban scientists in Guantánamo province in 1987 (in what is now the Parque Nacional Alejandro de Humboldt) and many observers now consider it extinct.

Hope was restored briefly in 2005 when a male woodpecker – distinguishable by its prominent head crest – was allegedly spotted in the US state of Arkansas, but these reports have so far remained unverified.

The species' decline is linked directly to deforestation in both Cuba and the US. Ivory-billed woodpeckers inhabit hardwood forests and require a spacious 25 sq km per pair to feed and survive.

If you want to join the search, head for the mountains around Baracoa where you'll need to look out for the bird's shiny black-and-white plumage, and 75cm wingspan (the ivory-billed woodpecker is the second-largest member of the woodpecker family). Even more distinctive is its characteristic bill drum, said to sound like a toy trumpet.

arms and the Cristal beer logo. It's believed there are 20 million royal palms in Cuba and locals will tell you that wherever you stand on the island, you'll always be within sight of one of them. Standing single file by the roadside or clumped on a hill, these majestic trees reach up to 40m in height and are easily identified by their lithesome trunk and green stalk at the top. There are also *cocotero* (coconut palm); *palma barrigona* (big-belly palm) with its characteristic bulge; and the extremely rare *palma corcho* (cork palm). The latter is a link with the Cretaceous period (between 65 and 135 million years ago) and is cherished as a living fossil. You can see examples of it on the grounds of the Museo de Ciencias Naturales Sandalio de Noda (p174) and La Ermita (p185), both in Pinar del Río province. All told, there are 90 palm-tree types in Cuba.

Other important trees include mangroves, in particular the spiderlike mangroves that protect the Cuban shoreline from erosion and provide an important habitat for small fish and birds. Mangroves account for 26% of Cuban forests and cover almost 5% of the island's coast; Cuba ranks ninth in the world in terms of mangrove density, and the most extensive swamps are situated in the Ciénaga de Zapata.

Main Cuban Crops

- » Bananas
- » Citrus fruit
- » Coffee
- » Mangos
- » Pineapples
- » Rice
- » Sugarcane
- » Tobacco

The largest native pine forests grow on Isla de la Juventud (the former Isle of Pines), in western Pinar del Río, in eastern Holguín (or more specifically the Sierra Cristal) and in central Guantánamo. These forests are especially susceptible to fire damage, and pine reforestation has been a particular headache for the island's environmentalists.

Rainforests exist at higher altitudes – between approximately 500m and 1500m – in the Sierra del Escambray, Sierra Maestra and Macizo de Sagua-Baracoa mountains. Original rainforest species include ebony and mahogany, but today most re-forestation is in eucalyptus, which is graceful and fragrant, but invasive.

Dotted liberally across the island, ferns, cacti and orchids contribute hundreds of species, many endemic, to Cuba's cornucopia of plant life. For the best concentrations check out the botanical gardens in Santiago de Cuba for ferns and cacti and Pinar del Río for orchids. Most orchids bloom from November to January, and one of the best places to see them is in the Reserva Sierra del Rosario. The national flower is the graceful *mariposa* (butterfly jasmine); you'll know it by its white floppy petals and strong perfume.

Medicinal plants are widespread in Cuba due largely to a chronic shortage of prescription medicines (banned under the US embargo). Pharmacies are well stocked with effective tinctures such as aloe (for cough and congestion) and a bee by-product called *propólio*, used for everything from stomach amoebas to respiratory infections. On the home front, every Cuban patio has a pot of *orégano de la tierra* (Cuban oregano) growing and if you start getting a cold you'll be whipped up a wonder elixir made from the fat, flat leaves mixed with lime juice, honey and hot water.

The Future of Cuba

What next? No serious Cuba-watcher dares proffer an answer to this seemingly innocuous question, though the international media have been less shy about speculating. An end to the embargo, an ignominious *adiós* to socialism, a bland return to the days of golf and gambling? The scenarios have been discussed, debated and updated for over 50 years.

Hovering above it all is the omnipresent obstacle of Fidel Castro. Like a movie script that never makes the final draft, the Cuban revolutionary's obituary has been trotted out with tedious regularity since the 1950s. In 1961 at the Bay of Pigs, in 1962 during the Cuban Missile Crisis, in 1991 when the country's Soviet creditors went AWOL, and in 2006 after a bout of diverticulitis had everyone assuming the graying guerrilla had one foot in his grave.

Yet, with or without a fully functioning Fidel, the political drama that defines Cuban–American relations has continued; two opposing governments pursuing the same long-held policies and reiterating platitudes which, for over 50 years now, have failed to move the dialogue forward.

And then, along came a possible breakthrough...

Foreign Tourist Arrivals 2010

- » **Total** 2,531,745
- » **Canada** 945,248
- » **UK** 174,343
- » **Italy** 112,298
- » **Spain** 104,948
- » **Germany** 93,136

New Economic Realities

The 2008–9 recession played havoc with Cuba's already weak economy, exacerbating change. It finally arrived in late 2010 when Raúl Castro made the surprisingly nonsocialistic move of laying off over half a million 'unproductive' government workers and loosening the laws that governed private enterprise. The plan initially left many ordinary Cubans flummoxed. For well over a generation, people in this tightly controlled socialist economy had been sheltered by a paternalistic state apparatus that infiltrated every aspect of their daily lives. The standard of living wasn't high, but at least citizens didn't have to worry about mortgages, start-up costs, or hefty tax returns. The new laws removed many of these comforting assurances, and, while most have welcomed the opportunity to open up long-dreamt-about businesses ventures, things aren't so easy when you can't advertise, arrange credit, or get access online.

Since 2011, private restaurants (paladars) have been able to seat more customers, employ people other than family members, and serve a wider variety of dishes.

As 2011 dawned, many new small businesses (everything from hairdressers to equestrian centers) were taking their first tentative steps in a newer, freer economy. It was a promising start. But, overshadowed by a government that has a habit of giving out with one hand while taking away with the other; the road ahead is unlikely to be smooth.

Fidel Redux

After three years of convalescence, an older and frailer Fidel resurfaced in 2010, debating on TV, pontificating in parliament, and speaking haltingly during a Havana rally. His presence confirmed two things most people already knew: that the views of the 'maximum leader' are still hugely important in Cuba, and that brother, Raúl – no spring chicken himself – is unlikely to do anything earth-shattering while his older sibling is still alive. Some observers were even starting to think the unthinkable: that Fidel might outlive Raúl. But, come what may, Castro senior is largely a one-man revolution. The question keeps getting thrown back. What next?

Some envisage Cuba becoming a larger, more independently minded version of Puerto Rico; others have pointed to Spain whose peaceful transition to democracy after the death of Franco astounded many. But Cuba is not like anywhere else. Over half a century of isolationism, coupled with the presence of a hostile and powerful US to the north, has had an indelible affect on the country's psyche. The influence isn't necessarily all bad. Outsiders routinely underestimate Cuba's innate patriotism. As writer Pico Iyer once observed, 'everyone here seems to spend half his time complaining about Castro, and half his time glorying in the country's autonomy.' The adage is largely true. Tap a person on the street in Havana and, after the usual groans of *no es fácil* (it ain't easy), they'll enthusiastically hijack you with verses from José Martí, or anecdotes about the genius of Cuban cinema.

Longevity runs in the Castro family. All of Fidel's six siblings are still alive, from Angela, three years his senior, to Agostina, 11 years his junior.

Yet, the issue remains. Is this country of groundbreaking healthcare and pathological contrarianism ready to sell its soul wholesale to corporate capitalism? Or can the world (and the future) learn at least *something* from the Cuban experience; about fortitude, survival, and life without shopping malls?

People in developing countries would like to think so. The perception of Cuba in poorer parts of the world, where the country has often been a beacon of hope for people denied healthcare, education and housing, is very different to that garnered by visitors from the West. Arrive on a plane from Toronto and Cuba can seem tatty, comically slow and grossly

TOURIST TRENDS

In 1958, eight out of 10 tourists who visited Havana came from the US. Tourism dropped off a cliff following the new US travel restrictions in 1961 and overall numbers didn't recover their 1950s levels until 1989 (minus the Americans, of course). Since 1994 and the initiation of a massive government-sanctioned tourist industry in Cuba, visitor numbers have quadrupled to over two million, a quarter of whom come from Canada. Rising like a phoenix from the recession, 2010 was a record year for tourism spearheaded in part by a dramatic increase in Cuban-Americans visiting the country post the 2009 relaxation in US travel laws.

Studies conducted by the Cuba Policy Foundation have predicted that Cuban tourism would top four million within five years of a full end to the US trade embargo and government-led plans in Cuba have allegedly been drawn up to deal with the influx. More resorts have been earmarked for the northern keys, and rumors have been circulating about a massive golf complex near Banes in Holguín province. Slightly more congruous are the local historians who have continued with their stoic work reviving the colonial cityscapes of Havana, Trinidad, Camagüey and Cienfuegos in order to generate tourist revenue.

But, challenged by other Caribbean nations, today's tourist market is a little different to the hedonistic '50s. In Havana's mafia heyday, Cuba had no real competition. Today there are strong tourist infrastructures in neighboring Jamaica, Puerto Rico, the Bahamas and the Dominican Republic all vying for attention. Cuba's primary problem in the future will be damping down its legendary reputation for bureaucracy in order to encourage these foreign investors, most of whom are understandably wary of operating in a country where normal business practices have been on hold since 1959.

inefficient. Step off a flight from economically challenged Angola and you might temporarily think you've arrived in the Promised Land.

The American Dream

Commentators in the US – including nearly two million Cuban exiles – have long harbored their own ideas about their southern neighbor. In 2003 the Bush administration created the Commission for Assistance to a Free Cuba whose Post-Castro transition plan (including $36 million to finance democratic opposition to Castro in Cuba) was broadly condemned as damaging and unconstructive. 'There's no transition and it's not your country' retorted José Miguel Insulza, head of the OAS (Organization of American States), and even dissidents inside Cuba were leery.

In 2010 the general assembly of the UN voted against the continuance of the US embargo on Cuba by 187 votes to three.

The Obama administration made some significant changes, revoking the Bush administration's travel restrictions on Cuban-Americans in April 2009, and permitting licenses to US religious and academic groups to visit Cuba in January 2011. But, the age-old sticking point remains: a powerful Cuban-American lobby in Florida clinging to the notion that you can advance freedom in one country (Cuba) by denying freedom to travel in another (the US).

The future offers a few rays of hope to anti-embargo activists. With economic migrants currently outnumbering older politicized exiles in the US, a small majority of Cuban-Americans is now less vociferously anti-Castro and more in favor of ending the embargo that has undoubtedly helped keep the man in power. But, after 50 years of squabbling, the Cubans remain a divided populace with a worrying number of unresolved issues in their closet. What part will the exile community play in a new Cuban government? How much are they in the pockets of the Americans? And how can/should Cuba compensate them for property and goods confiscated in 1960?

Cuba for the Cubans

One thing nearly all political theories leave out is the Cubans themselves. What do the supposedly poor, oppressed people of Havana and Nueva Gerona think about all this? In the absence of any elections or referendums, no one can be certain. There's the daily grumbling in the shop queues about food prices, and the surreptitious whispering on the buses about the unmentionable (by name) leader, but anti-government whining is endemic in any country, be it Belgium or Burkina Faso. As tired as people are of the brothers Castro, and as impervious as they might be to their lengthy speeches, many still grant them a grudging respect. Lest we forget, Fidel was the first person to offer Cuba true independence and, as an instantly recognizable global figure, he has ensured that the country has punched well above its weight on the international stage for over half a century.

The new privatization laws inaugurated in January 2011 have promised to issue self-employment licenses for up to 250,000 individuals in 178 different professions.

But, patriotism aside; some kind of post-Castro change in Cuba is inevitable. When you've been ruled by the same bearded fraternity for a generation, a desire for *anything* different becomes a prerequisite, especially among the young. As to 'what' or 'with who'; it's still anybody's guess. Castro's succession plans are a carefully guarded state secret, a fact confirmed by the surprise sacking of two possible heirs, Carlos Lage and Felipe Pérez Roque in 2009.

Survival Guide

Directory A-Z

Accommodations

Cuban accommodations run the gamut from CUC$10 beach cabins to five-star resorts. Solo travelers are penalized price-wise, paying 75% of the price of a double room.

Budget

In this price range, casas particulares are almost always better value than a hotel. Only the most deluxe casas particulares in Havana will be over CUC$45, and in these places you're assured quality amenities and attention. In cheaper casas particulares (CUC$15 to CUC$20), you may have to share a bathroom and will have a fan instead of air-con. In the rock-bottom places (campismos mostly), you'll be lucky if there are sheets and running water, though there are usually private bathrooms.

If you're staying in a place intended for Cubans, you'll compromise materially, but the memories are guaranteed to be platinum.

Midrange

The midrange category is a lottery, with some boutique colonial hotels and some awful places with spooky Soviet-like architecture and atmosphere. In midrange hotels you can expect air-con, private hot-water bathroom, clean linens, satellite TV, a restaurant and a swimming pool, although the architecture is often uninspiring and the food not exactly gourmet.

Top end

The most comfortable top-end hotels are usually partly foreign-owned and maintain international standards (although service can sometimes be a bit lax). Rooms have everything that a midrange hotel has, plus big, quality beds and linens; a minibar; international phone service; and perhaps a terrace or view. Havana has some real gems.

Price differentials

Factors influencing rates are time of year, location and hotel chain. Low season is generally mid-September to early December and February to May (except for Easter week). Christmas and New Year is what's called extreme high season, when rates are 25% more than high-season rates. Bargaining is sometimes possible in casas particulares – though as far as foreigners go, it's not really the done thing. The casa owners in any given area pay generic taxes, and the prices you will be quoted reflect this. You'll find very few casas in Cuba that aren't priced between CUC$15 to CUC$45, unless you're up for a long stay. Prearranging Cuban accommodation has become easier now that more Cubans (unofficially) have access to the internet.

Types of Accommodations

CAMPISMOS

Campismos are where Cubans go on vacation. There are more than 80 of them sprinkled throughout the country, and they are wildly popular (an estimated one million Cubans use them annually). Staying at a campismo is hardly 'camping,' though – most of these installations are simple concrete cabins with bunk beds, foam mattresses and cold showers. Campismos are the best place to meet Cubans, make friends and party in a natural setting.

Campismos are ranked either *nacional* or *internacional*. The former are (technically) only for Cubans, while the latter host both Cubans and foreigners and are more upscale, with air-con and/or linens. There are currently a dozen international campismos in Cuba ranging from the

BOOK YOUR STAY ONLINE

For more accommodations reviews by Lonely Planet authors, check out hotels.lonelyplanet.com/Cuba. You'll find independent reviews, as well as recommendations on the best places to stay. Best of all, you can book online.

ACCOMMODATIONS PRICES

In this book, accommodations use the following price brackets (for two people):

» **Budget ($)** Under CUC$50.

» **Midrange ($$)** From CUC$50 to CUC$100.

» **Top End ($$$)** Over CUC$100.

hotel-standard Aguas Claras (Pinar del Río) to the more basic Puerto Rico Libre (Holguín). In practice, campismo staff may rent out a *nacional* cabin (or tent space) to a foreigner subject to availability, but it depends on the installation. Many foreigners are turned away (not helpful when you've traveled to a way-out place on the expectation of getting accommodations). To avoid this situation, we've listed only international campismos in this book.

As far as international campismos go, contact the excellent **Cubamar** (☎7-833-2523/4; www.cubamarviajes.cu; Calle 3 btwn Calle 12 & Malecón, Vedado; ⏰8:30am-5pm Mon-Sat) in Havana for reservations. If you're adamant about trying to wing it in a campismo *nacional*, try the provincial Campismo Popular office to make a reservation closer to the installation proper (some office addresses can be found in the relevant regional chapters). Cabin accommodation in international campismos costs from CUC$10 to CUC$30 per bed.

Cubamar also rents mobile homes (campervans) called *autocaravanas*, which sleep four adults and two children. Prices are around CUC$165 per day (but vary according to type, season and number of days required) including insurance (plus CUC$400 refundable deposit). You can park these campers wherever it's legal to park a regular car. There are 21 campismos or hotels that have Campertour facilities giving you access to electricity and water. These are a great alternative for families.

CASAS PARTICULARES

Private rooms are the best option for independent travelers in Cuba and a great way of meeting the locals on their home turf. Furthermore, staying in these venerable, family-orientated establishments will give you a far more open and less censored view of the country, and your understanding and appreciation of Cuba will grow far richer as a result. Casa owners also often make excellent tour guides.

You'll know houses renting rooms by the blue insignia on the door marked 'Arrendador Divisa.' There are thousands of casas particulares all over Cuba; 3000 in Havana alone and nearly 400 in Trinidad. From penthouses to historical homes, all manner of rooms are available from CUC$15 to CUC$45. Although some houses will treat you like a business paycheck, the vast majority of casa owners are warm, open and impeccable hosts.

Government regulation has eased since 2011, and renters can now let out multiple rooms if they have space. Owners pay a monthly tax per room depending on location (plus extra for off-street parking) to post a sign advertising their rooms and to serve meals. These taxes must be paid whether the rooms are rented or not. Owners must keep a register of all guests and report each new arrival within 24 hours. For these reasons, you will find it hard to bargain for rooms. You will also be requested to produce your passport (not a photocopy). Penalties are high for infractions. Regular government inspections ensure that conditions inside casas remain clean, safe and secure. Most proprietors offer breakfast and dinner for an extra rate. Hot showers are a prerequisite. In general, rooms these days provide at least two beds (one is usually a double), fridge, air-con, fan and private bathroom. Bonuses could include a terrace or patio, private entrance, TV, security box, kitchenette and parking space.

Bookings & Further Information

Due to the plethora of casas particulares in Cuba, it has been impossible to include even a fraction of the total in this book. The ones chosen are a combination of reader recommendations and local research. If one casa is full, they'll almost always be able to recommend to you someone else down the road.

The following websites list a large of number of casas

HOTEL WEBSITES

Ninety-five percent of Cuba's hotels are run by one of the following companies. For more information see their websites.

» **Cubanacán** (www.cubanacan.com)

» **Gaviota** (www.gaviota-grupo.com)

» **Gran Caribe** (www.grancaribe.cu)

» **Habaguanex** (www.habaguanexhotels.com)

» **Islazul** (www.islazul.cu)

» **Sol Meliá** (www.solmeliacuba.com)

across the country and allow online booking.

Cubacasas (www.cubacasas.net) The best online source for casa particular information and booking; up to date, accurate and with colorful links to hundreds of private rooms across the island (in English and French).

Casa Particular Organization (www.casaparticularcuba.org) Reader-recommended website for pre-booking private rooms.

HOTELS

All tourist hotels and resorts are at least 51% owned by the Cuban government and are administered by one of five main organizations. Islazul is the cheapest and most popular with Cubans (who pay in Cuban pesos). Although the facilities can be variable at these establishments and the architecture a tad Sovietesque, Islazul hotels are invariably clean, cheap, friendly and, above all, Cuban. They're also more likely to be situated in the island's smaller provincial towns. One downside is the blaring on-site discos that often keep guests awake until the small hours. Cubanacán is a step up and offers a nice mix of budget and midrange options in both cities and resort areas. The company has recently developed a new clutch of affordable boutique-style hotels (the Encanto brand) in attractive city centers such as Sancti Spíritus, Baracoa, Remedios and Santiago. Gaviota manages higher-end resorts including glittering 933-room Playa Pesquero, though the chain also has a smattering of cheaper 'villas' in places such as Santiago and Cayo Coco. Gran Caribe does midrange to top-end hotels, including many of the all-inclusive resorts in Havana and Varadero. Lastly, Habaguanex is based solely in Havana and manages most of the fastidiously restored historic hotels in Habana Vieja. The profits from these ventures go toward restoring Habana Vieja, which is a Unesco World Heritage Site. Except for Islazul properties, tourist hotels are for guests paying in convertible pesos only. Since May 2008 Cubans have been allowed to stay in any tourist hotels, although financially most of them are still out of reach.

At the top end of the hotel chain you'll often find foreign chains such as Sol Meliá and Superclubs running hotels in tandem with Cubanacán, Gaviota or Gran Caribe – mainly in the resort areas. The standards and service at these types of places are not unlike resorts in Mexico and the rest of the Caribbean.

Business Hours

TYPE OF BUSINESS	STANDARD OPENING HOURS
Banks	9am-3pm Mon-Fri
Cadeca exchange offices	9am-6pm Mon-Sat; 9am-noon Sun
Pharmacies	8am-8pm daily
Post offices	8am-6pm Mon-Sat
Restaurants	10:30am-11pm daily
Shops	9am-5pm Mon-Sat; 9am-noon Sun

Customs Regulations

Cuban customs regulations are complicated. For the full scoop see www.aduana.co.cu.

Items You Are Allowed to Bring In

Travelers are allowed to bring in personal belongings (including photography equipment, binoculars, musical instrument, tape recorder, radio, personal computer, tent, fishing rod, bicycle, canoe and other sporting gear), and gifts up to CUC$50.

Items that do not fit into the categories mentioned above are subject to a 100% customs duty to a maximum of CUC$1000.

Prohibited Items

Items prohibited from entry into Cuba include narcotics, explosives, pornography, electrical appliances broadly defined, global positioning systems, endangered species and publications considered a threat to the general interests of the nation. Canned, processed and dried food are no problem, nor are pets.

Items You Are Allowed to Take Out

You are allowed to export 50 boxed cigars duty-free (or 23 singles), US$5000 (or equivalent) in cash and only CUC$200.

Exporting undocumented art and items of cultural patrimony is restricted and involves fees. Normally, when you buy art you will be given an official 'seal' at point of sale. Check this before you buy. If you don't get one, you'll need to obtain one from the **Registro Nacional de Bienes Culturales** (Calle 17 No 1009 btwn Calles 10 & 12, Vedado, Havana; ⌚9am-noon Mon-Fri) in Havana. Bring the objects here for inspection; fill in a form; pay a fee of between CUC$10 and CUC$30, which covers from one to five pieces of artwork; and return 24 hours later to pick up the certificate.

Discount Cards

Students who can provide proof of enrolment at a university or college are afforded longer visas and issued with a *carnet* – the identification document that allows foreigners to pay for museums, transport (including *colectivos* – collective taxis) and theater performances in Cuban pesos (CUP), thus saving a bundle of money.

Electricity

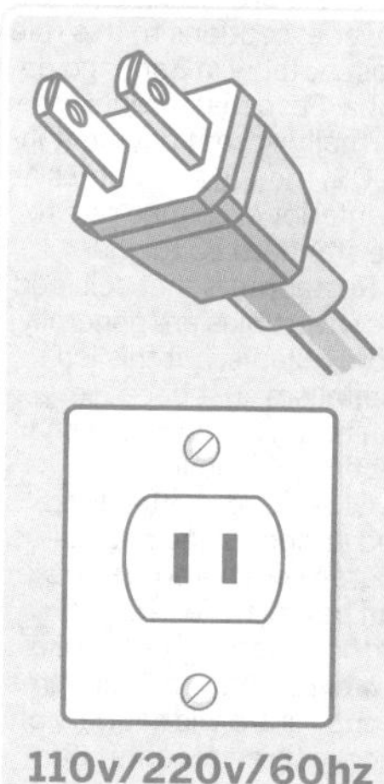

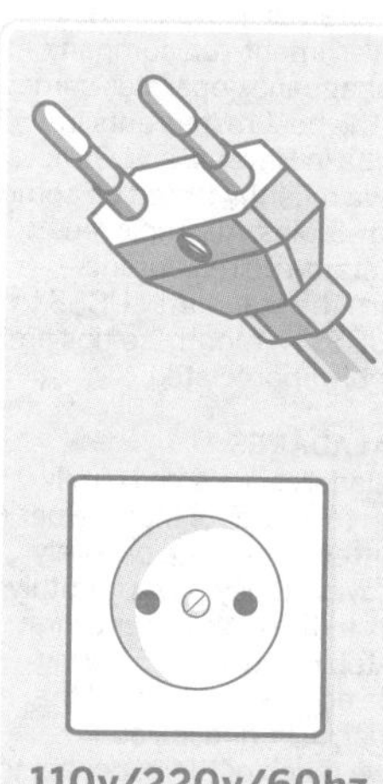

Climate

Havana

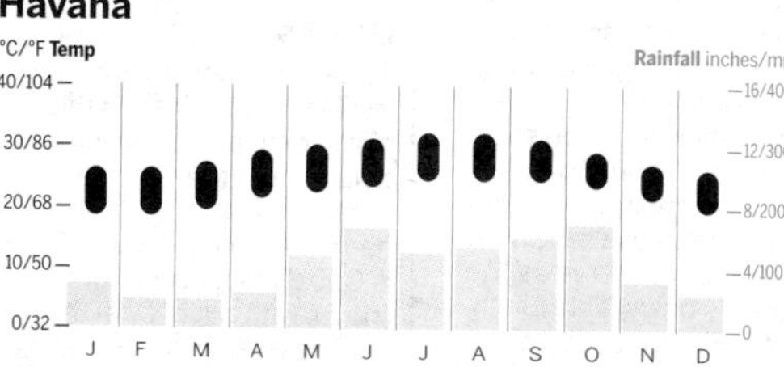

Sancti Spíritus

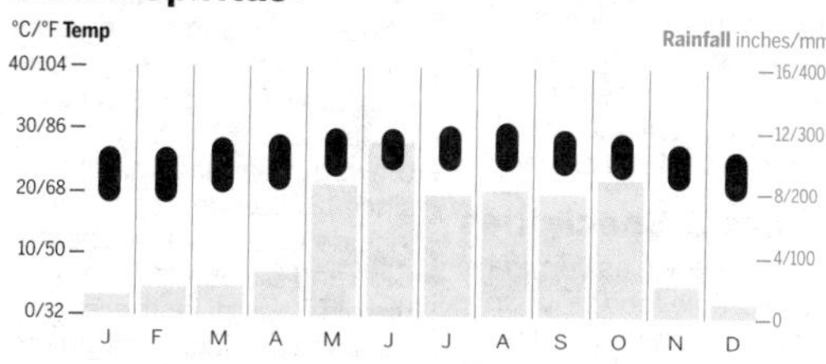

Santiago De Cuba

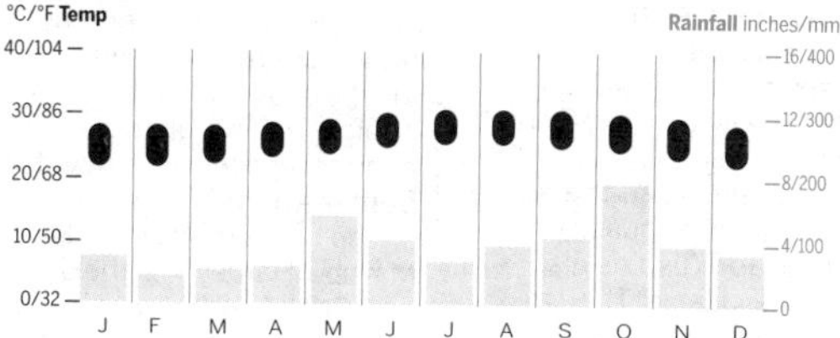

Embassies & Consulates

All embassies are in Havana, and most are open from 8am to noon on weekdays. Australia is represented in the Canadian Embassy. New Zealand is represented in the UK Embassy. The US is represented by a 'Special Interests Section.' Canada has additional consulates in Varadero and Guardalavaca. Most embassies are open from 8am to noon on weekdays.

Australia See Canada.

Austria (☎7-204-2825; Calle 4 No 101, Miramar)

Canada (☎7-204-2517; Calle 30 No 518, Playa) Also represents Australia.

Denmark (☎7-33-81-28; 4th fl, Paseo de Martí No 20, Centro Habana)

France (☎7-204-2308; Calle 14 No 312 btwn Avs 3 & 5, Miramar)

Germany (☎7-833-2539; Calle 13 No 652, Vedado)

Italy (☎7-204-5615; Av 5 No 402, Miramar)

Japan (☎7-204-3508; Miramar Trade Center, cnr Av 3 & Calle 80, Playa)

Mexico (☎7-204-7722; Calle 12 No 518, Miramar)

Netherlands (☎7-204-2511; Calle 8 No 307 btwn Avs 3 & 5, Miramar)

New Zealand See UK.

Spain (☎7-866-8029; Cárcel No 51, Habana Vieja)

Sweden (☎7-204-2831; fax 7-204-1194; Calle 34 No 510, Miramar)

Switzerland (☎7-204-2611; Av 5 No 2005 btwn Avs 20 & 22, Miramar)

UK (☎7-204-1771; Calle 34 No 708, Miramar) Also represents New Zealand.

USA (☎7-833-3026; US Interests Section, Calzada btwn Calles L & M, Vedado)

Food

For legions of gastronomes, Cuban cuisine has always been something of an international joke. From the empty-shelved ration shops of Centro Habana to the depressing ubiquity of soggy ham-and-cheese sandwiches, which seem to serve as the country's only viable lunch option, it's a question of less feast, more famine. But while celebrity chefs might remain scarce in many of Cuba's uninspiring government-run restaurants, simmering quietly on the sidelines a whole new pot of tricks is brewing.

Staples & Specialties

Popularly known as *comida criolla* (Creole food), Cuban meals are characterized by *congrí* (rice flecked with black beans), meat (primarily pork, closely followed by chicken and beef), fried plantains (green bananas), salad (limited to seasonal ingredients) and root vegetables, usually *Yuca* (cassava) and *calabaza* (pumpkin-like squash).

Pescado (fish) is also readily available. Though you'll come across dorado, *aguja* (swordfish), and occasionally octopus and crab in some of the specialist seafood places, you're more likely to see *pargo* (red snapper), lobster or prawns.

Cubans are also aficionados of ice cream and the nuances of different flavors are heatedly debated. Coppelia ice cream is legendary, but ridiculously cheap tubs of other brands (440g for CUC$1) can be procured almost everywhere, and even the machine-dispensed peso stuff ain't half bad.

Drinks

Cuba's rum cocktails are world famous. There's the minty mojito, the shaved ice daiquirí and the sugary Cuba *libres* (rum and Coke) to name but three. Havana Club is Cuba's most celebrated *ron* (rum), with Silver Dry (the cheapest) and three-year-old Carta Blanca used for mixed drinks, while five-year-old Carta de Oro and seven-year-old Añejo are best enjoyed in a highball. Cuba's finest rum is Matusalem Añejo Superior, brewed in Santiago de Cuba since 1872. Other top brands include Varadero, Caribbean Club and Caney (made at the old Bacardí factory in Santiago de Cuba, though the name Bacardí is anathema as the exiled family decided to sue the Cuban government under US embargo laws). Most Cubans drink their rum straight up and, on more informal occasions, straight from the bottle.

Top beer brands include Mayabe, Hatuey and the big two: Cristal and Bucanero. Imported beers include Lagarto, Bavaria and Heineken.

The quality of tap water is variable and many Cubans have gory amoebic tales, including giardia. To be safe you can drink *agua natural* (bottled water), but that gets expensive over longer trips.

Where to Eat & Drink

GOVERNMENT-RUN RESTAURANTS

Government-run restaurants operate in either pesos or convertibles. Peso restaurants are nearly always grim and are notorious for handing you a nine-page menu (in Spanish), when the only thing available is fried chicken. There are, however, a few newer exceptions to this rule, most notably in Santiago de Cuba. Peso restaurants will normally accept payment in CUC$, though sometimes at an inferior exchange rate to the standard 25 to one.

Restaurants that sell food in convertibles are generally more reliable, but this isn't capitalism: just because you're paying more doesn't necessarily mean better service. Food is often limp and unappetizing and discourse with bored waiters can be worthy of a *Monty Python* sketch. There are a few highlights. The Palmares group runs a wide variety of excellent restaurants countrywide from bog-standard beach shacks to the *New York Times*–lauded El Aljibe in Miramar, Havana. The government-run company Habaguanex operates some of the best restaurants in Cuba in Havana, and Gaviota have recently tarted up some old staples. All employees of state-run restaurants earn the standard CUC$8 to CUC$13 a month, so tips are highly appreciated.

PALADARES

Paladares are small family-run restaurants that are permitted to operate privately provided they pay a monthly tax to the government. First established in 1995 during the economic chaos of the Special Period, paladares owe much of their success to the sharp increase in tourist traffic on the island, coupled with the bold experimentation of local chefs who, despite a paucity of decent ingredients, have heroically managed to keep the age-old traditions of Cuban cooking alive. Paladar meals can cost anything between CUC$8 and CUC$25.

FOOD PRICES

It will be a very rare meal in Cuba that costs over CUC$25. In this book, restaurant listings use the following price brackets.

» **Budget ($)** Meals for under CUC$7.

» **Midrange ($$)** Meals for CUC$7 to CUC$15.

» **Top End ($$$)** Meals for over CUC$15.

Vegetarians

In a land of rationing and food shortages, strict vegetarians (ie no lard, no meat bullion, no fish) will have a hard time. Cubans don't really understand vegetarianism, and when they do (or when they *say* they do), it can be summarized rather adroitly with one key word: omelet – or, at a stretch, scrambled eggs. Cooks in casas particulares, who may already have had experience cooking meatless dishes for other travelers, are usually much better at accommodating vegetarians; just ask.

Gay & Lesbian Travelers

While Cuba can't be called a queer destination (yet), it's more tolerant than many other Latin American countries. The hit movie *Fresa y Chocolate* (Strawberry and Chocolate, 1994) sparked a national dialogue about homosexuality, and Cuba is pretty tolerant, all things considered. People from more accepting societies may find this tolerance too 'don't ask, don't tell' or tokenistic (everybody has a gay friend/relative/coworker, whom they'll mention when the topic arises), but what the hell, you have to start somewhere and Cuba is moving in the right direction.

Lesbianism is less tolerated and seldom discussed and you'll see very little open displays of gay pride between female lovers. There are occasional *fiestas para chicas* (not necessarily all-girl parties but close); ask around at the Cine Yara in Havana's gay cruising zone.

Cubans are physical with each other and you'll see men hugging, women holding hands and lots of friendly caressing. This type of casual touching shouldn't be a problem, but take care when that hug among friends turns overtly sensual in public.

See also boxed text, p109.

Health

From a medical point of view, Cuba is generally safe as long as you're reasonably careful about what you eat and drink. The most common travel-related diseases, such as dysentery and hepatitis, are acquired by the consumption of contaminated food and water. Mosquito-borne illnesses are not a significant concern on most of the islands within the Cuban archipelago.

Prevention is the key to staying healthy while traveling around Cuba. Travelers who receive the recommended vaccines and follow commonsense precautions usually come away with nothing more than a little diarrhea.

Insurance

Since May 2010, Cuba has made it obligatory for all foreign visitors to show proof of their medical insurance when entering the country (see p503).

Should you end up in hospital, call **Asistur** (☎7-866-4499, emergency 7-866-8527; www.asistur.cu; Paseo de Martín No 208, Centro Habana) for help with insurance and medical assistance. The company has regional offices in Havana, Varadero, Cienfuegos, Cayo Coco, Camagüey, Guardalavaca and Santiago de Cuba.

Outpatient treatment at international clinics is reasonably priced, but emergency and prolonged hospitalization gets expensive (the free medical system for Cubans should only be used when there is no other option).

If you're really concerned about your health, consider purchasing travel insurance at Asistur once you arrive. It has two types of coverage. For non-Americans the policy costs CUC$2.50 per day and covers up to CUC$700 in hotel costs, CUC$10,000 in medical expenses (for illness) and CUC$10,000 for repatriation of a sick person. For Americans, similar coverage costs CUC$8 per day. It's strongly recommended that you take car insurance if hiring one.

Worldwide travel insurance is available at www.lonelyplanet.com/travel_services.

Health Care for Foreigners in Cuba

The Cuban government has established a for-profit health system for foreigners called **Servimed** (☎7-24-01-41), which is entirely separate from the free, not-for-profit system that takes care of Cuban citizens. There are more than 40 Servimed health centers across the island, offering primary care as well as a variety of specialty and high-tech services. If you're staying in a hotel, the usual way to access the system is to ask the manager for a physician referral. Servimed

> **COMPULSORY MEDICAL TRAVEL INSURANCE**
>
> Since May 2010 it has been compulsory for all foreigners visiting Cuba to have medical travel insurance. You should bring proof of your policy with you and be prepared to show it with your other documents at Cuban customs. If you arrive without medical insurance, you will be obliged to purchase a policy in Cuba with government insurance company Asistur.

centers accept walk-ins. While Cuban hospitals provide some free emergency treatment for foreigners, this should only be used when there is no other option. Remember that in Cuba medical resources are scarce and the local populace should be given priority in free healthcare facilities.

Almost all doctors and hospitals expect payment in cash, regardless of whether you have travel health insurance or not. If you develop a life-threatening medical problem, you'll probably want to be evacuated to a country with state-of-the-art medical care. Since this may cost tens of thousands of dollars, be sure you have insurance to cover this before you depart.

There are special pharmacies for foreigners also run by the Servimed system, but all Cuban pharmacies are notoriously short on supplies, including pharmaceuticals. Be sure to bring along adequate quantities of all medications you might need, both prescription and over-the-counter. Also, be sure to bring along a fully stocked medical kit. Pharmacies marked *turno permanente* or *pilotos* are open 24 hours.

Water

Tap water in Cuba is not reliably safe to drink. Vigorous boiling for one minute is the most effective means of water purification.

You may also disinfect water with iodine pills. Pregnant women, those with a history of thyroid disease, and those allergic to iodine should not drink iodinated water.

A number of water filters are on the market. Follow the manufacturers' instructions carefully.

INTERNET RESOURCES

- **Australia** (www.smarttraveller.gov.au) Follow the link to Travel Health.
- **Canada** (www.travelhealth.gc.ca)
- **UK** (www.fco.gov.uk) Follow the link to Travel & Living Abroad on the Foreign & Commonwealth Office website.
- **USA** (www.cdc.gov/travel)

Internet Access

With state-run telecommunications company Etecsa re-establishing its monopoly as service provider, internet access is available all over the country in Etecsa's spanking new *telepuntos*. You'll find one of its swish, air-conditioned sales offices in almost every provincial town, and it is your best point of call for fast and reliable internet access. The drill is to buy a one-hour user card (CUC$6) with scratch-off *usuario* (code) and *contraseña* (password) and help yourself to an available computer. These cards are interchangeable in any *telepunto* across the country, so you don't have to use up your whole hour in one go.

The downside of the Etecsa monopoly is that there are few, if any, independent internet cafes outside the *telepuntos*. As a general rule, most three to five-star hotels (and all resort hotels) will have their own internet cafes, although the fees here are often higher (sometimes as much as CUC$12 per hour).

As internet access for Cubans is restricted (they're only allowed internet under supervision, eg in educational programs or if their job deems it necessary), you may be asked to show your passport when using a *telepunto* (although if you look obviously foreign, they won't bother). On the plus side, the Etecsa places are open long hours and are seldom crowded.

Wi-fi is almost nonexistent in Cuba outside Havana's better hotels. When it is available, it usually costs CUC$8 an hour and is rather slow.

Language Courses

Cuba's rich cultural tradition and the abundance of highly talented, trained professionals make it a great place to study Spanish. Technological and linguistic glitches, plus general unresponsiveness, make it hard to set up courses before arriving, but you can arrange everything once you get there. In Cuba, things are always better done face to face.

Options for US citizens to study in Cuba have opened up since the Obama administration started issuing more people-to-people (educational) travel licenses in 2011.

The largest organization offering study visits for foreigners is **UniversiTUR SA** (☎7-261-4939, 7-55-55-77; agencia@universitur.com; Calle 30 No 768-1 btwn Calle 41 & Av Kohly, Nuevo Vedado, Havana). UniversiTUR arranges regular study and working holidays at any of Cuba's universities and at many higher education or research institutes. Its most popular programs are intensive courses in Spanish language and Cuban culture at La Universidad de La Habana. UniversiTUR has 17 branch offices at various universities throughout Cuba, all providing the same services, though prices vary.

Students heading to Cuba should bring a good bilingual dictionary and a basic 'learn Spanish' textbook, as such books are scarce or expensive in Cuba. You might sign up for a two-week course at a university to get your feet wet and then jump into private classes once you've made some contacts.

Legal Matters

Cuban police are everywhere and they're usually very friendly – more likely to ask you for a date than a bribe. Corruption is a serious offense in Cuba, and typically no one wants to get messed up in it. Getting caught out without identification is never good; carry some around just in case (a driver's license, a copy of your passport or a student ID card should be sufficient).

Drugs are prohibited in Cuba, though you may still get offered marijuana and cocaine on the streets of Havana. Penalties for buying, selling, holding or taking drugs are serious, and Cuba is making a concerted effort to treat demand and curtail supply; it is only the foolish traveler who partakes while on a Cuban vacation.

Maps

Signage is awful in Cuba, so a good map is essential for drivers and cyclists alike. The comprehensive *Guía de Carreteras*, published in Italy, includes the best maps available in Cuba. It usually comes free when you hire a car, though some travelers have been asked to pay between CUC$5 and CUC$10. It has a complete index, a detailed Havana map and useful information in English, Spanish, Italian and French. Handier is the all-purpose *Automapa Nacional*, available at hotel shops and car-rental offices.

The best map published outside Cuba is the Freytag & Berndt 1:1.25 million *Cuba* map. The island map is good, and it has indexed town plans of Havana, Playas del Este, Varadero, Cienfuegos, Camagüey and Santiago de Cuba.

For good basic maps, pick up one of the provincial *Guías* available in Infotur offices.

Money

This is a tricky part of any Cuban trip, as the double economy takes some getting used to. Two currencies circulate in Cuba: convertible pesos (CUC$) and Cuban pesos (referred to as *moneda nacional*, abbreviated MN). Most things tourists pay for are in convertibles (eg accommodation, rental cars, bus tickets, museum admission and internet access). At the time of writing, Cuban pesos were selling at 25 to one convertible, and while there are many things you can't buy with *moneda nacional*, using them on certain occasions means you'll see a bigger slice of authentic Cuba. The prices in this book are in convertibles unless otherwise stated.

Making everything a little more confusing, euros are also accepted at the Varadero, Guardalavaca, Cayo Largo del Sur, Cayo Coco and Cayo Guillermo resorts, but once you leave the resort grounds, you'll still need convertibles.

The best currencies to bring to Cuba are euros, Canadian dollars or pounds sterling (all subject to an 8% to 11.25% commission). The worst is US dollars and – despite the prices you might see posted in bank windows – the commission you'll get charged is a whopping 20% (the normal 10% commission plus an extra 10% penalty – often not displayed). At the time of writing, traveler's checks issued by US banks could be exchanged at branches of Banco Financiero Internacional, but credit cards issued by US banks could not be used at all. Note that Australian dollars are not accepted anywhere in Cuba.

Cadeca branches in every city and town sell Cuban pesos. You won't need more than CUC$10 worth of pesos a week. There is almost always a branch at the local *agropecuario* (vegetable market). If you get caught without Cuban pesos and are drooling for that ice-cream cone, you can always use convertibles; in street transactions such as these, CUC$1 is equal to 25 pesos and you'll receive change in pesos. There is no black market in Cuba, only hustlers trying to fleece you with money-changing scams.

ATMs & Credit Cards

When the banks are open, the machines are working and the phone lines are live, credit cards are an option – as long as the cards are not issued by US banks. You will be charged an 11.25% fee on every credit-card transaction. This is made up of the 8% levy charged for all foreign currency exchanges (which must first be converted into US dollars), plus a standard 3.25% conversion fee. However, in reality, credit card and cash payments work out the same; with cash you pay the 11.25% levy when you exchange your foreign money into convertibles at the bank. Nonetheless, due to poor processing facilities, lack of electronic equipment and non-acceptance of many US-linked cards, cash is still by far the best option in Cuba.

Cash advances can be drawn from credit cards, but the commission is the same. Check with your home bank before you leave, as many banks won't authorize large withdrawals in foreign countries unless you notify them of your travel plans first.

ATMs are good for non-American credit cards and are the equivalent to obtaining a cash advance over the counter. In reality they're best avoided (especially when the banks are closed), as they are notorious for eating up people's cards.

Some, but not all, debit cards work in Cuba. Take care, as machines sometimes 'eat' these cards too.

Cash

Cuba is a cash economy and credit cards don't have the importance or ubiquity that they do elsewhere in the western hemisphere. Although carrying just cash is far riskier than the usual cash/credit-card/traveler's-check mix, it's infinitely more convenient. As long as you use a concealed money belt and keep the cash on you or in your hotel's safety deposit box at all times, you should be OK.

It's better to ask for CUC$20/10/5/3/1 bills when you're changing money, as many smaller Cuban businesses (taxis, restaurants etc) can't change anything bigger (ie CUC$50 or CUC$100 bills) and the words *no hay cambio* (no change) resonate everywhere. If desperate, you can always break big bills at hotels.

Denominations & Lingo

One of the most confusing parts of a double economy is terminology. Cuban pesos are called *moneda nacional* (abbreviated MN) or *pesos Cubanos* or simply pesos, while convertible pesos are called *pesos convertibles* (abbreviated CUC), or simply pesos (again!). More recently people have been referring to them as *Cucs*. Sometimes you'll be negotiating in pesos (Cubanos) and your counterpart will be negotiating in pesos (convertibles). It doesn't help that the notes look similar as well. Worse, the symbol for both convertibles and Cuban pesos is $. You can imagine the potential scams just working these combinations.

The Cuban peso comes in notes of one, five, 10, 20, 50 and 100 pesos; and coins of one (rare), five and 20 centavos, and one and three pesos. The five-centavo coin is called a *medio*, the 20-centavo coin a *peseta*. Centavos are also called *kilos*.

The convertible peso comes in multicolored notes of one, three, five, 10, 20, 50 and 100 pesos; and coins of five, 10, 25 and 50 centavos, and one peso.

Tipping

If you're not in the habit of tipping, you'll learn fast in Cuba. Wandering *son* (Cuban popular music) septets, parking attendants, ladies at bathroom entrances, restaurant wait staff, tour guides – they all work for hard-currency tips. Musicians who besiege tourists while they dine, converse or flirt will want a convertible, but only give what you feel the music is worth. Washroom attendants expect CUC$0.05 to CUC$0.10, while *parqueadores* (parking attendants) should get CUC$0.25 for a short watch and CUC$1 per 12 hours. For a day tour, CUC$2 per person is appropriate for a tour guide. Taxi drivers will appreciate 10% of the meter fare, but if you've negotiated a ride without the meter, don't tip as the whole fare is going straight into their wallets.

Tipping can quickly *resolver las cosas* (fix things up). If you want to stay beyond the hotel check-out time or enter a site after hours, for instance, small tips (CUC$1 to CUC$5) bend rules, open doors and have people looking the other way.

Traveler's Checks

While they add security and it makes sense to carry a few for that purpose, traveler's checks are a hassle in Cuba, although they work out to be better value than credit cards. Bear in mind that you'll pay commission at both the buying and selling ends (3% to 6%), and that some hotels and banks won't accept them, especially in the provinces. The Banco Financiero Internacional is your best bet for changing Amex checks, though a much safer all-round option is to bring Thomas Cook.

Post

Letters and postcards sent to Europe and the US take about a month to arrive. While *sellos* (stamps) are sold in Cuban pesos and convertibles, correspondence bearing the latter has a better chance of arriving. Postcards cost CUC$0.65 to all countries. Letters cost CUC$0.65 to the Americas, CUC$0.75 to Europe and CUC$0.85 to all other countries. Prepaid postcards, including international postage, are available at most hotel shops and post offices and are the surest bet for successful delivery. For important mail, you're better off using DHL, which is located in all the major cities; it costs CUC$55 for a 900g letter pack to Australia, or CUC$50 to Europe.

Public Holidays

Officially Cuba has nine public holidays (see list below). Other important national days to look out for include January 28 (anniversary of the birth of José Martí); April 19 (Bay of Pigs victory); October 8 (anniversary of the death of Che Guevara); October 28 (anniversary of the death of Camilo Cienfuegos); and December 7 (anniversary of the death of Antonio Maceo).

January 1 Triunfo de la Revolución (Liberation Day)

January 2 Día de la Victoria (Victory of the Armed Forces)

May 1 Día de los Trabajadores (International Worker's Day)

July 25 Commemoration of Moncada Attack

July 26 Día de la Rebeldía Nacional – Commemoration of Moncada Attack

July 27 Commemoration of Moncada Attack

October 10 Día de la Indepedencia (Independence Day)

December 25 Navidad (Christmas Day)

December 31 New Year's Eve

Safe Travel

Cuba is generally safer than most countries, and violent attacks are extremely rare. Petty theft (eg rifled luggage in hotel rooms or unattended shoes disappearing from the beach) is common, but preventative measures work wonders. Pickpocketing is preventable: wear your bag in front of you on crowded buses and at busy markets, and only take what money you'll need when you head out at night.

Begging is more widespread and is exacerbated by tourists who hand out money, soap, pens, chewing gum and other things to people on the street. If you truly want to do something to help, pharmacies and hospitals will accept medicine donations, schools happily take pens, paper, crayons etc, and libraries will gratefully accept books. Alternatively pass stuff onto your casa particular owner or leave it at a local church. Hustlers are called *jineteros/jineteras* (male/female touts), and can be a real nuisance.

Telephone

The Cuban phone system is still undergoing upgrades, so beware of phone-number changes. Normally a recorded message will inform you of recent upgrades.

Most of the country's Etecsa *telepuntos* have now been completely refurbished, which means there will be a spick-and-span (as well as air-conditioned) phone and internet office in almost every provincial town.

Cell Phones

Cuba's cell-phone company is called **Cubacel** (www.cubacel.com). While you may be able to use your own equipment, you have to pre-buy their services. Cubacel has more than 15 offices around the country (including at the Havana airport) where you can do this. Its plan costs approximately CUC$3 per day, or CUC$6 per day if you use their equipment. Local calls cost from CUC$0.10 (reduced) to CUC$0.45 (normal) per minute. Calls abroad are between CUC$1.40 and CUC$1.80 per minute.

Phone Codes

To call Cuba from abroad, dial your international access code, Cuba's country code (☎53), the city or area code (minus the '0,' which is used when dialing domestically between provinces), and the local number. In this book, area codes are indicated at the start of each chapter. To call internationally from Cuba, dial Cuba's international access code (☎119), the country code, the area code and the number. To the US, you just dial ☎119, then 1, the area code and the number.

To place a call through an international operator, dial ☎09, except to the US, which can be reached with an operator on ☎66-12-12. Not all private phones in Cuba have international service, in which case you'll want to call collect (reverse charges or *cobro revertido*). This service is available only to Argentina, Brazil, Canada, Chile, Colombia, Costa Rica, Dominican Republic, France, Italy, Mexico, Panama, Spain, the UK, the US and Venezuela. International operators are available 24 hours and speak English. You cannot call collect from public phones.

Phonecards

Etecsa is where you buy phonecards, send and receive faxes, use the internet and make international calls. Blue public Etecsa phones accepting magnetized or computer-chip cards are everywhere. The cards are sold in convertibles (CUC$5, CUC$10 and CUC$20), and in Cuban pesos (three, five and seven pesos). You can call nationally with either, but you can call internationally only with convertible cards. If you are mostly going to be making national and local calls, buy a peso card, as it's much more economical.

The best cards for calls from Havana are called Propia. They come in pesos (five- and 10-peso denominations) and convertibles (CUC$10 and CUC$25 denominations) and allow you to call from any phone – even ones permitting only emergency calls – using a personal code. The rates are the cheapest as well.

Phone Rates

Local calls cost five centavos per minute, while interprovincial calls cost from 35 centavos to one peso per minute (note that only the peso coins with the star work in pay phones). Since most coin phones don't return change, common courtesy means that you should push the 'R' button so that the next person in line can make their call with your remaining money.

International calls made with a card cost from CUC$2 per minute to the US and Canada and CUC$5 to Europe and Oceania. Calls placed through an operator cost slightly more.

Tourist Information

Cuba's official tourist information bureau is called **Infotur** (www.infotur.cu). It has offices in all the main provincial towns and desks in most of the bigger hotels and airports. Travel agencies, such as Cubanacán, Cubatur and Ecotur can usually supply some general information.

Travelers with Disabilities

Cuba's inclusive culture extends to disabled travelers, and while facilities may be lacking, the generous nature of Cubans generally compensates. Sight-impaired travelers will be helped across streets and given priority in lines. The same holds true for travelers in wheelchairs, who will find the few ramps ridiculously steep and will have trouble in colonial parts of town where sidewalks are narrow and streets are cobblestoned. Elevators are often out of order. Etecsa phone centers have telephone equipment for the hearing-impaired, and TV programs are broadcast with closed captioning.

Visas & Tourist Cards

Regular tourists who plan to spend up to two months in Cuba do not need visas. Instead, you get a *tarjeta de turista* (tourist card) valid for 30 days (Canadians get 90 days), which can be extended for once you're in Cuba. Those going 'air only' usually buy the tourist card from the travel agency or airline office that sells them the plane ticket (equivalent of US$15 extra). Package tourists receive their card with their other travel documents.

You are usually not allowed to board a plane to Cuba without this card, but if by some chance you are, you should be able to buy one at Aeropuerto Internacional José Martí in Havana – although this is a hassle (and risk) best avoided. Once in Havana, tourist-card extensions or replacements cost another CUC$25. You cannot leave Cuba without presenting your tourist card, so don't lose it. You are not permitted entry to Cuba without an onward ticket. Note that Cubans don't stamp your passport on either entry or exit; instead they stamp your tourist card.

The 'address in Cuba' line should be filled in, if only to avoid unnecessary questioning. As long as you are staying in a legal casa particular or hotel, you shouldn't have problems.

Business travelers and journalists need visas. Applications should be made through a consulate at least three weeks in advance (longer if you apply through a consulate in a country other than your own).

Visitors with visas or anyone who has stayed in Cuba longer than 90 days must apply for an exit permit from an immigration office. The Cuban consulate in London issues official visas (£32 plus two photos). They take two weeks to process, and the name of an official contact in Cuba is necessary.

Extensions

For most travelers, obtaining an extension once in Cuba is easy: you just go to the *inmigración* (immigration office) and present your documents and CUC$25 in stamps. Obtain these stamps from a branch of Bandec or Banco Financiero Internacional beforehand. You'll only receive an additional 30 days after your original 30 days (apart from Canadians who get an additional 90 days after their original 90), but you can exit and re-enter the country for 24 hours and start over again (some travel agencies in Havana have special deals for this type of trip). Attend to extensions at least a few business days before your visa is due to expire and never attempt travel around Cuba with an expired visa.

Cuban immigration offices

Nearly all provincial towns have an immigration office (closed Wednesday, Saturday and Sunday), though the staff rarely speak English and aren't always overly helpful. Try to avoid Havana's office if you can, as it gets ridiculously crowded.

Baracoa (Antonio Maceo No 48; ⏲8am-noon & 2-4pm Mon-Fri)

Bayamo (Carretera Central Km 2; ⏲9am-noon & 1:30-4pm Tue & Thu-Fri) In a big complex 200m south of the Hotel Sierra Maestra.

Camagüey (Calle 3 No 156 btwn Calles 8 & 10, Reparto Vista Hermosa; ⏲8-11:30am & 1-3pm Mon-Fri, except Wed)

Ciego de Ávila (cnr Delgado & Independencia; ⏲8am-noon & 1-5pm Mon & Tue, 8am-noon Wed-Fri)

Cienfuegos (☎43-52-10-17; Av 46 btwn Calles 29 & 31)

Guantánamo (Calle 1 Oeste btwn Calles 14 & 15 Norte; ⏲8:30am-noon & 2-4pm Mon-Thu) Directly behind Hotel Guantánamo.

Guardalavaca (☎24-43-02-26/7) In the police station at the entrance to the resort. Head here for visa extensions.

Havana (Desamparados No 110 btwn Habana & Compostela; ⏲8:30am-4pm Mon-Wed & Fri, 8:30-11am Thu & Sat)

Holguín (cnr General Marrero & General Vázquez; ⏲8am-noon & 2-4pm Mon-Fri) Arrive early – it gets crowded here.

Las Tunas (Av Camilo Cienfuegos, Reparto Buenavista) Northeast of the train station.

Sancti Spíritus (☎41-32-47-29; Independencia Norte No

107; 8:30am-noon & 1:30-3:30pm Mon-Thu)

Santa Clara (cnr Av Sandino & Sexta; 8am-noon & 1-3pm Mon-Thu) Three blocks east of Estadio Sandino.

Santiago de Cuba (22-69-36-07; Calle 13 No 6 btwn Av General Cebreco & Calle 4; 8:30am-noon & 2-4pm Mon-Fri, except Wed) Stamps for visa extensions are sold at the Banco de Crédito y Comercio at Felix Peña No 614 on Parque Céspedes.

Trinidad (Julio Cueva Díaz; 8am-5pm Tue-Thu) Off Paseo Agramonte.

Varadero (cnr Av 1 & Calle 39; 8am-3:30pm Mon-Fri)

Entry Permits for Cubans & Naturalized Citizens

Naturalized citizens of other countries who were born in Cuba require an *autorización de entrada* (entry permit) issued by a Cuban embassy or consulate. Called a *Vigencia de Viaje*, it allows Cubans resident abroad to visit Cuba as many times as they like over a two-year period. Persons hostile to the Revolution or with a criminal record are not eligible.

The Cuban government does not recognize dual citizenship. All persons born in Cuba are considered Cuban citizens unless they have formally renounced their citizenship at a Cuban diplomatic mission and the renunciation has been accepted. Cuban-Americans with questions about dual nationality can contact the Office of Overseas Citizens Services, Department of State, in Washington, DC 20520 (1-888-407-4747).

Licenses for US Visitors

In 1961 the US government imposed an order limiting the freedom of its citizens to visit Cuba, and airline offices and travel agencies in the US are forbidden to book tourist travel to Cuba via third countries. However, the Cuban government has never banned Americans from visiting Cuba, and it continues to welcome US passport holders under exactly the same terms as any other visitor.

Americans traditionally go to Cuba via Canada, Mexico, the Bahamas, or any other third country. Since American travel agents are prohibited from handling tourism arrangements, most Americans go through a foreign travel agency. Travel agents in those countries routinely arrange Cuban tourist cards, flight reservations and accommodation packages.

The US government has an 'Interests Section' in Havana, but American visitors are advised to go there only if something goes terribly wrong. Therefore, unofficial US visitors are especially careful not to lose their passports while in Cuba, as this would put them in a very difficult position. Many Cuban hotels rent security boxes (CUC$2 per day) to guests and nonguests alike, and you can carry a photocopy of your passport for identification on the street.

At the time of writing there were two types of licenses issued by the US government to visit Cuba: general licenses (typically for government officials, journalists and professional researchers) and specific licenses (for visiting family members, humanitarian projects, public performances, religious activities and educational activities).

In January 2011 the Obama administration revoked the George W Bush administration's clampdown on the issuing of legal licenses. This will pave the way for more educational, cultural and religious groups to apply for permission to visit the country through study abroad programs, people-to-people exchanges and research trips.

For the latest information, check with the **US Department of the Treasury** (www.treasury.gov/resource-center/sanctions/Programs/pages/cuba.aspx). Travel arrangements for those eligible for a license can be made by specialized US companies such as Marazul (see p515).

Under the Trading with the Enemy Act, goods originating in Cuba are prohibited from being brought into the US by anyone but licensed travelers. Cuban cigars, rum, coffee etc will be confiscated by US customs, and officials can create additional problems if they feel so inclined. Possession of Cuban goods inside the US or bringing them in from a third country is also banned.

The maximum penalty for 'unauthorized' Americans traveling to Cuba is US$250,000 and 10 years in prison. In practice, people are usually fined US$7500. It is estimated that close to 100,000 US citizens a year travel to Cuba illegally with no consequences. However, as long as these regulations remain in place, visiting Cuba certainly qualifies as soft adventure travel for Americans. There are many organizations, including a group of congress-people on Capitol Hill, working to lift the travel ban (see www.cubacentral.com for more information).

Volunteering

There are a number of bodies offering volunteer work in Cuba though it is always best to organize things in your home country first. Just turning up in Havana and volunteering can be difficult, if not impossible. Take a look at the following:

Canada-Cuba Farmer to Farmer Project (www.farmertofarmer.ca) Vancouver-based sustainable agriculture organization.

Canada World Youth (www.cwy-jcm.org) Head office in Montreal, Canada.

Cuban Solidarity Campaign (www.cuba-solidarity.org) Head office in London, UK.

Pastors for Peace (www.ifconews.org) Collects donations across the US to take to Cuba.

Witness for Peace (www.witnessforpeace.org) Looking for Spanish-speakers with a two-year commitment.

Women Travelers

In terms of personal safety, Cuba is a dream destination for women travelers. Most streets can be walked alone at night, violent crime is rare and the chivalrous part of machismo means you'll never step into oncoming traffic. But machismo cuts both ways, protecting on one side and pursuing – relentlessly – on the other. Cuban women are used to *piropos* (the whistles, kissing sounds and compliments constantly ringing in their ears), and might even reply with their own if they're feeling frisky. For foreign women, however, it can feel like an invasion.

Ignoring *piropos* is the first step. But sometimes ignoring isn't enough. Learn some rejoinders in Spanish so you can shut men up. *No me moleste* (don't bother me), *está bueno ya* (all right already) or *que falta respeto* (how disrespectful) are good ones, as is the withering 'don't you dare' stare that is also part of the Cuban woman's arsenal. Wearing plain, modest clothes might help lessen unwanted attention; topless sunbathing is out. An absent husband, invented or not, seldom has any effect. If you go to a disco, be very clear with Cuban dance partners what you are and are not interested in.

Transportation

GETTING THERE & AWAY

Entering the Country

Whether it's your first or 50th time, descending low into José Martí International Airport, over rust-red tobacco fields, is an exciting and unforgettable experience. Fortunately, entry procedures are relatively straightforward, and with in excess of 2.4 million visitors a year, immigration officials are used to dealing with foreign arrivals. See also p508 for further immigration information.

Outside Cuba, the capital city is called Havana, and this is how travel agents, airlines and other professionals will refer to it. Within Cuba, it's almost always called La Habana. For the sake of consistency, we have used the former spelling throughout this book.

Flights, tours and rail tickets can be booked online at www.lonelyplanet.com/travel_services.

Air

Airports

Cuba has 10 international airports. The largest by far is **José Martí** in Havana. The only other sizeable airport is **Juan Gualberto Gómez** in Varadero.

Charter flights for legally sanctioned Cuban-Americans currently fly into four Cuban airports from Miami and New York.

Airlines

In Havana most airline offices are situated in one of two clusters: the **Airline Building** (Calle 23 No 64) in Vedado, or in the **Miramar Trade Center** (Av 3 btwn Calles 76 & 80) in Playa.

Cubana (www.cubana.cu), the national carrier, operates regular flights to Bogotá, Buenos Aires, Mexico City, Cancún, Caracas, Guatemala City, London, Madrid, Paris, Toronto, Montreal, San José (Costa Rica) and Santo Domingo (Dominican Republic). Its modern fleet flies major routes and its airfares are usually among the cheapest. However, overbooking and delays are nagging problems. The airline has a zero-tolerance attitude toward overweight luggage, charging stiffly for every kilogram above the 20kg baggage allowance. In terms of safety, Cubana had back-to-back crashes in December 1999, with 39 fatalities, but it hasn't had any incidents since. You might want to check the latest at www.airsafe.com.

AFRICA

Direct flights from Africa originate in Luanda, Angola. From all other African countries you'll need to connect in London, Paris, Madrid, Amsterdam or Rome.

TAAG (www.taag.com) Weekly flights from Luanda to Havana.

ASIA & AUSTRALIA

There are no direct flights to Cuba from Asia or Australia. Travelers can connect through Europe, Canada, the US or Mexico.

DOCUMENTS REQUIRED ON ENTRY

- » Passport valid for at least one month beyond your departure date
- » Cuba 'tourist card' filled out correctly
- » Proof of travel medical insurance (obligatory since May 2010)
- » Evidence of sufficient funds for the duration of your stay
- » Return air ticket

CANADA

Flights from Canada serve 10 Cuban airports from 22 Canadian cities. Toronto and Montreal are the main hubs. Other cities are served by direct charter flights. **A Nash Travel** (www.anashtravel.com), based in Toronto, can sort out any flight/holiday queries.

Air Canada (www.aircanada.com) Flies to Havana, Cayo Largo del Sur, Holguín, Santa Clara and Varadero.

Air Transat (www.airtransat.com) Flies to Cayo Coco, Cayo Largo del Sur, Holguín and Santa Clara.

CanJet (www.canjet.com) Flies to Camagüey, Cayo Largo del Sur, Cienfuegos, Holguín, Santa Clara, Santiago de Cuba, Varadero and Havana.

Enerjet (www.enerjet.ca) Seasonal charters to Varadero from Calgary, Edmonton, Toronto and Vancouver.

Hola Sun (www.holasunholidays,ca) Cuba holiday specialist operating flights into Cayo Coco and Holguín.

Sunwing (www.flysunwing.com) Flies to Cayo Coco, Camagüey, Cayo Largo del Sur, Cienfuegos, Manzanillo, Holguín, Santiago de Cuba, Varadero and Havana.

Westjet (www.westjet.com) Flies to Cayo Coco, Holguín, Santa Clara and Varadero.

CARIBBEAN

Cubana and subsidiary **Aerocaribbean** (http://fly-aerocaribbean.com) are the main airlines. The other three are listed below.

Air Caraibes Airlines (www.aircaraibes.com) Direct flights from Pointe-a-Pitre on the French island of Guadeloupe to Havana.

Bahamasair (www.bahamasair.com) Nassau the Bahamas, to Havana.

Cayman Airways (www.caymanairways.com) Grand Cayman to Havana.

EUROPE

Regular flights to Cuba depart from Belgium, France, Germany, Italy, Russia, Spain, Switzerland and the Netherlands.

Aeroflot (www.aeroflot.ru) Moscow to Havana, twice weekly.

Air Berlin (www.airberlin.com) Dusseldorf, Munich and Berlin to Havana.

Air Europa (www.aireuropa.com) Twice weekly flights from Madrid to Havana.

Air France (www.airfrance.com) Daily flights from Paris-Charles de Gaulle to Havana.

Air Italy (www.alitalia.com) Milan and Rome to Varadero.

Arkefly (www.arkefly.nl) Amsterdam to Varadero.

Blue Panorama (www.blue-panorama.com) Milan and Rome to Cayo Coco, Cayo Largo del Sur, Holguín, Varadero and Havana.

Condor (www.condor.com) Frankfurt to Holguín, Varadero and Havana.

CUBA'S INTERNATIONAL AIRPORTS

AIRPORT NAME	LOCATION	AIRPORT CODE	DIRECT FLIGHTS FROM
Ignacio Agramonte	Camagüey	CMW	Canada, Miami
Jardines del Rey	Cayo Coco	CCC	UK, Canada, Italy
Vilo Acuña	Cayo Largo del Sur	CYO	Italy, Canada
Jaime González	Cienfuegos	CFG	Canada, Miami
José Martí	Havana	HAV	Russia, Mexico, UK, Spain, France, Miami, New York, Bahamas, Cayman Islands, Germany, Panama, Colombia, Angola, Peru, Argentina, Costa Rica, Canada, Dominican Republic, Jamaica, Guadeloupe, Venezuela, Guatemala, Holland
Frank País	Holguín	HOG	Canada, UK, Italy, Switzerland, Germany, Holland
Sierra Maestra	Manzanillo	MZO	Canada
Abel Santamaría	Santa Clara	SNU	Canada, UK
Antonio Maceo	Santiago de Cuba	SCU	Miami, Canada
Juan Gualberto Gómez	Varadero	VRA	Germany, Canada, Italy, Poland, Holland, Argentina, Switzerland, Belgium, Mexico, UK, Brazil

CLIMATE CHANGE & TRAVEL

Every form of transport that relies on carbon-based fuel generates CO^2, the main cause of human-induced climate change. Modern travel is dependent on aeroplanes, which might use less fuel per kilometer per person than most cars but travel much greater distances. The altitude at which aircraft emit gases (including CO^2) and particles also contributes to their climate change impact. Many websites offer 'carbon calculators' that allow people to estimate the carbon emissions generated by their journey and, for those who wish to do so, to offset the impact of the greenhouse gases emitted with contributions to portfolios of climate-friendly initiatives throughout the world. Lonely Planet offsets the carbon footprint of all staff and author travel.

Edelwiess (www.edelweissair.ch) From Zurich to Holguín and Varadero.

Iberia (www.iberia.com) Daily flights between Madrid and Havana.

Jetairfly (www.jetairfly.com) Charter flights from Brussels to Havana.

Martinair (www.martinair.com) Amsterdam to Varadero and Havana.

Neos (www.neosair.it) Charter linking Milan with Cayo Largo del Sur, Holguín and Varadero.

Rossiya Airlines (www.rossiya-airlines.com) St Petersburg to Varadero.

Transaero (www.transaero.com) Seasonal charter from St Petersburg and Moscow to Varadero.

MEXICO

Mexico City and Cancún are good places to connect with a wide number of US cities. Cuban travel company **Sol y Son México** (www.mx.solysonviajes.com), based in Mexico City and can help organize flights/packages.

Aeroméxico (www.aeromexico.com) Daily flights from Cancún and Mexico City to Havana.

Lan (www.lan.com) Cancún to Havana.

Magni (www.magnicharters.com.mx) Charter flights from Cancún and Monterrey to Varadero.

SOUTH & CENTRAL AMERICA

Copa Airlines (www.copaair.com) Daily flights from Bogotá, in Columbia, and Panama City to Havana.

Lan Chile (www.lan.com) Weekly flights from Santiago de Chile to Havana.

Taca Airlines (www.taca.com) Daily flights from San José, in Costa Rica, and Lima, in Peru, to Havana.

Whitejets (www.whitejets.com.br) Charters from Rio de Janeiro to Varadero.

UK

Thomas Cook (www.thomascook.com) Charter flights from London and Manchester to Holguín, Cayo Coco, Santa Clara and Varadero.

Thomson (www.thomson.so.uk) Charters from London and Manchester to Holguín and Varadero.

Virgin Atlantic (www.virgin-atlantic.com) Twice weekly flights from London Gatwick to Havana.

UNITED STATES

Since the Obama administration loosened travel restrictions for Cuban-Americans in 2009, a handful of regular charters from the US now fly to Cuba from Miami and New York. All flights to Havana's José Martí International Airport land at Terminal 2, rather than at Terminal 3, the main international portal.

DEPARTURE TAX

Everyone must pay a CUC$25 departure tax at the airport. It's payable in cash only.

American Eagle (www.aa.com) Miami to Havana, Camagüey, Cienfuegos and Santiago de Cuba.

Sky King (www.flyskyking.net) Charter from Miami and New York to Havana and Camagüey.

Vision (www.visionairlines.com) Charter from Miami and New York to Havana.

Tickets

Since Americans can't buy tickets to Cuba and can't use US-based travel agents, a host of businesses in Mexico, Canada and the Caribbean specialize in air-only deals. They sometimes won't sell you the first leg of your trip to the 'gateway' country for fear of embargo-related repercussions. When booking online, or if an agency requires financial acrobatics to steer clear of US embargo laws (which sometimes happens), be sure to confirm details, take contact names and clarify the procedure. You will need a Cuban tourist card and these agencies should arrange that. Except during peak holiday seasons, you can usually just arrive in Mexico, Jamaica or whatever gateway country and buy your round-trip ticket to Cuba there.

Sea

Cruises

Thanks to the US embargo, which prohibits vessels calling at Cuban ports from visiting the US for six months, few cruise ships include Cuba on

US CITIZENS & CUBA

In conjunction with the US embargo against Cuba, the US government currently enforces a 'travel ban,' preventing its citizens from visiting Cuba. Technically a treasury law prohibiting Americans from spending money in Cuba, it has largely squelched leisure travel for more than 45 years.

The 1996 Helms-Burton Act, which was signed into law by President Clinton on March 12, 1996, imposes *without judicial review* fines of up to US$50,000 on US citizens who visit Cuba without US government permission. It also allows for confiscation of their property. In addition, under the Trading with the Enemy Act, violators may face up to US$250,000 in fines and up to 10 years in prison. Fines levied under the George W Bush administration more than tripled, when fewer legal licenses were also issued, but under the Obama administration, a less hard-line approach has been followed. This was aided in April 2009 when travel restrictions were eased for Cuban-Americans, and again in January 2011 when the US government allowed more leniency in the granting of legal licenses.

Visit www.cubacentral.com to inform yourself of the latest legislation on Capitol Hill. See also p509 for further entry information for US travelers.

their itineraries. European lines, however, tired of being locked out, are starting to trickle in. Two worth trying are British-run **Thomson Cruises** (www.thomson.co.uk), who have offered Havana stops on three of their itineraries since December 2010, and the UK-based, Norwegian-owned **Fred Olsen Cruises** (www.fredolsencruises.com), which connects to Havana from Barbados.

Private Yacht

If you have your own private yacht or cruiser, Cuba has seven international entry ports equipped with customs facilities:

- Marina Hemingway (Havana)
- Marina Dásena (Varadero)
- Marina Cienfuegos
- Marina Cayo Guillermo
- Marina Santiago de Cuba
- Puerto de Vita (near Guardalavaca in Holguín province)
- Cayo Largo del Sur
- Cabo San Antonio (far western tip of Pinar del Río province)

Boat owners should communicate with Cuban coast guard on VHF 16 and 68 or the tourist network 19A. There are no scheduled ferry services to Cuba.

Tours

Cuba is popular on the organized-tour circuit, especially in the realm of soft adventure. There are also specialist tours focusing on culture, the environment, adventure, cycling, bird-watching, architecture, hiking, you name it...

Cuban Adventures (www.cubagrouptour.com) Australian-based company specializing in Cuba travel running small tours with mainly local guides.

Explore (www.explore.co.uk) Nine different trips including a hiking-focused 'revolutionary trails' excursion that ascends Pico Turquino.

Exodus (www.exodus.co.uk) British-based adventure-travel company offering over half-a-dozen regular Cuba trips, including family travel and a two-week cycling excursion.

GETTING AROUND

Air

Cubana de Aviación (www.cubana.cu) and its regional carrier Aerocaribbean have flights between Havana and 11 regional airports. There are no internal connections between the airports except via Havana. More details are listed in the table below.

One-way flights are half the price of round-trip flights and weight restrictions are strict (especially on Aerocaribbean's smaller planes). You can purchase tickets at most hotel tour desks and travel agencies for the same price as at the airline offices, which are often chaotic. Sol y Son is Cubana's own travel agency and is known for its customer service and efficiency.

Aerogaviota (www.aerogaviota.com; Av 47 No 2814 btwn Calles 28 & 34, Playa, Havana) runs more expensive charter flights to La Coloma and Cayo Levisa (Pinar del Río province), Nueva Gerona, Cayo Largo del Sur, Varadero, Cayo Las Brujas, Cayo Coco, Playa Santa Lucía and Santiago de Cuba.

Bicycle

Cuba is a cyclist's paradise, with bike lanes, bike workshops and drivers accustomed to sharing the road countrywide. Spare parts are difficult to find – you should bring important spares with you. Still, Cubans are grand masters at improvised repair, and though specific parts may not be available, something can surely be jury-rigged. *Poncheros* fix flat tires and provide air; every small town has one.

Helmets are unheard of in Cuba except at upscale resorts, so you should bring your own. A lock is imperative, as bicycle theft is rampant. *Parqueos* are bicycle parking lots located wherever crowds congregate (eg markets, bus terminals, downtown etc); they cost one peso.

Throughout the country, the 1m-wide strip of road to the extreme right is reserved for bicycles, even on highways. It's illegal to ride on sidewalks and against traffic on one-way streets and you'll be ticketed if caught. Road lighting is deplorable, so avoid riding after dark (over one-third of vehicular accidents in Cuba involve bicycles); carry lights with you just in case.

Trains with *coches de equipaje* or *bagones* (baggage carriages) should take bikes for around CUC$10 per trip. These compartments are guarded, but take your panniers with you and check over the bike when you arrive at your destination. Víazul buses also take bikes.

Purchase

Limited selection and high prices make buying a bike in Cuba through official channels unattractive. Better to ask around and strike a deal with an individual to buy their *chivo* (Cuban slang for bike) and trade it or resell it when you leave. With some earnest bargaining, you can get one for around CUC$30 – although the more you pay, the less your bones are likely to shake. Despite the obvious cost savings, bringing your own bike is still the best bet by far.

The bike shop El Orbe (p115) in Havana sell reasonably good Canadian-made bikes.

Rental

At the time of writing, there were no official bike-rental agencies in Cuba, though you can procure something roadworthy for between CUC$3 per hour or CUC$15 per day. Bikes are usually included as a perk in all-inclusive resort packages, but beware of bad brakes and zero gears.

Bus

Bus travel is a dependable way of getting around Cuba, at least in the more popular areas. **Víazul** (www.viazul.com) is the only long-distance bus company available to non-Cubans, with punctual, (over) air-conditioned coaches going to destinations of interest to travelers. Víazul charges for tickets in convertibles, and you can be confident you'll get where you're going on these buses – and on time. Buses schedule regular stops for lunch/dinner and always carry two drivers. They have daily departures and they're a good place to meet other foreigners.

Many of the popular tourist areas now have 'bus tours,' hop-on/hop-off buses that link all the main sights in a given area and charge CUC$5 for an all-day ticket. The services are run by government transport agency **Transtur** (☎7-831-7333). Havana and Varadero both have open-topped double-decker buses. Smaller minibuses are used in Vi-

TOURS FROM THE US

The Bush administration clamped down on organized legal travel between the United States and Cuba in 2003. However, the Obama administration reversed the order in January 2011. Legal tours are trickling back in.

» **Marazul Charters Inc** (www.marazulcharters.com) Has been facilitating travel to Cuba for over 30 years and can help place you on legal sponsored trips. The company can also book tickets on their own charter flights direct from Miami to Havana or Camagüey.

» **Center for Cuban Studies** (www.cubaupdate.org) A nonprofit educational institution located in New York that helps people involved in professional, humanitarian or religious work arrange trips to Cuba.

» **Global Exchange** (www.globalexchange.org) An NGO based in San Francisco that promotes human rights and social and economic justice around the world. Its Cuba arm organizes eco-exchanges exploring Cuba's sustainable development.

» **Witness for Peace** (www.witnessforpeace.org) This US-based organization focuses on Latin America and America's relationship with it. It organizes research trips to Cuba in tandem with Marazul Charters.

Americans traveling to Cuba are still subject to Treasury laws; see the **Department of the Treasury** (www.treas.gov) website for details (type the word 'Cuba' into the site search engine).

Air Routes

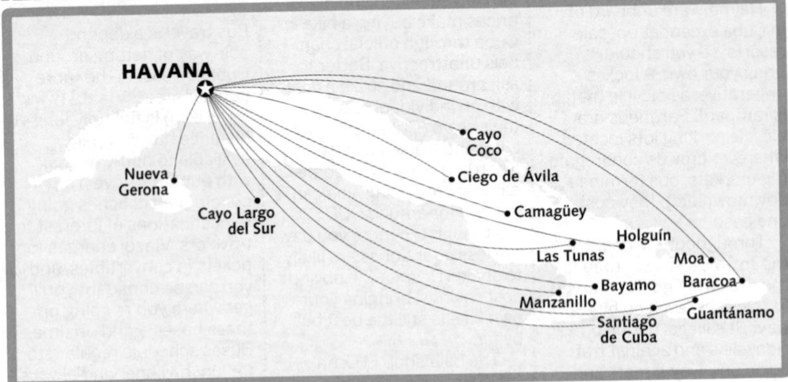

ñales, Trinidad, Cayo Coco, Guardalavaca and Baracoa (seasonal).

Cubans travel over shorter distances in provincial buses. These buses sell tickets in pesos and are a lot less comfortable and reliable than Víazul. They leave from the provincial bus stations in each province. Schedules and prices are usually chalked up on a board inside the terminal.

Reservations

Reservations with Víazul aren't always necessary, though it's advisable to check during peak travel periods (June to August, Christmas and Easter) and on popular routes (Havana–Trinidad, Trinidad–Santa Clara, and Santiago de Cuba–Baracoa). You can usually put your name down on a list a day or two beforehand. The buses have become popular with Cuban-Americans visiting the island in the wake of the lifting of travel restrictions in 2009.

The Víazul bus out of Baracoa is almost always booked, so reserve a seat on this service when you arrive. It is now possible to make reservations online at www.viazul.com.

Car

Renting a car in Cuba is easy, but once you've factored in gas, insurance, hire fees etc, it isn't cheap. Bank on paying CUC$70 per day minimum, even for a small car. It's actually cheaper to hire a taxi for distances of under 150km (at the time of writing taxis were charging CUC$0.50 per kilometer for inter-city routes).

Driver's License

Your home license is sufficient to rent and drive a car in Cuba.

Gas

Gas sold in convertibles (as opposed to peso gas) is widely available in stations all over the country (the north coast west of Havana being the notable exception). Gas stations are often open 24 hours and may have a small parts store on site. Gas is sold by the liter and comes in *regular* (CUC$1.10 per liter) and *especial* (CUC$1.30 per liter) varieties. Rental cars are advised to use *especial*. All gas stations have efficient pump attendants, usually in the form of *trabajadores sociales* (students in the process of studying for a degree).

Spare Parts

While you cannot count on spare parts per se to be available, Cubans have decades of experience keeping old wrecks on the road without factory parts and you'll see them do amazing things with cardboard, string, rubber and clothes hangers to keep a car mobile.

If you need air in your tires or you have a puncture, use a gas station or visit the local *ponchero*. They often don't have measures, so make sure they don't overinflate them.

Insurance

Rental cars come with an optional CUC$10 per day insurance, which covers everything but theft of the radio (which you'll need to put in the trunk of the car at night). You can choose to decline the insurance, but then the refundable deposit you must leave upon renting the car (in cash if you don't have a credit card issued by a non-US bank) soars from CUC$200 to CUC$500. If you do have an accident, you must get a copy of the *denuncia* (police report) to be eligible for the insurance coverage, a process which can take all day. If the police determine that you are the party responsible for the accident, say *adiós* to your deposit.

Rental

Renting a car in Cuba is straightforward. You'll need

WARNING: THIRD PARTY ACCIDENTS

Beware when driving a car in Cuba. Though the roads are ostensibly quiet, all kinds of hidden obstacles await the untrained eye. Bank on grazing goats, night-riding horse carts without lights, playing children, overgrown barely visible railway lines (and no level crossings), traffic-dyslexic cyclists, escaped chickens, jaywalkers, drunk drivers and more. Should you be involved in a car accident resulting in the death or injury of a third party, you will be detained in Cuba until the issue is resolved.

your passport, driver's license and a refundable CUC$200 deposit (in cash or non-US credit card). You can rent a car in one city and drop it off in another for a reasonable fee, which is handy. If you're on a tight budget, ask about diesel cars – some agencies stock a few and you'll save bundles in gas money considering a liter of non-diesel is CUC$1.15 while a liter of *petróleo* (diesel) is CUC$0.65. Note that there are very few rental cars with automatic transmission.

If you want to rent a car for three days or fewer, it will come with limited kilometers, while contracts for three days or more come with unlimited kilometers. In Cuba, you pay for the first tank of gas when you rent the car (CUC$1.15 per liter) and return it empty (a suicidal policy that sees many tight-fisted tourists running out of gas a kilometer or so from the drop-off point). Just to make it worse, you will not be refunded for any gas left in the tank. Petty theft of mirrors, antennas, taillights etc is common, so it's worth it to pay someone a convertible or two to watch your car for the night. If you lose your rental contract or keys you'll pay a CUC$50 penalty. Drivers under 25 pay a CUC$5 fee, while additional drivers on the same contract pay a CUC$15 surcharge.

Check over the car carefully with the rental agent before driving into the sunset, as you'll be responsible for any damage or missing parts. Make sure there is a spare tire of the correct size, a jack and a lug wrench. Check that there are seatbelts and that all the doors lock properly.

We have received many letters about poor or nonexistent customer service, bogus spare tires, forgotten reservations and other car-rental problems. Reservations are only accepted 15 days in advance and are still not guaranteed. While agents are usually accommodating, you might end up paying more than you planned or have to wait for hours until someone returns a car. The more Spanish you speak and the friendlier you are, the more likely problems will be resolved to everyone's satisfaction (tips to the agent might help). As with most Cuban travel, always have a Plan B.

Road Conditions

Driving here isn't just a different ballpark, it's a different sport. The first problem is that there are no signs – almost anywhere. Major junctions and turnoffs to important resorts or cities are often not indicated at all. Not only is this distracting, it's also incredibly time-consuming. The lack of signage also extends to highway instructions. Often a one-way street is not clearly indicated or a speed limit not highlighted, which can cause problems with the police (who won't understand your inability to telepathically absorb the road rules), and road markings are nonexistent everywhere.

The Autopista, Vía Blanca and Carretera Central are generally in a good state, but be prepared for roads suddenly deteriorating into chunks of asphalt and unexpected railroad crossings everywhere else (especially in the Oriente). Rail crossings are particularly problematic, as there are hundreds of them and there are never any safety gates. Beware: however overgrown the rails may look, you can pretty much assume that the line is still in use. Cuban trains, rather like its cars, defy all normal logic when it comes to mechanics.

While motorized traffic is refreshingly light, bicycles, pedestrians, oxcarts, horse carriages and livestock are a different matter. Many old cars and trucks lack rearview mirrors and traffic-unaware children run out of all kinds of nooks and crannies. Stay alert, drive with caution and use your horn when passing or on blind curves.

Driving at night is not recommended due to vari-

AIR TRAVEL WARNINGS

Some embassies – most notably the British – recommend against internal air travel in Cuba due to safety concerns. In November 2010, a French-Italian-manufactured twin-propeller plane operated by Cuban company Aerocaribbean crashed in Sancti Spíritus province en route from Santiago de Cuba to Havana, killing all 68 people on board. At the time of writing the causes of the crash were still being investigated.

able roads, drunk drivers, crossing cows and poor lighting. Drunk-driving remains a troublesome problem despite a government educational campaign. Late night in Havana is particularly dangerous, as it seems there's a passing lane, cruising lane and drunk lane.

Traffic lights are often busted or hard to pick out and right-of-way rules thrown to the wind. Take extra care.

Road Rules

Cubans drive how they want, where they want. It seems chaotic at first, but it has its rhythm. Seatbelts are supposedly required and maximum speed limits are technically 50km/h in the city, 90km/h on highways and 100km/h on the Autopista, but some cars can't even go that fast and those that can go faster still.

With so few cars on the road, it's hard not to put the pedal to the floor and just fly. Unexpected potholes are a hazard, however, as are police. There are some clever speed traps, particularly along the Autopista. Speeding tickets start at CUC$30 and are noted on your car contract; the fine is deducted from your deposit when you return the car. When pulled over by the cops, you're expected to get out of the car and walk over to them with your paperwork. An oncoming car flashing its lights means a hazard up ahead (usually the police).

The Cuban transport crisis means there are a lot of people waiting for rides by the side of the road. Giving a *botella* (a lift) to local hitchhikers has advantages aside from altruism. With a Cuban passenger you'll never get lost, you'll learn about secret spots not in any guidebook and you'll meet some great people. There are always risks associated with picking up hitchhikers; giving lifts to older people or families may reduce the risk factor. In the provinces, people waiting for rides are systematically queued by the *amarillos* (roadside traffic organizers), and they'll hustle the most needy folks into your car, usually an elderly couple or a pregnant woman.

Ferry

The most important ferry services for travelers are the catamaran from Surgidero de Batabanó to Nueva Gerona, **Isla de la Juventud** (☎7-878-1841), and the passenger ferry from Havana to Regla and **Casablanca** (☎7-867-3726). These ferries are generally safe, though in 1997 two hydrofoils crashed en route to Isla de la Juventud. In both 1994 and 2003, the Regla/Casablanca ferry was hijacked by Cubans trying to make their way to Florida. The 2003 incident involved tourists, so you can expect tight security.

Hitchhiking

The transport crisis, culture of solidarity and low crime levels make Cuba a popular hitchhiking destination. Here, hitchhiking is more like ride-sharing, and it's legally enforced. Traffic lights, railroad crossings and country crossroads are regular stops for people seeking rides. In the provinces and on the outskirts of Havana, the *amarillos* (official state-paid traffic supervisors, so-named for their mustard yellow uniforms) organize and prioritize ride seekers, and you're welcome to jump in line. Rides cost five

INTERNAL FLIGHTS FROM HAVANA

DESTINATION	FREQUENCY	DURATION
Baracoa	1 weekly	2½ hr
Bayamo	2 weekly	2 hr
Camagüey	daily	1½ hr
Cayo Coco	daily	1¼ hr
Cayo Largo del Sur	daily	40 min
Ciego de Ávila	1 weekly	1¼ hr
Guantánamo	5 weekly	2½ hr
Holguín	2-3 daily	1½ hr
Isla de la Juventud	2 daily	40 min
Manzanillo	1 weekly	2 hr
Moa	1 weekly	3 hr
Santiago de Cuba	2-3 daily	2¼ hr

VÍAZUL ROUTES

ROUTE	DURATION (HR)	PRICE (CUC$)	STOPS IN BETWEEN
Havana–Santiago de Cuba	15½	51	Entronque de Jaguey, Santa Clara, Sancti Spíritus, Ciego de Ávila, Camagüey, Las Tunas, Holguín, Bayamo
Trinidad–Santiago de Cuba	12	33	Sancti Spíritus, Ciego de Ávila, Camagüey, Las Tunas, Holguín, Bayamo
Havana–Viñales	3¼	12	Pinar del Río
Havana–Holguín	10½	44	Santa Clara, Sancti Spíritus, Ciego de Ávila, Camagüey, Las Tunas
Havana–Trinidad	5½	25	Entronque de Jaguey, Cienfuegos
Havana–Varadero	3	10	Matanzas, Varadero Airport
Santiago de Cuba–Baracoa	4¾	15	Guantánamo
Varadero–Santiago de Cuba	16	49	Cárdenas, Colón, Santa Clara, Sancti Spíritus, Ciego de Ávila, Camagüey, Las Tunas, Holguín, Bayamo
Trinidad–Varadero	6	20	Cárdenas, Colón, Entronque de Jaguey, Cienfuegos

to 20 pesos depending on distance. Travelers hitching rides will want a good map and some Spanish skills. Expect to wait two or three hours for rides in some cases. Hitchhiking is never entirely safe in any country in the world. Travelers who decide to hitchhike should understand that they are taking a small but potentially serious risk. People who do choose to hitchhike will be safer if they travel in pairs and let someone know where they are planning to go.

Local Transportation

Bici-taxi

Bici-taxis are big pedal-powered tricycles with a double seat behind the driver and are common in Havana, Camagüey, Holguín and a few other cities. In Havana they'll insist on a CUC$1 minimum fare (Cubans pay five or 10 pesos). Some bici-taxistas ask ridiculous amounts. The fare should be clearly understood before you hop aboard. By law, bici-taxis aren't allowed to take tourists (who are expected to use regular taxis), and they're taking a risk by carrying foreigners. Bici-taxi rules are more lax in the provinces and you should be able to get one for five pesos.

Boat

Some towns, such as Havana, Cienfuegos, Gibara and Santiago de Cuba, have local ferry services. Details are in the respective chapters.

Bus

Very crowded, very steamy, very challenging, very Cuban – *guaguas* (local buses) are useful in bigger cities. Buses work fixed routes, stopping at *paradas* (bus stops) that always have a line, even if it doesn't look like it. You have to shout out *¿el último?* to find out who was last in line before you showed up. You give this call when the next person arrives and then you know exactly where you fall in line, allowing you to go have a beer until the bus shows up.

Buses cost from 40 centavos to one peso. Havana and Santiago de Cuba have recently been kitted out with brand new fleets of Chinese-made metro buses. You must always walk as far back in the bus as you can and exit through the rear. Make room to pass by saying *permiso*, always wear your pack in front and watch your wallet.

Colectivo & Máquina

Colectivos are taxis running on fixed, long-distance routes, leaving when full. They are generally pre-1959 American cars that belch diesel fumes and can squash in at least three people across the front seat. State-owned taxis that charge in convertibles hanging about bus stations are faster and usually cheaper than the bus.

THE MAN IN SEAT SIXTY-ONE

A regularly updated précis of Cuban train times, types and nuances are available on the website **The Man in Seat Sixty-one** (www.seat61.com), run by Mark Smith in the UK. The website covers train travel across the globe, but has a decent printed run-down on Cuba's main train services – a rarity indeed!

Horse Carriage

Many provincial cities have *coches de caballo* (horse carriages) that trot on fixed routes, often between train/bus stations and city centers. Prices in Moneda Nacional cost around one peso.

Taxi

Car taxis are metered and cost CUC$1 to start and CUC$1 per kilometer. Taxi drivers are in the habit of offering foreigners a flat, off-meter rate that usually works out very close to what you'll pay with the meter. The difference is that with the meter, the money goes to the state to be divided up; without the meter it goes into the driver's pocket.

Tours

Of the many tourist agencies in Cuba, the following are the most useful:

Cubamar Viajes (☎7-833-2523/4; www.cubamar viajes.cu) Rents campismo cabins and mobile homes (caravans).

Cubanacán (☎7-873-2686; www.cubanacan.cu) General tour agency that also has divisions called Cubanacán Náutica (scuba diving, boating and fishing) and Turismo Y Salud (surgery, spas and rehabilitation).

Cubatur (☎7-835-4155)

Ecotur (☎7-204-5188)

Gaviota (☎7-204-4411; www.gaviota-grupo.com)

Havanatur (☎7-835-3720; www.havanatur.cu) Works with Marazul Tours in the US.

Paradiso (☎7-832-9538/9; paradis@paradiso.artex.com.cu) Multiday cultural and art tours.

San Cristóbal Agencia de Viajes (☎7-861-9171; www.viajessancristobal.cu)

Train

Public railways operated by Ferrocarriles de Cuba serve all of the provincial capitals and are a great way to experience Cuba, if you have time and patience. While train travel is safe, the departure information provided in this book is purely theoretical. Getting a ticket is usually no problem, as there's a quota for tourists paying in convertibles.

Foreigners must pay for their tickets in cash, but prices are reasonable and the carriages, though old and worn, are fairly comfortable. The toilets are foul – bring toilet paper. Watch your luggage on overnight trips and bring some of your own food. Only the Tren Francés has snack facilities, although vendors often come through the train selling coffee (you supply the cup).

Train Stations

Cuban train stations, despite their occasionally grandiose façades, are invariably dingy, chaotic places with little visible train information. Departure times are displayed on black chalkboards or handwritten notices; there are no electronic or printed timetables. Always check train info two to three days before your intended travel.

Classes

Trains are either *especial* (air-conditioned, faster trains with fewer departures), *regular* (slowish trains with daily departures) or *lecheros* (milk trains that stop at every little town on the line). Trains on major routes such as Havana–Santiago de Cuba will be *especial* or *regular* trains.

THE TREN FRANCÉS

Cuba's best and fastest train is the Tren Francés, which runs between Havana and Santiago de Cuba in both directions every third day (1st/2nd class CUC$62/50, 15½ hours, 861km). Train No 1 leaves Havana at 6.20pm, passing Santa Clara and Camagüey, before reaching Santiago de Cuba at 9.50am. Train 2 leaves Santiago de Cuba daily at 9pm and reaches Havana at 12.15pm. The trains use second-hand French carriages (hence the name), which formerly operated on the Paris–Brussels–Amsterdam European route. They were bought by the Cubans in 2001. The carriages are relatively comfortable, if a little worn, with frigid air-conditioning, a limited cafe, a purser (one per carriage) and decidedly dingy toilets. As with many things in Cuba, it's not so much the quality of the carriages that's the problem, but their upkeep – or lack thereof. The Tren Francés has two classes, *primera* amd *primera especial*. The latter is worth the extra CUC$12 investment.

CUBA'S TRAIN SERVICES FROM HAVANA

The following information is liable to change or cancellation. Always check ahead.

DESTINATION	TRAIN NO	FREQUENCY	PRICE (CUC$)
Pinar del Río	225	every other day	6.50
Bayamo	7	every 3rd day	26
Guantánamo	5	every 3rd day	32
Santiago de Cuba	1, 5	2 days out of 3	30-62
Matanzas	3, 5, 7, 9, 29	daily	3
Morón	29	daily	24
Manzanillo	28	every 3rd day	32
Cienfuegos	19	every other day	11
Santa Clara	1, 3, 5, 7, 9, 29	daily	10–21
Camagüey	1, 3, 5, 7	daily	19–41
Sancti Spíritus	9	every other day	13.50

Costs

Regular trains cost under CUC$3 per 100km, while *especial* trains cost closer to CUC$5.50 per 100km. The Hershey Train (p154) is priced like the *regular* trains.

Reservations

In most train stations, you just go to the ticket window and buy a ticket. In Havana, there's a separate waiting room and ticket window for passengers paying in convertibles in La Coubre train station. Be prepared to show your passport when purchasing tickets. It's always wise to check beforehand at the station for current departures because things change.

Rail Network

Cuba's train network is comprehensive, running almost the full length of the main island from Guane in Pinar del Río province to Caimanera, just south of the city of Guantánamo. There are also several branch lines heading out north and south and linking up places such as Manzanillo, Nuevitas, Morón and Cienfuegos. Baracoa is one of the few cities without a train connection. Other trainless enclaves are the Isla de la Juventud, the far west of Pinar del Río province and the northern keys. Trinidad has been detached from the main rail network since a storm brought down a bridge in 1992, though it has a small branch line that runs along the Valle del los Ingenios.

Services

Many additional local trains operate at least daily and some more frequently. There are also smaller trains linking Las Tunas and Holguín, Holguín and Santiago de Cuba, Santa Clara and Nuevitas, Cienfuegos and Sancti Spíritus, and Santa Clara and Caibarién. More information is provided in the regional chapters of this book.

The Hershey Train (p154) is the only electric railway in Cuba and was built by the Hershey Chocolate Company in the early years of the 20th century; it's a fun way to get between Havana and Matanzas. For schedules, see Havana and Matanzas chapters.

Truck

Camiones (trucks) are a cheap, fast way to travel within or between provinces. Every city has a provincial and municipal bus stop with *camiones* departures. They run on a (loose) schedule and you'll need to take your place in line by asking for *el último* to your destination; you pay as you board. A truck from Santiago de Cuba to Guantánamo costs five pesos (CUC$0.20), while the same trip on a Víazul bus costs CUC$6.

Camion traveling is hot, crowded and uncomfortable, but is a great way to meet local people, fast; a little Spanish will go a long way.

Sometimes terminal staff tell foreigners they're prohibited from traveling on trucks. As with anything in Cuba, never take 'no' as your final answer. Crying poor, striking up a conversation with the driver, appealing to other passengers for aid etc usually helps.

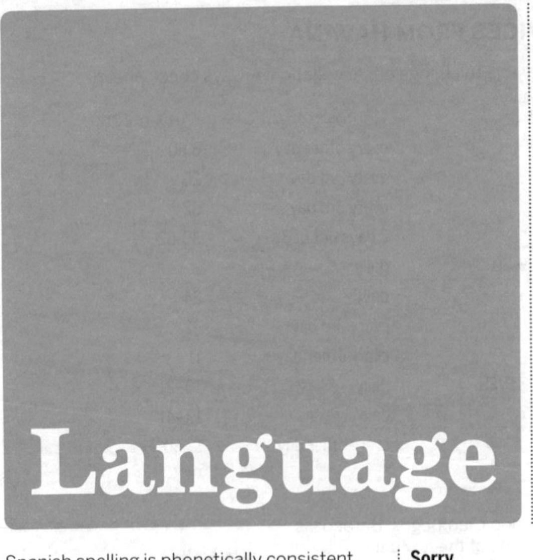

WANT MORE?

For in-depth language information and handy phrases, check out Lonely Planet's *Latin American Spanish Phrasebook*. You'll find it at **shop.lonelyplanet.com**, or you can buy Lonely Planet's iPhone phrasebooks at the Apple App Store.

Spanish spelling is phonetically consistent, meaning that there's a clear and consistent relationship between what you see in writing and how it's pronounced. Most Latin American Spanish sounds are pronounced the same as their English counterparts– if you read our blue pronunciation guides as if they were English, you'll be understood just fine. Note that the kh in our pronunciation guides is a throaty sound (like the 'ch' in the Scottish *loch*), v and b are similar to the English 'b' (but softer, between a 'v' and a 'b'), and r is strongly rolled. Some Spanish words are written with an acute accent (eg *días*) – this indicates a stressed syllable. In our pronunciation guides, the stressed syllables are in italics.

Spanish nouns are marked for gender (masculine or feminine). Endings for adjectives also change to agree with the gender of the noun they modify. Where necessary, both forms are given for the phrases in this chapter, separated by a slash and with the masculine form first, eg *perdido/a* (m/f).

When talking to people familiar to you or younger than you, use the informal form of 'you', *tú*, rather than the polite form *Usted*. In all other cases use the polite form. The polite form is used in the phrases provided in this chapter; where both options are given, they are indicated by the abbreviations 'pol' and 'inf'.

BASICS

Hello.	*Hola.*	o·la
Goodbye.	*Adiós.*	a·*dyos*
How are you?	*¿Qué tal?*	ke tal
Fine, thanks.	*Bien, gracias.*	byen *gra*·syas
Excuse me.	*Perdón.*	per·*don*
Sorry.	*Lo siento.*	lo *syen*·to
Yes./No.	*Sí./No.*	see/no
Please.	*Por favor.*	por fa·*vor*
Thank you.	*Gracias.*	*gra*·syas
You're welcome.	*De nada.*	de *na*·da

My name is ...
Me llamo ... — me *ya*·mo ...

What's your name?
¿Cómo se llama Usted? — *ko*·mo se *ya*·ma *oo*·ste (pol)
¿Cómo te llamas? — *ko*·mo te *ya*·mas (inf)

Do you speak English?
¿Habla inglés? — *a*·bla een·*gles* (pol)
¿Hablas inglés? — *a*·blas een·*gles* (inf)

I (don't) understand.
Yo (no) entiendo. — yo (no) en·*tyen*·do

ACCOMMODATIONS

I'd like to book a room.
Quisiera reservar una habitación. — kee·*sye*·ra re·ser·*var* *oo*·na a·bee·ta·*syon*

How much is it per night/person?
¿Cuánto cuesta por noche/persona? — *kwan*·to *kwes*·ta por *no*·che/per·*so*·na

Does it include breakfast?
¿Incluye el desayuno? — een·*kloo*·ye el de·sa·*yoo*·no

campsite	*terreno de cámping*	te·*re*·no de *kam*·peeng
hotel	*hotel*	o·*tel*
guesthouse	*pensión*	pen·*syon*
youth hostel	*albergue juvenil*	al·*ber*·ge khoo·ve·*neel*

KEY PATTERNS

To get by in Spanish, mix and match these simple patterns with words of your choice:

When's (the next flight)?
¿Cuándo sale (el próximo vuelo)? kwan·do sa·le (el prok·see·mo vwe·lo)

Where's (the station)?
¿Dónde está (la estación)? don·de es·ta (la es·ta·syon)

Where can I (buy a ticket)?
¿Dónde puedo (comprar un billete)? don·de pwe·do (kom·prar oon bee·ye·te)

Do you have (a map)?
¿Tiene (un mapa)? tye·ne (oon ma·pa)

Is there (a toilet)?
¿Hay (servicios)? ai (ser·vee·syos)

I'd like (a coffee).
Quisiera (un café). kee·sye·ra (oon ka·fe)

I'd like (to hire a car).
Quisiera (alquilar un coche). kee·sye·ra (al·kee·lar oon ko·che)

Can I (enter)?
¿Se puede (entrar)? se pwe·de (en·trar)

Could you please (help me)?
¿Puede (ayudarme), por favor? pwe·de (a·yoo·dar·me) por fa·vor

Do I have to (get a visa)?
¿Necesito (obtener un visado)? ne·se·see·to (ob·te·ner oon vee·sa·do)

I'd like a ... room.	*Quisiera una habitación ...*	kee·sye·ra oo·na a·bee·ta·syon ...
single	*individual*	een·dee·vee·dwal
double	*doble*	do·ble

air-con	*aire acondicionado*	ai·re a·kon·dee·syo·na·do
bathroom	*baño*	ba·nyo
bed	*cama*	ka·ma
window	*ventana*	ven·ta·na

DIRECTIONS

Where's ...?
¿Dónde está ...? don·de es·ta ...

What's the address?
¿Cuál es la dirección? kwal es la dee·rek·syon

Could you please write it down?
¿Puede escribirlo, por favor? pwe·de es·kree·beer·lo por fa·vor

Can you show me (on the map)?
¿Me lo puede indicar (en el mapa)? me lo pwe·de een·dee·kar (en el ma·pa)

at the corner	*en la esquina*	en la es·kee·na
at the traffic lights	*en el semáforo*	en el se·ma·fo·ro
behind ...	*detrás de ...*	de·tras de ...
far	*lejos*	le·khos
in front of ...	*enfrente de ...*	en·fren·te de ...
left	*izquierda*	ees·kyer·da
near	*cerca*	ser·ka
next to ...	*al lado de ...*	al la·do de ...
opposite ...	*frente a ...*	fren·te a ...
right	*derecha*	de·re·cha
straight ahead	*todo recto*	to·do rek·to

EATING & DRINKING

What would you recommend?
¿Qué recomienda? ke re·ko·myen·da

What's in that dish?
¿Que lleva ese plato? ke ye·va e·se pla·to

I don't eat ...
No como ... no ko·mo ...

That was delicious!
¡Estaba buenísimo! es·ta·ba bwe·nee·see·mo

Please bring the bill.
Por favor nos trae la cuenta. por fa·vor nos tra·e la kwen·ta

Cheers!
¡Salud! sa·loo

I'd like to book a table for ...	*Quisiera reservar una mesa para ...*	kee·sye·ra re·ser·var oo·na me·sa pa·ra ...
(eight) o'clock	*las (ocho)*	las (o·cho)
(two) people	*(dos) personas*	(dos) per·so·nas

Key Words

appetisers	*aperitivos*	a·pe·ree·tee·vos
bar	*bar*	bar
bottle	*botella*	bo·te·ya
bowl	*bol*	bol
breakfast	*desayuno*	de·sa·yoo·no
cafe	*café*	ka·fe
children's menu	*menú infantil*	me·noo een·fan·teel
(too) cold	*(muy) frío*	(mooy) free·o
dinner	*cena*	se·na
food	*comida*	ko·mee·da
fork	*tenedor*	te·ne·dor
glass	*vaso*	va·so
highchair	*trona*	tro·na

hot (warm)	*caliente*	kal·*yen*·te
knife	*cuchillo*	koo·*chee*·yo
lunch	*comida*	ko·*mee*·da
main course	*segundo plato*	se·*goon*·do *pla*·to
market	*mercado*	mer·*ka*·do
menu (in English)	*menú (en inglés)*	me·*noo* (en een·*gles*)
plate	*plato*	*pla*·to
restaurant	*restaurante*	res·tow·*ran*·te
spoon	*cuchara*	koo·*cha*·ra
supermarket	*supermercado*	soo·per·mer·*ka*·do
vegetarian food	*comida vegetariana*	ko·*mee*·da ve·khe·ta·*rya*·na
with/without	*con/sin*	kon/seen

Meat & Fish

beef	*carne de vaca*	*kar*·ne de *va*·ka
chicken	*pollo*	*po*·yo
duck	*pato*	*pa*·to
fish	*pescado*	pes·*ka*·do
lamb	*cordero*	kor·*de*·ro
pork	*cerdo*	*ser*·do
turkey	*pavo*	*pa*·vo
veal	*ternera*	ter·*ne*·ra

Fruit & Vegetables

apple	*manzana*	man·*sa*·na
apricot	*albaricoque*	al·ba·ree·*ko*·ke
artichoke	*alcachofa*	al·ka·*cho*·fa
asparagus	*espárragos*	es·*pa*·ra·gos
banana	*plátano*	*pla*·ta·no
beans	*judías*	khoo·*dee*·as
beetroot	*remolacha*	re·mo·*la*·cha
cabbage	*col*	kol
carrot	*zanahoria*	sa·na·o·rya
celery	*apio*	*a*·pyo
cherry	*cereza*	se·*re*·sa
corn	*maíz*	ma·*ees*
cucumber	*pepino*	pe·*pee*·no
fruit	*fruta*	*froo*·ta
grape	*uvas*	*oo*·vas
lemon	*limón*	lee·*mon*
lentils	*lentejas*	len·*te*·khas
lettuce	*lechuga*	le·*choo*·ga
mushroom	*champiñón*	cham·pee·*nyon*
nuts	*nueces*	*nwe*·ses
onion	*cebolla*	se·*bo*·ya
orange	*naranja*	na·*ran*·kha
peach	*melocotón*	me·lo·ko·*ton*
peas	*guisantes*	gee·*san*·tes
(red/green) pepper	*pimiento (rojo/verde)*	pee·*myen*·to (*ro*·kho/*ver*·de)
pineapple	*piña*	*pee*·nya
plum	*ciruela*	seer·*we*·la
potato	*patata*	pa·*ta*·ta
pumpkin	*calabaza*	ka·la·*ba*·sa
spinach	*espinacas*	es·pee·*na*·kas
strawberry	*fresa*	*fre*·sa
tomato	*tomate*	to·*ma*·te
vegetable	*verdura*	ver·*doo*·ra
watermelon	*sandía*	san·*dee*·a

Signs

Abierto	Open
Cerrado	Closed
Entrada	Entrance
Hombres/Varones	Men
Mujeres/Damas	Women
Prohibido	Prohibited
Salida	Exit
Servicios/Baños	Toilets

Other

bread	*pan*	pan
butter	*mantequilla*	man·te·*kee*·ya
cheese	*queso*	*ke*·so
egg	*huevo*	*we*·vo
honey	*miel*	myel
jam	*mermelada*	mer·me·*la*·da
oil	*aceite*	a·*sey*·te
pasta	*pasta*	*pas*·ta
pepper	*pimienta*	pee·*myen*·ta
rice	*arroz*	a·*ros*
salt	*sal*	sal
sugar	*azúcar*	a·*soo*·kar
vinegar	*vinagre*	vee·*na*·gre

Drinks

beer	*cerveza*	ser·*ve*·sa
coffee	*café*	ka·*fe*
(orange) juice	*zumo (de naranja)*	*soo*·mo (de na·*ran*·kha)
milk	*leche*	*le*·che
tea	*té*	te

(mineral) water	*agua (mineral)*	a·gwa (mee·ne·*ral*)
(red/white) wine	*vino (tinto/ blanco)*	*vee*·no (*teen*·to/ *blan*·ko)

EMERGENCIES

Help!	*¡Socorro!*	so·*ko*·ro
Go away!	*¡Vete!*	*ve*·te

Call ...!	*¡Llame a ...!*	*ya*·me a ...
a doctor	*un médico*	oon *me*·dee·ko
the police	*la policía*	la po·lee·*see*·a

I'm lost.
Estoy perdido/a. es·*toy* per·*dee*·do/a (m/f)

I had an accident.
He tenido un accidente. e te·*nee*·do oon ak·see·*den*·te

I'm ill.
Estoy enfermo/a. es·*toy* en·*fer*·mo/a (m/f)

It hurts here.
Me duele aquí. me *dwe*·le a·*kee*

I'm allergic to (antibiotics).
Soy alérgico/a a (los antibióticos). soy a·*ler*·khee·ko/a a (los an·tee·*byo*·tee·kos) (m/f)

SHOPPING & SERVICES

I'd like to buy ...
Quisiera comprar ... kee·*sye*·ra kom·*prar* ...

I'm just looking.
Sólo estoy mirando. *so*·lo es·*toy* mee·*ran*·do

May I look at it?
¿Puedo verlo? *pwe*·do *ver*·lo

I don't like it.
No me gusta. no me *goos*·ta

How much is it?
¿Cuánto cuesta? *kwan*·to *kwes*·ta

That's too expensive.
Es muy caro. es mooy *ka*·ro

Can you lower the price?
¿Podría bajar un poco el precio? po·*dree*·a ba·*khar* oon *po*·ko el *pre*·syo

There's a mistake in the bill.
Hay un error en la cuenta. ai oon e·*ror* en la *kwen*·ta

Question Words

How?	*¿Cómo?*	*ko*·mo
What?	*¿Qué?*	ke
When?	*¿Cuándo?*	*kwan*·do
Where?	*¿Dónde?*	*don*·de
Who?	*¿Quién?*	kyen
Why?	*¿Por qué?*	por ke

ATM	*cajero automático*	ka·*khe*·ro ow·to·*ma*·tee·ko
credit card	*tarjeta de crédito*	tar·*khe*·ta de *kre*·dee·to
internet cafe	*cibercafé*	see·ber·ka·*fe*
post office	*correos*	ko·*re*·os
tourist office	*oficina de turismo*	o·fee·*see*·na de too·*rees*·mo

TIME & DATES

What time is it?	*¿Qué hora es?*	ke *o*·ra es
It's (10) o'clock.	*Son (las diez).*	son (las dyes)
It's half past (one).	*Es (la una) y media.*	es (la *oo*·na) ee *me*·dya

morning	*mañana*	ma·*nya*·na
afternoon	*tarde*	*tar*·de
evening	*noche*	*no*·che
yesterday	*ayer*	a·*yer*
today	*hoy*	oy
tomorrow	*mañana*	ma·*nya*·na

Monday	*lunes*	*loo*·nes
Tuesday	*martes*	*mar*·tes
Wednesday	*miércoles*	*myer*·ko·les
Thursday	*jueves*	*khwe*·ves
Friday	*viernes*	*vyer*·nes
Saturday	*sábado*	*sa*·ba·do
Sunday	*domingo*	do·*meen*·go

January	*enero*	e·*ne*·ro
February	*febrero*	fe·*bre*·ro
March	*marzo*	*mar*·so
April	*abril*	a·*breel*
May	*mayo*	*ma*·yo
June	*junio*	*khoon*·yo
July	*julio*	*khool*·yo
August	*agosto*	a·*gos*·to
September	*septiembre*	sep·*tyem*·bre
October	*octubre*	ok·*too*·bre
November	*noviembre*	no·*vyem*·bre
December	*diciembre*	dee·*syem*·bre

TRANSPORTATION

Public Transportation

boat	*barco*	*bar*·ko
bus	*autobús*	ow·to·*boos*
plane	*avión*	a·*vyon*
train	*tren*	tren

Numbers

1	*uno*	oo·no
2	*dos*	dos
3	*tres*	tres
4	*cuatro*	*kwa*·tro
5	*cinco*	*seen*·ko
6	*seis*	seys
7	*siete*	*sye*·te
8	*ocho*	*o*·cho
9	*nueve*	*nwe*·ve
10	*diez*	dyes
20	*veinte*	*veyn*·te
30	*treinta*	*treyn*·ta
40	*cuarenta*	kwa·*ren*·ta
50	*cincuenta*	seen·*kwen*·ta
60	*sesenta*	se·*sen*·ta
70	*setenta*	se·*ten*·ta
80	*ochenta*	o·*chen*·ta
90	*noventa*	no·*ven*·ta
100	*cien*	syen
1000	*mil*	meel

first	*primero*	pree·*me*·ro
last	*último*	*ool*·tee·mo
next	*próximo*	*prok*·see·mo

I want to go to ...
Quisiera ir a ... kee·*sye*·ra eer a ...

Does it stop at ...?
¿Para en ...? *pa*·ra en ...

What stop is this?
¿Cuál es esta parada? kwal es *es*·ta pa·*ra*·da

What time does it arrive/leave?
¿A qué hora llega/ sale? a ke *o*·ra *ye*·ga/ *sa*·le

Please tell me when we get to ...
¿Puede avisarme cuando lleguemos a ...? *pwe*·de a·vee·*sar*·me *kwan*·do ye·*ge*·mos a ...

I want to get off here.
Quiero bajarme aquí. *kye*·ro ba·*khar*·me a·*kee*

a ... ticket	*un billete de ...*	oon bee·*ye*·te de ...
1st-class	*primera clase*	pree·*me*·ra *kla*·se
2nd-class	*segunda clase*	se·*goon*·da *kla*·se
one-way	*ida*	*ee*·da
return	*ida y vuelta*	*ee*·da ee *vwel*·ta

airport	*aeropuerto*	a·e·ro·*pwer*·to
aisle seat	*asiento de pasillo*	a·*syen*·to de pa·*see*·yo
bus stop	*parada de autobuses*	pa·*ra*·da de ow·to·*boo*·ses
cancelled	*cancelado*	kan·se·*la*·do
delayed	*retrasado*	re·tra·*sa*·do
platform	*plataforma*	pla·ta·*for*·ma
ticket office	*taquilla*	ta·*kee*·ya
timetable	*horario*	o·*ra*·ryo
train station	*estación de trenes*	es·ta·*syon* de *tre*·nes
window seat	*asiento junto a la ventana*	a·*syen*·to *khoon*·to a la ven·*ta*·na

Driving & Cycling

I'd like to hire a ...	*Quisiera alquilar ...*	kee·*sye*·ra al·kee·*lar* ...
4WD	*un todo-terreno*	oon to·do·te·*re*·no
bicycle	*una bicicleta*	*oo*·na bee·see·*kle*·ta
car	*un coche*	oon *ko*·che
motorcycle	*una moto*	*oo*·na *mo*·to

child seat	*asiento de seguridad para niños*	a·*syen*·to de se·goo·ree·*da* *pa*·ra *nee*·nyos
diesel	*petróleo*	pet·*ro*·le·o
helmet	*casco*	*kas*·ko
hitchhike	*hacer botella*	a·*ser* bo·*te*·ya
mechanic	*mecánico*	me·*ka*·nee·ko
petrol/gas	*gasolina*	ga·so·*lee*·na
service station	*gasolinera*	ga·so·lee·*ne*·ra
truck	*camion*	ka·*myon*

Is this the road to ...?
¿Se va a ... por esta carretera? se va a ... por *es*·ta ka·re·*te*·ra

(How long) Can I park here?
¿(Por cuánto tiempo) Puedo aparcar aquí? (por *kwan*·to *tyem*·po) *pwe*·do a·par·*kar* a·*kee*

The car has broken down (at ...).
El coche se ha averiado (en ...). el *ko*·che se a a·ve·*rya*·do (en ...)

I have a flat tyre.
Tengo un pinchazo. *ten*·go oon peen·*cha*·so

I've run out of petrol.
Me he quedado sin gasolina. me e ke·*da*·do seen ga·so·*lee*·na

agropecuario – vegetable market; also sells rice, fruit

aguardiente – fermented cane; literally 'firewater'

ama de llaves – housekeeper; see camarera

amarillo – a roadside traffic organizer in a yellow uniform

americano/a – a citizen of any Western hemisphere country (from Canada to Argentina); a US citizen is called a norteamericano/a or estado- unidense; see also gringo/a and yuma

Arawak – linguistically related Indian tribes that inhabited most of the Caribbean islands and northern South America

Autopista – the national highway

babalawo – a Santería priest; also babalao; see also santero

bahía – bay

balseros – rafters; used to describe the emigrants who escaped to the US in the 1990s on homemade rafts

barbuda – name given to Castro's rebel army; literally 'bearded one'

barrio – neighborhood

bici-taxi – bicycle taxi

bloqueo – Cuban term for the US embargo

bodega – stores distributing ration-card products

bohío – thatched hut

bolero – a love song

botella – hitchhiking; literally 'bottle'

cabaña – cabin, hut

cabildo – a town council during the colonial era; also an association of tribes in Cuban religions of African origin

cacique – chief; originally used to describe an Indian chief and today used to designate a petty tyrant

Cadeca – exchange booth

cafetal – coffee plantation

caliente – hot

calle – street

camión – truck

campesinos – people who live in the campo

campismo – national network of 82 camping installations, not all of which are open to foreigners

carnet – the identification document that allows foreigners to pay for museums, transport and theater performances in pesos

casa particular – private house that lets out rooms to foreigners (and sometimes Cubans); all legal casas display a green triangle on the door

casco histórico – historic center of a city

CDR – Comités de Defensa de la Revolución; neighborhood-watch bodies originally formed in 1960 to consolidate grassroots support for the Revolution; they now play a role in health, education, social, recycling and voluntary labor campaigns

chachachá – cha-cha; dance music in 4/4 meter derived from the rumba and mambo

Changó – the Santería deity signifying war and fire, twinned with Santa Barbara in Catholicism

chivo – Cuban slang for 'bike'

cimarrón – a runaway slave

claves – rhythm sticks used by musicians

Cohiba – native Indian name for a smoking implement; one of Cuba's top brands of cigar

colectivo – collective taxi that takes on as many passengers as possible; usually a classic American car

comida criolla – Creole food

compañero/a – companion or partner, with revolutionary connotations (ie 'comrade')

conseguir – to get, obtain

convertibles – convertible pesos

criollo – Creole; Spaniard born in the Americas

Cubanacán – soon after landing in Cuba, Christopher Columbus visited a Taíno village called Cubanacán (meaning 'in the center of the island'); a Cuban tourism company uses the name

danzón – a traditional Cuban ballroom dance, pioneered in Matanzas during the late 19th century

décima – the rhyming, eight-syllable verse that provides the lyrics for Cuban *son*

duende – spirit/charm; used in flamenco to describe the ultimate climax to the music

el imperio – 'the empire'; a term used in the official Cuban media to refer to the US, which is led by the imperialistas

El Líder Máximo – Maximum Leader; title often used to describe Fidel Castro

el último – literally 'the last'; this term is key to mastering Cuban queues (you must 'take' el último when joining a line and 'give it up' when someone new arrives)

entronque – crossroads in rural areas

espectacular – show/extravaganza

finca – farmhouse

Gitmo – American slang for Guantánamo US Naval Base

Granma – the yacht that carried Fidel and his companions from Mexico to Cuba in 1956 to launch the Revolution; in 1975 the name was adopted for the province where the *Granma* arrived; also name of Cuba's leading daily newspaper

gringo/a – any Caucasian; see also americano/a and yuma

guajiro/a – a country bumpkin or hick
guarapo – fresh sugarcane juice

habanero/a – someone from Havana
herbero – seller of herbs, natural medicines and concocter of remedies

ingenio – an antiquated term for a sugar mill; see central
inmigración – immigration office

jardín – garden
jinetera – a female tout; a woman who attaches herself to male foreigners
jinetero – a male tout who hustles tourists; literally 'jockey'

luchar – literally 'to struggle/fight'

M-26-7 – the '26th of July Movement,' Fidel Castro's revolutionary organization, was named for the abortive assault on the Moncada army barracks in Santiago de Cuba on July 26, 1953
maqueta – scale model
máquina – private peso taxi
mercado – market
mirador – lookout or viewpoint
mogote – a limestone monolith found at Viñales
Moncada – a former army barracks in Santiago de Cuba named for General Guillermo Moncada
moneda nacional – abbreviated to MN; Cuban pesos
mudéjar – Iberian Peninsula's Moorish-influenced style in architecture and decoration that lasted from the 12th to 16th centuries and combined elements of Islamic and Christian art

nueva trova – philosophical folk/guitar music popularized in the late '60s and early '70s by Silvio Rodríguez and Pablo Milanés

Operación Milagros – the pioneering medical program introduced in 2004 that offers free eye treatment for impoverished Venezuelans in Cuban hospitals
Oriente – the region comprised of Las Tunas, Holguín, Granma, Santiago de Cuba and Guantánamo provinces; literally 'the east'
orisha – a Santería deity

paladar – a privately owned restaurant
parada – bus stop
parque – park
PCC – Partido Comunista de Cuba; Cuba's only political party, formed in October 1965 by merging cadres from the Partido Socialista Popular and veterans of the guerrilla campaign
peña – musical performance or get-together in any genre; see also esquina
período especial – the 'Special Period in Time of Peace' (Cuba's economic reality post-1991)
pregón – a singsong manner of selling fruits, vegetables, brooms, whatever; often comic, they are belted out by pregoneros/as
puente – bridge

¿qué bola? – 'what's up?' (popular greeting, especially in the Oriente)
quinciñera – rite of passage for girls turning 15 (quince): they dress up like brides, have their photos taken, and then have a big party

ranchón – rural farm/restaurant
reggaetón – Cuban hip-hop
Regla de Ocha – set of related religious beliefs popularly known as Santería
resolver – to resolve or fix a problematic situation
río – river

salsa – Cuban music based on *son*
salsero – salsa singer
Santería – Afro-Cuban religion resulting from the syncretization of the Yoruba religion of West Africa and Spanish Catholicism
santero – a priest of Santería; see also babalawo
santiagüero – someone from Santiago de Cuba
s/n – sin número; indicates an address that has no street number
son – Cuba's basic form of popular music, originating in the late 19th century

Taíno – an Arawak-speaking tribe that inhabited much of Cuba prior to the Spanish conquest; the word itself means 'we the good people'
tambores – Santería drumming ritual
telenovela – soap opera
telepunto – Etecsa (Cuban state-run telecommunications company) telephone and internet shop/call center
temporada alta/baja – high/low season
terminal de ómnibus – bus station
tinajón – large earthenware jar; particularly common in the city of Camagüey
trova – traditional poetic singing/songwriting
trovador – traditional singer/songwriter

Uneac – Unión Nacional de Escritores y Artistas de Cuba (National Union of Cuban Writers and Artists)

vaquero – cowboy
VIH – virus de inmunodeficiencia humana; HIV

Yanqui – someone from the US
Yoruba – an ethno-linguistic group from West Africa
yuma – slang for someone from the US; can be used for any foreigner; see americano/a and gringo/a

behind the scenes

SEND US YOUR FEEDBACK

We love to hear from travelers – your comments keep us on our toes and help make our books better. Our well-traveled team reads every word on what you loved or loathed about this book. Although we cannot reply individually to postal submissions, we always guarantee that your feedback goes straight to the appropriate authors, in time for the next edition. Each person who sends us information is thanked in the next edition – and the most useful submissions are rewarded with a free book.

Visit **lonelyplanet.com/contact** to submit your updates and suggestions or to ask for help. Our award-winning website also features inspirational travel stories, news and discussions.

Note: We may edit, reproduce and incorporate your comments in Lonely Planet products such as guidebooks, websites and digital products, so let us know if you don't want your comments reproduced or your name acknowledged. For a copy of our privacy policy visit lonelyplanet.com/privacy.

OUR READERS

Many thanks to the travelers who used the last edition and wrote to us with helpful hints, useful advice and interesting anecdotes:

Renate Altenriederer, Javier Barba, Rowiena & Kate & Fabio Barros, Marie Belcredi, Joyce Berry, Jan Beukema, Per Bisgaard, Robert Blom, Marino Bravo, Jessica Buckley & Arthur Van Schie, Tim Büthe, Alexandre Cabanis, Sonya Calderbank, Kim Cameron, Aileen Chang, Penny Chiva s, Fabiano Cid, Laura Crawford, Stuart Cutts, Giuseppe de Amicis, Maria de Los Angeles Perez, Paul de Waal, Marjet Derix, Jacques Desjardins, Mark Dolley, Denise Domaille, Julian du Perron, Maartje Duin, Carl Durber, Barbara Easteal, Joyce Edling, David Eldon, Maria Elena, Jake Filush, Mikkel Franks, Reinhard Freiberg, Mike Fulham, Ger Garland, Polly Garnett, James Gayoso, Rich Geary, Lorenzo Ghielmetti, Christopher Gibson, Jeremy Gilling, Jolande Goddijn, Barbara Goodwin, Stephany Grasset, Sarah Green, Ian Gribler, Astrid Haldorsen, Audrey Hall, Glen Hansman, Carlotta Helwig, Janice Henly, Beth Henshall, Jorrit Herder, Rob Hoek, the Hollemeersch family, Jochen Hoppe, Anne Jaumees, Arjan Kemp, Mick Kemp, Dennis Kim, Florence Knosp, Henry Kvist, Guillaume Lahaye, Gilles Lalonde, Paul Lammens, Susan Laneville, Nicolas Le Carre, Cindy-Marie Leicester, Sam Leslie, Ana Liddie Navarro, Helle Lund-Pedersen, Olivia Lyons, Manuel Madrid, Simon Malcolm, Klas Malmberg, John Mann, Elaine Marshall, Sally Marshall, Erin McKenna, Andreas Mihaljinec, Jonathan Moss-Vernon, Dino Moutsopoulos, Wendy Myers, Louise Nielsen, Annemarie Nietlispach, Mark Nolan, Wade Novakovski, Meaghan O'Brien, Paolo Oliveri, Pier Paolo Radaelli, Claudia Peschel, Briony Potts, Nick Quinnell, Ramyji, Stefano Razio, Daniel Reiter, Raphael Richards, Dana Rodger-Bond, Gert-Jan Roozeboom, Toon Schellekens & Sophie Poell, Maria Scheller, Sonja Schoentag, Titus Schonberger, Kassandra Schreuder, Siegfried Schwab & Ina Schlude, Judy Sebba & Brian Parkinson, Alice Self, Ketan Shah, Bora Shnitman, Louise Soanes, Christoph Spallek, Debbie Spauls, Rins Spinhoven, Eric Stark, Andrew Swearingen, Charlie Tatman, Graham Taylor, Nicole Torti, Conrad & Paula Trujillo, Kariina Tshursin, Eric Van Balen, Suzanne Van Der Zanden, Hugo Van Ende, Hans Van Zwienen, John Varley, Antonio Vinals Taquechel, Jurgen Vogt, Dirk Vrints, Christoph Weizenauer, Mike Whitaker, Udo Winterhagen, Ken Woods, Harold Zukerman

AUTHOR THANKS

Brendan Sainsbury

Thanks to all the untold bus drivers, weather forecasters, paladar owners, wandering troubadours and innocent bystanders who helped me during my research. Special thanks to Julio Muñoz, Rafael Requejo, Nilson Guilaré, Angel Rodríguez, Victor in Trinidad, Maité and Idolka in Morón, Norberto Hernández in Havana and the bloke at Ecotur in Bayamo. On the work front, *muchas gracias* to coauthor Luke Waterson and commissioning editor Catherine Craddock-Carrillo. On the home front, well-deserved *besos* to my wife, Liz, and son, Kieran.

Luke Waterson

Here goes: thanks to Waldo and Alfonso in Cienfuegos, Angel and all the guys at the university in Santa Clara, Yoel in Matanzas, Luis Miguel in Havana (for resolving visa difficulties in particular), and Yoan, Yarelis and a certain '51 Plymouth in Viñales. *Abrazos* all round. Thank you also to my wonderful editor Catherine Craddock-Carrillo in Oakland, my coauthor Brendan Sainsbury and, crucially, my girlfriend, Poppy, for intrepid research for this book and generally tolerating a travel writer's erratic existence.

ACKNOWLEDGMENTS

Climate map data adapted from Peel MC, Finlayson BL & McMahon TA (2007) 'Updated World Map of the Köppen-Geiger Climate Classification', *Hydrology and Earth System Sciences*, 11, 163344.

Cover photograph: Taxi, Havana, Keith Levit Photography.

Many of the images in this guide are available for licensing from Lonely Planet Images: www.lonelyplanetimages.com.

THIS BOOK

This sixth edition of Lonely Planet's Cuba guidebook was researched and written by Brendan Sainsbury (coordinating author) and Luke Waterson. The previous two editions were researched and written by Brendan Sainsbury. This guidebook was commissioned in Lonely Planet's Melbourne office, and produced by the following:

Commissioning Editor Catherine Craddock-Carrillo
Coordinating Editors Bella Li, Martine Power
Coordinating Cartographer Valeska Cañas
Coordinating Layout Designer Wendy Wright
Managing Editors Bruce Evans, Annelies Mertens
Managing Cartographer Alison Lyall
Managing Layout Designer Jane Hart
Assisting Editors Asha Ioculari, Catherine Naghten, Monique Perrin, Matty Soccio, Simon Williamson
Assisting Cartographers Enes Basic, Ildiko Bogdanovits, Julie Dodkins, Mick Garrett, Mark Griffiths, Jennifer Johnston, Maritza Kolega, Joelene Kowalski, Andrew Smith, Brendan Streager
Assisting Layout Designers Yvonne Bischofberger, Carol Jackson, Paul Iacono
Cover & Internal Image Research Aude Vauconsant
Language Content Branislava Vladisavljevic

Thanks to Ryan Evans, Joshua Geoghegan, Lisa Knights, Katie Lynch, Wayne Murphy, Gabrielle Stefanos, Gina Tsarouhas, Gerard Walker, Juan Winata

index

000 Map pages
000 Photo pages

D

E

F

000 Map pages
000 Photo pages

G

H

000 Map pages
000 Photo pages

how to use this book

These symbols will help you find the listings you want:

- Sights
- Activities
- Courses
- Tours
- Festivals & Events
- Sleeping
- Eating
- Drinking
- Entertainment
- Shopping
- Information/Transport

These symbols give you the vital information for each listing:

- Telephone Numbers
- Opening Hours
- Parking
- Nonsmoking
- Air-Conditioning
- Internet Access
- Wi-Fi Access
- Swimming Pool
- Vegetarian Selection
- English-Language Menu
- Family-Friendly
- Pet-Friendly
- Bus
- Ferry
- Metro
- Subway
- London Tube
- Tram
- Train

Reviews are organised by author preference.

Look out for these icons:

TOP CHOICE Our author's recommendation

FREE No payment required

A green or sustainable option

Our authors have nominated these places as demonstrating a strong commitment to sustainability – for example by supporting local communities and producers, operating in an environmentally friendly way, or supporting conservation projects.

Map Legend

Sights
- Beach
- Buddhist
- Castle
- Christian
- Hindu
- Islamic
- Jewish
- Monument
- Museum/Gallery
- Ruin
- Winery/Vineyard
- Zoo
- Other Sight

Activities, Courses & Tours
- Diving/Snorkelling
- Canoeing/Kayaking
- Skiing
- Surfing
- Swimming/Pool
- Walking
- Windsurfing
- Other Activity/Course/Tour

Sleeping
- Sleeping
- Camping

Eating
- Eating

Drinking
- Drinking
- Cafe

Entertainment
- Entertainment

Shopping
- Shopping

Information
- Post Office
- Tourist Information

Transport
- Airport
- Border Crossing
- Bus
- Cable Car/Funicular
- Cycling
- Ferry
- Metro
- Monorail
- Parking
- S-Bahn
- Taxi
- Train/Railway
- Tram
- Tube Station
- U-Bahn
- Other Transport

Routes
- Tollway
- Freeway
- Primary
- Secondary
- Tertiary
- Lane
- Unsealed Road
- Plaza/Mall
- Steps
- Tunnel
- Pedestrian Overpass
- Walking Tour
- Walking Tour Detour
- Path

Boundaries
- International
- State/Province
- Disputed
- Regional/Suburb
- Marine Park
- Cliff
- Wall

Population
- Capital (National)
- Capital (State/Province)
- City/Large Town
- Town/Village

Geographic
- Hut/Shelter
- Lighthouse
- Lookout
- Mountain/Volcano
- Oasis
- Park
- Pass
- Picnic Area
- Waterfall

Hydrography
- River/Creek
- Intermittent River
- Swamp/Mangrove
- Reef
- Canal
- Water
- Dry/Salt/Intermittent Lake
- Glacier

Areas
- Beach/Desert
- Cemetery (Christian)
- Cemetery (Other)
- Park/Forest
- Sportsground
- Sight (Building)
- Top Sight (Building)

OUR STORY

A beat-up old car, a few dollars in the pocket and a sense of adventure. In 1972 that's all Tony and Maureen Wheeler needed for the trip of a lifetime – across Europe and Asia overland to Australia. It took several months, and at the end – broke but inspired – they sat at their kitchen table writing and stapling together their first travel guide, *Across Asia on the Cheap*. Within a week they'd sold 1500 copies. Lonely Planet was born.

Today, Lonely Planet has offices in Melbourne, London and Oakland, with more than 600 staff and writers. We share Tony's belief that 'a great guidebook should do three things: inform, educate and amuse'.

OUR WRITERS

Brendan Sainsbury

Coordinating Author, Havana, Sancti Spíritus Province, Ciego de Ávila Province, Camagüey Province, Las Tunas Province, Holguín Province, Granma Province, Santiago de Cuba Province, Guantánamo Province Brendan is a British freelance writer who lives in British Columbia, Canada. He first visited Cuba in the 1990s and returned in 2002, after a spell as a teacher in Angola, to work as a travel guide leading cultural and cycling trips around the country. He researched and wrote his first Lonely Planet Cuba guide in 2006, with his 3-month-old son in tow. Since then he has produced three more Cuba guides, written countless Cuba-related newspaper articles, given presentations and been interviewed by everyone from Rick Steves to USA Today. When not writing and researching, Brendan likes to relax by running unaided across deserts, playing flamenco guitar and teaching his son to cross-country ski. He has also contributed to Lonely Planet guides to Spain, Italy, Canada and the USA.

Read more about Brendan at:
lonelyplanet.com/members/brendansainsbury

Luke Waterson

Artemisa & Mayabeque Provinces, Isla de la Juventud (Special Municipality), Pinar del Río Province, Matanzas Province, Cienfuegos Province and Villa Clara Province Cruising the countryside in wheezing Cadillacs and Plymouths, smoking several dozen cigars, experiencing two drag shows, sinking a myriad mojitos and learning some (tentative) salsa moves while researching this edition helped Luke fall in love with Cuba all over again. He was first smitten with the country back in 2004, on a backpacking trip that coincided with the withdrawal of the dollar from circulation by Castro. Highlights since then have included bathing in a waterfall on a restricted military zone and seeing sea turtles nest. Travel-wise, Luke's passions are Latin America, Eastern Europe and Britain – yes, Britain: musings on his journeys to these places, and advice on what and what not to do in them, can be found at www.lukewaterson.co.uk.

Read more about Luke at:
lonelyplanet.com/members/lukewaterson

Published by Lonely Planet Publications Pty Ltd
ABN 36 005 607 983
6th edition – Oct 2011
ISBN 978 1 74179 802 9

10 9 8 7 6 5 4 3 2 1
Printed in China